D0529651

RSP FINANCIAL AID DIRECTORIES
OF INTEREST TO MINORITIES

College Student's Guide to Merit and Other No-Need Funding
Selected as one of the "Outstanding Titles of the Year" by *Choice,* this directory describes 1,300 no-need funding opportunities for college students. 490 pages. ISBN 1588412121. $32.50, plus $7 shipping.

Directory of Financial Aids for Women
There are 1,400+ funding programs set aside for women described in this biennial directory, which has been called "the cream of the crop" by *School Library Journal* and the "best available reference source" by *Guide to Reference.* 552 pages. ISBN 1588412164. $45, plus $7 shipping.

Financial Aid for African Americans
Nearly 1,300 funding opportunities open to African American college students, professionals, and postdoctorates are described in this award-winning directory. 490 pages. ISBN 1588412172. $42.50, plus $7 shipping.

Financial Aid for Asian Americans
This is the source to use if you are looking for funding for Asian Americans, from college-bound high school seniors to professionals and postdoctorates; more than 1,000 sources of free money are described here. 350 pages. ISBN 1588412180. $40, plus $7 shipping.

Financial Aid for Hispanic Americans
The 1,100 biggest and best sources of free money available to undergraduates, graduates students, professionals, and postdoctorates of Mexican, Puerto Rican, Central American, or other Latin American heritage are described here. 446 pages. ISBN 1588412199. $42.50, plus $7 shipping.

Financial Aid for Native Americans
Detailed information is provided on nearly 1,400 funding opportunities open to American Indians, Native Alaskans, and Native Pacific Islanders for college, graduate school, or professional activities. 506 pages. ISBN 1588412202. $45, plus $7 shipping.

Financial Aid for Research and Creative Activities Abroad
Described here are more than 1,000 scholarships, fellowships, grants, etc. available to support research, professional, or creative activities abroad. 422 pages. ISBN 1588412067. $45, plus $7 shipping.

Financial Aid for Study and Training Abroad
This directory, which the reviewers call "invaluable," describes nearly 1,000 financial aid opportunities available to support study abroad. 362 pages. ISBN 1588412059. $40, plus $7 shipping.

Financial Aid for Veterans, Military Personnel, & Their Families
According to *Reference Book Review,* this directory (with its 1,100 entries) is "the most comprehensive guide available on the subject." 436 pages. ISBN 1588412091. $40, plus $7 shipping.

High School Senior's Guide to Merit and Other No-Need Funding
Here's your guide to 1,100 funding programs that *never* look at income level when making awards to college-bound high school seniors. 416 pages. ISBN 1588412105. $29.95, plus $7 shipping.

Money for Graduate Students in the Arts & Humanities
Use this directory to identify 1,000 funding opportunities available to support graduate study and research in the arts/humanities. 292 pages. ISBN 1588411974. $42.50, plus $7 shipping

Money for Graduate Students in the Biological Sciences
This unique directory focuses solely on funding for graduate study/research in the biological sciences (800+ funding opportunities). 248 pages. ISBN 1588411982. $37.50, plus $7 shipping.

Money for Graduate Students in the Health Sciences
Described here are 1,000+ funding opportunities just for students interested in a graduate degree in dentistry, medicine, nursing, nutrition, pharmacology, etc. 304 pages. ISBN 1588411990. $42.50, plus $7 shipping.

Money for Graduate Students in the Physical & Earth Sciences
Nearly 900 funding opportunities for graduate students in the physical and earth sciences are described in detail here. 276 pages. ISBN 1588412008. $40, plus $7 shipping.

Money for Graduate Students in the Social & Behavioral Sciences
Looking for money for a graduate degree in the social/behavioral sciences? Here are 1,100 funding programs for you. 316 pages. ISBN 1588412016. $42.50, plus $7 shipping.

Financial Aid
for Native Americans
2012-2014

Financial Aid for Native Americans 2012-2014

Gail Ann Schlachter
R. David Weber

A Listing of Scholarships, Fellowships, Grants, Awards, Internships, and Other Sources of Free Money Available Primarily or Exclusively to Native Americans Plus a Set of Six Indexes (Program Title, Sponsoring Organization, Residency, Tenability, Subject, and Deadline Date)

Reference Service Press
El Dorado Hills, California

ISBN 10: 1588412202
ISBN 13: 9781588412201

10 9 8 7 6 5 4 3 2 1

Reference Service Press (RSP) began in 1977 with a single financial aid publication *(The Directory of Financial Aids for Women)* and now specializes in the development of financial aid resources in multiple formats, including books, large print books, print-on-demand reports, eBooks, and online sources. Long recognized as a leader in the field, RSP has been called by the *Samba Report on Directory Publishing* "a true success in the world of independent directory publishers." Both Kaplan Educational Centers and Military.com have hailed RSP as "the leading authority on scholarships."

Reference Service Press
El Dorado Hills Business Park
5000 Windplay Drive, Suite 4
El Dorado Hills, CA 95762-9319
    (916) 939-9620
    Fax: (916) 939-9626
    E-mail: info@rspfunding.com
Visit our web site: www.rspfunding.com

Manufactured in the United States of America
Price: $45, plus $7 shipping

ACADEMIC INSTITUTIONS, LIBRARIES, ORGANIZATIONS AND OTHER QUANTITY BUYERS:
Discounts on this book are available for bulk purchases. Write or call for information on our discount programs.

Contents

Introduction

WHY THIS DIRECTORY IS NEEDED

Despite our country's ongoing economic problems and increased college costs, the financial aid picture for minorities has never looked brighter. Currently, billions of dollars are set aside each year specifically for Native Americans, African Americans, Asian Americans, and Hispanic Americans. This funding is open to minorities at any level (high school through postdoctoral and professional) for a variety of activities, including study, research, travel, training, career development, and creative projects.

While numerous print or online listings have been prepared to identify and describe general financial aid opportunities (those open to all segments of society), those resources have never covered more than a small portion of the programs designed primarily or exclusively for minorities. As a result, many advisors, librarians, scholars, researchers, and students are often unaware of the extensive funding available to Native Americans and other minorities. But, with the ongoing publication of *Financial Aid for Native Americans* that has all changed. Here, in just one place, Native American students, professionals, and postdoctorates now have current and detailed information about the special resources set aside specifically for them.

Financial Aid for Native Americans is prepared biennially as part of Reference Service Press' four-volume *Minority Funding Set* (the other volumes in the set cover funding for Asian Americans, African Americans, and Hispanic Americans). Each of the volumes in this set is sold separately, or the complete set can be purchased at a discounted price; for more information, contact Reference Service Press's marketing department or visit www.rspfunding.com/prod_prodalpha.html.

No other source, in print or online, offers the extensive coverage provided by these titles. That's why the Grantsmanship Center labeled the set "a must for every organization serving minorities," *Reference Sources for Small and Medium-Sized Libraries* called the titles "the absolute best guides for finding funding," and *Reference Books Bulletin* selected each of the volumes in the *Minority Funding Set* as their "Editor's Choice." *Financial Aid for Native Americans,* itself, has also received rave reviews. According to *Choice,* "This is a unique and valuable resource" which is "highly recommended." *Reference Books Bulletin* calls it a "landmark resource" and *EMIE Bulletin* concluded that the directory is "definitely designed to ease what can be a very stressful process." Perhaps *American Reference Books Annual* sums up best the critical reaction to *Financial Aid for Native Americans:* "extraordinarily useful...absolutely essential."

WHAT'S UPDATED?

The preparation of each new edition of *Financial Aid for Native Americans* involves extensive updating and revision. To make sure that the information included here is both reliable and current, the editors at Reference Service Press 1) reviewed and updated all relevant programs covered in the previous edition of the directory, 2) collected information on all programs open to Native Americans that were added to Reference Service Press' funding database since the last edition of the directory, and then 3) searched extensively for new program leads in a variety of sources, including printed directories, news reports, journals, newsletters, house organs, annual reports, and sites on the Internet. We only include program descriptions that are written directly from information supplied by the sponsoring organization in print or online (no information is ever taken from secondary sources). When that information could not be found, we sent up to four collection letters (followed by up to three telephone or email inquiries, if necessary) to those sponsors. Despite our best efforts, however, some sponsoring organizations still failed to respond and, as a result, their programs are not included in this edition of the directory.

The 2012-2014 edition of *Financial Aid for Native Americans* completely revises and updates the previous (sixth) edition. Programs that have ceased operations have been dropped from the listing. Similarly, programs that have broadened their scope and no longer focus on Native Americans have also been removed from the listing. Profiles of continuing programs have been rewritten to reflect current requirements; more than 75 percent of the continuing programs reported substantive changes in their locations, requirements (particularly application deadline), benefits, or eligibility requirements since the 2009-2011 edition. In addition, more than 375 new entries have been added to the program section of the directory. The resulting listing describes the 1,350+ biggest and best sources of free money available to Native Americans, including scholarships, fellowships, grants, awards, and internships.

WHAT MAKES THIS DIRECTORY UNIQUE?

The 2012-2014 edition of *Financial Aid for Native Americans* will help American Indians, Native Alaskans (including Eskimos and Aleuts), and Native Hawaiians tap into the billions of dollars available to them, as minorities, for study, research, creative activities, past accomplishments, future projects, professional development, work experience, and many other activities. The listings cover every major subject area, are sponsored by nearly 900 different private and public agencies and organizations, and are open to Native Americans at any level, from college-bound high school students through professionals and postdoctorates.

Not only does *Financial Aid for Native Americans* provide the most comprehensive coverage of available funding (1,384 entries), but it also displays the most informative program descriptions (on the average, more than twice the detail found in any other listing). In addition to this extensive and focused coverage, *Financial Aid for Native Americans* also offers several other unique features. First of all, hundreds of funding opportunities listed here have never been covered in any other source. So, even if you have checked elsewhere, you will want to look at *Financial Aid for Native Americans* for additional leads. And, here's another plus: all of the funding programs in this edition of the directory offer "free" money; not one of the programs will ever require you to pay anything back (provided, of course, that you meet the program requirements).

Further, unlike other funding directories, which generally follow a straight alphabetical arrangement, *Financial Aid for Native Americans* groups entries by intended recipients (undergraduates, graduate students, or professionals/postdoctorates), to make it easy for you to search for appropriate programs. This same convenience is offered in the indexes, where program title, sponsoring organization, geographic, subject, and deadline date entries are each subdivided by recipient group.

Finally, we have tried to anticipate all the ways you might wish to search for funding. The volume is organized so you can identify programs not only by intended recipient, but also by subject focus, sponsoring organization, program title, residency requirements, where the money can be spent, and even deadline date. Plus, we've included all the information you'll need to decide if a program is right for you: purpose, eligibility requirements, financial data, duration, special features, limitations, number awarded, and application date. You even get fax numbers, toll-free numbers, e-mail addresses, and web sites (when available), along with complete contact information.

WHAT'S EXCLUDED?

While this book is intended to be the most comprehensive source of information on funding available to Native Americans, there are some programs we've specifically excluded from the directory:

- *Programs that do not accept applications from U.S. citizens or residents.* If a program is open only to foreign nationals or excludes Americans from applying, it is not covered.

- *Programs that are open equally to all segments of the population.* Only funding opportunities set aside primarily or exclusively for American Indians, Native Alaskans, and/or Native Hawaiians are included here.

SAMPLE ENTRY

(1) **[411]**

(2) **NATIVE AMERICAN LEADERSHIP IN EDUCATION (NALE) PROGRAM**

(3) Catching the Dream
8200 Mountain Road, N.E., Suite 203
8333 Greenwood Boulevard
Albuquerque, NM 87110-7835
(505) 262-2351   Fax: (505) 262-0534
E-mail: NScholarsh@aol.com
Web: www.catchingthedream.org/Scholarship.htm

(4) **Summary**   To provide financial assistance to American Indian paraprofessionals in the education field who wish to return to college or graduate school.

(5) **Eligibility**   This program is open to paraprofessionals who are working in Indian schools and who plan to return to college or graduate school to complete their degree in education, counseling, or school administration. Applicants must be able to provide proof that they are at least one-quarter Indian blood and a member of a U.S. tribe that is federally-recognized, state-recognized, or terminated. Along with their application, they must submit documentation of financial need, 3 letters of recommendation, copies of applications and responses from all other sources of funding for which they are eligible, official transcripts, standardized test scores (ACT, SAT, GRE, MCAT, LSAT, etc.), and an essay explaining their goals in life, college plans, and career plans (especially how those plans include working with and benefiting Indians). Selection is based on merit and potential for improving the lives of Indian people.

(6) **Financial data**   Stipends range from $500 to $5,000 per year.

(7) **Duration**   1 year; may be renewed.

(8) **Additional information**   The sponsor was formerly known as the Native American Scholarship Fund.

(9) **Number awarded**   Varies; generally, 15 or more each year.

(10) **Deadline**   April of each year for fall term; September of each year for spring and winter terms; March of each year for summer school.

DEFINITION

(1) **Entry number:** The consecutive number that is given to each entry and used to identify the entry in the index.

(2) **Program title:**   Title of scholarship, fellowship, grant, award, internship or other source of free money described in the directory.

(3) **Sponsoring organization:** Name, address, and telephone number, toll-free number, fax number, e-mail address, and/or web site (when information was available) for organization sponsoring the program.

(4) **Summary:** Identifies the major program requirements; read the rest of the entry for additional detail.

(5) **Eligibility:** Qualifications required of applicants, plus information on application procedure and selection process.

(6) **Financial data:** Financial details of the program, including fixed sum, average amount, or range of funds offered, expenses for which funds may and may not be applied, and cash-related benefits supplied (e.g., room and board).

(7) **Duration:** Period for which support is provided; renewal prospects.

(8) **Additional information:** Any unusual (generally nonmonetary) benefits, features, restrictions, or limitations associated with the program.

(9) **Number awarded:** Total number of recipients each year or other specified period.

(10) **Deadline:** The month by which applications must be submitted.

- *Money for study or research outside the United States.*   Since there are comprehensive and up-to-date directories that describe the available funding for study, research, or other activities abroad (see the list of Reference Service Press publications opposite the directory's title page), only programs that fund activities in the United States are covered here.

- *Very restrictive programs.*   In general, programs are excluded if they are open only to a limited geographic area (less than a state) or offer limited financial support (less than $1,000). Note, however, that the vast majority of programs included here go way beyond that, paying up to full tuition or stipends that exceed $25,000 a year!

- *Programs administered by individual academic institutions solely for their own students.*   The directory identifies "portable" programs—ones that can be used at any number of schools. Financial aid administered by individual schools specifically for their own students is not covered. Write directly to the schools you are considering to get information on their offerings.

- *Money that must be repaid.*   Only "free money" is identified here. If a program requires repayment or charges interest, it's not listed. Now you can find out about billions of dollars in aid and know (if you meet the program requirements) that not one dollar of that will ever need to be repaid.

HOW THE DIRECTORY IS ORGANIZED

Financial Aid for Native Americans is divided into two sections: 1) a detailed list of funding opportunities open to Native Americans and 2) a set of six indexes to help you pinpoint appropriate funding programs.

Financial Aid Programs Open to Native Americans.   The first section of the directory describes close to >2Q>1,400 sources of free money available to American Indians, Native Alaskans, and/or Native Hawaiians. The focus is on financial aid aimed at American citizens or residents to support study, research, or other activities in the United States. The programs listed here are sponsored by nearly 900 different government agencies, professional organizations, corporations, sororities and fraternities, foundations, religious groups, educational associations, and military/veterans organizations. All areas of the sciences, social sciences, and humanities are covered.

To help you focus your search, the entries in this section are grouped into the following three chapters:

- **Undergraduates:** Included here are nearly 650 scholarships, grants, awards, internships, and other sources of free money that support undergraduate study, training, research, or creative activities. These programs are open to high school seniors, high school graduates, currently-enrolled college students, and students returning to college after an absence. Money is available to support these students in any type of public or private postsecondary institution, ranging from technical schools and community colleges to major universities in the United States.

- **Graduate Students:** Described here are more than 525 fellowships, grants, awards, internships, and other sources of free money that support post-baccalaureate study, training, research, and creative activities. These programs are open to students applying to, currently enrolled in, or returning to a master's, doctoral, professional, or specialist program in public or private graduate schools in the United States.

- **Professionals/Postdoctorates:** Included here are more than 200 funding programs for U.S. citizens or residents who 1) are in professional positions (e.g., artists, writers), whether or not they have an advanced degree; 2) are master's or professional degree recipients; 3) have earned a doctoral degree or its equivalent (e.g., Ph.D., Ed.D., M.D.); or 4) have recognized stature as established scientists, scholars, academicians, or researchers.

Within each of these three chapters, entries appear alphabetically by program title. Since some of the programs supply assistance to more than one specific group, those are listed in all relevant chapters. For example, the Blossom Kalama Evans Memorial Scholarships support both undergraduate or graduate study, so the program is described in both the Undergraduates *and* Graduate Students chapters.

Each program entry has been designed to give you a concise profile that, as the sample on page 7 illustrates, includes Information (when available) on organization address and telephone numbers (including toll-free and fax numbers), e-mail addresses and web site, purpose, eligibility, money awarded, duration, special features, limitations, number of awards, and application deadline.

The information reported for each of the programs in this section was gathered from research conducted through the beginning of 2012. While the listing is intended to cover as comprehensively as possible the biggest and best sources of free money available to Native Americans, some sponsoring organizations did not post information online or respond to our research inquiries and, consequently, are not included in this edition of the directory.

Indexes. To help you find the aid you need, we have constructed six indexes; these will let you access the listings by program title, sponsoring organization, residency, tenability, subject focus, and deadline date. These indexes use a word-by-word alphabetical arrangement. Note: numbers in the index refer to entry numbers, not to page numbers in the book.

Program Title Index. If you know the name of a particular funding program and want to find out where it is covered in the directory, use the Program Title Index. To assist you in your search, every program is listed by all its known names, former names, and abbreviations. Since one program can be included in more than one place (e.g., a program providing assistance to both undergraduate and graduate students is described in both the first and second chapter), each entry number in the index has been coded to indicate the intended recipient group ("U" = Undergraduates; "G" = Graduate Students; "P" = Professionals/Postdoctorates). By using this coding system, you can avoid duplicate entries and turn directly to the programs that match your eligibility characteristics.

Sponsoring Organization Index. This index makes it easy to identify agencies that offer funding primarily or exclusively to Native Americans. Nearly 900 organizations are indexed here. As in the Program Title Index, we've used a code to help you determine which organizations sponsor programs that match your educational level.

Residency Index. Some programs listed in this book are restricted to Native Americans in a particular state or region. Others are open to Native Americans wherever they live. This index helps you identify programs available only to residents in your area as well as programs that have no residency requirements. Further, to assist you in your search, we've also indicated the recipient level for the funding offered to residents in each of the areas listed in the index.

Tenability Index. This index identifies the geographic locations where the funding described in *Financial Aid for Native Americans* may be used. Index entries (city, county, state, region) are arranged alphabetically (word by word) and subdivided by recipient group. Use this index when you are looking for money to support your activities in a particular geographic area.

Subject Index. This index allows you to identify the subject focus of each of the financial aid opportunities described in *Financial Aid for Native Americans*. More than 250 different subject terms are listed. Extensive "see" and "see also" references, as well as recipient group subdivisions, will help you locate appropriate funding opportunities.

Calendar Index. Since most financial aid programs have specific deadline dates, some may have closed by the time you begin to look for funding. You can use the Calendar Index to determine which programs are still open. This index is arranged by recipient group (Undergraduates, Graduate Students, and Professionals/Postdoctorates) and subdivided by month during which the deadline falls. Filing dates can and quite often do vary from year to year; consequently, this index should be used only as a guide for deadlines beyond 2014.

HOW TO USE THE DIRECTORY

Here are some tips to help you get the most out the funding opportunities listed in *Financial Aid for Native Americans*.

To Locate Funding by Recipient Group.   To bring together programs with a similar educational focus, this directory is divided into three chapters: Undergraduates, Graduate Students, and Professionals/Postdoctorates. If you want to get an overall picture of the sources of free money available to Native Americans in any of these categories, turn to the appropriate chapter and then review the entries there. Since each of these chapters functions as a self-contained entity, you can browse through any of them without having to first consulting an index.

To Find Information on a Particular Financial Aid Program.   If you know the name of a particular financial aid program, and the group eligible for that award, then go directly to the appropriate chapter in the directory (e.g., Undergraduates, Graduate Students), where you will find the program profiles arranged alphabetically by title. To save time, though, you should always check the Program Title Index first if you know the name of a specific award but are not sure in which chapter it has been listed. Plus, since we index each program by all its known names and abbreviations, you'll also be able to track down a program there when you only know the popular rather than official name.

To Locate Programs Sponsored by a Particular Organization.   The Sponsoring Organization Index makes it easy to identify agencies that provide financial assistance to Native Americans or to identify specific financial aid programs offered by a particular organization. Each entry number in the index is coded to identify recipient group (Undergraduates, Graduate Students, Professionals/Postdoctorates), so that you can easily target appropriate entries.

To Browse Quickly Through the Listings.   Look at the listings in the chapter that relates to you (Undergraduates, Graduate Students, or Professionals/Postdoctorates) and read the "Summary" paragraph in each entry. In seconds, you'll know if this is an opportunity that you might want to pursue. If it is, be sure to read the rest of the information in the entry, to make sure you meet all of the program requirements before writing or going online for an application form. Please save your time and energy. Don't apply if you don't qualify!

To Locate Funding Available to Native Americans from or Tenable in a Particular City, County, or State.   The Residency Index identifies financial aid programs open to Native Americans in a specific state, region, etc. The Tenability Index shows where the money can be spent. In both indexes, "see" and "see also" references are used liberally, and index entries for a particular geographic area are subdivided by recipient group (Undergraduates, Graduate Students, and Professionals/Postdoctorates) to help you identify the funding that's right for you. When using these indexes, always check the listings under the term "United States," since the programs indexed there have no geographic restrictions and can be used in any area.

To Locate Financial Aid Programs Open to Native Americans in a Particular Subject Area.   Turn to the Subject Index first if you are interested in identifying funding programs for Native Americans that are focused on a particular subject area (more than 250 different subject fields are listed there). To make your search easier, the intended recipient groups (Undergraduates, Graduate Students, Professionals/Postdoctorates) are clearly labeled in each of the subject listings. Extensive cross-references are also provided. Since a large number of programs are not restricted by subject, be sure to check the references listed under the "General programs" heading in the index, in addition to the specific terms that directly relate to your interest areas. The listings under "General programs" can be used to fund activities in any subject area (although the programs may be restricted in other ways).

To Locate Financial Aid Programs for Native Americans by Deadline Date.   If you are working with specific time constraints and want to weed out the financial aid programs whose filing dates you won't be able to meet, turn first to the Calendar Index and check the program references listed under the appropriate recipient group and month. Note: not all sponsoring organizations supplied deadline information; those programs are listed under the "Deadline not specified" entries in the index. To identify every relevant financial aid program, regardless of filing date, go the appropriate chapter and read through all the entries there that match your educational level.

To Locate Financial Aid Programs Open to All Segments of the Population. Only programs available to Native Americans are listed in this publication. However, there are thousands of other programs that are open equally to all segments of the population. To identify these programs, talk to your local librarian, check with your financial aid office on campus, look at the list of RSP print resources on the page opposite the title page in this directory, or see if your library subscribes to Reference Service Press' interactive online funding databases (for more information, go online to: www.rspfunding.com/esubscriptions.html).

PLANS TO UPDATE THE DIRECTORY

This volume, covering 2012-2014, is the seventh edition of *Financial Aid for Native Americans.* The next biennial edition will cover the years 2014-2016 and will be issued in mid-2014.

OTHER RELATED PUBLICATIONS

In addition to *Financial Aid for Native Americans,* Reference Service Press publishes several other titles dealing with fundseeking, including the award-winning *Directory of Financial Aids for Women; Financial Aid for the Disabled and Their Families;* and *Financial Aid for Veterans, Military Personnel, and Their Families.* Since each of these titles focuses on a separate population group, there is very little duplication in the listings. For more information on Reference Service Press' award-winning publications, write to the company at 5000 Windplay Drive, Suite 4, El Dorado Hills, CA 95762, give us a call at (916) 939-9620, fax us at (916) 939-9626, send us an e-mail at info@rspfunding.com, or visit our expanded web site: www.rspfunding.com.

ACKNOWLEDGEMENTS

A debt of gratitude is owed all the organizations that contributed information to the 2012-2014 edition of *Financial Aid for Native Americans.* Their generous cooperation has helped to make this publication a current and comprehensive survey of awards.

ABOUT THE AUTHORS

Dr. Gail Ann Schlachter has worked for more than three decades as a library manager, a library educator, and an administrator of library-related publishing companies. Among the reference books to her credit are the biennially-issued *Directory of Financial Aids for Women* and two award-winning bibliographic guides: *Minorities and Women: A Guide to Reference Literature in the Social Sciences* (which was chosen as an "outstanding reference book of the year" by *Choice)* and *Reference Sources in Library and Information Services* (which won the first Knowledge Industry Publications "Award for Library Literature"). She was the reference book review editor for *RQ* (now *Reference and User Services Quarterly)* for 10 years, is a past president of the American Library Association's Reference and User Services Association, is the former editor-in-chief of the *Reference and User Services Association Quarterly,* and is currently serving her fifth term on the American Library Association's governing council. In recognition of her outstanding contributions to reference service, Dr. Schlachter has been named the University of Wisconsin School of Library and Information Studies "Alumna of the Year" and has been awarded both the Isadore Gilbert Mudge Citation and the Louis Shores/Oryx Press Award.

Dr. R. David Weber taught history and economics at Los Angeles Harbor College (in Wilmington, California) for many years and continues to teach history as an emeritus professor. During his years of full-time teaching there, and at East Los Angeles College, he directed the Honors Program and was frequently chosen the "Teacher of the Year." He has written a number of critically-acclaimed reference works, including *Dissertations in Urban History* and the three-volume *Energy Information Guide.* With Gail Schlachter, he is the author of Reference Service Press' *Financial Aid for the Disabled and Their Families,* which was selected by *Library Journal* as one of the "best reference books of the year," and a number of other financial aid titles, including the *College Student's Guide to Merit and Other No-Need Funding,* which was chosen as one of the "outstanding reference books of the year" by *Choice.*

Financial Aid Programs
Open to Native Americans

Undergraduates ●

Graduate Students ●

Professionals/Postdoctorates ●

Undergraduates

Listed alphabetically by program title and described in detail here are 649 scholarships, grants, awards, internships, and other sources of "free money" set aside for college-bound high school seniors and continuing or returning undergraduate students of American Indian, Native Alaskan (including Eskimos and Aleuts), and Native Hawaiian descent. This funding is available to support study, training, research, and/or creative activities in the United States.

[1]
ADOLPH VAN PELT SCHOLARSHIPS

Association on American Indian Affairs, Inc.
Attn: Director of Scholarship Programs
966 Hungerford Drive, Suite 12-B
Rockville, MD 20850
(240) 314-7155   Fax: (240) 314-7159
E-mail: lw.aaia@verizon.net
Web: www.indian-affairs.org

Summary   To provide financial assistance to Native American undergraduate students.

Eligibility   This program is open to Native American students interested in working on an undergraduate degree on a full-time basis. Applicants must submit documentation of financial need, a Certificate of Indian Blood showing at least one-quarter Indian blood, proof of tribal enrollment, an essay on their educational goals, 2 letters of recommendation, and their most recent transcript. Selection is based on merit and need.

Financial data   The stipend is $1,500.

Duration   1 year; recipients may reapply.

Number awarded   Varies each year; recently, 4 new and 2 renewal scholarships were awarded.

Deadline   June of each year.

[2]
AGNES LARSEN DARNELL SCHOLARSHIP

The Aleut Corporation
Attn: Aleut Foundation
703 West Tudor Road, Suite 102
Anchorage, AK 99503-6650
(907) 646-1929   Toll Free: (800) 232-4882
Fax: (907) 646-1949   E-mail: taf@thealeutfoundation.org
Web: www.thealeutfoundation.org/ScholarshipGuide.aspx

Summary   To provide financial assistance to Native Alaskans who are 1) shareholders of The Aleut Corporation or their descendants and 2) high school seniors planning to attend college in any state.

Eligibility   This program is open to Native Alaskans who are original enrollees or descendants of original enrollees of The Aleut Corporation (TAC). Applicants must be graduating high school seniors and planning to attend a 4-year college or university in any state. They must have a GPA of 3.0 or higher.

Financial data   The stipend is $1,000 per year.

Duration   4 years.

Additional information   The Aleut Corporation is 1 of 13 Alaska Native Regional Corporations created under the Alaska Native Claims Settlement Act of 1971.

Number awarded   1 each year.

Deadline   March of each year.

[3]
AIGC ACCENTURE UNDERGRADUATE SCHOLARSHIPS

American Indian Graduate Center
Attn: Executive Director
4520 Montgomery Boulevard, N.E., Suite 1-B
Albuquerque, NM 87109-1291
(505) 881-4584   Toll Free: (800) 628-1920
Fax: (505) 884-0427   E-mail: aigc@aigc.com
Web: www.aigc.com

Summary   To provide financial assistance for college to Native American high school seniors interested in majoring in fields of business and technology.

Eligibility   This program is open to enrolled members of federally-recognized American Indian tribes and Alaska Native groups who can provide a Certificate of Indian Blood (CIB). Applicants must be entering freshmen at an accredited U.S. college or university, planning to work full time on a bachelor's degree in engineering, computer science, operations management, finance, marketing, management, or other business-oriented fields. They must have a GPA of 3.25 or higher. Along with their application, they must submit an essay describing their character, personal merit, and commitment to community and American Indian or Alaska Native heritage. Selection is based on academic excellence, demonstrated leadership, and commitment to preserving American Indian culture and communities.

Financial data   The stipend is $5,000 per year.

Duration   4 years.

Additional information   This program, established in 2005, is supported by Accenture.

Number awarded   3 each year.

Deadline   April of each year.

[4]
AIR PRODUCTS AND CHEMICALS SCHOLARSHIP FOR DIVERSITY IN ENGINEERING

Association of Independent Colleges and Universities of Pennsylvania
101 North Front Street
Harrisburg, PA 17101-1405
(717) 232-8649   Fax: (717) 233-8574
E-mail: info@aicup.org
Web: www.aicup.org

Summary   To provide financial assistance to Native Americans, other minorities, and women from any state who are enrolled at member institutions of the Association of Independent Colleges and Universities of Pennsylvania (AICUP) and majoring in designated fields of engineering.

Eligibility   This program is open to undergraduate students from any state enrolled full time at AICUP colleges and universities. Applicants must be women and/or members of the following minority groups: American Indians, Alaska Natives, Asians, Blacks/African Americans, Hispanics/Latinos, Native Hawaiians, or Pacific Islanders. They must be juniors majoring in chemical or mechanical engineering with a GPA of 2.7 or higher. Along with their application, they must submit an essay on their characteristics, accomplishments, primary interests, plans, goals, and uniqueness.

Financial data   The stipend is $7,500 per year.

Duration 1 year; may be renewed 1 additional year if the recipient maintains appropriate academic standards.

Additional information This program, sponsored by Air Products and Chemicals, Inc., is available at the 83 private colleges and universities in Pennsylvania that comprise the AICUP.

Number awarded 1 each year.

Deadline April of each year.

[5]
ALEUT FOUNDATION PART-TIME SCHOLARSHIPS

The Aleut Corporation
Attn: Aleut Foundation
703 West Tudor Road, Suite 102
Anchorage, AK 99503-6650
(907) 646-1929   Toll Free: (800) 232-4882
Fax: (907) 646-1949   E-mail: taf@thealeutfoundation.org
Web: www.thealeutfoundation.org/ScholarshipGuide.aspx

Summary To provide financial assistance for college or graduate school to Native Alaskans who are shareholders of The Aleut Corporation or their descendants and are enrolled part time.

Eligibility This program is open to Native Alaskans who are original enrollees or descendants of original enrollees of The Aleut Corporation (TAC). Applicants must be enrolled in an associate, bachelor's, or higher degree program as a part-time student (at least 3 credit hours). They must have a GPA of 2.0 or higher. Along with their application, they must include a letter of intent, up to 500 words in length, that describes their educational goals and objectives and their expected graduation date.

Financial data The stipend depends on the number of credit hours in the undergraduate or graduate program, to a maximum of $1,200 per year.

Duration 1 year.

Additional information The Aleut Corporation is 1 of 13 Alaska Native Regional Corporations created under the Alaska Native Claims Settlement Act of 1971. The foundation began awarding scholarships in 1987.

Number awarded Varies each year; recently, 2 of these scholarships were awarded.

Deadline June of each year for annual scholarships; November of each year for spring scholarships; April of each year for summer school.

[6]
ALEUT FOUNDATION SCHOLARSHIP PROGRAM

The Aleut Corporation
Attn: Aleut Foundation
703 West Tudor Road, Suite 102
Anchorage, AK 99503-6650
(907) 646-1929   Toll Free: (800) 232-4882
Fax: (907) 646-1949   E-mail: taf@thealeutfoundation.org
Web: www.thealeutfoundation.org/ScholarshipGuide.aspx

Summary To provide financial assistance to Native Alaskans who are shareholders of The Aleut Corporation or their descendants and plan to attend college in any state.

Eligibility This program is open to Native Alaskans who are original enrollees or descendants of original enrollees of The Aleut Corporation (TAC). Applicants must be enrolled or

planning to enroll full time at a college or university in any state to work on an undergraduate degree. They must have earned a GPA of 3.5 or higher for the Honors Scholarship, 3.0 or higher for the Exceptional Scholarship, 2.5 or higher for the Achievement Scholarship, or 2.0 or higher for the Merit Scholarship. Along with their application, they must include a letter of intent, up to 500 words in length, that describes their educational goals and objectives and their expected graduation date.

Financial data Annual stipends are $3,000 for Honors Scholarships, $2,500 for Exceptional Scholarships, $2,000 for Achievement Scholarships, or $1,500 for Merit Scholarships.

Duration 1 year; may be renewed.

Additional information The Aleut Corporation is 1 of 13 Alaska Native Regional Corporations created under the Alaska Native Claims Settlement Act of 1971. The foundation began awarding scholarships in 1987.

Number awarded Varies each year.

Deadline June of each year for annual scholarships; November of each year for spring scholarships; April of each year for summer school.

[7]
ALEUT FOUNDATION VOCATIONAL SCHOLARSHIPS

The Aleut Corporation
Attn: Aleut Foundation
703 West Tudor Road, Suite 102
Anchorage, AK 99503-6650
(907) 646-1929   Toll Free: (800) 232-4882
Fax: (907) 646-1949   E-mail: taf@thealeutfoundation.org
Web: www.thealeutfoundation.org/ScholarshipGuide.aspx

Summary To provide financial assistance for vocational school in any state to Native Alaskans who are shareholders of The Aleut Corporation or their descendants.

Eligibility This program is open to Native Alaskans who are original enrollees or descendants of original enrollees of The Aleut Corporation (TAC). Applicants must be enrolled in or accepted to a vocational program in any state on a full-time basis. Along with their application, they must include a letter of intent, up to 500 words in length, that describes their educational goals and objectives and their expected graduation date.

Financial data The stipend is $1,700 per year.

Duration 1 semester (at least 6 weeks); may be renewed.

Additional information The Aleut Corporation is 1 of 13 Alaska Native Regional Corporations created under the Alaska Native Claims Settlement Act of 1971. The foundation began awarding scholarships in 1987.

Number awarded Varies each year; recently, 4 of these scholarships were awarded.

Deadline June of each year for annual scholarships; November of each year for spring scholarships; April of each year for summer school.

[8]
ALLOGAN SLAGLE MEMORIAL SCHOLARSHIP

Association on American Indian Affairs, Inc.
Attn: Director of Scholarship Programs
966 Hungerford Drive, Suite 12-B
Rockville, MD 20850
(240) 314-7155   Fax: (240) 314-7159
E-mail: lw.aaia@verizon.net
Web: www.indian-affairs.org

Summary To provide financial assistance for college to Native American students whose tribe is not federally recognized.

Eligibility This program is open to American Indian and Native Alaskan full-time undergraduate students. Applicants must be members of tribes that are either state-recognized or that are not federally recognized but are seeking federal recognition. Along with their application, they must submit documentation of financial need, a Certificate of Indian Blood showing at least one-quarter Indian blood (if available) or other verification of tribal involvement, an essay on their educational goals, 2 letters of recommendation, and their most recent transcript. Selection is based on need.

Financial data The stipend is $1,500.

Duration 1 year; recipients may reapply.

Number awarded Varies each year; recently, 4 of these scholarships were awarded.

Deadline June of each year.

[9]
ALMA EXLEY SCHOLARSHIP

Community Foundation of Greater New Britain
Attn: Scholarship Manager
74A Vine Street
New Britain, CT 06052-1431
(860) 229-6018, ext. 305   Fax: (860) 225-2666
E-mail: cfarmer@cfgnb.org
Web: www.cfgnb.org

Summary To provide financial assistance to Native American and other minority college students in Connecticut who are interested in preparing for a teaching career.

Eligibility This program is open to students of color (African Americans, Asian Americans, Hispanic Americans, and Native Americans) enrolled in a teacher preparation program in Connecticut. Applicant must 1) have been admitted to a traditional teacher preparation program at an accredited 4-year college or university in the state; or 2) be participating in the Alternate Route to Certification (ARC) program sponsored by the Connecticut Department of Higher Education.

Financial data The stipend is $1,500 per year for students at a 4-year college or university or $500 for a student in the ARC program.

Duration 2 years for students at 4-year colleges or universities; 1 year for students in the ARC program.

Number awarded 2 each year: 1 to a 4-year student and 1 to an ARC student.

Deadline October of each year.

[10]
ALYESKA MATCH SCHOLARSHIPS

Cook Inlet Tribal Council, Inc.
Attn: Tribal Scholarships and Grants Program
3600 San Jeronimo Drive, Suite 286
Anchorage, AK 99508
(907) 793-3578   Toll Free: (877) 985-5900
Fax: (907) 793-3589   E-mail: scholarships@citci.com
Web: www.citci.com/content/alyeska-match-scholarship

Summary To provide financial assistance to Alaska Natives who are working on an undergraduate degree or certificate at a school in any state in fields that will prepare them for employment on the Trans-Alaska Pipeline System (TAPS).

Eligibility This program is open to Alaska Natives who are enrolled in college or a vocational training program in any state. Applicants must be studying a field specified by Alyeska Pipeline Service Company that relates to future employment on the TAPS. Recently, those were limited to engineering (civil, electrical, mechanical, safety, engineering technology) and information technology. Applicants must be able to demonstrate unmet financial need even though they are receiving other funding. Awards are granted on a first-come, first-served basis.

Financial data The maximum stipend is $5,000. Awards are intended to be applied to tuition, fees, course-required books and supplies, and on-campus housing and meal plans only.

Duration 1 year; may be renewed up to 4 additional years if the recipient maintains a GPA of 2.0 or higher.

Additional information Funding for this program is provided by Alyeska Pipeline Service Company as part of its commitment under Section 29 of the Right of Way Agreement to provide scholarships to Alaska Natives.

Number awarded Varies each year.

Deadline May of each year for fall; November of each year for spring.

[11]
AMERICAN ADVERTISING FEDERATION FOURTH DISTRICT MOSAIC SCHOLARSHIP

American Advertising Federation-District 4
c/o Tami L. Grimes, Education Chair
4712 Southwood Lane
Lakeland, FL 33813
(863) 648-5392   E-mail: tamilgrimes@yahoo.com
Web: www.4aaf.com/scholarships.cfm

Summary To provide financial assistance to Native American and other minority undergraduate and graduate students from any state who are enrolled at colleges and universities in Florida and interested in entering the field of advertising.

Eligibility This program is open to undergraduate and graduate students from any state enrolled at accredited colleges and universities in Florida who are U.S. citizens or permanent residents of African, African American, Hispanic, Hispanic American, Indian, Native American, Asian, Asian American, or Pacific Islander descent. Applicants must be working on a bachelor's or master's degree in advertising, marketing, communications, public relations, art, graphic arts, or a related field. They must have an overall GPA of 3.0 or higher. Along with their application, they must submit a 250-word essay on why multiculturalism, diversity, and inclusion are important in the advertising, marketing, and communications industry today. Preference is given to members of the American Advertising Federation.

Financial data The stipend is $1,000.

Duration 1 year.

Number awarded 1 or more each year.

Deadline May of each year.

[12]
AMERICAN CHEMICAL SOCIETY SCHOLARS PROGRAM

American Chemical Society
Attn: Department of Diversity Programs
1155 16th Street, N.W.
Washington, DC 20036
(202) 872-6250   Toll Free: (800) 227-5558, ext. 6250
Fax: (202) 872-4361   E-mail: scholars@acs.org
Web: portal.acs.org

Summary To provide financial assistance to Native American and other underrepresented minority students who have a strong interest in chemistry and a desire to prepare for a career in a chemically-related science.

Eligibility This program is open to 1) college-bound high school seniors; 2) freshmen, sophomores, and juniors enrolled full time at an accredited college or university; 3) community college graduates and transfer students who plan to study for a bachelor's degree; and 4) community college freshmen. Applicants must be African American, Hispanic/Latino, or American Indian. They must be majoring or planning to major in chemistry, biochemistry, chemical engineering, or other chemically-related fields, such as environmental science, materials science, or toxicology, in preparation for a career in the chemical sciences or chemical technology. Students planning careers in medicine or pharmacy are not eligible. U.S. citizenship or permanent resident status is required. Selection is based on academic record (GPA of 3.0 or higher), career objective, leadership ability, participation in school activities, community service, and financial need.

Financial data Stipends range up to $5,000 per year. Funds are sent directly to the recipient's college or university.

Duration 1 year; may be renewed.

Additional information This program was established in 1994.

Number awarded Approximately 135 new awards are granted each year.

Deadline February of each year.

[13]
AMERICAN DIETETIC ASSOCIATION BACCALAUREATE (DIDACTIC OR COORDINATED PROGRAM) SCHOLARSHIPS

American Dietetic Association
Attn: Commission on Accreditation for Dietetics Education
120 South Riverside Plaza, Suite 2000
Chicago, IL 60606-6995
(312) 899-0040   Toll Free: (800) 877-1600, ext. 5400
Fax: (312) 899-4817   E-mail: education@eatright.org
Web: www.eatright.org/CADE/content.aspx?id=7934

Summary To provide financial assistance to Native Americans and other undergraduate student members of the American Dietetic Association (ADA).

Eligibility This program is open to ADA members enrolled at a CADE-accredited/approved college or university program for at least junior status in the dietetics program. Applicants must be U.S. citizens or permanent residents and show promise of being a valuable, contributing member of the profession. Some scholarships require membership in a specific dietetic practice group, residency in a specific state, or underrepresented minority group status. The same application form can be used for all categories.

Financial data Stipends range from $500 to $3,000; most are for $1,000.

Duration 1 year.

Number awarded Varies each year, depending upon the funds available; recently, the sponsoring organization awarded 222 scholarships for all its programs.

Deadline February of each year.

[14]
AMERICAN HEALTH INFORMATION MANAGEMENT ASSOCIATION FOUNDATION DIVERSITY SCHOLARSHIPS

American Health Information Management Association
Attn: AHIMA Foundation
233 North Michigan Avenue, 21st Floor
Chicago, IL 60601-5809
(312) 233-1175   Fax: (312) 233-1475
E-mail: info@ahimafoundation.org
Web: www.ahimafoundation.org

Summary To provide financial assistance to Native American and other members of the American Health Information Management Association (AHIMA) who are interested in working on an undergraduate degree in health information administration or technology and who will contribute to diversity in the profession.

Eligibility This program is open to AHIMA members who are enrolled at least half time in a program accredited by the Commission on Accreditation of Allied Health Education Programs. Applicants must be working on an associate degree in health information technology or a bachelor's degree in health information administration. They must have a GPA of 3.0 or higher and at least 1 full semester remaining after the date of the award. To qualify for this support, applicants must demonstrate how they will contribute to diversity in the health information management profession; diversity is defined as differences in race, ethnicity, nationality, gender, sexual orientation, socioeconomic status, age, physical capabilities, and religious beliefs. Financial need is not considered in the selection process.

Financial data Stipends are $1,000 for students working on an associate degree or $1,200 for students working on a bachelor's degree.

Duration 1 year.

Number awarded Varies each year; recently, 8 of these scholarships were awarded.

Deadline April or October of each year.

[15]
AMERICAN INDIAN COLLEGE FUND FOUNDATION SCHOLARSHIP

American Indian College Fund
Attn: Scholarship Department
8333 Greenwood Boulevard
Denver, CO 80221
(303) 426-8900   Toll Free: (800) 776-FUND
Fax: (303) 426-1200
E-mail: scholarships@collegefund.org
Web: www.collegefund.org

Summary To provide financial assistance to Native American college students from California who are enrolled at mainstream colleges and universities in any state.

Eligibility This program is open to American Indians and Alaska Natives who have proof of enrollment or descendancy and are residents of California or members or descendants of a California-based tribe. Applicants must be enrolled full time at a mainstream college or university in any state. They must have a GPA of 2.5 or higher and be able to demonstrate exceptional academic achievement or financial need. Applications are available only online and include required essays on specified topics.

Financial data The stipend is $3,000.

Duration 1 year.

Number awarded 1 or more each year.

Deadline May of each year.

[16]
AMERICAN INDIAN COMMUNITY COLLEGE SCHOLARSHIP

Scholarship Administrative Services, Inc.
Attn: MEFUSA Program
457 Ives Terrace
Sunnyvale, CA 94087

Summary To provide financial assistance to American Indian high school seniors who are interested in attending a community college.

Eligibility This program is open to American Indian seniors graduating from high schools anywhere in the United States. Applicants must be enrolled members of a federally-recognized tribal organization and planning to attend a community college on a full-time basis. Along with their application, they must submit a 1,000-word essay on their educational and career goals, how a community college education will help them to achieve those goals, and how they plan to serve the American Indian community after completing their education. Selection is based on the essay, high school GPA (2.5 or higher), SAT or ACT scores, involvement in the American Indian community, and financial need.

Financial data The stipend is $5,000 per year.

Duration 1 year; may be renewed 1 additional year if the recipient maintains full-time enrollment and a GPA of 2.5 or higher.

Additional information This program is sponsored by the Minority Educational Foundation of the United States of America (MEFUSA) and administered by Scholarship Administrative Services, Inc. MEFUSA was established in 2001 to meet the needs of minority students who "show a determination to get a college degree," but who, for financial or other personal reasons, are not able to attend a 4-year college or university. Requests for applications should be accompanied by a self-addressed stamped envelope, the student's e-mail address, and the name of the source where they found the scholarship information.

Number awarded Up to 100 each year.

Deadline April of each year.

[17]
AMERICAN INDIAN EDUCATION AND OPPORTUNITY FUND SCHOLARSHIP

American Indian Chamber of Commerce of Texas
11245 Indian Trail, Second Floor
Dallas, TX 75229
(972) 241-6450   Fax: (972) 241-6454
E-mail: tmarshall@aicct.com
Web: www.aicct.com

Summary To provide financial assistance to American Indians from Texas who are interested in attending college in any state.

Eligibility This program is open to residents of Texas who are American Indians and at least 16 years of age. Applicants must be enrolled or planning to enroll full time at an accredited postsecondary educational institution in any state. They must have a GPA of 2.0 or higher in their previous course work. Along with their application, they must submit a 250-word essay on how their degree will help the American Indian community. Selection is based on GPA, planned major and how it will be used to aid American Indians or their community, community service (especially involving tribal culture, language, or heritage), recommendations, and financial need.

Financial data A stipend is awarded (amount not specified).

Duration 1 year; recipients may reapply.

Number awarded 1 or more each year.

Deadline May of each year.

[18]
AMERICAN INDIAN EDUCATION FOUNDATION SCHOLARSHIP PROGRAM

American Indian Education Foundation
2401 Eglin Street
Rapid City, SD 57703
Toll Free: (866) 866-8642   E-mail: mlee@nrc1.org
Web: www.nrcprograms.org

Summary To provide financial assistance for college to American Indian and Alaskan Native students.

Eligibility This program is open to full-time students of Native American or Alaskan Native descent who are currently attending or planning to attend a 2-year college, a 4-year college or university, or a vocational/technical school. Applicants may be either graduating high school seniors or undergraduates who are entering, continuing, or returning to school. Along with their application, they must submit a 4-page essay in which they describe themselves as a student, their ultimate career goals, their plans for working in or with the Indian community, and their participation in leadership and/or community service activities. A GPA between 2.0 and 3.4 is desirable, but all current or future undergraduate students are encouraged to apply. An ACT score of 14 or higher is desirable. Financial need is considered in the selection process.

Financial data   The stipend is $2,000 per year. Funds are paid directly to the recipient's college or university.

Duration   1 year; may be renewed, provided the recipient maintains a GPA of 2.0 or higher.

Number awarded   More than 225 each year.

Deadline   April of each year.

[19]
AMERICAN INDIAN MUSEUM FELLOWSHIP PROGRAM

Minnesota Humanities Center
Attn: Grant Program Staff
987 Ivy Avenue East
St. Paul, MN 55106-2046
(651) 774-0105   Toll Free: (866) 268-7293
Fax: (651) 774-0205   E-mail: chris.taylor@mnhs.org
Web: www.minnesotahumanities.org/museumfellowship

Summary   To provide an opportunity for American Indian students from any state to learn about tribal historic preservation and museum studies during a summer program at sites in Minnesota.

Eligibility   This program is open to American Indian undergraduates who may be residents of any state and are not required to be tribally enrolled. Applicants must be interested in a summer training program in tribal historic preservation and museum studies. Along with their application, they must submit brief descriptions of 1) why they are interested in this program and how they believe their participation might benefit their community; and 2) how their academic and personal experiences will contribute to seminar discussions related to tribal historic preservation and the representation of American Indian communities in historical organizations.

Financial data   The program provides payment of all travel expenses, housing, meals, and a $1,000 stipend upon completion.

Duration   15 days during the summer.

Additional information   This program operates as a partnership between the Minnesota Humanities Center and the Minnesota Historical Society. Activities take place at the Minnesota Humanities Center in St. Paul and the Mille Lacs Indian Museum in Onamia, Minnesota.

Number awarded   15 each year.

Deadline   February of each year.

[20]
AMERICAN INDIAN SCHOLARSHIPS

Daughters of the American Revolution-National Society
Attn: Committee Services Office, Scholarships
1776 D Street, N.W.
Washington, DC 20006-5303
(202) 628-1776
Web: www.dar.org/natsociety/edout_scholar.cfm

Summary   To provide supplementary financial assistance to Native American students who are interested in working on an undergraduate or graduate degree.

Eligibility   This program is open to Native Americans of any age, any tribe, in any state who are enrolled or planning to enroll in a college, university, or vocational school. Applicants must have a GPA of 2.75 or higher. Graduate students are eligible, but undergraduate students receive preference. Selection is based on academic achievement and financial need.

Financial data   The stipend is $1,000. The funds are paid directly to the recipient's college.

Duration   This is a 1-time award.

Number awarded   1 each year.

Deadline   March of each year.

[21]
AMERICAN INDIAN SCIENCE AND ENGINEERING SOCIETY INTERNSHIP PROGRAM

American Indian Science and Engineering Society
Attn: Program Officer
2305 Renard, S.E., Suite 200
P.O. Box 9828
Albuquerque, NM 87119-9828
(505) 765-1052, ext. 105   Fax: (505) 765-5608
E-mail: tina@aises.org
Web: www.aises.org

Summary   To provide summer work experience with federal agencies or other partner organizations to American Indian and Alaska Native college students who are members of the American Indian Science and Engineering Society (AISES).

Eligibility   This program is open to AISES members who are full-time college or university sophomores, juniors, seniors, or graduate students with a GPA of 3.0 or higher. Applicants must be American Indians or Alaska Natives interested in working at selected sites with a partner organization. They must submit an application that includes an essay on their reasons for participating in the program, how it relates to their academic and career goals, what makes them a strong candidate for the program, what they hope to learn and gain as a result, and their leadership skills and experience. U.S. citizenship is required for most positions, although permanent residents may be eligible at some agencies.

Financial data   Interns receive a weekly stipend, dormitory lodging, round-trip airfare or mileage to the internship site, and an allowance for local transportation.

Duration   10 weeks during the summer.

Additional information   Recently, internships were available at the Arctic Slope Regional Corporation Federal Holding Company (in Greenbelt, Maryland), AMERIND Rick Management Corporation (in Santa Ana Pueblo, New Mexico), NASA Goddard Space Flight Center (in Greenbelt, Maryland), NASA Glenn Research Center (in Cleveland, Ohio), the Bonneville Power Administration (in Portland, Oregon), and the U.S. Department of Veterans Affairs (in Washington, D.C. and other locations).

Number awarded   Varies each year.

Deadline   February of each year.

[22]
AMERICAN INDIAN SERVICES SCHOLARSHIP PROGRAM

American Indian Services
1902 North Canyon Road, Suite 100
Provo, UT 84604
(801) 375-1777   Toll Free: (888) 227-4120
Fax: (801) 375-1643
E-mail: ais@americanindianservices.org
Web: www.americanindianservices.org/students.html

Summary To provide financial assistance for college to Native Americans who demonstrate financial need.

Eligibility This program is open to undergraduate students who have completed no more than 150 semester credits at a university, college, junior college, or technical school with a GPA of 2.25 or higher. Applicants must be able to document their Indian heritage with a Certificate of Indian Blood (CIB), another official document, or an official document for their parent or grandparent. They must be at least one-quarter North American Native Indian blood. Along with their application, they must submit a 1-page letter about themselves, including their tribe, where they are from, the school they are attending, their area of study, their educational goals and future plans, and why they feel they need this scholarship. Selection is based on financial need, academic status, and availability of funds.

Financial data Students are expected to arrange for payment of half their tuition. This program pays the other half, from $200 to $1,500.

Duration 1 semester; may be renewed if the recipient maintains a GPA of 2.25 or higher.

Number awarded Recently, more than 1,500 of these scholarships were awarded.

Deadline February of each year for classes starting in April or May; May of each year for classes starting in June; August of each year for classes starting in August or September; November of each year for classes starting in January.

[23]
AMERICAN METEOROLOGICAL SOCIETY UNDERGRADUATE NAMED SCHOLARSHIPS

American Meteorological Society
Attn: Fellowship/Scholarship Program
45 Beacon Street
Boston, MA 02108-3693
(617) 227-2426, ext. 246   Fax: (617) 742-8718
E-mail: scholar@ametsoc.org
Web: www.ametsoc.org

Summary To provide financial assistance to undergraduates (particularly Native Americans, other underrepresented minorities, women, and individuals with disabilities) who are majoring in meteorology or an aspect of atmospheric sciences.

Eligibility This program is open to full-time students entering their final year of undergraduate study and majoring in meteorology or an aspect of the atmospheric or related oceanic and hydrologic sciences. Applicants must intend to make atmospheric or related sciences their career. They must be U.S. citizens or permanent residents enrolled at a U.S. institution and have a cumulative GPA of 3.25 or higher. Along with their application, they must submit 200-word essays on 1) their most important attributes and achievements that qualify them for this scholarship, and 2) their career goals in the atmospheric or related sciences. Financial need is considered in the selection process. The sponsor specifically encourages applications from women, minorities, and students with disabilities who are traditionally underrepresented in the atmospheric and related oceanic sciences.

Financial data Stipend amounts vary each year.

Duration 1 year.

Additional information All scholarships awarded through this program are named after individuals who have assisted the sponsor in various ways.

Number awarded Varies each year; recently, 20 of these scholarships were awarded.

Deadline February of each year.

[24]
AMY LOUISE HUNTER-WILSON, M.D. MEMORIAL SCHOLARSHIP

Wisconsin Medical Society
Attn: Executive Director, Wisconsin Medical Society Foundation
330 East Lakeside Street
P.O. Box 1109
Madison, WI 53701-1109
(608) 442-3722   Toll Free: (866) 442-3800, ext. 3722
Fax: (608) 442-3851   E-mail: eileen.wilson@wismed.org
Web: www.wisconsinmedicalsociety.org

Summary To provide financial assistance to American Indians interested in working on a degree in medicine, nursing, or allied health care.

Eligibility This program is open to members of federally-recognized American Indian tribes who are 1) full-time students enrolled in a health career program at an accredited institution, 2) adults returning to school in an allied health field, and 3) adults working in a non-professional health-related field returning for a professional license or degree. Applicants must be working on a degree or advanced training as a doctor of medicine, nurse, physician assistant, technician, or other health-related professional. Along with their application, they must submit a personal statement of 1 to 2 pages on their family background, achievements, current higher educational status, career goals, and financial need. Preference is given to residents of Wisconsin who are students at educational institutions in the state. U.S. citizenship is required. Selection is based on financial need, academic achievement, personal qualities and strengths, and letters of recommendation.

Financial data Stipends range from $1,000 to $4,000.

Duration 1 year.

Number awarded Varies each year.

Deadline January of each year.

[25]
ANA MULTICULTURAL EXCELLENCE SCHOLARSHIP

American Association of Advertising Agencies
Attn: AAAA Foundation
405 Lexington Avenue, 18th Floor
New York, NY 10174-1801
(212) 682-2500   Toll Free: (800) 676-9333
Fax: (212) 682-2028   E-mail: ameadows@aaaa.org
Web: www2.aaaa.org

Summary To provide financial assistance to Native American and other multicultural students who are working on an undergraduate degree in advertising.

Eligibility This program is open to undergraduate students who are U.S. citizens of proven multicultural heritage and have at least 1 grandparent of multicultural heritage. Applicants must be participating in the Multicultural Advertising

Intern Program (MAIP). They must be entering their senior year at an accredited college or university in the United States and have a GPA of 3.0 or higher. Selection is based on academic ability.

Financial data The stipend is $2,000.

Duration 1 year.

Additional information This program was established by the Association of National Advertisers (ANA) in 2001. The American Association of Advertising Agencies (AAAA) assumed administration in 2003.

Number awarded 3 each year.

Deadline Deadline not specified.

[26]
ANDREW GRONHOLDT SCHOLARSHIP AWARD

The Aleut Corporation
Attn: Aleut Foundation
703 West Tudor Road, Suite 102
Anchorage, AK 99503-6650
(907) 646-1929   Toll Free: (800) 232-4882
Fax: (907) 646-1949   E-mail: taf@thealeutfoundation.org
Web: www.thealeutfoundation.org/ScholarshipGuide.aspx

Summary To provide financial assistance to Native Alaskans who are shareholders of The Aleut Corporation or their descendants and working on a degree in the arts at a school in any state.

Eligibility This program is open to Native Alaskans who are original enrollees or descendants of original enrollees of The Aleut Corporation (TAC). Applicants must have completed at least 1 year of a bachelor's, 2- or 4-year vocational, or master's degree in the arts at a school in any state. They must be enrolled full time and have a GPA of 3.0 or higher. Along with their application, they must include a letter of intent, up to 500 words in length, that describes their educational goals and objectives and their expected graduation date.

Financial data A stipend is awarded (amount not specified).

Duration 1 year.

Additional information The Aleut Corporation is 1 of 13 Alaska Native Regional Corporations created under the Alaska Native Claims Settlement Act of 1971.

Number awarded 1 each year.

Deadline June of each year.

[27]
ANS ACCELERATOR APPLICATIONS DIVISION SCHOLARSHIP

American Nuclear Society
Attn: Scholarship Coordinator
555 North Kensington Avenue
La Grange Park, IL 60526-5592
(708) 352-6611   Toll Free: (800) 323-3044
Fax: (708) 352-0499   E-mail: outreach@ans.org
Web: www.ans.org/honors/scholarships/aad.html

Summary To provide financial assistance to undergraduate students (particularly Native Americans, other minorities, and women) who are interested in preparing for a career dealing with accelerator applications aspects of nuclear science or nuclear engineering.

Eligibility This program is open to students entering their junior year in physics, engineering, or materials science at an accredited institution in the United States. Applicants must submit a description of their long- and short-term professional objectives, including their research interests related to accelerator aspects of nuclear science and engineering. Selection is based on that statement, faculty recommendations, and academic performance. Special consideration is given to members of underrepresented groups (women and minorities), students who can demonstrate financial need, and applicants who have a record of service to the American Nuclear Society (ANS).

Financial data The stipend is $1,000 per year.

Duration 1 year (the junior year); may be renewed for the senior year.

Additional information This program is offered by the Accelerator Applications Division (AAD) of the ANS.

Number awarded 1 each year.

Deadline January of each year.

[28]
ANTHC SCHOLARSHIPS

Alaska Native Tribal Health Consortium
Attn: Education, Development and Training Department
4000 Ambassador Drive, Suite 114
Anchorage, AK 99508
(907) 729-1917   Toll Free: (800) 684-8361
Fax: (907) 729-1335   E-mail: anthceducation@anthc.org
Web: www.anthc.org/jt/int

Summary To provide financial assistance for college or graduate school to Alaska Natives and American Indians who are residents of Alaska and interested in a career in health care.

Eligibility This program is open to Alaska Natives and American Indians who are undergraduates or graduate students interested in preparing for a career in the field of health care. Applicants must be residents of Alaska enrolled full time. Along with their application, they must submit a resume, 3 letters of recommendation, documentation of financial need, and a 1-page personal statement that covers their personal and educational history, accomplishments, educational and career goals, involvement in the Native community, and how this scholarship and degree program contribute to their career goals.

Financial data The stipend is $5,000 per year.

Duration 1 year; may be renewed if they maintain a minimum GPA of 2.0 for undergraduates or 3.0 for graduate students.

Number awarded 10 each year: 5 for undergraduate students and 5 for graduate students.

Deadline February of each year.

[29]
ANTHC SUMMER INTERNSHIPS

Alaska Native Tribal Health Consortium
Attn: Education, Development and Training Department
4000 Ambassador Drive, Suite 114
Anchorage, AK 99508
(907) 729-1917   Toll Free: (800) 684-8361
Fax: (907) 729-1335   E-mail: anthceducation@anthc.org
Web: www.anthc.org/jt/int

Summary To provide summer work experience at the Alaska Native Tribal Health Consortium (ANTHC) to Native Alaskan and American Indian high school, undergraduate, and graduate students.

Eligibility This program is open to Alaska Natives and American Indians who are high school students, undergraduates, graduate students, and recipients during the past 6 months of a GED, diploma, or degree. Applicants must be residents of Alaska and interested in an internship at ANTHC in such areas as finance, human resources, health records, computer technology, engineering, maintenance, or housekeeping. Along with their application, they must submit a resume, documentation of financial need, and a 1-page personal statement that covers their personal and educational history, accomplishments, educational and career goals, involvement in the Native community, and how this internship corresponds with their career goals.

Financial data These are paid internships.

Duration 9 weeks during the summer.

Number awarded Approximately 25 each year: 20 for high school and undergraduate students and 5 for graduate students.

Deadline February of each year.

[30]
APS SCHOLARSHIPS FOR MINORITY UNDERGRADUATE PHYSICS MAJORS

American Physical Society
Attn: Committee on Minorities
One Physics Ellipse
College Park, MD 20740-3844
(301) 209-3232   Fax: (301) 209-0865
Web: www.aps.org

Summary To provide financial assistance to Native American and other underrepresented minority students interested in studying physics on the undergraduate level.

Eligibility Any Native American, African American, or Hispanic American who plans to major in physics and who is a high school senior or college freshman or sophomore may apply. U.S. citizenship or permanent resident status is required. The selection committee especially encourages applications from students who are attending or planning to attend institutions with historically or predominantly Black, Hispanic, or Native American enrollment. Selection is based on commitment to the study of physics and plans to work on a physics baccalaureate degree.

Financial data Stipends are $2,000 per year in the first year or $3,000 in the second year; funds must be used for tuition, room, and board. In addition, $500 is awarded to the host department.

Duration 1 year; renewable for 1 additional year with the approval of the APS selection committee.

Additional information APS conducts this program, which began in 1980 as the Corporate-Sponsored Scholarships for Minority Undergraduate Students Who Major in Physics, in conjunction with the Corporate Associates of the American Institute of Physics. Each scholarship is sponsored by a corporation, which is normally designated as the sponsor. A corporation generally sponsors from 1 to 10 scholarships, depending upon its size and utilization of physics in the business.

Number awarded Varies each year; recently, 40 of these scholarships were awarded.

Deadline February of each year.

[31]
AQQALUK TRUST SCHOLARSHIPS

Robert Aqqaluk Newlin, Sr. Memorial Trust
Attn: Education Coordinator
P.O. Box 509
Kotzebue, AK 99752
(907) 442-8143   Toll Free: (866) 442-1607
Fax: (907) 442-2289
E-mail: claudia.tiepelman@nana.com
Web: www.aqqaluktrust.com/pages/scholarship.html

Summary To provide financial assistance to Alaska Natives who are associated with the Northwest Alaska Native Association (NANA) Regional Corporation and interested in attending college in any state.

Eligibility This program is open to NANA shareholders, descendants of NANA shareholders, and dependents of NANA shareholders and their descendants. Applicants must have a GED or high school diploma with a cumulative GPA of 2.0 or higher and be enrolled or accepted for enrollment at an accredited or authorized college, university, or vocational technical skills program in any state. Along with their application, they must submit a statement that explains how they intend to use their education to enhance Inupiaq values and culture, summarizes their accomplishments, and describes their educational and career goals.

Financial data Stipends are $2,000 per semester for full-time students or $1,000 per semester for part-time students. Funds must be used for tuition, fees, books, course-related supplies, room, board, and similar expenses.

Duration 1 semester; recipients may reapply by providing a letter updating their educational and career goals, explaining how they are moving toward their goals, and reporting how the previous funds were spend.

Additional information The NANA Regional Corporation is 1 of 13 regional corporations established according to the terms of the Alaska Native Claims Settlement Act (ANCSA) of 1971. It originally administered its scholarship program, but later transferred its education department to the Robert Aqqaluk Newlin, Sr. Memorial Trust. Sponsors of the program include the NANA Regional Corporation, Teck Alaska Inc., and Qivliq, LLC.

Number awarded Varies each year, depending upon the availability of funds and qualified applicants.

Deadline College and university students must apply by July of each year for fall semester or quarter, October of each year for winter quarter, January of each year for spring semester, February of each year for spring quarter, or May of each year for summer school. Vocational/technical students must apply before the start of training.

[32]
ARAPAHO EDUCATIONAL TRUST SCHOLARSHIP

Northern Arapaho Tribe
Attn: Sky People Higher Education
P.O. Box 8480
Ethete, WY 82520
(307) 332-5286   Toll Free: (800) 815-6795
Fax: (307) 332-9104   E-mail: assistant@skypeopleed.org
Web: www.skypeopleed.org

Summary   To provide financial assistance to members of the Northern Arapaho Tribe who are working on an undergraduate or graduate degree in engineering, law, or the sciences.

Eligibility   This program is open to full-time undergraduate and graduate students who have an undergraduate GPA of 2.0 or higher or the graduate GPA required by their school. Applicants must be of at least one-fourth Northern Arapaho descent (enrolled or non-enrolled) and must submit a Certificate of Indian Blood or other verification of Northern Arapaho blood. They must be working on a degree in engineering, law, or the sciences. Along with their application, they must submit a 1-page personal statement that includes a brief history of their background, academic ability and achievement, work or leadership experience, participation in community-related activities, and career goals. Selection is based on that statement, potential to contribute to the community upon graduation, academic ability and achievement, and a letter of recommendation.

Financial data   The stipend is $1,500 per year.

Duration   1 year; may be renewed.

Additional information   The recipient is expected to apply for employment with the Northern Arapaho Tribe after graduation.

Number awarded   1 each year.

Deadline   June of each year.

[33]
ARAPAHO RANCH EDUCATIONAL TRUST SCHOLARSHIP

Northern Arapaho Tribe
Attn: Sky People Higher Education
P.O. Box 8480
Ethete, WY 82520
(307) 332-5286   Toll Free: (800) 815-6795
Fax: (307) 332-9104   E-mail: assistant@skypeopleed.org
Web: www.skypeopleed.org

Summary   To provide financial assistance to members of the Northern Arapaho Tribe who are working on an undergraduate or graduate degree in conservation-related fields.

Eligibility   This program is open to full-time undergraduate and graduate students who have an undergraduate GPA of 2.0 or higher or the graduate GPA required by their school. Applicants must be of at least one-fourth Northern Arapaho descent (enrolled or non-enrolled) and must submit a Certificate of Indian Blood or other verification of Northern Arapaho blood with at least one-fourth degree. They must be working on a degree in range conservation, forestry, animal sciences, or ranch and range management. Along with their application, they must submit a 1-page personal statement that includes a brief history of their background, academic ability and achievement, work or leadership experience, participa-

tion in community-related activities, and career goals. Selection is based on that statement, potential to contribute to the community upon graduation, academic ability and achievement, and a letter of recommendation.

Financial data   The stipend is $2,000 per year.

Duration   1 year; may be renewed.

Number awarded   1 each year.

Deadline   June of each year.

[34]
ARCTIC EDUCATION FOUNDATION SCHOLARSHIPS

Arctic Slope Regional Corporation
Attn: Arctic Education Foundation
P.O. Box 129
Barrow, AK 99723
(907) 852-8633   Toll Free: (800) 770-2772
Fax: (907) 852-2774   E-mail: mjkaleak@asrc.com
Web: www.articed.com

Summary   To provide financial assistance Inupiat Natives who are shareholders or descendants of shareholders of the Arctic Slope Regional Corporation (ASRC) and plan to attend college or graduate school in any state.

Eligibility   This program is open to U.S. citizens who are 1) a northern Alaskan Inupiat Native currently residing in the Arctic Slope region of Alaska; 2) an original shareholder of the ASRC; or 3) a direct lineal descendant of an original ASRC shareholder. Applicants must be attending or planning to attend a college, university, or vocational/technical school in any state as a full- or part-time undergraduate or graduate student. Along with their application, they must submit documentation of financial need and a short paragraph on their personal plans upon completion of study.

Financial data   For full-time students at 4-year colleges and universities, the maximum stipend is $6,000 per year. For students in vocational training programs, the maximum stipend is $2,500 per term ($5,000 per year).

Duration   1 year; may be renewed.

Additional information   The Arctic Slope Regional Corporation is 1 of 13 Alaska Native Regional Corporations created under the Alaska Native Claims Settlement Act of 1971.

Number awarded   Varies each year.

Deadline   February of each year for spring quarter or early summer; April of each year for summer school; July of each year for fall semester or quarter; or November of each year for spring semester or winter quarter.

[35]
ARKANSAS CONFERENCE ETHNIC LOCAL CHURCH CONCERNS SCHOLARSHIPS

United Methodist Church-Arkansas Conference
Attn: Committee on Ethnic Local Church Concerns
800 Daisy Bates Drive
Little Rock, AR 72202
(501) 324-8045   Toll Free: (877) 646-1816
Fax: (501) 324-8018   E-mail: mallen@arumc.org
Web: www.arumc.org

Summary   To provide financial assistance to Native American and other minority Methodist students from Arkansas who are interested in attending college or graduate school in any state.

Eligibility This program is open to ethnic minority undergraduate and graduate students who are active members of local congregations affiliated with the Arkansas Conference of the United Methodist Church (UMC). Applicants must be currently enrolled in an accredited institution of higher education in any state. Along with their application, they must submit a transcript (GPA of 2.0 or higher) and documentation of participation in local church activities. Preference is given to students attending a UMC-affiliated college or university.

Financial data The stipend is $500 per semester ($1,000 per year) for undergraduates or $1,000 per semester ($2,000 per year) for graduate students.

Duration 1 year; may be renewed.

Number awarded 1 or more each year.

Deadline September of each year.

[36]
ARKANSAS MINORITY TEACHERS SCHOLARSHIPS

Arkansas Department of Higher Education
Attn: Financial Aid Division
114 East Capitol Avenue
Little Rock, AR 72201-3818
(501) 371-2050   Toll Free: (800) 54-STUDY
Fax: (501) 371-2001   E-mail: finaid@adhe.edu
Web: www.adhe.edu

Summary To provide funding to Native American and other minority undergraduates in Arkansas who want to become teachers in the state.

Eligibility This program is open to minority (African American, Native American, Hispanic, or Asian American) residents of Arkansas who are U.S. citizens or permanent residents and enrolled full time as juniors or seniors in an approved teacher certification program at an Arkansas public or independent 4-year institution. Applicants must have a cumulative GPA of 2.5 or higher and be willing to teach in an Arkansas public school for at least 5 years after completion of their teaching certificate (3 years if the teaching is in 1 of the 42 counties of Arkansas designated as the Delta Region, or if the teaching is in a critical subject shortage area, or if the recipient is an African American male teaching at the elementary level).

Financial data Loans up to $5,000 per year are available. The loan will be forgiven at the rate of 20% for each year the recipient teaches full time in an Arkansas public school (or 33% per year if the obligation is fulfilled in 3 years). If the loan is not forgiven by service, it must be repaid with interest at 10%.

Duration 1 year; may be renewed for 1 additional year if the recipient remains enrolled full time with a GPA of 2.5 or higher.

Additional information Recently, the critical subject shortage areas included art (K-12), foreign language (French, German, Spanish), mathematics (secondary), middle childhood (4-8 mathematics and science, 4-8 English language arts or social studies), science (secondary life or physical), or special education (deaf education, visually impaired, instructional specialist).

Number awarded Varies each year; recently, 97 of these forgivable loans were approved.

Deadline May of each year.

[37]
ARMY MINORITY COLLEGE RELATIONS PROGRAM INTERNSHIPS

Vista Sciences Corporation
Attn: Intern Program Manager
7700 Alabama Street, Suite E
El Paso, TX 79904
(915) 757-3331   Fax: (915) 757-3371
E-mail: romy.ledesma@vistasciences.com
Web: www.vistasciences.com/services.asp?service=19

Summary To provide work experience at U.S. Army facilities to upper-division and graduate students at Tribal Colleges and Universities (TCUs) or other minority institutions.

Eligibility This program is open to students working on an undergraduate or graduate degree at Historically Black Colleges and Universities (HBCUs), Hispanic Serving Institutions (HSIs), or Tribal Colleges and Universities (TCUs). Applicants must be U.S. citizens currently enrolled as a junior or above and have a GPA of 2.5 or higher; recent (within 6 months) graduates are also eligible. They must be interested in an internship at an Army facility in such fields as engineering (civil, computer, construction, electrical, environmental), sciences (agronomy, biology, environmental, natural resources, safety), business (accounting, finance, legal, management, marketing, operations), computer science and engineering (data management, information systems, information technology, languages, programming, trouble shooting, website/webpage design and management), or other (communications, English, history, human resources, journalism, library sciences, mathematics, public administration, public relations, quality control, risk management, statistics, training development and management). Along with their application, they must submit a resume and a transcript.

Financial data Interns are paid a stipend of $500 per week and are reimbursed for housing and transportation costs.

Duration 10 weeks in the summer or 15 weeks in spring.

Additional information This program, which began in 1997, is currently administered by Vista Sciences Corporation under a contract with the Army. Recently, assignments were available at the Crane Army Ammunition Activity (Crane, Indiana), Sierra Army Depot (Herlong, California), McAlester Army Ammunition Plant (McAlester, Oklahoma), Blue Grass Army Depot (Richmond, Kentucky), Rock Island Arsenal (Rock Island, Illinois), Anniston Defense Munitions Center (Anniston, Alabama), Pine Bluff Arsenal (Pine Bluff, Arkansas), and Tooele Army Depot (Tooele, Utah).

Number awarded Varies each year.

Deadline May of each year for summer; November of each year for spring.

[38]
ASLA COUNCIL OF FELLOWS SCHOLARSHIPS

Landscape Architecture Foundation
Attn: Scholarship Program
818 18th Street, N.W., Suite 810
Washington, DC 20006-3520
(202) 331-7070   Fax: (202) 331-7079
E-mail: scholarships@lafoundation.org
Web: www.laprofession.org/financial/scholarships.htm

Summary To provide financial assistance to upper-division students, especially Native Americans and those from other disadvantaged and underrepresented groups, who are working on a degree in landscape architecture.

Eligibility This program is open to landscape architecture students in the third, fourth, or fifth year of undergraduate work. Preference is given to, and 1 scholarship is reserved for, members of underrepresented ethnic or cultural groups. Applicants must submit a 300-word essay on how they envision themselves contributing to the profession of landscape architecture, 2 letters of recommendation, documentation of financial need, and (for students applying for the scholarship reserved for underrepresented groups) a statement identifying their association with a specific ethnic or cultural group. U.S. citizenship or permanent resident status is required.

Financial data The stipend is $4,000. Students also receive a 1-year membership in the American Society of Landscape Architecture (ASLA), general registration fees for the ASLA annual meeting, and a travel stipend to attend the meeting.

Duration 1 year.

Additional information This program is sponsored by ASLA and administered by the Landscape Architecture Foundation.

Number awarded 2 each year.

Deadline February of each year.

[39]
ASSOCIATED FOOD AND PETROLEUM DEALERS MINORITY SCHOLARSHIPS

Associated Food and Petroleum Dealers
Attn: AFPD Foundation
30415 West 13 Mile Road
Farmington Hills, MI 48334
(248) 671-9600   Toll Free: (800) 666-6233
Fax: (248) 671-9610   E-mail: info@afdom.org
Web: www.afpdonline.org

Summary To provide financial assistance to Native American and other minority high school seniors and current college students from Michigan who are enrolled or planning to enroll at a college in any state.

Eligibility This program is open to Michigan residents who are high school seniors or college freshmen, sophomores, or juniors. Applicants must be members of 1 of the following minority groups: African American, Hispanic, Asian, Native American, or Arab/Chaldean. They must be enrolled or planning to enroll full time at a college or university in any state. Preferential consideration is given to applicants with a membership affiliation in the Associated Food and Petroleum Dealers (AFPD), although membership is not required. Selection is based on academic performance, leadership, and participation in school and community activities; college grades are considered if the applicant is already enrolled in college.

Financial data The stipend is $1,500.

Duration 1 year; nonrenewable.

Additional information This program is administered by International Scholarship and Tuition Services, Inc. The AFPD was formed in 2006 by a merger of the Associated Food Dealers of Michigan and the Great Lakes Petroleum Retailers and Allied Trades Association.

Number awarded At least 10 each year, of which at least 3 must be awarded to member customers.

Deadline March of each year.

[40]
ASSOCIATION FOR WOMEN IN SCIENCE INTERNSHIPS

Association for Women in Science
Attn: Internship Coordinator
1442 Duke Street
Alexandria, VA 22314
(703) 372-4380   Toll Free: (800) 886-AWIS
Fax: (703) 778-7807   E-mail: awis@awis.org
Web: www.awis.org/careers/internship.html

Summary To provide an opportunity for Native American and other underrepresented minority female undergraduates to gain summer work experience at the offices of the Association for Women in Science (AWIS) in the Washington, D.C. area.

Eligibility This program is open to women who are working on an undergraduate degree in a field of science, technology, engineering, or mathematics (STEM) and interested in a summer internship at AWIS. Applicants must be members of a group currently underrepresented in STEM fields (African Americans, Latinas/Hispanics, Native Americans, and Pacific Islanders). Along with their application, they must submit a resume, cover letter, writing sample, and letter of recommendation.

Financial data The stipend is $3,500.

Duration 10 weeks during the summer.

Additional information Interns may be assigned to publish the Washington Wire, contribute to the *AWIS Magazine,* develop content for the AWIS web site, advocate at Capitol Hill briefings, conduct research grants, perform special projects affiliated with AWIS committees, and interact with board members and top STEM professionals.

Number awarded Varies each year.

Deadline March of each year.

[41]
A.T. ANDERSON MEMORIAL SCHOLARSHIP PROGRAM

American Indian Science and Engineering Society
Attn: Program Officer
2305 Renard, S.E., Suite 200
P.O. Box 9828
Albuquerque, NM 87119-9828
(505) 765-1052, ext. 105   Fax: (505) 765-5608
E-mail: tina@aises.org
Web: www.aises.org

Summary To provide financial assistance to members of the American Indian Science and Engineering Society who are majoring in designated fields as undergraduate or graduate students.

Eligibility This program is open to members of the society who can furnish a Certificate of Indian Blood or proof of enrollment in an American Indian tribe or Alaskan Native group. Applicants must be full-time students at the undergraduate or graduate level attending an accredited 4-year college or university or a 2-year college leading to an academic degree in engineering, mathematics, medicine, natural resources, or the sciences. They must have a GPA of 3.0 or higher. Along with their application, they must submit a 500-word essay on their educational and career goals, including their interest in and motivation to continue higher education, an understanding of the importance of college and completing their educational and/or career goals, and a commitment to learning and giving back to the community. Selection is based on that essay (40%), GPA (35%), letters of recommendation (15%), and overall impression of the application (10%).

Financial data The annual stipend is $1,000 for undergraduates or $2,000 for graduate students.

Duration 1 year; nonrenewable.

Additional information This program was launched in 1983 in memory of A.T. Anderson, a Mohawk and a chemical engineer who worked with Albert Einstein. Anderson was 1 of the society's founders and was the society's first executive director. The program includes the following named awards: the Al Qöyawayma Award for an applicant who is majoring in science or engineering and also has a strong interest in the arts, the Norbert S. Hill, Jr. Leadership Award, the Polingaysi Qöyawayma Award for an applicant who is working on a teaching degree in order to teach mathematics or science in a Native community or an advanced degree for personal improvement or teaching at the college level, and the Robert W. Brocksbank Scholarship.

Number awarded Varies; generally, 200 or more each year, depending upon the availability of funds from corporate and other sponsors.

Deadline June of each year.

[42]
AT-LARGE TRIBAL COUNCIL AWARD

Cherokee Nation
Attn: Cherokee Nation Education Corporation
115 East Delaware Street
P.O. Box 948
Tahlequah, OK 74465-0948
(918) 207-0950   Fax: (918) 207-0951
E-mail: contact@cnec-edu.org
Web: cnec.cherokee.org

Summary To provide financial assistance to high school senior citizens of the Cherokee Nation who are planning to attend college in any state and who reside outside the tribal jurisdictional boundaries.

Eligibility This program is open to citizens of the Cherokee Nation who are graduating from high schools outside the jurisdictional area of the tribe. Applicants must be planning to enroll at a college, university, or vocational/technical school in any state. Along with their application, they must submit a 4-page personal essay that includes background information, their degree plan for higher education, why they have chosen that field of study, how they plan to serve Cherokee people when they complete higher education, and why they should be selected for this scholarship. Selection is based on the clarity and presentation of the essay; academic information (including transcripts and ACT scores); school, cultural and community activities; future plans to serve Cherokee people; and financial need.

Financial data The stipend is $1,500 per semester ($3,000 per year).

Duration 1 year. Renewal for the second semester requires the recipient to earn a GPA of 2.5 or higher in the first semester.

Additional information These scholarships were first awarded in 2008.

Number awarded Varies each year; recently, 5 of these scholarships were awarded.

Deadline April of each year.

[43]
AUSTIN FAMILY SCHOLARSHIP ENDOWMENT FOR TRIBAL COLLEGES

American Indian College Fund
Attn: Scholarship Department
8333 Greenwood Boulevard
Denver, CO 80221
(303) 426-8900   Toll Free: (800) 776-FUND
Fax: (303) 426-1200
E-mail: scholarships@collegefund.org
Web: www.collegefund.org/scholarships/schol_tcu.html

Summary To provide financial assistance to members of American Indian tribes in Oklahoma who are enrolled at Tribal Colleges and Universities (TCUs) in any state.

Eligibility This program is open to residents of Oklahoma who are members or descendants of an American Indian tribe in the state. Applicants must be enrolled full time at an eligible TCU in any state. Applications are available only online and include required essays on specified topics.

Financial data The stipend is $1,250.

Duration 1 year.

Number awarded 1 or more each year.

Deadline May of each year.

[44]
AWG MINORITY SCHOLARSHIP

Association for Women Geoscientists
Attn: AWG Foundation
12000 North Washington Street, Suite 285
Thornton, CO 80241
(303) 412-6219   Fax: (303) 253-9220
E-mail: minorityscholarship@awg.org
Web: www.awg.org/EAS/scholarships.html

Summary To provide financial assistance to Native American and other underrepresented minority women who are interested in working on an undergraduate degree in the geosciences.

Eligibility This program is open to women who are African American, Hispanic, or Native American (including Eskimo, Hawaiian, Samoan, or American Indian). Applicants must be full-time students working on, or planning to work on, an undergraduate degree in the geosciences (including geology, geophysics, geochemistry, hydrology, meteorology, physical oceanography, planetary geology, or earth science education). They must submit a 500-word essay on their academic and career goals, 2 letters of recommendation, high school and/or college transcripts, and SAT or ACT scores. Financial need is not considered in the selection process.

Financial data A total of $6,000 is available for this program each year.

Duration 1 year; may be renewed.

Additional information This program, first offered in 2004, is supported by ExxonMobil Foundation.

Number awarded 1 or more each year.

Deadline June of each year.

[45]
BAD RIVER ADULT VOCATIONAL TRAINING PROGRAM

Bad River Band of Lake Superior Chippewa Indians
Attn: Education Office
P.O. Box 39
Odanah, WI 54861
(715) 682-7111, ext. 1533   Fax: (715) 682-7118

Summary To provide financial assistance for vocational or technical training to tribal members of Bad River Band of Lake Superior Chippewa Indians who live in Wisconsin.

Eligibility This program is open to Bad River tribal members who are interested in vocational or technical training and are or will be working on a certificate, diploma, or associate degree. Applicants must be Wisconsin residents and able to document financial need.

Financial data The maximum stipend is $1,800 per year.

Duration Up to 24 months at a vocational technical training institution or 36 months at a school of nursing, provided the recipient maintains a GPA of 2.0 or higher.

Number awarded Varies each year.

Deadline July of each year.

[46]
BAD RIVER HIGHER EDUCATION GRANT PROGRAM

Bad River Band of Lake Superior Chippewa Indians
Attn: Education Office
P.O. Box 39
Odanah, WI 54861
(715) 682-7111, ext. 1533   Fax: (715) 682-7118

Summary To provide financial assistance for college or graduate school to tribal members of the Bad River Band of Lake Superior Chippewa Indians.

Eligibility This program is open to Bad River tribal members who are or will be working full time on an undergraduate degree or full or part time on a graduate degree. Applicants must be able to document financial need. Graduate students must document that they have been denied funding from the American Indian Graduate Center.

Financial data The maximum stipend is $1,800 per year for undergraduates or $3,600 per year for graduate students.

Duration Up to 10 semesters for undergraduate students or up to 6 semesters for graduate students, provided the recipient maintains a GPA of 2.0 or higher as an undergraduate or 3.0 or higher as a graduate student.

Number awarded Varies each year.

Deadline July of each year.

[47]
BANK2 BANKING SCHOLARSHIP

Chickasaw Foundation
110 West 12th Street
P.O. Box 1726
Ada, OK 74821-1726
(580) 421-9030   Fax: (580) 421-9031
E-mail: ChickasawFoundation@chickasaw.net
Web: www.chickasawfoundation.org/index_20.htm

Summary To provide financial assistance to members of the Chickasaw Nation who are preparing for a career in banking.

Eligibility This program is open to Chickasaw students who are currently enrolled at a 4-year college or university as a full-time undergraduate student. Applicants must be majoring in finance, business, or accounting and preparing for a career in banking. Along with their application, they must submit high school or college transcripts, 2 letters of recommendation, a copy of their Chickasaw Nation citizenship card, and a 1-page essay on their long-term goals and plans for achieving them. Financial need is not considered in the selection process.

Financial data The stipend is $4,000.

Duration 1 year.

Additional information This program is supported by Bank2, headquartered in Oklahoma City and owned by the Chickasaw Nation.

Number awarded 1 each year.

Deadline August of each year.

[48]
BANK2 TA-OSSAA-ASHA' SCHOLARSHIPS

Chickasaw Foundation
110 West 12th Street
P.O. Box 1726
Ada, OK 74821-1726
(580) 421-9030   Fax: (580) 421-9031
E-mail: ChickasawFoundation@chickasaw.net
Web: www.chickasawfoundation.org/index_20.htm

Summary To provide financial assistance to members of the Chickasaw Nation who are preparing for a career in banking.

Eligibility This program is open to Chickasaw students who are currently enrolled at an accredited institution of higher education as a full-time undergraduate student. Applicants must be majoring in finance, business, or accounting and preparing for a career in banking. Along with their application, they must submit high school or college transcripts, 2 letters of recommendation, a copy of their Chickasaw Nation citizenship card, and a 1-page essay on their long-term goals and plans for achieving them. Financial need is not considered in the selection process.

Financial data The stipend is $1,000.

Duration 1 year.

Additional information This program is supported by Bank2, headquartered in Oklahoma City and owned by the Chickasaw Nation.

Number awarded 4 each year.

Deadline August of each year.

[49]
BARRY AND DEANNA SNYDER, SR. CHAIRMAN'S SCHOLARSHIP

Seneca Diabetes Foundation
Attn: Lucille White
TIS Building 12837, Route 438
P.O. Box 309
Irving, NY 14081
(716) 532-4900   Fax: (716) 549-1629
E-mail: white@sni.org
Web: www.senecadiabetesfoundation.org

Summary To provide financial assistance to members of the Seneca Nation who are interested in attending college to prepare for a career in the health or social services professions and have experience in a leadership position.

Eligibility This program is open to members of the Seneca Nation who are interested in attending college to assist the Seneca people, especially in regard to the fight against diabetes, by working on a degree in health or social services. Applicants must be able to demonstrate experience in a leadership position. Along with their application, they must submit brief statements on 1) the professional, community, or cultural services and activities in which they have participated; 2) how this scholarship would help further their education; 3) their goals or plan for using their education and training to benefit the Seneca Nation and its people; and 4) an example of a time when they served in a leadership position, the successes and challenges that they faced, the lessons they learned, and how they can apply those lessons to other life experiences. In the selection process, primary consideration is given to financial need, but involvement in community and cultural activities, personal assets, and desire to improve the quality of life for the Seneca people are also considered.

Financial data The stipend is $5,000 per year.

Duration 2 years.

Number awarded Varies each year; recently, 4 of these scholarships were awarded.

Deadline May of each year.

[50]
BCA/ALAN COMPTON AND BOB STANLEY MINORITY AND INTERNATIONAL SCHOLARSHIP

Baptist Communicators Association
Attn: Scholarship Committee
1715-K South Rutherford Boulevard, Suite 295
Murfreesboro, TN 37130
(615) 904-0152   E-mail: bca.office@comcast.net
Web: www.baptistcommunicators.org/about/scholarship.cfm

Summary To provide financial assistance to Native Americans, other minorities, and international students who are working on an undergraduate degree to prepare for a career in Baptist communications.

Eligibility This program is open to undergraduate students of minority or international origin. Applicants must be majoring in communications, English, journalism, or public relations with a GPA of 2.5 or higher. Their vocational objective must be in Baptist communications. Along with their application, they must submit a statement explaining why they want to receive this scholarship.

Financial data The stipend is $1,000.

Duration 1 year; recipients may reapply.

Additional information This program was established in 1996.

Number awarded 1 each year.

Deadline December of each year.

[51]
BECHTEL UNDERGRADUATE FELLOWSHIP AWARD

National Action Council for Minorities in Engineering
Attn: University Programs
440 Hamilton Avenue, Suite 302
White Plains, NY 10601-1813
(914) 539-4010   Fax: (914) 539-4032
E-mail: scholarships@nacme.org
Web: www.nacme.org/NACME_D.aspx?pageid=105

Summary To provide financial assistance to Native American and other underrepresented minority college juniors majoring in construction engineering.

Eligibility This program is open to African American, Latino, and American Indian college juniors who have a GPA of 3.0 or higher and have demonstrated academic excellence, leadership skills, and a commitment to science and engineering as a career. Applicants must be enrolled full time at an ABET-accredited engineering program and preparing for a career in a construction-related engineering discipline.

Financial data The stipend is $2,500 per year. Funds are sent directly to the recipient's university.

Duration Up to 2 years.

Additional information This program was established by the Bechtel Group Foundation.

Number awarded 2 each year.

Deadline April of each year.

[52]
BERING STRAITS FOUNDATION HIGHER EDUCATION SCHOLARSHIPS

Bering Straits Native Corporation
Attn: Bering Straits Foundation
110 Front Street, Suite 300
P.O. Box 1008
Nome, AK 99762-1008
(907) 443-5252   Toll Free: (800) 478-5079 (within AK)
Fax: (907) 443-2985
E-mail: foundation@beringstraits.com
Web: beringstraits.com

Summary To provide financial assistance to Alaska Natives who are shareholders or descendants of shareholders of the Bering Straits Native Corporation and entering or enrolled in an undergraduate or graduate program in any state.

Eligibility This program is open to Native Alaskans who are shareholders or lineal descendants of shareholders of the Bering Straits Native Corporation. Applicants must be graduating or have graduated from high school with a GPA of 3.0 or higher (or have earned a GED). They must be accepted or currently enrolled (as an undergraduate or graduate student) at an accredited college or university in any state as a full-time student and be able to demonstrate financial need. Along with their application, they must submit a personal statement on their educational goals and objectives, their community and school activities, and honors and awards they have received.

Financial data The stipend is $1,000 per semester for students who maintain a GPA of 3.0 or higher or $400 per semester for students whose GPA is from 2.5 to 2.99. Funds are paid directly to the recipient's school.

Duration 1 semester; may be renewed if the recipient maintains a GPA of 2.0 or higher during the first semester and 2.5 or higher in succeeding semesters.

Additional information The Bering Straits Native Corporation is 1 of 13 Alaska Native Regional Corporations created under the Alaska Native Claims Settlement Act of 1971.

Number awarded Varies each year.

Deadline April of each year for high school seniors; June of each year for the fall semester for continuing undergraduates; December of each year for the spring semester; April of each year for summer school.

[53]
BERING STRAITS FOUNDATION VOCATIONAL TRAINING SCHOLARSHIPS

Bering Straits Native Corporation
Attn: Bering Straits Foundation
110 Front Street, Suite 300
P.O. Box 1008
Nome, AK 99762-1008
(907) 443-4305   Toll Free: (800) 478-5079 (within AK)
Fax: (907) 443-2985
E-mail: foundation@beringstraits.com
Web: beringstraits.com

Summary To provide financial assistance to Alaska Natives who are shareholders or descendants of shareholders of the Bering Straits Native Corporation and entering or enrolled in a vocational training program in any state.

Eligibility This program is open to Native Alaskans who are shareholders or lineal descendants of shareholders of the Bering Straits Native Corporation. Applicants must be high school graduates with a GPA of 2.5 or higher. They must be accepted or currently enrolled at an accredited vocational school in any state as a full-time student and be able to demonstrate financial need. Along with their application, they must submit a personal statement on their educational goals and objectives, their community and school activities, and honors and awards they have received.

Financial data The stipend is $500 per semester. Funds are paid directly to the recipient's school.

Duration 1 semester; may be renewed if the recipient maintains a GPA of 2.0 or higher during the first semester and 2.5 or higher in succeeding semesters.

Additional information The Bering Straits Native Corporation is 1 of 13 Alaska Native Regional Corporations created under the Alaska Native Claims Settlement Act of 1971.

Number awarded Varies each year.

Deadline Applications may be submitted at any time, but they must be received at least 2 weeks prior to the start of class.

[54]
BERNARD BOUSCHOR HONORARY SCHOLARSHIPS

Sault Tribe of Chippewa Indians
Attn: Higher Education Program-Memorial/Tributary
    Scholarships
523 Ashmun Street
Sault Ste. Marie, MI 49783
(906) 635-4944   Toll Free: (800) 793-0660
Fax: (906) 635-7785   E-mail: amatson@saulttribe.net
Web: www.saulttribe.com

Summary To provide financial assistance to members of the Sault Tribe of Chippewa Indians who are attending college in any state.

Eligibility This program is open to enrolled members of the Sault Tribe who are working full time on an undergraduate degree in any field at a 2- or 4-year college or university in any state. Applicants must submit an essay of 300 to 500 words on how this scholarship will help them realize their goals.

Financial data The stipend is $1,000 per year.

Duration 1 year.

Number awarded 10 each year.

Deadline May of each year.

[55]
BILL FRYREAR MEMORIAL SCHOLARSHIPS

Chickasaw Foundation
110 West 12th Street
P.O. Box 1726
Ada, OK 74821-1726
(580) 421-9030   Fax: (580) 421-9031
E-mail: ChickasawFoundation@chickasaw.net
Web: www.chickasawfoundation.org/index_20.htm

Summary To provide financial assistance to members of the Chickasaw Nation who are working on an undergraduate degree in art or history.

Eligibility This program is open to Chickasaw students who are currently enrolled at an accredited institution of higher education as a full-time undergraduate student. Applicants must be majoring in art or history. Along with their application, they must submit high school or college transcripts, 2 letters of recommendation, a copy of their Chickasaw Nation citizenship card, and a 1-page essay on their long-term goals and plans for achieving them. Financial need is not considered in the selection process.

Financial data The stipend is $1,000.

Duration 1 year.

Number awarded 1 each year.

Deadline August of each year.

[56]
BILL THUNDER, JR. MEMORIAL SCHOLARSHIP

Northern Arapaho Tribe
Attn: Sky People Higher Education
P.O. Box 8480
Ethete, WY 82520
(307) 332-5286   Toll Free: (800) 815-6795
Fax: (307) 332-9104   E-mail: assistant@skypeopleed.org
Web: www.skypeopleed.org

Summary To provide financial assistance to members of the Northern Arapaho Tribe who are working on an undergraduate or graduate degree in agriculture or a related field.
Eligibility This program is open to full-time undergraduate and graduate students who have an undergraduate GPA of 2.0 or higher or the graduate GPA required by their school. Applicants must be of at least one-fourth Northern Arapaho descent (enrolled or non-enrolled) and must submit a Certificate of Indian Blood or other verification of Northern Arapaho blood with at least one-fourth degree. They must be working on a degree in agriculture or a related field (agribusiness, veterinary studies, animal science, horticulture, resource economics, rangeland ecosystem science, or agronomy). Along with their application, they must submit a 1-page personal statement that includes a brief history of their background, academic ability and achievement, work or leadership experience, participation in community-related activities, and career goals. Selection is based on that statement, potential to contribute to the community upon graduation, academic ability and achievement, and a letter of recommendation.
Financial data The stipend is $2,500 per year.
Duration 1 year; may be renewed.
Additional information The recipient is expected to apply for employment with the Northern Arapaho Tribe after graduation.
Number awarded 1 each year.
Deadline June of each year.

[57]
BILLY L. CYPRESS SCHOLARSHIP

Seminole Tribe of Florida
Attn: Higher Education Advisor
3100 North 63 Avenue
Hollywood, FL 33024
(954) 989-6840, ext. 1311   Toll Free: (877) 592-6573
Fax: (954) 893-8856
Web: www.semtribe.com/Services/Education.aspx

Summary To provide financial assistance to members of the Seminole Tribe of Florida who plan to attend college in any state.
Eligibility This program is open to Seminole tribal members who are applying to or currently enrolled in a program of higher education at a college, university, or vocational school in any state.
Financial data The amount of the award depends on the availability of funds and the need of the recipient.
Duration 1 year; may be renewed.
Number awarded Varies each year.
Deadline June of each year for fall term; October of each year for spring term; March of each year for summer term.

[58]
BIOMEDICAL RESEARCH TRAINING PROGRAM FOR UNDERREPRESENTED GROUPS

National Heart, Lung, and Blood Institute
Attn: Office of Training and Minority Health
6701 Rockledge Drive, Suite 9180
Bethesda, MD 20892-7913
(301) 451-5081   Toll Free: (301) 451-0088
Fax: (301) 480-0862   E-mail: mishoeh@nhlbi.nih.gov
Web: www.nhlbi.nih.gov

Summary To provide training in fundamental biomedical sciences and clinical research disciplines to Native Americans and other undergraduates, graduate students, and postbaccalaureates from underrepresented groups.
Eligibility This program is open to underrepresented undergraduate and graduate students (and postbaccalaureate individuals) interested in receiving training in fundamental biomedical sciences and clinical research disciplines of interest to the National Heart, Lung, and Blood Institute (NHLBI) of the National Institutes of Health (NIH). Underrepresented individuals include African Americans, Hispanic Americans, Native Americans, Alaskan Natives, Native Hawaiians and Pacific Islanders, individuals with disabilities, and individuals from disadvantaged backgrounds. Applicants must be U.S. citizens or permanent residents; have completed academic course work relevant to biomedical, behavioral, or statistical research; be enrolled full time or have recently completed baccalaureate work; and have a GPA of 3.3 or higher. Research experiences are available in the NHLBI Division of Intramural Research (in its cardiology, hematology, vascular medicine, or pulmonary critical care medicine branches) and its Division of Cardiovascular Sciences (which provides training in the basic principles of design, implementation, and analysis of epidemiology studies and clinical trials).
Financial data Stipends are paid at the annual rate of $24,000 for sophomores, $25,200 for juniors, $26,400 for seniors, $27,200 for postbaccalaureate individuals, $27,600 for first-year graduate students, $31,200 for second-year graduate students, or $34,900 for third-year graduate students.
Duration 6 to 24 months over a 2-year period; training must be completed in increments during consecutive academic years.
Additional information Training is conducted in the laboratories of the NHLBI in Bethesda, Maryland.
Number awarded Varies each year.
Deadline January of each year for placements beginning in June; March of each year for post-baccalaureate research internships beginning from June through September.

[59]
BLACKFEET ADULT VOCATIONAL TRAINING GRANTS

Blackfeet Nation
Attn: Higher Education Program
1 Agency Square
P.O. Box 850
Browning, MT 59417
(406) 338-7539   Fax: (406) 338-7529
E-mail: bhep@3rivers.net
Web: www.blackfeetnation.com

Summary To provide financial assistance for vocational training to members of the Blackfeet and other tribes.
Eligibility This program is open to enrolled members of a federally-recognized tribe between 18 and 35 years of age in need of training to obtain reasonable and satisfactory employment. Applicants must be willing to accept full-time employment as soon as possible after completion of training. Along with their application they must submit high school or GED transcripts, college transcripts (if they have ever attended college), a copy of the admission letter from the school they plan to attend, a financial needs analysis, a Cer-

tificate of Indian Blood, a copy of their marriage license (if their spouse is claimed as financially dependent), a copy of birth certificates for any family members claimed as financially dependent, and military discharge papers (if applicable). Grants are awarded according to the following priorities: 1) Blackfeet tribal members residing on or near the Blackfeet Reservation; 2) Blackfeet tribal members residing off the Blackfeet Reservation; 3) members of other federally-recognized tribes (as funding permits); and 4) second training grant applicants (as funding permits).

Financial data The amount awarded varies, depending upon the recipient's educational requirements and financial needs. The maximum for an unmarried student with no dependents is $3,200 per year; for a student with 3 or more dependents; the maximum stipend is $3,800 per year. Funds are sent to the school's financial aid officer.

Duration Up to 24 months (36 months for registered nursing students) of full-time training.

Number awarded Varies each year.

Deadline February of each year.

[60]
BLACKFEET HIGHER EDUCATION GRANTS

Blackfeet Nation
Attn: Higher Education Program
P.O. Box 850
Browning, MT 59417
(406) 338-7539   Fax: (406) 338-7530
E-mail: bhep@3rivers.net
Web: www.blackfeetnation.com

Summary To provide financial assistance to members of the Blackfeet Tribe who are interested in working on an undergraduate degree at a college or university in any state.

Eligibility Applicants must be enrolled members of the Blackfeet Tribe and be enrolled or accepted for enrollment as an undergraduate at an academically recognized college or university in any state. They must submit a 1-page letter describing their career goals and academic plans, high school or GED transcripts, college transcripts (if they have previously attended college), a copy of the admission letter from the college or university they plan to attend, a financial needs analysis, and a Certificate of Indian Blood. Scholarships are awarded according to the following priorities: 1) renewal of grants to students currently funded who are in good academic and financial aid standing and submit the application packet on time; 2) college seniors not currently funded who can graduate within the current academic year; 3) 2-year degree graduates who apply within 1 year of earning their associate degree; 4) high school seniors who apply within 1 year of earning their high school diploma; 5) applicants previously funded who are in good academic and financial aid standing and submit the application packet in a timely manner; and 6) candidates who submit late applications (supported only if funding permits).

Financial data The amount awarded varies, depending upon the recipient's educational requirements and financial needs. The maximum for an unmarried student with no dependents is $3,200 per year; for a student with 3 or more dependents; the maximum stipend is $3,800 per year. Funds are sent to the school's financial aid officer.

Duration 1 year; may be renewed up to a total of 10 semesters or 15 quarters.

Additional information Recipients must enroll as full-time students and earn no less than 12 credit hours per term with a GPA of 2.0 or higher as freshmen, 13 credits and 2.2 as sophomores, 14 credits and 2.4 as juniors, and 15 credits and 2.6 as seniors. Students who attend private schools or institutions outside of Montana must pay the difference in tuition, unless no comparable program exists at Montana public institutions.

Number awarded Varies each year.

Deadline February for the academic year; March for summer term.

[61]
BLOSSOM KALAMA EVANS MEMORIAL SCHOLARSHIPS

Hawai'i Community Foundation
Attn: Scholarship Department
827 Fort Street Mall
Honolulu, HI 96813
(808) 537-6333   Toll Free: (888) 731-3863
Fax: (808) 521-6286
E-mail: scholarships@hcf-hawaii.org
Web: www.hawaiicommunityfoundation.org/scholarships

Summary To provide financial assistance to residents of Hawaii of native ancestry who are interested in working on an undergraduate or graduate degree at a school in any state.

Eligibility This program is open to residents of Hawaii who are of Hawaiian ancestry and enrolled as full-time juniors, seniors, or graduate students at a college or university in any state. Applicants must be able to demonstrate academic achievement (GPA of 2.7 or higher), good moral character, and financial need. Along with their application, they must submit a short statement indicating their reasons for attending college, their planned course of study, their career goals, what community service means to them, and how they plan to use their knowledge to serve the needs of the Native Hawaiian community.

Financial data The amounts of the awards depend on the availability of funds and the need of the recipient. Recently, the average value of each of the scholarships awarded by the foundation was $2,041.

Duration 1 year.

Number awarded Varies each year; recently, 9 of these scholarships were awarded.

Deadline February of each year.

[62]
BOIS FORTE HIGHER EDUCATION PROGRAM

Bois Forte Band of Chippewa
Attn: Department of Education and Training
5344 Lakeshore Drive
P.O. Box 16
Nett Lake, MN 55772
(218) 757-3261   Toll Free: (800) 221-8129
Fax: (218) 757-3312 E-mail: bmason@boisforte-NSN.gov
Web: www.boisforte.com/divisions/education.htm

Summary To provide financial assistance for undergraduate or graduate study to enrolled members of the Bois Forte Band of Chippewa Indians.

Eligibility Eligible to apply for this assistance are enrolled members of the Bois Forte Band of Chippewa Indians. Applicants must have been accepted at an institution of higher education and had their financial need determined by that institution based on the Free Application for Federal Student Aid (FAFSA). Minnesota residents must apply to the Indian Scholarship Assistance Program of the Minnesota Indian Scholarship Program. Applicants wishing to attend school outside of Minnesota must complete an out-of-state application form. Applicants must also apply for financial assistance from all other available sources, including but not limited to public and private grants and scholarships. They must not be in default of any tribal, federal, or state student education loan or in noncompliance with child support payments. Applicants are interviewed. Financial assistance is awarded on a first-come, first-served basis.

Financial data The maximum amount awarded is $5,000 per year for undergraduates or $6,250 per year for graduate students.

Duration 1 year; may be renewed for a total of 10 semesters of full-time enrollment or part-time equivalent provided recipients maintain a GPA of 2.0 or higher.

Additional information Students may receive financial assistance for summer school.

Number awarded Varies each year.

Deadline Applications may be submitted any time after January 1 but should be received no later than 8 weeks prior to the first day of school.

[63]
BONNEVILLE POWER ADMINISTRATION REGIONAL TRIBAL SCHOLARSHIPS

Bonneville Power Administration
Attn: Tribal Affairs Program
P.O. Box 3621
Portland, OR 97208-3621
(503) 230-7685   E-mail: tribalaffairs@bpa.gov
Web: www.bpa.gov

Summary To provide financial assistance to members of Indian tribes in the Pacific Northwest who are interested in working on an undergraduate or graduate degree in specified finance and science-related fields at a university in any state.

Eligibility This program is open to Indians who are enrolled members of federally-recognized tribes in the service area of the Bonneville Power Administration (BPA) in Washington, Oregon, Idaho, and Montana. Applicants must be attending or planning to attend a college or university in any state as a full-time student to prepare for a career in a field of interest to BPA, including 1) an academic degree in accounting, business, economics, electrical engineering, finance, natural resources, or statistics or 2) a technical degree in the electrical crafts. They must have a GPA of 2.5 or higher. Along with their application, they must submit an essay of 500-words on a topic that changes annually but relates to the work of BPA; recently, students were asked to complete the phrase, "Renewable Energy means." Selection is based on the essay and academic merit, including course work, major field of study, leadership, community service, academic achievements, and overcoming obstacles.

Financial data The stipend is $2,500.

Duration 1 year.

Number awarded 10 each year.

Deadline March of each year.

[64]
BOOKER T. WASHINGTON SCHOLARSHIPS

National FFA Organization
Attn: Scholarship Office
6060 FFA Drive
P.O. Box 68960
Indianapolis, IN 46268-0960
(317) 802-4419   Fax: (317) 802-5419
E-mail: scholarships@ffa.org
Web: www.ffa.org

Summary To provide financial assistance to Native American and other minority FFA members who are interested in studying agriculture in college.

Eligibility This program is open to members who are graduating high school seniors planning to enroll full time in college. Applicants must be members of a minority ethnic group (African American, Asian American, Pacific Islander, Hispanic, Alaska Native, or American Indian) planning to work on a 4-year degree in agriculture. Selection is based on academic achievement (10 points for GPA, 10 points for SAT or ACT score, 10 points for class rank), leadership in FFA activities (30 points), leadership in community activities (10 points), and participation in the Supervised Agricultural Experience (SAE) program (30 points). U.S. citizenship is required.

Financial data Scholarships are either $10,000 or $5,000. Funds are paid directly to the recipient.

Duration 1 year; nonrenewable.

Number awarded 4 each year: 1 at $10,000 and 3 at $5,000.

Deadline February of each year.

[65]
BOSTON UNIVERSITY SUMMER UNDERGRADUATE RESEARCH FELLOWSHIP PROGRAM

Boston University
Attn: Undergraduate Research Opportunities Program
143 Bay State Road
Boston, MA 02215-1719
(617) 353-2020   Fax: (617) 353-2056
E-mail: urop@bu.edu
Web: www.bu.edu/urop/surf-program/about

Summary To provide an opportunity for undergraduates, especially Native Americans and members of other underrepresented minority groups, to participate in scientific research projects during the summer at Boston University.

Eligibility This program is open to undergraduates who are entering their junior or senior year and have a GPA of 3.0 or higher. Applicants must be interested in working on a summer research project in biology, chemistry, computer science, engineering, or psychology under the mentorship of a Boston University professor. Along with their application, they must submit an essay of 400 to 1,000 words explaining why they wish to participate in the program. Preference is given to members of minority groups traditionally underrepresented in the sciences: African Americans, Hispanics, Native Americans and Native Alaskans, Pacific Islanders (including Native Hawaiians and Polynesians), and Asians (except Indians, Chinese, Japanese, Koreans, Filipinos, and Thais). U.S. citizenship or permanent resident status is required.

Financial data Participants receive a $4,500 stipend, a $600 supplies allowance, up to $550 in travel expenses, and housing in a Boston University dormitory.

Duration 10 weeks during the summer.

Additional information Support for this program is provided by the National Science Foundation (NSF) through its Research Experiences for Undergraduates (REU) program, the Department of Defense through its Awards to Stimulate and Support Undergraduate Research Experiences (ASSURE) program, and the Northeast Alliance for Graduate Education and the Professoriate.

Number awarded 10 to 20 each year, including 2 or 3 positions reserved for Boston University students who serve as peer mentors for the other participants.

Deadline February of each year.

[66]
BREAKTHROUGH TO NURSING SCHOLARSHIPS

National Student Nurses' Association
Attn: Foundation
45 Main Street, Suite 606
Brooklyn, NY 11201
(718) 210-0705   Fax: (718) 797-1186
E-mail: nsna@nsna.org
Web: www.nsna.org

Summary To provide financial assistance to Native American and other minority undergraduate and graduate students who wish to prepare for careers in nursing.

Eligibility This program is open to students currently enrolled in state-approved schools of nursing or pre-nursing associate degree, baccalaureate, diploma, generic master's, generic doctoral, R.N. to B.S.N., R.N. to M.S.N., or L.P.N./L.V.N. to R.N. programs. Graduating high school seniors are not eligible. Support for graduate education is provided only for a first degree in nursing. Applicants must be members of a racial or ethnic minority underrepresented among registered nurses (American Indian or Alaska Native, Hispanic or Latino, Native Hawaiian or other Pacific Islander, Black or African American, or Asian). They must be committed to providing quality health care services to underserved populations. Along with their application, they must submit a 200-word description of their professional and educational goals and how this scholarship will help them achieve those goals. Selection is based on academic achievement, financial need, and involvement in student nursing organizations and community health activities. U.S. citizenship or permanent resident status is required.

Financial data Stipends range from $1,000 to $2,500. A total of approximately $155,000 is awarded each year by the foundation for all its scholarship programs.

Duration 1 year.

Additional information Applications must be accompanied by a $10 processing fee.

Number awarded Varies each year; recently, 5 of these scholarships were awarded: 2 sponsored by the American Association of Critical-Care Nurses and 3 sponsored by the Mayo Clinic.

Deadline January of each year.

[67]
BRISTOL BAY NATIVE CORPORATION EDUCATION FOUNDATION HIGHER EDUCATION SCHOLARSHIPS

Bristol Bay Native Corporation
Attn: BBNC Education Foundation
111 West 16th Avenue, Suite 400
Anchorage, AK 99501
(907) 278-3602   Toll Free: (800) 426-3602
Fax: (907) 276-3925   E-mail: pelagiol@bbnc.net
Web: www.bbnc.net

Summary To provide financial assistance to shareholders of Bristol Bay Native Corporation (BBNC) who are interested in attending college in any state.

Eligibility This program is open to BBNC shareholders who have a high school diploma or equivalent and are enrolled or planning to enroll in an accredited college or university as a full-time student. Applicants must have a GPA of 2.0 or higher and be able to demonstrate financial need. Along with their application, they must submit an essay on how they became interested in their proposed field of study, any special circumstances they want to be considered, and their desire to work in the region or for a BBNC subsidiary company. Selection is based on the essay (35%), cumulative GPA (40%), financial need (20%), and letters of recommendation (5%).

Financial data Stipends recently ranged from $750 to $3,500 per year.

Duration 1 year.

Additional information The BBNC is 1 of 13 Alaska Native Regional Corporations created under the Alaska Native Claims Settlement Act of 1971.

Number awarded Approximately 100 each year.

Deadline March of each year.

[68]
BROOKHAVEN NATIONAL LABORATORY SCIENCE AND ENGINEERING PROGRAMS FOR WOMEN AND MINORITIES

Brookhaven National Laboratory
Attn: Diversity Office, Human Resources Division
Building 400B
P.O. Box 5000
Upton, New York 11973-5000
(631) 344-2703   Fax: (631) 344-5305
E-mail: palmore@bnl.gov
Web: www.bnl.gov/diversity/programs.asp

Summary To provide on-the-job training in scientific areas at Brookhaven National Laboratory (BNL) during the summer to Native Americans, other minorities, and women students.

Eligibility This program at BNL is open to women and underrepresented minority (African American/Black, Hispanic, Native American, or Pacific Islander) students who have completed their freshman, sophomore, or junior year of college. Applicants must be U.S. citizens or permanent residents, at least 18 years of age, and majoring in applied mathematics, biology, chemistry, computer science, engineering, high and low energy particle accelerators, nuclear medicine, physics, or scientific writing. Since no transportation or housing allowance is provided, preference is given to students who reside in the BNL area.

Financial data Participants receive a competitive stipend.

Duration 10 to 12 weeks during the summer.

Additional information Students work with members of the scientific, technical, and professional staff of BNL in an educational training program developed to give research experience.

Deadline April of each year.

[69]
BROWN AND CALDWELL MINORITY SCHOLARSHIP

Brown and Caldwell
Attn: Scholarship Program
201 North Civic Drive, Suite 115
P.O. Box 8045
Walnut Creek, CA 94596
(925) 937-9010 Fax: (925) 937-9026
E-mail: scholarships@brwncald.com
Web: www.brownandcaldwell.com/_Index_scholarships.htm

Summary To provide financial assistance and work experience to Native Americans and other minority students working on an undergraduate degree in an environmental or engineering field.

Eligibility This program is open to members of minority groups (African Americans, Hispanics, Asians, Pacific Islanders, Native Americans, and Alaska Natives) who are full-time students in their junior year at an accredited 4-year college or university. Applicants must have a GPA of 3.0 or higher and a declared major in civil, chemical, or environmental engineering or an environmental science (e.g., ecology, geology, hydrogeology). Along with their application, they must submit an essay (up to 250 words) on their future career goals in environmental science. They must be U.S. citizens or permanent residents and available to participate in a summer internship at a Brown and Caldwell office. Financial need is not considered in the selection process.

Financial data The stipend is $5,000.

Duration 1 year.

Additional information As part of the paid summer internship at a Brown and Caldwell office at 1 of more than 45 cities in the country, the program provides a mentor to guide the intern through the company's information and communications resources.

Number awarded 1 each year.

Deadline February of each year.

[70]
BUREAU OF INDIAN EDUCATION HIGHER EDUCATION GRANT PROGRAM

Bureau of Indian Affairs
Attn: Bureau of Indian Education
1849 C Street, N.W.
Mail Stop 3609 MIB
Washington, DC 20240
(202) 208-6123 Fax: (202) 208-3312
Web: www.bie.edu/ParentsStudents/Grants/index.htm

Summary To provide financial assistance to undergraduate students who belong to or are affiliated with federally-recognized Indian tribes.

Eligibility This program is open to 1) members of American Indian tribes who are eligible for the special programs

and services provided through the Bureau of Indian Affairs (BIA) because of their status as Indians, and 2) individuals who are at least one-quarter degree Indian blood descendants of those members. Applicants must be 1) enrolled or planning to enroll at an accredited college or university in a course of study leading to an associate of arts or bachelor's degree and 2) able to demonstrate financial need. Most tribes administer the grant program directly for their members, but other tribal members may contact the BIA Bureau of Indian Education to learn the name and address of the nearest Education Line Officer who can provide an application and assistance in completing it.

Financial data Individual awards depend on the financial need of the recipient; they range from $300 to $5,000 and average $2,800 per year. Recently, a total of $20 million was available for this program.

Duration 1 year; may be renewed for up to 4 additional years.

Additional information Funds may be used for either part-time or full-time study. This program was authorized by the Snyder Act of 1921.

Number awarded Approximately 9,500 students receive assistance through this program annually.

Deadline June of each year for fall term; October of each year for spring term; April of each year for summer school.

[71]
BURLINGTON NORTHERN SANTA FE FOUNDATION SCHOLARSHIP

American Indian Science and Engineering Society
Attn: Program Officer
2305 Renard, S.E., Suite 200
P.O. Box 9828
Albuquerque, NM 87119-9828
(505) 765-1052, ext. 105 Fax: (505) 765-5608
E-mail: tina@aises.org
Web: www.aises.org

Summary To provide financial assistance for college to outstanding American Indian and Alaskan Native high school seniors from designated states who are members of American Indian Science and Engineering Society (AISES).

Eligibility This program is open to AISES members who are seniors graduating from high schools in the service area of the Burlington Northern and Santa Fe Corporation (Arizona, California, Colorado, Kansas, Minnesota, Montana, New Mexico, North Dakota, Oklahoma, Oregon, South Dakota, and Washington). Applicants must be planning to attend an accredited 4-year college or university in any state and major in business, education, engineering, mathematics, medicine or health administration, natural or physical sciences, or technology. They must submit 1) a Certificate of Indian Blood or proof of enrollment in an American Indian tribe or Alaskan Native group; 2) a 500-word essay on their educational and career goals, including their interest in and motivation to continue higher education, an understanding of the importance of college and a commitment to completing their educational and/or career goals, and a commitment to learning and giving back to the community; and 3) school transcripts showing a GPA of 2.0 or higher. Selection is based on the essay (40%), GPA (35%), letters of recommendation (15%), and overall impression of the application (10%).

Financial data The stipend is $2,500 per year.

Duration 4 years or until completion of a baccalaureate degree, whichever occurs first.

Additional information This program is funded by the Burlington Northern Santa Fe Foundation and administered by AISES.

Number awarded 5 new awards are made each year.

Deadline April of each year.

[72]
CALIFORNIA DIETETIC ASSOCIATION AMERICAN INDIAN/ALASKA NATIVE SCHOLARSHIP

California Dietetic Association
Attn: CDA Foundation
7740 Manchester Avenue, Suite 102
Playa del Rey, CA 90293-8499
(310) 822-0177   Fax: (310) 823-0264
E-mail: patsmith@dietitian.org
Web: www.dietitian.org/cdaf_scholarships.htm

Summary To provide financial assistance to Native Americans from California who are members of the American Dietetic Association (ADA) and interested in working on an undergraduate degree at a school in any state.

Eligibility This program is open to enrolled members of federally-recognized Indian tribes and Native Alaskan villages who currently reside in California (although they may attend school in any state). Applicants must be juniors or seniors accepted into a Registered Dietetic Technician (DTR) program, a Didactic Program in Dietetics (DPD), a Coordinated Program (CP) in dietetics, or a Supervised Practice Program. They must have at least a "B" average in high school, a 2.75 or higher overall college GPA (for DTR students), or a GPA of 2.75 or higher in didactic courses for the DPD, CP, or Supervised Practice Program. ADA membership is required. Along with their application, they must submit a letter of application that includes a discussion of their career goals. Selection is based on that letter (15%), academic ability (25%), work or volunteer experience (15%), letters of recommendation (15%), extracurricular activities (5%), and financial need (25%).

Financial data The stipend is normally $1,000.

Duration 1 year.

Number awarded 1 each year.

Deadline February of each year.

[73]
CALIFORNIA PLANNING FOUNDATION OUTSTANDING DIVERSITY AWARD

American Planning Association-California Chapter
Attn: California Planning Foundation
c/o Paul Wack
P.O. Box 1086
Morro Bay, CA 93443-1086
(805) 756-6331   Fax: (805) 756-1340
E-mail: pwack@calpoly.edu
Web: www.californiaplanningfoundation.org

Summary To provide financial assistance to minority and other undergraduate and graduate students in accredited planning programs at California universities who will increase diversity in the profession.

Eligibility This program is open to students entering their final year for an undergraduate or master's degree in an accredited planning program at a university in California. Applicants must be students who will increase diversity in the planning profession. Selection is based on academic performance, professional promise, and financial need.

Financial data The stipend is $3,000. The award includes a 1-year student membership in the American Planning Association (APA) and payment of registration for the APA California Conference.

Duration 1 year.

Additional information The accredited planning programs are at 3 campuses of the California State University system (California State Polytechnic University at Pomona, California Polytechnic State University at San Luis Obispo, and San Jose State University), 3 campuses of the University of California (Berkeley, Irvine, and Los Angeles), and the University of Southern California.

Number awarded 1 each year.

Deadline March of each year.

[74]
CALISTA SCHOLARSHIP FUND

Calista Corporation
Attn: Calista Scholarship Fund
301 Calista Court, Suite A
Anchorage, AK 99518-3028
(907) 279-5516   Toll Free: (800) 277-5516
Fax: (907) 272-5060
E-mail: scholarships@calistacorp.com
Web: www.calistacorp.com/scholarships.html

Summary To provide financial assistance to Alaska Natives who are shareholders or descendants of shareholders of the Calista Corporation and interested in working on an undergraduate or graduate degree at a school in any state.

Eligibility This program is open to Alaska Natives who are shareholders or lineal descendants of shareholders of the Calista Corporation. Applicants must be at least a high school graduate or have earned a GED and be in good academic standing with a GPA of 2.0 or higher. They must be working on an undergraduate or graduate degree at a college or university in any state. Along with their application, they must submit a 1-page essay on their educational and career goals. Financial need is considered in the selection process.

Financial data The amount awarded for undergraduates depends upon the recipient's GPA: $500 per semester for a GPA of 2.0 to 2.49, $750 per semester for a GPA of 2.5 to 2.99, and $1,000 per semester a GPA of 3.0 or higher. For graduate students, the stipend is $1,500 per semester. The funds are paid in 2 equal installments; the second semester check is not issued until grades from the previous semester's work are received.

Duration 1 year; recipients may reapply.

Additional information The Calista Corporation is 1 of 13 Alaska Native Regional Corporations created under the Alaska Native Claims Settlement Act of 1971. This program was established in 1994.

Number awarded Varies each year; recently, 79 of these scholarships were awarded.

Deadline June of each year.

[75]
CANFIT PROGRAM UNDERGRADUATE SCHOLARSHIPS

California Adolescent Nutrition and Fitness Program
Attn: Scholarship Program
2140 Shattuck Avenue, Suite 610
Berkeley, CA 94704
(510) 644-1533   Toll Free: (800) 200-3131
Fax: (510) 644-1535   E-mail: info@canfit.org
Web: canfit.org/scholarships

Summary To provide financial assistance to Native American and other minority undergraduate students who are working on a degree in nutrition or physical education in California.

Eligibility This program is open to American Indians, Alaska Natives, African Americans, Asian Americans, Pacific Islanders, and Latinos/Hispanics from California who are enrolled in an approved bachelor's degree program in nutrition or physical education in the state. Applicants must have completed at least 50 semester units and have a GPA of 2.5 or higher. Along with their application, they must submit 1) documentation of financial need; 2) letters of recommendation from 2 individuals; 3) a 1-to 2-page letter describing their academic goals and involvement in community nutrition and/or physical education activities; and 4) an essay of 500 to 1,000 words on a topic related to healthy foods for youth from low-income communities of color.

Financial data A stipend is awarded (amount not specified).

Number awarded 1 or more each year.

Deadline March of each year.

[76]
CAP LATHROP ENDOWMENT SCHOLARSHIP FUND

Cook Inlet Region, Inc.
Attn: The CIRI Foundation
3600 San Jeronimo Drive, Suite 256
Anchorage, AK 99508-2870
(907) 793-3575   Toll Free: (800) 764-3382
Fax: (907) 793-3585   E-mail: tcf@thecirifoundation.org
Web: www.thecirifoundation.org/designated.htm

Summary To provide financial assistance for undergraduate or graduate studies in media-related fields to Alaska Natives and their lineal descendants.

Eligibility This program is open to Alaska Native enrollees under the Alaska Native Claims Settlement Act (ANCSA) of 1971 and their lineal descendants. Proof of eligibility must be submitted. Applicants may be enrollees of any of the 13 ANCSA regional corporations, but preference is given to original enrollees/descendants of Cook Inlet Region, Inc. (CIRI) who have a GPA of 3.0 or higher. There are no Alaska residency requirements or age limitations. Applicants must be accepted or enrolled full time in a 2-year undergraduate, 4-year undergraduate, or graduate degree program. They must be majoring in a media-related field (e.g., telecommunications, broadcast, business, engineering, journalism) and planning to work in the telecommunications or broadcast industry in Alaska after graduation. Along with their application, they must submit a 500-word statement on their educational and career goals and how they are contributing, or planning to contribute, to a positive Alaska Native community.

Selection is based on that statement, academic achievement, rigor of course work or degree program, student financial contribution, financial need, grade level, previous work performance, community service, and relationship of degree program to career goals.

Financial data The stipend is $3,500 per year. Funds must be used for tuition, university fees, books, required class supplies, and campus housing and meal plans for students who must live away from their permanent home to attend college. Checks are sent directly to the recipient's school.

Duration 1 year (2 semesters).

Additional information This program was established in 1997. Recipients must attend school on a full-time basis and must plan to work in the broadcast or telecommunications industry in Alaska upon completion of their academic degree.

Number awarded 1 each year.

Deadline May of each year.

[77]
CAREER TECHNOLOGY SCHOLARSHIP

Chickasaw Foundation
110 West 12th Street
P.O. Box 1726
Ada, OK 74821-1726
(580) 421-9030   Fax: (580) 421-9031
E-mail: ChickasawFoundation@chickasaw.net
Web: www.chickasawfoundation.org/index_20.htm

Summary To provide financial assistance for vocational school to employees of the Chickasaw Nation.

Eligibility This program is open to employees of the Chickasaw Nation who are currently enrolled at a career technology, vocational/technical, or trade school. Applicants must be at least 18 years of age and have a GPA of 2.0 or higher. Along with their application, they must submit high school or college transcripts, 2 letters of recommendation, a copy of their Chickasaw Nation citizenship card, a copy of their Chickasaw Nation employee identification badge, and a 1-page essay on their long-term goals and plans for achieving them. Financial need is not considered in the selection process.

Financial data The stipend is $1,000.

Duration 1 year.

Number awarded 1 each year.

Deadline August of each year.

[78]
CAREER UPGRADE GRANTS

Cook Inlet Region, Inc.
Attn: The CIRI Foundation
3600 San Jeronimo Drive, Suite 256
Anchorage, AK 99508-2870
(907) 793-3575   Toll Free: (800) 764-3382
Fax: (907) 793-3585   E-mail: tcf@thecirifoundation.org
Web: www.thecirifoundation.org/grants.htm

Summary To provide financial assistance for employment skills upgrades to Alaska Natives who are original enrollees to the Cook Inlet Region, Inc. (CIRI) and their lineal descendants.

Eligibility This program is open to Alaska Native enrollees to CIRI under the Alaska Native Claims Settlement Act (ANCSA) of 1971 and their lineal descendants. Applicants should have a high school diploma or GED, have a GPA of 2.5

or higher, be preparing to enter or reenter or upgrade in the job market upon completion of training, and be able to demonstrate the availability of employment. They must be accepted or enrolled part time in a course of study that directly contributes toward potential employment or employment upgrade. Alaska residency is not required. Along with their application, they must submit a 500-word statement on their educational and career goals and how they are contributing, or planning to contribute, to a positive Alaska Native community. Selection is based on that statement, academic achievement, rigor of course work or degree program, student financial contribution, financial need, grade level, previous work performance, community service, and relationship of degree program to career goals.

Financial data The maximum stipend is $4,500 per calendar year.

Duration 1 quarter; recipients may reapply.

Additional information Only part-time study is supported. Total course credits may not exceed 11 credit hours per application.

Number awarded Varies each year; recently, 70 of these grants were awarded.

Deadline March, June, September, or November of each year.

[79]
CAREERS IN TRANSPORTATION FOR YOUTH (CITY) INTERNSHIP PROGRAM

Conference of Minority Transportation Officials
Attn: Internship Program
818 18th Street, N.W., Suite 850
Washington, DC 20006
(202) 530-0551   Fax: (202) 530-0617
Web: www.comto.org/news-city.php

Summary To provide summer work experience in transportation-related fields to Native American and other underrepresented upper-division students.

Eligibility This program is open to full-time underrepresented students entering their junior or senior year with a GPA of 2.5 or higher. Applicants must be working on a degree related to public transportation. They must be interested in a summer internship with transit firms or agencies in Atlanta, Austin, San Francisco, or Washington, D.C. Along with their application, they must submit a 1-page essay on their transportation interests, including how participation in this internship will enhance their educational plan, their mid- and long-term professional goals, their specific transportation-related goal, the issues of interest to them, their plans to further their education and assist in making future contributions to their field of study, and their expectations for this internship experience. U.S. citizenship is required.

Financial data The stipend recently was $4,000.

Duration 10 weeks during the summer.

Additional information This program is managed by the Conference of Minority Transportation Officials (COMTO), with funding provided by the Federal Transit Administration. Interns work at transit agencies, private transit-related consulting firms, transportation service providers, manufacturers, and suppliers.

Number awarded 12 each year.

Deadline April of each year.

[80]
CARGILL SCHOLARSHIP PROGRAM FOR TRIBAL COLLEGES

American Indian College Fund
Attn: Scholarship Department
8333 Greenwood Boulevard
Denver, CO 80221
(303) 426-8900   Toll Free: (800) 776-FUND
Fax: (303) 426-1200
E-mail: scholarships@collegefund.org
Web: www.collegefund.org/scholarships/schol_tcu.html

Summary To provide financial assistance to Native American college students from any state who are working on a bachelor's degree in specified fields at Tribal Colleges and Universities (TCUs) in selected states.

Eligibility This program is open to American Indians, Alaska Natives, and Hawaiian Natives who have proof of enrollment or descendancy. Applicants must be enrolled full time at an eligible TCU in Kansas, Minnesota, North Dakota, South Dakota, or Wisconsin and be working on a bachelor's degree in agricultural studies, business, engineering, finance, mathematics, science, or technology. They must have a GPA of 3.0 or higher, be willing to commit to attend the "Backpacks to Briefcases" program, and have a record of leadership and service to the Native American community. Applications are available only online and include required essays on specified topics. Selection is based on exceptional academic achievement.

Financial data The stipend is $2,500.

Duration 1 year.

Additional information This program is funded by Cargill, Inc. in partnership with the American Indian College Fund.

Number awarded 1 or more each year.

Deadline May of each year.

[81]
CARL H. MARRS SCHOLARSHIP FUND

Cook Inlet Region, Inc.
Attn: The CIRI Foundation
3600 San Jeronimo Drive, Suite 256
Anchorage, AK 99508-2870
(907) 793-3575   Toll Free: (800) 764-3382
Fax: (907) 793-3585   E-mail: tcf@thecirifoundation.org
Web: www.thecirifoundation.org/designated.htm

Summary To provide financial assistance for undergraduate or graduate studies in business-related fields to Alaska Natives who are original enrollees to Cook Inlet Region, Inc. (CIRI) and their lineal descendants.

Eligibility This program is open to Alaska Native enrollees to CIRI under the Alaska Native Claims Settlement Act (ANCSA) of 1971 and their lineal descendants. There are no Alaska residency requirements or age limitations. Applicants must be accepted or enrolled full time in a 4-year undergraduate or a graduate degree program in business administration, economics, finance, organizational management, accounting, or a similar field. They must have a GPA of 3.7 or higher. Along with their application, they must submit a 500-word statement on their educational and career goals and how they are contributing, or planning to contribute, to a positive Alaska Native community. Selection is based on that statement, academic achievement, rigor of course work or degree program, student financial contribution, financial need, grade level, previous work performance, community service, and relationship of degree program to career goals.

Financial data The stipend is $20,000 per year.

Duration 1 year; may be renewed.

Additional information This program was established in 2001.

Number awarded Varies each year; recently, 2 of these scholarships were awarded.

Deadline May of each year.

[82]
CARMEN E. TURNER SCHOLARSHIPS

Conference of Minority Transportation Officials
Attn: National Scholarship Program
818 18th Street, N.W., Suite 850
Washington, DC 20006
(202) 530-0551   Fax: (202) 530-0617
Web: www.comto.org/news-youth.php

Summary To provide financial assistance for college or graduate school to Native American and other members of the Conference of Minority Transportation Officials (COMTO).

Eligibility This program is open to undergraduate and graduate students who have been members of COMTO for at least 1 year. Applicants must be working on a degree in a field related to transportation with a GPA of 2.5 or higher. Along with their application, they must submit a cover letter with a 500-word statement of career goals. Financial need is not considered in the selection process. U.S. citizenship is required.

Financial data The stipend is $3,500. Funds are paid directly to the recipient's college or university.

Duration 1 year.

Additional information COMTO was established in 1971 to promote, strengthen, and expand the roles of minorities in all aspects of transportation. Recipients are expected to attend the COMTO National Scholarship Luncheon.

Number awarded 2 each year.

Deadline April of each year.

[83]
CAROL HAYES TORIO MEMORIAL UNDERGRADUATE SCHOLARSHIP

California Dietetic Association
Attn: CDA Foundation
7740 Manchester Avenue, Suite 102
Playa del Rey, CA 90293-8499
(310) 822-0177   Fax: (310) 823-0264
E-mail: patsmith@dietitian.org
Web: www.dietitian.org/cdaf_scholarships.htm

Summary To provide financial assistance to minority and other residents of California who are members of the American Dietetic Association (ADA) and interested in working on an undergraduate degree at a school in any state.

Eligibility This program is open to California residents who are ADA members and 1) entering at least the second year of an accredited Coordinated Program (CP) or Didactic Program in Dietetics (DPD) in any state; or 2) accepted to an accredited Supervised Practice Program in any state to begin within 6 months. Along with their application, they must submit a letter of application that includes a discussion of their

career goals. Selection is based on that letter (15%), academic ability (25%), work or volunteer experience (15%), letters of recommendation (15%), extracurricular activities (5%), and financial need (25%). Applications are especially encouraged from ethnic minorities, men, and people with physical disabilities.

Financial data The stipend is normally $1,000.

Duration 1 year.

Number awarded 1 each year.

Deadline February of each year.

[84]
CAROLE SIMPSON RTDNF SCHOLARSHIP

Radio Television Digital News Foundation
Attn: RTDNF Fellowship Program
4121 Plank Road, Suite 512
Fredericksburg, VA 22407
(202) 467-5214   Fax: (202) 223-4007
E-mail: staceys@rtdna.org
Web: www.rtdna.org/pages/education/undergraduates.php

Summary To provide financial assistance to Native American and other minority undergraduate students who are interested in preparing for a career in electronic journalism.

Eligibility This program is open to sophomore or more advanced minority undergraduate students enrolled in an electronic journalism sequence at an accredited or nationally-recognized college or university. Applicants must submit 1 to 3 examples of their journalistic skills on audio CD or DVD (no more than 15 minutes total, accompanied by scripts); a description of their role on each story and a list of who worked on each story and what they did; a 1-page statement explaining why they are preparing for a career in electronic journalism with reference to their specific career preference (radio, television, online, reporting, producing, or newsroom management); a resume; and a letter of reference from their dean or faculty sponsor explaining why they are a good candidate for the award and certifying that they have at least 1 year of school remaining.

Financial data The stipend is $2,000, paid in semiannual installments of $1,000 each.

Duration 1 year.

Additional information The Radio Television Digital News Foundation (RTDNF) also provides an all-expense paid trip to the Radio Television Digital News Association (RTDNA) annual international conference. The RTDNF was formerly the Radio and Television News Directors Foundation (RTNDF). Previous winners of any RTDNF scholarship or internship are not eligible.

Number awarded 1 each year.

Deadline May of each year.

[85]
CECELIA SOMDAY EDUCATION FUND

Confederated Tribes of the Colville Reservation
Attn: Higher Education Office
P.O. Box 150
Nespelem, WA 99155-0150
(509) 634-2779   Fax: (509) 634-2790
E-mail: gloria.atkins@colvilletribes.com
Web: www.colvilletribes.com/cteap_higher_education.php

Summary To provide financial assistance to members of the Colville Confederated Tribes who wish to attend college or graduate school in any state.

Eligibility This program is open to enrolled members of the Confederated Tribes of the Colville Reservation who have a GPA of 3.0 or higher for their past 3 years of high school and/or college study. Applicants must be interested in attending a college, university, or vocational/technical school in any state to work full time on an undergraduate or graduate degree. They should be able to demonstrate strong involvement in school and community activities and a desire to have a positive future impact on the tribes. Along with their application, they must submit a 200-word essay describing their educational goals.

Financial data The stipend is $2,000 per year.

Duration 1 year; may be renewed.

Additional information The Colville Reservation was established in 1872 as a federation of 12 tribes: Colville, Nespelem, San Poil, Lake, Palus, Wenatchee, Chelan, Entiat, Methow, southern Okanogan, Moses Columbia, and Nez Perce. The reservation is located in north central Washington, primarily in Ferry and Okanogan counties.

Number awarded Varies each year.

Deadline April of each year.

[86]
CECIL SHOLL MEMORIAL SCHOLARSHIPS

Natives of Kodiak, Inc.
Attn: Scholarship Committee
215 Mission Road, Suite 201
Kodiak, AK 99615
(907) 486-3606   Toll Free: (800) 648-8462
Fax: (907) 486-2745   E-mail: nokinfo@alaska.com
Web: www.nativesofkodiak.com/shareholder.html

Summary To provide financial assistance to shareholders of Natives of Kodiak, Inc. and their dependents and descendants who are interested in attending college, graduate school, or vocational school in any state.

Eligibility This program is open to the shareholders, dependents of shareholders, and descendants of shareholders of Natives of Kodiak, Inc. Applicants must be enrolled or planning to enroll full time at a recognized or accredited college, university, or vocational school in any state to work on an undergraduate, graduate, or vocational degree. Along with their application, they must submit a 2-page essay about their future plans for education, special talents and abilities, community involvement, philosophy of life, and reasons for attending school. Selection is based on that essay (10 points), GPA (10 points), leadership abilities (10 points), educational goals (10 points), letters of recommendation (10 points), financial need (10 points), achievements, activities, and responsibilities (10 points), and neatness and grammar (10 points).

Financial data Stipends are $2,500, $2,000, or $1,000 per year.

Duration 1 year; recipients may reapply.

Number awarded 20 each year: 5 at $2,500, 10 at $2,000, and 5 at $1,000.

Deadline April of each year.

[87]
CENTER FOR STUDENT OPPORTUNITY SCHOLARSHIP

Center for Student Opportunity
Attn: Opportunity Scholarship
4903 Auburn Avenue
P.O. Box 30370
Bethesda, MD 20824
(301) 951-7101, ext. 214   Fax: (301) 951-7104
E-mail: scholarship@csopportunity.org
Web: www.csopportunity.org/ss/oppscholarship.aspx

Summary To provide financial assistance to first-generation, low-income, and/or Native American and other minority high school seniors who have participated in activities of the sponsoring organization and plan to attend selected universities.

Eligibility This program is open to graduating high school (or home-schooled) seniors who have participated in high school activities of the sponsoring organization. Applicants must be planning to attend a 4-year college or university that has a partnership arrangement with the sponsoring organization. They must be students whose parents did not go to or graduate from college, and/or students who need financial aid or scholarships to go to college, and/or students who identify as African American/Black, American Indian/Alaska Native, Hispanic/Latino, or Asian/Pacific Islander. Along with their application, they must submit 500-word essays on 1) the challenges they have faced in their college preparation, search, and application process; and 2) why they are deserving of this scholarship. There are no minimum academic requirements.

Financial data The stipend is $2,000 per year.

Duration 1 year; may be renewed up to 3 additional years.

Additional information The sponsor has partnership arrangements with more than 250 universities in nearly every state; most of them are private institutions, although some public universities are included. For a list, contact the sponsor. Recipients are invited to serve as monthly guest bloggers on the sponsor's web blog to share insight and perspective about their transition to college with high school participants in the sponsor's activities.

Number awarded 1 or more each year.

Deadline May of each year.

[88]
CESDA DIVERSITY SCHOLARSHIPS

Colorado Educational Services and Development
 Association
P.O. Box 40214
Denver, CO 80204
Web: www.cesda.org/664.html

Summary To provide financial assistance to high school seniors in Colorado who are planning to attend college in the state and are Native Americans, other minorities, or first-generation college students.

Eligibility This program is open to seniors graduating from high schools in Colorado who are 1) the first member of their family to attend college; 2) a member of an underrepresented ethnic or racial minority (African American, Asian/Pacific Islander, American Indian, Hispanic/Chicano/Latino); and/or 3) able to demonstrate financial need. Applicants must have a

GPA of 2.8 or higher and be planning to enroll at a 2- or 4-year college or university in Colorado. U.S. citizenship or permanent resident status is required. Selection is based on leadership and community service (particularly within minority communities), past academic performance, personal and professional accomplishments, personal attributes, special abilities, academic goals, and financial need.

Financial data The stipend is $1,000.

Duration 1 year; nonrenewable.

Number awarded Varies each year.

Deadline March of each year.

[89]
CH2M HILL SCHOLARSHIP PROGRAM

CH2M Hill Alaska, Inc.
Attn: Emily Cross
949 East 36th Avenue, Suite 500
Anchorage, AK 99508
(907) 762-1510   Fax: (907) 762-1600

Summary To provide financial assistance to Alaska Natives interested in attending college in any state to prepare for employment on the Trans-Alaska Pipeline System (TAPS).

Eligibility This program is open to Alaska Natives who are enrolled or planning to enrolled at a 2- or 4-year college or university in any state. Applicants must be interested in working on a degree in an engineering, design, or drafting field that corresponds to the services that CH2M Hill provides to the Alyeska Pipeline Service Company. Along with their application, they must submit a letter describing their goals and objectives, expected graduation date, and how their selected academic career will link directly to a position on TAPS.

Financial data A stipend is awarded (amount not specified).

Duration 1 year; recipients may reapply, provided they maintain a GPA of 2.0 or higher.

Additional information Funding for this program is provided by Alyeska Pipeline Service Company as part of its commitment under Section 29 of the Right of Way Agreement to provide scholarships to Alaska Natives.

Number awarded 1 or more each year.

Deadline July of each year.

[90]
CHEROKEE NATION PELL SCHOLARSHIPS

Cherokee Nation
Attn: College Resource Center
22361 Bald Hill Road
P.O. Box 948
Tahlequah, OK 74465
(918) 453-5000, ext. 5465
Toll Free: (800) 256-0671, ext. 5465 (within OK)
Fax: (918) 458-6195
E-mail: highereducation@cherokee.org
Web: www.cherokee.org/Services/297/Page/default.aspx

Summary To provide financial assistance to undergraduate students who belong to the Cherokee Nation and qualify for federal Pell Grants.

Eligibility This program is open to citizens of the Cherokee Nation, regardless of their permanent residence. Applicants who qualify for federal Pell Grant funding are eligible for this

additional assistance through the U.S. Bureau of Indian Affairs (BIA).

Financial data Available funding is divided equally among all Pell eligible students who complete the application process.

Duration Up to 8 semesters.

Number awarded Varies each year; nearly 1,600 students receive support from all Cherokee Nation Undergraduate Scholarship programs.

Deadline June of each year.

[91]
CHEYENNE AND ARAPAHO HIGHER EDUCATION GRANTS

Cheyenne and Arapaho Tribes of Oklahoma
Attn: Higher Education Program
P.O. Box 38
Concho, OK 73022
(405) 262-0345, ext. 27653   Toll Free: (800) 247-4612
Fax: (405) 262-5419   E-mail: heducation@c-a-tribes.org
Web: www.c-a-tribes.org/higher-education

Summary To provide financial assistance to enrolled Cheyenne-Arapaho tribal members who are interested in working on an undergraduate or graduate degree at a college in any state.

Eligibility This program is open to Cheyenne-Arapaho Indians who reside in any state and are at least a high school graduate (or the equivalent), approved for admission by a college or university, and in financial need. Applicants may be enrolled or planning to enroll at a 2- or 4-year college or university (not a vocational or technical school) in any state. The vast majority of students assisted under this program are at the undergraduate level, although graduate and/or married students are eligible for consideration and assistance. Summer and part-time students may apply as well, as long as application is made well in advance of enrollment and is accompanied by an official need evaluation.

Financial data The amount of the award depends on the need of the applicant.

Duration 1 year; renewable.

Number awarded 40 to 80 each year.

Deadline May of each year for fall semester; October for spring semester; or March for summer session.

[92]
CHEYENNE RIVER SIOUX TRIBE ADULT VOCATIONAL TRAINING PROGRAM

Cheyenne River Sioux Tribe
Attn: Education Services Office
2001 Main Street
P.O. Box 590
Eagle Butte, SD 57625
(605) 964-8311   E-mail: dal7882@lakotanetwork.com
Web: www.sioux.org/English/crst_higher_ed.php

Summary To provide financial assistance for vocational training in any state to members of the Cheyenne River Sioux Tribe and other tribal members who reside on the Cheyenne River Reservation.

Eligibility This program is open to enrolled Cheyenne River Sioux tribal members and other eligible Indian tribal members who reside on the Cheyenne River Reservation.

Applicants must be a high school graduate or GED recipient interested in a program of vocational training in any state. They must be able to demonstrate financial need.

Financial data A stipend is awarded (amount not specified).

Duration 1 year; may be renewed.

Additional information Funding for this program is provided by the U.S. Bureau of Indian Affairs (BIA).

Number awarded Varies each year.

Deadline Applications may be submitted at any time; awards are granted on a first-come, first-served basis.

[93]
CHEYENNE RIVER SIOUX TRIBE HIGHER EDUCATION PROGRAM

Cheyenne River Sioux Tribe
Attn: Education Services Office
2001 Main Street
P.O. Box 590
Eagle Butte, SD 57625
(605) 964-8311   E-mail: dal7882@lakotanetwork.com
Web: www.sioux.org/English/crst_higher_ed.php

Summary To provide financial assistance to members of the Cheyenne River Sioux Tribe who are interested in attending college in any state.

Eligibility This program is open to enrolled Cheyenne River Sioux tribal members who are attending or planning to attend a college, university, or vocational/technical school in any state. Applicants must be a high school graduate or GED recipient and planning to enroll full time. They must be able to demonstrate financial need. First priority is given to college seniors, then juniors, then sophomores, and then freshmen.

Financial data A stipend is awarded (amount not specified).

Duration 1 year; may be renewed, provided the recipient remains enrolled full time and maintains a GPA of 2.0 or higher.

Additional information Funding for this program is provided by the U.S. Bureau of Indian Affairs (BIA).

Number awarded Varies each year.

Deadline June of each year for the academic year; November of each year for spring semester only; April of each year for summer session.

[94]
CHEYENNE RIVER SIOUX TRIBE SCHOLARSHIP

Cheyenne River Sioux Tribe
Attn: Education Services Office
2001 Main Street
P.O. Box 590
Eagle Butte, SD 57625
(605) 964-8311   E-mail: dal7882@lakotanetwork.com
Web: www.sioux.org/English/crst_higher_ed.php

Summary To provide financial assistance to members of the Cheyenne River Sioux Tribe who are interested in attending college in any state but are not eligible for funding through other tribal programs.

Eligibility This program is open to enrolled Cheyenne River Sioux tribal members who are attending or planning to attend a college, university, or vocational/technical school in any state. Applicants must be a high school graduate or GED

recipient and planning to enroll full time. They must be eligible for the tribe's Higher Education Program, but they must have been denied funding because of 1) lack of funds available through that program; 2) inability to meet the financial need requirement of that program; or 3) exhaustion of the number of semesters allowed by that program.

Financial data A stipend is awarded (amount not specified).

Duration 1 year; may be renewed, provided the recipient remains enrolled full time and maintains a GPA of 2.0 or higher.

Number awarded Varies each year.

Deadline July of each year for the academic year; December of each year for spring semester only.

[95]
CHICKASAW FOUNDATION HEALTH PROFESSIONS SCHOLARSHIP

Chickasaw Foundation
110 West 12th Street
P.O. Box 1726
Ada, OK 74821-1726
(580) 421-9030   Fax: (580) 421-9031
E-mail: ChickasawFoundation@chickasaw.net
Web: www.chickasawfoundation.org/index_20.htm

Summary To provide financial assistance to members of the Chickasaw Nation who are interested in working on an undergraduate, graduate, or vocational/technical degree in a health-related field.

Eligibility This program is open to members of the Chickasaw Nation who are currently enrolled in an undergraduate, graduate, or vocational/technical program. Academic students must be preparing for a career as a dentist, dental hygienist, nurse, physician assistant, nurse practitioner, medical doctor, laboratory technologist, pharmacist, imaging technologist, behavioral health counselor, or biomedical engineer. Vocational students must be engaged in training as an emergency medical technician, licensed practical nurse, or electrician or plumber for the health arena. Applicants must have a GPA of 3.0 or higher. Along with their application, they must submit high school or college transcripts, 2 letters of recommendation, a copy of their Chickasaw Nation citizenship card, a copy of their Certificate of Indian Blood (CIB), and a 1-page essay on their long-term goals and plans for achieving them. Financial need is not considered in the selection process.

Financial data The stipend is $1,000.

Duration 1 year.

Number awarded 1 each year.

Deadline August of each year.

[96]
CHICKASAW NATION AGRICULTURE SCHOLASTIC PROGRAM

Oklahoma Youth Expo
Attn: Scholarship Program
431 N.E. 14th Street
Oklahoma City, OK 73104
(405) 235-0404   Fax: (405) 235-1727
Web: www.okyouthexpo.com/scholarships.htm

Summary To provide financial assistance to members of the Chickasaw Nation who are high school seniors, exhibit at the Oklahoma Youth Expo (OYE), and plan to attend college in Oklahoma to major in any subject.

Eligibility This program is open to members of the Chickasaw Nation who are high school seniors and exhibit at the OYE (membership in an Oklahoma 4-H Club or Oklahoma FFA chapter is required to exhibit). Applicants must be planning to enroll full time at an institution of higher education in Oklahoma where they may major in any subject field. They must have a Chickasaw Nation CIB card and a Chickasaw Nation Membership Card. Along with their application, they must submit 500-word essays on 1) how the junior livestock program has contributed to their higher educational and career pursuits, and 2) their 10-year goals in life and how those pursuits will help make Oklahoma a better place. Selection is based on financial need, academics, community involvement, and junior agriculture program participation.

Financial data The stipend is $2,500.

Duration 1 year; nonrenewable.

Additional information This program is sponsored by the Chickasaw Nation.

Number awarded 3 each year.

Deadline November of each year.

[97]
CHICKASAW NATION GENERAL SCHOLARSHIPS

Chickasaw Nation
Attn: Department of Education Services
300 Rosedale Road
Ada, OK 74820
(580) 421-7711　　　　　　Fax: (580) 436-3733
E-mail: education.services@chickasaw.net
Web: www.chickasaweducationservices.com/index_90.htm

Summary To provide financial assistance to members of the Chickasaw Nation who are working on an undergraduate or graduate degree at a school in any state.

Eligibility This program is open to members of the Chickasaw Nation who are working full or part time on an undergraduate, graduate, or doctoral degree at an accredited college or university in any state. Applicants must have a GPA of 3.0 or higher.

Financial data Stipends depend on the level of academic study, the number of units the recipients are taking, and their GPA. The range is from $150 per semester (for part-time freshmen and sophomores with a GPA of 3.0 to 3.49) to $550 per semester (for full-time graduate students with a GPA of 4.0).

Duration 1 semester; recipients may reapply.

Number awarded Varies each year.

Deadline January of each year for spring semester; June of each year for summer semester; August of each year for fall semester for continuing students; March of each year for high school seniors.

[98]
CHICKASAW NATION HIGHER EDUCATION GRANTS

Chickasaw Nation
Attn: Department of Education Services
300 Rosedale Road
Ada, OK 74820
(580) 421-7711　　　　　　Fax: (580) 436-3733
E-mail: education.services@chickasaw.net
Web: www.chickasaweducationservices.com/index_90.htm

Summary To provide financial assistance to needy members of the Chickasaw Nation who are working on an undergraduate or graduate degree at a school in any state.

Eligibility This program is open to members of the Chickasaw Nation who are working full or part time on an undergraduate, graduate, or doctoral degree at an accredited college or university in any state. Applicants must have a GPA of 2.0 or higher. They may be attending a community college, regional college or university, or research university.

Financial data For full-time undergraduates, stipends are $1,200 per semester at community colleges, $1,500 per semester at regional colleges and universities, or $2,400 per semester at research universities. For full-time graduate students, stipends are $2,400 per semester. For full-time doctoral students, stipends are $3,000 per semester. For part-time undergraduates, stipends are $100 per credit hour at community colleges, $125 per credit hour at regional colleges and universities, or $200 per credit hour at research universities. For part-time graduate students, stipends are $200 per credit hour at regional colleges and universities or $250 per credit hour at research universities. For part-time doctoral students, stipends are $250 per credit hour.

Duration 1 semester; recipients may reapply.

Number awarded Varies each year.

Deadline January of each year for spring semester; June of each year for summer semester; August of each year for fall semester for continuing students; March of each year for high school seniors.

[99]
CHIEF MANUELITO SCHOLARSHIP PROGRAM

Navajo Nation
Attn: Office of Navajo Nation Scholarship and Financial Assistance
P.O. Box 1870
Window Rock, AZ 86515-1870
(928) 871-7444　　　　Toll Free: (800) 243-2956
Fax: (928) 871-6742　　E-mail: onnsfacentral@navajo.org
Web: www.onnsfa.org

Summary To provide financial assistance to academically superior members of the Navajo Nation who are interested in working on an undergraduate degree.

Eligibility This program is open to enrolled members of the Navajo Nation who are attending or planning to enroll as full-time students at an accredited 4-year college or university. Applicants who are graduating high school seniors must have the following minimum combinations of ACT score and GPA: 21 and 3.8, 22 and 3.7, 23 and 3.6, 24 and 3.5, 25 and 3.4, 26 and 3.3, 27 and 3.2, 28 and 3.1, or 29 and 3.0. They must have completed in high school at least 1 unit of Navajo language and at least half a unit of Navajo government. Applicants who are current undergraduate students must have completed at least 24 semester credit hours with an overall GPA of 3.0 or higher.

Financial data The stipend is $7,000 per year.

Duration 1 year; may be renewed if the recipient maintains full-time status and a GPA of 3.0 or higher.

Additional information This program was established in 1980.

Number awarded Varies each year; recently, 79 of these scholarships were awarded.

Deadline April of each year.

[100]
CHIEF MOGUAGO SCHOLARSHIPS

Nottawaseppi Huron Band of Potawatomi
Attn: Education Director
2221 1-1/2 Mile Road
Fulton, MI 49052
(269) 729-5151, ext. 205   Fax: (269) 729-4837
E-mail: bphillips@nhbpi.com
Web: nhbpi.com/departments/education.html

Summary To provide financial assistance to members of the Nottawaseppi Huron Band of Potawatomi who are attending college in any state.

Eligibility This program is open to members of the Nottawaseppi Huron Band of Potawatomi who are currently enrolled at an accredited college or university in any state. Applicants must have a GPA of 3.0 or higher. Selection is based on academic accomplishment, personal character, leadership qualities, and community involvement.

Financial data A stipend is awarded (amount not specified).

Duration 1 year.

Additional information This program was established in 2004 to honor John Moguago, the Nottawaseppi Huron Band chief from 1839 to 1863 who led the tribe to settle along Pine Creek in Michigan.

Number awarded 2 or 3 each year.

Deadline June of each year.

[101]
CHIEF PUSHMATAHA COLLEGE SCHOLARSHIP FUND

Choctaw Nation
Attn: Scholarship Advisement Program
16th and Locust
P.O. Box 1210
Durant, OK 74702-1210
(580) 924-8280
Toll Free: (800) 522-6170, ext. 2523 (within OK)
Fax: (580) 920-3122
E-mail: scholarshipadvisement@choctawnation.com
Web: www.choctawnation-sap.com/cnoscholarship.shtml

Summary To provide financial assistance to members of the Choctaw Nation who are interested in attending college in any state and can demonstrate academic excellence.

Eligibility This program is open to members of the Choctaw Nation who are graduating high school seniors or currently attending a college or university in any state. Applicants must be able to demonstrate academic excellence (ACT of 30 or higher or SAT of 1340 or higher) and high potential. They

must register online with the Choctaw Scholarship Advisement Program.

Financial data The stipend is $20,000 per year.

Duration 4 years.

Number awarded 1 each year.

Deadline April of each year.

[102]
CHIEF TONY TANNER SCHOLARSHIP

Coquille Indian Tribe
Attn: Education Department
2611 Mexeye Loop
Coos Bay, OR 97420
(541) 756-0904   Toll Free: (800) 622-5869
Fax: (541) 888-2418
E-mail: lindamecum@coquilletribe.org
Web: www.coquilletribe.org

Summary To provide financial assistance to members of the Coquille Indian Tribe who are planning to attend college in any state.

Eligibility This program is open to enrolled members of the Coquille Indian Tribe who are currently sophomores or juniors at an accredited college or university in any state. Along with their application, they must submit a personal essay on their career goals, why they chose their educational field, and how they plan to use their education to benefit the Coquille Indian Tribe. Selection is based on academic achievement and/or community service and leadership.

Financial data The stipend is $5,000.

Duration 1 year; nonrenewable.

Number awarded 1 or more each year.

Deadline April of each year.

[103]
CHIPS QUINN SCHOLARS PROGRAM

Freedom Forum
Attn: Chips Quinn Scholars Program
555 Pennsylvania Avenue, N.W.
Washington, DC 20001
(202) 292-6271   Fax: (202) 292-6275
E-mail: kcatone@freedomforum.org
Web: www.chipsquinn.org

Summary To provide work experience to Native American and other minority college students or recent graduates who are majoring in journalism.

Eligibility This program is open to students of color who are college juniors, seniors, or recent graduates with journalism majors or career goals in newspapers. Candidates must be nominated or endorsed by journalism faculty, campus media advisers, editors of newspapers, or leaders of minority journalism associations. Along with their application, they must submit a resume, transcripts, 2 letters of recommendation, and an essay of 200 to 500 words on why they want to be a Chips Quinn Scholar. Reporters must also submit 6 samples of published articles they have written; photographers must submit 10 to 20 photographs on a CD. Applicants must have a car and be available to work as a full-time intern during the spring or summer. U.S. citizenship or permanent resident status is required. Campus newspaper experience is strongly encouraged.

Financial data Students chosen for this program receive a travel stipend to attend a Multimedia training program in Nashville, Tennessee prior to reporting for their internship, a $500 housing allowance from the Freedom Forum, and a competitive salary during their internship.

Duration Internships are for 10 to 12 weeks, in spring or summer.

Additional information This program was established in 1991 in memory of the late John D. Quinn Jr., managing editor of the *Poughkeepsie Journal*. Funding is provided by the Freedom Forum, formerly the Gannett Foundation. After graduating from college and obtaining employment with a newspaper, alumni of this program are eligible to apply for fellowship support to attend professional journalism development activities.

Number awarded Approximately 70 each year. Since the program began, more than 1,200 scholars have been selected.

Deadline October of each year.

[104]
CHOCTAW NATION AGRICULTURE SCHOLASTIC PROGRAM

Oklahoma Youth Expo
Attn: Scholarship Program
431 N.E. 14th Street
Oklahoma City, OK 73104
(405) 235-0404 Fax: (405) 235-1727
Web: www.okyouthexpo.com/scholarships.htm

Summary To provide financial assistance to members of the Choctaw Nation who are high school seniors, exhibit at the Oklahoma Youth Expo (OYE), and plan to attend college in Oklahoma to major in any subject.

Eligibility This program is open to members of the Choctaw Nation who are high school seniors and exhibit at the OYE (membership in an Oklahoma 4-H Club or Oklahoma FFA chapter is required to exhibit). Applicants must be planning to enroll full time at an institution of higher education in Oklahoma, where they may major in any subject field. They must have a Choctaw Nation CIB card and a Choctaw Nation Membership Card. Along with their application, they must submit 500-word essays on 1) how the junior livestock program has contributed to their higher educational and career pursuits, and 2) their 10-year goals in life and how those pursuits will help make Oklahoma a better place. Selection is based on financial need, academics, community involvement, and junior agriculture program participation.

Financial data The stipend is $2,500.

Duration 1 year; nonrenewable.

Additional information This program is sponsored by the Choctaw Nation.

Number awarded 2 each year.

Deadline November of each year.

[105]
CHOCTAW NATION HIGHER EDUCATION GRANTS

Choctaw Nation
Attn: Higher Education Department
16th and Locust
P.O. Box 1210
Durant, OK 74702-1210
(580) 924-8280
Toll Free: (800) 522-6170, ext. 2224 (within OK)
Fax: (580) 924-1267
Web: www.choctawnation.com/services/departments

Summary To provide financial assistance to Choctaw Indians who are interested in working on an undergraduate degree and can demonstrate financial need.

Eligibility This program is open to students who are attending or planning to attend an accredited college or university and have a Certificate of Indian Blood (CIB) and tribal membership card showing Choctaw descent. Students in vocational and technical schools or correspondence courses are not eligible. Applicants must be able to demonstrate financial need.

Financial data The stipend depends on the need, class level, and enrollment status of the recipient; maximum awards are $400 per semester for part-time students, $500 per semester for full-time freshmen, $600 per semester for full-time sophomores, $700 per semester for full-time juniors, or $800 per semester for full-time seniors.

Duration 1 year; may be renewed for up to 4 additional years as long as the recipient enrolls in at least 12 hours per semester (or at least 6 hours for part-time students) with a GPA of 2.0 or higher.

Additional information This program began in 1984 with funding from the Bureau of Indian Affairs.

Number awarded Varies each year.

Deadline September of each year for fall semester; February of each year for spring semester.

[106]
CHOCTAW NATION HIGHER EDUCATION SCHOLARSHIPS

Choctaw Nation
Attn: Higher Education Department
16th and Locust
P.O. Box 1210
Durant, OK 74702-1210
(580) 924-8280
Toll Free: (800) 522-6170, ext. 2224 (within OK)
Fax: (580) 924-1267
Web: www.choctawnation.com/services/departments

Summary To provide financial assistance to Choctaw Indians who are interested in working on an undergraduate degree.

Eligibility This program is open to students who are attending or planning to attend an accredited college or university and have a Certificate of Indian Blood (CIB) and tribal membership card showing Choctaw descent. Students in vocational and technical schools or correspondence courses are not eligible. Applicants must have a GPA of 2.5 or higher. Financial need is not considered in the selection process.

Financial data The stipend depends on GPA: $600 per semester for full-time students with a GPA of 2.50 to 2.99, $800 per semester for full-time students with a GPA of 3.00 to 3.49, or $1,000 per semester for full-time students with a GPA of 3.50 to 4.00. Part-time students receive $500 per semester regardless of GPA.

Duration 1 year; may be renewed for up to 4 additional years, as long as the recipient enrolls in at least 12 hours per semester (or at least 6 hours for part-time students) with a GPA of 2.5 or higher.

Additional information The Choctaw Nation established this program in 1998.

Number awarded Varies each year.

Deadline September of each year for fall semester; February of each year for spring semester.

[107]
CHUGACH HERITAGE FOUNDATION SCHOLARSHIPS

Chugach Alaska Corporation
Attn: Chugach Heritage Foundation
3800 Centerpoint Drive
Anchorage, AK 99503
(907) 563-8866   Toll Free: (800) 858-2768
Fax: (907) 550-4147
E-mail: scholarships@chugach-ak.com
Web: www.chugachheritagefoundation.org/application.asp

Summary To provide financial assistance to undergraduate and graduate students who are original enrollees of the Chugach Alaska Corporation or their descendants and attending college in any state.

Eligibility This program is open to original enrollees and the descendants of original enrollees of the Chugach Alaska Corporation. Applicants must be enrolled or planning to enroll at an accredited college, university, or vocational program in any state as an undergraduate or graduate student. They must have a GPA of 2.0 or higher.

Financial data For full-time students, stipends are $4,800 per year for students working on an associate degree or 1- or 2-year certificate, $6,000 per year for juniors and seniors, or $12,000 per year for graduate students. Stipends for part-time students are prorated appropriately. Undergraduates who earn a GPA of 3.5 or higher are eligible for a bonus of up to $1,200 per year.

Duration 1 year; may be renewed if the recipient maintains a GPA of 2.0 or higher.

Additional information The Chugach Alaska Corporation is 1 of 13 Alaska Native Regional Corporations created under the Alaska Native Claims Settlement Act of 1971.

Number awarded Varies each year.

Deadline August of each year.

[108]
CHUGACH HERITAGE FOUNDATION VOCATIONAL TRAINING FUNDING

Chugach Alaska Corporation
Attn: Chugach Heritage Foundation
3800 Centerpoint Drive
Anchorage, AK 99503
(907) 563-8866   Toll Free: (800) 858-2768
Fax: (907) 550-4147
E-mail: scholarships@chugach-ak.com
Web: www.chugachheritagefoundation.org/application.asp

Summary To provide financial assistance to students who are original enrollees of the Chugach Alaska Corporation or their descendants and enrolled in a vocational training program in any state.

Eligibility This program is open to original enrollees and the descendants of original enrollees of the Chugach Alaska Corporation. Applicants must be registered for training that will broaden their employment opportunities or maintain their skill level at a school in any state. They must have a GPA of 2.0 or higher.

Financial data The stipend is $4,000 per year.

Duration 1 year; may be renewed if the recipient maintains a GPA of 2.0 or higher.

Additional information The Chugach Alaska Corporation is 1 of 13 Alaska Native Regional Corporations created under the Alaska Native Claims Settlement Act of 1971.

Number awarded Varies each year.

Deadline Applications may be submitted at any time, but they must be received at least 30 days prior to the first day of class.

[109]
CIRI FOUNDATION ACHIEVEMENT SCHOLARSHIPS

Cook Inlet Region, Inc.
Attn: The CIRI Foundation
3600 San Jeronimo Drive, Suite 256
Anchorage, AK 99508-2870
(907) 793-3575   Toll Free: (800) 764-3382
Fax: (907) 793-3585   E-mail: tcf@thecirifoundation.org
Web: www.thecirifoundation.org/scholarships.htm

Summary To provide financial assistance for undergraduate or graduate studies to Alaska Natives who are original enrollees to Cook Inlet Region, Inc. (CIRI) and their lineal descendants.

Eligibility This program is open to Alaska Native enrollees to CIRI under the Alaska Native Claims Settlement Act (ANCSA) of 1971 and their lineal descendants. There are no Alaska residency requirements or age limitations. Applicants must be accepted or enrolled full time in a 4-year or graduate degree program. They must have a GPA of 3.0 or higher. Along with their application, they must submit a 500-word statement on their educational and career goals and how they are contributing, or planning to contribute, to a positive Alaska Native community. Selection is based on that statement, academic achievement, rigor of course work or degree program, student financial contribution, financial need, grade level, previous work performance, community service, and relationship of degree program to career goals.

Financial data The stipend is $8,000 per year.

Duration 1 year (2 semesters).
Number awarded Varies each year.
Deadline May of each year.

[110]
CIRI FOUNDATION EXCELLENCE SCHOLARSHIPS

Cook Inlet Region, Inc.
Attn: The CIRI Foundation
3600 San Jeronimo Drive, Suite 256
Anchorage, AK 99508-2870
(907) 793-3575   Toll Free: (800) 764-3382
Fax: (907) 793-3585   E-mail: tcf@thecirifoundation.org
Web: www.thecirifoundation.org/scholarships.htm

Summary To provide financial assistance for undergraduate or graduate studies to Alaska Natives who are original enrollees to Cook Inlet Region, Inc. (CIRI) and their lineal descendants.

Eligibility This program is open to Alaska Native enrollees to CIRI under the Alaska Native Claims Settlement Act (ANCSA) of 1971 and their lineal descendants. There are no Alaska residency requirements or age limitations. Applicants must be accepted or enrolled full time in a 4-year undergraduate or a graduate degree program. They must have a GPA of 3.5 or higher. Along with their application, they must submit a 500-word statement on their educational and career goals and how they are contributing, or planning to contribute, to a positive Alaska Native community. Selection is based on that statement, academic achievement, rigor of course work or degree program, student financial contribution, financial need, grade level, previous work performance, community service, and relationship of degree program to career goals.

Financial data The stipend is $10,000 per year.
Duration 1 year (2 semesters).
Number awarded Varies each year; recently, 7 of these scholarships were awarded.
Deadline May of each year.

[111]
CIRI FOUNDATION GENERAL SEMESTER SCHOLARSHIPS

Cook Inlet Region, Inc.
Attn: The CIRI Foundation
3600 San Jeronimo Drive, Suite 256
Anchorage, AK 99508-2870
(907) 793-3575   Toll Free: (800) 764-3382
Fax: (907) 793-3585   E-mail: tcf@thecirifoundation.org
Web: www.thecirifoundation.org/scholarships.htm

Summary To provide financial assistance for undergraduate or graduate studies to Alaska Natives who are original enrollees to Cook Inlet Region, Inc. (CIRI) and their lineal descendants.

Eligibility This program is open to Alaska Native enrollees to CIRI under the Alaska Native Claims Settlement Act (ANCSA) of 1971 and their lineal descendants. There are no Alaska residency requirements or age limitations. Applicants must be accepted or enrolled full time in a 2-year, 4-year, or graduate degree program. They must have a GPA of 2.5 or higher. Along with their application, they must submit a 500-word statement on their educational and career goals and how they are contributing, or planning to contribute, to a pos-

itive Alaska Native community. Selection is based on that statement, academic achievement, rigor of course work or degree program, student financial contribution, financial need, grade level, previous work performance, community service, and relationship of degree program to career goals.

Financial data The stipend is $2,500 per semester.
Duration 1 semester; recipients may reapply.
Number awarded Varies each year; recently, 213 of these scholarships were awarded.
Deadline May or November of each year.

[112]
CIRI FOUNDATION INTERNSHIP PROGRAM

Cook Inlet Region, Inc.
Attn: The CIRI Foundation
3600 San Jeronimo Drive, Suite 256
Anchorage, AK 99508-2870
(907) 793-3575   Toll Free: (800) 764-3382
Fax: (907) 793-3585   E-mail: tcf@thecirifoundation.org
Web: www.thecirifoundation.org/internships.htm

Summary To provide on-the-job training to Alaska Natives who are original enrollees to the Cook Inlet Region, Inc. (CIRI) and their lineal descendants.

Eligibility This program is open to Alaska Native enrollees to CIRI under the Alaska Native Claims Settlement Act (ANCSA) of 1971 and their lineal descendants. Applicants must 1) be enrolled in a 2- or 4-year academic or graduate degree program with a GPA of 3.0 or higher; 2) have recently completed an undergraduate or graduate degree program; or 3) be enrolled or have recently completed a technical skills training program at an accredited or otherwise approved postsecondary institution. Along with their application, they must submit a 500-word statement on their areas of interest, their educational and career goals, how their career goals relate to their educational goals, and the type of work experience they would like to gain as it relates to their career and educational goals.

Financial data The intern's wage is based on a trainee position and is determined by the employer of the intern with the approval of the foundation (which pays one half of the intern's wages).

Duration Internships are approved on a quarterly basis for 480 hours of part-time or full-time employment. Interns may reapply on a quarter-by-quarter basis, not to exceed 12 consecutive months.

Additional information The foundation and the intern applicant work together to identify an appropriate placement experience. The employer hires the intern. Placement may be with Cook Inlet Region, Inc., a firm related to the foundation, or a business or service organization located anywhere in the United States. The intern may be placed with more than 1 company during the internship period. Interns may receive academic credit.

Deadline March, June, September, or November of each year.

[113]
CIRI FOUNDATION SPECIAL EXCELLENCE SCHOLARSHIPS

Cook Inlet Region, Inc.
Attn: The CIRI Foundation
3600 San Jeronimo Drive, Suite 256
Anchorage, AK 99508-2870
(907) 793-3575   Toll Free: (800) 764-3382
Fax: (907) 793-3585   E-mail: tcf@thecirifoundation.org
Web: www.thecirifoundation.org/scholarships.htm

Summary   To provide financial assistance for undergraduate or graduate studies in selected fields to Alaska Natives who are original enrollees to Cook Inlet Region, Inc. (CIRI) and their lineal descendants.

Eligibility   This program is open to Alaska Native enrollees to CIRI under the Alaska Native Claims Settlement Act (ANCSA) of 1971 and their lineal descendants. There are no Alaska residency requirements or age limitations. Applicants must be accepted or enrolled full time in a 4-year undergraduate or a graduate degree program. They must have a GPA of 3.7 or higher. Preference is given to students working on a degree in business, education, mathematics, sciences, health services, or engineering. Along with their application, they must submit a 500-word statement on their educational and career goals and how they are contributing, or planning to contribute, to a positive Alaska Native community. Selection is based on that statement, academic achievement, rigor of course work or degree program, student financial contribution, financial need, grade level, previous work performance, community service, and relationship of degree program to career goals.

Financial data   The stipend is $20,000 per year.

Duration   1 year; may be renewed.

Additional information   This program was established in 1997.

Number awarded   1 or more each year.

Deadline   May of each year.

[114]
CIRI FOUNDATION VOCATIONAL TRAINING GRANTS

Cook Inlet Region, Inc.
Attn: The CIRI Foundation
3600 San Jeronimo Drive, Suite 256
Anchorage, AK 99508-2870
(907) 793-3575   Toll Free: (800) 764-3382
Fax: (907) 793-3585   E-mail: tcf@thecirifoundation.org
Web: www.thecirifoundation.org/grants.htm

Summary   To provide financial assistance for professional preparation after high school to Alaska Natives who are original enrollees to the Cook Inlet Region, Inc. (CIRI) and their lineal descendants.

Eligibility   This program is open to Alaska Native enrollees to CIRI under the Alaska Native Claims Settlement Act (ANCSA) of 1971 and their lineal descendants. Applicants should have a high school diploma or GED, have a GPA of 2.5 or higher, and be able to document the availability of employment upon completion of the training. They must be accepted or enrolled part or full time in a technical skills certificate or degree program, such as (but not limited to) craft/trade, automotive technology, office occupations, and computer technol-

ogy. Alaska residency is not required. Along with their application, they must submit a 500-word statement on their educational and career goals and how they are contributing, or planning to contribute, to a positive Alaska Native community. Selection is based on that statement, academic achievement, rigor of course work or degree program, student financial contribution, financial need, grade level, previous work performance, community service, and relationship of degree program to career goals.

Financial data   The maximum stipend is $4,500 per calendar year.

Duration   1 quarter; recipients may reapply.

Number awarded   Varies each year; recently, 42 of these grants were awarded.

Deadline   March, June, September, or November of each year.

[115]
CITI FOUNDATION SCHOLARSHIP PROGRAM

American Indian College Fund
Attn: Scholarship Department
8333 Greenwood Boulevard
Denver, CO 80221
(303) 426-8900   Toll Free: (800) 776-FUND
Fax: (303) 426-1200
E-mail: scholarships@collegefund.org
Web: www.collegefund.org/scholarships/schol_tcu.html

Summary   To provide financial assistance to Native American students from any state who are attending tribal colleges in South Dakota.

Eligibility   This program is open to American Indians or Alaska Natives from any state enrolled full time at eligible Tribal Colleges and Universities (TCUs) in South Dakota. Applicants must have a GPA of 3.0 or higher and be able to demonstrate exceptional academic achievement or financial need. They must be willing to work with other scholarship recipients at their campus to organize a professional development component called the Citi Foundation Career Exploration Day. Applications are available only online and include required essays on specified topics.

Financial data   The stipend is $4,000.

Duration   1 year.

Additional information   This scholarship is sponsored by the Citigroup Foundation in partnership with the American Indian College Fund.

Number awarded   1 or more each year.

Deadline   May of each year.

[116]
CITIZEN POTAWATOMI NATION TRIBAL ROLLS SCHOLARSHIPS

Citizen Potawatomi Nation
Attn: Office of Tribal Rolls
1601 South Gordon Cooper Drive
Shawnee, OK 74801-9002
(405) 878-5835   Toll Free: (800) 880-9880
Fax: (405) 878-4653
Web: www.potawatomi.org

Summary   To provide financial assistance for college or graduate school to members of the Citizen Potawatomi Nation.

Eligibility This program is open to enrolled members of the Citizen Potawatomi Nation who are attending or planning to attend an undergraduate or graduate degree program, vocational technical career courses, or other accredited educational program in any state. Applicants must have a GPA of 2.0 or higher and be able to demonstrate financial need.

Financial data Stipends are $1,500 per semester for full-time students or $750 per semester for part-time students.

Duration 1 semester; may be renewed, provided the recipient maintains a GPA of 2.0 or higher.

Number awarded Varies each year; recently, 125 of these scholarships were awarded, including 94 to undergraduates, 10 to vocational/technical students, and 21 to graduate students.

Deadline July of each year for the fall session, November for the spring or winter session, or May for summer session.

[117]
CLEM JUDD, JR. MEMORIAL SCHOLARSHIP

Hawai'i Hotel & Lodging Association
Attn: Hawaii Hotel Industry Foundation
2270 Kalakaua Avenue, Suite 1506
Honolulu, HI 96815
(808) 923-0407   Fax: (808) 924-3843
E-mail: hhla@hawaiihotels.org
Web: www.hawaiihotels.org/displaycommon.cfm?an=6

Summary To provide financial assistance to Native Hawaiians who are upper-division students working on a degree in hotel management at a school in any state.

Eligibility This program is open to Hawaii residents who can provide proof of their Hawaiian ancestry through birth certificates of their parents or grandparents. Applicants must be a junior or senior at an accredited college or university (in any state) and majoring in hotel management. They must have a GPA of 2.8 or higher. Financial need is not considered in the selection process.

Financial data The stipend ranges from $1,000 to $2,500.

Duration 1 year.

Additional information This program was established in 1996.

Number awarded 1 each year.

Deadline June of each year.

[118]
CLSA LEADERSHIP FOR DIVERSITY SCHOLARSHIP

California School Library Association
Attn: Executive Director
950 Glenn Drive, Suite 150
Folsom, CA 95630
(916) 447-2684   Fax: (916) 447-2695
E-mail: info@csla.net
Web: www.csla.net/awa/scholarships.htm

Summary To provide financial assistance to Native Americans and other students who reflect the diversity of California's population and are interested in earning a credential as a library media teacher in the state.

Eligibility This program is open to students who are members of a traditionally underrepresented group enrolled in a college or university library media teacher credential program in California. Applicants must intend to work as a library

media teacher in a California school library media center for a minimum of 3 years. Along with their application, they must submit a 250-word statement on their school library media career interests and goals, why they should be considered, what they can contribute, their commitment to serving the needs of multicultural and multilingual students, and their financial situation.

Financial data The stipend is $1,500.

Duration 1 year.

Number awarded 1 each year.

Deadline April of each year.

[119]
CNEC MISSION AWARD

Cherokee Nation
Attn: Cherokee Nation Education Corporation
115 East Delaware Street
P.O. Box 948
Tahlequah, OK 74465-0948
(918) 207-0950   Fax: (918) 207-0951
E-mail: contact@cnec-edu.org
Web: cnec.cherokee.org

Summary To provide financial assistance to citizens of the Cherokee Nation who are enrolled at a college or university in any state and working on an undergraduate or graduate degree in a field related to the Cherokee people.

Eligibility This program is open to citizens of the Cherokee Nation who are currently enrolled full time at a college or university in any state. Applicants must be working on an undergraduate or graduate degree that will prepare them for a career that will promote the revitalization of the language, culture, and history of Cherokee people. Along with their application, they must submit a 4-page personal essay that includes background information, their degree plan for higher education, why they have chosen that field of study, how they plan to serve Cherokee people when they complete higher education, and why they should be selected for this scholarship. Selection is based on the clarity and presentation of the essay; academic information (including transcripts and ACT scores); school, cultural and community activities; future plans to serve Cherokee people; and financial need.

Financial data The stipend is $1,500 per semester ($3,000 per year).

Duration 1 year. Renewal for the second semester requires the recipient to earn a GPA of 2.5 or higher in the first semester.

Number awarded 1 each year.

Deadline April of each year.

[120]
COCA-COLA FIRST GENERATION SCHOLARSHIP

American Indian College Fund
Attn: Scholarship Department
8333 Greenwood Boulevard
Denver, CO 80221
(303) 426-8900   Toll Free: (800) 776-FUND
Fax: (303) 426-1200
E-mail: scholarships@collegefund.org
Web: www.collegefund.org/scholarships/schol_tcu.html

Summary To provide financial assistance to Native Americans who are attending a Tribal College or University (TCU) and are the first in their family to attend college.

Eligibility This program is open to American Indians or Alaska Natives who are enrolled full time in their first or second semester at an eligible TCU. Applicants must have a GPA of 3.0 or higher and be able to demonstrate exceptional academic achievement or financial need. They must be the first in their immediate family to attend college. Applications are available only online and include required essays on specified topics.

Financial data The stipend is $5,000 per year.

Duration 1 year; may be renewed, provided the recipient maintains a GPA of 3.0 or higher and participates actively in campus and community life.

Additional information This program is sponsored by the Coca-Cola Company in partnership with the American Indian College Fund.

Number awarded 1 or more each year.

Deadline May of each year.

[121]
COCOPAH HIGHER EDUCATION GRANTS

Cocopah Indian Tribe
Attn: Education Department
County 15th and Avenue G
Somerton, AZ 85350
(928) 627-2101   Fax: (928) 627-3173
E-mail: cocopah@cocopah.com
Web: www.cocopah.com/education.html

Summary To provide financial assistance to members of the Cocopah Indian Nation who are attending or planning to attend college to work on an undergraduate degree.

Eligibility This program is open to enrolled members of the Cocopah Indian Nation who are enrolled at or accepted by an accredited college or university in the United States. Applicants with a GPA of 2.99 or lower must attend their local community college; applicants with a GPA of 3.0 or higher are allowed to attend their local community college or a university in the state in which they reside; applicants with a GPA of 3.5 or higher may attend an institution in any state. They must submit documentation of financial need, although awards are available to students who have no unmet need. Awards are granted in the following priority order: 1) continuing undergraduates in good academic standing; 2) continuing education new undergraduates; 3) higher education new undergraduates; and 4) non-financial need students.

Financial data For full-time students at in-state public universities and colleges who can document financial need, grants are intended to cover tuition, books, room and board, transportation, personal costs, and any other expenses deemed necessary by the institution's financial aid department. For full-time students at private and out-of state colleges and universities who can document financial need, assistance is based on average attendance costs at the institution, as determined by the tribal education department. Full-time students who cannot document financial need are eligible for assistance if funds are available; the amount of that assistance depends on the average attendance costs at their institution, as determined by the tribal education department. Part-time students receive payment of direct costs only (tuition, fees, and textbooks) for the program in which they are enrolled at an in-state public college or university.

Duration 1 year; may be renewed, provided the recipient maintains a GPA of 2.0 or higher.

Number awarded Varies each year.

Deadline April of each year for fall semester; September of each year for spring semester.

[122]
COCOPAH SUMMER TUITION ASSISTANCE

Cocopah Indian Tribe
Attn: Education Department
County 15th and Avenue G
Somerton, AZ 85350
(928) 627-2101   Fax: (928) 627-3173
E-mail: cocopah@cocopah.com
Web: www.cocopah.com/education.html

Summary To provide financial assistance to members of the Cocopah Indian Nation who are interested in working during the summer on an undergraduate or graduate degree.

Eligibility This program is open to enrolled members of the Cocopah Indian Nation who are enrolled at or accepted by an accredited college or university in the United States. Undergraduates should have a GPA of 2.0 or higher; graduate students should have a GPA of 3.0 or higher. Applicants must be interested in attending school during the summer. They must be able to document financial need.

Financial data Maximum grants are $2,500 for graduate students or $1,000 for undergraduates. Funds may be used for payment of direct costs only (tuition, fees, and textbooks).

Duration 1 summer term.

Number awarded Varies each year.

Deadline March of each year.

[123]
COLBERT "BUD" BAKER SCHOLARSHIP

Chickasaw Foundation
110 West 12th Street
P.O. Box 1726
Ada, OK 74821-1726
(580) 421-9030   Fax: (580) 421-9031
E-mail: ChickasawFoundation@chickasaw.net
Web: www.chickasawfoundation.org/index_20.htm

Summary To provide financial assistance to members of the Chickasaw Nation who are majoring or minoring in American history, education, or pre-law.

Eligibility This program is open to Chickasaw students who are currently enrolled full time at an accredited institution of higher education. Applicants must be classified as juniors or seniors at a 4-year college. They must be 1) majoring in history; or 2) majoring in education or pre-law with a minor in history. The history emphasis must be on Chickasaw tribal history or Native American studies. Along with their application, they must submit high school or college transcripts, 2 letters of recommendation, a copy of their Chickasaw Nation citizenship card, and a 1-page essay on their long-term goals and plans for achieving them. Financial need is not considered in the selection process.

Financial data The stipend is $1,200.

Duration 1 year.

Number awarded 3 each year.

Deadline August of each year.

[124]
COLGATE "BRIGHT SMILES, BRIGHT FUTURES" MINORITY SCHOLARSHIPS

American Dental Hygienists' Association
Attn: Institute for Oral Health
444 North Michigan Avenue, Suite 3400
Chicago, IL 60611-3980
(312) 440-8944   Toll Free: (800) 735-4916
Fax: (312) 467-1806   E-mail: institute@adha.net
Web: www.adha.org/ioh/programs/scholarships.htm

Summary To provide financial assistance to Native Americans, other minority students, and males of any race who are members of the Student American Dental Hygienists' Association (SADHA) or the American Dental Hygienists' Association (ADHA) and enrolled in certificate programs in dental hygiene.

Eligibility This program is open to members of groups currently underrepresented in the dental hygiene profession (Native Americans, African Americans, Hispanics, Asians, and males) who are active members of the SADHA or the ADHA. Applicants must have a GPA of 3.0 or higher, be able to document financial need of at least $1,500, and have completed at least 1 year of full-time enrollment in an accredited dental hygiene certificate program in the United States. Along with their application, they must submit a statement that covers their long-term career goals, their intended contribution to the dental hygiene profession, their professional interests, and how their extracurricular activities and their degree enhance the attainment of their goals.

Financial data The stipend ranges from $1,000 to $2,000.

Duration 1 year; nonrenewable.

Additional information These scholarships are sponsored by the Colgate-Palmolive Company.

Number awarded 2 each year.

Deadline January of each year.

[125]
COLLEGE SCHOLARSHIPS FOUNDATION MINORITY STUDENT SCHOLARSHIP

College Scholarships Foundation
5506 Red Robin Road
Raleigh, NC 27613
(919) 630-4895   Toll Free: (888) 501-9050
E-mail: info@collegescholarships.org
Web: www.collegescholarships.org

Summary To provide financial assistance to Native Americans and other minority undergraduate and graduate students.

Eligibility This program is open to full-time undergraduate and graduate students who are Black, Hispanic, Native American, or Pacific Islander. Applicants must have a GPA of 3.0 or higher. Along with their application, they must submit a 300-word essay on how being a minority affected their pre-college education, how being a minority has positively affected their character, and where they see themselves in 10 years. U.S. citizenship is required.

Financial data The stipend is $1,000.

Duration 1 year.

Additional information This scholarship was first awarded in 2006. The sponsor was formerly known as the Daniel Kovach Scholarship Foundation.

Number awarded 1 each year.

Deadline December of each year.

[126]
COLLEGE STUDENT PRE-COMMISSIONING INITIATIVE

U.S. Coast Guard
Attn: Recruiting Command
2300 Wilson Boulevard, Suite 500
Arlington, VA 22201
(703) 235-1775   Toll Free: (877) NOW-USCG
Fax: (703) 235-1881
E-mail: Margaret.A.Jackson@uscg.mil
Web: www.gocoastguard.com

Summary To provide financial assistance to college students at Tribal Colleges or Universities and other minority institutions who are willing to serve in the Coast Guard following graduation.

Eligibility This program is open to students entering their junior or senior year at a college or university designated as an Historically Black College or University (HBCU), Hispanic Serving Institution (HSI), Tribal College or University (TCU), or an institution located in Guam, Puerto Rico, or the U.S. Virgin Islands. Applicants must be U.S. citizens; have a GPA of 2.5 or higher; have scores of 1100 or higher on the critical reading and mathematics SAT, 23 or higher on the ACT, or 109 or higher on the ASVAB GT; be between 19 and 27 years of age; have no more than 2 dependents; and meet all physical requirements for a Coast Guard commission. They must agree to attend the Coast Guard Officer Candidate School following graduation and serve on active duty as an officer for at least 3 years.

Financial data Those selected to participate receive full payment of tuition, books, and fees; monthly housing and food allowances; medical and life insurance; special training in leadership, management, law enforcement, navigation, and marine science; 30 days of paid vacation per year; and a monthly salary of up to $2,200.

Duration Up to 2 years.

Number awarded Varies each year.

Deadline February of each year.

[127]
COLORADO EDUCATION ASSOCIATION ETHNIC MINORITY SCHOLARSHIPS

Colorado Education Association
Attn: Ethnic Minority Advisory Council
1500 Grant Street
Denver, CO 80203
(303) 837-1500   Toll Free: (800) 332-5939
Web: coloradoea.org/education/grants.aspx

Summary To provide financial assistance to Native American and other minority high school seniors in Colorado who are children of members of the Colorado Education Association (CEA) and planning to attend college in any state.

Eligibility This program is open to seniors graduating from high schools in Colorado who are members of a minority ethnic group, defined to include American Indians/Alaska

Natives, Asians, Blacks, Hispanics, Native Hawaiians/Pacific Islanders, and multi-ethnic. Applicants must be the dependent child of an active, retired, or deceased CEA member. They must be planning to attend an accredited institution of higher education in any state. Along with their application, they must submit brief statements on 1) their need for this scholarship; and 2) why they plan to pursue a college education.

Financial data The stipend is $1,000.

Duration 1 year; nonrenewable.

Number awarded 4 each year.

Deadline March of each year.

[128]
COLORADO INDIAN EDUCATION FOUNDATION SCHOLARS PROGRAM

Rocky Mountain Indian Chamber of Commerce
Attn: Colorado Indian Education Foundation
924 West Colfax Avenue, Suite 104F
Denver, CO 80204
(303) 629-0102   Fax: (720) 974-9450
E-mail: info@rmicc.org
Web: www.rmicc.org/foundation.html

Summary To provide financial assistance to American Indians from Colorado who are interested in attending college in the state.

Eligibility This program is open to American Indian residents of Colorado who can verify that they 1) are on a federal or state-recognized tribal roll and are identified by a tribal enrollment card; 2) have an official letter from a federal or state recognized tribe or agency stating tribal membership or Indian blood; 3) have a family tree and officially sealed birth certificates establishing that at least 1 parent is Indian; or 4) are an enrolled official member of a terminated tribe. Applicants must be enrolled or planning to enroll full time at an accredited college, university, or vocational/trade school in Colorado. They must have a GPA of 2.5 or higher. Along with their application, they must submit a 500-word essay describing their chosen field of study, educational goals, career goals, involvement in the Indian community, and how this scholarship will help them in furthering their education. Financial need is not considered in the selection process.

Financial data The stipend is $1,000.

Duration 1 year.

Number awarded Varies each year; recently, 15 of these scholarships were awarded.

Deadline September of each year.

[129]
COLORADO RIVER INDIAN TRIBES ADULT VOCATIONAL TRAINING PROGRAM

Colorado River Indian Tribes
Attn: Career Development Office
13390 North First Avenue
Parker, AZ 85344
(928) 669-5548   Toll Free: (800) 809-6207
Fax: (928) 669-5570   E-mail: critcdo@critcdo.com
Web: www.crit-cdo.com/index.htm

Summary To provide need-based financial assistance to members of the Colorado River Indian Tribes who are interested in obtaining adult vocational training at a school in any state.

Eligibility This program is open to enrolled members of the Colorado River Indian Tribes who are graduating high school seniors, GED recipients, or students already enrolled in at a junior college or vocational training facility in any state. Applicants must have a high school GPA of 2.0 or higher or a GED certificate with a composite score of 45% or higher. Financial need is considered in the selection process, and students must apply for all other available funding sources, such as Pell Grants and State Student Incentive Grants (SSIG).

Financial data A stipend is awarded (amount not specified).

Duration Up to 24 months (or 36 months for students in a nursing program).

Additional information The Colorado River Indian Tribes Reservation was established in 1865 for Indians who resided along the Colorado River in Arizona and California. It currently includes members of the Mohave, Chemehuevi, Hopi, and Navajo tribes. This program is supported by funding from the U.S. Bureau of Indian Affairs (BIA).

Number awarded Varies each year.

Deadline June of each year for fall semester; October of each year for spring semester.

[130]
COLORADO RIVER INDIAN TRIBES BIA GRANTS

Colorado River Indian Tribes
Attn: Career Development Office
13390 North First Avenue
Parker, AZ 85344
(928) 669-5548   Toll Free: (800) 809-6207
Fax: (928) 669-5570   E-mail: critcdo@critcdo.com
Web: www.crit-cdo.com/index.htm

Summary To provide need-based financial assistance to members of the Colorado River Indian Tribes who are interested in attending college or graduate school in any state.

Eligibility This program is open to enrolled members of the Colorado River Indian Tribes who are graduating high school seniors, GED recipients, or students already enrolled in college or graduate school. Applicants must be enrolled or planning to enroll at an accredited college or university in any state to work on an associate, bachelor's, master's, or doctoral degree. They must have a high school GPA of 2.5 or higher or a GED certificate with a composite score of 45% or higher. Financial need is considered in the selection process, and students must apply for all other available funding sources, such as Pell Grants and State Student Incentive Grants (SSIG).

Financial data A stipend is awarded (amount not specified).

Duration 1 year; may be renewed.

Additional information The Colorado River Indian Tribes Reservation was established in 1865 for Indians who resided along the Colorado River in Arizona and California. It currently includes members of the Mohave, Chemehuevi, Hopi, and Navajo tribes. This program is supported by funding from the U.S. Bureau of Indian Affairs (BIA).

Number awarded Varies each year.

Deadline June of each year for fall semester; October of each year for spring semester.

[131]
COLORADO RIVER INDIAN TRIBES TRIBAL SCHOLARSHIPS

Colorado River Indian Tribes
Attn: Career Development Office
13390 North First Avenue
Parker, AZ 85344
(928) 669-5548   Toll Free: (800) 809-6207
Fax: (928) 669-5570   E-mail: critcdo@critcdo.com
Web: www.crit-cdo.com/index.htm

Summary To provide merit-based financial assistance to members of the Colorado River Indian Tribes who are interested in attending college or graduate school in any state.

Eligibility This program is open to enrolled members of the Colorado River Indian Tribes who are graduating high school seniors, GED recipients, or students already enrolled in college or graduate school. Applicants must be enrolled or planning to enroll at an accredited college or university in any state to work on an associate, bachelor's, master's, or doctoral degree. They must have a high school GPA of 2.5 or higher or a GED certificate with a composite score of 45% or higher. Financial need is not considered in the selection process.

Financial data A stipend is awarded (amount not specified).

Duration 1 year; may be renewed.

Additional information The Colorado River Indian Tribes Reservation was established in 1865 for Indians who resided along the Colorado River in Arizona and California. It currently includes members of the Mohave, Chemehuevi, Hopi, and Navajo tribes. This program is supported by tribal funds.

Number awarded Varies each year.

Deadline June of each year for fall semester; October of each year for spring semester.

[132]
COMANCHE NATION ADULT VOCATIONAL TRAINING PROGRAM

Comanche Nation
Attn: Education Programs
584 N.W. Bingo Road
P.O. Box 908
Lawton, OK 73502
(580) 492-3363   Fax: (580) 492-4017
Web: www.comanchenation.com/education/index.html

Summary To provide financial assistance to adult members of the Comanche Nation who are interested in vocational training.

Eligibility This program is open to adult enrolled members of the Comanche Nation who are attending full-time programs offered by vocational schools in the state where they live. They must be seeking financial assistance and vocational counseling.

Financial data A stipend is awarded (amount not specified).

Duration Support is provided for at least 9 but not more than 24 months.

Number awarded Varies each year.

Deadline Deadline not specified.

[133]
COMANCHE NATION COLLEGE SCHOLARSHIP PROGRAM

Comanche Nation
Attn: Education Programs
584 N.W. Bingo Road
P.O. Box 908
Lawton, OK 73502
(580) 492-3363   Fax: (580) 492-4017
Web: www.comanchenation.com/education/index.html

Summary To provide financial assistance to members of the Comanche Nation who are interested in working on an undergraduate or graduate degree.

Eligibility This program is open to enrolled members of the Comanche Nation who are high school graduates or GED recipients and attending or planning to attend a college or university. Applicants must intend to work on a bachelor's, master's, or doctoral degree or be enrolled in a 2-year program that will transfer to a 4-year institution. They must be able to demonstrate financial need and provide a reasonable assurance that they will be able to complete their degree program.

Financial data A stipend is awarded (amount not specified).

Duration 1 year; may be renewed.

Number awarded Varies each year.

Deadline March of each year for summer; May of each year for fall; September of each year for spring.

[134]
COMMUNICATIONS INTERNSHIP AWARD FOR STUDENTS OF COLOR

College and University Public Relations Association of Pennsylvania
Calder Square
P.O. Box 10034
State College, PA 16805-0034
Fax: (814) 863-3428   E-mail: kathyettinger@psu.edu
Web: www.cuprap.org/default.aspx?pageid=16

Summary To provide an opportunity for Native Americans and other students of color at institutions that are members of the College and University Public Relations Association of Pennsylvania (CUPRAP) to complete an internship in communications.

Eligibility This program is open to students of color (i.e., African Americans, Asian/Pacific Islanders, Hispanics/Latinos, and Native Americans) who have completed the first year of college and are enrolled as a degree candidate in the second year or higher. Applicants must obtain and complete a verifiable internship of at least 150 hours in a communications-related field (e.g., print media, radio, television, public relations, advertising, graphic/web design). They must be enrolled full time at an accredited 2- or 4-year college or university that is a member of CUPRAP, but they are not required to be residents of Pennsylvania. Selection is based on financial need, academic ability, communication skills, and creativity as demonstrated through work samples.

Financial data The stipend is $1,500, paid upon confirmation of employment in an internship position.

Duration The internship award is presented annually; recipients may reapply.

Additional information This internship award was first presented in 1983.

Number awarded 1 each year.

Deadline January.

[135]
COMPUTERCRAFT CORPORATION SCHOLARSHIP

Chickasaw Foundation
110 West 12th Street
P.O. Box 1726
Ada, OK 74821-1726
(580) 421-9030   Fax: (580) 421-9031
E-mail: ChickasawFoundation@chickasaw.net
Web: www.chickasawfoundation.org/index_20.htm

Summary To provide financial assistance to members of the Chickasaw Nation who are majoring in fields of interest to ComputerCraft Corporation.

Eligibility This program is open to Chickasaw students who are currently enrolled full time as an undergraduate student. The sponsor recruits computer engineers, graphic designers, biologists, conference managers, and international trade specialists. Preference may be given to those majors, but all fields of study are eligible. Applicants must have a GPA of 2.5 or higher. Along with their application, they must submit high school or college transcripts, 2 letters of recommendation, a copy of their Chickasaw Nation citizenship card, and a 1-page essay on their long-term goals and plans for achieving them. Financial need is not considered in the selection process.

Financial data The stipend is $1,500.

Duration 1 year.

Number awarded 1 each year.

Deadline August of each year.

[136]
CONFEDERATED SALISH AND KOOTENAI TRIBES HIGHER EDUCATION SCHOLARSHIPS

Confederated Salish and Kootenai Tribes
Attn: Tribal Education Department
P.O. Box 278
Pablo, MT 59855
(406) 675-2700, ext. 1072   Toll Free: (877) 575-0086
Fax: (406) 275-2814   E-mail: tribaled@cskt.org
Web: www.cskt.org/services/education.htm

Summary To provide financial assistance to members of the Confederated Salish and Kootenai Tribes who are interested in attending college or graduate school in any state.

Eligibility This program is open to enrolled members of the Confederated Salish and Kootenai Tribes who are enrolled or accepted for enrollment at an accredited college, university or vocational/technical school. Applicants must be able to demonstrate financial need. Assistance is available to students in the following priority order: 1) continuing students in good standing; 2) new students who have never received tribal higher education funding; 3) returning students who have taken a break from school for 1 or more quarters or semesters; and 4) non-need students. A small fund is set aside for graduate students.

Financial data For students at public colleges and universities in Montana, stipends supplement other funding avail-able to the student to pay for tuition and fees, room and board, books, and miscellaneous expenses related to school. For students at private or out-of-state colleges and universities, support is limited to the level at public in-state colleges. Assistance for part-time students is capped at $3,000 per year and support for graduate students is limited to $2,000 per year.

Duration 1 year; may be renewed, provided recipients maintain a GPA of 2.0 or higher and full-time enrollment.

Number awarded Varies each year. Recently, 258 of these scholarships were awarded, including 141 to students at Salish Kootenai College, 39 to students at the University of Montana, 7 to students at the Bozeman or Billings campuses of Montana State University, 71 to students at colleges and universities outside Montana, and 10 to graduate students.

Deadline April of each year.

[137]
CONFEDERATED TRIBES OF THE UMATILLA INDIAN RESERVATION HIGHER EDUCATION SCHOLARSHIPS

Confederated Tribes of the Umatilla Indian Reservation
Attn: Education and Training Department
46411 Ti'mine Way
Pendleton, OR 97801
(541) 276-8120   Toll Free: (888) 809-8027
Fax: (541) 276-6543   E-mail: info@ctuir.com
Web: www.umatilla.nsn.us/ed.html

Summary To provide financial assistance for a bachelor's or master's degree to Indians affiliated with the Confederated Tribes of the Umatilla Indian Reservation (CTUIR).

Eligibility This program is open to tribal members enrolled or planning to enroll in a bachelor's degree program at an accredited college or university; support for a master's or doctoral degree is available only if funds are available. Applicants must submit a personal letter describing their educational goals and how their receipt of this scholarship will benefit the CTUIR. Financial need is considered in the selection process.

Financial data A stipend is awarded (amount not specified).

Duration 1 year; may be renewed.

Additional information The CTUIR was established in 1949 when the Cayuse, Walla Walla, and Umatilla tribes entered into an agreement regarding their reservation in northeastern Oregon and southeastern Washington.

Number awarded Varies each year.

Deadline June of each year for fall quarter or semester; October of each year of winter quarter or semester; January of each year for spring quarter; April of each year for summer quarter.

[138]
CONNECTICUT MINORITY TEACHER INCENTIVE PROGRAM

Connecticut Department of Higher Education
Attn: Office of Student Financial Aid
61 Woodland Street
Hartford, CT 06105-2326
(860) 947-1857   Fax: (860) 947-1838
E-mail: mtip@ctdhe.org
Web: www.ctdhe.org/SFA/default.htm

Summary To provide financial assistance and loan repayment to Native American and other minority upper-division college students in Connecticut who are interested in teaching at public schools in the state.

Eligibility This program is open to juniors and seniors enrolled full time in Connecticut college and university teacher preparation programs. Applicants must be members of a minority group, defined as African American, Hispanic/Latino, Asian American, or Native American. They must be nominated by the education dean at their institution.

Financial data The maximum stipend is $5,000 per year. In addition, if recipients complete a credential and begin teaching at a public school in Connecticut within 16 months of graduation, they may receive up to $2,500 per year, for up to 4 years, to help pay off college loans.

Duration Up to 2 years.

Number awarded Varies each year.

Deadline September of each year.

[139]
CONTINENTAL SOCIETY, DAUGHTERS OF INDIAN WARS SCHOLARSHIP

Continental Society, Daughters of Indian Wars
c/o Julia A. Farrigan, Scholarship Chair
326 South Oak Street
Jackson, GA 30233
E-mail: farrigan@bellsouth.net
Web: www.rootsweb.ancestry.com

Summary To provide financial assistance to Native American college students who are interested in preparing for a career in education or social service.

Eligibility This program is open to enrolled tribal members of a federally-recognized tribe who are accepted at or already attending an accredited college or university. Applicants must be planning to work with a tribe or nation in the field of education or social service. They must have a GPA of 3.0 or higher and be carrying at least 10 quarter hours or 8 semester hours. Preference is given to students entering their junior year. Financial need is considered in the selection process.

Financial data The stipend is $5,000 per year.

Duration 1 year; may be renewed.

Number awarded 1 each year.

Deadline June of each year.

[140]
COOK INLET TRIBAL COUNCIL TRIBAL HIGHER EDUCATION PROGRAM

Cook Inlet Tribal Council, Inc.
Attn: Tribal Scholarships and Grants Program
3600 San Jeronimo Drive, Suite 286
Anchorage, AK 99508
(907) 793-3578   Toll Free: (877) 985-5900
Fax: (907) 793-3589   E-mail: scholarships@citci.com
Web: www.citci.com/content/tribal-higher-education

Summary To provide financial assistance to Alaska Native shareholders of the Cook Inlet Region, Inc. (CIRI) and their descendants who are working on an undergraduate or graduate degree.

Eligibility This program is open to Alaska Native shareholders of CIRI and their descendants, regardless of residence, who are enrolled or planning to enroll full time at an accredited college, university, or vocational training facility. Applicants must be working on a certificate, associate, bachelor's, or graduate degree. Along with their application they must submit a letter of reference, a 200-word statement of purpose, their Certificate of Indian Blood (CIB), a letter of acceptance from the school, transcripts, their Student Aid Report, a budget forecast, and (for males) documentation of Selective Service registration. Awards are presented on a first-come, first-served basis as long as funds are available.

Financial data This program provides supplementary matching financial aid. Awards are intended to be applied to tuition, fees, course-required books and supplies, and on-campus housing and meal plans only. Total funding over a lifetime educational career is limited to $15,000.

Duration 1 year; may be renewed up to 4 additional years if the recipient maintains a GPA of 2.0 or higher.

Additional information Students whose CIB gives their village as Tyonek, Kenai, Ninilchik, Knik, or Salamatof must apply directly to their village organization.

Number awarded Varies each year, depending on the availability of funds.

Deadline May of each year for fall; November of each year for spring.

[141]
COPPER RIVER NATIVE ASSOCIATION ADULT VOCATIONAL TRAINING SCHOLARSHIP

Copper River Native Association
Attn: Higher Education Coordinator
Mile 104 Richardson Highway
Drawer H
Copper Center, AK 99573
(907) 822-5241   Fax: (907) 822-8801
Web: crnative.org

Summary To provide financial assistance for vocational training to Alaska Natives enrolled in the Ahtna Region.

Eligibility This program is open to enrolled members, or direct descendants eligible for enrollment with one-quarter or more Indian blood quantum, of 1) the villages of Cantwell, Gakona, or Tazlina in Alaska; or 2) other villages in the Ahtna Region and not enrolled in or receiving funding from any other tribal government. Applicants must have been accepted into an approved vocational training or apprenticeship program in any state and have reasonable assurance of a job offer upon completion of the training. Alaska residency is not required.

Financial data Stipends are disbursed directly to the school or training institution and applied towards tuition, fees, course-related books or supplies, and on-campus room and board.

Duration 1 year; may be renewed if the recipient maintains a GPA of 2.0 or higher.

Additional information The association is also known as Atna'T'Aene Nene.

Number awarded Varies each year.

Deadline Deadline not specified.

[142]
COPPER RIVER NATIVE ASSOCIATION HIGHER EDUCATION SCHOLARSHIP

Copper River Native Association
Attn: Higher Education Coordinator
Mile 104 Richardson Highway
Drawer H
Copper Center, AK 99573
(907) 822-5241   Fax: (907) 822-8801
Web: crnative.org

Summary To provide financial assistance for undergraduate or graduate studies in any state to Alaska Natives who are enrolled in villages in the Ahtna region.

Eligibility This program is open to enrolled members, or direct descendants eligible for enrollment with one-quarter or more Indian blood quantum, of 1) the villages of Cantwell, Gakona, or Tazlina in Alaska; or 2) other villages in the Ahtna Region and not enrolled or receiving funding from any other tribal government. Alaska residency is not required. Applicants must be enrolled or accepted as full-time students at an accredited college or university in any state on the undergraduate (4-year program) or graduate school level. They should have at least a 2.0 GPA. Along with their application, they must submit a 200-word personal statement of educational goals.

Financial data The stipend is $2,000 per semester. Funds are sent directly to the recipient's school to be used for tuition, university fees, course-related books and supplies, and campus housing and meal plans.

Duration 1 year; may be renewed if the recipient maintains a GPA of 2.0 or higher and full-time enrollment, but the lifetime educational support limit is $15,000.

Additional information The association is also known as Atna'T'Aene Nene.

Number awarded Varies each year.

Deadline September of each year for fall; January of each year for spring; June of each year for summer.

[143]
COQUILLE INDIAN TRIBE ADULT VOCATIONAL TRAINING GRANTS

Coquille Indian Tribe
Attn: Education Department
2611 Mexeye Loop
Coos Bay, OR 97420
(541) 756-0904   Toll Free: (800) 622-5869
Fax: (541) 888-2418
E-mail: lindamecum@coquilletribe.org
Web: www.coquilletribe.org

Summary To provide financial assistance to members of the Coquille Indian Tribe who are attending or planning to attend vocational school in any state.

Eligibility This program is open to enrolled members of the Coquille Indian Tribe who are entering or continuing at a vocational/technical school in any state. Along with their application, they must submit a personal essay on their vocational goals and how the tribe will benefit by sending them to school.

Financial data A stipend is awarded (amount not specified).

Duration 1 year; may be renewed, provided the recipient maintains a GPA of 2.0 or higher.

Number awarded Varies each year.

Deadline Deadline not specified.

[144]
COQUILLE INDIAN TRIBE COMPUTER EQUIPMENT PROGRAM

Coquille Indian Tribe
Attn: Education Department
2611 Mexeye Loop
Coos Bay, OR 97420
(541) 756-0904   Toll Free: (800) 622-5869
Fax: (541) 888-2418
E-mail: lindamecum@coquilletribe.org
Web: www.coquilletribe.org

Summary To provide funding for the purchase of computer equipment to members of the Coquille Indian Tribe who are working full time on an undergraduate or graduate degree.

Eligibility This program is open to enrolled members of the Coquille Indian Tribe who have been enrolled for at least 2 semester as full-time undergraduate or graduate students at an accredited college, university, or community college in any state. Applicants must be seeking funding for the purchase of computer equipment.

Financial data The grant is $1,200; funds must be used for purchase of computer equipment or programming, and not for training, shipping, and/or maintenance of equipment.

Duration This is a 1-time grant.

Number awarded Varies each year.

Deadline Deadline not specified.

[145]
COQUILLE INDIAN TRIBE HIGHER EDUCATION GRANTS

Coquille Indian Tribe
Attn: Education Department
2611 Mexeye Loop
Coos Bay, OR 97420
(541) 756-0904   Toll Free: (800) 622-5869
Fax: (541) 888-2418
E-mail: lindamecum@coquilletribe.org
Web: www.coquilletribe.org

Summary To provide financial assistance to members of the Coquille Indian Tribe who are attending or planning to attend college or graduate school in any state.

Eligibility This program is open to enrolled members of the Coquille Indian Tribe who are entering or continuing undergraduate or graduate students at an accredited college, university, or community college in any state. Along with their application, they must submit a personal statement on their educational goals, the schools they plan to attend, the degrees they plan to pursue, their plans after college graduation, and how the tribe will benefit by sending them to school. Financial need is also considered in the selection process.

Financial data Maximum stipends are $9,000 per year for full-time students at 4-year colleges and universities or $7,500 per year for students a 2-year community colleges. Part-time students are eligible to receive funding for books, fees, and tuition only.

Duration 1 year; may be renewed up to 4 additional years.

Number awarded Varies each year.

Deadline Deadline not specified.

[146]
COSTCO WHOLESALE SCHOLARSHIPS

Independent Colleges of Washington
600 Stewart Street, Suite 600
Seattle, WA 98101
(206) 623-4494   Fax: (206) 625-9621
E-mail: info@icwashington.org
Web: www.icwashington.org/scholarships/index.html

Summary To provide financial assistance to Native American and other underrepresented minority students enrolled at participating colleges and universities that are members of the Independent Colleges of Washington (ICW).

Eligibility This program is open to students enrolled at ICW-member colleges and universities. Applicants must be members of underrepresented minority populations and able to demonstrate financial need. No application is required; each ICW institution makes a selection from all of its students.

Financial data The stipend varies at each institution.

Duration 1 year; nonrenewable.

Additional information The participating ICW-member institutions are Pacific Lutheran University, Saint Martin's College, Seattle Pacific University, University of Puget Sound, Walla Walla University, Whitman College, and Whitworth University. This program is sponsored by Costco Wholesale.

Number awarded Varies each year; recently, 18 of these scholarships were awarded.

Deadline Each institution sets its own deadline.

[147]
CRACKER BARREL-MINORITY TEACHER EDUCATION SCHOLARSHIPS

Florida Fund for Minority Teachers, Inc.
Attn: Executive Director
G415 Norman Hall
P.O. Box 117045
Gainesville, FL 32611-7045
(352) 392-9196, ext. 21   Fax: (352) 846-3011
E-mail: info@ffmt.org
Web: www.ffmt.org

Summary To provide funding to Native American and other minorities who are Florida residents and preparing for a career as a teacher.

Eligibility This program is open to Florida residents who are African American/Black, Hispanic/Latino, Asian American/Pacific Islander, or American Indian/Alaskan Native. Applicants must be entering their junior year in a teacher education program at a participating college or university in Florida. Special consideration is given to community college graduates. Selection is based on writing ability, communication skills, overall academic performance, and evidence of commitment to the youth of America (preferably demonstrated through volunteer activities).

Financial data The stipend is $2,000 per year. Recipients are required to teach 1 year in a Florida public school for each year they receive the scholarship. If they fail to teach in a public school, they are required to repay the total amount of support received at an annual interest rate of 8%.

Duration Up to 2 consecutive years, provided the recipient remains enrolled full time with a GPA of 2.5 or higher.

Additional information For a list of the 16 participating public institutions and the 18 participating private institutions, contact the Florida Fund for Minority Teachers (FFMT). Recipients are also required to attend the annual FFMT recruitment and retention conference.

Number awarded Varies each year.

Deadline July of each year for fall semester; November of each year for spring semester.

[148]
CRAZY HORSE MEMORIAL JOURNALISM SCHOLARSHIP

Crazy Horse Memorial Foundation
12151 Avenue of the Chiefs
Crazy Horse, SD 57730-8900
(605) 673-4681   Fax: (605) 673-2185
E-mail: memorial@crazyhorse.org
Web: www.crazyhorsememorial.org/education

Summary To provide financial assistance to Native American students interested in preparing for a career in journalism.

Eligibility This program is open to Native American students enrolled or planning to enroll at a college or university. Applicants must be interested in preparing for a journalism career, although they are not required to major in journalism in college. They must attend the Native American Journalism Career Conference held at the Crazy Horse Memorial in South Dakota in April. Scholarship winners are selected at the conference. Along with their application, they must submit a 500-word essay explaining their interest in journalism and 2 letters of reference.

Financial data   The stipend is $1,000.

Duration   1 year.

Additional information   This program is funded by the Freedom Forum Diversity Institute with support from the South Dakota Newspaper Association, the Crazy Horse Memorial Foundation, the Native American Journalists Association, and the journalism programs at South Dakota State University and the University of South Dakota.

Number awarded   Varies each year; recently, 4 of these scholarships were awarded.

Deadline   March of each year.

[149]
CREEK NATION HIGHER EDUCATION SCHOLARSHIPS

Muscogee (Creek) Nation of Oklahoma
Attn: Higher Education Program
P.O. Box 580
Okmulgee, OK 74447
(918) 732-7688   Toll Free: (800) 482-1979, ext. 7688
Fax: (918) 732-7694
E-mail: jothill@muscogeenation-nsn.gov
Web: www.muscogeenation-nsn.gov

Summary   To provide financial assistance to needy Creek undergraduate students who plan to attend college in any state.

Eligibility   This program is open to Creek students of any degree of Indian blood who are attending or planning to attend an accredited institution of higher learning in any state. Applicants must be eligible to receive Pell Grants. They must submit copies of their Certificate of Indian Blood (CIB) and tribal enrollment card.

Financial data   Maximum stipends are $1,000 per semester for single students, $1,500 per semester for independent students, or $2,000 per semester for married or head of household students.

Duration   1 year; may be renewed for a maximum of 10 semesters of funding as long as the recipient enrolls in at least 15 hours per term and maintains a GPA of 2.0 or higher.

Additional information   The Muscogee (Creek) Nation of Oklahoma administers the Higher Education Program. This program expends funds appropriated by Congress for the education of Indian students and administered by the Bureau of Indian Affairs.

Number awarded   Varies each year.

Deadline   May of each year for fall semester; December of each year for spring semester.

[150]
CREEK NATION TRIBAL FUNDS GRANT PROGRAM

Muscogee (Creek) Nation of Oklahoma
Attn: Higher Education Program
P.O. Box 580
Okmulgee, OK 74447
(918) 732-7688   Toll Free: (800) 482-1979, ext. 7688
Fax: (918) 732-7694
E-mail: jothill@muscogeenation-nsn.gov
Web: www.muscogeenation-nsn.gov

Summary   To provide financial assistance to enrolled citizens of the Muscogee (Creek) Nation attending an accredited college or university in any state.

Eligibility   This program is open to enrolled citizens of the Muscogee (Creek) Nation (no minimum blood quantum required) who are enrolled or planning to enroll in an accredited college or university in any state. Applicants must submit copies of their Certificate of Indian Blood (CIB) and tribal enrollment card. Financial need is not required.

Financial data   The maximum stipend is $1,000 per semester for full-time students (12 credit hours or more per semester) or $500 per semester for part-time students (less than 12 hours). Support may not exceed $2,000 per year. The award may be used to supplement other financial aid sources.

Duration   1 semester; may be renewed up to 9 additional semesters (as long as the recipient maintains at least a 2.5 GPA).

Number awarded   Varies each year.

Deadline   May of each year for fall semester; December of each year for spring semester.

[151]
CREEK NATION TRIBAL INCENTIVE GRANT PROGRAM

Muscogee (Creek) Nation of Oklahoma
Attn: Higher Education Program
P.O. Box 580
Okmulgee, OK 74447
(918) 732-7688   Toll Free: (800) 482-1979, ext. 7688
Fax: (918) 732-7694
E-mail: jothill@muscogeenation-nsn.gov
Web: www.muscogeenation-nsn.gov

Summary   To provide financial assistance to enrolled citizens of the Muscogee (Creek) Nation who have an excellent academic record and are attending an accredited college or university in any state.

Eligibility   This program is open to enrolled citizens of the Muscogee (Creek) Nation (no minimum blood quantum required) who are enrolled or planning to enroll in an accredited college or university in any state. Applicants must have a GPA of 3.0 or higher. They must submit copies of their Certificate of Indian Blood (CIB) and tribal enrollment card.

Financial data   The maximum stipend is $700 per semester for full-time students (12 credit hours or more per semester) or $350 per semester for part-time students (less than 12 hours). Support may not exceed $1,400 per year. The award may be used to supplement other financial aid sources.

Duration   1 semester; may be renewed for up to 9 additional semesters.

Number awarded   Varies each year.

Deadline   May of each year for fall semester; December of each year for spring semester.

[152]
CULINARY ARTS SCHOLARSHIPS

California Adolescent Nutrition and Fitness Program
Attn: Scholarship Program
2140 Shattuck Avenue, Suite 610
Berkeley, CA 94704
(510) 644-1533   Toll Free: (800) 200-3131
Fax: (510) 644-1535   E-mail: info@canfit.org
Web: canfit.org/scholarships

Summary   To provide financial assistance to Native Americans and other minority culinary arts students in California.

Eligibility   This program is open to American Indians, Alaska Natives, African Americans, Asian Americans, Pacific Islanders, and Latinos/Hispanics from California who are enrolled at a culinary arts college in the state. Applicants are not required to have completed any college units. Along with their application, they must submit 1) documentation of financial need; 2) letters of recommendation from 2 individuals; 3) a 1-to 2-page letter describing their academic goals and involvement in community nutrition and/or physical education activities; and 4) an essay of 500 to 1,000 words on a topic related to healthy foods for youth from low-income communities of color.

Financial data   A stipend is awarded (amount not specified).

Number awarded   1 or more each year.

Deadline   March of each year.

[153]
CULTURAL RESOURCES DIVERSITY INTERNSHIP PROGRAM

Student Conservation Association, Inc.
Attn: Diversity Internships
1800 North Kent Street, Suite 102
Arlington, VA 22209
(703) 524-2441   Fax: (703) 524-2451
E-mail: jchow@thesca.org
Web: www.thesca.org/partners/special-initiatives

Summary   To provide summer work experience at U.S. National Park Service (NPS) facilities to 1) Native Americans and other ethnically diverse undergraduate and graduate students and 2) students with disabilities.

Eligibility   This program is open to currently-enrolled students at the sophomore or higher level. Applicants must be U.S. citizens or permanent residents with a GPA of 3.0 or higher. Although all students may apply, the program is designed to give ethnically diverse students and students with disabilities the opportunity to experience the diversity of careers in the federal sector. Applicants are assigned to a position within the NPS. Possible projects include editing publications, planning exhibits, participating in archaeological excavations, preparing research reports, cataloguing park and museum collections, providing interpretive programs on historical topics, developing community outreach, and writing lesson plans based on historical themes.

Financial data   Interns receive a salary of $225 per week, basic medical insurance coverage, a housing stipend of up to $800 per month, a $100 uniform allowance, travel expenses up to $630, and eligibility for an Americorps Educational Award of $1,000.

Duration   10 weeks in the summer (beginning in June).

Additional information   While participating in the internship, students engage in tri-weekly evening career and professional development events, ongoing career counseling, mentoring, and personal and career development services.

Number awarded   Approximately 15 each year.

Deadline   February of each year.

[154]
DAKOTA INDIAN FOUNDATION SCHOLARSHIP

Dakota Indian Foundation
P.O. Box 340
Chamberlain, SD 57325-0340
(605) 234-5472   Fax: (605) 234-5858
Web: www.dakotaindianfoundation.com

Summary   To provide financial assistance to American Indians (especially those of Sioux heritage) who are currently enrolled in college.

Eligibility   This program is open to American Indians (priority given to those of Sioux heritage) who are currently enrolled full time at a college or university in any state as a sophomore, junior, or senior. A copy of tribal registration must be provided. Applicants may be studying in any field. Along with their application, they must submit a personal statement that includes their qualifications for a scholarship, educational interest, career plans, extracurricular activities, and need for financial assistance.

Financial data   The stipend is $1,000 per semester ($2,000 per year).

Duration   1 semester; recipients may reapply.

Number awarded   Varies each year.

Deadline   July of each year for the fall semester; January of each year for the spring semester.

[155]
DAMON P. MOORE SCHOLARSHIP

Indiana State Teachers Association
Attn: Scholarships
150 West Market Street, Suite 900
Indianapolis, IN 46204-2875
(317) 263-3400   Toll Free: (800) 382-4037
Fax: (317) 655-3700   E-mail: mshoup@ista-in.org
Web: www.ista-in.org/dynamic.aspx?id=1212

Summary   To provide financial assistance to Native American and other ethnic minority high school seniors in Indiana who are interested in studying education in college.

Eligibility   This program is open to ethnic minority public high school seniors in Indiana who are interested in studying education in college. Selection is based on academic achievement, leadership ability as expressed through co-curricular activities and community involvement, recommendations, and a 300-word essay on their educational goals and how they plan to use this scholarship.

Financial data   The stipend is $1,000.

Duration   1 year; may be renewed for 2 additional years if the recipient maintains at least a "C+" GPA.

Additional information   This program was established in 1987.

Number awarded   1 each year.

Deadline   February of each year.

[156]
DAVID SANKEY MINORITY SCHOLARSHIP IN METEOROLOGY

National Weather Association
Attn: Executive Director
228 West Millbrook Road
Raleigh, NC 27609-4304
(919) 845-1546   Fax: (919) 845-2956
E-mail: exdir@nwas.org
Web: www.nwas.org

Summary   To provide financial assistance to Native Americans and other minorities working on an undergraduate or graduate degree in meteorology.

Eligibility   This program is open to members of minority groups who are either entering their sophomore or higher year of undergraduate study or enrolled as graduate students. Applicants must be working on a degree in meteorology. Along with their application, they must submit a 1-page statement explaining why they are applying for this scholarship. Selection is based on that statement, academic achievement, and 2 letters of recommendation.

Financial data   The stipend is $1,000.

Duration   1 year.

Additional information   This program was established in 2002.

Number awarded   1 each year.

Deadline   April of each year.

[157]
DEFENSE INTELLIGENCE AGENCY UNDERGRADUATE TRAINING ASSISTANCE PROGRAM

Defense Intelligence Agency
Attn: Human Resources, HCH-4
200 MacDill Boulevard, Building 6000
Bolling AFB, DC 20340-5100
(202) 231-8228   Fax: (202) 231-4889
TDD: (202) 231-5002   E-mail: staffing@dia.mil
Web: www.dia.mil/employment/student/index.htm

Summary   To provide funding and work experience to minority and other high school seniors and lower-division students interested in majoring in specified fields and working for the U.S. Defense Intelligence Agency (DIA).

Eligibility   This program is open to graduating high school seniors and college freshmen and sophomores interested in working full time on a baccalaureate degree in 1 of the following fields in college: biology, chemistry, computer science, engineering, foreign area studies, intelligence analysis, international relations, microbiology, pharmacology, physics, political science, or toxicology. High school seniors must have a GPA of 2.75 or higher and either 1) an SAT combined critical reading and mathematics score of 1000 or higher plus 500 or higher on the writing portion or 2) an ACT score of 21 or higher. College freshmen and sophomores must have a GPA of 3.0 or higher. All applicants must be able to demonstrate financial need (household income ceiling of $70,000 for a family of 4 or $80,000 for a family of 5 or more) and leadership abilities through extracurricular activities, civic involvement, volunteer work, or part-time employment. Students and all members of their immediate family must be U.S. citizens.

Minorities, women, and persons with disabilities are strongly encouraged to apply.

Financial data   Students accepted into this program receive tuition (up to $18,000 per year) at an accredited college or university selected by the student and endorsed by the sponsor; reimbursement for books and needed supplies; an annual salary to cover college room and board expenses and for summer employment; and a position at the sponsoring agency after graduation. Recipients must work for DIA after college graduation for at least 1 and a half times the length of study. For participants who leave DIA earlier than scheduled, the agency arranges for payments to reimburse DIA for the total cost of education (including the employee's pay and allowances).

Duration   4 years, provided the recipient maintains a GPA of 2.75 during the freshman year and 3.0 or higher in subsequent semesters.

Additional information   Recipients are provided a challenging summer internship and guaranteed a job at the agency in their field of study upon graduation.

Number awarded   Only a few are awarded each year.

Deadline   November of each year.

[158]
DELTA KAPPA GAMMA NATIVE AMERICAN PROJECT GRANTS

Delta Kappa Gamma Society International-Mu State
  Organization
c/o Beverly Staff, Native American Project
7407 Lillie Lane
Pensacola, FL 32526
(850) 944-3302   E-mail: leannjax@yahoo.com
Web: www.orgsites.com/fl/mustatedeltakappagamma

Summary   To provide financial assistance to female Native Americans from Florida who are working on a degree in education or conducting research into the history of Native Americans at a college or university in the state.

Eligibility   This program is open to women who are members of a recognized Native American tribe in Florida. Applicants must be enrolled at an accredited college or university in the state and either working on a degree in education or conducting research into the history of Native Americans in Florida. Along with their application, they must submit a brief statement with details of the purpose of the grant, a letter of recommendation from a tribal official, and a copy of high school or college transcripts.

Financial data   The stipend is $1,000.

Duration   1 year.

Number awarded   6 each year: 1 in each of the districts of the sponsoring organization in Florida.

Deadline   May of each year.

[159]
DENNIS WONG AND ASSOCIATES SCHOLARSHIP

Ke Ali'i Pauahi Foundation
Attn: Financial Aid & Scholarship Services
567 South King Street, Suite 160
Honolulu, HI 96813
(808) 534-3966   Toll Free: (800) 842-4682, ext. 43966
Fax: (808) 534-3890   E-mail: scholarships@pauahi.org
Web: www.pauahi.org/scholarships

Summary To provide financial assistance to undergraduate or graduate students in liberal arts or science, especially those of Native Hawaiian descent.

Eligibility This program is open to students working full time on an undergraduate degree in liberal arts or science or a graduate degree in a professional field. Applicants must have a GPA of 3.5 or higher and a well-rounded and balanced record of achievement in preparation for career objectives. Financial need is considered in the selection process. Residency in Hawaii is not required, but preference is given to Native Hawaiians (descendants of the aboriginal inhabitants of the Hawaiian Islands prior to 1778).

Financial data The stipend is $1,100.

Duration 1 year.

Number awarded 3 each year.

Deadline March of each year.

[160]
DEPARTMENT OF HOMELAND SECURITY SUMMER FACULTY AND STUDENT RESEARCH TEAM PROGRAM

Oak Ridge Institute for Science and Education
Attn: Science and Engineering Education
P.O. Box 117
Oak Ridge, TN 37831-0117
(865) 574-1447   Fax: (865) 241-5219
E-mail: Patti.Obenour@orau.gov
Web: see.orau.org

Summary To provide an opportunity for teams of students and faculty from Tribal Colleges or Universities (TCUs) and other minority serving educational institutions to conduct summer research in areas of interest to the Department of Homeland Security (DHS).

Eligibility This program is open to teams of up to 2 students (undergraduate and/or graduate) and 1 faculty from Historically Black Colleges and Universities (HBCUs), Hispanic Serving Institutions (HSIs), Tribal Colleges and Universities (TCUs), Alaska Native Serving Institutions (ANSIs), and Native Hawaiian Serving Institutions (NHSIs). Applicants must be interested in conducting research at designated DHS Centers of Excellence in science, technology, engineering, or mathematics related to homeland security (HS-STEM), including explosives detection, mitigation, and response; social, behavioral, and economic sciences; risk and decision sciences; human factors aspects of technology; chemical threats and countermeasures; biological threats and countermeasures; community, commerce, and infrastructure resilience; food and agricultural security; transportation security; border security; immigration studies; maritime and port security; infrastructure protection; natural disasters and related geophysical studies; emergency preparedness and response; communications and interoperability; or advanced data analysis and visualization. Faculty must have a full-time appointment at an eligible institution and have received a Ph.D. in an HS-STEM discipline no more than 7 years previously; at least 2 years of full-time research and/or teaching experience is preferred. Students must have a GPA of 3.0 or higher and be enrolled full time. Undergraduates must be entering their junior or senior year. U.S. citizenship is required. Selection is based on relevance and intrinsic merit of the research (40%), faculty applicant qualifications (30%), academic benefit to the faculty applicant and his/her institution (10%), and student applicant qualifications (20%).

Financial data Stipends are $1,200 per week for faculty, $600 per week for graduate students, and $500 per week for undergraduates. Faculty members who live more than 50 miles from their assigned site may receive a relocation allowance of $1,500 and travel expenses up to an additional $500. Limited travel expenses for 1 round trip are reimbursed for undergraduate and graduate students living more than 50 miles from their assigned site.

Duration 12 weeks during the summer.

Additional information This program is funded by DHS and administered by Oak Ridge Institute for Science and Education (ORISE). Recently, the available DHS Centers of Excellence were the Center for Advancing Microbial Risk Assessment (led by Michigan State University and Drexel University); the Center for Risk and Economic Analysis of Terrorism Events (led by University of Southern California); the National Center for Food Protection and Defense (led by University of Minnesota); the Center of Excellence for Foreign Animal and Zoonotic Disease Defense (led by Texas A&M University and Kansas State University); the National Center for the Study of Preparedness and Catastrophic Event Response (led by Johns Hopkins University); the National Consortium for the Study of Terrorism and Responses to Terrorism (led by University of Maryland); the Center of Excellence for Awareness and Location of Explosives-Related Threats (led by Northeastern University and University of Rhode Island); the National Center for Border Security and Immigration (led by the University of Arizona and the University of Texas at El Paso); the Center for Maritime, Island and Remote and Extreme Environment Security (led by the University of Hawaii and Stevens Institute of Technology); the Center for Natural Disasters, Coastal Infrastructure, and Emergency Management (led by the University of North Carolina at Chapel Hill and Jackson State University); the National Transportation Security Center of Excellence (consisting of 7 institutions); and the Center of Excellence in Command, Control, and Interoperability (led by Purdue University and Rutgers University).

Number awarded Approximately 12 teams are selected each year.

Deadline January of each year.

[161]
DEPARTMENT OF STATE STUDENT INTERN PROGRAM

Department of State
Attn: HR/REE
2401 E Street, N.W., Suite 518 H
Washington, DC 20522-0108
(202) 261-8888   Toll Free: (800) JOB-OVERSEAS
Fax: (301) 562-8968   E-mail: Careers@state.gov
Web: www.careers.state.gov/students/programs

Summary To provide a work/study opportunity to minority and other undergraduate and graduate students interested in foreign service.

Eligibility This program is open to full- and part-time continuing college and university juniors, seniors, and graduate students. Applications are encouraged from students with a broad range of majors, such as business or public administration, social work, economics, information management, journalism, and the biological, engineering, and physical sciences, as well as those majors more traditionally identified with international affairs. U.S. citizenship is required. The State Department particularly encourages eligible women and minority students with an interest in foreign affairs to apply.

Financial data Most internships are unpaid. A few paid internships are granted to applicants who can demonstrate financial need. If they qualify for a paid internship, they are placed at the GS-4 step 5 level (currently with an annual rate of $27,786). Interns placed abroad may also receive housing, medical insurance, a travel allowance, and a dependents' allowance.

Duration Paid internships are available only for 10 weeks during the summer. Unpaid internships are available for 1 semester or quarter during the academic year, or for 10 weeks during the summer.

Additional information About half of all internships are in Washington, D.C., or occasionally in other large cities in the United States. The remaining internships are at embassies and consulates abroad. Depending upon the needs of the department, interns are assigned junior-level professional duties, which may include research, preparing reports, drafting replies to correspondence, working in computer science, analyzing international issues, financial management, intelligence, security, or assisting in cases related to domestic and international law. Interns must agree to return to their schooling immediately upon completion of their internship.

Number awarded Approximately 800 internships are offered each year, but only about 5% of those are paid positions.

Deadline February of each year for fall internships; June of each year for spring internships; October of each year for summer internships.

[162]
DEPARTMENT OF THE INTERIOR DIVERSITY INTERN PROGRAM

Department of the Interior
Attn: Office of Educational Partnerships
1849 C Street, N.W., MS 5221 MIB
Washington, DC 20240
(202) 208-6403   Toll Free: (888) 447-4392
Fax: (202) 208-3620   TDD: (202) 208-5069
E-mail: ed_partners@ios.doi.gov
Web: www.doi.gov/hrm/dipfact.html

Summary To provide work experience at federal agencies involved with natural and cultural resources to 1) Native American and other minority college and graduate students and 2) students with disabilities.

Eligibility This program is open to currently-enrolled students at the sophomore or higher level at Historically Black Colleges and Universities (HBCUs), Hispanic-Serving Institutions (HSIs), Tribal Colleges and Universities (TCUs), and some other major institutions. Applicants must be U.S. citizens or permanent residents with a GPA of 3.0 or higher. Although all students may apply, the program is designed to give ethnically diverse students and students with disabilities the opportunity to experience the diversity of careers in the federal sector. Applicants are assigned to a position within the U.S. Department of the Interior (DOI). Possible placements include archaeology and anthropology; wildlife and fisheries biology; business administration, accounting, and finance; civil and environmental engineering; computer science, especially GIS applications; human resources; mining and petroleum engineering; communications and public relations; web site and database design; environmental and realty law; geology, hydrology, and geography; Native American studies; interpretation and environmental education; natural resource and range management; public policy and administration; and surveying and mapping.

Financial data The weekly stipend is $420 for sophomores and juniors, $450 for seniors, or $520 for law and graduate students. Other benefits include a pre-term orientation, transportation to the orientation and the work site, worker's compensation, and accident insurance.

Duration 10 weeks in the summer (beginning in June) or 15 weeks in the fall (beginning in September) or spring (beginning in January).

Additional information This program, which began in 1994, is administered through 5 nonprofit organizations: Hispanic Association of Colleges and Universities, Minority Access, Inc., Student Conservation Association, and National Association for Equal Opportunity in Higher Education. While participating in the internship, students engage in tri-weekly evening career and professional development events, ongoing career counseling, mentoring, and personal and career development services.

Number awarded Varies each year; since the program began, more than 700 interns have participated.

Deadline February of each year for summer; June of each year for fall; November of each year for spring.

[163]
DISPLACED HOMEMAKER SCHOLARSHIPS

Association on American Indian Affairs, Inc.
Attn: Director of Scholarship Programs
966 Hungerford Drive, Suite 12-B
Rockville, MD 20850
(240) 314-7155   Fax: (240) 314-7159
E-mail: lw.aaia@verizon.net
Web: www.indian-affairs.org

Summary To provide financial assistance to Native American displaced homemakers who are trying to complete their college education.

Eligibility This program is open to full-time college students who are Native Americans and have special needs because of family responsibilities. Examples of displaced homemakers include students who are attending college for the first time at the age of 40 because they have put off higher education to raise their children, students who are entering or returning to college after their children enter elementary school, and men or women who have been divorced and had to leave college to care for children and are now returning. Applicants must submit documentation of financial need, a Certificate of Indian Blood showing at least one-quarter Indian blood, proof of tribal enrollment, an essay on their educational goals and family responsibilities, 2 letters of recommendation, and their most recent transcript.

Financial data The stipend is $1,500. Awards are intended to assist recipients with child care, transportation, and some basic living expenses as well as educational costs.

Duration 1 year; recipients may reapply.

Number awarded Varies each year; recently, 6 of these scholarships were awarded.

Deadline June of each year.

[164]
DISTANCE DELIVERY SCHOLARSHIPS

The Aleut Corporation
Attn: Aleut Foundation
703 West Tudor Road, Suite 102
Anchorage, AK 99503-6650
(907) 646-1929   Toll Free: (800) 232-4882
Fax: (907) 646-1949   E-mail: taf@thealeutfoundation.org
Web: www.thealeutfoundation.org/ScholarshipGuide.aspx

Summary To provide financial assistance to Native Alaskans who are shareholders of The Aleut Corporation or their descendants and interested in working on a college degree through a distance delivery program.

Eligibility This program is open to Native Alaskans who are original enrollees or descendants of original enrollees of The Aleut Corporation (TAC). Applicants must have a GPA of 2.0 or higher and be enrolled in a distance delivery program. They may have been working on a college degree for some time or want to remain in their community while taking classes. Along with their application, they must include a letter of intent, up to 500 words in length, that describes their educational goals and objectives and their expected graduation date.

Financial data A stipend is awarded (amount not specified).

Duration 1 year; may be renewed.

Additional information The Aleut Corporation is 1 of 13 Alaska Native Regional Corporations created under the Alaska Native Claims Settlement Act of 1971. The foundation established this program in 2008.

Number awarded Varies each year.

Deadline June of each year for annual scholarships; November of each year for spring scholarships; April of each year for summer school.

[165]
DIVERSITY COMMITTEE SCHOLARSHIP

American Society of Safety Engineers
Attn: ASSE Foundation
1800 East Oakton Street
Des Plaines, IL 60018
(847) 768-3435   Fax: (847) 768-3434
E-mail: agabanski@asse.org
Web: www.asse.org

Summary To provide financial assistance to upper-division and graduate student members of the American Society of Safety Engineers (ASSE) who are Native American or come from other diverse groups.

Eligibility This program is open to ASSE student members who are working on an undergraduate or graduate degree in occupational safety, health, and environment or a closely-related field (e.g., industrial or environmental engineering, environmental science, industrial hygiene, occupational health nursing). Applicants must be full-time students who have completed at least 60 semester hours with a GPA of 3.0 or higher as undergraduates or at least 9 semester hours with a GPA of 3.5 or higher as graduate students. Along with their application, they must submit 2 essays of 300 words or less: 1) why they are seeking a degree in occupational safety and health or a closely-related field, a brief description of their current activities, and how those relate to their career goals and objectives; and 2) why they should be awarded this scholarship (including career goals and financial need). A goal of this program is to support individuals regardless of race, ethnicity, gender, religion, personal beliefs, age, sexual orientation, physical challenges, geographic location, university, or specific area of study. U.S. citizenship is not required.

Financial data The stipend is $1,000 per year.

Duration 1 year; recipients may reapply.

Number awarded 1 each year.

Deadline November of each year.

[166]
DIVERSITY SUMMER HEALTH-RELATED RESEARCH EDUCATION PROGRAM

Medical College of Wisconsin
Attn: Student Affairs/Diversity Program Coordinator
8701 Watertown Plank Road
Milwaukee, WI 53226
(414) 955-8735   Fax: (414) 955-0129
Web: www.mcw.edu/display/router.asp?docid=619

Summary To provide an opportunity for Native Americans and other undergraduates from diverse backgrounds to participate in a summer research training experience at the Medical College of Wisconsin.

Eligibility This program is open to U.S. citizens and permanent residents who come from diverse and economically and/or educationally disadvantaged backgrounds. Applicants must be interested in participating in a summer research training program at the Medical College of Wisconsin. They must have completed at least 1 year of undergraduate study at an accredited college or university (or be a community college student enrolled in at least 3 courses per academic term) and have a GPA of 3.0 or higher.

Financial data The stipend is $10 per hour for a 40-hour week. Housing is provided for students who live outside the Milwaukee area and travel expenses are paid for those who live outside Wisconsin.

Duration 10 weeks during the summer.

Additional information Students are "matched" with a full-time faculty investigator to participate in a research project addressing the causes, prevention, and treatment of cardiovascular, pulmonary, or hematological diseases. This program is funded by the National Heart, Lung, and Blood Institute (NHLBI) of the National Institutes of Health (NIH). Participants are required to prepare an abstract of their research and make a brief oral presentation of their project at the conclusion of the summer.

Number awarded Approximately 12 each year.

Deadline February of each year.

[167]
DIVISION ON AGING SCHOLARSHIP

Chickasaw Foundation
110 West 12th Street
P.O. Box 1726
Ada, OK 74821-1726
(580) 421-9030   Fax: (580) 421-9031
E-mail: ChickasawFoundation@chickasaw.net
Web: www.chickasawfoundation.org/index_20.htm

Summary To provide financial assistance to members of the Chickasaw Nation who are upper-division students majoring in geriatrics.

Eligibility This program is open to Chickasaw students who are currently enrolled full time at an accredited institution of higher education. Applicants must be classified as juniors or seniors at a 4-year college. They must be majoring in a field related to geriatrics. Along with their application, they must submit high school or college transcripts, 2 letters of recommendation, a copy of their Chickasaw Nation citizenship card, and a 1-page essay on their long-term goals and plans for achieving them. Financial need is not considered in the selection process.

Financial data The stipend is $1,000.

Duration 1 year.

Number awarded 1 each year.

Deadline August of each year.

[168]
DON CORP SCHOLARSHIP

Sault Tribe of Chippewa Indians
Attn: Higher Education Program-Memorial/Tributary
  Scholarships
523 Ashmun Street
Sault Ste. Marie, MI 49783
(906) 635-4944   Toll Free: (800) 793-0660
Fax: (906) 635-7785   E-mail: amatson@saulttribe.net
Web: www.saulttribe.com

Summary To provide financial assistance to members of the Sault Tribe of Chippewa Indians who are interested in working on an undergraduate degree in a field related to history.

Eligibility This program is open to enrolled members of the Sault Tribe who are enrolled or planning to enroll full time at a 2- or 4-year college or university in any state. Applicants must be interested in working on an undergraduate degree in history, museum studies, historical preservation, or other history-related field. Along with their application, they must submit an essay of 300 to 500 words on how this scholarship will help them realize their goals.

Financial data The stipend is $1,000.

Duration 1 year.

Number awarded 1 each year.

Deadline May of each year.

[169]
DON SAHLI–KATHY WOODALL MINORITY
STUDENT SCHOLARSHIP

Tennessee Education Association
801 Second Avenue North
Nashville, TN 37201-1099
(615) 242-8392   Toll Free: (800) 342-8367
Fax: (615) 259-4581   E-mail: wdickens@tea.nea.org
Web: www.teateachers.org

Summary To provide financial assistance to Native American and other minority high school seniors in Tennessee who are interested in majoring in education at a college or university in the state.

Eligibility This program is open to minority high school seniors in Tennessee who are planning to attend a college or university in the state and major in education. Application must be made either by a Future Teachers of America chapter affiliated with the Tennessee Education Association (TEA) or by the student with the recommendation of an active TEA member. Selection is based on academic record, leadership ability, financial need, and demonstrated interest in becoming a teacher.

Financial data The stipend is $1,000.

Duration 1 year.

Number awarded 1 each year.

Deadline February of each year.

[170]
DORA AMES LEE LEADERSHIP DEVELOPMENT
FUND

United Methodist Church
General Board of Global Ministries
Attn: United Methodist Committee on Relief
475 Riverside Drive, Room 1522
New York, NY 10115
(212) 870-3871   Toll Free: (800) UMC-GBGM
E-mail: jyoung@gbgm-umc.org
Web: gbgm-umc.org/health/doralee.cfm

Summary To provide financial assistance to Methodists and other Christians of Native American or Asian descent who are preparing for a career in a health-related field.

Eligibility This program is open to undergraduate and graduate students who are U.S. citizens of Asian American or Native American descent. Applicants must be professed

Christians, preferably United Methodists. They must be attending a college or university to enter or continue in a health-related field. Financial need is considered in the selection process.

Financial data The stipend is $2,000.

Duration 1 year.

Additional information This program was established in 1980.

Number awarded 5 each year.

Deadline June of each year.

[171]
DOYON FOUNDATION BASIC SCHOLARSHIPS

Doyon, Limited
Attn: Doyon Foundation
714 Fourth Avenue, Suite 302B
Fairbanks, AK 99701
(907) 459-2049   Toll Free: (888) 478-4755, ext. 2049
Fax: (907) 459-2065   E-mail: foundation@doyon.com
Web: www.doyonfoundation.com/static/scholarships.aspx

Summary To provide financial assistance to undergraduate and graduate students at schools in any state who are shareholders or descendants of shareholders of Doyon, Limited.

Eligibility This program is open to undergraduate or graduate students who are shareholders or the descendants of shareholders of Doyon, Limited. Applicants must be accepted or enrolled at an accredited college, university, technical institute, or vocational school. Both part-time and full-time students are eligible, but full-time students must be accepted into a degree program.

Financial data Stipends are $800 per semester for full-time students or $400 per semester for part-time students.

Duration 1 year. Undergraduate students may reapply if they maintain a GPA of 2.0 or higher; graduate or master's degree students may reapply if they maintain a GPA of 3.0 or higher; and specialist or doctoral students may reapply if they maintain a GPA of 3.25 or higher.

Additional information Doyon, Limited is 1 of 13 Alaska Native Regional Corporations created under the Alaska Native Claims Settlement Act of 1971.

Number awarded Varies each year; recently, scholarships were awarded to 228 full-time students and 40 part-time students.

Deadline March of each year for summer school, April of each year for fall semester, September of each year for winter term (vocational students only), November of each year for spring semester.

[172]
DOYON FOUNDATION COMPETITIVE SCHOLARSHIPS

Doyon, Limited
Attn: Doyon Foundation
1 Doyon Place, Suite 300
Fairbanks, AK 99701-2941
(907) 459-2049   Toll Free: (888) 478-4755, ext. 2049
Fax: (907) 459-2065   E-mail: foundation@doyon.com
Web: www.doyonfoundation.com/static/scholarships.aspx

Summary To provide financial assistance to undergraduate and graduate students at schools in any state who are shareholders or descendants of shareholders of Doyon, Limited.

Eligibility This program is open to undergraduate or graduate students who are shareholders or the descendants of shareholders of Doyon, Limited. Applicants must be accepted or enrolled at an accredited college, university, or vocational/technical school in a program that lasts at least 6 weeks. Along with their application, they must submit a personal essay on their educational goals, professional goals, extracurricular and community service activities or volunteerism, and cultural awareness and contributions to a healthy Native community. Selection is based on the essay (40 points), GPA (40 points), letters of recommendation (30 points), and personal impression (10 points).

Financial data Stipends range from $2,000 to $7,000 per year.

Duration 1 year. Undergraduate students may reapply if they maintain a GPA of 2.0 or higher; graduate or master's degree students may reapply if they maintain a GPA of 3.0 or higher; and specialist or doctoral students may reapply if they maintain a GPA of 3.25 or higher. Students can receive a total of $10,000 throughout their entire undergraduate or vocational career. Students who continue in a 1- or 2-year master's degree program are eligible to receive an additional $10,000, for a total maximum of $20,000. Students who work on a 3- to 5-year graduate degree (e.g., Ph.D., M.D., J.D.) can receive an additional $10,000, for a total maximum of $30,000.

Additional information Doyon, Limited is 1 of 13 Alaska Native Regional Corporations created under the Alaska Native Claims Settlement Act of 1971. This program includes the Morris Thompson Scholarship Fund and the Rosemarie Maher Memorial Fund. Recipients must attend school on a full-time basis. Scholarship recipients of $5,000 or more are encouraged to complete at least 1 summer internship during their 4 years of study. Scholarship recipients of less than $5,000 are encouraged to do 1 of the following: serve on a local or regional board or commission, volunteer at least 20 hours, or give presentations on their field of study. A written report detailing the internship or service and lessons learned is required upon completion of the internship.

Number awarded Varies each year; recently, 52 new and renewal scholarships, with a total value of $178,352, were awarded.

Deadline April of each year.

[173]
DR. HANS AND CLARA ZIMMERMAN FOUNDATION EDUCATION SCHOLARSHIPS

Hawai'i Community Foundation
Attn: Scholarship Department
827 Fort Street Mall
Honolulu, HI 96813
(808) 537-6333   Toll Free: (888) 731-3863
Fax: (808) 521-6286
E-mail: scholarships@hcf-hawaii.org
Web: www.hawaiicommunityfoundation.org/scholarships

Summary To provide financial assistance to Hawaii residents (particularly Native Hawaiians) who are nontraditional students planning to major in education at a school in any state.

Eligibility This program is open to Hawaii residents who have worked as a teacher for at least 2 years and are returning to school in any state as full-time students majoring in education. Applicants must be able to demonstrate academic achievement (GPA of 2.8 or higher), good moral character, and financial need. Along with their application, they must submit a short statement indicating their reasons for attending college, their planned course of study, their career goals, what community service means to them, their involvement in community service, why they are involved in those activities, their teaching philosophy, and how their philosophy is being applied in the classroom today. Preference is given to students of Hawaiian ancestry.

Financial data The amount of the award depends on the availability of funds and the need of the recipient. Recently, the average value of all scholarships awarded by the foundation was $2,041.

Duration 1 year.

Additional information This scholarship was established in 1997.

Number awarded Varies each year; recently, 28 of these scholarships were awarded.

Deadline February of each year.

[174]
DR. JO ANN OTA FUJIOKA SCHOLARSHIP

Phi Delta Kappa International
Attn: PDK Educational Foundation
408 North Union Street
P.O. Box 7888
Bloomington, IN 47407-7888
(812) 339-1156   Toll Free: (800) 766-1156
Fax: (812) 339-0018   E-mail: scholarships@pdkintl.org
Web: www.pdkintl.org/awards/prospective.htm

Summary To provide financial assistance to Native American and other high school seniors of color who plan to study education at a college in any state and have a connection to Phi Delta Kappa (PDK).

Eligibility This program is open to high school seniors of color who are planning to major in education and can meet 1 of the following criteria: 1) is a member of a Future Educators Association (FEA) chapter; 2) is the child or grandchild of a PDK member; 3) has a reference letter written by a PDK member; or 4) is selected to represent the local PDK chapter. Applicants must submit a 500-word essay on a topic related to education that changes annually; recently, they were invited to explain what caused them to choose a career in education, what they hope to accomplish during their career as an educator, and how they will measure their success. Selection is based on the essay, academic standing, letters of recommendation, service activities, educational activities, and leadership activities; financial need is not considered.

Financial data The stipend depends on the availability of funds; recently, it was $2,000.

Duration 1 year.

Additional information This program was established in 2006.

Number awarded 1 each year.

Deadline January of each year.

[175]
DR. PHILLIP R. LEE SCHOLARSHIP

California Rural Indian Health Board, Inc.
Attn: Administrative Services Department
4400 Auburn Boulevard, Second Floor
Sacramento, CA 95841
(916) 929-9761   Toll Free: (800) 274-4288
Fax: (916) 929-7246 E-mail: shelley.whitebear@crihb.net
Web: www.crihb.org/scholarship.htm

Summary To provide financial assistance to Indians, especially those from California, working on a degree in a health-related field at a school in California.

Eligibility This program is open to American Indians who are enrolled at an accredited college or university in California. Applicants must be working on a degree in a field related to health care (e.g., physician assistant, L.V.N., R.N., dentist, dental hygienist, dental assistant, pharmacist). They must submit certification from their tribe or the U.S. Bureau of Indian Affairs. Priority is given to applicants who are 1) employed by a California tribal health program; 2) enrolled in a nursing degree program; 3) within 1 or 2 years of graduating; and 4) from a community background that indicates the likelihood of long-term employment at a California Tribal Health Clinic. Financial need is considered in the selection process.

Financial data Stipends range up to $2,800 per semester.

Duration 1 semester; may be renewed, provided the recipient maintains a GPA of 3.0 or higher.

Additional information This program is supported by the California Wellness Foundation.

Number awarded Varies each year.

Deadline August of each year for fall; December of each year for spring.

[176]
DUKE UNIVERSITY SUMMER RESEARCH OPPORTUNITY PROGRAM

Duke University
Graduate School
2127 Campus Drive
Box 90070
Durham, NC 27708-0070
(919) 681-3257   Fax: (919) 681-8018
E-mail: SROP@duke.edu
Web: gradschool.duke.edu/gsa/srop

Summary To provide Native American and other undergraduate students from underrepresented groups with an opportunity to spend a summer learning research techniques in biomedical research laboratories at Duke University.

Eligibility This program is open to undergraduates who are seriously considering joining a Ph.D. graduate program following completion of their undergraduate degree. Applicants must be interested in participating in a summer program at Duke University, during which they will spend most of their time learning research techniques in a laboratory, mentored by faculty members who are actively engaged in conducting research and who would be particularly adept at training undergraduates from underrepresented groups. Eligible departments of study include biochemistry, biological and biologically inspired materials, biological chemistry, biology, biomedical engineering, cell and molecular biology, cell biology, computational biology and bioinformatics, developmental biology, ecology, environment, evolutionary anthropology, genetics and genomics, immunology, integrated toxicology, molecular cancer biology, molecular genetics and microbiology, neurobiology, pathology, pharmacology, and structural biology and biophysics. Along with their application, they must submit a 250-word essay on why they are interested in participating in this program, a 300-word essay on their career goals and how they plan to accomplish those goals, a 400-word description of past research experiences, and a 200-word description of current research interests. Both U.S. and international students are eligible.

Financial data Students receive an on-campus apartment, travel assistance, a food allowance, and a competitive stipend.

Duration 10 weeks during the summer.

Number awarded Approximately 15 each year.

Deadline February of each year.

[177]
DWIGHT DAVID EISENHOWER TRIBAL COLLEGES AND UNIVERSITIES TRANSPORTATION FELLOWSHIPS

Department of Transportation
Federal Highway Administration
Attn: Office of PCD, HPC-32
4600 North Fairfax Drive, Suite 800
Arlington, VA 22203-1553
(703) 235-0538   Toll Free: (877) 558-6873
Fax: (703) 235-0593   E-mail: transportationedu@dot.gov
Web: www.fhwa.dot.gov/ugp/index.htm

Summary To provide financial assistance to undergraduate students working on a degree in a transportation-related field at a Tribal College or University (TCU).

Eligibility This program is open to students enrolled at a TCU and working on a degree in a transportation-related field (i.e., engineering, accounting, business, architecture, environmental sciences). Applicants must be U.S. citizens or have an I-20 (foreign student) or I-551 (permanent resident) identification card. They must have a GPA of 3.0 or higher. Selection is based on their proposed plan of study, academic achievement (based on class standing, GPA, and transcripts), transportation work experience, and letters of recommendation.

Financial data Fellows receive payment of full tuition and fees (to a maximum of $10,000) and a monthly stipend of $1,450. They are also provided with a 1-time allowance of up to $1,500 to attend the annual Transportation Research Board (TRB) meeting.

Duration 1 year.

Additional information This program is administered by the participating TCUs.

Number awarded Varies each year.

Deadline January of each year.

[178]
ED BRADLEY SCHOLARSHIP

Radio Television Digital News Foundation
Attn: RTDNF Fellowship Program
4121 Plank Road, Suite 512
Fredericksburg, VA 22407
(202) 467-5214   Fax: (202) 223-4007
E-mail: staceys@rtdna.org
Web: www.rtdna.org/pages/education/undergraduates.php

Summary To provide financial assistance to Native American and other minority undergraduate students who are preparing for a career in electronic journalism.

Eligibility This program is open to sophomore or more advanced minority undergraduate students enrolled in an electronic journalism sequence at an accredited or nationally-recognized college or university. Applicants must submit 1 to 3 examples of their journalistic skills on audio CD or DVD (no more than 15 minutes total, accompanied by scripts); a description of their role on each story and a list of who worked on each story and what they did; a 1-page statement explaining why they are preparing for a career in electronic journalism with reference to their specific career preference (radio, television, online, reporting, producing, or newsroom management); a resume; and a letter of reference from their dean or faculty sponsor explaining why they are a good candidate for the award and certifying that they have at least 1 year of school remaining.

Financial data The stipend is $10,000, paid in semiannual installments of $5,000 each.

Duration 1 year.

Additional information The Radio Television Digital News Foundation (RTDNF) also provides an all-expense paid trip to the Radio Television Digital News Association (RTDNA) annual international conference. The RTDNF was formerly the Radio and Television News Directors Foundation (RTNDF). Previous winners of any RTDNF scholarship or internship are not eligible.

Number awarded 1 each year.

Deadline May of each year.

[179]
EDSA MINORITY SCHOLARSHIP

Landscape Architecture Foundation
Attn: Scholarship Program
818 18th Street, N.W., Suite 810
Washington, DC 20006-3520
(202) 331-7070   Fax: (202) 331-7079
E-mail: scholarships@lafoundation.org
Web: www.laprofession.org/financial/scholarships.htm

Summary To provide financial assistance to Native American and other minority college students who are interested in studying landscape architecture.

Eligibility This program is open to African American, Hispanic, Native American, and minority college students of other cultural and ethnic backgrounds. Applicants must be entering their final 2 years of undergraduate study in landscape architecture. Along with their application, they must submit a 500-word essay on a design or research effort they plan to pursue (explaining how it will contribute to the advancement of the profession and to their ethnic heritage), work samples, and 2 letters of recommendation. Selection is based on professional experience, community involvement, extracurricular activities, and financial need.

Financial data The stipend is $3,500.

Additional information This scholarship was formerly designated the Edward D. Stone, Jr. and Associates Minority Scholarship.

Number awarded 1 each year.

Deadline February of each year.

[180]
EDUCATION ASSISTANCE PROGRAM OF THE ACCOUNTANCY BOARD OF OHIO

Accountancy Board of Ohio
77 South High Street, 18th Floor
Columbus, OH 43215-6128
(614) 466-4135   Fax: (614) 466-2628
Web: acc.ohio.gov/educasst.htm

Summary To provide financial assistance to Native American or other minority/financially disadvantaged students enrolled in an accounting education program at Ohio academic institutions approved by the Accountancy Board of Ohio.

Eligibility This program is open to minority and financially disadvantaged Ohio residents who apply as full-time sophomores, juniors, or seniors in an accounting program at an accredited college or university in the state. Students who remain in good standing at their institutions and who enter a qualified fifth-year program are then eligible to receive these funds. Minority is defined as people with significant ancestry from Africa (excluding the Middle East), Asia (excluding the Middle East), Central America and the Caribbean islands, South America, and the islands of the Pacific Ocean; in addition, persons with significant ancestry from the original peoples of North America who are of non-European descent. Financial disadvantage is defined according to information provided on the Free Application for Federal Student Aid (FAFSA). U.S. citizenship or permanent resident status is required.

Financial data The amount of the stipend is determined annually but does not exceed the in-state tuition at Ohio public universities (currently, $10,426).

Duration 1 year (the fifth year of an accounting program). Funds committed to students who apply as sophomores must be used within 5 calendar years of the date of the award; funds committed to students who apply as juniors must be used within 4 years; and funds committed to students who apply as seniors must be used within 3 years. The award is nonrenewable and may only be used when the student enrolls in the fifth year of a program.

Number awarded Several each year.

Deadline Applications may be submitted at any time.

[181]
EDWIN MAHIAI COPP BEAMER SCHOLARSHIP

Ke Ali'i Pauahi Foundation
Attn: Financial Aid & Scholarship Services
567 South King Street, Suite 160
Honolulu, HI 96813
(808) 534-3966   Toll Free: (800) 842-4682, ext. 43966
Fax: (808) 534-3890   E-mail: scholarships@pauahi.org
Web: www.pauahi.org/scholarships

Summary To provide financial assistance to undergraduate students, especially those of Native Hawaiian descent, preparing for a career in music.

Eligibility This program is open to undergraduate students working on a degree in music, specifically piano and/or voice, with emphasis on Hawaiian music, opera, or musical theater. Applicants must be able to demonstrate a serious commitment to music training, a career in music, and dedication to artistic excellence. Along with their application, they must submit a personal essay describing their background, musical accomplishments, and educational goals. Finalists are asked to present an informal musical performance or (for non-Hawaii residents) to provide a video of their performance. Residency in Hawaii is not required, but preference is given to Native Hawaiians (descendants of the aboriginal inhabitants of the Hawaiian Islands prior to 1778).

Financial data The stipend is $1,000.

Duration 1 year.

Number awarded 1 each year.

Deadline March of each year.

[182]
EIGHT NORTHERN INDIAN PUEBLOS COUNCIL HIGHER EDUCATION GRANT PROGRAM

Eight Northern Indian Pueblos Council, Inc.
Attn: Higher Education Program
P.O. 969
San Juan, NM 87566
(505) 747-1593   Fax: (505) 747-9650
Web: www.enipc.org

Summary To provide financial assistance for college to members of designated Pueblos in New Mexico.

Eligibility This program is open to enrolled members of the following Pueblos: Tesuque, San Ildefonso, Nambe, Pojoaque, Ohkay Owingeh, Santa Clara, Taos, and Picuris. Applicants must be enrolled or planning to enroll full time in an associate or baccalaureate degree program and have a GPA of 2.0 or higher. They may major in any subject area. Financial need is considered in determining the amount of the award.

Financial data The amount awarded varies, depending upon the recipient's financial need, up to $5,000 per year. Generally, however, scholarships range between $1,000 and $1,800 per year.

Duration 1 year; may be renewed for up to 4 additional years.

Number awarded Varies each year.

Deadline June of each year for the fall term; December of each year for the spring term; April of each year for summer school (for seniors only).

[183]
EISENHOWER GRANTS FOR RESEARCH AND INTERN FELLOWSHIPS

Department of Transportation
Federal Highway Administration
Attn: Office of PCD, HPC-32
4600 North Fairfax Drive, Suite 800
Arlington, VA 22203-1553
(703) 235-0538   Toll Free: (877) 558-6873
Fax: (703) 235-0593   E-mail: transportationedu@dot.gov
Web: www.fhwa.dot.gov/ugp/grf_ann.htm

Summary To enable Native American and other students to participate in transportation-related research activities either at facilities of the U.S. Department of Transportation (DOT) Federal Highway Administration in the Washington, D.C. area or as interns for private or public organizations.

Eligibility This program is open to 1) students in their junior year of a baccalaureate program who will complete their junior year before being awarded a fellowship; 2) students in their senior year of a baccalaureate program; and 3) students who have completed their baccalaureate degree and are enrolled in a program leading to a master's, Ph.D., or equivalent degree. Applicants must be enrolled full time at an accredited U.S institution of higher education and planning to enter the transportation profession after completing their higher education. They must be U.S. citizens or have an I-20 (foreign student) or I-551 (permanent resident) identification card. For research fellowships, they select 1 or more projects from a current list of research activities underway at various DOT facilities; the research is conducted with academic supervision provided by a faculty adviser from their home university (which grants academic credit for the research project) and with technical direction provided by the DOT staff. Intern fellowships provide students with opportunities to perform transportation-related research, development, technology transfer, and other activities at public and private sector organizations. Specific requirements for the target projects vary; most require engineering backgrounds, but others involve transportation planning, information management, public administration, physics, materials science, statistical analysis, operations research, chemistry, economics, technology transfer, urban studies, geography, and urban and regional planning. The DOT encourages students at Historically Black Colleges and Universities (HBCUs), Hispanic Serving Institutions (HSIs), and Tribal Colleges and Universities (TCUs) to apply for these grants. Selection is based on match of the student's qualifications with the proposed research project (including the student's ability to accomplish the project in the available time), recommendation letters regarding the nominee's qualifications to conduct the research, academic records (including class standing, GPA, and transcripts), and transportation work experience (if any), including the employer's endorsement.

Financial data Fellows receive full tuition and fees that relate to the academic credits for the approved research project (to a maximum of $10,000) and a monthly stipend of $1,450 for undergraduates, $1,700 for master's students, or $2,000 for doctoral students. An allowance for travel to and from the DOT facility where the research is conducted is also provided, but selectees are responsible for their own housing accommodations. Recipients are also provided with a 1-time allowance of up to $1,500 to attend the annual Transportation Research Board (TRB) meeting.

Duration Projects normally range from 3 to 12 months.

Number awarded Varies each year; recently, 9 students participated in this program.

Deadline Applications remain open until each project is filled.

[184]
EKLUTNA, INCORPORATED SCHOLARSHIP AND GRANT PROGRAM

Cook Inlet Region, Inc.
Attn: The CIRI Foundation
3600 San Jeronimo Drive, Suite 256
Anchorage, AK 99508-2870
(907) 793-3575   Toll Free: (800) 764-3382
Fax: (907) 793-3585   E-mail: tcf@thecirifoundation.org
Web: www.thecirifoundation.org/village_scholarships.htm

Summary To provide financial assistance for professional preparation after high school to Alaska Natives who are original enrollees of Eklunta, Inc. and their lineal descendants.

Eligibility This program is open to Alaska Native enrollees to Eklunta, Inc. under the Alaska Native Claims Settlement Act (ANCSA) of 1971 and their lineal descendants. Applicants must be 1) accepted or enrolled full time in an accredited or otherwise approved postsecondary college or university; or 2) enrolled part or full time in a technical skills education program. They must have a GPA of 2.5 or higher. higher. Along with their application, they must submit a 500-word statement on their educational and career goals and how they are contributing, or planning to contribute, to a positive Alaska Native community. Selection is based on that statement, academic achievement, rigor of course work or degree program, student financial contribution, financial need, grade level, and community service.

Financial data Stipends are $1,000 or $500.

Duration 1 year.

Additional information This program was established in 2008. Funds are provided equally by Eklunta, Inc. and the CIRI Foundation.

Number awarded Varies each year.

Deadline Applications for scholarships (for academic study) must be submitted by May of each year. Applications for grants (for vocational or technical programs) are due by March, June, September, or November of each year.

[185]
ELI LILLY AND COMPANY/BLACK DATA PROCESSING ASSOCIATES SCHOLARSHIP

Black Data Processing Associates
Attn: BDPA Education Technology Foundation
4423 Lehigh Road, Number 277
College Park, MD 20740
(513) 284-4968   Fax: (202) 318-2194
E-mail: scholarships@betf.org
Web: www.betf.org/scholarships/eli-lilly.shtml

Summary To provide financial assistance to Native American and other minority high school seniors and current college students who are interested in studying information technology at a college in any state.

Eligibility This program is open to graduating high school seniors and current college undergraduates who are members of minority groups (African American, Hispanic, Asian, or Native American). Applicants must be enrolled or planning to enroll at an accredited 4-year college or university and work on a degree in information technology. They must have a GPA of 3.0 or higher. Along with their application, they must submit a 500-word essay on why information technology is important. Selection is based on that essay, academic achievement, leadership ability through academic or civic involvement, and participation in community service activities. U.S. citizenship or permanent resident status is required.

Financial data The stipend is $2,500. Funds may be used to pay for tuition, fees, books, room and board, or other college-related expenses.

Duration 1 year; nonrenewable.

Additional information The BDPA established its Education and Technology Foundation (BETF) in 1992 to advance the skill sets needed by African American and other minority adults and young people to compete in the information technology industry. This program is sponsored by Eli Lilly and Company.

Number awarded 1 or more each year.

Deadline July of each year.

[186]
ELIZABETH AND SHERMAN ASCHE MEMORIAL SCHOLARSHIP

Association on American Indian Affairs, Inc.
Attn: Director of Scholarship Programs
966 Hungerford Drive, Suite 12-B
Rockville, MD 20850
(240) 314-7155   Fax: (240) 314-7159
E-mail: lw.aaia@verizon.net
Web: www.indian-affairs.org

Summary To provide financial assistance to Native Americans interested in working on an undergraduate or graduate degree in public health.

Eligibility This program is open to American Indian and Alaskan Native full-time undergraduate and graduate students working on a degree in public health or science. Applicants must submit documentation of financial need, a Certificate of Indian Blood showing at least one-quarter Indian blood, proof of tribal enrollment, an essay on their educational goals, 2 letters of recommendation, and their most recent transcript. Selection is based on merit and need.

Financial data The stipend is $1,500.

Duration 1 year. Recipients may reapply.

Number awarded Varies each year; recently, 6 of these scholarships were awarded.

Deadline June of each year.

[187]
EMILIE HESEMEYER MEMORIAL SCHOLARSHIP

Association on American Indian Affairs, Inc.
Attn: Director of Scholarship Programs
966 Hungerford Drive, Suite 12-B
Rockville, MD 20850
(240) 314-7155   Fax: (240) 314-7159
E-mail: lw.aaia@verizon.net
Web: www.indian-affairs.org

Summary To provide financial assistance for college to Native American students, especially those interested in majoring in education.

Eligibility This program is open to American Indian and Native Alaskan full-time undergraduate students. Preference is given to students working on a degree in education. Applicants must submit documentation of financial need, a Certificate of Indian Blood showing at least one-quarter Indian blood, proof of tribal enrollment, an essay on their educational goals, 2 letters of recommendation, and their most recent transcript.

Financial data The stipend is $1,500 per year.

Duration 1 year; may be renewed up to 3 additional years or until completion of a degree, provided the recipient maintains satisfactory progress.

Number awarded Varies each year; recently, 3 new and 16 renewal scholarships were awarded.

Deadline June of each year.

[188]
ENCOURAGE MINORITY PARTICIPATION IN OCCUPATIONS WITH EMPHASIS ON REHABILITATION

Courage Center
Attn: EMPOWER Scholarship Program
3915 Golden Valley Road
Minneapolis, MN 55422
(763) 520-0214   Toll Free: (888) 8-INTAKE
Fax: (763) 520-0562   TDD: (763) 520-0245
E-mail: empower@couragecenter.org
Web: www.couragecenter.org

Summary To provide financial assistance to Native Americans and other students of color from Minnesota and western Wisconsin who are interested in attending college in any state to prepare for a career in the medical rehabilitation field.

Eligibility This program is open to ethnically diverse students accepted at or enrolled in an institution of higher learning in any state. Applicants must be residents of Minnesota or western Wisconsin (Burnett, Pierce, Polk, and St. Croix counties). They must be able to demonstrate a career interest in the medical rehabilitation field by a record of volunteer involvement related to health care and must have a GPA of 2.0 or higher. Along with their application, they must submit a 1-page essay that covers their experiences and interactions to date with the area of volunteering, what they have accomplished and gained from those experiences, how those experiences will assist them in their future endeavors, why education is important to them, how this scholarship will help them with their financial need and their future career goals.

Financial data The stipend is $1,500.

Duration 1 year.

Additional information This program, established in 1995, is also identified by its acronym as the EMPOWER Scholarship Award.

Number awarded 2 each year.

Deadline May of each year.

[189]
ENTERPRISE RANCHERIA HIGHER EDUCATION PROGRAM

Enterprise Rancheria
Attn: Education Department
3690 Olive Highway
Oroville, CA 95966
(530) 532-9214   Fax: (530) 532-1768
Web: enterpriserancheria.org

Summary To provide financial assistance to members of the Estom Yumeka Maidu tribe of Enterprise Rancheria in northern California who are interested in attending college or graduate school in any state.

Eligibility This program is open to enrolled members of Enterprise Rancheria who are attending or planning to attend a college, university, or community college in any state. Applicants must be interested in working on an undergraduate or graduate degree in any field. Along with their application, they must submit a brief essay on their educational goals and plans for utilizing their education. Financial need is considered in the selection process.

Financial data The stipend is $1,000 per year for undergraduate and graduate students at 4-year colleges and universities or $500 per year for students at community colleges. A book allowance of $500 per semester for 4-year institution students or $300 per semester for community college students is also provided. Transportation costs of $100 per month may be reimbursed and monthly living expenses may be paid if funds are available.

Duration 1 year; may be renewed, provided the recipient maintains a GPA of 2.0 or higher.

Number awarded Varies each year.

Deadline July of each year for academic year or fall semester; December of each year for spring semester only.

[190]
ENVIRONMENTAL PROTECTION AGENCY STUDENT DIVERSITY INTERNSHIP PROGRAM

United Negro College Fund Special Programs
   Corporation
Attn: NASA Science and Technology Institute
6402 Arlington Boulevard, Suite 600
Falls Church, VA 22042
(703) 677-3400   Toll Free: (800) 530-6232
Fax: (703) 205-7645   E-mail: portal@uncfsp.org
Web: www.uncfsp.org

Summary To provide an opportunity for Native Americans and other underrepresented undergraduate and graduate students to work on a summer research project at research sites of the U.S. Environmental Protection Agency (EPA).

Eligibility This program is open to rising college sophomores, juniors, and seniors and to full-time graduate students at accredited institutions who are members of underrepresented groups, including ethnic minorities (African Americans, Hispanic/Latinos, Native Americans, Asians, Alaskan Natives, and Native Hawaiians/Pacific Islanders) and persons with disabilities. Applicants must have a GPA of 2.8 or higher and be working on a degree in business, communications, economics, engineering, environmental science/management, finance, information technology, law, marketing, or science. They must be interested in working on a research proj-

ect during the summer at their choice of 23 EPA research sites (for a list, contact EPA). U.S. citizenship is required.

Financial data The stipend is $5,000 for undergraduates or $6,000 for graduate students. Interns also receive a travel and housing allowance, but they are responsible for covering their local transportation, meals, and miscellaneous expenses.

Duration 10 weeks during the summer.

Additional information This program is funded by EPA and administered by the United Negro College Fund Special Programs Corporation.

Number awarded Varies each year.

Deadline May of each year.

[191]
ETHEL CURRY SCHOLARSHIPS

Minnesota Department of Education
Attn: Manager, Minnesota Indian Education
1500 Highway 36 West
Roseville, MN 55113-4266
(651) 582-8862   Toll Free: (800) 657-3927
E-mail: mde.indian-education@state.mn.us
Web: education.state.mn.us

Summary To provide financial assistance to Native Americans in Minnesota who are interested in working on an undergraduate or graduate degree.

Eligibility This program is open to Indians who are enrolled in a Minnesota-based tribe or community. Applicants must be attending an accredited postsecondary institution in Minnesota as a junior, senior, or graduate student. They must have a GPA of 3.0 or higher. Selection is based on merit.

Financial data The stipend is $3,000 per year for undergraduates or $6,000 per year for graduate students.

Duration Up to 4 years.

Number awarded Varies each year; recently, 12 of these scholarships were awarded.

Deadline May of each year.

[192]
EXCELLENCE IN CARDIOVASCULAR SCIENCES SUMMER RESEARCH PROGRAM

Wake Forest University School of Medicine
Attn: Hypertension and Vascular Research Center
Medical Center Boulevard
Winston-Salem, NC 27157-1032
(336) 716-1080   Fax: (336) 716-2456
E-mail: nsarver@wfubmc.edu
Web: www.wfubmc.edu

Summary To provide Native Americans and other underrepresented students with an internship opportunity to engage in a summer research project in cardiovascular science at Wake Forest University in Winston-Salem, North Carolina.

Eligibility This program is open to undergraduates and master's degree students who are members of underrepresented minority groups (African Americans, Alaskan Natives, Asian Americans, Native Americans, Pacific Islanders, and Hispanics) or who come from disadvantaged backgrounds (e.g., rural areas, first generation college students). Applicants must be interested in participating in a program of summer research in the cardiovascular sciences that includes "hands-on" laboratory research, a lecture series by faculty and guest speakers, and a research symposium at which students present their research findings. U.S. citizenship or permanent resident status is required.

Financial data The stipend is $1,731 per month, housing in a university dormitory, and round-trip transportation expense.

Duration 2 months during the summer.

Additional information This program is sponsored by the National Heart, Lung, and Blood Institute (NHLBI) of the National Institutes of Health (NIH).

Number awarded Approximately 10 each year.

Deadline February of each year.

[193]
EYAK FOUNDATION SCHOLARSHIPS

Eyak Corporation
Attn: Eyak Foundation
901 LeFevre Street
P.O. Box 340
Cordova, AK 99574
(907) 424-7161 Fax: (907) 424-5161
Web: www.eyakcorporation.com

Summary To provide financial assistance to Native Alaskans who are shareholders of the Eyak Corporation or their descendants and are interested in working on an undergraduate or graduate degree in any state.

Eligibility This program is open to Native Alaskans who are shareholders of the Eyak Corporation or lineal descendants of a Native shareholder. Applicants must be enrolled or planning to enroll in an accredited undergraduate or graduate program at a college, university, vocational education school, or continuing education program in any state. They must have a GPA of 2.5 or higher and be able to demonstrate financial need. Along with their application, they must submit a personal history and statement of educational goals.

Financial data The stipend is $1,000.

Duration 1 year.

Additional information The Eyak Foundation was formerly named the Cordova Native Foundation.

Number awarded 5 each year.

Deadline June of each year.

[194]
FALLON PAIUTE SHOSHONE TRIBE ADULT VOCATIONAL EDUCATION PROGRAM

Fallon Paiute Shoshone Tribe
Attn: Education Office
565 Rio Vista Drive
Fallon, NV 89406
(775) 423-8065, ext. 224 Fax: (775) 423-8067
E-mail: education@fpst.org
Web: www.fpst.org

Summary To provide financial assistance to members of the Fallon Paiute Shoshone Tribe who are interested in attending vocational school in any state.

Eligibility This program is open to members of the Fallon Paiute Shoshone Tribe who are attending or planning to attend a vocational training program in any state. Applicants must submit a short essay describing the type of vocation in which they plan to enroll, the length of the course, why they

chose that field of study, and what they plan to do after completion of the course.

Financial data The program provides at least partial payment of the costs of tuition and books. Students who attend school away from home may also apply for payment of the costs associated with room and board.

Duration 1 year; nonrenewable.

Number awarded Varies each year.

Deadline March, June, September, or December of each year.

[195]
FALLON PAIUTE SHOSHONE TRIBE HIGHER EDUCATION PROGRAM

Fallon Paiute Shoshone Tribe
Attn: Education Office
565 Rio Vista Drive
Fallon, NV 89406
(775) 423-8065, ext. 224 Fax: (775) 423-8067
E-mail: education@fpst.org
Web: www.fpst.org

Summary To provide financial assistance to members of the Fallon Paiute Shoshone Tribe who are interested in attending college or graduate school in any state as a full-time student.

Eligibility This program is open to members of the Fallon Paiute Shoshone Tribe who are enrolled or planning to enroll as a full-time undergraduate or graduate student at a college or university in any state. Applicants must be able to demonstrate financial need.

Financial data A stipend is awarded (amount not specified).

Duration 1 year.

Additional information This program is funded, in part, by the U.S. Bureau of Indian Affairs.

Number awarded Varies each year.

Deadline May or September of each year.

[196]
FALLON PAIUTE SHOSHONE TRIBE HIGHER EDUCATION PROGRAM

Fallon Paiute Shoshone Tribe
Attn: Education Office
565 Rio Vista Drive
Fallon, NV 89406
(775) 423-8065, ext. 224 Fax: (775) 423-8067
E-mail: education@fpst.org
Web: www.fpst.org

Summary To provide financial assistance to members of the Fallon Paiute Shoshone Tribe who are interested in attending college in any state as a part-time student.

Eligibility This program is open to members of the Fallon Paiute Shoshone Tribe who are attending or planning to attend a college or university in any state. Applicants must enroll in 11 or fewer credit hours. Along with their application, they must submit a short statement explaining why they are taking the courses and what they plan to do after their courses are completed. If they enroll in 6 or more credit hours, they must also provide documentation of financial need.

Financial data The stipend depends on the need of the recipient and the cost of the program.

Duration 1 year.

Number awarded Varies each year.

Deadline May of each year for fall; September of each year for spring; March of each year for summer.

[197]
FINE ARTS SCHOLARSHIP

Chickasaw Foundation
110 West 12th Street
P.O. Box 1726
Ada, OK 74821-1726
(580) 421-9030   Fax: (580) 421-9031
E-mail: ChickasawFoundation@chickasaw.net
Web: www.chickasawfoundation.org/index_20.htm

Summary To provide financial assistance to members of the Chickasaw Nation interested in studying fine arts in college.

Eligibility This program is open to Chickasaw students who are currently enrolled full time as a junior or senior at an accredited 4-year college. Applicants must be majoring in fine arts (dance, dramatics, art, music) and have a GPA of 3.0 or higher. Along with their application, they must submit high school or college transcripts, 2 letters of recommendation, a copy of their Certificate of Indian Blood, a copy of their Chickasaw Nation citizenship card, and a 1-page essay on their long-term goals and plans for achieving them. Financial need is not considered in the selection process.

Financial data The stipend is $1,500.

Duration 1 year.

Number awarded 1 each year.

Deadline August of each year.

[198]
FIRST SERGEANT DOUGLAS AND CHARLOTTE DEHORSE SCHOLARSHIP

Catching the Dream
8200 Mountain Road, N.E., Suite 203
Albuquerque, NM 87110-7835
(505) 262-2351   Fax: (505) 262-0534
E-mail: NScholarsh@aol.com
Web: www.catchingthedream.org

Summary To provide financial assistance to American Indians who have ties to the military and are working on an undergraduate or graduate degree.

Eligibility This program is open to American Indians who 1) have completed 1 year of an Army, Navy, or Air Force Junior Reserve Officer Training (JROTC) program; 2) are enrolled in an Army, Navy, or Air Force Reserve Officer Training (ROTC) program; or 3) are a veteran of the U.S. Army, Navy, Air Force, Marines, Merchant Marine, or Coast Guard. Applicants must be enrolled in an undergraduate or graduate program of study. Along with their application, they must submit a personal essay, high school transcripts, and letters of recommendation.

Financial data A stipend is awarded (amount not specified).

Duration 1 year.

Additional information This program was established in 2007.

Number awarded 1 or more each year.

Deadline April of each year for fall semester or quarter; September of each year for spring semester or winter quarter.

[199]
FISHER COMMUNICATIONS SCHOLARSHIPS FOR MINORITIES

Fisher Communications
Attn: Minority Scholarship
100 Fourth Avenue North, Suite 510
Seattle, WA 98109
(206) 404-7000   Fax: (206) 404-6037
E-mail: Info@fsci.com
Web: www.fsci.com/scholarship.html

Summary To provide financial assistance to Native American and other minority college students in selected states who are interested in preparing for a career in broadcasting.

Eligibility This program is open to U.S. citizens of non-white origin who have a GPA of 2.5 or higher and are at least sophomores enrolled in 1) a broadcasting curriculum (radio, television, marketing, or broadcast technology) leading to a bachelor's degree at an accredited 4-year college or university; 2) a broadcast curriculum at an accredited community college, transferable to a 4-year baccalaureate degree program; or 3) a broadcast curriculum at an accredited vocational/technical school. Applicants must be either 1) residents of California, Washington, Oregon, Idaho, or Montana; or 2) attending a school in those states. They must submit an essay that explains their financial need, educational and career goals, any experience or interest they have in broadcast communications that they feel qualifies them for this scholarship, and involvement in school activities. Selection is based on need, academic achievement, and personal qualities.

Financial data A stipend is awarded (amount not specified).

Duration 1 year; recipients may reapply.

Additional information This program began in 1987.

Number awarded Varies; a total of $10,000 is available for this program each year.

Deadline May of each year.

[200]
FLANDREAU SANTEE SIOUX ADULT VOCATIONAL TRAINING GRANTS

Flandreau Santee Sioux Tribe
Attn: Education Coordinator
P.O. Box 283
Flandreau, SD 57028
(605) 997-2859   Fax: (605) 997-2951
E-mail: highered@fsst.org
Web: www.fsst.org/Agnesrossedu_main.html

Summary To provide financial assistance to members of the Flandreau Santee Sioux Tribe and other Indians who live near the reservation and are interested in attending vocational school.

Eligibility This program is open to enrolled members of the Flandreau Santee Sioux Tribe and members of other federally-recognized tribes who live within 50 miles of Tribal Headquarters. Applicants must be between 18 and 35 years of age and in need of training at a vocational/technical institute to obtain reasonable and satisfactory employment. They must apply for all available federal funding, using the Free Application for Student Aid (FAFSA). Awards are granted on a first-come, first-served basis.

Financial data The stipend is $500 per semester. Funds are for tuition and fees and are paid directly to the institution.

Duration Up to 24 months of full-time training or equivalent in part-time training is provided.

Additional information Funding for this program is provided by the U.S. Bureau of Indian Affairs (BIA).

Number awarded Varies each year.

Deadline July of each year for fall semester or quarter; December of each year for spring semester or winter quarter; January of each year for spring quarter; May of each year for summer session.

[201]
FLANDREAU SANTEE SIOUX BIA HIGHER EDUCATION GRANTS

Flandreau Santee Sioux Tribe
Attn: Education Coordinator
P.O. Box 283
Flandreau, SD 57028
(605) 997-2859   Fax: (605) 997-2951
E-mail: highered@fsst.org
Web: www.fsst.org/Agnesrossedu_main.html

Summary To provide financial assistance to members of the Flandreau Santee Sioux Tribe who are interested in attending college in any state.

Eligibility This program is open to enrolled members of the tribe who are attending or planning to attend a college or university in any state. Applicants must intend to complete a baccalaureate degree or an associate degree that leads to a baccalaureate degree. They must apply for all available federal funding, using the Free Application for Student Aid (FAFSA). In the selection process, first priority is given to continuing students, second to new students, and third to returning students. Within those categories, additional consideration is given to class rank (upper classmen are funded before lower classmen), financial need (students with unmet financial need are funded before students with no financial need), and residency (students who are on reservation are funded before students who are off reservation).

Financial data For the first semester of each year, full-time students receive $1,000 as freshmen, $1,100 as sophomores, $1,200 as juniors, or $1,300 as seniors. For the second semester of each year, full-time students who have a GPA of 2.0 to 3.0 during the first semester receive the same amounts; those who have less than 2.0 receive $800 as freshmen, $880 as sophomores, $960 as juniors, or $1,040 as seniors; those who have more than 3.0 receive $1,100 as freshmen, $1,200 as sophomores, $1,300 as juniors, or $1,400 as seniors. Part-time students receive stipends equal to half the amount of full-time students in the same category. Funds are for tuition and fees and are paid directly to the institution.

Duration 1 semester; may be renewed for a total of 89 semester credits for an associate degree or a total of 154 semester credits for a bachelor's degree (including funded associate degree credits). Renewal requires that recipients maintain a GPA of 2.0 or higher.

Additional information Funding for this program is provided by the U.S. Bureau of Indian Affairs (BIA).

Number awarded Varies each year.

Deadline July of each year for fall semester or quarter; December of each year for spring semester or winter quarter; January of each year for spring quarter; May of each year for summer session.

[202]
FLINTCO SCHOLARSHIP

Choctaw Nation
Attn: Scholarship Advisement Program
16th and Locust
P.O. Box 1210
Durant, OK 74702-1210
(580) 924-8280
Toll Free: (800) 522-6170, ext. 2523 (within OK)
Fax: (580) 920-3122
E-mail: scholarshipadvisement@choctawnation.com
Web: www.choctawnation-sap.com/cnoscholarship.shtml

Summary To provide financial assistance to Choctaw Indian high school seniors and current college students who are interested in working on an undergraduate degree in a field related to construction.

Eligibility This program is open to graduating high school seniors and current college students who are members of the Choctaw Nation and its Scholarship Advisement Program. Applicants must be enrolled or planning to enroll in a 4- or 5-year program in construction management, construction science, or a closely-related degree program. High school seniors must have an ACT score of at least 25; college students must have a GPA of 3.0 or higher.

Financial data The stipend is $2,500 per year.

Duration 1 year; may be renewed up to 4 additional years, provided the recipient maintains a GPA of 3.0 or higher.

Additional information This program is funded by Flintco, Inc.

Number awarded Varies each year; a total of $25,000 is available for this program annually.

Deadline April of each year.

[203]
FLORIDA FUND FOR MINORITY TEACHERS SCHOLARSHIPS

Florida Fund for Minority Teachers, Inc.
Attn: Executive Director
G415 Norman Hall
P.O. Box 117045
Gainesville, FL 32611-7045
(352) 392-9196, ext. 21   Fax: (352) 846-3011
E-mail: info@ffmt.org
Web: www.ffmt.org

Summary To provide funding to Native Americans and other minorities residing in Florida who are preparing for a career as a teacher.

Eligibility This program is open to Florida residents who are African American/Black, Hispanic/Latino, Asian American/Pacific Islander, or American Indian/Alaskan Native. Applicants must be entering their junior year in a teacher education program at a participating college or university in Florida. Special consideration is given to community college graduates. Selection is based on writing ability, communication skills, overall academic performance, and evidence of commitment to the youth of America (preferably demonstrated through volunteer activities).

Financial data The stipend is $4,000 per year. Recipients are required to teach 1 year in a Florida public school for each year they receive the scholarship. If they fail to teach in a public school, they are required to repay the total amount of support received at an annual interest rate of 8%.

Duration Up to 2 consecutive years, provided the recipient remains enrolled full time with a GPA of 2.5 or higher.

Additional information For a list of the 16 participating public institutions and the 18 participating private institutions, contact the Florida Fund for Minority Teachers (FFMT). Recipients are also required to attend the annual FFMT recruitment and retention conference.

Number awarded Varies each year.

Deadline July of each year for fall semester; November of each year for spring semester.

[204]
FORD MOTOR COMPANY SCHOLARSHIPS

American Indian College Fund
Attn: Scholarship Department
8333 Greenwood Boulevard
Denver, CO 80221
(303) 426-8900   Toll Free: (800) 776-FUND
Fax: (303) 426-1200
E-mail: scholarships@collegefund.org
Web: www.collegefund.org

Summary To provide financial assistance to Native American college students who are majoring in designated fields at mainstream colleges and universities.

Eligibility This program is open to American Indians and Alaska Natives who have proof of enrollment or descendancy and are enrolled full time in a bachelor's degree program at a mainstream institution. Applicants must have a GPA of 3.0 or higher and be able to demonstrate exceptional academic achievement or financial need. They must have declared a major in accounting, computer science, engineering, finance, marketing, or operations management. Applications are available only online and include required essays on specified topics.

Financial data The stipend is $10,000 per year.

Duration 1 year; may be renewed.

Additional information This program is funded by the Ford Motor Company in partnership with the American Indian College Fund.

Number awarded Varies each year.

Deadline May of each year.

[205]
FORD MOTOR COMPANY TRIBAL COLLEGE SCHOLARSHIP

American Indian College Fund
Attn: Scholarship Department
8333 Greenwood Boulevard
Denver, CO 80221
(303) 426-8900   Toll Free: (800) 776-FUND
Fax: (303) 426-1200
E-mail: scholarships@collegefund.org
Web: www.collegefund.org/scholarships/schol_tcu.html

Summary To provide financial assistance to Native Americans who are attending a Tribal College or University (TCU) and majoring in specified fields.

Eligibility This program is open to American Indians or Alaska Natives who are enrolled full time at an eligible TCU. Applicants must have a GPA of 3.0 or higher and be able to demonstrate exceptional academic achievement or financial need. They must have declared a major in mathematics, science, engineering, business, teacher training, or environmental science. Applications are available only online and include required essays on specified topics.

Financial data The stipend is $5,000.

Duration 1 year.

Additional information This program is funded by the Ford Motor Company in partnership with the American Indian College Fund.

Number awarded 1 or more each year.

Deadline May of each year.

[206]
FOREST COUNTY POTAWATOMI ADULT VOCATIONAL TRAINING PROGRAM

Forest County Potawatomi
Attn: Education Department
7695 Lois Crowe Lane
P.O. Box 340
Crandon, WI 54520
(715) 478-7355   Toll Free: (800) 960-5479
Fax: (715) 478-7352
Web: www.fcpotawatomi.com

Summary To provide financial assistance for vocational or technical training to tribal members of the Forest County Potawatomi.

Eligibility This program is open to enrolled Forest County Potawatomi members who are working on or planning to work on a diploma, certificate, or associate degree. Applicants must be able to demonstrate financial need.

Financial data The stipend depends on the need of the recipient, up to full payment of tuition, books, and required fees.

Duration Up to 24 months at a vocational technical training institution or 36 months at a school of nursing, provided the recipient maintains a GPA of 2.0 or higher.

Number awarded Varies each year.

Deadline May of each year.

[207]
FOREST COUNTY POTAWATOMI HIGHER EDUCATION PROGRAM

Forest County Potawatomi
Attn: Education Department
7695 Lois Crowe Lane
P.O. Box 340
Crandon, WI 54520
(715) 478-7355   Toll Free: (800) 960-5479
Fax: (715) 478-7352
Web: www.fcpotawatomi.com

Summary To provide financial assistance for college or graduate school to tribal members of the Forest County Potawatomi.

Eligibility This program is open to enrolled Forest County Potawatomi members who are working on or planning to work on an undergraduate or graduate degree. Applicants must be able to demonstrate financial need.

Financial data The stipend depends on the need of the recipient, up to full payment of tuition, books, and required fees.

Duration Up to 10 semesters for undergraduate students, up to 2 years for master's degree students, or up to 3 years for doctoral students, provided the recipient maintains a GPA of 2.0 or higher as an undergraduate or 3.0 or higher as a graduate student.

Number awarded Varies each year.

Deadline May of each year.

[208]
FORT PECK TRIBES SCHOLARSHIP GRANT ASSISTANCE

Fort Peck Assiniboine and Sioux Tribes
Attn: Education Department
501 Medicine Bear Road
P.O. Box 1027
Poplar, MT 59255-1027
(406) 768-5136   Toll Free: (800) 799-2926
Fax: (406) 768-3556
Web: www.fortpecktribes.org

Summary To provide financial assistance to members of the Fort Peck Assiniboine and Sioux Tribes who are interested in attending college in any state.

Eligibility This program is open to enrolled members of the Fort Peck Assiniboine and Sioux Tribes who have or will have a high school diploma or GED certificate. Applicants must be enrolled or planning to enroll at an institution of higher education in any state. They must be able to document financial need. Priority in funding is given to seniors, juniors, sophomores, and freshmen, in that order.

Financial data The maximum stipend is $3,600 per year for students who live off the reservation or $1,800 per year for students who live on the reservation. Funding is the same, regardless of whether the student attends school in Montana or another state.

Duration 1 year; may be renewed, provided the recipient maintains a GPA of 2.0 or higher.

Number awarded Varies each year.

Deadline July of each year for fall and spring semesters; April of each year for summer school.

[209]
FOUR DIRECTIONS SUMMER RESEARCH PROGRAM

Brigham and Women's Hospital
Office for Multicultural Faculty Careers
Attn: Elena Muench
1620 Tremont Street 3-014.04
Boston, MA 02120
(617) 525-7644   E-mail: FourDirections@partners.org
Web: www.fdsrp.org

Summary To provide an opportunity for Native American undergraduate and graduate students to participate in a summer research project at Harvard Medical School.

Eligibility This program is open to Native American undergraduate and graduate students who are interested in preparing for a career as a physician or in biomedical research. Applicants must have completed at least 1 year of undergraduate study and have taken at least 1 introductory science course (may include biology or chemistry). They must be interested in conducting a research project at Harvard Medical School under the supervision of a scientist engaged in medical or biomedical research, ranging from neurobiology and neuropathology to cell biology and molecular genetics. Selection is based on demonstrated commitment to the health of Native American communities and demonstrated interest in a career in medical sciences. Students from rural state colleges, tribal colleges, and community colleges are especially encouraged to apply.

Financial data The program provides a stipend of at least $2,500, airfare, transportation, and lodging expenses.

Duration 8 weeks during the summer.

Additional information This program, which began in 1994, is administered jointly by Harvard Medical School and Brigham and Women's Hospital. Funding is provided by the Aetna Foundation, the Mohegan Sun casino, and the Office of Minority Health of the U.S. Department of Health and Human Services. Participants may not take the summer MCAT, because the time constraints of this program do not allow time to study for that examination.

Number awarded 6 each year.

Deadline February of each year.

[210]
FRANCES CRAWFORD MARVIN AMERICAN INDIAN SCHOLARSHIP

Daughters of the American Revolution-National Society
Attn: Committee Services Office, Scholarships
1776 D Street, N.W.
Washington, DC 20006-5303
(202) 628-1776
Web: www.dar.org/natsociety/edout_scholar.cfm

Summary To provide financial assistance to Native American students who are working on an undergraduate degree.

Eligibility This program is open to Native Americans enrolled full time at a 2- or 4-year college or university. Applicants must have a GPA of 3.0 or higher. Selection is based on academic achievement and financial need.

Financial data The stipend depends on the availability of funds.

Duration 1 year; nonrenewable.

Number awarded 1 each year.

Deadline January of each year.

[211]
FRANCES JOHNSON MEMORIAL TRUST SCHOLARSHIP

Northern Arapaho Tribe
Attn: Sky People Higher Education
P.O. Box 8480
Ethete, WY 82520
(307) 332-5286   Toll Free: (800) 815-6795
Fax: (307) 332-9104   E-mail: assistant@skypeopleed.org
Web: www.skypeopleed.org

Summary To provide financial assistance to members of the Northern Arapaho Tribe who are working on an undergraduate or graduate degree in nursing or a health-related field.

Eligibility This program is open to full-time undergraduate and graduate students who have an undergraduate GPA of 2.0 or higher or the graduate GPA required by their school. Applicants must be at least one-fourth Northern Arapaho descent (enrolled or non-enrolled) and must submit a Certificate of Indian Blood or other verification of Northern Arapaho blood with at least one-fourth degree. They must be working on a degree in nursing or a health-related field. Along with their application, they must submit a 1-page personal statement that includes a brief history of their background, academic ability and achievement, work or leadership experience, participation in community-related activities, and career goals. Selection is based on that statement, potential to contribute to the community upon graduation, academic ability and achievement, and a letter of recommendation.

Financial data The stipend is $1,500 per year.

Duration 1 year; may be renewed.

Additional information The recipient is expected to apply for employment, after graduation, at the Tribal Health Program, Indian Health Services, at health care facilities on the Wind River Indian Reservation, or in the local communities of Lander or Riverton.

Number awarded 1 each year.

Deadline June of each year.

[212]
FRED L. HATCH MEMORIAL TEACHER EDUCATION SCHOLARSHIP

Sault Tribe of Chippewa Indians
Attn: Higher Education Program-Memorial/Tributary
  Scholarships
523 Ashmun Street
Sault Ste. Marie, MI 49783
(906) 635-4944   Toll Free: (800) 793-0660
Fax: (906) 635-7785   E-mail: amatson@saulttribe.net
Web: www.saulttribe.com

Summary To provide financial assistance to members of the Sault Tribe who are enrolled in a teacher education program at a college in Michigan.

Eligibility This program is open to members of the Sault Tribe who are college juniors or higher and are one-quarter Indian blood quantum or more. Applicants must be enrolled full time in a teacher education program at an accredited Michigan 4-year public college or university. They must have

a cumulative GPA of 3.0 or higher. Along with their application, they must submit an essay of 300 to 500 words on how this scholarship will help them realize their goals.

Financial data The stipend is $1,000 per year.

Duration 1 year; may be renewed.

Number awarded 1 each year.

Deadline May of each year.

[213]
FRED L. MCGHEE FIRST GENERATION INDIAN DESCENT SCHOLARSHIP PROGRAM

Poarch Band of Creek Indians
Attn: Tuition Program Coordinator
5811 Jack Springs Road
Atmore, AL 36502
(251) 368-9136, ext. 2241   Fax: (251) 368-4502
E-mail: sfisher@pci-nsn.gov
Web: www.poarchcreekindians.org

Summary To provide financial assistance to undergraduate and graduate students who are first-generation descendants of members of the Poarch Band of Creek Indians.

Eligibility This program is open to first-generation descendants of enrolled tribal members of the Poarch Band of Creek Indians. Applicants must be attending or planning to attend an approved postsecondary institution as an undergraduate or graduate student. They must have a GPA of 2.0 or higher and be able to document financial need.

Financial data The stipend depends on the need of the recipient, to an annual cap of $6,000.

Duration 1 year; may be renewed until the recipient reaches a lifetime benefit cap of $20,000.

Number awarded Varies each year.

Deadline Applications may be submitted at any time.

[214]
GABE STEPETIN SCHOLARSHIP AWARD

The Aleut Corporation
Attn: Aleut Foundation
703 West Tudor Road, Suite 102
Anchorage, AK 99503-6650
(907) 646-1929   Toll Free: (800) 232-4882
Fax: (907) 646-1949   E-mail: taf@thealeutfoundation.org
Web: www.thealeutfoundation.org/ScholarshipGuide.aspx

Summary To provide financial assistance to Native Alaskans who are shareholders of The Aleut Corporation or their descendants and working on a degree in business at a school in any state.

Eligibility This program is open to Native Alaskans who are original enrollees or descendants of original enrollees of The Aleut Corporation (TAC). Applicants must have completed at least 1 year of a bachelor's, 2- or 4-year vocational, or master's degree in business at a school in any state. They must be enrolled full time and have a GPA of 3.0 or higher. Along with their application, they must include a letter of intent, up to 500 words in length, that describes their educational goals and objectives and their expected graduation date.

Financial data A stipend is awarded (amount not specified).

Duration 1 year.

Additional information The Aleut Corporation is 1 of 13 Alaska Native Regional Corporations created under the Alaska Native Claims Settlement Act of 1971.

Number awarded 1 each year.

Deadline June of each year.

[215]
GATES MILLENNIUM SCHOLARS PROGRAM

Bill and Melinda Gates Foundation
P.O. Box 10500
Fairfax, VA 22031-8044
Toll Free: (877) 690-GMSP   Fax: (703) 205-2079
Web: www.gmsp.org

Summary To provide financial assistance to outstanding low-income Native Americans and other minorities, particularly those interested in majoring in specific fields in college.

Eligibility This program is open to African Americans, Alaska Natives, American Indians, Hispanic Americans, and Asian Pacific Islander Americans who are graduating high school seniors with a GPA of 3.3 or higher. Principals, teachers, guidance counselors, tribal higher education representatives, and other professional educators are invited to nominate students with outstanding academic qualifications, particularly those likely to succeed in the fields of computer science, education, engineering, library science, mathematics, public health, or science. Nominees should have significant financial need and have demonstrated leadership abilities through participation in community service, extracurricular, or other activities. U.S. citizenship, nationality, or permanent resident status is required. Nominees must be planning to enter an accredited college or university as a full-time, degree-seeking freshman in the following fall.

Financial data The program covers the cost of tuition, fees, books, and living expenses not paid for by grants and scholarships already committed as part of the recipient's financial aid package.

Duration 4 years or the completion of the undergraduate degree, if the recipient maintains at least a 3.0 GPA.

Additional information This program, established in 1999, is funded by the Bill and Melinda Gates Foundation and administered by the United Negro College Fund with support from the American Indian Graduate Center, the Hispanic Scholarship Fund, and the Asian & Pacific Islander American Scholarship Fund.

Number awarded 1,000 new scholarships are awarded each year.

Deadline January of each year.

[216]
GATEWAYS TO THE LABORATORY PROGRAM

Cornell University
Attn: Weill Cornell/Rockefeller/Sloan-Kettering Tri-
  Institutional MD-PhD Program
Gateways to the Laboratory Program
1300 York Avenue, Room C-103
New York, NY 10065-4805
(212) 746-6023   Fax: (212) 746-8678
E-mail: mdphd@med.cornell.edu
Web: www.med.cornell.edu/mdphd/summerprogram

Summary To provide Native American and other minority or disadvantaged college freshmen and sophomores with an opportunity to participate in a summer research internship in New York City through the Tri-Institutional MD-PhD Program of Weill Cornell Medical College, Rockefeller University, and Sloan-Kettering Institute.

Eligibility This program is open to college freshmen and sophomores who are defined by the National Institutes of Health (NIH) as in need of special recruitment and retention, i.e., members of racial and ethnic groups underrepresented in health-related sciences (American Indians or Alaska Natives, Blacks or African Americans, Hispanics or Latinos, and Native Hawaiians or Other Pacific Islanders), persons with disabilities, and individuals from disadvantaged backgrounds (low-income or from a rural or inner-city environment). Applicants must be interested in continuing on to a combined M.D./Ph.D. program following completion of their undergraduate degree. Along with their application, they must submit an essay summarizing their laboratory experience, research interests, and goals. U.S. citizenship or permanent resident status is required.

Financial data Students receive a stipend of $4,300 and reimbursement of travel expenses. At the end of the summer, 1 family member receives airfare and hotel accommodations to come to New York for the final presentations.

Duration 10 weeks, during the summer.

Additional information Participants work independently on a research project at Weill Cornell Medical College, Rockefeller University, or Memorial Sloan-Kettering Cancer Center, all located across the street from each other on the Upper East Side of New York City.

Number awarded 15 each year.

Deadline January of each year.

[217]
GENERAL MILLS FOUNDATION TRIBAL COLLEGE SCHOLARSHIP PROGRAM

American Indian College Fund
Attn: Scholarship Department
8333 Greenwood Boulevard
Denver, CO 80221
(303) 426-8900   Toll Free: (800) 776-FUND
Fax: (303) 426-1200
E-mail: scholarships@collegefund.org
Web: www.collegefund.org/scholarships/schol_tcu.html

Summary To provide financial assistance to Native American students from any state who are attending a Tribal College or University (TCU) in Minnesota or New Mexico.

Eligibility This program is open to American Indians and Alaska Natives from any state who are enrolled full time at an eligible TCU in Minnesota or New Mexico. Applicants must have a GPA of 2.5 or higher and be able to demonstrate exceptional academic achievement or financial need. Applications are available only online and include required essays on specified topics.

Financial data The stipend is $2,500.

Duration 1 year.

Additional information This scholarship is sponsored by the General Mills Foundation in partnership with the American Indian College Fund.

Number awarded 25 each year.

Deadline May of each year.

[218]
GEOCORPS AMERICAN INDIAN INTERNSHIPS

Geological Society of America
Attn: Program Officer, GeoCorps America
3300 Penrose Place
P.O. Box 9140
Boulder, CO 80301-9140
(303) 357-1025   Toll Free: (800) 472-1988, ext. 1025
Fax: (303) 357-1070   E-mail: mdawson@geosociety.org
Web: rock.geosociety.org/g.corps/index

Summary To provide work experience in national parks to American Indians and Native Alaskans who are student members of the Geological Society of America (GSA).

Eligibility This program is open to all GSA members, but applications are especially encouraged from American Indians, Alaska Natives, and persons with a strong connection to an American Indian tribe or community. Applicants must be interested in a summer work experience in facilities of the U.S. government, currently limited to the National Park Service but planned for expansion to the Forest Service and the Bureau of Land Management. Geoscience knowledge and skills are a significant requirement for most positions, but students from various disciplines (e.g., chemistry, physics, engineering, mathematics, computer science, ecology, hydrology, meteorology, the social sciences, and the humanities) are also invited to apply. Activities involve research; interpretation and education; inventory and monitoring; or mapping, surveying, and GIS. Prior interns are not eligible. U.S. citizenship or possession of a proper visa is required.

Financial data Each internship provides a $2,750 stipend. Free housing, or a housing allowance of $1,500 to $2,000, is also provided.

Duration 10 to 12 weeks during the summer.

Number awarded Deadline not specified.

Deadline January of each year.

[219]
GEORGE CAMPBELL, JR. FELLOWSHIP IN ENGINEERING

National Action Council for Minorities in Engineering
Attn: University Programs
440 Hamilton Avenue, Suite 302
White Plains, NY 10601-1813
(914) 539-4010   Fax: (914) 539-4032
E-mail: scholarships@nacme.org
Web: www.nacme.org/NACME_D.aspx?pageid=105

Summary To provide financial assistance to Native American and other underrepresented minority college sophomores majoring in engineering or related fields.

Eligibility This program is open to African American, Latino, and American Indian college sophomores who have a GPA of 3.0 or higher and have demonstrated academic excellence, leadership skills, and a commitment to science and engineering as a career. Applicants must be enrolled full time at an ABET-accredited engineering program. Fields of study include all areas of engineering as well as computer science, materials science, mathematics, operations research, or physics.

Financial data The stipend is $5,000 per year. Funds are sent directly to the recipient's university.

Duration Up to 3 years.

Number awarded 1 each year.

Deadline April of each year.

[220]
GEORGE GENG ON LEE MINORITIES IN LEADERSHIP SCHOLARSHIP

Capture the Dream, Inc.
Attn: Scholarship Program
484 Lake Park Avenue, Suite 15
Oakland, CA 94610
(510) 343-3635   E-mail: info@capturethedream.org
Web: www.capturethedream.org/programs/scholarship.php

Summary To provide financial assistance for college to Native Americans and other minorities who can demonstrate leadership.

Eligibility This program is open to members of minority groups who are graduating high school seniors or current full-time undergraduates at 4-year colleges and universities. Applicants must submit a 1,000-word essay on why they should be selected to receive this scholarship, using their experiences within school, work, and home to display the challenges they have faced as a minority and how they overcame adversity to assume a leadership role. They should also explain how their career goals and future aspirations will build them as a future minority leader. Financial need is considered in the selection process. U.S. citizenship or permanent resident status is required.

Financial data The stipend is $1,000.

Duration 1 year.

Number awarded 1 or more each year.

Deadline July of each year.

[221]
GEORGE K. NOLAN TRIBAL JUDICIAL SCHOLARSHIP

Sault Tribe of Chippewa Indians
Attn: Higher Education Program-Memorial/Tributary Scholarships
523 Ashmun Street
Sault Ste. Marie, MI 49783
(906) 635-4944   Toll Free: (800) 793-0660
Fax: (906) 635-7785   E-mail: amatson@saulttribe.net
Web: www.saulttribe.com

Summary To provide financial assistance to members of the Sault Tribe of Chippewa Indians who are working on a degree in a field related to law.

Eligibility This program is open to enrolled members of the Sault Tribe who are attending a 2- or 4-year college or university as a full-time sophomore or higher. Applicants must be majoring in law enforcement, legal studies, political science, public administration, or tribal law. Along with their application, they must submit an essay of 300 to 500 words on how this scholarship will help them realize their goals.

Financial data The stipend is $1,000.

Duration 1 year.

Number awarded 1 each year.

Deadline May of each year.

[222]
GERALDINE MEMMO SCHOLARSHIP

Seneca Diabetes Foundation
Attn: Lucille White
TIS Building 12837, Route 438
P.O. Box 309
Irving, NY 14081
(716) 532-4900   Fax: (716) 549-1629
E-mail: white@sni.org
Web: www.senecadiabetesfoundation.org

Summary To provide financial assistance to members of the Seneca Nation who are interested in attending college to prepare for a career in the health or social services professions and have also demonstrated an interest in Seneca and Native American history.

Eligibility This program is open to members of the Seneca Nation who are interested in attending college to assist the Seneca people, especially in regard to the fight against diabetes, by working on a degree in health or social services. Applicants must be able to demonstrate an interest in Seneca and Native American history. Along with their application, they must submit brief statements on 1) the professional, community, or cultural services and activities in which they have participated; 2) how this scholarship would help further their education; 3) their goals or plan for using their nursing experience to benefit the Seneca Nation and its people; and 4) how their interest in Seneca and Native American history came about, how they research the subject, how they have applied their knowledge, and the most interesting aspect to them of Seneca and Native American heritage. In the selection process, primary consideration is given to financial need, but involvement in community and cultural activities, interest in research on Seneca and Native American history and heritage, and desire to improve the quality of life for the Seneca people are also considered.

Financial data The stipend is $5,000.

Duration 1 year.

Number awarded 1 each year.

Deadline May of each year.

[223]
GLADYS KAMAKAKUOKALANI AINOA BRANDT SCHOLARSHIPS

Ke Ali'i Pauahi Foundation
Attn: Financial Aid & Scholarship Services
567 South King Street, Suite 160
Honolulu, HI 96813
(808) 534-3966   Toll Free: (800) 842-4682, ext. 43966
Fax: (808) 534-3890   E-mail: scholarships@pauahi.org
Web: www.pauahi.org/scholarships

Summary To provide financial assistance to undergraduate and graduate students, especially those of Native Hawaiian descent, who are preparing for a career in education.

Eligibility This program is open to full-time juniors, seniors, and graduate students who are planning to enter the education profession. Applicants must have a GPA of 2.5 or higher and be able to demonstrate financial need. Preference is given to Native Hawaiians (descendants of the aboriginal inhabitants of the Hawaiian Islands prior to 1778) and current or former residents of Kaua'i.

Financial data The stipend is $3,000.

Duration 1 year.

Number awarded Varies each year; recently, 4 of these scholarships were awarded.

Deadline March of each year.

[224]
GLENN GODFREY MEMORIAL SCHOLARSHIP

Koniag Incorporated
Attn: Koniag Education Foundation
4241 B Street, Suite 303B
Anchorage, AK 99503
(907) 562-9093   Toll Free: (888) 562-9093
Fax: (907) 562-9023
E-mail: scholarships@koniageducation.org
Web: www.koniageducation.org/scholarships

Summary To provide financial assistance to Alaska Natives who are Koniag Incorporated shareholders or descendants and have demonstrated leadership and plans to attend college in any state.

Eligibility This program is open to college sophomores, juniors, and seniors who are Alaska Native shareholders of Koniag Incorporated or descendants of those original enrollees. Applicants must be enrolled in or accepted at an accredited college, university, or vocational school in any state. They must have a GPA of 2.5 or higher and be able to demonstrate leadership in school, community, athletics, church, or Native culture activities. Along with their application, they must submit an essay of 300 to 600 words in the form of a thank you letter about their background, educational goals, work history, and/or achievements. Financial need is not considered in the selection process.

Financial data The stipend is $5,000. Funds are sent directly to the recipient's school and may be used for tuition, fees, books, and on-campus room and meals.

Duration 1 year; may be renewed up to 2 additional years, provided the recipient maintains a GPA of 2.5 or higher and participates in school, community, or church activities.

Additional information Koniag Incorporated is 1 of 13 Alaska Native Regional Corporations created under the Alaska Native Claims Settlement Act of 1971.

Number awarded 1 each year.

Deadline August of each year.

[225]
GLOBAL CHANGE SUMMER UNDERGRADUATE RESEARCH EXPERIENCE (SURE)

Oak Ridge Institute for Science and Education
Attn: Global Change Education Program
120 Badger Avenue, M.S. 36
P.O. Box 117
Oak Ridge, TN 37831-0117
(865) 576-7009   Fax: (865) 241-9445
E-mail: gcep@orau.gov
Web: www.atmos.anl.gov/GCEP/SURE/index.html

Summary To provide minority and other undergraduate students with an opportunity to conduct research during the summer on global change.

Eligibility This program is open to undergraduates in their sophomore and junior years, although outstanding freshman and seniors are also considered. Applicants must be proposing to conduct research in a program area within the Department of Energy's Office of Biological and Environmental Research (DOE-BER): the atmospheric science program, the environmental meteorology program, the atmospheric radiation measurement program, the terrestrial carbon processes effort, the program for ecosystem research, and studies carried out under the direction of the National Institute for Global Environmental Change. They must have a GPA of 3.0 or higher overall and in their major. Minority and female students are particularly encouraged to apply. U.S. citizenship is required.

Financial data Participants receive a weekly stipend of $475 and support for travel and housing.

Duration 10 weeks during the summer. Successful participants are expected to reapply for a second year of research with their mentors.

Additional information This program, funded by DOE-BER, began in summer 1999. The first week is spent in an orientation and focus session at a participating university. For the remaining 9 weeks, students conduct mentored research at 1 of the national laboratories or universities conducting BER-supported global change research.

Number awarded Approximately 20 each year.

Deadline December of each year.

[226]
GOLDMAN SACHS SCHOLARSHIP FOR EXCELLENCE

Goldman Sachs
Attn: Human Capital Management
30 Hudson Street, 34th Floor
Jersey City, NJ 07302
(212) 902-1000   E-mail: Julie.Mantilla@gs.com
Web: www2.goldmansachs.com

Summary To provide financial assistance and work experience to Native Americans and other underrepresented minority students preparing for a career in the financial services industry.

Eligibility This program is open to undergraduate students of Black, Latino, or Native American heritage. Applicants must be entering their sophomore or junior year with a GPA of 3.4 or higher. Students with all majors and disciplines are encouraged to apply, but they must be able to demonstrate an interest in the financial services industry. Along with their application, they must submit 2 essays of 500 words or fewer on the following topics: 1) why they are interested in the financial services industry; and 2) how they have demonstrated team-oriented leadership through their involvement with a campus-based or community-based organization. Selection is based on academic achievement, interest in the financial services industry, community involvement, and demonstrated leadership and teamwork capabilities.

Financial data Sophomores receive a stipend of $5,000, a summer internship at Goldman Sachs, an opportunity to receive a second award upon successful completion of the internship, and an offer to return for a second summer internship. Juniors receive a stipend of $10,000 and a summer internship at Goldman Sachs.

Duration Up to 2 years.

Additional information This program was initiated in 1994 when it served only students at 4 designated Historically Black Colleges and Universities: Florida A&M University, Howard University, Morehouse College, and Spelman Col-

lege. It has since been expanded to serve underrepresented minority students in all states.

Number awarded 1 or more each year.

Deadline December of each year.

[227]
GOOGLE SCHOLARSHIP

American Indian Science and Engineering Society
Attn: Program Officer
2305 Renard, S.E., Suite 200
P.O. Box 9828
Albuquerque, NM 87119-9828
(505) 765-1052, ext. 105   Fax: (505) 765-5608
E-mail: tina@aises.org
Web: www.aises.org

Summary To provide financial assistance to members of the American Indian Science and Engineering Society (AISES) who are working on an undergraduate or graduate degree in a computer-related field.

Eligibility This program is open to AISES members who are full-time undergraduate or graduate students at a 4-year college or university or a full-time student at a 2-year college enrolled in a program leading to a 4-year degree. Applicants must be majoring in computer science or computer engineering. They must have a GPA of 3.5 or higher and be able to document ancestry as an American Indian, Alaskan Native, or Native Hawaiian. Along with their application, they must submit a 500-word essay on their educational and/or career goals, interest in and motivation to continue higher education, understanding of the importance of college and commitment to completion, commitment to learning, and giving back to the community. U.S. citizenship is required. Selection is based on that essay (40%), GPA (35%), letters of recommendation (15%), and overall impression of the application (10%).

Financial data The total award is $10,000, disbursed equally over the recipient's course of study.

Duration Until completion of a degree.

Additional information This program, established in 2008, is funded by Google Inc.

Number awarded 20 each year.

Deadline June of each year.

[228]
GRAND PORTAGE SCHOLARSHIP PROGRAM

Grand Portage Tribal Council
Attn: Education Director
P.O. Box 428
Grand Portage, MN 55605
(218) 475-2812   Fax: (218) 475-2284
E-mail: gpeduc@boreal.org
Web: www.grandportage.com/program.php

Summary To provide financial assistance for undergraduate or graduate study to Minnesota Chippewa Tribe members.

Eligibility Applicants must be an enrolled member of the Grand Portage Band of Chippewa or have a parent who is enrolled. They must be enrolled at or accepted for enrollment at an accredited training program or degree-granting college or university and have applied for all other forms of financial aid. Residents of states other than Minnesota are eligible only for college or university study, not for vocational training.

Financial data The amount of the award is based on the need of the recipient.

Duration 1 year; may be renewed for a total of 10 semesters or 15 quarters to complete a 4-year degree program if recipients maintain full-time enrollment and a GPA of 2.0 or higher. Adjustments are considered for part-time and/or graduate study.

Number awarded Varies each year.

Deadline At least 8 weeks before school starts.

[229]
GROW YOUR OWN TEACHER SCHOLARSHIP PROGRAM

Idaho State Board of Education
Len B. Jordan Office Building
650 West State Street, Room 307
P.O. Box 83720
Boise, ID 83720-0037
(208) 332-1574   Fax: (208) 334-2632
E-mail: scholarshiphelp@osbe.idaho.gov
Web: www.boardofed.idaho.gov/scholarships/gyo.asp

Summary To provide financial assistance to Native Americans in Idaho who are interested in becoming teachers 1) of bilingual education or English as a Second Language (ESL) or 2) to Native American students.

Eligibility This program is open to Idaho school district employees and volunteers who are 1) interested in completing an associate and/or baccalaureate degree in education with a bilingual or ESL endorsement, or 2) Native Americans preparing to teach in Idaho school districts with a significant Native American student population. Applicants must be attending selected schools in Idaho: Boise State University, the College of Southern Idaho, Lewis-Clark State College, or Idaho State University.

Financial data The stipend is $3,000 per year for full-time students; the stipend for part-time students depends on the number of credit hours and the fee charged to part-time students at the participating college or university.

Duration 1 year.

Number awarded Varies each year.

Deadline Deadline not specified.

[230]
GTB ADULT VOCATIONAL TRAINING GRANTS

Grand Traverse Band of Ottawa and Chippewa Indians
Attn: Higher Education
845 Business Park Drive
Traverse City, MI 49686
(231) 534-7760   Toll Free: (866) 534-7760
Fax: (231) 534-7773
E-mail: joyce.wilson@gtbindians.com
Web: www.gtbindians.org/departments/index.html

Summary To provide financial assistance to members of the Grand Traverse Band (GTB) of Ottawa and Chippewa Indians who are interested in attending a vocational/technical institute in any state.

Eligibility This program is open to enrolled GTB members who are working on or planning to work on licensing or certification in a vocational field. Applicants must be able to document financial need. Along with their application, they must submit a personal statement on how they plan to serve their

Indian community after they have successfully completed their course of study.

Financial data Stipends are $5 per clock hour, to a maximum of $7,200 per year. Recipients are also entitled to a grant of up to $500 per year for licensing fees, certifications, and state board fees.

Duration Students must be able to complete their programs within 3 years.

Number awarded Varies each year.

Deadline Deadline not specified.

[231]
GTB HIGHER EDUCATION GRANTS

Grand Traverse Band of Ottawa and Chippewa Indians
Attn: Higher Education
845 Business Park Drive
Traverse City, MI 49686
(231) 534-7760   Toll Free: (866) 534-7760
Fax: (231) 534-7773
E-mail: joyce.wilson@gtbindians.com
Web: www.gtbindians.org/departments/index.html

Summary To provide financial assistance to members of the Grand Traverse Band (GTB) of Ottawa and Chippewa Indians who are interested in attending college or graduate school in any state.

Eligibility This program is open to enrolled GTB members who are working on or planning to work on an associate, bachelor's, master's, or doctoral degree at a college or university in any state. Applicants must be able to document financial need. Along with their application, they must submit a personal statement on how they plan to serve their Indian community after they have successfully completed their course of study.

Financial data Stipends for associate degree students are $200 per credit hour, to a maximum of $7,200 per year; stipends for bachelor's degree students are $250 per credit hour, to a maximum of $9,000 per year; stipends for graduate students are $600 per credit hour, to a maximum of $10,800 per year.

Duration 1 semester; may be renewed as long as the recipient maintains a GPA of 2.0 or higher. Support is provided for up to 12 credits above the number required for an undergraduate degree or up to 6 credits above the number required for a graduate degree.

Number awarded Varies each year.

Deadline Deadline not specified.

[232]
HANA SCHOLARSHIPS

United Methodist Church
Attn: General Board of Higher Education and Ministry
Office of Loans and Scholarships
1001 19th Avenue South
P.O. Box 340007
Nashville, TN 37203-0007
(615) 340-7344   Fax: (615) 340-7367
E-mail: umscholar@gbhem.org
Web: www.gbhem.org/loansandscholarships

Summary To provide financial assistance to upper-division and graduate Methodist students who are of Native American, Asian, Pacific Islander, or Hispanic ancestry.

Eligibility This program is open to full-time juniors, seniors, and graduate students at accredited colleges and universities in the United States who have been active, full members of a United Methodist Church (UMC) for at least 1 year prior to applying. Applicants must have at least 1 parent who is Asian, Hispanic, Native American, or Pacific Islander. They must be able to demonstrate involvement in their Hispanic, Asian, or Native American (HANA) community in the UMC. Selection is based on that involvement, academic ability (GPA of at least 2.85), and financial need. U.S. citizenship or permanent resident status is required.

Financial data The maximum stipend is $3,000 for undergraduates or $5,000 for graduate students.

Duration 1 year; recipients may reapply.

Number awarded 50 each year.

Deadline March of each year.

[233]
HARVARD SCHOOL OF PUBLIC HEALTH SUMMER PROGRAM IN BIOLOGICAL SCIENCES IN PUBLIC HEALTH

Harvard School of Public Health
Attn: Division of Biological Sciences
655 Huntington Avenue, Building 2-113
Boston, MA 02115
(617) 432-4397   Fax: (617) 432-0433
E-mail: aharmon@hsph.harvard.edu
Web: www.hsph.harvard.edu

Summary To enable Native American and other disadvantaged college science students to participate in a summer research internship in biological sciences at Harvard School of Public Health.

Eligibility This program is open to 1) members of ethnic groups underrepresented in graduate education (African Americans, Hispanics/Latinos, American Indians/Alaskan Natives, Pacific Islanders, and biracial/multiracial); 2) first-generation college students; and 3) low-income students. Applicants must be entering their junior or senior year and interested in preparing for a research career in the biological sciences. They must be interested in participating in a summer research project related to biological science questions that are important to the prevention of disease, especially such public health questions as cancer, infections (malaria, tuberculosis, parasites), lung diseases, common diseases of aging, diabetes, and obesity.

Financial data The program provides a stipend of at least $3,460, a travel allowance of up to $475, and free dormitory housing.

Duration 9 weeks, beginning in mid-June.

Additional information Interns conduct research under the mentorship of Harvard faculty members who are specialists in cancer cell biology, immunology and infectious diseases, molecular and cellular toxicology, environmental health sciences, nutrition, and cardiovascular research. Funding for this program is provided by the National Institutes of Health.

Number awarded Up to 6 each year.

Deadline January of each year.

[234]
HAWAIIAN CIVIC CLUB OF HONOLULU SCHOLARSHIP

Hawaiian Civic Club of Honolulu
Attn: Scholarship Committee
P.O. Box 1513
Honolulu, HI 96806
E-mail: newmail@hotbot.com
Web: www.hcchonolulu.org/scholarship

Summary To provide financial assistance for undergraduate or graduate studies to persons of Native Hawaiian descent.

Eligibility Applicants must be of Hawaiian descent (descendants of the aboriginal inhabitants of the Hawaiian Islands prior to 1778), residents of Hawaii, able to demonstrate academic achievement, and enrolled or planning to enroll full time in an accredited 2-year college, 4-year college, or graduate school. Graduating seniors and current undergraduate students must have a GPA of 2.5 or higher; graduate students must have at least a 3.0 GPA. Along with their application, they must submit a 2-page essay on a topic that changes annually but relates to issues of concern to the Hawaiian community; a recent topic related to the leadership, cultural and governmental, of the Hawaiian community. Selection is based on quality of the essay, academic standing, financial need, and completeness of the application package.

Financial data The amount of the stipend varies. Scholarship checks are made payable to the recipient and the institution and are mailed to the college or university financial aid office. Funds may be used for tuition, fees, books, and other educational expenses.

Duration 1 year.

Additional information Recipients may attend school in Hawaii or on the mainland. Information on this program is also available from Ke Ali'i Pauahi Foundation.

Number awarded Varies each year; recently, 50 of these scholarships, worth $72,000, were awarded.

Deadline May of each year.

[235]
HAWAIIAN HOMES COMMISSION SCHOLARSHIPS

Hawai'i Community Foundation
Attn: Scholarship Department
827 Fort Street Mall
Honolulu, HI 96813
(808) 537-6333   Toll Free: (888) 731-3863
Fax: (808) 521-6286
E-mail: scholarships@hcf-hawaii.org
Web: www.hawaiicommunityfoundation.org/scholarships

Summary To provide financial assistance to persons of Native Hawaiian descent who are interested in working on an undergraduate or graduate degree at a school in any state.

Eligibility Applicants must be 50% or more of Hawaiian descent (descendants of the aboriginal inhabitants of the Hawaiian Islands prior to 1778) or a Department of Hawaiian Home Lands (DHHL) homestead lessee. They must be U.S. citizens, enrolled in full-time study in an undergraduate or graduate degree program, and able to demonstrate financial need and academic excellence. Undergraduates must have a

GPA of 2.0 or higher. Graduate students must have a GPA of 3.0 or higher. Current Hawaiian residency is not required. Special consideration is given to applicants with exceptional academic merit and proven commitment to serving the Native Hawaiian community. Along with their application, they must submit a short statement indicating their reasons for attending college, their planned course of study, their career goals, and what community service means to them. Selection is based on academic achievement, good moral character, and financial need.

Financial data The amounts of the awards depend on the availability of funds and the need of the recipient. Recently, the average value of all scholarships awarded by the foundation was $2,041.

Duration 1 year.

Additional information This program is sponsored by the state Department of Hawaiian Home Lands.

Number awarded Varies each year; recently, 111 of these scholarships were awarded.

Deadline February of each year.

[236]
HAYNES/HETTING AWARD

Philanthrofund Foundation
Attn: Scholarship Committee
1409 Willow Street, Suite 210
Minneapolis, MN 55403-3251
(612) 870-1806　　　　　Toll Free: (800) 435-1402
Fax: (612) 871-6587　　　E-mail: info@PfundOnline.org
Web: www.pfundonline.org/scholarships.html

Summary To provide funds to Native American and African American students in Minnesota who are associated with gay, lesbian, bisexual, and transgender (GLBT) activities.

Eligibility This program is open to residents of Minnesota and students attending a Minnesota educational institution who are African American or Native American. Applicants must be self-identified as GLBT or from a GLBT family. They may be attending or planning to attend a trade school, technical college, college, or university (as an undergraduate or graduate student). Selection is based on the applicant's 1) affirmation of GLBT identity or commitment to GLBT communities; 2) evidence of experience and skills in service and leadership; and 3) evidence of service and leadership in GLBT communities, including serving as a role model, mentor, and/or adviser.

Financial data The stipend ranges up to $2,000. Funds must be used for tuition, books, fees, or dissertation expenses.

Duration 1 year.

Number awarded 1 or more each year.

Deadline January of each year.

[237]
HDR ENGINEERING SCHOLARSHIP FOR DIVERSITY IN ENGINEERING

Association of Independent Colleges and Universities of Pennsylvania
101 North Front Street
Harrisburg, PA 17101-1405
(717) 232-8649　　　　　Fax: (717) 233-8574
E-mail: info@aicup.org
Web: www.aicup.org

Summary To provide financial assistance to Native Americans, other minorities, and women from any state who are enrolled at member institutions of the Association of Independent Colleges and Universities of Pennsylvania (AICUP) and majoring in designated fields of engineering.

Eligibility This program is open to undergraduate students from any state enrolled full time at AICUP colleges and universities. Applicants must be women and/or members of the following minority groups: American Indians, Alaska Natives, Asians, Blacks/African Americans, Hispanics/Latinos, Native Hawaiians, or Pacific Islanders. They must be juniors majoring in civil, geotechnical, or structural engineering with a GPA of 3.0 or higher. Along with their application, they must submit a 2-page essay on their characteristics, accomplishments, primary interests, plans, and goals.

Financial data The stipend is $5,000 per year.

Duration 1 year; may be renewed 1 additional year if the recipient maintains appropriate academic standards.

Additional information This program, sponsored by HDR Engineering, Inc., is available at the 83 private colleges and universities in Pennsylvania that comprise the AICUP.

Number awarded 1 each year.

Deadline April of each year.

[238]
HEATHER CARDINAL MEMORIAL SCHOLARSHIP

Wisconsin Indian Education Association
Attn: Scholarship Coordinator
P.O. Box 910
Keshena, WI 54135
(715) 799-5110　　　　　Fax: (715) 799-5102
E-mail: vnuske@mitw.org
Web: www.wiea.org

Summary To provide financial assistance to members of Wisconsin Indian tribes who are working on an undergraduate degree in a health-related field or a medical degree.

Eligibility This program is open to residents of Wisconsin who can provide proof of tribal enrollment. Applicants must be either: 1) an undergraduate majoring in a health-related field at a college in any state; or 2) a student enrolled at a medical school in any state. Along with their application, they must submit a 1-page personal essay on how they will apply their education.

Financial data The stipend is $1,000.

Duration 1 year; nonrenewable.

Additional information Eligible tribes include Menominee, Oneida, Stockbridge-Munsee, Forest County Potowatomi, Ho-Chunk, Bad River Chippewa, Lac Courte Oreilles Ojibwe, St. Croix Chippewa, Red Cliff Chippewa, Sakoagon (Mole Lake) Chippewa, Brotherton, and Lac du Flambeau Chippewa.

Number awarded 1 each year.

Deadline March of each year.

[239]
HELEN K. AND ARTHUR E. JACKSON FOUNDATION SCHOLARSHIP

American Indian College Fund
Attn: Scholarship Department
8333 Greenwood Boulevard
Denver, CO 80221
(303) 426-8900   Toll Free: (800) 776-FUND
Fax: (303) 426-1200
E-mail: scholarships@collegefund.org
Web: www.collegefund.org/scholarships/schol_tcu.html

Summary To provide financial assistance to Native American college students from Colorado who are enrolled at Tribal Colleges and Universities (TCUs) in any state.

Eligibility This program is open to American Indians and Alaska Natives who have proof of enrollment or descendancy and are residents of Colorado or members or descendants of the Southern Ute or Ute Mountain tribe. Applicants must be enrolled full time at an eligible TCU in any state. They must have a GPA of 2.5 or higher. Applications are available only online and include required essays on specified topics.

Financial data The stipend is $2,500.

Duration 1 year.

Number awarded 1 or more each year.

Deadline May of each year.

[240]
HELEN TRUEHEART COX ART SCHOLARSHIP

National League of American Pen Women
1300 17th Street, N.W.
Washington, DC 20036-1973
(202) 785-1997   Fax: (202) 452-8868
E-mail: nlapw1@verizon.net
Web: www.americanpenwomen.org

Summary To provide financial assistance to Native American women interested in studying art in college.

Eligibility This program is open to women between 17 and 24 years of age who are members of a Native American tribe. Applicants must be interested in attending a college or university and majoring in art. They must submit 3 prints (4 by 6 inches) in any media (e.g., oil, water color, original works on paper, mixed media, acrylic) or 3 pictures (4 by 6 inches) of art work, sculpture, or photographic works. U.S. citizenship is required. Financial need is considered in the selection process.

Financial data A stipend is awarded (amount not specified).

Duration 1 year.

Number awarded 1 each even-numbered year.

Deadline January of even-numbered years.

[241]
HIGHER EDUCATION GRANTS FOR HOPI TRIBAL MEMBERS

Hopi Tribe
Attn: Grants and Scholarship Program
P.O. Box 123
Kykotsmovi, AZ 86039
(928) 734-3542   Toll Free: (800) 762-9630
Fax: (928) 734-9575   E-mail: tlomakema@hopi.nsn.us
Web: www.hopi-nsn.gov

Summary To provide financial assistance to students of Hopi ancestry who are working on an undergraduate, graduate, or postgraduate degree.

Eligibility This program is open to students who are working on an associate, baccalaureate, graduate, or postgraduate degree. Applicants must be enrolled members of the Hopi Tribe. They must have a GPA of 2.0 or higher and be able to demonstrate financial need.

Financial data The maximum grant is $2,500 per semester ($5,000 per year).

Duration 1 semester; may be renewed for up to 10 terms of undergraduate study or up to 5 terms of graduate study, provided the recipient remains enrolled full time.

Additional information This grant is awarded as a secondary source of financial aid to eligible students who are also receiving aid from the Bureau of Indian Affairs (BIA) Higher Education program.

Number awarded Varies each year.

Deadline June of each year for fall; October of each year for winter; November of each year for spring; April of each year for summer.

[242]
HIGHER EDUCATION PROGRAM OF THE AFOGNAK NATIVE CORPORATION

Afognak Native Corporation
215 Mission Road, Suite 212
Kodiak, AK 99615
(907) 486-6014   Toll Free: (800) 770-6014
Fax: (907) 486-2514   E-mail: scholarships@afognak.com
Web: www.afognak.com

Summary To provide financial assistance to shareholders of the Afognak Native Corporation in Alaska who are interested in enrolling in a traditional college, university, graduate school, or vocational program.

Eligibility This program is open to Alaska Natives who are original Afognak Native Corporation enrollees and their lineal descendants. Applicants must be high school graduates or GED recipients who have been accepted to or are enrolled at an accredited college, university, or vocational school to work on an associate, bachelor's, master's, or doctoral degree. Along with their application, they must submit a letter that provides a personal history (information about their family and their special talents and abilities, community involvement, plans for the future, philosophy of life), future plans for education, and how their education may benefit the Alutiiq people and their commitment to the Alutiiq community. Financial need is considered in the selection process.

Financial data A stipend is awarded (amount not specified).

Duration 1 year; may be renewed if the recipient maintains a GPA of 2.0 or higher.

Number awarded Varies each year.

Deadline April of each year.

[243]
HO-CHUNK NATION GRADUATION ACHIEVEMENT AWARDS

Ho-Chunk Nation
Attn: Higher Education Division
P.O. Box 667
Black River Falls, WI 54615
(715) 284-4915   Toll Free: (800) 362-4476
Fax: (715) 284-1760
E-mail: higher.education@ho-chunk.com
Web: www.ho-chunknation.com/?PageId=47

Summary To recognize and reward Ho-Chunk students who received financial assistance from the tribe and have completed an associate, bachelor's, graduate, or professional degree.

Eligibility Applicants must be enrolled in the Ho-Chunk Nation and have received financial assistance from the tribe in the past to work on a postsecondary degree. Funds are paid once they have completed any of the following degrees: 1-year certificate or diploma, associate degree (2 years), bachelor's degree (4 years), master's or professional degree, J.D. degree, or doctoral degree.

Financial data Awards are $300 for a 1-year certificate or degree, $750 for an associate degree, $1,000 for a bachelor's degree, $3,000 for a master's or professional degree, $4,000 for a J.D. degree, or $5,000 for a doctoral degree.

Duration Students are eligible for only 1 award per degree.

Number awarded Varies each year.

Deadline Applications must be submitted within 1 year of completion of the degree.

[244]
HO-CHUNK NATION HIGHER EDUCATION SCHOLARSHIPS

Ho-Chunk Nation
Attn: Higher Education Division
P.O. Box 667
Black River Falls, WI 54615
(715) 284-4915   Toll Free: (800) 362-4476
Fax: (715) 284-1760
E-mail: higher.education@ho-chunk.com
Web: www.ho-chunknation.com/?PageId=47

Summary To provide financial assistance to undergraduate or graduate students who are enrolled members of the Ho-Chunk Nation.

Eligibility Applicants must be enrolled members of the Ho-Chunk Nation who have been accepted at an accredited college, university, or vocational college in the United States as an undergraduate or graduate student. Applicants must intend to attend a nonprofit institution that is accredited by a regional agency and by the U.S. Department of Education as eligible to receive student financial aid funds. If they are determined by their school's financial aid office to have no financial need, they are eligible to receive non-need grants. If their school determines that they have financial need, they are eligible for need-based grants. Funds are awarded with the expectation that graduates will return to the Ho-Chunk Nation to use their knowledge and expertise to protect and strengthen the economic self-sufficiency and sovereignty of the nation.

Financial data Non-need grants cover direct costs of tuition, required fees, and books, up to the maximum award. Need-based grants are capped at $7,000 per academic year for full-time undergraduates or $12,000 per academic year for full-time graduate students. Awards for part-time students per academic year are for direct costs (tuition, required fees, and books) not covered by another source, to a maximum of $4,500 for undergraduates or $9,000 for graduate students. Funds are paid directly to the recipient's school.

Duration 1 year. Support is limited to 10 semesters for undergraduates, 6 semesters for master's degree students, or 10 semesters for doctoral students. Undergraduates must maintain a GPA of 2.0 or higher and graduate students 3.0 or higher in order to continue receiving funds.

Number awarded Varies each year.

Deadline April of each year or 4 months before the start of the term.

[245]
HO-CHUNK NATION SUMMER TUITION ASSISTANCE

Ho-Chunk Nation
Attn: Higher Education Division
P.O. Box 667
Black River Falls, WI 54615
(715) 284-4915   Toll Free: (800) 362-4476
Fax: (715) 284-1760
E-mail: higher.education@ho-chunk.com
Web: www.ho-chunknation.com/?PageId=47

Summary To provide financial assistance to Ho-Chunk undergraduate or graduate students who wish to continue their postsecondary studies during the summer.

Eligibility Applicants must be enrolled members of the Ho-Chunk Nation; have been accepted at an accredited public vocational or technical school, college, or university in the United States in an undergraduate or graduate program; and be interested in attending summer school on a full-time basis.

Financial data This program pays up to $2,500 to undergraduate recipients and up to $5,000 to graduate school recipients. Funds must be used for tuition, fees, or books. Funds are paid directly to the recipient's school.

Duration Summer months. May be renewed for a total of 6 summers of support.

Additional information Undergraduate recipients must earn a GPA of 2.0 or higher in the summer classes; graduate school recipients must earn 3.0 or higher.

Number awarded Varies each year.

Deadline The priority deadline is the end of April of each year.

[246]
HO-CHUNK NATION TRAINING AND EMPLOYMENT ASSISTANCE

Ho-Chunk Nation
Attn: Higher Education Division
P.O. Box 667
Black River Falls, WI 54615
(715) 284-4915   Toll Free: (800) 362-4476
Fax: (715) 284-1760
E-mail: higher.education@ho-chunk.com
Web: www.ho-chunknation.com/?PageId=47

Summary   To provide financial assistance to enrolled members of the Ho-Chunk Nation who are interested in obtaining a postsecondary diploma/certificate (1-year program) or associate of arts degree (2-year program).

Eligibility   Applicants must be enrolled members of the Ho-Chunk Nation and be planning to obtain either a diploma/certificate (1-year program) or an associate of arts degree (2-year program). They must intend to attend school on a full-time basis. Both need-based and non-need applicants are considered.

Financial data   The tribal grants do not exceed $5,000 per academic year. Students who receive funding under this program are considered either need-based or non-need students. Students who show financial need receive 2 equal payments each academic term; one half of their term award is sent at the beginning of the term and the second half is sent in the middle of their term after verification that they are still enrolled on a full-time basis. Students who are determined to have "no financial need" (no-need students) may be considered for a grant to cover direct costs (tuition, fees, and books) only up to the maximum award amount, based upon the availability of funds.

Duration   1 year; may be renewed for a total of 6 semesters, provided the recipient maintains a GPA of 2.0 or higher.

Deadline   April of each year or 4 months before the start of the term.

[247]
HOOPA BIA HIGHER EDUCATION GRANTS

Hoopa Valley Tribe
Attn: Hoopa Tribal Education Association
P.O. Box 428
Hoopa, CA 95546-0428
(530) 625-4413   Fax: (530) 625-5444
E-mail: hoopaeducation@gmail.com
Web: www.hoopa-nsn.gov

Summary   To provide financial assistance to members of the Hoopa Tribe who can demonstrate financial need and are attending or planning to attend college in any state.

Eligibility   This program is open to enrolled members of the Hoopa Tribe who are enrolled or planning to enroll full time at an accredited college or university in any state. Applicants must submit 1) an educational plan that outlines the course work required for completing their degree and an estimate of the time remaining until completion; 2) official transcripts; 3) a class schedule; and 4) a letter describing their educational goals and proposed course of study. They must be able to demonstrate financial need.

Financial data   A stipend is awarded (amount not specified).

Duration   1 semester; may be renewed up to a total of 3 years for a 2-year degree or 5 years for a 4-year.

Additional information   Funding for this program is provided by the U.S. Bureau of Indian Affairs (BIA).

Number awarded   Varies each year.

Deadline   July of each year.

[248]
HOOPA TRIBAL EDUCATION ASSOCIATION ADULT VOCATIONAL TRAINING AWARDS

Hoopa Valley Tribe
Attn: Hoopa Tribal Education Association
P.O. Box 428
Hoopa, CA 95546-0428
(530) 625-4413   Fax: (530) 625-5444
E-mail: hoopaeducation@gmail.com
Web: www.hoopa-nsn.gov

Summary   To provide financial assistance to members of the Hoopa Tribe who are attending or planning to attend a vocational/technical institute in any state.

Eligibility   This program is open to enrolled members of the Hoopa Tribe who are attending or planning to attend a vocational/technical institute in any state. Applicants must intend to work full time on a vocational certificate or license. They must be able to demonstrate financial need. Along with their application, they must submit a letter describing their vocational goals and an itemized list of expenses for the services they are requesting.

Financial data   A stipend is awarded (amount not specified).

Duration   1 semester; may be renewed up to a total of 3 years.

Number awarded   Varies each year.

Deadline   Deadline not specified.

[249]
HOOPA TRIBAL EDUCATION GRANTS

Hoopa Valley Tribe
Attn: Hoopa Tribal Education Association
P.O. Box 428
Hoopa, CA 95546-0428
(530) 625-4413   Fax: (530) 625-5444
E-mail: hoopaeducation@gmail.com
Web: www.hoopa-nsn.gov

Summary   To provide financial assistance to members of the Hoopa Tribe who are attending or planning to attend college in any state.

Eligibility   This program is open to enrolled members of the Hoopa Tribe who are 1) high school seniors or graduates with a GPA of 2.0 or higher; 2) current undergraduates with a GPA of 2.0 or higher; 3) students graduating from an alternative high school, with a GED, or a high school equivalency certificate with a grade that converts to the equivalent of a 2.0 GPA; 4) students enrolled in an approved vocational program; and 5) students enrolled in remedial or developmental classes that do not apply to general education requirements. Applicants must be enrolled or planning to enroll full or part time at an educational institution in any state. Along with their application, they must submit 1) an educational plan that outlines the course work required for completing their degree and an estimate of the time remaining until completion; 2) official transcripts; 3) a class schedule; and 4) a letter describing their educational goals and proposed course of study. Financial need is not considered in the selection process. Grants are awarded in the following priority order: continuing college students, new students, part-time students, special program students, enrichment/remediation students, and summer session students.

Financial data A stipend is awarded (amount not specified).

Duration 1 semester; may be renewed up to a total of 3 years for a 2-year degree, 5 years for a 4-year, until completion of a vocational program, or for 10 remedial or developmental classes.

Number awarded Varies each year.

Deadline June of each year for fall semester or academic year; November of each year for winter quarter; December of each year for spring semester; March of each year for spring quarter; May of each year for summer session.

[250]
HOOPA TRIBAL EDUCATION SCHOLARSHIPS

Hoopa Valley Tribe
Attn: Hoopa Tribal Education Association
P.O. Box 428
Hoopa, CA 95546-0428
(530) 625-4413   Fax: (530) 625-5444
E-mail: hoopaeducation@gmail.com
Web: www.hoopa-nsn.gov

Summary To provide financial assistance to members of the Hoopa Tribe who are attending or planning to attend college or graduate school in any state.

Eligibility This program is open to enrolled members of the Hoopa Tribe who are 1) high school seniors or graduates with a GPA of 3.0 or higher; 2) current undergraduates with a GPA of 2.5 or higher; or 3) graduate students. Applicants must be working or planning to work full time on an undergraduate or graduate degree at an accredited college or university in any state. Along with their application, they must submit 1) an educational plan that outlines the course work required for completing their degree and an estimate of the time remaining until completion; 2) official transcripts; 3) a class schedule; and 4) a letter describing their educational goals and proposed course of study. Financial need is not considered in the selection process.

Financial data A stipend is awarded (amount not specified).

Duration 1 semester; may be renewed up to a total of 3 years for a 2-year degree, 5 years for a 4-year, or until completion of a graduate degree.

Number awarded Varies each year.

Deadline June of each year for fall semester or academic year; November of each year for winter quarter; December of each year for spring semester; March of each year for spring quarter; May of each year for summer session.

[251]
HOPI ADULT VOCATIONAL TRAINING PROGRAM

Hopi Tribe
Attn: Department of Education
P.O. Box 123
Kykotsmovi, AZ 86039
(928) 734-3542   Toll Free: (800) 762-9630
Fax: (928) 734-9575   E-mail: tlomakema@hopi.nsn.us
Web: www.hopi-nsn.gov

Summary To provide financial assistance to members of the Hopi Tribe who are interested in vocational training.

Eligibility This program is open to enrolled members of the Hopi Tribe who are unskilled, unemployed, or underemployed. Applicants must be between 17 and 35 years of age and residing on or near the Hopi Reservation. They must be interested in full-time vocational training at an accredited private or public institution approved by the Hopi Tribe Adult Vocational Training Program to acquire marketable vocational skills.

Financial data A stipend is awarded (amount not specified).

Duration Support is provided until completion of the program.

Number awarded Varies each year.

Deadline Deadline not specified.

[252]
HOPI EDUCATION AWARDS PROGRAM

Hopi Tribe
Attn: Grants and Scholarship Program
P.O. Box 123
Kykotsmovi, AZ 86039
(928) 734-3542   Toll Free: (800) 762-9630
Fax: (928) 734-9575   E-mail: tlomakema@hopi.nsn.us
Web: www.hopi-nsn.gov

Summary To provide financial assistance to needy students of Hopi ancestry who are working on an undergraduate, graduate, or postgraduate degree.

Eligibility This program is open to students who are working on an associate, baccalaureate, graduate, or postgraduate degree. Applicants must be enrolled members of the Hopi Tribe. They must have a GPA of 2.5 or higher and be able to demonstrate financial need.

Financial data The maximum grant is $2,500 per semester ($5,000 per year).

Duration 1 semester; may be renewed for up to 10 terms of undergraduate study or up to 5 terms of graduate study, provided the recipient maintains a GPA of 2.5 or higher and full-time enrollment.

Additional information This grant is awarded as a secondary source of financial aid to eligible students who are also receiving aid from the Bureau of Indian Affairs (BIA) Higher Education program.

Number awarded Varies each year.

Deadline June of each year for fall; October of each year for winter; November of each year for spring; April of each year for summer.

[253]
HOPI SCHOLARSHIP

Hopi Tribe
Attn: Grants and Scholarship Program
P.O. Box 123
Kykotsmovi, AZ 86039
(928) 734-3542   Toll Free: (800) 762-9630
Fax: (928) 734-9575   E-mail: tlomakema@hopi.nsn.us
Web: www.hopi-nsn.gov

Summary   To provide financial assistance to academically outstanding students of Hopi ancestry who are interested in working on an undergraduate or graduate degree at a college in any state.

Eligibility   This program is open to enrolled members of the Hopi Tribe who are attending or planning to attend a college or university in any state. Entering freshmen must rank in the top 10% of their graduating class or have minimum scores of 930 on the combined critical reading and mathematics SAT or 21 on the ACT. Continuing undergraduates must have a cumulative GPA of 3.0 or higher. Graduate and professional students must have a cumulative GPA of 3.2 or higher. Selection is based on academic merit.

Financial data   The stipend is $1,000 per semester.

Duration   1 semester (fall semester only).

Number awarded   Varies each year.

Deadline   July of each year.

[254]
HOPI TRIBAL PRIORITY AWARDS

Hopi Tribe
Attn: Grants and Scholarship Program
P.O. Box 123
Kykotsmovi, AZ 86039
(928) 734-3542   Toll Free: (800) 762-9630
Fax: (928) 734-9575   E-mail: tlomakema@hopi.nsn.us
Web: www.hopi-nsn.gov

Summary   To provide funding to Hopi students who are interested in working on an undergraduate or graduate degree in an area of interest to the Hopi Tribe.

Eligibility   This program is open to enrolled members of the Hopi Tribe who are college juniors, seniors, or graduate students working on a degree in a subject area that is of priority interest to the Hopi Tribe. Currently, those areas are law, natural resources, education, medicine, health, engineering, or business. Applicants must have a GPA of 3.5 or higher. This is a highly competitive scholarship. Selection is based on academic merit and the likelihood that the applicants will use their training and expertise for tribal goals and objectives.

Financial data   This program provides payment of all tuition and fees, books and supplies, transportation, room and board, and a stipend of $1,500 per month. Recipients must agree to provide 1 year of professional services to the Hopi Tribe or other service agencies that serve the Hopi People for each year funding is awarded.

Duration   1 year; may be renewed, provided the recipient maintains a GPA of 3.5 or higher.

Additional information   Recipients must attend school on a full-time basis.

Number awarded   Up to 5 each year.

Deadline   July of each year.

[255]
HORACE AND SUSIE REVELS CAYTON SCHOLARSHIP

Public Relations Society of America-Puget Sound
  Chapter
c/o Diane Bevins
1006 Industry Drive
Seattle, WA 98188-4801
(206) 623-8632   E-mail: prsascholarship@asi-seattle.net
Web: www.prsapugetsound.org/scholars.html

Summary   To provide financial assistance to Native American and other minority upper-classmen from Washington who are interested in preparing for a career in public relations.

Eligibility   This program is open to U.S. citizens who are members of minority groups, defined as African Americans, Asian Americans, Hispanic/Latino Americans, Native Americans, and Pacific Islanders. Applicants must be full-time juniors or seniors attending a college in Washington or Washington students (who graduated from a Washington high school or whose parents live in the state year-round) attending college elsewhere. They must be able to demonstrate aptitude in public relations and related courses, activities, and/or internships. Along with their application, they must submit a description of their career goals and the skills that are most important in general to a public relations career (15 points in the selection process); a description of their activities in communications in class, on campus, in the community, or during internships, including 3 samples of their work (15 points); a statement on the value of public relations to an organization (10 points); a description of any barriers, financial or otherwise, they have encountered in pursuing their academic or personal goals and how they have addressed them (15 points); a discussion of their heritage, and how their cultural background and/or the discrimination they may have experienced has impacted them (15 points); a certified transcript (15 points); and 2 or more letters of recommendation (15 points).

Financial data   The stipend is $2,500.

Duration   1 year.

Additional information   This program was established in 1992.

Number awarded   1 each year.

Deadline   April of each year.

[256]
HOWARD KECK/WESTMIN ENDOWMENT SCHOLARSHIP FUND

Cook Inlet Region, Inc.
Attn: The CIRI Foundation
3600 San Jeronimo Drive, Suite 256
Anchorage, AK 99508-2870
(907) 793-3575   Toll Free: (800) 764-3382
Fax: (907) 793-3585   E-mail: tcf@thecirifoundation.org
Web: www.thecirifoundation.org/designated.htm

Summary   To provide financial assistance for undergraduate or graduate studies to Alaska Natives who are original enrollees to Cook Inlet Region, Inc. (CIRI) and their lineal descendants.

Eligibility   This program is open to Alaska Native enrollees to CIRI under the Alaska Native Claims Settlement Act

(ANCSA) of 1971 and their lineal descendants. There are no Alaska residency requirements or age limitations. Applicants must be accepted or enrolled full time in a 2-year undergraduate, 4-year undergraduate, or graduate degree program. They may be studying in any field but must have a GPA of 2.5 or higher. Along with their application, they must submit a 500-word statement on their educational and career goals and how they are contributing, or planning to contribute, to a positive Alaska Native community. Selection is based on that statement, academic achievement, rigor of course work or degree program, student financial contribution, financial need, grade level, previous work performance, community service, and relationship of degree program to career goals.

Financial data The stipend is $20,000 per year, $10,000 per year, $8,000 per year, or $2,500 per semester, depending on GPA.

Duration 1 semester or 1 year.

Additional information This fund was established in 1986.

Number awarded Varies each year; recently, 5 of these scholarships were awarded.

Deadline May of each year for annual scholarships; May or November of each year for semester scholarships.

[257]
HOWARD ROCK FOUNDATION UNDERGRADUATE SCHOLARSHIP PROGRAM

Cook Inlet Region, Inc.
Attn: The CIRI Foundation
3600 San Jeronimo Drive, Suite 256
Anchorage, AK 99508-2870
(907) 793-3575   Toll Free: (800) 764-3382
Fax: (907) 793-3585   E-mail: tcf@thecirifoundation.org
Web: www.thecirifoundation.org/designated.htm

Summary To provide financial assistance for undergraduate study to Alaska Natives and their lineal descendants.

Eligibility This program is open to Alaska Natives who are original enrollees or lineal descendants of a regional or village corporation under the Alaska Native Claims Settlement Act (ANCSA) of 1971 or a member of a tribal organization or other Native organization. The corporation or other Native organization with which the applicant is affiliated must be a current member of Alaska Village Initiatives, Inc. Applicants must have a GPA of 2.5 or higher and must be able to demonstrate financial need. They must be accepted or enrolled full time in a 4-year undergraduate program. Preference is given to juniors and seniors. Along with their application, they must submit a 500-word statement on their educational and career goals and how they are contributing, or planning to contribute, to a positive Alaska Native community.

Financial data The stipend is $2,500 per year. Funds are to be used for tuition, university fees, books, course-required supplies, and (for students who must live away from their permanent home in order to attend college) room and board. Checks are made payable to the student and the university and are sent directly to the student's university.

Duration 1 year.

Additional information This program, established in 1986, is funded by Alaska Village Initiatives, Inc. The CIRI Foundation assumed its administration in 1999.

Number awarded Varies each year.

Deadline March of each year.

[258]
HUNA HERITAGE FOUNDATION EDUCATION ASSISTANCE PROGRAM

Huna Totem Corporation
Attn: Huna Heritage Foundation
9301 Glacier Highway, Suite 210
Juneau, AK 99801
(907) 523-3682   Toll Free: (800) 428-8298
Fax: (907) 789-1896   E-mail: kmiller@hunaheritage.org
Web: www.hunaheritage.org/education.html

Summary To provide financial assistance to Huna Totem Corporation shareholders and their descendants who are attending or planning to attend college or graduate school in any state.

Eligibility This program is open to Huna Totem Corporation shareholders and descendants who have a high school diploma or GED certificate. Applicants must be accepted by or attending a college or university in any state as a full-time undergraduate or graduate student. Internships, apprenticeships, and on-the-job training may also be funded. Students must have applied to other programs before they apply for this assistance and be able to demonstrate unmet financial need. Proof of awards or denial by other programs must be supplied.

Financial data Stipends range up to $2,000 per year. Funding is intended to help pay for whatever costs other grant programs do not cover.

Duration 1 year; recipients may reapply.

Additional information The Huna Totem Corporation is an Alaska Native village corporation whose shareholders have aboriginal ties to the village of Hoonah in southeast Alaska.

Number awarded Varies each year.

Deadline September of each year for first or second quarter or fall semester; January of each year for third or fourth quarter or spring or summer semester.

[259]
HUNA HERITAGE FOUNDATION VOCATIONAL EDUCATION ASSISTANCE PROGRAM

Huna Totem Corporation
Attn: Huna Heritage Foundation
9301 Glacier Highway, Suite 210
Juneau, AK 99801
(907) 523-3682   Toll Free: (800) 428-8298
Fax: (907) 789-1896   E-mail: kmiller@hunaheritage.org
Web: www.hunaheritage.org/education.html

Summary To provide financial assistance to Huna Totem Corporation shareholders and their descendants who are interested in pursuing vocational education.

Eligibility This program is open to Huna Totem Corporation shareholders or descendants (as defined in accordance with the Alaska Native Claim Settlement Act Amendments of 1987) who are at least 18 years of age (high school students are eligible at 17 years of age) and either unemployed or underemployed. They must be in need of training in order to be employable. Applicants who are underemployed must show how the lack of additional training would result in hardship. All applicants must be interested in pursuing vocational education or apprenticeships that 1) are approved by the National Accreditation Association, the Alaska Department of Education's Division of Vocational Education, or the U.S. Bureau of Apprenticeship Training; 2) are enrolled full time (at least 30 hours of study per week and include shop practices as an integral component); and 3) lead to employment at the completion of training.

Financial data The amount of assistance depends on the nature of the program and the need of the recipient.

Duration 1 year. Recipients may be eligible for a second award only if they can demonstrate that they continue to be unemployed, underemployed, or unable to work in their primary occupation due to physical or other disability.

Additional information The Huna Totem Corporation is an Alaska Native village corporation whose shareholders have aboriginal ties to the village of Hoonah in southeast Alaska.

Number awarded Varies each year.

Deadline Applications may be submitted at any time, but they must be received in a timely manner to allow for trustee review.

[260]
HYATT HOTELS FUND FOR MINORITY LODGING MANAGEMENT STUDENTS

American Hotel & Lodging Educational Foundation
Attn: Manager of Foundation Programs
1201 New York Avenue, N.W., Suite 600
Washington, DC 20005-3931
(202) 289-3181   Fax: (202) 289-3199
E-mail: ahlef@ahlef.org
Web: www.ahlef.org/content.aspx?id=19828

Summary To provide financial assistance to Native Americans and other minority college students working on a degree in hotel management.

Eligibility This program is open to students majoring in hospitality management at a 4-year college or university as at least a sophomore. Applicants must be members of a minority group (African American, Hispanic, American Indian, Alaskan Native, Asian, or Pacific Islander). They must be enrolled full time. Along with their application, they must submit a 500-word essay on their personal background, including when they became interested in the hospitality field, what traits they possess or will need to succeed in the industry, and their plans as related to their educational and career objectives and future goals. Selection is based on industry-related work experience; financial need; academic record and educational qualifications; professional, community, and extracurricular activities; personal attributes, including career goals; the essay; and neatness and completeness of the application. U.S. citizenship or permanent resident status is required.

Financial data The stipend is $2,000.

Duration 1 year.

Additional information Funding for this program, established in 1988, is provided by Hyatt Hotels & Resorts.

Number awarded Varies each year; recently, 10 of these scholarships were awarded. Since this program was established, it has awarded scholarships worth $508,000 to approximately 255 minority students.

Deadline April of each year.

[261]
IDA M. POPE MEMORIAL SCHOLARSHIPS

Hawai'i Community Foundation
Attn: Scholarship Department
827 Fort Street Mall
Honolulu, HI 96813
(808) 537-6333   Toll Free: (888) 731-3863
Fax: (808) 521-6286
E-mail: scholarships@hcf-hawaii.org
Web: www.hawaiicommunityfoundation.org/scholarships

Summary To provide financial assistance to Native Hawaiian women who are interested in working on an undergraduate or graduate degree in designated fields at a school in any state.

Eligibility This program is open to female residents of Hawaii who are Native Hawaiian, defined as a descendant of the aboriginal inhabitants of the Hawaiian islands prior to 1778. Applicants must be enrolled at a school in any state in an accredited associate, bachelor's, or graduate degree program and working on a degree in health, science, or education (including counseling and social work). They must be able to demonstrate academic achievement (GPA of 3.5 or higher), good moral character, and financial need. Along with their application, they must submit a short statement indicating their reasons for attending college, their planned course of study, their career goals, and what community service means to them.

Financial data The amounts of the awards depend on the availability of funds and the needs of the recipient. Recently, the average value of all scholarships awarded by the foundation was $2,041.

Duration 1 year; may be renewed.

Number awarded Varies each year; recently, 61 of these scholarships were awarded.

Deadline February of each year.

[262]
IDAHO MINORITY AND "AT RISK" STUDENT SCHOLARSHIP

Idaho State Board of Education
Len B. Jordan Office Building
650 West State Street, Room 307
P.O. Box 83720
Boise, ID 83720-0037
(208) 332-1574   Fax: (208) 334-2632
E-mail: scholarshiphelp@osbe.idaho.gov
Web: www.boardofed.idaho.gov/scholarships/minority.asp

Summary To provide financial assistance to minorities and other "at risk" high school seniors in Idaho who plan to attend college in the state.

Eligibility This program is open to residents of Idaho who are graduates of high schools in the state. Applicants must meet at least 3 of the following 5 requirements: 1) have a disability; 2) be a member of an ethnic minority group historically underrepresented in higher education in Idaho; 3) have substantial financial need; 4) be a first-generation college student; 5) be a migrant farm worker or a dependent of a farm worker. U.S. citizenship is required.

Financial data The maximum stipend is $3,000 per year.

Duration 1 year; may be renewed for up to 3 additional years.

Additional information This program was established in 1991 by the Idaho state legislature. Information is also available from high school counselors and financial aid offices of colleges and universities in Idaho. Recipients must plan to attend or be attending 1 of 11 participating colleges and universities in the state on a full-time basis. For a list of those schools, write to the State of Idaho Board of Education.

Number awarded Approximately 40 each year.

Deadline Deadline not specified.

[263]
IHS HEALTH PROFESSIONS PRE-GRADUATE SCHOLARSHIP PROGRAM

Indian Health Service
Attn: Scholarship Program
801 Thompson Avenue, Suite 120
Rockville, MD 20852
(301) 443-6197   Fax: (301) 443-6048
Web: www.scholarship.ihs.gov

Summary To provide financial support to American Indian and Alaska Native students interested in majoring in pre-medicine, pre-podiatry, pre-optometry, or pre-dentistry in college.

Eligibility This program is open to American Indians and Alaska Natives who are members or descendants of members of state- or federally-recognized tribes. Applicants must be high school graduates or the equivalent; have the capacity to complete a health professions course of study; and be enrolled or accepted for enrollment in a baccalaureate degree program to prepare for entry into a school of medicine, podiatry, optometry, or dentistry. They must intend to serve Indian people upon completion of their professional health care education. Priority is given to students entering their junior or senior year; support is provided to freshmen and sophomores only if remaining funds are available. Along with their application, they must submit a brief narrative that includes why they are requesting the scholarship, their career goals, and how those goals will help to meet the health needs of American Indian and Alaska Native people. Selection is based on that narrative (30 points); academic performance (40 points); and faculty, employer, and tribal recommendations (30 points).

Financial data Awards provide a payment directly to the school for tuition and required fees.

Duration Up to 4 years of full-time study or up to 8 years of part-time study.

Number awarded Varies each year.

Deadline February of each year for continuing students; March of each year for new applicants.

[264]
IHS HEALTH PROFESSIONS PREPARATORY SCHOLARSHIP PROGRAM

Indian Health Service
Attn: Scholarship Program
801 Thompson Avenue, Suite 120
Rockville, MD 20852
(301) 443-6197   Fax: (301) 443-6048
Web: www.scholarship.ihs.gov

Summary To provide financial assistance to Native American students who need compensatory or preprofessional education to qualify for enrollment in a health professions school.

Eligibility This program is open to American Indians and Alaska Natives who are members or descendants of members of state- or federally-recognized tribes. Applicants must be high school graduates or the equivalent; have the capacity to complete a health professions course of study; and be enrolled or accepted for enrollment in a compensatory or pre-professional general education course or curriculum. The qualifying fields of study may vary annually, but recently they included pre-medical technology (for courses leading to a B.S. degree in medical technology), pre-dietetics (for courses leading to a B.S. degree in dietetics), pre-nursing (for courses leading to a B.S. degree in nursing), pre-pharmacy (for courses leading to a Pharm.D. degree), pre-physical therapy (for juniors and seniors preparing for an M.S. degree in physical therapy), pre-social work (for juniors and seniors preparing for an M.S. degree in social work), pre-occupational therapy (for juniors and seniors preparing for an M.S. degree in occupational therapy), and pre-clinical psychology (for juniors and seniors). They must intend to serve Indian people upon completion of their professional health care education as a health care provider in the discipline for which they are enrolled at the pregraduate level. Along with their application, they must submit a brief narrative that includes why they are requesting the scholarship, their career goals, and how those goals will help to meet the health needs of American Indian and Alaska Native people. Selection is based on that narrative (30 points); academic performance (40 points); and faculty, employer, and tribal recommendations (30 points).

Financial data Awards provide a payment directly to the school for tuition and required fees.

Duration Up to 2 years of full-time study or up to 4 years of part-time study.

Number awarded Varies each year.

Deadline February of each year for continuing students; March of each year for new applicants.

[265]
IHS HEALTH PROFESSIONS SCHOLARSHIP PROGRAM

Indian Health Service
Attn: Scholarship Program
801 Thompson Avenue, Suite 120
Rockville, MD 20852
(301) 443-6197   Fax: (301) 443-6048
E-mail: dawn.kelly@ihs.gov
Web: www.scholarship.ihs.gov

Summary To provide funding to American Indian and Alaska Native students enrolled in health professions and allied health professions programs.

Eligibility This program is open to American Indians and Alaska Natives who are members of federally-recognized tribes. Applicants must be at least high school graduates and enrolled in a full-time study program leading to a degree in a health-related professions school within the United States. Priority is given to upper-division and graduate students. Qualifying fields of study recently included chemical dependency counseling (bachelor's or master's degree), clinical psychology (Ph.D. only), dental hygiene (B.S.), dentistry (D.D.S. or D.M.D.), diagnostic radiology technology (certificate, associate, or B.S.), dietetics (B.S.), environmental health and engineering (B.S.), health records administration (R.H.I.T. or R.H.I.A.), medical technology (B.S.), allopathic and osteopathic medicine (M.D. or D.O.), nursing (A.D.N., B.S.N., C.R.N.A., geriatric nursing, nurse practitioner, pediatric nursing, psychiatric and mental health nursing, women's health nursing), occupational therapy (B.S. or M.S.), optometry (O.D.), pharmacy (Pharm.D.), physician assistant (P.A.C.), physical therapy (M.S. or D.P.T.), physical therapy assistant (associate degree), podiatry (D.P.M.), respiratory therapy (B.S.), social work (master's degree with concentration in mental health only), or ultrasonography (B.S. or certificate). Along with their application, they must submit a brief narrative that includes why they are requesting the scholarship, their career goals, and how those goals will help to meet the health needs of American Indian and Alaska Native people. Selection is based on that narrative (30 points); academic performance (40 points); and faculty, employer, and tribal recommendations (30 points).

Financial data Awards provide a payment directly to the school for tuition and required fees; a stipend for living expenses of approximately $1,250 per month for 10 months; a lump sum to cover the costs of books, laboratory expenses, and other necessary educational expenses; a payment of $300 for travel expenses; and up to $400 for approved tutorial costs. Upon completion of their program of study, recipients are required to provide payback service of 1 year for each year of scholarship support at the Indian Health Service, a tribal health program, an urban Indian health program, or in private practice in a designated health professional shortage area serving a substantial number of Indians. Recipients who fail to complete their service obligation must repay all funds received (although no interest is charged).

Duration 1 year; may be renewed for up to 3 additional years.

Number awarded Varies each year.

Deadline February of each year for continuing students; March of each year for new applicants.

[266]
ILLINOIS BROADCASTERS ASSOCIATION MULTICULTURAL INTERNSHIPS

Illinois Broadcasters Association
Attn: MIP Coordinator
200 Missouri Avenue
Carterville, IL 62918
(618) 985-5555   Fax: (618) 985-6070
E-mail: iba@ilba.org
Web: www.ilba.org

Summary To provide funding to Native American and other minority college students in Illinois who are majoring in broadcasting and interested in interning at a radio or television station in the state.

Eligibility This program is open to currently-enrolled minority students majoring in broadcasting at a college or university in Illinois. Applicants must be interested in a fall, spring, or summer internship at a radio or television station that is a member of the Illinois Broadcasters Association. Along with their application, they must submit 1) a 250-word essay on how they expect to benefit from a grant through this program, and 2) at least 2 letters of recommendation from a broadcasting faculty member or professional familiar with their career potential and 1 other letter. The president of the

sponsoring organization selects those students nominated by their schools who have the best opportunity to make it in the world of broadcasting and matches them with internship opportunities that would otherwise be unpaid.

Financial data This program provides a grant to pay the living expenses for the interns in the Illinois communities where they are assigned. The amount of the grant depends on the length of the internship.

Duration 16 weeks in the fall and spring terms or 12 weeks in the summer.

Number awarded 12 each year: 4 in each of the 3 terms.

Deadline Deadline not specified.

[267]
ILLINOIS NURSES ASSOCIATION CENTENNIAL SCHOLARSHIP

Illinois Nurses Association
Attn: Illinois Nurses Foundation
105 West Adams Street, Suite 2101
Chicago, IL 60603
(312) 419-2900   Fax: (312) 419-2920
E-mail: info@illinoisnurses.com
Web: www.illinoisnurses.com

Summary To provide financial assistance to nursing undergraduate and graduate students who are Native American or members of other underrepresented groups.

Eligibility This program is open to students working on an associate, bachelor's, or master's degree at an accredited NLNAC or CCNE school of nursing. Applicants must be members of a group underrepresented in nursing (African Americans, Hispanics, American Indians, Asians, and males). Undergraduates must have earned a passing grade in all nursing courses taken to date and have a GPA of 2.85 or higher. Graduate students must have completed at least 12 semester hours of graduate work and have a GPA of 3.0 or higher. All applicants must be willing to 1) act as a spokesperson to other student groups on the value of the scholarship to continuing their nursing education, and 2) be profiled in any media or marketing materials developed by the Illinois Nurses Foundation. Along with their application, they must submit a narrative of 250 to 500 words on how they, nurses, plan to affect policy at either the state or national level that impacts on nursing or health care generally, or how they believe they will impact the nursing profession in general.

Financial data A stipend is awarded (amount not specified).

Duration 1 year.

Number awarded 1 or more each year.

Deadline March of each year.

[268]
INCENTIVE AWARDS OF THE SEMINOLE NATION JUDGMENT FUND

Seminole Nation of Oklahoma
Attn: Judgment Fund Office
2007 West Wrangler Boulevard
Seminole, OK 74868
(405) 382-0549   Toll Free: (877) 382-0549
Fax: (405) 382-0571
Web: www.seminolenation.com/services_judgmentfund.htm

Summary To recognize and reward undergraduate student members of the Seminole Nation of Oklahoma who achieve high grades in college.

Eligibility This program is open to enrolled members of the Seminole Nation of Oklahoma who are descendants of a member of the Seminole Nation as it existed in Florida on September 18, 1823. Applicants must be attending a college or university as an undergraduate student. They must complete either 1) 12 units with a GPA of 3.5 or higher; or 2) 15 units with a GPA 3.0 or higher.

Financial data Students who complete 12 credit hours with a GPA of 3.5 or higher receive an award of $300 per semester. Students who complete 15 credit hours with a GPA of 3.0 or higher receive an award of $500 per semester. The total of all incentive awards to an applicant may not exceed $4,000.

Duration 1 semester; may be renewed each semester the student completes the required number of units with the required minimum GPA.

Additional information The General Council of the Seminole Nation of Oklahoma approved a plan for use of the Judgment Fund Award in 1990. This aspect of the program went into effect in September of 1991.

Number awarded Varies each year.

Deadline Applications must be submitted within 60 days of the end of the semester.

[269]
INDIAN MARKET AWARDS

Southwestern Association for Indian Arts, Inc.
3600 Cerrillos Road, Suite 712
P.O. Box 969
Santa Fe, NM 87504-0969
(505) 983-5220   Fax: (505) 983-7647
E-mail: info@swaia.org
Web: www.swaia.org/awards.php

Summary To recognize and reward outstanding Indian artists who participate in the Santa Fe Indian Market.

Eligibility This program is open to artists who have a Certificate of Indian Blood as an enrolled member of a federally-recognized tribe or Alaska Native corporation and a New Mexico Taxation and Revenue CRS Identification Number. Artists must be 18 years of age and older. The 10 divisions are 1) jewelry; 2) pottery; 3) paintings, drawings, graphics, and photography; 4) Pueblo wooden carvings; 5) sculpture; 6) textiles; 7) diverse art forms; 8) beadwork and quillwork; 9); moving images (subdivided into narrative shorts, documentary shorts, animation, and experimental); and 10) basketry. Along with their application, artists must submit slides of each medium that they wish to show at the annual Santa Fe Indian Market. The work must comply with standards of the Southwestern Association for Indian Arts (SWAIA) and be representative of the artwork they plan to sell at the Market.

Financial data A total of more than $100,000 in prize money is awarded each year. Awards vary each year, but they have included $1,000 for Best of Show and $500 for first place in each category.

Duration The Market is held on 2 days in August of each year.

Additional information Special awards include the IAIA Distinguished Alumni Award ($500), the Youth Smile Award ($100), the Artists' Choice Award ($300), and the Innovation Award ($2,500). Standards awards include the Tony Da Award for Pottery ($500), the Joe Cat<A3>3 Award for Beadmaking ($500), the Horse Tack and Attire Award ($500), the Miniature Award ($500), the Jean Seth Award for Basket Making ($500), the Jean Seth Award for Painting ($500), and the Traditional Pueblo Pot Award ($1,000). SWAIA endowed awards include the Helen Naha Award for Hopi Pottery ($200) and the Indian Arts Fund Award ($200). Artists are responsible for payment of a $25 application fee, a $10 city of Santa Fe business license fee, a $10 city of Santa Fe booth permit fee, and a booth fee of $400 to $650.

Number awarded Varies each year.

Deadline Applications must be submitted by January of each year.

[270]
INDIAN SUMMER RECENT HIGH SCHOOL GRADUATE SCHOLARSHIP

Indian Summer, Inc.
10809 West Lincoln Avenue, Suite 101
West Allis, WI 53227
(414) 774-7119   Fax: (414) 774-6810
E-mail: indiansummer@wi.rr.com
Web: www.indiansummer.org/education/scholarships.aspx

Summary To provide financial assistance to American Indian high school seniors from Wisconsin who are planning to attend college in any state.

Eligibility This program is open to Wisconsin residents who are American Indians by tribal enrollment or descendancy (having 1 or more ancestors who are tribally enrolled). Applicants must be accepted or in good standing at an institution of higher education in any state. They must submit a 1-page statement describing their educational goals, the reasons they feel they should receive the scholarship, their community service, and any special needs. Preference is given to applicants who have provided service to the Indian community and have not previously received a scholarship.

Financial data The stipend is $1,000.

Duration 1 year.

Additional information This program is offered in cooperation with American Indian Student Services at the University of Wisconsin at Milwaukee.

Number awarded 1 each year.

Deadline July of each year.

[271]
INDIANA INDUSTRY LIAISON GROUP SCHOLARSHIP

Indiana Industry Liaison Group
c/o Tony Pickell, Vice Chair
AAP Precision Planning, LLC
6215 Meridian Street West Drive
Indianapolis, IN 46260
(317) 590-4797
E-mail: tony.pickell@precisionplanningaap.com
Web: www.indianailg.org/scholardetails.html

Summary To provide financial assistance to Native American and other students from any state enrolled at colleges and universities in Indiana who have been involved in activities to promote diversity.

Eligibility This program is open to residents of any state currently enrolled at an accredited college or university in Indiana. Applicants must either 1) be studying programs or classes related to diversity/Affirmative Action (AA)/Equal Employment Opportunity (EEO), or 2) have work or volunteer experience for diversity/AA/EEO organizations. Along with their application, they must submit an essay of 400 to 500 words on 1 of the following topics: 1) their personal commitment to diversity/AA/EEO within their community or business; 2) a time or situation in which they were able to establish and/or sustain a commitment to diversity; 3) a time when they have taken a position in favor of affirmative action and/or diversity; or 4) activities in which they have participated within their community that demonstrate their personal commitment to moving the community's diversity agenda forward. Financial need is not considered in the selection process.

Financial data The stipend is $1,000.

Duration 1 year.

Number awarded 1 each year.

Deadline March of each year.

[272]
INDUSTRY MINORITY SCHOLARSHIPS

American Meteorological Society
Attn: Fellowship/Scholarship Program
45 Beacon Street
Boston, MA 02108-3693
(617) 227-2426, ext. 246   Fax: (617) 742-8718
E-mail: scholar@ametsoc.org
Web: www.ametsoc.org

Summary To provide financial assistance to Native American and other underrepresented minority students entering college and planning to major in meteorology or an aspect of atmospheric sciences.

Eligibility This program is open to members of minority groups traditionally underrepresented in the sciences (especially Hispanics, Native Americans, and Blacks/African Americans) who are entering their freshman year at a college or university and planning to work on a degree in the atmospheric or related oceanic and hydrologic sciences. Applicants must submit an official high school transcript showing grades from the past 3 years, a letter of recommendation from a high school teacher or guidance counselor, a copy of scores from an SAT or similar national entrance exam, and a 500-word essay on a topic that changes annually; recently, applicants were invited to write on global change and how they would use their college education in atmospheric science (or a closely-related field) to make their community a better place in which to live. Selection is based on the essay and academic performance in high school.

Financial data The stipend is $3,000 per year.

Duration 1 year; may be renewed for the second year of college study.

Additional information This program is funded by grants from industry and by donations to the American Meteorological Society (AMS) 21st Century Campaign. Requests for an application must be accompanied by a self-addressed stamped envelope.

Number awarded Varies each year; recently, 5 of these scholarships were awarded.

Deadline February of each year.

[273]
INROADS NATIONAL COLLEGE INTERNSHIPS

INROADS, Inc.
10 South Broadway, Suite 300
St. Louis, MO 63102
(314) 241-7488   Fax: (314) 241-9325
E-mail: info@inroads.org
Web: www.inroads.org

Summary To provide an opportunity for Native American and other young people of color to gain work experience in business or industry.

Eligibility This program is open to African Americans, Hispanics, and Native Americans who reside in the areas served by INROADS. Applicants must be interested in preparing for a career in business, computer and information sciences, engineering, health, marketing, retail store management, or sales. They must be 1) seniors in high school with a GPA of 3.0 or higher; or 2) freshmen or sophomores in 4-year colleges and universities with a GPA of 2.8 or higher. Citizenship is required.

Financial data Salaries vary, depending upon the specific internship assigned; recently, the range was from $170 to $750 per week.

Duration Up to 4 years.

Additional information INROADS places interns in Fortune 1000 companies, where training focuses on preparing them for corporate and community leadership. The INROADS organization offers internship opportunities through 35 local affiliates in 26 states, Canada, and Mexico.

Number awarded Approximately 2,000 high school and college students are currently working for more than 200 corporate sponsors nationwide.

Deadline March of each year.

[274]
INSPIRATIONAL EDUCATOR SCHOLARSHIP

Ke Ali'i Pauahi Foundation
Attn: Financial Aid & Scholarship Services
567 South King Street, Suite 160
Honolulu, HI 96813
(808) 534-3966   Toll Free: (800) 842-4682, ext. 43966
Fax: (808) 534-3890   E-mail: scholarships@pauahi.org
Web: www.pauahi.org/scholarships

Summary To provide financial assistance to undergraduate students, especially those of Native Hawaiian descent, preparing for a career in education.

Eligibility This program is open to students working full or part time on an undergraduate degree in education. Applicants must submit 1) an essay on their commitment to education and how they would use the scholarship funds for educational costs; and 2) letters of recommendation, especially from their prior and prospective employers in the Hawaiian community. Residency in Hawaii is not required, but preference is given to Native Hawaiians (descendants of the aboriginal inhabitants of the Hawaiian Islands prior to 1778).

Financial data The stipend is $1,200.

Duration 1 year.

Number awarded 2 each year.

Deadline March of each year.

[275]
INSTITUTE FOR INTERNATIONAL PUBLIC POLICY FELLOWSHIPS

United Negro College Fund Special Programs
 Corporation
Attn: Institute for International Public Policy
6402 Arlington Boulevard, Suite 600
Falls Church, VA 22042
(703) 677-3400   Toll Free: (800) 530-6232
Fax: (703) 205-7645   E-mail: iippl@uncfsp.org
Web: www.uncfsp.org

Summary To provide financial assistance and work experience to Native Americans and other minority students who are interested in preparing for a career in international affairs.

Eligibility This program is open to full-time sophomores at 4-year institutions who have a GPA of 3.2 or higher and are nominated by the president of their institution. Applicants must be African American, Hispanic/Latino American, Asian American, American Indian, Alaskan Native, Native Hawaiian, or Pacific Islander. They must be interested in participating in policy institutes, study abroad, language training, internships, and graduate education that will prepare them for a career in international service. U.S. citizenship or permanent resident status is required.

Financial data For the sophomore summer policy institute, fellows receive student housing and meals in a university facility, books and materials, all field trips and excursions, and a $1,050 stipend. For the junior year study abroad component, half of the expenses for 1 semester, to a maximum of $8,000, is provided. For the junior summer policy institute, fellows receive student housing and meals in a university facility, books and materials, travel to and from the institute, and a $1,000 stipend. For the summer language institute, fellows receive tuition and fees, books and materials, room and board, travel to and from the institute, and a $1,000 stipend. During the internship, a stipend of up to $3,500 is paid. During the graduate school period, fellowships are funded jointly by this program and the participating graduate school. The program provides $15,000 toward a master's degree in international affairs, with the expectation that the graduate school will provide $15,000 in matching funds.

Duration 2 years of undergraduate work and 2 years of graduate work, as well as the intervening summers.

Additional information This program consists of 6 components: 1) a sophomore year summer policy institute based at Howard University that introduces fellows to international policy development, foreign affairs, cultural competence, careers in those fields, and options for graduate study; 2) a junior year study abroad program at an accredited overseas institution; 3) a 7-week junior year summer institute at the University of Maryland's School of Public Policy; 4) for students without established foreign language competency, a summer language institute at Middlebury College Language Schools in Middlebury, Vermont following the senior year; 5) fellows with previously established foreign language competence participate in a post-baccalaureate internship to provide the practical experience needed for successful graduate studies in international affairs; and 6) a master's degree in international affairs (for students who are admitted to such a program). This program is administered by the United Negro College Fund Special Programs Corporation with funding provided by a grant from the U.S. Department of Education.

Number awarded 30 each year.
Deadline February of each year.

[276]
INTEL SCHOLARSHIP

American Indian Science and Engineering Society
Attn: Program Officer
2305 Renard, S.E., Suite 200
P.O. Box 9828
Albuquerque, NM 87119-9828
(505) 765-1052, ext. 105   Fax: (505) 765-5608
E-mail: tina@aises.org
Web: www.aises.org

Summary To provide financial assistance to members of the American Indian Science and Engineering Society (AISES) who are working on an undergraduate or graduate degree in a field of computer science or engineering.

Eligibility This program is open to AISES members who are full-time undergraduate or graduate students at an accredited 4-year college or university or at a 2-year college in a program leading to an academic degree. Applicants must have a GPA of 3.0 or higher and be members of an American Indian tribe or Alaskan Native group or otherwise considered to be an American Indian or Alaskan Native by the tribe or group with which affiliation is claimed. They must be majoring in computer science, computer engineering, or electrical engineering; students majoring in chemical engineering or material science may also be considered. Along with their application, they must submit a 500-word essay on their educational and career goals, including their interest in and motivation to continue higher education, an understanding of the importance of college and a commitment to completing their educational and/or career goals, and a commitment to learning and giving back to the community. Selection is based on that essay (40%), GPA (35%), letters of recommendation (15%), and overall impression of the application (10%).

Financial data The stipend is $5,000 for undergraduates or $10,000 for graduate students.

Duration 1 year; nonrenewable.

Additional information This program is funded by Intel.

Number awarded 1 or more each year.

Deadline June of each year.

[277]
INTERMOUNTAIN SECTION AWWA DIVERSITY SCHOLARSHIP

American Water Works Association-Intermountain
 Section
3430 East Danish Road
Sandy, UT 94093
(801) 712-1619   Fax: (801) 487-6699
E-mail: nicoleb@ims-awwa.org
Web: www.ims-awwa.org

Summary To provide financial assistance to Native Americans and other underrepresented undergraduate and graduate students working on a degree in the field of water quality, supply, and treatment at a university in Idaho or Utah.

Eligibility This program is open to women and students who identify as Hispanic or Latino, Black or African American, Native Hawaiian or other Pacific Islander, Asian, or American Indian or Alaska Native. Applicants must be entering or enrolled in an undergraduate or graduate program at a college or university in Idaho or Utah that relates to water quality, supply, or treatment. Along with their application, they must submit a 2-page essay on their academic interests and career goals and how those relate to water quality, supply, or treatment. Selection is based on that essay, letters of recommendation, and potential to contribute to the field of water quality, supply, and treatment in the Intermountain West.

Financial data The stipend is $1,000. The winner also receives a 1-year student membership in the Intermountain Section of the American Water Works Association (AWWA) and a 1-year subscription to *Journal AWWA*.

Duration 1 year; nonrenewable.

Number awarded 1 each year.

Deadline October of each year.

[278]
INTERPUBLIC GROUP SCHOLARSHIP AND INTERNSHIP

New York Women in Communications, Inc.
Attn: NYWICI Foundation
355 Lexington Avenue, 15th Floor
New York, NY 10017-6603
(212) 297-2133　　　　　　　　Fax: (212) 370-9047
E-mail: nywicipr@nywici.org
Web: www.nywici.org/foundation/scholarships

Summary To provide financial assistance and work experience to Native American and other minority women who are residents of designated eastern states and enrolled as juniors at a college in any state to prepare for a career in advertising or public relations.

Eligibility This program is open to female residents of New York, New Jersey, Connecticut, or Pennsylvania who are from ethnically diverse groups and currently enrolled as juniors at a college or university in any state. Also eligible are women who reside outside the 4 states but are currently enrolled at a college or university within 1 of the 5 boroughs of New York City. Applicants must be preparing for a career in advertising or public relations and have a GPA of 3.2 or higher. They must be available for a summer internship with Interpublic Group (IPG) in New York City. Along with their application, they must submit a 2-page resume that includes school and extracurricular activities, significant achievements, academic honors and awards, and community service work; a personal essay of 300 to 500 words on their choice of an assigned topic that changes annually; 2 letters of recommendation; and an official transcript. Selection is based on academic record, need, demonstrated leadership, participation in school and community activities, honors, work experience, goals and aspirations, and unusual personal and/or family circumstances. U.S. citizenship is required.

Financial data The scholarship stipend ranges up to $10,000; the internship is paid (amount not specified).

Duration 1 year.

Additional information This program is sponsored by IPG, a holding company for a large number of firms in the advertising industry.

Number awarded 1 each year.

Deadline January of each year.

[279]
INTER-TRIBAL COUNCIL OF AT&T EMPLOYEES SCHOLARSHIP PROGRAM

Inter-Tribal Council of AT&T Employees
c/o Carolyn Free
2528 Center West Parkway, Suite B
Augusta, GA 30909
(706) 729-5473　　　　　　　　E-mail: cf2735@att.com

Summary To provide financial assistance for college to Native American students.

Eligibility This program is open to Native Americans who are graduating high school seniors or undergraduates already enrolled full time at an accredited college or university. Applicants must submit a 300-word essay on a topic that changes annually but relates to issues of concern to Native Americans; recently, students were invited to write on their feelings, as a Native American, about legalized gambling on reservations. Selection is based on scholastic discipline, personal achievement, and community involvement. U.S. citizenship or permanent resident status is required.

Financial data The stipend is $1,000.

Duration 1 year; recipients may reapply.

Number awarded 1 or more each year.

Deadline April or September of each year.

[280]
IOLA M. HENHAWK NURSING SCHOLARSHIP

Seneca Nation of Indians
Attn: Allegany Education Department
P.O. Box 231
Salamanca, NY 14779
(716) 945-1790, ext. 3103　　　　Fax: (716) 945-7170
E-mail: dhoag@sni.org
Web: www.sni.org/node/34

Summary To provide financial assistance to members of the Seneca Nation of Indians who are interested in studying nursing in college.

Eligibility This program is open to enrolled Seneca Indians interested in preparing for a career in nursing. Both high school seniors and students already enrolled in college are eligible. Applicants must submit a certificate of tribal affiliation, letter of acceptance from the college, transcript, and personal letter describing their need and the proposed use of the funds.

Financial data The stipend is $1,000 per year. Funds are paid directly to the college financial aid office to be used for tuition or such course-related expenses as laboratory fees or books.

Duration 1 year.

Additional information This program was established in 1993.

Number awarded 1 or more each year.

Deadline June of each year.

[281]
IOWA TRIBE EDUCATION INCENTIVE AWARDS

Iowa Tribe of Oklahoma
Attn: Human Services
Route 1, Box 721
Perkins, OK 74059
(405) 547-2402   Toll Free: (888) 336-4692
Fax: (405) 547-1090
E-mail: HumanServices@iowanation.org
Web: www.iowanation.org

Summary To recognize and reward members of the Iowa Tribe of Oklahoma who have completed specified levels of education.

Eligibility This monetary award is available to Iowa tribal members when they graduate from eighth grade, high school, college, or graduate school, or when they complete a GED or 800 hours of vocational training.

Financial data The awards are $100 for eighth-grade graduates, $200 for high school graduates, $200 for completion of a GED, or $200 for completion of 800 hours of vocational training. For college graduates, the award is calculated by multiplying a dollar amount based on GPA by the credit hours passed; the amount is $70 for a GPA of 3.5 or higher, $65 for a GPA of 2.5 to 3.49, or $60 for a GPA of 2.0 to 2.49. For graduate students, the award is $92 times the credit hours passed.

Duration These are 1-time awards.

Number awarded Varies each year.

Deadline Applications must be submitted in the same year as completion of the education.

[282]
IOWA TRIBE HIGHER EDUCATION PROGRAM

Iowa Tribe of Oklahoma
Attn: Human Services
Route 1, Box 721
Perkins, OK 74059
(405) 547-2402, ext. 279   Toll Free: (888) 336-4692
Fax: (405) 547-1090
E-mail: HumanServices@iowanation.org
Web: www.iowanation.org

Summary To provide financial assistance for college to members of the Iowa Tribe of Oklahoma.

Eligibility This program is open to Iowa tribal members who are enrolled or planning to enroll at a 2- or 4-year college or university in any state. Applicants must submit their Iowa Tribe CIB, high school diploma or GED, a short paragraph explaining their academic goals, and a financial need analysis.

Financial data The stipend is $1,500 per semester for full-time students or $1,000 per semester for part-time students.

Duration 1 semester; may be renewed, provided the recipient maintains a GPA of 2.0 or higher.

Number awarded Varies each year.

Deadline July of each year for fall semester; December of each year for spring semester.

[283]
IRA L. AND MARY L. HARRISON MEMORIAL SCHOLARSHIP

Baptist Convention of New Mexico
Attn: Missions Mobilization Team
5325 Wyoming Boulevard, N.E.
P.O. Box 94485
Albuquerque, NM 87199-4485
(505) 924-2315   Toll Free: (800) 898-8544
Fax: (505) 924-2320   E-mail: cpairett@bcnm.com
Web: www.bcnm.com

Summary To provide financial assistance to Native American Southern Baptist students from New Mexico who are attending designated colleges or Baptist seminaries.

Eligibility This program is open to undergraduate and seminary students who are Native American members of churches affiliated with the Baptist Convention of New Mexico. Applicants must have a GPA of 2.0 or higher and be able to demonstrate financial need. Undergraduates must be attending Wayland Baptist University at its main campus in Plainview, Texas or at its New Mexico external campuses in Clovis or Albuquerque. Graduate students must be attending 1 of the 6 Southern Baptist seminaries: Southeastern Baptist Theological Seminary (Wake Forest, North Carolina); Southern Baptist Theological Seminary (Louisville, Kentucky); Southwestern Baptist Theological Seminary (Fort Worth, Texas); New Orleans Baptist Theological Seminary (New Orleans, Louisiana); Midwestern Baptist Theological Seminary (Kansas City, Missouri); or Golden Gate Baptist Theological Seminary (Mill Valley, California).

Financial data A stipend is awarded (amount not specified).

Duration 1 year; may be renewed.

Number awarded 1 or more each year.

Deadline June of each year for fall semester; November of each year for spring semester.

[284]
IRENE C. HOWARD MEMORIAL SCHOLARSHIPS

Chickasaw Foundation
110 West 12th Street
P.O. Box 1726
Ada, OK 74821-1726
(580) 421-9030   Fax: (580) 421-9031
E-mail: ChickasawFoundation@chickasaw.net
Web: www.chickasawfoundation.org/index_20.htm

Summary To provide financial assistance to members of the Chickasaw Nation who are working on a college degree in nutrition or other fields.

Eligibility This program is open to Chickasaw students who are currently enrolled at an accredited institution of higher education as a full-time undergraduate student. Applicants must be majoring in science, liberal arts, or nutrition science. They must have a GPA of 3.5 or higher. Along with their application, they must submit high school or college transcripts, 2 letters of recommendation, a copy of their Chickasaw Nation citizenship card, and a 1-page essay on their long-term goals and plans for achieving them. Financial need is not considered in the selection process.

Financial data The stipend is $8,000.

Duration 1 year.

Number awarded 1 each year.
Deadline August of each year.

[285]
J. PARIS MOSLEY SCHOLARSHIP

Cleveland Foundation
Attn: Scholarship Officer
1422 Euclid Avenue, Suite 1300
Cleveland, OH 44115-2001
(216) 861-3810   Fax: (216) 861-1729
E-mail: mbaker@clevefdn.org
Web: www.clevelandfoundation.org/Scholarships

Summary To provide financial assistance for college to Native American and other high school seniors in any state who are deaf or whose primary caregivers are deaf.

Eligibility This program is open to high school seniors in any state who are deaf or hard of hearing or the children or grandchildren of deaf or hard of hearing parents or grandparents. Applicants must be planning to attend a college, university, vocational school, or other postsecondary program in any state. They must use some form of sign language, have a GPA of 2.5 or higher, and be able to demonstrate financial need. Preference is given to students of African American, Latino American, or Native American descent.

Financial data A stipend is awarded (amount not specified).

Duration 1 year.

Number awarded 1 or more each year.

Deadline March of each year.

[286]
JACKIE ROBINSON SCHOLARSHIPS

Jackie Robinson Foundation
Attn: Education and Leadership Development Program
75 Varick Street, Second Floor
New York, NY 10013-1917
(212) 290-8600   Fax: (212) 290-8081
E-mail: general@jackierobinson.org
Web: www.jackierobinson.org

Summary To provide financial assistance for college to Native American and other minority high school seniors.

Eligibility This program is open to members of an ethnic minority group who are high school seniors accepted at a 4-year college or university. Applicants must have a mathematics and critical reading SAT score of 1000 or higher or ACT score of 21 or higher. Selection is based on academic achievement, financial need, dedication towards community service, and leadership potential. U.S. citizenship is required.

Financial data The maximum stipend is $7,500 per year.

Duration 4 years.

Additional information The program also offers personal and career counseling on a year-round basis, a week of interaction with other scholarship students from around the country, and assistance in obtaining summer jobs and permanent employment after graduation. It was established in 1973 by a grant from Chesebrough-Pond.

Number awarded 100 or more each year.

Deadline March of each year.

[287]
JACOBS ENGINEERING SCHOLARSHIP

Conference of Minority Transportation Officials
Attn: National Scholarship Program
818 18th Street, N.W., Suite 850
Washington, DC 20006
(202) 530-0551   Fax: (202) 530-0617
Web: www.comto.org/news-youth.php

Summary To provide financial assistance to Native American and other minority upper-division and graduate students in a field related to transportation.

Eligibility This program is open to minority juniors, seniors, and graduate students in fields related to transportation (e.g., civil engineering, construction engineering, environmental engineering, safety, transportation, urban planning). Undergraduates must have a GPA of 3.0 or higher; graduate students must have a GPA of at least 3.5. Applicants must submit a cover letter with a 500-word statement of career goals. Financial need is not considered in the selection process. U.S. citizenship is required.

Financial data The stipend is $4,000. Funds are paid directly to the recipient's college or university.

Duration 1 year.

Additional information The Conference of Minority Transportation Officials (COMTO) was established in 1971 to promote, strengthen, and expand the roles of minorities in all aspects of transportation. This program is sponsored by Jacobs Engineering Group Inc. Recipients are required to become members of COMTO and attend the COMTO National Scholarship Luncheon.

Number awarded 1 or more each year.

Deadline April of each year.

[288]
JAMES B. MORRIS SCHOLARSHIP

James B. Morris Scholarship Fund
Attn: Scholarship Selection Committee
525 S.W. Fifth Street, Suite A
Des Moines, IA 50309-4501
(515) 282-8192   Fax: (515) 282-9117
E-mail: morris@assoc-mgmt.com
Web: www.morrisscholarship.org

Summary To provide financial assistance to Native Americans and other minority undergraduate, graduate, and law students in Iowa.

Eligibility This program is open to minority students (African Americans, Asian/Pacific Islanders, Hispanics, or Native Americans) who are interested in studying at a college, graduate school, or law school. Applicants must be either Iowa residents and high school graduates who are attending a college or university anywhere in the United States or non-Iowa residents who are attending a college or university in Iowa; preference is given to native Iowans who are attending an Iowa college or university. Along with their application, they must submit an essay of 250 to 500 words on why they are applying for this scholarship, activities or organizations in which they are involved, and their future plans. Selection is based on the essay, academic achievement (GPA of 2.5 or higher), community service, and financial need. U.S. citizenship is required.

Financial data The stipend is $2,300 per year.

Duration   1 year; may be renewed.

Additional information   This fund was established in 1978 in honor of the J.B. Morris family, who founded the Iowa branch of the National Association for the Advancement of Colored People and published the *Iowa Bystander* newspaper.

Number awarded   Varies each year; recently, 24 of these scholarships were awarded.

Deadline   March of each year.

[289]
JAMES E. WEBB INTERNSHIPS

Smithsonian Institution
Attn: Office of Fellowships
470 L'Enfant Plaza, Suite 7102
P.O. Box 37012, MRC 902
Washington, DC 20013-7012
(202) 633-7070   Fax: (202) 633-7069
E-mail: siofg@si.edu
Web: www.si.edu/ofg/Applications/WEBB/WEBBapp.htm

Summary   To provide internship opportunities throughout the Smithsonian Institution to Native Americans and other minority upper-division and graduate students in business or public administration.

Eligibility   This program is open to minorities who are juniors, seniors, or graduate students majoring in areas of business or public administration (finance, human resource management, accounting, or general business administration). Applicants must have a GPA of 3.0 or higher. They must seek placement in offices, museums, and research institutes within the Smithsonian Institution.

Financial data   Interns receive a stipend of $550 per week and a travel allowance.

Duration   10 weeks during the summer, fall, or spring.

Number awarded   Varies each year; recently, 8 of these internships were awarded.

Deadline   January of each year for summer or fall; September of each year for spring.

[290]
JEWELL HILTON BONNER SCHOLARSHIP

Navy League of the United States
Attn: Scholarships
2300 Wilson Boulevard, Suite 200
Arlington, VA 22201-5424
(703) 528-1775   Toll Free: (800) 356-5760
Fax: (703) 528-2333
E-mail: scholarships@navyleague.org
Web: www.navyleague.org/scholarship

Summary   To provide financial assistance for college to Native American and other dependent children of sea service personnel.

Eligibility   This program is open to U.S. citizens who are 1) dependents or direct descendants of an active, Reserve, retired, or honorably discharged member of the U.S. sea service (including the Navy, Marine Corps, Coast Guard, or Merchant Marines), or 2) current active members of the Naval Sea Cadet Corps. Applicants must be entering their freshman year at an accredited college or university. They must have a GPA of 3.0 or higher. Along with their application, they must submit transcripts, 2 letters of recommendation, SAT/ACT

scores, documentation of financial need, proof of qualifying sea service duty, and a 1-page personal statement on why they should be considered for this scholarship. Preference is given to applicants of Native American heritage.

Financial data   The stipend is $2,500 per year.

Duration   4 years, provided the recipient maintains a GPA of 3.0 or higher.

Number awarded   1 each year.

Deadline   February of each year.

[291]
JOHN AND MURIEL LANDIS SCHOLARSHIPS

American Nuclear Society
Attn: Scholarship Coordinator
555 North Kensington Avenue
La Grange Park, IL 60526-5592
(708) 352-6611   Toll Free: (800) 323-3044
Fax: (708) 352-0499   E-mail: outreach@ans.org
Web: www.ans.org/honors/scholarships

Summary   To provide financial assistance to Native American and other undergraduate or graduate students who are interested in preparing for a career in nuclear-related fields.

Eligibility   This program is open to undergraduate and graduate students at colleges or universities located in the United States who are preparing for, or planning to prepare for, a career in nuclear science, nuclear engineering, or a nuclear-related field. Qualified high school seniors are also eligible. Applicants must have greater than average financial need and have experienced circumstances that render them disadvantaged. They must be sponsored by an organization (e.g., plant branch, local section, student section) within the American Nuclear Society (ANS). Along with their application, they must submit an essay on their academic and professional goals, experiences that have affected those goals, etc. Selection is based on that essay, academic achievement, letters of recommendation, and financial need. Women and members of minority groups are especially urged to apply. U.S. citizenship is not required.

Financial data   The stipend is $5,000, to be used to cover tuition, books, fees, room, and board.

Duration   1 year; nonrenewable.

Number awarded   Up to 8 each year.

Deadline   January of each year.

[292]
JOHN BENNETT HERRINGTON SCHOLARSHIP

Chickasaw Foundation
110 West 12th Street
P.O. Box 1726
Ada, OK 74821-1726
(580) 421-9030   Fax: (580) 421-9031
E-mail: ChickasawFoundation@chickasaw.net
Web: www.chickasawfoundation.org/index_20.htm

Summary   To provide financial assistance to members of the Chickasaw Nation who are preparing for a career in space aeronautics.

Eligibility   This program is open to Chickasaw students who are currently enrolled full time at an accredited institution of higher education. Applicants must be classified as juniors or seniors at a 4-year college and have a GPA of 2.5 or higher. They must be majoring in chemistry, engineering, geophysics, mathematics, natural science, physics, or a related field. Their career interest must relate to space aeronautics. Along with their application, they must submit high school or college transcripts, 2 letters of recommendation, a copy of their Chickasaw Nation citizenship card, and a 1-page essay on their long-term goals and plans for achieving them. Financial need is not considered in the selection process.

Financial data The stipend is $10,000 per year.

Duration Up to 2 years.

Number awarded 1 each year.

Deadline August of each year.

[293]
JOHN C. ROUILLARD AND ALICE TONEMAH MEMORIAL SCHOLARSHIPS

National Indian Education Association
Attn: Awards Committee
110 Maryland Avenue, N.E., Suite 104
Washington, DC 20002
(202) 544-7290   Fax: (202) 544-7293
E-mail: niea@niea.org
Web: www.niea.org/events/scholarship.php

Summary To provide financial assistance for college or graduate school to students nominated by members of the National Indian Education Association (NIEA).

Eligibility This program is open to American Indians, Native Hawaiians, and Alaska Natives working full time on an associate, bachelor's, master's, or doctoral degree. Applicants are not required to be members of NIEA, but they must be nominated by a member. They must have demonstrated leadership qualities, maintained high academic achievement, served as a role model for other students, and shown creativity or commitment in the following areas: 1) promoted an understanding and an appreciation of Native American culture in an educational setting; 2) demonstrated positive, active leadership in student affairs; 3) demonstrated and/or encouraged student involvement in educational or community activities; and/or 4) achieved their educational goals and objectives.

Financial data Stipends range from $1,000 to $2,500. Funds may be used for educational expenses not covered by other sources.

Duration 1 year.

Number awarded 1 or more each year.

Deadline August of each year.

[294]
JOHN C. SMITH SCHOLARSHIP

Choctaw Nation
Attn: Scholarship Advisement Program
16th and Locust
P.O. Box 1210
Durant, OK 74702-1210
(580) 924-8280
Toll Free: (800) 522-6170, ext. 2523 (within OK)
Fax: (580) 920-3122
E-mail: scholarshipadvisement@choctawnation.com
Web: www.choctawnation-sap.com/cnoscholarship.shtml

Summary To provide financial assistance to Choctaw Indian students who are interested in attending a university in any state.

Eligibility This program is open to entering freshmen at a college or university in any state who have a Choctaw Adult Membership card and are Choctaw Honors Scholars. Applicants must be able to demonstrate involvement with or measurable interests in Native American activities.

Financial data A private donor provides an annual stipend of $5,000 and the Choctaw Nation matches that so the total award is $10,000 per year.

Duration 1 year; may be renewed.

Number awarded 1 each year.

Deadline April of each year.

[295]
JOHN N. COLBERG ENDOWMENT SCHOLARSHIP FUND

Cook Inlet Region, Inc.
Attn: The CIRI Foundation
3600 San Jeronimo Drive, Suite 256
Anchorage, AK 99508-2870
(907) 793-3575   Toll Free: (800) 764-3382
Fax: (907) 793-3585   E-mail: tcf@thecirifoundation.org
Web: www.thecirifoundation.org/designated.htm

Summary To provide financial assistance for undergraduate or graduate studies leading to a career in the law to Alaska Natives who are original enrollees to Cook Inlet Region, Inc. (CIRI) and their lineal descendants.

Eligibility This program is open to Alaska Native enrollees to CIRI under the Alaska Native Claims Settlement Act (ANCSA) of 1971 and their lineal descendants. There are no Alaska residency requirements or age limitations. Applicants must be accepted or enrolled full time in a 4-year undergraduate or a graduate degree program. Preference is given to students who are working on a degree leading to the study of law and have a GPA of 2.5 or higher. Along with their application, they must submit a 500-word statement on their educational and career goals and how they are contributing, or planning to contribute, to a positive Alaska Native community. Selection is based on that statement, academic achievement, rigor of course work or degree program, student financial contribution, financial need, grade level, previous work performance, community service, and relationship of degree program to career goals.

Financial data The stipend is $2,500 per semester.

Duration 1 semester or 1 year.

Additional information This program was established in 2003.

Number awarded 1 or more each year.

Deadline May of each year.

[296]
JOHN SHURR JOURNALISM AWARD

Cherokee Nation
Attn: Cherokee Nation Education Corporation
115 East Delaware Street
P.O. Box 948
Tahlequah, OK 74465-0948
(918) 207-0950   Fax: (918) 207-0951
E-mail: contact@cnec-edu.org
Web: cnec.cherokee.org

Summary To provide financial assistance to citizens of the Cherokee Nation who are enrolled at a college or university in any state and working on an undergraduate or graduate degree in journalism.

Eligibility This program is open to citizens of the Cherokee Nation who are currently enrolled in an undergraduate or graduate program in journalism or mass communications at a college or university in any state. Applicants must have a GPA of 3.0 or higher. They are not required to reside in the Cherokee Nation area. Along with their application, they must submit a 4-page personal essay that includes background information, their degree plan for higher education, why they have chosen that field of study, how they plan to serve Cherokee people when they complete higher education, and why they should be selected for this scholarship. Selection is based on the clarity and presentation of the essay; academic information (including transcripts and ACT scores); school, cultural and community activities; future plans to serve Cherokee people; and financial need.

Financial data The stipend is $1,000 per semester ($2,000 per year).

Duration 1 year. Renewal for the second semester requires the recipient to earn a GPA of 3.0 or higher in the first semester.

Additional information Recipients are expected to apply for an 8-week paid internship with *The Cherokee Phoenix* newspaper in Tahlequah, Oklahoma during the summer following their scholarship year.

Number awarded 1 each year.

Deadline April of each year.

[297]
JOSEPH A. SOWA SCHOLARSHIP

Ke Ali'i Pauahi Foundation
Attn: Financial Aid & Scholarship Services
567 South King Street, Suite 160
Honolulu, HI 96813
(808) 534-3966   Toll Free: (800) 842-4682, ext. 43966
Fax: (808) 534-3890   E-mail: scholarships@pauahi.org
Web: www.pauahi.org/scholarships

Summary To provide financial assistance to undergraduate students, especially those of Native Hawaiian descent, who are preparing for a career in communications.

Eligibility This program is open to undergraduate students who are planning to major in communications. Applicants must have a GPA of 3.0 or higher and be able to demonstrate financial need. Along with their application, they must submit an essay describing their plan to maximize the potential of young people through communication as well as to demonstrate their leadership potential in the community. Residency in Hawaii is not required, but preference is given to Native Hawaiians (descendants of the aboriginal inhabitants of the Hawaiian Islands prior to 1778).

Financial data The stipend is $1,500.

Duration 1 year.

Additional information This program began in 2008.

Number awarded 1 each year.

Deadline March of each year.

[298]
JOSEPH K. LUMSDEN MEMORIAL SCHOLARSHIP

Sault Tribe of Chippewa Indians
Attn: Higher Education Program-Memorial/Tributary
  Scholarships
523 Ashmun Street
Sault Ste. Marie, MI 49783
(906) 635-4944   Toll Free: (800) 793-0660
Fax: (906) 635-7785   E-mail: amatson@saulttribe.net
Web: www.saulttribe.com

Summary To provide financial assistance to members of the Sault Tribe in Michigan who are upper-division or graduate students at a university in any state.

Eligibility This program is open to members of the Sault Tribe who are college juniors or higher and are one-quarter Indian blood quantum or more. Applicants must be enrolled full time at a 4-year college or university in any state and have a cumulative GPA of 3.0 or higher. Along with their application, they must submit an essay of 300 to 500 words on how this scholarship will help them realize their goals.

Financial data The stipend is $1,000 per year.

Duration 1 year; may be renewed.

Number awarded 1 each year.

Deadline May of each year.

[299]
JOSEPHINE NIPPER MEMORIAL SCHOLARSHIP

American Indian Education Foundation
2401 Eglin Street
Rapid City, SD 57703
Toll Free: (866) 866-8642   E-mail: mlee@nrc1.org
Web: www.nrcprograms.org

Summary To provide financial assistance for college to Native Americans who are interested in studying education or nursing.

Eligibility This program is open to full-time students of Native American descent who are currently attending or planning to attend a 2-year college, a 4-year college or university, or a vocational/technical school and major in education or nursing. Applicants may be either graduating high school seniors or undergraduates who are entering, continuing, or returning to school. They must be first-generation college students. Along with their application, they must submit a 4-page essay in which they describe themselves as a student, their ultimate career goals, their plans for working in or with the Indian community, and their participation in leadership and/or community service activities. A GPA of 2.0 to 3.4 is desirable, but all current or future undergraduate students are encouraged to apply. An ACT score of 14 or higher is desirable. Financial need is considered in the selection process.

Financial data The stipend is $2,000. Funds are paid directly to the recipient's college or university.

Duration 1 year.

Additional information This program was established in 2004.

Number awarded 1 each year.

Deadline April of each year.

[300]
JP MORGAN CHASE LAUNCHING LEADERS UNDERGRADUATE SCHOLARSHIP

JPMorgan Chase
Campus Recruiting
Attn: Launching Leaders
277 Park Avenue, Second Floor
New York, NY 10172
(212) 270-6000
E-mail: bronwen.x.baumgardner@jpmorgan.com
Web: www.jpmorgan.com

Summary To provide financial assistance and work experience to Native American and other underrepresented minority undergraduate students interested in a career in financial services.

Eligibility This program is open to Black, Hispanic, and Native American students enrolled as sophomores or juniors and interested in financial services. Applicants must have a GPA of 3.5 or higher. Along with their application, they must submit 500-word essays on 1) why they should be considered potential candidates for CEO of the sponsoring bank in 2020; and 2) the special background and attributes they would contribute to the sponsor's diversity agenda. They must be interested in a summer associate position in the sponsor's investment banking, sales and trading, or research divisions.

Financial data The stipend is $5,000 for recipients accepted as sophomores or $10,000 for recipients accepted as juniors. For students accepted as sophomores and whose scholarship is renewed for a second year, the stipend is $15,000. The summer internship is a paid position.

Duration 1 year; may be renewed 1 additional year if the recipient successfully completes the 10-week summer intern program and maintains a GPA of 3.5 or higher.

Number awarded Approximately 12 each year.

Deadline October of each year.

[301]
JUDITH MCMANUS PRICE SCHOLARSHIPS

American Planning Association
Attn: Leadership Affairs Associate
205 North Michigan Avenue, Suite 1200
Chicago, IL 60601
(312) 431-9100   Fax: (312) 786-6700
E-mail: fellowship@planning.org
Web: www.planning.org/scholarships/apa

Summary To provide financial assistance to Native Americans and other underrepresented students enrolled in undergraduate or graduate degree programs at recognized planning schools.

Eligibility This program is open to undergraduate and graduate students in urban and regional planning who are women or members of the following minority groups: African American, Hispanic American, or Native American. Applicants must be citizens of the United States and able to document financial need. They must intend to work as practicing planners in the public sector. Along with their application, they must submit a 2-page personal and background statement describing how their education will be applied to career goals and why they chose planning as a career path. Selection is based (in order of importance), on: 1) commitment to planning as reflected in their personal statement and on their resume; 2) academic achievement and/or improvement dur-

ing the past 2 years; 3) letters of recommendation; 4) financial need; and 5) professional presentation.

Financial data Stipends range from $2,000 to $4,000 per year. The money may be applied to tuition and living expenses only. Payment is made to the recipient's university and divided by terms in the school year.

Duration 1 year; recipients may reapply.

Additional information This program was established in 2002.

Number awarded Varies each year; recently, 3 of these scholarships were awarded.

Deadline April of each year.

[302]
JUDSON L. BROWN ENDOWMENT FUND SCHOLARSHIP

Sealaska Corporation
Attn: Sealaska Heritage Institute
One Sealaska Plaza, Suite 301
Juneau, AK 99801-1249
(907) 586-9170   Toll Free: (888) 311-4992
Fax: (907) 586-9293 E-mail: scholarship@sealaska.com
Web: www.sealaskaheritage.org

Summary To provide financial assistance to Native Alaskan upper-division students who have a connection to the to Sealaska Corporation.

Eligibility This program is open to 1) Alaska Natives who are shareholders of Sealaska Corporation, and 2) Native lineal descendants of Alaska Natives enrolled to Sealaska Corporation, whether or not they own Sealaska Corporation stock. Applicants must be entering their junior or senior year at a college or university in any state. They must be able to provide documentation of the involvement in tribal governments and Alaska Native organizations or programs that promote advancement of cultural, social, and economic development for Native Peoples. Along with their application, they must submit an essay on how they have been involved in Native activities and how they plan to use their education to promote the cultural, social, and economic well being of the Native Peoples and communities. Financial need is also considered in the selection process.

Financial data The stipend is $5,000.

Duration 1 year.

Additional information Sealaska Corporation is 1 of 13 Alaska Native Regional Corporations created under the Alaska Native Claims Settlement Act of 1971.

Number awarded 1 each year.

Deadline February of each year.

[303]
JUNE CURRAN PORCARO SCHOLARSHIP

Sault Tribe of Chippewa Indians
Attn: Higher Education Program-Memorial/Tributary
  Scholarships
523 Ashmun Street
Sault Ste. Marie, MI 49783
(906) 635-4944   Toll Free: (800) 793-0660
Fax: (906) 635-7785   E-mail: amatson@saulttribe.net
Web: www.saulttribe.com

Summary To provide financial assistance to members of the Sault Tribe of Chippewa Indians who have been homeless, displaced, or in the foster care system and are interested in attending college in any state to work on an undergraduate degree in human services.

Eligibility This program is open to enrolled members of the Sault Tribe who have been homeless, displaced, or in the foster care system. Applicants must be working on an undergraduate degree in human services at a college or university in any state to prepare for a career of helping people who are homeless, displaced, or involved in the foster care system. They must be able to demonstrate financial need. Along with their application, they must submit an essay of 300 to 500 words on how this scholarship will help them realize their goals.

Financial data The stipend is $1,000.

Duration 1 year.

Additional information Recipients must agree to provide at least 40 hours of volunteer service at an accredited homeless shelter during the school year for which they receive the award.

Number awarded 1 each year.

Deadline May of each year.

[304]
JUSTINE E. GRANNER MEMORIAL SCHOLARSHIP

Iowa United Methodist Foundation
2301 Rittenhouse Street
Des Moines, IA 50321
(515) 974-8927
Web: www.iumf.org/otherscholarships.html

Summary To provide financial assistance to Native Americans and other ethnic minorities in Iowa interested in majoring in a health-related field.

Eligibility This program is open to ethnic minority students preparing for a career in nursing, public health, or a related field at a college or school of nursing in Iowa. Applicants must have a GPA of 3.0 or higher. Preference is given to graduates of Iowa high schools. Financial need is considered in the selection process.

Financial data The stipend is $1,000.

Duration 1 year.

Number awarded 1 each year.

Deadline March of each year.

[305]
KAISER PERMANENTE COLORADO DIVERSITY SCHOLARSHIP PROGRAM

Kaiser Permanente
Attn: Multicultural Associations/Employee Resource
  Groups
P.O. Box 378066
Denver, CO 80247-8066
E-mail: co-diversitydevelopment@kp.org
Web: physiciancareers.kp.org

Summary To provide financial assistance to Colorado residents who are Native American or come from other diverse backgrounds and are interested in working on an undergraduate or graduate degree in a health care field at a school in any state.

Eligibility This program is open to all residents of Colorado, including those who identify as 1 or more of the follow-

ing: African American, Asian Pacific, Latino, lesbian, gay, bisexual, transgender, intersex, Native American, and/or a person with a disability. Applicants must be 1) a graduating high school senior with a GPA of 2.7 or higher and planning to enroll full time at a college or technical school in any state; 2) a GED recipient with a GED score of 520 or higher and planning to enroll full time at a college or technical school in any state; 3) a full-time undergraduate student at a college or technical school in any state; or 4) a full-time graduate or doctoral student at a school in any state. They must be preparing for a career in health care (e.g., doctor, nurse, surgeon, physician assistant, dentist), mental health, public health, or health policy. Along with their application, they must submit 300-word essays on 1) a personal setback in their life and how they responded and learned from it; 2) how they give back to their community; and 3) why they have chosen health care and/or public health for their educational and career path. Selection is based on academic achievement, character qualities, community outreach and volunteering, and financial need.

Financial data Stipends range from $1,400 to $2,600.

Duration 1 year.

Number awarded Varies each year; recently, 17 of these scholarships were awarded.

Deadline January of each year.

[306]
KA'IULANI HOME FOR GIRLS TRUST SCHOLARSHIP

Hawai'i Community Foundation
Attn: Scholarship Department
827 Fort Street Mall
Honolulu, HI 96813
(808) 537-6333   Toll Free: (888) 731-3863
Fax: (808) 521-6286
E-mail: scholarships@hcf-hawaii.org
Web: www.hawaiicommunityfoundation.org/scholarships

Summary To provide financial assistance to women of Native Hawaiian ancestry who are attending college in any state.

Eligibility This program is open to women of Native Hawaiian ancestry who are entering their freshman or sophomore year at a college or university in any state. Applicants must demonstrate academic achievement (GPA of 3.0 or higher), good moral character, and financial need. Along with their application, they must submit a short statement indicating their reasons for attending college, their planned course of study, their career goals, and what community service means to them.

Financial data The amounts of the awards depend on the availability of funds and the need of the recipient. Recently, the average value of all scholarships awarded by the foundation was $2,041.

Duration 1 year; may be renewed.

Additional information This fund was established in 1963 when the Ka'iulani Home for Girls, formerly used to provide boarding home facilities for young women of Hawaiian ancestry, was demolished and the property sold.

Number awarded Varies each year.

Deadline February of each year.

[307]
KANSAS ETHNIC MINORITY SCHOLARSHIP PROGRAM

Kansas Board of Regents
Attn: Student Financial Assistance
1000 S.W. Jackson Street, Suite 520
Topeka, KS 66612-1368
(785) 296-3517   Fax: (785) 296-0983
E-mail: dlindeman@ksbor.org
Web: www.kansasregents.org/scholarships_and_grants

Summary To provide financial assistance to Native Americans and other minority students in Kansas who are interested in attending college in the state.

Eligibility Eligible to apply are Kansas residents who fall into 1 of these minority groups: American Indian, Alaskan Native, African American, Asian, Pacific Islander, or Hispanic. Applicants may be current college students (enrolled in community colleges, colleges, or universities in Kansas), but high school seniors graduating in the current year receive priority consideration. Minimum academic requirements include 1 of the following: 1) ACT score of 21 or higher or combined mathematics and critical reading SAT score of 990 or higher; 2) cumulative GPA of 3.0 or higher; 3) high school rank in upper 33%; 4) completion of the Kansas Scholars Curriculum (4 years of English, 3 years of mathematics, 3 years of science, 3 years of social studies, and 2 years of foreign language); 5) selection by the National Merit Corporation in any category; or 6) selection by the College Board as a Hispanic Scholar. Selection is based primarily on financial need.

Financial data A stipend of up to $1,850 is provided, depending on financial need and availability of state funds.

Duration 1 year; may be renewed for up to 3 additional years (4 additional years for designated 5-year programs) if the recipient maintains a 2.0 cumulative GPA and has financial need.

Additional information There is a $10 application fee.

Number awarded Approximately 200 each year.

Deadline April of each year.

[308]
KANSAS SPJ MINORITY STUDENT SCHOLARSHIP

Society of Professional Journalists-Kansas Professional Chapter
c/o Denise Neil, Scholarship Committee
Wichita Eagle
825 East Douglas Avenue
P.O. Box 820
Wichita, KS 67201-0820
(316) 268-6327   E-mail: dneil@wichitaeagle.com
Web: www.spjchapters.org/kansas/gridiron.html

Summary To provide financial assistance to residents of any state enrolled at colleges and universities in Kansas who are Native American or members of another racial or ethnic minority group and interested in a career in journalism.

Eligibility This program is open to residents of any state who are members of a racial or ethnic minority group and entering their junior or senior year at colleges and universities in Kansas. Applicants do not have to be journalism or communication majors, but they must demonstrate a strong and sincere interest in print journalism, broadcast journalism,

online journalism, or photojournalism. They must have a GPA of 2.5 or higher. Along with their application, they must submit a professional resume, 4 to 6 examples of their best work (clips or stories, copies of photographs, tapes or transcripts of broadcasts, printouts of web pages) and a 1-page cover letter about themselves, how they came to be interested in journalism, their professional goals, and (if appropriate) their financial need for this scholarship.

Financial data The stipend is $1,000.

Duration 1 year.

Number awarded 1 each year.

Deadline April of each year.

[309]
KATU THOMAS R. DARGAN SCHOLARSHIP

KATU-TV
Attn: Human Resources
2153 N.E. Sandy Boulevard
P.O. Box 2
Portland, OR 97207-0002
(503) 231-4222
Web: www.katu.com/about/scholarship

Summary To provide financial assistance and work experience to Native American and other minority students from Oregon and Washington who are studying broadcasting or communications in college.

Eligibility This program is open to minority (Asian, Black/African American, Hispanic or Latino, Native Hawaiian or Pacific Islander, American Indian or Alaska Native) U.S. citizens currently enrolled as a sophomore or higher at a 4-year college or university or an accredited community college in Oregon or Washington. Residents of Oregon or Washington enrolled at a school in any state are also eligible. Applicants must be majoring in broadcasting or communications and have a GPA of 3.0 or higher. Community college students must be enrolled in a broadcast curriculum that is transferable to a 4-year accredited university. Finalists will be interviewed. Selection is based on financial need, academic achievement, and an essay on personal and professional goals.

Financial data The stipend is $6,000. Funds are sent directly to the recipient's school.

Duration 1 year; recipients may reapply if they have maintained a GPA of 3.0 or higher.

Additional information Winners are also eligible for a paid internship in selected departments at Fisher Broadcasting/KATU in Portland, Oregon.

Number awarded 1 each year.

Deadline April of each year.

[310]
KAW NATION ACADEMIC SCHOLARSHIP PROGRAM

Kaw Nation
Attn: Education and Social Services Department
698 Grandview Drive
Drawer 50
Kaw City, OK 74641
(580) 269-1186   Fax: (580) 269-2116
E-mail: khowe@kawnation.com
Web: www.kawnation.com

Summary To provide financial assistance for college to members of the Kaw Nation who can demonstrate academic achievement.

Eligibility This program is open to Kaw tribal members who are working on or planning to work on a college degree. Applicants must have a GPA of 3.0 or higher. Financial need is not considered in the selection process.

Financial data A stipend is awarded (amount not specified).

Duration 1 year; may be renewed, provided the recipient maintains a GPA of 3.0 or higher and full-time enrollment.

Number awarded Varies each year.

Deadline April of each year.

[311]
KAW NATION ADULT VOCATIONAL TRAINING PROGRAM

Kaw Nation
Attn: Education and Social Services Department
698 Grandview Drive
Drawer 50
Kaw City, OK 74641
(580) 269-1186   Fax: (580) 269-2116
E-mail: khowe@kawnation.com
Web: www.kawnation.com

Summary To provide financial assistance for vocational school to members of the Kaw Nation and other Native Americans living in the Kaw service area in Oklahoma who can demonstrate need.

Eligibility This program is open to Kaw tribal members and other Native Americans living within the Kaw Nation service area in Oklahoma. Applicants must be enrolled or planning to enroll at a vocational/technical school. They must be able to demonstrate financial need.

Financial data A stipend is awarded (amount not specified).

Duration 1 or 2 years.

Number awarded Varies each year.

Deadline Deadline not specified.

[312]
KAW NATION HIGHER EDUCATION GRANT PROGRAM

Kaw Nation
Attn: Education and Social Services Department
P.O. Box 50
Kaw City, OK 74641
(580) 269-1186   Fax: (580) 269-2116
E-mail: khowe@kawnation.com
Web: www.kawnation.com/Programs/edsvcs.html

Summary To provide financial assistance for college to members of the Kaw Nation who can demonstrate need.

Eligibility This program is open to Kaw tribal members who are working on or planning to work on a college degree. Applicants must be able to demonstrate financial need.

Financial data A stipend is awarded (amount not specified).

Duration 1 year; may be renewed.

Number awarded Varies each year.

Deadline May of each year for fall semester; October of each year for spring semester.

[313]
KAWERAK HIGHER EDUCATION SCHOLARSHIPS

Kawerak, Inc.
Attn: Education, Employment and Training Division
P.O. Box 948
Nome, AK 99762
(907) 443-4351   Toll Free: (800) 450-4341
Fax: (907) 443-4480   E-mail: wfd.spec@kawerak.org
Web: www.kawerak.org/servicedivisions/eet/hes/index.html

Summary To provide financial assistance to Alaska Natives from the Bering Straits region who are interested in attending college in any state.

Eligibility This program is open to tribally enrolled members of Native villages in the Bering Straits region of Alaska (although they are not required to reside in the area). Applicants must be enrolled or accepted for enrollment in a 2- or 4-year degree program at a college or university in any state. They be able to demonstrate financial need. Along with their application, they must submit a personal statement on their educational goals and objectives, their community and school activities, and honors and awards they have received.

Financial data The stipend is $1,500 per semester.

Duration 1 semester; may be renewed if the recipient remains enrolled full time with a GPA of 2.0 or higher.

Additional information This program is supported by funding from the U.S. Bureau of Indian Affairs (BIA).

Number awarded Varies each year.

Deadline July of each year for fall semester or quarter; December of each year for spring semester or winter quarter; February of each year for spring quarter; April of each year for summer semester or quarter.

[314]
KBIC BIA HIGHER EDUCATION GRANTS

Keweenaw Bay Indian Community-Lake Superior Band of Chippewa Indians
Attn: Education Department
16429 Bear Town Road
Baraga, MI 49908
(906) 353-4117   E-mail: amy@kbic-nsn.gov
Web: www.kbic-nsn.gov/html/education.htm

Summary To provide financial assistance to members of the Keeweenaw Bay Indian Community (KBIC) of the Lake Superior Band of Chippewa Indians who live in Michigan and are interested in attending college in the state.

Eligibility This program is open to enrolled KBIC tribal members who are residents of Michigan. Applicants must be attending or planning to attend a 2- or 4-year college or university in Michigan to work on an associate or bachelor's degree. They must be able to demonstrate financial need and apply for all other assistance for which they might be eligible.

Financial data A stipend is awarded (amount not specified).

Duration 1 semester; may be renewed.

Additional information This program is supported by the U.S. Bureau of Indian Affairs (BIA).

Number awarded Varies each year.

Deadline April of each year.

[315]
KEN KASHIWAHARA SCHOLARSHIP

Radio Television Digital News Foundation
Attn: RTDNF Fellowship Program
4121 Plank Road, Suite 512
Fredericksburg, VA 22407
(202) 467-5214   Fax: (202) 223-4007
E-mail: staceys@rtdna.org
Web: www.rtdna.org/pages/education/undergraduates.php

Summary To provide financial assistance to Native American and other minority undergraduate students who are interested in preparing for a career in electronic journalism.

Eligibility This program is open to sophomores or more advanced minority undergraduate students enrolled in an electronic journalism sequence at an accredited or nationally-recognized college or university. Applicants must submit 1 to 3 examples of their journalistic skills on audio CD or DVD (no more than 15 minutes total, accompanied by scripts); a description of their role on each story and a list of who worked on each story and what they did; a 1-page statement explaining why they are preparing for a career in electronic journalism with reference to their specific career preference (radio, television, online, reporting, producing, or newsroom management); a resume; and a letter of reference from their dean or faculty sponsor explaining why they are a good candidate for the award and certifying that they have at least 1 year of school remaining.

Financial data The stipend is $2,500, paid in semiannual installments of $1,250 each.

Duration 1 year.

Additional information The Radio Television Digital News Foundation (RTDNF) was formerly the Radio and Television News Directors Foundation (RTNDF). Previous winners of any RTDNF scholarship or internship are not eligible to apply for this program.

Number awarded 1 each year.

Deadline May of each year.

[316]
KENAITZE INDIAN TRIBE HIGHER EDUCATION GRANT PROGRAM

Kenaitze Indian Tribe
Attn: Education Services Coordinator
1104 Mission Avenue in Olde Town Kenai
P.O. Box 988
Kenai, AK 99611
(907) 335-0669   Fax: (907) 335-0989
E-mail: education@kenaitze.org
Web: www.kenaitze.org/education/index.html

Summary To provide financial assistance to members of recognized Native Alaskan Tribes who plan to attend college or graduate school in any state.

Eligibility This program is open to members of federally-recognized tribes and Native Alaskans of at least one-quarter degree blood. Applicants must be enrolled or planning to enroll full time at a college or university in any state and work on a baccalaureate degree. They are also expected to apply for federal financial aid through the FAFSA. Along with their application, they must submit a letter on their goals and educational plans, verification of Indian ancestry (CIB or tribal card), a letter of acceptance to the school they plan to attend, transcripts, a completed FAFSA application, and an Alaska driver's license. Limited support may be provided to graduate students if funds are available.

Financial data The amount awarded varies, depending upon the available funds and the recipient's unmet needs. Funds are paid directly to the educational institution.

Duration 1 year; may be renewed if the recipient maintains a GPA of 2.5 of higher.

Additional information This program is funded by the U.S. Bureau of Indian Affairs.

Number awarded Varies each year.

Deadline May of each year for fall; November of each year for spring or winter.

[317]
KIC SCHOLARSHIPS

Kikiktagruk Inupiat Corporation
Attn: KIC Scholarship Foundation
373A Second Avenue
P.O. Box 1050
Kotzebue, AK 99752
(907) 442-3165   Fax: (907) 442-2165
E-mail: info@kicorp.org
Web: www.kikiktagruk.com/kic/node/25

Summary To provide financial assistance for college or vocational school in any state to shareholders of the Kikiktagruk Inupiat Corporation (KIC) and their descendants.

Eligibility This program is open to KIC shareholders and their children who are attending or planning to attend a college or vocational school in any state as a full-time student. Applicants must submit a copy of their high school transcripts, 2 letters of recommendation, and a cover letter describing themselves and their goals. Awards are presented on a first-come, first-served basis.

Financial data The stipend is $500 per semester for full-time students or $250 per semester for part-time and short vocational program students.

Duration 1 semester; may be renewed for 1 additional semester per year if the recipient maintains a GPA of 2.0 or higher.

Additional information Kikiktagruk Inupiat Corporation was established in 1973 as a village corporation under the terms of the Alaska Native Claims Settlement Act (ANCSA) of 1971.

Number awarded Varies each semester.

Deadline Applications may be submitted at any time, but they must be received within 2 weeks after the semester starts.

[318]
KIOWA TRIBE OF OKLAHOMA ADULT VOCATIONAL TRAINING

Kiowa Tribe of Oklahoma
Attn: Education Programs Department
P.O. Box 369
Carnegie, OK 73015
(580) 654-2300, ext. 322   Fax: (580) 654-2406
E-mail: highereducation@kiowaok.com
Web: kiowatribe.net

Summary   To provide financial assistance to members of the Kiowa Tribe of Oklahoma who are interested in attending a vocational/technical school in any state.

Eligibility   This program is open to members of the Kiowa Tribe of Oklahoma who are enrolled or planning to enroll in a vocational training program in any state. Applicants must agree to abide by the attendance policy and all other rules of their school, to maintain a GPA of 2.6 or higher, and to remain in contact with the Kiowa Job Placement and Training staff. Along with their application, they must submit a copy of the Kiowa Certificate of Indian Blood (CIB), a letter of intent, a copy of their high school transcript or GED certificate, a copy of their birth certificate and Social Security card, the names of 3 references, and documentation of financial need.

Financial data   A stipend is paid (amount not specified).

Duration   Up to 24 months or until completion of the training program, whichever occurs first.

Number awarded   Varies each year.

Deadline   Applications must be submitted at any time.

[319]
KIOWA TRIBE OF OKLAHOMA HIGHER EDUCATION GRANT PROGRAM

Kiowa Tribe of Oklahoma
Attn: Education Programs Department
P.O. Box 369
Carnegie, OK 73015
(580) 654-2300, ext. 322   Fax: (580) 654-2406
E-mail: highereducation@kiowaok.com
Web: kiowatribe.net

Summary   To provide financial assistance to members of the Kiowa Tribe of Oklahoma who are interested in working on an associate or bachelor's degree at a college in any state.

Eligibility   This program is open to members of the Kiowa Tribe of Oklahoma who are enrolled or planning to enroll full time at a college or university in any state. Applicants must be interested in working on an associate or bachelor's degree in any field. Along with their application, they must submit a copy of the Kiowa Certificate of Indian Blood (CIB), a letter describing their educational goals, a current class schedule, and documentation of financial need.

Financial data   The maximum stipend is $5,000 per year.

Duration   1 semester; may be renewed for up to 5 additional semesters for completion of an associate degree or up to 9 additional semesters for completion of a bachelor's degree.

Number awarded   Varies each year.

Deadline   Applications must be submitted at the beginning of each academic year.

[320]
KIRBY MCDONALD EDUCATION ENDOWMENT SCHOLARSHIP FUND

Cook Inlet Region, Inc.
Attn: The CIRI Foundation
3600 San Jeronimo Drive, Suite 256
Anchorage, AK 99508-2870
(907) 793-3575   Toll Free: (800) 764-3382
Fax: (907) 793-3585   E-mail: tcf@thecirifoundation.org
Web: www.thecirifoundation.org/designated.htm

Summary   To provide financial assistance for undergraduate or graduate studies to Alaska Natives who are original enrollees to Cook Inlet Region, Inc. (CIRI) and their lineal descendants.

Eligibility   This program is open to Alaska Native enrollees to CIRI under the Alaska Native Claims Settlement Act (ANCSA) of 1971 and their lineal descendants. There are no Alaska residency requirements or age limitations. Applicants must be accepted or enrolled full time in a 4-year undergraduate or a graduate degree program. Preference is given to students in the culinary arts, business administration, or engineering. They must have a GPA of 2.5 or higher. Along with their application, they must submit a 500-word statement on their educational and career goals and how they are contributing, or planning to contribute, to a positive Alaska Native community. Selection is based on that statement, academic achievement, rigor of course work or degree program, student financial contribution, financial need, grade level, previous work performance, community service, and relationship of degree program to career goals.

Financial data   The stipend is $10,000 per year, $8,000 per year, or $2,500 per semester, depending on GPA.

Duration   1 semester or 1 year.

Additional information   This program was established in 1991.

Number awarded   1 or more each year.

Deadline   May of each year for annual scholarships; May or November of each year for semester scholarships.

[321]
KNIK TRIBAL COUNCIL HIGHER EDUCATION SCHOLARSHIPS

Knik Tribal Council
Attn: Education and Training Coordinator
901 West Commercial Drive
P.O. Box 871565
Wasilla, AK 99687
(907) 373-7991
Web: www.kniktribalcouncil.org

Summary   To provide financial assistance to Alaska Natives and American Indians in Alaska who are interested in attending college in any state.

Eligibility   This program is open to Alaska Natives and American Indians in Alaska who have a Tribal membership card or Certificate of Indian Blood (CIB) showing at least 25% native ancestry. Applicants must be attending or planning to attend a college, university, or vocational school in any state. Along with their application, they must submit an essay on their world view as an Alaska Native or American Indian and how funding will assist them and their community. Financial need is considered in the selection process.

Financial data The stipend depends on the unmet financial need of the recipient, to a maximum of $4,000 per year.

Duration 1 year; may be renewed, provided the recipient maintains a GPA of 2.0 or higher.

Number awarded Varies each year.

Deadline August of each year for fall; December of each year for spring.

[322]
KONIAG ANGAYUK SCHOLARSHIP AND INTERNSHIP

Koniag Incorporated
Attn: Koniag Education Foundation
4241 B Street, Suite 303B
Anchorage, AK 99503
(907) 562-9093   Toll Free: (888) 562-9093
Fax: (907) 562-9023
E-mail: scholarships@koniageducation.org
Web: www.koniageducation.org/scholarships

Summary To provide financial assistance and work experience to Alaska Natives who are Koniag Incorporated shareholders or descendants and interested in attending college in any state.

Eligibility This program is open to undergraduate students who are Alaska Native shareholders of Koniag Incorporated or descendants of those original enrollees. Applicants must have a GPA of 3.0 or higher and be working full time on a degree in any field. They must be interested in interning during the summer at a subsidiary of Koniag Development Corporation. Along with their application, they must submit an essay of 300 to 600 words in the form of a thank you letter about their background, educational goals, work history, and/or achievements. Financial need is not considered in the selection process.

Financial data The scholarship stipend is $10,000 per year. The internships provide a competitive salary and reimbursement of travel and lodging costs.

Duration The scholarship is for 1 academic year and may be renewed, provided the recipient maintains a GPA of 3.0 or higher and full-time status. The internship is for 6 to 10 weeks during the summer.

Additional information Koniag Incorporated is 1 of 13 Alaska Native Regional Corporations created under the Alaska Native Claims Settlement Act of 1971.

Number awarded 1 each year.

Deadline January of each year.

[323]
KONIAG EDUCATION FOUNDATION ACADEMIC SCHOLARSHIPS

Koniag Incorporated
Attn: Koniag Education Foundation
4241 B Street, Suite 303B
Anchorage, AK 99503
(907) 562-9093   Toll Free: (888) 562-9093
Fax: (907) 562-9023
E-mail: scholarships@koniageducation.org
Web: www.koniageducation.org/scholarships

Summary To provide financial assistance to Alaska Natives who are Koniag Incorporated shareholders or descendants and plan to attend college or graduate school in any state.

Eligibility This program is open to high school seniors, high school and GED graduates, college students, and graduate students who are Alaska Native shareholders of Koniag Incorporated or descendants of those original enrollees. Applicants must have a GPA of 3.0 or higher and be enrolled or planning to enroll at a college or university in any state. Along with their application, they must submit an essay of 300 to 600 words in the form of a thank you letter about their background, educational goals, work history, and/or achievements. Financial need is not considered in the selection process.

Financial data Stipends range up to $2,500 per year. Funds are sent directly to the recipient's school and may be used for tuition, books, supplies, room, board, and transportation.

Duration 1 year; may be renewed, provided recipients maintain a GPA of 3.0 or higher.

Additional information Koniag Incorporated is 1 of 13 Alaska Native Regional Corporations created under the Alaska Native Claims Settlement Act of 1971.

Number awarded Varies each year.

Deadline March of each year for summer term; May of each year for fall or spring term.

[324]
KONIAG EDUCATION FOUNDATION BASIC SCHOLARSHIPS

Koniag Incorporated
Attn: Koniag Education Foundation
4241 B Street, Suite 303B
Anchorage, AK 99503
(907) 562-9093   Toll Free: (888) 562-9093
Fax: (907) 562-9023
E-mail: scholarships@koniageducation.org
Web: www.koniageducation.org/scholarships

Summary To provide financial assistance to Alaska Natives who are Koniag Incorporated shareholders or descendants and plan to attend college in any state.

Eligibility This program is open to high school seniors, high school and GED graduates, and college students who are Alaska Native shareholders of Koniag Incorporated or descendants of those original enrollees. Applicants must have a GPA of 2.0 to 2.9 and be enrolled or planning to enroll at an accredited college or university in any state. Along with their application, they must submit an essay of 300 to 600 words in the form of a thank you letter about their background, educational goals, work history, and/or achievements. Financial need is not considered in the selection process.

Financial data Stipends range up to $1,000. Funds are sent directly to the recipient's school and may be used for tuition, books, supplies, room, board, and transportation.

Duration 1 year; may be renewed, provided recipients maintain a GPA of 2.0 or higher.

Additional information Koniag Incorporated is 1 of 13 Alaska Native Regional Corporations created under the Alaska Native Claims Settlement Act of 1971.

Number awarded Varies each year.

Deadline March of each year for summer term; May of each year for fall or spring term.

[325]
KONIAG EDUCATION FOUNDATION VOCATIONAL SCHOLARSHIPS

Koniag Incorporated
Attn: Koniag Education Foundation
4241 B Street, Suite 303B
Anchorage, AK 99503
(907) 562-9093   Toll Free: (888) 562-9093
Fax: (907) 562-9023
E-mail: scholarships@koniageducation.org
Web: www.koniageducation.org/scholarships

Summary To provide financial assistance to Alaska Natives who are Koniag Incorporated shareholders or descendants and interested in a program of vocational education.

Eligibility This program is open to high school seniors, high school graduates, and currently-enrolled vocational school students who are Alaska Native shareholders of Koniag Incorporated or descendants of those original enrollees. Applicants must have a GPA of 2.0 or higher and be enrolled or planning to enroll in a state-accredited or municipally-recognized vocational school. They must supply proof of eligibility; a demonstration of how the training will assist them in gaining employment, job security, and/or advancement; and documentation of financial need. Along with their application, they must submit an essay of 300 to 600 words in the form of a thank you letter about their background, educational goals, work history, and/or achievements. Financial need is not considered in the selection process.

Financial data Stipends range up to $2,500. Funds are sent directly to the recipient's school and may be used for tuition, books, supplies, room, board, and transportation.

Duration At least 6 weeks; may be renewed, provided the recipient maintains a GPA of 2.0 or higher.

Additional information Koniag Incorporated is 1 of 13 Alaska Native Regional Corporations created under the Alaska Native Claims Settlement Act of 1971.

Number awarded Varies each year.

Deadline March of each year for summer term; May of each year for fall or spring term.

[326]
KONIAG INCORPORATED EXXONMOBIL SCHOLARSHIP

Koniag Incorporated
Attn: Koniag Education Foundation
4241 B Street, Suite 303B
Anchorage, AK 99503
(907) 562-9093   Toll Free: (888) 562-9093
Fax: (907) 562-9023
E-mail: scholarships@koniageducation.org
Web: www.koniageducation.org/scholarships

Summary To provide financial assistance to Alaska Natives who are Koniag Incorporated shareholders or descendants and working on an undergraduate or graduate degree in science or mathematics related to the oil and gas industry.

Eligibility This program is open to undergraduate and graduate students who are Alaska Native shareholders of Koniag Incorporated or descendants of those original enrollees. Applicants must have a GPA of 3.0 or higher and be working full time on a degree in a field of science or mathematics related to the oil and gas industry. Along with their application, they must submit an essay of 300 to 600 words in the form of a thank you letter about their background, educational goals, work history, and/or achievements. Financial need is not considered in the selection process.

Financial data The stipend is $10,000 per year. Funds are sent directly to the recipient's school and may be used for tuition, books, supplies, room, board, and transportation.

Duration 1 year; may be renewed.

Additional information Koniag Incorporated is 1 of 13 Alaska Native Regional Corporations created under the Alaska Native Claims Settlement Act of 1971. This program is supported by ExxonMobil.

Number awarded 1 each year.

Deadline August of each year.

[327]
KURT KLUMB BUSINESS SCHOLARSHIP

Indian Summer, Inc.
10809 West Lincoln Avenue, Suite 101
West Allis, WI 53227
(414) 774-7119   Fax: (414) 774-6810
E-mail: indiansummer@wi.rr.com
Web: www.indiansummer.org/education/scholarships.aspx

Summary To provide financial assistance to American Indians from Wisconsin who are studying or planning to study business at a college in any state.

Eligibility This program is open to Wisconsin residents who are American Indians by tribal enrollment or descendancy (having 1 or more ancestors who are tribally enrolled). Applicants must be accepted or in good standing at an institution of higher education in any state and majoring in business. They must submit a 1-page statement describing their educational goals, the reasons they feel they should receive the scholarship, their community service, and any special needs. Preference is given to applicants who have provided service to the Indian community and have not previously received a scholarship.

Financial data The stipend is $1,000.

Duration 1 year.

Additional information This program is offered in cooperation with American Indian Student Services at the University of Wisconsin at Milwaukee.

Number awarded 1 each year.

Deadline July of each year.

[328]
LAC COURTE OREILLES ADULT VOCATIONAL TRAINING GRANTS

Lac Courte Oreilles Band of Ojibwe
Attn: Consolidated Education and Native Employment
  Works Program
13394 West Trepania Road
Hayward, WI 54843
(715) 634-8934, ext. 281   Toll Free: (800) 633-6093
Fax: (715) 634-4797
Web: www.lco-nsn.gov/entities.htm

Summary To provide financial assistance for vocational or technical training to tribal members of the Lac Courte Oreilles Band of Ojibwe.

Eligibility This program is open to enrolled members of the Lac Courte Oreilles who are working on or planning to work on a diploma, certificate, or associate degree. Applicants must be able to document financial need.

Financial data The maximum stipend is $1,500 per year.

Duration Up to 24 months at a vocational technical training institution or 36 months at a school of nursing, provided the recipient maintains a GPA of 2.0 or higher.

Number awarded Varies each year.

Deadline June of each year for fall term; October of each year for spring term.

[329]
LAC COURTE OREILLES HIGHER EDUCATION GRANTS

Lac Courte Oreilles Band of Ojibwe
Attn: Consolidated Education and Native Employment
  Works Program
13394 West Trepania Road
Hayward, WI 54843
(715) 634-8934, ext. 281   Toll Free: (800) 633-6093
Fax: (715) 634-4797
Web: www.lco-nsn.gov/entities.htm

Summary To provide financial assistance for college or graduate school to tribal members of the Lac Courte Oreilles Band of Ojibwe.

Eligibility This program is open to enrolled members of the Lac Courte Oreilles who are working on or planning to work on an undergraduate or graduate degree. Applicants must be able to document financial need.

Financial data The maximum stipend is $1,500 per year for undergraduates or $3,000 per year for graduate students.

Duration Up to 10 semesters for undergraduate students or up to 4 semesters for graduate students, provided the recipient maintains a GPA of 2.0 or higher as an undergraduate or 3.0 or higher as a graduate student.

Number awarded Varies each year.

Deadline June of each year for fall term; October of each year for spring term.

[330]
LAC DU FLAMBEAU ADULT VOCATIONAL TRAINING PROGRAM

Lac du Flambeau Band of Lake Superior Chippewa
  Indians
Attn: Education Coordinator
562 Peace Pipe Road
P.O. Box 189
Lac du Flambeau, WI 54538
(715) 588-7925   Fax: (715) 588-3903
E-mail: jbldfedu@nnex.net
Web: www.lacduflambeaunation.com/depts/Education.html

Summary To provide financial assistance for vocational or technical training to tribal members of the Lac du Flambeau Band of Lake Superior Chippewa Indians.

Eligibility This program is open to enrolled Lac du Flambeau members who are working on or planning to work on a diploma, certificate, or associate degree. Applicants must be able to demonstrate financial need.

Financial data The maximum stipend is $2,500 per year.

Duration Up to 24 months at a vocational technical training institution or 36 months at a school of nursing, provided the recipient maintains a GPA of 2.0 or higher.

Number awarded Varies each year.

Deadline July of each year.

[331]
LAC DU FLAMBEAU UNDERGRADUATE ASSISTANCE PROGRAM

Lac du Flambeau Band of Lake Superior Chippewa
  Indians
Attn: Education Coordinator
562 Peace Pipe Road
P.O. Box 189
Lac du Flambeau, WI 54538
(715) 588-7925   Fax: (715) 588-3903
E-mail: jbldfedu@nnex.net
Web: www.lacduflambeaunation.com/depts/Education.html

Summary To provide financial assistance to tribal members of the Lac du Flambeau Band of Lake Superior Chippewa Indians who are interested in working on an undergraduate degree.

Eligibility This program is open to enrolled Lac du Flambeau members who are working on or planning to work full or part time on an undergraduate degree. Applicants must be able to demonstrate financial need.

Financial data The maximum stipend is $3,000 per year.

Duration 1 year; may be renewed up to 4 additional years, provided the recipient maintains a GPA of 2.0 or higher.

Number awarded Varies each year.

Deadline July of each year.

[332]
LAGRANT FOUNDATION UNDERGRADUATE SCHOLARSHIPS

Lagrant Foundation
Attn: Programs Manager
626 Wilshire Boulevard, Suite 700
Los Angeles, CA 90071-2920
(323) 469-8680   Fax: (323) 469-8683
E-mail: erickaavila@lagrant.com
Web: www.lagrantfoundation.org/site/?page_id=3

Summary To provide financial assistance to Native American and other minority college students who are interested in majoring in advertising, public relations, or marketing.

Eligibility This program is open to African Americans, Asian Pacific Americans, Hispanics/Latinos, and Native Americans/Alaska Natives who are full-time students at a 4-year accredited institution. Applicants must have a GPA of 2.75 or higher and be either majoring in advertising, marketing, or public relations or minoring in communications with plans to prepare for a career in advertising, marketing, or public relations. Along with their application, they must submit 1) a 1- to 2-page essay outlining their career goals; what steps they will take to increase ethnic representation in the fields of advertising, marketing, and public relations; and the role of an advertising, marketing, or public relations practitioner; 2) a paragraph describing the college and/or community activities in which they are involved; 3) a brief paragraph describing any honors and awards they have received; 4) a letter of reference; 5) a resume; and 6) an official transcript. U.S. citizenship or permanent resident status is required.

Financial data The stipend is $5,000.

Duration 1 year.

Number awarded 10 each year.

Deadline February of each year.

[333]
LANDMARK SCHOLARS PROGRAM

Landmark Media Enterprises LLC
c/o Ann Morris, Managing Editor
Greensboro News & Record
200 East Market Street
Greensboro, NC 27401
(540) 981-3211   Toll Free: (800) 346-1234
E-mail: amorris@news-record.com
Web: company.news-record.com/intern.htm

Summary To provide work experience and financial aid to Native American and other minority undergraduates who are interested in preparing for a career in journalism.

Eligibility This program is open to minority (Asian, Hispanic, African American, Native American) college sophomores, preferably those with ties to the mid-Atlantic states (Delaware, Maryland, North Carolina, South Carolina, Virginia, and Washington, D.C.). Applicants must be full-time students with a GPA of 2.5 or higher in a 4-year degree program. They must be interested in preparing for a career in print journalism and participating in an internship in news, features, sports, copy editing, photography, or graphics/illustration. U.S. citizenship or permanent resident status is required. Selection is based on grades, work samples, recommendations, targeted selection interview skills, and financial need.

Financial data The stipend is $5,000 per year. During the summers following their sophomore and junior years, recipients are provided with paid internships. Following graduation, they are offered a 1-year internship with full benefits and the possibility of continued employment.

Duration 2 years (the junior and senior years of college).

Additional information The internships are offered at the *News & Record* in Greensboro, North Carolina, the *Virginian-Pilot* in Norfolk, Virginia, or the *Roanoke Times* in Roanoke, Virginia.

Number awarded 1 or more each year.

Deadline December of each year.

[334]
LARRY MATFAY SCHOLARSHIP

Koniag Incorporated
Attn: Koniag Education Foundation
4241 B Street, Suite 303B
Anchorage, AK 99503
(907) 562-9093   Toll Free: (888) 562-9093
Fax: (907) 562-9023
E-mail: scholarships@koniageducation.org
Web: www.koniageducation.org/scholarships

Summary To provide financial assistance to Alaska Natives who are Koniag Incorporated shareholders or descendants and enrolled in undergraduate or graduate study in a field related to Alutiiq culture.

Eligibility This program is open to college juniors, seniors, and graduate students who are Alaska Native shareholders of Koniag Incorporated or descendants of those original enrollees. Applicants must have a GPA of 2.5 or higher and be working full time on a degree in anthropology, history, Alaska Native or American Indian studies, or another discipline that involves research and learning about Alutiiq culture. Along with their application, they must submit an essay of 300 to 600 words in the form of a thank you letter about their background, educational goals, work history, and/or achievements. Financial need is not considered in the selection process.

Financial data The stipend is $1,000 per year. Funds are sent directly to the recipient's school and may be used for tuition, books, supplies, room, board, and transportation.

Duration 1 year; may be renewed.

Additional information Koniag Incorporated is 1 of 13 Alaska Native Regional Corporations created under the Alaska Native Claims Settlement Act of 1971.

Number awarded 1 each year.

Deadline August of each year.

[335]
LARRY W. MCCORMICK COMMUNICATIONS SCHOLARSHIP FOR UNDERREPRESENTED STUDENTS

The Lullaby Guild, Inc.
Attn: Scholarship Committee
6709 La Tijera, Suite 116
Los Angeles, CA 90045
(310) 335-5655   E-mail: mail@lullabyguild.org
Web: www.lullabyguild.org

Summary To provide financial assistance to Native American and other underrepresented upper-division students who are working on a degree in a field related to mass communications.

Eligibility This program is open to underrepresented (e.g., African American, Hispanic American, Native American, Alaskan American, Pacific Islander, Asian) students entering their junior or senior year at an accredited college or university. Applicants must be working on a degree in a field related to mass communications, including audiovisual and electronic and print journalism. Along with their application, they must submit a personal statement regarding their volunteer services, official transcripts, 3 letters of recommendation, 3 samples of their journalistic work, and a 500-word personal statement about their interest in journalism or mass communication. Selection is based on academic achievement, letters of recommendation, journalistic experience and/or evidence of journalistic talent, clarity of purpose in plans and goals for a future in journalism or mass communications, and involvement in volunteer community service.

Financial data The stipend is $2,500.

Duration 1 year.

Number awarded 1 each year.

Deadline February of each year.

[336]
LAURENCE R. FOSTER MEMORIAL UNDERGRADUATE SCHOLARSHIPS

Oregon Student Assistance Commission
Attn: Grants and Scholarships Division
1500 Valley River Drive, Suite 100
Eugene, OR 97401-2146
(541) 687-7395   Toll Free: (800) 452-8807, ext. 7395
Fax: (541) 687-7414   TDD: (800) 735-2900
E-mail: awardinfo@osac.state.or.us
Web: www.osac.state.or.us/osac_programs.html

Summary To provide financial assistance to minority and other undergraduate students from Oregon who are interested in enrolling at a school in any state to prepare for a public health career.

Eligibility This program is open to residents of Oregon who are enrolled at least half time at a 4-year college or university in any state to prepare for a career in public health (not private practice). Applicants must be entering the junior or senior year of a health program, including nursing, medical technology, and physician assistant. Preference is given to applicants from diverse environments. Along with their application, they must submit brief essays on 1) what public health means to them; 2) the public health aspect they intend to practice and the health and population issues impacted by that aspect; and 3) their experience living or working in diverse environments.

Financial data Stipend amounts vary; recently, they were at least $4,167.

Duration 1 year.

Additional information This program is administered by the Oregon Student Assistance Commission (OSAC) with funds provided by the Oregon Community Foundation.

Number awarded Varies each year; recently, 6 undergraduate and graduate scholarships were awarded.

Deadline February of each year.

[337]
LAWRENCE MATSON MEMORIAL ENDOWMENT FUND SCHOLARSHIPS

Cook Inlet Region, Inc.
Attn: The CIRI Foundation
3600 San Jeronimo Drive, Suite 256
Anchorage, AK 99508-2870
(907) 793-3575   Toll Free: (800) 764-3382
Fax: (907) 793-3585   E-mail: tcf@thecirifoundation.org
Web: www.thecirifoundation.org/designated.htm

Summary To provide financial assistance for undergraduate or graduate studies in selected liberal arts to Alaska Natives who are original enrollees to Cook Inlet Region, Inc. (CIRI) and their lineal descendants.

Eligibility This program is open to Alaska Native enrollees to CIRI under the Alaska Native Claims Settlement Act (ANCSA) of 1971 and their lineal descendants. There are no Alaska residency requirements or age limitations. Applicants must be accepted or enrolled full time in a 4-year undergraduate or a graduate degree program in the following liberal arts fields: language, education, social sciences, arts, communications, or law. They must have a GPA of 2.5 or higher. Along with their application, they must submit a 500-word statement on their educational and career goals and how they are contributing, or planning to contribute, to a positive Alaska Native community. Selection is based on that statement, academic achievement, rigor of course work or degree program, student financial contribution, financial need, grade level, previous work performance, community service, and relationship of degree program to career goals.

Financial data The stipend is $10,000 per year, $8,000 per year, or $2,500 per semester, depending on GPA.

Duration 1 semester or 1 year.

Additional information This fund was established in 1989.

Number awarded Varies each year; recently, 3 of these scholarships were awarded: 1 at $10,000 per year, 1 at $8,000 per year, and 1 at $2,500 per semester.

Deadline May of each year for annual scholarships; May or November of each year for semester scholarships.

[338]
LEADING WITH DILIGENCE SCHOLARSHIP

Choctaw Nation
Attn: Scholarship Advisement Program
16th and Locust
P.O. Box 1210
Durant, OK 74702-1210
(580) 924-8280
Toll Free: (800) 522-6170, ext. 2523 (within OK)
Fax: (580) 924-1267
E-mail: scholarshipadvisement@choctawnation.com
Web: www.choctawnation-sap.com/cnoscholarship.shtml

Summary To provide financial assistance to male Choctaw Indian high school seniors who plan to attend college to prepare for a career in public service.

Eligibility This program is open to male Choctaw students who are enrolled in the Scholarship Advisement Program (SAP). Applicants must be planning to enter a college or university in any state to prepare for a career in a field of public service, especially fields dealing with national security or diplomacy (such as the military). Preference is given to males entering their freshman year of college. They must have an ACT score of 25 or higher.

Financial data The stipend is $1,000.

Duration 1 year; nonrenewable.

Number awarded 1 each year.

Deadline September of each year.

[339]
LEECH LAKE POSTSECONDARY GRANT PROGRAM

Leech Lake Band of Ojibwe
Attn: Education Division
6530 US Highway 2 N.W.
Cass Lake, MN 56633
(218) 335-8253   Toll Free: (866) 638-7738
Fax: (218) 335-8339
Web: www.llojibwe.com/edu/postsecondary.html

Summary To provide financial assistance to Minnesota Chippewa Tribal members who are interested in undergraduate or graduate education at a school in any state.

Eligibility This program is open to enrolled members of the Leech Lake Band of Ojibwe who have been residents of Minnesota for at least 1 year. Applicants may be high school seniors or graduates, current undergraduates, short-term training students, or full- or part-time graduate students. They must be interested in attending a postsecondary institution in any state. Financial need is considered in the selection process.

Financial data Stipends range up to $3,000 per year, depending on need.

Duration 1 year; may be renewed.

Additional information Applicants for this program must also apply for the Minnesota Indian Scholarship Program, financial aid administered by their institution, and any other aid for which they may be eligible (e.g., work-study, Social Security, veteran's benefits).

Number awarded Varies each year.

Deadline For vocational school students, at least 8 weeks before school starts; for college or university students, June of each year.

[340]
LEONARD M. PERRYMAN COMMUNICATIONS SCHOLARSHIP FOR ETHNIC MINORITY STUDENTS

United Methodist Communications
Attn: Communications Resourcing Team
810 12th Avenue South
P.O. Box 320
Nashville, TN 37202-0320
(615) 742-5481   Toll Free: (888) CRT-4UMC
Fax: (615) 742-5485   E-mail: scholarships@umcom.org
Web: crt.umc.org/interior.asp?ptid=44&mid=10270

Summary To provide financial assistance to Native American and other minority United Methodist college students who are interested in careers in religious communications.

Eligibility This program is open to United Methodist ethnic minority students enrolled in accredited institutions of higher education as juniors or seniors. Applicants must be interested in preparing for a career in religious communications. For the

purposes of this program, "communications" is meant to cover audiovisual, electronic, and print journalism. Selection is based on Christian commitment and involvement in the life of the United Methodist church, academic achievement, journalistic experience, clarity of purpose, and professional potential as a religion communicator.

Financial data The stipend is $2,500 per year.

Duration 1 year.

Additional information The scholarship may be used at any accredited institution of higher education.

Number awarded 1 each year.

Deadline March of each year.

[341]
LIFE-TIME SCHOLARSHIPS

Chickasaw Nation
Attn: Department of Education Services
300 Rosedale Road
Ada, OK 74820
(580) 421-7711   Fax: (580) 436-3733
E-mail: education.services@chickasaw.net
Web: www.chickasaweducationservices.com/index_90.htm

Summary To provide funding to members of the Chickasaw Nation who are working on an undergraduate or graduate degree at a school in any state.

Eligibility This program is open to members of the Chickasaw Nation who have completed at least 24 hours of full-time college credit for an undergraduate, graduate, or doctoral degree at an accredited college or university in any state. Applicants must have a GPA of 3.0 or higher. Along with their application, they must submit a 2- to 3-page essay on their past accomplishments, future goals, tribal involvement, and community involvement. Finalists are interviewed.

Financial data The maximum stipend is $15,000 per semester for fall and spring semesters or $5,000 per term for summer school. Recipients must agree to provide service to the Chickasaw Nation of 1 year for each 2 years of support received. The Chickasaw Nation is not obliged to provide employment to a scholarship recipient; if it declines to do so, the service requirement is waived.

Duration 1 year; may be renewed provided the recipient maintains a GPA of 3.0 or higher.

Number awarded 5 each year.

Deadline June of each year.

[342]
LIGHTHORSE SCHOLARSHIP

Chickasaw Foundation
110 West 12th Street
P.O. Box 1726
Ada, OK 74821-1726
(580) 421-9030   Fax: (580) 421-9031
E-mail: ChickasawFoundation@chickasaw.net
Web: www.chickasawfoundation.org/index_20.htm

Summary To provide financial assistance to members of the Chickasaw Nation who are working on an undergraduate degree in a field related to law enforcement.

Eligibility This program is open to Chickasaw students who are currently enrolled full time at a 2- or 4-year college or university and working on an undergraduate degree in criminal justice, police science, or another field related to law enforcement. Applicants must have a GPA of 3.0 or higher. Along with their application, they must submit high school or college transcripts, 2 letters of recommendation, a copy of their Chickasaw Nation citizenship card, and a 1-page essay on their long-term goals and plans for achieving them. Financial need is not considered in the selection process.

Financial data The stipend is $1,000.

Duration 1 year.

Number awarded 1 each year.

Deadline August of each year.

[343]
LIKO A'E SCHOLARSHIPS

Liko A'e Native Hawaiian Scholarship Program
c/o UH Maui College
310 Ka'ahumanu Avenue
Kahului, HI 96732-1617
(808) 984-3553   Fax: (808) 984-3562
E-mail: maliad@hawaii.edu
Web: www.likoae.org/scholarship_info.asp

Summary To provide financial assistance to Native Hawaiian students who are interested in working on an undergraduate or graduate degree at a college in Hawaii or on the mainland.

Eligibility This program is open to U.S. citizens who are descendants of the aboriginal inhabitants of the Hawaiian Islands prior to 1778. Applicants must be enrolled or accepted as full- or part-time students in an accredited 2- or 4-year degree-granting institution of higher education in Hawaii or on the mainland. Undergraduates must have a GPA of 2.0 or higher and graduate students must have a GPA of 3.0 or higher. Selection is based on merit (as judged by GPA and responses to essay questions) and financial need.

Financial data A stipend is awarded (amount not specified). Child care assistance is also provided.

Duration 1 year.

Additional information This program was established in 2003 by a grant from the U.S. Department of Education and is administered by UH Maui College.

Number awarded Varies each year.

Deadline Deadlines are in April, July, October, or January.

[344]
LILLE HOPE MCGARVEY SCHOLARSHIP AWARD

The Aleut Corporation
Attn: Aleut Foundation
703 West Tudor Road, Suite 102
Anchorage, AK 99503-6650
(907) 646-1929   Toll Free: (800) 232-4882
Fax: (907) 646-1949   E-mail: taf@thealeutfoundation.org
Web: www.thealeutfoundation.org/ScholarshipGuide.aspx

Summary To provide financial assistance to Native Alaskans who are shareholders of The Aleut Corporation or their descendants and working on a degree in the medical field at a school in any state.

Eligibility This program is open to Native Alaskans who are original enrollees or descendants of original enrollees of The Aleut Corporation (TAC). Applicants must have completed at least 1 year of a bachelor's, 2- or 4-year vocational, or master's degree in a medical field at a school in any state. They must be enrolled full time and have a GPA of 3.0 or

higher. Along with their application, they must include a letter of intent, up to 500 words in length, that describes their educational goals and objectives and their expected graduation date.

Financial data A stipend is awarded (amount not specified).

Duration 1 year.

Additional information The Aleut Corporation is 1 of 13 Alaska Native Regional Corporations created under the Alaska Native Claims Settlement Act of 1971.

Number awarded 1 each year.

Deadline June of each year.

[345]
LILLIAN FOWLER MEMORIAL SCHOLARSHIP

Chickasaw Foundation
110 West 12th Street
P.O. Box 1726
Ada, OK 74821-1726
(580) 421-9030   Fax: (580) 421-9031
E-mail: ChickasawFoundation@chickasaw.net
Web: www.chickasawfoundation.org/index_20.htm

Summary To provide financial assistance to members of the Chickasaw Nation who are working on an undergraduate or graduate degree in health care or social work.

Eligibility This program is open to Chickasaw students who are currently working full time on an undergraduate or graduate degree in social work or a health care-related field. Applicants must have a GPA of 3.0 or higher. Along with their application, they must submit high school or college transcripts, 2 letters of recommendation, a copy of their Chickasaw Nation citizenship card, and a 1-page essay on their long-term goals and plans for achieving them. Financial need is not considered in the selection process.

Financial data The stipend is $1,000.

Duration 1 year.

Number awarded 1 each year.

Deadline August of each year.

[346]
LIN MEDIA MINORITY SCHOLARSHIP AND TRAINING PROGRAM

LIN Television Corporation
Attn: Vice President, Human Resources
One West Exchange Street, Suite 5A
Providence, RI 02903-1064
(401) 454-2880   Fax: (401) 454-6990
Web: www.linmedia.com/contact-us/careers.php

Summary To provide funding to Native Americans and other minority undergraduates interested in earning a degree in a field related to broadcast journalism and working at a station owned by LIN Television Corporation.

Eligibility This program is open to U.S. citizens of non-white origin who are enrolled as a sophomore or higher at a college or university. Applicants must have a declared major in broadcast journalism, mass communication, television production, or marketing and a GPA of 3.0 or higher. Along with their application, they must submit a list of organizations and activities in which they have held leadership positions, 3 references, a 50-word description of their career goals, a list of personal achievements and honors, and a 500-word essay about themselves. Financial need is not considered in the selection process.

Financial data The program pays for tuition and fees, books, and room and board, to a maximum of $20,000 per year. Recipients must sign an employment agreement that guarantees them part-time employment as an intern during school and a 2-year regular position at a television station owned by LIN Television Corporation following graduation. If they fail to honor the employment agreement, they must repay all scholarship funds received.

Duration 2 years.

Additional information LIN Television Corporation owns 28 television stations in 17 media markets in the United States. Recipients of these scholarships must work at a station selected by LIN management.

Number awarded 1 or more each year.

Deadline March of each year.

[347]
LINCOLN CULTURAL DIVERSITY SCHOLARSHIP

American Advertising Federation-Lincoln
Attn: Scholarship Chair
P.O. Box 80093
Lincoln, NE 68501-0093
Web: www.aaflincoln.org/resources/scholarships.htm

Summary To provide financial assistance to Native American and other minority residents of any state preparing for a career in a field related to advertising at a college in Nebraska.

Eligibility This program is open to minority residents of any state currently enrolled full time at an accredited college or university in Nebraska. Applicants must be working on a degree in advertising, marketing, public relations, communications, or commercial art. Along with their application, they must submit an essay describing their interest in receiving this scholarship and why they should be selected. They may also submit up to 3 samples of their work, although this is not required. Finalists are interviewed. Selection is based on ability, commitment and enthusiasm for the advertising profession, academic performance, participation in extracurricular activities, and career goals. U.S. citizenship is required.

Financial data The stipend is $1,000. Awards are provided in the form of a credit at the recipient's institution.

Duration 1 year.

Number awarded 1 each year.

Deadline October of each year.

[348]
LITTLE RIVER BAND OF OTTAWA INDIANS HIGHER EDUCATION SCHOLARSHIP

Little River Band of Ottawa Indians
Attn: Education Department
375 River Street
Manistee, MI 49660
(231) 723-8288   Toll Free: (888) 723-8288
Fax: (231) 398-2961   E-mail: vparsons@lrboi.com
Web: www.lrboi-nsn.gov

Summary To provide financial assistance to members of the Little River Band of Ottawa Indians who are interested in attending college or graduate school.

Eligibility This program is open to tribal citizens of the Little River Band of Ottawa Indians who are attending or planning to attend an accredited college or university. Applicants must be interested in working on an associate, bachelor's, master's, or Ph.D. degree. They must have applied for all other available financial aid and still show unmet need. In the selection process, priority is given first to residents of Michigan, second to students attending schools in Michigan, and third to students attending schools in other states.

Financial data The stipend is $3,500 per semester ($7,000 per year). Recipients are also eligible to apply for book stipends of $200 to $500 (depending on the number of credits in which they are enrolled). Funds are paid to the recipient's institution.

Duration 1 year; may be renewed, provided the recipient maintains a GPA of 2.0 or higher.

Number awarded Varies each year.

Deadline Deadline not specified.

[349]
LITTLE RIVER BAND OF OTTAWA INDIANS VOCATIONAL EDUCATION ASSISTANCE PROGRAM

Little River Band of Ottawa Indians
Attn: Education Department
375 River Street
Manistee, MI 49660
(231) 723-8288   Toll Free: (888) 723-8288
Fax: (231) 398-2961   E-mail: vparsons@lrboi.com
Web: www.lrboi-nsn.gov

Summary To provide financial assistance to members of the Little River Band of Ottawa Indians who are interested in attending vocational school.

Eligibility This program is open to tribal citizens of the Little River Band of Ottawa Indians who are at least 18 years of age. Applicants must be interested in attending an accredited vocational/technical program for training to obtain reasonable and satisfactory employment. They must have applied for all other available financial aid and still show unmet need. In the selection process, priority is given first to residents of Michigan, second to students attending schools in Michigan, and third to students attending schools in other states.

Financial data The stipend is $4,000 per term. Funds are paid to the recipient's institution.

Duration Recipients are entitled to a maximum of 24 months of support (or 36 months for nursing programs).

Number awarded Varies each year.

Deadline Deadline not specified.

[350]
LORI PIESTEWA VOCATIONAL/TECHNICAL OR 4-YEAR SCHOLARSHIP

Indian Summer, Inc.
10809 West Lincoln Avenue, Suite 101
West Allis, WI 53227
(414) 774-7119   Fax: (414) 774-6810
E-mail: indiansummer@wi.rr.com
Web: www.indiansummer.org/education/scholarships.aspx

Summary To provide financial assistance to American Indians from Wisconsin who are attending or planning to attend a vocational/technical school or 4-year college or university in any state.

Eligibility This program is open to Wisconsin residents who are American Indians by tribal enrollment or descendancy (having 1 or more ancestors who are tribally enrolled). Applicants must be accepted or in good standing at a 4-year college or university or vocational/technical school in any state. They must submit a 1-page statement describing their educational goals, the reasons they feel they should receive the scholarship, their community service, and any special needs. Preference is given to applicants who have provided service to the Indian community and have not previously received a scholarship.

Financial data The stipend is $1,000.

Duration 1 year.

Additional information This program is offered in cooperation with American Indian Student Services at the University of Wisconsin at Milwaukee.

Number awarded 1 each year.

Deadline July of each year.

[351]
LOU MOLLER SCHOLARSHIP FOR ACHIEVEMENT

American Indian Chamber of Commerce of Texas
11245 Indian Trail, Second Floor
Dallas, TX 75229
(972) 241-6450   Fax: (972) 241-6454
E-mail: tmarshall@aicct.com
Web: www.aicct.com

Summary To provide financial assistance to American Indians from Texas who are interested in attending college in any state.

Eligibility This program is open to residents of Texas who are American Indians between 18 and 35 years of age. Applicants must be enrolled or planning to enroll full time at an accredited institution of higher education in any state. They must have a GPA of 2.0 or higher in their previous course work. Along with their application, they must submit a 250-word essay on how their degree will help the American Indian community.

Financial data A stipend is awarded (amount not specified).

Duration 1 year.

Additional information Funding for this program is provided by RichHeape Films.

Number awarded 1 or more each year.

Deadline April of each year for the academic year; December of each year for spring semester.

[352]
LOUIE LEFLORE/GRANT FOREMAN SCHOLARSHIP

Choctaw Nation
Attn: Scholarship Advisement Program
16th and Locust
P.O. Box 1210
Durant, OK 74702-1210
(580) 924-8280
Toll Free: (800) 522-6170, ext. 2523 (within OK)
Fax: (580) 920-3122
E-mail: scholarshipadvisement@choctawnation.com
Web: www.choctawnation-sap.com/cnoscholarship.shtml

Summary To provide financial assistance to members of the Five Civilized Tribes who live in Oklahoma and plan to work on a health-related degree at a school in the state.

Eligibility This program is open to members of the Seminole Nation, Chickasaw Nation, Cherokee Nation, Creek Nation, and Choctaw Nation who reside within the jurisdictional boundaries of their tribe in Oklahoma. Applicants must have been accepted into an accredited program in nursing, pre-health professions, or health professions at a college or university in Oklahoma.

Financial data A stipend is awarded (amount not specified).

Duration 1 year; may be renewed.

Number awarded 1 each year.

Deadline April of each year.

[353]
LOUIS B. RUSSELL, JR. MEMORIAL SCHOLARSHIP

Indiana State Teachers Association
Attn: Scholarships
150 West Market Street, Suite 900
Indianapolis, IN 46204-2875
(317) 263-3400   Toll Free: (800) 382-4037
Fax: (317) 655-3700   E-mail: mshoup@ista-in.org
Web: www.ista-in.org/dynamic.aspx?id=1038

Summary To provide financial assistance to Native American and other minority high school seniors in Indiana who are interested in attending vocational school in any state.

Eligibility This program is open to ethnic minority high school seniors in Indiana who are interested in continuing their education in the area of industrial arts, vocational education, or technical preparation at an accredited postsecondary institution in any state. Selection is based on academic achievement, leadership ability as expressed through co-curricular activities and community involvement, recommendations, and a 300-word essay on their educational goals and how they plan to use this scholarship.

Financial data The stipend is $1,000.

Duration 1 year; may be renewed for 1 additional year, provided the recipient maintains a GPA of "C+" or higher.

Number awarded 1 each year.

Deadline February of each year.

[354]
LTK SCHOLARSHIP

Conference of Minority Transportation Officials
Attn: National Scholarship Program
818 18th Street, N.W., Suite 850
Washington, DC 20006
(202) 530-0551   Fax: (202) 530-0617
Web: www.comto.org/news-youth.php

Summary To provide financial assistance to Native American and other minority upper-division and graduate students in engineering or another field related to transportation.

Eligibility This program is open to full-time minority juniors, seniors, and graduate students in engineering of other technical transportation-related disciplines. Applicants must have a GPA of 3.0 or higher. Along with their application, they must submit a cover letter with a 500-word statement of career goals. Financial need is not considered in the selection process. U.S. citizenship is required.

Financial data The stipend is $6,000. Funds are paid directly to the recipient's college or university.

Duration 1 year.

Additional information The Conference of Minority Transportation Officials (COMTO) was established in 1971 to promote, strengthen, and expand the roles of minorities in all aspects of transportation. This program is sponsored by LTK Engineering Services. Recipients are required to become members of COMTO if they are not already members and attend the COMTO National Scholarship Luncheon.

Number awarded 1 or more each year.

Deadline April of each year.

[355]
MABEL SMITH MEMORIAL SCHOLARSHIP

Wisconsin Women of Color Network, Inc.
Attn: MSMS Committee
P.O. Box 2337
Madison, WI 53701-2337
E-mail: contact@womenofcolornetwork-wis.org
Web: www.womenofcolornetwork-wis.org/scholarship.html

Summary To provide financial assistance for vocation/technical school or community college to Native Americans and other minority residents of Wisconsin.

Eligibility This program is open to residents of Wisconsin who are high school or GED-equivalent graduating seniors planning to continue their education at a vocational/technical school or community college in any state. Applicants must be a member of 1 of the following groups: African American, Asian, American Indian, Hispanic, or biracial. They must have a GPA of 2.0 or higher and be able to demonstrate financial need. Along with their application, they must submit a 1-page essay on how this scholarship will help them accomplish their educational goal. U.S. citizenship is required.

Financial data A stipend is awarded (amount not specified).

Duration 1 year.

Additional information This program was established in 1990.

Number awarded 1 each year.

Deadline May of each year.

[356]
MAE LASSLEY/OSAGE SCHOLARSHIPS

Osage Scholarship Fund
c/o Roman Catholic Diocese of Tulsa
P.O. Box 690240
Tulsa, OK 74169-0240
(918) 294-1904   Fax: (918) 294-0920
E-mail: sarah.jameson@dioceseoftulsa.org
Web: www.osagetribe.com

Summary To provide financial assistance to Osage Indians who are Roman Catholics attending college or graduate school.

Eligibility This program is open to Roman Catholics who are attending or planning to attend a college or university as a full-time undergraduate or graduate student. Applicants must be Osage Indians on the rolls in Pawhuska, Oklahoma and have a copy of their Certificate of Indian Blood (CIB) or Osage tribal membership card. Selection is based on academic ability and financial need.

Financial data The stipend is $1,000 per year.

Duration 1 year; may be renewed if the recipient maintains full-time enrollment and a GPA of 2.5 or higher as an undergraduate or 3.0 or higher as a graduate student.

Number awarded Normally, 10 each year: 2 for students attending St. Gregory's University in Shawnee, Oklahoma as freshmen and 8 for any college or university.

Deadline April of each year.

[357]
MAGNEL LARSEN DRABEK SCHOLARSHIP

Koniag Incorporated
Attn: Koniag Education Foundation
4241 B Street, Suite 303B
Anchorage, AK 99503
(907) 562-9093   Toll Free: (888) 562-9093
Fax: (907) 562-9023
E-mail: scholarships@koniageducation.org
Web: www.koniageducation.org/scholarships

Summary To provide financial assistance to Alaska Natives who are Koniag Incorporated shareholders or descendants and working on an undergraduate or graduate degree in education, arts, or cultural studies.

Eligibility This program is open to undergraduate and graduate students who are Alaska Native shareholders of Koniag Incorporated or descendants of those original enrollees. Applicants must have a GPA of 2.0 or higher and be working full time on a degree in education, arts, or cultural studies. Along with their application, they must submit an essay of 300 to 600 words in the form of a thank you letter about their background, educational goals, work history, and/or achievements. Financial need is not considered in the selection process.

Financial data The stipend is $2,000 per year. Funds are sent directly to the recipient's school and may be used for tuition, books, supplies, room, board, and transportation.

Duration 1 year; may be renewed.

Additional information Koniag Incorporated is 1 of 13 Alaska Native Regional Corporations created under the Alaska Native Claims Settlement Act of 1971.

Number awarded 1 each year.

Deadline August of each year.

[358]

MARATHON OIL CORPORATION COLLEGE SCHOLARSHIP PROGRAM OF THE HISPANIC SCHOLARSHIP FUND

Hispanic Scholarship Fund
Attn: Selection Committee
55 Second Street, Suite 1500
San Francisco, CA 94105
(415) 808-2365   Toll Free: (877) HSF-INFO
Fax: (415) 808-2302   E-mail: scholar1@hsf.net
Web: www.hsf.net/Scholarships.aspx?id=464

Summary To provide financial assistance to Native Americans and other minority upper-division and graduate students working on a degree in a field related to the oil and gas industry.

Eligibility This program is open to U.S. citizens and permanent residents (must have a permanent resident card or a passport stamped I-551) who are of Hispanic American, African American, Asian Pacific Islander American, or American Indian/Alaskan Native heritage. Applicants must be currently enrolled full time at an accredited 4-year college or university in the United States, Puerto Rico, Guam, or the U.S. Virgin Islands with a GPA of 3.0 or higher. They must be 1) sophomores majoring in accounting, chemical engineering, civil engineering, computer engineering, computer science, electrical engineering, energy management or petroleum land management, environmental engineering, environmental health and safety, finance, geology, geophysics, geotechnical engineering, global procurement or supply chain management, information technology/management information systems, marketing, mechanical engineering, petroleum engineering, or transportation and logistics,; or 2) seniors planning to work on a master's degree in geology or geophysics. Selection is based on academic achievement, personal strengths, interest and commitment to a career in the oil and gas industry, leadership, and financial need.

Financial data The stipend is $15,000 per year.

Duration 2 years (the junior and senior undergraduate years or the first 2 years of a master's degree program).

Additional information This program is jointly sponsored by Marathon Oil Corporation and the Hispanic Scholarship Fund (HSF). Recipients may be offered a paid 8- to 10-week summer internship at various Marathon Oil Corporation locations.

Number awarded 1 or more each year.

Deadline November of each year.

[359]

MARTHA MILLER TRIBUTARY SCHOLARSHIP

Sault Tribe of Chippewa Indians
Attn: Higher Education Program-Memorial/Tributary
  Scholarships
523 Ashmun Street
Sault Ste. Marie, MI 49783
(906) 635-4944   Toll Free: (800) 793-0660
Fax: (906) 635-7785   E-mail: amatson@saulttribe.net
Web: www.saulttribe.com

Summary To provide financial assistance to members of the Sault Tribe of Chippewa Indians who are attending college in any state and working on an undergraduate or graduate degree in human services or social work.

Eligibility This program is open to enrolled members of the Sault Tribe who are enrolled full time at a 2- or 4-year college or university in any state. Applicants must be working on an undergraduate or graduate degree in human services or social work. Along with their application, they must submit an essay of 300 to 500 words on how this scholarship will help them realize their goals.

Financial data The stipend is $1,000.

Duration 1 year.

Number awarded 1 each year.

Deadline May of each year.

[360]

MARY HILL DAVIS ETHNIC/MINORITY STUDENT SCHOLARSHIP PROGRAM

Baptist General Convention of Texas
Attn: Institutional Ministries Department
333 North Washington
Dallas, TX 75246-1798
(214) 828-5252   Toll Free: (888) 244-9400
Fax: (214) 828-5261   E-mail: institutions@bgct.org
Web: texasbaptists.org

Summary To provide financial assistance for college to Native Americans and other minority residents of Texas who are members of Texas Baptist congregations.

Eligibility This program is open to members of Texas Baptist congregations who are of African American, Hispanic, Native American, Asian, or other intercultural heritage. Applicants must be attending or planning to attend a university affiliated with the Baptist General Convention of Texas to work on a bachelor's degree as preparation for service as a future lay or vocational ministry leader in a Texas Baptist ethnic/minority church. They must have been active in their respective ethnic/minority community. Along with their application, they must submit a letter of recommendation from their pastor and transcripts. Students still in high school must have a GPA of at least 3.0; students previously enrolled in a college must have at least a 2.0 GPA. U.S. citizenship or permanent resident status is required.

Financial data Stipends are $800 per semester ($1,600 per year) for full-time students or $400 per semester ($800 per year) for part-time students.

Duration 1 semester; may be renewed up to 7 additional semesters.

Additional information The scholarships are funded through the Week of Prayer and the Mary Hill Davis Offering for state missions sponsored annually by Women's Missionary Union of Texas. The eligible institutions are Baptist University of The Americas, Baylor University, Dallas Baptist University, East Texas Baptist University, Hardin Simmons University, Houston Baptist University, Howard Payne University, University of Mary Hardin Baylor, and Wayland Baptist University.

Number awarded Varies each year.

Deadline April of each year.

[361]
MARY K. MORELAND AND DANIEL T. JENKS SCHOLARSHIP

Chickasaw Foundation
110 West 12th Street
P.O. Box 1726
Ada, OK 74821-1726
(580) 421-9030   Fax: (580) 421-9031
E-mail: ChickasawFoundation@chickasaw.net
Web: www.chickasawfoundation.org/index_20.htm

Summary To provide financial assistance to members of the Chickasaw Nation interested in studying education in college.

Eligibility This program is open to Chickasaw students who are currently enrolled full time as an undergraduate at an accredited 4-year college or university. Applicants must be majoring in education and have a GPA of 3.0 or higher. Along with their application, they must submit high school or college transcripts, 2 letters of recommendation, a copy of their Chickasaw Nation citizenship card, and a 1-page essay on their long-term goals and plans for achieving them. Financial need is not considered in the selection process.

Financial data The stipend is $2,000.

Duration 1 year.

Number awarded 1 each year.

Deadline August of each year.

[362]
MASSACHUSETTS NATIVE AMERICAN TUITION WAIVER PROGRAM

Massachusetts Office of Student Financial Assistance
454 Broadway, Suite 200
Revere, MA 02151
(617) 727-9420   Fax: (617) 727-0667
E-mail: osfa@osfa.mass.edu
Web: www.osfa.mass.edu

Summary To provide financial assistance for college to Massachusetts residents who are Native Americans.

Eligibility Applicants for this assistance must have been permanent legal residents of Massachusetts for at least 1 year and certified by the Bureau of Indian Affairs as Native Americans. They may not be in default on any federal student loan.

Financial data Eligible students are exempt from any tuition payments for an undergraduate degree or certificate program at public colleges or universities in Massachusetts.

Duration Up to 4 academic years, for a total of 130 semester hours.

Additional information Recipients may enroll either part or full time in a Massachusetts publicly-supported institution.

Number awarded Varies each year.

Deadline April of each year.

[363]
MAUREEN L. AND HOWARD N. BLITMAN, P.E. SCHOLARSHIP TO PROMOTE DIVERSITY IN ENGINEERING

National Society of Professional Engineers
Attn: NSPE Educational Foundation
1420 King Street
Alexandria, VA 22314-2794
(703) 684-2833   Toll Free: (888) 285-NSPE
Fax: (703) 836-4875   E-mail: education@nspe.org
Web: www.nspe.org/Students/Scholarships/index.html

Summary To provide financial assistance for college to Native Americans and members of other underrepresented minority groups interested in preparing for a career in engineering.

Eligibility This program is open to members of underrepresented ethnic minorities (African Americans, Hispanics, or Native Americans) who are high school seniors accepted into an ABET-accredited engineering program at a 4-year college or university. Applicants must have a GPA of 3.5 or higher, verbal SAT score of 600 or higher, and math SAT score of 700 or higher (or English ACT score of 29 or higher and math ACT score of 29 or higher). They must submit brief essays on an experience they consider significant to their interest in engineering, how their study of engineering will contribute to their long-term career plans, how their ethnic background has influenced their personal development and perceptions, and anything special about them that they would like the selection committee to know. Selection is based on those essays, GPA, internship/co-op experience and community involvement, 2 faculty recommendations, and honors/scholarships/awards. U.S. citizenship is required.

Financial data The stipend is $5,000 per year; funds are paid directly to the recipient's institution.

Duration 1 year; nonrenewable.

Number awarded 1 each year.

Deadline February of each year.

[364]
MCGHEE-TULLIS TUITION ASSISTANCE PROGRAM

Poarch Band of Creek Indians
Attn: Tuition Program Coordinator
5811 Jack Springs Road
Atmore, AL 36502
(251) 368-9136, ext. 2241   Fax: (251) 368-4502
E-mail: sfisher@pci-nsn.gov
Web: www.poarchcreekindians.org

Summary To provide funding to members of the Poarch Band of Creek Indians for payment of tuition or repayment of educational loans.

Eligibility This program is open to enrolled members of the Poarch Band of Creek Indians who are enrolled or planning to enroll in 1) a certificate program leading to an increased chance of employment and/or increase in salary; 2) a vocational/technical school; or 3) a college or university program leading to an undergraduate, graduate, or professional degree. Applicants must be seeking funding 1) to pay the cost of tuition, books, and mandatory fees; or 2) to repay their educational loans incurred prior to their current enrollment.

Financial data Undergraduates may receive up to $10,000 per year for payment of tuition and fees or repayment of prior educational loans. Graduate and professional students may receive up to $12,000 for the same purposes. All tribal members are entitled to a lifetime tuition assistance allotment of $30,000. When that allotment is exhausted, they may request an additional sum of $10,000, which may be granted at the discretion of the tribal authorities. Tribal members may also apply for a supplemental grant of $500 per semester for purchase of specialized tools required for their program and a 1-time grant of $1,000 for the purchase of a laptop or desktop computer.

Duration Available funds are disbursed as requested, until exhaustion of the $30,000 allotment and the supplement of $10,000 (if approved by tribal authorities).

Number awarded Varies each year.

Deadline Applications may be submitted at any time.

[365]
MEDICAL SCIENTIST TRAINING PROGRAM

University of California at San Diego
Attn: School of Medicine
Summer Undergraduate Research Fellowship Program
9500 Gilman Drive, MC 0606
La Jolla, CA 92093-0606
(858) 822-5631   Toll Free: (800) 925-8704
Fax: (858) 534-8556   E-mail: mstp@ucsd.edu
Web: meded.ucsd.edu/asa/mstp/surf

Summary To provide an internship opportunity to Native Americans and other undergraduate students from underrepresented groups to work during the summer on a research project in the biomedical sciences at the University of California at San Diego (UCSD).

Eligibility This program is open to undergraduate students at colleges in any state who are members of an underrepresented group (racial and ethnic groups that have been shown to be underrepresented in health-related sciences, individuals with disabilities, or individuals from a disadvantaged background). Applicants must be interested in working on a research project in the laboratory of a UCSD faculty member in the biomedical sciences. Along with their application, they must submit brief essays on 1) why they consider themselves an individual from a disadvantaged ethnicity or background or are underrepresented in the biomedical sciences; 2) their past research experiences; 3) the areas of research they wish to pursue in the program; 4) their educational and career plans and how this program will advance them towards their goals; and 5) anything else that might help to evaluate their application.

Financial data The program provides a stipend of $1,600 per month, room (but not board), and a $500 travel allowance.

Duration 8 weeks during the summer.

Additional information This program is sponsored by the National Heart, Lung, and Blood Institute (NHLBI) of the National Institutes of Health (NIH).

Number awarded From 12 to 20 each year.

Deadline February of each year.

[366]
MELLEN SHEA MEMORIAL SCHOLARSHIP

Cook Inlet Tribal Council, Inc.
Attn: Tribal Scholarships and Grants Program
3600 San Jeronimo Drive, Suite 286
Anchorage, AK 99508
(907) 793-3578   Toll Free: (877) 985-5900
Fax: (907) 793-3589   E-mail: scholarships@citci.com
Web: www.citci.com

Summary To provide financial assistance to Alaska Natives and American Indians who are interested in attending college in any state to prepare for a career as a teacher.

Eligibility This program is open to Alaska Natives and American Indians who are enrolled in or admitted to a post-secondary undergraduate program in education in any state and preparing for a career as a teacher. Applicants must have a GPA of 2.0 or higher. Along with their application, they must submit a 600-word essay that details their educational experience to date and explains why they want to become a teacher. Selection is based on the quality and sincerity of that essay; financial need is not considered.

Financial data The stipend is $1,000.

Duration 1 year.

Additional information This program was established in 2006.

Number awarded 1 each year.

Deadline April of each year.

[367]
MENOMINEE INDIAN TRIBAL SCHOLARSHIPS

Menominee Indian Tribe of Wisconsin
Attn: Tribal Education Office
P.O. Box 910
Keshena, WI 54135
(715) 799-5110   Fax: (715) 799-5102
E-mail: vnuske@mitw.org
Web: menominee-nsn.gov

Summary To provide financial assistance for college or graduate school in any state to Menominee Indians.

Eligibility This program is open to enrolled members of the Menominee Indian Tribe of Wisconsin who are 1) graduating high school seniors; 2) undergraduates at 4-year colleges and universities; 3) technical college students; or 4) graduate students. Applicants must submit an essay of 1 to 2 pages on how their education will benefit them, including their community service and extracurricular activities. The essay should not discuss financial need, because the selection committee assumes that all students have financial need. Selection is based on the essay (30 points), a letter of support (5 points), and GPA (15 points if 3.5 or higher, 10 points if 3.00 to 3.49, or 5 points if 2.0 to 2.99).

Financial data The stipend is $500 per semester ($1,000 per year). Funds are sent directly to the recipient's school.

Duration Up to 10 semesters.

Number awarded 4 each year: 1 to each category of student.

Deadline March of each year.

[368]
MENOMINEE INDIAN TRIBE ADULT VOCATIONAL TRAINING PROGRAM

Menominee Indian Tribe of Wisconsin
Attn: Tribal Education Office
P.O. Box 910
Keshena, WI 54135
(715) 799-5110   Fax: (715) 799-5102
E-mail: vnuske@mitw.org
Web: menominee-nsn.gov

Summary To provide financial assistance to Menominee Indians who are interested in a program of vocational training.

Eligibility This program is open to adult enrolled members of the Menominee Indian Tribe of Wisconsin who are working on an associate degree, certificate, or technical college diploma. Applicants must be able to demonstrate financial need.

Financial data Stipends range from $550 to $2,200.

Duration The maximum training period for Adult Vocational Training students is 24 months. Training for nursing is 36 months. Renewal awards require the student to maintain a minimum GPA of 2.0 and to carry at least 12 credits per term.

Additional information Part-time study is not supported under this program.

Deadline February of each year for fall; October of each year for spring.

[369]
MENTORSHIP FOR ENVIRONMENTAL SCHOLARS

United Negro College Fund Special Programs
  Corporation
6402 Arlington Boulevard, Suite 600
Falls Church, VA 22042
(703) 677-3400   Toll Free: (800) 530-6232
Fax: (703) 205-7645   E-mail: portal@uncfsp.org
Web: www.uncfsp.org

Summary To provide an opportunity for upper-division students at Tribal Colleges and Universities and other Minority Institutions (MIs) to work on a summer research internship in a field of interest to the U.S. Department of Energy (DOE).

Eligibility This program is open to rising juniors and seniors at MIs (Historically Black Colleges and Universities, Hispanic Serving Institutions, and Tribal Colleges and Universities) who are members of underrepresented groups, including ethnic minorities and persons with disabilities. Applicants must be working on a degree in a science, technology, engineering, or mathematics (STEM) field of interest to DOE (e.g., biology, chemistry, physics, engineering, environmental science) and have a GPA of 3.0 or higher. They must be interested in working on a research project during the summer at a DOE laboratory or research facility. U.S. citizenship is required.

Financial data A stipend is provided (amount not specified).

Duration 9 weeks during the summer.

Additional information This program is funded by DOE and administered by the United Negro College Fund Special Programs Corporation.

Number awarded Varies each year.

Deadline February of each year.

[370]
MESBEC PROGRAM

Catching the Dream
8200 Mountain Road, N.E., Suite 203
Albuquerque, NM 87110-7835
(505) 262-2351   Fax: (505) 262-0534
E-mail: NScholarsh@aol.com
Web: www.catchingthedream.org/Scholarship.htm

Summary To provide financial assistance to American Indian students who are interested in working on an undergraduate or graduate degree in selected fields.

Eligibility This program is open to American Indians who can provide proof that they have at least one-quarter Indian blood and are a member of a U.S. tribe that is federally-recognized, state-recognized, or terminated. Applicants must be enrolled or planning to enroll full time and major in 1 of the following fields: mathematics, engineering, science (including medicine), business administration, education, or computer science. They may be entering freshmen, undergraduate students, graduate students, or Ph.D. candidates. Along with their application, they must submit documentation of financial need, 3 letters of recommendation, copies of applications and responses for all other sources of funding for which they are eligible, official transcripts, standardized test scores (ACT, SAT, GRE, MCAT, LSAT, etc.), and an essay explaining their goals in life, college plans, and career plans (especially how those plans include working with and benefiting Indians). Selection is based on merit and potential for improving the lives of Indian people.

Financial data Stipends range from $500 to $5,000 per year.

Duration 1 year; may be renewed.

Additional information MESBEC is an acronym that stands for the priority areas of this program: mathematics, engineering, science, business, education, and computers. The sponsor was formerly known as the Native American Scholarship Fund.

Number awarded Varies; generally, 30 to 35 each year.

Deadline April of each year for fall term; September of each year for spring and winter terms; March of each year for summer school.

[371]
MICHAEL BAKER CORPORATION SCHOLARSHIP PROGRAM FOR DIVERSITY IN ENGINEERING

Association of Independent Colleges and Universities of
  Pennsylvania
101 North Front Street
Harrisburg, PA 17101-1405
(717) 232-8649   Fax: (717) 233-8574
E-mail: info@aicup.org
Web: www.aicup.org/fundraising

Summary To provide financial assistance to Native Americans, other minorities, and women students from any state enrolled at member institutions of the Association of Independent Colleges and Universities of Pennsylvania (AICUP) who are majoring in designated fields of engineering.

Eligibility This program is open to full-time undergraduate students from any state enrolled at designated AICUP colleges and universities who are women and/or members of the following minority groups: American Indians, Alaska Natives,

Asians, Blacks/African Americans, Hispanics/Latinos, Native Hawaiians, or Pacific Islanders. Applicants must be juniors majoring in architectural, civil, or environmental engineering with a GPA of 3.0 or higher. Along with their application, they must submit a 2-page essay on what they believe will be the greatest challenge facing the engineering profession over the next decade, and why.

Financial data The stipend is $2,500 per year.

Duration 1 year; may be renewed 1 additional year if the recipient maintains appropriate academic standards.

Additional information This program, sponsored by the Michael Baker Corporation, is available at the 83 private colleges and universities in Pennsylvania that comprise the AICUP.

Number awarded 1 each year.

Deadline April of each year.

[372]
MICHIGAN INDIAN TUITION WAIVER PROGRAM

Michigan Department of Civil Rights
Attn: Michigan Indian Tuition Waiver
110 West Michigan Avenue, Suite 800
Lansing, MI 48933
(517) 241-7748   Fax: (517) 335-3882
TDD: (517) 335-3881
Web: www.michigan.gov

Summary To exempt members of Indian tribes from tuition at Michigan postsecondary institutions.

Eligibility This program is open to Michigan residents who have lived in the state for at least 12 months and can certify at least one-quarter North American Indian blood from a federally-recognized or state historic tribe. Applicants must be attending a public college, university, or community college in Michigan. The program includes full- and part-time study, academic-year and summer school, and undergraduate and graduate work.

Financial data All qualified applicants are entitled to a waiver of tuition at Michigan public institutions.

Duration Indian students are entitled to the waiver as long as they attend college in Michigan.

Additional information This program was established in 1976 as the result of an agreement between the state of Michigan and the federal government under which the state agreed to provide free tuition to North American Indians in exchange for the Mt. Pleasant Indian School, which the state acquired as a training facility for the developmentally disabled.

Number awarded Varies each year.

Deadline Deadline not specified.

[373]
MICKEY LELAND ENERGY FELLOWSHIPS

Department of Energy
Attn: Office of Fossil Energy
19901 Germantown Road, FE-6
Germantown, MD 20874
(301) 903-4293   E-mail: MLEF@hq.doe.gov
Web: fossil.energy.gov

Summary To provide summer work experience at fossil energy sites of the Department of Energy (DOE) to Native

Americans, other underrepresented minorities, and female students.

Eligibility This program is open to U.S. citizens currently enrolled full time at an accredited college or university. Applicants must be undergraduate, graduate, or postdoctoral students in mathematics, physical sciences, technology, or engineering and have a GPA of 3.0 or higher. They must be interested in a summer work experience at a DOE fossil energy research facility. Along with their application, they must submit a 100-word statement on why they want to participate in this program. A goal of the program is to recruit women and underrepresented minorities into careers related to fossil energy.

Financial data Weekly stipends are $500 for undergraduates, $650 for master's degree students, or $750 for doctoral and postdoctoral students. Travel costs for a round trip to and from the site and for a trip to a designated place for technical presentations are also paid.

Duration 10 weeks during the summer.

Additional information This program began as 3 separate activities: the Historically Black Colleges and Universities Internship Program, established in 1995; the Hispanic Internship Program, established in 1998; and the Tribal Colleges and Universities Internship Program, established in 2000. Those 3 programs were merged into the Fossil Energy Minority Education Initiative, renamed the Mickey Leland Energy Fellowship Program in 2000. Sites to which interns may be assigned include the Albany Research Center (Albany, Oregon), the National Energy Technology Laboratory (Morgantown, West Virginia and Pittsburgh, Pennsylvania), Pacific Northwest National Laboratory (Richland, Washington), Rocky Mountain Oilfield Testing Center (Casper, Wyoming), Strategic Petroleum Reserve Project Management Office (New Orleans, Louisiana), or U.S. Department of Energy Headquarters (Washington, D.C.).

Number awarded Varies each year; recently, 30 students participated in this program.

Deadline January of each year.

[374]
MICROBIOLOGY UNDERGRADUATE RESEARCH FELLOWSHIP

American Society for Microbiology
Attn: Education Board
1752 N Street, N.W.
Washington, DC 20036-2904
(202) 942-9283   Fax: (202) 942-9329
E-mail: fellowships@asmusa.org
Web: www.asm.org

Summary To provide Native Americans and other underrepresented minority college students with the opportunity to work on a summer research project in microbiology under the mentorship of a member of the American Society for Microbiology (ASM).

Eligibility This program is open to African Americans, Hispanics, Native Americans, Alaskan Natives, and Pacific Islanders who 1) are enrolled as full-time undergraduate students; 2) have taken introductory courses in biology, chemistry, and (preferably) microbiology prior to applying; 3) have a strong interest in obtaining a Ph.D. or M.D./Ph.D. in the microbiological sciences; 4) have laboratory research experience; and 5) are U.S. citizens or permanent residents. Applicants must be interested in conducting basic science research at a host institution during the summer under an ASM mentor. Selection is based on academic achievement, achievement in previous research experiences or independent projects, career goals as a research scientist, commitment to research, personal motivation to participate in the project, willingness to conduct summer research with an ASM member located at an institution other than their own, leadership skills, and involvement in activities that serve the needs of underrepresented groups.

Financial data Students receive $3,500 as a stipend, up to $1,000 for student lodging, up to $500 for round-trip travel to the host institution, 2-year student membership in the ASM, and travel support up to $1,000 if they present the results of the research project at the ASM general meeting the following year.

Duration 10 to 12 weeks during the summer.

Additional information This program was formerly named the American Society for Microbiology Minority Undergraduate Research Fellowship. In addition to their research activities, fellows participate in a weekly seminar series, journal club, GRE preparatory course, graduate admission counseling, and career counseling.

Number awarded 5 to 8 students are placed at each institution.

Deadline January of each year.

[375]
MIEA SCHOLARSHIP

Michigan Indian Elders Association
c/o Clinton Pelcher, President
Director, 7th Generations Program
7070 East Broadway
Mt. Pleasant, MI 48858
(989) 775-4780   Fax: (989) 775-4781
E-mail: cpelder2@sagchip.org
Web: www.michiganindianelders.org

Summary To provide financial assistance to members of constituent tribes and bands of the Michigan Indian Elders Association (MIEA) who are interested in attending college in any state.

Eligibility This program is open to enrolled members of the 12 MIEA constituent tribes and bands and their direct descendants. Applicants must be 1) graduating high school seniors who have a GPA of 3.0 or higher; 2) students currently enrolled in college, university, or trade school who have a GPA of 3.0 or higher; or 3) holders of a GED certificate who passed all 5 GED equivalency tests with a minimum score of at least 40 and an average score of at least 45. They must be attending or planning to attend a public college, university, or trade school in any state as a full-time student. Financial need is not considered in the selection process.

Financial data Stipends are $1,000 or $500.

Duration 1 year.

Additional information The constituent tribes and bands are the Bay Mills Indian Community, Grand Traverse Band of Ottawa and Chippewa Indians, Hannahville Band of Potawatomi Indians, Keweenaw Bay Indian Community, Lac Vieux Desert Band of Lake Superior Chippewa Indians, Little River Band of Ottawa Indians, Little Traverse Bay Band of Odawa Indians, Match-E-Be-Nash-She-Wish Band of Potawatomi Indians, Nottawaseppi Huron Band of Potawatomi, Pokagon

Band of Potawatomi Indians, Saginaw Chippewa Indian Tribe, and Sault Ste. Marie Tribe of Chippewa Indians.

Number awarded At least 5 each year, including 1 at $1,000 and at least 4 at $500.

Deadline June of each year.

[376]
MILLE LACS BAND ACADEMIC ACHIEVEMENT AWARDS

Mille Lacs Band of Ojibwe
Attn: Higher Education Office
43408 Oodena Avenue
Onamia, MN 56359-2236
(320) 495-3702   Toll Free: (866) 916-5282
Fax: (320) 495-3707
E-mail: mlb.inquiries@millelacsband.com
Web: www.millelacsband.org/Page_Education.aspx

Summary To recognize and reward members of the Mille Lacs Band of Ojibwe after they complete a degree.

Eligibility This program is open to enrolled members of the band, their non-enrolled biological children, and legally adopted children of enrolled band members. Applicants must have just completed their GED certificate or high school diploma, a vocational/technical diploma or certificate (for a program 9 months or more in length), an associate degree, a bachelor's degree, or a graduate (master's or doctoral) degree.

Financial data Awards are $500 for completion of a GED certificate or high school diploma, $1,000 for a vocational/technical diploma or certificate, $1,250 for an associate degree, $1,500 for a bachelor's degree, or $2,000 for a graduate degree.

Duration Awards are presented whenever a student completes a diploma, certificate, or degree.

Number awarded Varies each year.

Deadline Applications may be submitted as soon as an eligible student has completed an educational degree.

[377]
MILLE LACS BAND SCHOLARSHIP PROGRAM

Mille Lacs Band of Ojibwe
Attn: Higher Education Office
43408 Oodena Avenue
Onamia, MN 56359-2236
(320) 495-3702   Toll Free: (866) 916-5282
Fax: (320) 495-3707
E-mail: mlb.inquiries@millelacsband.com
Web: www.millelacsband.org/Page_Education.aspx

Summary To provide financial assistance for college to members of the Mille Lacs Band of Ojibwe.

Eligibility This program is open to enrolled members of the band, their non-enrolled biological children, and legally adopted children of enrolled band members. Applicants may be attending a 2- or 4-year college, university, or vocational/technical school. Financial need is required. Applicants for this program must also apply for financial aid administered by their institution and any other aid for which they may be eligible (e.g., work-study, Social Security, veteran's benefits).

Financial data This program provides a stipend of up to $9,000 per year and an allowance of up to $375 per semester for books and supplies.

Duration Students at 2-year institutions are eligible for 8 quarters or 5 semesters of support; students at 4-year institutions are allowed 15 quarters or 10 semesters to complete their program.

Number awarded Varies each year.

Deadline September of each year for fall semester or quarter; January of each year for winter quarter or spring semester or quarter; June of each year for summer school.

[378]
MINNESOTA INDIAN SCHOLARSHIP PROGRAM

Minnesota Office of Higher Education
Attn: Manager of State Financial Aid Programs
1450 Energy Park Drive, Suite 350
St. Paul, MN 55108-5227
(651) 642-0567   Toll Free: (800) 657-3866
Fax: (651) 642-0675   TDD: (800) 627-3529
E-mail: Ginny.Dodds@state.mn.us
Web: www.ohe.state.mn.us

Summary To provide financial assistance to Native Americans in Minnesota who are interested in working on an undergraduate or graduate degree in any field.

Eligibility Applicants must be at least one-fourth degree Indian ancestry; members of a recognized Indian tribe; at least high school graduates (or approved equivalent); accepted by an accredited college, university, or vocational school in Minnesota; and residents of Minnesota for at least 1 year. Undergraduates must be attending college at least three-fourths time; graduate students must be enrolled at least half time.

Financial data The stipend depends on need, to a maximum of $4,000 per year for undergraduates or $6,600 per year for graduate students. Awards are paid directly to the student's school or college.

Duration 1 year; may be renewed up to 4 additional years, provided the recipient maintains a GPA of 2.0 or higher and sends official grade transcripts to the office for review after each quarter or semester.

Number awarded Approximately 700 each year.

Deadline June of each year.

[379]
MINORITIES IN HOSPITALITY SCHOLARS PROGRAM

International Franchise Association
Attn: IFA Educational Foundation
1501 K Street, N.W., Suite 350
Washington, DC 20005
(202) 662-0784   Fax: (202) 628-0812
E-mail: mbrewer@franchise.org
Web: www.franchise.org/Scholarships.aspx

Summary To provide financial assistance to Native Americans and other minority students working on an undergraduate degree related to hospitality.

Eligibility This program is open to college sophomores, juniors, and seniors who are U.S. citizens and members of a minority group (defined as African Americans, American Indians, Hispanic Americans, and Asian Americans). Applicants must be working on a degree in a field related to the hospitality industry. Along with their application, they must submit a 500-word essay on why they should be selected to receive

this scholarship. Financial need is not considered in the selection process.

Financial data The stipend is $2,000.

Duration 1 year.

Additional information This program is cosponsored by the IFA Educational Foundation and Choice Hotels International.

Number awarded 1 or more each year.

Deadline January of each year.

[380]
MINORITY ACCESS INTERNSHIP

Minority Access, Inc.
Attn: Directory of Internship Program
5214 Baltimore Avenue
Hyattsville, MD 20781
(301) 779-7100   Fax: (301) 779-9812
Web: www.minorityaccess.org

Summary To provide work experience to Native American and other minority undergraduate and graduate students interested in internships at participating entities in Washington, D.C. and throughout the United States.

Eligibility This program is open to full-time undergraduate and graduate students who have a GPA of 3.0 or higher. Applicants must be U.S. citizens for most positions. All academic majors are eligible. Interns are selected by participating federal government and other agencies. Most of these are located in Washington, D.C., but placements may be made anywhere in the United States.

Financial data The weekly stipend is $450 for sophomores and juniors, $500 for seniors, or $550 for graduate and professional students. In addition, most internships include paid round-trip travel between home and the internship location.

Duration Spring internships are 5 months, starting in January; summer internships are 3 months, starting in August; fall internships are 4 months, starting in September.

Additional information Minority Access, Inc. is committed to the diversification of institutions, federal agencies, and corporations of all kinds and to improving their recruitment, retention, and enhancement of minorities. The majority of interns are placed in the Washington, D.C. metropolitan area. Both full-time and part-time internships are awarded. Students may receive academic credit for full-time internships. Students are expected to pay all housing costs. They are required to attend a pre-employment session in Washington, D.C., all seminars and workshops hosted by Minority Access, and any mandatory activities sponsored by the host agency.

Number awarded Varies each year.

Deadline February of each year for summer internships; June of each year for fall internships; and November of each year for spring internships.

[381]
MINORITY AFFAIRS COMMITTEE AWARD FOR OUTSTANDING SCHOLASTIC ACHIEVEMENT

American Institute of Chemical Engineers
Attn: Minority Affairs Committee
Three Park Avenue
New York, NY 10016-5991
(646) 495-1348   Fax: (646) 495-1504
E-mail: awards@aiche.org
Web: www.aiche.org/About/Awards/MACScholastic.aspx

Summary To recognize and reward Native Americans and other underrepresented minority students majoring in chemical engineering who serve as role models for other minority students.

Eligibility Members of the American Institute of Chemical Engineers (AIChE) may nominate any chemical engineering student who serves as a role model for minority students in that field. Nominees must be members of a minority group that is underrepresented in chemical engineering (i.e., African American, Hispanic, Native American, Alaskan Native). They must have a GPA of 3.0 or higher. Along with their application, they must submit a 300-word essay on their immediate plans after graduation, areas of chemical engineering of most interest, and long-range career plans. Selection is based on that essay, academic record, participation in AIChE student chapter and professional or civic activities, and financial need.

Financial data The award consists of a plaque and a $1,500 honorarium.

Duration The award is presented annually.

Additional information This award was first presented in 1996.

Number awarded 1 each year.

Deadline Nominations must be submitted by May of each year.

[382]
MINORITY ENTREPRENEURS SCHOLARSHIP PROGRAM

International Franchise Association
Attn: IFA Educational Foundation
1501 K Street, N.W., Suite 350
Washington, DC 20005
(202) 662-0784   Fax: (202) 628-0812
E-mail: mbrewer@franchise.org
Web: www.franchise.org/Scholarships.aspx

Summary To provide financial assistance to Native Americans and other minority students or adult entrepreneurs enrolled in academic or professional development programs related to franchising.

Eligibility This program is open to 1) college students enrolled at an accredited college or university, and 2) adult entrepreneurs who have at least 5 years of business ownership or managerial experience. Applicants must be U.S. citizens and members of a minority group (defined as African Americans, American Indians, Hispanic Americans, and Asian Americans). Students should be enrolled in courses or programs relating to business, finance, marketing, hospitality, franchising, or entrepreneurship. Adult entrepreneurs should be enrolled in professional development courses related to franchising, such as those recognized by the Institute of Cer-

tified Franchise Executives (ICFE). All applicants must submit a 500-word essay on why they want the scholarship and their career goals. Financial need is not considered in the selection process.

Financial data The stipend is $3,000.

Duration 1 year.

Additional information This program is cosponsored by the IFA Educational Foundation and Marriott International.

Number awarded 5 each year.

Deadline June of each year.

[383]
MINORITY GEOSCIENCE STUDENT SCHOLARSHIPS

American Geological Institute
Attn: Minority Participation Program
4220 King Street
Alexandria, VA 22302-1502
(703) 379-2480, ext. 227   Fax: (703) 379-7563
E-mail: mpp@agiweb.org
Web: www.agiweb.org/mpp/index.html

Summary To provide financial assistance to Native Americans and other underrepresented minority undergraduate and graduate students interested in working on a degree in the geosciences.

Eligibility This program is open to members of ethnic minority groups underrepresented in the geosciences (Blacks, Hispanics, American Indians, Eskimos, Hawaiians, and Samoans). U.S. citizenship is required. Applicants must be full-time students enrolled in an accredited institution working on an undergraduate or graduate degree in the geosciences, including geology, geochemistry, geophysics, hydrology, meteorology, physical oceanography, planetary geology, or earth science education; students in other natural sciences, mathematics, or engineering are not eligible. Selection is based on a 250-word essay on career goals and why the applicant has chosen a geoscience as a major, work experience, recommendations, honors and awards, extracurricular activities, and financial need.

Financial data Stipends range from $500 to $3,000 per year.

Duration 1 academic year; renewable if the recipient maintains satisfactory performance.

Additional information Funding for this program is provided by ExxonMobil Corporation, ConocoPhillips, ChevronTexaco Corporation, Marathon Corporation, and the Seismological Society of America.

Number awarded Varies each year; recently, 18 of these scholarships were awarded.

Deadline March of each year.

[384]
MINORITY SCHOLARSHIP AWARD FOR ACADEMIC EXCELLENCE IN PHYSICAL THERAPY

American Physical Therapy Association
Attn: Honors and Awards Program
1111 North Fairfax Street
Alexandria, VA 22314-1488
(703) 684-APTA   Toll Free: (800) 999-APTA
Fax: (703) 684-7343   TDD: (703) 683-6748
E-mail: executivedept@apta.org
Web: www.apta.org

Summary To provide financial assistance to Native Americans and other minority students who are interested in becoming a physical therapist or physical therapy assistant.

Eligibility This program is open to U.S. citizens and permanent residents who are members of the following minority groups: African American or Black, Asian, Native Hawaiian or other Pacific Islander, American Indian or Alaska Native, or Hispanic/Latino. Applicants must be in the final year of a professional physical therapy or physical therapy assistant education program. They must submit a personal essay outlining their professional goals and minority service. U.S. citizenship or permanent resident status is required. Selection is based on 1) demonstrated evidence of contributions in the area of minority affairs and services with an emphasis on contributions made while enrolled in a physical therapy program; 2) potential to contribute to the profession of physical therapy; and 3) scholastic achievement.

Financial data The stipend varies; recently, minimum awards were $6,000 for physical therapy students or $2,500 for physical therapy assistant students.

Duration 1 year.

Number awarded Varies each year; recently, 8 of these awards were granted: 7 to professional physical therapy students and 1 to a physical therapy assistant student.

Deadline November of each year.

[385]
MINORITY SCHOLARSHIP AWARDS FOR COLLEGE STUDENTS IN CHEMICAL ENGINEERING

American Institute of Chemical Engineers
Attn: Minority Affairs Committee
Three Park Avenue
New York, NY 10016-5991
(646) 495-1348   Fax: (646) 495-1504
E-mail: awards@aiche.org
Web: www.aiche.org/Students/Scholarships/index.aspx

Summary To provide financial assistance for the undergraduate study of chemical engineering to Native Americans and other underrepresented minority student members of the American Institute of Chemical Engineers (AIChE).

Eligibility This program is open to undergraduate student AIChE members who are also members of a minority group that is underrepresented in chemical engineering (African Americans, Hispanics, Native Americans, and Alaskan Natives). They must have a GPA of 3.0 or higher. Along with their application, they must submit a 300-word essay on their immediate plans after graduation, areas of chemical engineering of most interest, and long-range career plans. Selec-

tion is based on that essay, academic record, participation in AIChE student chapter and professional or civic activities, and financial need.

Financial data The stipend is $1,000.

Duration 1 year; nonrenewable.

Number awarded Approximately 10 each year.

Deadline June of each year.

[386]
MINORITY SCHOLARSHIP AWARDS FOR INCOMING COLLEGE FRESHMEN IN CHEMICAL ENGINEERING

American Institute of Chemical Engineers
Attn: Minority Affairs Committee
Three Park Avenue
New York, NY 10016-5991
(646) 495-1348   Fax: (646) 495-1504
E-mail: awards@aiche.org
Web: www.aiche.org/Students/Scholarships/index.aspx

Summary To provide financial assistance to Native Americans and other incoming minority freshmen who are interested in studying science or engineering in college.

Eligibility Eligible are members of a minority group that is underrepresented in chemical engineering (African Americans, Hispanics, Native Americans, and Alaskan Natives). Applicants must be graduating high school seniors planning to enroll at a 4-year university with a major in science or engineering. They must be nominated by an American Institute of Chemical Engineers (AIChE) local section. Selection is based on academic record (including a GPA of 3.0 or higher), participation in school and work activities, a 300-word letter outlining the reasons for choosing science or engineering, and financial need.

Financial data The stipend is $1,000.

Duration 1 year; nonrenewable.

Number awarded Approximately 10 each year.

Deadline Nominations must be submitted by June of each year.

[387]
MINORITY SCIENCE WRITERS INTERNSHIP

American Association for the Advancement of Science
Directorate for Education and Human Resources
Attn: Minority Science Writers Internship
1200 New York Avenue, N.W., Room 639
Washington, DC 20005-3920
(202) 326-6441   Fax: (202) 371-9849
E-mail: raculver@aaas.org
Web: www.aaas.org

Summary To provide summer work experience at *Science* magazine to Native American and other minority undergraduate students.

Eligibility This program is open to minority undergraduates with a serious interest in science writing. Preference is given to students majoring in journalism. Applicants must be interested in a summer internship at *Science* magazine, the journal of the American Association for the Advancement of Science (AAAS). Along with their application, they must submit an 800-word essay on their commitment to journalism, their career goals, their thoughts about science and science writing, and what they hope to get out of this opportunity. A telephone interview is conducted of semifinalists.

Financial data Interns receive a salary and reimbursement of travel expenses to the work site in Washington, D.C.

Duration 10 weeks during the summer.

Number awarded Varies each year.

Deadline February of each year.

[388]
MINORITY TEACHERS OF ILLINOIS SCHOLARSHIP PROGRAM

Illinois Student Assistance Commission
Attn: Scholarship and Grant Services
1755 Lake Cook Road
Deerfield, IL 60015-5209
(847) 948-8550   Toll Free: (800) 899-ISAC
Fax: (847) 831-8549   TDD: (800) 526-0844
E-mail: collegezone@isac.org
Web: www.collegezone.com/studentzone/407_655.htm

Summary To provide funding to Native Americans and other minority students in Illinois who plan to become teachers at the preschool, elementary, or secondary level.

Eligibility Applicants must be Illinois residents, U.S. citizens or eligible noncitizens, members of a minority group (African American/Black, Hispanic American, Asian American, or Native American), and high school graduates or holders of a General Educational Development (GED) certificate. They must be enrolled in college full time at the sophomore level or above, have a GPA of 2.5 or higher, not be in default on any student loan, and be enrolled or accepted for enrollment in a teacher education program. U.S. citizenship or eligible noncitizenship status is required.

Financial data Grants up to $5,000 per year are awarded. This is a scholarship/loan program. Recipients must agree to teach full time 1 year for each year of support received. The teaching agreement may be fulfilled at a public, private, or parochial preschool, elementary school, or secondary school in Illinois; at least 30% of the student body at those schools must be minority. It must be fulfilled within the 5-year period following the completion of the undergraduate program for which the scholarship was awarded. The time period may be extended if the recipient serves in the U.S. armed forces, enrolls full time in a graduate program related to teaching, becomes temporarily disabled, is unable to find employment as a teacher at a qualifying school, or takes additional courses on at least a half-time basis to obtain certification as a teacher in Illinois. Recipients who fail to honor this work obligation must repay the award with 5% interest.

Duration 1 year; may be renewed for a total of 8 semesters or 12 quarters.

Number awarded Varies each year.

Deadline Priority consideration is given to applications received by February of each year.

[389]
MIRIAM WEINSTEIN PEACE AND JUSTICE EDUCATION AWARD

Philanthrofund Foundation
Attn: Scholarship Committee
1409 Willow Street, Suite 210
Minneapolis, MN 55403-3251
(612) 870-1806   Toll Free: (800) 435-1402
Fax: (612) 871-6587   E-mail: info@PfundOnline.org
Web: www.pfundonline.org/scholarships.html

Summary To provide financial assistance to Native Americans and other minority students from Minnesota who are associated with gay, lesbian, bisexual, and transgender (GLBT) activities and interested in working on a degree in education.

Eligibility This program is open to residents of Minnesota and students attending a Minnesota educational institution who are members of a religious, racial, or ethnic minority. Applicants must be self-identified as GLBT or from a GLBT family and have demonstrated a commitment to peace and justice issues. They may be attending or planning to attend trade school, technical college, college, or university (as an undergraduate or graduate student). Preference is given to students who have completed at least 2 years of college and are working on a degree in education. Selection is based on the applicant's 1) affirmation of GLBT identity or commitment to GLBT communities; 2) participation and leadership in community and/or GLBT activities; and 3) service as role model, mentor, and/or adviser for the GLBT community.

Financial data The stipend is $3,000. Funds must be used for tuition, books, fees, or dissertation expenses.

Duration 1 year.

Number awarded 1 each year.

Deadline January of each year.

[390]
MISS INDIAN USA SCHOLARSHIP PROGRAM

American Indian Heritage Foundation
P.O. Box 750
Pigeon Forge, TN 37868
(703) 819-0979   E-mail: MissIndianUSA@indians.org
Web: www.indians.org/miss-indian-usa-program.html

Summary To recognize and reward the most beautiful and talented Indian women.

Eligibility American Indian women between the ages of 18 and 26 are eligible to enter this national contest if they are high school graduates and have never been married, cohabited with the opposite sex, been pregnant, or had children. U.S. citizenship is required. Selection is based on public appearance (20%), a traditional interview (15%), a contemporary interview (15%), beauty of spirit (15%), a cultural presentation (10%), scholastic achievement (10%), a platform question (10%), and a finalist question (5%).

Financial data Awards vary each year; recently, Miss Indian USA received an academic scholarship of $4,000 plus a cash grant of $6,500, a wardrobe allowance of $2,000, appearance fees of $3,000, a professional photo shoot worth $500, gifts worth more than $4,000, honoring gifts worth more than $2,000, promotional materials worth more than $2,000, and travel to Washington, D.C. with a value of approximately $2,000; the total value of the prize was more than

$26,000. Members of her court received scholarships of $2,000 for the first runner-up, $1,500 for the second runner-up, $1,000 for the third runner-up, and $500 for the fourth runner-up.

Duration This competition is held annually.

Additional information The program involves a week-long competition in the Washington, D.C. metropolitan area that includes seminars, interviews, cultural presentations, and many public appearances. The application fee is $100 if submitted prior to mid-April or $200 if submitted later. In addition, a candidate fee of $750 is required.

Number awarded 1 winner and 4 runners-up are selected each year.

Deadline May of each year.

[391]
MISSOURI MINORITY TEACHER EDUCATION SCHOLARSHIP PROGRAM

Missouri Department of Higher Education
Attn: Student Financial Assistance
3515 Amazonas Drive
Jefferson City, MO 65109-5717
(573) 751-2361   Toll Free: (800) 473-6757
Fax: (573) 751-6635   E-mail: info@dhe.mo.gov
Web: www.dhe.mo.gov/minorityteaching.html

Summary To provide funding to Native American and other minority high school seniors, high school graduates, and college students in Missouri who are interested in preparing for a teaching career in mathematics or science.

Eligibility This program is open to Missouri residents who are African American, Asian American, Hispanic American, or Native American. Applicants must be 1) high school seniors, college students, or returning adults (without a degree) who rank in the top 25% of their high school class and scored at or above the 75th percentile on the ACT or SAT examination; 2) individuals who have completed 30 college hours and have a cumulative GPA of 3.0 or better; or 3) baccalaureate degree-holders who are returning to an approved mathematics or science teacher education program. They must be a U.S. citizen or permanent resident or otherwise lawfully present in the United States. All applicants must be enrolled full time in an approved teacher education program at a community college, 4-year college, or university in Missouri. Selection is based on academic performance, the quantity and quality of school and community activities, range of interests and activities, leadership abilities, interpersonal skills, and desire to enter the field of education.

Financial data The stipend is $3,000 per year, of which $2,000 is provided by the state as a forgivable loan and $1,000 is provided by the school as a scholarship. Recipients must commit to teaching in a Missouri public elementary or secondary school for 5 years following graduation. If they fail to fulfill that obligation, they must repay the state portion of the scholarship with interest at 9.5%.

Duration Up to 4 years.

Number awarded Up to 100 each year.

Deadline February of each year.

[392]
MITCH SPERRY MEMORIAL LAW SCHOLARSHIP

Chickasaw Foundation
110 West 12th Street
P.O. Box 1726
Ada, OK 74821-1726
(580) 421-9030   Fax: (580) 421-9031
E-mail: ChickasawFoundation@chickasaw.net
Web: www.chickasawfoundation.org/index_20.htm

Summary To provide financial assistance to members of the Chickasaw Nation who are interested in working on an undergraduate or graduate degree in a field related to law.

Eligibility This program is open to Chickasaw students who are currently enrolled at an accredited 4-year college or university as a full-time undergraduate or law student. Applicants must be working on a degree in law, pre-law, legal studies, paralegal, or any major associated with law or a bachelor's degree obtained with the intention of pursuing a law degree. They must have a GPA of 3.2 or higher. Along with their application, they must submit high school or college transcripts, 2 letters of recommendation, a copy of their Chickasaw Nation citizenship card, and a 1-page essay on their long-term goals and plans for achieving them. Financial need is not considered in the selection process.

Financial data A stipend is awarded (amount not specified).

Duration 1 year.

Number awarded 1 each year.

Deadline August of each year.

[393]
MOHAWK HIGHER EDUCATION PROGRAM

St. Regis Mohawk Tribe
Attn: Higher Education
Community Building
412 State Route 37
Akwesasne, NY 13655-3109
(518) 358-2272, ext. 215   Toll Free: (800) 800-8679
Fax: (518) 358-3337   E-mail: rcook@srmt-nsn.gov
Web: srmt-nsn.gov/divisions/education

Summary To provide financial assistance to members of the St. Regis Mohawk Tribe who are interested in attending college in any state.

Eligibility This program is open to members of the St. Regis Mohawk Tribe who are enrolled full time at an accredited 2- or 4-year college or university in any state. Applicants must be able to demonstrate unmet financial need after receipt of all other financial aid (e.g., federal Pell Grants, New York TAP Awards). First priority is given to enrolled members who live on the reservation, second to enrolled members who live near the reservation, and third to one-quarter degree descendants of enrolled members who live in any state. Awards are presented on a first-come, first-served basis.

Financial data The stipend depends on the need of the recipient.

Duration 1 year; may be renewed as long as the recipient maintains a GPA of 2.0 or higher as a freshman or 2.5 or higher afterwards.

Additional information This program has been in operation since 1986.

Number awarded   Varies each year.

Deadline   July of each year for fall or academic year; October of each year for spring.

[394]
MONTANA AMERICAN INDIAN STUDENT WAIVER

Montana Guaranteed Student Loan Program
2500 Broadway
P.O. Box 203101
Helena, MT 59620-3101
(406) 444-6570   Toll Free: (800) 537-7508
Fax: (406) 444-1869
E-mail: scholarships@mgslp.state.mt.us
Web: www.mgslp.state.mt.us

Summary   To provide financial assistance to Montana Indians interested in attending college or graduate school in the state.

Eligibility   Eligible to apply are Native American students (one-quarter Indian blood or more) who have been residents of Montana for at least 1 year prior to application, have graduated from an accredited high school or federal Indian school, and can demonstrate financial need.

Financial data   Students eligible for this benefit are entitled to attend any unit of the Montana University System without payment of undergraduate or graduate registration or incidental fees.

Duration   Students are eligible for continued fee waiver as long as they maintain reasonable academic progress and full-time status (12 or more credits for undergraduates, 9 or more credits for graduate students).

Number awarded   Varies; more than $1 million in waivers are approved each year.

Deadline   Deadline not specified.

[395]
MORGAN STANLEY SCHOLARS PROGRAM

American Indian College Fund
Attn: Scholarship Department
8333 Greenwood Boulevard
Denver, CO 80221
(303) 426-8900   Toll Free: (800) 776-FUND
Fax: (303) 426-1200
E-mail: scholarships@collegefund.org
Web: www.collegefund.org

Summary   To provide financial assistance to American Indian students at mainstream 4-year institutions who are preparing for a career in the business and financial services industry.

Eligibility   This program is open to American Indians or Alaska Natives who are currently enrolled full time in a bachelor's degree program at a mainstream institution in the United States. Applicants must be interested in preparing for a career in the financial services industry (e.g., information technology, investment banking, investment management, marketing, branch operations, financial advising, financial accounting, credit card services). They must have a GPA of 3.0 or higher. Applications are available only online and include required essays on specified topics. Selection is based on exceptional academic achievement.

Financial data   The stipend is $10,000.

Duration   1 year.

Additional information   This scholarship is sponsored by Morgan Stanley, in partnership with the American Indian College Fund. Selected students may also be considered for internship opportunities with Morgan Stanley.

Number awarded   5 each year.

Deadline   May of each year.

[396]
MORGAN STANLEY TRIBAL SCHOLARS PROGRAM

American Indian College Fund
Attn: Scholarship Department
8333 Greenwood Boulevard
Denver, CO 80221
(303) 426-8900   Toll Free: (800) 776-FUND
Fax: (303) 426-1200
E-mail: scholarships@collegefund.org
Web: www.collegefund.org/scholarships/schol_tcu.html

Summary   To provide financial assistance to Native American students currently enrolled full time at a Tribal College or University (TCU) to prepare for a career in business and the financial services industry.

Eligibility   This program is open to American Indians and Alaska Natives who are enrolled full time at an eligible TCU. Applicants must have declared a major in business or a related field and have a GPA of 3.0 or higher. Applications are available only online and include required essays on specified topics. Selection is based on exceptional academic achievement.

Financial data   The stipend is $2,500.

Duration   1 year.

Additional information   This scholarship is sponsored by Morgan Stanley, in partnership with the American Indian College Fund.

Number awarded   10 each year.

Deadline   May of each year.

[397]
MORRIS K. UDALL SCHOLARSHIPS

Morris K. Udall and Stewart L. Udall Foundation
Attn: Program Manager, Scholarship Program
130 South Scott Avenue
Tucson, AZ 85701-1922
(520) 901-8562   Fax: (520) 670-5530
E-mail: info@udall.gov
Web: www.udall.gov

Summary   To provide financial assistance to 1) college sophomores and juniors who intend to prepare for a career in environmental public policy and 2) Native American and Alaska Native students who intend to prepare for a career in health care or tribal public policy.

Eligibility   Each 2- and 4-year college and university in the United States and its possessions may nominate up to 6 sophomores or juniors for either or both categories of this program: 1) students who intend to prepare for a career in environmental public policy, and 2) Native American and Alaska Native students who intend to prepare for a career in health care or tribal public policy. For the first category, the program seeks future leaders across a wide spectrum of environmental fields, such as policy, engineering, science, education, urban planning and renewal, business, health, justice, and economics. For the second category, the program seeks future Native American and Alaska Native leaders in public and community health care, tribal government, and public policy affecting Native American communities, including land and resource management, economic development, and education. Nominees must be U.S. citizens, nationals, or permanent residents with a GPA of 3.0 or higher. Along with their application, they must submit an 800-word essay discussing a significant public speech, legislative act, or public policy statement by Congressman Morris K. Udall or Secretary of Interior Stewart L. Udall and its impact on their field of study, interests, and career goals. Selection is based on demonstrated commitment to 1) environmental issues through participation in 1 or more of the following: campus activities, research, community service, or public service; or 2) tribal public policy or Native American health through participation in 1 or more of the following: campus activities, tribal involvement, community or public service, or research; a course of study and proposed career likely to lead to positions where the nominee can make significant contributions to the shaping of environmental, tribal public policy, or Native American health care issues, whether through scientific advances, public or political service, or community action; or leadership, character, desire to make a difference, and general well-roundedness.

Financial data The maximum stipend for scholarship winners is $5,000 per year. Funds are to be used for tuition, fees, books, room, and board. Honorable mention stipends are $350.

Duration 1 year; recipients nominated as sophomores may be renominated in their junior year.

Number awarded Approximately 80 scholarships and 50 honorable mentions are awarded each year.

Deadline Faculty representatives must submit their nominations by early March of each year.

[398]
MULTICULTURAL ADVERTISING INTERN PROGRAM

American Association of Advertising Agencies
Attn: Manager of Diversity Programs
405 Lexington Avenue, 18th Floor
New York, NY 10174-1801
(212) 850-0732   Toll Free: (800) 676-9333
Fax: (212) 682-2028   E-mail: maip@aaaa.org
Web: www2.aaaa.org

Summary To provide Native Americans and other minority students with summer work experience in advertising agencies and to present them with an overview of the agency business.

Eligibility This program is open to U.S. citizens and permanent residents who are Black/African American, Asian/Asian American, Pacific Islander, Hispanic, North American Indian/Native American, or multiracial and either 1) college juniors, seniors, or graduate students at an accredited college or university, or 2) students at any academic level attending a portfolio school of the sponsor. Applicants may be majoring in any field, but they must be able to demonstrate a serious commitment to preparing for a career in advertising. They must have a GPA of 3.0 or higher. Students with a cumulative

GPA of 2.7 to 2.9 are encouraged to apply, but they must complete an additional essay question.

Financial data Interns are paid a salary of at least $70 per day. If they do not live in the area of their host agencies, they may stay in housing arranged by the sponsor. They are responsible for a percentage of the cost of housing and materials.

Duration 10 weeks during the summer.

Additional information Interns may be assigned duties in the following departments: account management, broadcast production, media buying/planning, creative (art direction or copywriting), digital/interactive technologies, print production, strategic/account planning, or traffic. The portfolio schools are the AdCenter at Virginia Commonwealth University, the Creative Circus and the Portfolio Center in Atlanta, the Miami Ad School, the University of Texas at Austin, Pratt Institute, the Minneapolis College of Art and Design, and the Art Center College of Design in Pasadena, California.

Number awarded 70 to 100 each year.

Deadline December of each year.

[399]
MUTUAL OF OMAHA ACTUARIAL SCHOLARSHIP FOR MINORITY STUDENTS

Mutual of Omaha
Attn: Strategic Staffing-Actuarial Recruitment
Mutual of Omaha Plaza
Omaha, NE 68175
(402) 351-3300   E-mail: diversity@mutualofomaha.com
Web: www.mutualofomaha.com

Summary To provide financial assistance and work experience to Native Americans and other minority undergraduate students who are preparing for an actuarial career.

Eligibility This program is open to members of minority groups (African American, Hispanic, Native American, Asian or Pacific Islander, or Alaskan Eskimo) who have completed at least 24 semester hours of full-time study. Applicants must be working on an actuarial or mathematics-related degree with the goal of preparing for an actuarial career. They must have a GPA of 3.0 or higher and have passed at least 1 actuarial examination. Prior to accepting the award, they must be available to complete a summer internship at the sponsor's home office in Omaha, Nebraska. Along with their application, they must submit a 1-page personal statement on why they are interested in becoming an actuary and how they are preparing themselves for an actuarial career. Status as a U.S. citizen, permanent resident, or asylee or refugee must be established.

Financial data The scholarship stipend is $5,000 per year. Funds are paid directly to the student. For the internship, students receive an hourly rate of pay, subsidized housing, and financial incentives for successful examination results received during the internship period.

Duration 1 year. Recipients may reapply if they maintain a cumulative GPA of 3.0 or higher.

Number awarded Varies each year.

Deadline October of each year.

[400]
MYAAMIA SCHOLARSHIP

Miami Nation
Attn: Education Committee
202 South Eight Tribes Trail
P.O. Box 1326
Miami, OK 74355
(918) 542-1445   Fax: (918) 542-7260
E-mail: edu@miamination.com
Web: www.miamination.com/mto/edu.html

Summary To provide financial assistance to high school seniors who are enrolled members of the Miami Nation of Oklahoma and planning to attend college in any state.

Eligibility This program is open to graduating high school seniors who are enrolled members of the Miami Nation of Oklahoma. Applicants must have a GPA of 3.0 or higher and be planning to enroll full time at a college or university in any state. Along with their application, they must submit a high school transcript or equivalent (GED), 3 letters of recommendation, documentation of financial need, and a 1-page essay with the title, "Tell Us About Yourself."

Financial data The stipend is $1,000 per semester.

Duration 1 semester; may be renewed up to 7 additional semesters if the recipient remains enrolled full time with a college GPA of 3.0 or higher.

Number awarded 10 students may be receiving this scholarship at any given time.

Deadline April of each year.

[401]
MYRON AND LAURA THOMPSON SCHOLARSHIP

Ke Ali'i Pauahi Foundation
Attn: Financial Aid & Scholarship Services
567 South King Street, Suite 160
Honolulu, HI 96813
(808) 534-3966   Toll Free: (800) 842-4682, ext. 43966
Fax: (808) 534-3890   E-mail: scholarships@pauahi.org
Web: www.pauahi.org/scholarships

Summary To provide financial assistance to undergraduate or graduate students, especially those of Native Hawaiian descent, who are working on a degree in early childhood education.

Eligibility This program is open to full-time undergraduate and graduate students working on a degree in early childhood education. Applicants must be able to demonstrate financial need; an interest in the Hawaiian language, culture, history, and values; and commitment to contribute to the greater community. Preference is given to Native Hawaiians (descendants of the aboriginal inhabitants of the Hawaiian Islands prior to 1778) and to students who demonstrate an interest in working with Hawaiian children in Hawaii after completion of their education.

Financial data The stipend is $1,300.

Duration 1 year.

Number awarded 2 each year.

Deadline March each year.

[402]
NACME PRE-ENGINEERING STUDENT SCHOLARSHIPS

National Action Council for Minorities in Engineering
Attn: University Programs
440 Hamilton Avenue, Suite 302
White Plains, NY 10601-1813
(914) 539-4010   Fax: (914) 539-4032
E-mail: scholarships@nacme.org
Web: www.nacmebacksme.org/NBM_C.aspx?pageid=153

Summary To provide financial assistance to Native American and other underrepresented minority high school seniors interested in studying engineering or related fields in college.

Eligibility This program is open to African American, Latino, and American Indian high school seniors who are in the top 10% of their graduating class and have demonstrated academic excellence, leadership skills, and a commitment to science and engineering as a career. Candidates must have been accepted as a full-time student at an ABET-accredited engineering program. They must be nominated by their school (each high school may nominate only 1 student). Fields of study include all areas of engineering as well as computer science, materials science, mathematics, operations research, or physics. Letters of nomination must be accompanied by a transcript, SAT or ACT report form, resume, and 100-word statement of why the student should receive this scholarship.

Financial data The stipend is $1,500. Funds are sent directly to the recipient's university.

Duration 1 year.

Number awarded Varies each year; recently, 95 of these scholarships were awarded.

Deadline April of each year.

[403]
NASA MOTIVATING UNDERGRADUATES IN SCIENCE AND TECHNOLOGY (MUST) SCHOLARSHIP PROGRAM

National Aeronautics and Space Administration
Attn: Vanessa R. Webbs, MUST Project Manager
NASA John H. Glenn Research Center at Lewis Field
2100 Brookpark Road, M.S. 500-107
Cleveland, OH 44135
(216) 433-3768   Fax: (216) 433-3344
E-mail: vanessa.r.webbs@nasa.gov
Web: www.nasa.gov

Summary To provide financial assistance to Native Americans and members of other underrepresented groups who are working on an undergraduate degree in a field of science, technology, engineering, or mathematics (STEM).

Eligibility This program is open to U.S. citizens from an underrepresented group, including women, African Americans, Hispanic Americans, Native Americans, and persons with disabilities. Applicants must be entering their sophomore or junior year at an accredited college or university in the 50 states or Puerto Rico as a full-time student. They must have a GPA of 3.0 or higher and a major in a STEM field of study.

Financial data Stipends provide payment of 50% of the tuition and fees at the recipient's institution, to a maximum of $10,000.

Duration 1 year; may be renewed 1 additional year.

Deadline January of each year.

[404]
NASA SCIENCE AND TECHNOLOGY INSTITUTE (NSTI) SUMMER SCHOLARS PROGRAM

United Negro College Fund Special Programs
 Corporation
Attn: NASA Science and Technology Institute
6402 Arlington Boulevard, Suite 600
Falls Church, VA 22042
(703) 677-3400 Toll Free: (800) 530-6232
Fax: (703) 205-7645 E-mail: portal@uncfsp.org
Web: www.uncfsp.org

Summary To provide an internship opportunity to Native Americans and other underrepresented undergraduate students interested in working on a summer research project at designated research centers of the U.S. National Aeronautics and Space Administration (NASA).

Eligibility This program is open to current college freshmen, sophomores, and juniors at accredited institutions who are members of underrepresented groups, including women, ethnic minorities, and persons with disabilities. Applicants must be working on a degree in a science, technology, engineering, or mathematics (STEM) field and have a GPA of 3.0 or higher. They must be interested in working on a research project during the summer at Ames Research Center (Moffett Field, California), Johnson Space Center (Houston, Texas), or Glenn Research Center (Cleveland, Ohio). U.S. citizenship is required.

Financial data A stipend is provided (amount not specified).

Duration 10 weeks during the summer.

Additional information This program, which began in 2006, is funded by NASA and administered by the United Negro College Fund Special Programs Corporation.

Number awarded Varies each year.

Deadline January of each year.

[405]
NATIONAL MUSEUM OF THE AMERICAN INDIAN 10-WEEK INTERNSHIPS IN CONSERVATION

National Museum of the American Indian
Attn: Head of Conservation
Cultural Resources Center
4220 Silver Hill Road, MRC 538
Suitland, MD 20746-2863
(301) 238-1415 Fax: (301) 238-3201
E-mail: kaminitzm@si.edu
Web: www.nmai.si.edu

Summary To provide undergraduate and graduate students with an opportunity to learn more about conservation during an internship at the Smithsonian Institution's National Museum of the American Indian (NMAI).

Eligibility This program is open to undergraduate and graduate students with a background in studio art, anthropology, art history, museum studies, chemistry, or biology. Native American students interested in conservation and museum care practices are especially welcome. Applicants must be interested in participating in a program at the NMAI Cultural Resources Center in Suitland, Maryland that involves collab-

oration with Native people in developing appropriate methods of handling, preserving, and interpreting cultural materials.

Financial data Interns receive a stipend (amount not specified).

Duration 10 weeks, in summer or winter.

Number awarded Varies each year.

Deadline January of each year for summer; September of each year for winter.

[406]
NATIONAL PRESS CLUB SCHOLARSHIP FOR JOURNALISM DIVERSITY

National Press Club
Attn: General Manager's Office
529 14th Street, N.W.
Washington, DC 20045
(202) 662-7599
Web: www.press.org/activities/aboutscholarship.cfm

Summary To provide funding to Native Americans and other high school seniors who will bring diversity to the field and are planning to major in journalism in college.

Eligibility This program is open to high school seniors who have been accepted to college and plan to prepare for a career in journalism. Applicants must submit 1) a 500-word essay explaining how they would add diversity to U.S. journalism; 2) up to 5 work samples demonstrating an ongoing interest in journalism through work on a high school newspaper or other media; 3) letters of recommendation from 3 people; 4) a copy of their high school transcript; 5) documentation of financial need; 6) a letter of acceptance from the college or university of their choice; and 7) a brief description of how they have pursued journalism in high school.

Financial data The stipend is $2,000 for the first year and $2,500 for each subsequent year. The program also provides an additional $500 book stipend, designated the Ellen Masin Persina Scholarship, for the first year.

Duration 4 years.

Additional information The program began in 1990.

Number awarded 1 each year.

Deadline February of each year.

[407]
NATIONAL SPACE GRANT COLLEGE AND FELLOWSHIP PROGRAM

National Aeronautics and Space Administration
Attn: Office of Education
300 E Street, S.W.
Mail Suite 6M35
Washington, DC 20546-0001
(202) 358-1069 Fax: (202) 358-7097
E-mail: Diane.D.DeTroye@nasa.gov
Web: www.nasa.gov

Summary To provide financial assistance to Native Americans and other undergraduate and graduate students interested in preparing for a career in a space-related field.

Eligibility This program is open to undergraduate and graduate students at colleges and universities that participate in the National Space Grant program of the U.S. National Aeronautics and Space Administration (NASA) through their state consortium. Applicants must be interested in a program of study and/or research in a field of science, technology, engineering, or mathematics (STEM) related to space. A specific goal of the program is to increase preparation by members of underrepresented groups (minorities, women, and persons with disabilities) for STEM space-related careers. Financial need is not considered in the selection process.

Financial data Each consortium establishes the terms of the fellowship program in its state.

Additional information NASA established the Space Grant program in 1989. It operates through 52 consortia in each state, the District of Columbia, and Puerto Rico. Each consortium includes selected colleges and universities in that state as well as other affiliates from industry, museums, science centers, and state and local agencies.

Number awarded Varies each year.

Deadline Each consortium sets its own deadlines.

[408]
NATIONAL TRIBAL GAMING COMMISSIONS/ REGULATORS SCHOLARSHIPS

National Tribal Gaming Commissions/Regulators
Attn: Scholarship Committee
P.O. Box 454
Oneida, WI 54155
E-mail: dawn@thehillgroup.org
Web: www.ntgcr.com/scholarships.php

Summary To provide financial assistance to Native Americans interested in working on an undergraduate or graduate degree in a field related to the gaming industry.

Eligibility This program is open to enrolled members of federally-recognized American Indian tribes and Alaska Native groups. Applicants must be high school seniors, rising undergraduates, or potential graduate students enrolled or planning to enroll full time at an accredited college or university in the United States and have a GPA of 2.5 or higher. They must be preparing for a career in the gaming, business, financial, or hospitality industries. Along with their application, they must submit a 4-page essay on their personal background (including whether they speak their tribal language or are learning their tribal language and other cultural skills), their degree plan for higher education, why they have chosen that field of study, how they plan to serve their tribal people when they complete their higher education, and why they should be selected for this scholarship. Selection is based on the essay, academic ability (judged on GPA, class rank, SAT and/or ACT scores, and curriculum rigor), leadership, honors and awards received, community involvement, 3 letters of recommendation, intellectual skills beyond the classroom, accomplishments, professional development, and financial need.

Financial data The stipend is $5,000.

Duration 1 year.

Number awarded 3 each year.

Deadline June of each year for fall semester; October of each year for spring semester.

[409]
NATIVE AMERICAN EDUCATION GRANTS

Presbyterian Church (USA)
Attn: Office of Financial Aid for Studies
100 Witherspoon Street, Room M-052
Louisville, KY 40202-1396
(502) 569-5776   Toll Free: (888) 728-7228, ext. 5776
Fax: (502) 569-8766   E-mail: finaid@pcusa.org
Web: www.pcusa.org

Summary To provide financial assistance to Native American students, especially members of the Presbyterian Church (USA), who are interested in continuing their college education.

Eligibility This program is open to Alaska Native and Native American students who have completed at least 2 years of full-time study at an accredited institution in the United States and have a GPA of 2.5 or higher. Applicants must be making satisfactory progress toward a degree, able to provide proof of tribal membership, U.S. citizens or permanent residents, recommended by their church pastor, and able to demonstrate financial need. Students from all faith traditions are encouraged to apply, but preference is given to members of the PCUSA.

Financial data Stipends range from $500 to $1,500 per year, depending upon the recipient's financial need.

Duration 1 year; may be renewed.

Number awarded Varies each year.

Deadline June of each year.

[410]
NATIVE AMERICAN JOURNALISTS ASSOCIATION SCHOLARSHIPS

Native American Journalists Association
c/o University of Oklahoma
Gaylord College
395 West Lindsey Street
Norman, OK 73019-4201
(405) 325-9008   Fax: (405) 325-6945
E-mail: info@naja.com
Web: www.naja.com/index.php/students/naja-scholarships

Summary To provide financial assistance to student members of the Native American Journalists Association (NAJA) who are interested in a career in journalism or journalism education.

Eligibility This program is open to NAJA members who are high school seniors, undergraduates, or graduate students working on or planning to work on a degree in journalism. Applicants must include proof of enrollment in a federal- or state-recognized tribe; work samples; transcripts; a cover letter on their financial need, area of interest (print, broadcast, photojournalism, new media, journalism education), and reasons for preparing for a career in journalism; and 2 letters of recommendation.

Financial data The stipends range from $500 to $5,000.

Duration 1 year.

Additional information Support for this program is provided by the James M. Cox Foundation, the Samuel I. Newhouse Foundation, and CNN.

Number awarded Varies each year; recently, 11 of these scholarships were awarded.

Deadline March of each year.

[411]
NATIVE AMERICAN LEADERSHIP IN EDUCATION (NALE) PROGRAM

Catching the Dream
8200 Mountain Road, N.E., Suite 203
Albuquerque, NM 87110-7835
(505) 262-2351   Fax: (505) 262-0534
E-mail: NScholarsh@aol.com
Web: www.catchingthedream.org/Scholarship.htm

Summary To provide financial assistance to American Indian paraprofessionals in the education field who wish to return to college or graduate school.

Eligibility This program is open to paraprofessionals who are working in Indian schools and who plan to return to college or graduate school to complete their degree in education, counseling, or school administration. Applicants must be able to provide proof that they are at least one-quarter Indian blood and a member of a U.S. tribe that is federally-recognized, state-recognized, or terminated. Along with their application, they must submit documentation of financial need, 3 letters of recommendation, copies of applications and responses from all other sources of funding for which they are eligible, official transcripts, standardized test scores (ACT, SAT, GRE, MCAT, LSAT, etc.), and an essay explaining their goals in life, college plans, and career plans (especially how those plans include working with and benefiting Indians). Selection is based on merit and potential for improving the lives of Indian people.

Financial data Stipends range from $500 to $5,000 per year.

Duration 1 year; may be renewed.

Additional information The sponsor was formerly known as the Native American Scholarship Fund.

Number awarded Varies; generally, 15 or more each year.

Deadline April of each year for fall term; September of each year for spring and winter terms; March of each year for summer school.

[412]
NATIVE AMERICAN SCIENCE SCHOLARSHIPS

Denver Museum of Nature & Science
Attn: Department of Anthropology
Native American Science Programs
2001 Colorado Boulevard
Denver, CO 80205
(303) 370-6313   E-mail: nascience@dmns.org
Web: www.dmns.org/nascience

Summary To provide financial assistance to Native Americans from Colorado who are interested in preparing for a science career.

Eligibility This program is open to students who have demonstrated leadership, academic achievement, and an interest in a science career. Preference is given to Native Americans who are either 1) seniors graduating from a high school in Colorado and planning to major in science at a college or university in any state; or 2) undergraduates currently majoring in science at a college or university in Colorado. Applicants must submit 150-word essays on 1) their academic achievements; 2) their educational and career goals; and 3) why they should be selected for the program.

Financial data A stipend is awarded (amount not specified).

Duration 1 year.

Number awarded 1 or more each year.

Deadline September of each year.

[413]
NATIVE HAWAIIAN CHAMBER OF COMMERCE SCHOLARSHIPS

Ke Ali'i Pauahi Foundation
Attn: Financial Aid & Scholarship Services
567 South King Street, Suite 160
Honolulu, HI 96813
(808) 534-3966   Toll Free: (800) 842-4682, ext. 43966
Fax: (808) 534-3890   E-mail: scholarships@pauahi.org
Web: www.pauahi.org/scholarships

Summary To provide financial assistance to students, especially Native Hawaiians, who are interested in working on an undergraduate or graduate degree in business at a school in any state.

Eligibility This program is open to undergraduate and graduate students who are working on a degree in business administration at a college or university in any state. Applicants must have a GPA of 3.0 or higher. Residency in Hawaii is not required, but preference is given to Native Hawaiians (descendants of the aboriginal inhabitants of the Hawaiian Islands prior to 1778).

Financial data The stipend is $1,100.

Duration 1 year.

Additional information This program is sponsored by the Native Hawaiian Chamber of Commerce.

Number awarded Varies each year; recently, 7 of these scholarships were awarded.

Deadline March of each year.

[414]
NATIVE VISION SCHOLARSHIPS

Native Vision
c/o Johns Hopkins University
Center for American Indian Health
621 North Washington Street
Baltimore, MD 21205
(410) 955-6931   Fax: (410) 955-2010
E-mail: mhammen@jhsph.edu
Web: www.nativevision.org

Summary To provide financial assistance for college to American Indian high school seniors who participate in a sports camp.

Eligibility This program is open to graduating high school seniors who are enrolled members of a federally-recognized tribe. Applicants must have been admitted to an accredited community college or 4-year undergraduate program. They must be able to demonstrate a sustained involvement in the community, an applied interest in American Indian concerns and initiatives, a GPA of 3.0 or higher, and involvement in extracurricular and/or athletic activities. Along with their application, they must submit a high school transcript, 2 letters of recommendation, and a 200-word essay on their goals for the future and how this scholarship will help them achieve their dreams; their essay should emphasize how their goals relate to their continued involvement in American Indian communities. The program is intended for students who also participate in the sponsor's summer Sports and Life Skills camp.

Financial data The stipend is $5,000.

Duration 1 year.

Additional information Native Vision was established in 2001 by the Center for American Indian Health at the Johns Hopkins Bloomberg School of Public Health and the National Football League Players Association. Each year, it sponsors a Sports and Life Skills camp, hosted by a tribal organization, for approximately 800 Native American students. In addition to training clinics in baseball, football, basketball, soccer, volleyball, and track, it conducts workshops on such topics as financial aid for college, leadership, crafts, and drunk driving prevention.

Number awarded 2 or 3 each year.

Deadline May of each year.

[415]
NAVAJO GENERATING STATION SCHOLARSHIP

Salt River Project
Navajo Generating Station
Attn: Linda Dawavendewa (NGS 640)
P.O. Box 850
Page, AZ 86040
(928) 645-6539 E-mail: Linda.Dawavendewa@srpnet.com
Web: www.srpnet.com/education/grants/navajo.aspx

Summary To provide financial assistance to members of the Navajo Nation who have completed at least 2 years of college, particularly those who are majoring in selected sciences.

Eligibility This program is open to enrolled members of the Navajo Nation who are full-time students at an accredited college or university. Applicants must be entering their junior year of college and have a GPA of 3.0 or higher. Preference is given to students majoring in mathematics, engineering, or environmental studies. Along with their application, they must submit a 1-page letter explaining their career goals, reasons for selecting that field of study, and why they believe the sponsor should provide funds; a current resume; official transcripts; 2 letters of recommendation; documentation of financial need; and a Certificate of Indian Blood. Selection is based on field of study, academic excellence, and achievement.

Financial data The stipend depends on the need of the recipient.

Duration 1 year; may be renewed until completion of a bachelor's degree.

Additional information This program was established in 1976.

Number awarded Varies each year; recently, 7 of these scholarships were awarded.

Deadline April of each year.

[416]
NAVAJO NATION COLLEGE DEVELOPMENTAL STUDIES PROGRAM

Navajo Nation
Attn: Office of Navajo Nation Scholarship and Financial
     Assistance
P.O. Box 1870
Window Rock, AZ 86515-1870
(928) 871-7444   Toll Free: (800) 243-2956
Fax: (928) 871-6742   E-mail: onnsfacentral@navajo.org
Web: www.onnsfa.org

Summary To provide financial assistance to members of the Navajo Nation who require remedial education at the college level.

Eligibility This program is open to enrolled members of the Navajo Nation who are taking developmental studies courses to improve deficiencies in math, reading, or writing skills. Preference is given to students at Diné College. Selection is based on financial need.

Financial data The amount of the award depends on the needs of the recipient.

Duration Recipients may enroll in up to 12 semester credit hours of college development courses during their first year in college.

Deadline June of each year for fall term; November of each year for winter or spring terms; April of each year for summer session.

[417]
NAVAJO NATION FINANCIAL NEED-BASED ASSISTANCE PROGRAM

Navajo Nation
Attn: Office of Navajo Nation Scholarship and Financial
     Assistance
P.O. Box 1870
Window Rock, AZ 86515-1870
(928) 871-7444   Toll Free: (800) 243-2956
Fax: (928) 871-6742   E-mail: onnsfacentral@navajo.org
Web: www.onnsfa.org

Summary To provide financial assistance for college to members of the Navajo Nation.

Eligibility This program is open to enrolled members of the Navajo Nation who have proof of one-quarter or more Navajo Indian blood quantum on their Certificate of Indian Blood. Applicants must be attending or planning to attend an accredited institution of higher education to work on an associate or baccalaureate degree. Financial need must be demonstrated.

Financial data The stipend is $1,500 per year.

Duration 1 year; may be renewed (if the recipient maintains at least a 2.0 GPA) for up to a total of 10 semesters of full-time undergraduate study, 5 academic terms or 64 semester credit hours at 2-year institutions, or 50 semester credit hours of part-time undergraduate study.

Number awarded Varies each year; recently, 3,714 of these scholarships were awarded.

Deadline June of each year for fall term; November of each year for winter or spring terms; April of each year for summer session.

[418]
NAVAJO NATION VOCATIONAL EDUCATION PROGRAM

Navajo Nation
Attn: Office of Navajo Nation Scholarship and Financial
  Assistance
P.O. Box 1870
Window Rock, AZ 86515-1870
(928) 871-7444   Toll Free: (800) 243-2956
Fax: (928) 871-6742   E-mail: onnsfacentral@navajo.org
Web: www.onnsfa.org

Summary   To provide financial assistance for vocational education to members of the Navajo Nation.

Eligibility   This program is open to enrolled members of the Navajo Nation who are enrolled or planning to enroll full time at a regionally accredited vocational institution. Applicants must be interested in working on an associate of applied science degree or a vocational certificate. Selection is based on financial need.

Financial data   The amount of the award depends on the need of the recipient.

Duration   1 year; may be renewed.

Number awarded   Varies each year.

Deadline   June of each year for fall term; November of each year for winter or spring terms; April of each year for summer session.

[419]
NAVAJO TIMES INTERNSHIPS

Navajo Times
Attn: Publisher
P.O. Box 310
Window Rock, AZ 86515-0310
(928) 871-1130   Fax: (928) 871-1159
E-mail: tarviso@navajotimes.com
Web: www.navajotimes.com/jobs/internships.php

Summary   To provide summer work experience at the *Navajo Times* to college students, especially Navajos and other Native Americans.

Eligibility   This program is open to college students members who are majoring in journalism, communications, graphic arts, or printing. Preference is given to Navajo and other Native American students. Applicants must submit a current resume; samples of any articles, photographs, graphic art work, or other examples of their writing, especially any that have been previously published; and a letter of interest that explains why they want the internship, what they hope to learn, and what they can provide to the paper.

Financial data   A stipend is paid (amount not specified).

Duration   Summer months.

Number awarded   1 or more each year.

Deadline   April of each year.

[420]
NAVAJO TRIBAL UTILITY AUTHORITY ENHANCED SCHOLARSHIPS

Navajo Tribal Utility Authority
Attn: Human Resources Division/Training Department
P.O. Box 170
Fort Defiance, AZ 86504
(928) 729-5721, ext. 2152
Web: www.ntua.com/Scholar/Scholarship.html

Summary   To provide financial assistance to enrolled members of the Navajo Nation who are interested in working on a bachelor's or master's degree to prepare for a career in the multi-service utility industry and complete an internship at the Navajo Tribal Utility Authority (NTUA).

Eligibility   This program is open to enrolled members of the Navajo Nation who are graduating high school seniors, high school graduates, GED recipients, or continuing full-time undergraduate or graduate students with a GPA of 2.0 or higher. Applicants must have successfully completed a 2-month summer internship with NTUA. They must be interested in working on a bachelor's or master's degree in a field related to the multi-service utility industry, including accounting, administration, business, engineering (civil, electrical, environmental), environment, information technology, or management. In the selection process to hire interns, priority is given to recipients of standard NTUA scholarships.

Financial data   The stipend is $2,500 per year.

Duration   1 year; may be renewed, provided the recipient maintains a GPA of 2.0 or higher and completes another 2-month summer internship with NTUA.

Number awarded   Varies each year.

Deadline   April of each year.

[421]
NAVY/MARINE CORPS JROTC SCHOLARSHIP

National Naval Officers Association-Washington, D.C.
  Chapter
Attn: Scholarship Program
2701 Park Center Drive, A1108
Alexandria, VA 22302
(703) 566-3840   Fax: (703) 566-3813
E-mail: Stephen.Williams@Navy.mil
Web: dcnnoa.memberlodge.com

Summary   To provide financial assistance to Native American and other minority high school seniors from the Washington, D.C. area who have participated in Navy or Marine Corps Junior Reserve Officers Training Corps (JROTC) and are planning to attend college in any state.

Eligibility   This program is open to minority seniors graduating from high schools in the Washington, D.C. metropolitan area who have participated in Navy or Marine Corps JROTC. Applicants must be planning to enroll full time at an accredited 2- or 4-year college or university in any state. They must have a GPA of 2.5 or higher. Selection is based on academic achievement, community involvement, and financial need.

Financial data   The stipend is $1,000.

Duration   1 year; nonrenewable.

Additional information   Recipients are not required to join or affiliate with the military in any way after college.

Number awarded   1 each year.

Deadline   March of each year.

[422]
NCAI YOUTH AMBASSADOR LEADERSHIP PROGRAM SCHOLARSHIPS

National Congress of American Indians
Attn: Internship Program
1516 P Street, N.W.
Washington, DC 20005
(202) 466-7767   Fax: (2020 466-7797
E-mail: ncai@ncai.org
Web: www.ncai.org/Youth.418.0.html

Summary To provide financial assistance to undergraduates and graduate students who participate in the Youth Commission Ambassador Leadership Program (ALP) of the National Congress of American Indians (NCAI).

Eligibility This program is open to youth between 17 and 25 years of age who are eligible for NCAI membership. Applicants must be graduating high school seniors or full-time undergraduate or graduate students and have a GPA of 2.0 or higher. They must have support from their tribal council. Males and females are considered separately. Recipients are selected at the Congress on the basis of an oration, contemporary dress, extemporaneous question, cultural presentation, and debate; GPA and recommendations are also considered.

Financial data The stipend is $2,500. Funds are paid directly to the academic institution.

Duration The stipend is for 1 year; recipients serve as Youth Ambassadors for 2 years.

Additional information This program was established in 2006. Students selected as Youth Ambassadors lead the NCAI Youth Commission in its meetings and represent NCAI Youth when their presence is requested.

Number awarded 2 (1 male and 1 female) each even-numbered year.

Deadline September of even-numbered years.

[423]
NEW JERSEY UTILITIES ASSOCIATION EQUAL EMPLOYMENT OPPORTUNITY SCHOLARSHIPS

New Jersey Utilities Association
50 West State Street, Suite 1117
Trenton, NJ 08608
(609) 392-1000   Fax: (609) 396-4231
Web: www.njua.org/html/njua_eeo_scholarship.cfm

Summary To provide financial assistance to Native American, minority, female, and disabled high school seniors in New Jersey interested in attending college in any state.

Eligibility This program is open to seniors graduating from high schools in New Jersey who are women, minorities (Black or African American, Hispanic or Latino, American Indian or Alaska Native, Asian, Native Hawaiian or Pacific Islander, or 2 or more races), and persons with disabilities. Applicants must be planning to work on a bachelor's degree at a college or university in any state. They must be able to demonstrate financial need. Children of employees of any New Jersey Utilities Association-member company are ineligible. Selection is based on overall academic excellence and demonstrated financial need. U.S. citizenship or permanent resident status is required.

Financial data The stipend is $1,500 per year.

Duration 4 years.

Number awarded 2 each year.

Deadline March of each year.

[424]
NEW YORK AID TO NATIVE AMERICANS

New York State Education Department
Attn: Native American Education Unit
Education Building Annex, Room 374
Albany, NY 12234
(518) 474-0537   Fax: (518) 474-3666
E-mail: emscosigen@mail.nysed.gov
Web: www.emsc.nysed.gov/rss/natamer/studentaidinfo.html

Summary To provide financial assistance to American Indians in New York who are interested in attending college in the state.

Eligibility This program is open to Native Americans who meet these qualifications: are on official tribal rolls of a New York State tribe or are the child of an enrolled member; are residents of New York State; and are or will be graduates of an accredited high school or have a New York State General Equivalency Diploma or are enrolled in college credit programs working for the State High School Equivalency Diploma. Recipients must be accepted by an approved accredited postsecondary institution within New York State.

Financial data The stipend is $2,000 per year for full-time study (at least 12 credit hours per semester or 24 credit hours per year); students registering for less than full-time study are funded on a prorated basis. Funding is available for summer course work on a special needs basis. Funds spent for summer school are deducted from the recipient's maximum entitlement.

Duration 1 year; renewable for up to 3 additional years (4 additional years for specific programs requiring 5 years to complete degree requirements).

Additional information The New York State tribes include members of the Iroquoian tribes (St. Regis Mohawk, Oneida, Onondaga, Cayuga, Seneca Nation, Tonawanda Band of Seneca, and Tuscarora), the Shinnecock tribe, and the Poospatuck tribe. Remedial, noncredit, and college preparation courses are not funded.

Number awarded Varies; approximately 500 each year.

Deadline July of each year for fall semester; December of each year for spring semester; May of each year for summer session.

[425]
NEWMONT MINING CORPORATION TRIBAL SCHOLARS PROGRAM

American Indian College Fund
Attn: Scholarship Department
8333 Greenwood Boulevard
Denver, CO 80221
(303) 426-8900   Toll Free: (800) 776-FUND
Fax: (303) 426-1200
E-mail: scholarships@collegefund.org
Web: www.collegefund.org/scholarships/schol_tcu.html

Summary To provide financial assistance to Native American college students from Colorado who are enrolled at Tribal Colleges and Universities (TCUs) in any state.

Eligibility This program is open to American Indians and Alaska Natives who have proof of enrollment or descendancy and are residents of Colorado. Applicants must be enrolled full time at an eligible TCU in any state. They must have a GPA of 2.5 or higher. Applications are available only online and include required essays on specified topics.

Financial data The stipend is $2,000.

Duration 1 year.

Additional information This program is funded by the Newmont Mining Corporation in partnership with the American Indian College Fund.

Number awarded 1 or more each year.

Deadline May of each year.

[426]
NEZ PERCE HIGHER EDUCATION GRANTS

Nez Perce Tribe
Attn: Higher Education
116 Veterans Drive
P.O. Box 365
Lapwai, ID 83540
(206) 621-4610   Fax: (206) 843-7387
E-mail: education@nezperce.org
Web: www.nezperce.org/Official/highereducation.htm

Summary To provide financial assistance to members of the Nez Perce Tribe who are interested in attending college or graduate school in any state.

Eligibility This program is open to enrolled members of the Nez Perce Tribe who are attending or planning to attend a college, university, or vocational/technical school in any state to work on a vocational certificate or an associate, bachelor's, master's, or doctoral/professional degree. Applicants must submit documentation of financial need and a personal letter describing their educational goals and future plans.

Financial data Tribal scholarship funds (including the Isaac Broncheau Memorial Fund and the Nez Perce Tribal Tobacco Tax Revenue Funds) provide stipends of $1,600 per year for undergraduates (including vocational/technical students) or $3,000 per year for graduate students. Funding from the Bureau of Indian Affairs (BIA) is generally available only for undergraduate students and provides stipends of $3,120 per year.

Duration 1 semester; may be renewed up to 4 additional semesters for a 2-year degree, up to 9 additional semesters for a 4-year degree, up to 5 additional semesters for a master's degree, or up to 9 additional semesters for a doctoral/professional degree.

Number awarded Varies each year.

Deadline September of each year for fall semester or quarter; January of each year for spring semester or winter quarter; March of each year for spring quarter.

[427]
NICKERSON WEST SHAKESPEARE/ARAPAHO FARM TRUST UNDERGRADUATE SCHOLARSHIP

Northern Arapaho Tribe
Attn: Sky People Higher Education
P.O. Box 8480
Ethete, WY 82520
(307) 332-5286   Toll Free: (800) 815-6795
Fax: (307) 332-9104   E-mail: assistant@skypeopleed.org
Web: www.skypeopleed.org

Summary To provide financial assistance to members of the Northern Arapaho Tribe who are working on an undergraduate degree in accounting or agribusiness.

Eligibility This program is open to full-time undergraduate students who have an undergraduate GPA of 2.0 or higher. Applicants must be of at least one-fourth Northern Arapaho descent (enrolled or non-enrolled) and must submit a Certificate of Indian Blood or other verification of Northern Arapaho blood with at least one-fourth degree. They must be working on a degree in accounting or agribusiness. Along with their application, they must submit a 1-page personal statement that includes a brief history of their background, academic ability and achievement, work or leadership experience, participation in community-related activities, and career goals. Selection is based on that statement, potential to contribute to the community upon graduation, academic ability and achievement, and a letter of recommendation.

Financial data The stipend is $1,500 per year.

Duration 1 year; may be renewed.

Additional information Recipients are expected to apply for employment with the Northern Arapaho Tribe after graduation.

Number awarded 2 each year.

Deadline June of each year.

[428]
NIDDK/OMHRC SUMMER INTERNSHIP PROGRAM FOR UNDERREPRESENTED MINORITIES

National Institute of Diabetes and Digestive and Kidney Diseases
Attn: Office of Minority Health Research Coordination
6707 Democracy Boulevard, Room 906A
Bethesda, MD 20892-5454
(301) 435-2988   Fax: (301) 594-9358
E-mail: MartinezW@mail.nih.gov
Web: www2.niddk.nih.gov/Funding

Summary To provide Native Americans and other underrepresented minority undergraduate students with an opportunity to conduct research in the laboratory of a National Institute of Diabetes and Digestive and Kidney Diseases (NIDDK) intramural scientist during the summer.

Eligibility This program is open to undergraduate students who are members of underrepresented minority groups (African Americans, Hispanic Americans, Native Americans, Native Hawaiians, other Pacific Islanders, and Alaska Natives). Applicants must be interested in participating in a research project conducted at an intramural research laboratory of NIDDK in Bethesda, Maryland or Phoenix, Arizona. They must have completed at least 1 year at an accredited institution and have a GPA of 3.0 or higher. Along with their application, they must submit a 2-page personal statement of their research interest, career goals, and reasons for applying to training at NIDDK. U.S. citizenship or permanent resident status is required.

Financial data Students receive a stipend of $2,500, housing, and (for those who live outside the Washington metropolitan area or the state of Arizona) a travel allowance of $500.

Duration 10 weeks during the summer.

Deadline February of each year.

[429]
NIHEWAN SCHOLARSHIPS

Nihewan Foundation for Native American Education
9595 Wilshire Boulevard, Suite 1020
Beverly Hills, CA 90212
(808) 822-3111   Fax: (310) 278-0238
E-mail: info@nihewan.org
Web: www.nihewan.org/programs.html

Summary   To provide financial assistance to Native Americans interested in studying about their culture in college.

Eligibility   This program is open to enrolled members of a Native American tribe or Canadian First nation. Applicants must be interested in working on a college degree in Native American/indigenous studies. Along with their application, they must include 3 essays: 1) their goals with regard to Native American/indigenous studies; 2) other foundations that are helping finance their studies (must have applied to at least 2 other foundations and still have unmet need); and 3) their current school expenses.

Financial data   A stipend is awarded (amount not specified).

Duration   1 year.

Additional information   The Nihewan Foundation was established by singer-songwriter Buffy Sainte-Marie in 1969.

Number awarded   1 or more each year.

Deadline   Deadline not specified.

[430]
NINILCHIK NATIVE ASSOCIATION SCHOLARSHIP AND VOCATIONAL GRANT

Cook Inlet Region, Inc.
Attn: The CIRI Foundation
3600 San Jeronimo Drive, Suite 256
Anchorage, AK 99508-2870
(907) 793-3575   Toll Free: (800) 764-3382
Fax: (907) 793-3585   E-mail: tcf@thecirifoundation.org
Web: www.thecirifoundation.org/village_scholarships.htm

Summary   To provide financial assistance for professional preparation after high school to Alaska Natives who are original enrollees or descendants of the Ninilchik Native Association.

Eligibility   This program is open to 1) Alaska Native enrollees of the Ninilchik Native Association under the Alaska Native Claims Settlement Act (ANCSA) of 1971; and 2) their lineal descendants. Proof of eligibility must be submitted. There is no residency requirement. Applicants for the scholarships must be accepted or enrolled full time in an accredited or otherwise approved postsecondary college or university; applicants for the grants may be enrolled either part or full time in a technical skills certificate or degree program. All applicants should have a GPA of 2.5 or higher. Along with their application, they must submit a 500-word statement on their educational and career goals and how they are contributing, or planning to contribute, to a positive Alaska Native community. Selection is based on that statement, academic achievement, rigor of course work or degree program, student financial contribution, financial need, grade level, previous work performance, community service, and relationship of degree program to career goals.

Financial data   The stipend depends on the availability of funds.

Duration   1 semester for the general scholarship and 1 calendar year for the vocational technical grant; recipients may reapply.

Additional information   This program was established in 1992.

Number awarded   Varies each year.

Deadline   May or November of each year for scholarships; June of each year for grants.

[431]
NISSAN NORTH AMERICA SCHOLARSHIP

American Indian College Fund
Attn: Scholarship Department
8333 Greenwood Boulevard
Denver, CO 80221
(303) 426-8900   Toll Free: (800) 776-FUND
Fax: (303) 426-1200
E-mail: scholarships@collegefund.org
Web: www.collegefund.org

Summary   To provide financial assistance to Native American students enrolling in a bachelor's degree program at a mainstream college.

Eligibility   This program is open to American Indians and Alaska Natives who can document proof of enrollment or descendancy. Applicants must be enrolled or planning to enroll full time in a bachelor's degree program at a mainstream institution. They must have a GPA of 2.5 GPA or higher and be able to demonstrate leadership and commitment to an American Indian community. Applications are available only online and include required essays on specified topics. Selection is based on exceptional academic achievement.

Financial data   The stipend is $5,000 per year.

Duration   1 year; may be renewed.

Additional information   This scholarship is sponsored by Nissan North America, Inc., in partnership with the American Indian College Fund.

Number awarded   20 each year.

Deadline   May of each year.

[432]
NISSAN NORTH AMERICA TRIBAL COLLEGE SCHOLARSHIP PROGRAM

American Indian College Fund
Attn: Scholarship Department
8333 Greenwood Boulevard
Denver, CO 80221
(303) 426-8900   Toll Free: (800) 776-FUND
Fax: (303) 426-1200
E-mail: scholarships@collegefund.org
Web: www.collegefund.org/scholarships/schol_tcu.html

Summary   To provide financial assistance to Native Americans who are attending or planning to attend a Tribal College or University (TCU).

Eligibility   This program is open to American Indians or Alaska Natives who are enrolled or planning to enroll full time at an eligible TCU. Applicants must have a GPA of 2.5 or higher and be able to demonstrate leadership and commitment to an American Indian community. Applications are available only online and include required essays on specified topics. Selection is based on exceptional academic achievement.

Financial data The stipend is $3,000.

Duration 1 year.

Additional information This scholarship is sponsored by Nissan North America, Inc., in partnership with the American Indian College Fund.

Number awarded 1 or more each year.

Deadline May of each year.

[433]
NMAI INTERNSHIP PROGRAM

National Museum of the American Indian
Attn: Internship Program
Cultural Resources Center
4220 Silver Hill Road
Suitland, MD 20746-2863
(301) 238-1540   Fax: (301) 238-3200
E-mail: NMAIinterns@si.edu
Web: americanindian.si.edu

Summary To provide work and/or research opportunities for Native American students in the area of museum practice and related programming at the Smithsonian Institution's National Museum of the American Indian (NMAI).

Eligibility These internships are intended primarily for American Indian, Native Hawaiian, and Alaska Native students currently enrolled in undergraduate or graduate academic programs with a cumulative GPA of 3.0 or higher. Applicants must be interested in guided work/research experiences using the resources of the NMAI or other Smithsonian Institution facilities. Along with their application, they must submit a personal statement on their interest in the museum field, what they hope to accomplish through an internship, how it would relate to their academic and professional development, and what in particular about the NMAI interests them and leads them to apply for an internship.

Financial data Travel, housing, and stipends (from $300 to $400 per week) are provided on a limited basis.

Duration 3 sessions of 10 weeks each are held annually.

Additional information Intern projects vary by department. Most projects provide the intern with museum practice and program development experience. Some projects may be more research oriented. Interns who receive a stipend must work 40 hours per week. Positions are available at the Cultural Resources Center in Suitland, Maryland, the George Gustav Heye Center in New York, or the administrative offices in Washington, D.C.

Number awarded Varies each year. More than 100 students have participated in the program since it began in 1994.

Deadline February of each year for summer; July of each year for fall; November of each year for spring.

[434]
NNALEA ACADEMIC SCHOLARSHIP PROGRAM

National Native American Law Enforcement Association
Attn: Academic Scholarship Program
1300 Pennsylvania Avenue, N.W., Suite 700
P.O. Box 171
Washington, DC 20044
(202) 204-3065   Fax: (866) 506-7631
E-mail: info@nnalea.org
Web: www.nnalea.org

Summary To provide financial assistance to Native American high school seniors, undergraduates, and graduate students who have an interest in law enforcement.

Eligibility This program is open to Native Americans who are working on or planning to work on an undergraduate or graduate degree in law enforcement at a 4-year college or university. Applicants must have a GPA of 2.5 or higher. Along with their application, they must provide transcripts and a 200-word essay on Indian Country law enforcement and its impact on tribal communities.

Financial data Stipends are $2,500 or $2,000.

Duration 1 year.

Additional information This program includes 2 named awards: the Jimmy Wooten Memorial Scholarship and the Don Leonard Memorial Scholarship.

Number awarded 2 each year: the Jimmy Wooten Memorial Scholarship at $2,500 and the Don Leonard Memorial Scholarship at $2,000.

Deadline November of each year.

[435]
NOME ESKIMO COMMUNITY HIGHER EDUCATION SCHOLARSHIPS

Nome Eskimo Community
Attn: Tribal Services
P.O. Box 1090
Nome, AK 99762
(907) 443-2246   Fax: (907) 443-3539
E-mail: marshasloan@gci.net
Web: www.necalaska.org/services.html

Summary To provide financial assistance to Alaska Natives and American Indians who are members of a tribe affiliated with the Nome Eskimo Community and interested in attending college or graduate school in any state.

Eligibility This program is open to high school seniors and current college students who are members of an Alaska Native or American Indian tribe or organization affiliated with the Nome Eskimo Community, regardless of their current residence. Applicants must be enrolled or planning to enroll at an accredited college or university in any state to work on an associate, bachelor's, or (if funding is available) master's degree. They must have graduated or will graduate from high school with a GPA of 2.0 or higher.

Financial data A stipend is awarded (amount not specified). Funding is considered supplemental and will not cover the total financial need of students.

Duration 1 year; may be renewed until completion of a degree, provided the recipient maintains acceptable academic progress and a satisfactory GPA.

Additional information Members of the Nome Eskimo Community reflect the heritages of the Bering Straits region of Alaska, including Central Yupik, Inupiaq, St. Lawrence Island Yupik, and American Indians whose lineage derives from tribes in the lower 48 states.

Number awarded Varies each year.

Deadline April of each year for high school seniors entering college as first-year students; July of each year for continuing students for fall semester or quarter; December of each year for spring semester or winter quarter; February or each year for spring quarter; May of each year for summer term.

[436]
NONPROFIT MANAGEMENT SCHOLARSHIP

Chickasaw Foundation
110 West 12th Street
P.O. Box 1726
Ada, OK 74821-1726
(580) 421-9030   Fax: (580) 421-9031
E-mail: ChickasawFoundation@chickasaw.net
Web: www.chickasawfoundation.org/index_20.htm

Summary To provide financial assistance to members of the Chickasaw Nation interested in studying a field related to nonprofit management.

Eligibility This program is open to members of the Chickasaw Nation who are currently enrolled as full-time undergraduates at a 4-year college or university. Applicants must be working on nonprofit management certification or another field of study related to the nonprofit sector. They must have a GPA of 3.0 or higher. Along with their application, they must submit high school or college transcripts, 2 letters of recommendation, a copy of their Chickasaw Nation citizenship card, and a 1-page essay on their long-term goals and plans for achieving them. Financial need is not considered in the selection process.

Financial data The stipend is $1,000.

Duration 1 year.

Number awarded 1 each year.

Deadline August of each year.

[437]
NORTH DAKOTA INDIAN SCHOLARSHIP PROGRAM

North Dakota University System
Attn: Coordinator of Multicultural Education
1815 Schafer Street, Suite 202
Bismarck, ND 58501
(701) 224-2497   Fax: (701) 224-2500
E-mail: rhonda_schauer@ndus.nodak.edu
Web: www.ndus.nodak.edu

Summary To provide financial assistance to Native American students in North Dakota colleges and universities.

Eligibility Applicants must have at least one-quarter degree Indian blood, be residents of North Dakota or enrolled members of a tribe resident in North Dakota, and be accepted as full-time undergraduate students by an institution of higher learning or vocational education in North Dakota. They must have at least a 2.0 GPA, although priority in funding is given to those with a GPA of 3.5 or higher. Participants in internship, student teaching, teaching assistance, or cooperative education programs are eligible only if participation in that program is required for the degree and only if tuition must be paid for the credits earned.

Financial data The amount of the stipend varies from $700 to $2,000 depending on scholastic ability, funds available, total number of applicants, and financial need. The award is divided into semester or quarter payments. The money is to be used to pay registration, health fees, board, room, books, and other necessary items handled by the institution. Any remaining balance may be used to cover the student's personal expenses.

Duration 1 academic year; renewable up to 3 additional years, if the recipient maintains a 2.0 GPA and continues to be in financial need.

Number awarded Varies; approximately 150 to 175 each year.

Deadline July of each year.

[438]
NORTHERN ARAPAHO TRIBAL SCHOLARSHIPS

Northern Arapaho Tribe
Attn: Sky People Higher Education
P.O. Box 8480
Ethete, WY 82520
(307) 332-5286   Toll Free: (800) 815-6795
Fax: (307) 332-9104   E-mail: assistant@skypeopleed.org
Web: www.skypeopleed.org

Summary To provide financial assistance for college to members of the Northern Arapaho Tribe.

Eligibility This program is open to anyone who can certify at least one-fourth degree Northern Arapaho Indian Blood, but preference is given to enrolled members of the Northern Arapaho tribe. Funding priorities are 1) college seniors ready to graduate; 2) continuing students with a GPA of 2.25 or higher; 3) high school or GED graduates; and 4) late applicants.

Financial data The amount of the awards depends on the financial need of the recipients.

Duration 1 year; may be renewed for a total of 5 academic years.

Additional information The scholarships may be used at any accredited college, university, or vocational/technical school. Recipients must attend college full time.

Number awarded Varies each year.

Deadline June of each year for the academic year; November of each year for the spring semester; April of each year for summer school.

[439]
NORTHERN ARAPAHO TRIBE ALFRED J. DURAN SR. TRUST SCHOLARSHIP

Northern Arapaho Tribe
Attn: Sky People Higher Education
P.O. Box 8480
Ethete, WY 82520
(307) 332-5286   Toll Free: (800) 815-6795
Fax: (307) 332-9104   E-mail: assistant@skypeopleed.org
Web: www.skypeopleed.org

Summary To provide financial assistance to members of the Northern Arapaho Tribe who are working on an undergraduate or graduate degree in any field.

Eligibility This program is open to full-time undergraduate and graduate students who have an undergraduate GPA of 2.0 or higher or the graduate GPA required by their school. Applicants must be at least one-fourth Northern Arapaho (enrolled or non-enrolled) and must submit a Certificate of Indian Blood or other verification of Northern Arapaho blood with at least one-fourth degree. They may be working on a degree in any field. Along with their application, they must submit a 1-page personal statement that includes a brief history of their background, academic ability and achievement, work or leadership experience, participation in community-related activities, and career goals. Selection is based on that statement, potential to contribute to the community upon graduation, academic ability and achievement, and a letter of recommendation.

Financial data The stipend is $1,000 per year.

Duration 1 year; may be renewed.

Additional information Recipients are expected to apply for employment with the Northern Arapaho Tribe after graduation.

Number awarded 2 each year.

Deadline June of each year.

[440]
NORTHERN CHEYENNE HIGHER EDUCATION SCHOLARSHIP PROGRAM

Northern Cheyenne Nation
Attn: Tribal Education Department
P.O. Box 307
Lame Deer, MT 59043
(406) 477-6770   Toll Free: (800) 353-8183
Fax: (406) 477-8150   E-mail: darleneh@rangeweb.net
Web: www.cheyennenation.com/education.html

Summary To provide financial assistance to Northern Cheyenne tribal members who are interested in attending college or graduate school in any state.

Eligibility This program is open to enrolled Northern Cheyenne tribal members who have been accepted to a degree program at an accredited college or university in any state. The priority order for awards is 1) continuing and former college students in good standing; 2) graduating high school seniors in good standing or first-time adult college applicants not previously funded; 3) students or other individuals who have previously failed to meet the requirements of the scholarship program; and 4) graduate students (if funds are still available). Applicants must be able to demonstrate financial need. Along with their application, they must submit a 1-page statement on their educational goals, including need for the scholarship, choice of college, major, entry date, and plans after graduation.

Financial data The stipend depends on the need of the recipient, to a maximum of $6,000 per year. These awards are intended to supplement other available sources of funding. The scholarship must be used for tuition, subsistence, required fees, and textbooks.

Duration 1 year; may be renewed if the recipient maintains a GPA of 2.0 or higher and completes at least 14 quarter or 16 semester units as a freshman and sophomore and at least 16 quarter or 18 semester units as a junior or senior.

Number awarded Approximately 80 each year.

Deadline February of each year for fall quarter or semester; September of each year for winter quarter, spring semester, or spring quarter; March of each year for summer school.

[441]
NORTHERN CHEYENNE JOB TRAINING AND PLACEMENT GRANTS

Northern Cheyenne Nation
Attn: Tribal Education Department
P.O. Box 307
Lame Deer, MT 59043
(406) 477-6770   Toll Free: (800) 353-8183
Fax: (406) 477-8150   E-mail: darleneh@rangeweb.net
Web: www.cheyennenation.com/education.html

Summary To provide financial assistance to Northern Cheyenne tribal members and other American Indians residing on the Northern Cheyenne reservation who are interested in vocational training.

Eligibility This program is open to 1) enrolled members of the Northern Cheyenne tribe who reside on or near the reservation; 2) enrolled Northern Cheyenne tribal members who reside outside the service area, provided funding is not available from other tribal or Bureau of Indian Affairs job training and placement programs; and 3) enrolled members of other Indian tribes residing on the Northern Cheyenne reservation, provided they have applied to their home agency and been denied. Applicants must be enrolled or planning to enroll at an accredited institution in any state that provides vocational training. Along with their application, they must submit a 1-page statement on their educational goals, including need for the scholarship, choice of vocational institution, reason for choice, type of training, and entry date. Awards are made according to the following priorities: 1) renewal of grants to continuing students in good standing; 2) new applicants who are enrolled Northern Cheyenne residing on or near the Northern Cheyenne Indian Reservation; 3) enrolled Northern Cheyenne new applicants who reside outside the service area of the reservation; 4) other Indian enrolled tribal members residing on the Northern Cheyenne Indian Reservation; and 5) individuals requesting retraining.

Financial data Funding under this program is supplemental to any other income. Grants are intended to cover living expenses, tuition, books, and supplies related directly to the course.

Duration Support is provided for up to 24 months (up to 36 months for nursing training). Recipients must complete at least 12 units each semester or quarter with a GPA of 2.0 or higher.

Number awarded Varies each year.

Deadline February of each year for fall quarter or semester; September of each year for winter quarter, spring semester, or spring quarter; March of each year for summer school.

[442]
NORTHWEST INDIAN HOUSING ASSOCIATION SCHOLARSHIPS

Northwest Indian Housing Association
Attn: Educational Scholarship Committee
P.O. Box 3785
Seattle, WA 98124-3785
(206) 290-5498　　　　　　　　　　Fax: (206) 526-8662
Web: www.nwiha.org

Summary To provide financial assistance to members of Indian tribes in the Pacific Northwest who are interested in attending college in any state.

Eligibility This program is open to enrolled members of Indian tribes in the Pacific Northwest who are younger than 24 years of age. Applicants must be attending or planning to attend a 2- or 4-year college or university in any state. They must be sponsored by a member organization of the Northwest Indian Housing Association (NWIHA), including a tribal department, an Indian housing authority, or a Tribally Designated Housing Entity (TDHE). Along with their application, they must submit an essay on their need for funds, how the funds will be used, and how the educational activity or training will improve their life.

Financial data A stipend is awarded (amount not specified).

Duration 1 year.

Number awarded 1 or more each year.

Deadline March of each year.

[443]
NORTHWEST JOURNALISTS OF COLOR SCHOLARSHIP AWARDS

Northwest Journalists of Color
c/o Caroline Li
14601 Ninth Avenue N.E.
Shoreline, WA 98155
E-mail: editor@earthwalkersmag.com
Web: www.aajaseattle.org

Summary To provide financial assistance to Native Americans and other minority students from Washington state who are interested in careers in journalism.

Eligibility This program is open to members of minority groups (Asian American, African American, Native American, and Latino) who are 1) residents of Washington attending an accredited college or university in any state; 2) residents of any state attending a Washington college or university; or 3) seniors graduating from Washington high schools. Applicants must be planning a career in broadcast, photo, or print journalism. Along with their application, they must submit 1) a brief essay about themselves, including why they want to be a journalist, challenges they foresee, how they think they can contribute to the profession, and the influence their ethnic heritage might have on their perspective as a working journalist; 2) a current resume; 3) up to 3 work samples; 4) reference letters; and 5) documentation of financial need.

Financial data Stipends range up to $2,500 per year.

Duration 1 year; may be renewed.

Additional information This program, established in 1986, is sponsored by the Seattle chapters of the Asian American Journalists Association, the Native American Journalists Association, the National Association of Black Journalists, and the Latino Media Association. It includes the Walt and Milly Woodward Memorial Scholarship donated by the Western Washington Chapter of the Society of Professional Journalists.

Number awarded Varies each year.

Deadline April of each year.

[444]
NOTTAWASEPPI HURON BAND OF POTAWATOMI HIGHER EDUCATION SCHOLARSHIPS

Nottawaseppi Huron Band of Potawatomi
Attn: Education Director
2221 1-1/2 Mile Road
Fulton, MI 49052
(269) 729-5151, ext. 205　　　　　Fax: (269) 729-4837
E-mail: bphillips@nhbpi.com
Web: nhbpi.com/departments/education.html

Summary To provide financial assistance to members of the Nottawaseppi Huron Band of Potawatomi who are interested in attending college, graduate school, or vocational training in any state.

Eligibility This program is open to members of the Nottawaseppi Huron Band of Potawatomi who are working on or planning to work on a vocational certificate or an associate, bachelor's, or graduate degree at a school in any state. Applicants may be planning to enroll full or part time. They must be able to demonstrate financial need.

Financial data A stipend is awarded (amount not specified).

Duration 1 year; may be renewed.

Number awarded Varies each year.

Deadline July of each year for fall quarter or semester; November of each year for winter quarter or spring semester.

[445]
OFFICE OF HAWAIIAN AFFAIRS SCHOLARSHIPS

Hawai'i Community Foundation
Attn: Scholarship Department
827 Fort Street Mall
Honolulu, HI 96813
(808) 537-6333　　　　　　　　Toll Free: (888) 731-3863
Fax: (808) 521-6286
E-mail: scholarships@hcf-hawaii.org
Web: www.hawaiicommunityfoundation.org/scholarships

Summary To provide financial assistance for college or graduate school to Native Hawaiian residents of any state.

Eligibility This program is open to residents of any state who can document Hawaiian ancestry through the Office of Hawaiian Affairs Hawaiian Registry Program. Applicants must be enrolled full or part time at an accredited 2- or 4-year college or university as an undergraduate or graduate student. They must be able to demonstrate academic achievement (GPA of 2.0 or higher for undergraduates or 3.0 or higher for graduate students), good moral character, and financial need. Along with their application, they must submit a short statement indicating their reasons for attending college, their planned course of study, their career goals, and what community service means to them.

Financial data The amounts of the awards depend on the availability of funds and the need of the recipient. Recently,

the average value of all scholarships awarded by the foundation was $2,041.
Duration 1 year; may be renewed.
Number awarded Varies each year.
Deadline February of each year.

[446]
OGLALA SIOUX TRIBE HIGHER EDUCATION GRANT PROGRAM

Oglala Sioux Tribe
Attn: Higher Education
P.O. Box 562
Pine Ridge, SD 57770-0562
(605) 867-5338　　　Toll Free: (800) 832-3651
Fax: (605) 867-1390　　　E-mail: highered@gwtc.net
Web: www.osthighered.com/index.html

Summary To provide financial assistance to members of the Oglala Sioux Tribe who are interested in working on a baccalaureate degree at a college in any state.

Eligibility This program is open to members of the Oglala Sioux Tribe who are enrolled or planning to enroll at a 4-year college or university in any state. Applicants must be interested in working on a baccalaureate degree in any field; certificate and diploma programs do not qualify. Along with their application, they must submit their Certificate of Indian Blood, a letter of acceptance from the college they will attend, college transcripts of an official grade report, and a financial needs analysis form. Awards are granted on a first-come, first-served basis, contingent upon academic progress, financial need, and availability of funds.

Financial data A stipend is awarded (amount not specified).
Duration 1 year; may be renewed up to 4 additional years.
Number awarded Varies each year.
Deadline June of each year for academic year and fall semester or quarter; November of each year for spring term; March of each year for summer sessions.

[447]
OHIO NEWSPAPERS FOUNDATION MINORITY SCHOLARSHIPS

Ohio Newspapers Foundation
1335 Dublin Road, Suite 216-B
Columbus, OH 43215-7038
(614) 486-6677　　　Fax: (614) 486-4940
E-mail: ariggs@ohionews.org
Web: www.ohionews.org/students/scholarships

Summary To provide financial assistance to Native American and other minority high school seniors in Ohio planning to attend college in the state to prepare for a career in journalism.

Eligibility This program is open to high school seniors in Ohio who are members of minority groups (African American, Hispanic, Asian American, or American Indian) and planning to prepare for a career in newspaper journalism. Applicants must have a high school GPA of 2.5 or higher and demonstrate writing ability in an autobiography of 750 to 1,000 words that describes their academic and career interests, awards, extracurricular activities, and journalism-related activities. They must be planning to attend a college or university in Ohio.

Financial data The stipend is $1,500.
Duration 1 year; nonrenewable.
Additional information This program was established in 1990.
Number awarded 1 each year.
Deadline March of each year.

[448]
OLIVE WHITMAN MEMORIAL SCHOLARSHIP

Daughters of the American Revolution-New York State Organization
c/o Theresa Willemsen, Recording Secretary
1248 McKoons Road
Richfield Springs, NY 13438-4101
E-mail: sportster_harley@hotmail.com
Web: www.nydar.org/education.html

Summary To provide financial assistance for college to Native American women in New York.

Eligibility This program is open to females who are at least 50% Native American and graduating seniors at high schools in New York. Applicants must be planning to attend an accredited 4-year college or university in the state.

Financial data The stipend is $2,000.
Duration 1 year.
Number awarded 1 each year.
Deadline January of each year.

[449]
ONEIDA TOTAL INTEGRATED ENTERPRISES COLLEGE SCHOLARSHIP PROGRAM

Oneida Tribe of Indians of Wisconsin
Attn: Oneida Total Integrated Enterprises
1033 North Mayfair Road, Suite 200
Milwaukee, WI 53226
(414) 257-4200　　　Fax: (414) 777-5899
E-mail: hcotey@otie.com
Web: www.oneidanation.org/HigherEd/page.aspx?is=568

Summary To provide financial assistance to members of the Oneida Tribe of Indians of Wisconsin who are high school seniors planning to study engineering or earth/natural sciences at a school in any state.

Eligibility This program is open to enrolled members of the Oneida Tribe of Indians of Wisconsin who are high school seniors accepted into a full-time undergraduate degree program at an accredited college or university in any state. Applicants must be planning to work on a degree in a field of engineering or earth/natural sciences. They must have a GPA of 3.4 or higher. Along with their application, they must submit a 1-page essay describing why they are interested in engineering or science. Selection is based on that essay, transcripts, and involvement in extracurricular and community activities; financial need is not considered.

Financial data The stipend is $5,000.
Duration 1 year.
Additional information Oneida Total Integrated Enterprises, owned by the Oneida Tribe of Indians of Wisconsin, provides environmental, remediation, construction, engineering, and emergency response services nationwide and internationally.

Number awarded Up to 2 each year.

Deadline June of each year.

[450]
ONEIDA TRIBE HIGHER EDUCATION GRANT PROGRAM

Oneida Tribe of Indians of Wisconsin
Attn: Higher Education Office
N7210 Seminary Road, North Wing
P.O. Box 365
Oneida, WI 54155-0365
(920) 869-4033   Toll Free: (800) 236-2214, ext. 4033
Fax: (920) 869-4039 E-mail: highered@oneidanation.org
Web: www.oneidanation.org/highered

Summary To provide financial assistance for undergraduate or graduate study to members of the Oneida Tribe of Indians of Wisconsin.

Eligibility This program is open to enrolled members of the Oneida Tribe of Indians of Wisconsin who have a high school diploma, HSED diploma, or GED. Applicants must be working on or planning to work on a vocational/technical, undergraduate, graduate, or doctoral degree at a college, university, or vocational school in any state. They must be able to demonstrate financial need.

Financial data Stipends range up to $20,000 per year, depending on the need of the recipient.

Duration The total length of eligibility is 6 terms for vocation/technical students, 10 terms for undergraduate students, 6 terms for graduate students, and 10 terms for doctoral students. To be eligible for renewal, vocational/technical students and undergraduates must maintain a GPA of 2.0 or higher and graduate and doctoral students must maintain a GPA of 3.0 or higher.

Number awarded Varies each year, depending upon the availability of funds.

Deadline Applications must be submitted by April of each year for the fall term, by September of each year for the spring term, or by April of each year for the summer term.

[451]
OPERATION JUMP START III SCHOLARSHIPS

American Association of Advertising Agencies
Attn: AAAA Foundation
405 Lexington Avenue, 18th Floor
New York, NY 10174-1801
(212) 682-2500   Toll Free: (800) 676-9333
Fax: (212) 682-2028   E-mail: ameadows@aaaa.org
Web: www2.aaaa.org

Summary To provide financial assistance to Native American and other multicultural art directors and copywriters interested in working on an undergraduate or graduate degree in advertising.

Eligibility This program is open to African Americans, Asian Americans, Hispanic Americans, and Native Americans who are U.S. citizens or permanent residents. Applicants must be incoming graduate students at 1 of 6 designated portfolio schools or full-time juniors at 1 of 2 designated colleges. They must be able to demonstrate extreme financial need, creative talent, and promise. Along with their application, they must submit 10 samples of creative work in their respective field of expertise.

Financial data The stipend is $5,000 per year.

Duration Most awards are for 2 years.

Additional information Operation Jump Start began in 1997 and was followed by Operation Jump Start II in 2002. The current program began in 2006. The 6 designated portfolio schools are the AdCenter at Virginia Commonwealth University, the Creative Circus in Atlanta, the Portfolio Center in Atlanta, the Miami Ad School, the University of Texas at Austin, and Pratt Institute. The 2 designated colleges are the Minneapolis College of Art and Design and the Art Center College of Design at Pasadena, California.

Number awarded 20 each year.

Deadline Deadline not specified.

[452]
OREGON NATIVE AMERICAN CHAMBER OF COMMERCE SCHOLARSHIPS

Oregon Native American Chamber of Commerce
c/o Kelly Anne Ilagan
P.O. Box 69593
Portland, OR 97239
E-mail: kellyanne@onacc.org
Web: www.onacc.org/scholarship.htm

Summary To provide financial assistance to Native American students from Oregon and southwestern Washington who are attending college in any state.

Eligibility This program is open to Native American residents of Oregon and southwestern Washington who are currently enrolled at an accredited community college or 4-year college or university in any state. Applicants must submit 250-word statements on how receiving this scholarship would benefit them and their educational needs, how they are involved in their Native American community on or off campus, what they plan to do with their education to help "give back" to Native Americans after graduation, and how they view their Native American heritage and its importance to them. Financial need is not considered in the selection process.

Financial data The stipend is $1,000.

Duration 1 year.

Additional information This program began in 2000. Recipients must attend the sponsor's annual gathering to receive their awards.

Number awarded Varies each year; recently, 5 of these scholarships were awarded.

Deadline September of each year.

[453]
OSAGE HIGHER EDUCATION GRANTS

Osage Nation Department of Education
Attn: Scholarship Program
105 Buffalo Avenue
Hominy, OK 74035
(918) 287-5301   Fax: (918) 885-2136
E-mail: scholarship@osagetribe.com
Web: www.osagetribe.com

Summary To provide financial assistance for college or graduate school to members of the Osage Tribe.

Eligibility This program is open to Osage tribal students who are enrolled or planning to enroll in a 2- or 4-year college or university. A point system is used to rank applicants, including such factors as student status (freshman through graduate student), number of previous full-time semesters in college, GPA from previous semester, full-time or part-time enrollment, qualification for federal Pell Grant, and Osage blood quantum.

Financial data The amount of the award depends on the number of points earned by the recipient.

Duration 1 semester; may be renewed.

Number awarded Varies each year.

Deadline July of each year for fall semester; December of each year for spring semester; April of each year for summer term.

[454]
OSAGE TRIBAL EDUCATION COMMITTEE PROGRAM

Osage Tribal Education Committee
c/o Oklahoma Area Education Office
200 N.W. Fourth, Suite 4049
Oklahoma City, OK 73102
(405) 605-6051, ext. 304   Fax: (405) 605-6057
Web: www.osagetribe.com/education/info.aspx

Summary To provide financial assistance to undergraduate and graduate Osage students.

Eligibility This program is open to students who can prove Osage Indian blood in any degree. Applicants must be working on or planning to work on an undergraduate or graduate degree at an accredited college, university, or technical vocational program. They may be residents of any state.

Financial data The amount of the award depends on the financial need of the recipient.

Duration 1 year; may be renewed for up to 4 additional years, provided the recipient reapplies each semester and maintains a GPA of 2.0 or higher.

Number awarded Varies each year.

Deadline June of each year for fall term; December of each year for spring term.

[455]
OTTAWA TRIBE HIGHER EDUCATION GRANTS

Ottawa Tribe of Oklahoma
c/o Oklahoma Area Education Office
200 N.W. Fourth, Suite 4049
Oklahoma City, OK 73102
(405) 605-6051, ext. 304   Fax: (405) 605-6057
Web: ottawatribe.org/heducation.htm

Summary To provide financial assistance to members of the Ottawa Tribe of Oklahoma who plan to attend college or graduate school in any state.

Eligibility This program is open to enrolled members of the Ottawa Tribe of Oklahoma who have been accepted at an accredited institution of higher education in any state as a full- or part-time undergraduate or graduate student. Applicants must be able to document financial need. Along with their application, they must submit a copy of their tribal enrollment card, a copy of their high school and/or college transcripts, documentation of financial need, and a letter of intent explaining why they wish to attend college.

Financial data The amount of the award depends on the financial need of the recipient.

Duration 1 year; may be renewed for up to 4 additional years, provided the recipient reapplies each semester and maintains a GPA of 2.0 or higher.

Number awarded Varies each year.

Deadline July of each year.

[456]
OUZINKIE TRIBAL COUNCIL BIA HIGHER EDUCATION SCHOLARSHIP GRANT

Ouzinkie Tribal Council
Attn: Education Director
P.O. Box 130
Ouzinkie, AK 99644
(907) 680-2323   Fax: (907) 680-2214
E-mail: scholarships@ouzinkie.org
Web: www.ouzinkie.org/scholarships.php

Summary To provide financial assistance to members of the Ouzinkie Tribe of Native Alaskans who are interested in attending college in any state.

Eligibility This program is open to Native Alaskans who are enrolled to the Ouzinkie Tribe. Applicants must be enrolled to planning to enroll full time at an accredited 4-year college or university in any state. Along with their application, they must submit a brief statement of the long-range career goals and how their educational experience will help them achieve those. In the selection process, heavy emphasis is placed on financial need.

Financial data A stipend is awarded (amount not specified).

Duration 1 year; may be renewed, provided the recipient remains enrolled full time and maintains a GPA of 2.0 or higher.

Additional information This program is supported by funding from the U.S. Bureau of Indian Affairs (BIA).

Number awarded Varies each year.

Deadline May of each year for fall term; November of each year for spring term.

[457]
PACIFIC TEACHER SCHOLARSHIP

Pacific Resources for Education and Learning
Attn: Pacific Teacher Scholarship
900 Fort Street Mall, Suite 1300
Honolulu, HI 96813-3718
(808) 441-1300   Toll Free: (800) 377-4773
Fax: (808) 441-1416   E-mail: scholarships@prel.org
Web: www.prel.org

Summary To provide financial assistance to residents of the U.S.-affiliated Pacific who are enrolled in a teacher preparation program and plan to teach at a school in the region following graduation.

Eligibility This program is open to residents of American Samoa, the Commonwealth of the Northern Mariana Islands, the Federated States of Micronesia, Guam, the Republic of Palau, and the Republic of the Marshall Islands. Applicants must be enrolled in the second, third, or fourth year of an accredited teacher preparation program at a college or university in any state. They must have a GPA of 2.5 or higher and plans to teach in a school in the U.S.-affiliated Pacific following graduation. Along with their application, they must submit a personal statement that covers why they chose to be a teacher, their experience working in schools, where in the U.S.-affiliated Pacific they intend to work, the grade level and subject area in which they plan to concentrate, and relevant financial information.

Financial data   The stipend ranges from $750 to $1,000. Funds are disbursed directly to the recipient's college or university.

Duration   1 year.

Number awarded   Varies each year; recently, 6 of these scholarships were awarded.

Deadline   March of each year.

[458]
PAGE EDUCATION FOUNDATION GRANTS

Page Education Foundation
P.O. Box 581254
Minneapolis, MN 55458-1254
(612) 332-0406   E-mail: info@page-ed.org
Web: www.page-ed.org

Summary   To provide funding to Native Americans and other high school seniors of color in Minnesota who plan to attend college in the state.

Eligibility   This program is open to students of color who are graduating from high schools in Minnesota and planning to enroll full time at a postsecondary school in the state. Applicants must submit a 500-word essay that deals with why they believe education is important, their plans for the future, and the service-to-children project they would like to complete in the coming school year. Selection is based on the essay, 3 letters of recommendation, and financial need.

Financial data   Stipends range from $1,000 to $2,500 per year.

Duration   1 year; may be renewed up to 3 additional years.

Additional information   This program was founded in 1988 by Alan Page, a former football player for the Minnesota Vikings. While attending college, the Page Scholars fulfill a 50-hour service-to-children contract that brings them into contact with K-8 students of color.

Number awarded   Varies each year; recently, 560 Page Scholars (218 new recipients and 342 renewals) were enrolled, of whom 337 were African American, 114 Asian American, 63 Chicano/Latino, and 16 American Indian.

Deadline   April of each year.

[459]
PARSONS BRINCKERHOFF ENGINEERING SCHOLARSHIP

Conference of Minority Transportation Officials
Attn: National Scholarship Program
818 18th Street, N.W., Suite 850
Washington, DC 20006
(202) 530-0551   Fax: (202) 530-0617
Web: www.comto.org/news-youth.php

Summary   To provide financial assistance to Native American and other members of the Conference of Minority Transportation Officials (COMTO) who are working on an undergraduate degree in engineering.

Eligibility   This program is open to undergraduate students who have been members of COMTO for at least 1 year. Applicants must be working on a degree in engineering with a GPA of 3.0 or higher. Along with their application, they must submit

a cover letter with a 500-word statement of career goals. Financial need is not considered in the selection process. U.S. citizenship is required.

Financial data   The stipend is $5,000. Funds are paid directly to the recipient's college or university.

Duration   1 year.

Additional information   COMTO was established in 1971 to promote, strengthen, and expand the roles of minorities in all aspects of transportation. This program is sponsored by Parsons Brinckerhoff, Inc. Recipients are expected to attend the COMTO National Scholarship Luncheon.

Number awarded   1 or more each year.

Deadline   April of each year.

[460]
PARSONS BRINCKERHOFF GOLDEN APPLE SCHOLARSHIP

Conference of Minority Transportation Officials
Attn: National Scholarship Program
818 18th Street, N.W., Suite 850
Washington, DC 20006
(202) 530-0551   Fax: (202) 530-0617
Web: www.comto.org/news-youth.php

Summary   To provide financial assistance to Native American and other members of the Conference of Minority Transportation Officials (COMTO) who are high school seniors planning to attend college to prepare for a career in the business aspects of the transportation industry.

Eligibility   This program is open to graduating high school seniors who have been members of COMTO for at least 1 year. Applicants must be planning to attend an accredited college, university, or vocational/technical institution to prepare for a career in transportation in the fields of communications, finance, or marketing. They must have a GPA of 2.0 or higher. Along with their application, they must submit a cover letter with a 500-word statement of career goals. Financial need is not considered in the selection process. U.S. citizenship is required.

Financial data   The stipend is $2,500. Funds are paid directly to the recipient's college or university.

Duration   1 year.

Additional information   COMTO was established in 1971 to promote, strengthen, and expand the roles of minorities in all aspects of transportation. This program is sponsored by Parsons Brinckerhoff, Inc. Recipients are expected to attend the COMTO National Scholarship Luncheon.

Number awarded   1 or more each year.

Deadline   April of each year.

[461]
PASCUA YAQUI HIGHER EDUCATION SCHOLARSHIP

Pascua Yaqui Tribe
Attn: Higher Education Program
7474 South Camino de Oeste
Tucson, AZ 85757
(520) 883-5706   Toll Free: (800) 5-PASCUA
Fax: (520) 883-5021
Web: www.pascuayaqui-nsn.gov

Summary To provide financial assistance to members of the Pascua Yaqui Tribe who are interested in attending college or graduate school in any state.

Eligibility This program is open to enrolled members of the Pascua Yaqui Tribe who are attending or planning to attend a public college, university, or vocational/technical institute in any state. Applicants must apply for all other available aid and still have unmet financial need. They may be planning to work on an undergraduate or graduate degree on a full- or part-time basis.

Financial data A stipend is awarded (amount not specified).

Duration 1 semester; may be renewed for a total of 6 semesters of full-time work on an associate degree; 72 credits of part-time work on an associate degree, 12 semesters of full-time work on a bachelor's degree, 130 credit hours of part-time work on a bachelor's degree, 5 semesters of full-time work on a master's or doctoral degree, the required credits of the program for part-time graduate students, or an additional 2 semesters for doctoral students to completed their dissertation. Renewal requires that recipients maintain a GPA of 2.0 or higher as an undergraduate or 3.0 or higher as a graduate student.

Number awarded Varies each year.

Deadline July of each year for fall; December of each year for spring.

[462]
PAUL AND EMILY SHAGEN SCHOLARSHIP

Chippewa County Community Foundation
P.O. Box 1979
Sault Ste. Marie, MI 49783
(906) 635-1046   Fax: (775) 417-7368
E-mail: cccf@lighthouse.net
Web: www.cccf4good4ever.org/main.asp?id=7

Summary To provide financial assistance to members of the Sault Ste. Marie Tribe of Chippewa Indians who are interested in attending college or graduate school in any state.

Eligibility This program is open to enrolled members of the Sault Ste. Marie Tribe of Chippewa Indians who have been accepted for enrollment as a full-time undergraduate, graduate, or professional student at an accredited college, university, vocational school, or community college in any state. Applicants must submit an essay of 300 to 500 words on how they plan to use the education or training to contribute to the community, including the tribe. Selection is based on that essay, academic performance and progress, and financial need.

Financial data A stipend is awarded (amount not specified).

Duration 1 year.

Number awarded Varies each year.

Deadline June or November of each year.

[463]
PAUL FRANCIS MEMORIAL SCHOLARSHIP

American Indian Education Foundation
2401 Eglin Street
Rapid City, SD 57703
Toll Free: (866) 866-8642   E-mail: mlee@nrc1.org
Web: www.nrcprograms.org

Summary To provide financial assistance for college to Native Americans who demonstrate a commitment to helping their community.

Eligibility This program is open to full-time students of Native American descent who are currently attending or planning to attend a 2-year college, a 4-year college or university, or a vocational/technical school. Applicants may be either graduating high school seniors or undergraduates who are entering, continuing, or returning to school. Along with their application, they must submit a 4-page essay in which they describe themselves as a student, their ultimate career goals, their plans for working in or with the Indian community, and their participation in leadership and/or community service activities. A GPA of 2.0 to 3.4 is desirable, but all current or future undergraduate students are encouraged to apply. An ACT score of 14 or higher is desirable. Financial need is considered in the selection process. This scholarship is designated for applicants who demonstrate a commitment to helping their community.

Financial data The stipend is $2,000. Funds are paid directly to the recipient's college or university.

Duration 1 year.

Additional information This program was established in 2003.

Number awarded 1 each year.

Deadline April of each year.

[464]
PAWNEE NATION HIGHER EDUCATION PROGRAM

Pawnee Nation of Oklahoma
Attn: Education Division
657 Harrison Street
P.O. Box 470
Pawnee, OK 74058
(918) 762-3227   Fax: (918) 762-3662
E-mail: ftippeconnie@pawneenationa.org
Web: www.pawneenation.org/divisions/program/20

Summary To provide financial assistance for college to members of the Pawnee Nation of Oklahoma.

Eligibility This program is open to members of the Pawnee Nation who are enrolled or planning to enroll full time at an accredited institution of higher education in any state. Applicants must be interested in working on a bachelor's degree, either at a 4-year university or at a 2-year college or university with definite plans to transfer to a 4-year school. Along with their application, they must submit an essay on their future educational goals. Financial need is a major factor in the selection process.

Financial data A stipend is awarded (amount not specified).

Duration 1 year; may be renewed, provided the student remains enrolled full time and maintains a GPA of 2.0 or higher.

Number awarded Varies each year.

Deadline July of each year for fall; December of each year for spring.

[465]
PBS&J ACHIEVEMENT SCHOLARSHIP

Conference of Minority Transportation Officials
Attn: National Scholarship Program
818 18th Street, N.W., Suite 850
Washington, DC 20006
(202) 530-0551   Fax: (202) 530-0617
Web: www.comto.org/news-youth.php

Summary To provide financial assistance to Native American and other minority high school seniors, undergraduates, and graduate students interested in studying the field of transportation.

Eligibility This program is open to minority graduating high school seniors, current undergraduates, and graduate students interested in the field of transportation. Applicants must be enrolled or planning to enroll full time at an accredited college, university, or vocational/technical institution. They must have a GPA of 2.0 or higher. Along with their application, they must submit a cover letter with a 500-word statement of career goals. Financial need is not considered in the selection process. U.S. citizenship is required.

Financial data The stipend is $4,000. Funds are paid directly to the recipient's college or university.

Duration 1 year.

Additional information The Conference of Minority Transportation Officials (COMTO) was established in 1971 to promote, strengthen, and expand the roles of minorities in all aspects of transportation. This program is sponsored by the engineering, architecture, and sciences company PBS&J. Recipients are expected to attend the COMTO National Scholarship Luncheon.

Number awarded 1 or more each year.

Deadline April of each year.

[466]
PEARL CARTER SCOTT AVIATION SCHOLARSHIP

Chickasaw Foundation
110 West 12th Street
P.O. Box 1726
Ada, OK 74821-1726
(580) 421-9030   Fax: (580) 421-9031
E-mail: ChickasawFoundation@chickasaw.net
Web: www.chickasawfoundation.org/index_20.htm

Summary To provide financial assistance to members of the Chickasaw Nation who are working on an undergraduate or graduate degree in a field related to aviation.

Eligibility This program is open to Chickasaw students who are currently enrolled at a college, university, or recognized private aviation school. Applicants must be working full time on an undergraduate or graduate degree in a field related to aviation (e.g., aviation maintenance technology, flight training, aviation law, air traffic control, aeronautical engineering, aerospace mechanical engineering, manufacturing engineering with an aviation emphasis, airline and airport operations, airport management, meteorology, aviation technology management, or a related field). Along with their application, they must submit high school or college transcripts, 2 letters of recommendation, a copy of their Chickasaw Nation citizenship card, and a 1-page essay on their

long-term goals and plans for achieving them. Financial need is not considered in the selection process.

Financial data The stipend is $1,250 per year.

Duration 1 year; may be renewed if the recipient demonstrates appropriate progress toward a degree in an aviation program.

Number awarded 1 each year.

Deadline August of each year.

[467]
PEDRO BAY SCHOLARSHIP

Bristol Bay Native Corporation
Attn: BBNC Education Foundation
111 West 16th Avenue, Suite 400
Anchorage, AK 99501
(907) 278-3602   Toll Free: (800) 426-3602
Fax: (907) 276-3925   E-mail: pelagiol@bbnc.net
Web: www.bbnc.net

Summary To provide financial assistance to shareholders of Pedro Bay Corporation who are working on an undergraduate or graduate degree at a college in any state.

Eligibility This program is open to Pedro Bay Corporation shareholders who are enrolled full time as a junior, senior, or advanced degree student at an accredited college or university in any state. Applicants must have a GPA of 2.0 or higher and be able to demonstrate financial need. Along with their application, they must submit an essay on how they became interested in their proposed field of study, any special circumstances they want to be considered, and their desire to work in the region. Selection is based on the essay (35%), cumulative GPA (40%), financial need (20%), and letters of recommendation (5%).

Financial data The stipend is $3,000.

Duration 1 year.

Additional information This program is funded by Pedro Bay Benefits Corporation and administered by the Bristol Bay Native Corporation Education Foundation.

Deadline March of each year.

[468]
PENNSYLVANIA DIETETIC ASSOCIATION FOUNDATION DIVERSITY SCHOLARSHIP

Pennsylvania Dietetic Association
Attn: Foundation
96 Northwoods Boulevard, Suite B2
Columbus, OH 43235
(614) 436-6136
Web: www.eatrightpa.org/scholarships/applications.htm

Summary To provide financial assistance to Native American and other minority members of the Pennsylvania Dietetic Association (PDA) who are working on an associate or bachelor's degree in dietetics.

Eligibility This program is open to PDA members who are Black, Hispanic, Asian or Pacific Islander, or Native American (Alaskan Native, American Indian, or Hawaiian Native). Applicants must be 1) enrolled in the first year of study in an accredited dietetic technology program; or 2) enrolled in the third year of study in an accredited undergraduate or coordinated program in dietetics. They must have a GPA of 2.5 or higher. Along with their application, they must submit a letter indicating their intent and the reason they are applying for the scholarship, including a description of their personal financial situation. Selection is based on academic achievement (20%), commitment to the dietetic profession (30%), leadership ability (30%), and financial need (20%).

Financial data The stipend is $1,000.

Duration 1 year.

Number awarded 1 or more each year.

Deadline March of each year.

[469]
PENOBSCOT NATION ADULT VOCATIONAL TRAINING

Penobscot Nation
Attn: Department of Education and Career Services
6 River Road
Indian Island, ME 04468
(207) 827-1649, ext. 148   Fax: (207) 827-2088
E-mail: pnhec@penobscotnation.org
Web: www.penobscotnation.org/Education/education.htm

Summary To provide financial assistance to members of the Penobscot Nation who are working on 2-year degrees or training programs at schools in any state.

Eligibility This program is open to students who are members of the Penobscot Nation and are enrolled full time in an associate degree, diploma, or certificate training program at a school in any state. Awards are granted on the basis of financial need (as determined by the institution the student is attending).

Financial data The amount awarded varies, depending upon the needs of the recipient.

Duration 1 year or more.

Additional information Funding for this program is provided to the Penobscot Nation through the Bureau of Indian Affairs.

Number awarded Varies each year.

Deadline June of each year.

[470]
PENOBSCOT NATION HIGHER EDUCATION GRANT PROGRAM

Penobscot Nation
Attn: Department of Education and Career Services
6 River Road
Indian Island, ME 04468
(207) 827-1649, ext. 148   Fax: (207) 827-2088
E-mail: pnhec@penobscotnation.org
Web: www.penobscotnation.org/Education/education.htm

Summary To provide financial assistance to members of the Penobscot Nation who are or will be working on a 4-year degree at a college in any state.

Eligibility This program is open to students who are members of the Penobscot Nation and are enrolled (or going to be enrolled) full time in a 4-year degree program in any state. Awards are granted on the basis of financial need, as determined by the institution the student is attending.

Financial data The amount awarded varies, depending upon the needs of the recipient. Funds may be used to pay for tuition, fees, room, board, books, or living expenses.

Duration 1 year or more.

Additional information Funding for this program is provided to the Penobscot Nation through the Bureau of Indian Affairs.

Number awarded Varies each year.

Deadline June of each year.

[471]
PEORIA TRIBAL EDUCATION PROGRAM

Peoria Tribe of Indians of Oklahoma
Attn: Education Program
118 South Eight Tribes Trail
P.O. Box 1527
Miami, OK 74355
(918) 540-2535, ext. 10   Toll Free: (800) 259-9987
Fax: (918) 540-2538
Web: www.peoriatribe.com/programs/education.php

Summary To provide financial assistance to members of the Peoria Tribe of Indians of Oklahoma who are interested in attending college in any state.

Eligibility This program is open to enrolled members of the Peoria Tribe of Indians of Oklahoma who have been accepted by an accredited college or vocational school in any state as a full- or part-time student. Applicants must have a GPA of 2.5 or higher. They must submit high school transcripts, a copy of SAT or ACT scores, 2 letters of recommendation, and a short essay outlining their academic goals. Selection is based on academic achievement and the probability of completing the academic program; financial need is not considered.

Financial data The stipend is $3,500 per semester for full-time students or $1,750 per semester for part-time students.

Duration 1 semester; may be renewed up to 7 additional semesters if the recipient maintains a GPA of 2.5 or higher.

Number awarded Varies each year; recently, 136 of these scholarships (37 new awards, 91 renewals, and 8 part-time scholarships) were awarded.

Deadline July of each year for the fall semester; January of each year for the spring semester.

[472]
PETER DOCTOR MEMORIAL INDIAN SCHOLARSHIP GRANTS

Peter Doctor Memorial Indian Scholarship Foundation, Inc.
c/o Clara Hill, Treasurer
P.O. Box 731
Basom, NY 14013
(716) 542-2025   E-mail: cehill@wnynet.net

Summary To provide financial assistance to New York Iroquois Indians currently enrolled at a college in any state on the undergraduate or graduate school level.

Eligibility This program is open to enrolled New York Iroquois Indian students who have completed at least 1 year at a technical school, college, or university in any state. Both undergraduate and graduate students are eligible. There are no age limits or GPA requirements. Interviews may be required. Applicants must have tribal certification. Selection is based on need.

Financial data Stipends range up to $1,500.

Duration 2 years for medical students; 1 year for all other recipients.

Deadline May of each year.

[473]
PETER KALIFORNSKY MEMORIAL ENDOWMENT SCHOLARSHIP FUND

Cook Inlet Region, Inc.
Attn: The CIRI Foundation
3600 San Jeronimo Drive, Suite 256
Anchorage, AK 99508-2870
(907) 793-3575   Toll Free: (800) 764-3382
Fax: (907) 793-3585   E-mail: tcf@thecirifoundation.org
Web: www.thecirifoundation.org/designated.htm

Summary   To provide financial assistance for undergraduate or graduate studies to Alaska Natives who are original enrollees to Cook Inlet Region, Inc. (CIRI) and their lineal descendants.

Eligibility   This program is open to Alaska Native enrollees to CIRI under the Alaska Native Claims Settlement Act (ANCSA) of 1971 and their lineal descendants. There are no Alaska residency requirements or age limitations. Applicants must be accepted or enrolled full time in a 4-year undergraduate or a graduate degree program. Preference is given to students in Alaska Native studies. They must have a GPA of 2.5 or higher. Along with their application, they must submit a 500-word statement on their educational and career goals and how they are contributing, or planning to contribute, to a positive Alaska Native community. Selection is based on that statement, academic achievement, rigor of course work or degree program, student financial contribution, financial need, grade level, previous work performance, community service, and relationship of degree program to career goals.

Financial data   The stipend is $10,000 per year, $8,000 per year, or $2,500 per semester, depending on GPA.

Duration   1 semester or 1 year.

Additional information   This program was established in 1993.

Number awarded   Varies each year.

Deadline   May of each year for annual scholarships; May or November of each year for semester scholarships.

[474]
PGA TOUR DIVERSITY INTERNSHIP PROGRAM

PGA Tour, Inc.
Attn: Minority Internship Program
100 PGA Tour Boulevard
Ponte Vedra Beach, FL 32082
(904) 285-3700
Web: www.pgatour.com/company/internships.html

Summary   To provide summer work experience to Native Americans and other undergraduate and graduate students who are interested in learning about the business side of golf and will contribute to diversity in the profession.

Eligibility   This program is open to students who either have completed at least their sophomore year at an accredited 4-year college or university or are enrolled in graduate school. Applicants should be able to enrich the PGA Tour and its partnering organizations through diversity. They must have a GPA of 2.8 or higher. International students are eligible if they are legally permitted to work in the United States. Although all interns work in the business side of golf, the ability to play golf or knowledge of the game is not required for many positions.

Financial data   Interns receive competitive wages and up to $500 for travel expenses to orientation in Ponte Vedra Beach, Florida or their initial work location. Depending on position and location, other benefits include subsidized housing, discounts on company merchandise, access to company training seminars, and possible golf privileges.

Duration   Most assignments are for 10 to 12 weeks during the summer.

Additional information   This program was established in 1992. Positions are available in accounting, corporate marketing, business development, international TV, information systems, event management, tournament services, tournament operations, retail licensing, sales, human resources, new media, and other areas within the PGA Tour. Most assignments are in Ponte Vedra Beach, Florida.

Number awarded   Approximately 30 each year.

Deadline   February of each year.

[475]
PHILLIP D. REED UNDERGRADUATE ENDOWMENT FELLOWSHIP

National Action Council for Minorities in Engineering
Attn: University Programs
440 Hamilton Avenue, Suite 302
White Plains, NY 10601-1813
(914) 539-4010   Fax: (914) 539-4032
E-mail: scholarships@nacme.org
Web: www.nacme.org/NACME_D.aspx?pageid=105

Summary   To provide financial assistance to Native American and other underrepresented minority college sophomores majoring in engineering or related fields.

Eligibility   This program is open to African American, Latino, and American Indian college sophomores who have a GPA of 3.0 or higher and have demonstrated academic excellence, leadership skills, and a commitment to science and engineering as a career. Applicants must be enrolled full time at an ABET-accredited engineering program. Fields of study include all areas of engineering as well as computer science, materials science, mathematics, operations research, or physics.

Financial data   The stipend is $5,000 per year. Funds are sent directly to the recipient's university.

Duration   Up to 3 years.

Number awarded   1 each year.

Deadline   April of each year.

[476]
PI STATE NATIVE AMERICAN GRANTS-IN-AID

Delta Kappa Gamma Society International-Pi State
 Organization
c/o Harlene Gilbert
5338 East Lake Road
Romulus, NY 14541
(315) 585-6691   E-mail: hgilbert@happiness.org
Web: www.deltakappagamma.org/NY/ASaGiA.html

Summary   To provide funding to Native American women from New York who plan to work in education or another service field.

Eligibility   This program is open to Native American women from New York who are attending a 2- or 4-year college in the state. Applicants must be planning to work in education or another service field, but preference is given to those majoring in education. Both undergraduate and graduate students are eligible.

Financial data The grant is $500 per semester ($1,000 per year). Funds may be used for any career-related purpose, including purchase of textbooks.

Duration 1 semester; may be renewed for a total of 5 years and a total of $5,000 over a recipient's lifetime.

Number awarded Up to 5 each year.

Deadline July or December of each year.

[477]
P.O. PISTILLI SCHOLARSHIPS

Design Automation Conference
c/o Cherrice Traver
Union College
Steinmetz Hall, Room 202
Schenectady, NY 12308
(518) 388-6326   Fax: (518) 388-6789
E-mail: traverc@union.edu
Web: doc.union.edu/acsee.html

Summary To provide financial assistance to Native American, other minority, female, or disabled high school seniors who are interested in preparing for a career in computer science or electrical engineering.

Eligibility This program is open to graduating high school seniors who are members of underrepresented groups: women, African Americans, Hispanics, Native Americans, and persons with disabilities. Applicants must be interested in preparing for a career in electrical engineering, computer engineering, or computer science. They must have at least a 3.0 GPA, have demonstrated high achievements in math and science courses, have demonstrated involvement in activities associated with the underrepresented group they represent, and be able to demonstrate significant financial need. U.S. citizenship is not required, but applicants must be U.S. residents when they apply and must plan to attend an accredited U.S. college or university. Along with their application, they must submit 3 letters of recommendation, official transcripts, ACT/SAT and/or PSAT scores, a personal statement outlining future goals and why they think they should receive this scholarship, and documentation of financial need.

Financial data Stipends are $4,000 per year. Awards are paid each year in 2 equal installments.

Duration 1 year; renewable for up to 4 additional years.

Additional information This program is funded by the Design Automation Conference of the Association for Computing Machinery's Special Interest Group on Design Automation.

Number awarded 2 to 7 each year.

Deadline January of each year.

[478]
POARCH BAND OF CREEK INDIANS ACADEMIC ACHIEVEMENT BONUS

Poarch Band of Creek Indians
Attn: Tuition Program Coordinator
5811 Jack Springs Road
Atmore, AL 36502
(251) 368-9136, ext. 2241   Fax: (251) 368-4502
E-mail: sfisher@pci-nsn.gov
Web: www.poarchcreekindians.org

Summary To recognize and reward members of the Poarch Band of Creek Indians who achieve academic excellence while working on an undergraduate or graduate degree.

Eligibility These awards are presented to enrolled members of the Poarch Band of Creek Indians who are enrolled full time in an associate, bachelor's, or master's degree program at a college or university in any state. To qualify, they must maintain a GPA of 3.5 or higher each semester of the academic year.

Financial data The award is $2,000 for associate degree students, $4,000 for bachelor's degree students, or $2,000 for master's degree students. Other professional degree students are evaluated on a case-by-case basis.

Duration The awards are presented annually.

Number awarded Varies each year.

Deadline Deadline not specified.

[479]
POKAGON BAND HIGHER EDUCATION SCHOLARSHIP

Pokagon Band of Potawatomi Indians
Attn: Department of Education
58620 Sink Road
P.O. Box 180
Dowagiac, MI 49047
(269) 782-0887   Toll Free: (888) 330-1234
Fax: (269) 782-0985
E-mail: joseph.avance@pokagon.com
Web: www.pokagon.com/education/edu-highered.htm

Summary To provide financial assistance to members of the Pokagon Band of Potawatomi Indians who are interested in working on an undergraduate or graduate degree at a college in any state.

Eligibility This program is open to enrolled members of the Pokagon Band who are attending or planning to attend an accredited college or university in any state to work on an associate, bachelor's, master's, or doctoral degree. Applicants must apply for all campus-based financial aid for which they are eligible and be able to document that they still have an unmet financial need. If they plan to attend a public college or university in Michigan and have an Indian blood level of one-quarter or more, they must also apply for a Michigan Indian Tuition Waiver.

Financial data The stipend is $100 per credit hour for associate degree students (to a maximum of 18 credit hours per semester), $200 per credit hour for bachelor's degree students (to a maximum of 18 credit hours per semester), or $300 per credit hour for graduate students (to a maximum of 12 credit hours per semester).

Duration 1 semester; may be renewed for a total of 3 years of study for an associate degree, 5 years of study for a bachelor's degree, or 5 years of study for a graduate degree.

Number awarded Varies each year.

Deadline Deadline not specified.

[480]
PONCA NATION HIGHER EDUCATION GRANT PROGRAM

Ponca Tribe of Oklahoma
Attn: Higher Education
20 White Eagle Drive
Ponca City, OK 74601
(580) 763-0120   Fax: (580) 763-0126
E-mail: pted@poncacity.net
Web: ponca.com/9801/29458.html

Summary To provide financial assistance for college to members of the Ponca Tribe of Oklahoma.

Eligibility This program is open to students entering college who are at least one-quarter degree enrolled members of the Ponca Tribe of Oklahoma. Applicants must submit documentation of financial need.

Financial data A stipend is awarded (amount not specified).

Duration 1 year; may be renewed.

Number awarded Varies each year.

Deadline May of each year for fall semester; November of each year for spring semester; March of each year for summer school.

[481]
PONCA TRIBE OF NEBRASKA EDUCATIONAL GRANTS

Ponca Tribe of Nebraska
Attn: Director of Education
1800 Syracuse Avenue
Norfolk, NE 68701
(402) 371-8834   Fax: (402) 371-7564
E-mail: pate@poncatribe-ne.org
Web: www.poncatribe-ne.org/departments_education.php

Summary To provide financial assistance to members of the Ponca Tribe of Nebraska who are interested in attending an undergraduate, graduate, or vocational school in any state.

Eligibility This program is open to enrolled members of the Ponca Tribe of Nebraska who are attending or planning to attend a college, university, or vocational/technical school in any state. Applicants must submit a letter of admission from the school they plan to attend, a Certificate of Indian Blood (CIB), and documentation of financial need.

Financial data A stipend is awarded (amount not specified).

Duration 1 semester or year. Full-time students may reapply each academic year (or summer session if they wish to attend summer school). Part-time students may reapply each semester or quarter. Renewals are approved if the student maintains a GPA of 2.0 or higher as an undergraduate or vocational student or 3.0 or higher as a graduate student.

Number awarded Varies each year.

Deadline August of each year for fall quarter or semester; November of each year for winter quarter; December of each year for spring quarter or semester; May of each year for summer session.

[482]
POUHANA HOKELE SCHOLARSHIP

Ke Ali'i Pauahi Foundation
Attn: Financial Aid & Scholarship Services
567 South King Street, Suite 160
Honolulu, HI 96813
(808) 534-3966   Toll Free: (800) 842-4682, ext. 43966
Fax: (808) 534-3890   E-mail: scholarships@pauahi.org
Web: www.pauahi.org/scholarships

Summary To provide financial assistance to high school seniors in Hawaii, especially those of Native Hawaiian descent, who plan to attend college in any state to prepare for a career in Hawaii's lodging industry.

Eligibility This program is open to seniors graduating from high schools in Hawaii who have a GPA of 2.8 or higher. Applicants must be planning to enroll in a travel industry management program at a 2- or 4-year college or university in any state. They must demonstrate a desire to work in the Hawaii lodging industry after graduation. Preference is given to Native Hawaiians (descendants of the aboriginal inhabitants of the Hawaiian Islands prior to 1778).

Financial data The stipend is $1,000.

Duration 1 year.

Number awarded 5 each year.

Deadline March of each year.

[483]
PRAIRIE BAND POTAWATOMI NATION ADULT VOCATIONAL TRAINING GRANT

Prairie Band Potawatomi Nation
Attn: Higher Education
16281 Q Road
Mayetta, KS 66509-8970
(785) 966-2960   Toll Free: (877) 715-6789
Fax: (785) 966-2956   E-mail: info@pbpnation.org
Web: www.pbpindiantribe.com/education.aspx

Summary To provide financial assistance to members of the Prairie Band Potawatomi Nation who are interested in attending an adult vocational training program in any state.

Eligibility This program is open to members of the Prairie Band Potawatomi Nation who have a Certificate of Indian Blood. Applicants must be enrolled or planning to enroll in an adult vocational training program in any state. They may be attending a traditional (9 to 12 months) or nontraditional (less than 9 months) program. Along with their application, they must submit a letter explaining why they need the grant and how it will be used.

Financial data Grants provide partial payment of tuition and other costs. Funds may be used for tuition, fees, and books. Part-time students are eligible for exact costs only.

Duration 1 semester; may be renewed.

Number awarded Varies each year.

Deadline Applications must be submitted at least 2 months prior to beginning of attendance or payment due date, whichever occurs first.

[484]
PRAIRIE BAND POTAWATOMI NATION HIGHER EDUCATION UNDERGRADUATE PROGRAM

Prairie Band Potawatomi Nation
Attn: Higher Education
16281 Q Road
Mayetta, KS 66509-8970
(785) 966-2960　　　Toll Free: (877) 715-6789
Fax: (785) 966-2956　　E-mail: info@pbpnation.org
Web: www.pbpindiantribe.com/education.aspx

Summary To provide financial assistance to members of the Prairie Band Potawatomi Nation who are interested in attending college in any state.

Eligibility This program is open to members of the Prairie Band Potawatomi Nation who have a Certificate of Indian Blood. Applicants must be enrolled or planning to enroll at a college or university in any state to work on a bachelor's degree. Along with their application, they must submit a letter explaining why they need the grant and how it will be used.

Financial data Full-time students receive a stipend of up to $3,000 per semester as a freshman, $3,500 per semester as a sophomore, $4,000 per semester as a junior, or $4,500 per semester as a senior. Funds may be used for tuition, fees, and books. Part-time students are eligible for exact costs only.

Duration 1 semester; may be renewed.

Number awarded Varies each year.

Deadline June of each year for fall semester; October of each year for spring semester.

[485]
PRE-MED ENRICHMENT PROGRAM FOR UNDERREPRESENTED MINORITY UNDERGRADUATES

University of Pennsylvania Health System
Attn: Center of Excellence for Diversity in Health Education and Research
3508 Market Street, Suite 234
Philadelphia, PA 19104-3357
(215) 898-3913　　　　Fax: (215) 573-2793
E-mail: taylor2@mail.med.upenn.edu
Web: www.uphs.upenn.edu/coeomh/premed.htm

Summary To provide an opportunity for Native Americans and other underrepresented minority undergraduates to gain research experience in medicine during a summer program at the University of Pennsylvania.

Eligibility This program is open to undergraduate students who are members of ethnic or racial groups underrepresented in medicine. Applicants must have completed at least 60 credits of a premedical program and have a GPA of 2.75 or higher. They must be interested in participating in a program at the University of Pennsylvania that includes research, clinical observations, classroom exercises, and teaching observation designed to stimulate and cultivate their interest in academic medicine. U.S. citizenship or permanent resident status is required.

Financial data The program provides a stipend (amount not specified), housing, and 2 meals per day.

Duration 10 weeks during the summer.

Additional information This program, which began in 1993, is sponsored by the Bureau of Health Professions of the U.S. Health Resources and Services Administration.

Number awarded 10 to 12 each year.

Deadline January of each year.

[486]
PRINCE KUHI'O HAWAIIAN CIVIC CLUB SCHOLARSHIP

Prince Kuhi'o Hawaiian Civic Club
Attn: Scholarship Chair
P.O. Box 4728
Honolulu, HI 96812
E-mail: pkhcc64@gmail.com
Web: www.pkhcc.com/scholarship.html

Summary To provide financial assistance for undergraduate or graduate studies to persons of Native Hawaiian descent.

Eligibility This program is open to high school seniors and full-time undergraduate or graduate students who are of Hawaiian descent (descendants of the aboriginal inhabitants of the Hawaiian Islands prior to 1778). Graduating high school seniors and current undergraduate students must have a GPA of 2.5 or higher; graduate students must have at least a 3.3 GPA. Along with their application, they must submit an essay on how they will apply their education toward the well-being of the Hawaiian community. Priority is given to members of the Prince Kuhi'o Hawaiian Civic Club in good standing, including directly-related family members. Special consideration is given to applicants majoring in Hawaiian studies, Hawaiian language, education, or journalism. Selection is based on academic achievement and leadership potential.

Financial data Stipends range from $500 to $1,000 per year.

Duration 1 year; may be renewed.

Number awarded Varies each year.

Deadline March of each year.

[487]
PROFESSIONAL GOLF MANAGEMENT DIVERSITY SCHOLARSHIP

Professional Golfers' Association of America
Attn: PGA Foundation
100 Avenue of the Champions
Palm Beach Gardens, FL 33418
Toll Free: (888) 532-6661
Web: www.pgafoundation.com

Summary To provide financial assistance to Native Americans, other minorities, and women who are interested in attending a designated college or university to prepare for a career as a golf professional.

Eligibility This program is open to women and minorities interested in becoming a licensed PGA Professional. Applicants must be interested in attending 1 of 20 colleges and universities that offer the Professional Golf Management (PGM) curriculum sanctioned by the PGA.

Financial data The stipend is $3,000 per year.

Duration 1 year; may be renewed.

Additional information This program began in 1993. Programs are offered at Arizona State University (Mesa, Arizona), Campbell University (Buies Creek, North Carolina), Clemson University (Clemson, South Carolina), Coastal Carolina University (Conway, South Carolina), Eastern Kentucky University (Richmond, Kentucky), Ferris State University (Big Rapids, Michigan), Florida Gulf Coast University (Fort Myers, Florida), Florida State University (Tallahassee, Florida), Methodist College (Fayetteville, North Carolina), Mississippi State University (Mississippi State, Mississippi), New Mexico State University (Las Cruces, New Mexico), North Carolina State University (Raleigh, North Carolina), Pennsylvania State University (University Park, Pennsylvania), Sam Houston State University (Huntsville, Texas), University of Central Oklahoma (Edmond, Oklahoma), University of Colorado (Colorado Springs, Colorado), University of Idaho (Moscow, Idaho), University of Maryland Eastern Shore (Princess Anne, Maryland), University of Nebraska (Lincoln, Nebraska), and University of Nevada (Las Vegas, Nevada).

Number awarded Varies each year; recently, 20 of these scholarships were awarded.

Deadline Deadline not specified.

[488]
PROJECT SEED SCHOLARSHIPS

American Chemical Society
Attn: Education Division
1155 16th Street, N.W.
Washington, DC 20036
(202) 872-4380   Toll Free: (800) 227-5558, ext. 4380
E-mail: projectseed@acs.org
Web: portal.acs.org

Summary To provide financial assistance for college to underrepresented minorities and other high school students who participated in the American Chemical Society's Project SEED: Summer Education Experience for the Disadvantaged.

Eligibility Applicants for Project SEED must have completed the junior or senior year in high school, live within commuting distance of a sponsoring institution, have completed a course in high school chemistry, and come from an economically disadvantaged family. Preference is given to students whose family income is below $34,340 or does not exceed 200% of the federal poverty guidelines based on family size; family income may be up to $48,260 if the student is a member of an ethnic group underrepresented in the sciences (African American, Hispanic, American Indian), if their parents did not attend college, if they live in a single parent household, or if they are a member of a large family. Participants in the Project SEED program are eligible to apply for these scholarships during their senior year in high school if they plan to major in college in a chemical science or engineering field, such as chemistry, chemical engineering, biochemistry, materials science, or another closely-related field.

Financial data Stipends up to $5,000 per year are available.

Duration 1 year; nonrenewable.

Number awarded Varies each year; recently, 37 of these scholarships were awarded.

Deadline March of each year.

[489]
PUBLIC RELATIONS SOCIETY OF AMERICA MULTICULTURAL AFFAIRS SCHOLARSHIPS

Public Relations Student Society of America
Attn: Vice President of Member Services
33 Maiden Lane, 11th Floor
New York, NY 10038-5150
(212) 460-1474   Fax: (212) 995-0757
E-mail: prssa@prsa.org
Web: www.prssa.org/awards/awardMulticultural.aspx

Summary To provide financial assistance to Native American and other minority college students who are interested in preparing for a career in public relations.

Eligibility This program is open to minority (African American/Black, Hispanic/Latino, Asian, Native American, Alaskan Native, or Pacific Islander) students who are at least juniors at an accredited 4-year college or university. Applicants must be enrolled full time, be able to demonstrate financial need, and have earned a GPA of 3.0 or higher. Membership in the Public Relations Student Society of America is preferred but not required. A major or minor in public relations is preferred; students who attend a school that does not offer a public relations degree or program must be enrolled in a communications degree program (e.g., journalism, mass communications).

Financial data The stipend is $1,500.

Duration 1 year.

Additional information This program was established in 1989.

Number awarded 2 each year.

Deadline April of each year.

[490]
PUEBLO OF ACOMA HIGHER EDUCATION GRANT PROGRAM

Pueblo of Acoma
Attn: Higher Education Coordinator
P.O. Box 307
Acoma, NM 87034
(505) 552-5121   Fax: (505) 552-6812
E-mail: highered@puebloofacoma.org
Web: puebloofacoma.org/Higher_Ed_Service.aspx

Summary To provide financial assistance to Pueblo of Acoma enrolled members who are interested in attending college in any state.

Eligibility This program is open to members of the Pueblo of Acoma who are enrolled or planning to enroll full or part time at an accredited college or university in any state to work on an associate or bachelor's degree. Applicants must submit their Certificate of Indian Blood (CIB) and tribal enrollment, 2 letters of recommendation, high school or college transcripts, ACT or SAT scores, a copy of their class schedule, and documentation of financial need.

Financial data The amount awarded varies, depending upon the recipient's financial need. Generally, scholarships are considered supplemental funds.

Duration 1 year; may be renewed, provided the recipient maintains a GPA of 2.0 or higher.

Number awarded Varies each year.

Deadline April of each year for the fall term; September of each year for the spring term.

[491]
PUEBLO OF ISLETA HIGHER EDUCATION PROGRAM

Pueblo of Isleta
Attn: Higher Education Program
P.O. Box 1270
Isleta, NM 87022
(505) 924-3186   Fax: (505) 869-7692
E-mail: poi08090@isletapueblo.com
Web: www.isletapueblo.com/highered2.html

Summary To provide financial assistance to members of the Pueblo of Isleta who are interested in attending college or graduate school in any state.

Eligibility This program is open to undergraduate and graduate students who can document tribal membership in the Pueblo of Isleta or at least one-quarter Isleta blood. Applicants must have a GPA of 2.5 or higher and be able to demonstrate financial need. They must have applied for federal aid by submitting a Free Application for Federal Student Aid (FAFSA).

Financial data The stipend depends on the need of the recipient.

Duration 1 year; may be renewed if the recipient maintains a GPA of 2.5 or higher.

Number awarded Varies each year.

Deadline June of each year for the fall semester; October of each year for the spring semester or winter quarter; March of each year for summer term.

[492]
PUEBLO OF JEMEZ SCHOLARSHIP PROGRAM

Pueblo of Jemez
Attn: Higher Education Center
P.O. Box 100
Jemez Pueblo, NM 87024
(505) 834-9102   Toll Free: (888) 834-3936
Fax: (505) 834-7900
E-mail: Higher_Ed@jemezpueblo.org
Web: www.jemezpueblo.org/Education.aspx

Summary To provide financial assistance to Jemez Pueblo students who are interested in earning a college degree at a school in any state.

Eligibility This program is open to Jemez Pueblo students working on or planning to work on an associate or bachelor's degree at an accredited institution of higher education in any state as a full-time student. Applicants must be at least one quarter Jemez and recognized by the Jemez Pueblo census office (a Certificate of Indian Blood must be provided). They must submit 2 letters of recommendation, a copy of their letter of acceptance from the institution they are or are planning to attend, and an official transcript from the high school or college they last attended. It is required that all students fill out the Free Application for Federal Student Aid (FAFSA) and apply for aid from the college they plan to attend.

Financial data The stipend depends on the need of the recipient.

Duration 1 semester; may be renewed if the recipient remains enrolled full time with a GPA of 2.0 or higher.

Number awarded Varies each year.

Deadline January of each year.

[493]
PUEBLO OF LAGUNA HIGHER EDUCATION PROGRAM

Pueblo of Laguna
Attn: Laguna Higher Education
P.O. Box 207
Laguna, NM 87026
(505) 552-7182   Fax: (505) 552-7235
E-mail: m.conant@lagunaed.net
Web: www.ldoe.org/pfs_programs.html

Summary To provide financial assistance to regular members of the Pueblo of Laguna who are interested in attending college or graduate school in any state.

Eligibility This program is open to regular enrolled members of the Pueblo of Laguna. Applicants must have a high school diploma or GED certificate and be working on a bachelor's, transferable associate, or graduate degree. They must have been accepted by an accredited college or university in the United States as a full-time student. Along with their application, they must submit documentation of financial need, a 1-page personal statement on their purpose in working on a degree in their chosen field of study and their career or professional goals, high school and/or college transcripts, ACT scores, and verification of tribal membership or Indian blood. Vocational students, part-time students, and "naturalized" Laguna tribal members are not eligible.

Financial data Stipends are intended to cover unmet financial need, to a maximum of $8,000 per year. Most awards range from $2,000 to $5,000 per academic year.

Duration 1 year; may be renewed for a maximum of 4 academic years (students may submit an appeal for a fifth year of study), provided the recipient maintains a GPA of 2.0 or higher and full-time enrollment.

Number awarded Varies each year.

Deadline May of each year for the fall term or academic year; October of each year for the winter/spring term; April of each year for the summer term.

[494]
PURCELL POWLESS SCHOLARSHIP

Indian Summer, Inc.
10809 West Lincoln Avenue, Suite 101
West Allis, WI 53227
(414) 774-7119   Fax: (414) 774-6810
E-mail: indiansummer@wi.rr.com
Web: www.indiansummer.org/education/scholarships.aspx

Summary To provide financial assistance to American Indians from Wisconsin who are studying or planning to study a medical field in college in any state.

Eligibility This program is open to Wisconsin residents who are American Indians by tribal enrollment or descendancy (having 1 or more ancestors who are tribally enrolled). Applicants must be accepted or in good standing at an institution of higher education in any state and majoring in a medical field. They must submit a 1-page statement describing their educational goals, the reasons they feel they should receive the scholarship, their community service, and any special needs. Preference is given to applicants who have provided service to the Indian community and have not previously received a scholarship.

Financial data The stipend is $1,000.

Duration   1 year.

Additional information   This program is offered in cooperation with American Indian Student Services at the University of Wisconsin at Milwaukee.

Number awarded   1 each year.

Deadline   July of each year.

[495]
PWC EXCEED SCHOLARSHIP PROGRAM

PricewaterhouseCoopers LLP
Attn: Campus Recruiting Manager
125 High Street
Boston, MA 02110
(617) 530-5349   Fax: (813) 741-8595
Web: www.pwc.com

Summary   To provide financial assistance to Native Americans and other underrepresented minority undergraduate students interested in preparing for a career in public accounting.

Eligibility   This program is open to African American, Native American, and Hispanic American students entering their sophomore, junior, or senior year of college. Applicants must have a GPA of 3.4 or higher, be able to demonstrate interpersonal skills and leadership ability, and be working on a bachelor's degree in accounting, computer information systems, management information systems, finance, economics, or actuarial science. Along with their application, they must submit a 300-word essay on how they have demonstrated the core values of PricewaterhouseCoopers (PwC) of achieving excellence, developing teamwork, and inspiring leadership in their academic and/or professional career.

Financial data   The stipend is $3,000.

Duration   1 year; nonrenewable.

Additional information   Recipients also participate in the annual Diversity in Business Leadership Conference (held in New York City), are considered for an internship position with PwC, and engage in a mentoring program. This program began in 1990.

Number awarded   Varies each year; recently, 81 of these scholarships were awarded.

Deadline   December of each year.

[496]
PYRAMID LAKE PAIUTE TRIBE CONSOLIDATED HIGHER EDUCATION SCHOLARSHIP

Pyramid Lake Paiute Tribe
Attn: Consolidated Higher Education Office
P.O. Box 256
Nixon, NV 89424
(775) 574-0300   Fax: (775) 574-0302
E-mail: asampson@plpt.nsn.us
Web: www.plpt.nsn.us/highed/index.html

Summary   To provide financial assistance to members of the Pyramid Lake Paiute Tribe who are interested in working full time on an undergraduate degree at a school in any state.

Eligibility   This program is open to enrolled members of the Pyramid Lake Paiute Tribe who are working on or planning to work on an undergraduate degree at a college or university in any state. Applicants must be enrolled full time and be able to demonstrate financial need.

Financial data   Stipends depend on the unmet financial need (as determined by the FAFSA) of the recipient. Recently, the program has attempted to provide 30% of the recipient's documented unmet financial need.

Duration   1 year; may be renewed, provided the recipient maintains a GPA of 2.0 or higher.

Additional information   This program is funded both by the U.S. Bureau of Indian Affairs and the Pyramid Lake Paiute Tribal General Fund.

Number awarded   Varies each year.

Deadline   June of each year for fall; November of each year for spring.

[497]
PYRAMID LAKE PAIUTE TRIBE ENRICHMENT SCHOLARSHIP

Pyramid Lake Paiute Tribe
Attn: Consolidated Higher Education Office
P.O. Box 256
Nixon, NV 89424
(775) 574-0300   Fax: (775) 574-0302
E-mail: asampson@plpt.nsn.us
Web: www.plpt.nsn.us/highed/index.html

Summary   To provide financial assistance to members of the Pyramid Lake Paiute Tribe who are interested in working part time on an undergraduate or graduate degree.

Eligibility   This program is open to enrolled members of the Pyramid Lake Paiute Tribe who are working on or planning to work on an associate, bachelor's, master's, or doctoral (including law and medicine) degree. Applicants may take up to 9 credits per term (or 12 credits for law and medical students). They must have a GPA of 2.0 or higher for their most recent semester. Along with their application, they must submit a 75-word essay on how they will benefit from the courses they are taking.

Financial data   The stipend is $1,000 per semester (or $2,000 per semester for law and medical students). A supplemental grant of $250 is provided for books and supplies.

Duration   1 semester; may be renewed, provided the recipient maintains a GPA of 2.0 or higher.

Number awarded   Varies each year.

Deadline   June of each year for fall; November of each year for spring.

[498]
QUAPAW TRIBAL EDUCATIONAL FUND PROGRAM

Quapaw Tribe of Oklahoma
Office of Educational Funds
P.O. Box 765
Quapaw, OK 74363
(918) 542-1853, ext. 211   Toll Free: (888) 642-4724
Fax: (918) 542-4694   E-mail: pleptich@quapawtribe.com
Web: quapawtribe.com/site/view/73841_Eduction.pml

Summary   To provide financial assistance for college or graduate school to members of the Quapaw Tribe of Oklahoma.

Eligibility   This program is open to enrolled members of the Quapaw Tribe who are or will be high school graduates or GED recipients. Applicants must be attending or planning to attend an accredited college, university, or vocational school in any state at the undergraduate or graduate level. Along with their application, they must submit an essay of 150 to 600 words on their educational goals and plans for utilizing their educational funding.

Financial data Participating students receive $100 per credit hour, to a maximum of $2,100 per semester.

Duration 1 semester; may be renewed, provided the recipient maintains a GPA of 2.0 or higher.

Number awarded Varies each year.

Deadline September of each year for fall semester; January of each year for spring semester; August of each year for summer school.

[499]
RACE RELATIONS MULTIRACIAL STUDENT SCHOLARSHIP

Christian Reformed Church
Attn: Office of Race Relations
2850 Kalamazoo Avenue, S.E.
Grand Rapids, MI 49560-0200
(616) 241-1691   Toll Free: (877) 279-9994
Fax: (616) 224-0803   E-mail: crcna@crcna.org
Web: www.crcna.org/pages/racerelations_scholar.cfm

Summary To provide financial assistance to Native American and other undergraduate and graduate minority students interested in attending colleges related to the Christian Reformed Church in North America (CRCNA).

Eligibility Students of color in the United States and Canada are eligible to apply. Normally, applicants are expected to be members of CRCNA congregations who plan to pursue their educational goals at Calvin Theological Seminary or any of the colleges affiliated with the CRCNA. Students who have no prior history with the CRCNA must attend a CRCNA-related college or seminary for a full academic year before they are eligible to apply for this program. Students entering their sophomore year must have earned a GPA of 2.0 or higher as freshmen; students entering their junior year must have earned a GPA of 2.3 or higher as sophomores; students entering their senior year must have earned a GPA of 2.6 or higher as juniors.

Financial data First-year students receive $500 per semester. Other levels of students may receive up to $2,000 per academic year.

Duration 1 year.

Additional information This program was first established in 1971 and revised in 1991. Recipients are expected to train to engage actively in the ministry of racial reconciliation in church and in society. They must be able to work in the United States or Canada upon graduating and must consider working for 1 of the agencies of the CRCNA.

Number awarded Varies each year; recently, 31 students received a total of $21,000 in support.

Deadline March of each year.

[500]
RACIAL ETHNIC EDUCATIONAL SCHOLARSHIPS

Synod of the Trinity
Attn: Scholarships
3040 Market Street
Camp Hill, PA 17011-4599
(717) 737-0421, ext. 233
Toll Free: (800) 242-0534, ext. 233
Fax: (717) 737-8211   E-mail: mhumer@syntrinity.org
Web: www.syntrinity.org

Summary To provide financial assistance to Native Americans and other minority students in Pennsylvania, West Virginia, and designated counties in Ohio who are interested in attending college in any state.

Eligibility This program is open to members of a racial minority group (African American, Asian, Hispanic, Latino, Middle Eastern, or Native American) who are enrolled or planning to enroll full time at an accredited college or vocational school in any state. Applicants may be of any religious denomination, but they must be residents of the area served by the Presbyterian Church (USA) Synod of the Trinity, which covers all of Pennsylvania; West Virginia except for the counties of Berkeley, Grant, Hampshire, Hardy, Jefferson, Mineral, Morgan, and Pendleton; and the Ohio counties of Belmont, Harrison, Jefferson, Monroe, and the southern sector of Columbiana. They must have total income of less than $85,000 for a family of 4. U.S. citizenship or permanent resident status is required.

Financial data Awards range from $100 to $1,000 per year, depending on the need of the recipient.

Duration 1 year; recipients may reapply.

Number awarded Varies each year.

Deadline April of each year.

[501]
RAE ROYER MEMORIAL SCHOLARSHIP FUND

Rosebud Sioux Tribe
Attn: Higher Education Grant Program
P.O. Box 130
Rosebud, SD 57570-0130
(605) 747-2375   Toll Free: (877) 808-3283
Fax: (605) 747-5274   E-mail: rstedav@gwtc.net
Web: www.gwtc.net/~rsted/index_files/Page599.html

Summary To provide financial assistance to members of the Rosebud Sioux Tribe who are interested in attending college or graduate school in any state and returning to the reservation to work for the tribe.

Eligibility This program is open to members of the Rosebud Sioux Tribe who are enrolled or planning to enroll at a college or university in any state to work on an undergraduate or graduate degree. Undergraduates may enroll full or part time, but only full-time graduate students are eligible. Applicants must be able to demonstrate financial need. They must indicate a willingness to commit to a 1-year or 1-semester internship of service to the tribe for each year of funding received. In the selection process, half the awards are reserved for students who live within the boundaries of the Rosebud Reservation in south central South Dakota and half to those who live off the reservation.

Financial data For undergraduates, the maximum stipend is $1,500 per term for students with no dependents or $3,000 per term for students with dependents. For graduate students, the maximum stipend is $6,000 per term.

Duration 1 year; may be renewed, provided recipients earn a GPA of 2.0 or higher as a freshman and sophomore, 2.5 or higher as a junior and senior, or 3.5 or higher as a graduate student.

Number awarded Varies each year.

Deadline July of each year for fall semester; October of each year for winter quarter; November of each year for spring semester; January of each year for spring quarter; March of each year for summer school.

[502]
RALPH BUNCHE SUMMER INSTITUTE

American Political Science Association
Attn: Ralph Bunch Summer Institute
1527 New Hampshire Avenue, N.W.
Washington, DC 20036-1206
(202) 483-2512   Fax: (202) 483-2657
E-mail: minority@apsanet.org
Web: www.apsanet.org/content_6002.cfm

Summary To introduce Native Americans and other underrepresented minority undergraduate students to the world of graduate study and to encourage their eventual application to a Ph.D. program in political science.

Eligibility This program is open to African American, Latino(a), Native American, and Pacific Islander college students completing their junior year. Applicants must be interested in attending graduate school and working on a degree in a field related to political science. Along with their application, they must submit a 2-page personal statement on their reasons for wanting to participate in this program and their future academic and professional plans. U.S. citizenship is required.

Financial data Participants receive a stipend of $200 per week plus full support of tuition, transportation, room, board, books, and instructional materials.

Duration 5 weeks during the summer.

Additional information The institute includes 2 transferable credit courses (1 in quantitative analysis and the other on race and American politics). In addition, guest lecturers and recruiters from Ph.D. programs visit the students. Classes are held on the campus of Duke University. Most students who attend the institute excel in their senior year and go on to graduate school, many with full graduate fellowships and teaching assistantships. This program is funded by the National Science Foundation.

Number awarded 20 each year.

Deadline January of each year.

[503]
RDW GROUP, INC. MINORITY SCHOLARSHIP FOR COMMUNICATIONS

Rhode Island Foundation
Attn: Funds Administrator
One Union Station
Providence, RI 02903
(401) 427-4017   Fax: (401) 331-8085
E-mail: lmonahan@rifoundation.org
Web: www.rifoundation.org

Summary To provide financial assistance to Native Americans and other undergraduate and graduate students of color in Rhode Island who are interested in preparing for a career in communications at a school in any state.

Eligibility This program is open to undergraduate and graduate students at colleges and universities in any state who are Rhode Island residents of color. Applicants must intend to work on a degree in communications (including computer graphics, art, cinematography, or other fields that would prepare them for a career in advertising). They must be able to demonstrate financial need and a commitment to a career in communications. Along with their application, they must submit an essay (up to 300 words) on the impact they would like to have on the communications field.

Financial data The stipend ranges from $1,000 to $2,500 per year.

Duration 1 year; recipients may reapply.

Additional information This program is sponsored by the RDW Group, Inc.

Number awarded 1 each year.

Deadline April of each year.

[504]
RED CLIFF BAND ADULT VOCATIONAL TRAINING PROGRAM

Red Cliff Band of Lake Superior Chippewa
Attn: Education Department
88385 Pike Road, Highway 13
Bayfield, WI 54814
(715) 779-3706, ext. 229   Fax: (715) 779-3704
E-mail: Carmen.VanderVenter@redcliff-nsn.gov
Web: redcliff-nsn.gov

Summary To provide financial assistance for technical or vocational training to members of the Red Cliff Band of Lake Superior Chippewa.

Eligibility This program is open to enrolled tribal members of the Red Cliff Band who are working on or planning to work on a diploma, certificate, or associate degree. Applicants must be able to demonstrate financial need.

Financial data The maximum stipend is $1,800 per year.

Duration Up to 24 months at a vocational technical training institution or 36 months at a school of nursing, provided the recipient maintains a GPA of 2.0 or higher.

Number awarded Varies each year.

Deadline June of each year.

[505]
RED CLIFF BAND HIGHER EDUCATION GRANTS PROGRAM

Red Cliff Band of Lake Superior Chippewa
Attn: Education Department
88385 Pike Road, Highway 13
Bayfield, WI 54814
(715) 779-3706, ext. 229   Fax: (715) 779-3704
E-mail: Carmen.VanderVenter@redcliff-nsn.gov
Web: redcliff-nsn.gov

Summary To provide financial assistance for college or graduate school to members of the Red Cliff Band of Lake Superior Chippewa.

Eligibility This program is open to enrolled tribal members of the Red Cliff Band who are working on or planning to work on an undergraduate or graduate degree. Applicants must be able to demonstrate financial need.

Financial data The maximum stipend for undergraduate students is $1,800 per year. The stipend for graduate students depends on the availability of funds.

Duration 1 year; may be renewed for a total of 10 semesters, provided the recipient maintains a GPA of 2.0 or higher as an undergraduate or 3.0 or higher as a graduate student.

Number awarded Varies each year.

Deadline June of each year.

[506]
RESEARCH INTERNSHIPS IN SCIENCE OF THE ENVIRONMENT

Arkansas State University
Attn: Department of Chemistry and Physics
P.O. Box 419
State University, AR 72467
(870) 972-3298　　　　　　　　Fax: (870) 972-3089
E-mail: jpratte@astate.edu
Web: www2.astate.edu

Summary To provide an opportunity for Native American and other minority undergraduates to participate in a summer research activity at Arkansas State University in Jonesboro.

Eligibility This program is open to underrepresented minority undergraduate students who have completed at least 1 course sequence in environmental science (including biology, chemistry, or geology), have a GPA of 2.5 or higher in their major, and are U.S. citizens or permanent residents. Applicants must be interested in participating in a summer research experience centered on exploring the relationships between agricultural land use and ecosystem function. Along with their application, they must submit a brief essay on their career goals after completing their bachelor's degree, their interests related to environmental science, any specific research interests, and how a research internship will contribute to their career goals.

Financial data Interns receive a stipend of $4,000; housing and travel to the site are also provided.

Duration 10 weeks during the summer.

Additional information This program is funded by the National Science Foundation as part of its Research Experiences for Undergraduates program.

Number awarded Approximately 12 each year.

Deadline March of each year.

[507]
RICHARD HAGEN-MINERVA HARVEY MEMORIAL SCHOLARSHIP

South Dakota Department of Education
Attn: Office of the Secretary
700 Governors Drive
Pierre, SD 57501
(605) 773-3134　　　　　　　　Fax: (605) 773-6139
Web: doe.sd.gov/scholarships/hagen

Summary To provide financial assistance for college to American Indians whose reservation is located in South Dakota.

Eligibility This program is open to enrolled members of American Indian tribes whose reservation is located in whole or part in South Dakota. Applicants must be attending or plan-

ning to attend a public or non-public accredited college, university, or technical institute in South Dakota. They must apply within 5 years after high school graduation or within 1 year after release from active military duty (if that release is within 5 years of high school graduation). Along with their application, they must submit high school and/or college transcripts, verification of tribal enrollment, ACT scores, and an essay explaining why they deserve to receive this scholarship.

Financial data The stipend is at least $1,000 per year for the first 2 years of college, at least $1,500 for the third year, and at least $2,500 for the fourth year.

Duration 4 years, provided the recipient maintains a cumulative GPA of 2.5 or higher.

Number awarded Up to 7 each year.

Deadline April of each year.

[508]
RICHARD HECKERT FELLOWSHIP

National Action Council for Minorities in Engineering
Attn: University Programs
440 Hamilton Avenue, Suite 302
White Plains, NY 10601-1813
(914) 539-4010　　　　　　　　Fax: (914) 539-4032
E-mail: scholarships@nacme.org
Web: www.nacme.org/NACME_D.aspx?pageid=105

Summary To provide financial assistance to Native American and other underrepresented minority high school seniors interested in studying engineering or related fields in college.

Eligibility This program is open to African American, Latino, and American Indian high school seniors who are in the top 10% of their graduating class, have a GPA of 3.0 or higher, and have demonstrated academic excellence, leadership skills, and a commitment to science and engineering as a career. Candidates must have been accepted as a full-time student at an ABET-accredited engineering program. They must be nominated by their school (each high school may nominate only 1 student). Fields of study include all areas of engineering as well as computer science, materials science, mathematics, operations research, or physics. Letters of nomination must be accompanied by a transcript, SAT or ACT report form, resume, and 100-word statement of why the student should receive this scholarship.

Financial data The stipend is $5,000 per year. Funds are sent directly to the recipient's university.

Duration 4 years.

Number awarded 1 each year.

Deadline April of each year.

[509]
RICHARD MARKS EDUCATIONAL FUND

Ke Ali'i Pauahi Foundation
Attn: Financial Aid & Scholarship Services
567 South King Street, Suite 160
Honolulu, HI 96813
(808) 534-3966　　　Toll Free: (800) 842-4682, ext. 43966
Fax: (808) 534-3890　　　E-mail: scholarships@pauahi.org
Web: www.pauahi.org/scholarships

Summary To provide financial assistance to students, especially Native Hawaiians, who are interested in working on an undergraduate degree in a medical field at a school in Hawaii.

Eligibility This program is open to students working full time on a 4-year undergraduate degree in a medical field at a college or university in Hawaii; preference is given to Native Hawaiians (descendants of the aboriginal inhabitants of the Hawaiian Islands prior to 1778).

Financial data The stipend is $1,000.

Duration 1 year.

Additional information This scholarship was first offered in 2010.

Number awarded 1 each year.

Deadline March of each year.

[510]
RICHARD S. SMITH SCHOLARSHIP

United Methodist Church
Attn: General Board of Discipleship
Division on Ministries with Young People
P.O. Box 340003
Nashville, TN 37203-0003
(615) 340-7184   Toll Free: (877) 899-2780, ext. 7184
Fax: (615) 340-7063   E-mail: youngpeople@gbod.org
Web: www.gbod.org

Summary To provide financial assistance to Native American and other minority high school seniors who wish to prepare for a Methodist church-related career.

Eligibility This program is open to graduating high school seniors who are members of racial/ethnic minority groups and have been active members of a United Methodist Church for at least 1 year. Applicants must have been admitted to an accredited college or university to prepare for a church-related career. They must have maintained at least a "C" average throughout high school and be able to demonstrate financial need. Along with their application, they must submit brief essays on their participation in church projects and activities, a leadership experience, the role their faith plays in their life, the church-related vocation to which God is calling them, and their extracurricular interests and activities. U.S. citizenship or permanent resident status is required.

Financial data The stipend is $1,000.

Duration 1 year; nonrenewable.

Additional information This scholarship was first awarded in 1997. Recipients must enroll full time in their first year of undergraduate study.

Number awarded 2 each year.

Deadline May of each year.

[511]
RICHARD W. TANNER SCHOLARSHIP FUND

Saint Paul Foundation
Attn: Program Assistant
55 Fifth Street East, Suite 600
St. Paul, MN 55101-1797
(651) 325-4202   Toll Free: (800) 875-6167
Fax: (651) 224-8123
E-mail: jmu@saintpaulfoundation.org
Web: www.saintpaulfoundation.org/scholarships

Summary To provide financial assistance to Indians who belong to a Minnesota tribe and are interested in attending college in any state.

Eligibility This program is open to members of Indian tribes in Minnesota who are full-time juniors or seniors at a college or university in any state. Applicants must submit a 250-word essay describing their involvement in the Indian community and how the accomplishment of their educational goals will benefit the American Indian community. Financial need is not considered in the selection process.

Financial data The stipend is $1,000.

Duration 1 year; nonrenewable.

Number awarded 1 each year.

Deadline June of each year.

[512]
ROBERT J. AND EVELYN CONLEY AWARD

Cherokee Nation
Attn: Cherokee Nation Education Corporation
115 East Delaware Street
P.O. Box 948
Tahlequah, OK 74465-0948
(918) 207-0950   Fax: (918) 207-0951
E-mail: contact@cnec-edu.org
Web: cnec.cherokee.org

Summary To provide financial assistance to citizens of several Cherokee nations who are enrolled at a college or university in any state and working on an undergraduate or graduate degree in English or creative writing.

Eligibility This program is open to citizens of the Cherokee Nation, the United Keetoowah Band, or the Eastern Band of Cherokee Indians. Applicants must be currently enrolled in an undergraduate or graduate program in English or creative writing at a college or university in any state. They are not required to reside in the Cherokee Nation area. Along with their application, they must submit a 4-page personal essay that includes background information, their degree plan for higher education, why they have chosen that field of study, how they plan to serve Cherokee people when they complete their higher education, and why they should be selected for this scholarship. Selection is based on the clarity and presentation of the essay; academic information (including transcripts and ACT scores); school, cultural and community activities; future plans to serve Cherokee people; and financial need.

Financial data The stipend is $1,000 per semester ($2,000 per year).

Duration 1 year. Renewal for the second semester requires the recipient to earn a GPA of 2.5 or higher in the first semester.

Number awarded 1 each year.

Deadline April of each year.

[513]
RODNEY T. MATHEWS, JR. MEMORIAL SCHOLARSHIP FOR CALIFORNIA INDIANS

Morongo Band of Mission Indians
Attn: Scholarship Coordinator
11545 Potrero Road
Banning, CA 92220
(951) 572-6185   E-mail: trisha.smith@morongo.org
Web: www.morongonation.org

Summary To provide financial assistance for college or graduate school in any state to California Indians.

Eligibility This program is open to enrolled members of federally-recognized California Indian tribes who have been actively involved in the Native American community. Applicants must submit documentation of financial need, an academic letter of recommendation, and a letter of recommendation from the American Indian community. They must be enrolled full time at an accredited college or university in any state. Undergraduates must have a GPA of 2.75 or higher; graduate students must have a GPA of 3.5 or higher. Along with their application, they must submit 1) a 2-page personal statement on their academic, career, and personal goals; any extenuating circumstances they wish to have considered; how they view their Native American heritage and its importance to them; how they plan to "give back" to Native Americans after graduation; and their on-going active involvement in the Native American community both on and off campus; and 2) a 2-page essay, either on what they feel are the most critical issues facing tribal communities today and how they see themselves working in relationship to those issues, or on where they see Native people in the 21st century in terms of survival, governance, and cultural preservation, and what role they see themselves playing in that future.

Financial data The maximum stipend is $10,000 per year. Funds are paid directly to the recipient's school for tuition, housing, textbooks, and required fees.

Duration 1 year; may be renewed 1 additional year.

Additional information Recipients are required to complete 60 hours of service with a designated California Indian community agency: California Indian Museum and Cultural Center, Indian Health Care Services, National Indian Justice Center, California Indian Legal Services, California Indian Professors Association, California Indian Culture and Awareness Conference, or California Democratic Party Native American Caucus.

Number awarded 4 each year.

Deadline March of each year.

[514]
ROSEBUD SIOUX TRIBE HIGHER EDUCATION GRANT PROGRAM

Rosebud Sioux Tribe
Attn: Higher Education Grant Program
P.O. Box 130
Rosebud, SD 57570-0130
(605) 747-2375   Toll Free: (877) 808-3283
Fax: (605) 747-5274   E-mail: rstedav@gwtc.net
Web: www.gwtc.net/~rsted/index_files/Page599.html

Summary To provide financial assistance for college to members of the Rosebud Sioux Tribe.

Eligibility This program is open to members of the Rosebud Sioux Tribe who are enrolled or planning to enroll full time at a college or university in any state. Licensure and diploma programs do not qualify. Applicants must have applied for a Pell Grant and be eligible for federal financial aid. In the selection process, first priority is given to continuing students who currently are receiving this assistance; second to students who received their high school diploma or GED certification from within the boundaries of the Rosebud Reservation in south central South Dakota; third to students from South Dakota but outside the reservation; and fourth to out-of-state students.

Financial data A stipend is awarded (amount not specified).

Duration 1 year; may be renewed.

Additional information This program is funded by the U.S. Bureau of Indian Affairs (BIA).

Number awarded Varies each year.

Deadline July of each year for fall semester or quarter; October of each year for winter quarter; November of each year for spring semester; January of each year for spring quarter; March of each year for summer school.

[515]
ROSEMARY GASKIN SCHOLARSHIP

Chippewa County Community Foundation
P.O. Box 1979
Sault Ste. Marie, MI 49783
(906) 635-1046   Fax: (775) 417-7368
E-mail: cccf@lighthouse.net
Web: www.cccf4good4ever.org/main.asp?id=7

Summary To provide financial assistance to members of the Sault Ste. Marie Tribe of Chippewa Indians who are interested in attending a public college in any state.

Eligibility This program is open to enrolled members of the Sault Ste. Marie Tribe of Chippewa Indians who have been accepted for enrollment at a public institution of higher education in any state. Applicants are not required to demonstrate financial need, to enroll full time, or to have a minimum blood quantum level. Along with their application, they must submit a 500-word essay on their choice of the following topics: equality, American Indian rights, education, or reviving Indian culture and traditional beliefs.

Financial data The stipend is $1,000.

Duration 1 year.

Number awarded 1 each year.

Deadline July of each year.

[516]
ROY M. HUHNDORF ENDOWMENT SCHOLARSHIP FUND

Cook Inlet Region, Inc.
Attn: The CIRI Foundation
3600 San Jeronimo Drive, Suite 256
Anchorage, AK 99508-2870
(907) 793-3575   Toll Free: (800) 764-3382
Fax: (907) 793-3585   E-mail: tcf@thecirifoundation.org
Web: www.thecirifoundation.org/designated.htm

Summary To provide financial assistance for undergraduate or graduate studies in health science to Alaska Natives who are original enrollees to Cook Inlet Region, Inc. (CIRI) and their lineal descendants.

Eligibility This program is open to Alaska Native enrollees to CIRI under the Alaska Native Claims Settlement Act (ANCSA) of 1971 and their lineal descendants. There are no Alaska residency requirements or age limitations. Applicants must be accepted or enrolled full time in a 4-year undergraduate or a graduate degree program. They must be working on a degree in health science and have a GPA of 2.5 or higher. Along with their application, they must submit a 500-word statement on their educational and career goals and how they are contributing, or planning to contribute, to a positive Alaska Native community. Selection is based on that statement, academic achievement, rigor of course work or degree program, student financial contribution, financial need, grade level, previous work performance, community service, and relationship of degree program to career goals.

Financial data The stipend is $10,000 per year, $8,000 per year, or $2,500 per semester, depending on GPA.

Duration 1 semester or 1 year.

Additional information This program was established in 1995.

Number awarded Varies each year.

Deadline May of each year for annual scholarships; May or November of each year for semester scholarships.

[517]
RUSS DENOMIE CRIMINAL JUSTICE/SOCIAL WELFARE SCHOLARSHIP

Indian Summer, Inc.
10809 West Lincoln Avenue, Suite 101
West Allis, WI 53227
(414) 774-7119   Fax: (414) 774-6810
E-mail: indiansummer@wi.rr.com
Web: www.indiansummer.org/education/scholarships.aspx

Summary To provide financial assistance to American Indians from Wisconsin who are studying or planning to study criminal justice or social welfare at a college in any state.

Eligibility This program is open to Wisconsin residents who are American Indians by tribal enrollment or descendancy (having 1 or more ancestors who are tribally enrolled). Applicants must be accepted or in good standing at an institution of higher education in any state and majoring in criminal justice or social welfare. They must submit a 1-page statement describing their educational goals, the reasons they feel they should receive the scholarship, their community service, and any special needs. Preference is given to applicants who have provided service to the Indian community and have not previously received a scholarship.

Financial data The stipend is $1,000.

Duration 1 year.

Additional information This program is offered in cooperation with American Indian Student Service at the University of Wisconsin at Milwaukee.

Number awarded 1 each year.

Deadline July of each year.

[518]
RUTH GOODE NURSING SCHOLARSHIP

Seneca Diabetes Foundation
Attn: Lucille White
TIS Building 12837, Route 438
P.O. Box 309
Irving, NY 14081
(716) 532-4900   Fax: (716) 549-1629
E-mail: white@sni.org
Web: www.senecadiabetesfoundation.org

Summary To provide financial assistance to members of the Seneca Nation who are interested in attending college to work on a degree in nursing.

Eligibility This program is open to members of the Seneca Nation who are interested in attending college to work on a degree in nursing. Applicants must submit brief statements on 1) the professional, community, or cultural services and

activities in which they have participated; 2) how this scholarship would help further their education; 3) their goals or plan for using their nursing experience to benefit the Seneca Nation and its people; and 4) the qualities about Ruth Goode's life, both personal and professional, they identify with the most. In the selection process, primary consideration is given to financial need, but involvement in community and cultural activities, personal assets, and desire to improve the quality of life for the Seneca people are also considered.

Financial data The stipend is $5,000.

Duration 1 year.

Number awarded 1 each year.

Deadline May of each year.

[519]
SAC AND FOX NATION HIGHER EDUCATION GRANTS

Sac and Fox Nation
Attn: Higher Education Department
920883 South Highway 99, Building A
Stroud, OK 74079
(918) 968-0509   Fax: (918) 968-0542
Web: www.sacandfoxnation.com

Summary To provide financial assistance for college or graduate school to members of the Sac and Fox Nation.

Eligibility This program is open to enrolled members of the Sac and Fox Nation who are enrolled or planning to enroll at an accredited college or university. Applicants must submit a personal letter describing the college major they plan to pursue and their career goals after graduation. They must be able to demonstrate financial need. Limited funding is available for graduate students.

Financial data Stipends are $800 per semester for full-time students, $400 per semester for part-time students, or $400 per semester for graduate students.

Duration 1 semester; may be renewed up to 9 additional semester for students at 4-year institutions, up to 5 additional semesters for students at 2-year institutions, or up to 5 additional semesters for graduate students. Freshmen and sophomores must earn a GPA of 2.0 to remain eligible; juniors and seniors must earn at GPA of 2.25 to remain eligible.

Number awarded Varies each year.

Deadline June of each year for fall semester; November of each year for spring semester.

[520]
SAC AND FOX NATION VOCATIONAL TECHNICAL SCHOOL INCENTIVE

Sac and Fox Nation
Attn: Higher Education Department
920883 South Highway 99, Building A
Stroud, OK 74079
(918) 968-0509   Fax: (918) 968-0542
Web: www.sacandfoxnation.com

Summary To provide financial assistance for adult vocational training to members of the Sac and Fox Nation.

Eligibility This program is open to enrolled members of the Sac and Fox Nation. Applicants must be working on or planning to work on an associate degree or certificate at an accredited vocational/technical school. They must have a

GPA of 3.0 or higher and be able to demonstrate financial need.

Financial data Full-time students enrolled in a program of 1 to 2 years receive $500 per term (semester, quarter, trimester). Full-time students enrolled in a program of 9 months or less receive a 1-time grant of $500. Part-time students receive a 1-time grant of $250.

Duration 1 term; may be renewed up to 3 additional terms of full-time study or 7 additional terms of part-time study.

Number awarded Varies each year.

Deadline Applications may be submitted at any time; awards are granted on a first-come, first-served basis.

[521]
SAGINAW CHIPPEWA INDIAN TRIBE SCHOLARSHIP PROGRAM

Saginaw Chippewa Indian Tribe of Michigan
Attn: Higher Education Coordinator
7070 East Broadway
Mt. Pleasant, MI 48858
(989) 775-4505   E-mail: skutt@sagchip.org
Web: www.sagchip.org

Summary To provide financial assistance for college, graduate school, or vocational training to members of the Saginaw Chippewa Indian Tribe of Michigan.

Eligibility This program is open to enrolled members of the Saginaw Chippewa Indian Tribe of Michigan who are attending or planning to attend an accredited 2- or 4-year college, university, or vocational/trade institution in any state. Applicants must be interested in working on an undergraduate or graduate degree or vocational certificate as a full- or part-time student. They must apply for all available financial aid using the FAFSA standard form; residents of Michigan who plan to attend college in that state must also apply for the Michigan Indian Tuition Waiver. U.S. citizenship is required.

Financial data A stipend is awarded (amount not specified).

Duration 1 year; may be renewed, provided the recipient maintains a GPA of 2.0 or higher.

Number awarded Varies each year.

Deadline Deadline not specified.

[522]
SALAMATOF NATIVE ASSOCIATION, INC. SCHOLARSHIP PROGRAM

Cook Inlet Region, Inc.
Attn: The CIRI Foundation
3600 San Jeronimo Drive, Suite 256
Anchorage, AK 99508-2870
(907) 793-3575   Toll Free: (800) 764-3382
Fax: (907) 793-3585   E-mail: tcf@thecirifoundation.org
Web: www.thecirifoundation.org/village_scholarships.htm

Summary To provide financial assistance for undergraduate or graduate studies to Alaska Natives who are original enrollees of the Salamatof Native Association, Inc. (SNAI) and their spouses and lineal descendants.

Eligibility This program is open to Alaska Native enrollees to SNAI under the Alaska Native Claims Settlement Act (ANCSA) of 1971 and their spouses and lineal descendants. There are no Alaska residency requirements or age limitations. Applicants must be accepted or enrolled full time in a 2-year, 4-year undergraduate, or graduate degree program. They must have a GPA of 2.5 or higher. Along with their application, they must submit a 500-word statement on their educational and career goals and how they are contributing, or planning to contribute, to a positive Alaska Native community. Selection is based on that statement, academic achievement, rigor of course work or degree program, student financial contribution, financial need, grade level, previous work performance, community service, and relationship of degree program to career goals.

Financial data The stipend depends on the availability of funds.

Duration 1 year; recipients must reapply each year.

Additional information This program was established in 1992 by the Salamatof Native Association, Inc. which provides funds matched by the CIRI Foundation.

Number awarded Varies each year; recently, 3 of these scholarships were awarded.

Deadline May of each year.

[523]
SAN CARLOS APACHE TRIBE HIGHER EDUCATION GRANTS

San Carlos Apache Tribe
Attn: Department of Education
P.O. Box O
San Carlos, AZ 85550
(928) 475-2336   Fax: (928) 475-2507
Web: scateducationdepartment.com/scholarships.html

Summary To provide financial assistance for college or graduate school in any state to members of the San Carlos Apache Tribe.

Eligibility This program is open to members of the San Carlos Apache Tribe who are attending or planning to attend an accredited 2- or 4-year college or university in any state. Applicants must be interested in working on an associate, baccalaureate, or graduate degree as a full- or part-time student. They must be able to demonstrate financial need and have 1) a GPA of 2.0 or higher or a GED score of 45 or higher; and 2) an ACT score of 22 or higher or an SAT combined critical reading and mathematics score of 930 or higher. In the selection process, awards are presented in the following priority order: first, full-time undergraduate students who reside on the San Carlos Reservation in southeastern Arizona; second, graduate students who reside on the reservation; third, part-time students who reside on the reservation; fourth, students who reside off the reservation; and fifth, students who do not demonstrate financial need (assisted only if funds are available).

Financial data The stipend depends on the financial need of the recipient, to a maximum of $4,000 per semester at a 2-year college or $5,000 per semester at a 4-year college or university.

Duration 1 year; may be renewed up to a total of 64 credit hours at a 2-year college, up to 125 credit hours at a 4-year college or university. Renewal requires the recipient to maintain a GPA of 2.0 or higher as an undergraduate or 3.0 or higher as a graduate student.

Number awarded Varies each year.

Deadline June of each year for fall semester; November of each year for spring semester.

[524]
SANDRA R. SPAULDING MEMORIAL SCHOLARSHIPS

California Nurses Association
Attn: Scholarship Fund
2000 Franklin Street, Suite 300
Oakland, CA 94612
(510) 273-2200, ext. 344   Fax: (510) 663-1625
E-mail: membershipbenefits@calnurses.org
Web: www.calnurses.org/membership

Summary   To provide financial assistance to Native Americans and other students from diverse ethnic backgrounds who are enrolled in an associate degree in nursing (A.D.N.) program in California.

Eligibility   This program is open to students who have been admitted to a second-year accredited A.D.N. program in California and plan to complete the degree within 2 years. Along with their application, they must submit a 1-page essay describing their personal and professional goals. Selection is based on that essay, commitment and active participation in nursing and health-related organizations, professional vision and direction, and financial need. A goal of this scholarship program is to encourage ethnic and socioeconomic diversity in nursing.

Financial data   A stipend is awarded (amount not specified).

Duration   1 year; nonrenewable.

Additional information   This program was established in 1985.

Number awarded   1 or more each year.

Deadline   June of each year.

[525]
SAULT HIGHER EDUCATION GRANT PROGRAM

Sault Tribe of Chippewa Indians
Attn: Education Department
523 Ashmun Street
Sault Ste. Marie, MI 49783
(906) 635-7784   Toll Free: (800) 793-0660
Fax: (906) 635-7785   E-mail: amatson@saulttribe.net
Web: www.saulttribe.com

Summary   To provide financial assistance for college to members of the Sault Tribe in Michigan.

Eligibility   This program is open to members of the Sault Tribe who have been accepted at an accredited Michigan public college or university and have entered or will enter full time into a certificate- or degree-granting program. Students must apply for all institutional and governmental financial aid before tribal grant funds can be awarded.

Financial data   The amounts of the awards depend on the availability of funds and the need of the recipient. Funds must be used for tuition, fees, books, supplies, room, and board.

Duration   1 year; may be renewed if the recipient maintains a GPA of 2.0 or higher.

Number awarded   Varies each year.

Deadline   February of each year.

[526]
SAULT TRIBE HIGHER EDUCATION SELF SUFFICIENCY FUND

Sault Tribe of Chippewa Indians
Attn: Education Department
523 Ashmun Street
Sault Ste. Marie, MI 49783
(906) 635-7784   Toll Free: (800) 793-0660
Fax: (906) 635-7785   E-mail: amatson@saulttribe.net
Web: www.saulttribe.com

Summary   To recognize and reward members of the Sault Tribe in Michigan who complete college-level courses at a school in any state.

Eligibility   This monetary award is available to members of the Sault Tribe who are enrolled in a certificate- or degree-granting program at a community college, 4-year college, or university in the United States, regardless of blood quantum or financial need. Applicants must be in good academic standing and making satisfactory progress toward completion of a degree.

Financial data   For full-time students (12 credits or more), the award is $500 per semester or $333 per quarter. For part-time students (11 credits or less), the award is $40 per semester credit or $26.65 per quarter credit. The maximum award is $1,000 for a calendar year.

Duration   The awards are granted each term the students complete their programs successfully.

Additional information   Recipients need to complete their academic program successfully each term to receive funding.

Number awarded   Varies each year.

Deadline   October of each year.

[527]
SAULT TRIBE HIGHER EDUCATION VOCATIONAL TRAINING PROGRAM

Sault Tribe of Chippewa Indians
Attn: Education Department
523 Ashmun Street
Sault Ste. Marie, MI 49783
(906) 635-7784   Toll Free: (800) 793-0660, ext. 56536
Fax: (906) 635-7785   E-mail: amatson@saulttribe.net
Web: www.saulttribe.com

Summary   To provide financial assistance to members of the Sault Tribe in Michigan who wish to attend a vocational school.

Eligibility   This program is open to members of the Sault Tribe who are 18 years of age or older and have a family income less than 200% of the federal poverty guideline. Applicants must have been accepted at a state-licensed vocational school in the United States. They may not be participating in the tribe's tributary/memorial scholarship programs, higher education grant program, or higher education self-sufficiency program.

Financial data   The maximum stipend is $3,000 for a calendar year.

Duration   1 year.

Number awarded   Varies each year.

Deadline   Applications may be submitted at any time, but they must be received at least 30 days before the program starts.

[528]
SAULT TRIBE SPECIAL NEEDS SCHOLARSHIPS

Sault Tribe of Chippewa Indians
Attn: Higher Education Program-Memorial/Tributary
  Scholarships
523 Ashmun Street
Sault Ste. Marie, MI 49783
(906) 635-4944   Toll Free: (800) 793-0660
Fax: (906) 635-7785   E-mail: amatson@saulttribe.net
Web: www.saulttribe.com

Summary To provide financial assistance for education at any level to members of the Sault Tribe of Chippewa Indians who have a disability.

Eligibility This program is open to enrolled members of the Sault Tribe who have a documented physical or emotional disability. Applicants must be enrolled in an educational program at any level. Along with their application, they must submit a letter from themselves or a parent describing the proposed use of the funds and an itemized list of the expected costs.

Financial data The stipend is $1,000.

Duration 1 year.

Number awarded 4 each year: 2 for students under 18 years of age and 2 for students 18 years of age or older.

Deadline May of each year.

[529]
SCHOLARSHIP FOR DIVERSITY IN TEACHING

Mid-Atlantic Association for Employment in Education
c/o Kerri G. Gardi
Kutztown University
Director, Career Development Center
P.O. Box 730
Kutztown, PA 19530
(610) 683-4647   E-mail: gardi@kutztown.edu
Web: www.maeeonline.org/pages/scholarships_jump.aspx

Summary To provide financial assistance to Native American and other minority upper-division students at universities in the Mid-Atlantic region who are preparing for a career as a teacher.

Eligibility This program is open to members of racial and ethnic minority groups who have completed between 48 and 90 credits at a college or university in Delaware, Maryland, New Jersey, New York, Pennsylvania, Virginia, Washington, D.C., or West Virginia. Applicants must be enrolled full time majoring in a field to prepare for a career in teaching. Along with their application, they must submit a 1-page essay on why they have chosen to become a teacher and what they hope to accomplish as an educator. Selection is based on academic success, service to college and/or community, and potential to achieve excellence as a teacher. U.S. citizenship is required.

Financial data The stipend is $1,000.

Duration 1 year; nonrenewable.

Number awarded 1 each year.

Deadline November of each year.

[530]
SCHOLARSHIPS FOR MINORITY ACCOUNTING STUDENTS

American Institute of Certified Public Accountants
Attn: Academic and Career Development Division
220 Leigh Farm Road
Durham, NC 27707-8110
(919) 402-4931   Fax: (919) 419-4705
E-mail: MIC_Programs@aicpa.org
Web: www.aicpa.org/members/div/career/mini/smas.htm

Summary To provide financial assistance to Native Americans and other minorities interested in studying accounting at the undergraduate or graduate school level.

Eligibility This program is open to minority undergraduate and graduate students, enrolled full time, who have a GPA of 3.3 or higher (both cumulatively and in their major) and intend to pursue a C.P.A. credential. Undergraduates must have completed at least 30 semester hours, including at least 6 semester hours of a major in accounting. Graduate students must be working on a master's degree in accounting, finance, taxation, or a related program. Applicants must be U.S. citizens or permanent residents and student affiliate members of the American Institute of Certified Public Accountants (AICPA). The program defines minority students as those whose heritage is Black or African American, Hispanic or Latino, Native American, or Asian American.

Financial data Stipends range from $1,500 to $3,000 per year. Funds are disbursed directly to the recipient's school.

Duration 1 year; may be renewed up to 3 additional years or until completion of a bachelor's or master's degree, whichever is earlier.

Additional information This program is administered by The Center for Scholarship Administration, E-mail: allison-lee@bellsouth.net. The most outstanding applicant for this program is awarded the Stuart A. Kessler Scholarship for Minority Students.

Number awarded Varies each year; recently, 94 students received funding through this program.

Deadline March of each year.

[531]
SCHOLARSHIPS FOR SOCIAL JUSTICE

Higher Education Consortium for Urban Affairs
Attn: Student Services
2233 University Avenue West, Suite 210
St. Paul, MN 55114-1698
(651) 646-8831   Toll Free: (800) 554-1089
Fax: (651) 659-9421   E-mail: hecua@hecua.org
Web: www.hecua.org/scholarships.php

Summary To provide financial assistance to Native Americans and other students from targeted groups who are enrolled in programs of the Higher Education Consortium for Urban Affairs (HECUA) at participating colleges and universities.

Eligibility This program is open to students at member colleges and universities who are participating in HECUA programs. Applicants must be a first-generation college student, from a low-income family, or a student of color. Along with their application, they must submit a reflective essay, drawing on their life experiences and their personal and academic goals, on what they believe they can contribute to the mission of HECUA to equip students with the knowledge, experiences, tools, and passion to address issues of social justice and social change. The essay should also explain how the HECUA program will benefit them and the people, issues, and communities they care about.

Financial data The stipend is $1,500. Funds are applied as a credit to the student's HECUA program fees for the semester.

Duration 1 semester.

Additional information This program was established in 2006. Consortium members include Augsburg College (Minneapolis, Minnesota), Augustana College (Sioux Falls, South Dakota), Carleton College (Northfield, Minnesota), College of Saint Scholastica (Duluth, Minnesota), Colorado College (Colorado Springs, Colorado), Denison University (Granville, Ohio), Gustavus Adolphus College (St. Peter, Minnesota), Hamline University (St. Paul, Minnesota), Macalester College (St. Paul, Minnesota), Saint Mary's University (Winona, Minnesota), Saint Catherine University (St. Paul, Minnesota), Saint Olaf College (Northfield, Minnesota), Swarthmore College (Swarthmore, Pennsylvania), University of Minnesota (Minneapolis, Minnesota), University of Saint Thomas (St. Paul, Minnesota), and Viterbo University (La Crosse, Wisconsin).

Number awarded 2 each year.

Deadline April of each year for summer and fall programs; November of each year for January and spring programs.

[532]
SCIENCE APPLICATIONS INTERNATIONAL CORPORATION ENGINEERING SCHOLARSHIP

National Naval Officers Association-Washington, D.C. Chapter
Attn: Scholarship Program
2701 Park Center Drive, A1108
Alexandria, VA 22302
(703) 566-3840　　　　　　　　Fax: (703) 566-3813
E-mail: Stephen.Williams@Navy.mil
Web: dcnnoa.memberlodge.com

Summary To provide financial assistance to Native American and other minority high school seniors from the Washington, D.C. area who are interested in majoring in engineering at a college in any state.

Eligibility This program is open to minority seniors graduating from high schools in the Washington, D.C. metropolitan area who plan to enroll full time in an engineering program at an accredited 2- or 4-year college or university in any state. Applicants must have a GPA of 2.5 or higher and be U.S. citizens or permanent residents. Selection is based on academic achievement, community involvement, and financial need.

Financial data The stipend is $4,500.

Duration 1 year; nonrenewable.

Additional information Recipients are not required to join or affiliate with the military in any way. This program is sponsored by Science Applications International Corporation.

Number awarded 1 each year.

Deadline March of each year.

[533]
SCIENCE APPLICATIONS INTERNATIONAL CORPORATION SCIENCE AND MATHEMATICS SCHOLARSHIP

National Naval Officers Association-Washington, D.C. Chapter
Attn: Scholarship Program
2701 Park Center Drive, A1108
Alexandria, VA 22302
(703) 566-3840　　　　　　　　Fax: (703) 566-3813
E-mail: Stephen.Williams@Navy.mil
Web: dcnnoa.memberlodge.com

Summary To provide financial assistance to Native American and other minority high school seniors from the Washington, D.C. area who are interested in majoring in science or mathematics at a college in any state.

Eligibility This program is open to minority seniors graduating from high schools in the Washington, D.C. metropolitan area who plan to enroll full time at an accredited 2- or 4-year college or university in any state and major in science or mathematics. Applicants must have a GPA of 2.5 or higher and be U.S. citizens or permanent residents. Selection is based on academic achievement, community involvement, and financial need.

Financial data The stipend is $4,500.

Duration 1 year; nonrenewable.

Additional information Recipients are not required to join or affiliate with the military in any way. This program is sponsored by Science Applications International Corporation.

Number awarded 1 each year.

Deadline March of each year.

[534]
SCIENCE TEACHER PREPARATION PROGRAM

Alabama Alliance for Science, Engineering, Mathematics, and Science Education
Attn: Project Director
University of Alabama at Birmingham
Campbell Hall, Room 401
1300 University Boulevard
Birmingham, AL 35294-1170
(205) 934-8762　　　　　　　　Fax: (205) 934-1650
E-mail: LDale@uab.edu
Web: www.uab.edu/istp/alabama.html

Summary To provide financial assistance to Native Americans and other underrepresented students at designated institutions in Alabama who are interested in preparing for a career as a science teacher.

Eligibility This program is open to members of underrepresented minority groups who have been unconditionally admitted to a participating Alabama college or university. Applicants must be interested in becoming certified to teach science and mathematics in K-12 schools. They may be 1) entering freshmen enrolling in a science education program leading to a bachelor's degree and certification; 2) students transferring from a community college and enrolling in a science education program leading to a bachelor's degree and certification; 3) students with a bachelor's degree in mathematics, science, or education and enrolling in a certification program; or 4) students with a bachelor's degree in mathematics, science, or education and enrolling in a fifth-year program leading to a master's degree and certification.

Financial data The stipend is $1,000 per year.

Duration 1 year; may be renewed.

Additional information Support for this program is provided by the National Science Foundation. The participating institutions are Alabama A&M University, Alabama State University, Auburn University, Miles College, Stillman College, Talladega College, Tuskegee University, University of Alabama at Birmingham, and University of Alabama in Huntsville.

Number awarded Varies each year.

Deadline Deadline not specified.

[535]
SCOTTS COMPANY SCHOLARS PROGRAM

Golf Course Superintendents Association of America
Attn: Environmental Institute for Golf
1421 Research Park Drive
Lawrence, KS 66049-3859
(785) 832-4445   Toll Free: (800) 472-7878, ext. 4445
Fax: (785) 832-4448   E-mail: mwright@gcsaa.org
Web: www.gcsaa.org/students/Scholarships.aspx

Summary To provide financial assistance and summer work experience to high school seniors and college students, particularly those from diverse backgrounds, who are preparing for a career in golf management.

Eligibility This program is open to high school seniors and college students (freshmen, sophomores, and juniors) who are interested in preparing for a career in golf management (the "green industry"). Applicants should come from diverse ethnic, cultural, or socioeconomic backgrounds, defined to include women, minorities, and people with disabilities. Selection is based on cultural diversity, academic achievement, extracurricular activities, leadership, employment potential, essay responses, and letters of recommendation. Financial need is not considered. Finalists are selected for summer internships and then compete for scholarships.

Financial data The finalists receive a $500 award to supplement their summer internship income. Scholarship stipends are $2,500.

Duration 1 year.

Additional information The program is funded from a permanent endowment established by Scotts Company. Finalists are responsible for securing their own internships.

Number awarded 5 finalists, of whom 2 receive scholarships, are selected each year.

Deadline February of each year.

[536]
SEALASKA CORPORATION INTERNSHIPS

Sealaska Corporation
Attn: Intern Program Coordinator
One Sealaska Plaza, Suite 400
Juneau, AK 99801-1276
(907) 586-9134   Toll Free: (800) 848-5921
Fax: (907) 586-2304
E-mail: ken.southerland@sealaska.com
Web: www.sealaska.com

Summary To provide work experience during the summer to Native Alaskan college students affiliated with Sealaska Corporation.

Eligibility This program is open to Sealaska Corporation shareholders and direct descendants of originally-enrolled shareholders. Applicants must have completed at least 2 years of college, have a GPA of 2.5 or higher, and be attending college in the following fall. They must be interested in working with Sealaska Corporation (for students majoring in accounting, administration, communications, finance, legal, marketing, or natural resources); Sealaska Timber Corporation (for students majoring in computer science, forestry, or engineering); Sealaska Heritage Institute (for students majoring in anthropology, business administration, or education); Synergy Systems (for students majoring in business administration); or other Sealaska business associates.

Financial data A competitive salary is paid, along with a housing stipend, transportation, and tuition for summer credit for the internship.

Duration Summer months.

Additional information Sealaska Corporation is 1 of 13 Alaska Native Regional Corporations created under the Alaska Native Claims Settlement Act of 1971.

Number awarded Varies each year.

Deadline March of each year.

[537]
SEALASKA ENDOWMENT SCHOLARSHIPS

Sealaska Corporation
Attn: Sealaska Heritage Institute
One Sealaska Plaza, Suite 301
Juneau, AK 99801-1249
(907) 586-9170   Toll Free: (888) 311-4992
Fax: (907) 586-9293 E-mail: scholarship@sealaska.com
Web: www.sealaskaheritage.org

Summary To provide financial assistance for undergraduate or graduate study in any state to Native Alaskans who have a connection to Sealaska Corporation.

Eligibility This program is open to 1) Alaska Natives who are shareholders of Sealaska Corporation, and 2) Native lineal descendants of Alaska Natives enrolled to Sealaska Corporation, whether or not they own Sealaska Corporation stock. Applicants must be enrolled or accepted for enrollment as full-time undergraduate or graduate students at a college or university in any state. Along with their application, they must submit 2 essays: 1) their personal history and educational goals, and 2) their expected contributions to the Alaska Native or Native American community. Financial need is also considered in the selection process.

Financial data The amount of the award depends on the availability of funds, the number of qualified applicants, class standing, and cumulative GPA.

Duration 1 year; may be renewed up to 5 years for a bachelor's degree, up to 3 years for a master's degree, up to 2 years for a doctorate, or up to 3 years for vocational study. The maximum total support is limited to 9 years. Renewal depends on recipients' maintaining full-time enrollment and a GPA of 2.0 or higher as an undergraduate or 3.0 or higher as a graduate student.

Additional information   Sealaska Corporation is 1 of 13 Alaska Native Regional Corporations created under the Alaska Native Claims Settlement Act of 1971.

Number awarded   Varies each year.

Deadline   February of each year.

[538]
SEALASKA HERITAGE INSTITUTE 7(I) SCHOLARSHIPS

Sealaska Corporation
Attn: Sealaska Heritage Institute
One Sealaska Plaza, Suite 301
Juneau, AK 99801-1249
(907) 586-9170   Toll Free: (888) 311-4992
Fax: (907) 586-9293   E-mail: scholarship@sealaska.com
Web: www.sealaskaheritage.org

Summary   To provide financial assistance for undergraduate or graduate study in any state to Native Alaskans who have a connection to Sealaska Corporation and are majoring in designated fields.

Eligibility   This program is open to 1) Alaska Natives who are shareholders of Sealaska Corporation, and 2) Native lineal descendants of Alaska Natives enrolled to Sealaska Corporation, whether or not the applicant owns Sealaska Corporation stock. Applicants must be enrolled or accepted for enrollment as full-time undergraduate or graduate students at a college or university in any state. Along with their application, they must submit 2 essays: 1) their personal history and educational goals, and 2) their expected contributions to the Alaska Native or Native American community. Financial need is also considered in the selection process. The following areas of study qualify for these awards: natural resources (environmental sciences, engineering, conservation biology, environmental law, fisheries, forestry, geology, marine science/biology, mining technology, wildlife management); business administration (accounting, computer information systems, economics, finance, human resources management, industrial management, information systems management, international business, international commerce and trade, and marketing); and other special fields (cadastral surveys, chemistry, equipment/machinery operators, industrial safety specialists, health specialists, plastics engineers, trade specialists, physics, mathematics, and marine trades and occupations).

Financial data   The amount of the award depends on the availability of funds, the number of qualified applicants, class standing, and cumulative GPA.

Duration   1 year; may be renewed up to 5 years for a bachelor's degree, up to 3 years for a master's degree, up to 2 years for a doctorate, or up to 3 years for vocational study. The maximum total support is limited to 9 years. Renewal depends on recipients' maintaining full-time enrollment and a GPA of 2.0 or higher.

Additional information   Funding for this program is provided from Alaska Native Claims Settlement Act (ANSCA) Section 7(i) revenue sharing provisions. Sealaska Corporation is 1 of 13 Alaska Native Regional Corporations created under the Alaska Native Claims Settlement Act of 1971.

Number awarded   Varies each year.

Deadline   February of each year.

[539]
SEMESTER INTERNSHIPS IN GEOSCIENCE PUBLIC POLICY

American Geological Institute
Attn: Government Affairs Program
4220 King Street
Alexandria, VA 22302-1502
(703) 379-2480   Fax: (703) 379-7563
E-mail: govt@agiweb.org
Web: www.agiweb.org/gap/interns/index.html

Summary   To provide work experience to Native American and other geoscience students who have a strong interest in federal science policy.

Eligibility   This program is open to geoscience students who are interested in working with Congress and federal agencies to promote sound public policy in areas that affect geoscientists, including water, energy, and mineral resources; geologic hazards; environmental protection, and federal funding for geoscience research and education. Applicants must submit official copies of college transcripts, a resume with the names and contact information for 2 references, and a statement of their science and policy interests and what they feel they can contribute to the program. Native Americans, other minorities, and women are especially encouraged to apply.

Financial data   The stipend is $5,000.

Duration   14 weeks, during the fall or spring semester. The sponsor also offers a similar program for summer internships.

Additional information   This program is jointly funded by the American Geological Institute (AGI) and the American Association of Petroleum Geologists (AAPG). Activities for the interns include monitoring and analyzing geoscience-related legislation in Congress, updating legislative and policy information on AGI's web site, attending House and Senate hearings and preparing summaries, responding to information requests from AGI's member societies, and attending meetings with policy-level staff members in Congress, federal agencies, and non-governmental organizations.

Number awarded   1 each semester.

Deadline   April of each year for fall internships; October of each year for spring internships.

[540]
SENECA GAMING CORPORATION SCHOLARSHIP

Seneca Diabetes Foundation
Attn: Lucille White
TIS Building 12837, Route 438
P.O. Box 309
Irving, NY 14081
(716) 532-4900   Fax: (716) 549-1629
E-mail: white@sni.org
Web: www.senecadiabetesfoundation.org

Summary   To provide financial assistance to members of the Seneca Nation who are interested in attending college to prepare for a career in the health or social services professions and have demonstrated a commitment to community service and volunteerism.

Eligibility   This program is open to members of the Seneca Nation who are interested in attending college to assist the Seneca people, especially in regard to the fight against diabetes, by working on a degree in health or social services. Applicants must be able to demonstrate a commitment to community service and volunteerism. Along with their application, they must submit brief statements on 1) the professional, community, or cultural services and activities in which they have participated; 2) how this scholarship would help further their education; 3) their goals or plan for using their education and training to benefit the Seneca Nation and its people; and 4) what they would say to a friend who doesn't see a need to volunteer in the community and how they would convince the friend that community service is a rewarding experience. In the selection process, primary consideration is given to financial need, but involvement in community and cultural activities, personal assets, and desire to improve the quality of life for the Seneca people are also considered.

Financial data The stipend is $5,000.

Duration 1 year.

Number awarded 1 each year.

Deadline May of each year.

[541]
SENECA NATION HIGHER EDUCATION PROGRAM

Seneca Nation of Indians
Attn: Higher Education Department, Cattaraugus Territory
12861 Route 438
Irving, NY 14081
(716) 532-3341   Fax: (716) 532-3269
E-mail: carrie.peterson@sni.org
Web: www.sni.org/node/34

Summary To provide financial assistance for college or graduate school to members of the Seneca Nation of Indians in New York.

Eligibility This program is open to members of the Seneca Nation of Indians who are enrolled or planning to enroll in an associate, bachelor's, master's, or doctoral program. They must have applied for all other forms of financial aid for which they qualify, e.g., full-time undergraduates who are New York residents must apply for New York State Indian Aid (NYSIA) and the New York State Tuition Assistance Program (TAP); part-time undergraduates who are New York residents must apply for Aid for Part-Time Study (APTS); non-residents of New York must apply for funding from their state of residence; graduate students must apply for an American Indian Graduate Center (AIGC) fellowship. Applicants with permanent residence on the reservation qualify for level 1 awards; those with permanent residence within New York state qualify for level 2 awards; those with permanent residence outside New York state qualify for level 3 awards. Financial need is considered in the selection process.

Financial data Maximum awards per academic year for tuition and fees are $11,000 for level 1 students, $8,000 for level 2 students, or $6,000 for level 3 students. Other benefits for all recipients include $1,000 per year for books and supplies for full-time students or $100 per 3-credit hours for part-time students; payment of room and board in dormitories or college-approved housing for full-time students; a transportation allowance for commuters of $900 per year for full-time students or $85 per 3-credit hours for part-time students; and a personal expense allowance of $500 per year for full-time students or $50 per 3-credit hours for part-time students.

Duration 1 year; may be renewed.

Number awarded Varies each year.

Deadline June of each year for fall semester; July of each year for fall quarter; October of each year for winter quarter; November of each year for spring semester; January of each year for spring quarter; April of each year for summer semester or quarter.

[542]
SENECA-CAYUGA EDUCATION FELLOWSHIP PROGRAM

Seneca-Cayuga Tribe of Oklahoma
Attn: Tribal Claims Committee
23701 South 655 Road (Highway 10)
Grove, OK 74344
(918) 786-5576   Fax: (918) 786-9245
E-mail: claims@sctribe.com
Web: www.sctribe.com

Summary To provide financial assistance for college or graduate school to members of the Seneca-Cayuga Tribe of Oklahoma.

Eligibility This program is open to Seneca-Cayuga tribal members who are enrolled or planning to enroll as full-time undergraduate or graduate students at a college, university, or vocational training school in any state. Applicants must submit a copy of their tribal membership card; a letter of estimated graduation date from their school; a copy of their class schedule; and either 1) a copy of their high school diploma or GED score; or 2) a college transcript.

Financial data The stipend is $2,500 for the academic year or $1,250 for the summer term. All students also qualify for a 1-time educational supply payment of $1,000. All funds are paid directly to the student.

Duration 1 year; may be renewed, provided the recipient maintains a GPA of 2.0 or higher.

Number awarded Varies each year.

Deadline September of each year for fall semester; January of each year for spring semester; June of each year for summer semester.

[543]
SEO CAREER PROGRAM

Sponsors for Educational Opportunity
Attn: Career Program
55 Exchange Place
New York, NY 10005
(212) 979-2040   Toll Free: (800) 462-2332
Fax: (646) 706-7113
E-mail: careerprogram@seo-usa.org
Web: www.seo-usa.org/Career/Career_Program_Overview

Summary To provide Native Americans and other undergraduate students of color with an opportunity to gain summer work experience in selected fields.

Eligibility This program is open to sophomores, juniors, and seniors of color at colleges and universities in the United States. Applicants must be interested in a summer internship in 1 of the following fields: corporate financial leadership, banking and asset management (including accounting/finance, asset management, information technology, investment banking, investment research, sales and trading, or transaction services), or nonprofit sector. They should be able to demonstrate analytical and quantitative skills, interpersonal and community skills, maturity, and a cumulative GPA of 3.0 or higher. Along with their application, they must submit 1) information on their extracurricular and employment experience; 2) an essay of 75 to 100 words on how the program area to which they are applying relates to their professional goals; and 3) an essay of 250 to 400 words on either an example of a time when they had to operate outside their "comfort zone" or their definition of success. Personal interviews are required.

Financial data   Interns receive a competitive stipend.

Duration   10 weeks during the summer.

Additional information   This program was established in 1980. Most banking and asset management internships are available in the New York City metropolitan area (including Connecticut and New Jersey), but corporate financial leadership and nonprofit sector placements are nationwide.

Number awarded   Varies each year; recently, more than 300 internships were available at more than 40 firms.

Deadline   October of each year for most programs; December of each year for sales and trading or nonprofit sector.

[544]
SHEE ATIKA ACADEMIC SCHOLARSHIPS

Shee Atiká, Incorporated
Attn: Shee Atiká Benefits Trust
315 Lincoln Street, Suite 300
Sitka, AK 99835
(907) 747-3534   Toll Free: (800) 478-3534
Fax: (907) 747-5727
E-mail: scholarships@sheeatika.com
Web: www.sheeatika.com

Summary   To provide financial assistance to shareholders of Shee Atiká, Incorporated interested in attending college or graduate school in any state.

Eligibility   This program is open to Shee Atiká Class A and Class B shareholders enrolled or planning to enroll at a college, university, graduate school, or trade or vocational school in any state. Relatives of shareholders are eligible only if they receive at least 1 share of stock from their family member allowed to make a gift under ANSCA. Students interested in a program of concentrated vocational training may petition for that status. Applicants must submit a statement covering their personal and professional goals, honors and activities, and how this scholarship will assist them. Selection is based on that statement, academic achievement, and financial need.

Financial data   The maximum annual stipend is $2,400 for undergraduates, $4,800 for graduate students, or $7,200 for students enrolled in concentrated vocational training.

Duration   1 year; may be renewed up to 3 additional years of undergraduate study or 2 years of graduate study. The maximum that any shareholder may receive for both undergraduate and graduate study is $28,800.

Additional information   Shee Atiká, Incorporated is an urban corporation organized under the Alaska Native Claims Settlement Act (ANSCA) to serve the people of the Sitka area of Alaska.

Number awarded   Varies each year.

Deadline   March, July, October, or November of each year.

[545]
SHELL INCENTIVE FUND SCHOLARSHIPS

Shell Oil Company
Attn: Scholarship Administrator
910 Louisiana, Suite 4476C
Houston, TX 77002
(713) 241-0514
Web: www.shell.com.sg

Summary   To provide financial assistance to Native Americans and other underrepresented minority students majoring in specified engineering and geosciences fields at designated universities.

Eligibility   This program is open to students enrolled full time as sophomores, juniors, or seniors at 21 participating universities. Applicants must be U.S. citizens or authorized to work in the United States and members of a race or ethnicity underrepresented in the technical and scientific academic areas (Black, Hispanic/Latino, American Indian, or Alaskan Native). They must have a GPA of 3.2 or higher with a major in engineering (chemical, civil, electrical, geological, geophysical, mechanical, or petroleum) or geosciences (geology, geophysics, or physics). Along with their application, they must submit a 100-word essay on the kind of work they plan to be doing in 10 years, both in their career and in their community. Financial need is not considered in the selection process.

Financial data   The stipend is $5,000 per year.

Duration   1 year; may be renewed up to 3 additional years, provided the recipient remains qualified and accepts a Shell Oil Company internship (if offered).

Additional information   This program is administered by Educational Testing Service's Scholarship and Recognition Programs. The participating institutions are Colorado School of Mines, Cornell University, Florida A&M University, Georgia Institute of Technology, Louisiana State University, Massachusetts Institute of Technology, Michigan State University, North Carolina A&T State University, Ohio State University, Pennsylvania State University, Prairie View A&M University, Purdue University, Rice University, Texas A&M University, University of Colorado at Boulder, University of Houston, University of Illinois at Urbana-Champaign, University of Michigan, University of Oklahoma, University of Texas at Austin, and University of Texas at El Paso.

Number awarded   Approximately 20 each year.

Deadline   February of each year.

[546]
SITKA TRIBE OF ALASKA HIGHER EDUCATION PROGRAM

Sitka Tribe of Alaska
Attn: Education Department
456 Katlian Street
Sitka, AK 99835
(907) 747-6478   Toll Free: (800) 746-3207
Fax: (907) 747-4915   E-mail: education@sitkatribe.org
Web: www.sitkatribe.org/depts/edu/Scholarships.htm

Summary   To provide financial assistance to enrolled members of the Sitka Tribe of Alaska who are interested in attending college or graduate school in any state.

Eligibility   This program is open to enrolled members of the Sitka Tribe of Alaska as documented by the Bureau of Indian

Affairs. Members of other federally-recognized tribes may also be eligible if funds are available. Applicants must be enrolled full time at an accredited 2-year college (credits must be transferable to a 4-year school) or a 4-year college or university in any state. They must have a high school diploma or GED and be able to demonstrate financial need. Priority is given to eligible Sitka Tribe of Alaska students who have met the minimum requirements in the following order: 1) college seniors; 2) college juniors; 3) college sophomores; 4) entering freshmen; 5) graduate students (provided funds are available); and 6) other qualified applicants (provided funds are available).

Financial data The maximum stipend is $3,000 per year. Payments are made to students through the financial aid office at the college or university they attend.

Duration Up to 10 semesters for students working on a 4-year degree or up to 5 semesters for students working on a 2-year degree. Recipients must maintain a GPA of at least 2.0 as freshmen, 2.2 as sophomores, 2.25 as juniors, and 2.5 as seniors to remain eligible. Graduate students must remain enrolled full time and maintain minimum standards as set by their institution.

Number awarded Varies each year.

Deadline April of each year for students attending the fall semester/quarter or the full year; September of each year for students beginning the spring/winter semester/quarter.

[547]
SMITHSONIAN NATIVE AMERICAN INTERNSHIPS

Smithsonian Institution
Attn: Office of Fellowships
470 L'Enfant Plaza, Suite 7102
P.O. Box 37012, MRC 902
Washington, DC 20013-7012
(202) 633-7070   Fax: (202) 633-7069
E-mail: siofg@si.edu
Web: www.si.edu/ofg/Applications/NAP/NAPapp.htm

Summary To support Native American students interested in conducting projects related to Native American topics that require the use of Native American resources at the Smithsonian Institution.

Eligibility Applicants must be Native American students who are actively engaged in graduate or undergraduate study and are interested in working with Native American resources at the Smithsonian Institution. Along with their application, they must submit a 2- to 4-page essay in which they describe their past and present academic history and other experiences which they feel have prepared them for an internship, what they hope to accomplish through an internship and how it would relate to their academic and career goals, and what about the Smithsonian in particular interests them and leads them to apply for the internship.

Financial data Interns receive a stipend of $550 per week and a travel allowance.

Duration 10 weeks.

Additional information Interns pursue directed research projects supervised by Smithsonian staff members. Recipients must be in residence at the Smithsonian Institution for the duration of the program.

Number awarded Varies each year.

Deadline January of each year for summer residency; May of each year for fall residency; September of each year for spring residency.

[548]
SNA FOUNDATION SCHOLARSHIPS

Seldovia Native Association, Inc.
Attn: SNA Foundation
P.O. Drawer L
Seldovia, AK 99663
(907) 234-7625   Toll Free: (800) 478-7898
Fax: (907) 234-7637
Web: www.snai.com/shareholders/sna-foundation.html

Summary To provide financial assistance to Alaska Natives 1) who are shareholders in Seldovia Native Association (SNA) or their family members and 2) who wish to attend college or graduate school in any state.

Eligibility This program is open to Alaska Natives who are enrolled as shareholders in SNA, their spouses, and their descendants. Applicants must be enrolled or accepted for enrollment as full-time undergraduate or graduate students at an accredited 2- or 4-year college or university in any state. They must have a GPA of 3.0 or higher for achievement scholarships or 2.0 or higher for general scholarships. Along with their application, they must submit a statement of purpose that includes their personal history, a summary of accomplishments, a description of their career goals, and how their degree program fits with their education and career plans. Selection is based on that statement, academic achievement, previous work experience, educational and community involvement, recommendations, seriousness of purpose, major field of study, practicality of educational and professional goals, completeness of the application, and financial need. Alaska residency is not required.

Financial data Achievement scholarships are $2,500 per year; general scholarships are $500 per year.

Duration 1 year; may be renewed.

Number awarded Varies each year.

Deadline June of each year.

[549]
SOKAOGON CHIPPEWA COMMUNITY ADULT VOCATIONAL TRAINING PROGRAM

Sokaogon Chippewa Community
Attn: Higher Education Director
10808 Sokaogon Drive
Crandon, WI 54520
(715) 478-3830   Fax: (715) 478-0980
Web: www.sokaogonchippewa.com

Summary To provide financial assistance for vocational or technical training to members of the Sokaogon Chippewa Community.

Eligibility This program is open to enrolled tribal members of the Sokaogon Chippewa Community who are working on or planning to work on a diploma or vocational degree. Applicants must be able to demonstrate financial need.

Financial data The maximum stipend is $1,200 per year.

Duration Up to 24 months at a vocational technical training institution or 36 months at a school of nursing, provided the recipient maintains a GPA of 2.0 or higher.

Number awarded Varies each year.

Deadline June of each year.

[550]
SOKAOGON CHIPPEWA COMMUNITY HIGHER EDUCATION GRANTS PROGRAM

Sokaogon Chippewa Community
Attn: Higher Education Director
10808 Sokaogon Drive
Crandon, WI 54520
(715) 478-3830   Fax: (715) 478-0980
Web: www.sokaogonchippewa.com

Summary To provide financial assistance for college or graduate school to members of the Sokaogon Chippewa Community.

Eligibility This program is open to enrolled tribal members of the Sokaogon Chippewa Community who are working on or planning to work on an undergraduate or graduate degree. Applicants must be able to demonstrate financial need.

Financial data The maximum stipend is $1,200 per year.

Duration 1 year; undergraduate grants may be renewed for a total of 10 semesters; graduate grants may be renewed if funding is available; all renewals require the recipient to maintain a GPA of 2.0 or higher.

Number awarded Varies each year.

Deadline June of each year.

[551]
SOUTHERN UTE INDIAN TRIBE FULL-TIME SCHOLARSHIP PROGRAM

Southern Ute Indian Tribe
Attn: Department of Higher Education
P.O. Box 737
Ignacio, CO 81137
(970) 563-0100, ext. 2780   Fax: (970) 563-0382
Web: www.southern-ute.nsn.us/education

Summary To provide financial assistance to Southern Ute Indians and selected other Native Americans who are attending college on a full-time basis.

Eligibility This program is open to all Native Americans residing within the exterior boundaries of the Southern Ute Reservation. They may be high school seniors or currently-enrolled college students. They must be attending or planning to attend college on a full-time basis.

Financial data This program covers 100% of tuition and provides a monthly stipend for books, fees, and living expenses.

Duration 1 year; may be renewed for up to 4 additional years.

Number awarded Varies each year.

Deadline June of each year.

[552]
SOUTHERN UTE INDIAN TRIBE PART-TIME SCHOLARSHIP PROGRAM

Southern Ute Indian Tribe
Attn: Department of Higher Education
P.O. Box 737
Ignacio, CO 81137
(970) 563-0100, ext. 2780   Fax: (970) 563-0382
Web: www.southern-ute.nsn.us/education

Summary To provide financial assistance to Southern Ute Indians and selected other Native Americans who are attending college on a part-time basis.

Eligibility This program is open to all Native Americans residing within the exterior boundaries of the Southern Ute Reservation. They may be high school seniors or currently-enrolled college students. They must be attending or planning to attend college on a part-time basis.

Financial data This program covers 100% of all expenses for tuition, fees, and books. In addition, recipients are reimbursed for 70% of their mileage.

Duration 1 year; may be renewed for up to 4 additional years.

Number awarded Varies each year.

Deadline Applications may be submitted at any time.

[553]
SOVEREIGN NATIONS SCHOLARSHIP FUND FOR MAINSTREAM UNIVERSITIES

American Indian College Fund
Attn: Scholarship Department
8333 Greenwood Boulevard
Denver, CO 80221
(303) 426-8900   Toll Free: (800) 776-FUND
Fax: (303) 426-1200
E-mail: scholarships@collegefund.org
Web: www.collegefund.org

Summary To provide financial assistance to Native American students who are interested in attending a mainstream university and working for a tribe or Indian organization after graduation.

Eligibility This program is open to American Indians and Alaska Natives who can document proof of enrollment or descendancy. Applicants must be planning to 1) enroll full time in a bachelor's degree program at a mainstream institution, and 2) work for their tribe or an Indian organization after graduation. They must have a GPA of 3.0 or higher and be able to demonstrate exceptional academic achievement. Applications are available only online and include required essays on specified topics.

Financial data The stipend is $2,000 per year.

Duration 1 year; may be renewed.

Number awarded Varies each year.

Deadline May of each year.

[554]
SOVEREIGN NATIONS SCHOLARSHIP FUND FOR TRIBAL COLLEGES

American Indian College Fund
Attn: Scholarship Department
8333 Greenwood Boulevard
Denver, CO 80221
(303) 426-8900   Toll Free: (800) 776-FUND
Fax: (303) 426-1200
E-mail: scholarships@collegefund.org
Web: www.collegefund.org/scholarships/schol_tcu.html

Summary To provide financial assistance for college to Native American students who are interested in attending a Tribal College or University (TCU) and working for a tribe or Indian organization after graduation.

Eligibility This program is open to American Indians and Alaska Natives who can document proof of enrollment or descendancy. Applicants must be planning to 1) enroll full time at a TCU, and 2) work for their tribe or an Indian organization after graduation. They must have a GPA of 3.0 or higher and be able to demonstrate exceptional academic achievement. Applications are available only online and include required essays on specified topics.

Financial data The stipend is $2,000 per year.

Duration 1 year; may be renewed.

Number awarded Varies each year.

Deadline May of each year.

[555]
SPIRIT OF SOVEREIGNTY FOUNDATION TRIBAL SCHOLARS PROGRAM

American Indian College Fund
Attn: Scholarship Department
8333 Greenwood Boulevard
Denver, CO 80221
(303) 426-8900   Toll Free: (800) 776-FUND
Fax: (303) 426-1200
E-mail: scholarships@collegefund.org
Web: www.collegefund.org/scholarships/schol_tcu.html

Summary To provide financial assistance to Native American students enrolled at a Tribal College or University (TCU), especially those majoring in designated fields.

Eligibility This program is open to American Indians and Alaska Natives who are enrolled full time at an eligible TCU. Applicants may be majoring in any field, but preference is given to business, hospitality, information technology, or marketing. They must have a GPA of 3.0 or higher. Applications are available only online and include required essays on specified topics.

Financial data The stipend is $2,000.

Duration 1 year.

Additional information This scholarship is sponsored by the Spirit of Sovereignty Foundation of the National Indian Gaming Association, in partnership with the American Indian College Fund.

Number awarded 1 or more each year.

Deadline May of each year.

[556]
ST. CROIX CHIPPEWA INDIANS HIGHER EDUCATION GRANTS PROGRAM

St. Croix Chippewa Indians of Wisconsin
Attn: Education Coordinator
24663 Angeline Avenue
Webster, WI 54893
(715) 349-7709   Toll Free: (800) 236-2195
Fax: (715) 349-7905
Web: www.stcciw.com

Summary To provide financial assistance for college or graduate school to tribal members of the St. Croix Chippewa Indians of Wisconsin.

Eligibility This program is open to enrolled tribal members of the St. Croix Chippewa Indians who are working on or planning to work on an undergraduate or graduate degree. Applicants must be able to demonstrate financial need.

Financial data Stipends range up to $8,000 per year.

Duration 1 year; may be renewed for a total of 10 semesters, provided the recipient maintains a GPA of 2.0 or higher as an undergraduate or 3.0 or higher as a graduate student.

Number awarded Varies each year.

Deadline July of each year for fall term; November of each year for winter term; January of each year for spring term; May of each year for summer term.

[557]
ST. CROIX CHIPPEWA INDIANS VOCATIONAL GRANTS PROGRAM

St. Croix Chippewa Indians of Wisconsin
Attn: Education Coordinator
24663 Angeline Avenue
Webster, WI 54893
(715) 349-7709   Toll Free: (800) 236-2195
Fax: (715) 349-7905
Web: www.stcciw.com

Summary To provide financial assistance for technical or vocational training to tribal members of the St. Croix Chippewa Indians of Wisconsin.

Eligibility This program is open to enrolled tribal members of the St. Croix Chippewa Indians who are working on or planning to work on a vocational degree. Applicants must be able to demonstrate financial need.

Financial data Stipends range up to $4,000 per year.

Duration Up to 24 months at a vocational technical training institution or 36 months at a school of nursing, provided the recipient maintains a GPA of 2.0 or higher.

Number awarded Varies each year.

Deadline July of each year for fall term; November of each year for winter term; January of each year for spring term; May of each year for summer term.

[558]
STABLES EDUCATION AWARD

Miami Nation
Attn: Education Committee
202 South Eight Tribes Trail
P.O. Box 1326
Miami, OK 74355
(918) 542-1445   Fax: (918) 542-7260
E-mail: edu@miamination.com
Web: www.miamination.com/mto/edu.html

Summary To provide financial assistance to enrolled members of the Miami Nation of Oklahoma who are interested in attending college in any state.

Eligibility This program is open to enrolled members of the Miami Nation of Oklahoma who are entering or attending a college or university in any state as a full-time student. Applicants must have a GPA of 2.5 or higher. Along with their application, they must submit a high school and/or college transcript, 3 letters of recommendation, documentation of financial need, and a 1-page essay with the title, "Tell Us About Yourself."

Financial data The stipend is $1,500.

Duration 1 year; nonrenewable.

Number awarded 1 or more each year.

Deadline April of each year.

[559]
STACIE LYNN HAYS MEMORIAL SCHOLARSHIP

Chickasaw Foundation
110 West 12th Street
P.O. Box 1726
Ada, OK 74821-1726
(580) 421-9030   Fax: (580) 421-9031
E-mail: ChickasawFoundation@chickasaw.net
Web: www.chickasawfoundation.org/index_20.htm

Summary To provide financial assistance to members of the Chickasaw Nation who are working on an undergraduate degree in counseling.

Eligibility This program is open to Chickasaw students who are currently enrolled full time at a 2- or 4-year college or university and working on an undergraduate degree in counseling. Preference is given to students focusing on domestic violence prevention. Applicants must have a GPA of 2.5 or higher. Along with their application, they must submit high school or college transcripts, 2 letters of recommendation, a copy of their Chickasaw Nation citizenship card, and a 1-page essay on their long-term goals and plans for achieving them. Financial need is not considered in the selection process.

Financial data The stipend is $1,000.

Duration 1 year.

Number awarded 1 each year.

Deadline August of each year.

[560]
STANDING ROCK SIOUX TRIBE HIGHER EDUCATION SCHOLARSHIPS

Standing Rock Sioux Tribe
Standing Rock Administrative Service Center
Attn: Office of Higher Education
P.O. Box D
Fort Yates, ND 58538
(701) 854-8545   Fax: (701) 854-2175
Web: www.standingrock.org

Summary To provide financial assistance for college to members of the Standing Rock Sioux Tribe.

Eligibility This program is open to enrolled members of the Standing Rock Sioux Tribe in North Dakota and South Dakota. Applicants must be attending or planning to attend an accredited college or university. They must be able to demonstrate financial need.

Financial data The stipend depends on the needs of the recipient.

Duration 1 semester; may be renewed until completion of an undergraduate degree.

Number awarded Varies each year.

Deadline May of each year for fall semester; November of each year for spring semester; April of each year for summer school.

[561]
STANFORD SUMMER RESEARCH PROGRAM/ AMGEN SCHOLARS PROGRAM

Stanford University
School of Medicine
Attn: Office of Graduate Affairs
M.S.O.B. Second Floor
251 Campus Drive
Stanford, CA 94305-5421
(650) 725-8791   E-mail: ssrpmail@stanford.edu
Web: ssrp.stanford.edu

Summary To provide Native American and other underrepresented undergraduate students with a summer research experience at Stanford University in biological and biomedical sciences.

Eligibility This program is open to sophomores, juniors, and non-graduating seniors at 4-year colleges and universities in the United States, Puerto Rico, and U.S. territories. Students from all ethnic backgrounds are eligible, but the program especially encourages applications from Black/African Americans, Latino/Chicano Americans, Native Americans, Pacific Islanders, and other undergraduates who, by reason of their culture, class, race, ethnicity, background, work and life experiences, skills, and interests would bring diversity to graduate study in the biological and biomedical sciences (biochemistry, bioengineering, biology, biomedical informatics, biophysics, cancer biology, chemistry, chemical and systems biology, chemical engineering, developmental biology, earth sciences, genetics, immunology, microbiology, molecular and cellular physiology, neurosciences, statistics, and structural biology). Applicants must have at least 1 year of undergraduate education remaining before graduation and should be planning to prepare for and enter a Ph.D. program in the biological or biomedical sciences. They must have a GPA of 3.2

or higher. U.S. citizenship or permanent resident status is required.

Financial data The program provides a stipend of $3,400, housing, meals, and transportation to and from the San Francisco Bay area.

Duration 8 weeks during the summer.

Additional information This program currently serves as the Stanford component of the Amgen Scholars Program, which operates at 9 other U.S. universities and is funded by the Amgen Foundation.

Number awarded Up to 25 each year.

Deadline January of each year.

[562]
STANLEY AND JANET ZISK SCHOLARSHIP

Ke Ali'i Pauahi Foundation
Attn: Financial Aid & Scholarship Services
567 South King Street, Suite 160
Honolulu, HI 96813
(808) 534-3966   Toll Free: (800) 842-4682, ext. 43966
Fax: (808) 534-3890   E-mail: scholarships@pauahi.org
Web: www.pauahi.org/scholarships

Summary To provide financial assistance to residents of any state, especially Native Hawaiians, who are attending college in Hawaii.

Eligibility This program is open to residents of any state who are currently enrolled at an accredited college or university in Hawaii. Applicants must have a GPA of 2.0 to 3.5 and be able to demonstrate financial need. Preference is given to Native Hawaiians (descendants of the aboriginal inhabitants of the Hawaiian Islands prior to 1778).

Financial data The stipend is $1,000.

Duration 1 year.

Number awarded 1 each year.

Deadline March of each year.

[563]
STOCKBRIDGE-MUNSEE HIGHER EDUCATION GRANT PROGRAM

Stockbridge-Munsee Community
Attn: Education and Cultural Affairs Director
W13447 Camp 14 Road
P.O. Box 70
Bowler, WI 54416
(715) 793-4060   Toll Free: (800) 720-2790
Fax: (715) 793-4830
E-mail: jolene.bowman@mohican-nsn.gov
Web: www.mohican-nsn.gov

Summary To provide financial assistance to members of the Stockbridge-Munsee Community Band of Mohican Indians who are interested in attending college or graduate school in any state.

Eligibility This program is open to members of the Stockbridge-Munsee Community Band of Mohican Indians who are interested in working on an associate, baccalaureate, or graduate degree at a college or university in any state. Applicants must be able to demonstrate financial need. In the selection process, priority is given to students in the following order: continuing current students, new students, part-time students, students for whom the educational institution has

made a determination of no financial need, and students who are repeating a degree level.

Financial data Stipends for full-time study are $2,650 per semester for 2-year college students, $5,000 per semester for 4-year baccalaureate students, or $6,670 per semester for graduate students. Stipends for part-time study are prorated appropriately.

Duration 1 semester; may be renewed up to 4 additional semesters for associate degree students, up to 9 additional semesters for baccalaureate students, up to 4 additional semesters for students in a 2-year graduate program, up to 6 additional semesters for students in a 3-year graduate program, or up to 8 additional semesters for students in a 4-year graduate program. Renewals require students to remain enrolled full time and to maintain a GPA of 2.0 or higher as an undergraduate or 3.0 or higher as a graduate student. Part-time students may renew proportionally.

Additional information This program is offered under contract with the U.S. Bureau of Indian Affairs. Wisconsin residents who attend school in the state must also apply for a Wisconsin Indian Student Assistance Grant.

Number awarded Varies each year.

Deadline May of each year for fall term; September of each year for spring term; April of each year for summer term.

[564]
STUART BROTMAN STUDENT RESEARCH FELLOWSHIP AWARDS

American Gastroenterological Association
Attn: AGA Research Foundation
Research Awards Manager
4930 Del Ray Avenue
Bethesda, MD 20814-2512
(301) 222-4012   Fax: (301) 654-5920
E-mail: awards@gastro.org
Web: www.gastro.org/aga-foundation/grants

Summary To provide funding for research on digestive diseases or nutrition to high school and undergraduate students, especially those who are Native Americans or other minorities).

Eligibility This program is open to high school and undergraduate students at accredited institutions in North America. Applicants must be interested in conducting research on digestive diseases or nutrition. They may not hold similar salary support awards from other agencies (e.g., American Liver Foundation, Crohn's and Colitis Foundation). Research must be conducted under the supervision of a preceptor who is a full-time faculty member at a North American institution, directing a research project in a gastroenterology-related area, and a member of the American Gastroenterological Association (AGA). The program includes awards reserved for underprivileged and underrepresented undergraduates, including (but not limited to) Black Americans, Hispanic or Latino Americans, Native Americans, and Pacific Islanders. Selection is based on novelty, feasibility, and significance of the proposal; attributes of the candidate; record of the preceptor; evidence of institutional commitment; and laboratory environment.

Financial data The grant is $2,500. No indirect costs are allowed. The award is paid directly to the student and is to be used as a stipend.

Duration At least 10 weeks. The work may take place at any time during the year.

Number awarded 11 high school students and 24 undergraduates (of whom 10 must be underprivileged or underrepresented students) are supported each year.

Deadline March of each year.

[565]
STUDENT OPPORTUNITY SCHOLARSHIPS FOR ETHNIC MINORITY GROUPS

Presbyterian Church (USA)
Attn: Office of Financial Aid for Studies
100 Witherspoon Street, Room M-052
Louisville, KY 40202-1396
(502) 569-5224   Toll Free: (888) 728-7228, ext. 5224
Fax: (502) 569-8766   E-mail: finaid@pcusa.org
Web: www.pcusa.org

Summary To provide financial assistance to minority and other upper-division college students who are Presbyterians and majoring in selected fields.

Eligibility This program is open to members of the Presbyterian Church (USA), especially those from racial/ethnic minority groups (Asian American, African American, Hispanic American, Native American, Alaska Native). Applicants must be able to demonstrate financial need, be entering their junior or senior year of college as full-time students, and have a GPA of 2.5 or higher. Preference is given to applicants who are majoring in the following fields of interest to missions of the church: education, health services and sciences, religious studies, sacred music, social services, and social sciences.

Financial data Stipends range up to $3,000 per year, depending upon the financial need of the recipient.

Duration 1 year; may be renewed for up to 3 additional years if the recipient continues to need financial assistance and demonstrates satisfactory academic progress.

Number awarded Varies each year.

Deadline June of each year.

[566]
SUMMER DIVERSITY INTERNSHIP PROGRAM

Ad Club
Attn: Director of Content and Programming
9 Hamilton Place, Second Floor
Boston, MA 02108
(617) 262-1100, ext. 103   Fax: (617) 456-1772
E-mail: kate@adclub.org
Web: www.adclub.org/div_int

Summary To provide summer work experience in advertising or a related industry to upper-division students, especially Native American or members of other minority groups, at agencies in New England.

Eligibility This program is open to advertising and marketing students who have junior standing or above and a GPA of 3.0 or higher. Special consideration is given to students who are African American, Asian American, Indian American, Hispanic American, Native American, biracial, or multiracial. Applicants must be interested in a summer internship at an advertising agency in New England. Positions are available in account management, branding, creative, design, digital, and system operations/IT.

Financial data The stipend is $3,500.

Duration 10 weeks during the summer.

Number awarded 12 each year.

Deadline April of each year.

[567]
SUMMER HONORS UNDERGRADUATE RESEARCH PROGRAM

Harvard Medical School
Attn: Division of Medical Sciences
Diversity Programs Office
260 Longwood Avenue, Room 432
Boston, MA 02115-5720
(617) 432-1342   Toll Free: (800) 367-9019
Fax: (617) 432-2644   E-mail: SHURP@hms.harvard.edu
Web: www.hms.harvard.edu

Summary To provide an opportunity for Native Americans and other underrepresented minority students to engage in research at Harvard Medical School during the summer.

Eligibility This program at Harvard Medical School is open to undergraduate students belonging to minority groups that are underrepresented in the sciences. Applicants must have had at least 1 summer (or equivalent) of experience in a research laboratory and have taken at least 1 upper-level biology course that includes molecular biology. They should be considering a career in biological or biomedical research. U.S. citizenship or permanent resident status is required.

Financial data The program provides a stipend of $420 per week, dormitory housing, travel costs, a meal card, and health insurance if it is needed.

Duration 10 weeks during the summer.

Number awarded Varies each year.

Deadline January of each year.

[568]
SUMMER PROGRAM IN QUANTITATIVE SCIENCES FOR PUBLIC HEALTH RESEARCH

Harvard School of Public Health
Department of Biostatistics
Attn: Diversity Program Coordinator
655 Huntington Avenue, SPH2, Fourth Floor
Boston, MA 02115
(617) 432-3175   Fax: (617) 432-5619
E-mail: biostat_diversity@hsph.harvard.edu
Web: www.hsph.harvard.edu/biostats/diversity/summer

Summary To enable Native Americans and other underrepresented or disadvantaged science undergraduates to participate in a summer research internship at Harvard School of Public Health that focuses on biostatistics, epidemiology, and health and social behavior.

Eligibility This program is open to 1) members of ethnic groups underrepresented in the sciences (African Americans, Hispanics, Native American, Pacific Islanders, biracial/multiracial); 2) first-generation college students; 3) low-income students; or 4) individuals with a disability. Applicants must be current undergraduates interested in participating in a summer program on the use of quantitative methods for biological, environmental, and medical research as preparation for graduate studies in public health, biostatistics, or epidemiology. They must have a GPA of 3.0 or higher, including course work in calculus, but prior exposure to statistics is not required. U.S. citizenship or permanent resident status is required.

Financial data Funding covers travel, housing, course materials, and a stipend to cover meals and incidental.

Duration 4 weeks, in June.

Additional information Interns participate in seminars, led by faculty members from various departments at the Harvard School of Public Health and Harvard Medical School, that are designed to broaden a participant's understanding of the relationship of biostatistics to human health. They also attend non-credit classes in biostatistics, epidemiology, and health and social behavior.

Number awarded Varies each year.

Deadline February of each year.

[569]
SUMMER RESEARCH DIVERSITY FELLOWSHIPS IN LAW AND SOCIAL SCIENCE FOR UNDERGRADUATE STUDENTS

American Bar Foundation
Attn: Summer Research Diversity Fellowship
750 North Lake Shore Drive
Chicago, IL 60611-4403
(312) 988-6560   Fax: (312) 988-6579
E-mail: fellowships@abfn.org
Web: www.americanbarfoundation.org

Summary To provide an opportunity for Native Americans and other undergraduate students from diverse backgrounds to work on a summer research project in the field of law and social science.

Eligibility This program is open to U.S. citizens and permanent residents who are African Americans, Hispanic/Latinos, Puerto Ricans, Native Americans, or other individuals who will add diversity to the field of law and social science. Applicants must be sophomores or juniors in college, have a GPA of 3.0 or higher, be majoring in the social sciences or humanities, and be willing to consider an academic or research career. Along with their application, they must submit a 200-word essay on their future plans and why this fellowship would contribute to them, another essay on an assigned topic, official transcripts, and a letter of recommendation from a faculty member familiar with their work.

Financial data Participants receive a stipend of $3,600.

Duration 35 hours per week for 8 weeks during the summer.

Additional information Students are assigned to an American Bar Foundation Research Professor who involves the student in the design and conduct of the professor's research project and who acts as mentor during the student's tenure.

Number awarded 4 each year.

Deadline February of each year.

[570]
SUMMER TRANSPORTATION INTERNSHIP PROGRAM FOR DIVERSE GROUPS

Department of Transportation
Attn: Summer Transportation Internship Program for
  Diverse Groups
HAHR-40, Room E63-433
1200 New Jersey Avenue, S.E.
Washington, DC 20590
(202) 366-2907   E-mail: lafayette.melton@dot.gov
Web: www.fhwa.dot.gov/education/stipdg.htm

Summary To enable Native American and other undergraduate, graduate, and law students from diverse groups to gain work experience during the summer at facilities of the U.S. Department of Transportation (DOT).

Eligibility This program is open to all qualified applicants, but it is designed to provide women, persons with disabilities, and members of diverse social and ethnic groups with summer opportunities in transportation. Applicants must be U.S. citizens currently enrolled in a degree-granting program of study at an accredited institution of higher learning at the undergraduate (community or junior college, university, college, or Tribal College or University) or graduate level. Undergraduates must be entering their junior or senior year; students attending a Tribal or community college must have completed their first year of school; law students must be entering their second or third year of school. Students who will graduate during the spring or summer are not eligible unless they have been accepted for enrollment in graduate school. The program accepts applications from students in all majors who are interested in working on transportation-related topics and issues. Preference is given to students with a GPA of 3.0 or higher. Undergraduates must submit a 1-page essay on their transportation interests and how participation in this program will enhance their educational and career plans and goals. Graduate students must submit a writing sample representing their educational and career plans and goals. Law students must submit a legal writing sample.

Financial data The stipend is $4,000 for undergraduates or $5,000 for graduate and law students. The program also provides housing and reimbursement of travel expenses from interns' homes to their assignment location.

Duration 10 weeks during the summer.

Additional information Assignments are at the DOT headquarters in Washington, D.C., a selected modal administration, or selected field offices around the country.

Number awarded 80 to 100 each year.

Deadline January of each year.

[571]
SUSIE QIMMIQSAK BEVINS ENDOWMENT SCHOLARSHIP FUND

Cook Inlet Region, Inc.
Attn: The CIRI Foundation
3600 San Jeronimo Drive, Suite 256
Anchorage, AK 99508-2870
(907) 793-3575   Toll Free: (800) 764-3382
Fax: (907) 793-3585   E-mail: tcf@thecirifoundation.org
Web: www.thecirifoundation.org/designated.htm

Summary To provide financial assistance for undergraduate or graduate studies in the literary, performing, and visual arts to Alaska Natives who are original enrollees to Cook Inlet Region, Inc. (CIRI) and their lineal descendants.

Eligibility This program is open to Alaska Native enrollees to CIRI under the Alaska Native Claims Settlement Act (ANCSA) of 1971 and their lineal descendants. There are no Alaska residency requirements or age limitations. Applicants must be accepted or enrolled full time in a 2-year, 4-year, or graduate degree program in the literary, visual, or performing arts. They should have a GPA of 2.5 or higher. Along with their application, they must submit a 500-word statement on their educational and career goals and how they are contributing, or planning to contribute, to a positive Alaska Native community. Selection is based on that statement, academic achievement, rigor of course work or degree program, student financial contribution, financial need, grade level, previous work performance, community service, and relationship of degree program to career goals.

Financial data The stipend is $2,000 per semester.

Duration 1 semester; recipients may reapply.

Additional information This program was established in 1990.

Number awarded Varies each year.

Deadline May or November of each year.

[572]
TANADGUSIX CORPORATION SCHOLARSHIPS

Tanadgusix Corporation
Attn: TDX Foundation
4300 B Street, Suite 402
Anchorage, AK 99502
(907) 278-2312   Fax: (907) 278-2316
E-mail: info@tanadgusix.com
Web: www.tanadgusix.com/SHR/index.html

Summary To provide financial assistance to Native Alaskans who are shareholders or descendants of shareholders of the Tanadgusix Corporation (TDX) and interested in attending college in any state.

Eligibility This program is open to TDX shareholders and their lineal descendants who are enrolled or planning to enroll full time at a college or university in any state. Applicants must have a GPA of 2.0 or higher. Along with their application, they must submit a letter of intent that includes their motivation for continuing their education and obtaining a degree or certificate, plans to use their education, involvement in Native affairs, and perceived benefits to the community of St. Paul, the Aleut region, or the state of Alaska.

Financial data A stipend is awarded (amount not specified).

Duration 1 year; may be renewed, provided the recipient remains enrolled full time and maintains a GPA of 2.0 or higher.

Additional information The TDX Corporation is an Alaska Native village corporation that serves the Aleut people of St. Paul Island in the Pribilof chain.

Number awarded Varies each year.

Deadline July of each year.

[573]
TANANA CHIEFS CONFERENCE HIGHER EDUCATION GRANTS

Tanana Chiefs Conference
Attn: Education Department
122 First Avenue, Suite 600
Fairbanks, AK 99701-4897
(907) 452-8251, ext. 3184
Toll Free: (800) 478-6822 (within AK)
Fax: (907) 459-3885
Web: www.tananachiefs.org/Higher_Education.shtm

Summary To provide financial assistance to Native Alaskans who have a tie to the Tanana Chiefs Conference (TCC) and are interested in attending college or graduate school in any state.

Eligibility This program is open to Alaska Natives who are enrolled to Doyon, Limited or a member of a tribe or village served by TCC. Applicants must be attending or planning to attend an accredited college, university, graduate school, or vocational training program in any state. They must be able to demonstrate financial need and to apply for all other available financial aid.

Financial data A stipend is awarded (amount not specified).

Duration 1 semester; may be renewed if the recipient maintains a GPA of 2.0 or higher and full-time enrollment.

Additional information TCC serves the following villages in interior Alaska: Birch Creek, Huslia, Minto, Nenana, Nikolai, Rampart, and Tetlin. It also provides funding to 28 other villages that administer the program for students enrolled to their tribe or corporation.

Number awarded More than 200 each year.

Deadline April of each year for fall semester or quarter; November of each year for spring semester or winter or spring quarter; February of each year for summer school.

[574]
TANAQ FOUNDATION SCHOLARSHIPS

St. George Tanaq Corporation
Attn: Tanaq Foundation
4141 B Street, Suite 301
Anchorage, AK 99503
(907) 272-9886   Toll Free: (888) 811-9886
Fax: (907) 272-9855
Web: stgeorgetanaq.com/foundation.html

Summary To provide financial assistance to Native Alaskans who are shareholders or descendants of shareholders of the St. George Tanaq Corporation and interested in attending college or graduate school in any state.

Eligibility This program is open to shareholders of the St. George Tanaq Corporation and their lineal descendants who are enrolled or planning to enroll full time at a college or university in any state. Applicants must be interested in working on an associate, bachelor's, or master's degree in any field. They must have a GPA of 2.0 or higher. Along with their application, they must submit a 500-word letter of intent that explains how they are doing, their goals, and their expected date of graduation. Financial need is not considered in the selection process.

Financial data Stipends are $2,000 or $1,000. Funds are disbursed directly to the financial aid office of the recipient's school.

Duration 1 year; may be renewed.

Additional information The St. George Tanaq Corporation is an Alaska Native village corporation that serves the island of St. George in the Aleutian chain.

Number awarded Varies each year; recently, 5 of these scholarships (4 at $2,000 and 1 at $1,000) were awarded.

Deadline June of each year for the school year; November of each year for spring semester only.

[575]
TANAQ FOUNDATION VOCATIONAL EDUCATION SCHOLARSHIPS

St. George Tanaq Corporation
Attn: Tanaq Foundation
4141 B Street, Suite 301
Anchorage, AK 99503
(907) 272-9886   Toll Free: (888) 811-9886
Fax: (907) 272-9855
Web: stgeorgetanaq.com/foundation.html

Summary To provide financial assistance to Native Alaskans who are shareholders or descendants of shareholders of the St. George Tanaq Corporation and interested in attending vocational school in any state.

Eligibility This program is open to shareholders of the St. George Tanaq Corporation and their lineal descendants who are enrolled or planning to enroll full time at a vocational school in any state. Applicants must have a GPA of 2.0 or higher. Along with their application, they must submit a 500-word letter of intent that explains how they are doing, their goals, and their expected date of graduation. Financial need is not considered in the selection process.

Financial data The stipend recently was $1,500. Funds are disbursed directly to the financial aid office of the recipient's school.

Duration 1 year; may be renewed.

Additional information The St. George Tanaq Corporation is an Alaska Native village corporation that serves the island of St. George in the Aleutian chain.

Number awarded 1 or more each year.

Deadline June of each year for the school year; November of each year for the spring semester only.

[576]
TARGETED OPPORTUNITY PROGRAM (TOPJOBS)

Wisconsin Office of State Employment Relations
Attn: Division of Affirmative Action Workforce Planning
101 East Wilson Street, Fourth Floor
P.O. Box 7855
Madison, WI 53707-7855
(608) 267-1005   Fax: (608) 267-1020
E-mail: Claire.Dehnert@wisconsin.gov
Web: oser.state.wi.us/category.asp?linkcatid=342

Summary To provide an opportunity for Native Americans and other underrepresented students to gain summer work experience with agencies of the state of Wisconsin.

Eligibility This program is open to ethnic/racial minorities (Black or African American, Asian, Native Hawaiian or other

Pacific Islander, American Indian or Alaska Native, or Hispanic or Latino), women, and persons with disabilities. Applicants must be juniors, seniors, or graduate students at an accredited 4-year college or university or second-year students in the second year of a 2-year technical or vocational school program. They must be 1) Wisconsin residents enrolled full time at a school in Wisconsin or any other state, or 2) residents of other states who are enrolled full time at a school in Wisconsin.

Financial data Most internships provide a competitive stipend.

Duration Summer months.

Additional information This program was established in 1974. Relevant fields of study include, but are not limited to, the liberal arts and sciences (e.g., history, mathematics, library science, political science, philosophy, physics, psychology, social services, social work, sociology, women's studies); agriculture and natural resources (e.g., animal and dairy science, biology, botany, chemistry, geography, entomology, environmental studies, horticulture, landscape architecture, microbiology, plant pathology, soil science, urban planning, water resources management, wildlife ecology); business (e.g., accounting, business management, economics, finance, human resources, marketing, public administration, real estate); criminal justice; education; health care (including nursing); engineering; information systems and computers; journalism and communications; and law.

Number awarded Varies each year. Since the program was established, it has placed more than 2,500 students with more than 30 different agencies and universities throughout the state.

Deadline February of each year.

[577]
TBM PROGRAM

Catching the Dream
8200 Mountain Road, N.E., Suite 203
Albuquerque, NM 87110-7835
(505) 262-2351   Fax: (505) 262-0534
E-mail: NScholarsh@aol.com
Web: www.catchingthedream.org/Scholarship.htm

Summary To provide financial assistance to American Indian undergraduate and graduate students interested in studying a field related to economic development for tribes.

Eligibility This program is open to American Indians who can provide proof that they are at least one-quarter Indian blood and a member of a U.S. tribe that is federally-recognized, state-recognized, or terminated. Applicants must be enrolled or planning to enroll full time and major in the 1 of the following fields: business administration, finance, management, economics, banking, hotel management, or other fields related to economic development for tribes. They may be entering freshmen, undergraduate students, graduate students, or Ph.D. candidates. Along with their application, they must submit documentation of financial need, 3 letters of recommendation, copies of applications and responses for all other sources of funding for which they are eligible, official transcripts, standardized test scores (ACT, SAT, GRE, MCAT, LSAT, etc.), and an essay explaining their goals in life, college plans, and career plans (especially how those plans include working with and benefiting Indians). Selection is based on merit and potential for improving the lives of Indian people.

Financial data Stipends range from $500 to $5,000 per year.

Duration 1 year.

Additional information The sponsor was formerly known as the Native American Scholarship Fund. This program was established in 2003.

Number awarded Varies; generally, 30 to 35 each year.

Deadline April of each year for fall term; September of each year for spring and winter terms; March of each year for summer school.

[578]
TEACHER QUEST SCHOLARSHIP

Brown Foundation for Educational Equity, Excellence and Research
Attn: Scholarship Committee
1515 S.E. Monroe
Topeka, KS 66615
(785) 235-3939   Fax: (785) 235-1001
E-mail: brownfound@juno.com
Web: brownvboard.org

Summary To provide financial assistance to Native Americans and other undergraduate and graduate students of color who are interested in preparing for a teaching career.

Eligibility This program is open to members of minority groups who are enrolled at least half time at an institution of higher education with an accredited teacher education program. Applicants must be enrolled at the undergraduate, graduate, or post-baccalaureate level and have a GPA of 3.0 or higher. Along with their application, they must submit brief essays on 1) their involvement in school, community, and/or other activities and how those activities have prepared them to be an educator; 2) why they aspire to a career in education, their goals, and the level at which they plan to teach; and 3) how they think *Brown v. Board of Education* has influenced their own life experiences. Selection is based on the essays; GPA; school, community, and leisure activities; career plans and goals in education; and recommendations.

Financial data The stipend is $1,000 per year.

Duration 2 years.

Additional information The first Brown Foundation Scholarships were awarded in 1989. The current program replaced the Brown Foundation Academic Scholarships in 2009.

Number awarded Varies each year; recently, 5 of these scholarships were awarded.

Deadline March of each year.

[579]
TENNESSEE MINORITY TEACHING FELLOWS PROGRAM

Tennessee Student Assistance Corporation
Parkway Towers
404 James Robertson Parkway, Suite 1510
Nashville, TN 37243-0820
(615) 741-1346   Toll Free: (800) 342-1663
Fax: (615) 741-6101   E-mail: TSAC.Aidinfo@tn.gov
Web: www.tn.gov

Summary To provide funding to Native Americans and other minority residents of Tennessee who wish to attend college in the state to prepare for a career in the teaching field.

Eligibility This program is open to minority residents of Tennessee who are either high school seniors planning to enroll full time at a college or university in the state or continuing college students at a Tennessee college or university. High school seniors must have a GPA of 2.75 or higher and an ACT score of at least 18, a combined mathematics and critical reading SAT score of at least 860, or a rank in the top 25% of their high school class. Continuing college students must have a college GPA of 2.5 or higher. All applicants must agree to teach at the K-12 level in a Tennessee public school following graduation from college. Along with their application, they must submit a 250-word essay on why they chose teaching as a profession. U.S. citizenship is required.

Financial data The funding is $5,000 per year. Recipients incur an obligation to teach at the preK-12 level in a Tennessee public school 1 year for each year the award is received.

Duration 1 year; may be renewed for up to 3 additional years, provided the recipient maintains full-time enrollment and a cumulative GPA of 2.5 or higher.

Additional information This program was established in 1989.

Number awarded 20 new awards are granted each year.

Deadline April of each year.

[580]
THE HILL GROUP SCHOLARSHIP

Chickasaw Foundation
110 West 12th Street
P.O. Box 1726
Ada, OK 74821-1726
(580) 421-9030   Fax: (580) 421-9031
E-mail: ChickasawFoundation@chickasaw.net
Web: www.chickasawfoundation.org/index_20.htm

Summary To provide financial assistance to members of the Chickasaw Nation who are interested in working on an undergraduate degree.

Eligibility This program is open to Chickasaw students who are currently enrolled at an accredited institution of higher education as a full-time undergraduate student. Applicants may be majoring in any field, but they must have a GPA of 2.0 or higher. Along with their application, they must submit high school or college transcripts, 2 letters of recommendation, a copy of their Chickasaw Nation citizenship card, and a 1-page essay on their long-term goals and plans for achieving them. Financial need is not considered in the selection process.

Financial data The stipend is $2,000.

Duration 1 year.

Number awarded 2 each year.

Deadline August of each year.

[581]
TIME WARNER TRIBAL SCHOLARS PROGRAM

American Indian College Fund
Attn: Scholarship Department
8333 Greenwood Boulevard
Denver, CO 80221
(303) 426-8900   Toll Free: (800) 776-FUND
Fax: (303) 426-1200
E-mail: scholarships@collegefund.org
Web: www.collegefund.org/scholarships/schol_tcu.html

Summary To provide financial assistance to Native Americans who are attending or planning to attend a Tribal College or University (TCU).

Eligibility This program is open to American Indians or Alaska Natives who are enrolled or planning to enroll full time at an eligible TCU. Applicants must have a GPA of 2.5 or higher. Applications are available only online and include required essays on specified topics. Selection is based on exceptional academic achievement.

Financial data The stipend is $2,500.

Duration 1 year.

Additional information This scholarship is sponsored by Time Warner in partnership with the American Indian College Fund.

Number awarded 1 or more each year.

Deadline May of each year.

[582]
TRAILBLAZER SCHOLARSHIPS

Conference of Minority Transportation Officials
Attn: National Scholarship Program
818 18th Street, N.W., Suite 850
Washington, DC 20006
(202) 530-0551   Fax: (202) 530-0617
Web: www.comto.org/news-youth.php

Summary To provide financial assistance to Native American and other undergraduate and graduate minority students working on a degree in a field related to transportation.

Eligibility This program is open to undergraduate and graduate students who are working on a degree in a field related to transportation with a GPA of 2.5 or higher. Along with their application, they must submit a cover letter with a 500-word statement of career goals. Financial need is not considered in the selection process. U.S. citizenship is required.

Financial data The stipend is $2,500. Funds are paid directly to the recipient's college or university.

Duration 1 year.

Additional information The Conference of Minority Transportation Officials (COMTO) was established in 1971 to promote, strengthen, and expand the roles of minorities in all aspects of transportation. Recipients are expected to attend the COMTO National Scholarship Luncheon.

Number awarded 2 each year.

Deadline April of each year.

[583]
TRAVELER'S FOUNDATION SCHOLARSHIP

American Indian College Fund
Attn: Scholarship Department
8333 Greenwood Boulevard
Denver, CO 80221
(303) 426-8900   Toll Free: (800) 776-FUND
Fax: (303) 426-1200
E-mail: scholarships@collegefund.org
Web: www.collegefund.org

Summary To provide financial assistance to Native American college students from Kansas, Minnesota, Montana, or Washington who are enrolled at mainstream colleges and universities in designated cities.

Eligibility This program is open to American Indians and Alaska Natives from Kansas, Minnesota, Montana, or Washington who have proof of enrollment or descendancy. Applicants must be enrolled full time at a mainstream college or university in St. Paul or Minneapolis (Minnesota), Seattle (Washington), Spokane (Washington), or Kansas City (Kansas). They must have a GPA of 2.5 or higher, be able to demonstrate exceptional academic achievement or financial need, and be willing to commit to leadership development by attending a 2-day Traveler's career day. Business majors are given preference, but all majors are eligible. Applications are available only online and include required essays on specified topics.

Financial data The stipend is $2,500.

Duration 1 year.

Additional information This program is funded by the Traveler's Foundation in partnership with the American Indian College Fund.

Number awarded 1 or more each year.

Deadline May of each year.

[584]
TRAVELER'S FOUNDATION TRIBAL COLLEGE SCHOLARSHIP

American Indian College Fund
Attn: Scholarship Department
8333 Greenwood Boulevard
Denver, CO 80221
(303) 426-8900   Toll Free: (800) 776-FUND
Fax: (303) 426-1200
E-mail: scholarships@collegefund.org
Web: www.collegefund.org/scholarships/schol_tcu.html

Summary To provide financial assistance to Native American college students from Kansas, Minnesota, Montana, or Washington who are enrolled at designated Tribal Colleges and Universities (TCUs) in those states.

Eligibility This program is open to American Indians and Alaska Natives from Kansas, Minnesota, Montana, or Washington who have proof of enrollment or descendancy. Applicants must be enrolled full time at 1 of the following TCUs: Fond du Lac Tribal and Community College, Leech Lake Tribal College, White Earth Tribal and Community College, Northwest Indian College, Salish Kootenai College, Blackfeet Community College, or Haskell Indian Nations University. They must have a GPA of 2.5 or higher, be able to demonstrate exceptional academic achievement or financial need, and be willing to commit to leadership development by attending a 2-day Traveler's career day. Business majors are given preference, but all majors are eligible. Applications are available only online and include required essays on specified topics.

Financial data The stipend is $2,500.

Duration 1 year.

Additional information This program is funded by the Traveler's Foundation in partnership with the American Indian College Fund.

Number awarded 1 or more each year.

Deadline May of each year.

[585]
TRIBAL COLLEGE SCHOLARSHIP

American Indian College Fund
Attn: Scholarship Department
8333 Greenwood Boulevard
Denver, CO 80221
(303) 426-8900   Toll Free: (800) 776-FUND
Fax: (303) 426-1200
E-mail: scholarships@collegefund.org
Web: www.collegefund.org/scholarships/schol_tcu.html

Summary   To provide financial assistance to Native American college students from California who are enrolled at Tribal Colleges and Universities (TCUs) in any state.

Eligibility   This program is open to American Indians and Alaska Natives who have proof of enrollment or descendancy and are residents of California or members or descendants of a California-based tribe. Applicants must be enrolled full time at an eligible TCU in any state. They must have a GPA of 2.5 or higher and be able to demonstrate exceptional academic achievement or financial need. Applications are available only online and include required essays on specified topics.

Financial data   The stipend is $2,600.

Duration   1 year.

Number awarded   1 or more each year.

Deadline   May of each year.

[586]
TRIBAL ENERGY PROGRAM SUMMER INTERNSHIP PROGRAM

Sandia National Laboratories
Attn: Photovoltaics and Grid Integration Program
MS-0734
P.O. Box 5800
Albuquerque, NM 87185-0734
(505) 844-5418   TDD: (505) 844-7786
E-mail: skbegay@sandia.gov
Web: apps1.eere.energy.gov/tribalenergy/internships.cfm

Summary   To provide an opportunity for Native Americans to learn more about renewable energy and energy self-sufficiency during a summer internship at Sandia National Laboratories.

Eligibility   This program is open to members of federally-recognized tribes, Alaska villages, and Alaska corporations; members of state-recognized tribes, members of bands or groups, and first peoples of Hawaii or Guam are not eligible. Applicants must be upper-division or graduate students and familiar with Native American cultural and tribal issues. They must be interested in summer employment at Sandia in Albuquerque to learn more about economic development and employment on tribal lands through the use of renewable energy and energy efficient technologies. Along with their application, they must submit a resume indicating their GPA (minimum of 3.2 for bachelor's students, 3.5 for master's students, or 3.7 for doctoral candidates) and 5 essays of 250 words each on assigned topics related to their background and interest in renewable energy at Sandia.

Financial data   The stipend depends on the number of credit hours completed.

Duration   12 weeks during the summer.

Additional information   This program is sponsored by the Energy Efficiency and Renewable Energy Program of the U.S. Department of Energy.

Number awarded   Varies each year; recently, 4 students received these internships.

Deadline   February of each year.

[587]
TRUMAN D. PICARD SCHOLARSHIP PROGRAM

Intertribal Timber Council
Attn: Education Committee
1112 N.E. 21st Avenue, Suite 4
Portland, OR 97232-2114
(503) 282-4296   Fax: (503) 282-1274
E-mail: itc1@teleport.com
Web: www.itcnet.org/about_us/scholarships.html

Summary   To provide financial assistance to American Indians or Alaskan Natives who are interested in studying natural resources in college.

Eligibility   This program is open to 1) graduating high school seniors, and 2) currently-enrolled college students. Applicants must be enrolled in a federally-recognized tribe or Native Alaska corporation. They must be majoring or planning to major in natural resources. Selection is based on interest in natural resources; commitment to education, community, and culture; academic merit; and financial need.

Financial data   The stipend is $1,500 for high school seniors entering college or $2,000 for students already enrolled in college.

Duration   1 year.

Additional information   Recipients who attend the University of Washington (Seattle) or Salish Kootenai College (Pablo, Montana) are also eligible for additional scholarships and tuition waivers.

Number awarded   Varies each year; recently, 21 of these scholarships were awarded.

Deadline   March of each year.

[588]
TURTLE MOUNTAIN BAND OF CHIPPEWA INDIANS SCHOLARSHIP PROGRAM

Turtle Mountain Band of Chippewa Indians
Attn: Tribal Scholarship Office
P.O. Box 900
Belcourt, ND 58316
(701) 477-8102   Fax: (701) 477-8053
Web: www.tmbci.net

Summary   To provide financial assistance for full-time undergraduate or graduate study in any state to enrolled members of the Turtle Mountain Band of Chippewa.

Eligibility   Applicants must be enrolled members of the Turtle Mountain Band of Chippewa, be full-time students enrolled in an academic program at an accredited postsecondary institution in any state on either the undergraduate or graduate school level, and have a GPA of 2.0 or higher. Undergraduate applicants must be enrolled for at least 12 quarter or 12 semester credit hours (or 6 semester/quarter hours for a summer session); graduate school applicants must be enrolled for at least 1 course. Along with their application, they must submit a Certificate of Indian Blood, a letter of acceptance/admission from their college, the award notice sent by the college's financial aid office, a high school transcript or GED certificate, and any college transcripts. Priority is given to applicants in the following order: seniors who need to attend summer school in order to graduate, juniors who need summer school in order to become seniors, students who need summer school to acquire their 2-year degree, sophomores, freshmen, and graduate students.

Financial data A stipend is awarded (amount not specified).

Duration The maximum number of terms the scholarship program will fund a student for an undergraduate degree is 10 semesters or 15 quarters; the maximum number of terms for a student at a 2-year college is 3 years, 6 semesters, or 9 quarters.

Additional information Once recipients earn 65 or more credit hours at a 2-year college, they must transfer to a 4-year institution.

Number awarded Varies each year.

Deadline August of each year.

[589]
TUSCARORA SCHOLARSHIP PROGRAM

New York Power Authority
c/o Jamie Gilbert
Niagara-Wheatfield Central School District
6700 Schultz Street
Niagara Falls, NY 14304
(716) 215-3100, ext. 2344   E-mail: jgilbert@nwcsd.org
Web: niagara.nypa.gov

Summary To provide financial assistance to members of the Tuscarora Nation who are interested in attending a college in the State University of New York (SUNY) system.

Eligibility This program is open to enrolled members of the Tuscarora Nation who are attending or planning to attend a community college or university in the SUNY system. Applicants must submit an essay of 200 to 300 words on their educational and future goals. They must also submit a description of a community involvement project for the Tuscarora Nation that they propose to conduct over the course of 4 years if they are selected to receive a scholarship; the project may be in the areas of environment, education, health and well being, culture, administration, recreation, or history and the arts.

Financial data The program provides recipients with full payment of tuition at any SUNY college or university.

Duration 4 years.

Additional information This program was established in 2007 as part of the relicensing agreement between the Power Authority of the State of New York and the Tuscarora Nation. Funding is provided by the Power Authority, but the Tuscarora Nation has sole responsibility for selecting the recipients.

Number awarded 2 each year.

Deadline March of each year.

[590]
TVSHKA CHUNKASH (HEART OF A WARRIOR) SCHOLARSHIP

Choctaw Nation
Attn: Scholarship Advisement Program
16th and Locust
P.O. Box 1210
Durant, OK 74702-1210
(580) 924-8280
Toll Free: (800) 522-6170, ext. 2523 (within OK)
Fax: (580) 920-3122
E-mail: scholarshipadvisement@choctawnation.com
Web: www.choctawnation-sap.com/cnoscholarship.shtml

Summary To provide financial assistance to Choctaw Indian students who are attending a university in any state and who submit an outstanding essay on the impact of the wars in Iraq and Afghanistan on their lives.

Eligibility This program is open to Choctaw students who are currently enrolled at an accredited college or university in any state and are enrolled in its Scholarship Advisement Program. Applicants must submit a 500-word essay on 1) how the war in Iraq or Afghanistan has affected their outlook on life or their future (including a personal impact, such as a family or friend, a specific political event, or a cultural situation or event that has impacted their life); 2) how the event impacted their educational goals; and 3) their future goals. Selection is based on the essay's content (40%), originality (20%), structure and writing (20%), and grammar and spelling (20%).

Financial data The stipend is $1,000.

Duration 1 year; nonrenewable.

Number awarded 1 each year.

Deadline September of each year.

[591]
TWO FEATHERS ENDOWMENT AMERICAN INDIAN SCHOLARSHIPS

Saint Paul Foundation
Attn: Program Assistant
55 Fifth Street East, Suite 600
St. Paul, MN 55101-1797
(651) 325-4202   Toll Free: (800) 875-6167
Fax: (651) 224-8123
E-mail: jmu@saintpaulfoundation.org
Web: www.saintpaulfoundation.org/scholarships

Summary To provide financial assistance to Indians who belong to a Minnesota tribe and are interested in attending college in any state.

Eligibility This program is open to members of Indian tribes in Minnesota who are enrolled or planning to enroll full time at a college or university in any state. Applicants must submit a 250-word essay describing their involvement in the Indian community and how the accomplishment of their educational goals will benefit the American Indian community. Financial need is considered in the selection process.

Financial data The stipend is $1,000.

Duration 1 year; nonrenewable.

Number awarded Up to 5 each year.

Deadline June of each year.

[592]
TWO FEATHERS FUND HEALTH INITIATIVE SCHOLARSHIP

Saint Paul Foundation
Attn: Program Assistant
55 Fifth Street East, Suite 600
St. Paul, MN 55101-1797
(651) 325-4202   Toll Free: (800) 875-6167
Fax: (651) 224-8123
E-mail: jmu@saintpaulfoundation.org
Web: www.saintpaulfoundation.org/scholarships

Summary   To provide financial assistance to Indians who belong to a Minnesota tribe and are interested in studying a health-related field at a college in any state.

Eligibility   This program is open to members of Indian tribes in Minnesota who are enrolled full time at a college or university in any state in a field of study related to health. Applicants must submit a 250-word essay describing their involvement in the Indian community and how the accomplishment of their educational goals will benefit the American Indian community. Financial need is considered in the selection process.

Financial data   The stipend is $5,000.

Duration   1 year; nonrenewable.

Number awarded   Several each year.

Deadline   June of each year.

[593]
TYONEK NATIVE CORPORATION UNDERGRADUATE SCHOLARSHIPS

Tebughna Foundation
1689 C Street, Suite 221
Anchorage, AK 99501
(907) 272-0707   Toll Free: (877) 862-6667
Fax: (907) 274-7125   E-mail: tebughna@tyonek.com
Web: www.tebughnafoundation.com

Summary   To provide financial assistance to original enrollees of the Tyonek Native Corporation (TNC) and their lineal descendants who are interested in attending college in any state.

Eligibility   This program is open to Alaska Native enrollees to TNC under the Alaska Native Claims Settlement Act (ANCSA) of 1971 and their lineal descendants. Applicants must be accepted or enrolled part or full time in an undergraduate degree program at an accredited college or university in any state. Along with their application, they must submit a 500-word statement on their educational and career goals, how their degree program fits with their career plans, and how their degree program will contribute to a positive Alaska Native community. Selection is based on that statement, academic achievement, and financial need.

Financial data   The full-time stipend is $2,000 per semester ($4,000 per academic year) for students at 4-year colleges and universities or $1,000 per semester ($2,000 per academic year) for students at 2-year colleges. Stipends for part-time students are prorated appropriately.

Duration   1 semester; students may receive funding for a second semester if the maintain a GPA of 2.0 or higher, but they must reapply for a third semester.

Number awarded   Varies each year.

Deadline   June or November of each year.

[594]
TYONEK NATIVE CORPORATION VOCATIONAL/ TECHNICAL TRAINING SCHOLARSHIPS

Tebughna Foundation
1689 C Street, Suite 221
Anchorage, AK 99501
(907) 272-0707   Toll Free: (877) 862-6667
Fax: (907) 274-7125   E-mail: tebughna@tyonek.com
Web: www.tebughnafoundation.com

Summary   To provide financial assistance to original enrollees of the Tyonek Native Corporation (TNC) and their lineal descendants who are interested in attending a vocational/technical school in any state.

Eligibility   This program is open to Alaska Native enrollees to TNC under the Alaska Native Claims Settlement Act (ANCSA) of 1971 and their lineal descendants. Applicants must be accepted or enrolled at a vocational/technical school in any state. Along with their application, they must submit a 500-word statement on their educational and career goals, how their degree program fits with their career plans, and how their degree program will contribute to a positive Alaska Native community. Selection is based on that statement, academic achievement, and financial need.

Financial data   Stipends are available in 2 levels: 1) for students taking up to 2 classes a year, a total of $1,000; or 2) for students taking more than 2 classes a year, 33.3% of the enrollment fee, to a maximum of $2,500.

Duration   1 calendar year.

Number awarded   Varies each year.

Deadline   Applications may be submitted at any time, but they must be received at least 30 days prior to the start date of the training program.

[595]
UDALL FOUNDATION NATIVE AMERICAN CONGRESSIONAL INTERNSHIPS

Morris K. Udall and Stewart L. Udall Foundation
Attn: Program Manager, Internship Program
130 South Scott Avenue
Tucson, AZ 85701-1922
(520) 901-8568   Fax: (520) 670-5530
E-mail: info@udall.gov
Web: www.udall.gov

Summary   To provide an opportunity for Native American upper-division students, graduate students, and recent graduates to work in a Congressional office during the summer.

Eligibility   This program is open to American Indians and Alaska Natives who are enrolled members of recognized tribes and have an interest in tribal government and policy. Applicants must have a GPA of 3.0 or higher as a junior, senior, graduate student, law student, or recent graduate of a tribal or 4-year college. They must be able to participate in an internship in Washington, D.C., where they will gain practical experience in the legislative process, Congressional matters, and governmental proceedings that specifically relate to Native American issues. Fields of study of previous interns have included American Indian studies, political science, law and pre-law, psychology, social work, history, business and public administration, anthropology, community and urban planning, architecture, communications, health sciences, public health, biology, engineering, sociology, environmental studies and natural resources, economics, and justice studies. Applicants must demonstrate strong research and writing skills; organizational abilities and time management skills; maturity, responsibility, and flexibility; interest in learning how the federal government "really works;" commitment to their tribal community; knowledge of Congressman Morris K. Udall's legacy with regard to Native Americans; and awareness of issues and challenges currently facing Indian Country.

Financial data Interns receive round-trip airfare to Washington, D.C.; dormitory lodging at a local university; a daily allowance sufficient for meals, transportation, and incidentals; and an educational stipend of $1,200 to be paid at the conclusion of the internship.

Duration 10 weeks during the summer.

Additional information These internships were first offered in 1996.

Number awarded 12 each year.

Deadline January of each year.

[596]
UIC FOUNDATION SCHOLARSHIPS

Ukpeagvik Inupiat Corporation
Attn: UIC Foundation
P.O. Box 890
Barrow, AK 99723
(907) 852-4460   Fax: (907) 852-4459
E-mail: UICFoundation@ukpik.com
Web: www.ukpik.com

Summary To provide financial assistance to Native Alaskans who are shareholders or descendants of shareholders of the Ukpeagvik Inupiat Corporation and interested in attending college in any state.

Eligibility This program is open to shareholders of the corporation and their descendants who are attending or planning to attend a college, university, or vocational school in any state. Applicants must have a GPA of 2.0 or higher and be able to demonstrate financial need. Along with their application, they must submit a personal statement describing their future career plans and participation in extracurricular and community service activities.

Financial data The stipend is $900 per semester ($1,800 per year) for full-time students or $450 per semester ($900 per year) for part-time students. Full-time students who live away from home are also eligible for rent support (up to $1,500 per term) and a food allowance of $150 per month.

Duration 1 semester; may be renewed, provided the recipient maintains a GPA of 2.0 or higher.

Number awarded Varies each year.

Deadline July of each year for fall semester or quarter; November of each year for spring semester or winter quarter; February of each year for spring quarter; April of each year for summer semester or quarter.

[597]
UNDERGRADUATE AWARDS OF THE SEMINOLE NATION JUDGMENT FUND

Seminole Nation of Oklahoma
Attn: Judgment Fund Office
2007 West Wrangler Boulevard
Seminole, OK 74868
(405) 382-0549   Toll Free: (877) 382-0549
Fax: (405) 382-0571
Web: www.seminolenation.com/services_judgmentfund.htm

Summary To provide financial assistance for undergraduate study to members of the Seminole Nation of Oklahoma.

Eligibility This program is open to enrolled members of the Seminole Nation of Oklahoma who are descendants of a member of the Seminole Nation as it existed in Florida on September 18, 1823. Applicants must be attending or planning to attend a college or university to work on an undergraduate degree. Along with their application, they must submit copies of their tribal membership card, Certificate of Indian Blood (CIB), class schedule and grades from previous classes, and official college transcript.

Financial data The stipend for full-time students is $1,000 per year for freshmen, $1,200 per year for sophomores, $1,600 per year for juniors, or $1,800 for seniors. Part-time students receive the actual cost of tuition, books, and fees, to a maximum of $300 per semester. The total of all undergraduate degree awards to a student may not exceed $5,600.

Duration 1 year; may be renewed as long as the recipient maintains a GPA of 2.0 or higher.

Additional information The General Council of the Seminole Nation of Oklahoma approved a plan for use of the Judgment Fund Award in 1990. This aspect of the program went into effect in September of 1991.

Number awarded Varies each year.

Deadline November of each year for fall semester; April of each year for spring semester.

[598]
UNDERGRADUATE STUDENT INDUSTRIAL FELLOWSHIPS/TRAINEESHIPS

National Science Foundation
Directorate for Engineering
Attn: Division of Industrial Innovation and Partnerships
4201 Wilson Boulevard, Room 550S
Arlington, VA 22230
(703) 292-7082   Fax: (703) 292-9056
TDD: (800) 281-8749   E-mail: dsenich@nsf.gov
Web: www.nsf.gov/funding/pgm_summ.jsp?pims_id=13706

Summary To provide an opportunity for underrepresented minorities and other undergraduate students to work in industry as part of the Grant Opportunities for Academic Liaison with Industry (GOALI) program of the National Science Foundation (NSF).

Eligibility This program is open to undergraduate students in science, engineering, and mathematics fields of interest to NSF. Applicants must be U.S. citizens, nationals, or permanent residents. They must be proposing a program of full- or part-time work in industry in an area related to their academic program under the guidance of an academic adviser and an industrial mentor. The program encourages applications from underrepresented minorities and persons with disabilities.

Financial data Undergraduate students may receive stipends from $500 to $800 per week; they may also receive some assistance with housing or travel expenses, or both. No indirect costs are allowed. The total award may be up to $10,000 for a fellowship for a single student.

Duration Support may be provided for a summer project, or for 1 or 2 semesters of part- or full-time work.

Additional information This program is also offered by most other NSF directorates. Check the web site for a name and e-mail address of the contact person in each directorate.

Number awarded A total of 60 to 80 grants for all GOALI programs is awarded each year; total funding is approximately $5 million.

Deadline Applications may be submitted at any time.

[599]
UNITED HEALTH FOUNDATION AICF SCHOLARSHIP

American Indian College Fund
Attn: Scholarship Department
8333 Greenwood Boulevard
Denver, CO 80221
(303) 426-8900   Toll Free: (800) 776-FUND
Fax: (303) 426-1200
E-mail: scholarships@collegefund.org
Web: www.collegefund.org

Summary To provide financial assistance to Native American college students who are majoring in health-related fields at mainstream colleges and universities in Arizona.

Eligibility This program is open to American Indians and Alaska Natives from any state who have proof of enrollment or descendancy and are enrolled full time in a bachelor's degree program at a mainstream institution in Arizona. Applicants must have a GPA of 3.0 or higher and be able to demonstrate exceptional academic achievement or financial need. They must have declared a major in health or a related field (not including social work). Applications are available only online and include required essays on specified topics.

Financial data The stipend is $5,000.

Duration 1 year.

Additional information This program is funded by the United Health Foundation in partnership with the American Indian College Fund (AICF).

Number awarded 1 or more each year.

Deadline May of each year.

[600]
UNITED KEETOOWAH BAND OF CHEROKEE INDIANS EDUCATIONAL SCHOLARSHIPS

United Keetoowah Band of Cherokee Indians
Attn: Department of Education
P.O. Box 746
Tahlequah, OK 74465
(918) 453-2569   Toll Free: (800) 259-0093
Fax: (918) 453-1267
Web: www.unitedkeetoowahband.org

Summary To provide financial assistance for vocational school, college, or graduate school to members of the United Keetoowah Band of Cherokee Indians.

Eligibility This program is open to students who have been enrolled members of the United Keetoowah Band of Chero-

kee Indians for at least 6 months. Applicants must be working on or planning to work on a vocational certificate, bachelor's degree, master's degree, doctoral degree, or law degree. Along with their application, they must submit a copy of their tribal membership card, a copy of their Social Security card, an official transcript, a class schedule, and documentation of financial need.

Financial data For full-time undergraduate and graduate students, the stipend is $1,500 per semester; for part-time undergraduate and graduate students, the stipend is $750 per semester; for vocational students, the stipend is $1,000 per year.

Duration 1 semester; may be renewed, provided the recipient maintains a GPA of 2.0 or higher.

Number awarded Varies each year.

Deadline August of each year for fall semester; January of each year for spring semester.

[601]
UNITED METHODIST HIGHER EDUCATION FOUNDATION NATIVE ALASKAN FUND

United Methodist Higher Education Foundation
Attn: Scholarships Administrator
1001 19th Avenue South
P.O. Box 340005
Nashville, TN 37203-0005
(615) 340-7385   Toll Free: (800) 811-8110
Fax: (615) 340-7330
E-mail: umhefscholarships@gbhem.org
Web: www.umhef.org/receive.php?id=endowed_funds

Summary To provide financial assistance to Native Alaskan Methodist undergraduate and graduate students at Methodist-related colleges and universities.

Eligibility This program is open to Native Alaskans enrolling as full-time undergraduate or graduate students at United Methodist-related colleges and universities. Preference is given to United Methodist students at Alaska Pacific University. Applicants must have been active, full members of a United Methodist Church for at least 1 year prior to applying. They must have a GPA of 3.0 or higher and be able to demonstrate financial need. Along with their application, they must submit a 200-word essay on their involvement and/or leadership responsibilities in their church, school, and community within the last 3 years. U.S. citizenship or permanent resident status is required.

Financial data The stipend is at least $1,000 per year.

Duration 1 year; nonrenewable.

Number awarded Varies each year; recently, 2 of these scholarships were awarded.

Deadline May of each year.

[602]
UNITED PARCEL SERVICE SCHOLARSHIP FOR MINORITY STUDENTS

Institute of Industrial Engineers
Attn: Scholarship Coordinator
3577 Parkway Lane, Suite 200
Norcross, GA 30092
(770) 449-0461, ext. 105   Toll Free: (800) 494-0460
Fax: (770) 441-3295   E-mail: bcameron@iienet.org
Web: www.iienet2.org/Details.aspx?id=857

Summary To provide financial assistance to Native American and other minority undergraduates who are studying industrial engineering at a school in the United States, Canada, or Mexico.

Eligibility Eligible to be nominated are minority undergraduate students enrolled at any school in the United States and its territories, Canada, or Mexico, provided the school's engineering program is accredited by an agency recognized by the Institute of Industrial Engineers (IIE) and the student is pursuing a full-time course of study in industrial engineering with a GPA of at least 3.4. Nominees must have at least 5 full quarters or 3 full semesters remaining until graduation. Students may not apply directly for these awards; they must be nominated by the head of their industrial engineering department. Nominees must be IIE members. Selection is based on scholastic ability, character, leadership, potential service to the industrial engineering profession, and need for financial assistance.

Financial data The stipend is $4,000.

Duration 1 year.

Additional information Funding for this program is provided by the UPS Foundation.

Number awarded 1 each year.

Deadline Schools must submit nominations by November of each year.

[603]
UNIVERSITY OF NORTH CAROLINA CAMPUS SCHOLARSHIPS

North Carolina State Education Assistance Authority
Attn: Scholarship and Grant Services
10 Alexander Drive
P.O. Box 14103
Research Triangle Park, NC 27709-4103
(919) 549-8614   Toll Free: (800) 700-1775
Fax: (919) 549-8481   E-mail: information@ncseaa.edu
Web: www.ncseaa.edu

Summary To provide financial assistance to Native American and other students at University of North Carolina (UNC) constituent institutions whose enrollment contributes to the diversity of the undergraduate or graduate population.

Eligibility This program is open to undergraduate and doctoral students who are enrolled or planning to enroll full time at 1 of the 16 UNC institutions. Applicants must have graduated in the top 40% of their high school class, have a weighted GPA of 3.0 or higher, have an SAT score higher than the SAT score of the previous freshman class, and have a record of positive involvement in extracurricular activities. They must be able to demonstrate "exceptional financial need." Their enrollment must "contribute to the intellectual experiences and diversity of the undergraduate population." A portion of the funds are reserved specifically for American Indian students who can provide evidence of tribal affiliation.

Financial data The amount of the award depends upon the financial need of the recipient and the availability of funds; recently, stipends averaged more than $1,900.

Duration 1 year; may be renewed.

Additional information This program was established in 2002 as a replacement for the former North Carolina Minority Presence Grants, North Carolina Freshmen Scholars Program, North Carolina Incentive Scholarship Program, North

Carolina Legislative College Opportunity Program, and North Carolina Incentive Scholarship and Grant Program for Native Americans. Students must submit applications to the constituent institution's financial aid office rather than directly to the North Carolina State Education Assistance Authority.

Number awarded Varies each year; recently, a total of 2,793 of these scholarships, with a total value of $5,435,826, were awarded.

Deadline Deadline dates vary; check with the appropriate constituent institution.

[604]
UPS DIVERSITY SCHOLARSHIPS

American Society of Safety Engineers
Attn: ASSE Foundation
1800 East Oakton Street
Des Plaines, IL 60018
(847) 768-3435   Fax: (847) 768-3434
E-mail: agabanski@asse.org
Web: www.asse.org

Summary To provide financial assistance to Native American and other minority upper-division student members of the American Society of Safety Engineers (ASSE).

Eligibility This program is open to ASSE student members who are U.S. citizens and members of minority ethnic or racial groups. Applicants must be majoring in occupational safety, health, and environment or a closely-related field (e.g., industrial or environmental engineering, environmental science, industrial hygiene, occupational health nursing). They must be full-time students who have completed at least 60 semester hours with a GPA of 3.0 or higher. Along with their application, they must submit 2 essays of 300 words or less: 1) why they are seeking a degree in occupational safety and health or a closely-related field, a brief description of their current activities, and how those relate to their career goals and objectives; and 2) why they should be awarded this scholarship (including career goals and financial need).

Financial data The stipend is $5,250 per year.

Duration 1 year; recipients may reapply.

Additional information Funding for this program is provided by the UPS Foundation.

Number awarded 2 each year.

Deadline November of each year.

[605]
VANGUARD MINORITY SCHOLARSHIP PROGRAM

Scholarship America
Attn: Scholarship Management Services
One Scholarship Way
P.O. Box 297
St. Peter, MN 56082
(507) 931-1682   Toll Free: (800) 537-4180
Fax: (507) 931-9168
Web: sms.scholarshipamerica.org/vanguard

Summary To provide financial assistance to Native American and other minority students working on an undergraduate degree in specified fields.

Eligibility This program is open to U.S. citizens and permanent residents who are members of racial or ethnic minorities. Applicants must be entering their junior or senior year as a full-time student at an accredited 4-year college or university in the United States and have a GPA of 3.0 or higher. They must be working on a degree in accounting, business, economics, or finance. Selection is based on academic record, demonstrated leadership and participation in school and community activities, honors, work experience, a statement of goals and aspirations, unusual personal or family circumstances, recommendations, and a resume; financial need is not considered. Students who attended a 2-year college while working on a bachelor's degree are not eligible.

Financial data The stipend ranges up to $10,000.

Duration 1 year; nonrenewable.

Additional information This program, established in 2004, is sponsored by Vanguard Group, Inc.

Number awarded Up to 10 each year.

Deadline November of each year.

[606]
VIC MATSON, SR. TRIBUTARY SCHOLARSHIP

Sault Tribe of Chippewa Indians
Attn: Higher Education Program-Memorial/Tributary
  Scholarships
523 Ashmun Street
Sault Ste. Marie, MI 49783
(906) 635-4944   Toll Free: (800) 793-0660
Fax: (906) 635-7785   E-mail: amatson@saulttribe.net
Web: www.saulttribe.com

Summary To provide financial assistance to members of the Sault Tribe of Chippewa Indians interested in attending college in any state to work on an undergraduate or graduate degree in a field related to fisheries or natural resources.

Eligibility This program is open to enrolled members of the Sault Tribe who are enrolled full time at a 2- or 4-year college or university in any state. Applicants must be working on an undergraduate or graduate degree in the field of fisheries or natural resources management or a related area. Along with their application, they must submit an essay of 300 to 500 words on how this scholarship will help them realize their goals.

Financial data The stipend is $1,000.

Duration 1 year.

Number awarded 1 each year.

Deadline May of each year.

[607]
VIRGINIA D. WILSON SCHOLARSHIP

Navajo Nation
Attn: Office of Navajo Nation Scholarship and Financial
  Assistance
P.O. Box 1870
Window Rock, AZ 86515-1870
(928) 871-7444   Toll Free: (800) 243-2956
Fax: (928) 871-6742   E-mail: onnsfacentral@navajo.org
Web: www.onnsfa.org/corplist.asp

Summary To provide financial assistance to Navajo high school seniors in New Mexico who plan to attend college in any state.

Eligibility This program is open to high school seniors who are enrolled members of the Navajo Nation, reside in New Mexico, and are planning to enroll full time at a college or uni-

versity in any state. They may major in any field. Financial need is not considered in the selection process.

Financial data The stipend is $2,000 per year.

Duration 1 year; may be renewed if the recipient maintains a GPA of 2.0 or higher and enrolls in at least 12 credit hours per semester.

Number awarded 1 or more each year.

Deadline Deadline not specified.

[608]
VOCATIONAL SCHOOL AWARDS OF THE SEMINOLE NATION JUDGMENT FUND

Seminole Nation of Oklahoma
Attn: Judgment Fund Office
2007 West Wrangler Boulevard
Seminole, OK 74868
(405) 382-0549   Toll Free: (877) 382-0549
Fax: (405) 382-0571
Web: www.seminolenation.com/services_judgmentfund.htm

Summary To provide financial assistance for vocational school to members of the Seminole Nation of Oklahoma.

Eligibility This program is open to enrolled members of the Seminole Nation of Oklahoma who are descendants of a member of the Seminole Nation as it existed in Florida on September 18, 1823. Applicants must be attending or planning to attend a vocational school. Along with their application, they must submit a copy of their tribal membership card, a copy of their Certificate of Indian Blood (CIB), and verification of attendance at the vocational training program.

Financial data The grant is $1,200 per year for the actual cost of tuition, books, and fees. Funds are paid to the training facility if application is made prior to the date classes begin or as reimbursement to students who make application after classes begin. Full-time students also receive a stipend of $25 per week and part-time students also receive a stipend of $12 per week. Other benefits include a grant of $100 or the actual cost, whichever is less, of the fee to obtain a license upon completion of a vocational course. Students who take correspondence courses may receive up to $400 per year or the actual cost of tuition, books, or fees, whichever is less; no stipend is provided to those students. The total of all vocational school awards to an applicant may not exceed $2,400.

Duration 1 year; may be renewed for 1 additional year.

Additional information The General Council of the Seminole Nation of Oklahoma approved a plan for use of the Judgment Fund Award in 1990. This aspect of the program went into effect in September of 1991.

Number awarded Varies each year.

Deadline Applications must be submitted within 30 days of the completion of a vocational course.

[609]
WAH-TIAH-KAH SCHOLARSHIP

Osage Minerals Council
813 Grandview
P.O. Box 779
Pawhuska, OK 74056
(918) 287-5433
Web: www.osagetribe.com/education/info.aspx

Summary To provide financial assistance to Osage students who are interested in attending college or graduate school to prepare for a career in the petroleum industry.

Eligibility This program is open to full-time undergraduate and graduate students who can prove Osage Indian blood in any degree. Applicants must be working on or planning to work on a degree in a field related to petroleum. Along with their application, they must submit a copy of their Certificate of Osage Indian Blood, transcripts, 2 letters of recommendation, ACT or SAT scores, and a personal statement of their educational and career goals.

Financial data A stipend is awarded (amount not specified).

Duration 1 semester; may be renewed for up to 7 additional semesters, provided the recipient reapplies each semester and maintains a GPA of 2.0 or higher.

Number awarded Varies each year.

Deadline June of each year for fall term; December of each year for spring term.

[610]
WALTER CHARLEY MEMORIAL SCHOLARSHIPS

Ahtna, Incorporated
Attn: Ahtna Heritage Foundation
P.O. Box 213
Glennallen, AK 99588
(907) 822-5778   Fax: (907) 822-5338
E-mail: ahtnaheritage@yahoo.com
Web: www.ahtna-inc.com

Summary To provide financial assistance to shareholders of Ahtna, Incorporated in Alaska and their descendants who plan to attend college in any state.

Eligibility This program is open to Ahtna shareholders (original, gifted, inherited, or Class L) who are high school graduates or GED recipients. Applicants must be 1) attending or planning to attend a college, university, or vocational school in any state; or 2) accepted in a program specializing in a recognized area or field of study. They must have a GPA of 2.0 or higher and be able to demonstrate financial need.

Financial data The stipend is $2,000 per semester ($4,000 per year) for full-time students or $1,000 per semester ($2,000 per year) for part-time students.

Duration 1 year; may be renewed, provided the recipient maintains a GPA of 2.0 or higher.

Additional information Ahtna, Incorporated is 1 of 13 regional corporations established according to the terms of the Alaska Native Claims Settlement Act (ANCSA) of 1971.

Number awarded Varies each year.

Deadline July of each year for fall semester; December of each year for spring semester.

[611]
WAMPANOAG HIGHER EDUCATION SCHOLARSHIP PROGRAM

Wampanoag Tribe of Gay Head
Attn: Education Director
20 Black Brook Road
Aquinnah, MA 02535-1546
(508) 645-9265   Toll Free: (800) 332-7707
Fax: (508) 645-3790
Web: www.wampanoagtribe.net

Summary To provide financial assistance to members of the Wampanoag Tribe of Gay Head who are interested in attending college or graduate school in any state.

Eligibility This program is open to enrolled members of the Wampanoag Tribe of Gay Head who are working on or planning to work full time on a baccalaureate or advanced degree. Applicants must submit a brief essay describing their family ties to Martha's Vineyard (Massachusetts) and their personal reflections about their Wampanoag Heritage.

Financial data A stipend is awarded (amount not specified).

Duration 1 year; may be renewed.

Number awarded Varies each year.

Deadline June of each year.

[612]
WARNER NORCROSS & JUDD PARALEGAL ASSISTANT SCHOLARSHIP

Grand Rapids Community Foundation
Attn: Education Program Officer
185 Oakes Street S.W.
Grand Rapids, MI 49503-4008
(616) 454-1751, ext. 103   Fax: (616) 454-6455
E-mail: rbishop@grfoundation.org
Web: www.grfoundation.org/scholarships

Summary To provide financial assistance to Native American and other minority residents of Michigan who are interested in working on a paralegal studies degree at an institution in the state.

Eligibility This program is open to residents of Michigan who are students of color attending or planning to attend an accredited public or private 2- or 4-year college or university in the state. Applicants must have a declared major in paralegal/legal assistant studies. They must be U.S. citizens or permanent residents and have a GPA of 2.5 or higher. Financial need is considered in the selection process.

Financial data The stipend is $2,000. Funds are paid directly to the recipient's institution.

Duration 1 year.

Additional information Funding for this program is provided by the law firm Warner Norcross & Judd LLP.

Number awarded 1 each year.

Deadline March of each year.

[613]
WASHINGTON ADMIRAL'S FUND SCHOLARSHIP

National Naval Officers Association-Washington, D.C.
  Chapter
Attn: Scholarship Program
2701 Park Center Drive, A1108
Alexandria, VA 22302
(703) 566-3840   Fax: (703) 566-3813
E-mail: Stephen.Williams@Navy.mil
Web: dcnnoa.memberlodge.com

Summary To provide financial assistance to Native American and other minority high school seniors from the Washington, D.C. area who are interested in attending a college or university in any state and enrolling in the Navy Reserve Officers Training Corps (NROTC) program.

Eligibility This program is open to minority seniors graduating from high schools in the Washington, D.C. metropolitan area who plan to enroll full time at an accredited 2- or 4-year college or university in any state. Applicants must be planning to enroll in the NROTC program. They must have a GPA of 2.5 or higher and be U.S. citizens or permanent residents. Selection is based on academic achievement, community involvement, and financial need.

Financial data The stipend is $1,000.

Duration 1 year; nonrenewable.

Additional information If the recipient fails to enroll in the NROTC unit, all scholarship funds must be returned.

Number awarded 1 each year.

Deadline March of each year.

[614]
WASHINGTON AMERICAN INDIAN ENDOWED SCHOLARSHIP PROGRAM

Washington Higher Education Coordinating Board
917 Lakeridge Way
P.O. Box 43430
Olympia, WA 98504-3430
(360) 753-7843   Toll Free: (888) 535-0747
Fax: (360) 753-7808   TDD: (360) 753-7809
E-mail: aies@hecb.wa.gov
Web: www.hecb.wa.gov/Paying/waaidprgm/aies.asp

Summary To provide financial assistance to American Indian undergraduate and graduate students in Washington.

Eligibility This program is open to Washington residents who have close social and cultural ties to an American Indian tribe and/or community in the state. Applicants must demonstrate financial need and be enrolled, or planning to enroll, as a full-time undergraduate or graduate student at a Washington state public or independent college, university, or career school. They must agree to use their education to benefit other American Indians. Students who are working on a degree in religious, seminarian, or theological academic studies are not eligible. Selection is based on academic merit, financial need, and documented commitment to return service to the state's American Indian community.

Financial data Stipends range from about $500 to $2,000 per year.

Duration 1 year, may be renewed up to 4 additional years.

Additional information This program was created by the Washington legislature in 1990 with a state appropriation to an endowment fund and matching contributions from tribes, individuals, and organizations.

Number awarded Approximately 15 new and 10 renewal scholarships are awarded each year.

Deadline January of each year.

[615]
WASHINGTON, D.C. CHAPTER SCHOLARSHIP PROGRAM

National Naval Officers Association-Washington, D.C.
  Chapter
Attn: Scholarship Program
2701 Park Center Drive, A1108
Alexandria, VA 22302
(703) 566-3840   Fax: (703) 566-3813
E-mail: Stephen.Williams@Navy.mil
Web: dcnnoa.memberlodge.com

Summary To provide financial assistance to Native American and other minority high school seniors from the Washington, D.C. area who plan to attend college in any state.

Eligibility This program is open to minority seniors graduating from high schools in the Washington, D.C. metropolitan area who plan to enroll full time at an accredited 2- or 4-year college or university in any state. Applicants must have a GPA of 2.5 or higher (depending upon the specific scholarship). U.S. citizenship or permanent resident status is required. Selection is based on academic achievement, community involvement, and financial need.

Financial data The stipend is $1,000.

Duration 1 year; nonrenewable.

Additional information Recipients are not required to join or affiliate with the military in any way. A number of named scholarship are awarded, including the Capstone Corporation Scholarship Award and the Captain Willie Evans Scholarship, the Cochran/Greene Scholarship, the Ester Boone Memorial Scholarship, and the Madison/Kalathas/Davis Scholarship Award.

Number awarded Several each year.

Deadline March of each year.

[616]
WASHINGTON INDIAN GAMING ASSOCIATION SCHOLARSHIPS

Washington Indian Gaming Association
1110 Capitol Way South, Suite 404
Olympia, WA 98501
(360) 352-3248   Fax: (360) 352-4819
Web: www.washingtonindiangaming.org

Summary To provide financial assistance to members of Indian tribes in Washington who are interested in attending college or graduate school in any state.

Eligibility This program is open to Washington residents who are enrolled members of tribes affiliated with the Washington Indian Gaming Association (WIGA) and to urban Indian students in the state. Applicants must be attending or accepted at a community college, undergraduate institution, or graduate school in any state. Native American students from outside Washington who attend college in the state are also eligible. Along with their application, they must submit a 250-word personal essay on topics that change annually; recently, students were asked to explain why they were considering their intended major, how it would help them reach future career objectives, and how their education would benefit their home community (whether urban or rural). Financial need is also considered in the selection process.

Financial data Stipends are $2,000 per year for graduate or professional students, $1,500 per year for undergraduates at 4-year institutions, or $1,100 per year for students at community colleges or technical schools.

Duration 1 year; may be renewed.

Number awarded Up to 8 graduate and professional scholarships, up to 16 scholarships for 4-year institutions, and up to 9 community college or technical school scholarships are awarded each year.

Deadline March of each year.

[617]
WASHINGTON INTERNSHIPS FOR NATIVE STUDENTS

American University
Attn: Washington Internships for Native Students (WINS)
4400 Massachusetts Avenue, N.W.
Washington, DC 20016-8083
(202) 895-4900   Toll Free: (800) 853-3076
Fax: (202) 895-4882   E-mail: wins@american.edu
Web: www.american.edu/wins

Summary To provide an opportunity for Native American and Alaska Native undergraduate and graduate students to gain work experience at a federal agency in Washington, D.C.

Eligibility This program is open to members of recognized tribes of Native Americans and Alaska Natives. Applicants must be enrolled at a college or university as a sophomore, junior, senior, or graduate student with a GPA of 2.5 or higher. They must be interested in living in Washington D.C. for a semester or summer and interning at a federal government agency. Along with their application, they must submit transcripts, a letter of nomination from their tribe, a faculty letter of recommendation, a resume, proof of tribal membership, and a 500-word essay on why they want to participate in the program and the contributions they can offer a potential employer.

Financial data Interns receive round-trip travel to Washington, D.C., books, tuition, housing, meals, local transportation, insurance, and a stipend of $140 per week.

Duration Fall and spring internships are for 4 months; summer internships are 2 months.

Additional information This program began in 1994 as a small summer activity and was expanded to a full summer internship in 1999. Spring and fall programs were added in 2001. In addition to work assignments at participating federal agencies, interns take courses on topics of interest to Native communities and receive academic credit.

Number awarded Approximately 25 in each of the semester programs and approximately 100 in the summer.

Deadline May of each year for fall; September of each year for spring; January of each year for summer.

[618]
WASHOE TRIBE HIGHER EDUCATION GRANT PROGRAM

Washoe Tribe
Attn: Education Department
919 Highway 395 South
Gardnerville, NV 89410
(775) 265-4191, ext. 1136   Toll Free: (800) 76-WASHOE
Fax: (775) 265-6240   E-mail: education@washoetribe.us
Web: www.washoetribe.us

Summary To provide financial assistance for college or graduate school to members of the Washoe Tribe in Nevada and California.

Eligibility Eligible to apply for these scholarships are members of the Washoe Tribe who are working on (or planning to work on) an associate, bachelor's, or graduate degree. Applicants are required to seek all other sources of funding, in addition to applying for this program. In the process, they must complete a Free Application for Federal Student Aid (FAFSA) and receive a Student Aid Report. Awards are

grants in the following priority order: 1) continuing students with acceptable grades; 2) new students who reside near or within the boundaries of Washoe tribal colonies (Woodfords, Dresslerville, Carson, Stewart, Reno) and other Nevada and California residents; 3) students outside of Nevada and California; 4) graduate students; and 5) students who have a 4-year degree and are working to obtain a 4-year degree in a different field.

Financial data Recently, stipends were $1,005.

Duration 1 year; may be renewed if the recipient remains enrolled full time with a GPA of 1.8 or higher as a freshman and 2.0 or higher as a sophomore through senior.

Number awarded Varies each year; recently, 10 of these scholarships were awarded.

Deadline July or November of each year.

[619]
WASHOE TRIBE INCENTIVE SCHOLARSHIPS

Washoe Tribe
Attn: Education Department
919 Highway 395 South
Gardnerville, NV 89410
(775) 265-8600, ext. 1136   Toll Free: (800) 76-WASHOE
Fax: (775) 265-6240   E-mail: education@washoetribe.us
Web: www.washoetribe.us

Summary To provide financial assistance to members of the Washoe Tribe working on an undergraduate or graduate degree at a school in any state.

Eligibility This program is open to members of the Washoe Tribe who are currently working full time on an associate, baccalaureate, graduate, or postgraduate degree at a school in any state. Applicants must have a GPA of 3.0 or higher. Along with their application they must submit proof of Washoe enrollment, a copy of their college grade report, and a copy of their current class schedule. Selection is based on a first-come, first-served basis; financial need is not considered.

Financial data The stipend varies each year; recently, stipends were $1,225 in the spring semester and $890 in the fall semester.

Duration 1 year; recipients may reapply.

Number awarded Varies each year; recently, 8 of these scholarships were awarded in the spring semester and 11 in the fall semester.

Deadline January or September of each year.

[620]
WATSON MIDWIVES OF COLOR SCHOLARSHIP

American College of Nurse-Midwives
Attn: ACNM Foundation, Inc.
8403 Colesville Road, Suite 1550
Silver Spring, MD 20910-6374
(240) 485-1850   Fax: (240) 485-1818
Web: www.midwife.org/foundation_award.cfm

Summary To provide financial assistance for midwifery education to Native Americans and other students of color who belong to the American College of Nurse-Midwives (ACNM).

Eligibility This program is open to ACNM members of color who are currently enrolled in an accredited basic midwife education program and have successfully completed 1 academic or clinical semester/quarter or clinical module.

Applicants must submit a 150-word essay on their 5-year midwifery career plans and a 100-word essay on their intended future participation in the local, regional, and/or national activities of the ACNM. Selection is based on leadership potential, financial need, academic history, and potential for future professional contribution to the organization.

Financial data The stipend is $3,000.

Duration 1 year.

Number awarded Varies each year; recently, 3 of these scholarships were awarded.

Deadline March of each year.

[621]
WEISMAN SCHOLARSHIPS

Connecticut Department of Higher Education
Attn: Office of Student Financial Aid
61 Woodland Street
Hartford, CT 06105-2326
(860) 947-1857   Fax: (860) 947-1838
E-mail: mtip@ctdhe.org
Web: www.ctdhe.org/SFA/default.htm

Summary To provide financial assistance to Native American and other minority upper-division college students from any state who are enrolled at a college in Connecticut and interested in teaching mathematics or science at public middle and high schools in the state.

Eligibility This program is open to residents of any state who are enrolled full time as juniors or seniors at Connecticut colleges and universities and preparing to become a mathematics or science teacher at the middle or high school level. Applicants must be members of a minority group, defined as African American, Hispanic/Latino, Asian American, or Native American. They must be nominated by the education dean at their institution.

Financial data The maximum stipend is $5,000 per year. In addition, if recipients complete a credential and begin teaching at a public school in Connecticut within 16 months of graduation, they may receive up to $2,500 per year, for up to 4 years, to help pay off college loans.

Number awarded Varies each year.

Deadline September of each year.

[622]
WELLS FARGO UNDERGRADUATE SCHOLARSHIPS

American Indian Graduate Center
Attn: Executive Director
4520 Montgomery Boulevard, N.E., Suite 1-B
Albuquerque, NM 87109-1291
(505) 881-4584   Toll Free: (800) 628-1920
Fax: (505) 884-0427   E-mail: aigc@aigc.com
Web: www.aigc.com

Summary To provide financial assistance to Native American upper-division students working on a business-related degree.

Eligibility This program is open to enrolled members of federally-recognized American Indian tribes and Alaska Native groups who can provide a Certificate of Indian Blood (CIB). Applicants must be entering their junior or senior year as a full-time student and working on a degree to prepare for a career in banking, resort management, gaming operations,

or management and administration, including accounting, finance, human resources, and information systems. They must have a GPA of 3.0 or higher. Along with their application, they must submit an essay on their personal, educational, and professional goals. Financial need is also considered in the selection process.

Financial data A stipend is awarded (amount not specified).

Duration 1 year.

Additional information This program is supported by Wells Fargo Bank.

Number awarded 1 or more each year.

Deadline April of each year.

[623]
WELLS FARGO-BBNC SCHOLARSHIP FUND

Bristol Bay Native Corporation
Attn: BBNC Education Foundation
111 West 16th Avenue, Suite 400
Anchorage, AK 99501
(907) 278-3602   Toll Free: (800) 426-3602
Fax: (907) 276-3925   E-mail: pelagiol@bbnc.net
Web: www.bbnc.net

Summary To provide financial assistance to shareholders of Bristol Bay Native Corporation (BBNC) who are majoring in banking at a college in any state.

Eligibility This program is open to BBNC shareholders who are enrolled full time as a junior or senior at a college or university in any state to prepare for a career in banking. Applicants must have a GPA of 2.0 or higher and be able to demonstrate financial need. Along with their application, they must submit an essay on how they became interested in their proposed field of study, any special circumstances they want to be considered, and their desire to work in the region or for a BBNC subsidiary company. Selection is based on the essay (35%), cumulative GPA (40%), financial need (20%), and letters of recommendation (5%).

Financial data The stipend is $5,000.

Duration 1 year.

Additional information The BBNC is 1 of 13 Alaska Native Regional Corporations created under the Alaska Native Claims Settlement Act of 1971. The funding for this program is provided equally by Wells Fargo Bank and the BBNC Education Foundation.

Deadline March of each year.

[624]
WHITE EARTH SCHOLARSHIP PROGRAM

White Earth Indian Reservation Tribal Council
Attn: Scholarship Program
P.O. Box 418
White Earth, MN 56591
(218) 983-3285, ext. 5304   Toll Free: (800) 950-3248
Fax: (218) 983-3705   E-mail: highered@whiteearth.com
Web: www.whiteearth.com/education.htm

Summary To provide financial assistance to Minnesota Chippewa Tribe members who are interested in attending college, vocational school, or graduate school in any state.

Eligibility This program is open to enrolled members of the White Earth Band of the Minnesota Chippewa Tribe who can demonstrate financial need. Applicants must be attending or planning to attend a college, university, or vocational school in any state. Graduate students in the fields of business, education, human services, law, and medicine are also eligible.

Financial data A stipend is awarded (amount not specified).

Duration 1 year; may be renewed, provided undergraduates maintain a GPA of 2.0 or higher and graduate students maintain a GPA of 3.0 or higher.

Additional information Applicants for this program must also apply for financial aid administered by their institution and any other aid for which they may be eligible (e.g., work-study, Social Security, veteran's benefits).

Number awarded Varies each year.

Deadline May of each year.

[625]
WHITE MOUNTAIN APACHE TRIBAL SCHOLARSHIPS

White Mountain Apache Tribe
Attn: Office of Higher Education
205 West Fatco Road
P.O. Box 250
Whiteriver, AZ 85941
(928) 338-5800   Fax: (928) 338-1869
E-mail: harriethosetoavit@wmat.us
Web: www.wmat.nsn.us/high_ed.html

Summary To provide financial assistance to members of the White Mountain Apache Tribe who are interested in attending college or graduate school in any state.

Eligibility This program is open to members of the White Mountain Apache Tribe who are enrolled or planning to enroll at a college, university, or vocational/technical school in any state. Applicants must be interested in working on an undergraduate or graduate degree. Along with their application, they must submit verification of tribal enrollment, a letter of admission from the college they are attending (graduate students must submit an acceptance letter from their specific graduate program), high school or college transcripts, ACT test scores, and documentation of financial need.

Financial data A stipend is awarded (amount not specified).

Duration 1 year; may be renewed.

Additional information This program is funded by the U.S. Bureau of Indian Affairs (BIA).

Number awarded Varies each year.

Deadline June of each year for fall semester, quarter, or trimester; November of each year for spring semester, quarter, or trimester; May of each year for summer session.

[626]
WICHITA HIGHER EDUCATION PROGRAM

Wichita and Affiliated Tribes
Attn: Higher Education
P.O. Box 729
Anadarko, OK 73005
(405) 247-2425, ext. 106   Fax: (405) 247-5687
Web: www.wichitatribe.com/education.htm

Summary To provide financial assistance for college to Wichita tribal members.

Eligibility This program is open to Wichita tribal members who have been accepted to a college or university as a full-time student. Applicants must submit high school and/or college transcripts, tribal identification, and a letter of intent. Preference is given to students who are eligible for federal Pell grants.

Financial data Stipends depend on the need of the recipient.

Duration 1 year; may be renewed as long as the recipient remains enrolled full time with a GPA of 2.0 or higher.

Number awarded Varies each year.

Deadline Deadline not specified.

[627]
WIEA SCHOLARSHIPS

Wisconsin Indian Education Association
Attn: Scholarship Coordinator
P.O. Box 910
Keshena, WI 54135
(715) 799-5110   Fax: (715) 799-5102
E-mail: vnuske@mitw.org
Web: www.wiea.org

Summary To provide financial assistance for undergraduate or graduate study to members of Wisconsin Indian tribes.

Eligibility This program is open to residents of Wisconsin who can provide proof of tribal enrollment. Applicants must fall into 1 of the following categories: 1) entering freshman at a 4-year college or university; 2) new or continuing student at a tribal college or technical/vocational school; 3) undergraduate student at a 4-year college or university; or 4) graduate or Ph.D. student. All applicants must be full-time students. Along with their application, they must submit a 1-page personal essay on how they will apply their education. Selection is based on that essay (25 points), letters of recommendation (10 points), and GPA (15 points if 3.5 or higher, 10 points if 3.00 to 3.49, 5 points if 2.50 to 2.99). Financial need is not considered.

Financial data The stipend is $1,000.

Duration 1 year; nonrenewable.

Additional information Eligible tribes include Menominee, Oneida, Stockbridge-Munsee, Forest County Potowatomi, Ho-Chunk, Bad River Chippewa, Lac Courte Oreilles Ojibwe, St. Croix Chippewa, Red Cliff Chippewa, Sakoagon (Mole Lake) Chippewa, Brotherton, and Lac du Flambeau Chippewa.

Number awarded 4 each year: 1 in each of the 4 categories.

Deadline March of each year.

[628]
WILLIAM K. SCHUBERT M.D. MINORITY NURSING SCHOLARSHIP PROGRAM

Cincinnati Children's Hospital Medical Center
Attn: Office of Diversity and Inclusion, MLC 9008
3333 Burnet Avenue
Cincinnati, OH 45229-3039
(513) 803-6416   Toll Free: (800) 344-2462
Fax: (513) 636-5643   TDD: (513) 636-4900
E-mail: owen.burke@cchmc.org
Web: www.cincinnatichildrens.org

Summary To provide financial assistance to Native Americans and members of other underrepresented groups interested in working on a bachelor's or master's degree in nursing to prepare for licensure in Ohio.

Eligibility   This program is open to members of groups underrepresented in the nursing profession (males, American Indians or Alaska Natives, Blacks or African Americans, Hawaiian Natives or other Pacific Islanders, Hispanics or Latinos, or Asians). Applicants must be enrolled or accepted in a professional bachelor's or master's registered nurse program at an accredited school of nursing to prepare for initial licensure in Ohio. They must have a GPA of 2.75 or higher. Along with their application, they must submit a 750-word essay that covers 1) their long-range personal, educational, and professional goals and why they chose nursing as a profession; 2) any unique qualifications, experiences, or special talents that demonstrate their creativity; and 3) if they are able to pay any college expenses through work and how their work experience has contributed to their personal development.

Financial data   The stipend is $2,750 per year.

Duration   1 year. May be renewed up to 3 additional years for students working on a bachelor's degree or 1 additional year for students working on a master's degree; renewal requires that students maintain a GPA of 2.75 or higher.

Number awarded   1 or more each year.

Deadline   April of each year.

[629]
WILLIAM RANDOLPH HEARST ENDOWMENT SCHOLARSHIPS

National Action Council for Minorities in Engineering
Attn: University Programs
440 Hamilton Avenue, Suite 302
White Plains, NY 10601-1813
(914) 539-4010   Fax: (914) 539-4032
E-mail: scholarships@nacme.org
Web: www.nacme.org/NACME_D.aspx?pageid=105

Summary   To provide financial assistance to Native American and other underrepresented college freshmen or sophomores majoring in engineering or related fields.

Eligibility   This program is open to African American, Latino, and American Indian college freshmen and sophomores who have a GPA of 2.8 or higher and have demonstrated academic excellence, leadership skills, and a commitment to science and engineering as a career. Applicants must be enrolled full time at an ABET-accredited engineering program. Fields of study include all areas of engineering as well as computer science, materials science, mathematics, operations research, or physics.

Financial data   The stipend is $2,500 per year. Funds are sent directly to the recipient's university.

Duration   Up to 4 years.

Additional information   This program was established by the William Randolph Hearst Foundation.

Number awarded   2 each year.

Deadline   April of each year.

[630]
WILLIAM ZEITLER SCHOLARSHIPS

National Action Council for Minorities in Engineering
Attn: University Programs
440 Hamilton Avenue, Suite 302
White Plains, NY 10601-1813
(914) 539-4010   Fax: (914) 539-4032
E-mail: scholarships@nacme.org
Web: www.nacme.org/NACME_D.aspx?pageid=105

Summary   To provide financial assistance to Native American and other minority college sophomores majoring in engineering or related fields.

Eligibility   This program is open to African American, Latino, and American Indian college sophomores who have a GPA of 3.0 or higher and have demonstrated academic excellence, leadership skills, and a commitment to science and engineering as a career. Applicants must be enrolled full time at an ABET-accredited engineering program. Fields of study include all areas of engineering as well as computer science, materials science, mathematics, operations research, and physics.

Financial data   The stipend is $5,000 per year. Funds are sent directly to the recipient's university.

Duration   Up to 4 years.

Number awarded   2 each year.

Deadline   April of each year.

[631]
WILSON J. BROWN MEMORIAL SCHOLARSHIP

Chickasaw Foundation
110 West 12th Street
P.O. Box 1726
Ada, OK 74821-1726
(580) 421-9030   Fax: (580) 421-9031
E-mail: ChickasawFoundation@chickasaw.net
Web: www.chickasawfoundation.org/index_20.htm

Summary   To provide financial assistance to members of the Chickasaw Nation who are working on an undergraduate degree in criminal justice or Native American studies.

Eligibility   This program is open to Chickasaw students who are currently enrolled full time at a 2- or 4-year college or university and working on an undergraduate degree in criminal justice or Native American studies. Applicants must have a GPA of 3.0 or higher. Along with their application, they must submit high school or college transcripts, 2 letters of recommendation, a copy of their Chickasaw Nation citizenship card, and a 1-page essay on their long-term goals and plans for achieving them. Financial need is not considered in the selection process.

Financial data   The stipend is $1,000.

Duration   1 year.

Number awarded   1 each year.

Deadline   August of each year.

[632]
WINNEBAGO TRIBE HIGHER EDUCATION ASSISTANCE

Winnebago Tribe of Nebraska
Attn: Education Department
100 Bluff Street
P.O. Box 687
Winnebago, NE 68071
(402) 878-3202   Fax: (402) 878-2632
E-mail: education@winnebagotribe.com
Web: www.winnebagotribe.com/winbagoFrameset=1.htm

Summary   To provide financial assistance to members of the Winnebago Tribe of Nebraska who are interested in attending college or graduate school in any state.

Eligibility   This program is open to enrolled members of the Winnebago Tribe of Nebraska who are attending or planning to attend an institution of higher education in any state. Applicants must be working on an associate, bachelor's, master's, or doctoral degree or certificate. They must submit a copy of their Certificate of Indian Blood (CIB), transcripts, and documentation of financial need.

Financial data   A stipend is awarded (amount not specified). Funding is intended only to supplement other assistance available to the student.

Duration   1 semester; may be renewed.

Number awarded   Varies each year.

Deadline   April of each year for fall, academic year, or summer school; October of each year for spring or winter.

[633]
WISCONSIN INDIAN STUDENT ASSISTANCE GRANTS

Wisconsin Higher Educational Aids Board
131 West Wilson Street, Suite 902
P.O. Box 7885
Madison, WI 53707-7885
(608) 266-0888   Fax: (608) 267-2808
E-mail: Sandy.Thomas@wisconsin.gov
Web: heab.state.wi.us/programs.html

Summary   To provide financial assistance to Native Americans in Wisconsin who are interested in attending college or graduate school in the state.

Eligibility   Wisconsin residents who have at least 25% Native American blood (of a certified tribe or band) are eligible to apply if they are able to demonstrate financial need and are interested in attending college on the undergraduate or graduate school level. Applicants must attend a Wisconsin institution (public, independent, or proprietary). They may be enrolled either full or part time.

Financial data   The stipend ranges from $250 to $1,100 per year. Additional funds are available on a matching basis from the U.S. Bureau of Indian Affairs.

Duration   Up to 5 years.

Deadline   Generally, applications can be submitted at any time.

[634]
WISCONSIN MINORITY TEACHER LOANS

Wisconsin Higher Educational Aids Board
131 West Wilson Street, Suite 902
P.O. Box 7885
Madison, WI 53707-7885
(608) 267-2212   Fax: (608) 267-2808
E-mail: Mary.Kuzdas@wisconsin.gov
Web: heab.state.wi.us/programs.html

Summary   To provide funding to Native Americans and other minorities in Wisconsin who are interested in teaching in Wisconsin school districts with large minority enrollments.

Eligibility   This program is open to residents of Wisconsin who are African Americans, Hispanic Americans, American Indians, or southeast Asians (students who were admitted to the United States after December 31, 1975 and who are a former citizen of Laos, Vietnam, or Cambodia or whose ancestor was a citizen of 1 of those countries). Applicants must be enrolled at least half time as juniors, seniors, or graduate students at an independent or public institution in the state in a program leading to teaching licensure and have a GPA of 2.5 or higher. They must agree to teach in a Wisconsin school district in which minority students constitute at least 29% of total enrollment or in a school district participating in the interdistrict pupil transfer program. Financial need is not considered in the selection process.

Financial data   forgivable loans are provided up to $2,500 per year. For each year the student teaches in an eligible school district, 25% of the loan is forgiven; if the student does not teach in an eligible district, the loan must be repaid at an interest rate of 5%.

Duration   1 year; may be renewed 1 additional year.

Additional information   Eligible students should apply through their school's financial aid office.

Number awarded   Varies each year.

Deadline   Deadline dates vary by institution; check with your school's financial aid office.

[635]
WISCONSIN MINORITY UNDERGRADUATE RETENTION GRANTS

Wisconsin Higher Educational Aids Board
131 West Wilson Street, Suite 902
P.O. Box 7885
Madison, WI 53707-7885
(608) 267-2212   Fax: (608) 267-2808
E-mail: Mary.Kuzdas@wisconsin.gov
Web: heab.state.wi.us/programs.html

Summary   To provide financial assistance to Native Americans and other minorities in Wisconsin who are currently enrolled at a college in the state.

Eligibility   This program is open to residents of Wisconsin who are African Americans, Hispanic Americans, American Indians, or southeast Asians (students who were admitted to the United States after December 31, 1975 and who are a former citizen of Laos, Vietnam, or Cambodia or whose ancestor was a citizen of 1 of those countries). Applicants must be enrolled at least half time as sophomores, juniors, seniors, or fifth-year undergraduates at a Wisconsin technical college, tribal college, or independent college or university in the state. They must be nominated by their institution and be able to demonstrate financial need.

Financial data Stipends range from $250 to $2,500 per year, depending on the need of the recipient.

Duration Up to 4 years.

Additional information The Wisconsin Higher Educational Aids Board administers this program for students at private nonprofit institutions, technical colleges, and tribal colleges. The University of Wisconsin has a similar program for students attending any of the branches of that system. Eligible students should apply through their school's financial aid office.

Number awarded Varies each year.

Deadline Deadline dates vary by institution; check with your school's financial aid office.

[636]
WISCONSIN PUBLIC SERVICE FOUNDATION BUSINESS AND TECHNOLOGY SCHOLARSHIPS

Wisconsin Public Service Corporation
Attn: Wisconsin Public Service Foundation
c/o Scholarship Assessment Service
P.O. Box 997
Appleton, WI 54912-0997
(920) 832-8322
Web: www.wisconsinpublicservice.com

Summary To provide financial assistance to Native Americans, other minorities, and women who are upper-division students and majoring in business or engineering at universities in selected states.

Eligibility This program is open to women and African American, Native American, Asian American, and Hispanic students from any state who are enrolled full time as a junior or senior with a GPA of 2.8 or higher. Applicants must be attending a college or university in Illinois, Indiana, Iowa, Michigan, Minnesota, or Wisconsin. They must be majoring in business or engineering (chemical, civil, computer, electrical, environmental, industrial, or mechanical). Along with their application, they must submit 250-word essays on 1) their educational goals and why they have chosen their major; and 2) how they have demonstrated their leadership skills.

Financial data The stipend is $1,500 per year.

Duration 1 year; may be renewed if the recipient remains in good academic standing.

Number awarded Varies each year; recently, 15 of these scholarships were awarded.

Deadline February of each year.

[637]
WISCONSIN TALENT INCENTIVE PROGRAM (TIP) GRANTS

Wisconsin Higher Educational Aids Board
131 West Wilson Street, Suite 902
P.O. Box 7885
Madison, WI 53707-7885
(608) 266-1665   Fax: (608) 267-2808
E-mail: colettem1.brown@wi.gov
Web: heab.state.wi.us/programs.html

Summary To provide financial assistance for college to Native Americans and other needy or educationally disadvantaged students in Wisconsin.

Eligibility This program is open to residents of Wisconsin entering a college or university in the state who meet the requirements of both financial need and educational disadvantage. Financial need qualifications include 1) family contribution (a dependent student whose expected parent contribution is $200 or less, an independent student with dependents whose academic year contribution is $200 or less, or an independent student with no dependents whose maximum contribution is $200 or less); 2) Temporary Assistance to Needy Families (TANF) or Wisconsin Works (W2) benefits (a dependent student whose family is receiving TANF or W2 benefits or an independent student who is receiving TANF or W2 benefits); or 3) unemployment (a dependent student whose parents are ineligible for unemployment compensation and have no current income from employment, or an independent student and spouse, if married, who are ineligible for unemployment compensation and have no current income from employment). Educational disadvantage qualifications include students who are 1) minorities (African American, Native American, Hispanic, or southeast Asian); 2) enrolled in a special academic support program due to insufficient academic preparation; 3) a first-generation college student (neither parent graduated from a 4-year college or university); 4) disabled according to the Department of Workforce Development, the Division of Vocational Rehabilitation, or a Wisconsin college or university that uses the Americans with Disabilities Act definition; 5) currently or formerly incarcerated in a correctional institution; or 6) from an environmental and academic background that deters the pursuit of educational plans. Students already in college are not eligible.

Financial data Stipends range up to $1,800 per year.

Duration 1 year; may be renewed up to 4 additional years, provided the recipient continues to be a Wisconsin resident enrolled at least half time in a degree or certificate program, makes satisfactory academic progress, demonstrates financial need, and remains enrolled continuously from semester to semester and from year to year. If recipients withdraw from school or cease to attend classes for any reason (other than medical necessity), they may not reapply.

Number awarded Varies each year.

Deadline Deadline not specified.

[638]
WOKSAPE OYATE: "WISDOM OF THE PEOPLE" DISTINGUISHED SCHOLAR AWARD

American Indian College Fund
Attn: Scholarship Department
8333 Greenwood Boulevard
Denver, CO 80221
(303) 426-8900   Toll Free: (800) 776-FUND
Fax: (303) 426-1200
E-mail: scholarships@collegefund.org
Web: www.collegefund.org/scholarships/schol_tcu.html

Summary To provide financial assistance to Native American high school seniors who are the valedictorian or salutatorian of their class and planning to attend a Tribal College or University (TCU).

Eligibility This program is open to American Indians or Alaska Natives who are graduating from high school as the valedictorian or salutatorian of their class. Applicants must be planning to enroll full time at an eligible TCU. Applications are available only online and include required essays on specified topics. Selection is based on exceptional academic achievement.

Financial data The stipend is $8,000. Funding is available only if the recipient maintains a GPA of 3.5 or higher.

Duration 1 year.

Additional information This program was established in 2006 with an endowment grant from the Lilly Foundation.

Number awarded 1 each year.

Deadline May of each year.

[639]
WOKSAPE OYATE: "WISDOM OF THE PEOPLE" KEEPERS OF THE NEXT GENERATION AWARD

American Indian College Fund
Attn: Scholarship Department
8333 Greenwood Boulevard
Denver, CO 80221
(303) 426-8900   Toll Free: (800) 776-FUND
Fax: (303) 426-1200
E-mail: scholarships@collegefund.org
Web: www.collegefund.org/scholarships/schol_tcu.html

Summary To provide financial assistance to Native Americans who are single parents and attending or planning to attend a Tribal College or University (TCU).

Eligibility This program is open to American Indians or Alaska Natives who are single parents and enrolled or planning to enroll full time at an eligible TCU. Applicants must have a GPA of 3.5 or higher. Applications are available only online and include required essays on specified topics. Selection is based on exceptional academic achievement.

Financial data The stipend is $8,000.

Duration 1 year.

Additional information This program was established in 2006 with an endowment grant from the Lilly Foundation.

Number awarded 1 each year.

Deadline May of each year.

[640]
WOODS HOLE OCEANOGRAPHIC INSTITUTION MINORITY FELLOWSHIPS

Woods Hole Oceanographic Institution
Attn: Academic Programs Office
Clark Laboratory 223, MS 31
360 Woods Hole Road
Woods Hole, MA 02543-1541
(508) 289-2219   Fax: (508) 457-2188
E-mail: education@whoi.edu
Web: www.whoi.edu/page.do?pid=36375

Summary To provide work experience to Native Americans and other minorities who are interested in preparing for careers in the marine sciences, oceanographic engineering, or marine policy.

Eligibility This program is open to ethnic minority undergraduates enrolled in U.S. colleges or universities who have completed at least 2 semesters of study and who are interested in the physical or natural sciences, mathematics, engineering, or marine policy. Applicants must be U.S. citizens or permanent residents and African American or Black; Asian American; Chicano, Mexican American, Puerto Rican or other Hispanic; or Native American, Alaska Native, or Native Hawaiian. They must be interested in participating in a program of study and research at Woods Hole Oceanographic Institution.

Financial data The stipend is $488 per week; trainees may also receive additional support for travel to Woods Hole.

Duration 10 to 12 weeks during the summer or 1 semester during the academic year; renewable.

Additional information Trainees are assigned advisers who supervise their research programs and supplementary study activities. Some traineeships involve field work or research cruises. This program is conducted with support from and in cooperation with the Center for Marine and Coastal Geology of the U.S. Geological Survey.

Number awarded 4 to 5 each year.

Deadline For a summer appointment, applications must be submitted in February of each year. For the remaining portion of the year, applications may be submitted at any time, but they must be received at least 2 months before the anticipated starting date.

[641]
WYANDOTTE NATION ADULT VOCATIONAL TRAINING PROGRAM

Wyandotte Nation of Oklahoma
Attn: Department of Education
64790 East Highway 60
Wyandotte, OK 74370
(918) 678-2297, ext. 230
Toll Free: (800) 256-2539, ext. 230
E-mail: info@wyandotte-nation.org
Web: www.wyandotte-nation.org/community/education

Summary To provide financial assistance for vocational training to members of the Wyandotte Nation of Oklahoma.

Eligibility This program is open to Wyandotte tribal members who are attending or will be attending a vocational training program. Applicants must be able to demonstrate financial need.

Financial data A stipend is awarded (amount not specified).

Duration Up to 2 years.

Number awarded Varies each year.

Deadline Deadline not specified.

[642]
WYANDOTTE NATION HIGHER EDUCATION SCHOLARSHIPS

Wyandotte Nation of Oklahoma
Attn: Department of Education
64790 East Highway 60
Wyandotte, OK 74370
(918) 678-2297, ext. 230
Toll Free: (800) 256-2539, ext. 230
E-mail: info@wyandotte-nation.org
Web: www.wyandotte-nation.org/community/education

Summary To provide financial assistance to members of the Wyandotte Nation of Oklahoma who are interested in attending college in any state to work on an undergraduate or master's degree.

Eligibility This program is open to Wyandotte tribal members who are attending or will be attending an accredited college or university in any state to work on an undergraduate or master's degree. Applicants must be able to demonstrate financial need.

Financial data The stipend is $1,500 per semester ($3,000 per year).

Duration 1 semester; may be renewed up to 7 additional semesters by undergraduates or 2 additional semesters by master's degree students.

Number awarded Varies each year.

Deadline Deadline not specified.

[643]
XEROX TECHNICAL MINORITY SCHOLARSHIP PROGRAM

Xerox Corporation
Attn: Technical Minority Scholarship Program
150 State Street, Fourth Floor
Rochester, NY 14614
(585) 422-7689   E-mail: xtmsp@rballiance.com
Web: www.xeroxstudentcareers.com

Summary To provide financial assistance to Native Americans and other minorities interested in undergraduate or graduate education in the sciences and/or engineering.

Eligibility This program is open to minorities (people of African American, Asian, Pacific Islander, Native American, Native Alaskan, or Hispanic descent) working full time on a bachelor's, master's, or doctoral degree in chemistry, computing and software systems, engineering (chemical, computer, electrical, imaging, manufacturing, mechanical, optical, or software), information management, laser optics, materials science, physics, or printing management science. Applicants must be U.S. citizens or permanent residents with a GPA of 3.0 or higher and attending a 4-year college or university.

Financial data Stipends range from $1,000 to $10,000.

Duration 1 year.

Number awarded Varies each year, recently, 125 of these scholarships were awarded.

Deadline September of each year.

[644]
YAKAMA NATION HIGHER EDUCATION SCHOLARSHIP

Yakama Nation
Department of Human Services
Attn: Higher Education Program
401 Fort Road
P.O. Box 151
Toppenish, WA 98948
(509) 865-5121, ext. 519   Toll Free: (800) 543-2802
Fax: (509) 865-6994
Web: www.yakama.us/programs.php

Summary To provide financial assistance to Yakama tribal members interested in working on an undergraduate or graduate degree at a school in any state.

Eligibility This program is open to enrolled members of the Yakama nation who are enrolled or planning to enroll in a postsecondary institution in any state. Applicants must be interested in working on an undergraduate or graduate degree on a part-time or full-time basis. Along with their application, they must submit a personal letter describing their

educational and employment goals. Financial need is considered in the selection process.

Financial data The stipend is $2,000 per year.

Duration 1 year; may be renewed.

Number awarded Varies each year.

Deadline April of each year for high school seniors; June of each year for current undergraduate and graduate students.

[645]
YAVAPAI-APACHE NATION HIGHER EDUCATION GRANTS

Yavapai-Apache Nation
Attn: Higher Education Department
2400 West Datsi Street
Camp Verde, AZ 86322
(928) 649-7111   Fax: (928) 567-6485
Web: Yavapai-apache.org/departments.html

Summary To provide financial assistance for college or graduate school to members of the Yavapai-Apache Nation.

Eligibility This program is open to members of the Yavapai-Apache Nation who are enrolled or planning to enroll at an accredited institution of higher education in any state. Applicants must be interested in working full or part time on a vocational certificate or an associate, bachelor's, master's, or doctoral degree. Along with their application, they must submit 1) an academic plan that specifies their course of study or declared major, all classes required for their program, and the expected graduation date; 2) a brief essay on their educational goals and how they will utilize their education; 3) verification of tribal enrollment; 4) copy of high school diploma or GED certificate; and 5) current transcript. Full-time students must also submit documentation of financial need.

Financial data For full-time students, the stipend depends on the need of the recipient. For part-time students, support is limited to tuition, fees, textbooks, supplies, and transportation.

Duration 1 semester; may be renewed up to 5 additional full-time semesters for students working on an associate degree or 9 additional part-time semesters for students working on a bachelor's degree. Renewal requires the recipient to maintain a GPA of 2.0 or higher.

Number awarded Varies each year.

Deadline June of each year for fall and academic year; September of each year for spring only; March of each year for summer; August of each year for vocational/technical school.

[646]
YOUNG NATIVE WRITERS ESSAY CONTEST

Holland & Knight Charitable Foundation, Inc.
201 North Franklin Street, 11th Floor
P.O. Box 2877
Tampa, FL 33601-2877
(813) 227-8500   Toll Free: (866) HK-CARES
E-mail: indian@hklaw.com
Web: nativewriters.hklaw.com

Summary To recognize and reward, with college scholarships, Native American high school students who submit outstanding essays on issues impacting their tribal communities.

Eligibility This competition is open to Native American high school students in grades 9-12 who have a significant and current relationship with a tribal community. Applicants must submit a 1,200-word essay in which they describe a crucial issue confronting their tribal community today and how they hope to help their tribal community respond to that challenge and improve its future. Selection is based on 1) evidence of relevant reading and thoughtful use of resource materials; 2) treatment of the assigned theme; 3) clear and effective language, mechanics, and grammar; and 4) a coherent plan of organization.

Financial data First-place winners receive an all-expense paid trip to Washington, D.C. to visit the National Museum of the American Indian and other prominent sites. They also receive scholarships of $2,500 that are paid to their colleges or universities after they graduate from high school and upon receipt of proof of registration.

Duration The competition is held annually.

Additional information This program, which began in 2006, is sponsored by the National Museum of the American Indian.

Number awarded 5 each year.

Deadline March of each year.

[647]
YUROK TRIBE ADULT VOCATIONAL TRAINING PROGRAM

Yurok Tribe
Attn: Education Department
190 Klamath Boulevard
P.O. Box 1027
Klamath, CA 95548
(707) 482-1350   Fax: (707) 482-0760
Web: www.yuroktribe.org

Summary To provide financial assistance for vocational school to members of the Yurok Tribe.

Eligibility This program is open to enrolled members of the Yurok Tribe who are interested in attending an accredited vocational training program or school in any state. Applicants must submit a detailed budget, information on the length of the training program, evidence that they have applied for federal financial aid using the FAFSA, and an acceptance letter from the training program or school. They may be of any age.

Financial data The grant is $5,000.

Duration This is a 1-time grant.

Number awarded Varies each year.

Deadline October of each year.

[648]
YUROK TRIBE HIGHER EDUCATION PROGRAM

Yurok Tribe
Attn: Education Department
190 Klamath Boulevard
P.O. Box 1027
Klamath, CA 95548
(707) 482-1350   Fax: (707) 482-0760
Web: www.yuroktribe.org

Summary To provide financial assistance for college or graduate school to members of the Yurok Tribe.

Eligibility This program is open to enrolled members of the Yurok Tribe who are attending or planning to attend an accredited college or university in any state. Applicants must be interested in working full or part time on an undergraduate or graduate degree. They must apply for federal financial aid using the FAFSA. Awards are granted on a first-come, first-served basis.

Financial data A stipend is awarded (amount not specified). Part-time students are funded at half the level of full-time students.

Duration 1 year; may be renewed as long as recipients remain in good standing with their college or university and maintain a GPA of 2.0 or higher.

Number awarded Varies each year.

Deadline Applications may be submitted at any time.

[649]
ZUNI HIGHER EDUCATION SCHOLARSHIPS

Pueblo of Zuni
Attn: Education and Career Development Center
P.O. Box 339
Zuni, NM 87327
(505) 782-7178   Fax: (505) 782-7223
E-mail: jlucio@ashiwi.org
Web: www.ashiwi.org/highered/higheredhome.htm

Summary To provide financial assistance for college or graduate school in any state to members of the Pueblo of Zuni.

Eligibility This program is open to enrolled members of the Pueblo of Zuni who are high school seniors or graduates. Applicants must have earned a GPA of 2.0 or higher and be interested in working on an associate, bachelor's, or graduate degree as a full-time student at a college or university in any state. They must have also applied for a federal Pell Grant.

Financial data The amount awarded depends on the need of the recipient, up to $5,000 per year.

Duration 1 year; may be renewed if the recipient maintains a GPA of 2.0 or higher.

Number awarded Varies each year.

Deadline June of each year for the fall semester; October of each year for the spring semester; April of each year for the summer session.

Graduate Students

Listed alphabetically by program title and described in detail here are 528 fellowships, grants, awards, internships, and other sources of "free money" set aside for incoming, continuing, or returning graduate students of American Indian, Native Alaskan (including Eskimos and Aleuts), and Native Hawaiian descent who are working on a master's. doctoral, or professional degree. This funding is available to support study, training, research, and/or creative activities in the United States.

[650]
ACCENTURE GRADUATE FELLOWSHIPS

American Indian Graduate Center
Attn: Executive Director
4520 Montgomery Boulevard, N.E., Suite 1-B
Albuquerque, NM 87109-1291
(505) 881-4584   Toll Free: (800) 628-1920
Fax: (505) 884-0427   E-mail: aigc@aigc.com
Web: www.aigc.com

Summary   To provide financial assistance to Native American students interested in working on a graduate or professional degree in fields related to engineering, high technology, or business.

Eligibility   This program is open to enrolled members of federally-recognized American Indian tribes and Alaska Native groups who can provide a Certificate of Indian Blood (CIB). Applicants must be entering their first year as a full-time student in a graduate or professional school in the United States and have a GPA of 3.25 or higher. They must be planning to work on a master's, doctoral, or professional degree in engineering, computer science, operations management, finance, marketing, management, or other business-oriented fields. Along with their application, they must submit an essay describing their character, personal merit, and commitment to community and American Indian or Alaska Native heritage. Selection is based on academic excellence, demonstrated leadership, and commitment to preserving American Indian culture and communities.

Financial data   The stipend is $7,500 per year.

Duration   2 years.

Additional information   This program, established in 2005, is supported by Accenture.

Number awarded   2 each year.

Deadline   May of each year.

[651]
ACOUSTICAL SOCIETY OF AMERICA MINORITY FELLOWSHIP

Acoustical Society of America
Attn: Office Manager
2 Huntington Quadrangle, Suite 1NO1
Melville, NY 11747-4502
(516) 576-2360   Fax: (516) 576-2377
E-mail: asa@aip.org
Web: asa.aip.org/fellowships.html

Summary   To provide financial assistance to Native Americans and other underrepresented minorities who are working on a graduate degree involving acoustics.

Eligibility   This program is open to U.S. and Canadian citizens and permanent residents who are members of a minority group that is underrepresented in the sciences (Hispanic, African American, or Native American). Applicants must be enrolled in or accepted to a graduate degree program as a full-time student. Their program of study may be in any field of pure or applied science and engineering directly related to acoustics, including acoustical oceanography, architectural acoustics, animal bioacoustics, biomedical ultrasound and bioresponse to vibration, engineering acoustics, musical acoustics, noise, physical acoustics, psychological acoustics, physiological acoustics, signal processing in acoustics, speech communication, structural acoustics and vibration, and underwater acoustics. Along with their application, student must submit a statement on why they are enrolled in their present academic program, including how they intend to use their graduate education to develop a career and how the study of acoustics is relevant to their career objectives.

Financial data   The stipend is $20,000 per year. The sponsor strongly encourages the host educational institution to waive all tuition costs and assessed fees. Fellows also receive $1,000 for travel to attend a national meeting of the sponsor.

Duration   1 year; may be renewed for 1 additional year if the recipient is making normal progress toward a degree and is enrolled full time.

Additional information   This program was established in 1992.

Number awarded   1 each year.

Deadline   April of each year.

[652]
ADLER POLLOCK & SHEEHAN DIVERSITY SCHOLARSHIP

Adler Pollock & Sheehan P.C.
Attn: Diversity Committee Chair
175 Federal Street
Boston, MA 02110-2210
(617) 482-0600   Fax: (617) 482-0604
E-mail: Diversitycomm@apslaw.com
Web: www.apslaw.com/firm-diversity.html

Summary   To provide financial assistance to Native American and other residents of Massachusetts and Rhode Island who are members of diverse groups and plan to attend law school in any state.

Eligibility   This program is open to residents of Massachusetts and Rhode Island who are members of a diverse group, including African American, American Indian, Hispanic, Asian/Pacific Islander, gay/lesbian, or other minority group. Applicants must be entering their first year at an ABA-accredited law school anywhere in the United States. They must be able to demonstrate academic achievement, a desire to work and reside in Massachusetts or Rhode Island after graduation, a demonstrated commitment to the community, a vision of contributions to the profession and community after graduation, and financial need.

Financial data   The stipend is $10,000.

Duration   1 year.

Number awarded   1 each year.

Deadline   May of each year.

[653]
ADRIENNE M. AND CHARLES SHELBY ROOKS FELLOWSHIP FOR RACIAL AND ETHNIC THEOLOGICAL STUDENTS

United Church of Christ
Attn: Local Church Ministries
700 Prospect Avenue East
Cleveland, OH 44115-1100
(216) 736-3865   Toll Free: (866) 822-8224, ext. 3848
Fax: (216) 736-3783   E-mail: lcm@ucc.org
Web: www.ucc.org/seminarians/ucc-scholarships-for.html

Summary   To provide financial assistance to Native American and other minority students who are either enrolled at an accredited seminary preparing for a career of service in the United Church of Christ (UCC) or working on a doctoral degree in the field of religion.

Eligibility This program is open to members of underrepresented ethnic groups (African American, Hispanic American, Asian American, Native American Indian, or Pacific Islander) who have been a member of a UCC congregation for at least 1 year. Applicants must be either 1) enrolled in an accredited school of theology in the United States or Canada and working on an M.Div. degree with the intent of becoming a pastor or teacher within the UCC, or 2) doctoral (Ph.D., Th.D., or Ed.D.) students within a field related to religious studies. Seminary students must have a GPA in all postsecondary work of 3.0 or higher and must have begun the in-care process; preference is given to students who have demonstrated leadership (through a history of service to the church) and scholarship (through exceptional academic performance). For doctoral students, preference is given to applicants who have demonstrated academic excellence, teaching effectiveness, and commitment to the UCC and who intend to become professors in colleges, seminaries, or graduate schools.

Financial data Grants range from $500 to $5,000 per year.

Duration 1 year; may be renewed.

Number awarded Varies each year; recently, 11 of these scholarships, including 8 for M.Div. students and 3 for doctoral students, were awarded.

Deadline February of each year.

[654]
ADVANCED DEGREE SCHOLARSHIP FUND OF THE SEMINOLE NATION JUDGMENT FUND

Seminole Nation of Oklahoma
Attn: Judgment Fund Office
2007 West Wrangler Boulevard
Seminole, OK 74868
(405) 382-0549   Toll Free: (877) 382-0549
Fax: (405) 382-0571
Web: www.seminolenation.com/services_judgmentfund.htm

Summary To provide financial assistance for graduate study to members of the Seminole Nation of Oklahoma.

Eligibility This program is open to enrolled members of the Seminole Nation who are descendants of a member of the Seminole Nation as it existed in Florida on September 18, 1823. Applicants must be attending or planning to attend a college or university to work on a master's degree, Ph.D., J.D., medical degree, pharmacist degree, or other advanced degree. Along with their application, they must submit copies of their tribal membership card, Certificate of Indian Blood (CIB), class schedule and grades from previous classes, and official college transcript.

Financial data The stipend for full-time students is $1,700 per year. Part-time students receive the actual cost of tuition, books, and fees, to a maximum of $250 per semester. Students attending summer school receive $500 per semester. The total of all advanced degree awards to an applicant may not exceed $5,100.

Duration 1 year; may be renewed 2 additional years, provided the recipient maintains a GPA of 2.0 or higher.

Additional information The General Council of the Seminole Nation of Oklahoma approved a plan for use of the Judgment Fund Award in 1990. This aspect of the program went into effect in September of 1991.

Number awarded Varies each year.

Deadline November of each year for fall semester; April of each year for spring semester.

[655]
AGING RESEARCH DISSERTATION AWARDS TO INCREASE DIVERSITY

National Institute on Aging
Attn: Office of Extramural Affairs
7201 Wisconsin Avenue, Suite 2C-218
Bethesda, MD 20814
(301) 402-7713   Fax: (301) 402-2945
TDD: (301) 451-0088
E-mail: michael-david.kerns@nih.hhs.gov
Web: www.nia.nih.gov

Summary To provide financial assistance to Native Americans and other underrepresented doctoral candidates who wish to conduct research on aging.

Eligibility This program is open to doctoral candidates conducting research on a dissertation with an aging-related focus, including the 4 extramural programs within the National Institute on Aging (NIA): the biology of aging program, the behavioral and social research on aging program, the neuroscience and neuropsychology of aging program, and the geriatrics and clinical gerontology program. Applicants must be 1) Native Americans and members of other ethnic or racial groups underrepresented in biomedical or behavioral research; 2) individuals with disabilities; or 3) individuals from socially, culturally, economically, or educationally disadvantaged backgrounds that have inhibited their ability to prepare for a career in health-related research. They must be U.S. citizens, nationals, or permanent residents.

Financial data Grants provide $21,180 per year for stipend and up to $15,000 for additional expenses. No funds may be used to pay for tuition or fees associated with completion of doctoral studies. The institution may receive up to 8% of direct costs as facilities and administrative costs per year.

Duration Up to 2 years.

Number awarded Up to 5 each year.

Deadline Letters of intent must be submitted by February, June, or October of each year.

[656]
ALASKA LIBRARY ASSOCIATION GRADUATE LIBRARY STUDIES SCHOLARSHIP

Alaska Library Association
Attn: Scholarship Committee
c/o Alaska State Library
P.O. Box 110571
Juneau, AK 99811-0571
(907) 465-2458   Fax: (907) 465-2665
E-mail: aja_razumny@alaska.gov
Web: www.akla.org/scholarships/index.html

Summary To provide financial assistance to Alaska residents (particularly those with Alaska Native ethnicity) who are interested in working on a graduate library degree at a school in any state and, upon graduation, working in a library in Alaska.

Eligibility This program is open to Alaska residents who have earned a bachelor's degree or higher from an accredited college or university. Applicants must be eligible for acceptance or currently enrolled in an accredited graduate degree program in any state in library and information science; full-time students during the academic year, semester, or quarter for which the scholarship is awarded; and willing to make a commitment to work in an Alaska library for at least 1 year after graduation as a paid employee or volunteer. Preference is given to applicants meeting the federal definition of Alaska Native ethnicity. Selection is based on financial need, demonstrated scholastic ability and writing skills, an essay on professional goals and objectives, and 3 letters of recommendation (at least 1 of which must be from a librarian).

Financial data The stipend is $3,000.

Duration 1 year.

Number awarded 1 each year.

Deadline January of each year.

[657]
ALEUT FOUNDATION GRADUATE SCHOLARSHIPS

The Aleut Corporation
Attn: Aleut Foundation
703 West Tudor Road, Suite 102
Anchorage, AK 99503-6650
(907) 646-1929   Toll Free: (800) 232-4882
Fax: (907) 646-1949   E-mail: taf@thealeutfoundation.org
Web: www.thealeutfoundation.org/ScholarshipGuide.aspx

Summary To provide financial assistance to Native Alaskans who are shareholders of The Aleut Corporation or their descendants and plan to attend graduate school in any state.

Eligibility This program is open to Native Alaskans who are original enrollees or descendants of original enrollees of The Aleut Corporation (TAC). Applicants must be enrolled for at least 6 credit hours in a graduate degree program. They must have a GPA of 3.0 or higher. Along with their application, they must include a letter of intent, up to 500 words in length, that describes their educational goals and objectives and their expected graduation date.

Financial data The stipend is $3,000 per year.

Duration 1 year; may be renewed.

Additional information The Aleut Corporation is 1 of 13 Alaska Native Regional Corporations created under the Alaska Native Claims Settlement Act of 1971. The foundation established this program in 2008.

Number awarded Varies each year.

Deadline June of each year for annual scholarships; November of each year for spring scholarships; April of each year for summer school.

[658]
ALEUT FOUNDATION PART-TIME SCHOLARSHIPS

The Aleut Corporation
Attn: Aleut Foundation
703 West Tudor Road, Suite 102
Anchorage, AK 99503-6650
(907) 646-1929   Toll Free: (800) 232-4882
Fax: (907) 646-1949   E-mail: taf@thealeutfoundation.org
Web: www.thealeutfoundation.org/ScholarshipGuide.aspx

Summary To provide financial assistance for college or graduate school to Native Alaskans who are shareholders of

The Aleut Corporation or their descendants and are enrolled part time.

Eligibility This program is open to Native Alaskans who are original enrollees or descendants of original enrollees of The Aleut Corporation (TAC). Applicants must be enrolled in an associate, bachelor's, or higher degree program as a part-time student (at least 3 credit hours). They must have a GPA of 2.0 or higher. Along with their application, they must include a letter of intent, up to 500 words in length, that describes their educational goals and objectives and their expected graduation date.

Financial data The stipend depends on the number of credit hours in the undergraduate or graduate program, to a maximum of $1,200 per year.

Duration 1 year.

Additional information The Aleut Corporation is 1 of 13 Alaska Native Regional Corporations created under the Alaska Native Claims Settlement Act of 1971. The foundation began awarding scholarships in 1987.

Number awarded Varies each year; recently, 2 of these scholarships were awarded.

Deadline June of each year for annual scholarships; November of each year for spring scholarships; April of each year for summer school.

[659]
AMA FOUNDATION MINORITY SCHOLARS AWARDS

American Medical Association
Attn: AMA Foundation
515 North State Street
Chicago, IL 60610
(312) 464-4193   Fax: (312) 464-4142
E-mail: amafoundation@ama-assn.org
Web: www.ama-assn.org

Summary To provide financial assistance to Native Americans and other underrepresented minorities who are enrolled in medical school.

Eligibility This program is open to first- and second-year medical students who are members of the following minority groups: African American/Black, American Indian, Native Hawaiian, Alaska Native, or Hispanic/Latino. Only nominations are accepted. Each medical school is invited to submit 2 nominees. U.S. citizenship or permanent resident status is required.

Financial data The stipend is $10,000.

Duration 1 year.

Additional information This program is offered by the AMA Foundation of the American Medical Association in collaboration with the Minority Affairs Consortium (MAC) and with support from the Pfizer Medical Humanities Initiative.

Number awarded 12 each year.

Deadline April of each year.

[660]
AMERICAN ADVERTISING FEDERATION FOURTH DISTRICT MOSAIC SCHOLARSHIP

American Advertising Federation-District 4
c/o Tami L. Grimes, Education Chair
4712 Southwood Lane
Lakeland, FL 33813
(863) 648-5392   E-mail: tamilgrimes@yahoo.com
Web: www.4aaf.com/scholarships.cfm

Summary   To provide financial assistance to Native American and other minority undergraduate and graduate students from any state who are enrolled at colleges and universities in Florida and interested in entering the field of advertising.

Eligibility   This program is open to undergraduate and graduate students from any state enrolled at accredited colleges and universities in Florida who are U.S. citizens or permanent residents of African, African American, Hispanic, Hispanic American, Indian, Native American, Asian, Asian American, or Pacific Islander descent. Applicants must be working on a bachelor's or master's degree in advertising, marketing, communications, public relations, art, graphic arts, or a related field. They must have an overall GPA of 3.0 or higher. Along with their application, they must submit a 250-word essay on why multiculturalism, diversity, and inclusion are important in the advertising, marketing, and communications industry today. Preference is given to members of the American Advertising Federation.

Financial data   The stipend is $1,000.

Duration   1 year.

Number awarded   1 or more each year.

Deadline   May of each year.

[661]
AMERICAN BAR ASSOCIATION LEGAL OPPORTUNITY SCHOLARSHIP

American Bar Association
Attn: Fund for Justice and Education
321 North Clark Street
Chicago, IL 60654-7598
(312) 988-5415   Fax: (312) 988-6392
E-mail: legalosf@staff.abanet.org
Web: www.abanet.org/fje/losfpage.html

Summary   To provide financial assistance to Native Americans and other minority students who are interested in attending law school.

Eligibility   This program is open to racial and ethnic minority college graduates who are interested in attending an ABA-accredited law school. Only students beginning law school may apply; students who have completed 1 or more semesters of law school are not eligible. Applicants must have a cumulative GPA of 2.5 or higher and be citizens or permanent residents of the United States. Along with their application, they must submit a 1,000-word statement describing their personal and family background, community service activities, and other connections to their racial and ethnic minority community. Financial need is also considered in the selection process.

Financial data   The stipend is $5,000 per year.

Duration   1 year; may be renewed for 2 additional years if satisfactory performance in law school has been achieved.

Additional information   This program began in the 2000-01 academic year.

Number awarded   Approximately 20 each year.

Deadline   February of each year.

[662]
AMERICAN DIETETIC ASSOCIATION GRADUATE SCHOLARSHIPS

American Dietetic Association
Attn: Commission on Accreditation for Dietetics Education
120 South Riverside Plaza, Suite 2000
Chicago, IL 60606-6995
(312) 899-0040   Toll Free: (800) 877-1600, ext. 5400
Fax: (312) 899-4817   E-mail: education@eatright.org
Web: www.eatright.org/CADE/content.aspx?id=7934

Summary   To provide financial assistance to Native Americans and other graduate student members of the American Dietetic Association (ADA).

Eligibility   This program is open to ADA members who are enrolled or planning to enroll in a master's or doctoral degree program in dietetics. Applicants who are currently completing a dietetic internship or preprofessional practice program that is combined with a graduate program may also apply. The graduate scholarships are available only to U.S. citizens and permanent residents. Applicants should intend to practice in the field of dietetics. Some scholarships require specific areas of study (e.g., public health nutrition, food service administration) and status as a registered dietitian. Others may require membership in a specific dietetic practice group, residency in a specific state, or underrepresented minority group status. The same application form can be used for all categories.

Financial data   Stipends range from $500 to $3,000; most are for $1,000.

Duration   1 year.

Number awarded   Varies each year, depending upon the funds available; recently, the sponsoring organization awarded 222 scholarships for all its programs.

Deadline   February of each year.

[663]
AMERICAN INDIAN EDUCATION FOUNDATION GRADUATE SCHOLARSHIPS

American Indian Education Foundation
2401 Eglin Street
Rapid City, SD 57703
Toll Free: (866) 866-8642   E-mail: mlee@nrc1.org
Web: www.nrcprograms.org

Summary   To provide financial assistance for graduate school to American Indian, Alaskan Native, and Native Hawaiian students.

Eligibility   This program is open to students of Native American, Alaskan Native, or Native Hawaiian descent who are currently enrolled in between 6 and 18 credits in a master's or doctoral degree program. Students enrolled in online courses or at the ABD (all but dissertation) level are not eligible. Applicants should have a GPA between 2.5 and 3.5. Along with their application, they must submit a 500-word statement that includes why they should receive this scholarship, their most significant accomplishments and contributions, the impact of their selected studies or research, their financial need, and their tribal affiliation.

Financial data   The stipend ranges from $1,000 to $2,000 per year. Funds are paid directly to the recipient's institution.

Duration   1 year; may be renewed.

Number awarded   Varies each year.

Deadline   April of each year.

[664]
AMERICAN INDIAN GRADUATE CENTER FELLOWSHIPS

American Indian Graduate Center
Attn: Executive Director
4520 Montgomery Boulevard, N.E., Suite 1-B
Albuquerque, NM 87109-1291
(505) 881-4584   Toll Free: (800) 628-1920
Fax: (505) 884-0427   E-mail: aigc@aigc.com
Web: www.aigc.com/02scholarships/aigc/fellowship.htm

Summary   To provide financial assistance to Native American students interested in attending graduate school.

Eligibility   This program is open to enrolled members of federally-recognized American Indian tribes and Alaska Native groups and other students who can document one-fourth degree federally-recognized Indian blood. Applicants must be enrolled as full-time students in a graduate or professional school in the United States working on a master's, doctoral, or professional degree in any field. Along with their application, they must submit a 500-word essay on their extracurricular activities as they relate to American Indian programs at their institution, volunteer and community work as related to American Indian communities, tribal and community involvement, and plans to make positive changes in the American Indian community with their college education. Financial need is also considered in the selection process.

Financial data   Stipends range from $1,000 to $5,000 per academic year, depending on the availability of funds and the recipient's unmet financial need.

Duration   1 year; may be renewed up to 1 additional year for master's degree students; up to 2 additional years for M.F.A. students; up to 3 additional years for doctoral degree students; up to 3 additional years for medicine, osteopathic medicine, dentistry, chiropractic, or veterinary degree students; or up to 2 additional years for law degree students.

Additional information   This program is funded by the U.S. Bureau of Indian Affairs. The application fee is $15. Since this a supplemental program, students must apply in a timely manner for federal financial aid and campus-based aid at the college they are attending to be considered for this program. Failure to apply will disqualify an applicant.

Number awarded   Approximately 350 each year; a total of $1.2 million is available for this program annually.

Deadline   May of each year.

[665]
AMERICAN INDIAN LAW REVIEW WRITING COMPETITION

American Indian Law Review
Attn: Writing Competition Editor
University of Oklahoma Law Center
Andrew M. Coats Hall
300 Timberdell Road
Norman, OK 73019-0701
(405) 325-2840   Fax: (405) 325-6282
E-mail: mwaters@ou.edu
Web: adams.law.ou.edu/ailr/competition.cfm

Summary   To recognize and reward outstanding unpublished papers written by Native American and other law students on American Indian law.

Eligibility   This competition is open to students at accredited law schools in the United States or Canada. They may submit an unpublished paper (from 20 to 50 pages in length) on any issue concerning American Indian law (although topics recently published in the *American Indian Law Review* are not encouraged). Selection is based on originality and timeliness of topic, knowledge and use of applicable legal principles, proper and articulate analysis of the issues, use of authorities, extent of research, logic and reasoning in analysis, ingenuity and ability to argue by analogy, clarity and organization, correctness of format and citations, grammar and writing style, and strength and logic of conclusions.

Financial data   First prize is $1,000 and publication of the paper in the *American Indian Law Review*. Second prize is $500. Third prize is $250.

Duration   The competition is held annually.

Number awarded   3 each year.

Deadline   January of each year.

[666]
AMERICAN INDIAN LIBRARY ASSOCIATION LIBRARY SCHOOL SCHOLARSHIP

American Indian Library Association
c/o Holly Tomren, Scholarship Review Board Chair
University of California at Irvine Libraries, Cataloging
  Department
326 Science Library
P.O. Box 19557
Irvine, CA 92623-9557
(949) 824-3837   Fax: (949) 824-2059
E-mail: htomren@uci.edu
Web: www.ailanet.org/activities/lss.htm

Summary   To provide financial assistance to American Indians interested in working on a master's degree in library and/or information science.

Eligibility   This program is open to enrolled members of a federally-recognized American Indian tribe who live and work in the American Indian community. Applicants must have been admitted to a master's degree program in library and/or information science accredited by the American Library Association. They must be able to demonstrate sustained involvement in the American Indian community and sustained commitment to American Indian concerns and initiatives. Preference is give to applicants who are employed in a tribal library or who are currently employed in a library serving American

Indian populations. Financial need is considered in the selection process.

Financial data   The stipend is $2,000.

Duration   1 year; may be renewed 1 additional year.

Additional information   The first scholarship was awarded in 2002.

Number awarded   1 each year.

Deadline   April of each year.

[667]
AMERICAN INDIAN SCHOLARSHIPS

Daughters of the American Revolution-National Society
Attn: Committee Services Office, Scholarships
1776 D Street, N.W.
Washington, DC 20006-5303
(202) 628-1776
Web: www.dar.org/natsociety/edout_scholar.cfm

Summary   To provide supplementary financial assistance to Native American students who are interested in working on an undergraduate or graduate degree.

Eligibility   This program is open to Native Americans of any age, any tribe, in any state who are enrolled or planning to enroll in a college, university, or vocational school. Applicants must have a GPA of 2.75 or higher. Graduate students are eligible, but undergraduate students receive preference. Selection is based on academic achievement and financial need.

Financial data   The stipend is $1,000. The funds are paid directly to the recipient's college.

Duration   This is a 1-time award.

Number awarded   1 each year.

Deadline   March of each year.

[668]
AMERICAN INDIAN SCIENCE AND ENGINEERING SOCIETY INTERNSHIP PROGRAM

American Indian Science and Engineering Society
Attn: Program Officer
2305 Renard, S.E., Suite 200
P.O. Box 9828
Albuquerque, NM 87119-9828
(505) 765-1052, ext. 105   Fax: (505) 765-5608
E-mail: tina@aises.org
Web: www.aises.org

Summary   To provide summer work experience with federal agencies or other partner organizations to American Indian and Alaska Native college students who are members of the American Indian Science and Engineering Society (AISES).

Eligibility   This program is open to AISES members who are full-time college or university sophomores, juniors, seniors, or graduate students with a GPA of 3.0 or higher. Applicants must be American Indians or Alaska Natives interested in working at selected sites with a partner organization. They must submit an application that includes an essay on their reasons for participating in the program, how it relates to their academic and career goals, what makes them a strong candidate for the program, what they hope to learn and gain as a result, and their leadership skills and experience. U.S. citizenship is required for most positions, although permanent residents may be eligible at some agencies.

Financial data   Interns receive a weekly stipend, dormitory lodging, round-trip airfare or mileage to the internship site, and an allowance for local transportation.

Duration   10 weeks during the summer.

Additional information   Recently, internships were available at the Arctic Slope Regional Corporation Federal Holding Company (in Greenbelt, Maryland), AMERIND Rick Management Corporation (in Santa Ana Pueblo, New Mexico), NASA Goddard Space Flight Center (in Greenbelt, Maryland), NASA Glenn Research Center (in Cleveland, Ohio), the Bonneville Power Administration (in Portland, Oregon), and the U.S. Department of Veterans Affairs (in Washington, D.C. and other locations).

Number awarded   Varies each year.

Deadline   February of each year.

[669]
AMERICAN POLITICAL SCIENCE ASSOCIATION MINORITY FELLOWS PROGRAM

American Political Science Association
Attn: APSA Minority Fellows Program
1527 New Hampshire Avenue, N.W.
Washington, DC 20036-1206
(202) 483-2512, ext. 123   Fax: (202) 483-2657
E-mail: apsa@apsanet.org
Web: www.apsanet.org/content_3284.cfm

Summary   To provide financial assistance to Native Americans and other underrepresented minorities interested in working on a doctoral degree in political science.

Eligibility   This program is open to African Americans, Asian Pacific Americans, Latino(a)s, and Native Americans who are in their senior year at a college or university or currently enrolled in a master's degree program. Applicants must be planning to enroll in a doctoral program in political science to prepare for a career in teaching and research. They must be U.S. citizens and able to demonstrate financial need. Along with their application, they must submit a 500-word personal statement that includes why they are interested in attending graduate school in political science, what specific fields within the discipline they plan to study, and how they intend to contribute to research within the discipline. Selection is based on interest in teaching and potential for research in political science.

Financial data   The stipend is $2,000 per year.

Duration   2 years.

Additional information   In addition to the fellows who receive stipends from this program, students who are selected as fellows without stipend are recommended for admission and financial support to every doctoral political science program in the country. This program was established in 1969.

Number awarded   Up to 12 fellows receive stipends each year.

Deadline   October of each year.

[670]
AMERICAN SPEECH-LANGUAGE-HEARING FOUNDATION SCHOLARSHIP FOR MINORITY STUDENTS

American Speech-Language-Hearing Foundation
Attn: Program Assistant
2200 Research Boulevard
Rockville, MD 20850-3289
(301) 296-8703   Toll Free: (800) 498-2071, ext. 8703
E-mail: foundationprograms@asha.org
Web: www.ashfoundation.org/grants/GraduateScholarships

Summary To provide financial assistance to Native American and other minority graduate students in communication sciences and disorders programs.

Eligibility This program is open to full-time graduate students who are enrolled in communication sciences and disorders programs, with preference given to U.S. citizens who are members of a racial or ethnic minority group. Applicants must submit an essay, up to 5 pages in length, on a topic that relates to the future of leadership in the discipline. Selection is based on academic promise and outstanding academic achievement.

Financial data The stipend ranges from $2,000 to $4,000. Funds must be used for educational support (e.g., tuition, books, school living expenses), not for personal or conference travel.

Duration 1 year.

Number awarded 1 each year.

Deadline June of each year.

[671]
AMY LOUISE HUNTER-WILSON, M.D. MEMORIAL SCHOLARSHIP

Wisconsin Medical Society
Attn: Executive Director, Wisconsin Medical Society
  Foundation
330 East Lakeside Street
P.O. Box 1109
Madison, WI 53701-1109
(608) 442-3722   Toll Free: (866) 442-3800, ext. 3722
Fax: (608) 442-3851   E-mail: eileen.wilson@wismed.org
Web: www.wisconsinmedicalsociety.org

Summary To provide financial assistance to American Indians interested in working on a degree in medicine, nursing, or allied health care.

Eligibility This program is open to members of federally-recognized American Indian tribes who are 1) full-time students enrolled in a health career program at an accredited institution, 2) adults returning to school in an allied health field, and 3) adults working in a non-professional health-related field returning for a professional license or degree. Applicants must be working on a degree or advanced training as a doctor of medicine, nurse, physician assistant, technician, or other health-related professional. Along with their application, they must submit a personal statement of 1 to 2 pages on their family background, achievements, current higher educational status, career goals, and financial need. Preference is given to residents of Wisconsin who are students at educational institutions in the state. U.S. citizenship is required. Selection is based on financial need, academic achievement, personal qualities and strengths, and letters of recommendation.

Financial data Stipends range from $1,000 to $4,000.

Duration 1 year.

Number awarded Varies each year.

Deadline January of each year.

[672]
ANAPATA DIVERSITY SCHOLARSHIP CONTEST

Ms. JD
Attn: Executive Director
1659 Lyman Place
Los Angeles, CA 90027
(917) 446-8991   E-mail: kornberg@ms-jd.org
Web: ms-jd.org/anapata-student-scholarship

Summary To provide financial assistance to Native American law students and members of other groups traditionally underrepresented in the legal profession.

Eligibility This program is open to students currently enrolled at ABA-approved law schools in the United States. Members of groups traditionally underrepresented in the legal profession are especially encouraged to apply. They must submit a resume, transcript, personal introduction paragraph, 2 recommendations, and a 750-word essay demonstrating their personal philosophy regarding diversity in the legal profession. Selection is based on academic achievement, leadership ability, writing and interpersonal skills, and interest in promoting diversity in the legal profession.

Financial data The stipend is $1,000.

Duration 1 year.

Additional information This program is offered by Ms. JD in partnership with Anapata, Inc.

Number awarded 1 or more each year.

Deadline February of each year.

[673]
ANDREW GRONHOLDT SCHOLARSHIP AWARD

The Aleut Corporation
Attn: Aleut Foundation
703 West Tudor Road, Suite 102
Anchorage, AK 99503-6650
(907) 646-1929   Toll Free: (800) 232-4882
Fax: (907) 646-1949   E-mail: taf@thealeutfoundation.org
Web: www.thealeutfoundation.org/ScholarshipGuide.aspx

Summary To provide financial assistance to Native Alaskans who are shareholders of The Aleut Corporation or their descendants and working on a degree in the arts at a school in any state.

Eligibility This program is open to Native Alaskans who are original enrollees or descendants of original enrollees of The Aleut Corporation (TAC). Applicants must have completed at least 1 year of a bachelor's, 2- or 4-year vocational, or master's degree in the arts at a school in any state. They must be enrolled full time and have a GPA of 3.0 or higher. Along with their application, they must include a letter of intent, up to 500 words in length, that describes their educational goals and objectives and their expected graduation date.

Financial data A stipend is awarded (amount not specified).

Duration 1 year.

Additional information The Aleut Corporation is 1 of 13 Alaska Native Regional Corporations created under the Alaska Native Claims Settlement Act of 1971.

Number awarded 1 each year.

Deadline June of each year.

[674]
ANDREW W. MELLON ADVANCED TRAINING PROGRAM IN OBJECT AND TEXTILE CONSERVATION INTERNSHIPS

National Museum of the American Indian
Attn: Head of Conservation
Cultural Resources Center
4220 Silver Hill Road, MRC 538
Suitland, MD 20746-2863
(301) 238-1415   Fax: (301) 238-3201
E-mail: kaminitzm@si.edu
Web: www.nmai.si.edu

Summary To provide students and professionals involved in conservation of museum collections with an opportunity to participate in a training program at the Smithsonian Institution's National Museum of the American Indian (NMAI).

Eligibility This program is open to 1) students currently enrolled in a graduate program in conservation; 2) recent graduates of such a program; and 3) practicing conservation professionals. Applicants must be preparing for a career in the conservation of material culture of the indigenous peoples of North, Central, and South America. They must be interested in participating in a training program at the NMAI Cultural Resources Center in Suitland, Maryland that involves collaboration with Native people in developing appropriate methods of caring for and interpreting cultural materials. The program is intended to cultivate practical skills as well as foster a solid understanding of the contexts of material culture, the philosophies of conservation at NMAI, and the ethics of the conservation profession. Proficiency in English is required.

Financial data Interns receive a stipend (amount not specified) and funds for housing.

Duration 10 weeks, in summer or winter.

Number awarded Varies each year.

Deadline January of each year for summer; September of each year for winter.

[675]
ANDREW W. MELLON FOUNDATION/ACLS DISSERTATION COMPLETION FELLOWSHIPS

American Council of Learned Societies
Attn: Office of Fellowships and Grants
633 Third Avenue
New York, NY 10017-6795
(212) 697-1505   Fax: (212) 949-8058
E-mail: fellowships@acls.org
Web: www.acls.org/programs/dcf

Summary To provide research funding to doctoral candidates (especially Native Americans, other minorities, and women) in all disciplines of the humanities and the humanities-related social sciences who are ready to complete their doctoral dissertations.

Eligibility This program is open to doctoral candidates in a humanities or humanities-related social science discipline at

a U.S. institution. Applicants must have completed all requirements for the Ph.D. except the dissertation. They may have completed no more than 6 years in the degree program. Research may be conducted at the home institution, abroad, or another appropriate site. Appropriate fields of specialization include, but are not limited to, American studies; anthropology; archaeology; art and architectural history; classics; economics; film; geography; history; languages and literatures; legal studies; linguistics; musicology; philosophy; political science; psychology; religious studies; rhetoric, communication, and media studies; sociology; and theater, dance, and performance studies. Proposals in the social sciences are eligible only if they employ predominantly humanistic approaches (e.g., economic history, law and literature, political philosophy). Proposals in interdisciplinary and cross-disciplinary studies are welcome, as are proposals focused on a geographic region or on a cultural or linguistic group. Applications are particularly invited from women and members of minority groups.

Financial data Grants provide a stipend of $25,000, funds for research costs up to $3,000, and payment of university fees up to $5,000.

Duration 1 academic year. Grantees may accept this fellowship no later than their seventh year.

Additional information This program, which began in 2006, is supported by funding from the Andrew W. Mellon Foundation and administered by the American Council of Learned Societies (ACLS).

Number awarded 65 each year.

Deadline November of each year.

[676]
ANTHC SCHOLARSHIPS

Alaska Native Tribal Health Consortium
Attn: Education, Development and Training Department
4000 Ambassador Drive, Suite 114
Anchorage, AK 99508
(907) 729-1917   Toll Free: (800) 684-8361
Fax: (907) 729-1335   E-mail: anthceducation@anthc.org
Web: www.anthc.org/jt/int

Summary To provide financial assistance for college or graduate school to Alaska Natives and American Indians who are residents of Alaska and interested in a career in health care.

Eligibility This program is open to Alaska Natives and American Indians who are undergraduates or graduate students interested in preparing for a career in the field of health care. Applicants must be residents of Alaska enrolled full time. Along with their application, they must submit a resume, 3 letters of recommendation, documentation of financial need, and a 1-page personal statement that covers their personal and educational history, accomplishments, educational and career goals, involvement in the Native community, and how this scholarship and degree program contribute to their career goals.

Financial data The stipend is $5,000 per year.

Duration 1 year; may be renewed if they maintain a minimum GPA of 2.0 for undergraduates or 3.0 for graduate students.

Number awarded 10 each year: 5 for undergraduate students and 5 for graduate students.

Deadline February of each year.

[677]
ANTHC SUMMER INTERNSHIPS

Alaska Native Tribal Health Consortium
Attn: Education, Development and Training Department
4000 Ambassador Drive, Suite 114
Anchorage, AK 99508
(907) 729-1917   Toll Free: (800) 684-8361
Fax: (907) 729-1335   E-mail: anthceducation@anthc.org
Web: www.anthc.org/jt/int

Summary To provide summer work experience at the Alaska Native Tribal Health Consortium (ANTHC) to Native Alaskan and American Indian high school, undergraduate, and graduate students.

Eligibility This program is open to Alaska Natives and American Indians who are high school students, undergraduates, graduate students, and recipients during the past 6 months of a GED, diploma, or degree. Applicants must be residents of Alaska and interested in an internship at ANTHC in such areas as finance, human resources, health records, computer technology, engineering, maintenance, or housekeeping. Along with their application, they must submit a resume, documentation of financial need, and a 1-page personal statement that covers their personal and educational history, accomplishments, educational and career goals, involvement in the Native community, and how this internship corresponds with their career goals.

Financial data These are paid internships.

Duration 9 weeks during the summer.

Number awarded Approximately 25 each year: 20 for high school and undergraduate students and 5 for graduate students.

Deadline February of each year.

[678]
APA MINORITY MEDICAL STUDENT SUMMER MENTORING PROGRAM

American Psychiatric Association
Attn: Department of Minority and National Affairs
1000 Wilson Boulevard, Suite 1825
Arlington, VA 22209-3901
(703) 907-8653   Toll Free: (888) 35-PSYCH
Fax: (703) 907-7852   E-mail: mking@psych.org
Web: www.psych.org/Resources/OMNA/MFP.aspx

Summary To provide funding to Native American and other minority medical students who are interested in working on a summer project with a psychiatrist mentor.

Eligibility This program is open to minority medical students who are interested in psychiatric issues. Minorities include American Indians, Alaska Natives, Native Hawaiians, Asian Americans, Hispanic/Latinos, and African Americans. Applicants must be interested in working with a psychiatrist mentor, primarily on clinical work with underserved minority populations and mental health care disparities. Work settings may be in a research, academic, or clinical environment. Most of them are inner-city or rural and dealing with psychiatric subspecialties, particularly substance abuse and geriatrics. Selection is based on interest of the medical student and

specialty of the mentor, practice setting, and geographic proximity of the mentor to the student. U.S. citizenship or permanent resident status is required.

Financial data Fellowships provide $1,500 for living and out-of-pocket expenses directly related to the conduct of the fellowship.

Duration Summer months.

Additional information This program is funded by the Substance Abuse and Mental Health Services Administration.

Number awarded Varies each year.

Deadline February of each year.

[679]
APA PLANNING FELLOWSHIPS

American Planning Association
Attn: Leadership Affairs Associate
205 North Michigan Avenue, Suite 1200
Chicago, IL 60601
(312) 431-9100   Fax: (312) 786-6700
E-mail: fellowship@planning.org
Web: www.planning.org/scholarships/apa

Summary To provide financial assistance to Native American and other underrepresented minority students enrolled in master's degree programs at recognized planning schools.

Eligibility This program is open to first- and second-year graduate students in urban and regional planning who are members of the following minority groups: African American, Hispanic American, or Native American. Applicants must be citizens of the United States and able to document financial need. They must intend to work as practicing planners in the public sector. Along with their application, they must submit a 2- to 5-page personal statement describing how their graduate education will be applied to career goals and why they chose planning as a career path. Selection is based (in order of importance) on 1) commitment to planning as reflected in the personal statement and resume; 2) academic achievement and/or improvement during the past 2 years; 3) letters of recommendation; 4) financial need; and 5) professional presentation.

Financial data Stipends range from $1,000 to $5,000 per year. The money may be applied to tuition and living expenses only. Payment is made to the recipient's university and divided by terms in the school year.

Duration 1 year; recipients may reapply.

Additional information The fellowship program started in 1970 as a Ford Foundation Minority Fellowship Program.

Number awarded Varies each year; recently, 6 of these fellowships were awarded.

Deadline April of each year.

[680]
ARAPAHO EDUCATIONAL TRUST SCHOLARSHIP

Northern Arapaho Tribe
Attn: Sky People Higher Education
P.O. Box 8480
Ethete, WY 82520
(307) 332-5286   Toll Free: (800) 815-6795
Fax: (307) 332-9104   E-mail: assistant@skypeopleed.org
Web: www.skypeopleed.org

Summary   To provide financial assistance to members of the Northern Arapaho Tribe who are working on an undergraduate or graduate degree in engineering, law, or the sciences.

Eligibility   This program is open to full-time undergraduate and graduate students who have an undergraduate GPA of 2.0 or higher or the graduate GPA required by their school. Applicants must be of at least one-fourth Northern Arapaho descent (enrolled or non-enrolled) and must submit a Certificate of Indian Blood or other verification of Northern Arapaho blood. They must be working on a degree in engineering, law, or the sciences. Along with their application, they must submit a 1-page personal statement that includes a brief history of their background, academic ability and achievement, work or leadership experience, participation in community-related activities, and career goals. Selection is based on that statement, potential to contribute to the community upon graduation, academic ability and achievement, and a letter of recommendation.

Financial data   The stipend is $1,500 per year.

Duration   1 year; may be renewed.

Additional information   The recipient is expected to apply for employment with the Northern Arapaho Tribe after graduation.

Number awarded   1 each year.

Deadline   June of each year.

[681]
ARAPAHO RANCH EDUCATIONAL TRUST SCHOLARSHIP

Northern Arapaho Tribe
Attn: Sky People Higher Education
P.O. Box 8480
Ethete, WY 82520
(307) 332-5286   Toll Free: (800) 815-6795
Fax: (307) 332-9104   E-mail: assistant@skypeopleed.org
Web: www.skypeopleed.org

Summary   To provide financial assistance to members of the Northern Arapaho Tribe who are working on an undergraduate or graduate degree in conservation-related fields.

Eligibility   This program is open to full-time undergraduate and graduate students who have an undergraduate GPA of 2.0 or higher or the graduate GPA required by their school. Applicants must be of at least one-fourth Northern Arapaho descent (enrolled or non-enrolled) and must submit a Certificate of Indian Blood or other verification of Northern Arapaho blood with at least one-fourth degree. They must be working on a degree in range conservation, forestry, animal sciences, or ranch and range management. Along with their application, they must submit a 1-page personal statement that includes a brief history of their background, academic ability and achievement, work or leadership experience, participation in community-related activities, and career goals. Selection is based on that statement, potential to contribute to the community upon graduation, academic ability and achievement, and a letter of recommendation.

Financial data   The stipend is $2,000 per year.

Duration   1 year; may be renewed.

Number awarded   1 each year.

Deadline   June of each year.

[682]
ARCTIC EDUCATION FOUNDATION SCHOLARSHIPS

Arctic Slope Regional Corporation
Attn: Arctic Education Foundation
P.O. Box 129
Barrow, AK 99723
(907) 852-8633   Toll Free: (800) 770-2772
Fax: (907) 852-2774   E-mail: mjkaleak@asrc.com
Web: www.arcticed.com

Summary   To provide financial assistance Inupiat Natives who are shareholders or descendants of shareholders of the Arctic Slope Regional Corporation (ASRC) and plan to attend college or graduate school in any state.

Eligibility   This program is open to U.S. citizens who are 1) a northern Alaskan Inupiat Native currently residing in the Arctic Slope region of Alaska; 2) an original shareholder of the ASRC; or 3) a direct lineal descendant of an original ASRC shareholder. Applicants must be attending or planning to attend a college, university, or vocational/technical school in any state as a full- or part-time undergraduate or graduate student. Along with their application, they must submit documentation of financial need and a short paragraph on their personal plans upon completion of study.

Financial data   For full-time students at 4-year colleges and universities, the maximum stipend is $6,000 per year. For students in vocational training programs, the maximum stipend is $2,500 per term ($5,000 per year).

Duration   1 year; may be renewed.

Additional information   The Arctic Slope Regional Corporation is 1 of 13 Alaska Native Regional Corporations created under the Alaska Native Claims Settlement Act of 1971.

Number awarded   Varies each year.

Deadline   February of each year for spring quarter or early summer; April of each year for summer school; July of each year for fall semester or quarter; or November of each year for spring semester or winter quarter.

[683]
ARENT FOX DIVERSITY SCHOLARSHIPS

Arent Fox LLP
Attn: Attorney Recruitment and Professional Development Coordinator
1050 Connecticut Avenue, N.W.
Washington, DC 20036-5339
(202) 715-8503   Fax: (202) 857-6395
E-mail: lawrecruit@arentfox.com
Web: www.arentfox.com

Summary   To provide financial assistance and work experience to Native American and other minority law students.

Eligibility   This program is open to first-year law students who are members of a diverse population that historically has been underrepresented in the legal profession. Applicants must be U.S. citizens or otherwise authorized to work in the United States. They must also be willing to work as a summer intern at the sponsoring law firm's offices in Los Angeles, New York City, or Washington, D.C. Along with their application, they must submit a resume, an undergraduate transcript and law school grades when available, a 5- to 10-page legal writing sample, 3 letters of recommendation, and an essay on how their background, skills, experience, and interest equip them to meet the sponsor's goal of commitment to diversity. Selection is based on academic performance during college and law school, oral and writing communication skills, leadership qualities, and community involvement.

Financial data The scholarship stipend is $15,000. The summer salary is $2,500 per week.

Duration 1 year.

Additional information These scholarships were first offered in 2006. Recipients are also offered summer internships with Arent Fox: 1 in Los Angeles, 1 in New York City, and 1 in Washington, D.C.

Number awarded 3 each year.

Deadline January of each year.

[684]
ARKANSAS CONFERENCE ETHNIC LOCAL CHURCH CONCERNS SCHOLARSHIPS

United Methodist Church-Arkansas Conference
Attn: Committee on Ethnic Local Church Concerns
800 Daisy Bates Drive
Little Rock, AR 72202
(501) 324-8045   Toll Free: (877) 646-1816
Fax: (501) 324-8018   E-mail: mallen@arumc.org
Web: www.arumc.org

Summary To provide financial assistance to Native American and other minority Methodist students from Arkansas who are interested in attending college or graduate school in any state.

Eligibility This program is open to ethnic minority undergraduate and graduate students who are active members of local congregations affiliated with the Arkansas Conference of the United Methodist Church (UMC). Applicants must be currently enrolled in an accredited institution of higher education in any state. Along with their application, they must submit a transcript (GPA of 2.0 or higher) and documentation of participation in local church activities. Preference is given to students attending a UMC-affiliated college or university.

Financial data The stipend is $500 per semester ($1,000 per year) for undergraduates or $1,000 per semester ($2,000 per year) for graduate students.

Duration 1 year; may be renewed.

Number awarded 1 or more each year.

Deadline September of each year.

[685]
ARKANSAS MINORITY MASTERS FELLOWS PROGRAM

Arkansas Department of Higher Education
Attn: Financial Aid Division
114 East Capitol Avenue
Little Rock, AR 72201-3818
(501) 371-2050   Toll Free: (800) 54-STUDY
Fax: (501) 371-2001   E-mail: finaid@adhe.edu
Web: www.adhe.edu

Summary To provide funding to Native American and other minority graduate students in Arkansas who want to become teachers in the state.

Eligibility This program is open to minority (African American, Hispanic, Native American, or Asian American) residents of Arkansas who are U.S. citizens or permanent residents and enrolled in a master's degree program in education

(other than administration) at an Arkansas public or independent institution. Applicants must have a cumulative GPA of 2.75 or higher. They must be willing to teach in an Arkansas public school or public institution of higher education for at least 2 years after completion of their education. Preference is given to applicants who completed their baccalaureate degrees within the previous 2 years.

Financial data The loan is $1,250 per 3-credit course, to a maximum of $3,750 per semester or $7,500 over a lifetime. The loan will be forgiven if the recipient teaches full time in an Arkansas public school or public institution of higher education for 2 years. If the recipient withdraws from an approved teacher education program or does not fulfill the required teaching obligation, the loan must be repaid in full with 10% interest.

Duration 1 semester; may be renewed until the recipient completes 3 years of study, earns a master's degree, or reaches the maximum lifetime loan limit, whichever comes first. Renewal requires the recipient to maintain a GPA of 3.0 or higher.

Number awarded Varies each year; recently, 25 of these forgivable loans were approved.

Deadline May of each year.

[686]
ARMY MINORITY COLLEGE RELATIONS PROGRAM INTERNSHIPS

Vista Sciences Corporation
Attn: Intern Program Manager
7700 Alabama Street, Suite E
El Paso, TX 79904
(915) 757-3331   Fax: (915) 757-3371
E-mail: romy.ledesma@vistasciences.com
Web: www.vistasciences.com/services.asp?service=19

Summary To provide work experience at U.S. Army facilities to upper-division and graduate students at Tribal Colleges and Universities (TCUs) or other minority institutions.

Eligibility This program is open to students working on an undergraduate or graduate degree at Historically Black Colleges and Universities (HBCUs), Hispanic Serving Institutions (HSIs), or Tribal Colleges and Universities (TCUs). Applicants must be U.S. citizens currently enrolled as a junior or above and have a GPA of 2.5 or higher; recent (within 6 months) graduates are also eligible. They must be interested in an internship at an Army facility in such fields as engineering (civil, computer, construction, electrical, environmental), sciences (agronomy, biology, environmental, natural resources, safety), business (accounting, finance, legal, management, marketing, operations), computer science and engineering (data management, information systems, information technology, languages, programming, trouble shooting, website/webpage design and management), or other (communications, English, history, human resources, journalism, library sciences, mathematics, public administration, public relations, quality control, risk management, statistics, training development and management). Along with their application, they must submit a resume and a transcript.

Financial data Interns are paid a stipend of $500 per week and are reimbursed for housing and transportation costs.

Duration 10 weeks in the summer or 15 weeks in spring.

Additional information This program, which began in 1997, is currently administered by Vista Sciences Corporation under a contract with the Army. Recently, assignments were available at the Crane Army Ammunition Activity (Crane, Indiana), Sierra Army Depot (Herlong, California), McAlester Army Ammunition Plant (McAlester, Oklahoma), Blue Grass Army Depot (Richmond, Kentucky), Rock Island Arsenal (Rock Island, Illinois), Anniston Defense Munitions Center (Anniston, Alabama), Pine Bluff Arsenal (Pine Bluff, Arkansas), and Tooele Army Depot (Tooele, Utah).

Number awarded Varies each year.

Deadline May of each year for summer; November of each year for spring.

[687]
ASA MINORITY FELLOWSHIP PROGRAM

American Sociological Association
Attn: Minority Affairs Program
1430 K Street, N.W., Suite 600
Washington, DC 20005-2504
(202) 383-9005, ext. 322   Fax: (202) 638-0882
TDD: (202) 638-0981 E-mail: minority.affairs@asanet.org
Web: www.asanet.org/funding/mfp.cfm

Summary To provide financial assistance to Native American and other minority doctoral students in sociology.

Eligibility This program is open to U.S. citizens, permanent residents, and non-citizen nationals who are Blacks/African Americans, Latinos (e.g., Mexican Americans, Puerto Ricans, Cubans), American Indians or Alaskan Natives, Asian Americans (e.g., southeast Asians, Japanese, Chinese, Koreans), or Pacific Islanders (e.g., Filipinos, Samoans, Hawaiians, Guamanians). Applicants must be entering or continuing students in sociology at the doctoral level. Along with their application, they must submit 3-page essays on 1) the reasons why they decided to undertake graduate study in sociology, their primary research interests, and why they hope to do with a Ph.D. in sociology; and 2) what led them to select the doctoral program they attend or hope to attend and how they see that doctoral program preparing them for a professional career in sociology. Selection is based on commitment to research, focus of research experience, academic achievement, writing ability, research potential, and financial need.

Financial data The stipend is $18,000 per year.

Duration 1 year; may be renewed up to 2 additional years.

Additional information This program, which began in 1974, is supported by individual members of the American Sociological Association (ASA) and by several affiliated organizations (Alpha Kappa Delta, Sociologists for Women in Society, the Association of Black Sociologists, and the Southwestern Sociological Association).

Number awarded Varies each year; since the program began, approximately 500 of these fellowships have been awarded.

Deadline January of each year.

[688]
ASCO MEDICAL STUDENT ROTATION

American Society of Clinical Oncology
Attn: Conquer Cancer Foundation of ASCO
2318 Mill Road, Suite 800
Alexandria, VA 22314
(571) 483-1700
E-mail: grants@conquercancerfoundation.org
Web: www.conquercancerfoundation.org

Summary To provide funding to Native American and other minority medical students interested in a clinical research oncology rotation.

Eligibility This program is open to U.S. citizens, nationals, and permanent residents who are currently enrolled at a U.S. medical school. Applicants must be a member of a group currently underrepresented in medicine, defined as American Indian/Alaska Native, Black/African American, Hispanic/Latino, or Native Hawaiian/Pacific Islander. They must be interested in a rotation either in a patient cancer care setting or a clinical cancer research setting; the rotation may take place either at their own school or another institution but must have a faculty member who belongs to the American Society of Clinical Oncology (ASCO) and is willing to serve as a mentor. Selection is based on interest in preparing for a career in oncology and academic standing.

Financial data Students receive a stipend of $5,000 plus $1,500 for future travel to the annual meeting of the American Society of Clinical Oncology (ASCO). Their mentor receives a grant of $2,000.

Duration 8 to 10 weeks.

Additional information This program, which began in 2009, is sponsored by Susan G. Komen for the Cure.

Number awarded Varies each year; recently, 6 of these grants were awarded.

Deadline January of each year.

[689]
ASSOCIATION OF RESEARCH LIBRARIES CAREER ENHANCEMENT PROGRAM

Association of Research Libraries
Attn: Director of Diversity Programs
21 Dupont Circle, N.W., Suite 800
Washington, DC 20036
(202) 296-2296   Fax: (202) 872-0884
E-mail: mpuente@arl.org
Web: www.arl.org/diversity/cep/index.shtml

Summary To provide financial assistance for further study and an opportunity for Native Americans and other minorities to gain work experience at a library that is a member of the Association of Research Libraries (ARL).

Eligibility This program is open to members of racial and ethnic minority groups that are underrepresented as professionals in academic and research libraries (American Indian or Alaska Native, Asian, Black or African American, Native Hawaiian or other Pacific Islander, or Hispanic or Latino). Applicants must have completed at least 12 credit hours of an M.L.I.S. degree program at an ALA-accredited institution. They must be interested in an internship at 1 of 7 ARL member institutions. Along with their application, they must submit a 400-word essay on what attracts them to an internship opportunity in an ARL library, their professional interests as related to the internship, and their goals for the internship.

Financial data Fellows receive a stipend of $4,800 for the internship, an academic stipend of up to $2,500, a housing stipend of up to $2,000, a travel stipend of up to $1,000 for transportation expenses to and from the internship site, and financial support (approximately $1,000) to attend the annual ARL Leadership Institute.

Duration The internship lasts 6 to 12 weeks (or 240 hours). The academic stipend is for 1 year.

Additional information This program is funded by the Institute of Museum and Library Services. Recently, the 7 participating ARL institutions were the University of Arizona, University of California at San Diego, Columbia University, University of Kentucky, National Library of Medicine, North Carolina State University, and University of Washington.

Number awarded Varies each year; recently, 18 of these fellows were selected.

Deadline October of each year.

[690]
A.T. ANDERSON MEMORIAL SCHOLARSHIP PROGRAM

American Indian Science and Engineering Society
Attn: Program Officer
2305 Renard, S.E., Suite 200
P.O. Box 9828
Albuquerque, NM 87119-9828
(505) 765-1052, ext. 105   Fax: (505) 765-5608
E-mail: tina@aises.org
Web: www.aises.org

Summary To provide financial assistance to members of the American Indian Science and Engineering Society who are majoring in designated fields as undergraduate or graduate students.

Eligibility This program is open to members of the society who can furnish a Certificate of Indian Blood or proof of enrollment in an American Indian tribe or Alaskan Native group. Applicants must be full-time students at the undergraduate or graduate level attending an accredited 4-year college or university or a 2-year college leading to an academic degree in engineering, mathematics, medicine, natural resources, or the sciences. They must have a GPA of 3.0 or higher. Along with their application, they must submit a 500-word essay on their educational and career goals, including their interest in and motivation to continue higher education, an understanding of the importance of college and completing their educational and/or career goals, and a commitment to learning and giving back to the community. Selection is based on that essay (40%), GPA (35%), letters of recommendation (15%), and overall impression of the application (10%).

Financial data The annual stipend is $1,000 for undergraduates or $2,000 for graduate students.

Duration 1 year; nonrenewable.

Additional information This program was launched in 1983 in memory of A.T. Anderson, a Mohawk and a chemical engineer who worked with Albert Einstein. Anderson was 1 of the society's founders and was the society's first executive director. The program includes the following named awards: the Al Qöyawayma Award for an applicant who is majoring in science or engineering and also has a strong interest in the arts, the Norbert S. Hill, Jr. Leadership Award, the Polingaysi

Qöyawayma Award for an applicant who is working on a teaching degree in order to teach mathematics or science in a Native community or an advanced degree for personal improvement or teaching at the college level, and the Robert W. Brocksbank Scholarship.

Number awarded Varies; generally, 200 or more each year, depending upon the availability of funds from corporate and other sponsors.

Deadline June of each year.

[691]
AT&T LABORATORIES FELLOWSHIP PROGRAM

AT&T Laboratories
Attn: Fellowship Administrator
180 Park Avenue, Room C103
P.O. Box 971
Florham Park, NJ 07932-0971
(973) 360-8109   Fax: (973) 360-8881
E-mail: recruiting@research.att.com
Web: www.research.att.com

Summary To provide financial assistance and work experience to Native Americans and other underrepresented minority and women students who are working on a doctoral degree in computer and technology-related fields.

Eligibility This program is open to minorities underrepresented in the sciences (African Americans, Hispanics, and Native Americans) and to women. Applicants must be U.S. citizens or permanent residents who are graduating college seniors or graduate students enrolled in their first or second year. They must be working on or planning to work on a Ph.D. in a field of study relevant to the business of AT&T; currently, those include computer science, electrical engineering, industrial engineering, mathematics, operations research, systems engineering, statistics, and related fields. Along with their application, they must submit a personal statement on why they are enrolled in their present academic program and how they intend to use their technical training, official transcripts, 3 academic references, and GRE scores. Selection is based on potential for success in scientific research.

Financial data This program covers all educational expenses during the school year, including tuition, books, fees, and approved travel expenses; educational expenses for summer study or university research; a stipend for living expenses (recently, $2,380 per month); and support for attending approved scientific conferences.

Duration 1 year; may be renewed for up to 2 additional years, as long as the fellow continues making satisfactory progress toward the Ph.D.

Additional information The AT&T Laboratories Fellowship Program (ALFP) provides a mentor who is a staff member at AT&T Labs as well as a summer research internship with AT&T Labs during the first summer. The ALFP replaces the Graduate Research Program for Women (GRPW) and the Cooperative Research Fellowship Program (CRFP) run by the former AT&T Bell Laboratories. If recipients accept other support, the tuition payment and stipend received from that fellowship will replace the funds provided by this program. The other provisions of this fellowship will remain in force and the stipend will be replaced by an annual grant of $2,000.

Number awarded Approximately 8 each year.

Deadline January of each year.

[692]
BAD RIVER HIGHER EDUCATION GRANT PROGRAM

Bad River Band of Lake Superior Chippewa Indians
Attn: Education Office
P.O. Box 39
Odanah, WI 54861
(715) 682-7111, ext. 1533　　　　Fax: (715) 682-7118

Summary　To provide financial assistance for college or graduate school to tribal members of the Bad River Band of Lake Superior Chippewa Indians.

Eligibility　This program is open to Bad River tribal members who are or will be working full time on an undergraduate degree or full or part time on a graduate degree. Applicants must be able to document financial need. Graduate students must document that they have been denied funding from the American Indian Graduate Center.

Financial data　The maximum stipend is $1,800 per year for undergraduates or $3,600 per year for graduate students.

Duration　Up to 10 semesters for undergraduate students or up to 6 semesters for graduate students, provided the recipient maintains a GPA of 2.0 or higher as an undergraduate or 3.0 or higher as a graduate student.

Number awarded　Varies each year.

Deadline　July of each year.

[693]
BAKER & DANIELS DIVERSITY SCHOLARSHIPS

Baker & Daniels LLP
Attn: Diversity and Pro Bono Coordinator
300 North Meridian Street, Suite 2700
Indianapolis, IN 46204
(317) 237-8298　　　　Fax: (317) 237-1000
E-mail: brita.horvath@bakerd.com
Web: www.bakerdaniels.com/AboutUs/recruitment.aspx

Summary　To provide financial assistance and summer work experience to Native Americans and other students from diverse backgrounds entering the second year of law school in Indiana.

Eligibility　This program is open to residents of any state who are entering their second year at selected law schools in Indiana. Applicants must reflect diversity, defined to mean that they come from varied ethnic, racial, cultural, and lifestyle backgrounds, as well as those with disabilities or unique viewpoints. They must also be interested in a place in the sponsor's summer associate program. Along with their application, they must submit a personal statement that includes an explanation of how this scholarship would benefit them, an overview of their background and interests, an explanation of what diversity they would bring to the firm, and any other financial assistance they are receiving. Selection is based primarily on academic excellence.

Financial data　The stipend is $10,000.

Duration　1 year.

Additional information　The eligible law schools are those at Indiana University at Bloomington, Indiana University at Indianapolis, and the University of Notre Dame.

Number awarded　2 each year.

Deadline　June of each year.

[694]
BAKER DONELSON DIVERSITY SCHOLARSHIPS

Baker, Donelson, Bearman, Caldwell & Berkowitz, P.C.
Attn: Director of Attorney Recruiting
3414 Peachtree Road N.E.
Atlanta, GA 30326
(404) 577-6000　　　　Fax: (404) 221-6501
E-mail: lklein@bakerdonelson.com
Web: www.bakerdonelson.com

Summary　To provide financial assistance to law students who are Native Americans or members of other groups underrepresented at large law firms.

Eligibility　This program is open to students who have completed the first year at an ABA-accredited law school. Applicants must be members of a group traditionally underrepresented at large law firms (American Indian or Alaskan Native, Native Hawaiian or Pacific Islander, Hispanic or Latino, Black, or Asian). Along with their application, they must submit a 10-page legal writing sample and a 1-page personal statement on challenges they have faced in pursuit of their legal career that have helped them to understand the value of diversity and its inclusion in the legal profession. Finalists are interviewed.

Financial data　The stipend is $10,000.

Duration　1 year.

Additional information　Recipients are also offered summer internships at Baker Donelson offices in Atlanta (Georgia), Baton Rouge (Louisiana), Birmingham (Alabama), Chattanooga (Tennessee), Jackson (Mississippi), Johnson City (Tennessee), Knoxville (Tennessee), Memphis (Tennessee), Nashville (Tennessee), and New Orleans (Louisiana).

Number awarded　3 each year.

Deadline　June of each year.

[695]
BAKER HOSTETLER DIVERSITY FELLOWSHIP PROGRAM

Baker Hostetler LLP
Attn: Attorney Recruitment and Development Manager
PNC Center
1900 East Ninth Street, Suite 3200
Cleveland, OH 44114-3482
(216) 621-0200　　　　Fax: (216) 696-0740
E-mail: ddriscole@bakerlaw.com
Web: www.bakerlaw.com/diversity/fellowshipprogram

Summary　To provide summer work experience to Native American and other minority law school students.

Eligibility　This program is open to full-time second-year students at ABA-accredited law schools who are members of underrepresented groups (Black/African American, Hispanic, Asian American/Pacific Islander, American Indian/Alaskan Native, 2 or more races, or gay, lesbian, bisexual, transgender). Applicants must be interested in a summer associate position with Baker Hostetler and possible full-time employment following graduation. They must be U.S. citizens or otherwise authorized to work in the United States. Along with their application, they must submit a 500-word personal statement presenting their views of or experience with diversity, including why they are interested in Baker Hostetler and how they will be able to contribute to the diversity objectives of the firm. Selection is based on academic performance in college and law school, personal achievements, community involvement, oral and written communication skills, demonstrated leadership achievements, and a sincere interest and commitment to join Baker Hostetler.

Financial data The stipend is $25,000, of which $10,000 is paid within the first 30 days of starting a summer associate position with the firm and the remaining $15,000 is contingent upon receiving and accepting a full-time offer with the firm.

Duration Summer associate positions are for 8 weeks.

Additional information Summer associate positions may be performed at any of the firm's offices in Chicago, Cincinnati, Cleveland, Columbus, Costa Mesa, Denver, Houston, Los Angeles, New York, Orlando, or Washington, D.C.

Number awarded 1 or more each year.

Deadline October of each year.

[696]
BALFOUR PHI DELTA PHI MINORITY SCHOLARSHIP PROGRAM

Phi Delta Phi International Legal Fraternity
1426 21st Street, N.W., First Floor
Washington, DC 20036
(202) 223-6801   Toll Free: (800) 368-5606
Fax: (202) 223-6808   E-mail: info@phideltaphi.org
Web: www.phideltaphi.org

Summary To provide financial assistance to Native Americans and other minorities who are members of Phi Delta Phi International Legal Fraternity.

Eligibility All ethnic minority members of the legal fraternity are eligible to apply for this scholarship. Selection is based on participation, ethics, and scholastics.

Financial data The stipend is $3,000.

Duration 1 year.

Additional information This scholarship was established in 1997. Funding for this scholarship comes from the Lloyd G. Balfour Foundation.

Number awarded 1 each year.

Deadline October of each year.

[697]
BERDACH RESEARCH GRANTS

Gay Indian Studies Association
Attn: Foundation
13730 Loumont Street
Whittier, CA 90601

Summary To provide financial assistance to American Indian graduate students interested in conducting research on the phenomenon of berdaches in the southwestern United States.

Eligibility This program is open to graduate students who wish to conduct research (for a master's degree thesis or a doctoral dissertation) on the topic of berdaches (male Indians who lived as women) among the tribes of the southwestern United States. Applicants must be gay males who are enrolled members of a federally-recognized Indian tribal organization in the United States. They must be able to demonstrate a "congruence between their own personal experiences and the topic of their proposed research."

Financial data The grant is $10,000. Funds must be used for research purposes only; the research may be historical (in libraries and archives) or contemporary (involving field studies as well as library research).

Duration This is a 1-time grant.

Additional information Funding for this program is provided by the National Science Foundation. Requests for applications should be accompanied by a self-addressed stamped envelope, the student's e-mail address, and the source where they found the scholarship information.

Number awarded 2 or more each year.

Deadline December of each year.

[698]
BERING STRAITS FOUNDATION HIGHER EDUCATION SCHOLARSHIPS

Bering Straits Native Corporation
Attn: Bering Straits Foundation
110 Front Street, Suite 300
P.O. Box 1008
Nome, AK 99762-1008
(907) 443-5252   Toll Free: (800) 478-5079 (within AK)
Fax: (907) 443-2985
E-mail: foundation@beringstraits.com
Web: beringstraits.com

Summary To provide financial assistance to Alaska Natives who are shareholders or descendants of shareholders of the Bering Straits Native Corporation and entering or enrolled in an undergraduate or graduate program in any state.

Eligibility This program is open to Native Alaskans who are shareholders or lineal descendants of shareholders of the Bering Straits Native Corporation. Applicants must be graduating or have graduated from high school with a GPA of 3.0 or higher (or have earned a GED). They must be accepted or currently enrolled (as an undergraduate or graduate student) at an accredited college or university in any state as a full-time student and be able to demonstrate financial need. Along with their application, they must submit a personal statement on their educational goals and objectives, their community and school activities, and honors and awards they have received.

Financial data The stipend is $1,000 per semester for students who maintain a GPA of 3.0 or higher or $400 per semester for students whose GPA is from 2.5 to 2.99. Funds are paid directly to the recipient's school.

Duration 1 semester; may be renewed if the recipient maintains a GPA of 2.0 or higher during the first semester and 2.5 or higher in succeeding semesters.

Additional information The Bering Straits Native Corporation is 1 of 13 Alaska Native Regional Corporations created under the Alaska Native Claims Settlement Act of 1971.

Number awarded Varies each year.

Deadline April of each year for high school seniors; June of each year for the fall semester for continuing undergraduates; December of each year for the spring semester; April of each year for summer school.

[699]
BILL BERNBACH DIVERSITY SCHOLARSHIPS

American Association of Advertising Agencies
Attn: AAAA Foundation
405 Lexington Avenue, 18th Floor
New York, NY 10174-1801
(212) 682-2500   Toll Free: (800) 676-9333
Fax: (212) 682-2028   E-mail: ameadows@aaaa.org
Web: www2.aaaa.org

Summary To provide financial assistance to Native American and other multicultural students interested in working on a graduate degree in advertising at designated schools.

Eligibility This program is open to African Americans, Asian Americans, Hispanic Americans, and Native Americans who are interested in studying the advertising creative arts at designated institutions. Applicants must have already received an undergraduate degree and be able to demonstrate creative talent and promise. Along with their application, they must submit 10 samples of creative work in their respective field of expertise. U.S. citizenship or permanent resident status is required.

Financial data The stipend is $5,000.

Duration 1 year.

Additional information This program, which began in 1998, is currently sponsored by DDB Worldwide. The participating schools are the AdCenter at Virginia Commonwealth University, the Creative Circus and the Portfolio Center in Atlanta, the Miami Ad School, the University of Texas at Austin, and the Art Center College of Design in Pasadena, California.

Number awarded 5 each year.

Deadline Deadline not specified.

[700]
BILL THUNDER, JR. MEMORIAL SCHOLARSHIP

Northern Arapaho Tribe
Attn: Sky People Higher Education
P.O. Box 8480
Ethete, WY 82520
(307) 332-5286   Toll Free: (800) 815-6795
Fax: (307) 332-9104 E-mail: assistant@skypeopleed.org
Web: www.skypeopleed.org

Summary To provide financial assistance to members of the Northern Arapaho Tribe who are working on an undergraduate or graduate degree in agriculture or a related field.

Eligibility This program is open to full-time undergraduate and graduate students who have an undergraduate GPA of 2.0 or higher or the graduate GPA required by their school. Applicants must be of at least one-fourth Northern Arapaho descent (enrolled or non-enrolled) and must submit a Certificate of Indian Blood or other verification of Northern Arapaho blood with at least one-fourth degree. They must be working on a degree in agriculture or a related field (agribusiness, veterinary studies, animal science, horticulture, resource economics, rangeland ecosystem science, or agronomy). Along with their application, they must submit a 1-page personal statement that includes a brief history of their background, academic ability and achievement, work or leadership experience, participation in community-related activities, and career goals. Selection is based on that statement, potential to con-

tribute to the community upon graduation, academic ability and achievement, and a letter of recommendation.

Financial data The stipend is $2,500 per year.

Duration 1 year; may be renewed.

Additional information The recipient is expected to apply for employment with the Northern Arapaho Tribe after graduation.

Number awarded 1 each year.

Deadline June of each year.

[701]
BIOMEDICAL RESEARCH TRAINING PROGRAM FOR UNDERREPRESENTED GROUPS

National Heart, Lung, and Blood Institute
Attn: Office of Training and Minority Health
6701 Rockledge Drive, Suite 9180
Bethesda, MD 20892-7913
(301) 451-5081   Toll Free: (301) 451-0088
Fax: (301) 480-0862   E-mail: mishoeh@nhlbi.nih.gov
Web: www.nhlbi.nih.gov

Summary To provide training in fundamental biomedical sciences and clinical research disciplines to Native Americans and other undergraduates, graduate students, and postbaccalaureates from underrepresented groups.

Eligibility This program is open to underrepresented undergraduate and graduate students (and postbaccalaureate individuals) interested in receiving training in fundamental biomedical sciences and clinical research disciplines of interest to the National Heart, Lung, and Blood Institute (NHLBI) of the National Institutes of Health (NIH). Underrepresented individuals include African Americans, Hispanic Americans, Native Americans, Alaskan Natives, Native Hawaiians and Pacific Islanders, individuals with disabilities, and individuals from disadvantaged backgrounds. Applicants must be U.S. citizens or permanent residents; have completed academic course work relevant to biomedical, behavioral, or statistical research; be enrolled full time or have recently completed baccalaureate work; and have a GPA of 3.3 or higher. Research experiences are available in the NHLBI Division of Intramural Research (in its cardiology, hematology, vascular medicine, or pulmonary critical care medicine branches) and its Division of Cardiovascular Sciences (which provides training in the basic principles of design, implementation, and analysis of epidemiology studies and clinical trials).

Financial data Stipends are paid at the annual rate of $24,000 for sophomores, $25,200 for juniors, $26,400 for seniors, $27,200 for postbaccalaureate individuals, $27,600 for first-year graduate students, $31,200 for second-year graduate students, or $34,900 for third-year graduate students.

Duration 6 to 24 months over a 2-year period; training must be completed in increments during consecutive academic years.

Additional information Training is conducted in the laboratories of the NHLBI in Bethesda, Maryland.

Number awarded Varies each year.

Deadline January of each year for placements beginning in June; March of each year for post-baccalaureate research internships beginning from June through September.

[702]
BISHOP THOMAS HOYT, JR. FELLOWSHIP

St. John's University
Attn: Collegeville Institute for Ecumenical and Cultural
  Research
14027 Fruit Farm Road
Box 2000
Collegeville, MN 56321-2000
(320) 363-3366   Fax: (320) 363-3313
E-mail: staff@CollegevilleInstitute.org
Web: collegevilleinstitute.org/res-fellowships

Summary To provide funding to Native Americans and
other students of color who wish to complete their doctoral
dissertation while in residence at the Collegeville Institute for
Ecumenical and Cultural Research of St. John's University in
Collegeville, Minnesota.

Eligibility This program is open to people of color completing a doctoral dissertation in ecumenical and cultural
research. Applicants must be interested in a residency at the
Collegeville Institute for Ecumenical and Cultural Research of
St. John's University. Along with their application, they must
submit a 1,000-word description of the research project they
plan to complete while in residence at the Institute.

Financial data The stipend covers the residency fee of
$2,000, which includes housing and utilities.

Duration 1 year.

Additional information Residents at the Institute engage
in study, research, and publication on the important intersections between faith and culture. They seek to discern and
communicate the meaning of Christian identity and unity in a
religiously and culturally diverse world.

Number awarded 1 each year.

Deadline October of each year.

[703]
BLOSSOM KALAMA EVANS MEMORIAL SCHOLARSHIPS

Hawai'i Community Foundation
Attn: Scholarship Department
827 Fort Street Mall
Honolulu, HI 96813
(808) 537-6333   Toll Free: (888) 731-3863
Fax: (808) 521-6286
E-mail: scholarships@hcf-hawaii.org
Web: www.hawaiicommunityfoundation.org/scholarships

Summary To provide financial assistance to residents of
Hawaii of native ancestry who are interested in working on an
undergraduate or graduate degree at a school in any state.

Eligibility This program is open to residents of Hawaii who
are of Hawaiian ancestry and enrolled as full-time juniors,
seniors, or graduate students at a college or university in any
state. Applicants must be able to demonstrate academic
achievement (GPA of 2.7 or higher), good moral character,
and financial need. Along with their application, they must
submit a short statement indicating their reasons for attending college, their planned course of study, their career goals,
what community service means to them, and how they plan to
use their knowledge to serve the needs of the Native Hawaiian community.

Financial data The amounts of the awards depend on the
availability of funds and the need of the recipient. Recently,

the average value of each of the scholarships awarded by the
foundation was $2,041.

Duration 1 year.

Number awarded Varies each year; recently, 9 of these
scholarships were awarded.

Deadline February of each year.

[704]
BOIS FORTE HIGHER EDUCATION PROGRAM

Bois Forte Band of Chippewa
Attn: Department of Education and Training
5344 Lakeshore Drive
P.O. Box 16
Nett Lake, MN 55772
(218) 757-3261   Toll Free: (800) 221-8129
Fax: (218) 757-3312 E-mail: bmason@boisforte-NSN.gov
Web: www.boisforte.com/divisions/education.htm

Summary To provide financial assistance for undergraduate or graduate study to enrolled members of the Bois Forte
Band of Chippewa Indians.

Eligibility Eligible to apply for this assistance are enrolled
members of the Bois Forte Band of Chippewa Indians. Applicants must have been accepted at an institution of higher
education and had their financial need determined by that
institution based on the Free Application for Federal Student
Aid (FAFSA). Minnesota residents must apply to the Indian
Scholarship Assistance Program of the Minnesota Indian
Scholarship Program. Applicants wishing to attend school
outside of Minnesota must complete an out-of-state application form. Applicants must also apply for financial assistance
from all other available sources, including but not limited to
public and private grants and scholarships. They must not be
in default of any tribal, federal, or state student education loan
or in noncompliance with child support payments. Applicants
are interviewed. Financial assistance is awarded on a first-
come, first-served basis.

Financial data The maximum amount awarded is $5,000
per year for undergraduates or $6,250 per year for graduate
students.

Duration 1 year; may be renewed for a total of 10 semesters of full-time enrollment or part-time equivalent provided
recipients maintain a GPA of 2.0 or higher.

Additional information Students may receive financial
assistance for summer school.

Number awarded Varies each year.

Deadline Applications may be submitted any time after
January 1 but should be received no later than 8 weeks prior
to the first day of school.

[705]
BONNEVILLE POWER ADMINISTRATION REGIONAL TRIBAL SCHOLARSHIPS

Bonneville Power Administration
Attn: Tribal Affairs Program
P.O. Box 3621
Portland, OR 97208-3621
(503) 230-7685   E-mail: tribalaffairs@bpa.gov
Web: www.bpa.gov

Summary To provide financial assistance to members of
Indian tribes in the Pacific Northwest who are interested in

working on an undergraduate or graduate degree in specified finance and science-related fields at a university in any state.

Eligibility This program is open to Indians who are enrolled members of federally-recognized tribes in the service area of the Bonneville Power Administration (BPA) in Washington, Oregon, Idaho, and Montana. Applicants must be attending or planning to attend a college or university in any state as a full-time student to prepare for a career in a field of interest to BPA, including 1) an academic degree in accounting, business, economics, electrical engineering, finance, natural resources, or statistics or 2) a technical degree in the electrical crafts. They must have a GPA of 2.5 or higher. Along with their application, they must submit an essay of 500-words on a topic that changes annually but relates to the work of BPA; recently, students were asked to complete the phrase, "Renewable Energy means." Selection is based on the essay and academic merit, including course work, major field of study, leadership, community service, academic achievements, and overcoming obstacles.

Financial data The stipend is $2,500.

Duration 1 year.

Number awarded 10 each year.

Deadline March of each year.

[706]
BREAKTHROUGH TO NURSING SCHOLARSHIPS

National Student Nurses' Association
Attn: Foundation
45 Main Street, Suite 606
Brooklyn, NY 11201
(718) 210-0705   Fax: (718) 797-1186
E-mail: nsna@nsna.org
Web: www.nsna.org

Summary To provide financial assistance to Native American and other minority undergraduate and graduate students who wish to prepare for careers in nursing.

Eligibility This program is open to students currently enrolled in state-approved schools of nursing or pre-nursing associate degree, baccalaureate, diploma, generic master's, generic doctoral, R.N. to B.S.N., R.N. to M.S.N., or L.P.N./L.V.N. to R.N. programs. Graduating high school seniors are not eligible. Support for graduate education is provided only for a first degree in nursing. Applicants must be members of a racial or ethnic minority underrepresented among registered nurses (American Indian or Alaska Native, Hispanic or Latino, Native Hawaiian or other Pacific Islander, Black or African American, or Asian). They must be committed to providing quality health care services to underserved populations. Along with their application, they must submit a 200-word description of their professional and educational goals and how this scholarship will help them achieve those goals. Selection is based on academic achievement, financial need, and involvement in student nursing organizations and community health activities. U.S. citizenship or permanent resident status is required.

Financial data Stipends range from $1,000 to $2,500. A total of approximately $155,000 is awarded each year by the foundation for all its scholarship programs.

Duration 1 year.

Additional information Applications must be accompanied by a $10 processing fee.

Number awarded Varies each year; recently, 5 of these scholarships were awarded: 2 sponsored by the American Association of Critical-Care Nurses and 3 sponsored by the Mayo Clinic.

Deadline January of each year.

[707]
BROADCAST SALES ASSOCIATE PROGRAM

International Radio and Television Society Foundation
Attn: Director, Special Projects
420 Lexington Avenue, Suite 1601
New York, NY 10170-0101
(212) 867-6650   Toll Free: (888) 627-1266
Fax: (212) 867-6653   E-mail: apply@irts.org
Web: irts.org/broadcast-sales-associate-program.html

Summary To provide summer work experience to Native American and other minority graduate students interested in working in broadcast sales in the New York City area.

Eligibility This program is open to graduate students at 4-year colleges and universities who are members of a minority (Black, Hispanic, Asian/Pacific Islander, American Indian/Alaskan Native) group. Applicants must be interested in working during the summer in a sales training program traditionally reserved for actual station group employees. They must be a communications major or have demonstrated a strong interest in the field through extracurricular activities or other practical experience, but they are not required to have experience in broadcast sales.

Financial data Travel, housing, and a living allowance are provided.

Duration 9 weeks during the summer.

Additional information The program consists of a 1-week orientation to the media and entertainment business, followed by an 8-week internship experience in the sales division of a network stations group.

Number awarded Varies each year.

Deadline February of each year.

[708]
BULLIVANT HOUSER BAILEY LAW STUDENT DIVERSITY FELLOWSHIP PROGRAM

Bullivant Houser Bailey PC
Attn: Recruitment and Diversity Manager
888 S.W. Fifth Avenue, Suite 300
Portland, OR 97204-2089
(503) 499-4558   Toll Free: (800) 654-8972
Fax: (503) 295-0915   E-mail: jill.valentine@bullivant.com
Web: www.bullivant.com/diversity

Summary To provide financial assistance and work experience to Native American and other law students who come from a minority or disadvantaged background.

Eligibility This program is open to first-year law students who are members of a minority group (including any group underrepresented in the legal profession) and/or students coming from a disadvantaged educational or economic background. Applicants must have 1) a record of academic achievement and leadership in college and law school; 2) a willingness to complete a 12-week summer associateship at an office of the firm; and 3) a record of contributions to the community that promote diversity within society, the legal community, and/or law school.

Financial data The program provides a salaried associate position at an office of the firm during the summer following the first year of law school and a stipend of $7,500 for the second year.

Duration 1 year.

Number awarded 2 each year: 1 assigned to an associateship in the Sacramento office and 1 assigned to an associateship in the Portland office.

Deadline January of each year.

[709]
BUREAU OF INDIAN EDUCATION LOAN FOR SERVICE PROGRAM

American Indian Graduate Center
Attn: Executive Director
4520 Montgomery Boulevard, N.E., Suite 1-B
Albuquerque, NM 87109-1291
(505) 881-4584   Toll Free: (800) 628-1920
Fax: (505) 884-0427   E-mail: aigc@aigc.com
Web: www.aigc.com/02scholarships/bie/bie.htm

Summary To provide funding to Native American students interested in attending graduate school and working for organizations affiliated with the Bureau of Indian Affairs (BIA) or tribal governments.

Eligibility This program is open to enrolled members of federally-recognized American Indian tribes and Alaska Native groups and other students who can document one-fourth degree federally-recognized Indian blood. Applicants must be enrolled as full-time students in a graduate or professional school in the United States working on a master's, doctoral, or professional degree in any field. They must have a GPA of 3.0 or higher. Along with their application, they must submit a 500-word statement of intent describing their educational and/or career goals and expressing their commitment and willingness to give back to American Indian communities. Selection is based on that statement, academic achievement, and financial need.

Financial data These fellowship/loans are based on each applicant's unmet financial need. No interest is charged. Loan repayment may be cancelled at the rate of 1 year of loan payment for 1 year of employment with the BIA, the Bureau of Indian Education, a BIA-funded organization (on or off a reservation), or a tribal government.

Duration 1 year; may be renewed up to 1 additional year for master's degree students; up to 2 additional years for M.F.A. students; up to 3 additional years for doctoral degree students; up to 3 additional years for medicine, osteopathic medicine, dentistry, chiropractic, or veterinary degree students; or up to 2 additional years for law degree students.

Additional information This program is funded by the Bureau of Indian Education of the BIA. The application fee is $15.

Number awarded Varies each year.

Deadline May of each year.

[710]
BUTLER RUBIN DIVERSITY SCHOLARSHIP

Butler Rubin Saltarelli & Boyd LLP
Attn: Diversity Partner
70 West Madison Street, Suite 1800
Chicago, IL 60602
(312) 242-4120   Fax: (312) 444-9843
E-mail: kborg@butlerrubin.com
Web: www.butlerrubin.com/web/br.nsf/diversity

Summary To provide financial assistance and summer work experience to Native American and other minority law students who are interested in the area of business litigation.

Eligibility This program is open to law students of racial and ethnic backgrounds that will contribute to diversity in the legal profession. Applicants must be interested in the private practice of law in the area of business litigation and in a summer associateship in that field with Butler Rubin Saltarelli & Boyd in Chicago. Selection is based on academic performance and achievement, intention to remain in the Chicago area following graduation, and interpersonal and communication skills.

Financial data The stipend is $10,000 per year; funds are to be used for tuition and other expenses associated with law school. For the summer associateship, a stipend is paid.

Duration 1 year; may be renewed.

Additional information This program was established in 2006.

Number awarded 1 each year.

Deadline Deadline not specified.

[711]
CALIFORNIA BAR FOUNDATION DIVERSITY SCHOLARSHIPS

State Bar of California
Attn: California Bar Foundation
180 Howard Street
San Francisco, CA 94105-1639
(415) 856-0780, ext. 302   Fax: (415) 856-0788
E-mail: jguillory@calbarfoundation.org
Web: www.calbarfoundation.org

Summary To provide financial assistance to law students from any state who are Native Americans or members of other ethnic groups historically underrepresented in the legal profession and entering law school in California.

Eligibility This program to open to residents of any state who are entering their first year at a law school in California. Applicants must self-identify as being from a racial or ethnic group that historically has been underrepresented in the legal profession (Latino, African American, Asian and Pacific Islander, and Native American). They must be committed to making an impact in the community through leadership. Along with their application, they must submit a 500-word essay describing their commitment to serving the community and, if applicable, any significant obstacles or hurdles they have overcome to attend law school. Financial need is considered in the selection process.

Financial data Stipends for named awards are $7,500. Other stipends are $5,000 or $2,500.

Duration 1 year.

Additional information These scholarships were first awarded in 2008. Each year, the foundation grants awards named after sponsors that donate funding for the scholarships. Recipients are required to attend a reception in their honor in October of the year of their award and to submit a report on their progress at the end of that year.

Number awarded Varies each year; recently, the foundation awarded 28 of these scholarships: 20 named awards at $7,500, 4 awards at $5,000, and 4 awards at $2,500.

Deadline June of each year.

[712]
CALIFORNIA DIVERSITY FELLOWSHIPS IN ENVIRONMENTAL LAW

American Bar Association
Attn: Section of Environment, Energy, and Resources
321 North Clark Street
Chicago, IL 60654-7598
(312) 988-5602   Fax: (312) 988-5572
E-mail: jonusaid@staff.abanet.org
Web: www.abanet.org

Summary To provide funding to Native American and other law students from underrepresented groups who are interested in working on a summer project in environmental, energy, or resources law in California.

Eligibility This program is open to first- and second-year law students and third-year night students who are members of underrepresented and underserved groups, such as minority or low-income populations. Students may be residents of any state and attending school in any state; preference is given to residents of California and to students who are enrolled at law schools in California or who have a strong interest in the state. Applicants must be interested in working during the summer at a government agency or public interest organization on a project in California, with an emphasis on air quality issues in the Los Angeles basin and the Central Valley. Selection is based on interest in environmental issues, academic record, personal qualities, and leadership abilities.

Financial data The stipend is $5,000.

Duration 8 to 10 weeks during the summer.

Additional information This program is cosponsored by the State Bar of California's Environmental Law Section and the William and Flora Hewlett Foundation.

Number awarded Varies each year; recently, 13 of these fellowships were awarded.

Deadline April of each year.

[713]
CALIFORNIA INDIAN LAW ASSOCIATION ALLOGAN SLAGLE SCHOLARSHIP

California Indian Law Association
13223-1 Black Mountain Road, Suite 284
San Diego, CA 92129
Toll Free: (800) 690-1558   Fax: (760) 553-9473
E-mail: Christine@williamsjd.com
Web: www.calindianlaw.org

Summary To provide financial assistance to American Indian and Native Alaskan law students.

Eligibility This program is open to American Indians and Native Alaskans who are full-time law students. Preference is given to applicants in the following order: 1) entering law students who are enrolled or otherwise accepted members of federally-recognized or nonrecognized California Indian

nations; 2) entering law students who are enrolled members of federally-recognized Indian nations outside California but attending law school in California; 3) continuing law students who are enrolled or otherwise accepted members of federally-recognized or nonrecognized California Indian nations; 4) continuing law students who are enrolled members of federally-recognized Indian nations outside California but attending law school in California; and 5) entering or continuing law students of demonstrated Native ancestry who will be or are attending law school in California. Along with their application, they must submit an essay on their educational goals. Selection is based on academic achievement, financial need, and community involvement.

Financial data The stipend is $2,000.

Duration 1 year. Recipients may reapply.

Additional information This program, established in 2004, is managed by the California Community Foundation.

Number awarded 1 or more each year.

Deadline October of each year.

[714]
CALIFORNIA PLANNING FOUNDATION OUTSTANDING DIVERSITY AWARD

American Planning Association-California Chapter
Attn: California Planning Foundation
c/o Paul Wack
P.O. Box 1086
Morro Bay, CA 93443-1086
(805) 756-6331   Fax: (805) 756-1340
E-mail: pwack@calpoly.edu
Web: www.californiaplanningfoundation.org

Summary To provide financial assistance to minority and other undergraduate and graduate students in accredited planning programs at California universities who will increase diversity in the profession.

Eligibility This program is open to students entering their final year for an undergraduate or master's degree in an accredited planning program at a university in California. Applicants must be students who will increase diversity in the planning profession. Selection is based on academic performance, professional promise, and financial need.

Financial data The stipend is $3,000. The award includes a 1-year student membership in the American Planning Association (APA) and payment of registration for the APA California Conference.

Duration 1 year.

Additional information The accredited planning programs are at 3 campuses of the California State University system (California State Polytechnic University at Pomona, California Polytechnic State University at San Luis Obispo, and San Jose State University), 3 campuses of the University of California (Berkeley, Irvine, and Los Angeles), and the University of Southern California.

Number awarded 1 each year.

Deadline March of each year.

[715]
CALISTA SCHOLARSHIP FUND

Calista Corporation
Attn: Calista Scholarship Fund
301 Calista Court, Suite A
Anchorage, AK 99518-3028
(907) 279-5516   Toll Free: (800) 277-5516
Fax: (907) 272-5060
E-mail: scholarships@calistacorp.com
Web: www.calistacorp.com/scholarships.html

Summary To provide financial assistance to Alaska Natives who are shareholders or descendants of shareholders of the Calista Corporation and interested in working on an undergraduate or graduate degree at a school in any state.

Eligibility This program is open to Alaska Natives who are shareholders or lineal descendants of shareholders of the Calista Corporation. Applicants must be at least a high school graduate or have earned a GED and be in good academic standing with a GPA of 2.0 or higher. They must be working on an undergraduate or graduate degree at a college or university in any state. Along with their application, they must submit a 1-page essay on their educational and career goals. Financial need is considered in the selection process.

Financial data The amount awarded for undergraduates depends upon the recipient's GPA: $500 per semester for a GPA of 2.0 to 2.49, $750 per semester for a GPA of 2.5 to 2.99, and $1,000 per semester a GPA of 3.0 or higher. For graduate students, the stipend is $1,500 per semester. The funds are paid in 2 equal installments; the second semester check is not issued until grades from the previous semester's work are received.

Duration 1 year; recipients may reapply.

Additional information The Calista Corporation is 1 of 13 Alaska Native Regional Corporations created under the Alaska Native Claims Settlement Act of 1971. This program was established in 1994.

Number awarded Varies each year; recently, 79 of these scholarships were awarded.

Deadline June of each year.

[716]
CANFIT PROGRAM GRADUATE SCHOLARSHIPS

California Adolescent Nutrition and Fitness Program
Attn: Scholarship Program
2140 Shattuck Avenue, Suite 610
Berkeley, CA 94704
(510) 644-1533   Toll Free: (800) 200-3131
Fax: (510) 644-1535   E-mail: info@canfit.org
Web: canfit.org/scholarships

Summary To provide financial assistance to Native American and other minority students who are working on a graduate degree in nutrition, physical education, or public health in California.

Eligibility This program is open to American Indians, Alaska Natives, African Americans, Asian Americans, Pacific Islanders, and Latinos/Hispanics from California who are enrolled in 1) an approved master's or doctoral program in nutrition, public health, or physical education in the state, or 2) a preprofessional practice program approved by the American Dietetic Association at an accredited university in the state. Applicants must have completed 12 to 15 units of grad-

uate course work and have a cumulative GPA of 3.0 or higher. Along with their application, they must submit 1) documentation of financial need; 2) letters of recommendation from 2 individuals; 3) a 1-to 2-page letter describing their academic goals and involvement in community nutrition and/or physical education activities; and 4) an essay of 500 to 1,000 words on a topic related to healthy foods for youth from low-income communities of color.

Financial data A stipend is awarded (amount not specified).

Number awarded 1 or more each year.

Deadline March of each year.

[717]
CAP LATHROP ENDOWMENT SCHOLARSHIP FUND

Cook Inlet Region, Inc.
Attn: The CIRI Foundation
3600 San Jeronimo Drive, Suite 256
Anchorage, AK 99508-2870
(907) 793-3575   Toll Free: (800) 764-3382
Fax: (907) 793-3585   E-mail: tcf@thecirifoundation.org
Web: www.thecirifoundation.org/designated.htm

Summary To provide financial assistance for undergraduate or graduate studies in media-related fields to Alaska Natives and their lineal descendants.

Eligibility This program is open to Alaska Native enrollees under the Alaska Native Claims Settlement Act (ANCSA) of 1971 and their lineal descendants. Proof of eligibility must be submitted. Applicants may be enrollees of any of the 13 ANCSA regional corporations, but preference is given to original enrollees/descendants of Cook Inlet Region, Inc. (CIRI) who have a GPA of 3.0 or higher. There are no Alaska residency requirements or age limitations. Applicants must be accepted or enrolled full time in a 2-year undergraduate, 4-year undergraduate, or graduate degree program. They must be majoring in a media-related field (e.g., telecommunications, broadcast, business, engineering, journalism) and planning to work in the telecommunications or broadcast industry in Alaska after graduation. Along with their application, they must submit a 500-word statement on their educational and career goals and how they are contributing, or planning to contribute, to a positive Alaska Native community. Selection is based on that statement, academic achievement, rigor of course work or degree program, student financial contribution, financial need, grade level, previous work performance, community service, and relationship of degree program to career goals.

Financial data The stipend is $3,500 per year. Funds must be used for tuition, university fees, books, required class supplies, and campus housing and meal plans for students who must live away from their permanent home to attend college. Checks are sent directly to the recipient's school.

Duration 1 year (2 semesters).

Additional information This program was established in 1997. Recipients must attend school on a full-time basis and must plan to work in the broadcast or telecommunications industry in Alaska upon completion of their academic degree.

Number awarded 1 each year.

Deadline May of each year.

[718]
CARL H. MARRS SCHOLARSHIP FUND

Cook Inlet Region, Inc.
Attn: The CIRI Foundation
3600 San Jeronimo Drive, Suite 256
Anchorage, AK 99508-2870
(907) 793-3575   Toll Free: (800) 764-3382
Fax: (907) 793-3585   E-mail: tcf@thecirifoundation.org
Web: www.thecirifoundation.org/designated.htm

Summary To provide financial assistance for undergraduate or graduate studies in business-related fields to Alaska Natives who are original enrollees to Cook Inlet Region, Inc. (CIRI) and their lineal descendants.

Eligibility This program is open to Alaska Native enrollees to CIRI under the Alaska Native Claims Settlement Act (ANCSA) of 1971 and their lineal descendants. There are no Alaska residency requirements or age limitations. Applicants must be accepted or enrolled full time in a 4-year undergraduate or a graduate degree program in business administration, economics, finance, organizational management, accounting, or a similar field. They must have a GPA of 3.7 or higher. Along with their application, they must submit a 500-word statement on their educational and career goals and how they are contributing, or planning to contribute, to a positive Alaska Native community. Selection is based on that statement, academic achievement, rigor of course work or degree program, student financial contribution, financial need, grade level, previous work performance, community service, and relationship of degree program to career goals.

Financial data The stipend is $20,000 per year.

Duration 1 year; may be renewed.

Additional information This program was established in 2001.

Number awarded Varies each year; recently, 2 of these scholarships were awarded.

Deadline May of each year.

[719]
CARMEN E. TURNER SCHOLARSHIPS

Conference of Minority Transportation Officials
Attn: National Scholarship Program
818 18th Street, N.W., Suite 850
Washington, DC 20006
(202) 530-0551   Fax: (202) 530-0617
Web: www.comto.org/news-youth.php

Summary To provide financial assistance for college or graduate school to Native American and other members of the Conference of Minority Transportation Officials (COMTO).

Eligibility This program is open to undergraduate and graduate students who have been members of COMTO for at least 1 year. Applicants must be working on a degree in a field related to transportation with a GPA of 2.5 or higher. Along with their application, they must submit a cover letter with a 500-word statement of career goals. Financial need is not considered in the selection process. U.S. citizenship is required.

Financial data The stipend is $3,500. Funds are paid directly to the recipient's college or university.

Duration 1 year.

Additional information COMTO was established in 1971 to promote, strengthen, and expand the roles of minorities in

all aspects of transportation. Recipients are expected to attend the COMTO National Scholarship Luncheon.

Number awarded 2 each year.

Deadline April of each year.

[720]
CATHY L. BROCK MEMORIAL SCHOLARSHIP

Institute for Diversity in Health Management
Attn: Executive Assistant
One North Franklin Street, 30th Floor
Chicago, IL 60606
(312) 422-2630   Toll Free: (800) 233-0996
Fax: (312) 895-4511   E-mail: ejohnson@aha.org
Web: www.applicantsoft.com

Summary To provide financial assistance to Native American and other minority graduate students in health care management, especially those focusing on financial operations.

Eligibility This program is open to members of ethnic minority groups who are accepted or enrolled in an accredited graduate program in health care administration. Applicants must have a GPA of 3.0 or higher. They must demonstrate commitment to a career in health care administration. Along with their application, they must submit a personal statement of 300 to 500 words on their interest in health care management and their career goals. Selection is based on academic achievement, leadership potential, financial need, community involvement, commitment to health care administration, and overall professional maturity. Preference is given to applicants studying financial operations. U.S. citizenship is required.

Financial data The stipend ranges from $500 to $1,000.

Duration 1 year.

Number awarded 1 or more each year, depending on the availability of funds.

Deadline December of each year.

[721]
CDC/PRC MINORITY FELLOWSHIPS

Association of Schools of Public Health
Attn: Senior Manager, Graduate Training Programs
1101 15th Street, N.W., Suite 910
Washington, DC 20005
(202) 296-1099   Fax: (202) 296-1252
E-mail: TrainingPrograms@asph.org
Web: www.asph.org

Summary To provide an opportunity for Native American and other minority doctoral students to conduct research at Prevention Research Centers (PRCs) funded by the U.S. Centers for Disease Control and Prevention (CDC).

Eligibility This program is open to minority (African American/Black American, Hispanic/Latino, American Indian/ Alaska Native, and Asian/Pacific Islander) students working on a doctoral degree at a school of public health with a CDC-funded PRC. Applicants must be proposing to conduct a research project that is related to the PRC activities and is endorsed by the PRC director. Along with their application, they must submit a personal statement (2 pages or less) on why they are interested in this fellowship, including specifics regarding their interest in the opportunity, benefits they expect to receive from the fellowship experience, how the experience will shape their future career plans, and how the proposed project will advance the field of public health prevention research. Selection is based on the personal statement (30 points), curriculum vitae and transcripts (20 points), and project proposal (50 points). U.S. citizenship or permanent resident status is required.

Financial data The stipend is $22,500 per year. Fellows are also reimbursed up to $3,000 per year for health-related expenses, project-related travel, tuition, journal subscriptions, and association dues.

Duration 2 years.

Number awarded Varies each year; recently, 11 of these fellowships were awarded.

Deadline March of each year.

[722]
CECELIA SOMDAY EDUCATION FUND

Confederated Tribes of the Colville Reservation
Attn: Higher Education Office
P.O. Box 150
Nespelem, WA 99155-0150
(509) 634-2779   Fax: (509) 634-2790
E-mail: gloria.atkins@colvilletribes.com
Web: www.colvilletribes.com/cteap_higher_education.php

Summary To provide financial assistance to members of the Colville Confederated Tribes who wish to attend college or graduate school in any state.

Eligibility This program is open to enrolled members of the Confederated Tribes of the Colville Reservation who have a GPA of 3.0 or higher for their past 3 years of high school and/ or college study. Applicants must be interested in attending a college, university, or vocational/technical school in any state to work full time on an undergraduate or graduate degree. They should be able to demonstrate strong involvement in school and community activities and a desire to have a positive future impact on the tribes. Along with their application, they must submit a 200-word essay describing their educational goals.

Financial data The stipend is $2,000 per year.

Duration 1 year; may be renewed.

Additional information The Colville Reservation was established in 1872 as a federation of 12 tribes: Colville, Nespelem, San Poil, Lake, Palus, Wenatchee, Chelan, Entiat, Methow, southern Okanogan, Moses Columbia, and Nez Perce. The reservation is located in north central Washington, primarily in Ferry and Okanogan counties.

Number awarded Varies each year.

Deadline April of each year.

[723]
CECIL SHOLL MEMORIAL SCHOLARSHIPS

Natives of Kodiak, Inc.
Attn: Scholarship Committee
215 Mission Road, Suite 201
Kodiak, AK 99615
(907) 486-3606   Toll Free: (800) 648-8462
Fax: (907) 486-2745   E-mail: nokinfo@alaska.com
Web: www.nativesofkodiak.com/shareholder.html

Summary To provide financial assistance to shareholders of Natives of Kodiak, Inc. and their dependents and descendants who are interested in attending college, graduate school, or vocational school in any state.

Eligibility This program is open to the shareholders, dependents of shareholders, and descendants of shareholders of Natives of Kodiak, Inc. Applicants must be enrolled or planning to enroll full time at a recognized or accredited college, university, or vocational school in any state to work on an undergraduate, graduate, or vocational degree. Along with their application, they must submit a 2-page essay about their future plans for education, special talents and abilities, community involvement, philosophy of life, and reasons for attending school. Selection is based on that essay (10 points), GPA (10 points), leadership abilities (10 points), educational goals (10 points), letters of recommendation (10 points), financial need (10 points), achievements, activities, and responsibilities (10 points), and neatness and grammar (10 points).

Financial data Stipends are $2,500, $2,000, or $1,000 per year.

Duration 1 year; recipients may reapply.

Number awarded 20 each year: 5 at $2,500, 10 at $2,000, and 5 at $1,000.

Deadline April of each year.

[724]
CHARLES A. EASTMAN DISSERTATION FELLOWSHIP FOR NATIVE AMERICAN SCHOLARS

Dartmouth College
Attn: Office of Graduate Studies
6062 Wentworth Hall, Room 304
Hanover, NH 03755-3526
(603) 646-2106   Fax: (603) 646-8762
Web: graduate.dartmouth.edu

Summary To provide funding to Native American and other doctoral students who are interested in working on their dissertation at Dartmouth College.

Eligibility This program is open to doctoral candidates who have completed all requirements for the Ph.D. except the dissertation and are planning a career in higher education. Applicants must be Native Americans or other graduate students with a demonstrated commitment and ability to advance educational diversity. They must be interested in working on their dissertation at Dartmouth College. All academic fields that are taught in the Dartmouth undergraduate Arts and Sciences curriculum are eligible. Selection is based on academic achievement and promise; demonstrated commitment to increasing opportunities for underrepresented minorities and increasing cross-racial understanding; and potential for serving as an advocate and mentor for minority undergraduate and graduate students.

Financial data The stipend is $25,000. In addition, fellows receive office space, library privileges, and a $2,500 research allowance.

Duration 1 year, beginning in September.

Additional information The fellows are affiliated with a department or program at Dartmouth College. Fellows are expected to be in residence at Dartmouth College for the duration of the program and to complete their dissertation during that time. They are also expected to teach a course, either as the primary instructor or as part of a team.

Number awarded 1 each year.

Deadline January of each year.

[725]
CHEYENNE AND ARAPAHO HIGHER EDUCATION GRANTS

Cheyenne and Arapaho Tribes of Oklahoma
Attn: Higher Education Program
P.O. Box 38
Concho, OK 73022
(405) 262-0345, ext. 27653　　Toll Free: (800) 247-4612
Fax: (405) 262-5419　E-mail: heducation@c-a-tribes.org
Web: www.c-a-tribes.org/higher-education

Summary To provide financial assistance to enrolled Chey-enne-Arapaho tribal members who are interested in working on an undergraduate or graduate degree at a college in any state.

Eligibility This program is open to Cheyenne-Arapaho Indians who reside in any state and are at least a high school graduate (or the equivalent), approved for admission by a col-lege or university, and in financial need. Applicants may be enrolled or planning to enroll at a 2- or 4-year college or uni-versity (not a vocational or technical school) in any state. The vast majority of students assisted under this program are at the undergraduate level, although graduate and/or married students are eligible for consideration and assistance. Sum-mer and part-time students may apply as well, as long as application is made well in advance of enrollment and is accompanied by an official need evaluation.

Financial data The amount of the award depends on the need of the applicant.

Duration 1 year; renewable.

Number awarded 40 to 80 each year.

Deadline May of each year for fall semester; October for spring semester; or March for summer session.

[726]
CHICKASAW FOUNDATION HEALTH PROFESSIONS SCHOLARSHIP

Chickasaw Foundation
110 West 12th Street
P.O. Box 1726
Ada, OK 74821-1726
(580) 421-9030　　　　　　　Fax: (580) 421-9031
E-mail: ChickasawFoundation@chickasaw.net
Web: www.chickasawfoundation.org/index_20.htm

Summary To provide financial assistance to members of the Chickasaw Nation who are interested in working on an undergraduate, graduate, or vocational/technical degree in a health-related field.

Eligibility This program is open to members of the Chicka-saw Nation who are currently enrolled in an undergraduate, graduate, or vocational/technical program. Academic stu-dents must be preparing for a career as a dentist, dental hygienist, nurse, physician assistant, nurse practitioner, med-ical doctor, laboratory technologist, pharmacist, imaging technologist, behavioral health counselor, or biomedical engi-neer. Vocational students must be engaged in training as an emergency medical technician, licensed practical nurse, or electrician or plumber for the health arena. Applicants must have a GPA of 3.0 or higher. Along with their application, they must submit high school or college transcripts, 2 letters of recommendation, a copy of their Chickasaw Nation citizen-ship card, a copy of their Certificate of Indian Blood (CIB),

and a 1-page essay on their long-term goals and plans for achieving them. Financial need is not considered in the selec-tion process.

Financial data The stipend is $1,000.

Duration 1 year.

Number awarded 1 each year.

Deadline August of each year.

[727]
CHICKASAW NATION GENERAL SCHOLARSHIPS

Chickasaw Nation
Attn: Department of Education Services
300 Rosedale Road
Ada, OK 74820
(580) 421-7711　　　　　　　Fax: (580) 436-3733
E-mail: education.services@chickasaw.net
Web: www.chickasaweducationservices.com/index_90.htm

Summary To provide financial assistance to members of the Chickasaw Nation who are working on an undergraduate or graduate degree at a school in any state.

Eligibility This program is open to members of the Chicka-saw Nation who are working full or part time on an undergrad-uate, graduate, or doctoral degree at an accredited college or university in any state. Applicants must have a GPA of 3.0 or higher.

Financial data Stipends depend on the level of academic study, the number of units the recipients are taking, and their GPA. The range is from $150 per semester (for part-time freshmen and sophomores with a GPA of 3.0 to 3.49) to $550 per semester (for full-time graduate students with a GPA of 4.0).

Duration 1 semester; recipients may reapply.

Number awarded Varies each year.

Deadline January of each year for spring semester; June of each year for summer semester; August of each year for fall semester for continuing students; March of each year for high school seniors.

[728]
CHICKASAW NATION HIGHER EDUCATION GRANTS

Chickasaw Nation
Attn: Department of Education Services
300 Rosedale Road
Ada, OK 74820
(580) 421-7711　　　　　　　Fax: (580) 436-3733
E-mail: education.services@chickasaw.net
Web: www.chickasaweducationservices.com/index_90.htm

Summary To provide financial assistance to needy mem-bers of the Chickasaw Nation who are working on an under-graduate or graduate degree at a school in any state.

Eligibility This program is open to members of the Chicka-saw Nation who are working full or part time on an undergrad-uate, graduate, or doctoral degree at an accredited college or university in any state. Applicants must have a GPA of 2.0 or higher. They may be attending a community college, regional college or university, or research university.

Financial data For full-time undergraduates, stipends are $1,200 per semester at community colleges, $1,500 per semester at regional colleges and universities, or $2,400 per semester at research universities. For full-time graduate students, stipends are $2,400 per semester. For full-time doctoral students, stipends are $3,000 per semester. For part-time undergraduates, stipends are $100 per credit hour at community colleges, $125 per credit hour at regional colleges and universities, or $200 per credit hour at research universities. For part-time graduate students, stipends are $200 per credit hour at regional colleges and universities or $250 per credit hour at research universities. For part-time doctoral students, stipends are $250 per credit hour.

Duration 1 semester; recipients may reapply.

Number awarded Varies each year.

Deadline January of each year for spring semester; June of each year for summer semester; August of each year for fall semester for continuing students; March of each year for high school seniors.

[729]
CHRISTOPHER B. DURO GRADUATE FELLOWSHIP

Southern California Tribal Education Institute
Attn: Fellowship Coordinator
28940 Greenspot Road, Suite 228
Highland, CA 92346
E-mail: sctei@yahoo.com
Web: sctei.org

Summary To provide funding for dissertation research to Native Americans from North America who are working on a doctoral degree in any field.

Eligibility This program is open to doctoral candidates who have direct lineage and continued relationship to an Indigenous/Native community within North America. Applicants must be enrolled full time in an accredited doctoral degree program and be conducting research on their dissertation. Along with their application, they must submit a 2-page statement of purpose that includes their primary academic goals and research interests, how receipt of this fellowship will assist them in developing those goals and interests (especially how it will benefit indigenous communities), and how participation as a fellow will contribute to their academic, professional, and personal development. Financial need is considered in the selection process. An interview may be requested.

Financial data The grant ranges up to $25,000.

Duration 1 year.

Additional information This program was established in 2010. Recipients are required to perform community service with the sponsor and publish a scholarly article dealing with their research.

Number awarded 1 each year.

Deadline May of each year.

[730]
CHUGACH HERITAGE FOUNDATION SCHOLARSHIPS

Chugach Alaska Corporation
Attn: Chugach Heritage Foundation
3800 Centerpoint Drive
Anchorage, AK 99503
(907) 563-8866   Toll Free: (800) 858-2768
Fax: (907) 550-4147
E-mail: scholarships@chugach-ak.com
Web: www.chugachheritagefoundation.org/application.asp

Summary To provide financial assistance to undergraduate and graduate students who are original enrollees of the Chugach Alaska Corporation or their descendants and attending college in any state.

Eligibility This program is open to original enrollees and the descendants of original enrollees of the Chugach Alaska Corporation. Applicants must be enrolled or planning to enroll at an accredited college, university, or vocational program in any state as an undergraduate or graduate student. They must have a GPA of 2.0 or higher.

Financial data For full-time students, stipends are $4,800 per year for students working on an associate degree or 1- or 2-year certificate, $6,000 per year for juniors and seniors, or $12,000 per year for graduate students. Stipends for part-time students are prorated appropriately. Undergraduates who earn a GPA of 3.5 or higher are eligible for a bonus of up to $1,200 per year.

Duration 1 year; may be renewed if the recipient maintains a GPA of 2.0 or higher.

Additional information The Chugach Alaska Corporation is 1 of 13 Alaska Native Regional Corporations created under the Alaska Native Claims Settlement Act of 1971.

Number awarded Varies each year.

Deadline August of each year.

[731]
CIRI FOUNDATION ACHIEVEMENT SCHOLARSHIPS

Cook Inlet Region, Inc.
Attn: The CIRI Foundation
3600 San Jeronimo Drive, Suite 256
Anchorage, AK 99508-2870
(907) 793-3575   Toll Free: (800) 764-3382
Fax: (907) 793-3585   E-mail: tcf@thecirifoundation.org
Web: www.thecirifoundation.org/scholarships.htm

Summary To provide financial assistance for undergraduate or graduate studies to Alaska Natives who are original enrollees to Cook Inlet Region, Inc. (CIRI) and their lineal descendants.

Eligibility This program is open to Alaska Native enrollees to CIRI under the Alaska Native Claims Settlement Act (ANCSA) of 1971 and their lineal descendants. There are no Alaska residency requirements or age limitations. Applicants must be accepted or enrolled full time in a 4-year or graduate degree program. They must have a GPA of 3.0 or higher. Along with their application, they must submit a 500-word statement on their educational and career goals and how they are contributing, or planning to contribute, to a positive Alaska Native community. Selection is based on that statement, academic achievement, rigor of course work or degree program, student financial contribution, financial need, grade level, previous work performance, community service, and relationship of degree program to career goals.

Financial data   The stipend is $8,000 per year.

Duration   1 year (2 semesters).

Number awarded   Varies each year.

Deadline   May of each year.

[732]
CIRI FOUNDATION EXCELLENCE SCHOLARSHIPS

Cook Inlet Region, Inc.
Attn: The CIRI Foundation
3600 San Jeronimo Drive, Suite 256
Anchorage, AK 99508-2870
(907) 793-3575   Toll Free: (800) 764-3382
Fax: (907) 793-3585   E-mail: tcf@thecirifoundation.org
Web: www.thecirifoundation.org/scholarships.htm

Summary   To provide financial assistance for undergraduate or graduate studies to Alaska Natives who are original enrollees to Cook Inlet Region, Inc. (CIRI) and their lineal descendants.

Eligibility   This program is open to Alaska Native enrollees to CIRI under the Alaska Native Claims Settlement Act (ANCSA) of 1971 and their lineal descendants. There are no Alaska residency requirements or age limitations. Applicants must be accepted or enrolled full time in a 4-year undergraduate or a graduate degree program. They must have a GPA of 3.5 or higher. Along with their application, they must submit a 500-word statement on their educational and career goals and how they are contributing, or planning to contribute, to a positive Alaska Native community. Selection is based on that statement, academic achievement, rigor of course work or degree program, student financial contribution, financial need, grade level, previous work performance, community service, and relationship of degree program to career goals.

Financial data   The stipend is $10,000 per year.

Duration   1 year (2 semesters).

Number awarded   Varies each year; recently, 7 of these scholarships were awarded.

Deadline   May of each year.

[733]
CIRI FOUNDATION GENERAL SEMESTER SCHOLARSHIPS

Cook Inlet Region, Inc.
Attn: The CIRI Foundation
3600 San Jeronimo Drive, Suite 256
Anchorage, AK 99508-2870
(907) 793-3575   Toll Free: (800) 764-3382
Fax: (907) 793-3585   E-mail: tcf@thecirifoundation.org
Web: www.thecirifoundation.org/scholarships.htm

Summary   To provide financial assistance for undergraduate or graduate studies to Alaska Natives who are original enrollees to Cook Inlet Region, Inc. (CIRI) and their lineal descendants.

Eligibility   This program is open to Alaska Native enrollees to CIRI under the Alaska Native Claims Settlement Act (ANCSA) of 1971 and their lineal descendants. There are no Alaska residency requirements or age limitations. Applicants must be accepted or enrolled full time in a 2-year, 4-year, or graduate degree program. They must have a GPA of 2.5 or higher. Along with their application, they must submit a 500-word statement on their educational and career goals and how they are contributing, or planning to contribute, to a positive Alaska Native community. Selection is based on that statement, academic achievement, rigor of course work or degree program, student financial contribution, financial need, grade level, previous work performance, community service, and relationship of degree program to career goals.

Financial data   The stipend is $2,500 per semester.

Duration   1 semester; recipients may reapply.

Number awarded   Varies each year; recently, 213 of these scholarships were awarded.

Deadline   May or November of each year.

[734]
CIRI FOUNDATION INTERNSHIP PROGRAM

Cook Inlet Region, Inc.
Attn: The CIRI Foundation
3600 San Jeronimo Drive, Suite 256
Anchorage, AK 99508-2870
(907) 793-3575   Toll Free: (800) 764-3382
Fax: (907) 793-3585   E-mail: tcf@thecirifoundation.org
Web: www.thecirifoundation.org/internships.htm

Summary   To provide on-the-job training to Alaska Natives who are original enrollees to the Cook Inlet Region, Inc. (CIRI) and their lineal descendants.

Eligibility   This program is open to Alaska Native enrollees to CIRI under the Alaska Native Claims Settlement Act (ANCSA) of 1971 and their lineal descendants. Applicants must 1) be enrolled in a 2- or 4-year academic or graduate degree program with a GPA of 3.0 or higher; 2) have recently completed an undergraduate or graduate degree program; or 3) be enrolled or have recently completed a technical skills training program at an accredited or otherwise approved postsecondary institution. Along with their application, they must submit a 500-word statement on their areas of interest, their educational and career goals, how their career goals relate to their educational goals, and the type of work experience they would like to gain as it relates to their career and educational goals.

Financial data   The intern's wage is based on a trainee position and is determined by the employer of the intern with the approval of the foundation (which pays one half of the intern's wages).

Duration   Internships are approved on a quarterly basis for 480 hours of part-time or full-time employment. Interns may reapply on a quarter-by-quarter basis, not to exceed 12 consecutive months.

Additional information   The foundation and the intern applicant work together to identify an appropriate placement experience. The employer hires the intern. Placement may be with Cook Inlet Region, Inc., a firm related to the foundation, or a business or service organization located anywhere in the United States. The intern may be placed with more than 1 company during the internship period. Interns may receive academic credit.

Deadline   March, June, September, or November of each year.

[735]
CIRI FOUNDATION SPECIAL EXCELLENCE SCHOLARSHIPS

Cook Inlet Region, Inc.
Attn: The CIRI Foundation
3600 San Jeronimo Drive, Suite 256
Anchorage, AK 99508-2870
(907) 793-3575   Toll Free: (800) 764-3382
Fax: (907) 793-3585   E-mail: tcf@thecirifoundation.org
Web: www.thecirifoundation.org/scholarships.htm

Summary To provide financial assistance for undergraduate or graduate studies in selected fields to Alaska Natives who are original enrollees to Cook Inlet Region, Inc. (CIRI) and their lineal descendants.

Eligibility This program is open to Alaska Native enrollees to CIRI under the Alaska Native Claims Settlement Act (ANCSA) of 1971 and their lineal descendants. There are no Alaska residency requirements or age limitations. Applicants must be accepted or enrolled full time in a 4-year undergraduate or a graduate degree program. They must have a GPA of 3.7 or higher. Preference is given to students working on a degree in business, education, mathematics, sciences, health services, or engineering. Along with their application, they must submit a 500-word statement on their educational and career goals and how they are contributing, or planning to contribute, to a positive Alaska Native community. Selection is based on that statement, academic achievement, rigor of course work or degree program, student financial contribution, financial need, grade level, previous work performance, community service, and relationship of degree program to career goals.

Financial data The stipend is $20,000 per year.

Duration 1 year; may be renewed.

Additional information This program was established in 1997.

Number awarded 1 or more each year.

Deadline May of each year.

[736]
CITIZEN POTAWATOMI NATION TRIBAL ROLLS SCHOLARSHIPS

Citizen Potawatomi Nation
Attn: Office of Tribal Rolls
1601 South Gordon Cooper Drive
Shawnee, OK 74801-9002
(405) 878-5835   Toll Free: (800) 880-9880
Fax: (405) 878-4653
Web: www.potawatomi.org

Summary To provide financial assistance for college or graduate school to members of the Citizen Potawatomi Nation.

Eligibility This program is open to enrolled members of the Citizen Potawatomi Nation who are attending or planning to attend an undergraduate or graduate degree program, vocational technical career courses, or other accredited educational program in any state. Applicants must have a GPA of 2.0 or higher and be able to demonstrate financial need.

Financial data Stipends are $1,500 per semester for full-time students or $750 per semester for part-time students.

Duration 1 semester; may be renewed, provided the recipient maintains a GPA of 2.0 or higher.

Number awarded Varies each year; recently, 125 of these scholarships were awarded, including 94 to undergraduates, 10 to vocational/technical students, and 21 to graduate students.

Deadline July of each year for the fall session, November for the spring or winter session, or May for summer session.

[737]
CLSA LEADERSHIP FOR DIVERSITY SCHOLARSHIP

California School Library Association
Attn: Executive Director
950 Glenn Drive, Suite 150
Folsom, CA 95630
(916) 447-2684   Fax: (916) 447-2695
E-mail: info@csla.net
Web: www.csla.net/awa/scholarships.htm

Summary To provide financial assistance to Native Americans and other students who reflect the diversity of California's population and are interested in earning a credential as a library media teacher in the state.

Eligibility This program is open to students who are members of a traditionally underrepresented group enrolled in a college or university library media teacher credential program in California. Applicants must intend to work as a library media teacher in a California school library media center for a minimum of 3 years. Along with their application, they must submit a 250-word statement on their school library media career interests and goals, why they should be considered, what they can contribute, their commitment to serving the needs of multicultural and multilingual students, and their financial situation.

Financial data The stipend is $1,500.

Duration 1 year.

Number awarded 1 each year.

Deadline April of each year.

[738]
CNEC MISSION AWARD

Cherokee Nation
Attn: Cherokee Nation Education Corporation
115 East Delaware Street
P.O. Box 948
Tahlequah, OK 74465-0948
(918) 207-0950   Fax: (918) 207-0951
E-mail: contact@cnec-edu.org
Web: cnec.cherokee.org

Summary To provide financial assistance to citizens of the Cherokee Nation who are enrolled at a college or university in any state and working on an undergraduate or graduate degree in a field related to the Cherokee people.

Eligibility This program is open to citizens of the Cherokee Nation who are currently enrolled full time at a college or university in any state. Applicants must be working on an undergraduate or graduate degree that will prepare them for a career that will promote the revitalization of the language, culture, and history of Cherokee people. Along with their application, they must submit a 4-page personal essay that includes background information, their degree plan for higher education, why they have chosen that field of study, how they plan to serve Cherokee people when they complete higher education, and why they should be selected for this scholarship. Selection is based on the clarity and presentation of the essay; academic information (including transcripts and ACT scores); school, cultural and community activities; future plans to serve Cherokee people; and financial need.

Financial data The stipend is $1,500 per semester ($3,000 per year).

Duration 1 year. Renewal for the second semester requires the recipient to earn a GPA of 2.5 or higher in the first semester.

Number awarded 1 each year.

Deadline April of each year.

[739]
COCOPAH GRADUATE FELLOWSHIPS

Cocopah Indian Tribe
Attn: Education Department
County 15th and Avenue G
Somerton, AZ 85350
(928) 627-2101   Fax: (928) 627-3173
E-mail: cocopah@cocopah.com
Web: www.cocopah.com/education.html

Summary To provide financial assistance to members of the Cocopah Indian Nation who are attending or planning to attend a university to work on an graduate degree.

Eligibility This program is open to enrolled members of the Cocopah Indian Nation who are working full time on a master's or doctoral degree at an accredited public college or university in the United States. Applicants must be able to document financial need. Along with their application, they must submit an essay of 500 to 1,000 words discussing their academic and career goals and how those goals will contribute to the long-term goals of the Cocopah Indian Nation.

Financial data Grants are intended to cover tuition, books, room and board, transportation, personal costs, and any other expenses deemed necessary by the institution's financial aid department.

Duration 1 year; may be renewed, provided the recipient maintains a GPA of 3.0 or higher and full-time enrollment.

Number awarded Varies each year.

Deadline April of each year for fall semester; September of each year for spring semester.

[740]
COCOPAH SUMMER TUITION ASSISTANCE

Cocopah Indian Tribe
Attn: Education Department
County 15th and Avenue G
Somerton, AZ 85350
(928) 627-2101   Fax: (928) 627-3173
E-mail: cocopah@cocopah.com
Web: www.cocopah.com/education.html

Summary To provide financial assistance to members of the Cocopah Indian Nation who are interested in working during the summer on an undergraduate or graduate degree.

Eligibility This program is open to enrolled members of the Cocopah Indian Nation who are enrolled at or accepted by an accredited college or university in the United States. Undergraduates should have a GPA of 2.0 or higher; graduate students should have a GPA of 3.0 or higher. Applicants must be

interested in attending school during the summer. They must be able to document financial need.

Financial data Maximum grants are $2,500 for graduate students or $1,000 for undergraduates. Funds may be used for payment of direct costs only (tuition, fees, and textbooks).

Duration 1 summer term.

Number awarded Varies each year.

Deadline March of each year.

[741]
COLLEGE SCHOLARSHIPS FOUNDATION MINORITY STUDENT SCHOLARSHIP

College Scholarships Foundation
5506 Red Robin Road
Raleigh, NC 27613
(919) 630-4895   Toll Free: (888) 501-9050
E-mail: info@collegescholarships.org
Web: www.collegescholarships.org

Summary To provide financial assistance to Native Americans and other minority undergraduate and graduate students.

Eligibility This program is open to full-time undergraduate and graduate students who are Black, Hispanic, Native American, or Pacific Islander. Applicants must have a GPA of 3.0 or higher. Along with their application, they must submit a 300-word essay on how being a minority affected their pre-college education, how being a minority has positively affected their character, and where they see themselves in 10 years. U.S. citizenship is required.

Financial data The stipend is $1,000.

Duration 1 year.

Additional information This scholarship was first awarded in 2006. The sponsor was formerly known as the Daniel Kovach Scholarship Foundation.

Number awarded 1 each year.

Deadline December of each year.

[742]
COLORADO RIVER INDIAN TRIBES BIA GRANTS

Colorado River Indian Tribes
Attn: Career Development Office
13390 North First Avenue
Parker, AZ 85344
(928) 669-5548   Toll Free: (800) 809-6207
Fax: (928) 669-5570   E-mail: critcdo@critcdo.com
Web: www.crit-cdo.com/index.htm

Summary To provide need-based financial assistance to members of the Colorado River Indian Tribes who are interested in attending college or graduate school in any state.

Eligibility This program is open to enrolled members of the Colorado River Indian Tribes who are graduating high school seniors, GED recipients, or students already enrolled in college or graduate school. Applicants must be enrolled or planning to enroll at an accredited college or university in any state to work on an associate, bachelor's, master's, or doctoral degree. They must have a high school GPA of 2.5 or higher or a GED certificate with a composite score of 45% or higher. Financial need is considered in the selection process, and students must apply for all other available funding sources, such as Pell Grants and State Student Incentive Grants (SSIG).

Financial data A stipend is awarded (amount not specified).

Duration 1 year; may be renewed.

Additional information The Colorado River Indian Tribes Reservation was established in 1865 for Indians who resided along the Colorado River in Arizona and California. It currently includes members of the Mohave, Chemehuevi, Hopi, and Navajo tribes. This program is supported by funding from the U.S. Bureau of Indian Affairs (BIA).

Number awarded Varies each year.

Deadline June of each year for fall semester; October of each year for spring semester.

[743]
COLORADO RIVER INDIAN TRIBES TRIBAL SCHOLARSHIPS

Colorado River Indian Tribes
Attn: Career Development Office
13390 North First Avenue
Parker, AZ 85344
(928) 669-5548   Toll Free: (800) 809-6207
Fax: (928) 669-5570   E-mail: critcdo@critcdo.com
Web: www.crit-cdo.com/index.htm

Summary To provide merit-based financial assistance to members of the Colorado River Indian Tribes who are interested in attending college or graduate school in any state.

Eligibility This program is open to enrolled members of the Colorado River Indian Tribes who are graduating high school seniors, GED recipients, or students already enrolled in college or graduate school. Applicants must be enrolled or planning to enroll at an accredited college or university in any state to work on an associate, bachelor's, master's, or doctoral degree. They must have a high school GPA of 2.5 or higher or a GED certificate with a composite score of 45% or higher. Financial need is not considered in the selection process.

Financial data A stipend is awarded (amount not specified).

Duration 1 year; may be renewed.

Additional information The Colorado River Indian Tribes Reservation was established in 1865 for Indians who resided along the Colorado River in Arizona and California. It currently includes members of the Mohave, Chemehuevi, Hopi, and Navajo tribes. This program is supported by tribal funds.

Number awarded Varies each year.

Deadline June of each year for fall semester; October of each year for spring semester.

[744]
COMANCHE NATION COLLEGE SCHOLARSHIP PROGRAM

Comanche Nation
Attn: Education Programs
584 N.W. Bingo Road
P.O. Box 908
Lawton, OK 73502
(580) 492-3363   Fax: (580) 492-4017
Web: www.comanchenation.com/education/index.html

Summary To provide financial assistance to members of the Comanche Nation who are interested in working on an undergraduate or graduate degree.

Eligibility This program is open to enrolled members of the Comanche Nation who are high school graduates or GED recipients and attending or planning to attend a college or university. Applicants must intend to work on a bachelor's, master's, or doctoral degree or be enrolled in a 2-year program that will transfer to a 4-year institution. They must be able to demonstrate financial need and provide a reasonable assurance that they will be able to complete their degree program.

Financial data A stipend is awarded (amount not specified).

Duration 1 year; may be renewed.

Number awarded Varies each year.

Deadline March of each year for summer; May of each year for fall; September of each year for spring.

[745]
COMMERCIAL AND FEDERAL LITIGATION SECTION MINORITY FELLOWSHIP

The New York Bar Foundation
One Elk Street
Albany, NY 12207
(518) 487-5651   Fax: (518) 487-5699
E-mail: foundation@tnybf.org
Web: www.tnybf.org/restrictedfunds.htm

Summary To provide an opportunity for Native American and other minority residents of any state attending law school in New York to gain summer work experience in a litigation position in the public sector in the state.

Eligibility This program is open to minority students from any state who are enrolled in the first year at a law school in New York state. Applicants must have demonstrated an interest in commercial and federal litigation. They must be interested in working in a litigation position during the summer in the public sector in New York.

Financial data The stipend is $5,000.

Duration 10 weeks during the summer.

Additional information This program was established in 2007 by the Commercial and Federal Litigation Section of the New York State Bar Association. It is administered by The New York Bar Foundation.

Number awarded 1 each year.

Deadline January of each year.

[746]
COMMITTEE ON ETHNIC MINORITY RECRUITMENT SCHOLARSHIP

United Methodist Church-California-Pacific Annual
   Conference
Attn: Board of Ordained Ministry
1720 East Linfield Street
Glendora, CA 91740
(626) 335-6629   Fax: (626) 335-5750
E-mail: cathy.adminbom@gmail.com
Web: www.calpacordainedministry.org/523451

Summary To provide financial assistance to Native Americans and other minorities in the California-Pacific Annual Conference of the United Methodist Church (UMC) who are attending a seminary in any state to qualify for ordination as an elder or deacon.

Eligibility This program is open to members of ethnic minority groups in the UMC California-Pacific Annual Conference who are enrolled at a seminary in any state approved by the UMC University Senate. Applicants must have been approved as certified candidates by their district committee and be seeking Probationary Deacon or Elder's Orders. They may apply for 1 or more types of assistance: tuition scholarships, grants for books and school supplies (including computers), or emergency living expense grants.

Financial data Tuition stipends are $1,000 per year; books and supplies grants range up to $1,000 per year; emergency living expense grants depend on need and the availability of funds.

Duration 1 year; may be renewed up to 2 additional years.

Additional information The California-Pacific Annual Conference includes churches in southern California, Hawaii, Guam, and Saipan.

Number awarded Varies each year.

Deadline August of each year for fall term; December of each year for spring term.

[747]
CONFEDERATED SALISH AND KOOTENAI TRIBES HIGHER EDUCATION SCHOLARSHIPS

Confederated Salish and Kootenai Tribes
Attn: Tribal Education Department
P.O. Box 278
Pablo, MT 59855
(406) 675-2700, ext. 1072   Toll Free: (877) 575-0086
Fax: (406) 275-2814   E-mail: tribaled@cskt.org
Web: www.cskt.org/services/education.htm

Summary To provide financial assistance to members of the Confederated Salish and Kootenai Tribes who are interested in attending college or graduate school in any state.

Eligibility This program is open to enrolled members of the Confederated Salish and Kootenai Tribes who are enrolled or accepted for enrollment at an accredited college, university or vocational/technical school. Applicants must be able to demonstrate financial need. Assistance is available to students in the following priority order: 1) continuing students in good standing; 2) new students who have never received tribal higher education funding; 3) returning students who have taken a break from school for 1 or more quarters or semesters; and 4) non-need students. A small fund is set aside for graduate students.

Financial data For students at public colleges and universities in Montana, stipends supplement other funding available to the student to pay for tuition and fees, room and board, books, and miscellaneous expenses related to school. For students at private or out-of-state colleges and universities, support is limited to the level at public in-state colleges. Assistance for part-time students is capped at $3,000 per year and support for graduate students is limited to $2,000 per year.

Duration 1 year; may be renewed, provided recipients maintain a GPA of 2.0 or higher and full-time enrollment.

Number awarded Varies each year. Recently, 258 of these scholarships were awarded, including 141 to students at Salish Kootenai College, 39 to students at the University of Montana, 7 to students at the Bozeman or Billings campuses

of Montana State University, 71 to students at colleges and universities outside Montana, and 10 to graduate students.

Deadline April of each year.

[748]
CONFEDERATED TRIBES OF THE UMATILLA INDIAN RESERVATION HIGHER EDUCATION SCHOLARSHIPS

Confederated Tribes of the Umatilla Indian Reservation
Attn: Education and Training Department
46411 Ti'mine Way
Pendleton, OR 97801
(541) 276-8120   Toll Free: (888) 809-8027
Fax: (541) 276-6543   E-mail: info@ctuir.com
Web: www.umatilla.nsn.us/ed.html

Summary To provide financial assistance for a bachelor's or master's degree to Indians affiliated with the Confederated Tribes of the Umatilla Indian Reservation (CTUIR).

Eligibility This program is open to tribal members enrolled or planning to enroll in a bachelor's degree program at an accredited college or university; support for a master's or doctoral degree is available only if funds are available. Applicants must submit a personal letter describing their educational goals and how their receipt of this scholarship will benefit the CTUIR. Financial need is considered in the selection process.

Financial data A stipend is awarded (amount not specified).

Duration 1 year; may be renewed.

Additional information The CTUIR was established in 1949 when the Cayuse, Walla Walla, and Umatilla tribes entered into an agreement regarding their reservation in northeastern Oregon and southeastern Washington.

Number awarded Varies each year.

Deadline June of each year for fall quarter or semester; October of each year of winter quarter or semester; January of each year for spring quarter; April of each year for summer quarter.

[749]
CONNECTICUT COMMUNITY COLLEGE MINORITY FELLOWSHIP PROGRAM

Connecticut Community College System
Attn: System Officer for Diversity Awareness
61 Woodland Street
Hartford, CT 06105-9949
(860) 244-7606   Fax: (860) 566-6624
E-mail: karmstrong@commnet.edu
Web: www.commnet.edu/minority_fellowship.asp

Summary To provide financial assistance and work experience to graduate students in Connecticut, especially Native Americans and other minorities, who are interested in preparing for a career in community college teaching or administration.

Eligibility This program is open to graduate students who have completed at least 6 credits of graduate work and have indicated an interest in a career in community colleges. Current employees of the Connecticut Community Colleges are also eligible. Applicants must be willing to commit to at least 1 year of employment in the Connecticut Community College System. Although all qualified graduate students are eligible, the program encourages applicants to register who strengthen the racial and cultural diversity of the minority fellow registry. That includes, in particular, making all possible efforts to recruit from historically underrepresented groups.

Financial data Non-employee fellows receive a stipend of $3,500 per semester. Fellows who are current employees are reassigned time from their responsibilities.

Duration 1 year; may be renewed.

Additional information Teaching fellows are expected to spend 6 hours per week in teaching-related activities under the supervision of the mentor; those activities may include assisting the mentor. Administrative fellows spend at least 6 hours per week in structured administrative activity. In addition, all fellows are expected to spend at least 3 hours per week in additional assigned activities, including (but not limited to) attendance at Minority Fellowship Program and campus orientation activities, attendance at relevant faculty and staff meetings, participation in other system and college meetings or professional development activities, and evaluation of the fellowship experience at the end of the academic year.

Number awarded Up to 13 each year: 1 at each of the 12 colleges in the system and 1 in the chancellor's office.

Deadline July of each year.

[750]
CONSORTIUM FOR GRADUATE STUDY IN MANAGEMENT FELLOWSHIPS

Consortium for Graduate Study in Management
5585 Pershing Avenue, Suite 240
St. Louis, MO 63112-1795
(314) 877-5500   Toll Free: (888) 658-6814
Fax: (314) 877-5505   E-mail: recruiting@cgsm.org
Web: www.cgsm.org

Summary To provide financial assistance and work experience to Native Americans and other underrepresented minorities interested in preparing for a management career in business.

Eligibility This program is open to African Americans, Hispanic Americans (Chicanos, Cubans, Dominicans, and Puerto Ricans), and Native Americans who have graduated from college and are interested in preparing for a career in business. Other U.S. citizens and permanent residents who can demonstrate a commitment to the sponsor's mission of enhancing diversity in business education are also eligible. An undergraduate degree in business or economics is not required. Applicants must be planning to work on an M.B.A. degree at 1 of the consortium's 17 schools. Preference is given to applicants under 31 years of age.

Financial data The fellowship pays full tuition and required fees. Summer internships with the consortium's cooperative sponsors, providing paid practical experience, are also offered.

Duration Up to 4 semesters.

Additional information This program was established in 1966. The participating schools are Carnegie Mellon University, Cornell University, Dartmouth College, Emory University, Indiana University, University of Michigan, New York University, University of California at Berkeley, University of California at Los Angeles, University of North Carolina at Chapel Hill, University of Rochester, University of Southern Califor-

nia, University of Texas at Austin, University of Virginia, Washington University, University of Wisconsin at Madison, and Yale. Fellowships are tenable at member schools only. Application fees are $150 for students applying to 1 or 2 schools, $200 for 3 schools, $240 for 4 schools, $275 for 5 schools, or $300 for 6 schools.

Number awarded Varies each year; recently, more than 330 of these fellowships were awarded.

Deadline March of each year.

[751]
CONSTANGY, BROOKS & SMITH DIVERSITY SCHOLARS AWARD

Constangy, Brooks & Smith LLC
Attn: Chair, Diversity Council
200 West Forsyth Street, Suite 1700
Jacksonville, FL 32202-4317
(904) 356-8900   Fax: (904) 356-8200
E-mail: mzabijaka@constangy.com
Web: www.constangy.com/f-4.html

Summary To provide financial assistance to minority and other students enrolled in law schools in selected states.

Eligibility This program is open to second-year students enrolled in accredited law schools located in 1 of 3 regions: South (Alabama, Florida, Georgia, Tennessee), Midwest/West Coast (California, Illinois, Missouri, Texas, Wisconsin), or East (Massachusetts, New Jersey, North Carolina, South Carolina, Virginia/Washington, D.C.). Applicants must submit a personal statement on why diversity is important to them personally and in the legal profession. They must have a GPA of 2.7 or higher. Selection is based on academic achievement, commitment to diversity, and personal achievement in overcoming obstacles.

Financial data The stipend is $3,000.

Duration 1 year.

Number awarded 3 each year: 1 in each region.

Deadline November of each year.

[752]
CONSUELO W. GOSNELL MEMORIAL SCHOLARSHIPS

National Association of Social Workers
Attn: NASW Foundation
750 First Street, N.E., Suite 700
Washington, DC 20002-4241
(202) 408-8600, ext. 504   Fax: (202) 336-8292
E-mail: naswfoundation@naswdc.org
Web: www.naswfoundation.org/gosnell.asp

Summary To provide financial assistance to Native Americans, Hispanic Americans, and other students interested in working on a master's degree in social work.

Eligibility This program is open to students who have applied to or been accepted into an accredited M.S.W. program. Applicants must have demonstrated a commitment to work with, or have a special affinity with, American Indian, Alaska Native, or Hispanic/Latino populations in the United States. They must be members of the National Association of Social Workers (NASW), have the potential for completing an M.S.W. program, and have a GPA of 3.0 or higher. Applicants who have demonstrated a commitment to working with public or voluntary nonprofit agencies or with local grassroots groups in the United States are also eligible. Financial need is considered in the selection process.

Financial data The stipends range up to $2,000 per year.

Duration Up to 1 year; may be renewed for 1 additional year.

Number awarded Up to 10 each year.

Deadline March of each year.

[753]
COOK INLET TRIBAL COUNCIL TRIBAL HIGHER EDUCATION PROGRAM

Cook Inlet Tribal Council, Inc.
Attn: Tribal Scholarships and Grants Program
3600 San Jeronimo Drive, Suite 286
Anchorage, AK 99508
(907) 793-3578   Toll Free: (877) 985-5900
Fax: (907) 793-3589   E-mail: scholarships@citci.com
Web: www.citci.com/content/tribal-higher-education

Summary To provide financial assistance to Alaska Native shareholders of the Cook Inlet Region, Inc. (CIRI) and their descendants who are working on an undergraduate or graduate degree.

Eligibility This program is open to Alaska Native shareholders of CIRI and their descendants, regardless of residence, who are enrolled or planning to enroll full time at an accredited college, university, or vocational training facility. Applicants must be working on a certificate, associate, bachelor's, or graduate degree. Along with their application they must submit a letter of reference, a 200-word statement of purpose, their Certificate of Indian Blood (CIB), a letter of acceptance from the school, transcripts, their Student Aid Report, a budget forecast, and (for males) documentation of Selective Service registration. Awards are presented on a first-come, first-served basis as long as funds are available.

Financial data This program provides supplementary matching financial aid. Awards are intended to be applied to tuition, fees, course-required books and supplies, and on-campus housing and meal plans only. Total funding over a lifetime educational career is limited to $15,000.

Duration 1 year; may be renewed up to 4 additional years if the recipient maintains a GPA of 2.0 or higher.

Additional information Students whose CIB gives their village as Tyonek, Kenai, Ninilchik, Knik, or Salamatof must apply directly to their village organization.

Number awarded Varies each year, depending on the availability of funds.

Deadline May of each year for fall; November of each year for spring.

[754]
COPPER RIVER NATIVE ASSOCIATION HIGHER EDUCATION SCHOLARSHIP

Copper River Native Association
Attn: Higher Education Coordinator
Mile 104 Richardson Highway
Drawer H
Copper Center, AK 99573
(907) 822-5241   Fax: (907) 822-8801
Web: crnative.org

Summary To provide financial assistance for undergraduate or graduate studies in any state to Alaska Natives who are enrolled in villages in the Ahtna region.

Eligibility This program is open to enrolled members, or direct descendants eligible for enrollment with one-quarter or more Indian blood quantum, of 1) the villages of Cantwell, Gakona, or Tazlina in Alaska; or 2) other villages in the Ahtna Region and not enrolled or receiving funding from any other tribal government. Alaska residency is not required. Applicants must be enrolled or accepted as full-time students at an accredited college or university in any state on the undergraduate (4-year program) or graduate school level. They should have at least a 2.0 GPA. Along with their application, they must submit a 200-word personal statement of educational goals.

Financial data The stipend is $2,000 per semester. Funds are sent directly to the recipient's school to be used for tuition, university fees, course-related books and supplies, and campus housing and meal plans.

Duration 1 year; may be renewed if the recipient maintains a GPA of 2.0 or higher and full-time enrollment, but the lifetime educational support limit is $15,000.

Additional information The association is also known as Atna'T'Aene Nene.

Number awarded Varies each year.

Deadline September of each year for fall; January of each year for spring; June of each year for summer.

[755]
COQUILLE INDIAN TRIBE COMPUTER EQUIPMENT PROGRAM

Coquille Indian Tribe
Attn: Education Department
2611 Mexeye Loop
Coos Bay, OR 97420
(541) 756-0904   Toll Free: (800) 622-5869
Fax: (541) 888-2418
E-mail: lindamecum@coquilletribe.org
Web: www.coquilletribe.org

Summary To provide funding for the purchase of computer equipment to members of the Coquille Indian Tribe who are working full time on an undergraduate or graduate degree.

Eligibility This program is open to enrolled members of the Coquille Indian Tribe who have been enrolled for at least 2 semester as full-time undergraduate or graduate students at an accredited college, university, or community college in any state. Applicants must be seeking funding for the purchase of computer equipment.

Financial data The grant is $1,200; funds must be used for purchase of computer equipment or programming, and not for training, shipping, and/or maintenance of equipment.

Duration This is a 1-time grant.

Number awarded Varies each year.

Deadline Deadline not specified.

[756]
COQUILLE INDIAN TRIBE HIGHER EDUCATION GRANTS

Coquille Indian Tribe
Attn: Education Department
2611 Mexeye Loop
Coos Bay, OR 97420
(541) 756-0904   Toll Free: (800) 622-5869
Fax: (541) 888-2418
E-mail: lindamecum@coquilletribe.org
Web: www.coquilletribe.org

Summary To provide financial assistance to members of the Coquille Indian Tribe who are attending or planning to attend college or graduate school in any state.

Eligibility This program is open to enrolled members of the Coquille Indian Tribe who are entering or continuing undergraduate or graduate students at an accredited college, university, or community college in any state. Along with their application, they must submit a personal statement on their educational goals, the schools they plan to attend, the degrees they plan to pursue, their plans after college graduation, and how the tribe will benefit by sending them to school. Financial need is also considered in the selection process.

Financial data Maximum stipends are $9,000 per year for full-time students at 4-year colleges and universities or $7,500 per year for students a 2-year community colleges. Part-time students are eligible to receive funding for books, fees, and tuition only.

Duration 1 year; may be renewed up to 4 additional years.

Number awarded Varies each year.

Deadline Deadline not specified.

[757]
CREEK NATION POST GRADUATE PROGRAM

Muscogee (Creek) Nation of Oklahoma
Attn: Higher Education Program
P.O. Box 580
Okmulgee, OK 74447
(918) 732-7688   Toll Free: (800) 482-1979, ext. 7688
Fax: (918) 732-7694
E-mail: jothill@muscogeenation-nsn.gov
Web: www.muscogeenation-nsn.gov

Summary To provide financial assistance to enrolled citizens of the Muscogee (Creek) Nation interested in working on a graduate degree at a college or university in any state.

Eligibility This program is open to enrolled citizens of the Muscogee (Creek) Nation (no minimum blood quantum required) who are enrolled or planning to enroll in an accredited college or university in any state to work on a master's, doctoral, or professional degree. Applicants must have a GPA of 3.0 or higher. They must submit copies of their Certificate of Indian Blood (CIB) and tribal enrollment card.

Financial data The maximum award is $2,000 per semester for full-time study or $1,000 per semester for part-time study.

Duration 1 year; may be renewed for up to 1 additional year (for master's degree students) or up to 2 additional years (for doctoral students).

Number awarded Varies each year.

Deadline June of each year for summer; October of each year for fall.

[758]
CROWELL & MORING DIVERSITY IN THE LEGAL PROFESSION SCHOLARSHIP

Crowell & Moring LLP
Attn: Diversity in the Legal Profession Scholarship
1001 Pennsylvania Avenue, N.W.
Washington, DC 20004-2595
(202) 624-2500   Fax: (202) 628-5116
E-mail: scholarship@crowell.com
Web: www.crowell.com/Careers/DiversityScholarship.aspx

Summary To provide financial assistance to Native Americans and members of other racial and ethnic groups from any state who are underrepresented in the legal profession and attending law school in the District of Columbia.

Eligibility This program is open to underrepresented racial and ethnic minorities (American Indians/Alaskan Natives, Blacks/African Americans or Africans, Hispanics/Latinos, or Asians/Pacific Islanders) from any state currently working on a J.D. degree and enrolled in their second year at an accredited law school in the District of Columbia. Applicants must have overcome significant obstacles, disadvantages, or challenges in their pursuit of a legal education. Selection is based on academic performance, demonstrated leadership skills, relevant work experience, community service, special accomplishments and honors, and financial need. Finalists are interviewed.

Financial data Stipends are $10,000 or $7,500.

Duration 1 year; nonrenewable.

Number awarded 3 each year: 1 at $10,000 and 2 at $7,500.

Deadline December of each year.

[759]
CULTURAL RESOURCES DIVERSITY INTERNSHIP PROGRAM

Student Conservation Association, Inc.
Attn: Diversity Internships
1800 North Kent Street, Suite 102
Arlington, VA 22209
(703) 524-2441   Fax: (703) 524-2451
E-mail: jchow@thesca.org
Web: www.thesca.org/partners/special-initiatives

Summary To provide summer work experience at U.S. National Park Service (NPS) facilities to 1) Native Americans and other ethnically diverse undergraduate and graduate students and 2) students with disabilities.

Eligibility This program is open to currently-enrolled students at the sophomore or higher level. Applicants must be U.S. citizens or permanent residents with a GPA of 3.0 or higher. Although all students may apply, the program is designed to give ethnically diverse students and students with disabilities the opportunity to experience the diversity of careers in the federal sector. Applicants are assigned to a position within the NPS. Possible projects include editing publications, planning exhibits, participating in archaeological excavations, preparing research reports, cataloguing park and museum collections, providing interpretive programs on historical topics, developing community outreach, and writing lesson plans based on historical themes.

Financial data Interns receive a salary of $225 per week, basic medical insurance coverage, a housing stipend of up to

$800 per month, a $100 uniform allowance, travel expenses up to $630, and eligibility for an Americorps Educational Award of $1,000.

Duration 10 weeks in the summer (beginning in June).

Additional information While participating in the internship, students engage in tri-weekly evening career and professional development events, ongoing career counseling, mentoring, and personal and career development services.

Number awarded Approximately 15 each year.

Deadline February of each year.

[760]
DAVID HILLIARD EATON SCHOLARSHIP

Unitarian Universalist Association
Attn: Ministerial Credentialing Office
25 Beacon Street
Boston, MA 02108-2800
(617) 948-6403   Fax: (617) 742-2875
E-mail: mco@uua.org
Web: www.uua.org

Summary To provide financial assistance to Native American and other minority women preparing for the Unitarian Universalist (UU) ministry.

Eligibility This program is open to women from historically marginalized groups who are currently enrolled or planning to enroll full or at least half time in a UU ministerial training program with aspirant or candidate status. Applicants must be citizens of the United States or Canada. Priority is given first to those who have demonstrated outstanding ministerial ability and secondarily to students with the greatest financial need (especially persons of color).

Financial data The stipend ranges from $1,000 to $11,000 per year.

Duration 1 year.

Number awarded Varies each year; recently, 2 of these scholarships were awarded.

Deadline April of each year.

[761]
DAVID SANKEY MINORITY SCHOLARSHIP IN METEOROLOGY

National Weather Association
Attn: Executive Director
228 West Millbrook Road
Raleigh, NC 27609-4304
(919) 845-1546   Fax: (919) 845-2956
E-mail: exdir@nwas.org
Web: www.nwas.org

Summary To provide financial assistance to Native Americans and other minorities working on an undergraduate or graduate degree in meteorology.

Eligibility This program is open to members of minority groups who are either entering their sophomore or higher year of undergraduate study or enrolled as graduate students. Applicants must be working on a degree in meteorology. Along with their application, they must submit a 1-page statement explaining why they are applying for this scholarship. Selection is based on that statement, academic achievement, and 2 letters of recommendation.

Financial data The stipend is $1,000.

Duration 1 year.

Additional information This program was established in 2002.

Number awarded 1 each year.

Deadline April of each year.

[762]
DAVIS WRIGHT TREMAINE 1L DIVERSITY SCHOLARSHIP PROGRAM

Davis Wright Tremaine LLP
Attn: Diversity Scholarship Program
1201 Third Avenue, Suite 2200
Seattle, WA 98101-3045
(206) 622-3150   Toll Free: (877) 398-8416
Fax: (206) 757-7700   E-mail: carolyuly@dwt.com
Web: www.dwt.com

Summary To provide financial assistance and summer work experience to Native Americans and other law students of color.

Eligibility This program is open to first-year law students of color and others of diverse backgrounds. Applicants must have a record of academic achievement as an undergraduate and in the first year of law school that demonstrates promise for a successful career in law, a commitment to civic involvement that promotes diversity and will continue after entering the legal profession, and a willingness to become an associate in the sponsor's Seattle or Portland office during the summer between their first and second year of law school. They must submit a current resume, a complete undergraduate transcript, grades from the first semester of law school, a 1-page essay describing their eligibility for and interest in the scholarship, a legal writing sample, and 2 or 3 references. Although demonstrated need may be taken into account, applicants need not disclose their financial circumstances.

Financial data The award consists of a $7,500 stipend for second-year tuition and expenses and a paid summer clerkship.

Duration 1 academic year and summer.

Number awarded 2 each year: 1 in the Seattle office and 1 in the Portland office.

Deadline January of each year.

[763]
DELTA KAPPA GAMMA NATIVE AMERICAN PROJECT GRANTS

Delta Kappa Gamma Society International-Mu State
   Organization
c/o Beverly Staff, Native American Project
7407 Lillie Lane
Pensacola, FL 32526
(850) 944-3302   E-mail: leannjax@yahoo.com
Web: www.orgsites.com/fl/mustatedeltakappagamma

Summary To provide financial assistance to female Native Americans from Florida who are working on a degree in education or conducting research into the history of Native Americans at a college or university in the state.

Eligibility This program is open to women who are members of a recognized Native American tribe in Florida. Applicants must be enrolled at an accredited college or university in the state and either working on a degree in education or conducting research into the history of Native Americans in Florida. Along with their application, they must submit a brief statement with details of the purpose of the grant, a letter of recommendation from a tribal official, and a copy of high school or college transcripts.

Financial data The stipend is $1,000.

Duration 1 year.

Number awarded 6 each year: 1 in each of the districts of the sponsoring organization in Florida.

Deadline May of each year.

[764]
DENNIS WONG AND ASSOCIATES SCHOLARSHIP

Ke Ali'i Pauahi Foundation
Attn: Financial Aid & Scholarship Services
567 South King Street, Suite 160
Honolulu, HI 96813
(808) 534-3966   Toll Free: (800) 842-4682, ext. 43966
Fax: (808) 534-3890   E-mail: scholarships@pauahi.org
Web: www.pauahi.org/scholarships

Summary To provide financial assistance to undergraduate or graduate students in liberal arts or science, especially those of Native Hawaiian descent.

Eligibility This program is open to students working full time on an undergraduate degree in liberal arts or science or a graduate degree in a professional field. Applicants must have a GPA of 3.5 or higher and a well-rounded and balanced record of achievement in preparation for career objectives. Financial need is considered in the selection process. Residency in Hawaii is not required, but preference is given to Native Hawaiians (descendants of the aboriginal inhabitants of the Hawaiian Islands prior to 1778).

Financial data The stipend is $1,100.

Duration 1 year.

Number awarded 3 each year.

Deadline March of each year.

[765]
DEPARTMENT OF HOMELAND SECURITY SUMMER FACULTY AND STUDENT RESEARCH TEAM PROGRAM

Oak Ridge Institute for Science and Education
Attn: Science and Engineering Education
P.O. Box 117
Oak Ridge, TN 37831-0117
(865) 574-1447   Fax: (865) 241-5219
E-mail: Patti.Obenour@orau.gov
Web: see.orau.org

Summary To provide an opportunity for teams of students and faculty from Tribal Colleges or Universities (TCUs) and other minority serving educational institutions to conduct summer research in areas of interest to the Department of Homeland Security (DHS).

Eligibility This program is open to teams of up to 2 students (undergraduate and/or graduate) and 1 faculty from Historically Black Colleges and Universities (HBCUs), Hispanic Serving Institutions (HSIs), Tribal Colleges and Universities (TCUs), Alaska Native Serving Institutions (ANSIs), and Native Hawaiian Serving Institutions (NHSIs). Applicants must be interested in conducting research at designated DHS Centers of Excellence in science, technology, engineering, or mathematics related to homeland security (HS-STEM),

including explosives detection, mitigation, and response; social, behavioral, and economic sciences; risk and decision sciences; human factors aspects of technology; chemical threats and countermeasures; biological threats and countermeasures; community, commerce, and infrastructure resilience; food and agricultural security; transportation security; border security; immigration studies; maritime and port security; infrastructure protection; natural disasters and related geophysical studies; emergency preparedness and response; communications and interoperability; or advanced data analysis and visualization. Faculty must have a full-time appointment at an eligible institution and have received a Ph.D. in an HS-STEM discipline no more than 7 years previously; at least 2 years of full-time research and/or teaching experience is preferred. Students must have a GPA of 3.0 or higher and be enrolled full time. Undergraduates must be entering their junior or senior year. U.S. citizenship is required. Selection is based on relevance and intrinsic merit of the research (40%), faculty applicant qualifications (30%), academic benefit to the faculty applicant and his/her institution (10%), and student applicant qualifications (20%).

Financial data Stipends are $1,200 per week for faculty, $600 per week for graduate students, and $500 per week for undergraduates. Faculty members who live more than 50 miles from their assigned site may receive a relocation allowance of $1,500 and travel expenses up to an additional $500. Limited travel expenses for 1 round trip are reimbursed for undergraduate and graduate students living more than 50 miles from their assigned site.

Duration 12 weeks during the summer.

Additional information This program is funded by DHS and administered by Oak Ridge Institute for Science and Education (ORISE). Recently, the available DHS Centers of Excellence were the Center for Advancing Microbial Risk Assessment (led by Michigan State University and Drexel University); the Center for Risk and Economic Analysis of Terrorism Events (led by University of Southern California); the National Center for Food Protection and Defense (led by University of Minnesota); the Center of Excellence for Foreign Animal and Zoonotic Disease Defense (led by Texas A&M University and Kansas State University); the National Center for the Study of Preparedness and Catastrophic Event Response (led by Johns Hopkins University); the National Consortium for the Study of Terrorism and Responses to Terrorism (led by University of Maryland); the Center of Excellence for Awareness and Location of Explosives-Related Threats (led by Northeastern University and University of Rhode Island); the National Center for Border Security and Immigration (led by the University of Arizona and the University of Texas at El Paso); the Center for Maritime, Island and Remote and Extreme Environment Security (led by the University of Hawaii and Stevens Institute of Technology); the Center for Natural Disasters, Coastal Infrastructure, and Emergency Management (led by the University of North Carolina at Chapel Hill and Jackson State University); the National Transportation Security Center of Excellence (consisting of 7 institutions); and the Center of Excellence in Command, Control, and Interoperability (led by Purdue University and Rutgers University).

Number awarded Approximately 12 teams are selected each year.

Deadline January of each year.

[766]
DEPARTMENT OF STATE STUDENT INTERN PROGRAM

Department of State
Attn: HR/REE
2401 E Street, N.W., Suite 518 H
Washington, DC 20522-0108
(202) 261-8888   Toll Free: (800) JOB-OVERSEAS
Fax: (301) 562-8968   E-mail: Careers@state.gov
Web: www.careers.state.gov/students/programs

Summary   To provide a work/study opportunity to minority and other undergraduate and graduate students interested in foreign service.

Eligibility   This program is open to full- and part-time continuing college and university juniors, seniors, and graduate students. Applications are encouraged from students with a broad range of majors, such as business or public administration, social work, economics, information management, journalism, and the biological, engineering, and physical sciences, as well as those majors more traditionally identified with international affairs. U.S. citizenship is required. The State Department particularly encourages eligible women and minority students with an interest in foreign affairs to apply.

Financial data   Most internships are unpaid. A few paid internships are granted to applicants who can demonstrate financial need. If they qualify for a paid internship, they are placed at the GS-4 step 5 level (currently with an annual rate of $27,786). Interns placed abroad may also receive housing, medical insurance, a travel allowance, and a dependents' allowance.

Duration   Paid internships are available only for 10 weeks during the summer. Unpaid internships are available for 1 semester or quarter during the academic year, or for 10 weeks during the summer.

Additional information   About half of all internships are in Washington, D.C., or occasionally in other large cities in the United States. The remaining internships are at embassies and consulates abroad. Depending upon the needs of the department, interns are assigned junior-level professional duties, which may include research, preparing reports, drafting replies to correspondence, working in computer science, analyzing international issues, financial management, intelligence, security, or assisting in cases related to domestic and international law. Interns must agree to return to their schooling immediately upon completion of their internship.

Number awarded   Approximately 800 internships are offered each year, but only about 5% of those are paid positions.

Deadline   February of each year for fall internships; June of each year for spring internships; October of each year for summer internships.

[767]
DEPARTMENT OF THE INTERIOR DIVERSITY INTERN PROGRAM

Department of the Interior
Attn: Office of Educational Partnerships
1849 C Street, N.W., MS 5221 MIB
Washington, DC 20240
(202) 208-6403   Toll Free: (888) 447-4392
Fax: (202) 208-3620   TDD: (202) 208-5069
E-mail: ed_partners@ios.doi.gov
Web: www.doi.gov/hrm/dipfact.html

Summary   To provide work experience at federal agencies involved with natural and cultural resources to 1) Native American and other minority college and graduate students and 2) students with disabilities.

Eligibility   This program is open to currently-enrolled students at the sophomore or higher level at Historically Black Colleges and Universities (HBCUs), Hispanic-Serving Institutions (HSIs), Tribal Colleges and Universities (TCUs), and some other major institutions. Applicants must be U.S. citizens or permanent residents with a GPA of 3.0 or higher. Although all students may apply, the program is designed to give ethnically diverse students and students with disabilities the opportunity to experience the diversity of careers in the federal sector. Applicants are assigned to a position within the U.S. Department of the Interior (DOI). Possible placements include archaeology and anthropology; wildlife and fisheries biology; business administration, accounting, and finance; civil and environmental engineering; computer science, especially GIS applications; human resources; mining and petroleum engineering; communications and public relations; web site and database design; environmental and realty law; geology, hydrology, and geography; Native American studies; interpretation and environmental education; natural resource and range management; public policy and administration; and surveying and mapping.

Financial data   The weekly stipend is $420 for sophomores and juniors, $450 for seniors, or $520 for law and graduate students. Other benefits include a pre-term orientation, transportation to the orientation and the work site, worker's compensation, and accident insurance.

Duration   10 weeks in the summer (beginning in June) or 15 weeks in the fall (beginning in September) or spring (beginning in January).

Additional information   This program, which began in 1994, is administered through 5 nonprofit organizations: Hispanic Association of Colleges and Universities, Minority Access, Inc., Student Conservation Association, and National Association for Equal Opportunity in Higher Education. While participating in the internship, students engage in tri-weekly evening career and professional development events, ongoing career counseling, mentoring, and personal and career development services.

Number awarded   Varies each year; since the program began, more than 700 interns have participated.

Deadline   February of each year for summer; June of each year for fall; November of each year for spring.

[768]
DICKSTEIN SHAPIRO DIVERSITY SCHOLARSHIP

Dickstein Shapiro LLP
Attn: Director of Professional Development and Attorney Recruiting
1825 Eye Street, N.W.
Washington, DC 20006-5403
(202) 420-4880   Fax: (202) 420-2201
E-mail: careers@dicksteinshapiro.com
Web: www.dicksteinshapiro.com/careers/diversity

Summary To provide financial assistance and summer work experience at Dickstein Shapiro in Washington, D.C. or New York City to Native Americans and other diverse law students from any state.

Eligibility This program is open to second-year diverse law students, including 1) members of the lesbian, gay, bisexual, and transgender (LGBT) community; 2) members of minority ethnic and racial groups (Blacks, Hispanics and Latinos, Asians, American Indians and Native Alaskans, and Native Hawaiians and Pacific Islanders); and 3) students with disabilities. Applicants must be interested in a summer associateship with Dickstein Shapiro in Washington, D.C. or New York City. Selection is based on academic and professional experience as well as the extent to which they reflect the core values of the firm: excellence, loyalty, respect, initiative, and integrity.

Financial data The stipend is $25,000, including $15,000 upon completion of the summer associate program and $10,000 upon acceptance of a full-time offer of employment following graduation.

Duration The associateship takes place during the summer following the second year of law school and the stipend covers the third year of law school.

Additional information This program was established in 2006.

Number awarded 1 or more each year.

Deadline September of each year.

[769]
DINSMORE & SHOHL LLP DIVERSITY SCHOLARSHIP PROGRAM

Dinsmore & Shohl LLP
Attn: Manager of Legal Recruiting
255 East Fifth Street, Suite 1900
Cincinnati, OH 45202
(513) 977-8488   Fax: (513) 977-8141
E-mail: dinsmore.legalrecruiting@dinslaw.com
Web: www.dinslaw.com/careers/diversityscholarship

Summary To provide financial assistance and summer work experience to Native Americans and other law students from groups traditionally underrepresented in the legal profession.

Eligibility This program is open to first- and second-year law students who are members of groups traditionally underrepresented in the legal profession. Applicants must have a demonstrated record of academic or professional achievement and leadership qualities. They must also be interested in a summer associateship with Dinsmore & Shohl LLP. Along with their application, they must submit a 500-word personal statement explaining their interest in the scholarship program and how diversity has impacted their life.

Financial data The program provides an academic scholarship of $10,000 and a paid associateship at the firm.

Duration The academic scholarship is for 1 year. The summer associateship is for 12 weeks.

Additional information Associateships are available at firm offices in Charleston (West Virginia), Cincinnati (Ohio), Columbus (Ohio), Lexington (Kentucky), or Louisville (Kentucky). The program includes 1 associateship in which the student spends 6 weeks as a clerk in the legal department of the Procter & Gamble Company's worldwide headquarters in Cincinnati and 6 weeks at Dinsmore & Shohl's Cincinnati office. All associates are assigned to an attorney with the firm who serves as a mentor.

Number awarded Varies each year.

Deadline September of each year for second-year students; December of each year for first-year students.

[770]
DISSERTATION FELLOWSHIPS IN EAST EUROPEAN STUDIES

American Council of Learned Societies
Attn: Office of Fellowships and Grants
633 Third Avenue
New York, NY 10017-6795
(212) 697-1505   Fax: (212) 949-8058
E-mail: fellowships@acls.org
Web: www.acls.org/grants/Default.aspx?id=532

Summary To provide funding to minority and other doctoral candidates interested in conducting dissertation research in the social sciences and humanities relating to eastern Europe.

Eligibility This program is open to U.S. citizens or permanent residents who are working on a dissertation in the humanities or social sciences as related to eastern Europe, including Albania, Bosnia and Herzegovina, Bulgaria, Croatia, Czech Republic, Estonia, Hungary, Latvia, Lithuania, Former Yugoslav Republic of Macedonia, Kosovo, Montenegro, Poland, Romania, Serbia, Slovakia, and Slovenia. Applicants may be proposing projects comparing more than 1 country of eastern Europe or relating eastern European societies to those of other parts of the world. They may be seeking support for research fellowships (for use in eastern Europe to conduct fieldwork or archival investigations) or writing fellowships (for use in the United States, after all research is complete, to write the dissertation). Selection is based on the scholarly potential of the applicant, the quality and scholarly importance of the proposed work, and its importance to the development of scholarship on eastern Europe. Applications are particularly invited from women and members of minority groups.

Financial data The maximum stipend is $18,000. Recipients' home universities are required (consistent with their policies and regulations) to provide or to waive normal academic year tuition payments or to provide alternative cost-sharing support.

Duration 1 year. Students may apply for 1-year research and writing fellowships in sequence, but they may not apply for a second year of funding in either category.

Additional information This program is sponsored jointly by the American Council of Learned Societies, (ACLS) and the Social Science Research Council, funded by the U.S. Department of State under the Research and Training for

Eastern Europe and the Independent States of the Former Soviet Union Act of 1983 (Title VIII) but administered by ACLS.

Number awarded   Varies each year; recently, 8 of these fellowships were awarded.

Deadline   November of each year.

[771]
DISSERTATION FELLOWSHIPS OF THE FORD FOUNDATION DIVERSITY FELLOWSHIP PROGRAM

National Research Council
Attn: Fellowships Office, Keck 576
500 Fifth Street, N.W.
Washington, DC 20001
(202) 334-2872   Fax: (202) 334-3419
E-mail: infofell@nas.edu
Web: www.nationalacademies.org

Summary   To provide funding for dissertation research to Native Americans and other graduate students whose success will increase the racial and ethnic diversity of U.S. colleges and universities.

Eligibility   This program is open to citizens and nationals of the United States who are Ph.D. or Sc.D. degree candidates committed to a career in teaching and research at the college or university level. Applicants must be completing a degree in fields of the arts, sciences, humanities, and social sciences, but not for most practice-oriented areas, terminal master's degrees, other doctoral degrees (e.g., Ed.D., D.F.A., Psy.D.), professional degrees (e.g., medicine, law, public health), or joint degrees (e.g., M.D./Ph.D., J.D./Ph.D., M.F.A./Ph.D). The following are considered as positive factors in the selection process: evidence of superior academic achievement; promise of continuing achievement as scholars and teachers; membership in a group whose underrepresentation in the American professoriate has been severe and longstanding, including Black/African Americans, Puerto Ricans, Mexican Americans/Chicanos/Chicanas, Native American Indians, Alaska Natives (Eskimos, Aleuts, and other indigenous people of Alaska), and Native Pacific Islanders (Hawaiians, Micronesians, or Polynesians); capacity to respond in pedagogically productive ways to the learning needs of students from diverse backgrounds; sustained personal engagement with communities that are underrepresented in the academy and an ability to bring this asset to learning, teaching, and scholarship at the college and university level; and likelihood of using the diversity of human experience as an educational resource in teaching and scholarship.

Financial data   The stipend is $21,000 per year; stipend payments are made through fellowship institutions.

Duration   9 to 12 months.

Additional information   The competition for this program is conducted by the National Research Council on behalf of the Ford Foundation. Fellows may not accept remuneration from another fellowship or similar external award while supported by this program; however, supplementation from institutional funds, educational benefits from the Department of Veterans Affairs, or educational incentive funds may be received concurrently with Ford Foundation support. Dissertation fellows are required to submit an interim progress report 6 months after the start of the fellowship and a final report at the end of the 12 month tenure.

Number awarded   Approximately 35 each year.

Deadline   November of each year.

[772]
DISSERTATION FELLOWSHIPS OF THE MINORITY SCHOLAR-IN-RESIDENCE PROGRAM

Consortium for Faculty Diversity at Liberal Arts Colleges
c/o DePauw University
Academic Affairs Office
305 Harrison Hall
7 East Larabee Street
Greencastle, IN 46135
(765) 658-6595   E-mail: jgriswold@depauw.edu
Web: www.depauw.edu

Summary   To provide an opportunity for Native Americans and other minority students to work on their dissertation while in residence at selected liberal arts colleges.

Eligibility   This program is open to African American, Asian American, Hispanic American, and Native American doctoral candidates who have completed all the requirements for the Ph.D. or M.F.A. except the dissertation. Applicants must be interested in a residency at a member institution of the Consortium for Faculty Diversity at Liberal Arts Colleges during which they will complete their dissertation. They must be U.S. citizens or permanent residents.

Financial data   Dissertation fellows receive a stipend based on the average salary paid to instructors at the participating college. Modest funds are made available to finance the fellow's proposed research, subject to the usual institutional procedures.

Duration   1 year.

Additional information   The following schools are participating in the program: Agnes Scott College, Bard College at Simon's Rock, Bowdoin College, Bryn Mawr College, Carleton College, Centre College, College of Wooster, Colorado College, Denison University, DePauw University, Dickinson College, Gettysburg College, Goucher College, Grinnell College, Hamilton College, Harvey Mudd College, Haverford College, Hobart and William Smith Colleges, Kalamazoo College, Lafayette College, Lawrence University, Luther College, Macalester College, Mount Holyoke College, Muhlenberg College, New College of Florida, Oberlin College, Pomona College, Reed College, Rhodes College, University of Richmond, Scripps College, St. Olaf College, Sewanee: The University of the South, Skidmore College, Smith College, Southwestern University, Swarthmore College, Trinity College, Vassar College, Wellesley College, Whitman College, and Willamette University. Fellows are expected to teach at least 1 course, participate in departmental seminars, and interact with students.

Number awarded   Varies each year.

Deadline   October of each year.

[773]
DISSERTATION PROPOSAL DEVELOPMENT FELLOWSHIP PROGRAM

Social Science Research Council
Attn: DPDF Program
One Pierrepont Plaza, 15th Floor
Brooklyn, NY 11201
(212) 377-2700   Fax: (212) 377-2727
E-mail: dpdf@ssrc.org
Web: www.ssrc.org/fellowships/dpdf-fellowship

Summary To provide an opportunity for minority and other doctoral students in the social sciences and humanities to formulate their dissertation proposals and conduct predissertation research.

Eligibility This program is open to full-time graduate students in the second or third year of a doctoral program who have not yet had their dissertation proposals accepted by their thesis directors and their home institutions. Each year, the program selects 6 subdisciplinary and interdisciplinary fields within the social sciences and humanities, and students apply to participate in 1 of those fields. They must be able to attend a workshop in the spring to prepare to undertake predissertation research, spend the summer conducting that research, and then attend another workshop in the fall to synthesize their summer research and draft proposals for dissertation funding. Workshop participants are selected on the basis of the originality and appropriateness of their dissertation topic, the preparation of the student, and the quality of the summer predissertation research plan. Minorities and women are particularly encouraged to apply.

Financial data For all fellows, expenses to attend the workshops (airfare, hotel, meals, ground transport) are paid. Those fellows who are selected for summer predissertation research receive $5,000 grants.

Duration The program extends over 1 calendar year.

Additional information Funding for this program is provided by the Andrew W. Mellon Foundation. Recently, the designated research fields were: new approaches to religion and modernity; discrimination studies; interdisciplinary approaches to the study of contentious politics; multiculturalism, immigration, and identity in western Europe and the United States; spaces of inquiry; and virtual worlds.

Number awarded Each research field accepts 10 to 12 graduate students.

Deadline January of each year.

[774]
DISSERTATION YEAR VISITING DIVERSITY FELLOWSHIPS FOR ADVANCED GRADUATE STUDENTS

Northeast Consortium for Faculty Diversity
Attn: JoAnn Moody
13345 Benchley Road
San Diego, CA 92130-1247
E-mail: joann.moody@earthlink.net
Web: www.diversityoncampus.com/id15.html

Summary To provide an opportunity for Native American and other doctoral candidates from underrepresented minority groups to complete their dissertation while in residence at participating colleges and universities in the Northeast.

Eligibility This program is open to members of underrepresented minority groups who are at the dissertation writing stage of their doctoral program in any field. Applicants may be working at a university anywhere in the country. but they must be interested in completing their dissertation at a college or university in the Northeast. They must be able to demonstrate that they can complete the dissertation while at the host campus. There is no application form; interested students must submit a curriculum vitae, a statement of scholarship and teaching goals, 3 letters of recommendation (including 1 from the dissertation advisor at their home campus), a copy of the dissertation prospectus, and a graduate school transcript. U.S. citizenship is required.

Financial data The stipend ranges from $25,000 to $33,000. The host campus will provide computer and library privileges, office space, and health insurance.

Duration 12 months.

Additional information This program began in 2001. Recently, the host campuses were Northeastern University, Colgate University, Allegheny College, and the University of Rochester. Although the scholars have no formal teaching assignment, they are expected to present their work-in-progress at 2 or 3 campus-wide or department-wide forums during the year and to teach or co-teach a course.

Number awarded Varies each year. Each participating college or university hosts 1 or more dissertation scholars.

Deadline February of each year.

[775]
DISTRICT OF COLUMBIA-ELI DIVERSITY FELLOWSHIPS IN ENVIRONMENTAL LAW

American Bar Association
Attn: Section of Environment, Energy, and Resources
321 North Clark Street
Chicago, IL 60654-7598
(312) 988-5602   Fax: (312) 988-5572
E-mail: jonusaid@staff.abanet.org
Web: www.abanet.org

Summary To provide funding to Native American and other law students from traditionally underrepresented groups who are interested in working on a summer project at the Environmental Law Institute (ELI) in Washington, D.C.

Eligibility This program is open to first- and second-year law students and third-year night students who come from minority or other disadvantaged households. Students may be residents of any state and attending school in any state; preference is given to residents of the District of Columbia and to students who are enrolled at law schools in the District or who have a strong interest in the District. Applicants must be interested in a summer internship at ELI, where they work on projects involving domestic and international environmental law. Subject areas include wetlands and watershed policy, sustainable land use, biodiversity, environmental enforcement, long-term management of hazardous sites, public participation, and international environmental policy. Selection is based on research and writing skills, academic performance, and communication skills.

Financial data The stipend is $5,000.

Duration 8 to 10 weeks during the summer.

Additional information This program is cosponsored by ELI, Additional support is provided by Pfizer Inc. and Beveridge & Diamond PC.

Number awarded 2 each year.

Deadline November of each year.

[776]
DIVERSIFIED INVESTMENT ADVISORS LEADERS IN HEALTHCARE SCHOLARSHIP

Institute for Diversity in Health Management
Attn: Executive Assistant
One North Franklin Street, 30th Floor
Chicago, IL 60606
(312) 422-2630   Toll Free: (800) 233-0996
Fax: (312) 895-4511   E-mail: ejohnson@aha.org
Web: www.applicantsoft.com

Summary To provide financial assistance to Native Americans and other minority graduate students in health services management.

Eligibility This program is open to members of ethnic minority groups who are accepted or enrolled in a graduate program in health care administration. Applicants must have a GPA of 3.0 or higher. They must demonstrate commitment to a career in health care administration. Along with their application, they must submit a personal statement of 300 to 500 words on their interest in health care management and their career goals. Selection is based on academic achievement, leadership potential, financial need, community involvement, commitment to health care administration, and overall professional maturity. U.S. citizenship is required.

Financial data The stipend is $5,000.

Duration 1 year.

Additional information This program was established in 2007 by Diversified Investment Advisors.

Number awarded 2 each year.

Deadline December of each year.

[777]
DIVERSITY COMMITTEE SCHOLARSHIP

American Society of Safety Engineers
Attn: ASSE Foundation
1800 East Oakton Street
Des Plaines, IL 60018
(847) 768-3435   Fax: (847) 768-3434
E-mail: agabanski@asse.org
Web: www.asse.org

Summary To provide financial assistance to upper-division and graduate student members of the American Society of Safety Engineers (ASSE) who are Native American or come from other diverse groups.

Eligibility This program is open to ASSE student members who are working on an undergraduate or graduate degree in occupational safety, health, and environment or a closely-related field (e.g., industrial or environmental engineering, environmental science, industrial hygiene, occupational health nursing). Applicants must be full-time students who have completed at least 60 semester hours with a GPA of 3.0 or higher as undergraduates or at least 9 semester hours with a GPA of 3.5 or higher as graduate students. Along with their application, they must submit 2 essays of 300 words or less: 1) why they are seeking a degree in occupational safety and health or a closely-related field, a brief description of their current activities, and how those relate to their career goals and objectives; and 2) why they should be awarded this

scholarship (including career goals and financial need). A goal of this program is to support individuals regardless of race, ethnicity, gender, religion, personal beliefs, age, sexual orientation, physical challenges, geographic location, university, or specific area of study. U.S. citizenship is not required.

Financial data The stipend is $1,000 per year.

Duration 1 year; recipients may reapply.

Number awarded 1 each year.

Deadline November of each year.

[778]
DIVERSITY SCHOLARSHIP

Academic Library Association of Ohio
c/o Ken Burhanna, Diversity Committee Chair
Kent State University, Instructional Services
P.O. Box 5190
Kent, OH 44242-0001
(330) 672-1660   E-mail: kburhann@kent.edu
Web: www.alaoweb.org

Summary To provide financial assistance to Native Americans and other residents of Ohio who are working on a master's degree in library science at a school in any state and will contribute to diversity in the profession.

Eligibility This program is open to residents of Ohio who are enrolled or entering an ALA-accredited program for a master's degree in library science, either on campus or via distance education. Applicants must be able to demonstrate how they will contribute to diversity in the profession, including (but not limited to) race or ethnicity, sexual orientation, life experience, physical ability, and a sense of commitment to those and other diversity issues. Along with their application, they must submit 1) a list of participation in honor societies or professional organizations, awards, scholarships, prizes, honors, or class offices; 2) a list of community, civic, organizational, or volunteer experiences; and 3) an essay on their understanding of and commitment to diversity in libraries, including how they, as library school students and future professionals, might address the issue.

Financial data The stipend is $1,500.

Duration 1 year.

Number awarded 1 each year.

Deadline March of each year.

[779]
DOCTORAL DISSERTATION IMPROVEMENT GRANTS IN THE DIRECTORATE FOR BIOLOGICAL SCIENCES

National Science Foundation
Directorate for Biological Sciences
Attn: Division of Environmental Biology
4201 Wilson Boulevard
Arlington, VA 22230
(703) 292-8480   TDD: (800) 281-8749
E-mail: ddig-deb@nsf.gov
Web: www.nsf.gov/funding/pgm_summ.jsp?pims_id=5234

Summary To provide partial support to underrepresented minorities and other students for dissertation research in selected areas supported by the National Science Foundation (NSF) Directorate for Biological Sciences (DBS).

Eligibility Applications may be submitted through regular university channels by dissertation advisers on behalf of graduate students who have advanced to candidacy and have begun or are about to begin dissertation research. Students must be enrolled at U.S. institutions but need not be U.S. citizens. Proposals should focus on the ecology, ecosystems, systematics, or population biology programs in the DBS Division of Environmental Biology, or the animal behavior or ecological and evolutionary physiology programs in the DBS Division of Integrative Organismal Systems. The program encourages applications from underrepresented minorities and persons with disabilities.

Financial data Grants range up to $15,000; funds may be used for travel to specialized facilities or field research locations, specialized research equipment, purchase of supplies and services not otherwise available, fees for computerized or other forms of data, and rental of environmental chambers or other research facilities. Funding is not provided for stipends, tuition, textbooks, journals, allowances for dependents, travel to scientific meetings, publication costs, dissertation preparation or reproduction, or indirect costs.

Duration Normally 2 years.

Number awarded 100 to 120 each year; approximately $1,600,000 is available for this program each year.

Deadline November of each year.

[780]
DOCTORAL FELLOWSHIPS IN ARCHIVAL STUDIES

UCLA Center for Information as Evidence
c/o Department of Information Studies
GSEIS Building 208A
P.O. Box 951520
Los Angeles, CA 90095-1520
(310) 825-7310　　　　　　　　Fax: (310) 206-4460
E-mail: aeri@gseis.ucla.edu
Web: aeri.gseis.ucla.edu/fellowships.htm

Summary To provide financial assistance to Native American and other students entering a doctoral program in archival studies at designated universities.

Eligibility This program is open to students entering a doctoral program in archival studies at the University of California at Los Angeles, University of Michigan, University of Pittsburgh, University of North Carolina at Chapel Hill, Simmons College, University of Maryland, University of Texas at Austin, or University of Wisconsin at Madison. Applicants are not required to have received a master's degree in archival studies, library and information studies, or a related field, but they must be able to exhibit evidence of the ability to excel as a scholar and educator in the field. Selection is based on commitment to archival studies education, potential to make a strong scholarly contribution to the field of archival studies, and commitment to diversity within archival studies education and scholarship. Applications are particularly encouraged from students of American Indian/Alaska Native, Asian, Black/African American, Hispanic/Latino, or Native Hawaiian/other Pacific Islander heritage. U.S. citizenship or permanent resident status is required.

Financial data The program provides payment of full tuition and a stipend of $20,000 per year.

Duration 2 years; the partner universities provide full tuition and stipends to their fellows for 2 additional years of study.

Additional information These fellowships were first awarded in 2010. Funding for the program is provided by a grant from the Laura Bush 21st Century Librarian Program of the Institute of Museum and Library Services.

Number awarded At least 2 each year.

Deadline January of each year.

[781]
DONALD W. BANNER DIVERSITY SCHOLARSHIP

Banner & Witcoff, Ltd.
Attn: Christopher Hummel
1100 13th Street, N.W., Suite 1200
Washington, DC 20005-4051
(202) 824-3000　　　　　　　　Fax: (202) 824-3001
E-mail: chummel@bannerwitcoff.com
Web: www.bannerwitcoff.com

Summary To provide financial assistance to Native Americans and other law students who come from groups historically underrepresented in intellectual property law.

Eligibility This program is open to students enrolled in the first or second year of a J.D. program at an ABA-accredited law school in the United States. Applicants must come from a group historically underrepresented in intellectual property law; that underrepresentation may be the result of race, sex, ethnicity, sexual orientation, or disability. Selection is based on academic merit, commitment to the pursuit of a career in intellectual property law, written communication skills, oral communication skills (determined through an interview), leadership qualities, and community involvement.

Financial data The stipend is $5,000 per year.

Duration 1 year (the second or third year of law school); students who accept and successfully complete the firm's summer associate program may receive an additional $5,000 for a subsequent semester of law school.

Number awarded 2 each year.

Deadline October of each year.

[782]
DORA AMES LEE LEADERSHIP DEVELOPMENT FUND

United Methodist Church
General Board of Global Ministries
Attn: United Methodist Committee on Relief
475 Riverside Drive, Room 1522
New York, NY 10115
(212) 870-3871　　　　　　　　Toll Free: (800) UMC-GBGM
E-mail: jyoung@gbgm-umc.org
Web: gbgm-umc.org/health/doralee.cfm

Summary To provide financial assistance to Methodists and other Christians of Native American or Asian descent who are preparing for a career in a health-related field.

Eligibility This program is open to undergraduate and graduate students who are U.S. citizens of Asian American or Native American descent. Applicants must be professed Christians, preferably United Methodists. They must be attending a college or university to enter or continue in a health-related field. Financial need is considered in the selection process.

Financial data The stipend is $2,000.

Duration 1 year.

Additional information This program was established in 1980.

Number awarded 5 each year.

Deadline June of each year.

[783]
DORSEY & WHITNEY DIVERSITY FELLOWSHIPS

Dorsey & Whitney LLP
Attn: Recruiting Manager
50 South Sixth Street, Suite 1500
Minneapolis, MN 55402-1498
(612) 340-2600   Toll Free: (800) 759-4929
Fax: (612) 340-2868 E-mail: forsmark.claire@dorsey.com
Web: www.dorsey.com/diversity_fellowship_12111

Summary To provide financial assistance for law school to Native Americans and other students from diverse backgrounds who are interested in working during the summer at offices of the sponsoring law firm.

Eligibility This program is open to first-year students at ABA-accredited law schools who have accepted a summer associate position at an office of the sponsor in Denver, Minneapolis, or Seattle. Applicants must be able to demonstrate academic achievement and a commitment to promoting diversity in the legal community. Along with their application, they must submit a personal statement on the ways in which they have promoted and will continue to promote diversity in the legal community, what diversity means to them, and why they are interested in the sponsoring law firm.

Financial data Fellows receive a stipend of $7,500 for the second year of law school and, if they complete a summer associate position in the following summer, another stipend of $7,500 for the third year of law school. If they join the firm following graduation, they receive an additional $5,000.

Duration 1 year; may be renewed for 1 additional year.

Additional information This program was established in 2006.

Number awarded 1 or more each year.

Deadline January of each year.

[784]
DOYON FOUNDATION BASIC SCHOLARSHIPS

Doyon, Limited
Attn: Doyon Foundation
714 Fourth Avenue, Suite 302B
Fairbanks, AK 99701
(907) 459-2049   Toll Free: (888) 478-4755, ext. 2049
Fax: (907) 459-2065   E-mail: foundation@doyon.com
Web: www.doyonfoundation.com/static/scholarships.aspx

Summary To provide financial assistance to undergraduate and graduate students at schools in any state who are shareholders or descendants of shareholders of Doyon, Limited.

Eligibility This program is open to undergraduate or graduate students who are shareholders or the descendants of shareholders of Doyon, Limited. Applicants must be accepted or enrolled at an accredited college, university, technical institute, or vocational school. Both part-time and full-time students are eligible, but full-time students must be accepted into a degree program.

Financial data Stipends are $800 per semester for full-time students or $400 per semester for part-time students.

Duration 1 year. Undergraduate students may reapply if they maintain a GPA of 2.0 or higher; graduate or master's degree students may reapply if they maintain a GPA of 3.0 or higher; and specialist or doctoral students may reapply if they maintain a GPA of 3.25 or higher.

Additional information Doyon, Limited is 1 of 13 Alaska Native Regional Corporations created under the Alaska Native Claims Settlement Act of 1971.

Number awarded Varies each year; recently, scholarships were awarded to 228 full-time students and 40 part-time students.

Deadline March of each year for summer school, April of each year for fall semester, September of each year for winter term (vocational students only), November of each year for spring semester.

[785]
DOYON FOUNDATION COMPETITIVE SCHOLARSHIPS

Doyon, Limited
Attn: Doyon Foundation
1 Doyon Place, Suite 300
Fairbanks, AK 99701-2941
(907) 459-2049   Toll Free: (888) 478-4755, ext. 2049
Fax: (907) 459-2065   E-mail: foundation@doyon.com
Web: www.doyonfoundation.com/static/scholarships.aspx

Summary To provide financial assistance to undergraduate and graduate students at schools in any state who are shareholders or descendants of shareholders of Doyon, Limited.

Eligibility This program is open to undergraduate or graduate students who are shareholders or the descendants of shareholders of Doyon, Limited. Applicants must be accepted or enrolled at an accredited college, university, or vocational/technical school in a program that lasts at least 6 weeks. Along with their application, they must submit a personal essay on their educational goals, professional goals, extracurricular and community service activities or volunteerism, and cultural awareness and contributions to a healthy Native community. Selection is based on the essay (40 points), GPA (40 points), letters of recommendation (30 points), and personal impression (10 points).

Financial data Stipends range from $2,000 to $7,000 per year.

Duration 1 year. Undergraduate students may reapply if they maintain a GPA of 2.0 or higher; graduate or master's degree students may reapply if they maintain a GPA of 3.0 or higher; and specialist or doctoral students may reapply if they maintain a GPA of 3.25 or higher. Students can receive a total of $10,000 throughout their entire undergraduate or vocational career. Students who continue in a 1- or 2-year master's degree program are eligible to receive an additional $10,000, for a total maximum of $20,000. Students who work on a 3- to 5-year graduate degree (e.g., Ph.D., M.D., J.D.) can receive an additional $10,000, for a total maximum of $30,000.

Additional information Doyon, Limited is 1 of 13 Alaska Native Regional Corporations created under the Alaska Native Claims Settlement Act of 1971. This program includes the Morris Thompson Scholarship Fund and the Rosemarie Maher Memorial Fund. Recipients must attend school on a full-time basis. Scholarship recipients of $5,000 or more are encouraged to complete at least 1 summer internship during their 4 years of study. Scholarship recipients of less than $5,000 are encouraged to do 1 of the following: serve on a local or regional board or commission, volunteer at least 20 hours, or give presentations on their field of study. A written report detailing the internship or service and lessons learned is required upon completion of the internship.

Number awarded Varies each year; recently, 52 new and renewal scholarships, with a total value of $178,352, were awarded.

Deadline April of each year.

[786]
DR. GEORGE BLUE SPRUCE FELLOWSHIP

American Indian Graduate Center
Attn: Executive Director
4520 Montgomery Boulevard, N.E., Suite 1-B
Albuquerque, NM 87109-1291
(505) 881-4584 Toll Free: (800) 628-1920
Fax: (505) 884-0427 E-mail: aigc@aigc.com
Web: www.aigc.com/02scholarships/scholarships.htm

Summary To provide financial assistance to Native American students interested in working on a degree in dentistry.

Eligibility This program is open to enrolled members of federally-recognized American Indian tribes and Alaska Native groups and students who can document one-fourth degree federally-recognized Indian blood. Applicants must be enrolled full time at a dental school in the United States. Along with their application, they must submit a 500-word essay on their extracurricular activities as they relate to American Indian programs at their institution, volunteer and community work as related to American Indian communities, tribal and community involvement, and plans to make positive changes in the American Indian community with their college education. Financial need is also considered in the selection process.

Financial data Stipends range from $1,000 to $5,000 per academic year, depending on the availability of funds and the recipient's unmet financial need.

Duration 1 year; may be renewed.

Additional information The application fee is $15. Since this a supplemental program, students must apply in a timely manner for federal financial aid and campus-based aid at the college they are attending to be considered for this program. Failure to apply will disqualify an applicant.

Number awarded 1 each year.

Deadline May of each year.

[787]
DRI LAW STUDENT DIVERSITY SCHOLARSHIP

DRI-The Voice of the Defense Bar
Attn: Deputy Executive Director
55 West Monroe Street, Suite 2000
Chicago, IL 60603
(312) 795-1101 Fax: (312) 795-0747
E-mail: dri@dri.org
Web: www.dri.org/open/About.aspx

Summary To provide financial assistance to Native Americans, other minorities. and female law students.

Eligibility This program is open to students entering their second or third year of law school who are African American,

Hispanic, Asian, Pan Asian, Native American, or female. Applicants must submit an essay, up to 1,000 words, on a topic that changes annually but relates to the work of defense attorneys. Selection is based on that essay, demonstrated academic excellence, service to the profession, service to the community, and service to the cause of diversity. Students affiliated with the American Association for Justice as members, student members, or employees are not eligible. Finalists are invited to participate in personal interviews.

Financial data The stipend is $10,000.

Duration 1 year.

Additional information This program was established in 2004.

Number awarded 2 each year.

Deadline May of each year.

[788]
EAST EUROPEAN LANGUAGE GRANTS TO INDIVIDUALS FOR SUMMER STUDY

American Council of Learned Societies
Attn: Office of Fellowships and Grants
633 Third Avenue
New York, NY 10017-6795
(212) 697-1505 Fax: (212) 949-8058
E-mail: fellowships@acls.org
Web: www.acls.org/grants/Default.aspx?id=540

Summary To provide financial support to minority and other graduate students, professionals, and postdoctorates interested in studying eastern European languages during the summer.

Eligibility Applicants must have completed at least a 4-year college degree. They must be interested in a program of training in the languages of eastern Europe, including Albanian, Bosnian-Croatian-Serbian, Bulgarian, Czech, Estonian, Hungarian, Latvian, Lithuanian, Macedonian, Polish, Romanian, Slovak, or Slovene. The language course may be at the beginning, intermediate, or advanced level. Normally, requests for beginning and intermediate level training should be for attendance at intensive courses offered by institutions in the United States; proposals for study at the advanced level are ordinarily for courses in eastern Europe. Applications are particularly encouraged from women and members of minority groups.

Financial data Grants up to $2,500 are available.

Duration Summer months.

Additional information This program, reinstituted in 2002, is supported by the U.S. Department of State under the Research and Training for Eastern Europe and the Independent States of the Former Soviet Union Act of 1983 (Title VIII).

Number awarded Approximately 15 each year.

Deadline January of each year.

[789]
EDWARD L. KRUGER MEMORIAL *ITTISH AAISHA* SCHOLARSHIP

Chickasaw Foundation
110 West 12th Street
P.O. Box 1726
Ada, OK 74821-1726
(580) 421-9030   Fax: (580) 421-9031
E-mail: ChickasawFoundation@chickasaw.net
Web: www.chickasawfoundation.org/index_20.htm

Summary To provide financial assistance to members of the Chickasaw Nation who are working on a graduate degree in pharmacy.

Eligibility This program is open to Chickasaw students who are currently enrolled full time in a graduate school of pharmacy. Applicants must have a GPA of 3.0 or higher. Along with their application, they must submit high school or college transcripts, 2 letters of recommendation, a copy of their Chickasaw Nation citizenship card, and a 1-page essay on their long-term goals and plans for achieving them. Financial need is not considered in the selection process.

Financial data The stipend is $1,000.

Duration 1 year.

Number awarded 1 each year.

Deadline August of each year.

[790]
EISENHOWER GRADUATE TRANSPORTATION FELLOWSHIPS

Department of Transportation
Federal Highway Administration
Attn: Office of PCD, HPC-32
4600 North Fairfax Drive, Suite 800
Arlington, VA 22203-1553
(703) 235-0538   Toll Free: (877) 558-6873
Fax: (703) 235-0593   E-mail: transportationedu@dot.gov
Web: www.fhwa.dot.gov/ugp/index.htm

Summary To provide financial assistance to Native American and other graduate students working on a master's or doctoral degree in transportation-related fields.

Eligibility This program is open to students enrolled or planning to enroll full time to work on a master's or doctoral degree in a field of study directly related to transportation. Applicants must be planning to enter the transportation profession after completing their higher level education. They must be U.S. citizens or have an I-20 (foreign student) or I-551 (permanent resident) identification card. Selection is based on the proposed plan of study, academic records (class standing, GPA, and official transcripts), transportation work experience (including employer's endorsement), and recommendations. Students at Historically Black Colleges and Universities (HBCUs), Hispanic Serving Institutions (HSIs), and Tribal Colleges and Universities (TCUs) are especially encouraged to apply.

Financial data Fellows receive tuition and fees (to a maximum of $10,000 per year), monthly stipends of $1,700 for master's degree students or $2,000 for doctoral students, and a 1-time allowance of up to $1,500 for travel to an annual meeting of the Transportation Research Board.

Duration For master's degree students, 24 months, and the degree must be completed within 3 years; for doctoral stu-

dents, 36 months, and the degree must be completed within 5 years.

Number awarded Approximately 100 to 150 each year.

Deadline March of each year.

[791]
EISENHOWER GRANTS FOR RESEARCH AND INTERN FELLOWSHIPS

Department of Transportation
Federal Highway Administration
Attn: Office of PCD, HPC-32
4600 North Fairfax Drive, Suite 800
Arlington, VA 22203-1553
(703) 235-0538   Toll Free: (877) 558-6873
Fax: (703) 235-0593   E-mail: transportationedu@dot.gov
Web: www.fhwa.dot.gov/ugp/grf_ann.htm

Summary To enable Native American and other students to participate in transportation-related research activities either at facilities of the U.S. Department of Transportation (DOT) Federal Highway Administration in the Washington, D.C. area or as interns for private or public organizations.

Eligibility This program is open to 1) students in their junior year of a baccalaureate program who will complete their junior year before being awarded a fellowship; 2) students in their senior year of a baccalaureate program; and 3) students who have completed their baccalaureate degree and are enrolled in a program leading to a master's, Ph.D., or equivalent degree. Applicants must be enrolled full time at an accredited U.S institution of higher education and planning to enter the transportation profession after completing their higher education. They must be U.S. citizens or have an I-20 (foreign student) or I-551 (permanent resident) identification card. For research fellowships, they select 1 or more projects from a current list of research activities underway at various DOT facilities; the research is conducted with academic supervision provided by a faculty adviser from their home university (which grants academic credit for the research project) and with technical direction provided by the DOT staff. Intern fellowships provide students with opportunities to perform transportation-related research, development, technology transfer, and other activities at public and private sector organizations. Specific requirements for the target projects vary; most require engineering backgrounds, but others involve transportation planning, information management, public administration, physics, materials science, statistical analysis, operations research, chemistry, economics, technology transfer, urban studies, geography, and urban and regional planning. The DOT encourages students at Historically Black Colleges and Universities (HBCUs), Hispanic Serving Institutions (HSIs), and Tribal Colleges and Universities (TCUs) to apply for these grants. Selection is based on match of the student's qualifications with the proposed research project (including the student's ability to accomplish the project in the available time), recommendation letters regarding the nominee's qualifications to conduct the research, academic records (including class standing, GPA, and transcripts), and transportation work experience (if any), including the employer's endorsement.

Financial data Fellows receive full tuition and fees that relate to the academic credits for the approved research project (to a maximum of $10,000) and a monthly stipend of $1,450 for undergraduates, $1,700 for master's students, or

$2,000 for doctoral students. An allowance for travel to and from the DOT facility where the research is conducted is also provided, but selectees are responsible for their own housing accommodations. Recipients are also provided with a 1-time allowance of up to $1,500 to attend the annual Transportation Research Board (TRB) meeting.

Duration Projects normally range from 3 to 12 months.

Number awarded Varies each year; recently, 9 students participated in this program.

Deadline Applications remain open until each project is filled.

[792]
ELIZABETH AND SHERMAN ASCHE MEMORIAL SCHOLARSHIP

Association on American Indian Affairs, Inc.
Attn: Director of Scholarship Programs
966 Hungerford Drive, Suite 12-B
Rockville, MD 20850
(240) 314-7155   Fax: (240) 314-7159
E-mail: lw.aaia@verizon.net
Web: www.indian-affairs.org

Summary To provide financial assistance to Native Americans interested in working on an undergraduate or graduate degree in public health.

Eligibility This program is open to American Indian and Alaskan Native full-time undergraduate and graduate students working on a degree in public health or science. Applicants must submit documentation of financial need, a Certificate of Indian Blood showing at least one-quarter Indian blood, proof of tribal enrollment, an essay on their educational goals, 2 letters of recommendation, and their most recent transcript. Selection is based on merit and need.

Financial data The stipend is $1,500.

Duration 1 year. Recipients may reapply.

Number awarded Varies each year; recently, 6 of these scholarships were awarded.

Deadline June of each year.

[793]
ELIZABETH FURBUR FELLOWSHIP

American Indian Graduate Center
Attn: Executive Director
4520 Montgomery Boulevard, N.E., Suite 1-B
Albuquerque, NM 87109-1291
(505) 881-4584   Toll Free: (800) 628-1920
Fax: (505) 884-0427   E-mail: aigc@aigc.com
Web: www.aigc.com/02scholarships/scholarships.htm

Summary To provide financial assistance to female Native American graduate students interested in working on a degree related to the arts.

Eligibility This program is open to women who are enrolled members of federally-recognized American Indian tribes and Alaska Native groups or who can document one-fourth degree federally-recognized Indian blood. Applicants must be enrolled full time in a graduate program in the creative fine arts, visual works, crafts, music, performing, dance, literary arts, creative writing, or poetry. Along with their application, they must submit a 500-word essay on their extracurricular activities as they relate to American Indian programs at their institution, volunteer and community work as related

to American Indian communities, tribal and community involvement, and plans to make positive changes in the American Indian community with their college education. Financial need is also considered in the selection process.

Financial data Stipends range from $1,000 to $5,000 per academic year, depending on the availability of funds and the recipient's unmet financial need.

Duration 1 year; may be renewed.

Additional information The application fee is $15. Since this a supplemental program, students must apply in a timely manner for federal financial aid and campus-based aid at the college they are attending to be considered for this program. Failure to apply will disqualify an applicant.

Number awarded 1 each year.

Deadline May of each year.

[794]
ELLIOTT C. ROBERTS, SR. SCHOLARSHIP

Institute for Diversity in Health Management
Attn: Executive Assistant
One North Franklin Street, 30th Floor
Chicago, IL 60606
(312) 422-2630   Toll Free: (800) 233-0996
Fax: (312) 895-4511   E-mail: ejohnson@aha.org
Web: www.applicantsoft.com

Summary To provide financial assistance to Native American and other minority graduate students in health services management.

Eligibility This program is open to members of ethnic minority groups who are accepted or enrolled in a graduate program in health care administration. Applicants must have a GPA of 3.0 or higher. They must demonstrate commitment to a career in health care administration. Along with their application, they must submit a personal statement of 300 to 500 words on their interest in health care management and their career goals. Selection is based on academic achievement, leadership potential, financial need, community involvement, commitment to health care administration, and overall professional maturity. U.S. citizenship is required.

Financial data The stipend ranges from $500 to $1,000.

Duration 1 year.

Number awarded 1 or more each year, depending on the availability of funds.

Deadline December of each year.

[795]
ENTERPRISE RANCHERIA HIGHER EDUCATION PROGRAM

Enterprise Rancheria
Attn: Education Department
3690 Olive Highway
Oroville, CA 95966
(530) 532-9214   Fax: (530) 532-1768
Web: enterpriserancheria.org

Summary To provide financial assistance to members of the Estom Yumeka Maidu tribe of Enterprise Rancheria in northern California who are interested in attending college or graduate school in any state.

Eligibility This program is open to enrolled members of Enterprise Rancheria who are attending or planning to attend a college, university, or community college in any state. Applicants must be interested in working on an undergraduate or graduate degree in any field. Along with their application, they must submit a brief essay on their educational goals and plans for utilizing their education. Financial need is considered in the selection process.

Financial data　The stipend is $1,000 per year for undergraduate and graduate students at 4-year colleges and universities or $500 per year for students at community colleges. A book allowance of $500 per semester for 4-year institution students or $300 per semester for community college students is also provided. Transportation costs of $100 per month may be reimbursed and monthly living expenses may be paid if funds are available.

Duration　1 year; may be renewed, provided the recipient maintains a GPA of 2.0 or higher.

Number awarded　Varies each year.

Deadline　July of each year for academic year or fall semester; December of each year for spring semester only.

[796]
ENVIRONMENTAL PROTECTION AGENCY STUDENT DIVERSITY INTERNSHIP PROGRAM

United Negro College Fund Special Programs
　Corporation
Attn: NASA Science and Technology Institute
6402 Arlington Boulevard, Suite 600
Falls Church, VA 22042
(703) 677-3400　　　　　　Toll Free: (800) 530-6232
Fax: (703) 205-7645　　　　　E-mail: portal@uncfsp.org
Web: www.uncfsp.org

Summary　To provide an opportunity for Native Americans and other underrepresented undergraduate and graduate students to work on a summer research project at research sites of the U.S. Environmental Protection Agency (EPA).

Eligibility　This program is open to rising college sophomores, juniors, and seniors and to full-time graduate students at accredited institutions who are members of underrepresented groups, including ethnic minorities (African Americans, Hispanic/Latinos, Native Americans, Asians, Alaskan Natives, and Native Hawaiians/Pacific Islanders) and persons with disabilities. Applicants must have a GPA of 2.8 or higher and be working on a degree in business, communications, economics, engineering, environmental science/management, finance, information technology, law, marketing, or science. They must be interested in working on a research project during the summer at their choice of 23 EPA research sites (for a list, contact EPA). U.S. citizenship is required.

Financial data　The stipend is $5,000 for undergraduates or $6,000 for graduate students. Interns also receive a travel and housing allowance, but they are responsible for covering their local transportation, meals, and miscellaneous expenses.

Duration　10 weeks during the summer.

Additional information　This program is funded by EPA and administered by the United Negro College Fund Special Programs Corporation.

Number awarded　Varies each year.

Deadline　May of each year.

[797]
EPISCOPAL COUNCIL OF INDIAN MINISTRIES SCHOLARSHIPS

Episcopal Church Center
Attn: Domestic and Foreign Missionary Society
Episcopal Council of Indian Ministries
815 Second Avenue, Seventh Floor
New York, NY 10017-4503
(212) 716-6175　　　　　　Toll Free: (800) 334-7626
Fax: (212) 867-0395　　E-mail: dcoy@episcopalchurch.org
Web: www.episcopalchurch.org/native_american.htm

Summary　To provide financial assistance to Native Americans interested in theological education within the Episcopal Church in the United States of America (ECUSA).

Eligibility　Applicants must be seminarians of American Indian/Alaska Native descent attending an accredited Episcopal institution. They must submit documentation of tribal membership, diocesan endorsement with a statement signed by the bishop that the applicant is in track for ordination, and a signed statement that the applicant intends to serve in Indian ministry upon completion of study.

Financial data　The amount of the award depends on the needs of the recipient and the availability of funds, to a maximum of $2,000 per year.

Additional information　The Episcopal Council of Indian Ministries (ECIM) also awards the David Oakerhater Merit Fellowship to a middler with outstanding achievement and the Oakerhater Award of $2,500 to a seminarian pursuing a Ph.D. This program relies on funds established as early as 1879 and includes the Episcopal Legacy Fund for Scholarships Honoring the Memory of the Rev. Dr. Martin Luther King, Jr., established in 1991.

Number awarded　Varies each year.

Deadline　May of each year for fall semester or October of each year for spring semester.

[798]
ESTHER NGAN-LING CHOW AND MAREYJOYCE GREEN SCHOLARSHIP

Sociologists for Women in Society
Attn: Executive Officer
University of Rhode Island
Department of Sociology
10 Chafee Road
Kingston, RI 02881
(401) 874-9510　　　　　　　　　Fax: (401) 874-2588
E-mail: swseo@socwomen.org
Web: www.socwomen.org/page.php?sss=115

Summary　To provide funding to Native American and other women of color who are conducting dissertation research in sociology.

Eligibility　This program is open to women from a racial/ethnic group that faces racial discrimination in the United States. Applicants must be in the early stages of writing a doctoral dissertation in sociology on a topic relating to the concerns that women of color face domestically and/or internationally. They must be able to demonstrate financial need. Both domestic and international students are eligible to apply. Along with their application, they must submit a personal statement that details their short- and long-term career and research goals; a resume or curriculum vitae; 2 letters of recommendation; and a 5-page dissertation proposal that includes the purpose of the research, the work to be accomplished through support from this scholarship, and a time line for completion.

Financial data The stipend is $15,000. An additional grant of $500 is provided to enable the recipient to attend the winter meeting of Sociologists for Women in Society (SWS), and travel expenses to attend the summer meeting are reimbursed.

Duration 1 year.

Additional information This program was established in 2007 and originally named the Women of Color Dissertation Scholarship.

Number awarded 1 each year.

Deadline March of each year.

[799]
ETHEL BOLDEN MINORITY SCHOLARSHIP

Richland County Public Library Foundation
Attn: Development Manager
1431 Assembly Street
Columbia, SC 29201
(803) 929-3424   E-mail: tgills@myrcpl.com
Web: www.myrcpl.com/foundation/bolden

Summary To provide financial assistance to Native Americans and other minority residents of South Carolina who are interested in working on a master's degree in library and information science at a school in any state.

Eligibility This program is open to residents of South Carolina who are members of ethnic and racial groups underrepresented in the field of library and information science (American Indians, African Americans, Asian Americans, or Hispanic Americans). Applicants must have been admitted to an ALA-accredited school of library and information science in any state. Along with their application, they must submit a 300-word essay describing their interest and any work in the field of librarianship and the specific competencies or characteristics they believe they can contribute to the library profession. Selection is based on academic performance and demonstrated leadership abilities through participation in community service or other activities.

Financial data The stipend is $2,500.

Duration 1 year.

Additional information This program was established in 2010.

Number awarded 1 each year.

Deadline March of each year.

[800]
ETHEL CURRY SCHOLARSHIPS

Minnesota Department of Education
Attn: Manager, Minnesota Indian Education
1500 Highway 36 West
Roseville, MN 55113-4266
(651) 582-8862   Toll Free: (800) 657-3927
E-mail: mde.indian-education@state.mn.us
Web: education.state.mn.us

Summary To provide financial assistance to Native Americans in Minnesota who are interested in working on an undergraduate or graduate degree.

Eligibility This program is open to Indians who are enrolled in a Minnesota-based tribe or community. Applicants must be attending an accredited postsecondary institution in Minnesota as a junior, senior, or graduate student. They must have a GPA of 3.0 or higher. Selection is based on merit.

Financial data The stipend is $3,000 per year for undergraduates or $6,000 per year for graduate students.

Duration Up to 4 years.

Number awarded Varies each year; recently, 12 of these scholarships were awarded.

Deadline May of each year.

[801]
ETHNIC MINORITY ADMINISTRATOR IN TRAINING INTERNSHIP

Indiana Health Care Association
Attn: Executive Director
One North Capitol, Suite 100
Indianapolis, IN 46204
(317) 636-6406   Toll Free: (800) 466-IHCA
Fax: (877) 298-3749   E-mail: dhenry@ihca.org
Web: www.ihca.org

Summary To provide work experience to Native Americans and other minority residents of Indiana interested in gaining work experience at the Indiana Health Care Association (IHCA).

Eligibility This program is open to residents of Indiana who are members of ethnic minority groups (African Americans, Hispanics, American Indians, Asian Americans). Applicants must have a bachelor's degree or higher and an employment history that reflects management or leadership skills. They must be interested in preparing for a career in long-term care as a health facility administrator by working under a preceptor at IHCA. Preference is given to applicants interested in working with elderly or disabled populations. An interview at IHCA headquarters is required.

Financial data This is a paid internship (stipend not specified).

Duration 6 months.

Number awarded 1 each year.

Deadline July of each year.

[802]
ETHNIC MINORITY POSTGRADUATE SCHOLARSHIP FOR CAREERS IN ATHLETICS

Black Coaches Association
Attn: Director of Operations and Administration
Pan American Plaza
201 South Capitol Avenue, Suite 495
Indianapolis, IN 46225-1089
(317) 829-5619   Toll Free: (877) 789-1222
Fax: (317) 829-5601
Web: bcasports.cstv.com

Summary To provide financial assistance to Native Americans and other minorities who participated in college athletics and are interested in working on a graduate degree in athletic administration.

Eligibility This program is open to former student-athletes on the college level who are of ethnic minority origin. Applicants must be entering or enrolled full time in a graduate program in sports administration or a related field to prepare for a career in athletics. They must have performed with distinction as student body members at their undergraduate institution and have a GPA of 2.5 or higher. U.S. citizenship is required. Selection is based on academic course work, extracurricular activities, commitment to preparing for a career in athletics, and promise of success in their career.

Financial data The stipend is $2,500. Funds are paid to the college or university of the recipient's choice.

Duration 1 year; nonrenewable.

Additional information This program was established in 1995.

Number awarded Varies each year; recently, 6 of these scholarships were awarded.

Deadline April of each year.

[803]
EURASIA DISSERTATION SUPPORT FELLOWSHIPS

Social Science Research Council
Attn: Eurasia Program
One Pierrepont Plaza, 15th Floor
Brooklyn, NY 11201
(212) 377-2700   Fax: (212) 377-2727
E-mail: eurasia@ssrc.org
Web: www.ssrc.org/fellowships/Eurasia-fellowship

Summary To provide funding to minority and other graduate students completing a dissertation dealing with Eurasia.

Eligibility This program is open to students who have completed field research for their doctoral dissertation and who plan to work on writing it during the next academic year. Applicants must have been conducting research in a discipline of the social sciences or humanities that deals with the Russian Empire, the Soviet Union, or the New States of Eurasia. Research related to the non-Russian states, regions, and peoples is particularly encouraged. Regions and countries currently supported by the program include Armenia, Azerbaijan, Belarus, Georgia, Kazakhstan, Kyrgyzstan, Moldova, Russian Federation, Tajikistan, Turkmenistan, Ukraine, and Uzbekistan; funding is not presently available for research on the Baltic states. U.S. citizenship or permanent resident status is required. Minorities and women are particularly encouraged to apply.

Financial data Grants up to $25,000 are available.

Duration Up to 1 year.

Additional information Funding for this program is provided by the U.S. Department of State under the Program for Research and Training on Eastern Europe and the Independent States of the Former Soviet Union (Title VIII).

Number awarded Varies each year; recently, 7 of these fellowships were awarded.

Deadline December of each year.

[804]
EXCELLENCE IN CARDIOVASCULAR SCIENCES SUMMER RESEARCH PROGRAM

Wake Forest University School of Medicine
Attn: Hypertension and Vascular Research Center
Medical Center Boulevard
Winston-Salem, NC 27157-1032
(336) 716-1080   Fax: (336) 716-2456
E-mail: nsarver@wfubmc.edu
Web: www.wfubmc.edu

Summary To provide Native Americans and other under-represented students with an internship opportunity to engage in a summer research project in cardiovascular science at Wake Forest University in Winston-Salem, North Carolina.

Eligibility This program is open to undergraduates and master's degree students who are members of underrepresented minority groups (African Americans, Alaskan Natives, Asian Americans, Native Americans, Pacific Islanders, and Hispanics) or who come from disadvantaged backgrounds (e.g., rural areas, first generation college students). Applicants must be interested in participating in a program of summer research in the cardiovascular sciences that includes "hands-on" laboratory research, a lecture series by faculty and guest speakers, and a research symposium at which students present their research findings. U.S. citizenship or permanent resident status is required.

Financial data The stipend is $1,731 per month, housing in a university dormitory, and round-trip transportation expense.

Duration 2 months during the summer.

Additional information This program is sponsored by the National Heart, Lung, and Blood Institute (NHLBI) of the National Institutes of Health (NIH).

Number awarded Approximately 10 each year.

Deadline February of each year.

[805]
EYAK FOUNDATION SCHOLARSHIPS

Eyak Corporation
Attn: Eyak Foundation
901 LeFevre Street
P.O. Box 340
Cordova, AK 99574
(907) 424-7161   Fax: (907) 424-5161
Web: www.eyakcorporation.com

Summary To provide financial assistance to Native Alaskans who are shareholders of the Eyak Corporation or their descendants and are interested in working on an undergraduate or graduate degree in any state.

Eligibility This program is open to Native Alaskans who are shareholders of the Eyak Corporation or lineal descendants of a Native shareholder. Applicants must be enrolled or planning to enroll in an accredited undergraduate or graduate program at a college, university, vocational education school, or continuing education program in any state. They must have a GPA of 2.5 or higher and be able to demonstrate financial need. Along with their application, they must submit a personal history and statement of educational goals.

Financial data The stipend is $1,000.

Duration 1 year.

Additional information The Eyak Foundation was formerly named the Cordova Native Foundation.

Number awarded 5 each year.

Deadline June of each year.

[806]
FAEGRE & BENSON DIVERSITY SCHOLARSHIP

Faegre & Benson LLP
Attn: Manager of Junior Legal Talent Recruitment
2200 Wells Fargo Center
90 South Seventh Street
Minneapolis, MN 55402-3901
(612) 766-8952   Toll Free: (800) 328-4393
Fax: (612) 766-1600   E-mail: tselden@faegre.com
Web: www.faegre.com/12399

Summary To provide financial assistance and work experience to Native American and other law students who will contribute to diversity in the legal profession.

Eligibility This program is open to students enrolled in the first year at an accredited law school in the United States. Applicants must submit a 500-word personal statement explaining their interest in the scholarship program, how diversity has influenced their life, and how it impacts the legal profession. Selection is based on that statement, a resume, undergraduate transcripts, a legal writing sample, and 2 professional recommendations.

Financial data The stipend is $6,000 per year.

Duration 2 years: the second and third year of law school.

Additional information Recipients are also offered an associateship during the summer between the first and second year at an office of the firm in Minneapolis, Denver, Boulder, or Des Moines. An attorney from the firm is assigned as a mentor to help them adjust to the firm and to the legal profession.

Number awarded 2 each year.

Deadline January of each year.

[807]
FALLON PAIUTE SHOSHONE TRIBE HIGHER EDUCATION PROGRAM

Fallon Paiute Shoshone Tribe
Attn: Education Office
565 Rio Vista Drive
Fallon, NV 89406
(775) 423-8065, ext. 224   Fax: (775) 423-8067
E-mail: education@fpst.org
Web: www.fpst.org

Summary To provide financial assistance to members of the Fallon Paiute Shoshone Tribe who are interested in attending college or graduate school in any state as a full-time student.

Eligibility This program is open to members of the Fallon Paiute Shoshone Tribe who are enrolled or planning to enroll as a full-time undergraduate or graduate student at a college or university in any state. Applicants must be able to demonstrate financial need.

Financial data A stipend is awarded (amount not specified).

Duration 1 year.

Additional information This program is funded, in part, by the U.S. Bureau of Indian Affairs.

Number awarded Varies each year.

Deadline May or September of each year.

[808]
FASSE/CUFA INQUIRY GRANT

National Council for the Social Studies
Attn: Program Manager, External Relations
8555 16th Street, Suite 500
Silver Spring, MD 20910-2844
(301) 588-1800, ext. 106   Fax: (301) 588-2049
E-mail: excellence@ncss.org
Web: www.socialstudies.org/getinvolved/awards/fasse-cufa

Summary To provide funding to minorities and other faculty and graduate student members of the National Council for the Social Studies (NCSS) who are interested in conducting research projects in "citizenship education."

Eligibility This program is open to members of the council who are assistant, associate, or full professors or graduate students with the demonstrated support of a university mentor/adviser. Graduate student applicants must have a mentor/adviser who is also an NCSS member. Researchers from underrepresented groups are encouraged to apply. They must be interested in a project in "citizenship education" that affirms social, cultural, and racial diversity and that addresses issues of equality, equity, and social justice. Proposals that address aims for citizen action are preferred. All proposals should be relevant to school, university, or community-based educational settings. They should either 1) serve student bodies that are socially, culturally, and racially diverse; or 2) involve teachers or prospective teachers who work or will work with diverse student populations. They can address a range of educational levels and settings, from K-12 to collegiate levels, and from school to community settings.

Financial data Grants up to $10,000 are available.

Duration Funded projects must be completed within 1 academic year.

Additional information This program is sponsored by the College and University Faculty Assembly (CUFA) and the Fund for the Advancement of Social Studies Education (FASSE), established by the NCAA in 1984.

Number awarded 1 every 2 or 3 years.

Deadline June of the years in which grants are offered.

[809]
FELLOWSHIPS FOR MINORITY DOCTORAL STUDENTS

American Institute of Certified Public Accountants
Attn: Academic and Career Development Division
220 Leigh Farm Road
Durham, NC 27707-8110
(919) 402-4931   Fax: (919) 419-4705
E-mail: MIC_Programs@aicpa.org
Web: www.aicpa.org/members/div/career/mini/fmds.htm

Summary To provide financial assistance to Native Americans and other underrepresented minority doctoral students who wish to prepare for a career teaching accounting at the college level.

Eligibility This program is open to underrepresented minority students who have applied to and/or been accepted into a doctoral program with a concentration in accounting. Applicants must have earned a master's degree or completed a minimum of 3 years of full-time work in accounting. They must be attending or planning to attend school full time and agree not to work full time in a paid position, teach more than 1 course as a teaching assistant, or work more than 25% as a research assistant. U.S. citizenship or permanent resident status is required. Preference is given to applicants who have attained a C.P.A. designation and/or are members of the American Institute of Certified Public Accountants (AICPA) and those who perform AICPA committee service. For purposes of this program, the AICPA defines minority students as those whose heritage is Black or African American, Hispanic or Latino, or Native American. Selection is based on academic and professional achievement, commitment to earning an accounting doctoral degree, and financial need.

Financial data The stipend is $12,000 per year.

Duration 1 year; may be renewed up to 4 additional years.

Number awarded Varies each year; recently, 21 of these fellowships were awarded.

Deadline March of each year.

[810]
FELLOWSHIPS IN SCIENCE AND INTERNATIONAL AFFAIRS

Harvard University
John F. Kennedy School of Government
Belfer Center for Science and International Affairs
Attn: Fellowship Coordinator
79 John F. Kennedy Street
Cambridge, MA 02138
(617) 495-8806   Fax: (617) 495-8963
E-mail: bcsia_fellowships@ksg.harvard.edu
Web: belfercenter.ksg.harvard.edu/fellowships

Summary To provide funding to Native American and other professionals, postdoctorates, and doctoral students with diverse backgrounds who are interested in conducting research in areas of concern to the Belfer Center for Science and International Affairs at Harvard University in Cambridge, Massachusetts.

Eligibility The postdoctoral fellowship is open to recent recipients of the Ph.D. or equivalent degree, university faculty members, and employees of government, military, international, humanitarian, and private research institutions who have appropriate professional experience. Applicants for predoctoral fellowships must have passed their general examinations. Lawyers, economists, political scientists, those in the natural sciences, and others of diverse disciplinary backgrounds are also welcome to apply. The program especially encourages applications from women, minorities, and citizens of all countries. All applicants must be interested in conducting research in 1 of the 3 major program areas of the center: 1) the International Security Program (ISP), including Religion in International Affairs; 2) the Science, Technology, and Public Policy Program (STPP), including information and communications technology, energy and water policy, managing the atom project, and the energy technology innovation policy research group; 3) and the Dubai initiative.

Financial data The stipend is $34,000 for postdoctoral research fellows or $20,000 for predoctoral research fellows. Health insurance is also provided.

Duration 10 months.

Number awarded A limited number each year.

Deadline January of each year.

[811]
FINNEGAN HENDERSON DIVERSITY SCHOLARSHIP

Finnegan, Henderson, Farabow, Garrett & Dunner, LLP
Attn: Attorney Recruitment Manager
901 New York Avenue, N.W.
Washington, DC 20001-4413
(202) 408-4034   Fax: (202) 408-4400
E-mail: diversityscholarship@finnegan.com
Web: www.finnegan.com/careers/summerprogram/overview

Summary To provide financial assistance and work experience to Native American and other underrepresented minority law students interested in a career in intellectual property law.

Eligibility This program is open to law students from underrepresented minority groups who have demonstrated a commitment to a career in intellectual property law and are currently enrolled either as a first-year full-time student or second-year part-time student. The sponsor defines underrepresented minorities to include American Indians/Alaskan Natives, Blacks/African Americans, Asian Americans, Native Hawaiians or other Pacific Islanders, and Hispanics/Latinos. Applicants must have earned an undergraduate degree in life sciences, engineering, or computer science, or have substantial prior trademark experience. Selection is based on academic performance at the undergraduate, graduate (if applicable), and law school level; relevant work experience; community service; leadership skills; and special accomplishments.

Financial data The stipend is $15,000 per year.

Duration 1 year; may be renewed 1 additional year as long as the recipient completes a summer associateship with the sponsor and maintains of GPA of 3.0 or higher.

Additional information The sponsor, the world's largest intellectual property law firm, established this scholarship in 2003. Summer associateships are available at its offices in Washington, D.C.; Atlanta, Georgia; Cambridge, Massachusetts; Palo Alto, California; or Reston, Virginia.

Number awarded 1 each year.

Deadline February of each year.

[812]
FIRST SERGEANT DOUGLAS AND CHARLOTTE DEHORSE SCHOLARSHIP

Catching the Dream
8200 Mountain Road, N.E., Suite 203
Albuquerque, NM 87110-7835
(505) 262-2351   Fax: (505) 262-0534
E-mail: NScholarsh@aol.com
Web: www.catchingthedream.org

Summary To provide financial assistance to American Indians who have ties to the military and are working on an undergraduate or graduate degree.

Eligibility This program is open to American Indians who 1) have completed 1 year of an Army, Navy, or Air Force Junior Reserve Officer Training (JROTC) program; 2) are enrolled in an Army, Navy, or Air Force Reserve Officer Training (ROTC) program; or 3) are a veteran of the U.S. Army,

Navy, Air Force, Marines, Merchant Marine, or Coast Guard. Applicants must be enrolled in an undergraduate or graduate program of study. Along with their application, they must submit a personal essay, high school transcripts, and letters of recommendation.

Financial data A stipend is awarded (amount not specified).

Duration 1 year.

Additional information This program was established in 2007.

Number awarded 1 or more each year.

Deadline April of each year for fall semester or quarter; September of each year for spring semester or winter quarter.

[813]
FIRST-YEAR INTERNSHIP PROGRAM OF THE OREGON STATE BAR

Oregon State Bar
Attn: Affirmative Action Program
16037 S.W. Upper Boones Ferry Road
P.O. Box 231935
Tigard, OR 97281-1935
(503) 431-6338
Toll Free: (800) 452-8260, ext. 338 (within OR)
Fax: (503) 598-6938　　　　E-mail: eyip@osbar.org
Web: www.osbar.org/aap

Summary To provide work experience to Native American and other minority law students in Oregon.

Eligibility This program is open to ethnic minority students from any state who are completing the first year of law school in Oregon. Applicants must be interested in a summer internship at a law firm in the state. Along with their application, they must submit 1) a resume that includes their community activities; 2) up to 10 pages of a first-semester legal writing assignment; and 3) a 2-page personal statement that covers their past and present ties to ethnic minority communities in Oregon and elsewhere, diversity issues that inspired them to become a lawyer, and their expectations of this internship experience. Participating employers receive a catalog with all application packets; they select students whom they wish to interview and make the final hiring decisions.

Financial data Employers who hire interns through this program pay competitive stipends.

Duration Summer months.

Number awarded Varies each year.

Deadline January of each year.

[814]
FISH & RICHARDSON DIVERSITY FELLOWSHIP PROGRAM

Fish & Richardson P.C.
Attn: Recruiting Department
One Marina Park Drive
Boston, MA 02110
(617) 542-5070　　　　Fax: (617) 542-8906
E-mail: Kiley@fr.com
Web: www.fr.com/careers/diversity

Summary To provide financial assistance for law school to Native Americans and other students who will contribute to diversity in the legal profession.

Eligibility This program is open to students enrolled in the first year at a law school anywhere in the country. Applicants must be African American/Black, American Indian/Alaskan, Hispanic/Latino, Native Hawaiian/Pacific Islander, Asian, 2 or more races, disabled, or openly homosexual, bisexual, and/or transgender. Along with their application, they must submit a 500-word essay describing their background, what led them to the legal field, their interest in the sponsoring law firm, and what they could contribute to its practice and the profession. They must also indicate their first 3 choices of an office of the firm where they are interested in a summer associate clerkship.

Financial data The stipend is $5,000.

Duration 1 year: the second year of law school.

Additional information Recipients are also offered a paid associate clerkship during the summer following their first year of law school at an office of the firm in the location of their choice in Atlanta, Boston, Dallas, Delaware, Houston, New York, San Diego, Silicon Valley, Twin Cities, or Washington, D.C. This program began in 2005.

Number awarded 1 or more each year.

Deadline January of each year.

[815]
FIVE COLLEGE FELLOWSHIP PROGRAM

Five Colleges, Incorporated
Attn: Five Colleges Fellowship Program Committee
97 Spring Street
Amherst, MA 01002-2324
(413) 256-8316　　　　Fax: (413) 256-0249
E-mail: neckert@fivecolleges.edu
Web: www.fivecolleges.edu

Summary To provide funding to Native Americans and other graduate students from underrepresented groups who have completed all the requirements for the Ph.D. except the dissertation and are interested in teaching at selected colleges in Massachusetts.

Eligibility Fellows are chosen by the host department in each of the 5 participating campuses (Amherst, Hampshire, Mount Holyoke, Smith, and the University of Massachusetts). Applicants must be graduate students at an accredited school who have completed all doctoral requirements except the dissertation and are interested in devoting full time to the completion of the dissertation. The chief goal of the program is to support scholars from underrepresented groups and/or scholars "with unique interests and histories whose engagement in the Academy will enrich scholarship and teaching."

Financial data The program provides a stipend of $30,000, a research grant, fringe benefits, office space, library privileges, and housing assistance.

Duration 1 academic year; nonrenewable.

Additional information Although the primary goal is completion of the dissertation, each fellow also has many opportunities to experience working with students and faculty colleagues on the host campus as well as with those at the other colleges. The fellows are also given an opportunity to teach (generally as a team teacher, in a section of a core course, or in a component within a course). Fellows meet monthly with each other to share their experiences. At Smith College, this program is named Mendenhall Fellowships.

Number awarded 4 each year.
Deadline January of each year.

[816]
FLORENCE YOUNG MEMORIAL SCHOLARSHIP

Association on American Indian Affairs, Inc.
Attn: Director of Scholarship Programs
966 Hungerford Drive, Suite 12-B
Rockville, MD 20850
(240) 314-7155   Fax: (240) 314-7159
E-mail: lw.aaia@verizon.net
Web: www.indian-affairs.org

Summary To provide financial assistance to Native Americans interested in working on a graduate degree in specified fields.

Eligibility This program is open to American Indian and Alaskan Native full-time students working on a graduate degree in art, public health, or law. Applicants must submit documentation of financial need, a Certificate of Indian Blood showing at least one-quarter Indian blood, proof of tribal enrollment, an essay on their educational goals, 2 letters of recommendation, and their most recent transcript. Selection is based on merit and need.

Financial data The stipend is $1,500.

Duration 1 year; recipients may reapply.

Number awarded Varies each year; recently, 3 of these scholarships were awarded.

Deadline June of each year.

[817]
FLORIDA DIVERSITY FELLOWSHIPS IN ENVIRONMENTAL LAW

American Bar Association
Attn: Section of Environment, Energy, and Resources
321 North Clark Street
Chicago, IL 60654-7598
(312) 988-5602   Fax: (312) 988-5572
E-mail: jonusaid@staff.abanet.org
Web: www.abanet.org

Summary To provide funding to Native American and other law students from underrepresented and underserved groups who are interested in working on a summer project in environmental, energy, or natural resources law in Florida.

Eligibility This program is open to first- and second-year law students and third-year night students who are members of underrepresented and underserved groups, such as minority or low-income populations. Students may be residents of any state and attending school in any state; preference is given to residents of Florida and to students who are enrolled at law schools in Florida or who have a strong interest in the state. Applicants must be interested in working during the summer at a government agency or public interest organization on a project in Florida in the areas of environmental, energy, or natural resources law. Selection is based on interest in environmental issues, academic record, personal qualities, and leadership abilities.

Financial data The stipend is $5,000.

Duration 8 to 10 weeks during the summer.

Additional information This program is cosponsored by the Florida Department of Environmental Protection and the

Florida Bar Association's Environmental and Land Use Law Section.

Number awarded 2 each year.

Deadline March of each year.

[818]
FLORIDA LIBRARY ASSOCIATION MINORITY SCHOLARSHIPS

Florida Library Association
164 N.W. Madison Street, Suite 104
P.O. Box 1571
Lake City, FL 32056-1571
(336) 438-5795   Fax: (336) 438-5796
Web: www.flalib.org/scholarships.php

Summary To provide financial assistance to Native Americans and other minority students working on a graduate degree in library and information science in Florida.

Eligibility This program is open to residents of Florida who are working on a graduate degree in library and information science at schools in the state. Applicants must be members of a minority group: Black/African American, American Indian/Alaska Native, Asian/Pacific Islander, or Hispanic/Latino. They must have some experience in a Florida library, must be a member of the Florida Library Association, and must commit to working in a Florida library for at least 1 year after graduation. Along with their application, they must submit 1) a list of activities, honors, awards, and/or offices held during college and outside college; and 2) a statement of their reasons for entering librarianship and their career goals with respect to Florida libraries. Financial need is considered in the selection process.

Financial data The stipend is $2,000.

Duration 1 year.

Number awarded 1 each year.

Deadline February of each year.

[819]
FOCUS PROFESSIONS GROUP FELLOWSHIPS

American Association of University Women
Attn: AAUW Educational Foundation
301 ACT Drive, Department 60
P.O. Box 4030
Iowa City, IA 52243-4030
(319) 337-1716, ext. 60   Fax: (319) 337-1204
E-mail: aauw@act.org
Web: www.aauw.org/learn/fellowships_grants/selected.cfm

Summary To aid Native American and other women of color who are in their final year of graduate training in the fields of business administration, law, or medicine.

Eligibility This program is open to women who are working full time on a degree in fields in which women of color have been historically underrepresented: business administration (M.B.A.), law (J.D.), or medicine (M.D., D.O.). They must be African Americans, Mexican Americans, Puerto Ricans and other Hispanics, Native Americans, Alaska Natives, Asian Americans, or Pacific Islanders. U.S. citizenship or permanent resident status is required. Applicants in business administration must be entering their second year of study; applicants in law must be entering their third year of study; applicants in medicine may be entering their third or fourth year of study. Special consideration is given to applicants who

1) demonstrate their intent to enter professional practice in disciplines in which women are underrepresented, to serve underserved populations and communities, or to pursue public interest areas; and 2) are nontraditional students. Selection is based on professional promise and personal attributes (50%), academic excellence and related academic success indicators (40%), and financial need (10%).

Financial data Stipends range from $5,000 to $18,000.

Duration 1 academic year, beginning in September.

Additional information The filing fee is $35.

Number awarded Varies each year.

Deadline January of each year.

[820]
FOREST COUNTY POTAWATOMI HIGHER EDUCATION PROGRAM

Forest County Potawatomi
Attn: Education Department
7695 Lois Crowe Lane
P.O. Box 340
Crandon, WI 54520
(715) 478-7355   Toll Free: (800) 960-5479
Fax: (715) 478-7352
Web: www.fcpotawatomi.com

Summary To provide financial assistance for college or graduate school to tribal members of the Forest County Potawatomi.

Eligibility This program is open to enrolled Forest County Potawatomi members who are working on or planning to work on an undergraduate or graduate degree. Applicants must be able to demonstrate financial need.

Financial data The stipend depends on the need of the recipient, up to full payment of tuition, books, and required fees.

Duration Up to 10 semesters for undergraduate students, up to 2 years for master's degree students, or up to 3 years for doctoral students, provided the recipient maintains a GPA of 2.0 or higher as an undergraduate or 3.0 or higher as a graduate student.

Number awarded Varies each year.

Deadline May of each year.

[821]
FOUR DIRECTIONS SUMMER RESEARCH PROGRAM

Brigham and Women's Hospital
Office for Multicultural Faculty Careers
Attn: Elena Muench
1620 Tremont Street 3-014.04
Boston, MA 02120
(617) 525-7644   E-mail: FourDirections@partners.org
Web: www.fdsrp.org

Summary To provide an opportunity for Native American undergraduate and graduate students to participate in a summer research project at Harvard Medical School.

Eligibility This program is open to Native American undergraduate and graduate students who are interested in preparing for a career as a physician or in biomedical research. Applicants must have completed at least 1 year of undergraduate study and have taken at least 1 introductory science course (may include biology or chemistry). They must be

interested in conducting a research project at Harvard Medical School under the supervision of a scientist engaged in medical or biomedical research, ranging from neurobiology and neuropathology to cell biology and molecular genetics. Selection is based on demonstrated commitment to the health of Native American communities and demonstrated interest in a career in medical sciences. Students from rural state colleges, tribal colleges, and community colleges are especially encouraged to apply.

Financial data The program provides a stipend of at least $2,500, airfare, transportation, and lodging expenses.

Duration 8 weeks during the summer.

Additional information This program, which began in 1994, is administered jointly by Harvard Medical School and Brigham and Women's Hospital. Funding is provided by the Aetna Foundation, the Mohegan Sun casino, and the Office of Minority Health of the U.S. Department of Health and Human Services. Participants may not take the summer MCAT, because the time constraints of this program do not allow time to study for that examination.

Number awarded 6 each year.

Deadline February of each year.

[822]
FRANCES C. ALLEN FELLOWSHIPS

Newberry Library
Attn: McNickle Center for American Indian History
60 West Walton Street
Chicago, IL 60610-3305
(312) 255-3564   Fax: (312) 255-3696
E-mail: mcnickle@newberry.org
Web: www.newberry.org/mcnickle/frances.html

Summary To provide funding to Native American women graduate students who wish to use the resources of the D'Arcy McNickle Center for the History of the American Indian at the Newberry Library.

Eligibility This program is open to women of American Indian heritage who are interested in using the library for a project appropriate to its collections. Applicants must be enrolled in a graduate or pre-professional program, especially in the humanities or social sciences. Recommendations are required; at least 2 must come from academic advisers or instructors who can comment on the significance of the applicant's proposed project and explain how it will help in the achievement of professional goals.

Financial data The basic stipend is $1,600 per month; supplemental funding may be available on a case-by-case basis.

Duration From 1 month to 1 year.

Additional information These grants were first awarded in 1983. Fellows must spend a significant portion of their time at the library's D'Arcy McNickle Center.

Number awarded Varies each year; recently, 2 of these fellowships were awarded.

Deadline February of each year.

[823]
FRANCES JOHNSON MEMORIAL TRUST SCHOLARSHIP

Northern Arapaho Tribe
Attn: Sky People Higher Education
P.O. Box 8480
Ethete, WY 82520
(307) 332-5286   Toll Free: (800) 815-6795
Fax: (307) 332-9104   E-mail: assistant@skypeopleed.org
Web: www.skypeopleed.org

Summary To provide financial assistance to members of the Northern Arapaho Tribe who are working on an undergraduate or graduate degree in nursing or a health-related field.

Eligibility This program is open to full-time undergraduate and graduate students who have an undergraduate GPA of 2.0 or higher or the graduate GPA required by their school. Applicants must be at least one-fourth Northern Arapaho descent (enrolled or non-enrolled) and must submit a Certificate of Indian Blood or other verification of Northern Arapaho blood with at least one-fourth degree. They must be working on a degree in nursing or a health-related field. Along with their application, they must submit a 1-page personal statement that includes a brief history of their background, academic ability and achievement, work or leadership experience, participation in community-related activities, and career goals. Selection is based on that statement, potential to contribute to the community upon graduation, academic ability and achievement, and a letter of recommendation.

Financial data The stipend is $1,500 per year.

Duration 1 year; may be renewed.

Additional information The recipient is expected to apply for employment, after graduation, at the Tribal Health Program, Indian Health Services, at health care facilities on the Wind River Indian Reservation, or in the local communities of Lander or Riverton.

Number awarded 1 each year.

Deadline June of each year.

[824]
FRANCHISE LAW DIVERSITY SCHOLARSHIP AWARD

International Franchise Association
Attn: President, Educational Foundation
1501 K Street, N.W., Suite 350
Washington, DC 20005
(202) 662-0764   Fax: (202) 628-0812
E-mail: jreynolds@franchise.org
Web: www.franchise.org/files/Scholarships.aspx

Summary To provide financial assistance to Native American and other diverse law students who are interested in taking courses related to franchise law.

Eligibility This program is open to second- and third-year students who are enrolled at ABA-accredited law schools and a member of a diverse group (defined as African Americans, American Indians, Hispanic Americans, Asian Americans, or gays/lesbians). Applicants must be enrolled in at least 1 course oriented toward franchise law (e.g., torts, unfair trade practices, trade secrets, antitrust, trademarks, contracts, agency, or securities). Along with their application, they must submit current transcript, an essay explaining their interest in franchise law, and 2 letters of recommendation.

Financial data The stipend is $4,000. Funds are paid to the recipient's law school and are to be used for tuition.

Duration 1 year.

Additional information This award is cosponsored by the IFA Educational Foundation and DLA Piper US LLP. It may not be used by the recipient's law school to reduce the amount of any institutionally-awarded financial aid.

Number awarded 1 or more each year.

Deadline October of each year.

[825]
FRED L. MCGHEE FIRST GENERATION INDIAN DESCENT SCHOLARSHIP PROGRAM

Poarch Band of Creek Indians
Attn: Tuition Program Coordinator
5811 Jack Springs Road
Atmore, AL 36502
(251) 368-9136, ext. 2241   Fax: (251) 368-4502
E-mail: sfisher@pci-nsn.gov
Web: www.poarchcreekindians.org

Summary To provide financial assistance to undergraduate and graduate students who are first-generation descendants of members of the Poarch Band of Creek Indians.

Eligibility This program is open to first-generation descendants of enrolled tribal members of the Poarch Band of Creek Indians. Applicants must be attending or planning to attend an approved postsecondary institution as an undergraduate or graduate student. They must have a GPA of 2.0 or higher and be able to document financial need.

Financial data The stipend depends on the need of the recipient, to an annual cap of $6,000.

Duration 1 year; may be renewed until the recipient reaches a lifetime benefit cap of $20,000.

Number awarded Varies each year.

Deadline Applications may be submitted at any time.

[826]
GABE STEPETIN SCHOLARSHIP AWARD

The Aleut Corporation
Attn: Aleut Foundation
703 West Tudor Road, Suite 102
Anchorage, AK 99503-6650
(907) 646-1929   Toll Free: (800) 232-4882
Fax: (907) 646-1949   E-mail: taf@thealeutfoundation.org
Web: www.thealeutfoundation.org/ScholarshipGuide.aspx

Summary To provide financial assistance to Native Alaskans who are shareholders of The Aleut Corporation or their descendants and working on a degree in business at a school in any state.

Eligibility This program is open to Native Alaskans who are original enrollees or descendants of original enrollees of The Aleut Corporation (TAC). Applicants must have completed at least 1 year of a bachelor's, 2- or 4-year vocational, or master's degree in business at a school in any state. They must be enrolled full time and have a GPA of 3.0 or higher. Along with their application, they must include a letter of intent, up to 500 words in length, that describes their educational goals and objectives and their expected graduation date.

Financial data A stipend is awarded (amount not specified).

Duration 1 year.

Additional information The Aleut Corporation is 1 of 13 Alaska Native Regional Corporations created under the Alaska Native Claims Settlement Act of 1971.

Number awarded 1 each year.

Deadline June of each year.

[827]
GAIUS CHARLES BOLIN DISSERTATION AND POST-MFA FELLOWSHIPS

Williams College
Attn: Dean of the Faculty
Hopkins Hall, Third Floor
P.O. Box 141
Williamstown, MA 01267
(413) 597-4351   Fax: (413) 597-3553
E-mail: gburda@williams.edu
Web: dean-faculty.williams.edu/graduate-fellowships

Summary To provide financial assistance to Native Americans and members of other underrepresented groups who are interested in teaching courses at Williams College while working on their doctoral dissertation or building their post-M.F.A. professional portfolio.

Eligibility This program is open to members of underrepresented groups, including ethnic minorities, first-generation college students, women in predominantly male fields, and scholars with disabilities. Applicants must be 1) doctoral candidates in any field who have completed all work for a Ph.D. except for the dissertation; or 2) artists who completed an M.F.A. degree within the past 2 years and are building their professional portfolio. They must be willing to teach a course at Williams College. Along with their application, they must submit a full curriculum vitae, a graduate school transcript, 3 letters of recommendation, a copy of their dissertation prospectus or samples of their artistic work, and a description of their teaching interests within a department or program at Williams College. U.S. citizenship or permanent resident status is required.

Financial data Fellows receive $33,000 for the academic year, plus housing assistance, office space, computer and library privileges, and a research allowance of up to $4,000.

Duration 2 years.

Additional information Bolin fellows are assigned a faculty advisor in the appropriate department. This program was established in 1985. Fellows are expected to teach a 1-semester course each year. They must be in residence at Williams College for the duration of the fellowship.

Number awarded 3 each year.

Deadline November of each year.

[828]
GEM M.S. ENGINEERING FELLOWSHIP PROGRAM

National Consortium for Graduate Degrees for Minorities in Engineering and Science (GEM)
Attn: Manager, Fellowships Administration
1430 Duke Street
Alexandria, VA 22314
(703) 562-3639   Fax: (202) 207-3518
E-mail: info@gemfellowship.org
Web: www.gemfellowship.org/gem-fellowship

Summary To provide financial assistance and summer work experience to Native Americans and other underrepresented minority students interested in working on a master's degree in engineering or computer science.

Eligibility This program is open to U.S. citizens and permanent residents who are members of ethnic groups underrepresented in engineering: American Indians/Native Americans, Blacks/African Americans, or Latinos/Hispanic Americans. Applicants must be a junior, senior, or graduate of an ABET-accredited engineering or computer science program and have an academic record that indicates the ability to pursue graduate studies in engineering (including a GPA of 2.8 or higher). They must agree to apply to at least 3 of the 104 GEM member universities that offer a master's degree and to intern during summers with a sponsoring GEM employer.

Financial data The fellowship pays tuition, fees, and a stipend of $10,000 over its lifetime. In addition, each participant receives a salary during the summer work assignment as a GEM summer intern. Employer members reimburse GEM participants for travel expenses to and from the summer work site.

Duration Up to 3 semesters or 4 quarters, plus summer work internships lasting 10 to 14 weeks for up to 3 summers, depending on whether the student applies as a junior, senior, or college graduate; recipients begin their internship upon acceptance into the program and work each summer until completion of their master's degree.

Additional information During the summer internship, each fellow is assigned an engineering project in a research setting. Each project is based on the fellow's interest and background and is carried out under the supervision of an experienced engineer. At the conclusion of the internship, each fellow writes a project report. Recipients must work on a master's degree in the same engineering discipline as their baccalaureate degree.

Number awarded Approximately 300 each year.

Deadline November of each year.

[829]
GEM PH.D. ENGINEERING FELLOWSHIP PROGRAM

National Consortium for Graduate Degrees for Minorities in Engineering and Science (GEM)
Attn: Manager, Fellowships Administration
1430 Duke Street
Alexandria, VA 22314
(703) 562-3639   Fax: (202) 207-3518
E-mail: info@gemfellowship.org
Web: www.gemfellowship.org/gem-fellowship

Summary To provide financial assistance and summer work experience to Native Americans and other underrepresented minority students interested in obtaining a Ph.D. degree in engineering.

Eligibility This program is open to U.S. citizens and permanent residents who are members of ethnic groups underrepresented in engineering: American Indians/Native Americans, Blacks/African Americans, and Latinos/Hispanic Americans. Applicants must be college seniors, master's degree students, or graduates of an ABET-accredited program in engineering and have an academic record that indicates the ability to work on a doctoral degree in engineering (including a GPA of 3.0 or higher). They must agree to apply to at least 3 of the 100 GEM member universities that offer a doctoral degree in engineering and to intern during summer with a sponsoring GEM employer.

Financial data The stipend is $14,000 for the first year; in subsequent years, fellows receive full payment of tuition and fees plus a stipend and assistantship from their university that is equivalent to funding received by other doctoral students in their department.

Duration 3 to 5 years for the fellowship; 12 weeks during the summer immediately after sponsorship for the internship.

Additional information This program is valid only at 1 of the 105 participating GEM member universities; write to GEM for a list. The fellowship award is designed to support the student in the first year of the doctoral program without working. Subsequent years are subsidized by the respective universities and will usually include either a teaching or research assistantship. Recipients must participate in the GEM summer internship; failure to agree to accept the internship cancels the fellowship.

Number awarded Approximately 50 each year.

Deadline November of each year.

[830]
GEM PH.D. SCIENCE FELLOWSHIP PROGRAM

National Consortium for Graduate Degrees for Minorities
 in Engineering and Science (GEM)
Attn: Manager, Fellowships Administration
1430 Duke Street
Alexandria, VA 22314
(703) 562-3639   Fax: (202) 207-3518
E-mail: info@gemfellowship.org
Web: www.gemfellowship.org/gem-fellowship

Summary To provide financial assistance and summer work experience to Native American and other underrepresented minority students interested in working on a Ph.D. degree in the life sciences, mathematics, or physical sciences.

Eligibility This program is open to U.S. citizens and permanent residents who are members of ethnic groups underrepresented in the natural sciences: American Indians/Native Americans, Blacks/African Americans, and Latinos/Hispanic Americans. Applicants must be college seniors, master's degree students, or recent graduates in the biological sciences, mathematics, or physical sciences (chemistry, computer science, earth sciences, and physics) with an academic record that indicates the ability to pursue doctoral studies (including a GPA of 3.0 or higher). They must agree to apply to at least 3 of the 100 GEM member universities that offer a

doctoral degree in science and to intern during summer with a sponsoring GEM employer.

Financial data The stipend is $14,000 for the first year; in subsequent years, fellows receive full payment of tuition and fees plus a stipend and assistantship from their university that is equivalent to funding received by other doctoral students in their department.

Duration 3 to 5 years for the fellowship; 12 weeks during the summer immediately after sponsorship for the internship.

Additional information This program is valid only at 1 of 105 participating GEM member universities; write to GEM for a list. The fellowship award is designed to support the student in the first year of the doctoral program without working. Subsequent years are subsidized by the respective university and will usually include either a teaching or research assistantship. Recipients must participate in the GEM summer internship; failure to agree to accept the internship cancels the fellowship. Recipients must enroll in the same scientific discipline as their undergraduate major.

Number awarded Approximately 40 each year.

Deadline November of each year.

[831]
GEOCORPS AMERICAN INDIAN INTERNSHIPS

Geological Society of America
Attn: Program Officer, GeoCorps America
3300 Penrose Place
P.O. Box 9140
Boulder, CO 80301-9140
(303) 357-1025   Toll Free: (800) 472-1988, ext. 1025
Fax: (303) 357-1070   E-mail: mdawson@geosociety.org
Web: rock.geosociety.org/g.corps/index

Summary To provide work experience in national parks to American Indians and Native Alaskans who are student members of the Geological Society of America (GSA).

Eligibility This program is open to all GSA members, but applications are especially encouraged from American Indians, Alaska Natives, and persons with a strong connection to an American Indian tribe or community. Applicants must be interested in a summer work experience in facilities of the U.S. government, currently limited to the National Park Service but planned for expansion to the Forest Service and the Bureau of Land Management. Geoscience knowledge and skills are a significant requirement for most positions, but students from various disciplines (e.g., chemistry, physics, engineering, mathematics, computer science, ecology, hydrology, meteorology, the social sciences, and the humanities) are also invited to apply. Activities involve research; interpretation and education; inventory and monitoring; or mapping, surveying, and GIS. Prior interns are not eligible. U.S. citizenship or possession of a proper visa is required.

Financial data Each internship provides a $2,750 stipend. Free housing, or a housing allowance of $1,500 to $2,000, is also provided.

Duration 10 to 12 weeks during the summer.

Number awarded Deadline not specified.

Deadline January of each year.

[832]
GEORGE A. STRAIT MINORITY SCHOLARSHIP ENDOWMENT

American Association of Law Libraries
Attn: Chair, Scholarships Committee
105 West Adams Street, Suite 3300
Chicago, IL 60603
(312) 939-4764   Fax: (312) 431-1097
E-mail: scholarships@aall.org
Web: www.aallnet.org/services/sch_strait.asp

Summary To provide financial assistance to Native American and other minority college seniors or college graduates who are interested in becoming law librarians.

Eligibility This program is open to college graduates with meaningful law library experience who are members of minority groups and intend to have a career in law librarianship. Applicants must be degree candidates at an ALA-accredited library school or an ABA-accredited law school. Along with their application, they must submit a personal statement that discusses their interest in law librarianship, reason for applying for this scholarship, career goals as a law librarian, etc.

Financial data The stipend is $3,500.

Duration 1 year.

Additional information This program, established in 1990, is currently supported by Thomson West.

Number awarded Varies each year; recently, 5 of these scholarships were awarded.

Deadline March of each year.

[833]
GEORGE HI'ILANI MILLS SCHOLARSHIP

Ke Ali'i Pauahi Foundation
Attn: Financial Aid & Scholarship Services
567 South King Street, Suite 160
Honolulu, HI 96813
(808) 534-3966   Toll Free: (800) 842-4682, ext. 43966
Fax: (808) 534-3890   E-mail: scholarships@pauahi.org
Web: www.pauahi.org/scholarships

Summary To provide financial assistance to students, especially Native Hawaiians, who are interested in working on a graduate degree in medicine or allied health.

Eligibility This program is open to students working full time on a graduate degree in medicine or the allied health-related fields. Applicants must be able to demonstrate financial need. Residency in Hawaii is not required, but preference is given to Native Hawaiians (descendants of the aboriginal inhabitants of the Hawaiian Islands prior to 1778).

Financial data The stipend is $1,700.

Duration 1 year.

Number awarded Varies each year; recently, 3 of these fellowships were awarded.

Deadline March of each year.

[834]
GEORGE V. POWELL DIVERSITY SCHOLARSHIP

Lane Powell Spears Lubersky LLP
Attn: Manager of Attorney Recruiting
1420 Fifth Avenue, Suite 4100
Seattle, WA 98101-2338
(206) 223-6123   Fax: (206) 223-7107
E-mail: rodenl@lanepowell.com
Web: www.lanepowell.com/422/diversity-scholarship

Summary To provide financial assistance and work experience to Native American and other law students who will contribute to the diversity of the legal community.

Eligibility This program is open to second-year students in good standing at an ABA-accredited law school. Applicants must be able to contribute meaningfully to the diversity of the legal community and have a demonstrated desire to work, live, and eventually practice law in Seattle or Portland. They must submit a cover letter that includes a statement indicating eligibility to participate in the program, a resume, a current copy of law school transcript, a legal writing sample, and a list of 2 or 3 professional or academic references. Selection is based on academic achievement and record of leadership abilities, community service, and involvement in community issues.

Financial data The program provides a stipend of $7,500 for the third year of law school and a paid summer associate clerkship.

Duration 1 year, including the summer.

Additional information This program was established in 2005. Clerkships are provided at the offices of the sponsor in Seattle or Portland.

Number awarded 1 each year.

Deadline September of each year.

[835]
GERALD PEET FELLOWSHIP

American Indian Graduate Center
Attn: Executive Director
4520 Montgomery Boulevard, N.E., Suite 1-B
Albuquerque, NM 87109-1291
(505) 881-4584   Toll Free: (800) 628-1920
Fax: (505) 884-0427   E-mail: aigc@aigc.com
Web: www.aigc.com/02scholarships/scholarships.htm

Summary To provide financial assistance to Native American students interested in working on a graduate degree in medicine or other health-related field.

Eligibility This program is open to enrolled members of federally-recognized American Indian tribes and Alaska Native groups and students who can document one-fourth degree federally-recognized Indian blood. Applicants must be enrolled full time at a graduate or medical school in the United States and working on a degree in medicine or other health-related field. Along with their application, they must submit a 500-word essay on their extracurricular activities as they relate to American Indian programs at their institution, volunteer and community work as related to American Indian communities, tribal and community involvement, and plans to make positive changes in the American Indian community with their college education. Financial need is also considered in the selection process.

Financial data Stipends range from $1,000 to $5,000 per academic year, depending on the availability of funds and the recipient's unmet financial need.

Duration 1 year; may be renewed.

Additional information The application fee is $15. Since this a supplemental program, students must apply in a timely manner for federal financial aid and campus-based aid at the college they are attending to be considered for this program. Failure to apply will disqualify an applicant.

Number awarded 1 each year.

Deadline May of each year.

[836]
GLADYS KAMAKAKUOKALANI AINOA BRANDT SCHOLARSHIPS

Ke Ali'i Pauahi Foundation
Attn: Financial Aid & Scholarship Services
567 South King Street, Suite 160
Honolulu, HI 96813
(808) 534-3966   Toll Free: (800) 842-4682, ext. 43966
Fax: (808) 534-3890   E-mail: scholarships@pauahi.org
Web: www.pauahi.org/scholarships

Summary To provide financial assistance to undergraduate and graduate students, especially those of Native Hawaiian descent, who are preparing for a career in education.

Eligibility This program is open to full-time juniors, seniors, and graduate students who are planning to enter the education profession. Applicants must have a GPA of 2.5 or higher and be able to demonstrate financial need. Preference is given to Native Hawaiians (descendants of the aboriginal inhabitants of the Hawaiian Islands prior to 1778) and current or former residents of Kaua'i.

Financial data The stipend is $3,000.

Duration 1 year.

Number awarded Varies each year; recently, 4 of these scholarships were awarded.

Deadline March of each year.

[837]
GOLDMAN SACHS/MATSUO TAKABUKI COMMEMORATIVE SCHOLARSHIPS

Ke Ali'i Pauahi Foundation
Attn: Financial Aid & Scholarship Services
567 South King Street, Suite 160
Honolulu, HI 96813
(808) 534-3966   Toll Free: (800) 842-4682, ext. 43966
Fax: (808) 534-3890   E-mail: scholarships@pauahi.org
Web: www.pauahi.org/scholarships

Summary To provide financial assistance to students, especially Native Hawaiians, who are interested in working on a graduate degree in business or related fields.

Eligibility This program is open to graduate students working full time on a degree in business or other field related to financial services. Preference is given to Native Hawaiians (descendants of the aboriginal inhabitants of the Hawaiian Islands prior to 1778), current residents of Hawaii, and applicants who can demonstrate financial need.

Financial data The stipend is $5,000.

Duration 1 year; may be renewed.

Additional information This program is sponsored by Goldman Sachs, a global investment banking and securities firm.

Number awarded Varies each year; recently, 9 of these scholarships were awarded.

Deadline March of each year.

[838]
GOLDMAN SACHS MBA FELLOWSHIP

Goldman Sachs
Attn: Human Capital Management
30 Hudson Street, 34th Floor
Jersey City, NJ 07302
(212) 902-1000   E-mail: holly.jackson@gs.com
Web: www2.goldmansachs.com

Summary To provide financial assistance and work experience to Native Americans and other underrepresented minority students interested in working on an M.B.A. degree.

Eligibility This program is open to graduate students of Black, Latino, or Native American descent who are interested in working on an M.B.A. degree. Applicants must be preparing for a career in the financial services industry. Along with their application, they must submit 2 essays of 500 words or less on the following topics: 1) why they are preparing for a career in the financial services industry; and 2) their current involvement with a community-based organization. Selection is based on analytical skills and the ability to identify significant problems, gather facts, and analyze situations in depth; interpersonal skills, including, but not limited to, poise, confidence, and professionalism; academic record; evidence of hard work and commitment; ability to work well with others; and commitment to community involvement.

Financial data Fellows receive $15,000 toward payment of tuition and living expenses for the first year of business school; an internship at a domestic office of Goldman Sachs during the summer after the first year of business school; and (after successful completion of the summer internship and acceptance of an offer to return to the firm after graduation as a full-time regular employee) either payment of tuition costs for the second year of business school or an additional $15,000 toward tuition and living costs.

Duration Up to 2 years.

Additional information This program was initiated in 1997.

Number awarded 1 or more each year.

Deadline December of each year.

[839]
GOODWIN PUBLIC INTEREST FELLOWSHIPS FOR LAW STUDENTS OF COLOR

Goodwin Procter LLP
Attn: Recruiting Manager
53 State Street
Boston, MA 02109
(617) 570-8156 E-mail: fellowships@goodwinprocter.com
Web: www.goodwinprocter.com

Summary To provide financial assistance to Native Americans and other minority students who are interested in public interest law.

Eligibility This program is open to students of color entering their second year at a law school in any state. Applicants must actively express an interest in working in the sponsoring firm's summer program in public interest law. If they are applying for the Goodwin MassMutual Diversity, they must express an interest in working with MassMutual's legal department in Springfield, Massachusetts for 2 weeks as part of the summer program and specializing in the investment or insurance business or in a legal focus to advance business objectives. Selection is based on academic performance, leadership abilities, involvement in minority student organizations, commitment to community service, interpersonal skills, other special achievements and honors, and interest in working with the firm during the summer.

Financial data The stipend is $7,500.

Duration 1 year; nonrenewable.

Additional information This program was established in 2005. In 2007, it added the Goodwin MassMutual Diversity Fellowship, created in conjunction with its long-standing client, Massachusetts Mutual Life Insurance Company (Mass-Mutual). Summer positions are available at the firm's offices in Boston, Los Angeles, New York, Palo Alto, San Diego, San Francisco, and Washington, D.C.

Number awarded 3 each year, including 1 Goodwin MassMutual Diversity Fellowship.

Deadline October of each year.

[840]
GOOGLE SCHOLARSHIP

American Indian Science and Engineering Society
Attn: Program Officer
2305 Renard, S.E., Suite 200
P.O. Box 9828
Albuquerque, NM 87119-9828
(505) 765-1052, ext. 105   Fax: (505) 765-5608
E-mail: tina@aises.org
Web: www.aises.org

Summary To provide financial assistance to members of the American Indian Science and Engineering Society (AISES) who are working on an undergraduate or graduate degree in a computer-related field.

Eligibility This program is open to AISES members who are full-time undergraduate or graduate students at a 4-year college or university or a full-time student at a 2-year college enrolled in a program leading to a 4-year degree. Applicants must be majoring in computer science or computer engineering. They must have a GPA of 3.5 or higher and be able to document ancestry as an American Indian, Alaskan Native, or Native Hawaiian. Along with their application, they must submit a 500-word essay on their educational and/or career goals, interest in and motivation to continue higher education, understanding of the importance of college and commitment to completion, commitment to learning, and giving back to the community. U.S. citizenship is required. Selection is based on that essay (40%), GPA (35%), letters of recommendation (15%), and overall impression of the application (10%).

Financial data The total award is $10,000, disbursed equally over the recipient's course of study.

Duration Until completion of a degree.

Additional information This program, established in 2008, is funded by Google Inc.

Number awarded 20 each year.

Deadline June of each year.

[841]
GRACE WALL BARREDA MEMORIAL FELLOWSHIP

American Indian Graduate Center
Attn: Executive Director
4520 Montgomery Boulevard, N.E., Suite 1-B
Albuquerque, NM 87109-1291
(505) 881-4584   Toll Free: (800) 628-1920
Fax: (505) 884-0427   E-mail: aigc@aigc.com
Web: www.aigc.com/02scholarships/scholarships.htm

Summary To provide financial assistance to Native American students interested in working on a graduate degree in environmental studies or public health.

Eligibility This program is open to enrolled members of federally-recognized American Indian tribes and Alaska Native groups and students who can document one-fourth degree federally-recognized Indian blood. Applicants must be enrolled full time at a graduate school in the United States and working on a degree in environmental studies or public health. Along with their application, they must submit a 500-word essay on their extracurricular activities as they relate to American Indian programs at their institution, volunteer and community work as related to American Indian communities, tribal and community involvement, and plans to make positive changes in the American Indian community with their college education. Financial need is also considered in the selection process.

Financial data Stipends range from $1,000 to $5,000 per academic year, depending on the availability of funds and the recipient's unmet financial need.

Duration 1 year; may be renewed.

Additional information The application fee is $15. Since this a supplemental program, students must apply in a timely manner for federal financial aid and campus-based aid at the college they are attending to be considered for this program. Failure to apply will disqualify an applicant.

Number awarded 1 each year.

Deadline May of each year.

[842]
GRADUATE RESEARCH FELLOWSHIP PROGRAM OF THE NATIONAL SCIENCE FOUNDATION

National Science Foundation
Directorate for Education and Human Resources
Attn: Division of Graduate Education
4201 Wilson Boulevard, Room 875S
Arlington, VA 22230
(703) 292-8694   Toll Free: (866) NSF-GRFP
Fax: (703) 292-9048   E-mail: grfp@nsf.gov
Web: www.nsf.gov/funding/pgm_summ.jsp?pims_id=6201

Summary To provide financial assistance to minority and other graduate students interested in working on a master's or doctoral degree in fields supported by the National Science Foundation (NSF).

Eligibility This program is open to U.S. citizens, nationals, and permanent residents who wish to work on research-based master's or doctoral degrees in a field of science (including social science), technology, engineering, or mathematics (STEM) supported by NSF. Other work in medical, dental, law, public health, or practice-oriented professional degree programs, or in joint science-professional degree programs, such as M.D./Ph.D. and J.D./Ph.D. programs, is not eligible. Other categories of ineligible support include 1) clinical, counseling, business, or management fields; 2) education (except science and engineering education); 3) history (except the history of science); 4) social work; 5) medical sciences or research with disease-related goals, including work on the etiology, diagnosis, or treatment of physical or mental disease, abnormality, or malfunction in human beings or animals; 6) research involving animal models with disease-related goals; and 7) testing of drugs or other procedures for disease-related goals. Applications normally should be submitted during the senior year in college or in the first year of graduate study; eligibility is limited to those who have completed no more than 12 months of graduate study since completion of a baccalaureate degree. Applicants who have already earned an advanced degree in science, engineering, or medicine (including an M.D., D.D.S., or D.V.M.) are ineligible. Selection is based on 1) intellectual merit of the proposed activity (strength of the academic record, proposed plan of research, previous research experience, references, appropriateness of the choice of institution); and 2) broader impacts of the proposed activity (how well does the activity advance discovery and understanding, how well does it broaden the participation of underrepresented groups (e.g., gender, ethnicity, disability, geographic), to what extent will it enhance the infrastructure for research and education, will the results be disseminated broadly to enhance scientific and technological understanding, what may be the benefits of the proposed activity to society).

Financial data The stipend is $30,000 per year; an additional $10,500 cost-of-education allowance is provided to the recipient's institution. If a fellow affiliates with a foreign institution, tuition and fees are reimbursed to the fellow up to a maximum of $10,500 per tenure year and an additional international research travel allowance of $1,000 is provided.

Duration Up to 3 years, usable over a 5-year period.

Additional information Fellows may choose as their fellowship institution any appropriate nonprofit U.S. or foreign institution of higher education.

Number awarded Approximately 2,000 each year.

Deadline November of each year.

[843]
GRADUATE STUDENT INDUSTRIAL FELLOWSHIPS/TRAINEESHIPS

National Science Foundation
Directorate for Engineering
Attn: Division of Industrial Innovation and Partnerships
4201 Wilson Boulevard, Room 550S
Arlington, VA 22230
(703) 292-7082   Fax: (703) 292-9056
TDD: (800) 281-8749   E-mail: dsenich@nsf.gov
Web: www.nsf.gov/funding/pgm_summ.jsp?pims_id=13706

Summary To provide an opportunity for underrepresented minorities and other graduate students to work in industry as part of the Grant Opportunities for Academic Liaison with Industry (GOALI) program of the National Science Foundation (NSF).

Eligibility This program is open to graduate students (preferably Ph.D. students) in science, engineering, and mathematics fields of interest to NSF. Applicants must be U.S. citizens, nationals, or permanent residents. They must be proposing a program of full- or part-time work in industry in an area related to their research under the guidance of an academic adviser and an industrial mentor. The program encourages applications from underrepresented minorities and persons with disabilities.

Financial data Graduate students may receive stipends from $1,500 to $1,800 per month, plus transportation expenses. The faculty adviser may receive 10% of the total award for research-related expenses, excluding equipment. No indirect costs are allowed. The total award may be up to $30,000 for a fellowship for a single student.

Duration Up to 1 year.

Additional information This program is also offered by most other NSF directorates. Check the web site for a name and e-mail address of the contact person in each directorate.

Number awarded A total of 60 to 80 grants for all GOALI programs is awarded each year; total funding is approximately $5 million.

Deadline Applications may be submitted at any time.

[844]
GRAND PORTAGE SCHOLARSHIP PROGRAM

Grand Portage Tribal Council
Attn: Education Director
P.O. Box 428
Grand Portage, MN 55605
(218) 475-2812   Fax: (218) 475-2284
E-mail: gpeduc@boreal.org
Web: www.grandportage.com/program.php

Summary To provide financial assistance for undergraduate or graduate study to Minnesota Chippewa Tribe members.

Eligibility Applicants must be an enrolled member of the Grand Portage Band of Chippewa or have a parent who is enrolled. They must be enrolled at or accepted for enrollment at an accredited training program or degree-granting college or university and have applied for all other forms of financial aid. Residents of states other than Minnesota are eligible only for college or university study, not for vocational training.

Financial data The amount of the award is based on the need of the recipient.

Duration 1 year; may be renewed for a total of 10 semesters or 15 quarters to complete a 4-year degree program if recipients maintain full-time enrollment and a GPA of 2.0 or higher. Adjustments are considered for part-time and/or graduate study.

Number awarded Varies each year.

Deadline At least 8 weeks before school starts.

[845]
GTB HIGHER EDUCATION GRANTS

Grand Traverse Band of Ottawa and Chippewa Indians
Attn: Higher Education
845 Business Park Drive
Traverse City, MI 49686
(231) 534-7760   Toll Free: (866) 534-7760
Fax: (231) 534-7773
E-mail: joyce.wilson@gtbindians.com
Web: www.gtbindians.org/departments/index.html

Summary To provide financial assistance to members of the Grand Traverse Band (GTB) of Ottawa and Chippewa Indians who are interested in attending college or graduate school in any state.

Eligibility This program is open to enrolled GTB members who are working on or planning to work on an associate, bachelor's, master's, or doctoral degree at a college or university in any state. Applicants must be able to document financial need. Along with their application, they must submit a personal statement on how they plan to serve their Indian community after they have successfully completed their course of study.

Financial data Stipends for associate degree students are $200 per credit hour, to a maximum of $7,200 per year; stipends for bachelor's degree students are $250 per credit hour, to a maximum of $9,000 per year; stipends for graduate students are $600 per credit hour, to a maximum of $10,800 per year.

Duration 1 semester; may be renewed as long as the recipient maintains a GPA of 2.0 or higher. Support is provided for up to 12 credits above the number required for an undergraduate degree or up to 6 credits above the number required for a graduate degree.

Number awarded Varies each year.

Deadline Deadline not specified.

[846]
HANA SCHOLARSHIPS

United Methodist Church
Attn: General Board of Higher Education and Ministry
Office of Loans and Scholarships
1001 19th Avenue South
P.O. Box 340007
Nashville, TN 37203-0007
(615) 340-7344   Fax: (615) 340-7367
E-mail: umscholar@gbhem.org
Web: www.gbhem.org/loansandscholarships

Summary To provide financial assistance to upper-division and graduate Methodist students who are of Native American, Asian, Pacific Islander, or Hispanic ancestry.

Eligibility This program is open to full-time juniors, seniors, and graduate students at accredited colleges and universities in the United States who have been active, full members of a United Methodist Church (UMC) for at least 1 year prior to applying. Applicants must have at least 1 parent who is Asian, Hispanic, Native American, or Pacific Islander. They must be able to demonstrate involvement in their Hispanic, Asian, or Native American (HANA) community in the UMC. Selection is based on that involvement, academic ability (GPA of at least 2.85), and financial need. U.S. citizenship or permanent resident status is required.

Financial data The maximum stipend is $3,000 for undergraduates or $5,000 for graduate students.

Duration 1 year; recipients may reapply.

Number awarded 50 each year.

Deadline March of each year.

[847]
HAWAII DIVERSITY FELLOWSHIPS IN ENVIRONMENTAL LAW

American Bar Association
Attn: Section of Environment, Energy, and Resources
321 North Clark Street
Chicago, IL 60654-7598
(312) 988-5602   Fax: (312) 988-5572
E-mail: jonusaid@staff.abanet.org
Web: www.abanet.org

Summary To provide funding to Native Americans and other law students from underrepresented and underserved groups who are interested in working on a summer project in environmental, energy, or natural resources law in Hawaii.

Eligibility This program is open to first- and second-year law students and third-year night students who 1) are either enrolled at a law school in Hawaii or residents of Hawaii enrolled at a law school in another state; and 2) will contribute to increasing diversity in the Hawaii environmental bar. Applicants must be interested in working during the summer at a government agency or public interest organization in Hawaii in the field of environmental, energy, or natural resources law. Selection is based on interest in environmental issues, academic record, personal qualities, leadership abilities, and ability to contribute to diversity in the Hawaii environmental bar.

Financial data The stipend is $5,000.

Duration 8 to 10 weeks during the summer.

Additional information This program is cosponsored by the Hawai'i State Bar Association's Natural Resources Section.

Number awarded 1 each year.

Deadline April of each year.

[848]
HAWAIIAN CIVIC CLUB OF HONOLULU SCHOLARSHIP

Hawaiian Civic Club of Honolulu
Attn: Scholarship Committee
P.O. Box 1513
Honolulu, HI 96806
E-mail: newmail@hotbot.com
Web: www.hcchonolulu.org/scholarship

Summary To provide financial assistance for undergraduate or graduate studies to persons of Native Hawaiian descent.

Eligibility Applicants must be of Hawaiian descent (descendants of the aboriginal inhabitants of the Hawaiian Islands prior to 1778), residents of Hawaii, able to demonstrate academic achievement, and enrolled or planning to enroll full time in an accredited 2-year college, 4-year college, or graduate school. Graduating seniors and current undergraduate students must have a GPA of 2.5 or higher; graduate students must have at least a 3.0 GPA. Along with their application, they must submit a 2-page essay on a topic that changes annually but relates to issues of concern to the Hawaiian community; a recent topic related to the leadership, cultural and governmental, of the Hawaiian community. Selection is based on quality of the essay, academic standing, financial need, and completeness of the application package.

Financial data The amount of the stipend varies. Scholarship checks are made payable to the recipient and the institution and are mailed to the college or university financial aid office. Funds may be used for tuition, fees, books, and other educational expenses.

Duration 1 year.

Additional information Recipients may attend school in Hawaii or on the mainland. Information on this program is also available from Ke Ali'i Pauahi Foundation.

Number awarded Varies each year; recently, 50 of these scholarships, worth $72,000, were awarded.

Deadline May of each year.

[849]
HAWAIIAN HOMES COMMISSION SCHOLARSHIPS

Hawai'i Community Foundation
Attn: Scholarship Department
827 Fort Street Mall
Honolulu, HI 96813
(808) 537-6333   Toll Free: (888) 731-3863
Fax: (808) 521-6286
E-mail: scholarships@hcf-hawaii.org
Web: www.hawaiicommunityfoundation.org/scholarships

Summary To provide financial assistance to persons of Native Hawaiian descent who are interested in working on an undergraduate or graduate degree at a school in any state.

Eligibility Applicants must be 50% or more of Hawaiian descent (descendants of the aboriginal inhabitants of the Hawaiian Islands prior to 1778) or a Department of Hawaiian Home Lands (DHHL) homestead lessee. They must be U.S. citizens, enrolled in full-time study in an undergraduate or graduate degree program, and able to demonstrate financial need and academic excellence. Undergraduates must have a GPA of 2.0 or higher. Graduate students must have a GPA of 3.0 or higher. Current Hawaiian residency is not required. Special consideration is given to applicants with exceptional academic merit and proven commitment to serving the Native Hawaiian community. Along with their application, they must submit a short statement indicating their reasons for attending college, their planned course of study, their career goals, and what community service means to them. Selection is based on academic achievement, good moral character, and financial need.

Financial data The amounts of the awards depend on the availability of funds and the need of the recipient. Recently, the average value of all scholarships awarded by the foundation was $2,041.

Duration 1 year.

Additional information This program is sponsored by the state Department of Hawaiian Home Lands.

Number awarded Varies each year; recently, 111 of these scholarships were awarded.

Deadline February of each year.

[850]
HAYNES/HETTING AWARD

Philanthrofund Foundation
Attn: Scholarship Committee
1409 Willow Street, Suite 210
Minneapolis, MN 55403-3251
(612) 870-1806   Toll Free: (800) 435-1402
Fax: (612) 871-6587   E-mail: info@PfundOnline.org
Web: www.pfundonline.org/scholarships.html

Summary To provide funds to Native American and African American students in Minnesota who are associated with gay, lesbian, bisexual, and transgender (GLBT) activities.

Eligibility This program is open to residents of Minnesota and students attending a Minnesota educational institution who are African American or Native American. Applicants must be self-identified as GLBT or from a GLBT family. They may be attending or planning to attend a trade school, technical college, college, or university (as an undergraduate or graduate student). Selection is based on the applicant's 1) affirmation of GLBT identity or commitment to GLBT communities; 2) evidence of experience and skills in service and leadership; and 3) evidence of service and leadership in GLBT communities, including serving as a role model, mentor, and/or adviser.

Financial data The stipend ranges up to $2,000. Funds must be used for tuition, books, fees, or dissertation expenses.

Duration 1 year.

Number awarded 1 or more each year.

Deadline January of each year.

[851]
HEATHER CARDINAL MEMORIAL SCHOLARSHIP

Wisconsin Indian Education Association
Attn: Scholarship Coordinator
P.O. Box 910
Keshena, WI 54135
(715) 799-5110   Fax: (715) 799-5102
E-mail: vnuske@mitw.org
Web: www.wiea.org

Summary To provide financial assistance to members of Wisconsin Indian tribes who are working on an undergraduate degree in a health-related field or a medical degree.

Eligibility This program is open to residents of Wisconsin who can provide proof of tribal enrollment. Applicants must be either: 1) an undergraduate majoring in a health-related field at a college in any state; or 2) a student enrolled at a medical school in any state. Along with their application, they must submit a 1-page personal essay on how they will apply their education.

Financial data The stipend is $1,000.

Duration 1 year; nonrenewable.

Additional information Eligible tribes include Menominee, Oneida, Stockbridge-Munsee, Forest County Potowatomi, Ho-Chunk, Bad River Chippewa, Lac Courte Oreilles Ojibwe, St. Croix Chippewa, Red Cliff Chippewa, Sakoagon (Mole Lake) Chippewa, Brotherton, and Lac du Flambeau Chippewa.

Number awarded 1 each year.

Deadline March of each year.

[852]
HIGHER EDUCATION GRANTS FOR HOPI TRIBAL MEMBERS

Hopi Tribe
Attn: Grants and Scholarship Program
P.O. Box 123
Kykotsmovi, AZ 86039
(928) 734-3542   Toll Free: (800) 762-9630
Fax: (928) 734-9575   E-mail: tlomakema@hopi.nsn.us
Web: www.hopi-nsn.gov

Summary To provide financial assistance to students of Hopi ancestry who are working on an undergraduate, graduate, or postgraduate degree.

Eligibility This program is open to students who are working on an associate, baccalaureate, graduate, or postgraduate degree. Applicants must be enrolled members of the Hopi Tribe. They must have a GPA of 2.0 or higher and be able to demonstrate financial need.

Financial data The maximum grant is $2,500 per semester ($5,000 per year).

Duration 1 semester; may be renewed for up to 10 terms of undergraduate study or up to 5 terms of graduate study, provided the recipient remains enrolled full time.

Additional information This grant is awarded as a secondary source of financial aid to eligible students who are also receiving aid from the Bureau of Indian Affairs (BIA) Higher Education program.

Number awarded Varies each year.

Deadline June of each year for fall; October of each year for winter; November of each year for spring; April of each year for summer.

[853]
HIGHER EDUCATION PROGRAM OF THE AFOGNAK NATIVE CORPORATION

Afognak Native Corporation
215 Mission Road, Suite 212
Kodiak, AK 99615
(907) 486-6014   Toll Free: (800) 770-6014
Fax: (907) 486-2514   E-mail: scholarships@afognak.com
Web: www.afognak.com

Summary To provide financial assistance to shareholders of the Afognak Native Corporation in Alaska who are interested in enrolling in a traditional college, university, graduate school, or vocational program.

Eligibility This program is open to Alaska Natives who are original Afognak Native Corporation enrollees and their lineal descendants. Applicants must be high school graduates or GED recipients who have been accepted to or are enrolled at an accredited college, university, or vocational school to work on an associate, bachelor's, master's, or doctoral degree. Along with their application, they must submit a letter that provides a personal history (information about their family and their special talents and abilities, community involvement, plans for the future, philosophy of life), future plans for education, and how their education may benefit the Alutiiq people and their commitment to the Alutiiq community. Financial need is considered in the selection process.

Financial data A stipend is awarded (amount not specified).

Duration 1 year; may be renewed if the recipient maintains a GPA of 2.0 or higher.

Number awarded Varies each year.

Deadline April of each year.

[854]
HILLIS CLARK MARTIN & PETERSON DIVERSITY FELLOWSHIP

Hillis Clark Martin & Peterson P.S.
Attn: Recruiting and Marketing Coordinator
1221 Second Avenue, Suite 500
Seattle, WA 98101-2925
(206) 623-1745   Fax: (206) 623-7789
E-mail: abt@hcmp.com
Web: www.hcmp.com

Summary To provide financial assistance to Native American and other law students who have a diverse background and life experiences.

Eligibility This program is open to students enrolled in the first year at an ABA-accredited law school. Applicants must have a diverse background and life experiences and demonstrate the capacity to contribute meaningfully to the diversity of the legal community. Along with their application, they must submit a resume, transcripts, a personal statement of 1 to 2 pages describing their background and addressing the selection criteria, a legal writing sample, and a list of 3 references. Selection is based on distinction in academic performance, accomplishments and activities, commitment to community service, leadership ability, and financial need.

Financial data The stipend is $7,500.

Duration 1 year.

Additional information The program includes a salaried summer associate position following the first year of law school.

Number awarded 1 or more each year.

Deadline January of each year.

[855]
HO-CHUNK NATION GRADUATION ACHIEVEMENT AWARDS

Ho-Chunk Nation
Attn: Higher Education Division
P.O. Box 667
Black River Falls, WI 54615
(715) 284-4915   Toll Free: (800) 362-4476
Fax: (715) 284-1760
E-mail: higher.education@ho-chunk.com
Web: www.ho-chunknation.com/?PageId=47

Summary To recognize and reward Ho-Chunk students who received financial assistance from the tribe and have completed an associate, bachelor's, graduate, or professional degree.

Eligibility Applicants must be enrolled in the Ho-Chunk Nation and have received financial assistance from the tribe in the past to work on a postsecondary degree. Funds are paid once they have completed any of the following degrees: 1-year certificate or diploma, associate degree (2 years), bachelor's degree (4 years), master's or professional degree, J.D. degree, or doctoral degree.

Financial data Awards are $300 for a 1-year certificate or degree, $750 for an associate degree, $1,000 for a bachelor's degree, $3,000 for a master's or professional degree, $4,000 for a J.D. degree, or $5,000 for a doctoral degree.

Duration Students are eligible for only 1 award per degree.

Number awarded Varies each year.

Deadline Applications must be submitted within 1 year of completion of the degree.

[856]
HO-CHUNK NATION HIGHER EDUCATION SCHOLARSHIPS

Ho-Chunk Nation
Attn: Higher Education Division
P.O. Box 667
Black River Falls, WI 54615
(715) 284-4915   Toll Free: (800) 362-4476
Fax: (715) 284-1760
E-mail: higher.education@ho-chunk.com
Web: www.ho-chunknation.com/?PageId=47

Summary To provide financial assistance to undergraduate or graduate students who are enrolled members of the Ho-Chunk Nation.

Eligibility Applicants must be enrolled members of the Ho-Chunk Nation who have been accepted at an accredited college, university, or vocational college in the United States as an undergraduate or graduate student. Applicants must intend to attend a nonprofit institution that is accredited by a regional agency and by the U.S. Department of Education as eligible to receive student financial aid funds. If they are determined by their school's financial aid office to have no financial need, they are eligible to receive non-need grants. If their school determines that they have financial need, they are eligible for need-based grants. Funds are awarded with the expectation that graduates will return to the Ho-Chunk Nation to use their knowledge and expertise to protect and strengthen the economic self-sufficiency and sovereignty of the nation.

Financial data Non-need grants cover direct costs of tuition, required fees, and books, up to the maximum award. Need-based grants are capped at $7,000 per academic year for full-time undergraduates or $12,000 per academic year for full-time graduate students. Awards for part-time students per academic year are for direct costs (tuition, required fees, and books) not covered by another source, to a maximum of $4,500 for undergraduates or $9,000 for graduate students. Funds are paid directly to the recipient's school.

Duration 1 year. Support is limited to 10 semesters for undergraduates, 6 semesters for master's degree students, or 10 semesters for doctoral students. Undergraduates must maintain a GPA of 2.0 or higher and graduate students 3.0 or higher in order to continue receiving funds.

Number awarded Varies each year.

Deadline April of each year or 4 months before the start of the term.

[857]
HO-CHUNK NATION SUMMER TUITION ASSISTANCE

Ho-Chunk Nation
Attn: Higher Education Division
P.O. Box 667
Black River Falls, WI 54615
(715) 284-4915   Toll Free: (800) 362-4476
Fax: (715) 284-1760
E-mail: higher.education@ho-chunk.com
Web: www.ho-chunknation.com/?PageId=47

Summary To provide financial assistance to Ho-Chunk undergraduate or graduate students who wish to continue their postsecondary studies during the summer.

Eligibility Applicants must be enrolled members of the Ho-Chunk Nation; have been accepted at an accredited public vocational or technical school, college, or university in the United States in an undergraduate or graduate program; and be interested in attending summer school on a full-time basis.

Financial data This program pays up to $2,500 to undergraduate recipients and up to $5,000 to graduate school recipients. Funds must be used for tuition, fees, or books. Funds are paid directly to the recipient's school.

Duration Summer months. May be renewed for a total of 6 summers of support.

Additional information Undergraduate recipients must earn a GPA of 2.0 or higher in the summer classes; graduate school recipients must earn 3.0 or higher.

Number awarded Varies each year.

Deadline The priority deadline is the end of April of each year.

[858]
HOOPA TRIBAL EDUCATION SCHOLARSHIPS

Hoopa Valley Tribe
Attn: Hoopa Tribal Education Association
P.O. Box 428
Hoopa, CA 95546-0428
(530) 625-4413   Fax: (530) 625-5444
E-mail: hoopaeducation@gmail.com
Web: www.hoopa-nsn.gov

Summary To provide financial assistance to members of the Hoopa Tribe who are attending or planning to attend college or graduate school in any state.

Eligibility This program is open to enrolled members of the Hoopa Tribe who are 1) high school seniors or graduates with a GPA of 3.0 or higher; 2) current undergraduates with a GPA of 2.5 or higher; or 3) graduate students. Applicants must be working or planning to work full time on an undergraduate or graduate degree at an accredited college or university in any state. Along with their application, they must submit 1) an educational plan that outlines the course work required for completing their degree and an estimate of the time remaining until completion; 2) official transcripts; 3) a class schedule; and 4) a letter describing their educational goals and proposed course of study. Financial need is not considered in the selection process.

Financial data A stipend is awarded (amount not specified).

Duration 1 semester; may be renewed up to a total of 3 years for a 2-year degree, 5 years for a 4-year, or until completion of a graduate degree.

Number awarded Varies each year.

Deadline June of each year for fall semester or academic year; November of each year for winter quarter; December of each year for spring semester; March of each year for spring quarter; May of each year for summer session.

[859]
HOPI EDUCATION AWARDS PROGRAM

Hopi Tribe
Attn: Grants and Scholarship Program
P.O. Box 123
Kykotsmovi, AZ 86039
(928) 734-3542   Toll Free: (800) 762-9630
Fax: (928) 734-9575   E-mail: tlomakema@hopi.nsn.us
Web: www.hopi-nsn.gov

Summary To provide financial assistance to needy students of Hopi ancestry who are working on an undergraduate, graduate, or postgraduate degree.

Eligibility This program is open to students who are working on an associate, baccalaureate, graduate, or postgraduate degree. Applicants must be enrolled members of the Hopi Tribe. They must have a GPA of 2.5 or higher and be able to demonstrate financial need.

Financial data The maximum grant is $2,500 per semester ($5,000 per year).

Duration 1 semester; may be renewed for up to 10 terms of undergraduate study or up to 5 terms of graduate study, provided the recipient maintains a GPA of 2.5 or higher and full-time enrollment.

Additional information This grant is awarded as a secondary source of financial aid to eligible students who are also receiving aid from the Bureau of Indian Affairs (BIA) Higher Education program.

Number awarded Varies each year.

Deadline June of each year for fall; October of each year for winter; November of each year for spring; April of each year for summer.

[860]
HOPI TRIBAL PRIORITY AWARDS

Hopi Tribe
Attn: Grants and Scholarship Program
P.O. Box 123
Kykotsmovi, AZ 86039
(928) 734-3542   Toll Free: (800) 762-9630
Fax: (928) 734-9575   E-mail: tlomakema@hopi.nsn.us
Web: www.hopi-nsn.gov

Summary To provide funding to Hopi students who are interested in working on an undergraduate or graduate degree in an area of interest to the Hopi Tribe.

Eligibility This program is open to enrolled members of the Hopi Tribe who are college juniors, seniors, or graduate students working on a degree in a subject area that is of priority interest to the Hopi Tribe. Currently, those areas are law, natural resources, education, medicine, health, engineering, or business. Applicants must have a GPA of 3.5 or higher. This is a highly competitive scholarship. Selection is based on aca-

demic merit and the likelihood that the applicants will use their training and expertise for tribal goals and objectives.

Financial data This program provides payment of all tuition and fees, books and supplies, transportation, room and board, and a stipend of $1,500 per month. Recipients must agree to provide 1 year of professional services to the Hopi Tribe or other service agencies that serve the Hopi People for each year funding is awarded.

Duration 1 year; may be renewed, provided the recipient maintains a GPA of 3.5 or higher.

Additional information Recipients must attend school on a full-time basis.

Number awarded Up to 5 each year.

Deadline July of each year.

[861]
HOWARD KECK/WESTMIN ENDOWMENT SCHOLARSHIP FUND

Cook Inlet Region, Inc.
Attn: The CIRI Foundation
3600 San Jeronimo Drive, Suite 256
Anchorage, AK 99508-2870
(907) 793-3575   Toll Free: (800) 764-3382
Fax: (907) 793-3585   E-mail: tcf@thecirifoundation.org
Web: www.thecirifoundation.org/designated.htm

Summary To provide financial assistance for undergraduate or graduate studies to Alaska Natives who are original enrollees to Cook Inlet Region, Inc. (CIRI) and their lineal descendants.

Eligibility This program is open to Alaska Native enrollees to CIRI under the Alaska Native Claims Settlement Act (ANCSA) of 1971 and their lineal descendants. There are no Alaska residency requirements or age limitations. Applicants must be accepted or enrolled full time in a 2-year undergraduate, 4-year undergraduate, or graduate degree program. They may be studying in any field but must have a GPA of 2.5 or higher. Along with their application, they must submit a 500-word statement on their educational and career goals and how they are contributing, or planning to contribute, to a positive Alaska Native community. Selection is based on that statement, academic achievement, rigor of course work or degree program, student financial contribution, financial need, grade level, previous work performance, community service, and relationship of degree program to career goals.

Financial data The stipend is $20,000 per year, $10,000 per year, $8,000 per year, or $2,500 per semester, depending on GPA.

Duration 1 semester or 1 year.

Additional information This fund was established in 1986.

Number awarded Varies each year; recently, 5 of these scholarships were awarded.

Deadline May of each year for annual scholarships; May or November of each year for semester scholarships.

[862]
HOWARD ROCK FOUNDATION GRADUATE SCHOLARSHIP PROGRAM

Cook Inlet Region, Inc.
Attn: The CIRI Foundation
3600 San Jeronimo Drive, Suite 256
Anchorage, AK 99508-2870
(907) 793-3575   Toll Free: (800) 764-3382
Fax: (907) 793-3585   E-mail: tcf@thecirifoundation.org
Web: www.thecirifoundation.org/designated.htm

Summary To provide financial assistance for graduate study to Alaska Natives and their lineal descendants.

Eligibility This program is open to Alaska Natives who are original enrollees or lineal descendants of a regional or village corporation under the Alaska Native Claims Settlement Act (ANCSA) of 1971 or a member of a tribal organization or other Native organization. The corporation or other Native organization with which the applicant is affiliated must be a current member of Alaska Village Initiatives, Inc. Applicants must have a GPA of 3.0 or higher and must be able to demonstrate financial need. They must be accepted or enrolled full time in a graduate degree program. Along with their application, they must submit a 500-word statement on their educational and career goals and how they are contributing, or planning to contribute, to a positive Alaska Native community.

Financial data The stipend is $5,000 per year. Funds are to be used for tuition, university fees, books, course-required supplies, and (for students who must live away from their permanent home in order to attend college) room and board. Checks are made payable to the student and the university and are sent directly to the student's university.

Duration 1 year.

Additional information This program, established in 1986, is funded by Alaska Village Initiatives, Inc. The CIRI Foundation assumed its administration in 1999.

Number awarded Varies each year.

Deadline March of each year.

[863]
HUD DOCTORAL DISSERTATION RESEARCH GRANT PROGRAM

Department of Housing and Urban Development
Attn: Office of University Partnerships
451 Seventh Street, S.W., Room 8226
Washington, DC 20410
(202) 708-3852   Fax: (202) 708-0309
E-mail: oup@oup.org
Web: www.oup.org/programs/aboutDDRG.asp

Summary To provide funding to minority and other doctoral candidates interested in conducting dissertation research related to housing and urban development issues.

Eligibility This program is open to currently-enrolled doctoral candidates in an academic discipline that provides policy-relevant insight on issues in housing and urban development. Applicants must have fully-developed and approved dissertation proposals that can be completed within 2 years and must have completed all written and oral Ph.D. requirements. Examples of eligible topics include increasing homeownership opportunities; promoting decent affordable housing; strengthening communities; ensuring equal opportunity in housing; embracing high standards of ethics, management, and accountability; and promoting participation of faith-based and community organizations. U.S. citizenship or permanent resident status is required.

Financial data The grant is $25,000. Funds must be used to support direct costs incurred in completing the project, including stipends, computer software, purchase of data, travel expenses to collect data, transcription services, or compensation for interviews. Funds may not be used for tuition, computer hardware, or meals.

Duration Up to 24 months.

Additional information This program was established in 1994.

Number awarded Varies each year; recently, 12 of these grants were awarded.

Deadline June of each year.

[864]
HUGH J. ANDERSEN MEMORIAL SCHOLARSHIPS

National Medical Fellowships, Inc.
Attn: Scholarship Program
347 Fifth Avenue, Suite 510
New York, NY 10016
(212) 483-8880   Toll Free: (877) NMF-1DOC
Fax: (212) 483-8897   E-mail: info@nmfonline.org
Web: www.nmfonline.org

Summary To provide financial assistance to Native American and other underrepresented minority medical students who reside or attend school in Minnesota.

Eligibility This program is open to African Americans, Mexican Americans, Native Hawaiians, Alaska Natives, American Indians, Vietnamese, Cambodians, and mainland Puerto Ricans who have completed at least 1 year of medical school. Applicants must be Minnesota residents enrolled in an accredited U.S. medical school or residents of other states attending medical school in Minnesota. Selection is based on leadership, community service, and financial need. Direct applications are not accepted; candidates must be nominated by medical school deans.

Financial data The award is $2,500.

Duration 1 year.

Additional information This award was established in 1982.

Number awarded Up to 5 each year.

Deadline Nominations must be submitted by March of each year.

[865]
HUNA HERITAGE FOUNDATION EDUCATION ASSISTANCE PROGRAM

Huna Totem Corporation
Attn: Huna Heritage Foundation
9301 Glacier Highway, Suite 210
Juneau, AK 99801
(907) 523-3682   Toll Free: (800) 428-8298
Fax: (907) 789-1896   E-mail: kmiller@hunaheritage.org
Web: www.hunaheritage.org/education.html

Summary To provide financial assistance to Huna Totem Corporation shareholders and their descendants who are attending or planning to attend college or graduate school in any state.

Eligibility This program is open to Huna Totem Corporation shareholders and descendants who have a high school diploma or GED certificate. Applicants must be accepted by or attending a college or university in any state as a full-time undergraduate or graduate student. Internships, apprenticeships, and on-the-job training may also be funded. Students must have applied to other programs before they apply for this assistance and be able to demonstrate unmet financial need. Proof of awards or denial by other programs must be supplied.

Financial data Stipends range up to $2,000 per year. Funding is intended to help pay for whatever costs other grant programs do not cover.

Duration 1 year; recipients may reapply.

Additional information The Huna Totem Corporation is an Alaska Native village corporation whose shareholders have aboriginal ties to the village of Hoonah in southeast Alaska.

Number awarded Varies each year.

Deadline September of each year for first or second quarter or fall semester; January of each year for third or fourth quarter or spring or summer semester.

[866]
IBM PHD FELLOWSHIP PROGRAM

IBM Corporation
Attn: University Relations
1133 Westchester Avenue
White Plains, NY 10604
Toll Free: (800) IBM-4YOU   TDD: (800) IBM-3383
E-mail: phdfellow@us.ibm.com
Web: www.ibm.com

Summary To provide funding and work experience to minority and other students working on a Ph.D. in a research area of broad interest to IBM.

Eligibility Students nominated for this fellowship should be enrolled full time at an accredited college or university in any country and should have completed at least 1 year of graduate study in the following fields: business sciences (including financial services, risk management, marketing, communication, and learning/knowledge management); computer science and engineering; electrical and mechanical engineering; management; mathematical sciences (including analytics, statistics, operations research, and optimization); physical sciences (including chemistry, materials sciences, and physics); or service science, management, and engineering (SSME). They should be planning a career in research. Nominations must be made by a faculty member and endorsed by the department head. The program values diversity, and encourages nominations of women, minorities, and others who contribute to that diversity. Selection is based on the applicants' potential for research excellence, the degree to which their technical interests align with those of IBM, and academic progress to date. Preference is given to students who have had an IBM internship or have closely collaborated with technical or services people from IBM.

Financial data Fellowships pay tuition, fees, and a stipend of $17,500 per year.

Duration 1 year; may be renewed up to 2 additional years, provided the recipient is renominated, interacts with IBM's technical community, and demonstrates continued progress and achievement.

Additional information Recipients are offered an internship at 1 of the IBM Research Division laboratories and are given an IBM computer.

Number awarded Varies each year; recently, 57 of these scholarships were awarded.

Deadline October of each year.

[867]
IDA M. POPE MEMORIAL SCHOLARSHIPS

Hawai'i Community Foundation
Attn: Scholarship Department
827 Fort Street Mall
Honolulu, HI 96813
(808) 537-6333   Toll Free: (888) 731-3863
Fax: (808) 521-6286
E-mail: scholarships@hcf-hawaii.org
Web: www.hawaiicommunityfoundation.org/scholarships

Summary To provide financial assistance to Native Hawaiian women who are interested in working on an undergraduate or graduate degree in designated fields at a school in any state.

Eligibility This program is open to female residents of Hawaii who are Native Hawaiian, defined as a descendant of the aboriginal inhabitants of the Hawaiian islands prior to 1778. Applicants must be enrolled at a school in any state in an accredited associate, bachelor's, or graduate degree program and working on a degree in health, science, or education (including counseling and social work). They must be able to demonstrate academic achievement (GPA of 3.5 or higher), good moral character, and financial need. Along with their application, they must submit a short statement indicating their reasons for attending college, their planned course of study, their career goals, and what community service means to them.

Financial data The amounts of the awards depend on the availability of funds and the needs of the recipient. Recently, the average value of all scholarships awarded by the foundation was $2,041.

Duration 1 year; may be renewed.

Number awarded Varies each year; recently, 61 of these scholarships were awarded.

Deadline February of each year.

[868]
IHS HEALTH PROFESSIONS SCHOLARSHIP PROGRAM

Indian Health Service
Attn: Scholarship Program
801 Thompson Avenue, Suite 120
Rockville, MD 20852
(301) 443-6197   Fax: (301) 443-6048
E-mail: dawn.kelly@ihs.gov
Web: www.scholarship.ihs.gov

Summary To provide funding to American Indian and Alaska Native students enrolled in health professions and allied health professions programs.

Eligibility This program is open to American Indians and Alaska Natives who are members of federally-recognized tribes. Applicants must be at least high school graduates and enrolled in a full-time study program leading to a degree in a health-related professions school within the United States.

Priority is given to upper-division and graduate students. Qualifying fields of study recently included chemical dependency counseling (bachelor's or master's degree), clinical psychology (Ph.D. only), dental hygiene (B.S.), dentistry (D.D.S. or D.M.D.), diagnostic radiology technology (certificate, associate, or B.S.), dietetics (B.S.), environmental health and engineering (B.S.), health records administration (R.H.I.T. or R.H.I.A.), medical technology (B.S.), allopathic and osteopathic medicine (M.D. or D.O.), nursing (A.D.N., B.S.N., C.R.N.A., geriatric nursing, nurse practitioner, pediatric nursing, psychiatric and mental health nursing, women's health nursing), occupational therapy (B.S. or M.S.), optometry (O.D.), pharmacy (Pharm.D.), physician assistant (P.A.C.), physical therapy (M.S. or D.P.T.), physical therapy assistant (associate degree), podiatry (D.P.M.), respiratory therapy (B.S.), social work (master's degree with concentration in mental health only), or ultrasonography (B.S. or certificate). Along with their application, they must submit a brief narrative that includes why they are requesting the scholarship, their career goals, and how those goals will help to meet the health needs of American Indian and Alaska Native people. Selection is based on that narrative (30 points); academic performance (40 points); and faculty, employer, and tribal recommendations (30 points).

Financial data Awards provide a payment directly to the school for tuition and required fees; a stipend for living expenses of approximately $1,250 per month for 10 months; a lump sum to cover the costs of books, laboratory expenses, and other necessary educational expenses; a payment of $300 for travel expenses; and up to $400 for approved tutorial costs. Upon completion of their program of study, recipients are required to provide payback service of 1 year for each year of scholarship support at the Indian Health Service, a tribal health program, an urban Indian health program, or in private practice in a designated health professional shortage area serving a substantial number of Indians. Recipients who fail to complete their service obligation must repay all funds received (although no interest is charged).

Duration 1 year; may be renewed for up to 3 additional years.

Number awarded Varies each year.

Deadline February of each year for continuing students; March of each year for new applicants.

[869]
ILLINOIS NURSES ASSOCIATION CENTENNIAL SCHOLARSHIP

Illinois Nurses Association
Attn: Illinois Nurses Foundation
105 West Adams Street, Suite 2101
Chicago, IL 60603
(312) 419-2900   Fax: (312) 419-2920
E-mail: info@illinoisnurses.com
Web: www.illinoisnurses.com

Summary To provide financial assistance to nursing undergraduate and graduate students who are Native American or members of other underrepresented groups.

Eligibility This program is open to students working on an associate, bachelor's, or master's degree at an accredited NLNAC or CCNE school of nursing. Applicants must be members of a group underrepresented in nursing (African Americans, Hispanics, American Indians, Asians, and males).

Undergraduates must have earned a passing grade in all nursing courses taken to date and have a GPA of 2.85 or higher. Graduate students must have completed at least 12 semester hours of graduate work and have a GPA of 3.0 or higher. All applicants must be willing to 1) act as a spokesperson to other student groups on the value of the scholarship to continuing their nursing education, and 2) be profiled in any media or marketing materials developed by the Illinois Nurses Foundation. Along with their application, they must submit a narrative of 250 to 500 words on how they, nurses, plan to affect policy at either the state or national level that impacts on nursing or health care generally, or how they believe they will impact the nursing profession in general.

Financial data A stipend is awarded (amount not specified).

Duration 1 year.

Number awarded 1 or more each year.

Deadline March of each year.

[870]
INDIAN LEGAL SCHOLARSHIP PROGRAM

Northwest Indian Bar Association
c/o Gabriel Galanda
Williams Kastner and Gibbs
601 Union Street, Suite 4100
Seattle, WA 98101
(206) 628-2780   Fax: (206) 628-6611
E-mail: ggalanda@wkg.com
Web: www.nwiba.org

Summary To provide financial assistance to Native Americans from the Northwest who are interested in attending law school in the area.

Eligibility This program is open to residents of Alaska, British Columbia, Idaho, Oregon, Washington, and the Yukon Territory who are attending or planning to attend an accredited law school in the area. Applicants must have a tribal affiliation as an American Indian, Canadian First Nation, or Alaska Native. They must intend to work in the field of American Indian or Alaska Native law or policy in the area. Along with their application, they must submit a 1-page essay describing their commitment and career goals as they will benefit or provide service to American Indian, Canadian First Nation, or Alaska Native people.

Financial data Stipends recently ranged from $750 to $2,000.

Duration 1 year.

Additional information This program began in 2003. It is funded by several Native tribal organizations and the Indian Law Section of the Washington State Bar Association.

Number awarded Varies each year; recently, 6 of these scholarships were awarded. Since the program began, it has awarded more than $125,000 in scholarships.

Deadline November.

[871]
INDIANA CLEO FELLOWSHIPS

Indiana Supreme Court
Attn: Division of State Court Administration
115 West Washington Street, Suite 1080
Indianapolis, IN 46204-3417
(317) 232-2542 Toll Free: (800) 452-9963
Fax: (317) 233-6586
Web: www.in.gov/judiciary/cleo

Summary To provide financial assistance to Native Americans and other minority or disadvantaged college seniors from any state interested in attending law school in Indiana.

Eligibility This program is open to graduating college seniors who have applied to a law school in Indiana. Selected applicants are invited to participate in the Indiana Conference for Legal Education Opportunity (Indiana CLEO) Summer Institute, held at a law school in the state. Admission to that program is based on GPA, LSAT scores, 3 letters of recommendation, a resume, a personal statement, and financial need. Students who successfully complete the Institute and become certified graduates of the program may be eligible to receive a fellowship.

Financial data All expenses for the Indiana CLEO Summer Institute are paid. The fellowship stipend is $6,500 per year for students who attend a public law school or $9,000 per year for students who attend a private law school.

Duration The Indiana CLEO Summer Institute lasts 6 weeks. Fellowships are for 1 year and may be renewed up to 2 additional years.

Additional information The first Summer Institute was held in 1997.

Number awarded 30 students are invited to participate in the summer institute; the number of those selected to receive a fellowship varies each year.

Deadline March of each year.

[872]
INDUSTRY/GOVERNMENT GRADUATE FELLOWSHIPS

American Meteorological Society
Attn: Fellowship/Scholarship Coordinator
45 Beacon Street
Boston, MA 02108-3693
(617) 227-2426, ext. 246 Fax: (617) 742-8718
E-mail: scholar@ametsoc.org
Web: www.ametsoc.org

Summary To encourage Native Americans and other underrepresented students entering their first year of graduate school to work on an advanced degree in the atmospheric and related oceanic and hydrologic sciences.

Eligibility This program is open to students entering their first year of graduate study who wish to pursue advanced degrees in the atmospheric or related oceanic or hydrologic sciences. Applicants must be U.S. citizens or permanent residents and have a GPA of 3.25 or higher. Along with their application, they must submit 200-word essays on 1) their most important achievements that qualify them for this scholarship, and 2) their career goals in the atmospheric or related sciences. Selection is based on academic record as an undergraduate. The sponsor specifically encourages applications from women, minorities, and students with disabilities who are traditionally underrepresented in the atmospheric and related oceanic sciences.

Financial data The stipend is $24,000 per academic year.

Duration 9 months.

Additional information This program was initiated in 1991. It is funded by high-technology firms and government agencies.

Number awarded Varies each year; recently, 13 of these scholarships were awarded.

Deadline February of each year.

[873]
INITIATIVE TO RECRUIT A DIVERSE WORKFORCE

Association of Research Libraries
Attn: Director of Diversity Programs
21 Dupont Circle, N.W., Suite 800
Washington, DC 20036
(202) 296-2296 Fax: (202) 872-0884
E-mail: mpuente@arl.org
Web: www.arl.org/diversity/init/index.shtml

Summary To provide financial assistance to Native Americans and other minorities interested in preparing for a career as an academic or research librarian.

Eligibility This program is open to members of racial and ethnic minority groups that are underrepresented as professionals in academic and research libraries (American Indian or Alaska Native, Asian, Black or African American, Native Hawaiian or other Pacific Islander, or Hispanic or Latino). Applicants must be interested in working on an M.L.I.S. degree at an ALA-accredited program. Along with their application, they must submit a 350-word essay on what attracts them to a career in a research library. The essays are judged on clarity and content of form, clear goals and benefits, enthusiasm, potential growth perceived, and professional goals.

Financial data The stipend is $5,000 per year.

Duration 2 years.

Additional information This program began in 2000. Funding is currently provided by the Institute of Museum and Library Services and by the contributions of 52 libraries that are members of the Association of Research Libraries (ARL). Recipients must agree to work for at least 2 years in an ARL library after completing their degree.

Number awarded 20 each year.

Deadline August of each year.

[874]
INSTITUTE FOR INTERNATIONAL PUBLIC POLICY FELLOWSHIPS

United Negro College Fund Special Programs
  Corporation
Attn: Institute for International Public Policy
6402 Arlington Boulevard, Suite 600
Falls Church, VA 22042
(703) 677-3400 Toll Free: (800) 530-6232
Fax: (703) 205-7645 E-mail: iippl@uncfsp.org
Web: www.uncfsp.org

Summary To provide financial assistance and work experience to Native Americans and other minority students who are interested in preparing for a career in international affairs.

Eligibility This program is open to full-time sophomores at 4-year institutions who have a GPA of 3.2 or higher and are nominated by the president of their institution. Applicants must be African American, Hispanic/Latino American, Asian American, American Indian, Alaskan Native, Native Hawaiian, or Pacific Islander. They must be interested in participating in policy institutes, study abroad, language training, internships, and graduate education that will prepare them for a career in international service. U.S. citizenship or permanent resident status is required.

Financial data For the sophomore summer policy institute, fellows receive student housing and meals in a university facility, books and materials, all field trips and excursions, and a $1,050 stipend. For the junior year study abroad component, half of the expenses for 1 semester, to a maximum of $8,000, is provided. For the junior summer policy institute, fellows receive student housing and meals in a university facility, books and materials, travel to and from the institute, and a $1,000 stipend. For the summer language institute, fellows receive tuition and fees, books and materials, room and board, travel to and from the institute, and a $1,000 stipend. During the internship, a stipend of up to $3,500 is paid. During the graduate school period, fellowships are funded jointly by this program and the participating graduate school. The program provides $15,000 toward a master's degree in international affairs, with the expectation that the graduate school will provide $15,000 in matching funds.

Duration 2 years of undergraduate work and 2 years of graduate work, as well as the intervening summers.

Additional information This program consists of 6 components: 1) a sophomore year summer policy institute based at Howard University that introduces fellows to international policy development, foreign affairs, cultural competence, careers in those fields, and options for graduate study; 2) a junior year study abroad program at an accredited overseas institution; 3) a 7-week junior year summer institute at the University of Maryland's School of Public Policy; 4) for students without established foreign language competency, a summer language institute at Middlebury College Language Schools in Middlebury, Vermont following the senior year; 5) fellows with previously established foreign language competence participate in a post-baccalaureate internship to provide the practical experience needed for successful graduate studies in international affairs; and 6) a master's degree in international affairs (for students who are admitted to such a program). This program is administered by the United Negro College Fund Special Programs Corporation with funding provided by a grant from the U.S. Department of Education.

Number awarded 30 each year.

Deadline February of each year.

[875]
INTEL SCHOLARSHIP

American Indian Science and Engineering Society
Attn: Program Officer
2305 Renard, S.E., Suite 200
P.O. Box 9828
Albuquerque, NM 87119-9828
(505) 765-1052, ext. 105   Fax: (505) 765-5608
E-mail: tina@aises.org
Web: www.aises.org

Summary To provide financial assistance to members of the American Indian Science and Engineering Society (AISES) who are working on an undergraduate or graduate degree in a field of computer science or engineering.

Eligibility This program is open to AISES members who are full-time undergraduate or graduate students at an accredited 4-year college or university or at a 2-year college in a program leading to an academic degree. Applicants must have a GPA of 3.0 or higher and be members of an American Indian tribe or Alaskan Native group or otherwise considered to be an American Indian or Alaskan Native by the tribe or group with which affiliation is claimed. They must be majoring in computer science, computer engineering, or electrical engineering; students majoring in chemical engineering or material science may also be considered. Along with their application, they must submit a 500-word essay on their educational and career goals, including their interest in and motivation to continue higher education, an understanding of the importance of college and a commitment to completing their educational and/or career goals, and a commitment to learning and giving back to the community. Selection is based on that essay (40%), GPA (35%), letters of recommendation (15%), and overall impression of the application (10%).

Financial data The stipend is $5,000 for undergraduates or $10,000 for graduate students.

Duration 1 year; nonrenewable.

Additional information This program is funded by Intel.

Number awarded 1 or more each year.

Deadline June of each year.

[876]
INTELLECTUAL PROPERTY LAW SECTION WOMEN AND MINORITY SCHOLARSHIP

State Bar of Texas
Attn: Intellectual Property Law Section
c/o Bhaveeni D. Parmar, Scholarship Selection
   Committee
Klemchuk Kubasta LLP
Campbell Centre II
9150 North Central Expressway, Suite 1150
Dallas, TX 75206
(214) 367-6000   E-mail: bhaveeni@kk-llp.com
Web: www.texasbariplaw.org/index.htm

Summary To provide financial assistance to Native Americans, other minorities, and female students at law schools in Texas who plan to practice intellectual property law.

Eligibility This program is open to women and members of minority groups (African Americans, Hispanics, Asian Americans, and Native Americans) from any state who are currently enrolled at an ABA-accredited law school in Texas. Applicants must be planning to practice intellectual property law in Texas. Along with their application, they must submit a 2-page essay explaining why they plan to prepare for a career in intellectual property law in Texas, any qualifications they believe are relevant for their consideration for this scholarship, and (optionally) any issues of financial need they wish to have considered.

Financial data The stipend is $2,500.

Duration 1 year.

Number awarded 2 each year: 1 to a women and 1 to a minority.

Deadline April of each year.

[877]
INTERMOUNTAIN SECTION AWWA DIVERSITY SCHOLARSHIP

American Water Works Association-Intermountain
  Section
3430 East Danish Road
Sandy, UT 94093
(801) 712-1619   Fax: (801) 487-6699
E-mail: nicoleb@ims-awwa.org
Web: www.ims-awwa.org

Summary To provide financial assistance to Native Americans and other underrepresented undergraduate and graduate students working on a degree in the field of water quality, supply, and treatment at a university in Idaho or Utah.

Eligibility This program is open to women and students who identify as Hispanic or Latino, Black or African American, Native Hawaiian or other Pacific Islander, Asian, or American Indian or Alaska Native. Applicants must be entering or enrolled in an undergraduate or graduate program at a college or university in Idaho or Utah that relates to water quality, supply, or treatment. Along with their application, they must submit a 2-page essay on their academic interests and career goals and how those relate to water quality, supply, or treatment. Selection is based on that essay, letters of recommendation, and potential to contribute to the field of water quality, supply, and treatment in the Intermountain West.

Financial data The stipend is $1,000. The winner also receives a 1-year student membership in the Intermountain Section of the American Water Works Association (AWWA) and a 1-year subscription to *Journal AWWA.*

Duration 1 year; nonrenewable.

Number awarded 1 each year.

Deadline October of each year.

[878]
IOWA TRIBE EDUCATION INCENTIVE AWARDS

Iowa Tribe of Oklahoma
Attn: Human Services
Route 1, Box 721
Perkins, OK 74059
(405) 547-2402   Toll Free: (888) 336-4692
Fax: (405) 547-1090
E-mail: HumanServices@iowanation.org
Web: www.iowanation.org

Summary To recognize and reward members of the Iowa Tribe of Oklahoma who have completed specified levels of education.

Eligibility This monetary award is available to Iowa tribal members when they graduate from eighth grade, high school, college, or graduate school, or when they complete a GED or 800 hours of vocational training.

Financial data The awards are $100 for eighth-grade graduates, $200 for high school graduates, $200 for completion of a GED, or $200 for completion of 800 hours of vocational training. For college graduates, the award is calculated by multiplying a dollar amount based on GPA by the credit hours passed; the amount is $70 for a GPA of 3.5 or higher,

$65 for a GPA of 2.5 to 3.49, or $60 for a GPA of 2.0 to 2.49. For graduate students, the award is $92 times the credit hours passed.

Duration These are 1-time awards.

Number awarded Varies each year.

Deadline Applications must be submitted in the same year as completion of the education.

[879]
IRA L. AND MARY L. HARRISON MEMORIAL SCHOLARSHIP

Baptist Convention of New Mexico
Attn: Missions Mobilization Team
5325 Wyoming Boulevard, N.E.
P.O. Box 94485
Albuquerque, NM 87199-4485
(505) 924-2315   Toll Free: (800) 898-8544
Fax: (505) 924-2320   E-mail: cpairett@bcnm.com
Web: www.bcnm.com

Summary To provide financial assistance to Native American Southern Baptist students from New Mexico who are attending designated colleges or Baptist seminaries.

Eligibility This program is open to undergraduate and seminary students who are Native American members of churches affiliated with the Baptist Convention of New Mexico. Applicants must have a GPA of 2.0 or higher and be able to demonstrate financial need. Undergraduates must be attending Wayland Baptist University at its main campus in Plainview, Texas or at its New Mexico external campuses in Clovis or Albuquerque. Graduate students must be attending 1 of the 6 Southern Baptist seminaries: Southeastern Baptist Theological Seminary (Wake Forest, North Carolina); Southern Baptist Theological Seminary (Louisville, Kentucky); Southwestern Baptist Theological Seminary (Fort Worth, Texas); New Orleans Baptist Theological Seminary (New Orleans, Louisiana); Midwestern Baptist Theological Seminary (Kansas City, Missouri); or Golden Gate Baptist Theological Seminary (Mill Valley, California).

Financial data A stipend is awarded (amount not specified).

Duration 1 year; may be renewed.

Number awarded 1 or more each year.

Deadline June of each year for fall semester; November of each year for spring semester.

[880]
ISAAC J. "IKE" CRUMBLY MINORITIES IN ENERGY GRANT

American Association of Petroleum Geologists
  Foundation
Attn: Grants-in-Aid Program
1444 South Boulder Avenue
P.O. Box 979
Tulsa, OK 74101-0979
(918) 560-2644   Toll Free: (888) 945-2274, ext. 644
Fax: (918) 560-2642   E-mail: tcampbell@aapg.org
Web: foundation.aapg.org/gia/crumbly.cfm

Summary To provide funding to Native Americans, other minorities, and female graduate students who are interested in conducting research related to earth science aspects of the petroleum industry.

Eligibility This program is open to women and ethnic minorities (Black, Hispanic, Asian, or Native American, including American Indian, Eskimo, Hawaiian, or Samoan) who are working on a master's or doctoral degree. Applicants must be interested in conducting research related to the search for and development of petroleum and energy-minerals resources and to related environmental geology issues. Selection is based on merit and, in part, on financial need. Factors weighed in selecting the successful applicants include: the applicant's past academic performance, originality and imagination of the proposed project, departmental support, and significance of the project to petroleum, energy minerals, and related environmental geology.

Financial data Grants range from $500 to $3,000. Funds are to be applied to research-related expenses (e.g., a summer of field work). They may not be used to purchase capital equipment or to pay salaries, tuition, room, or board.

Duration 1 year. Doctoral candidates may receive a 1-year renewal.

Number awarded 1 each year.

Deadline January of each year.

[881]
IWALANI CARPENTER SOWA SCHOLARSHIP

Ke Ali'i Pauahi Foundation
Attn: Financial Aid & Scholarship Services
567 South King Street, Suite 160
Honolulu, HI 96813
(808) 534-3966   Toll Free: (800) 842-4682, ext. 43966
Fax: (808) 534-3890   E-mail: scholarships@pauahi.org
Web: www.pauahi.org/scholarships

Summary To provide financial assistance to graduate students, especially Native Hawaiians, who are preparing for a career in Protestant Christian ministry.

Eligibility This program is open to graduate students working full time on a degree that will prepare them for a career in Protestant Christian ministry. Applicants must express a desire to minister in Hawaii. Preference is given to Native Hawaiians (descendants of the aboriginal inhabitants of the Hawaiian Islands prior to 1778), graduates of Kamehameha Schools, and applicants who can demonstrate financial need.

Financial data The stipend is $1,400.

Duration 1 year.

Number awarded 1 each year.

Deadline March of each year.

[882]
JACOBS ENGINEERING SCHOLARSHIP

Conference of Minority Transportation Officials
Attn: National Scholarship Program
818 18th Street, N.W., Suite 850
Washington, DC 20006
(202) 530-0551   Fax: (202) 530-0617
Web: www.comto.org/news-youth.php

Summary To provide financial assistance to Native American and other minority upper-division and graduate students in a field related to transportation.

Eligibility This program is open to minority juniors, seniors, and graduate students in fields related to transportation (e.g., civil engineering, construction engineering, environmental engineering, safety, transportation, urban planning). Under-graduates must have a GPA of 3.0 or higher; graduate students must have a GPA of at least 3.5. Applicants must submit a cover letter with a 500-word statement of career goals. Financial need is not considered in the selection process. U.S. citizenship is required.

Financial data The stipend is $4,000. Funds are paid directly to the recipient's college or university.

Duration 1 year.

Additional information The Conference of Minority Transportation Officials (COMTO) was established in 1971 to promote, strengthen, and expand the roles of minorities in all aspects of transportation. This program is sponsored by Jacobs Engineering Group Inc. Recipients are required to become members of COMTO and attend the COMTO National Scholarship Luncheon.

Number awarded 1 or more each year.

Deadline April of each year.

[883]
JAMES B. MORRIS SCHOLARSHIP

James B. Morris Scholarship Fund
Attn: Scholarship Selection Committee
525 S.W. Fifth Street, Suite A
Des Moines, IA 50309-4501
(515) 282-8192   Fax: (515) 282-9117
E-mail: morris@assoc-mgmt.com
Web: www.morrisscholarship.org

Summary To provide financial assistance to Native Americans and other minority undergraduate, graduate, and law students in Iowa.

Eligibility This program is open to minority students (African Americans, Asian/Pacific Islanders, Hispanics, or Native Americans) who are interested in studying at a college, graduate school, or law school. Applicants must be either Iowa residents and high school graduates who are attending a college or university anywhere in the United States or non-Iowa residents who are attending a college or university in Iowa; preference is given to native Iowans who are attending an Iowa college or university. Along with their application, they must submit an essay of 250 to 500 words on why they are applying for this scholarship, activities or organizations in which they are involved, and their future plans. Selection is based on the essay, academic achievement (GPA of 2.5 or higher), community service, and financial need. U.S. citizenship is required.

Financial data The stipend is $2,300 per year.

Duration 1 year; may be renewed.

Additional information This fund was established in 1978 in honor of the J.B. Morris family, who founded the Iowa branch of the National Association for the Advancement of Colored People and published the *Iowa Bystander* newspaper.

Number awarded Varies each year; recently, 24 of these scholarships were awarded.

Deadline March of each year.

[884]
JAMES E. WEBB INTERNSHIPS

Smithsonian Institution
Attn: Office of Fellowships
470 L'Enfant Plaza, Suite 7102
P.O. Box 37012, MRC 902
Washington, DC 20013-7012
(202) 633-7070   Fax: (202) 633-7069
E-mail: siofg@si.edu
Web: www.si.edu/ofg/Applications/WEBB/WEBBapp.htm

Summary To provide internship opportunities throughout the Smithsonian Institution to Native Americans and other minority upper-division and graduate students in business or public administration.

Eligibility This program is open to minorities who are juniors, seniors, or graduate students majoring in areas of business or public administration (finance, human resource management, accounting, or general business administration). Applicants must have a GPA of 3.0 or higher. They must seek placement in offices, museums, and research institutes within the Smithsonian Institution.

Financial data Interns receive a stipend of $550 per week and a travel allowance.

Duration 10 weeks during the summer, fall, or spring.

Number awarded Varies each year; recently, 8 of these internships were awarded.

Deadline January of each year for summer or fall; September of each year for spring.

[885]
JEANETTE ELMER GRADUATE FELLOWSHIP

American Indian Graduate Center
Attn: Executive Director
4520 Montgomery Boulevard, N.E., Suite 1-B
Albuquerque, NM 87109-1291
(505) 881-4584   Toll Free: (800) 628-1920
Fax: (505) 884-0427   E-mail: aigc@aigc.com
Web: www.aigc.com/02scholarships/scholarships.htm

Summary To provide financial assistance to Native American students from tribes in designated states who are interested in working on a graduate degree in any field.

Eligibility This program is open to enrolled members of federally-recognized American Indian tribes in Arizona, New Mexico, or Wisconsin. Applicants must be enrolled full time at a graduate school in the United States. Along with their application, they must submit a 500-word essay on their extracurricular activities as they relate to American Indian programs at their institution, volunteer and community work as related to American Indian communities, tribal and community involvement, and plans to make positive changes in the American Indian community with their college education. Financial need is also considered in the selection process.

Financial data Stipends range from $1,000 to $5,000 per academic year, depending on the availability of funds and the recipient's unmet financial need.

Duration 1 year; may be renewed.

Additional information The application fee is $15. Since this a supplemental program, students must apply in a timely manner for federal financial aid and campus-based aid at the college they are attending to be considered for this program. Failure to apply will disqualify an applicant.

Number awarded 1 each year.
Deadline May of each year.

[886]
JEANNE SPURLOCK MINORITY MEDICAL STUDENT CLINICAL FELLOWSHIP IN CHILD AND ADOLESCENT PSYCHIATRY

American Academy of Child and Adolescent Psychiatry
Attn: Department of Research, Training, and Education
3615 Wisconsin Avenue, N.W.
Washington, DC 20016-3007
(202) 966-7300, ext. 117   Fax: (202) 364-5925
E-mail: training@aacap.org
Web: www.aacap.org/cs/awards

Summary To provide funding to Native American and other minority medical students who are interested in working with a child and adolescent psychiatrist during the summer.

Eligibility This program is open to African American, Asian American, Native American, Alaska Native, Mexican American, Hispanic, and Pacific Islander students in accredited U.S. medical schools. Applicants must present a plan for a clinical training experience that involves significant contact between the student and a mentor. The plan should include program planning discussions, instruction in treatment planning and implementation, regular meetings with the mentor and other treatment providers, and assigned readings. Clinical assignments may include responsibility for part of the observation or evaluation, conducting interviews or tests, using rating scales, and psychological or cognitive testing of patients. The training plan should also include discussion of ethical issues in treatment. U.S. citizenship or permanent resident status is required.

Financial data The stipend is $3,500. Fellows also receive reimbursement of travel expenses to attend the annual meeting of the American Academy of Child and Adolescent Psychiatry.

Duration 12 weeks during the summer.

Additional information Upon completion of the training program, the student is required to submit a brief paper summarizing the clinical experience. The fellowship pays expenses for the fellow to attend the academy's annual meeting and present this paper. This program is supported by the Center for Mental Health Services of the Substance Abuse and Mental Health Services Administration.

Number awarded Up to 14 each year.

Deadline February of each year.

[887]
JEANNE SPURLOCK RESEARCH FELLOWSHIP IN SUBSTANCE ABUSE AND ADDICTION FOR MINORITY MEDICAL STUDENTS

American Academy of Child and Adolescent Psychiatry
Attn: Department of Research, Training, and Education
3615 Wisconsin Avenue, N.W.
Washington, DC 20016-3007
(202) 966-7300, ext. 117   Fax: (202) 364-5925
E-mail: training@aacap.org
Web: www.aacap.org/cs/awards

Summary To provide funding to Native American and other minority medical students who are interested in working on the topics of drug abuse and addiction with a child and adolescent psychiatrist researcher-mentor during the summer.

Eligibility This program is open to African American, Asian American, Native American, Alaska Native, Mexican American, Hispanic, and Pacific Islander students in accredited U.S. medical schools. Applicants must present a plan for a program of research training in drug abuse and addiction that involves significant contact with a mentor who is an experienced child and adolescent psychiatrist researcher. The plan should include program planning discussions; instruction in research planning and implementation; regular meetings with the mentor, laboratory director, and the research group; and assigned readings. The mentor must be a member of the American Academy of Child and Adolescent Psychiatry (AACAP). Research assignments may include responsibility for part of the observation or evaluation, developing specific aspects of the research mechanisms, conducting interviews or tests, using rating scales, and psychological or cognitive testing of subjects. The training plan also should include discussion of ethical issues in research, such as protocol development, informed consent, collection and storage of raw data, safeguarding data, bias in analyzing data, plagiarism, protection of patients, and ethical treatment of animals. U.S. citizenship or permanent resident status is required.

Financial data The stipend is $3,500. Fellows also receive reimbursement of travel expenses to attend the annual meeting of the American Academy of Child and Adolescent Psychiatry.

Duration 12 weeks during the summer.

Additional information Upon completion of the training program, the student is required to submit a brief paper summarizing the research experience. The fellowship pays expenses for the fellow to attend the academy's annual meeting and present this paper. This program is co-sponsored by the National Institute on Drug Abuse.

Number awarded Up to 5 each year.

Deadline February of each year.

[888]
JEFFREY CAMPBELL GRADUATE FELLOWS PROGRAM

St. Lawrence University
Attn: Human Resources/Office of Equity Programs
Jeffrey Campbell Graduate Fellowship Program
23 Romoda Drive
Canton, NY 13617
(315) 229-5509   E-mail: humanresources@stlawu.edu
Web: www.stlawu.edu

Summary To provide funding to Native Americans and other minority graduate students who have completed their course work and are interested in conducting research at St. Lawrence University in New York.

Eligibility This program is open to graduate students who are members of racial or ethnic groups historically underrepresented at the university and in American higher education. Applicants must have completed their course work and preliminary examinations for the Ph.D. They must be interested in working on their dissertations or terminal degree projects while in residence at the University.

Financial data The stipend is $28,500 per academic year. Additional funds may be available to support travel to confer-

ences and professional meetings. Office space and a personal computer are provided.

Duration 1 academic year.

Additional information This program is named for 1 of the university's early African American graduates. Recipients must teach 1 course a semester in a department or program at St. Lawrence University related to their research interests. In addition, they must present a research-based paper in the fellows' lecture series each semester.

Deadline January of each year.

[889]
JO MORSE SCHOLARSHIP

Alaska Library Association
Attn: Scholarship Committee
c/o Alaska State Library
P.O. Box 110571
Juneau, AK 99811-0571
(907) 465-2458   Fax: (907) 465-2665
E-mail: aja_razumny@alaska.gov
Web: www.akla.org/scholarships/index.html

Summary To provide financial assistance to Alaska Natives and other Alaska residents who are interested in working on a certificate in school librarianship and, upon graduation, working in a school library in Alaska.

Eligibility This program is open to Alaska residents who hold a State of Alaska teaching certificate. Applicants must be eligible for acceptance or currently enrolled in a graduate school library media specialist certificate program during the academic year, semester, or quarter for which the scholarship is awarded and be willing to make a commitment to work in an Alaska school library for at least 1 year after graduation as a paid employee or volunteer. Preference is given to applicants meeting the federal definition of Alaska Native ethnicity. Selection is based on financial need, demonstrated scholastic ability and writing skills, an essay on professional goals and objectives in pursuing a library media specialist certificate, and 3 letters of recommendation (at least 1 of which must be from a librarian).

Financial data The stipend is $3,000.

Duration 1 year.

Number awarded 1 each year.

Deadline January of each year.

[890]
JOHN AND MURIEL LANDIS SCHOLARSHIPS

American Nuclear Society
Attn: Scholarship Coordinator
555 North Kensington Avenue
La Grange Park, IL 60526-5592
(708) 352-6611   Toll Free: (800) 323-3044
Fax: (708) 352-0499   E-mail: outreach@ans.org
Web: www.ans.org/honors/scholarships

Summary To provide financial assistance to Native American and other undergraduate or graduate students who are interested in preparing for a career in nuclear-related fields.

Eligibility This program is open to undergraduate and graduate students at colleges or universities located in the United States who are preparing for, or planning to prepare for, a career in nuclear science, nuclear engineering, or a nuclear-related field. Qualified high school seniors are also eligible. Applicants must have greater than average financial need and have experienced circumstances that render them disadvantaged. They must be sponsored by an organization (e.g., plant branch, local section, student section) within the American Nuclear Society (ANS). Along with their application, they must submit an essay on their academic and professional goals, experiences that have affected those goals, etc. Selection is based on that essay, academic achievement, letters of recommendation, and financial need. Women and members of minority groups are especially urged to apply. U.S. citizenship is not required.

Financial data The stipend is $5,000, to be used to cover tuition, books, fees, room, and board.

Duration 1 year; nonrenewable.

Number awarded Up to 8 each year.

Deadline January of each year.

[891]
JOHN C. ROUILLARD AND ALICE TONEMAH MEMORIAL SCHOLARSHIPS

National Indian Education Association
Attn: Awards Committee
110 Maryland Avenue, N.E., Suite 104
Washington, DC 20002
(202) 544-7290   Fax: (202) 544-7293
E-mail: niea@niea.org
Web: www.niea.org/events/scholarship.php

Summary To provide financial assistance for college or graduate school to students nominated by members of the National Indian Education Association (NIEA).

Eligibility This program is open to American Indians, Native Hawaiians, and Alaska Natives working full time on an associate, bachelor's, master's, or doctoral degree. Applicants are not required to be members of NIEA, but they must be nominated by a member. They must have demonstrated leadership qualities, maintained high academic achievement, served as a role model for other students, and shown creativity or commitment in the following areas: 1) promoted an understanding and an appreciation of Native American culture in an educational setting; 2) demonstrated positive, active leadership in student affairs; 3) demonstrated and/or encouraged student involvement in educational or community activities; and/or 4) achieved their educational goals and objectives.

Financial data Stipends range from $1,000 to $2,500. Funds may be used for educational expenses not covered by other sources.

Duration 1 year.

Number awarded 1 or more each year.

Deadline August of each year.

[892]
JOHN D. VOELKER FOUNDATION NATIVE AMERICAN SCHOLARSHIP

John D. Voelker Foundation
P.O. Box 15222
Lansing, MI 48901-5222
Web: www.voelkerfdn.org/Scholarships.asp

Summary To provide financial assistance to students enrolled in Wisconsin or Michigan tribes who live in any state and are interested in working on a law degree.

Eligibility This program is open to students who are enrolled members of a federally-recognized Michigan or Wisconsin tribe (applicants may live in any state) and are interested in studying law to prepare for a career that will benefit Native American people. Applicants do not need to be currently enrolled in law school, but if they apply as undergraduates they must ultimately intend to attend law school. Selection is based on academic achievements and financial need (preference is given to applicants with the greatest need).

Financial data The amount awarded varies annually; recently, the scholarships were at least $4,000 each.

Duration 1 year.

Additional information Recipients must provide an annual report on their progress.

Number awarded 1 or more each year.

Deadline Deadline not specified.

[893]
JOHN HOPE FRANKLIN DISSERTATION FELLOWSHIP

American Philosophical Society
Attn: Committee on Research
104 South Fifth Street
Philadelphia, PA 19106-3387
(215) 440-3429   Fax: (215) 440-3436
E-mail: LMusumeci@amphilsoc.org
Web: www.amphilsoc.org/grants/johnhopefranklin

Summary To provide funding to Native Americans and other underrepresented minority graduate students conducting research for a doctoral dissertation.

Eligibility This program is open to African American, Hispanic American, and Native American graduate students working on a degree at a Ph.D. granting institution in the United States. Other talented students who have a demonstrated commitment to eradicating racial disparities and enlarging minority representation in academia are also eligible. Applicants must have completed all course work and examinations preliminary to the doctoral dissertation and be able to devote full-time effort, with no teaching obligations, to researching or writing their dissertation. The proposed research should relate to a topic in which the holdings of the Library of the American Philosophical Society (APS) are particularly strong: quantum mechanics, nuclear physics, computer development, the history of genetics and eugenics, the history of medicine, Early American political and cultural history, natural history in the 18th and 19th centuries, the development of cultural anthropology, or American Indian culture and linguistics.

Financial data The grant is $25,000; an additional grant of $5,000 is provided to support the cost of residency in Philadelphia.

Duration 12 months, to begin at the discretion of the grantee.

Additional information This program was established in 2005. Recipients are expected to spend a significant amount of time in residence at the APS Library.

Number awarded 1 each year.

Deadline March of each year.

[894]
JOHN N. COLBERG ENDOWMENT SCHOLARSHIP FUND

Cook Inlet Region, Inc.
Attn: The CIRI Foundation
3600 San Jeronimo Drive, Suite 256
Anchorage, AK 99508-2870
(907) 793-3575   Toll Free: (800) 764-3382
Fax: (907) 793-3585   E-mail: tcf@thecirifoundation.org
Web: www.thecirifoundation.org/designated.htm

Summary To provide financial assistance for undergraduate or graduate studies leading to a career in the law to Alaska Natives who are original enrollees to Cook Inlet Region, Inc. (CIRI) and their lineal descendants.

Eligibility This program is open to Alaska Native enrollees to CIRI under the Alaska Native Claims Settlement Act (ANCSA) of 1971 and their lineal descendants. There are no Alaska residency requirements or age limitations. Applicants must be accepted or enrolled full time in a 4-year undergraduate or a graduate degree program. Preference is given to students who are working on a degree leading to the study of law and have a GPA of 2.5 or higher. Along with their application, they must submit a 500-word statement on their educational and career goals and how they are contributing, or planning to contribute, to a positive Alaska Native community. Selection is based on that statement, academic achievement, rigor of course work or degree program, student financial contribution, financial need, grade level, previous work performance, community service, and relationship of degree program to career goals.

Financial data The stipend is $2,500 per semester.

Duration 1 semester or 1 year.

Additional information This program was established in 2003.

Number awarded 1 or more each year.

Deadline May of each year.

[895]
JOHN RAINER GRADUATE FELLOWSHIP

American Indian Graduate Center
Attn: Executive Director
4520 Montgomery Boulevard, N.E., Suite 1-B
Albuquerque, NM 87109-1291
(505) 881-4584   Toll Free: (800) 628-1920
Fax: (505) 884-0427   E-mail: aigc@aigc.com
Web: www.aigc.com/02scholarships/rainer.htm

Summary To provide financial assistance to Native American students interested in working on a graduate degree in any field.

Eligibility This program is open to enrolled members of federally-recognized American Indian tribes and Alaska Native groups and students who can document one-fourth degree federally-recognized Indian blood. Applicants must be enrolled full time at a graduate school in the United States. Along with their application, they must submit a 500-word essay on their extracurricular activities as they relate to American Indian programs at their institution, volunteer and community work as related to American Indian communities, tribal and community involvement, and plans to make positive changes in the American Indian community with their college education. Financial need is also considered in the selection process. Males and females are considered separately.

Financial data The stipend is $1,000, of which $500 may be applied to the cost of education and $500 must be use to support participation in volunteer activities that afford an opportunity to develop leadership skills.

Duration 1 year; nonrenewable.

Additional information The application fee is $15. Since this a supplemental program, students must apply in a timely manner for federal financial aid and campus-based aid at the college they are attending to be considered for this program. Failure to apply will disqualify an applicant.

Number awarded 2 each year: 1 to a male and 1 to a female.

Deadline May of each year.

[896]
JOHN SHURR JOURNALISM AWARD

Cherokee Nation
Attn: Cherokee Nation Education Corporation
115 East Delaware Street
P.O. Box 948
Tahlequah, OK 74465-0948
(918) 207-0950   Fax: (918) 207-0951
E-mail: contact@cnec-edu.org
Web: cnec.cherokee.org

Summary To provide financial assistance to citizens of the Cherokee Nation who are enrolled at a college or university in any state and working on an undergraduate or graduate degree in journalism.

Eligibility This program is open to citizens of the Cherokee Nation who are currently enrolled in an undergraduate or graduate program in journalism or mass communications at a college or university in any state. Applicants must have a GPA of 3.0 or higher. They are not required to reside in the Cherokee Nation area. Along with their application, they must submit a 4-page personal essay that includes background information, their degree plan for higher education, why they have chosen that field of study, how they plan to serve Cherokee people when they complete higher education, and why they should be selected for this scholarship. Selection is based on the clarity and presentation of the essay; academic information (including transcripts and ACT scores); school, cultural and community activities; future plans to serve Cherokee people; and financial need.

Financial data The stipend is $1,000 per semester ($2,000 per year).

Duration 1 year. Renewal for the second semester requires the recipient to earn a GPA of 3.0 or higher in the first semester.

Additional information Recipients are expected to apply for an 8-week paid internship with *The Cherokee Phoenix* newspaper in Tahlequah, Oklahoma during the summer following their scholarship year.

Number awarded 1 each year.

Deadline April of each year.

[897]
JOHN STANFORD MEMORIAL WLMA SCHOLARSHIP

Washington Library Media Association
c/o Jeanne Staley
711 Scenic Bluff
Yakima, WA 98908
(509) 972-5899   E-mail: scholarships@wlma.org
Web: www.wlma.org/scholarships

Summary To provide financial assistance to Native Americans and other ethnic minorities in Washington who are interested in preparing for a library media career.

Eligibility This program is open to residents of Washington who are working toward a library media endorsement or graduate degree in the field. Applicants must be members of an ethnic minority group. They must be working or planning to work in a school library. Along with their application, they must submit a brief description of their reasons for applying, goals as a teacher librarian, plans for the future, interest in librarianship, plans for further education, and interest in this award. Financial need is considered in the selection process.

Financial data The stipend is $1,000.

Duration 1 year.

Number awarded 1 each year.

Deadline March of each year.

[898]
JOHNSON & JOHNSON CAMPAIGN FOR NURSING'S FUTURE-AMERICAN ASSOCIATION OF COLLEGES OF NURSING MINORITY NURSE FACULTY SCHOLARS PROGRAM

American Association of Colleges of Nursing
One Dupont Circle, N.W., Suite 530
Washington, DC 20036
(202) 463-6930   Fax: (202) 785-8320
E-mail: scholarship@aacn.nche.edu
Web: www.aacn.nche.edu/Education/financialaid.htm

Summary To provide funding to Native American and other minority students who are working on a graduate degree in nursing to prepare for a career as a faculty member.

Eligibility This program is open to members of racial and ethnic minority groups (Alaska Native, American Indian, Black or African American, Native Hawaiian or other, Pacific Islander, Hispanic or Latino, or Asian American) who are enrolled full time at a school of nursing. Applicants must be working on 1) a doctoral nursing degree (e.g., Ph.D., D.N.P.), or 2) a clinically-focused master's degree in nursing (e.g., M.S.N., M.S.). They must commit to 1) serve in a teaching capacity at a nursing school for a minimum of 1 year for each year of support they receive; 2) provide 6-month progress reports to the American Association of Colleges of Nursing (AACN) throughout the entire funding process and during the payback period; 3) agree to work with an assigned mentor throughout the period of the scholarship grant; and 4) attend an annual leadership training conference to connect with their mentor, fellow scholars, and colleagues. Selection is based on ability to contribute to nursing education; leadership potential; development of goals reflecting education, research, and professional involvement; ability to work with a mentor/adviser throughout the award period; proposed research and/or practice projects that are significant and show commitment to improving nursing education and clinical nursing practice in the United States; and evidence of commitment to a career in nursing education and to recruiting, mentoring, and retaining future underrepresented minority nurses. Preference is given to students enrolled in doctoral nursing programs. Applicants must be U.S. citizens, permanent residents, refugees, or qualified immigrants.

Financial data The stipend is $18,000 per year. The award includes $1,500 that is held in escrow to cover the costs for the recipient to attend the leadership training conference. Recipients are required to sign a letter of commitment that they will provide 1 year of service in a teaching capacity at a nursing school in the United States for each year of support received; if they fail to complete that service requirement, they must repay all funds received.

Duration 1 year; may be renewed 1 additional year.

Additional information This program, established in 2007, is sponsored by the Johnson & Johnson Campaign for Nursing's Future.

Number awarded 5 each year.

Deadline May of each year.

[899]
JOSEPH K. LUMSDEN MEMORIAL SCHOLARSHIP

Sault Tribe of Chippewa Indians
Attn: Higher Education Program-Memorial/Tributary
  Scholarships
523 Ashmun Street
Sault Ste. Marie, MI 49783
(906) 635-4944   Toll Free: (800) 793-0660
Fax: (906) 635-7785   E-mail: amatson@saulttribe.net
Web: www.saulttribe.com

Summary To provide financial assistance to members of the Sault Tribe in Michigan who are upper-division or graduate students at a university in any state.

Eligibility This program is open to members of the Sault Tribe who are college juniors or higher and are one-quarter Indian blood quantum or more. Applicants must be enrolled full time at a 4-year college or university in any state and have a cumulative GPA of 3.0 or higher. Along with their application, they must submit an essay of 300 to 500 words on how this scholarship will help them realize their goals.

Financial data The stipend is $1,000 per year.

Duration 1 year; may be renewed.

Number awarded 1 each year.

Deadline May of each year.

[900]
JOSEPH NAWAHI SCHOLARSHIP

Ke Ali'i Pauahi Foundation
Attn: Financial Aid & Scholarship Services
567 South King Street, Suite 160
Honolulu, HI 96813
(808) 534-3966   Toll Free: (800) 842-4682, ext. 43966
Fax: (808) 534-3890   E-mail: scholarships@pauahi.org
Web: www.pauahi.org/scholarships

Summary To provide financial assistance to graduate students at universities in Hawaii, especially those of Native Hawaiian descent, who are working on a degree in designated fields.

Eligibility This program is open to full-time graduate students at colleges and universities in Hawaii. Applicants must be working on a degree in Hawaiian studies, Hawaiian politics, law (specific to Hawaiian legal issues), or communications and journalism (specific to Hawaiian history, culture, and politics). Applicants must have a GPA of 3.2 or higher and be able to demonstrate financial need. Along with their application, they must submit an essay describing their plan to maximize the potential of young people through communication as well as to demonstrate their leadership potential in the community. Preference is given to Native Hawaiians (descendants of the aboriginal inhabitants of the Hawaiian Islands prior to 1778).

Financial data The stipend is $1,500.

Duration 1 year.

Additional information This program began in 2008.

Number awarded 2 each year.

Deadline March of each year.

[901]
JOSEPHINE FORMAN SCHOLARSHIP

Society of American Archivists
Attn: Chair, Awards Committee
17 North State Street, Suite 1425
Chicago, IL 60602-3315
(312) 606-0722   Toll Free: (866) 722-7858
Fax: (312) 606-0728   E-mail: info@archivists.org
Web: www2.archivists.org

Summary To provide financial assistance to Native Americans and other minority graduate students working on a degree in archival science.

Eligibility This program is open to members of minority groups (American Indian/Alaska Native, Asian, Black/African American, Hispanic/Latino, or Native Hawaiian/other Pacific Islander) currently enrolled in or accepted to a graduate program or a multi-course program in archival administration. The program must offer at least 3 courses in archival science and students may have completed no more than half of the credit requirements toward their graduate degree. Selection is based on potential for scholastic and personal achievement and commitment both to the archives profession and to advancing diversity concerns within it. U.S. citizenship or permanent resident status is required.

Financial data The stipend is $10,000.

Duration 1 year.

Additional information Funding for this program, established in 2011, is provided by the General Commission on Archives and History of the United Methodist Church.

Number awarded 1 each year.

Deadline February of each year.

[902]
JOSEPHINE P. WHITE EAGLE GRADUATE FELLOWSHIP

Ho-Chunk Nation
Attn: Higher Education Division
P.O. Box 667
Black River Falls, WI 54615
(715) 284-4915   Toll Free: (800) 362-4476
Fax: (715) 284-1760
E-mail: higher.education@ho-chunk.com
Web: www.ho-chunknation.com/?PageId=47

Summary To provide funding to enrolled members of the Ho-Chunk Nation who are working on a master's or doctoral degree in selected fields.

Eligibility This program is open to enrolled members of the Ho-Chunk Nation who have been accepted at an accredited college or university in the United States. Applicants must be working on a master's or doctoral degree in law, health professions, education, business, or social services. Along with their application, they must submit an essay of 500 to 1,000 words on their long term educational and professional goals, including achievements, career goals, financial need, and how their field of study will contribute to the long-term goals of the Ho-Chunk Nation. Law students must be attending an ABA-accredited school. Selection is based on their essay, academic achievement, prior work experience, and anticipated graduation date.

Financial data The program pays full tuition, books, and fees for the length of the recipient's program. Living expenses are capped at $1,800 per month; $400 per month is added to that for each dependent child. Spouses are not included in this calculation. This is a scholarship/loan program; recipients must work for the Ho-Chunk Nation for 1 year for each year funding was awarded (a minimum of 2 years).

Duration 1 year; will be renewed for the length of the recipient's program, if the student remains enrolled full time and has a GPA of 3.0 or higher.

Deadline April of each year for the fall term; October of each year for the spring term; January of each year for the summer session.

[903]
JTBF JUDICIAL EXTERNSHIP PROGRAM

Just the Beginning Foundation
c/o Paula Lucas, Executive Director
Schiff Hardin LLP
233 South Wacker Drive, Suite 6600
Chicago, IL 60606
(312) 258-5930   E-mail: plucas@jtbf.org
Web: www.jtbf.org

Summary To provide work experience to Native American and other underrepresented law students who plan to seek judicial clerkships after graduation.

Eligibility This program is open to students currently enrolled in their second or third year of law school who are members of minority or economically disadvantaged groups. Applicants must intend to work as a clerk in the federal or state judiciary upon graduation or within 5 years of graduation.

Financial data Program externs receive a quarterly or summer stipend in an amount determined by the sponsor.

Duration The academic year externships require a 1- or 2-year commitment, beginning each September and ending in May or June. During the academic year, participants are expected to work a minimum of 10 hours per week on externship assignments. The summer externships require students to perform at least 35 hours per week of work for at least 8 weeks during the summer.

Additional information This program began in 2005. Law students are matched with federal and state judges across the country who provide assignments to the participants that will enhance their legal research, writing, and analytical skills (e.g., drafting memoranda). Students are expected to complete at least 1 memorandum of law or other key legal document each semester of the externship. Course credit may be offered, but students may not receive academic credit and a stipend simultaneously.

Number awarded Varies each year.

Deadline February of each year for summer and fall appointments.

[904]
JUDICIAL INTERN OPPORTUNITY PROGRAM

American Bar Association
Attn: Section of Litigation
321 North Clark Street
Chicago, IL 60654-7598
(312) 988-6348   Fax: (312) 988-6234
E-mail: howardg@staff.abanet.org
Web: www.abanet.org/litigation/jiop

Summary To provide an opportunity for Native American and other traditionally underrepresented law students to gain experience as judicial interns in selected courts during the summer.

Eligibility This program is open to first- and second-year students at ABA-accredited law schools who are 1) members racial or ethnic groups that are traditionally underrepresented in the legal profession (African Americans, Asians, Hispanics/Latinos, Native Americans); 2) students with disabilities; 3) students who are economically disadvantaged; or 4) students who identify themselves as lesbian, gay, bisexual, or transgender. Applicants must be interested in a judicial internship at courts in selected areas and communities. They may indicate a preference for the area in which they wish to work, but they may not specify a court or a judge. Along with their application, they must submit a current resume, a 10-page legal writing sample, and a 2-page statement of interest that outlines their qualifications for the internship. Screening interviews are conducted by staff of the American Bar Association, either in person or by telephone. Final interviews are conducted by the judges with whom the interns will work. Some spots are reserved for students with an interest in intellectual property law.

Financial data The stipend is $1,500.

Duration 6 weeks during the summer.

Additional information Recently, internships were available in the following locations: Chicago and surrounding suburbs; central and southern Illinois; Houston, Dallas, southern, and eastern Texas; Miami, Florida; Phoenix, Arizona; Los Angeles, California; Philadelphia, Pennsylvania; San Francisco, California; and Washington, D.C. Some internships in Chicago, Los Angeles, Texas, and Washington, D.C. are reserved for students with an interest in intellectual property law.

Number awarded Varies each year; recently, 171 of these internships were awarded, including 9 at courts in Arizona, 36 in California, 12 in Florida, 51 in Illinois, 17 in Pennsylvania, 33 in Texas, and 13 in Washington, D.C.

Deadline January of each year.

[905]
JUDITH MCMANUS PRICE SCHOLARSHIPS

American Planning Association
Attn: Leadership Affairs Associate
205 North Michigan Avenue, Suite 1200
Chicago, IL 60601
(312) 431-9100   Fax: (312) 786-6700
E-mail: fellowship@planning.org
Web: www.planning.org/scholarships/apa

Summary To provide financial assistance to Native Americans and other underrepresented students enrolled in undergraduate or graduate degree programs at recognized planning schools.

Eligibility This program is open to undergraduate and graduate students in urban and regional planning who are women or members of the following minority groups: African American, Hispanic American, or Native American. Applicants must be citizens of the United States and able to document financial need. They must intend to work as practicing planners in the public sector. Along with their application, they must submit a 2-page personal and background statement describing how their education will be applied to career goals and why they chose planning as a career path. Selection is based (in order of importance), on: 1) commitment to planning as reflected in their personal statement and on their resume; 2) academic achievement and/or improvement during the past 2 years; 3) letters of recommendation; 4) financial need; and 5) professional presentation.

Financial data Stipends range from $2,000 to $4,000 per year. The money may be applied to tuition and living expenses only. Payment is made to the recipient's university and divided by terms in the school year.

Duration 1 year; recipients may reapply.

Additional information This program was established in 2002.

Number awarded Varies each year; recently, 3 of these scholarships were awarded.

Deadline April of each year.

[906]
JUNE M. SENECA SCHOLARSHIP

Seneca Diabetes Foundation
Attn: Lucille White
TIS Building 12837, Route 438
P.O. Box 309
Irving, NY 14081
(716) 532-4900   Fax: (716) 549-1629
E-mail: white@sni.org
Web: www.senecadiabetesfoundation.org

Summary To provide financial assistance to members of the Seneca Nation who are interested in working on a master's degree in social or health services.

Eligibility This program is open to members of the Seneca Nation who are interested in attending college to assist the Seneca people, especially in regard to the fight against diabetes, by working on a master's degree in health or social services. Applicants must be able to demonstrate how their area of health or social services interest would benefit the Seneca people. Along with their application, they must submit brief statements on 1) the professional, community, or cultural services and activities in which they have participated; 2) how this scholarship would help further their education; and 3) their goals or plan for using their education and training to benefit the Seneca Nation and its people. In the selection process, primary consideration is given to financial need, but involvement in community and cultural activities, personal assets, and desire to improve the quality of life for the Seneca people are also considered.

Financial data The stipend is $5,000.

Duration 1 year.

Number awarded 2 each year.

Deadline May of each year.

[907]
KAISER PERMANENTE COLORADO DIVERSITY SCHOLARSHIP PROGRAM

Kaiser Permanente
Attn: Multicultural Associations/Employee Resource
 Groups
P.O. Box 378066
Denver, CO 80247-8066
E-mail: co-diversitydevelopment@kp.org
Web: physiciancareers.kp.org

Summary To provide financial assistance to Colorado residents who are Native American or come from other diverse backgrounds and are interested in working on an undergraduate or graduate degree in a health care field at a school in any state.

Eligibility This program is open to all residents of Colorado, including those who identify as 1 or more of the following: African American, Asian Pacific, Latino, lesbian, gay, bisexual, transgender, intersex, Native American, and/or a person with a disability. Applicants must be 1) a graduating high school senior with a GPA of 2.7 or higher and planning to enroll full time at a college or technical school in any state; 2) a GED recipient with a GED score of 520 or higher and planning to enroll full time at a college or technical school in any state; 3) a full-time undergraduate student at a college or technical school in any state; or 4) a full-time graduate or doctoral student at a school in any state. They must be preparing for a career in health care (e.g., doctor, nurse, surgeon, physician assistant, dentist), mental health, public health, or health policy. Along with their application, they must submit 300-word essays on 1) a personal setback in their life and how they responded and learned from it; 2) how they give back to their community; and 3) why they have chosen health care and/or public health for their educational and career path. Selection is based on academic achievement, character qualities, community outreach and volunteering, and financial need.

Financial data Stipends range from $1,400 to $2,600.

Duration 1 year.

Number awarded Varies each year; recently, 17 of these scholarships were awarded.

Deadline January of each year.

[908]
KATRIN H. LAMON FELLOWSHIP

School for Advanced Research
Attn: Director of Scholar Programs
660 Garcia Street
P.O. Box 2188
Santa Fe, NM 87504-2188
(505) 954-7201   E-mail: scholar@sarsf.org
Web: sarweb.org/index.php?resident_scholars

Summary To provide funding to Native American pre- and postdoctoral scholars interested in conducting research in the social sciences or humanities while in residence at the School for Advanced Research (SAR) in Santa Fe, New Mexico.

Eligibility This program is open to Native American Ph.D. candidates and scholars with doctorates who are interested in conducting research at SAR in the humanities or the social sciences. Applicants must submit a 150-word abstract describing the purpose, goals, and objectives of their research project; a 4-page proposal; a bibliography; a curriculum vitae; a brief statement of tribal affiliation; and 3 letters of recommendation. Predoctoral applicants must also submit a brief letter of nomination from their department. Preference is given to applicants whose field work or basic research and analysis are complete and who need time to write up their research.

Financial data The fellowship provides an apartment and office on the school's campus, a stipend of up to $40,000 for scholars or $30,000 for Ph.D. candidates, library assistance, and other benefits.

Duration 9 months, beginning in September.

Additional information Funding for this program is provided by the Katrin H. Lamon Endowment for Native American Art and Education. Participants must spend their 9-month residency at the school in New Mexico.

Number awarded 1 each year.

Deadline October of each year.

[909]
KATRIN LAMON FUND

American Indian Graduate Center
Attn: Executive Director
4520 Montgomery Boulevard, N.E., Suite 1-B
Albuquerque, NM 87109-1291
(505) 881-4584   Toll Free: (800) 628-1920
Fax: (505) 884-0427   E-mail: aigc@aigc.com
Web: www.aigc.com/02scholarships/scholarships.htm

Summary To provide financial assistance to Native American students interested in working on a graduate degree in literature, journalism, or communications.

Eligibility This program is open to enrolled members of federally-recognized American Indian tribes and Alaska Native groups, as well as students who can document one-fourth degree federally-recognized Indian blood. Applicants must be enrolled full time at a graduate school in the United States and working on a degree in literature, journalism, or communications. Along with their application, they must submit a 500-word essay on their extracurricular activities as they relate to American Indian programs at their institution, their volunteer and community work as related to American Indian communities, their tribal and community involvement, and plans to make positive changes in the American Indian community with their college education. Financial need is also considered in the selection process.

Financial data Stipends range from $1,000 to $5,000 per academic year, depending on the availability of funds and the recipient's unmet financial need.

Duration 1 year; may be renewed.

Additional information The application fee is $15. Since this a supplemental program, students must apply in a timely manner for federal financial aid and campus-based aid at the college they are attending to be considered for this program. Failure to apply will disqualify an applicant.

Number awarded 1 each year.

Deadline May of each year.

[910]
KATTEN MUCHIN ROSENMAN MINORITY SCHOLARSHIPS

Katten Muchin Rosenman LLP
Attn: Legal Recruiting Coordinator
525 West Monroe Street
Chicago, IL 60661-3693
(312) 577-8406   Fax: (312) 577-4572
E-mail: grace.johnson@kattenlaw.com
Web: www.kattenlaw.com

Summary To provide financial assistance and summer work experience in Chicago or New York City to Native American and other minority law students from any state.

Eligibility This program is open to minority students from any state who have completed their first year of law school. Applicants must have applied for and been accepted as a summer associate at the sponsoring law firm's Chicago or New York office. Along with their application, they must submit 250-word statements on 1) their strongest qualifications for this award; 2) their reasons for preparing for law as a profession; and 3) their views on diversity and how their personal experience and philosophy will be an asset to the firm. Selection is based on academic achievement, leadership experience, and personal qualities that reflect the potential for outstanding contributions to the firm and the legal profession.

Financial data Participants receive the standard salary for the summer internship and a stipend of $15,000 for the academic year.

Duration 1 year.

Number awarded 1 each year.

Deadline October of each year.

[911]
KAW NATION GRADUATE PROGRAM

Kaw Nation
Attn: Education and Social Services Department
P.O. Box 50
Kaw City, OK 74641
(580) 269-1186   Fax: (580) 269-2116
E-mail: khowe@kawnation.com
Web: www.kawnation.com/Programs/edsvcs.html

Summary To provide financial assistance for graduate school to members of the Kaw Nation who can demonstrate need.

Eligibility This program is open to Kaw tribal members who are working on or planning to work on a graduate degree. Applicants must be able to demonstrate financial need and be eligible for other types of assistance, such as loans.

Financial data A stipend is awarded (amount not specified).

Duration 1 year; may be renewed.

Number awarded Varies each year.

Deadline May of each year for fall semester; October of each year for spring semester.

[912]
KEGLER, BROWN, HILL & RITTER MINORITY MERIT SCHOLARSHIP

Kegler, Brown, Hill & Ritter
Attn: Human Resources Manager
Capitol Square, Suite 1800
65 East State Street
Columbus, OH 43215
(614) 462-5467   Fax: (614) 464-2634
E-mail: ctammaro@keglerbrown.com
Web: www.keglerbrown.com

Summary To provide financial assistance and summer work experience at Kegler, Brown, Hill & Ritter in Columbus, Ohio to Native American and other minority students at law schools in any state.

Eligibility This program is open to first-year students of minority descent at law schools in any state. Applicants must be interested in a summer clerkship with the firm following their first year of law school. Along with their application, they must submit brief essays on 1) a major accomplishment that has shaped their life, how it influenced their decision to prepare for a career in law, and how it prepared them for a future as a lawyer; 2) what diversity means to them; 3) why they have applied for the scholarship; and 4) any training and/or experience they believe to be relevant to the clerkship. Selection is based on academic performance, accomplishments, activities, and potential contributions to the legal community.

Financial data The program provides a $5,000 stipend for law school tuition and a paid summer clerkship position.

Duration 1 year.

Additional information This program began in 2004.

Number awarded 1 each year.

Deadline January of each year.

[913]
KENAITZE INDIAN TRIBE HIGHER EDUCATION GRANT PROGRAM

Kenaitze Indian Tribe
Attn: Education Services Coordinator
1104 Mission Avenue in Olde Town Kenai
P.O. Box 988
Kenai, AK 99611
(907) 335-0669   Fax: (907) 335-0989
E-mail: education@kenaitze.org
Web: www.kenaitze.org/education/index.html

Summary To provide financial assistance to members of recognized Native Alaskan Tribes who plan to attend college or graduate school in any state.
Eligibility This program is open to members of federally-recognized tribes and Native Alaskans of at least one-quarter degree blood. Applicants must be enrolled or planning to enroll full time at a college or university in any state and work on a baccalaureate degree. They are also expected to apply for federal financial aid through the FAFSA. Along with their application, they must submit a letter on their goals and educational plans, verification of Indian ancestry (CIB or tribal card), a letter of acceptance to the school they plan to attend, transcripts, a completed FAFSA application, and an Alaska driver's license. Limited support may be provided to graduate students if funds are available.
Financial data The amount awarded varies, depending upon the available funds and the recipient's unmet needs. Funds are paid directly to the educational institution.
Duration 1 year; may be renewed if the recipient maintains a GPA of 2.5 of higher.
Additional information This program is funded by the U.S. Bureau of Indian Affairs.
Number awarded Varies each year.
Deadline May of each year for fall; November of each year for spring or winter.

[914]
KING & SPALDING DIVERSITY FELLOWSHIP PROGRAM

King & Spalding
Attn: Diversity Fellowship Program
1180 Peachtree Street
Atlanta, GA 30309
(404) 572-4643   Fax: (404) 572-5100
E-mail: fellowship@kslaw.com
Web: www.kslaw.com

Summary To provide financial assistance and summer work experience at U.S. offices of the sponsoring law firm to Native American and other law students who will contribute to the diversity of the legal community.
Eligibility This program is open to second-year law students who 1) come from a minority ethnic or racial group (American Indian/Alaskan Native, Asian American/Pacific Islander, Black/African American, Hispanic, or multi-racial); 2) are a member of the gay, lesbian, bisexual, or transgender (GLBT) community; or 3) have a disability. Applicants must receive an offer of a clerkship at a U.S. office of King & Spalding during their second-year summer. Along with their application, they must submit a 500-word personal statement that describes their talents, qualities, and experiences and how they would contribute to the diversity of the firm.
Financial data Fellows receive a stipend of $10,000 for their second year of law school and a paid summer associate clerkship at a U.S. office of the firm during the following summer.
Duration 1 year.
Additional information The firm's U.S. offices are located in Atlanta, Charlotte, Houston, New York, San Francisco, Silicon Valley, and Washington.
Number awarded Up to 4 each year.
Deadline August of each year.

[915]
KIRBY MCDONALD EDUCATION ENDOWMENT SCHOLARSHIP FUND

Cook Inlet Region, Inc.
Attn: The CIRI Foundation
3600 San Jeronimo Drive, Suite 256
Anchorage, AK 99508-2870
(907) 793-3575   Toll Free: (800) 764-3382
Fax: (907) 793-3585   E-mail: tcf@thecirifoundation.org
Web: www.thecirifoundation.org/designated.htm

Summary To provide financial assistance for undergraduate or graduate studies to Alaska Natives who are original enrollees to Cook Inlet Region, Inc. (CIRI) and their lineal descendants.
Eligibility This program is open to Alaska Native enrollees to CIRI under the Alaska Native Claims Settlement Act (ANCSA) of 1971 and their lineal descendants. There are no Alaska residency requirements or age limitations. Applicants must be accepted or enrolled full time in a 4-year undergraduate or a graduate degree program. Preference is given to students in the culinary arts, business administration, or engineering. They must have a GPA of 2.5 or higher. Along with their application, they must submit a 500-word statement on their educational and career goals and how they are contributing, or planning to contribute, to a positive Alaska Native community. Selection is based on that statement, academic achievement, rigor of course work or degree program, student financial contribution, financial need, grade level, previous work performance, community service, and relationship of degree program to career goals.
Financial data The stipend is $10,000 per year, $8,000 per year, or $2,500 per semester, depending on GPA.
Duration 1 semester or 1 year.
Additional information This program was established in 1991.
Number awarded 1 or more each year.
Deadline May of each year for annual scholarships; May or November of each year for semester scholarships.

[916]
KIRKLAND & ELLIS LLP DIVERSITY FELLOWSHIP PROGRAM

Kirkland & Ellis LLP
Attn: Attorney Recruiting Manager
333 South Hope Street
Los Angeles, CA 90071
(213) 680-8436   Fax: (213) 680-8500
E-mail: cherie.conrad@kirkland.com
Web: www.kirkland.com

Summary To provide financial assistance and summer work experience at an office of Kirkland & Ellis to Native American and other minority law students from any state.
Eligibility This program is open to second-year students at ABA-accredited law schools who meet the racial and ethnic categories established by the Equal Employment Opportunity Commission. Applicants must have been accepted as summer associates at a domestic office of the sponsoring law firm (Chicago, Los Angeles, New York, Palo Alto, San Francisco, Washington, D.C.) and be likely to practice at 1 of those offices after graduation. Along with their application, they must submit a 1-page personal statement that describes

ways in which they have promoted and will continue to promote diversity in the legal community, along with their interest in the firm. Selection is based on merit.

Financial data Fellows receive a salary during their summer associateship and a $15,000 stipend at the conclusion of the summer. Stipend funds are to be used for payment of educational expenses during the third year of law school.

Duration 1 year.

Additional information This program, which replaced the Kirkland & Ellis Minority Fellowship Program, was established at 14 law schools in 2004. In 2006, it began accepting a limited number of applications from students at all ABA-accredited law schools.

Number awarded Varies each year; recently, 14 of these fellowships were awarded.

Deadline September of each year.

[917]
K&L GATES DIVERSITY FELLOWSHIP

Kirkpatrick & Lockhart Preston Gates Ellis LLP
Attn: Regional Recruiting Manager
925 Fourth Avenue, Suite 2900
Seattle, WA 98104
(206) 370-5744   E-mail: dana.mills@klgates.com
Web: www.klgates.com/lawstudents/studentsdiversity

Summary To provide financial assistance and summer work experience in Seattle to Native American and other law students from any state who come from diverse racial and ethnic backgrounds.

Eligibility This program is open to first-year students at ABA-accredited law schools in the United States. Applicants must be members of minority racial and ethnic groups. Along with their application, they must submit a 500-word personal statement describing the contribution they would make to the legal profession and the sponsoring firm in particular.

Financial data Fellows receive a paid associateship with the Seattle office of the sponsoring firm during the summer following their first year of law school and an academic scholarship of $10,000 for their second year of law school.

Duration 1 year.

Number awarded 1 each year.

Deadline January of each year.

[918]
KONIAG EDUCATION FOUNDATION ACADEMIC SCHOLARSHIPS

Koniag Incorporated
Attn: Koniag Education Foundation
4241 B Street, Suite 303B
Anchorage, AK 99503
(907) 562-9093   Toll Free: (888) 562-9093
Fax: (907) 562-9023
E-mail: scholarships@koniageducation.org
Web: www.koniageducation.org/scholarships

Summary To provide financial assistance to Alaska Natives who are Koniag Incorporated shareholders or descendants and plan to attend college or graduate school in any state.

Eligibility This program is open to high school seniors, high school and GED graduates, college students, and graduate students who are Alaska Native shareholders of Koniag

Incorporated or descendants of those original enrollees. Applicants must have a GPA of 3.0 or higher and be enrolled or planning to enroll at a college or university in any state. Along with their application, they must submit an essay of 300 to 600 words in the form of a thank you letter about their background, educational goals, work history, and/or achievements. Financial need is not considered in the selection process.

Financial data Stipends range up to $2,500 per year. Funds are sent directly to the recipient's school and may be used for tuition, books, supplies, room, board, and transportation.

Duration 1 year; may be renewed, provided recipients maintain a GPA of 3.0 or higher.

Additional information Koniag Incorporated is 1 of 13 Alaska Native Regional Corporations created under the Alaska Native Claims Settlement Act of 1971.

Number awarded Varies each year.

Deadline March of each year for summer term; May of each year for fall or spring term.

[919]
KONIAG INCORPORATED EXXONMOBIL SCHOLARSHIP

Koniag Incorporated
Attn: Koniag Education Foundation
4241 B Street, Suite 303B
Anchorage, AK 99503
(907) 562-9093   Toll Free: (888) 562-9093
Fax: (907) 562-9023
E-mail: scholarships@koniageducation.org
Web: www.koniageducation.org/scholarships

Summary To provide financial assistance to Alaska Natives who are Koniag Incorporated shareholders or descendants and working on an undergraduate or graduate degree in science or mathematics related to the oil and gas industry.

Eligibility This program is open to undergraduate and graduate students who are Alaska Native shareholders of Koniag Incorporated or descendants of those original enrollees. Applicants must have a GPA of 3.0 or higher and be working full time on a degree in a field of science or mathematics related to the oil and gas industry. Along with their application, they must submit an essay of 300 to 600 words in the form of a thank you letter about their background, educational goals, work history, and/or achievements. Financial need is not considered in the selection process.

Financial data The stipend is $10,000 per year. Funds are sent directly to the recipient's school and may be used for tuition, books, supplies, room, board, and transportation.

Duration 1 year; may be renewed.

Additional information Koniag Incorporated is 1 of 13 Alaska Native Regional Corporations created under the Alaska Native Claims Settlement Act of 1971. This program is supported by ExxonMobil.

Number awarded 1 each year.

Deadline August of each year.

[920]
LAC COURTE OREILLES HIGHER EDUCATION GRANTS

Lac Courte Oreilles Band of Ojibwe
Attn: Consolidated Education and Native Employment
  Works Program
13394 West Trepania Road
Hayward, WI 54843
(715) 634-8934, ext. 281   Toll Free: (800) 633-6093
Fax: (715) 634-4797
Web: www.lco-nsn.gov/entities.htm

Summary To provide financial assistance for college or graduate school to tribal members of the Lac Courte Oreilles Band of Ojibwe.

Eligibility This program is open to enrolled members of the Lac Courte Oreilles who are working on or planning to work on an undergraduate or graduate degree. Applicants must be able to document financial need.

Financial data The maximum stipend is $1,500 per year for undergraduates or $3,000 per year for graduate students.

Duration Up to 10 semesters for undergraduate students or up to 4 semesters for graduate students, provided the recipient maintains a GPA of 2.0 or higher as an undergraduate or 3.0 or higher as a graduate student.

Number awarded Varies each year.

Deadline June of each year for fall term; October of each year for spring term.

[921]
LAC DU FLAMBEAU GRADUATE ASSISTANCE PROGRAM

Lac du Flambeau Band of Lake Superior Chippewa
  Indians
Attn: Education Coordinator
562 Peace Pipe Road
P.O. Box 189
Lac du Flambeau, WI 54538
(715) 588-7925   Fax: (715) 588-3903
E-mail: jbldfedu@nnex.net
Web: www.lacduflambeaunation.com/depts/Education.html

Summary To provide financial assistance to tribal members of the Lac du Flambeau Band of Lake Superior Chippewa Indians who are interested in working on a graduate degree.

Eligibility This program is open to enrolled Lac du Flambeau members who are working on or planning to work full or part time on a master's or doctoral degree. Applicants must be able to demonstrate financial need.

Financial data The maximum stipend is $7,500 per year for full-time work; the stipend for part-time work is prorated.

Duration 1 year; may be renewed up to 1 additional year of full-time master's degree study (3 additional years of part-time study) or 3 additional years of full-time doctoral study (7 additional years of part-time study); renewal is granted only if the recipient maintains a GPA of 3.0 or higher.

Number awarded Varies each year.

Deadline July of each year.

[922]
LAGRANT FOUNDATION GRADUATE SCHOLARSHIPS

Lagrant Foundation
Attn: Programs Manager
626 Wilshire Boulevard, Suite 700
Los Angeles, CA 90071-2920
(323) 469-8680   Fax: (323) 469-8683
E-mail: erickaavila@lagrant.com
Web: www.lagrantfoundation.org/site/?page_id=3

Summary To provide financial assistance to Native American and other minority graduate students who are working on a degree in advertising, public relations, or marketing.

Eligibility This program is open to African Americans, Asian Pacific Americans, Hispanics/Latinos, and Native Americans/Alaska Natives who are full-time graduate students at an accredited institution. Applicants must have a GPA of 3.2 or higher and be working on a master's degree in advertising, marketing, or public relations. They must have at least 2 academic semesters remaining to complete their degree. Along with their application, they must submit 1) a 1- to 2-page essay outlining their career goals; why it is important to increase ethnic representation in the fields of advertising, marketing, and public relations; and the role of an advertising, marketing, or public relations practitioner; 2) a paragraph describing the graduate school and/or community activities in which they are involved; 3) a brief paragraph describing any honors and awards they have received; 4) a letter of reference; 5) a resume; and 6) an official transcript. U.S. citizenship or permanent resident status is required.

Financial data The stipend is $10,000 per year.

Duration 1 year.

Number awarded 5 each year.

Deadline February of each year.

[923]
LARRY MATFAY SCHOLARSHIP

Koniag Incorporated
Attn: Koniag Education Foundation
4241 B Street, Suite 303B
Anchorage, AK 99503
(907) 562-9093   Toll Free: (888) 562-9093
Fax: (907) 562-9023
E-mail: scholarships@koniageducation.org
Web: www.koniageducation.org/scholarships

Summary To provide financial assistance to Alaska Natives who are Koniag Incorporated shareholders or descendants and enrolled in undergraduate or graduate study in a field related to Alutiiq culture.

Eligibility This program is open to college juniors, seniors, and graduate students who are Alaska Native shareholders of Koniag Incorporated or descendants of those original enrollees. Applicants must have a GPA of 2.5 or higher and be working full time on a degree in anthropology, history, Alaska Native or American Indian studies, or another discipline that involves research and learning about Alutiiq culture. Along with their application, they must submit an essay of 300 to 600 words in the form of a thank you letter about their background, educational goals, work history, and/or achievements. Financial need is not considered in the selection process.

Financial data The stipend is $1,000 per year. Funds are sent directly to the recipient's school and may be used for tuition, books, supplies, room, board, and transportation.

Duration 1 year; may be renewed.

Additional information Koniag Incorporated is 1 of 13 Alaska Native Regional Corporations created under the Alaska Native Claims Settlement Act of 1971.

Number awarded 1 each year.

Deadline August of each year.

[924]
LATHAM & WATKINS DIVERSITY SCHOLARS PROGRAM

Latham & Watkins LLP
Attn: Diversity Scholars Program Selection Panel
12636 High Bluff Drive, Suite 400
San Diego, CA 92130
(858) 523-5459   Fax: (858) 523-5450
E-mail: heather.sardinha@lw.com
Web: www.lw.com/AboutLatham.aspx?page=Diversity

Summary To provide financial assistance to Native American and other minority law students interested in working for a global law firm.

Eligibility Applicants must be second-year law students at an ABA-accredited law school and plan to practice law in a major city in the United States. Students who have received a similar scholarship from another sponsor are not eligible to apply. Applicants must submit a 500-word personal statement that describes their ability to contribute to the diversity objects of global law firms; the life experiences that have shaped their values and that provide them with a unique perspective, including any obstacles or challenges they have overcome; their academic and/or leadership achievements; and their intent to practice in a global law firm environment.

Financial data The stipend is $10,000.

Duration 1 year; nonrenewable.

Additional information This program was established in 2005. Recipients are not required to work for Latham & Watkins after graduation.

Number awarded 4 each year.

Deadline September of each year.

[925]
LAUNCHING LEADERS MBA SCHOLARSHIP

JPMorgan Chase
Campus Recruiting
Attn: Launching Leaders
277 Park Avenue, Second Floor
New York, NY 10172
(212) 270-6000
E-mail: bronwen.x.baumgardner@jpmorgan.com
Web: www.jpmorgan.com

Summary To provide financial assistance and work experience to Native American and other underrepresented minority students enrolled in the first year of an M.B.A. program.

Eligibility This program is open to Black, Hispanic, and Native American students enrolled in the first year of an M.B.A. program. Applicants must have a demonstrated commitment to working in financial services. Along with their application, they must submit essays on 1) a hypothetical proposal on how to use $50 million from a donor to their school to

benefit all of its students; and 2) the special background and attributes they would contribute to the sponsor's diversity agenda and their motivation for applying to this scholarship program. They must be interested in a summer associate position in the sponsor's investment banking, sales and trading, or research divisions.

Financial data The stipend is $40,000 for the first year of study; a paid summer associate position is also provided.

Duration 1 year; may be renewed 1 additional year if the recipient successfully completes the 10-week summer associate program.

Number awarded Varies each year.

Deadline October of each year.

[926]
LAWRENCE MATSON MEMORIAL ENDOWMENT FUND SCHOLARSHIPS

Cook Inlet Region, Inc.
Attn: The CIRI Foundation
3600 San Jeronimo Drive, Suite 256
Anchorage, AK 99508-2870
(907) 793-3575   Toll Free: (800) 764-3382
Fax: (907) 793-3585   E-mail: tcf@thecirifoundation.org
Web: www.thecirifoundation.org/designated.htm

Summary To provide financial assistance for undergraduate or graduate studies in selected liberal arts to Alaska Natives who are original enrollees to Cook Inlet Region, Inc. (CIRI) and their lineal descendants.

Eligibility This program is open to Alaska Native enrollees to CIRI under the Alaska Native Claims Settlement Act (ANCSA) of 1971 and their lineal descendants. There are no Alaska residency requirements or age limitations. Applicants must be accepted or enrolled full time in a 4-year undergraduate or a graduate degree program in the following liberal arts fields: language, education, social sciences, arts, communications, or law. They must have a GPA of 2.5 or higher. Along with their application, they must submit a 500-word statement on their educational and career goals and how they are contributing, or planning to contribute, to a positive Alaska Native community. Selection is based on that statement, academic achievement, rigor of course work or degree program, student financial contribution, financial need, grade level, previous work performance, community service, and relationship of degree program to career goals.

Financial data The stipend is $10,000 per year, $8,000 per year, or $2,500 per semester, depending on GPA.

Duration 1 semester or 1 year.

Additional information This fund was established in 1989.

Number awarded Varies each year; recently, 3 of these scholarships were awarded: 1 at $10,000 per year, 1 at $8,000 per year, and 1 at $2,500 per semester.

Deadline May of each year for annual scholarships; May or November of each year for semester scholarships.

[927]
LEECH LAKE POSTSECONDARY GRANT PROGRAM

Leech Lake Band of Ojibwe
Attn: Education Division
6530 US Highway 2 N.W.
Cass Lake, MN 56633
(218) 335-8253   Toll Free: (866) 638-7738
Fax: (218) 335-8339
Web: www.llojibwe.com/edu/postsecondary.html

Summary To provide financial assistance to Minnesota Chippewa Tribal members who are interested in undergraduate or graduate education at a school in any state.

Eligibility This program is open to enrolled members of the Leech Lake Band of Ojibwe who have been residents of Minnesota for at least 1 year. Applicants may be high school seniors or graduates, current undergraduates, short-term training students, or full- or part-time graduate students. They must be interested in attending a postsecondary institution in any state. Financial need is considered in the selection process.

Financial data Stipends range up to $3,000 per year, depending on need.

Duration 1 year; may be renewed.

Additional information Applicants for this program must also apply for the Minnesota Indian Scholarship Program, financial aid administered by their institution, and any other aid for which they may be eligible (e.g., work-study, Social Security, veteran's benefits).

Number awarded Varies each year.

Deadline For vocational school students, at least 8 weeks before school starts; for college or university students, June of each year.

[928]
LIFE-TIME SCHOLARSHIPS

Chickasaw Nation
Attn: Department of Education Services
300 Rosedale Road
Ada, OK 74820
(580) 421-7711   Fax: (580) 436-3733
E-mail: education.services@chickasaw.net
Web: www.chickasaweducationservices.com/index_90.htm

Summary To provide funding to members of the Chickasaw Nation who are working on an undergraduate or graduate degree at a school in any state.

Eligibility This program is open to members of the Chickasaw Nation who have completed at least 24 hours of full-time college credit for an undergraduate, graduate, or doctoral degree at an accredited college or university in any state. Applicants must have a GPA of 3.0 or higher. Along with their application, they must submit a 2- to 3-page essay on their past accomplishments, future goals, tribal involvement, and community involvement. Finalists are interviewed.

Financial data The maximum stipend is $15,000 per semester for fall and spring semesters or $5,000 per term for summer school. Recipients must agree to provide service to the Chickasaw Nation of 1 year for each 2 years of support received. The Chickasaw Nation is not obliged to provide employment to a scholarship recipient; if it declines to do so, the service requirement is waived.

Duration 1 year; may be renewed provided the recipient maintains a GPA of 3.0 or higher.

Number awarded 5 each year.

Deadline June of each year.

[929]
LIKO A'E SCHOLARSHIPS

Liko A'e Native Hawaiian Scholarship Program
c/o UH Maui College
310 Ka'ahumanu Avenue
Kahului, HI 96732-1617
(808) 984-3553   Fax: (808) 984-3562
E-mail: maliad@hawaii.edu
Web: www.likoae.org/scholarship_info.asp

Summary To provide financial assistance to Native Hawaiian students who are interested in working on an undergraduate or graduate degree at a college in Hawaii or on the mainland.

Eligibility This program is open to U.S. citizens who are descendants of the aboriginal inhabitants of the Hawaiian Islands prior to 1778. Applicants must be enrolled or accepted as full- or part-time students in an accredited 2- or 4-year degree-granting institution of higher education in Hawaii or on the mainland. Undergraduates must have a GPA of 2.0 or higher and graduate students must have a GPA of 3.0 or higher. Selection is based on merit (as judged by GPA and responses to essay questions) and financial need.

Financial data A stipend is awarded (amount not specified). Child care assistance is also provided.

Duration 1 year.

Additional information This program was established in 2003 by a grant from the U.S. Department of Education and is administered by UH Maui College.

Number awarded Varies each year.

Deadline Deadlines are in April, July, October, or January.

[930]
LILLE HOPE MCGARVEY SCHOLARSHIP AWARD

The Aleut Corporation
Attn: Aleut Foundation
703 West Tudor Road, Suite 102
Anchorage, AK 99503-6650
(907) 646-1929   Toll Free: (800) 232-4882
Fax: (907) 646-1949   E-mail: taf@thealeutfoundation.org
Web: www.thealeutfoundation.org/ScholarshipGuide.aspx

Summary To provide financial assistance to Native Alaskans who are shareholders of The Aleut Corporation or their descendants and working on a degree in the medical field at a school in any state.

Eligibility This program is open to Native Alaskans who are original enrollees or descendants of original enrollees of The Aleut Corporation (TAC). Applicants must have completed at least 1 year of a bachelor's, 2- or 4-year vocational, or master's degree in a medical field at a school in any state. They must be enrolled full time and have a GPA of 3.0 or higher. Along with their application, they must include a letter of intent, up to 500 words in length, that describes their educational goals and objectives and their expected graduation date.

Financial data A stipend is awarded (amount not specified).

Duration 1 year.

Additional information The Aleut Corporation is 1 of 13 Alaska Native Regional Corporations created under the Alaska Native Claims Settlement Act of 1971.

Number awarded 1 each year.

Deadline June of each year.

[931]
LILLIAN FOWLER MEMORIAL SCHOLARSHIP

Chickasaw Foundation
110 West 12th Street
P.O. Box 1726
Ada, OK 74821-1726
(580) 421-9030   Fax: (580) 421-9031
E-mail: ChickasawFoundation@chickasaw.net
Web: www.chickasawfoundation.org/index_20.htm

Summary To provide financial assistance to members of the Chickasaw Nation who are working on an undergraduate or graduate degree in health care or social work.

Eligibility This program is open to Chickasaw students who are currently working full time on an undergraduate or graduate degree in social work or a health care-related field. Applicants must have a GPA of 3.0 or higher. Along with their application, they must submit high school or college transcripts, 2 letters of recommendation, a copy of their Chickasaw Nation citizenship card, and a 1-page essay on their long-term goals and plans for achieving them. Financial need is not considered in the selection process.

Financial data The stipend is $1,000.

Duration 1 year.

Number awarded 1 each year.

Deadline August of each year.

[932]
LIONEL C. BARROW MINORITY DOCTORAL STUDENT SCHOLARSHIP

Association for Education in Journalism and Mass
   Communication
Attn: Communication Theory and Methodology Division
234 Outlet Pointe Boulevard, Suite A
Columbia, SC 29210-5667
(803) 798-0271   Fax: (803) 772-3509
E-mail: aejmc@aejmc.org
Web: aejmcctm.blogspot.com

Summary To provide financial assistance to Native Americans and other minorities who are interested in working on a doctorate in mass communication.

Eligibility This program is open to minority students enrolled in a Ph.D. program in journalism and/or mass communication. Applicants must submit 2 letters of recommendation, a resume, and a brief letter outlining their research interests and career plans. Membership in the association is not required, but applicants must be U.S. citizens or permanent residents. Selection is based on the likelihood that the applicant's work will contribute to communication theory and/or methodology.

Financial data The stipend is $1,400.

Duration 1 year.

Additional information This program began in 1972.

Number awarded 1 each year.

Deadline May of each year.

[933]
LITTLE RIVER BAND OF OTTAWA INDIANS HIGHER EDUCATION SCHOLARSHIP

Little River Band of Ottawa Indians
Attn: Education Department
375 River Street
Manistee, MI 49660
(231) 723-8288   Toll Free: (888) 723-8288
Fax: (231) 398-2961   E-mail: vparsons@lrboi.com
Web: www.lrboi-nsn.gov

Summary To provide financial assistance to members of the Little River Band of Ottawa Indians who are interested in attending college or graduate school.

Eligibility This program is open to tribal citizens of the Little River Band of Ottawa Indians who are attending or planning to attend an accredited college or university. Applicants must be interested in working on an associate, bachelor's, master's, or Ph.D. degree. They must have applied for all other available financial aid and still show unmet need. In the selection process, priority is given first to residents of Michigan, second to students attending schools in Michigan, and third to students attending schools in other states.

Financial data The stipend is $3,500 per semester ($7,000 per year). Recipients are also eligible to apply for book stipends of $200 to $500 (depending on the number of credits in which they are enrolled). Funds are paid to the recipient's institution.

Duration 1 year; may be renewed, provided the recipient maintains a GPA of 2.0 or higher.

Number awarded Varies each year.

Deadline Deadline not specified.

[934]
LLOYD M. JOHNSON, JR. SCHOLARSHIP PROGRAM

United Negro College Fund
Attn: Scholarships and Grants Department
8260 Willow Oaks Corporate Drive
P.O. Box 10444
Fairfax, VA 22031-8044
(703) 205-3466   Toll Free: (800) 331-2244
Fax: (703) 205-3574
Web: www.uncf.org

Summary To provide financial assistance to Native American and other law students who will contribute to diversity in the legal profession.

Eligibility Applicants must be U.S. citizens, have a strong academic record (at least a 3.2 GPA), have been accepted to an ABA-accredited law school, be able to demonstrate community service and leadership qualities, have an interest in diversity, be financially disadvantaged, plan to study on a full-time basis, and have an interest in corporate law, including working in a corporate law department and/or law firm. Applicants must submit a current transcript, a resume, 2 letters of recommendation, a personal statement, and a diversity essay (1 page). All students are eligible, but the sponsor expects that most recipients will be students of color.

Financial data The stipend is $10,000 per year.

Duration 1 year. Full scholarships may be renewed for up to 2 additional years, provided the recipient maintains a GPA of 3.2 or higher. Other scholarships are for 1 year only.

Additional information The Minority Corporate Counsel Association first began this program in 2005 and now cosponsors it with the United Negro College Fund. Mentoring and internship experiences are also offered to the winners.

Number awarded Varies each year; recently, 17 of these scholarships were awarded.

Deadline May of each year.

[935]
LTK SCHOLARSHIP

Conference of Minority Transportation Officials
Attn: National Scholarship Program
818 18th Street, N.W., Suite 850
Washington, DC 20006
(202) 530-0551   Fax: (202) 530-0617
Web: www.comto.org/news-youth.php

Summary To provide financial assistance to Native American and other minority upper-division and graduate students in engineering or another field related to transportation.

Eligibility This program is open to full-time minority juniors, seniors, and graduate students in engineering of other technical transportation-related disciplines. Applicants must have a GPA of 3.0 or higher. Along with their application, they must submit a cover letter with a 500-word statement of career goals. Financial need is not considered in the selection process. U.S. citizenship is required.

Financial data The stipend is $6,000. Funds are paid directly to the recipient's college or university.

Duration 1 year.

Additional information The Conference of Minority Transportation Officials (COMTO) was established in 1971 to promote, strengthen, and expand the roles of minorities in all aspects of transportation. This program is sponsored by LTK Engineering Services. Recipients are required to become members of COMTO if they are not already members and attend the COMTO National Scholarship Luncheon.

Number awarded 1 or more each year.

Deadline April of each year.

[936]
MAE LASSLEY/OSAGE SCHOLARSHIPS

Osage Scholarship Fund
c/o Roman Catholic Diocese of Tulsa
P.O. Box 690240
Tulsa, OK 74169-0240
(918) 294-1904   Fax: (918) 294-0920
E-mail: sarah.jameson@dioceseoftulsa.org
Web: www.osagetribe.com

Summary To provide financial assistance to Osage Indians who are Roman Catholics attending college or graduate school.

Eligibility This program is open to Roman Catholics who are attending or planning to attend a college or university as a full-time undergraduate or graduate student. Applicants must be Osage Indians on the rolls in Pawhuska, Oklahoma and have a copy of their Certificate of Indian Blood (CIB) or Osage tribal membership card. Selection is based on academic ability and financial need.

Financial data The stipend is $1,000 per year.

Duration 1 year; may be renewed if the recipient maintains full-time enrollment and a GPA of 2.5 or higher as an undergraduate or 3.0 or higher as a graduate student.

Number awarded Normally, 10 each year: 2 for students attending St. Gregory's University in Shawnee, Oklahoma as freshmen and 8 for any college or university.

Deadline April of each year.

[937]
MAGNEL LARSEN DRABEK SCHOLARSHIP

Koniag Incorporated
Attn: Koniag Education Foundation
4241 B Street, Suite 303B
Anchorage, AK 99503
(907) 562-9093   Toll Free: (888) 562-9093
Fax: (907) 562-9023
E-mail: scholarships@koniageducation.org
Web: www.koniageducation.org/scholarships

Summary To provide financial assistance to Alaska Natives who are Koniag Incorporated shareholders or descendants and working on an undergraduate or graduate degree in education, arts, or cultural studies.

Eligibility This program is open to undergraduate and graduate students who are Alaska Native shareholders of Koniag Incorporated or descendants of those original enrollees. Applicants must have a GPA of 2.0 or higher and be working full time on a degree in education, arts, or cultural studies. Along with their application, they must submit an essay of 300 to 600 words in the form of a thank you letter about their background, educational goals, work history, and/or achievements. Financial need is not considered in the selection process.

Financial data The stipend is $2,000 per year. Funds are sent directly to the recipient's school and may be used for tuition, books, supplies, room, board, and transportation.

Duration 1 year; may be renewed.

Additional information Koniag Incorporated is 1 of 13 Alaska Native Regional Corporations created under the Alaska Native Claims Settlement Act of 1971.

Number awarded 1 each year.

Deadline August of each year.

[938]
MAKIA AND ANN MALO SCHOLARSHIP

Hawai'i Community Foundation
Attn: Scholarship Department
827 Fort Street Mall
Honolulu, HI 96813
(808) 537-6333   Toll Free: (888) 731-3863
Fax: (808) 521-6286
E-mail: scholarships@hcf-hawaii.org
Web: www.hawaiicommunityfoundation.org/scholarships

Summary To provide financial assistance to residents of Hawaii, especially Native Hawaiians, who are working on a degree in law at a school in the state.

Eligibility This program is open to Hawaii residents who are entering the second or third year at a law school in the state. Preference is given to Native Hawaiians who demonstrate a desire to contribute to the Hawaiian community after earning their law degree. Applicants must be able to demonstrate academic achievement (GPA of 2.7 or higher), good moral character, and financial need. Along with their application, they must submit a short statement indicating their reasons for attending college, their planned course of study, their career goals, and what community service means to them). They must also submit a brief essay about their Hawaiian identity and plans to contribute to the community.

Financial data The amounts of the awards depend on the availability of funds and the need of the recipient. Recently, the average value of all scholarships awarded by the foundation was $2,041.

Duration 1 year.

Additional information This program began in 2001.

Number awarded 1 or more each year.

Deadline February of each year.

[939]
MARATHON OIL CORPORATION COLLEGE SCHOLARSHIP PROGRAM OF THE HISPANIC SCHOLARSHIP FUND

Hispanic Scholarship Fund
Attn: Selection Committee
55 Second Street, Suite 1500
San Francisco, CA 94105
(415) 808-2365   Toll Free: (877) HSF-INFO
Fax: (415) 808-2302   E-mail: scholar1@hsf.net
Web: www.hsf.net/Scholarships.aspx?id=464

Summary To provide financial assistance to Native Americans and other minority upper-division and graduate students working on a degree in a field related to the oil and gas industry.

Eligibility This program is open to U.S. citizens and permanent residents (must have a permanent resident card or a passport stamped I-551) who are of Hispanic American, African American, Asian Pacific Islander American, or American Indian/Alaskan Native heritage. Applicants must be currently enrolled full time at an accredited 4-year college or university in the United States, Puerto Rico, Guam, or the U.S. Virgin Islands with a GPA of 3.0 or higher. They must be 1) sophomores majoring in accounting, chemical engineering, civil engineering, computer engineering, computer science, electrical engineering, energy management or petroleum land management, environmental engineering, environmental health and safety, finance, geology, geophysics, geotechnical engineering, global procurement or supply chain management, information technology/management information systems, marketing, mechanical engineering, petroleum engineering, or transportation and logistics,; or 2) seniors planning to work on a master's degree in geology or geophysics. Selection is based on academic achievement, personal strengths, interest and commitment to a career in the oil and gas industry, leadership, and financial need.

Financial data The stipend is $15,000 per year.

Duration 2 years (the junior and senior undergraduate years or the first 2 years of a master's degree program).

Additional information This program is jointly sponsored by Marathon Oil Corporation and the Hispanic Scholarship Fund (HSF). Recipients may be offered a paid 8- to 10-week summer internship at various Marathon Oil Corporation locations.

Number awarded 1 or more each year.

Deadline November of each year.

[940]
MARK T. BANNER SCHOLARSHIP FOR LAW STUDENTS

Richard Linn American Inn of Court
c/o Cynthia M. Ho, Programs Chair
Loyola University School of Law
25 East Pearson Street, Room 1324
Chicago, IL 60611
(312) 915-7148
Web: www.linninn.org/marktbanner.htm

Summary To provide financial assistance to Native Americans and other law students who are members of a group historically underrepresented in intellectual property law.

Eligibility This program is open to students at ABA-accredited law schools in the United States who are members of groups historically underrepresented (by race, sex, ethnicity, sexual orientation, or disability) in intellectual property law. Applicants must submit a 1-page statement on how they have focused on ethics, civility, and professionalism and how diversity has impacted them; transcripts; a writing sample; and contact information for 3 references. Selection is based on academic merit, written and oral communication skills (determined in part through a telephone interview), leadership qualities, community involvement, and commitment to the pursuit of a career in intellectual property law.

Financial data The stipend is $5,000.

Duration 1 year.

Number awarded 1 each year.

Deadline November of each year.

[941]
MARTHA MILLER TRIBUTARY SCHOLARSHIP

Sault Tribe of Chippewa Indians
Attn: Higher Education Program-Memorial/Tributary
  Scholarships
523 Ashmun Street
Sault Ste. Marie, MI 49783
(906) 635-4944   Toll Free: (800) 793-0660
Fax: (906) 635-7785   E-mail: amatson@saulttribe.net
Web: www.saulttribe.com

Summary To provide financial assistance to members of the Sault Tribe of Chippewa Indians who are attending college in any state and working on an undergraduate or graduate degree in human services or social work.

Eligibility This program is open to enrolled members of the Sault Tribe who are enrolled full time at a 2- or 4-year college or university in any state. Applicants must be working on an undergraduate or graduate degree in human services or social work. Along with their application, they must submit an essay of 300 to 500 words on how this scholarship will help them realize their goals.

Financial data The stipend is $1,000.

Duration 1 year.

Number awarded 1 each year.

Deadline May of each year.

[942]
MARY BALL CARRERA SCHOLARSHIP

National Medical Fellowships, Inc.
Attn: Scholarship Program
347 Fifth Avenue, Suite 510
New York, NY 10016
(212) 483-8880   Toll Free: (877) NMF-1DOC
Fax: (212) 483-8897   E-mail: info@nmfonline.org
Web: www.nmfonline.org

Summary To provide financial assistance to Native American women who are attending medical school.

Eligibility This program is open to Native American women who are enrolled in the first or second year of an accredited medical school in the United States. Applicants must be able to demonstrate academic achievement, leadership, and community service, but selection is based primarily on financial need.

Financial data The stipend is $2,500.

Duration 1 year; nonrenewable.

Number awarded 1 or more each year.

Deadline August of each year.

[943]
MCANDREWS DIVERSITY IN PATENT LAW FELLOWSHIP

McAndrews, Held & Malloy, Ltd.
Attn: Diversity Fellowship
500 West Madison Street, 34th Floor
Chicago, IL 60661
(312) 775-8000   Fax: (312) 775-8100
E-mail: info@mcandrews-ip.com
Web: www.mcandrews-ip.com/diversity_fellowship.html

Summary To provide financial assistance to Native American and other law students who come from a diverse background and are interested in patent law.

Eligibility This program is open to first-year students at ABA-accredited law schools who come from a diverse background. Applicants must have a degree in science or engineering and be planning to practice patent law in the Chicago area. Along with their application, they must submit a 500-word personal statement on why they wish to prepare for a career in patent law, why they are interested in the sponsoring firm as a place to work, and how their background and/or life experiences would improved diversity in the field of intellectual property law. Selection is based on that statement, a resume (including their science or engineering educational credentials), a legal writing sample, undergraduate transcript, and at least 1 letter of recommendation.

Financial data The stipend is $5,000.

Duration 1 year (the second year of law school).

Additional information This fellowship was first awarded in 2008. It includes a paid clerkship position at McAndrews, Held & Malloy during the summer after the first year of law school and possibly another clerkship during the summer after the second year.

Number awarded 1 each year.

Deadline January of each year.

[944]
MCDERMOTT MINORITY SCHOLARSHIP

McDermott Will & Emery
Attn: Recruiting Coordinator
227 West Monroe Street
Chicago, IL 60606
(312) 984-6470   Fax: (312) 984-7700
E-mail: mcdermottscholarship@mwe.com
Web: www.mwe.com

Summary To provide financial assistance and work experience to Native American and other minority law students.

Eligibility This program is open to second-year minority (African American, Asian, Hispanic, Middle Eastern, Native American) law students at ABA-accredited U.S. law schools. Applicants must be able to demonstrate leadership, community involvement, and a commitment to improving diversity in the legal community. They must be interested in participating in the sponsor's summer program and be able to meet its hiring criteria. Along with their application, they must submit an essay of 1 to 2 pages that provides ideas they have on how the number of minority students in law schools can be increased and how they have improved and intend to help improve diversity in the legal profession throughout their law school and legal career.

Financial data The stipend is $15,000.

Duration 1 year.

Additional information Recipients also participate in a summer program at the sponsor's offices in Boston, Chicago, Houston, Los Angeles, Miami, New York, Orange County, San Diego, Silicon Valley, or Washington, D.C.

Number awarded 2 each year.

Deadline October of each year.

[945]
MCGHEE-TULLIS TUITION ASSISTANCE PROGRAM

Poarch Band of Creek Indians
Attn: Tuition Program Coordinator
5811 Jack Springs Road
Atmore, AL 36502
(251) 368-9136, ext. 2241   Fax: (251) 368-4502
E-mail: sfisher@pci-nsn.gov
Web: www.poarchcreekindians.org

Summary To provide funding to members of the Poarch Band of Creek Indians for payment of tuition or repayment of educational loans.

Eligibility This program is open to enrolled members of the Poarch Band of Creek Indians who are enrolled or planning to enroll in 1) a certificate program leading to an increased chance of employment and/or increase in salary; 2) a vocational/technical school; or 3) a college or university program leading to an undergraduate, graduate, or professional degree. Applicants must be seeking funding 1) to pay the cost of tuition, books, and mandatory fees; or 2) to repay their educational loans incurred prior to their current enrollment.

Financial data Undergraduates may receive up to $10,000 per year for payment of tuition and fees or repayment of prior educational loans. Graduate and professional students may receive up to $12,000 for the same purposes. All tribal members are entitled to a lifetime tuition assistance allotment of $30,000. When that allotment is exhausted, they may request an additional sum of $10,000, which may be granted at the discretion of the tribal authorities. Tribal members may also apply for a supplemental grant of $500 per semester for purchase of specialized tools required for their program and a 1-time grant of $1,000 for the purchase of a laptop or desktop computer.

Duration Available funds are disbursed as requested, until exhaustion of the $30,000 allotment and the supplement of $10,000 (if approved by tribal authorities).

Number awarded Varies each year.

Deadline Applications may be submitted at any time.

[946]
MENOMINEE INDIAN TRIBAL SCHOLARSHIPS

Menominee Indian Tribe of Wisconsin
Attn: Tribal Education Office
P.O. Box 910
Keshena, WI 54135
(715) 799-5110   Fax: (715) 799-5102
E-mail: vnuske@mitw.org
Web: menominee-nsn.gov

Summary To provide financial assistance for college or graduate school in any state to Menominee Indians.

Eligibility This program is open to enrolled members of the Menominee Indian Tribe of Wisconsin who are 1) graduating high school seniors; 2) undergraduates at 4-year colleges and universities; 3) technical college students; or 4) graduate students. Applicants must submit an essay of 1 to 2 pages on how their education will benefit them, including their community service and extracurricular activities. The essay should not discuss financial need, because the selection committee assumes that all students have financial need. Selection is based on the essay (30 points), a letter of support (5 points), and GPA (15 points if 3.5 or higher, 10 points if 3.00 to 3.49, or 5 points if 2.0 to 2.99).

Financial data The stipend is $500 per semester ($1,000 per year). Funds are sent directly to the recipient's school.

Duration Up to 10 semesters.

Number awarded 4 each year: 1 to each category of student.

Deadline March of each year.

[947]
MENTAL HEALTH DISSERTATION RESEARCH GRANT TO INCREASE DIVERSITY

National Institute of Mental Health
Attn: Division of Extramural Activities
6001 Executive Boulevard, Room 6138
Bethesda, MD 20892-9609
(301) 443-3534   Fax: (301) 443-4720
TDD: (301) 451-0088   E-mail: armstrda@mail.nih.gov
Web: www.nimh.nih.gov

Summary To provide research funding to Native American doctoral candidates and those from other underrepresented groups who are planning to prepare for a research career in any area relevant to mental health and/or mental disorders.

Eligibility This program is open to doctoral candidates conducting dissertation research in a field related to mental health and/or mental disorders at a university, college, or professional school with an accredited doctoral degree granting program. Applicants must be 1) members of an ethnic or racial group that has been determined by their institution to be underrepresented in biomedical or behavioral research; 2) individuals with disabilities; or 3) individuals from socially, culturally, economically, or educationally disadvantaged backgrounds that have inhibited their ability to prepare for a career in health-related research. They must be U.S. citizens, nationals, or permanent residents.

Financial data The stipend is $21,180. An additional grant up to $15,000 is provided for additional research expenses, fringe benefits (including health insurance), travel to scientific meetings, and research costs of the dissertation. Facilities and administrative costs are limited to 8% of modified total direct costs.

Duration Up to 2 years; nonrenewable.

Number awarded Varies each year.

Deadline April, August, or December of each year.

[948]
MESBEC PROGRAM

Catching the Dream
8200 Mountain Road, N.E., Suite 203
Albuquerque, NM 87110-7835
(505) 262-2351   Fax: (505) 262-0534
E-mail: NScholarsh@aol.com
Web: www.catchingthedream.org/Scholarship.htm

Summary To provide financial assistance to American Indian students who are interested in working on an undergraduate or graduate degree in selected fields.

Eligibility This program is open to American Indians who can provide proof that they have at least one-quarter Indian blood and are a member of a U.S. tribe that is federally-recognized, state-recognized, or terminated. Applicants must be enrolled or planning to enroll full time and major in 1 of the following fields: mathematics, engineering, science (including medicine), business administration, education, or computer science. They may be entering freshmen, undergraduate students, graduate students, or Ph.D. candidates. Along with their application, they must submit documentation of financial need, 3 letters of recommendation, copies of applications and responses for all other sources of funding for which they are eligible, official transcripts, standardized test scores (ACT, SAT, GRE, MCAT, LSAT, etc.), and an essay explaining their goals in life, college plans, and career plans (especially how those plans include working with and benefiting Indians). Selection is based on merit and potential for improving the lives of Indian people.

Financial data Stipends range from $500 to $5,000 per year.

Duration 1 year; may be renewed.

Additional information MESBEC is an acronym that stands for the priority areas of this program: mathematics, engineering, science, business, education, and computers. The sponsor was formerly known as the Native American Scholarship Fund.

Number awarded Varies; generally, 30 to 35 each year.

Deadline April of each year for fall term; September of each year for spring and winter terms; March of each year for summer school.

[949]
METROPOLITAN LIFE FOUNDATION AWARDS PROGRAM FOR ACADEMIC EXCELLENCE IN MEDICINE

National Medical Fellowships, Inc.
Attn: Scholarship Program
347 Fifth Avenue, Suite 510
New York, NY 10016
(212) 483-8880   Toll Free: (877) NMF-1DOC
Fax: (212) 483-8897   E-mail: info@nmfonline.org
Web: www.nmfonline.org

Summary To provide financial assistance to Native American and other underrepresented minority medical students who reside or attend school in designated cities throughout the country.

Eligibility This program is open to African American, mainland Puerto Rican, Mexican American, Native Hawaiian, Alaska Native, Vietnamese, Cambodian, or American Indian medical students in their second through fourth year who are nominated by their dean. Nominees must be enrolled in medical schools located in (or be residents of) designated cities that change annually. Selection is based on demonstrated financial need, outstanding academic achievement, leadership, and potential for distinguished contributions to medicine.

Financial data The stipend is $4,000.

Duration 1 year; nonrenewable.

Additional information Funding for this program, established in 1987, is provided by the Metropolitan Life Foundation of New York, New York.

Number awarded 17 each year.

Deadline March of each year.

[950]
MIAMI NATION OF OKLAHOMA CRANE AWARD

Miami Nation
Attn: Education Committee
202 South Eight Tribes Trail
P.O. Box 1326
Miami, OK 74355
(918) 542-1445   Fax: (918) 542-7260
E-mail: edu@miamination.com
Web: www.miamination.com/mto/edu.html

Summary To provide financial assistance for graduate study to enrolled members of the Miami Nation of Oklahoma.

Eligibility This program is open to enrolled members of the Miami Nation of Oklahoma who are working on or planning to work on a master's or doctoral degree. Applicants must submit a college transcript, 3 letters of recommendation, documentation of financial need, and a 1-page essay with the title, "Tell Us About Yourself."

Financial data The stipend is $1,500.

Duration 1 year; nonrenewable.

Number awarded 1 or more each year.

Deadline April of each year.

[951]
MICHIGAN INDIAN TUITION WAIVER PROGRAM

Michigan Department of Civil Rights
Attn: Michigan Indian Tuition Waiver
110 West Michigan Avenue, Suite 800
Lansing, MI 48933
(517) 241-7748   Fax: (517) 335-3882
TDD: (517) 335-3881
Web: www.michigan.gov

Summary To exempt members of Indian tribes from tuition at Michigan postsecondary institutions.

Eligibility This program is open to Michigan residents who have lived in the state for at least 12 months and can certify at least one-quarter North American Indian blood from a federally-recognized or state historic tribe. Applicants must be attending a public college, university, or community college in Michigan. The program includes full- and part-time study, academic-year and summer school, and undergraduate and graduate work.

Financial data All qualified applicants are entitled to a waiver of tuition at Michigan public institutions.

Duration Indian students are entitled to the waiver as long as they attend college in Michigan.

Additional information This program was established in 1976 as the result of an agreement between the state of Michigan and the federal government under which the state agreed to provide free tuition to North American Indians in exchange for the Mt. Pleasant Indian School, which the state acquired as a training facility for the developmentally disabled.

Number awarded Varies each year.

Deadline Deadline not specified.

[952]
MICKEY LELAND ENERGY FELLOWSHIPS

Department of Energy
Attn: Office of Fossil Energy
19901 Germantown Road, FE-6
Germantown, MD 20874
(301) 903-4293   E-mail: MLEF@hq.doe.gov
Web: fossil.energy.gov

Summary To provide summer work experience at fossil energy sites of the Department of Energy (DOE) to Native Americans, other underrepresented minorities, and female students.

Eligibility This program is open to U.S. citizens currently enrolled full time at an accredited college or university. Applicants must be undergraduate, graduate, or postdoctoral students in mathematics, physical sciences, technology, or engineering and have a GPA of 3.0 or higher. They must be interested in a summer work experience at a DOE fossil energy research facility. Along with their application, they must submit a 100-word statement on why they want to participate in this program. A goal of the program is to recruit women and underrepresented minorities into careers related to fossil energy.

Financial data Weekly stipends are $500 for undergraduates, $650 for master's degree students, or $750 for doctoral and postdoctoral students. Travel costs for a round trip to and from the site and for a trip to a designated place for technical presentations are also paid.

Duration 10 weeks during the summer.

Additional information This program began as 3 separate activities: the Historically Black Colleges and Universities Internship Program, established in 1995; the Hispanic Internship Program, established in 1998; and the Tribal Colleges and Universities Internship Program, established in 2000. Those 3 programs were merged into the Fossil Energy Minority Education Initiative, renamed the Mickey Leland Energy Fellowship Program in 2000. Sites to which interns may be assigned include the Albany Research Center (Albany, Oregon), the National Energy Technology Laboratory (Morgantown, West Virginia and Pittsburgh, Pennsylvania), Pacific Northwest National Laboratory (Richland, Washington), Rocky Mountain Oilfield Testing Center (Casper, Wyoming), Strategic Petroleum Reserve Project Management Office (New Orleans, Louisiana), or U.S. Department of Energy Headquarters (Washington, D.C.).

Number awarded Varies each year; recently, 30 students participated in this program.

Deadline January of each year.

[953]
MILBANK DIVERSITY SCHOLARS PROGRAM

Milbank, Tweed, Hadley & McCloy LLP
Attn: Manager of Law School Recruiting
One Chase Manhattan Plaza
New York, NY 10005
(212) 530-5757　　　　　　　　Fax: (212) 822-5757
E-mail: alevitt@milbank.com
Web: www.milbank.com/careers

Summary To provide financial assistance and work experience to Native Americans and other law students who are members of groups underrepresented at large law firms.

Eligibility This program is open to students who have completed their first year of a full-time J.D. program at an ABA-accredited law school. Joint degree candidates must have successfully completed 2 years of a J.D. program. Applications are particularly encouraged from members of groups traditionally underrepresented at large law firms. Applicants must submit a 500-word essay on 1) the challenges they have faced in pursuit of a legal career that have helped them understand the value of diversity and inclusion in the legal profession; and 2) the personal contributions they would make to furthering the diversity objectives of the sponsoring law firm. Selection is based on academic achievement, demonstrated leadership ability, writing and interpersonal skills, and interest in the firm's practice.

Financial data The stipend is $25,000. A paid associate position during the summer after the second year of law school is also provided. If the student is offered and accepts a permanent position with the firm after graduation, an additional $25,000 scholarship stipend is also awarded.

Duration 1 year (the third year of law school).

Additional information Scholars may be offered a permanent position with the firm, but there is no guarantee of such an offer.

Number awarded At least 2 each year.

Deadline August of each year.

[954]
MILLE LACS BAND ACADEMIC ACHIEVEMENT AWARDS

Mille Lacs Band of Ojibwe
Attn: Higher Education Office
43408 Oodena Avenue
Onamia, MN 56359-2236
(320) 495-3702　　　　　　　Toll Free: (866) 916-5282
Fax: (320) 495-3707
E-mail: mlb.inquiries@millelacsband.com
Web: www.millelacsband.org/Page_Education.aspx

Summary To recognize and reward members of the Mille Lacs Band of Ojibwe after they complete a degree.

Eligibility This program is open to enrolled members of the band, their non-enrolled biological children, and legally adopted children of enrolled band members. Applicants must have just completed their GED certificate or high school diploma, a vocational/technical diploma or certificate (for a program 9 months or more in length), an associate degree, a bachelor's degree, or a graduate (master's or doctoral) degree.

Financial data Awards are $500 for completion of a GED certificate or high school diploma, $1,000 for a vocational/technical diploma or certificate, $1,250 for an associate degree, $1,500 for a bachelor's degree, or $2,000 for a graduate degree.

Duration Awards are presented whenever a student completes a diploma, certificate, or degree.

Number awarded Varies each year.

Deadline Applications may be submitted as soon as an eligible student has completed an educational degree.

[955]
MILLE LACS BAND POST GRADUATE DEGREE PROGRAM

Mille Lacs Band of Ojibwe
Attn: Higher Education Office
43408 Oodena Avenue
Onamia, MN 56359-2236
(320) 495-3702　　　　　　　Toll Free: (866) 916-5282
Fax: (320) 495-3707
E-mail: mlb.inquiries@millelacsband.com
Web: www.millelacsband.org/Page_Education.aspx

Summary To provide financial assistance to members of the Mille Lacs Band of Ojibwe interested in working on a graduate degree in any field.

Eligibility This program is open to enrolled members of the band, their non-enrolled biological children, and legally adopted children of enrolled band members. Applicants must have received a baccalaureate degree from an accredited college or university and have been accepted at an accredited graduate degree program. They must be able to demonstrate financial need.

Financial data This program provides a stipend of up to $12,000 per year and an allowance of up to $375 per semester for books and supplies.

Duration 1 year; may be renewed, provided the recipient maintains a GPA of 2.75 or higher.

Number awarded Varies each year.

Deadline Applications may be submitted at any time, but they must be received at least 1 month prior to the start of the graduate program.

[956]
MILLER JOHNSON WEST MICHIGAN DIVERSITY LAW SCHOOL SCHOLARSHIP

Grand Rapids Community Foundation
Attn: Education Program Officer
185 Oakes Street S.W.
Grand Rapids, MI 49503-4008
(616) 454-1751, ext. 103   Fax: (616) 454-6455
E-mail: rbishop@grfoundation.org
Web: www.grfoundation.org/scholarships

Summary To provide financial assistance to Native Americans and other minorities from Michigan who are attending law school in any state.

Eligibility This program is open to U.S. citizens and permanent residents who are students of color and residents of Michigan. Preference is given to residents of western Michigan. Applicants must be attending an accredited law school in any state. They must have a GPA of 3.0 or higher and be able to demonstrate financial need.

Financial data The stipend is $5,000. Funds are paid directly to the recipient's institution.

Duration 1 year.

Number awarded 1 each year.

Deadline March of each year.

[957]
MILLER NASH LAW STUDENT DIVERSITY FELLOWSHIP PROGRAM

Miller Nash LLP
Attn: Director of Recruiting and Professional Development
3400 U.S. Bancorp Tower
111 S.W. Fifth Avenue
Portland, OR 97204-3699
(503) 224-5858   Fax: (503) 224-0155
E-mail: michelle.baird-johnson@millernash.com
Web: www.millernash.com/fellowship.aspx

Summary To provide financial assistance and work experience to Native American and other law students who will contribute to diversity and are interested in living and working in the Pacific Northwest following graduation from law school.

Eligibility This program is open to first- and second-year students at ABA-accredited law schools in any state. Applicants must be able to demonstrate academic excellence, interpersonal skills, leadership qualities, contributions to diversity, and meaningful contributions to the community. They must intend to work, live, and practice law in the Pacific Northwest. Along with their application, they must submit a personal statement of 2 to 4 pages that includes a description of organizations or projects in which they currently participate or have participated that address diversity issues or support diversity in their legal, business, or local communities.

Financial data Fellows receive a paid summer clerk position and a stipend of $7,500 for law school.

Duration 1 year (including 12 weeks for the summer clerk position); nonrenewable.

Additional information Summer clerk positions may be offered (depending on availability) at the sponsoring law firm's offices in Portland (Oregon), Seattle (Washington), or Vancouver (Washington).

Number awarded Up to 2 each year.

Deadline September of each year for second-year students; January of each year for first-year students.

[958]
MINNESOTA AMERICAN INDIAN BAR ASSOCIATION LAW STUDENT SCHOLARSHIPS

Minnesota American Indian Bar Association
Attn: MAIBA Scholarship Committee
P.O. Box 3712
Minneapolis, MN 55403
(612) 596-1805   Fax: (612) 348-2025
E-mail: jodi.drews@co.hennepin.mn.us
Web: www.maiba.org/scholarship.html

Summary To provide financial assistance to Native American students from any state who are enrolled at law schools in Minnesota.

Eligibility This program is open to students who are enrolled members of an Indian tribe or band or recognized by their community of residence or origin as being Indian. Applicants must be a second- or third-year law student at a Minnesota law school, demonstrate that they are currently in academic good standing, demonstrate that they have unmet financial need, submit a written personal statement, and submit at least 1 letter of recommendation.

Financial data The stipend ranges from $500 to $3,000.

Duration 1 year.

Number awarded Varies each year; recently, 3 of these scholarships were awarded.

Deadline October of each year.

[959]
MINNESOTA INDIAN SCHOLARSHIP PROGRAM

Minnesota Office of Higher Education
Attn: Manager of State Financial Aid Programs
1450 Energy Park Drive, Suite 350
St. Paul, MN 55108-5227
(651) 642-0567   Toll Free: (800) 657-3866
Fax: (651) 642-0675   TDD: (800) 627-3529
E-mail: Ginny.Dodds@state.mn.us
Web: www.ohe.state.mn.us

Summary To provide financial assistance to Native Americans in Minnesota who are interested in working on an undergraduate or graduate degree in any field.

Eligibility Applicants must be at least one-fourth degree Indian ancestry; members of a recognized Indian tribe; at least high school graduates (or approved equivalent); accepted by an accredited college, university, or vocational school in Minnesota; and residents of Minnesota for at least 1 year. Undergraduates must be attending college at least three-fourths time; graduate students must be enrolled at least half time.

Financial data The stipend depends on need, to a maximum of $4,000 per year for undergraduates or $6,600 per year for graduate students. Awards are paid directly to the student's school or college.

Duration 1 year; may be renewed up to 4 additional years, provided the recipient maintains a GPA of 2.0 or higher and sends official grade transcripts to the office for review after each quarter or semester.

Number awarded Approximately 700 each year.

Deadline June of each year.

[960]
MINORITY ACCESS INTERNSHIP

Minority Access, Inc.
Attn: Directory of Internship Program
5214 Baltimore Avenue
Hyattsville, MD 20781
(301) 779-7100   Fax: (301) 779-9812
Web: www.minorityaccess.org

Summary To provide work experience to Native American and other minority undergraduate and graduate students interested in internships at participating entities in Washington, D.C. and throughout the United States.

Eligibility This program is open to full-time undergraduate and graduate students who have a GPA of 3.0 or higher. Applicants must be U.S. citizens for most positions. All academic majors are eligible. Interns are selected by participating federal government and other agencies. Most of these are located in Washington, D.C., but placements may be made anywhere in the United States.

Financial data The weekly stipend is $450 for sophomores and juniors, $500 for seniors, or $550 for graduate and professional students. In addition, most internships include paid round-trip travel between home and the internship location.

Duration Spring internships are 5 months, starting in January; summer internships are 3 months, starting in August; fall internships are 4 months, starting in September.

Additional information Minority Access, Inc. is committed to the diversification of institutions, federal agencies, and corporations of all kinds and to improving their recruitment, retention, and enhancement of minorities. The majority of interns are placed in the Washington, D.C. metropolitan area. Both full-time and part-time internships are awarded. Students may receive academic credit for full-time internships. Students are expected to pay all housing costs. They are required to attend a pre-employment session in Washington, D.C., all seminars and workshops hosted by Minority Access, and any mandatory activities sponsored by the host agency.

Number awarded Varies each year.

Deadline February of each year for summer internships; June of each year for fall internships; and November of each year for spring internships.

[961]
MINORITY FACULTY DEVELOPMENT SCHOLARSHIP AWARD IN PHYSICAL THERAPY

American Physical Therapy Association
Attn: Honors and Awards Program
1111 North Fairfax Street
Alexandria, VA 22314-1488
(703) 684-APTA   Toll Free: (800) 999-APTA
Fax: (703) 684-7343   TDD: (703) 683-6748
E-mail: executivedept@apta.org
Web: www.apta.org

Summary To provide financial assistance to Native American and other minority faculty members in physical therapy who are interested in working on a doctoral degree.

Eligibility This program is open to U.S. citizens and permanent residents who are members of the following minority groups: African American or Black, Asian, Native Hawaiian or other Pacific Islander, American Indian or Alaska Native, or Hispanic/Latino. Applicants must be full-time faculty members, teaching in an accredited or developing professional physical therapist education program, who will have completed the equivalent of 2 full semesters of post-professional doctoral course work. They must possess a license to practice physical therapy in a U.S. jurisdiction and be enrolled as a student in an accredited post-professional doctoral program whose content has a demonstrated relationship to physical therapy. Along with their application, they must submit a personal essay on their professional goals, including their plans to contribute to the profession and minority services. Selection is based on 1) commitment to minority affairs and services; 2) commitment to further the physical therapy profession through teaching and research; and 3) scholastic achievement.

Financial data A stipend is awarded (amount not specified).

Duration 1 year.

Additional information This program was established in 1999.

Number awarded 1 or more each year.

Deadline November of each year.

[962]
MINORITY FELLOWSHIPS IN EDUCATION RESEARCH

American Educational Research Association
1430 K Street, N.W., Suite 1200
Washington, DC 20005
(202) 238-3200   Fax: (202) 238-3250
E-mail: fellowships@aera.net
Web: www.aera.net

Summary To provide funding to Native American and other minority doctoral students writing their dissertation on educational research.

Eligibility This program is open to U.S. citizens and permanent residents who have advanced to candidacy and successfully defended their Ph.D./Ed.D. dissertation research proposal. Applicants must plan to work full time on their dissertation in educational research. This program is targeted for members of groups historically underrepresented in higher education (African Americans, American Indians, Alaskan Natives, Asian Americans, Native Hawaiian or Pacific Islanders, and Hispanics or Latinos). Selection is based on scholarly achievements and publications, letters of recommendation, quality and significance of the proposed research, and commitment of the applicant's faculty mentor to the goals of the program.

Financial data The grant is $12,000. Up to $1,000 is provided to pay for travel to the sponsor's annual conference.

Duration 1 year; nonrenewable.

Additional information This program was established in 1991.

Number awarded Up to 3 each year.

Deadline December of each year.

[963]
MINORITY GEOSCIENCE STUDENT SCHOLARSHIPS

American Geological Institute
Attn: Minority Participation Program
4220 King Street
Alexandria, VA 22302-1502
(703) 379-2480, ext. 227   Fax: (703) 379-7563
E-mail: mpp@agiweb.org
Web: www.agiweb.org/mpp/index.html

Summary To provide financial assistance to Native Americans and other underrepresented minority undergraduate and graduate students interested in working on a degree in the geosciences.

Eligibility This program is open to members of ethnic minority groups underrepresented in the geosciences (Blacks, Hispanics, American Indians, Eskimos, Hawaiians, and Samoans). U.S. citizenship is required. Applicants must be full-time students enrolled in an accredited institution working on an undergraduate or graduate degree in the geosciences, including geology, geochemistry, geophysics, hydrology, meteorology, physical oceanography, planetary geology, or earth science education; students in other natural sciences, mathematics, or engineering are not eligible. Selection is based on a 250-word essay on career goals and why the applicant has chosen a geoscience as a major, work experience, recommendations, honors and awards, extracurricular activities, and financial need.

Financial data Stipends range from $500 to $3,000 per year.

Duration 1 academic year; renewable if the recipient maintains satisfactory performance.

Additional information Funding for this program is provided by ExxonMobil Corporation, ConocoPhillips, ChevronTexaco Corporation, Marathon Corporation, and the Seismological Society of America.

Number awarded Varies each year; recently, 18 of these scholarships were awarded.

Deadline March of each year.

[964]
MINORITY MEDICAL STUDENT ELECTIVE IN HIV PSYCHIATRY

American Psychiatric Association
Attn: Office of HIV Psychiatry
1000 Wilson Boulevard, Suite 1825
Arlington, VA 22209-3901
(703) 907-8668   Toll Free: (888) 357-7849
Fax: (703) 907-1089   E-mail: dpennessi@psych.org
Web: www.psych.org/Resources/OMNA/MFP.aspx

Summary To provide an opportunity for Native Americans and other minority medical students to spend an elective residency learning about HIV psychiatry.

Eligibility This program is open to medical students entering their fourth year at an accredited M.D. or D.O. degree-granting institution. Preference is given to minority candidates and those who have primary interests in services related to HIV/AIDS and substance abuse and its relationship to the mental health or the psychological well being of ethnic minorities. Applicants should be interested in a psychiatry, internal medicine, pediatrics, or research career. They must be interested in participating in a program that includes intense training in HIV mental health (including neuropsychiatry), a clinical and/or research experience working with a mentor, and participation in the Committee on AIDS of the American Psychiatric Association (APA). U.S. citizenship is required.

Financial data A stipend is provided (amount not specified).

Duration 1 year.

Additional information The heart of the program is in establishing a mentor relationship at 1 of 5 sites, becoming involved with a cohort of medical students interested in HIV medicine/psychiatry, participating in an interactive didactic/experimental learning program, and developing expertise in areas related to ethnic minority mental health research or psychiatric services. Students selected for the program who are not APA members automatically receive membership.

Number awarded Varies each year.

Deadline March of each year.

[965]
MINORITY MEDICAL STUDENT SUMMER EXTERNSHIP IN ADDICTION PSYCHIATRY

American Psychiatric Association
Attn: Department of Minority and National Affairs
1000 Wilson Boulevard, Suite 1825
Arlington, VA 22209-3901
(703) 907-8653   Toll Free: (888) 35-PSYCH
Fax: (703) 907-7852   E-mail: mking@psych.org
Web: www.psych.org/Resources/OMNA/MFP.aspx

Summary To provide funding to Native Americans and other minority medical students who are interested in working on a research externship during the summer with a mentor who specializes in addiction psychiatry.

Eligibility This program is open to minority medical students who have a specific interest in services related to substance abuse treatment and prevention. Minorities include American Indians, Alaska Natives, Native Hawaiians, Asian Americans, Hispanic/Latinos, and African Americans. Applicants must be interested in working with a mentor who specializes in addiction psychiatry. Work settings provide an emphasis on working clinically with or studying underserved minority populations and issues of co-occurring disorders, substance abuse treatment, and mental health disparity. Most of them are in inner-city or rural settings.

Financial data Externships provide $1,500 for travel expenses to go to the work setting of the mentor and up to another $1,500 for out-of-pocket expenses directly related to the conduct of the externship.

Duration 1 month during the summer.

Additional information Funding for this program is provided by the Substance Abuse and Mental Health Services Administration (SAMHSA).

Number awarded 10 each year.

Deadline February of each year.

[966]
MINORITY VISITING STUDENT AWARDS PROGRAM

Smithsonian Institution
Attn: Office of Fellowships
470 L'Enfant Plaza, Suite 7102
P.O. Box 37012, MRC 902
Washington, DC 20013-7012
(202) 633-7070   Fax: (202) 633-7069
E-mail: siofg@si.edu
Web: www.si.edu/ofg/Applications/MIP/MIPapp.htm

Summary To provide funding to Native American and other minority graduate students interested in conducting research at the Smithsonian Institution.

Eligibility This program is open to members of U.S. minority groups underrepresented in the Smithsonian's scholarly programs. Applicants must be advanced graduate students interested in conducting research in the Institution's disciplines and in the museum field.

Financial data Students receive a grant of $550 per week.

Duration Up to 10 weeks.

Additional information Recipients must carry out independent research projects in association with the Smithsonian's research staff. Eligible fields of study currently include animal behavior, ecology, and environmental science (including an emphasis on the tropics); anthropology (including archaeology); astrophysics and astronomy; earth sciences and paleobiology; evolutionary and systematic biology; history of science and technology; history of art (especially American, contemporary, African, Asian, and 20th-century art); American crafts and decorative arts; social and cultural history of the United States; and folklife. Students are required to be in residence at the Smithsonian for the duration of the fellowship.

Number awarded Varies each year.

Deadline January of each year for summer and fall residency; September of each year for spring residency.

[967]
MIRIAM WEINSTEIN PEACE AND JUSTICE EDUCATION AWARD

Philanthrofund Foundation
Attn: Scholarship Committee
1409 Willow Street, Suite 210
Minneapolis, MN 55403-3251
(612) 870-1806   Toll Free: (800) 435-1402
Fax: (612) 871-6587   E-mail: info@PfundOnline.org
Web: www.pfundonline.org/scholarships.html

Summary To provide financial assistance to Native Americans and other minority students from Minnesota who are associated with gay, lesbian, bisexual, and transgender (GLBT) activities and interested in working on a degree in education.

Eligibility This program is open to residents of Minnesota and students attending a Minnesota educational institution who are members of a religious, racial, or ethnic minority. Applicants must be self-identified as GLBT or from a GLBT family and have demonstrated a commitment to peace and justice issues. They may be attending or planning to attend trade school, technical college, college, or university (as an undergraduate or graduate student). Preference is given to students who have completed at least 2 years of college and are working on a degree in education. Selection is based on the applicant's 1) affirmation of GLBT identity or commitment to GLBT communities; 2) participation and leadership in community and/or GLBT activities; and 3) service as role model, mentor, and/or adviser for the GLBT community.

Financial data The stipend is $3,000. Funds must be used for tuition, books, fees, or dissertation expenses.

Duration 1 year.

Number awarded 1 each year.

Deadline January of each year.

[968]
MITCH SPERRY MEMORIAL LAW SCHOLARSHIP

Chickasaw Foundation
110 West 12th Street
P.O. Box 1726
Ada, OK 74821-1726
(580) 421-9030   Fax: (580) 421-9031
E-mail: ChickasawFoundation@chickasaw.net
Web: www.chickasawfoundation.org/index_20.htm

Summary To provide financial assistance to members of the Chickasaw Nation who are interested in working on an undergraduate or graduate degree in a field related to law.

Eligibility This program is open to Chickasaw students who are currently enrolled at an accredited 4-year college or university as a full-time undergraduate or law student. Applicants must be working on a degree in law, pre-law, legal studies, paralegal, or any major associated with law or a bachelor's degree obtained with the intention of pursuing a law degree. They must have a GPA of 3.2 or higher. Along with their application, they must submit high school or college transcripts, 2 letters of recommendation, a copy of their Chickasaw Nation citizenship card, and a 1-page essay on their long-term goals and plans for achieving them. Financial need is not considered in the selection process.

Financial data A stipend is awarded (amount not specified).

Duration 1 year.

Number awarded 1 each year.

Deadline August of each year.

[969]
MLA/NLM SPECTRUM SCHOLARSHIPS

Medical Library Association
Attn: Awards, Grants, and Scholarships
65 East Wacker Place, Suite 1900
Chicago, IL 60601-7246
(312) 419-9094   Fax: (312) 419-8950
E-mail: info@mlahq.org
Web: www.mlanet.org

Summary To provide financial assistance to Native Americans and other minorities interested in preparing for a career as a medical librarian.

Eligibility This program is open to members of minority groups (African Americans, Hispanics, Asian, Native Americans, and Pacific Islanders) who are attending library schools accredited by the American Library Association (ALA). Applicants must be interested in preparing for a career as a health sciences information professional.

Financial data The stipend is $3,250.

Duration 1 year.

Additional information This program, established in 2001, is jointly sponsored by the Medical Library Association (MLA) and the National Library of Medicine (NLM) of the U.S. National Institutes of Health (NIH). It operates as a component of the Spectrum Initiative Scholarship program of the ALA.

Number awarded 2 each year.

Deadline February of each year.

[970]
MLA SCHOLARSHIP FOR MINORITY STUDENTS

Medical Library Association
Attn: Professional Development Department
65 East Wacker Place, Suite 1900
Chicago, IL 60601-7246
(312) 419-9094, ext. 28   Fax: (312) 419-8950
E-mail: mlapd2@mlahq.org
Web: www.mlanet.org/awards/grants/minstud.html

Summary To assist Native Americans and other minority students interested in preparing for a career in medical librarianship.

Eligibility This program is open to racial minority students (Asians, African Americans, Hispanics, Native Americans, or Pacific Islander Americans) who are entering an ALA-accredited graduate program in librarianship or who have completed less than half of their academic requirements for the master's degree in library science. They must be interested in preparing for a career in medical librarianship. Selection is based on academic record, letters of reference, professional potential, and the applicant's statement of career objectives. U.S. or Canadian citizenship or permanent resident status is required.

Financial data The stipend is $5,000.

Duration 1 year.

Additional information This scholarship was first awarded in 1973.

Number awarded 1 each year.

Deadline November of each year.

[971]
MONTANA AMERICAN INDIAN STUDENT WAIVER

Montana Guaranteed Student Loan Program
2500 Broadway
P.O. Box 203101
Helena, MT 59620-3101
(406) 444-6570   Toll Free: (800) 537-7508
Fax: (406) 444-1869
E-mail: scholarships@mgslp.state.mt.us
Web: www.mgslp.state.mt.us

Summary To provide financial assistance to Montana Indians interested in attending college or graduate school in the state.

Eligibility Eligible to apply are Native American students (one-quarter Indian blood or more) who have been residents of Montana for at least 1 year prior to application, have graduated from an accredited high school or federal Indian school, and can demonstrate financial need.

Financial data Students eligible for this benefit are entitled to attend any unit of the Montana University System without

payment of undergraduate or graduate registration or incidental fees.

Duration Students are eligible for continued fee waiver as long as they maintain reasonable academic progress and full-time status (12 or more credits for undergraduates, 9 or more credits for graduate students).

Number awarded Varies; more than $1 million in waivers are approved each year.

Deadline Deadline not specified.

[972]
MULTICULTURAL ADVERTISING INTERN PROGRAM

American Association of Advertising Agencies
Attn: Manager of Diversity Programs
405 Lexington Avenue, 18th Floor
New York, NY 10174-1801
(212) 850-0732   Toll Free: (800) 676-9333
Fax: (212) 682-2028   E-mail: maip@aaaa.org
Web: www2.aaaa.org

Summary To provide Native Americans and other minority students with summer work experience in advertising agencies and to present them with an overview of the agency business.

Eligibility This program is open to U.S. citizens and permanent residents who are Black/African American, Asian/Asian American, Pacific Islander, Hispanic, North American Indian/Native American, or multiracial and either 1) college juniors, seniors, or graduate students at an accredited college or university, or 2) students at any academic level attending a portfolio school of the sponsor. Applicants may be majoring in any field, but they must be able to demonstrate a serious commitment to preparing for a career in advertising. They must have a GPA of 3.0 or higher. Students with a cumulative GPA of 2.7 to 2.9 are encouraged to apply, but they must complete an additional essay question.

Financial data Interns are paid a salary of at least $70 per day. If they do not live in the area of their host agencies, they may stay in housing arranged by the sponsor. They are responsible for a percentage of the cost of housing and materials.

Duration 10 weeks during the summer.

Additional information Interns may be assigned duties in the following departments: account management, broadcast production, media buying/planning, creative (art direction or copywriting), digital/interactive technologies, print production, strategic/account planning, or traffic. The portfolio schools are the AdCenter at Virginia Commonwealth University, the Creative Circus and the Portfolio Center in Atlanta, the Miami Ad School, the University of Texas at Austin, Pratt Institute, the Minneapolis College of Art and Design, and the Art Center College of Design in Pasadena, California.

Number awarded 70 to 100 each year.

Deadline December of each year.

[973]
MYRON AND LAURA THOMPSON SCHOLARSHIP

Ke Ali'i Pauahi Foundation
Attn: Financial Aid & Scholarship Services
567 South King Street, Suite 160
Honolulu, HI 96813
(808) 534-3966   Toll Free: (800) 842-4682, ext. 43966
Fax: (808) 534-3890   E-mail: scholarships@pauahi.org
Web: www.pauahi.org/scholarships

Summary To provide financial assistance to undergraduate or graduate students, especially those of Native Hawaiian descent, who are working on a degree in early childhood education.

Eligibility This program is open to full-time undergraduate and graduate students working on a degree in early childhood education. Applicants must be able to demonstrate financial need; an interest in the Hawaiian language, culture, history, and values; and commitment to contribute to the greater community. Preference is given to Native Hawaiians (descendants of the aboriginal inhabitants of the Hawaiian Islands prior to 1778) and to students who demonstrate an interest in working with Hawaiian children in Hawaii after completion of their education.

Financial data The stipend is $1,300.

Duration 1 year.

Number awarded 2 each year.

Deadline March each year.

[974]
NASA GRADUATE STUDENT RESEARCHERS PROGRAM

National Aeronautics and Space Administration
Attn: Acting National GSRP Project Manager
Jet Propulsion Laboratory
4800 Oak Grove Drive
Pasadena, CA 91109-8099
(818) 354-3274   Fax: (818) 393-4977
E-mail: Linda.L.Rodgers@jpl.nasa.gov
Web: fellowships.nasaprs.com/gsrp/nav

Summary To provide funding to minority and other graduate students interested in conducting research in fields of interest to the U.S. National Aeronautics and Space Administration (NASA).

Eligibility This program is open to full-time students enrolled or planning to enroll in an accredited graduate program at a U.S. college or university. Applicants must be citizens of the United States, sponsored by a faculty adviser or department chair, and interested in conducting research in a field of science, mathematics, or engineering related to NASA research and development. Students who are interested in becoming teaching or education administrators are also eligible. Selection is based on academic qualifications, quality of the proposed research and its relevance to NASA's program, proposed utilization of center research facilities (except for NASA headquarters), and ability of the student to accomplish the defined research. Individuals from underrepresented groups in science, technology, engineering, or mathematics (STEM) fields (African Americans, Native Americans, Alaskan Natives, Mexican Americans, Puerto Ricans, Native Pacific Islanders, women, and persons with disabilities) are strongly urged to apply.

Financial data The program provides a $20,000 student stipend, a $6,000 student travel allowance, up to $1,000 for health insurance, and a $3,000 university allowance. The student stipend may cover tuition, room and board, books, software, meal plans, school and laboratory supplies, and other related expenses. The student travel allowance may be used for national and international conferences and data collection. The university allowance is a discretionary award that typically goes to the research adviser. If the student already has health insurance, that $1,000 grant may be added to the student stipend or student travel allowance.

Duration 1 year; may be renewed for up to 1 additional year for master's degree students or 2 additional years for doctoral students.

Additional information This program was established in 1980. Students are required to participate in a 10-week research experience at NASA headquarters in Washington, D.C. or at 1 of 10 NASA centers.

Number awarded This program supports approximately 180 graduate students each year.

Deadline February of each year.

[975]
NASP MINORITY SCHOLARSHIP

National Association of School Psychologists
Attn: Education and Research Trust
4340 East-West Highway, Suite 402
Bethesda, MD 20814
(301) 657-0270, ext. 234   Toll Free: (866) 331-NASP
Fax: (301) 657-0275   TDD: (301) 657-4155
E-mail: kbritton@naspweb.org
Web: www.nasponline.org/about_nasp/minority.aspx

Summary To provide financial assistance to Native American and other minority graduate students who are members of the National Association of School Psychologists (NASP) and enrolled in a school psychology program.

Eligibility This program is open to minority students who are NASP members enrolled in a regionally-accredited school psychology program in the United States. Applicants must have a GPA of 3.0 or higher. Doctoral candidates are not eligible. Applications must be accompanied by 1) a resume that includes undergraduate and/or graduate schools attended, awards and honors, student and professional activities, work and volunteer experiences, research and publications, workshops or other presentations, and any special skills, training, or experience, such as bilingualism, teaching experience, or mental health experience; 2) a statement, up to 1,000 words, of professional goals; 3) at least 2 letters of recommendation, including at least 1 from a faculty member from their undergraduate or graduate studies (if a first-year student) or at least 1 from a faculty member of their school psychology program (if a second- or third-year student); 4) a completed financial statement; 5) an official transcript of all graduate course work (first-year students may submit an official undergraduate transcript); 6) other personal accomplishments that the applicant wishes to be considered; and 7) a letter of acceptance from a school psychology program for first-year applicants. U.S. citizenship is required.

Financial data The stipend is $5,000 per year.

Duration 1 year; may be renewed up to 2 additional years.

Number awarded Varies each year; recently, 4 of these scholarships were awarded.

Deadline October of each year.

[976]
NATIONAL ASSOCIATION OF BOND LAWYERS GOVERNMENTAL AFFAIRS SUMMER ASSOCIATE PROGRAM

National Association of Bond Lawyers
Attn: Governmental Affairs Office
601 13th Street, N.W., Suite 800 South
Washington, DC 20005-3875
(202) 682-1498   Fax: (202) 637-0217
E-mail: internship@nabl.org
Web: www.nabl.org/about/Governmental-Affairs.html

Summary To provide an opportunity for law students, especially Native Americans and those from other diverse backgrounds, to learn about municipal bond law during a summer internship at the Governmental Affairs Office of the National Association of Bond Lawyers (NABL) in Washington, D.C.

Eligibility This program is open to students currently enrolled in law school and interested in municipal bond law; diverse candidates are especially encouraged to apply. Applicants must be interested in a summer internship at the NABL Governmental Affairs Office in Washington, D.C. They should be able to demonstrate a high regard for honesty, integrity, and professional ethics; excellent organization, time management, and coordination skills and judgment; strong interpersonal skills; ability to communicate effectively, both orally and in writing; strong personal computer and data processing skills; proven attention to detail; a basic knowledge of the structure of government; and an ability to work effectively in member-driven associations.

Financial data The stipend is $4,000.

Duration 3 months during the summer.

Number awarded 1 each year.

Deadline May of each year.

[977]
NATIONAL DEFENSE SCIENCE AND ENGINEERING GRADUATE FELLOWSHIP PROGRAM

American Society for Engineering Education
Attn: NDSEG Fellowship Program
1818 N Street, N.W., Suite 600
Washington, DC 20036-2479
(202) 331-3516   Fax: (202) 265-8504
E-mail: ndseg@asee.org
Web: ndseg.asee.org

Summary To provide financial assistance to minority and other doctoral students in areas of science and engineering that are of military importance.

Eligibility This program is open to U.S. citizens and nationals entering or enrolled in the early stages of a doctoral program in aeronautical and astronautical engineering; biosciences, including toxicology; chemical engineering; chemistry; civil engineering; cognitive, neural, and behavioral sciences; computer and computational sciences; electrical engineering; geosciences, including terrain, water, and air; materials science and engineering; mathematics; mechanical engi-

neering; naval architecture and ocean engineering; oceanography; or physics, including optics. Applications are particularly encouraged from women, members of ethnic minority groups (American Indians, African Americans, Hispanics or Latinos, Native Hawaiians, Alaska Natives, Asians, and Pacific Islanders), and persons with disabilities. Selection is based on all available evidence of ability, including academic records, letters of recommendation, and GRE scores.

Financial data The annual stipend is $30,500 for the first year, $31,000 for the second year; and $31,500 for the third year; the program also pays the recipient's institution full tuition and required fees (not to include room and board). Medical insurance is covered up to $1,000 per year. An additional allowance may be considered for a student with a disability.

Duration 3 years, as long as satisfactory academic progress is maintained.

Additional information This program is sponsored by the Army Research Office, the Air Force Office of Scientific Research, and the Office of Naval Research. Recipients do not incur any military or other service obligation. They must attend school on a full-time basis.

Number awarded Approximately 200 each year.

Deadline January of each year.

[978]
NATIONAL MEDICAL FELLOWSHIPS EMERGENCY SCHOLARSHIP FUND

National Medical Fellowships, Inc.
Attn: Scholarship Program
347 Fifth Avenue, Suite 510
New York, NY 10016
(212) 483-8880   Toll Free: (877) NMF-1DOC
Fax: (212) 483-8897   E-mail: info@nmfonline.org
Web: www.nmfonline.org/programs.php

Summary To provide financial assistance to Native American and other minority medical students who are facing financial emergencies.

Eligibility This program is open to U.S. citizens who are enrolled in the third or fourth year of an accredited M.D. or D.O. degree-granting program in the United States and are facing extreme financial difficulties because of unforeseen training-related expenses. Applicants must be African Americans, Mexican Americans, Native Hawaiians, Alaska Natives, American Indians, Vietnamese, Cambodians, or mainland Puerto Ricans who permanently reside in the United States. They must be interested in primary care practice in underserved communities.

Financial data Assistance ranges up to $20,000.

Duration Awards are available semi-annually.

Additional information This program was established in 2008, with support from the Kellogg Foundation.

Number awarded Varies each year; recently, 3 of these scholarships were awarded.

Deadline August of each year.

[979]
NATIONAL MEDICAL FELLOWSHIPS NEED-BASED SCHOLARSHIP PROGRAM

National Medical Fellowships, Inc.
Attn: Scholarship Program
347 Fifth Avenue, Suite 510
New York, NY 10016
(212) 483-8880   Toll Free: (877) NMF-1DOC
Fax: (212) 483-8897   E-mail: info@nmfonline.org
Web: www.nmfonline.org/programs.php

Summary To provide financial assistance to Native American and other underrepresented minority medical students who demonstrate financial need.

Eligibility This program is open to U.S. citizens enrolled in the first or second year of an accredited M.D. or D.O. degree-granting program in the United States. Applicants must be African Americans, Mexican Americans, Native Hawaiians, Alaska Natives, American Indians, Vietnamese, Cambodians, or mainland Puerto Ricans who permanently reside in the United States. Along with their application, they must submit a 600-word essay on their motivation for a career in medicine and their personal and professional goals over the next 10 years. Selection is based primarily on financial need.

Financial data The amount of the award depends on the student's total resources (including parental and spousal support), cost of education, and receipt of additional scholarships; recently, individual awards ranged from $1,000 to $10,000 per year.

Duration 1 year for first-year students; may be renewed for the second year only.

Number awarded Varies each year; recently, 70 of these scholarships were awarded.

Deadline August of each year.

[980]
NATIONAL MINORITY STEM FELLOWSHIPS

Educational Advancement Alliance, Inc.
Attn: National Minority STEM Fellowship Program
4548 Market Street, Suite LL-04
Philadelphia, PA 19139
(215) 895-4003   E-mail: info@nmsfp.org
Web: www.nmsfp.org

Summary To provide financial assistance to Native American and other residents of designated states who are working on a master's degree in fields of science, technology, engineering, or mathematics (STEM) at colleges in those states.

Eligibility This program is open to U.S. citizens who are residents of Delaware, Maryland, New Jersey, Pennsylvania, or Washington, D.C. Members of cultural, racial, geographic, and socioeconomic backgrounds that are currently underrepresented in graduate education are especially encouraged to apply; those are defined to include Hispanics or Latinos, American Indians or Alaska Natives, Asians, Native Hawaiians or other Pacific Islanders, or Blacks. Applicants must be enrolled full time at colleges or universities in those states and working on a master's degree in a field of STEM, including physics, chemistry, non-medical biology, mathematics, computer science, or environmental science. Their degree requirements must include a research thesis. Students working on other graduate degrees (e.g., joint B.S./M.S., M.B.A., D.V.M., M.D., joint M.D./Ph.D., J.D., joint J.D./Ph.D.) are not

eligible. Along with their application, they must submit a 1,000-word essay on their qualifications for the fellowship and their career goals, college transcripts, information on extracurricular activities, a copy of their GRE scores, 3 letters of recommendation, and information on their financial situation.

Financial data The program provides a stipend of $18,000 per year and up to $20,500 per year as tuition support.

Duration 2 years.

Additional information This program is funded by the U.S. Department of Energy Office of Science and administered by the Educational Advancement Alliance, Inc.

Number awarded Up to 40 each year.

Deadline March of each year.

[981]
NATIONAL MUSEUM OF THE AMERICAN INDIAN 10-WEEK INTERNSHIPS IN CONSERVATION

National Museum of the American Indian
Attn: Head of Conservation
Cultural Resources Center
4220 Silver Hill Road, MRC 538
Suitland, MD 20746-2863
(301) 238-1415   Fax: (301) 238-3201
E-mail: kaminitzm@si.edu
Web: www.nmai.si.edu

Summary To provide undergraduate and graduate students with an opportunity to learn more about conservation during an internship at the Smithsonian Institution's National Museum of the American Indian (NMAI).

Eligibility This program is open to undergraduate and graduate students with a background in studio art, anthropology, art history, museum studies, chemistry, or biology. Native American students interested in conservation and museum care practices are especially welcome. Applicants must be interested in participating in a program at the NMAI Cultural Resources Center in Suitland, Maryland that involves collaboration with Native people in developing appropriate methods of handling, preserving, and interpreting cultural materials.

Financial data Interns receive a stipend (amount not specified).

Duration 10 weeks, in summer or winter.

Number awarded Varies each year.

Deadline January of each year for summer; September of each year for winter.

[982]
NATIONAL MUSEUM OF THE AMERICAN INDIAN CONSERVATION 6-MONTH PRE-PROGRAM INTERNSHIP

National Museum of the American Indian
Attn: Head of Conservation
Cultural Resources Center
4220 Silver Hill Road, MRC 538
Suitland, MD 20746-2863
(301) 238-1415   Fax: (301) 238-3201
E-mail: kaminitzm@si.edu
Web: www.nmai.si.edu

Summary To provide an opportunity for students planning to enter a graduate training program in art conservation to learn more about the field during an internship at the Smithsonian Institution's National Museum of the American Indian (NMAI).

Eligibility This program is open to students preparing to apply to a graduate level training program in art conservation. Applicants must be interested in participating in a program at the NMAI Cultural Resources Center in Suitland, Maryland that will provide them with an understanding of Native American ethnographic and archaeological materials and approaches to conservation. They must have a GPA of 3.0 or higher. Along with their application, they must submit a personal statement that includes why they want to become a conservator, what they hope to accomplish through this internship, how it would relate to their academic achievement and professional development, and what in particular about NMAI interests them and leads them to apply for the internship.

Financial data Interns receive a stipend (amount not specified).

Duration 6 months, beginning in September or October.

Additional information Interns perform supervised condition examinations, write reports and treatment proposals, perform photo documentation, and treat objects requested for exhibitions or loans.

Number awarded 1 each year.

Deadline February of each year.

[983]
NATIONAL PHYSICAL SCIENCE CONSORTIUM DISSERTATION SUPPORT PROGRAM

National Physical Science Consortium
c/o University of Southern California
3716 South Hope Street, Suite 348
Los Angeles, CA 90007-4344
(213) 743-2409   Toll Free: (800) 854-NPSC
Fax: (213) 743-2407   E-mail: npschq@npsc.org
Web: www.npsc.org

Summary To provide funding to Native Americans and other underrepresented minorities and women conducting dissertation research in designated science and engineering fields.

Eligibility This program is open to U.S. citizens who are enrolled in a doctoral program and about to begin dissertation research. Eligible fields of study are generally limited to astronomy, chemistry, computer science, geology, materials science, mathematical sciences, physics, their subdisciplines, and related engineering fields (chemical, computer, electrical, environmental, and mechanical). The program welcomes applications from all qualified students and continues to emphasize the recruitment of underrepresented minority (African American, Hispanic, Native American Indian, Eskimo, Aleut, and Pacific Islander) and women physical science and engineering students. Fellowships are provided to students at the 119 universities that are members of the consortium. Selection is based on academic standing (GPA), undergraduate and graduate course work and grades, university and/or industry research experience, letters of recommendation, and GRE scores.

Financial data The fellowship pays tuition and fees plus an annual stipend of $20,000.

Duration Up to 4 years.

Number awarded Varies each year.

Deadline November of each year.

[984]
NATIONAL PHYSICAL SCIENCE CONSORTIUM GRADUATE FELLOWSHIPS

National Physical Science Consortium
c/o University of Southern California
3716 South Hope Street, Suite 348
Los Angeles, CA 90007-4344
(213) 743-2409   Toll Free: (800) 854-NPSC
Fax: (213) 743-2407   E-mail: npschq@npsc.org
Web: www.npsc.org/students/info.html

Summary To provide financial assistance and summer work experience to Native Americans and other underrepresented minorities and women interested in working on a Ph.D. in designated science and engineering fields.

Eligibility This program is open to U.S. citizens who are seniors graduating from college with a GPA of 3.0 or higher, enrolled in the first year of a doctoral program, completing a terminal master's degree, or returning from the workforce and holding no more than a master's degree. Students currently in the third or subsequent year of a Ph.D. program or who already have a doctoral degree in any field (Ph.D., M.D., J.D., Ed.D.) are ineligible. Applicants must be interested in working on a Ph.D. in the physical sciences or related fields of science or engineering. The program welcomes applications from all qualified students and continues to emphasize the recruitment of underrepresented minority (African American, Hispanic, Native American Indian, Eskimo, Aleut, and Pacific Islander) and women physical science and engineering students. Fellowships are provided to students at the 119 universities that are members of the consortium. Selection is based on academic standing (GPA), course work taken in preparation for graduate school, university and/or industry research experience, letters of recommendation, and GRE scores.

Financial data The fellowship pays tuition and fees plus an annual stipend of $20,000. It also provides on-site paid summer employment to enhance technical experience. The exact value of the fellowship depends on academic standing, summer employment, and graduate school attended; the total amount generally exceeds $200,000.

Duration Support is initially provided for 2 or 3 years, depending on the employer-sponsor. If the fellow makes satisfactory progress and continues to meet the conditions of the award, support may continue for a total of up to 6 years or completion of the Ph.D., whichever comes first.

Additional information This program began in 1989. Tuition and fees are provided by the participating universities. Stipends and summer internships are provided by sponsoring organizations. Students must submit separate applications for internships, which may have additional eligibility requirements. Internships are currently available at Lawrence Livermore National Laboratory in Livermore, California (astronomy, chemistry, computer science, geology, materials science, mathematics, and physics); National Security Agency in Fort Meade, Maryland (astronomy, chemistry, computer science, geology, materials science, mathematics, and physics); Sandia National Laboratory in Livermore, California (biology, chemistry, computer science, environmental science, geology, materials science, mathematics, and physics); and Sandia National Laboratory in Albuquerque, New Mexico (chemical engineering, chemistry, computer science, materials science, mathematics, mechanical engineering, and physics). Fellows must submit a separate application for dissertation support in the year prior to the beginning of their dissertation research program, but not until they can describe their intended research in general terms.

Number awarded Varies each year; recently, 11 of these fellowships were awarded.

Deadline November of each year.

[985]
NATIONAL SPACE GRANT COLLEGE AND FELLOWSHIP PROGRAM

National Aeronautics and Space Administration
Attn: Office of Education
300 E Street, S.W.
Mail Suite 6M35
Washington, DC 20546-0001
(202) 358-1069   Fax: (202) 358-7097
E-mail: Diane.D.DeTroye@nasa.gov
Web: www.nasa.gov

Summary To provide financial assistance to Native Americans and other undergraduate and graduate students interested in preparing for a career in a space-related field.

Eligibility This program is open to undergraduate and graduate students at colleges and universities that participate in the National Space Grant program of the U.S. National Aeronautics and Space Administration (NASA) through their state consortium. Applicants must be interested in a program of study and/or research in a field of science, technology, engineering, or mathematics (STEM) related to space. A specific goal of the program is to increase preparation by members of underrepresented groups (minorities, women, and persons with disabilities) for STEM space-related careers. Financial need is not considered in the selection process.

Financial data Each consortium establishes the terms of the fellowship program in its state.

Additional information NASA established the Space Grant program in 1989. It operates through 52 consortia in each state, the District of Columbia, and Puerto Rico. Each consortium includes selected colleges and universities in that state as well as other affiliates from industry, museums, science centers, and state and local agencies.

Number awarded Varies each year.

Deadline Each consortium sets its own deadlines.

[986]
NATIONAL TRIBAL GAMING COMMISSIONS/ REGULATORS SCHOLARSHIPS

National Tribal Gaming Commissions/Regulators
Attn: Scholarship Committee
P.O. Box 454
Oneida, WI 54155
E-mail: dawn@thehillgroup.org
Web: www.ntgcr.com/scholarships.php

Summary To provide financial assistance to Native Americans interested in working on an undergraduate or graduate degree in a field related to the gaming industry.

Eligibility This program is open to enrolled members of federally-recognized American Indian tribes and Alaska Native groups. Applicants must be high school seniors, rising

undergraduates, or potential graduate students enrolled or planning to enroll full time at an accredited college or university in the United States and have a GPA of 2.5 or higher. They must be preparing for a career in the gaming, business, financial, or hospitality industries. Along with their application, they must submit a 4-page essay on their personal background (including whether they speak their tribal language or are learning their tribal language and other cultural skills), their degree plan for higher education, why they have chosen that field of study, how they plan to serve their tribal people when they complete their higher education, and why they should be selected for this scholarship. Selection is based on the essay, academic ability (judged on GPA, class rank, SAT and/or ACT scores, and curriculum rigor), leadership, honors and awards received, community involvement, 3 letters of recommendation, intellectual skills beyond the classroom, accomplishments, professional development, and financial need.

Financial data The stipend is $5,000.

Duration 1 year.

Number awarded 3 each year.

Deadline June of each year for fall semester; October of each year for spring semester.

[987]
NATIVE AMERICAN JOURNALISTS ASSOCIATION SCHOLARSHIPS

Native American Journalists Association
c/o University of Oklahoma
Gaylord College
395 West Lindsey Street
Norman, OK 73019-4201
(405) 325-9008   Fax: (405) 325-6945
E-mail: info@naja.com
Web: www.naja.com/index.php/students/naja-scholarships

Summary To provide financial assistance to student members of the Native American Journalists Association (NAJA) who are interested in a career in journalism or journalism education.

Eligibility This program is open to NAJA members who are high school seniors, undergraduates, or graduate students working on or planning to work on a degree in journalism. Applicants must include proof of enrollment in a federal- or state-recognized tribe; work samples; transcripts; a cover letter on their financial need, area of interest (print, broadcast, photojournalism, new media, journalism education), and reasons for preparing for a career in journalism; and 2 letters of recommendation.

Financial data The stipends range from $500 to $5,000.

Duration 1 year.

Additional information Support for this program is provided by the James M. Cox Foundation, the Samuel I. Newhouse Foundation, and CNN.

Number awarded Varies each year; recently, 11 of these scholarships were awarded.

Deadline March of each year.

[988]
NATIVE AMERICAN LEADERSHIP IN EDUCATION (NALE) PROGRAM

Catching the Dream
8200 Mountain Road, N.E., Suite 203
Albuquerque, NM 87110-7835
(505) 262-2351   Fax: (505) 262-0534
E-mail: NScholarsh@aol.com
Web: www.catchingthedream.org/Scholarship.htm

Summary   To provide financial assistance to American Indian paraprofessionals in the education field who wish to return to college or graduate school.

Eligibility   This program is open to paraprofessionals who are working in Indian schools and who plan to return to college or graduate school to complete their degree in education, counseling, or school administration. Applicants must be able to provide proof that they are at least one-quarter Indian blood and a member of a U.S. tribe that is federally-recognized, state-recognized, or terminated. Along with their application, they must submit documentation of financial need, 3 letters of recommendation, copies of applications and responses from all other sources of funding for which they are eligible, official transcripts, standardized test scores (ACT, SAT, GRE, MCAT, LSAT, etc.), and an essay explaining their goals in life, college plans, and career plans (especially how those plans include working with and benefiting Indians). Selection is based on merit and potential for improving the lives of Indian people.

Financial data   Stipends range from $500 to $5,000 per year.

Duration   1 year; may be renewed.

Additional information   The sponsor was formerly known as the Native American Scholarship Fund.

Number awarded   Varies; generally, 15 or more each year.

Deadline   April of each year for fall term; September of each year for spring and winter terms; March of each year for summer school.

[989]
NATIVE AMERICAN RIGHTS FUND CLERKSHIPS

Native American Rights Fund
Attn: Clerkship Program
1506 Broadway
Boulder, CO 80302-6296
(303) 447-8760   Fax: (303) 443-7776
E-mail: anderson@narf.org
Web: www.narf.org/contact/clerk.htm

Summary   To provide work experience at offices of the Native American Rights Fund (NARF) to law students with an interest in Indian law.

Eligibility   This program is open to law students who are experienced in Indian law or have a background in Indian affairs. Applicants for summer clerkships must have completed their second year of law school and be able to work at NARF offices in Boulder (Colorado), Anchorage (Alaska), or Washington, D.C. Applicants for semester clerkships must be attending law school near 1 of those 3 offices and be enrolled in their second year.

Financial data   Salaries are competitive with those of the federal government and nonprofit law firms.

Duration   Summer clerks work full time for 10 to 12 weeks. Semester clerks work part time.

Additional information   Law clerk projects consist primarily of legal research and writing.

Number awarded   Varies each year.

Deadline   October of each year for summer clerkships; applications for semester clerkships are accepted at any time.

[990]
NATIVE AMERICAN SUPPLEMENTAL GRANTS

Presbyterian Church (USA)
Attn: Office of Financial Aid for Studies
100 Witherspoon Street, Room M-052
Louisville, KY 40202-1396
(502) 569-5224   Toll Free: (888) 728-7228, ext. 5224
Fax: (502) 569-8766   E-mail: finaid@pcusa.org
Web: www.pcusa.org/financialaid/programs/grants.htm

Summary   To provide financial assistance to Native American students interested in preparing for church occupations within the Presbyterian Church (USA).

Eligibility   This program is open to Native American and Alaska Native students who are enrolled full time at a PCUSA seminary or accredited theological institution approved by their presbytery's Committee on Preparation for Ministry (CPM). Applicants must be working on 1) an M.Div. degree and enrolled as an inquirer or candidate by a PCUSA presbytery, or 2) an M.A.C.E. degree and preparing for a church occupation. They must be PCUSA members, U.S. citizens or permanent residents, able to demonstrate financial need, and recommended by the financial aid officer at their theological institution. Along with their application, they must submit a 1,000-word essay on what they believe God is calling them to do in ministry.

Financial data   Stipends range from $500 to $1,500 per year. Funds are intended as supplements to students who have been awarded a Presbyterian Study Grant but still demonstrate remaining financial need.

Duration   1 year; may be renewed up to 2 additional years.

Number awarded   Varies each year.

Deadline   June of each year.

[991]
NATIVE AMERICAN VISITING STUDENT AWARDS

Smithsonian Institution
Attn: Office of Fellowships
470 L'Enfant Plaza, Suite 7102
P.O. Box 37012, MRC 902
Washington, DC 20013-7012
(202) 633-7070   Fax: (202) 633-7069
E-mail: siofg@si.edu
Web: www.si.edu/ofg/Applications/NAP/NAPapp.htm

Summary   To provide funding to Native American graduate students interested in working on a project related to Native American topics at the Smithsonian Institution.

Eligibility   Native Americans who are formally or informally related to a Native American community are eligible to apply. Applicants must be advanced graduate students who are proposing to undertake a project that is related to a Native American topic and requires the use of Native American resources at the Smithsonian Institution.

Financial data Students receive a grant of $150 per day for short-term awards or $550 per week for long-term awards. Also provided are allowances for travel and research.

Duration Up to 21 days for short-term awards; 3 to 10 weeks for long-term awards.

Additional information Recipients carry out independent research projects in association with the Smithsonian's research staff. Fellows are required to be in residence at the Smithsonian for the duration of the fellowship.

Number awarded Varies each year.

Deadline January of each year for summer residency; May of each year for fall residency; September of each year for winter or spring residency.

[992]
NATIVE HAWAIIAN CHAMBER OF COMMERCE SCHOLARSHIPS

Ke Ali'i Pauahi Foundation
Attn: Financial Aid & Scholarship Services
567 South King Street, Suite 160
Honolulu, HI 96813
(808) 534-3966   Toll Free: (800) 842-4682, ext. 43966
Fax: (808) 534-3890   E-mail: scholarships@pauahi.org
Web: www.pauahi.org/scholarships

Summary To provide financial assistance to students, especially Native Hawaiians, who are interested in working on an undergraduate or graduate degree in business at a school in any state.

Eligibility This program is open to undergraduate and graduate students who are working on a degree in business administration at a college or university in any state. Applicants must have a GPA of 3.0 or higher. Residency in Hawaii is not required, but preference is given to Native Hawaiians (descendants of the aboriginal inhabitants of the Hawaiian Islands prior to 1778).

Financial data The stipend is $1,100.

Duration 1 year.

Additional information This program is sponsored by the Native Hawaiian Chamber of Commerce.

Number awarded Varies each year; recently, 7 of these scholarships were awarded.

Deadline March of each year.

[993]
NAVAJO NATION DISSERTATION FUNDING

Navajo Nation
Attn: Office of Navajo Nation Scholarship and Financial Assistance
P.O. Box 1870
Window Rock, AZ 86515-1870
(928) 871-7444   Toll Free: (800) 243-2956
Fax: (928) 871-6742   E-mail: onnsfacentral@navajo.org
Web: www.onnsfa.org

Summary To provide financial assistance to members of the Navajo Nation who are working on a doctoral dissertation.

Eligibility This program is open to enrolled members of the Navajo Nation who are conducting dissertation research for a doctoral degree. Applicants must have completed all course work and have been advanced to candidacy. They must submit an itemized dissertation budget.

Financial data Funding is limited to direct costs for field work and research necessary to complete the dissertation.

Duration 1 year; may be renewed if the recipient is making satisfactory progress on the dissertation.

Deadline April of each year.

[994]
NAVAJO NATION GRADUATE TRUST FUND AND FELLOWSHIP

Navajo Nation
Attn: Office of Navajo Nation Scholarship and Financial Assistance
P.O. Box 1870
Window Rock, AZ 86515-1870
(928) 871-7444   Toll Free: (800) 243-2956
Fax: (928) 871-6742   E-mail: onnsfacentral@navajo.org
Web: www.onnsfa.org

Summary To provide financial assistance to members of the Navajo Nation who wish to work on a graduate degree.

Eligibility This program is open to enrolled members of the Navajo Nation who are enrolled or planning to enroll as graduate students. Preference is given to students at institutions that provide matching funds to the Navajo Nation or its student participants. Candidates for a second graduate degree at the same level (master's, education terminal degree, or doctorate) are not eligible. Applicants must submit transcripts and documentation of financial need.

Financial data Stipends for full-time graduate students range from $5,000 to $10,000 per year, depending on the need of the recipient; for part-time graduate students, the stipend is $500 per 3 semester credit hours or an equivalent amount of quarter credit hours.

Duration 1 year; may be renewed for a total of 5 semesters (6 semesters for law students) provided the recipient maintains a GPA of at least 3.0 (or 2.0 for medical, veterinary, and law students).

Deadline April of each year.

[995]
NAVAJO TRIBAL UTILITY AUTHORITY ENHANCED SCHOLARSHIPS

Navajo Tribal Utility Authority
Attn: Human Resources Division/Training Department
P.O. Box 170
Fort Defiance, AZ 86504
(928) 729-5721, ext. 2152
Web: www.ntua.com/Scholar/Scholarship.html

Summary To provide financial assistance to enrolled members of the Navajo Nation who are interested in working on a bachelor's or master's degree to prepare for a career in the multi-service utility industry and complete an internship at the Navajo Tribal Utility Authority (NTUA).

Eligibility This program is open to enrolled members of the Navajo Nation who are graduating high school seniors, high school graduates, GED recipients, or continuing full-time undergraduate or graduate students with a GPA of 2.0 or higher. Applicants must have successfully completed a 2-month summer internship with NTUA. They must be interested in working on a bachelor's or master's degree in a field related to the multi-service utility industry, including accounting, administration, business, engineering (civil, electrical, environmental), environment, information technology, or management. In the selection process to hire interns, priority is given to recipients of standard NTUA scholarships.

Financial data   The stipend is $2,500 per year.

Duration   1 year; may be renewed, provided the recipient maintains a GPA of 2.0 or higher and completes another 2-month summer internship with NTUA.

Number awarded   Varies each year.

Deadline   April of each year.

[996]
NCAA ETHNIC MINORITY POSTGRADUATE SCHOLARSHIP PROGRAM

National Collegiate Athletic Association
Attn: Office for Diversity and Inclusion
1802 Alonzo Watford Sr. Drive
P.O. Box 6222
Indianapolis, IN 46206-6222
(317) 917-6222   Fax: (317) 917-6888
E-mail: tstrum@ncaa.org
Web: www.ncaa.org

Summary   To provide funding to Native Americans and other minority graduate students who are interested in preparing for a career in intercollegiate athletics.

Eligibility   This program is open to members of minority groups who have been accepted into a program at a National Collegiate Athletic Association (NCAA) member institution that will prepare them for a career in intercollegiate athletics (athletics administrator, coach, athletic trainer, or other career that provides a direct service to intercollegiate athletics). Applicants must be U.S. citizens, have performed with distinction as a student body member at their respective undergraduate institution, and be entering the first semester or term of full-time postgraduate study. Selection is based on the applicant's involvement in extracurricular activities, course work, commitment to preparing for a career in intercollegiate athletics, and promise for success in that career. Financial need is not considered.

Financial data   The stipend is $6,000; funds are paid to the college or university of the recipient's choice.

Duration   1 year; nonrenewable.

Number awarded   13 each year.

Deadline   November of each year.

[997]
NCAI YOUTH AMBASSADOR LEADERSHIP PROGRAM SCHOLARSHIPS

National Congress of American Indians
Attn: Internship Program
1516 P Street, N.W.
Washington, DC 20005
(202) 466-7767   Fax: (2020 466-7797
E-mail: ncai@ncai.org
Web: www.ncai.org/Youth.418.0.html

Summary   To provide financial assistance to undergraduates and graduate students who participate in the Youth Commission Ambassador Leadership Program (ALP) of the National Congress of American Indians (NCAI).

Eligibility   This program is open to youth between 17 and 25 years of age who are eligible for NCAI membership. Applicants must be graduating high school seniors or full-time

undergraduate or graduate students and have a GPA of 2.0 or higher. They must have support from their tribal council. Males and females are considered separately. Recipients are selected at the Congress on the basis of an oration, contemporary dress, extemporaneous question, cultural presentation, and debate; GPA and recommendations are also considered.

Financial data   The stipend is $2,500. Funds are paid directly to the academic institution.

Duration   The stipend is for 1 year; recipients serve as Youth Ambassadors for 2 years.

Additional information   This program was established in 2006. Students selected as Youth Ambassadors lead the NCAI Youth Commission in its meetings and represent NCAI Youth when their presence is requested.

Number awarded   2 (1 male and 1 female) each even-numbered year.

Deadline   September of even-numbered years.

[998]
NELL B. BROWN MEMORIAL AWARD

Cherokee Nation
Attn: Cherokee Nation Education Corporation
115 East Delaware Street
P.O. Box 948
Tahlequah, OK 74465-0948
(918) 207-0950   Fax: (918) 207-0951
E-mail: contact@cnec-edu.org
Web: cnec.cherokee.org

Summary   To provide financial assistance to graduate student citizens of the Cherokee Nation who are working on a degree in a field related to American Indian or Cherokee studies at a university in any state.

Eligibility   This program is open to citizens of the Cherokee Nation who live within or outside the jurisdictional area of the tribe. Applicants must be working on a graduate degree in history, anthropology, or archaeology with an emphasis on American Indian or Cherokee studies. Along with their application, they must submit a 4-page personal essay that includes background information, their degree plan for higher education, why they have chosen that field of study, how they plan to serve Cherokee people when they complete higher education, and why they should be selected for this scholarship. Selection is based on the clarity and presentation of the essay; academic information (including transcripts and ACT scores); school, cultural and community activities; future plans to serve Cherokee people; and financial need.

Financial data   The stipend is $1,000 per semester ($2,000 per year).

Duration   1 year. Renewal for the second semester requires the recipient to earn a GPA of 3.0 or higher in the first semester.

Number awarded   1 or 2 each year.

Deadline   April of each year.

[999]
NEW JERSEY LIBRARY ASSOCIATION DIVERSITY SCHOLARSHIP

New Jersey Library Association
4 Lafayette Street
P.O. Box 1534
Trenton, NJ 08607
(609) 394-8032   Fax: (609) 394-8164
E-mail: ptumulty@njla.org
Web: www.njla.org/honorsawards/scholarship

Summary To provide financial assistance to New Jersey residents who are Native Americans or members of other minority groups and interested in working on a graduate or postgraduate degree in public librarianship at a school in any state.

Eligibility This program is open to residents of New Jersey and individuals who have worked in a New Jersey library for at least 12 months. Applicants must be members of a minority group (African American, Asian/Pacific Islander, Latino/Hispanic, or Native American/Native Alaskan). They must be enrolled or planning to enroll at an ALA-accredited school of library science in any state to work on a graduate or postgraduate degree in librarianship. Along with their application, they must submit an essay of 150 to 250 words explaining their choice of librarianship as a profession. An interview is required. Selection is based on academic ability and financial need.

Financial data The stipend is $1,300.

Duration 1 year.

Number awarded 1 each year.

Deadline February of each year.

[1000]
NEW MEXICO DIVERSITY FELLOWSHIPS IN ENVIRONMENTAL LAW

American Bar Association
Attn: Section of Environment, Energy, and Resources
321 North Clark Street
Chicago, IL 60654-7598
(312) 988-5602   Fax: (312) 988-5572
E-mail: jonusaid@staff.abanet.org
Web: www.abanet.org

Summary To provide funding to Native American and other law students from traditionally underrepresented groups who are interested in working on a summer project in environmental, energy, or natural resources law in New Mexico.

Eligibility This program is open to first- and second-year law students and third-year night students who are residents of New Mexico or residents of other states with a demonstrated interest in practicing law in New Mexico. Preference is given to students at law schools in New Mexico. Applicants must be members of minority and traditionally underrepresented groups preparing for a career in environmental, energy, or natural resources law. They must be interested in working during the summer at a government agency or public interest organization in New Mexico. Selection is based on interest in environmental and natural resource issues, academic record, personal qualities, and leadership abilities.

Financial data The stipend is $5,000.

Duration 8 to 10 weeks during the summer.

Additional information This program is supported by the New Mexico Environment Department.

Number awarded 1 each year.

Deadline February of each year.

[1001]
NEW MEXICO MINORITY DOCTORAL LOAN-FOR-SERVICE PROGRAM

New Mexico Higher Education Department
Attn: Financial Aid Division
2048 Galisteo Street
Santa Fe, NM 87505-2100
(505) 476-8411   Toll Free: (800) 279-9777
Fax: (505) 476-8454 E-mail: Theresa.acker@state.nm.us
Web: hed.state.nm.us

Summary To provide funding to 1) Native Americans, 2) other underrepresented minorities, and 3) women who reside in New Mexico and are interested in working on a doctoral degree in selected fields.

Eligibility This program is open to ethnic minorities and women who are residents of New Mexico and have received a baccalaureate degree from a public 4-year college or university in the state in mathematics, engineering, the physical or life sciences, or any other academic discipline in which ethnic minorities and women are demonstrably underrepresented in New Mexico academic institutions. Applicants must have been admitted as a full-time doctoral student at an approved university in any state. They must be sponsored by a New Mexico institution of higher education which has agreed to employ them in a tenure-track faculty position after they obtain their degree. U.S. citizenship is required.

Financial data Students can receive $25,000 per year, but the average is $15,000. This is a loan-for-service program; for every year of service as a college faculty member in New Mexico, a portion of the loan is forgiven. If the entire service agreement is fulfilled, 100% of the loan is eligible for forgiveness. Penalties may be assessed if the service agreement is not satisfied.

Duration 1 year; may be renewed up to 3 additional years.

Number awarded Up to 12 each year.

Deadline March of each year.

[1002]
NEW YORK MINORITY FELLOWSHIP IN ENVIRONMENTAL LAW

American Bar Association
Attn: Section of Environment, Energy, and Resources
321 North Clark Street
Chicago, IL 60654-7598
(312) 988-5602   Fax: (312) 988-5572
E-mail: jonusaid@staff.abanet.org
Web: www.abanet.org

Summary To provide funding to Native American and other law students from traditionally underrepresented groups who are interested in working on a summer project related to environmental, energy, or natural resources law in New York.

Eligibility This program is open to first- and second-year law students and third-year night students who are African American, Latino, Native American, Alaskan Native, Asian, or Pacific Islander. Applicants may be enrolled at a law school in New York or be residents of New York and enrolled at a law school in another state. They must be interested in a summer internship at a government agency or public interest organization in New York in the field of environmental, energy, or natural resources law. Selection is based on interest in environmental issues, academic record, personal qualities, financial need, and leadership abilities.

Financial data The stipend is $6,000.

Duration At least 10 weeks during the summer.

Additional information This program is cosponsored by the Environmental Law Section of the New York State Bar Association and the Committee on Environmental Law of the New York City Bar Association.

Number awarded 1 or more each year.

Deadline November of each year.

[1003]
NEWBERRY CONSORTIUM IN AMERICAN INDIAN AND INDIGENOUS STUDIES GRADUATE STUDENT FELLOWSHIPS

Newberry Library
Attn: McNickle Center for American Indian History
60 West Walton Street
Chicago, IL 60610-3305
(312) 255-3564   Fax: (312) 255-3696
E-mail: mcnickle@newberry.org
Web: www.newberry.org/mcnickle/NCAISFellows.html

Summary To provide funding to doctoral students at member institutions of the Newberry Consortium in American Indian and Indigenous Studies (NCAIS) who wish to conduct dissertation research in American Indian studies at the D'Arcy McNickle Center for the History of the American Indian at the Newberry Library.

Eligibility This program is open to advanced graduate students at NCAIS institutions who are interested in conducting dissertation research in American Indian studies at the Newberry Library. Applicants must submit their curriculum vitae, 2 letters of recommendation, and a 2- to 3-page summary of an approved dissertation proposal, including a discussion of the methodology to be employed and the specific Newberry or other library collections to be consulted.

Financial data Grants provide a stipend of $2,500 per month.

Duration From 1 to 2 months.

Additional information The Newberry Library inaugurated the NCAIS in 2009, following the end of its partnership with the 13 universities of Committee on Institutional Cooperation (CIC). It is limited to 18 universities in the United States and Canada; for a list of those universities, contact the Newberry. Fellows are expected to present their research at the consortium's annual graduate student conference or at a Newberry-sponsored seminar in American Indian and Indigenous studies.

Number awarded Varies each year; recently, 7 of these fellowships were awarded.

Deadline February of each year.

[1004]
NEXSEN PRUET DIVERSITY SCHOLARSHIPS

Nexsen Pruet
Attn: Diversity Scholarship
1230 Main Street, Suite 700
P.O. Drawer 2426
Columbia, SC 29202-2426
(803) 771-8900   Fax: (803) 727-1469
E-mail: diversity@nexsenpruet.com
Web: www.nexsenpruet.com/firm-diversity.html

Summary To provide financial assistance to Native Americans and members of other minority groups attending designated law schools in North and South Carolina.

Eligibility This program is open to minority students currently enrolled in the first year at the University of North Carolina School of Law, University of South Carolina School of Law, Wake Forest University School of Law, North Carolina Central University School of Law, Charleston School of Law, or Charlotte School of Law. Applicants must be interested in practicing law in North or South Carolina after graduation. Along with their application, they must submit information on their academic achievements; their contributions to promoting diversity in their community, school, or work environment; and their ability to overcome challenges in the pursuit of their goals. They must also submit essays of 250 words each on 1) their reasons for preparing for a legal career; 2) their interest in the private practice of law in North Carolina and/or South Carolina; 3) any obstacles, including but not limited to financial obstacles, that the scholarship will help them overcome; and 4) what they see as potential obstacles, issues, and opportunities facing new minority lawyers.

Financial data The stipend is $3,000 per year.

Duration 1 year; recipients may reapply.

Additional information Recipients are considered for summer employment in an office of the firm after completion of their first year of law school.

Number awarded Varies each year; recently, 3 of these scholarships were awarded.

Deadline October of each year.

[1005]
NEZ PERCE HIGHER EDUCATION GRANTS

Nez Perce Tribe
Attn: Higher Education
116 Veterans Drive
P.O. Box 365
Lapwai, ID 83540
(206) 621-4610   Fax: (206) 843-7387
E-mail: education@nezperce.org
Web: www.nezperce.org/Official/highereducation.htm

Summary To provide financial assistance to members of the Nez Perce Tribe who are interested in attending college or graduate school in any state.

Eligibility This program is open to enrolled members of the Nez Perce Tribe who are attending or planning to attend a college, university, or vocational/technical school in any state to work on a vocational certificate or an associate, bachelor's, master's, or doctoral/professional degree. Applicants must submit documentation of financial need and a personal letter describing their educational goals and future plans.

Financial data Tribal scholarship funds (including the Isaac Broncheau Memorial Fund and the Nez Perce Tribal Tobacco Tax Revenue Funds) provide stipends of $1,600 per year for undergraduates (including vocational/technical students) or $3,000 per year for graduate students. Funding from the Bureau of Indian Affairs (BIA) is generally available only for undergraduate students and provides stipends of $3,120 per year.

Duration 1 semester; may be renewed up to 4 additional semesters for a 2-year degree, up to 9 additional semesters for a 4-year degree, up to 5 additional semesters for a master's degree, or up to 9 additional semesters for a doctoral/professional degree.

Number awarded Varies each year.

Deadline September of each year for fall semester or quarter; January of each year for spring semester or winter quarter; March of each year for spring quarter.

[1006]
NICKERSON WEST SHAKESPEARE/ARAPAHO FARM TRUST GRADUATE SCHOLARSHIP

Northern Arapaho Tribe
Attn: Sky People Higher Education
P.O. Box 8480
Ethete, WY 82520
(307) 332-5286   Toll Free: (800) 815-6795
Fax: (307) 332-9104   E-mail: assistant@skypeopleed.org
Web: www.skypeopleed.org

Summary To provide financial assistance to members of the Northern Arapaho Tribe who are working on a graduate degree in any field.

Eligibility This program is open to full-time graduate students who have the GPA required by their school. Applicants must be of at least one-fourth Northern Arapaho descent (enrolled or non-enrolled) and must submit a Certificate of Indian Blood or other verification of Northern Arapaho blood with at least one-fourth degree. They may be working on a degree in any field. Along with their application, they must submit a 1-page personal statement that includes a brief history of their background, academic ability and achievement, work or leadership experience, participation in community-related activities, and career goals. Selection is based on that statement, potential to contribute to the community upon graduation, academic ability and achievement, and a letter of recommendation.

Financial data The stipend is $1,500 per year.

Duration 1 year; may be renewed.

Additional information Recipients are expected to apply for employment with the Northern Arapaho Tribe after graduation.

Number awarded 2 each year.

Deadline June of each year.

[1007]
NMAI INTERNSHIP PROGRAM

National Museum of the American Indian
Attn: Internship Program
Cultural Resources Center
4220 Silver Hill Road
Suitland, MD 20746-2863
(301) 238-1540   Fax: (301) 238-3200
E-mail: NMAIinterns@si.edu
Web: americanindian.si.edu

Summary To provide work and/or research opportunities for Native American students in the area of museum practice and related programming at the Smithsonian Institution's National Museum of the American Indian (NMAI).

Eligibility These internships are intended primarily for American Indian, Native Hawaiian, and Alaska Native students currently enrolled in undergraduate or graduate academic programs with a cumulative GPA of 3.0 or higher. Applicants must be interested in guided work/research experiences using the resources of the NMAI or other Smithsonian Institution facilities. Along with their application, they must submit a personal statement on their interest in the museum field, what they hope to accomplish through an internship, how it would relate to their academic and professional development, and what in particular about the NMAI interests them and leads them to apply for an internship.

Financial data Travel, housing, and stipends (from $300 to $400 per week) are provided on a limited basis.

Duration 3 sessions of 10 weeks each are held annually.

Additional information Intern projects vary by department. Most projects provide the intern with museum practice and program development experience. Some projects may be more research oriented. Interns who receive a stipend must work 40 hours per week. Positions are available at the Cultural Resources Center in Suitland, Maryland, the George Gustav Heye Center in New York, or the administrative offices in Washington, D.C.

Number awarded Varies each year. More than 100 students have participated in the program since it began in 1994.

Deadline February of each year for summer; July of each year for fall; November of each year for spring.

[1008]
NNALEA ACADEMIC SCHOLARSHIP PROGRAM

National Native American Law Enforcement Association
Attn: Academic Scholarship Program
1300 Pennsylvania Avenue, N.W., Suite 700
P.O. Box 171
Washington, DC 20044
(202) 204-3065   Fax: (866) 506-7631
E-mail: info@nnalea.org
Web: www.nnalea.org

Summary To provide financial assistance to Native American high school seniors, undergraduates, and graduate students who have an interest in law enforcement.

Eligibility This program is open to Native Americans who are working on or planning to work on an undergraduate or graduate degree in law enforcement at a 4-year college or university. Applicants must have a GPA of 2.5 or higher. Along with their application, they must provide transcripts and a

200-word essay on Indian Country law enforcement and its impact on tribal communities.

Financial data Stipends are $2,500 or $2,000.

Duration 1 year.

Additional information This program includes 2 named awards: the Jimmy Wooten Memorial Scholarship and the Don Leonard Memorial Scholarship.

Number awarded 2 each year: the Jimmy Wooten Memorial Scholarship at $2,500 and the Don Leonard Memorial Scholarship at $2,000.

Deadline November of each year.

[1009]
NNALSA WRITING COMPETITION

National Native American Law Students Association
Attn: Stephanie Gassert, Competition Administrator
c/o Meg Daniels
875 Summit Avenue
St. Paul, MN 55105-3076
E-mail: stephanie.gassert@wmitchell.edu
Web: nationalnalsa.org

Summary To recognize and reward members of the National Native American Law Students Association (NNALSA) who submit outstanding articles on Indian law.

Eligibility This competition is open to NNALSA members who submit articles, from 25 to 50 pages in length in standard legal essay format, on a topic of importance to Indians, including federal Indian law and policy, tribal law and policy, international law and policy concerning indigenous peoples, or intertribal or government-to-government studies. Selection is based on originality, timeliness of topic, quality and creativity of analysis, knowledge and use of relevant law, grammar, punctuation, and citation style.

Financial data The first-place winner receives $1,000 and publication in the *William Mitchell Law Review*. The second-place winner receives $500 and the third-place winner receives $250.

Duration The competition is held annually.

Additional information This competition was first held in 2002.

Number awarded 3 each year.

Deadline January of each year.

[1010]
NOME ESKIMO COMMUNITY HIGHER EDUCATION SCHOLARSHIPS

Nome Eskimo Community
Attn: Tribal Services
P.O. Box 1090
Nome, AK 99762
(907) 443-2246   Fax: (907) 443-3539
E-mail: marshasloan@gci.net
Web: www.necalaska.org/services.html

Summary To provide financial assistance to Alaska Natives and American Indians who are members of a tribe affiliated with the Nome Eskimo Community and interested in attending college or graduate school in any state.

Eligibility This program is open to high school seniors and current college students who are members of an Alaska Native or American Indian tribe or organization affiliated with the Nome Eskimo Community, regardless of their current res-idence. Applicants must be enrolled or planning to enroll at an accredited college or university in any state to work on an associate, bachelor's, or (if funding is available) master's degree. They must have graduated or will graduate from high school with a GPA of 2.0 or higher.

Financial data A stipend is awarded (amount not specified). Funding is considered supplemental and will not cover the total financial need of students.

Duration 1 year; may be renewed until completion of a degree, provided the recipient maintains acceptable academic progress and a satisfactory GPA.

Additional information Members of the Nome Eskimo Community reflect the heritages of the Bering Straits region of Alaska, including Central Yupik, Inupiaq, St. Lawrence Island Yupik, and American Indians whose lineage derives from tribes in the lower 48 states.

Number awarded Varies each year.

Deadline April of each year for high school seniors entering college as first-year students; July of each year for continuing students for fall semester or quarter; December of each year for spring semester or winter quarter; February or each year for spring quarter; May of each year for summer term.

[1011]
NORTH AMERICAN DOCTORAL FELLOWSHIPS

The Fund for Theological Education, Inc.
Attn: North American Doctoral Fellows Program
825 Houston Mill Road, Suite 100
Atlanta, GA 30329
(404) 727-1450   Fax: (404) 727-1490
Web: www.fteleaders.org/pages/NAD-fellowships

Summary To provide financial assistance to Native Americans and other minority students enrolled in a doctoral program in religious or theological studies.

Eligibility This program is open to continuing students enrolled full time in a Ph.D. or Th.D. program in religious or theological studies. Applicants must be citizens or permanent residents of the United States or Canada who are racial or ethnic minority students traditionally underrepresented in graduate education (e.g., African Americans, Asian Americans, Native Hawaiians, Native Americans, Alaska Natives, Hispanics). D.Min. students are ineligible. Preference is given to students nearing completion of their degree. Selection is based on commitment to teaching and scholarship, academic achievement, capacity for leadership in theological scholarship, and financial need.

Financial data Stipends range from $5,000 to $10,000 per year, depending on financial need.

Duration 1 year; may be renewed up to 2 additional years.

Additional information Funding for this program is provided by the National Council of Churches, proceeds from the book *Stony the Road We Trod: African American Biblical Interpretation,* an endowment from the Hearst Foundation, and the previously established FTE Black Doctoral Program supported by Lilly Endowment, Inc.

Number awarded Varies each year; recently, 12 of these fellowships were awarded.

Deadline February of each year.

[1012]
NORTH CAROLINA DIVERSITY FELLOWSHIPS IN ENVIRONMENTAL LAW

American Bar Association
Attn: Section of Environment, Energy, and Resources
321 North Clark Street
Chicago, IL 60654-7598
(312) 988-5602   Fax: (312) 988-5572
E-mail: jonusaid@staff.abanet.org
Web: www.abanet.org

Summary To provide funding to Native Americans and other law students from traditionally underrepresented groups who are interested in working on a summer project related to environmental, energy, or natural resources law in North Carolina.

Eligibility This program is open to first- and second-year law students and third-year night students who are members of underrepresented and underserved groups, such as minority or low-income populations. Students may be residents of any state and attending school in any state; preference is given to residents of North Carolina and to students who are enrolled at law schools in North Carolina or who have a strong interest in the state. Applicants must be interested in a summer internship at a government agency or public interest organization in North Carolina and working on an environmental project. Selection is based on interest in environmental issues, academic record, personal qualities, and leadership abilities.

Financial data The stipend is $5,000.

Duration 8 to 10 weeks during the summer.

Additional information This program is cosponsored by the Environment, Energy and Natural Resources Law Section of the North Carolina Bar Association.

Number awarded 2 each year.

Deadline February of each year.

[1013]
NORTHERN ARAPAHO TRIBE ALFRED J. DURAN SR. TRUST SCHOLARSHIP

Northern Arapaho Tribe
Attn: Sky People Higher Education
P.O. Box 8480
Ethete, WY 82520
(307) 332-5286   Toll Free: (800) 815-6795
Fax: (307) 332-9104   E-mail: assistant@skypeopleed.org
Web: www.skypeopleed.org

Summary To provide financial assistance to members of the Northern Arapaho Tribe who are working on an undergraduate or graduate degree in any field.

Eligibility This program is open to full-time undergraduate and graduate students who have an undergraduate GPA of 2.0 or higher or the graduate GPA required by their school. Applicants must be at least one-fourth Northern Arapaho (enrolled or non-enrolled) and must submit a Certificate of Indian Blood or other verification of Northern Arapaho blood with at least one-fourth degree. They may be working on a degree in any field. Along with their application, they must submit a 1-page personal statement that includes a brief history of their background, academic ability and achievement, work or leadership experience, participation in community-related activities, and career goals. Selection is based on that

statement, potential to contribute to the community upon graduation, academic ability and achievement, and a letter of recommendation.

Financial data The stipend is $1,000 per year.

Duration 1 year; may be renewed.

Additional information Recipients are expected to apply for employment with the Northern Arapaho Tribe after graduation.

Number awarded 2 each year.

Deadline June of each year.

[1014]
NORTHERN CHEYENNE HIGHER EDUCATION SCHOLARSHIP PROGRAM

Northern Cheyenne Nation
Attn: Tribal Education Department
P.O. Box 307
Lame Deer, MT 59043
(406) 477-6770   Toll Free: (800) 353-8183
Fax: (406) 477-8150   E-mail: darleneh@rangeweb.net
Web: www.cheyennenation.com/education.html

Summary To provide financial assistance to Northern Cheyenne tribal members who are interested in attending college or graduate school in any state.

Eligibility This program is open to enrolled Northern Cheyenne tribal members who have been accepted to a degree program at an accredited college or university in any state. The priority order for awards is 1) continuing and former college students in good standing; 2) graduating high school seniors in good standing or first-time adult college applicants not previously funded; 3) students or other individuals who have previously failed to meet the requirements of the scholarship program; and 4) graduate students (if funds are still available). Applicants must be able to demonstrate financial need. Along with their application, they must submit a 1-page statement on their educational goals, including need for the scholarship, choice of college, major, entry date, and plans after graduation.

Financial data The stipend depends on the need of the recipient, to a maximum of $6,000 per year. These awards are intended to supplement other available sources of funding. The scholarship must be used for tuition, subsistence, required fees, and textbooks.

Duration 1 year; may be renewed if the recipient maintains a GPA of 2.0 or higher and completes at least 14 quarter or 16 semester units as a freshman and sophomore and at least 16 quarter or 18 semester units as a junior or senior.

Number awarded Approximately 80 each year.

Deadline February of each year for fall quarter or semester; September of each year for winter quarter, spring semester, or spring quarter; March of each year for summer school.

[1015]
NOTTAWASEPPI HURON BAND OF POTAWATOMI HIGHER EDUCATION SCHOLARSHIPS

Nottawaseppi Huron Band of Potawatomi
Attn: Education Director
2221 1-1/2 Mile Road
Fulton, MI 49052
(269) 729-5151, ext. 205   Fax: (269) 729-4837
E-mail: bphillips@nhbpi.com
Web: nhbpi.com/departments/education.html

Summary To provide financial assistance to members of the Nottawaseppi Huron Band of Potawatomi who are interested in attending college, graduate school, or vocational training in any state.

Eligibility This program is open to members of the Nottawaseppi Huron Band of Potawatomi who are working on or planning to work on a vocational certificate or an associate, bachelor's, or graduate degree at a school in any state. Applicants may be planning to enroll full or part time. They must be able to demonstrate financial need.

Financial data A stipend is awarded (amount not specified).

Duration 1 year; may be renewed.

Number awarded Varies each year.

Deadline July of each year for fall quarter or semester; November of each year for winter quarter or spring semester.

[1016]
OFFICE OF HAWAIIAN AFFAIRS SCHOLARSHIPS

Hawai'i Community Foundation
Attn: Scholarship Department
827 Fort Street Mall
Honolulu, HI 96813
(808) 537-6333   Toll Free: (888) 731-3863
Fax: (808) 521-6286
E-mail: scholarships@hcf-hawaii.org
Web: www.hawaiicommunityfoundation.org/scholarships

Summary To provide financial assistance for college or graduate school to Native Hawaiian residents of any state.

Eligibility This program is open to residents of any state who can document Hawaiian ancestry through the Office of Hawaiian Affairs Hawaiian Registry Program. Applicants must be enrolled full or part time at an accredited 2- or 4-year college or university as an undergraduate or graduate student. They must be able to demonstrate academic achievement (GPA of 2.0 or higher for undergraduates or 3.0 or higher for graduate students), good moral character, and financial need. Along with their application, they must submit a short statement indicating their reasons for attending college, their planned course of study, their career goals, and what community service means to them.

Financial data The amounts of the awards depend on the availability of funds and the need of the recipient. Recently, the average value of all scholarships awarded by the foundation was $2,041.

Duration 1 year; may be renewed.

Number awarded Varies each year.

Deadline February of each year.

[1017]
OLIVER GOLDSMITH, M.D. SCHOLARSHIP

Kaiser Permanente Southern California
Attn: Resident Recruitment and Outreach
393 East Walnut Street
Pasadena, CA 91188
Toll Free: (877) 574-0002   Fax: (626) 405-6581
E-mail: socal.residency@kp.org
Web: residency.kp.org

Summary To provide financial assistance to Native American and other medical students who will help bring diversity to the profession.

Eligibility This program is open to students entering their third or fourth year of allopathic or osteopathic medical school. Applicants must have demonstrated their commitment to diversity through community service, clinical volunteering, or research. They may be attending medical school in any state, but they must intend to practice in southern California and they must be available to participate in a mentoring program and a clinical rotation at a Kaiser Permanente facility in that region.

Financial data The stipend is $5,000.

Duration 1 year.

Additional information These scholarships were first awarded in 2004.

Number awarded 12 each year.

Deadline February of each year.

[1018]
OLIVER W. HILL SCHOLARSHIP

LeClairRyan
Attn: Director, Recruiting and Diversity
Riverfront Plaza, East Tower
951 East Byrd Street, Eighth Floor
Richmond, VA 23219
(804) 783-7597   Fax: (804) 783-2294
E-mail: george.braxton@leclairryan.com
Web: www.leclairryan.com

Summary To provide financial assistance to Native Americans and other students of color at law schools in Virginia and Washington, D.C.

Eligibility This program is open to students of color who have completed at least 1 semester at a law school in Virginia or Washington, D.C. Applicants must be planning to practice in Virginia after graduation. They must have a GPA of 2.5 or higher. Along with their application, they must submit a 2,000-word essay presenting their ideas of pursuing social justice through the law.

Financial data The stipend is $5,000.

Duration 1 year.

Additional information This program was established in 2009.

Number awarded 1 each year.

Deadline March of each year.

[1019]
ONEIDA TRIBE HIGHER EDUCATION GRANT PROGRAM

Oneida Tribe of Indians of Wisconsin
Attn: Higher Education Office
N7210 Seminary Road, North Wing
P.O. Box 365
Oneida, WI 54155-0365
(920) 869-4033   Toll Free: (800) 236-2214, ext. 4033
Fax: (920) 869-4039 E-mail: highered@oneidanation.org
Web: www.oneidanation.org/highered

Summary To provide financial assistance for undergraduate or graduate study to members of the Oneida Tribe of Indians of Wisconsin.

Eligibility This program is open to enrolled members of the Oneida Tribe of Indians of Wisconsin who have a high school diploma, HSED diploma, or GED. Applicants must be working on or planning to work on a vocational/technical, undergraduate, graduate, or doctoral degree at a college, university, or vocational school in any state. They must be able to demonstrate financial need.

Financial data Stipends range up to $20,000 per year, depending on the need of the recipient.

Duration The total length of eligibility is 6 terms for vocation/technical students, 10 terms for undergraduate students, 6 terms for graduate students, and 10 terms for doctoral students. To be eligible for renewal, vocational/technical students and undergraduates must maintain a GPA of 2.0 or higher and graduate and doctoral students must maintain a GPA of 3.0 or higher.

Number awarded Varies each year, depending upon the availability of funds.

Deadline Applications must be submitted by April of each year for the fall term, by September of each year for the spring term, or by April of each year for the summer term.

[1020]
OPERATION JUMP START III SCHOLARSHIPS

American Association of Advertising Agencies
Attn: AAAA Foundation
405 Lexington Avenue, 18th Floor
New York, NY 10174-1801
(212) 682-2500   Toll Free: (800) 676-9333
Fax: (212) 682-2028   E-mail: ameadows@aaaa.org
Web: www2.aaaa.org

Summary To provide financial assistance to Native American and other multicultural art directors and copywriters interested in working on an undergraduate or graduate degree in advertising.

Eligibility This program is open to African Americans, Asian Americans, Hispanic Americans, and Native Americans who are U.S. citizens or permanent residents. Applicants must be incoming graduate students at 1 of 6 designated portfolio schools or full-time juniors at 1 of 2 designated colleges. They must be able to demonstrate extreme financial need, creative talent, and promise. Along with their application, they must submit 10 samples of creative work in their respective field of expertise.

Financial data The stipend is $5,000 per year.

Duration Most awards are for 2 years.

Additional information Operation Jump Start began in 1997 and was followed by Operation Jump Start II in 2002. The current program began in 2006. The 6 designated portfolio schools are the AdCenter at Virginia Commonwealth University, the Creative Circus in Atlanta, the Portfolio Center in Atlanta, the Miami Ad School, the University of Texas at Austin, and Pratt Institute. The 2 designated colleges are the Minneapolis College of Art and Design and the Art Center College of Design at Pasadena, California.

Number awarded 20 each year.

Deadline Deadline not specified.

[1021]
OREGON DIVERSITY FELLOWSHIPS IN ENVIRONMENTAL LAW

American Bar Association
Attn: Section of Environment, Energy, and Resources
321 North Clark Street
Chicago, IL 60654-7598
(312) 988-5602   Fax: (312) 988-5572
E-mail: jonusaid@staff.abanet.org
Web: www.abanet.org

Summary To provide funding to Native American and other law students from underrepresented groups who are interested in working on a summer project related to environmental, energy, or natural resources law in Oregon.

Eligibility This program is open to first- and second-year law students and third-year night students who are members of underrepresented and underserved groups, such as minority or low-income populations. Students may be residents of any state and attending school in any state; preference is given to residents of Oregon and to students who are enrolled at law schools in Oregon or who have a strong interest in the state. Applicants must be interested in a summer internship at a government agency or public interest organization in Oregon and working on a project in the fields of environmental, energy, or natural resources law. Selection is based on interest in environmental issues, academic record, personal qualities, and leadership abilities.

Financial data The stipend is $5,000.

Duration 8 to 10 weeks during the summer.

Additional information This program is cosponsored by the Affirmative Action Program of the Oregon State Bar.

Number awarded 1 each year.

Deadline January of each year.

[1022]
OREGON STATE BAR SCHOLARSHIPS

Oregon State Bar
Attn: Affirmative Action Program
16037 S.W. Upper Boones Ferry Road
P.O. Box 231935
Tigard, OR 97281-1935
(503) 431-6338
Toll Free: (800) 452-8260, ext. 338 (within OR)
Fax: (503) 598-6938   E-mail: eyip@osbar.org
Web: www.osbar.org/aap

Summary To provide financial assistance to Native American and other entering and continuing students from any state enrolled at law schools in Oregon, especially those who will help the Oregon State Bar achieve its Affirmative Action objectives.

Eligibility This program is open to students entering or continuing at 1 of the law schools in Oregon (Willamette, University of Oregon, and Lewis and Clark). Preference is given to students who will contribute to the Oregon State Bar's Affirmative Action Program to "increase the diversity of the Oregon bench and bar to reflect the diversity of the people of Oregon." Applicants must submit 1) a personal statement on their history of disadvantage or barriers to educational advancement, personal experiences of discrimination, extraordinary financial obligations, composition of immediate family, extraordinary health or medical needs, and languages in which they are fluent as well as barriers they have experienced because English is a second language; and 2) a state bar statement on why they chose to attend an Oregon law school; if they are not committed but are considering practicing in Oregon, what would help them to decide to practice in the state; and how they will improve the quality of legal service or increase access to justice in Oregon. Selection is based on financial need (30%), the personal statement (25%), the state bar statement (25%), community activities (10%), and employment history (10%).

Financial data The stipend is $2,000 per year. Funds are credited to the recipient's law school tuition account.

Duration 1 year; recipients may reapply.

Number awarded 10 each year.

Deadline March of each year.

[1023]
OSAGE HIGHER EDUCATION GRANTS

Osage Nation Department of Education
Attn: Scholarship Program
105 Buffalo Avenue
Hominy, OK 74035
(918) 287-5301   Fax: (918) 885-2136
E-mail: scholarship@osagetribe.com
Web: www.osagetribe.com

Summary To provide financial assistance for college or graduate school to members of the Osage Tribe.

Eligibility This program is open to Osage tribal students who are enrolled or planning to enroll in a 2- or 4-year college or university. A point system is used to rank applicants, including such factors as student status (freshman through graduate student), number of previous full-time semesters in college, GPA from previous semester, full-time or part-time enrollment, qualification for federal Pell Grant, and Osage blood quantum.

Financial data The amount of the award depends on the number of points earned by the recipient.

Duration 1 semester; may be renewed.

Number awarded Varies each year.

Deadline July of each year for fall semester; December of each year for spring semester; April of each year for summer term.

[1024]
OSAGE TRIBAL EDUCATION COMMITTEE PROGRAM

Osage Tribal Education Committee
c/o Oklahoma Area Education Office
200 N.W. Fourth, Suite 4049
Oklahoma City, OK 73102
(405) 605-6051, ext. 304   Fax: (405) 605-6057
Web: www.osagetribe.com/education/info.aspx

Summary To provide financial assistance to undergraduate and graduate Osage students.

Eligibility This program is open to students who can prove Osage Indian blood in any degree. Applicants must be working on or planning to work on an undergraduate or graduate degree at an accredited college, university, or technical vocational program. They may be residents of any state.

Financial data The amount of the award depends on the financial need of the recipient.

Duration 1 year; may be renewed for up to 4 additional years, provided the recipient reapplies each semester and maintains a GPA of 2.0 or higher.

Number awarded Varies each year.

Deadline June of each year for fall term; December of each year for spring term.

[1025]
OTTAWA TRIBE HIGHER EDUCATION GRANTS

Ottawa Tribe of Oklahoma
c/o Oklahoma Area Education Office
200 N.W. Fourth, Suite 4049
Oklahoma City, OK 73102
(405) 605-6051, ext. 304   Fax: (405) 605-6057
Web: ottawatribe.org/heducation.htm

Summary To provide financial assistance to members of the Ottawa Tribe of Oklahoma who plan to attend college or graduate school in any state.

Eligibility This program is open to enrolled members of the Ottawa Tribe of Oklahoma who have been accepted at an accredited institution of higher education in any state as a full- or part-time undergraduate or graduate student. Applicants must be able to document financial need. Along with their application, they must submit a copy of their tribal enrollment card, a copy of their high school and/or college transcripts, documentation of financial need, and a letter of intent explaining why they wish to attend college.

Financial data The amount of the award depends on the financial need of the recipient.

Duration 1 year; may be renewed for up to 4 additional years, provided the recipient reapplies each semester and maintains a GPA of 2.0 or higher.

Number awarded Varies each year.

Deadline July of each year.

[1026]
PASCUA YAQUI HIGHER EDUCATION SCHOLARSHIP

Pascua Yaqui Tribe
Attn: Higher Education Program
7474 South Camino de Oeste
Tucson, AZ 85757
(520) 883-5706   Toll Free: (800) 5-PASCUA
Fax: (520) 883-5021
Web: www.pascuayaqui-nsn.gov

Summary To provide financial assistance to members of the Pascua Yaqui Tribe who are interested in attending college or graduate school in any state.

Eligibility This program is open to enrolled members of the Pascua Yaqui Tribe who are attending or planning to attend a public college, university, or vocational/technical institute in any state. Applicants must apply for all other available aid and still have unmet financial need. They may be planning to work on an undergraduate or graduate degree on a full- or part-time basis.

Financial data A stipend is awarded (amount not specified).

Duration 1 semester; may be renewed for a total of 6 semesters of full-time work on an associate degree; 72 credits of part-time work on an associate degree, 12 semesters of full-time work on a bachelor's degree, 130 credit hours of part-time work on a bachelor's degree, 5 semesters of full-time work on a master's or doctoral degree, the required credits of the program for part-time graduate students, or an additional 2 semesters for doctoral students to completed their dissertation. Renewal requires that recipients maintain a GPA of 2.0 or higher as an undergraduate or 3.0 or higher as a graduate student.

Number awarded Varies each year.

Deadline July of each year for fall; December of each year for spring.

[1027]
PATRICK D. MCJULIEN MINORITY GRADUATE SCHOLARSHIP

Association for Educational Communications and
  Technology
Attn: ECT Foundation
1800 North Stonelake Drive, Suite 2
Bloomington, IN 47408
(812) 335-7675   Toll Free: (877) 677-AECT
Fax: (812) 335-7678
Web: www.aect.org/Foundation/Awards/McJulien.asp

Summary To provide financial assistance to Native American and other minority members of the Association for Educational Communications and Technology (AECT) working on a graduate degree in the field of educational communications and technology.

Eligibility This program is open to AECT members who are members of minority groups. Applicants must be full-time graduate students enrolled in a degree-granting program in educational technology at the master's (M.S.), specialist (Ed.S.), or doctoral (Ph.D., Ed.D.) levels. They must have a GPA of 3.0 or higher.

Financial data A stipend is awarded (amount not specified).

Duration 1 year.

Number awarded 1 each year.

Deadline July of each year.

[1028]
PAUL AND EMILY SHAGEN SCHOLARSHIP

Chippewa County Community Foundation
P.O. Box 1979
Sault Ste. Marie, MI 49783
(906) 635-1046   Fax: (775) 417-7368
E-mail: cccf@lighthouse.net
Web: www.cccf4good4ever.org/main.asp?id=7

Summary To provide financial assistance to members of the Sault Ste. Marie Tribe of Chippewa Indians who are interested in attending college or graduate school in any state.

Eligibility This program is open to enrolled members of the Sault Ste. Marie Tribe of Chippewa Indians who have been accepted for enrollment as a full-time undergraduate, graduate, or professional student at an accredited college, university, vocational school, or community college in any state. Applicants must submit an essay of 300 to 500 words on how they plan to use the education or training to contribute to the community, including the tribe. Selection is based on that essay, academic performance and progress, and financial need.

Financial data A stipend is awarded (amount not specified).

Duration 1 year.

Number awarded Varies each year.

Deadline June or November of each year.

[1029]
PAUL D. WHITE SCHOLARSHIP

Baker Hostetler LLP
Attn: Attorney Recruitment and Development Manager
PNC Center
1900 East Ninth Street, Suite 3200
Cleveland, OH 44114-3482
(216) 621-0200   Fax: (216) 696-0740
E-mail: ddriscole@bakerlaw.com
Web: www.bakerlaw.com/firmdiversity/scholarship

Summary To provide financial assistance and summer work experience to American Indian and other minority law school students.

Eligibility This program is open to first- and second-year law students of African American, Hispanic, Asian American, or American Indian descent. Selection is based on law school performance, demonstrated leadership abilities (as evidenced by community and collegiate involvement), collegiate academic record, extracurricular activities, work experience, and a written personal statement.

Financial data The program provides a stipend of $7,500 for the scholarship and a paid summer clerkship with the sponsoring firm. To date, the firm has expended nearly $2.0 million in scholarships and clerkships.

Duration 1 year, including the following summer.

Additional information This program was established in 1997. Clerkships may be performed at any of the firm's offices in Chicago, Cincinnati, Cleveland, Columbus, Costa Mesa, Denver, Houston, Los Angeles, New York, Orlando, or Washington, D.C.

Number awarded   1 or more each year.
Deadline   January of each year.

[1030]
PBS&J ACHIEVEMENT SCHOLARSHIP

Conference of Minority Transportation Officials
Attn: National Scholarship Program
818 18th Street, N.W., Suite 850
Washington, DC 20006
(202) 530-0551   Fax: (202) 530-0617
Web: www.comto.org/news-youth.php

Summary   To provide financial assistance to Native American and other minority high school seniors, undergraduates, and graduate students interested in studying the field of transportation.

Eligibility   This program is open to minority graduating high school seniors, current undergraduates, and graduate students interested in the field of transportation. Applicants must be enrolled or planning to enroll full time at an accredited college, university, or vocational/technical institution. They must have a GPA of 2.0 or higher. Along with their application, they must submit a cover letter with a 500-word statement of career goals. Financial need is not considered in the selection process. U.S. citizenship is required.

Financial data   The stipend is $4,000. Funds are paid directly to the recipient's college or university.

Duration   1 year.

Additional information   The Conference of Minority Transportation Officials (COMTO) was established in 1971 to promote, strengthen, and expand the roles of minorities in all aspects of transportation. This program is sponsored by the engineering, architecture, and sciences company PBS&J. Recipients are expected to attend the COMTO National Scholarship Luncheon.

Number awarded   1 or more each year.

Deadline   April of each year.

[1031]
PEARL CARTER SCOTT AVIATION SCHOLARSHIP

Chickasaw Foundation
110 West 12th Street
P.O. Box 1726
Ada, OK 74821-1726
(580) 421-9030   Fax: (580) 421-9031
E-mail: ChickasawFoundation@chickasaw.net
Web: www.chickasawfoundation.org/index_20.htm

Summary   To provide financial assistance to members of the Chickasaw Nation who are working on an undergraduate or graduate degree in a field related to aviation.

Eligibility   This program is open to Chickasaw students who are currently enrolled at a college, university, or recognized private aviation school. Applicants must be working full time on an undergraduate or graduate degree in a field related to aviation (e.g., aviation maintenance technology, flight training, aviation law, air traffic control, aeronautical engineering, aerospace mechanical engineering, manufacturing engineering with an aviation emphasis, airline and airport operations, airport management, meteorology, aviation technology management, or a related field). Along with their application, they must submit high school or college tran-

scripts, 2 letters of recommendation, a copy of their Chickasaw Nation citizenship card, and a 1-page essay on their long-term goals and plans for achieving them. Financial need is not considered in the selection process.

Financial data   The stipend is $1,250 per year.

Duration   1 year; may be renewed if the recipient demonstrates appropriate progress toward a degree in an aviation program.

Number awarded   1 each year.

Deadline   August of each year.

[1032]
PEDRO BAY SCHOLARSHIP

Bristol Bay Native Corporation
Attn: BBNC Education Foundation
111 West 16th Avenue, Suite 400
Anchorage, AK 99501
(907) 278-3602   Toll Free: (800) 426-3602
Fax: (907) 276-3925   E-mail: pelagiol@bbnc.net
Web: www.bbnc.net

Summary   To provide financial assistance to shareholders of Pedro Bay Corporation who are working on an undergraduate or graduate degree at a college in any state.

Eligibility   This program is open to Pedro Bay Corporation shareholders who are enrolled full time as a junior, senior, or advanced degree student at an accredited college or university in any state. Applicants must have a GPA of 2.0 or higher and be able to demonstrate financial need. Along with their application, they must submit an essay on how they became interested in their proposed field of study, any special circumstances they want to be considered, and their desire to work in the region. Selection is based on the essay (35%), cumulative GPA (40%), financial need (20%), and letters of recommendation (5%).

Financial data   The stipend is $3,000.

Duration   1 year.

Additional information   This program is funded by Pedro Bay Benefits Corporation and administered by the Bristol Bay Native Corporation Education Foundation.

Deadline   March of each year.

[1033]
PENOBSCOT NATION FELLOWSHIP

Penobscot Nation
Attn: Department of Education and Career Services
6 River Road
Indian Island, ME 04468
(207) 827-1649, ext. 148   Fax: (207) 827-2088
E-mail: pnhec@penobscotnation.org
Web: www.penobscotnation.org/Education/education.htm

Summary   To provide financial assistance to members of the Penobscot Nation who are working on a graduate degree at a college or university in any state.

Eligibility   This program is open to students who are members of the Penobscot Nation and are enrolled either full or part time in a graduate degree program at a college or university in any state. Selection is not based on financial need.

Financial data   A stipend is awarded (amount not specified). Funds may be used for any educational expense.

Duration   1 year or more.

Number awarded Varies each year.

Deadline June of each year.

[1034]
PEORIA TRIBE MASTER'S PROGRAM SCHOLARSHIP

Peoria Tribe of Indians of Oklahoma
Attn: Education Program
118 South Eight Tribes Trail
P.O. Box 1527
Miami, OK 74355
(918) 540-2535, ext. 10   Toll Free: (800) 259-9987
Fax: (918) 540-2538
Web: www.peoriatribe.com/programs/education.php

Summary To provide financial assistance to members of the Peoria Tribe of Indians of Oklahoma who are interested in working on a master's degree at a university in any state.

Eligibility This program is open to enrolled members of the Peoria Tribe of Indians of Oklahoma who have been accepted by an accredited college or university in any state as a full- or part-time student. Applicants must be planning to work on a master's degree. They must submit a copy of their tribal card and proof of acceptance into a master's degree program. Selection is based on academic achievement and the probability of completing the academic program; financial need is not considered.

Financial data The stipend is $3,000 per semester for full-time students or $1,500 per semester for part-time students.

Duration 1 semester; may be renewed up to 3 additional semesters.

Number awarded Varies each year.

Deadline July of each year for the fall semester; January of each year for the spring semester.

[1035]
PERKINS COIE DIVERSITY STUDENT FELLOWSHIPS

Perkins Coie LLP
Attn: Chief Diversity Officer
131 South Dearborn Street, Suite 1700
Chicago, IL 60603-5559
(312) 324-8593   Fax: (312) 324-9400
E-mail: TCropper@perkinscoie.com
Web: www.perkinscoie.com/diversity/Diversity.aspx

Summary To provide financial assistance and work experience to Native American and other law students who reflect the diversity of communities in the country.

Eligibility This program is open to students enrolled in the first year of a J.D. program at an ABA-accredited law school. Applicants must contribute meaningfully to the diversity of the law school student body and the legal profession. Diversity is defined broadly to include members of racial, ethnic, disabled, and sexual orientation minority groups, as well as those who may be the first person in their family to pursue higher education. Applicants must submit a 1-page personal statement that describes their unique personal history, a legal writing sample, a current resume, and undergraduate and law school transcripts. They are not required to disclose their financial circumstances, but a demonstrated need for financial assistance may be taken into consideration.

Financial data The stipend is $7,500.

Duration 1 year.

Additional information Fellows are also offered a summer associateship at their choice of the firm's offices in Anchorage, Bellevue, Boise, Chicago, Dallas, Los Angeles, Madison, Palo Alto, Phoenix, Portland, San Diego, San Francisco, Seattle, or Washington, D.C.

Number awarded Varies each year; recently, 7 of these fellowships were awarded.

Deadline January of each year.

[1036]
PETER DOCTOR MEMORIAL INDIAN SCHOLARSHIP GRANTS

Peter Doctor Memorial Indian Scholarship Foundation, Inc.
c/o Clara Hill, Treasurer
P.O. Box 731
Basom, NY 14013
(716) 542-2025   E-mail: cehill@wnynet.net

Summary To provide financial assistance to New York Iroquois Indians currently enrolled at a college in any state on the undergraduate or graduate school level.

Eligibility This program is open to enrolled New York Iroquois Indian students who have completed at least 1 year at a technical school, college, or university in any state. Both undergraduate and graduate students are eligible. There are no age limits or GPA requirements. Interviews may be required. Applicants must have tribal certification. Selection is based on need.

Financial data Stipends range up to $1,500.

Duration 2 years for medical students; 1 year for all other recipients.

Deadline May of each year.

[1037]
PETER KALIFORNSKY MEMORIAL ENDOWMENT SCHOLARSHIP FUND

Cook Inlet Region, Inc.
Attn: The CIRI Foundation
3600 San Jeronimo Drive, Suite 256
Anchorage, AK 99508-2870
(907) 793-3575   Toll Free: (800) 764-3382
Fax: (907) 793-3585   E-mail: tcf@thecirifoundation.org
Web: www.thecirifoundation.org/designated.htm

Summary To provide financial assistance for undergraduate or graduate studies to Alaska Natives who are original enrollees to Cook Inlet Region, Inc. (CIRI) and their lineal descendants.

Eligibility This program is open to Alaska Native enrollees to CIRI under the Alaska Native Claims Settlement Act (ANCSA) of 1971 and their lineal descendants. There are no Alaska residency requirements or age limitations. Applicants must be accepted or enrolled full time in a 4-year undergraduate or a graduate degree program. Preference is given to students in Alaska Native studies. They must have a GPA of 2.5 or higher. Along with their application, they must submit a 500-word statement on their educational and career goals and how they are contributing, or planning to contribute, to a positive Alaska Native community. Selection is based on that statement, academic achievement, rigor of course work or degree program, student financial contribution, financial need, grade level, previous work performance, community service, and relationship of degree program to career goals.

Financial data The stipend is $10,000 per year, $8,000 per year, or $2,500 per semester, depending on GPA.

Duration 1 semester or 1 year.

Additional information This program was established in 1993.

Number awarded Varies each year.

Deadline May of each year for annual scholarships; May or November of each year for semester scholarships.

[1038]
PGA TOUR DIVERSITY INTERNSHIP PROGRAM

PGA Tour, Inc.
Attn: Minority Internship Program
100 PGA Tour Boulevard
Ponte Vedra Beach, FL 32082
(904) 285-3700
Web: www.pgatour.com/company/internships.html

Summary To provide summer work experience to Native Americans and other undergraduate and graduate students who are interested in learning about the business side of golf and will contribute to diversity in the profession.

Eligibility This program is open to students who either have completed at least their sophomore year at an accredited 4-year college or university or are enrolled in graduate school. Applicants should be able to enrich the PGA Tour and its partnering organizations through diversity. They must have a GPA of 2.8 or higher. International students are eligible if they are legally permitted to work in the United States. Although all interns work in the business side of golf, the ability to play golf or knowledge of the game is not required for many positions.

Financial data Interns receive competitive wages and up to $500 for travel expenses to orientation in Ponte Vedra Beach, Florida or their initial work location. Depending on position and location, other benefits include subsidized housing, discounts on company merchandise, access to company training seminars, and possible golf privileges.

Duration Most assignments are for 10 to 12 weeks during the summer.

Additional information This program was established in 1992. Positions are available in accounting, corporate marketing, business development, international TV, information systems, event management, tournament services, tournament operations, retail licensing, sales, human resources, new media, and other areas within the PGA Tour. Most assignments are in Ponte Vedra Beach, Florida.

Number awarded Approximately 30 each year.

Deadline February of each year.

[1039]
PHILLIPS FUND GRANTS FOR NATIVE AMERICAN RESEARCH

American Philosophical Society
Attn: Committee on Research
104 South Fifth Street
Philadelphia, PA 19106-3387
(215) 440-3429   Fax: (215) 440-3436
E-mail: LMusumeci@amphilsoc.org
Web: www.amphilsoc.org/grants/phillips

Summary To provide funding to graduate students and scholars interested in conducting research on North American Indian anthropological linguistics and ethnohistory.

Eligibility Eligible to apply are scholars, preferably young scholars, working in the fields of Native American linguistics and ethnohistory and the history of Native Americans in the continental United States and Canada. Applications are not accepted for projects in archaeology, ethnography, psycholinguistics, or for the preparation of pedagogical materials. Graduate students may apply for support for research on their master's or doctoral dissertations.

Financial data The grants average $2,500 and rarely exceed $3,500. These funds are intended for such extra costs as travel, tapes, films, and informants' fees, but not for general maintenance or the purchase of books or permanent equipment.

Duration 1 year.

Number awarded Varies each year; recently, 18 of these grants were awarded.

Deadline February of each year.

[1040]
PI STATE NATIVE AMERICAN GRANTS-IN-AID

Delta Kappa Gamma Society International-Pi State
    Organization
c/o Harlene Gilbert
5338 East Lake Road
Romulus, NY 14541
(315) 585-6691   E-mail: hgilbert@happiness.org
Web: www.deltakappagamma.org/NY/ASaGiA.html

Summary To provide funding to Native American women from New York who plan to work in education or another service field.

Eligibility This program is open to Native American women from New York who are attending a 2- or 4-year college in the state. Applicants must be planning to work in education or another service field, but preference is given to those majoring in education. Both undergraduate and graduate students are eligible.

Financial data The grant is $500 per semester ($1,000 per year). Funds may be used for any career-related purpose, including purchase of textbooks.

Duration 1 semester; may be renewed for a total of 5 years and a total of $5,000 over a recipient's lifetime.

Number awarded Up to 5 each year.

Deadline July or December of each year.

[1041]
POARCH BAND OF CREEK INDIANS ACADEMIC ACHIEVEMENT BONUS

Poarch Band of Creek Indians
Attn: Tuition Program Coordinator
5811 Jack Springs Road
Atmore, AL 36502
(251) 368-9136, ext. 2241   Fax: (251) 368-4502
E-mail: sfisher@pci-nsn.gov
Web: www.poarchcreekindians.org

Summary To recognize and reward members of the Poarch Band of Creek Indians who achieve academic excellence while working on an undergraduate or graduate degree.

Eligibility These awards are presented to enrolled members of the Poarch Band of Creek Indians who are enrolled full time in an associate, bachelor's, or master's degree program at a college or university in any state. To qualify, they must maintain a GPA of 3.5 or higher each semester of the academic year.

Financial data The award is $2,000 for associate degree students, $4,000 for bachelor's degree students, or $2,000 for master's degree students. Other professional degree students are evaluated on a case-by-case basis.

Duration The awards are presented annually.

Number awarded Varies each year.

Deadline Deadline not specified.

[1042]
POKAGON BAND HIGHER EDUCATION SCHOLARSHIP

Pokagon Band of Potawatomi Indians
Attn: Department of Education
58620 Sink Road
P.O. Box 180
Dowagiac, MI 49047
(269) 782-0887   Toll Free: (888) 330-1234
Fax: (269) 782-0985
E-mail: joseph.avance@pokagon.com
Web: www.pokagon.com/education/edu-highered.htm

Summary To provide financial assistance to members of the Pokagon Band of Potawatomi Indians who are interested in working on an undergraduate or graduate degree at a college in any state.

Eligibility This program is open to enrolled members of the Pokagon Band who are attending or planning to attend an accredited college or university in any state to work on an associate, bachelor's, master's, or doctoral degree. Applicants must apply for all campus-based financial aid for which they are eligible and be able to document that they still have an unmet financial need. If they plan to attend a public college or university in Michigan and have an Indian blood level of one-quarter or more, they must also apply for a Michigan Indian Tuition Waiver.

Financial data The stipend is $100 per credit hour for associate degree students (to a maximum of 18 credit hours per semester), $200 per credit hour for bachelor's degree students (to a maximum of 18 credit hours per semester), or $300 per credit hour for graduate students (to a maximum of 12 credit hours per semester).

Duration 1 semester; may be renewed for a total of 3 years of study for an associate degree, 5 years of study for a bachelor's degree, or 5 years of study for a graduate degree.

Number awarded Varies each year.

Deadline Deadline not specified.

[1043]
PONCA TRIBE OF NEBRASKA EDUCATIONAL GRANTS

Ponca Tribe of Nebraska
Attn: Director of Education
1800 Syracuse Avenue
Norfolk, NE 68701
(402) 371-8834   Fax: (402) 371-7564
E-mail: pate@poncatribe-ne.org
Web: www.poncatribe-ne.org/departments_education.php

Summary To provide financial assistance to members of the Ponca Tribe of Nebraska who are interested in attending an undergraduate, graduate, or vocational school in any state.

Eligibility This program is open to enrolled members of the Ponca Tribe of Nebraska who are attending or planning to attend a college, university, or vocational/technical school in any state. Applicants must submit a letter of admission from the school they plan to attend, a Certificate of Indian Blood (CIB), and documentation of financial need.

Financial data A stipend is awarded (amount not specified).

Duration 1 semester or year. Full-time students may reapply each academic year (or summer session if they wish to attend summer school). Part-time students may reapply each semester or quarter. Renewals are approved if the student maintains a GPA of 2.0 or higher as an undergraduate or vocational student or 3.0 or higher as a graduate student.

Number awarded Varies each year.

Deadline August of each year for fall quarter or semester; November of each year for winter quarter; December of each year for spring quarter or semester; May of each year for summer session.

[1044]
PORTER PHYSIOLOGY DEVELOPMENT AWARDS

American Physiological Society
Attn: Education Office
9650 Rockville Pike, Room 3111
Bethesda, MD 20814-3991
(301) 634-7132   Fax: (301) 634-7098
E-mail: education@the-aps.org
Web: www.the-aps.org

Summary To provide research funding to Native Americans and other minorities who are members of the American Physiological Society (APS) interested in working on a doctoral degree in physiology.

Eligibility This program is open to U.S. citizens and permanent residents who are members of racial or ethnic minority groups (Hispanic or Latino, American Indian or Alaska Native, Asian, Black or African American, or Native Hawaiian or other Pacific Islander). Applicants must be currently enrolled in or accepted to a doctoral program in physiology at a university as full-time students. They must be APS members. Selection is based on the applicant's potential for success (academic record, statement of interest, previous awards and experiences, letters of recommendation); applicant's proposed training environment (including quality of preceptor); and applicant's research and training plan (clarity and quality).

Financial data The stipend is $28,300. No provision is made for a dependency allowance or tuition and fees.

Duration 1 year; may be renewed for 1 additional year and, in exceptional cases, for a third year.

Additional information This program is supported by the William Townsend Porter Foundation (formerly the Harvard Apparatus Foundation). The first Porter Fellowship was awarded in 1920. In 1966 and 1967, the American Physiological Society established the Porter Physiology Development Committee to award fellowships to minority students engaged in graduate study in physiology.

Number awarded Varies each year; recently, 8 of these fellowships were awarded.

Deadline January of each year.

[1045]
PRAIRIE BAND POTAWATOMI NATION HIGHER EDUCATION GRADUATE PROGRAM

Prairie Band Potawatomi Nation
Attn: Higher Education
16281 Q Road
Mayetta, KS 66509-8970
(785) 966-2960   Toll Free: (877) 715-6789
Fax: (785) 966-2956   E-mail: info@pbpnation.org
Web: www.pbpindiantribe.com/education.aspx

Summary To provide financial assistance to members of the Prairie Band Potawatomi Nation who are interested in attending graduate school in any state.

Eligibility This program is open to members of the Prairie Band Potawatomi Nation who have a Certificate of Indian Blood. Applicants must be enrolled or planning to enroll at a college or university in any state to work on a master's or doctoral degree. Along with their application, they must submit a letter explaining why they need the grant and how it will be used.

Financial data Full-time students receive a stipend of up to $5,000 per semester. Funds may be used for tuition, fees, and books. Part-time students are eligible for exact costs only.

Duration 1 semester; may be renewed.

Number awarded Varies each year.

Deadline Applications must be submitted at least 2 months prior to beginning of attendance or payment due date, whichever occurs first.

[1046]
PREDOCTORAL FELLOWSHIP IN MENTAL HEALTH AND SUBSTANCE ABUSE SERVICES

American Psychological Association
Attn: Minority Fellowship Program
750 First Street, N.E.
Washington, DC 20002-4242
(202) 336-6127   Fax: (202) 336-6012
TDD: (202) 336-6123   E-mail: mfp@apa.org
Web: www.apa.org

Summary To provide financial assistance to minority and other doctoral students committed to providing mental health and substance abuse services to ethnic minority populations.

Eligibility Applicants must be U.S. citizens or permanent residents, enrolled full time in an accredited doctoral program, and committed to a career in psychology related to ethnic minority mental health and substance abuse services. Members of ethnic minority groups (African Americans, His-

panics/Latinos, American Indians, Alaskan Natives, Asian Americans, Native Hawaiians, and other Pacific Islanders) are especially encouraged to apply. Preference is given to students specializing in clinical, school, and counseling psychology. Students of any other specialty will be considered if they plan careers in which their training will lead to delivery of mental health or substance abuse services to ethnic minority populations. Selection is based on commitment to ethnic minority health and substance abuse services, knowledge of ethnic minority psychology or mental health issues, the fit between career goals and training environment selected, potential to become a culturally competent mental health service provider as demonstrated through accomplishments and goals, scholarship and grades, and letters of recommendation.

Financial data The stipend varies but is based on the amount established by the National Institutes of Health for predoctoral students; recently that was $21,600 per year.

Duration 1 academic or calendar year; may be renewed for up to 2 additional years.

Additional information Funding is provided by the U.S. Substance Abuse and Mental Health Services Administration.

Number awarded Varies each year.

Deadline January of each year.

[1047]
PREDOCTORAL FELLOWSHIPS OF THE FORD FOUNDATION DIVERSITY FELLOWSHIP PROGRAM

National Research Council
Attn: Fellowships Office, Keck 576
500 Fifth Street, N.W.
Washington, DC 20001
(202) 334-2872   Fax: (202) 334-3419
E-mail: infofell@nas.edu
Web: www.nationalacademies.org

Summary To provide financial assistance for graduate school to Native Americans and other students whose success will increase the racial and ethnic diversity of U.S. colleges and universities.

Eligibility This program is open to citizens and nationals of the United States who are enrolled or planning to enroll full time in a Ph.D. or Sc.D. degree program and are committed to a career in teaching and research at the college or university level. Applicants may be undergraduates in their senior year, individuals who have completed undergraduate study or some graduate study, or current Ph.D. or Sc.D. students who can demonstrate that they can fully utilize a 3-year fellowship award. They must be working on or planning to work on a degree in most areas of the arts, sciences, humanities, and social sciences or in interdisciplinary ethnic or area studies. Support is not provided to students working on a degree in most practice-oriented areas, terminal master's degrees, other doctoral degrees (e.g., Ed.D., D.F.A., Psy.D.), professional degrees (e.g., medicine, law, public health), or joint degrees (e.g., M.D./Ph.D., J.D./Ph.D., M.F.A./Ph.D) The following are considered as positive factors in the selection process: evidence of superior academic achievement; promise of continuing achievement as scholars and teachers; membership in a group whose underrepresentation in the American professoriate has been severe and longstanding, including Black/African Americans, Puerto Ricans, Mexican Americans/Chicanos/Chicanas, Native American Indians, Alaska Natives (Eskimos, Aleuts, and other indigenous people of Alaska), and Native Pacific Islanders (Hawaiians, Micronesians, or Polynesians); capacity to respond in pedagogically productive ways to the learning needs of students from diverse backgrounds; sustained personal engagement with communities that are underrepresented in the academy and an ability to bring this asset to learning, teaching, and scholarship at the college and university level; and likelihood of using the diversity of human experience as an educational resource in teaching and scholarship.

Financial data The program provides a stipend to the student of $20,000 per year and an award to the host institution of $2,000 per year in lieu of tuition and fees.

Duration 3 years of support is provided, to be used within a 5-year period.

Additional information The competition for this program is conducted by the National Research Council on behalf of the Ford Foundation. Applicants who merit receiving the fellowship but to whom awards cannot be made because of insufficient funds are given Honorable Mentions; this recognition does not carry with it a monetary award but honors applicants who have demonstrated substantial academic achievement. The National Research Council publishes a list of those Honorable Mentions who wish their names publicized. Fellows may not accept remuneration from another fellowship or similar external award while on this program; however, supplementation from institutional funds, educational benefits from the Department of Veterans Affairs, or educational incentive funds may be received concurrently with Ford Foundation support. Predoctoral fellows are required to submit an interim progress report 6 months after the start of the fellowship and a final report at the end of the 12 month tenure.

Number awarded Approximately 60 each year.

Deadline November of each year.

[1048]
PRINCE KUHI'O HAWAIIAN CIVIC CLUB SCHOLARSHIP

Prince Kuhi'o Hawaiian Civic Club
Attn: Scholarship Chair
P.O. Box 4728
Honolulu, HI 96812
E-mail: pkhcc64@gmail.com
Web: www.pkhcc.com/scholarship.html

Summary To provide financial assistance for undergraduate or graduate studies to persons of Native Hawaiian descent.

Eligibility This program is open to high school seniors and full-time undergraduate or graduate students who are of Hawaiian descent (descendants of the aboriginal inhabitants of the Hawaiian Islands prior to 1778). Graduating high school seniors and current undergraduate students must have a GPA of 2.5 or higher; graduate students must have at least a 3.3 GPA. Along with their application, they must submit an essay on how they will apply their education toward the well-being of the Hawaiian community. Priority is given to members of the Prince Kuhi'o Hawaiian Civic Club in good standing, including directly-related family members. Special consideration is given to applicants majoring in Hawaiian studies, Hawaiian language, education, or journalism. Selec-

tion is based on academic achievement and leadership potential.

Financial data Stipends range from $500 to $1,000 per year.

Duration 1 year; may be renewed.

Number awarded Varies each year.

Deadline March of each year.

[1049]
PUBLIC HONORS FELLOWSHIPS OF THE OREGON STATE BAR

Oregon State Bar
Attn: Affirmative Action Program
16037 S.W. Upper Boones Ferry Road
P.O. Box 231935
Tigard, OR 97281-1935
(503) 431-6338
Toll Free: (800) 452-8260, ext. 338 (within OR)
Fax: (503) 598-6938   E-mail: eyip@osbar.org
Web: www.osbar.org/aap

Summary To provide Native American and other law students in Oregon with summer work experience in public interest law, especially those who will help the Oregon State Bar achieve its Affirmative Action objectives.

Eligibility This program is open to students at Oregon's law schools (Willamette, University of Oregon, and Lewis and Clark) who are not in the first or final year of study. Each school may nominate up to 5 students. Nominees must have demonstrated a career goal in public interest or public sector law. Preference is given to students who will contribute to the Oregon State Bar's Affirmative Action Program and "increase the diversity of the Oregon bench and bar to reflect the diversity of the people of Oregon." They must be interested in working in a law office during the summer; the employment should be in Oregon, although exceptions will be made if the job offers the student special experience not available within the state. Along with their application, they must submit 1) a personal statement on their history of disadvantage or barriers to educational advancement, personal experiences of discrimination, extraordinary financial obligations, composition of immediate family, extraordinary health or medical needs, and languages in which they are fluent as well as barriers they have experienced because English is a second language; and 2) a state bar statement on why they chose to attend an Oregon law school; if they are not committed but are considering practicing in Oregon, what would help them to decide to practice in the state; and how they will improve the quality of legal service or increase access to justice in Oregon. From the nominees of each school, 2 students are selected on the basis of financial need (30%), the personal statement (25%), the state bar statement (25%), and public service (20%). The information on those students is forwarded to prospective employers in Oregon and they arrange to interview the selectees.

Financial data Fellows receive a stipend of $4,800.

Duration 3 months during the summer.

Additional information There is no guarantee that all students selected by the sponsoring organization will receive fellowships at Oregon law firms.

Number awarded 6 each year: 2 from each of the law schools.

Deadline Each law school sets its own deadline.

[1050]
PUEBLO OF ISLETA HIGHER EDUCATION PROGRAM

Pueblo of Isleta
Attn: Higher Education Program
P.O. Box 1270
Isleta, NM 87022
(505) 924-3186   Fax: (505) 869-7692
E-mail: poi08090@isletapueblo.com
Web: www.isletapueblo.com/highered2.html

Summary To provide financial assistance to members of the Pueblo of Isleta who are interested in attending college or graduate school in any state.

Eligibility This program is open to undergraduate and graduate students who can document tribal membership in the Pueblo of Isleta or at least one-quarter Isleta blood. Applicants must have a GPA of 2.5 or higher and be able to demonstrate financial need. They must have applied for federal aid by submitting a Free Application for Federal Student Aid (FAFSA).

Financial data The stipend depends on the need of the recipient.

Duration 1 year; may be renewed if the recipient maintains a GPA of 2.5 or higher.

Number awarded Varies each year.

Deadline June of each year for the fall semester; October of each year for the spring semester or winter quarter; March of each year for summer term.

[1051]
PUEBLO OF LAGUNA HIGHER EDUCATION PROGRAM

Pueblo of Laguna
Attn: Laguna Higher Education
P.O. Box 207
Laguna, NM 87026
(505) 552-7182   Fax: (505) 552-7235
E-mail: m.conant@lagunaed.net
Web: www.ldoe.org/pfs_programs.html

Summary To provide financial assistance to regular members of the Pueblo of Laguna who are interested in attending college or graduate school in any state.

Eligibility This program is open to regular enrolled members of the Pueblo of Laguna. Applicants must have a high school diploma or GED certificate and be working on a bachelor's, transferable associate, or graduate degree. They must have been accepted by an accredited college or university in the United States as a full-time student. Along with their application, they must submit documentation of financial need, a 1-page personal statement on their purpose in working on a degree in their chosen field of study and their career or professional goals, high school and/or college transcripts, ACT scores, and verification of tribal membership or Indian blood. Vocational students, part-time students, and "naturalized" Laguna tribal members are not eligible.

Financial data Stipends are intended to cover unmet financial need, to a maximum of $8,000 per year. Most awards range from $2,000 to $5,000 per academic year.

Duration 1 year; may be renewed for a maximum of 4 academic years (students may submit an appeal for a fifth year of study), provided the recipient maintains a GPA of 2.0 or higher and full-time enrollment.

Number awarded Varies each year.

Deadline May of each year for the fall term or academic year; October of each year for the winter/spring term; April of each year for the summer term.

[1052]
PYRAMID LAKE PAIUTE TRIBE ENRICHMENT SCHOLARSHIP

Pyramid Lake Paiute Tribe
Attn: Consolidated Higher Education Office
P.O. Box 256
Nixon, NV 89424
(775) 574-0300   Fax: (775) 574-0302
E-mail: asampson@plpt.nsn.us
Web: www.plpt.nsn.us/highed/index.html

Summary To provide financial assistance to members of the Pyramid Lake Paiute Tribe who are interested in working part time on an undergraduate or graduate degree.

Eligibility This program is open to enrolled members of the Pyramid Lake Paiute Tribe who are working on or planning to work on an associate, bachelor's, master's, or doctoral (including law and medicine) degree. Applicants may take up to 9 credits per term (or 12 credits for law and medical students). They must have a GPA of 2.0 or higher for their most recent semester. Along with their application, they must submit a 75-word essay on how they will benefit from the courses they are taking.

Financial data The stipend is $1,000 per semester (or $2,000 per semester for law and medical students). A supplemental grant of $250 is provided for books and supplies.

Duration 1 semester; may be renewed, provided the recipient maintains a GPA of 2.0 or higher.

Number awarded Varies each year.

Deadline June of each year for fall; November of each year for spring.

[1053]
QUAPAW TRIBAL EDUCATIONAL FUND PROGRAM

Quapaw Tribe of Oklahoma
Office of Educational Funds
P.O. Box 765
Quapaw, OK 74363
(918) 542-1853, ext. 211   Toll Free: (888) 642-4724
Fax: (918) 542-4694   E-mail: pleptich@quapawtribe.com
Web: quapawtribe.com/site/view/73841_Eduction.pml

Summary To provide financial assistance for college or graduate school to members of the Quapaw Tribe of Oklahoma.

Eligibility This program is open to enrolled members of the Quapaw Tribe who are or will be high school graduates or GED recipients. Applicants must be attending or planning to attend an accredited college, university, or vocational school in any state at the undergraduate or graduate level. Along with their application, they must submit an essay of 150 to 600 words on their educational goals and plans for utilizing their educational funding.

Financial data Participating students receive $100 per credit hour, to a maximum of $2,100 per semester.

Duration 1 semester; may be renewed, provided the recipient maintains a GPA of 2.0 or higher.

Number awarded Varies each year.

Deadline September of each year for fall semester; January of each year for spring semester; August of each year for summer school.

[1054]
RACE RELATIONS MULTIRACIAL STUDENT SCHOLARSHIP

Christian Reformed Church
Attn: Office of Race Relations
2850 Kalamazoo Avenue, S.E.
Grand Rapids, MI 49560-0200
(616) 241-1691   Toll Free: (877) 279-9994
Fax: (616) 224-0803   E-mail: crcna@crcna.org
Web: www.crcna.org/pages/racerelations_scholar.cfm

Summary To provide financial assistance to Native American and other undergraduate and graduate minority students interested in attending colleges related to the Christian Reformed Church in North America (CRCNA).

Eligibility Students of color in the United States and Canada are eligible to apply. Normally, applicants are expected to be members of CRCNA congregations who plan to pursue their educational goals at Calvin Theological Seminary or any of the colleges affiliated with the CRCNA. Students who have no prior history with the CRCNA must attend a CRCNA-related college or seminary for a full academic year before they are eligible to apply for this program. Students entering their sophomore year must have earned a GPA of 2.0 or higher as freshmen; students entering their junior year must have earned a GPA of 2.3 or higher as sophomores; students entering their senior year must have earned a GPA of 2.6 or higher as juniors.

Financial data First-year students receive $500 per semester. Other levels of students may receive up to $2,000 per academic year.

Duration 1 year.

Additional information This program was first established in 1971 and revised in 1991. Recipients are expected to train to engage actively in the ministry of racial reconciliation in church and in society. They must be able to work in the United States or Canada upon graduating and must consider working for 1 of the agencies of the CRCNA.

Number awarded Varies each year; recently, 31 students received a total of $21,000 in support.

Deadline March of each year.

[1055]
RACIAL ETHNIC SUPPLEMENTAL GRANTS

Presbyterian Church (USA)
Attn: Office of Financial Aid for Studies
100 Witherspoon Street, Room M-052
Louisville, KY 40202-1396
(502) 569-5224   Toll Free: (888) 728-7228, ext. 5224
Fax: (502) 569-8766   E-mail: finaid@pcusa.org
Web: www.pcusa.org/financialaid/programs/grant.htm

Summary To provide financial assistance to Native Americans and other minority graduate students who are Presbyterian Church (USA) members interested in preparing for church occupations.

Eligibility This program is open to racial/ethnic graduate students (Asian American, African American, Hispanic American, Native American, or Alaska Native) who are enrolled full time at a PCUSA seminary or accredited theological institution approved by their Committee on Preparation for Ministry. Applicants must be working on 1) an M.Div. degree and enrolled as an inquirer or candidate by a PCUSA presbytery, or 2) an M.A.C.E. degree and preparing for a church occupation. They must be PCUSA members, U.S. citizens or permanent residents, able to demonstrate financial need, and recommended by the financial aid officer at their theological institution. Along with their application, they must submit a 1,000-word essay on what they believe God is calling them to do in ministry.

Financial data Stipends range from $500 to $1,000 per year. Funds are intended as supplements to students who have been awarded a Presbyterian Study Grant but still demonstrate remaining financial need.

Duration 1 year; may be renewed up to 2 additional years.

Number awarded Varies each year.

Deadline June of each year.

[1056]
RAE ROYER MEMORIAL SCHOLARSHIP FUND

Rosebud Sioux Tribe
Attn: Higher Education Grant Program
P.O. Box 130
Rosebud, SD 57570-0130
(605) 747-2375   Toll Free: (877) 808-3283
Fax: (605) 747-5274   E-mail: rstedav@gwtc.net
Web: www.gwtc.net/~rsted/index_files/Page599.html

Summary To provide financial assistance to members of the Rosebud Sioux Tribe who are interested in attending college or graduate school in any state and returning to the reservation to work for the tribe.

Eligibility This program is open to members of the Rosebud Sioux Tribe who are enrolled or planning to enroll at a college or university in any state to work on an undergraduate or graduate degree. Undergraduates may enroll full or part time, but only full-time graduate students are eligible. Applicants must be able to demonstrate financial need. They must indicate a willingness to commit to a 1-year or 1-semester internship of service to the tribe for each year of funding received. In the selection process, half the awards are reserved for students who live within the boundaries of the Rosebud Reservation in south central South Dakota and half to those who live off the reservation.

Financial data For undergraduates, the maximum stipend is $1,500 per term for students with no dependents or $3,000 per term for students with dependents. For graduate students, the maximum stipend is $6,000 per term.

Duration 1 year; may be renewed, provided recipients earn a GPA of 2.0 or higher as a freshman and sophomore, 2.5 or higher as a junior and senior, or 3.5 or higher as a graduate student.

Number awarded Varies each year.

Deadline July of each year for fall semester; October of each year for winter quarter; November of each year for spring semester; January of each year for spring quarter; March of each year for summer school.

[1057]
RALPH K. FRASIER SCHOLARSHIP

Porter Wright Morris & Arthur LLP
Huntington Center
41 South High Street
Columbus, OH 43215
(614) 227-2000   Toll Free: (800) 533-2794
Fax: (614) 227-2100
Web: www.porterwright.com/diversity_statement

Summary To provide financial assistance and summer work experience to Native American and other minority students from any state who are enrolled at designated law schools in Ohio.

Eligibility This program is open to minority students enrolled in the first year at the following law schools: Ohio State University Moritz College of Law, Capital University Law School, Case Western Reserve University School of Law, Cleveland-Marshall College of Law, University of Cincinnati College of Law, University of Dayton School of Law, and University of Toledo College of Law. Applicants must submit undergraduate and law school transcripts, a resume, and an essay in the form of a legal memorandum on a hypothetical law case. They must also indicate their choice of the sponsoring firm's offices in Cleveland and Columbus for a summer clerkship.

Financial data The program provides a competitive salary for the summer clerkship and a stipend of $5,000 for the second year of law school.

Duration 1 year.

Additional information This program was established in 2005.

Number awarded 2 each year: 1 for a clerkship in Cleveland and 1 for a clerkship in Columbus.

Deadline January of each year.

[1058]
RALPH W. SHRADER DIVERSITY SCHOLARSHIPS

Armed Forces Communications and Electronics
  Association
Attn: AFCEA Educational Foundation
4400 Fair Lakes Court
Fairfax, VA 22033-3899
(703) 631-6149   Toll Free: (800) 336-4583, ext. 6149
Fax: (703) 631-4693   E-mail: scholarship@afcea.org
Web: www.afcea.org

Summary To provide financial assistance to minority and other master's degree students in fields related to communications and electronics.

Eligibility This program is open to U.S. citizens working on a master's degree at an accredited college or university in the United States. Applicants must be enrolled full time and studying computer science, computer technology, engineering (chemical, electrical, electronic, communications, or systems), mathematics, physics, management information systems, or a field directly related to the support of U.S. national security or intelligence enterprises. At least 1 of these scholarships is set aside for a woman or a minority. Selection is based primarily on academic excellence.

Financial data The stipend is $3,000. Funds are paid directly to the recipient.

Duration 1 year.

Additional information This program is sponsored by Booz Allen Hamilton.

Number awarded Up to 5 each year, at least 1 of which is for a woman or minority candidate.

Deadline February of each year.

[1059]
RDW GROUP, INC. MINORITY SCHOLARSHIP FOR COMMUNICATIONS

Rhode Island Foundation
Attn: Funds Administrator
One Union Station
Providence, RI 02903
(401) 427-4017   Fax: (401) 331-8085
E-mail: lmonahan@rifoundation.org
Web: www.rifoundation.org

Summary To provide financial assistance to Native Americans and other undergraduate and graduate students of color in Rhode Island who are interested in preparing for a career in communications at a school in any state.

Eligibility This program is open to undergraduate and graduate students at colleges and universities in any state who are Rhode Island residents of color. Applicants must intend to work on a degree in communications (including computer graphics, art, cinematography, or other fields that would prepare them for a career in advertising). They must be able to demonstrate financial need and a commitment to a career in communications. Along with their application, they must submit an essay (up to 300 words) on the impact they would like to have on the communications field.

Financial data The stipend ranges from $1,000 to $2,500 per year.

Duration 1 year; recipients may reapply.

Additional information This program is sponsored by the RDW Group, Inc.

Number awarded 1 each year.

Deadline April of each year.

[1060]
REAL PROPERTY LAW SECTION MINORITY FELLOWSHIP

The New York Bar Foundation
One Elk Street
Albany, NY 12207
(518) 487-5651   Fax: (518) 487-5699
E-mail: foundation@tnybf.org
Web: www.tnybf.org/restrictedfunds.htm

Summary To provide an opportunity for Native American and other minority residents of any state attending law school in New York to gain summer work experience at a public interest organization that represents tenants in local landlord/tenant cases.

Eligibility This program is open to minority students from any state who are enrolled at a law school in New York state. Students must be interested in working during the summer for a public interest legal organization in the state that represents tenants in local landlord/tenant cases. Applications must be submitted by the organization, which must be located in New York City or on Long Island.

Financial data The stipend is $3,333.

Duration 8 weeks during the summer.

Additional information This program was established in 2007 by the Real Property Law Section of the New York State Bar Association. It is administered by The New York Bar Foundation.

Number awarded 1 or more each year.

Deadline October of each year.

[1061]
RED CLIFF BAND HIGHER EDUCATION GRANTS PROGRAM

Red Cliff Band of Lake Superior Chippewa
Attn: Education Department
88385 Pike Road, Highway 13
Bayfield, WI 54814
(715) 779-3706, ext. 229   Fax: (715) 779-3704
E-mail: Carmen.VanderVenter@redcliff-nsn.gov
Web: redcliff-nsn.gov

Summary To provide financial assistance for college or graduate school to members of the Red Cliff Band of Lake Superior Chippewa.

Eligibility This program is open to enrolled tribal members of the Red Cliff Band who are working on or planning to work on an undergraduate or graduate degree. Applicants must be able to demonstrate financial need.

Financial data The maximum stipend for undergraduate students is $1,800 per year. The stipend for graduate students depends on the availability of funds.

Duration 1 year; may be renewed for a total of 10 semesters, provided the recipient maintains a GPA of 2.0 or higher as an undergraduate or 3.0 or higher as a graduate student.

Number awarded Varies each year.

Deadline June of each year.

[1062]
REED SMITH DIVERSE SCHOLARS PROGRAM

Reed Smith LLP
Attn: U.S. Director of Legal Recruiting
2500 One Liberty Place
1650 Market Street
Philadelphia, PA 19103
(215) 851-8100   E-mail: dlevin@reedsmith.com
Web: diversity.reedsmith.com

Summary To provide financial assistance and summer work experience to Native American and other law students who are committed to diversity.

Eligibility This program is open to students completing their first year of law school. Applicants must be able to demonstrate a record of academic excellence and a commitment to diversity, inclusion, and community. Along with their application, they must submit 500-word statements on 1) the goals of diversity and inclusion in the legal profession and how their life experiences will enable them to contribute to those goals; and 2) their community involvement and/or volunteer efforts.

Financial data The stipend is $10,000. Recipients are also offered a summer associate position at their choice of 8 of the firm's U.S. offices after completion of their second year of law school.

Duration 1 year (the second year of law school).

Additional information The firm established this program in 2008 as part of its commitment to promote diversity in the legal profession.

Number awarded Several each year.

Deadline July of each year.

[1063]
RICHARD AND HELEN BROWN COREM SCHOLARSHIPS

United Church of Christ
Parish Life and Leadership Ministry Team
Attn: COREM Administrator
700 Prospect Avenue East
Cleveland, OH 44115-1100
(216) 736-2113   Toll Free: (866) 822-8224, ext. 2113
Fax: (216) 736-3783
Web: www.ucc.org/seminarians/ucc-scholarships-for.html

Summary To provide financial assistance to Native American and other minority seminary students who are interested in becoming a pastor in the United Church of Christ (UCC).

Eligibility This program is open to students at accredited seminaries who have been members of a UCC congregation for at least 1 year. Applicants must work through 1 of the member bodies of the Council for Racial and Ethnic Ministries (COREM): United Black Christians (UBC), Ministers for Racial, Social and Economic Justice (MRSEJ), Council for Hispanic Ministries (CHM), Pacific Islander and Asian American Ministries (PAAM), or Council for American Indian Ministries (CAIM). They must 1) have a GPA of 3.0 or higher, 2) be enrolled in a course of study leading to ordained ministry, 3) be in care of an association or conference at the time of application, and 4) demonstrate leadership ability through participation in their local church, association, conference, or academic environment.

Financial data Stipends are approximately $10,000 per year.

Duration 1 year.

Number awarded Varies each year; recently, 4 scholarships were awarded by UBC, 3 by MRSEJ, and 2 by CHM.

Deadline Deadline not specified.

[1064]
RICHARD D. HAILEY AAJ LAW STUDENT SCHOLARSHIPS

American Association for Justice
Attn: Minority Caucus
777 Sixth Street, N.W., Suite 200
Washington, DC 20001
(202) 965-3500, ext. 8302
Toll Free: (800) 424-2725, ext. 8302
Fax: (202) 965-0355
E-mail: brandon.grubesky@justice.org
Web: www.justice.org/cps/rde/xchg/justice/hs.xsl/1737.htm

Summary To provide financial assistance for law school to Native American and other minority student members of the American Association for Justice (AAJ).

Eligibility This program is open to African American, Hispanic, Asian American, Native American, and biracial members of the association who are entering the first, second, or third year of law school. Applicants must submit a 500-word essay on how they meet the selection criteria: commitment to the association, involvement in student chapter and minority caucus activities, desire to represent victims, interest and proficiency of skills in trial advocacy, and financial need.

Financial data The stipend is $1,000.

Duration 1 year.

Additional information The American Association for Justice was formerly the Association of Trial Lawyers of America.

Number awarded Up to 6 each year.

Deadline May of each year.

[1065]
ROBERT D. WATKINS GRADUATE RESEARCH FELLOWSHIP

American Society for Microbiology
Attn: Education Board
1752 N Street, N.W.
Washington, DC 20036-2904
(202) 942-9283   Fax: (202) 942-9329
E-mail: fellowships@asmusa.org
Web: www.asm.org

Summary To provide funding for research in microbiology to Native Americans and other underrepresented minority doctoral students who are members of the American Society for Microbiology (ASM).

Eligibility This program is open to African Americans, Hispanics, Native Americans, Alaskan Natives, and Pacific Islanders enrolled as full-time graduate students who have completed their first year of doctoral study and who are members of the society. Applicants must propose a joint research plan in collaboration with a society member scientist. They must have completed all graduate course work requirements for the doctoral degree by the date of the activation of the fellowship. U.S. citizenship or permanent resident status is required. Selection is based on academic achievement, evidence of a successful research plan developed in collabora-

tion with a research adviser/mentor, relevant career goals in the microbiological sciences, and involvement in activities that serve the needs of underrepresented groups.

Financial data Students receive $21,000 per year as a stipend; funds may not be used for tuition or fees.

Duration 3 years.

Number awarded Varies each year.

Deadline April of each year.

[1066]
ROBERT J. AND EVELYN CONLEY AWARD

Cherokee Nation
Attn: Cherokee Nation Education Corporation
115 East Delaware Street
P.O. Box 948
Tahlequah, OK 74465-0948
(918) 207-0950   Fax: (918) 207-0951
E-mail: contact@cnec-edu.org
Web: cnec.cherokee.org

Summary To provide financial assistance to citizens of several Cherokee nations who are enrolled at a college or university in any state and working on an undergraduate or graduate degree in English or creative writing.

Eligibility This program is open to citizens of the Cherokee Nation, the United Keetoowah Band, or the Eastern Band of Cherokee Indians. Applicants must be currently enrolled in an undergraduate or graduate program in English or creative writing at a college or university in any state. They are not required to reside in the Cherokee Nation area. Along with their application, they must submit a 4-page personal essay that includes background information, their degree plan for higher education, why they have chosen that field of study, how they plan to serve Cherokee people when they complete their higher education, and why they should be selected for this scholarship. Selection is based on the clarity and presentation of the essay; academic information (including transcripts and ACT scores); school, cultural and community activities; future plans to serve Cherokee people; and financial need.

Financial data The stipend is $1,000 per semester ($2,000 per year).

Duration 1 year. Renewal for the second semester requires the recipient to earn a GPA of 2.5 or higher in the first semester.

Number awarded 1 each year.

Deadline April of each year.

[1067]
RODNEY T. MATHEWS, JR. MEMORIAL SCHOLARSHIP FOR CALIFORNIA INDIANS

Morongo Band of Mission Indians
Attn: Scholarship Coordinator
11545 Potrero Road
Banning, CA 92220
(951) 572-6185   E-mail: trisha.smith@morongo.org
Web: www.morongonation.org

Summary To provide financial assistance for college or graduate school in any state to California Indians.

Eligibility This program is open to enrolled members of federally-recognized California Indian tribes who have been actively involved in the Native American community. Applicants must submit documentation of financial need, an academic letter of recommendation, and a letter of recommendation from the American Indian community. They must be enrolled full time at an accredited college or university in any state. Undergraduates must have a GPA of 2.75 or higher; graduate students must have a GPA of 3.5 or higher. Along with their application, they must submit 1) a 2-page personal statement on their academic, career, and personal goals; any extenuating circumstances they wish to have considered; how they view their Native American heritage and its importance to them; how they plan to "give back" to Native Americans after graduation; and their on-going active involvement in the Native American community both on and off campus; and 2) a 2-page essay, either on what they feel are the most critical issues facing tribal communities today and how they see themselves working in relationship to those issues, or on where they see Native people in the 21st century in terms of survival, governance, and cultural preservation, and what role they see themselves playing in that future.

Financial data The maximum stipend is $10,000 per year. Funds are paid directly to the recipient's school for tuition, housing, textbooks, and required fees.

Duration 1 year; may be renewed 1 additional year.

Additional information Recipients are required to complete 60 hours of service with a designated California Indian community agency: California Indian Museum and Cultural Center, Indian Health Care Services, National Indian Justice Center, California Indian Legal Services, California Indian Professors Association, California Indian Culture and Awareness Conference, or California Democratic Party Native American Caucus.

Number awarded 4 each year.

Deadline March of each year.

[1068]
RONALD M. DAVIS SCHOLARSHIP

American Medical Association
Attn: AMA Foundation
515 North State Street
Chicago, IL 60610
(312) 464-4193 Fax: (312) 464-4142
E-mail: amafoundation@ama-assn.org
Web: www.ama-assn.org

Summary To provide financial assistance to Native American and other underrepresented medical students who are planning to become a primary care physician.

Eligibility This program is open to first- and second-year medical students who are members of the following minority groups: African American/Black, American Indian, Native Hawaiian, Alaska Native, or Hispanic/Latino. Candidates must have an interest in becoming a primary care physician. Only nominations are accepted. Each medical school is invited to submit 2 nominees. U.S. citizenship or permanent resident status is required.

Financial data The stipend is $10,000.

Duration 1 year.

Additional information This program is offered by the AMA Foundation of the American Medical Association in collaboration with the National Business Group on Health.

Number awarded 12 each year.

Deadline April of each year.

[1069]
ROSEMARY GASKIN SCHOLARSHIP

Chippewa County Community Foundation
P.O. Box 1979
Sault Ste. Marie, MI 49783
(906) 635-1046 Fax: (775) 417-7368
E-mail: cccf@lighthouse.net
Web: www.cccf4good4ever.org/main.asp?id=7

Summary To provide financial assistance to members of the Sault Ste. Marie Tribe of Chippewa Indians who are interested in attending a public college in any state.

Eligibility This program is open to enrolled members of the Sault Ste. Marie Tribe of Chippewa Indians who have been accepted for enrollment at a public institution of higher education in any state. Applicants are not required to demonstrate financial need, to enroll full time, or to have a minimum blood quantum level. Along with their application, they must submit a 500-word essay on their choice of the following topics: equality, American Indian rights, education, or reviving Indian culture and traditional beliefs.

Financial data The stipend is $1,000.

Duration 1 year.

Number awarded 1 each year.

Deadline July of each year.

[1070]
ROY M. HUHNDORF ENDOWMENT SCHOLARSHIP FUND

Cook Inlet Region, Inc.
Attn: The CIRI Foundation
3600 San Jeronimo Drive, Suite 256
Anchorage, AK 99508-2870
(907) 793-3575 Toll Free: (800) 764-3382
Fax: (907) 793-3585 E-mail: tcf@thecirifoundation.org
Web: www.thecirifoundation.org/designated.htm

Summary To provide financial assistance for undergraduate or graduate studies in health science to Alaska Natives who are original enrollees to Cook Inlet Region, Inc. (CIRI) and their lineal descendants.

Eligibility This program is open to Alaska Native enrollees to CIRI under the Alaska Native Claims Settlement Act (ANCSA) of 1971 and their lineal descendants. There are no Alaska residency requirements or age limitations. Applicants must be accepted or enrolled full time in a 4-year undergraduate or a graduate degree program. They must be working on a degree in health science and have a GPA of 2.5 or higher. Along with their application, they must submit a 500-word statement on their educational and career goals and how they are contributing, or planning to contribute, to a positive Alaska Native community. Selection is based on that statement, academic achievement, rigor of course work or degree program, student financial contribution, financial need, grade level, previous work performance, community service, and relationship of degree program to career goals.

Financial data The stipend is $10,000 per year, $8,000 per year, or $2,500 per semester, depending on GPA.

Duration 1 semester or 1 year.

Additional information This program was established in 1995.

Number awarded Varies each year.

Deadline May of each year for annual scholarships; May or November of each year for semester scholarships.

[1071]
RUDEN MCCLOSKY DIVERSITY SCHOLARSHIP PROGRAM

Community Foundation of Sarasota County
Attn: Scholarship Manager
2635 Fruitville Road
P.O. Box 49587
Sarasota, FL 34230-6587
(941) 556-7156   Fax: (941) 556-7157
E-mail: mimi@cfsarasota.org
Web: www.cfsarasota.org/Default.aspx?tabid=263

Summary To provide financial assistance to Native American and other minority students from any state attending designated law schools (most of which are in Florida).

Eligibility This program is open to racial and ethnic minority students from any state who are members of groups traditionally underrepresented in the legal profession. Applicants must be entering their second year of full-time study at the University of Florida Levin College of Law, Florida State University College of Law, Stetson University College of Law, Nova Southeastern University Shepard Broad Law Center, St. Thomas University School of Law, Florida A&M University College of Law, Howard University College of Law, Texas Southern University Thurgood Marshall School of Law, Florida Coastal School of Law, Florida International University College of Law, or Barry University Dwayne O. Andreas School of Law. They must have a GPA of 2.6 or higher. Along with their application, they must submit a 1,000-word personal statement that describes their personal strengths, their contributions through community service, any special or unusual circumstances that may have affected their academic performance, or their personal and family history of educational or socioeconomic disadvantage; it must include their plans for practicing law in Florida after graduation. Applicants may also include information about their financial circumstances if they wish to have those considered in the selection process. U.S. citizenship or permanent resident status is required.

Financial data The stipend is $2,500 per semester.

Duration 1 semester (the spring semester of the second year of law school); may be renewed 1 additional semester (the fall semester of the third year).

Additional information This program is sponsored by the Florida law firm Ruden McClosky, which makes the final selection of recipients, and administered by the Community Foundation of Sarasota County.

Number awarded 1 or more each year.

Deadline July of each year.

[1072]
RUTH L. KIRSCHSTEIN NATIONAL RESEARCH SERVICE AWARDS FOR INDIVIDUAL PREDOCTORAL FELLOWSHIPS TO PROMOTE DIVERSITY IN HEALTH-RELATED RESEARCH

National Institutes of Health
Office of Extramural Research
Attn: Grants Information
6705 Rockledge Drive, Suite 4090
Bethesda, MD 20892-7983
(301) 435-0714   Fax: (301) 480-0525
TDD: (301) 451-5936   E-mail: GrantsInfo@nih.gov
Web: grants.nih.gov/grants/guide/pa-files/PA-11-112.html

Summary To provide financial assistance to Native American and other students from underrepresented groups who are interested in working on a doctoral degree and preparing for a career in biomedical and behavioral research.

Eligibility This program is open to students enrolled or accepted for enrollment in a Ph.D. or equivalent research degree program; a formally combined M.D./Ph.D. program; or other combined professional doctoral/research Ph.D. program in the biomedical, behavioral, health, or clinical sciences. Students in health professional degree programs (e.g., M.D., D.O., D.D.S., D.V.M.) are not eligible. Applicants must be 1) members of an ethnic or racial group underrepresented in biomedical or behavioral research; 2) individuals with disabilities; or 3) individuals from socially, culturally, economically, or educationally disadvantaged backgrounds that have inhibited their ability to prepare for a career in health-related research. They must be U.S. citizens, nationals, or permanent residents.

Financial data The fellowship provides an annual stipend of $21,180, a tuition and fee allowance (60% of costs up to $16,000 or 60% of costs up to $21,000 for dual degrees), and an institutional allowance of $4,200 ($3,100 at for-profit and federal institutions) for travel to scientific meetings, health insurance, and laboratory and other training expenses.

Duration Up to 5 years.

Additional information These fellowships are offered by most components of the National Institutes of Health (NIH). Check with the sponsor for a list of names and telephone numbers of responsible officers at each component.

Number awarded Varies each year.

Deadline April, August, or December of each year.

[1073]
RUTH MUSKRAT BRONSON FELLOWSHIP

American Indian Graduate Center
Attn: Executive Director
4520 Montgomery Boulevard, N.E., Suite 1-B
Albuquerque, NM 87109-1291
(505) 881-4584   Toll Free: (800) 628-1920
Fax: (505) 884-0427   E-mail: aigc@aigc.com
Web: www.aigc.com/02scholarships/scholarships.htm

Summary To provide financial assistance to Native American students interested in working on a graduate degree in nursing or other health-related field.

Eligibility This program is open to enrolled members of federally-recognized American Indian tribes and Alaska Native groups who can document one-fourth degree federally-recognized Indian blood. Applicants must be enrolled full time at a graduate school in the United States. First priority is given to nursing students; second priority is given to students in other health-related fields. Along with their application, they must submit a 500-word essay on their extracurricular activities as they relate to American Indian programs at their institution, volunteer and community work as related to American Indian communities, tribal and community involvement, and plans to make positive changes in the American Indian community with their college education. Financial need is also considered in the selection process.

Financial data Stipends range from $1,000 to $5,000 per academic year, depending on the availability of funds and the recipient's unmet financial need.

Duration 1 year; may be renewed.

Additional information The application fee is $15. Since this a supplemental program, students must apply in a timely manner for federal financial aid and campus-based aid at the college they are attending to be considered for this program. Failure to apply will disqualify an applicant.

Number awarded 1 or 2 each year.

Deadline May of each year.

[1074]
SAC AND FOX NATION HIGHER EDUCATION GRANTS

Sac and Fox Nation
Attn: Higher Education Department
920883 South Highway 99, Building A
Stroud, OK 74079
(918) 968-0509   Fax: (918) 968-0542
Web: www.sacandfoxnation.com

Summary To provide financial assistance for college or graduate school to members of the Sac and Fox Nation.

Eligibility This program is open to enrolled members of the Sac and Fox Nation who are enrolled or planning to enroll at an accredited college or university. Applicants must submit a personal letter describing the college major they plan to pursue and their career goals after graduation. They must be able to demonstrate financial need. Limited funding is available for graduate students.

Financial data Stipends are $800 per semester for full-time students, $400 per semester for part-time students, or $400 per semester for graduate students.

Duration 1 semester; may be renewed up to 9 additional semester for students at 4-year institutions, up to 5 additional semesters for students at 2-year institutions, or up to 5 additional semesters for graduate students. Freshmen and sophomores must earn a GPA of 2.0 to remain eligible; juniors and seniors must earn at GPA of 2.25 to remain eligible.

Number awarded Varies each year.

Deadline June of each year for fall semester; November of each year for spring semester.

[1075]
SAGINAW CHIPPEWA INDIAN TRIBE SCHOLARSHIP PROGRAM

Saginaw Chippewa Indian Tribe of Michigan
Attn: Higher Education Coordinator
7070 East Broadway
Mt. Pleasant, MI 48858
(989) 775-4505   E-mail: skutt@sagchip.org
Web: www.sagchip.org

Summary To provide financial assistance for college, graduate school, or vocational training to members of the Saginaw Chippewa Indian Tribe of Michigan.

Eligibility This program is open to enrolled members of the Saginaw Chippewa Indian Tribe of Michigan who are attending or planning to attend an accredited 2- or 4-year college, university, or vocational/trade institution in any state. Applicants must be interested in working on an undergraduate or graduate degree or vocational certificate as a full- or part-time student. They must apply for all available financial aid using the FAFSA standard form; residents of Michigan who plan to attend college in that state must also apply for the Michigan Indian Tuition Waiver. U.S. citizenship is required.

Financial data A stipend is awarded (amount not specified).

Duration 1 year; may be renewed, provided the recipient maintains a GPA of 2.0 or higher.

Number awarded Varies each year.

Deadline Deadline not specified.

[1076]
SALAMATOF NATIVE ASSOCIATION, INC. SCHOLARSHIP PROGRAM

Cook Inlet Region, Inc.
Attn: The CIRI Foundation
3600 San Jeronimo Drive, Suite 256
Anchorage, AK 99508-2870
(907) 793-3575   Toll Free: (800) 764-3382
Fax: (907) 793-3585   E-mail: tcf@thecirifoundation.org
Web: www.thecirifoundation.org/village_scholarships.htm

Summary To provide financial assistance for undergraduate or graduate studies to Alaska Natives who are original enrollees of the Salamatof Native Association, Inc. (SNAI) and their spouses and lineal descendants.

Eligibility This program is open to Alaska Native enrollees to SNAI under the Alaska Native Claims Settlement Act (ANCSA) of 1971 and their spouses and lineal descendants. There are no Alaska residency requirements or age limitations. Applicants must be accepted or enrolled full time in a 2-year, 4-year undergraduate, or graduate degree program. They must have a GPA of 2.5 or higher. Along with their application, they must submit a 500-word statement on their educational and career goals and how they are contributing, or planning to contribute, to a positive Alaska Native community. Selection is based on that statement, academic achievement, rigor of course work or degree program, student financial contribution, financial need, grade level, previous work performance, community service, and relationship of degree program to career goals.

Financial data The stipend depends on the availability of funds.

Duration 1 year; recipients must reapply each year.

Additional information This program was established in 1992 by the Salamatof Native Association, Inc. which provides funds matched by the CIRI Foundation.

Number awarded Varies each year; recently, 3 of these scholarships were awarded.

Deadline May of each year.

[1077]
SAN CARLOS APACHE TRIBE HIGHER EDUCATION GRANTS

San Carlos Apache Tribe
Attn: Department of Education
P.O. Box O
San Carlos, AZ 85550
(928) 475-2336   Fax: (928) 475-2507
Web: scateducationdepartment.com/scholarships.html

Summary To provide financial assistance for college or graduate school in any state to members of the San Carlos Apache Tribe.

Eligibility This program is open to members of the San Carlos Apache Tribe who are attending or planning to attend an accredited 2- or 4-year college or university in any state. Applicants must be interested in working on an associate, baccalaureate, or graduate degree as a full- or part-time student. They must be able to demonstrate financial need and have 1) a GPA of 2.0 or higher or a GED score of 45 or higher; and 2) an ACT score of 22 or higher or an SAT combined critical reading and mathematics score of 930 or higher. In the selection process, awards are presented in the following priority order: first, full-time undergraduate students who reside on the San Carlos Reservation in southeastern Arizona; second, graduate students who reside on the reservation; third, part-time students who reside on the reservation; fourth, students who reside off the reservation; and fifth, students who do not demonstrate financial need (assisted only if funds are available).

Financial data The stipend depends on the financial need of the recipient, to a maximum of $4,000 per semester at a 2-year college or $5,000 per semester at a 4-year college or university.

Duration 1 year; may be renewed up to a total of 64 credit hours at a 2-year college, up to 125 credit hours at a 4-year college or university. Renewal requires the recipient to maintain a GPA of 2.0 or higher as an undergraduate or 3.0 or higher as a graduate student.

Number awarded Varies each year.

Deadline June of each year for fall semester; November of each year for spring semester.

[1078]
SANDIA MASTER'S FELLOWSHIP PROGRAM

Sandia National Laboratories
Attn: Staffing Department 3535
MS-1023
P.O. Box 5800
Albuquerque, NM 87185-1023
(505) 844-3441   Fax: (505) 844-6636
E-mail: empsite@sandia.gov
Web: www.sandia.gov/careers/fellowships.html

Summary To enable Native Americans and other minority students to obtain a master's degree in engineering or computer science and also work at Sandia National Laboratories.

Eligibility This program is open to minority (American Indian, Asian, Black, or Hispanic) students who have a bachelor's degree in engineering or computer science and a GPA of 3.2 or higher. Participants must apply to 3 schools jointly selected by the program and themselves. They must be prepared to obtain a master's degree within 1 year. The fields of study (not all fields are available at all participating universities) include computer science, electrical engineering, mechanical engineering, civil engineering, chemical engineering, nuclear engineering, materials sciences, and petroleum engineering. Applicants must be interested in working at the sponsor's laboratories during the summer between graduation from college and the beginning of their graduate program, and then following completion of their master's degree. U.S. citizenship is required.

Financial data Participants receive a competitive salary while working at the laboratories on a full-time basis and a stipend while attending school.

Duration 1 year.

Additional information During their summer assignment, participants work at the laboratories, either in Albuquerque, New Mexico or in Livermore, California. Upon successful completion of the program, they return to Sandia's hiring organization as a full-time member of the technical staff. This program began in 1968. Application to schools where students received their undergraduate degree is not recommended. After the schools accept an applicant, the choice of a school is made jointly by the laboratories and the participant.

Number awarded Varies each year; since the program began, more than 350 engineers and computer scientists have gone to work at Sandia with master's degrees.

Deadline Deadline not specified.

[1079]
SAULT TRIBE SPECIAL NEEDS SCHOLARSHIPS

Sault Tribe of Chippewa Indians
Attn: Higher Education Program-Memorial/Tributary
  Scholarships
523 Ashmun Street
Sault Ste. Marie, MI 49783
(906) 635-4944   Toll Free: (800) 793-0660
Fax: (906) 635-7785   E-mail: amatson@saulttribe.net
Web: www.saulttribe.com

Summary To provide financial assistance for education at any level to members of the Sault Tribe of Chippewa Indians who have a disability.

Eligibility This program is open to enrolled members of the Sault Tribe who have a documented physical or emotional disability. Applicants must be enrolled in an educational program at any level. Along with their application, they must submit a letter from themselves or a parent describing the proposed use of the funds and an itemized list of the expected costs.

Financial data The stipend is $1,000.

Duration 1 year.

Number awarded 4 each year: 2 for students under 18 years of age and 2 for students 18 years of age or older.
Deadline May of each year.

[1080]
SBE DOCTORAL DISSERTATION RESEARCH IMPROVEMENT GRANTS

National Science Foundation
Attn: Directorate for Social, Behavioral, and Economic
  Sciences
4201 Wilson Boulevard, Room 905N
Arlington, VA 22230
(703) 292-8700   Fax: (703) 292-9083
TDD: (800) 281-8749
Web: www.nsf.gov/funding/pgm_summ.jsp?pims_id=13453

Summary To provide partial support to minority and other doctoral candidates conducting dissertation research in areas of interest to the Directorate for Social, Behavioral, and Economic Sciences (SBE) of the National Science Foundation (NSF).

Eligibility Applications may be submitted through regular university channels by dissertation advisers on behalf of graduate students who have advanced to candidacy and have begun or are about to begin dissertation research. Students must be enrolled at U.S. institutions, but they need not be U.S. citizens. The proposed research must relate to SBE's Division of Behavioral and Cognitive Sciences (archaeology, cultural anthropology, geography and spatial sciences, linguistics, or physical anthropology); Division of Social and Economic Sciences (decision, risk, and management science; economics; law and social science; methodology, measurement, and statistics; political science; sociology; or science, technology, and society); Division of Science Resources Statistics (research on science and technology surveys and statistics); or Office of Multidisciplinary Activities (science and innovation policy). Women, minorities, and persons with disabilities are strongly encouraged to apply.

Financial data Grants have the limited purpose of providing funds to enhance the quality of dissertation research. They are to be used exclusively for necessary expenses incurred in the actual conduct of the dissertation research, including (but not limited to) conducting field research in settings away from campus that would not otherwise be possible, data collection and sample survey costs, payments to subjects or informants, specialized research equipment, analysis and services not otherwise available, supplies, travel to archives, travel to specialized facilities or field research locations, and partial living expenses for conducting necessary research away from the student's U.S. academic institution. Funding is not provided for stipends, tuition, textbooks, journals, allowances for dependents, travel to scientific meetings, publication costs, dissertation preparation or reproduction, or indirect costs.

Duration Up to 2 years.

Number awarded 200 to 300 each year. Approximately $2.5 million is available for this program annually.

Deadline Deadline dates for the submission of dissertation improvement grant proposals differ by program within the divisions of the SBE Directorate; applicants should obtain information regarding target dates for proposals from the relevant program.

[1081]
SCHOLARSHIPS FOR MINORITY ACCOUNTING STUDENTS

American Institute of Certified Public Accountants
Attn: Academic and Career Development Division
220 Leigh Farm Road
Durham, NC 27707-8110
(919) 402-4931   Fax: (919) 419-4705
E-mail: MIC_Programs@aicpa.org
Web: www.aicpa.org/members/div/career/mini/smas.htm

Summary To provide financial assistance to Native Americans and other minorities interested in studying accounting at the undergraduate or graduate school level.

Eligibility This program is open to minority undergraduate and graduate students, enrolled full time, who have a GPA of 3.3 or higher (both cumulatively and in their major) and intend to pursue a C.P.A. credential. Undergraduates must have completed at least 30 semester hours, including at least 6 semester hours of a major in accounting. Graduate students must be working on a master's degree in accounting, finance, taxation, or a related program. Applicants must be U.S. citizens or permanent residents and student affiliate members of the American Institute of Certified Public Accountants (AICPA). The program defines minority students as those whose heritage is Black or African American, Hispanic or Latino, Native American, or Asian American.

Financial data Stipends range from $1,500 to $3,000 per year. Funds are disbursed directly to the recipient's school.

Duration 1 year; may be renewed up to 3 additional years or until completion of a bachelor's or master's degree, whichever is earlier.

Additional information This program is administered by The Center for Scholarship Administration, E-mail: allison-lee@bellsouth.net. The most outstanding applicant for this program is awarded the Stuart A. Kessler Scholarship for Minority Students.

Number awarded Varies each year; recently, 94 students received funding through this program.

Deadline March of each year.

[1082]
SCHWABE, WILLIAMSON & WYATT SUMMER ASSOCIATE DIVERSITY SCHOLARSHIP

Schwabe, Williamson & Wyatt, Attorneys at Law
Attn: Attorney Recruiting Administrator
1211 S.W. Fifth Avenue, Suite 1500-2000
Portland, OR 97204
(503) 796-2889   Fax: (503) 796-2900
E-mail: dcphillips@schwabe.com
Web: www.schwabe.com/recruitdiversity.aspx

Summary To provide financial assistance and summer work experience in Portland, Oregon to Native American and other law students who will contribute to the diversity of the legal profession.

Eligibility This program is open to first-year students working on a J.D. degree at an ABA-accredited law school. Applicants must 1) contribute to the diversity of the law school student body and the legal community; 2) possess a record of academic achievement, capacity, and leadership as an undergraduate and in law school that indicates promise for a successful career in the legal profession; and 3) demonstrate a commitment to practice law in the Pacific Northwest upon completion of law school. They must be interested in a paid summer associateship at the sponsoring law firm's office in Portland, Oregon. Along with their application, they must submit a resume, undergraduate and law school transcripts, a legal writing sample, and a 1- to 2-page personal statement explaining their interest in the scholarship and how they will contribute to diversity in the legal community.

Financial data The program provides a paid summer associateship during the summer following completion of the first year of law school and an academic scholarship of $7,500 to help pay tuition and other expenses during the recipient's second year of law school.

Duration 1 year.

Number awarded 1 each year.

Deadline January of each year.

[1083]
SCIENCE TEACHER PREPARATION PROGRAM

Alabama Alliance for Science, Engineering, Mathematics, and Science Education
Attn: Project Director
University of Alabama at Birmingham
Campbell Hall, Room 401
1300 University Boulevard
Birmingham, AL 35294-1170
(205) 934-8762   Fax: (205) 934-1650
E-mail: LDale@uab.edu
Web: www.uab.edu/istp/alabama.html

Summary To provide financial assistance to Native Americans and other underrepresented students at designated institutions in Alabama who are interested in preparing for a career as a science teacher.

Eligibility This program is open to members of underrepresented minority groups who have been unconditionally admitted to a participating Alabama college or university. Applicants must be interested in becoming certified to teach science and mathematics in K-12 schools. They may be 1) entering freshmen enrolling in a science education program leading to a bachelor's degree and certification; 2) students transferring from a community college and enrolling in a science education program leading to a bachelor's degree and certification; 3) students with a bachelor's degree in mathematics, science, or education and enrolling in a certification program; or 4) students with a bachelor's degree in mathematics, science, or education and enrolling in a fifth-year program leading to a master's degree and certification.

Financial data The stipend is $1,000 per year.

Duration 1 year; may be renewed.

Additional information Support for this program is provided by the National Science Foundation. The participating institutions are Alabama A&M University, Alabama State University, Auburn University, Miles College, Stillman College, Talladega College, Tuskegee University, University of Alabama at Birmingham, and University of Alabama in Huntsville.

Number awarded Varies each year.

Deadline Deadline not specified.

[1084]
SEALASKA ENDOWMENT SCHOLARSHIPS

Sealaska Corporation
Attn: Sealaska Heritage Institute
One Sealaska Plaza, Suite 301
Juneau, AK 99801-1249
(907) 586-9170   Toll Free: (888) 311-4992
Fax: (907) 586-9293   E-mail: scholarship@sealaska.com
Web: www.sealaskaheritage.org

Summary To provide financial assistance for undergraduate or graduate study in any state to Native Alaskans who have a connection to Sealaska Corporation.

Eligibility This program is open to 1) Alaska Natives who are shareholders of Sealaska Corporation, and 2) Native lineal descendants of Alaska Natives enrolled to Sealaska Corporation, whether or not they own Sealaska Corporation stock. Applicants must be enrolled or accepted for enrollment as full-time undergraduate or graduate students at a college or university in any state. Along with their application, they must submit 2 essays: 1) their personal history and educational goals, and 2) their expected contributions to the Alaska Native or Native American community. Financial need is also considered in the selection process.

Financial data The amount of the award depends on the availability of funds, the number of qualified applicants, class standing, and cumulative GPA.

Duration 1 year; may be renewed up to 5 years for a bachelor's degree, up to 3 years for a master's degree, up to 2 years for a doctorate, or up to 3 years for vocational study. The maximum total support is limited to 9 years. Renewal depends on recipients' maintaining full-time enrollment and a GPA of 2.0 or higher as an undergraduate or 3.0 or higher as a graduate student.

Additional information Sealaska Corporation is 1 of 13 Alaska Native Regional Corporations created under the Alaska Native Claims Settlement Act of 1971.

Number awarded Varies each year.

Deadline February of each year.

[1085]
SEALASKA HERITAGE INSTITUTE 7(I) SCHOLARSHIPS

Sealaska Corporation
Attn: Sealaska Heritage Institute
One Sealaska Plaza, Suite 301
Juneau, AK 99801-1249
(907) 586-9170   Toll Free: (888) 311-4992
Fax: (907) 586-9293   E-mail: scholarship@sealaska.com
Web: www.sealaskaheritage.org

Summary To provide financial assistance for undergraduate or graduate study in any state to Native Alaskans who have a connection to Sealaska Corporation and are majoring in designated fields.

Eligibility This program is open to 1) Alaska Natives who are shareholders of Sealaska Corporation, and 2) Native lineal descendants of Alaska Natives enrolled to Sealaska Corporation, whether or not the applicant owns Sealaska Corporation stock. Applicants must be enrolled or accepted for enrollment as full-time undergraduate or graduate students at a college or university in any state. Along with their application, they must submit 2 essays: 1) their personal history and educational goals, and 2) their expected contributions to the

Alaska Native or Native American community. Financial need is also considered in the selection process. The following areas of study qualify for these awards: natural resources (environmental sciences, engineering, conservation biology, environmental law, fisheries, forestry, geology, marine science/biology, mining technology, wildlife management); business administration (accounting, computer information systems, economics, finance, human resources management, industrial management, information systems management, international business, international commerce and trade, and marketing); and other special fields (cadastral surveys, chemistry, equipment/machinery operators, industrial safety specialists, health specialists, plastics engineers, trade specialists, physics, mathematics, and marine trades and occupations).

Financial data The amount of the award depends on the availability of funds, the number of qualified applicants, class standing, and cumulative GPA.

Duration 1 year; may be renewed up to 5 years for a bachelor's degree, up to 3 years for a master's degree, up to 2 years for a doctorate, or up to 3 years for vocational study. The maximum total support is limited to 9 years. Renewal depends on recipients' maintaining full-time enrollment and a GPA of 2.0 or higher.

Additional information Funding for this program is provided from Alaska Native Claims Settlement Act (ANSCA) Section 7(i) revenue sharing provisions. Sealaska Corporation is 1 of 13 Alaska Native Regional Corporations created under the Alaska Native Claims Settlement Act of 1971.

Number awarded Varies each year.

Deadline February of each year.

[1086]
SECTION OF BUSINESS LAW DIVERSITY CLERKSHIP PROGRAM

American Bar Association
Attn: Section of Business Law
321 North Clark Street
Chicago, IL 60654-7598
(312) 988-5588   Fax: (312) 988-5578
E-mail: businesslaw@abanet.org
Web: www.abanet.org/buslaw/students/clerkship.shtml

Summary To provide summer work experience in business law to Native American and other student members of the American Bar Association (ABA) and its Section of Business Law who will help the section to fulfill its goal of promoting diversity.

Eligibility This program is open to first- and second-year students at ABA-accredited law schools who are interested in a summer business court clerkship. Applicants must 1) be a member of an underrepresented group (student of color, woman, student with disabilities, gay, lesbian, bisexual, or transgender); or 2) have overcome social or economic disadvantages, such as a physical disability, financial constraints, or cultural impediments to becoming a law student. They must be able to demonstrate financial need. Along with their application, they must submit a 500-word essay that covers why they are interested in this clerkship program, what they would gain from the program, how it would positively influence their future professional goals as a business lawyer, and how they meet the program's criteria. Membership in the ABA and its Section of Business Law are required.

Financial data The stipend is $6,000.

Duration Summer months.

Additional information This program began in 2008. Assignments vary, but have included the Philadelphia Commerce Court, the Prince George's District Court in Upper Marlboro, Maryland, and the Delaware Court of Chancery.

Number awarded 9 each year.

Deadline January of each year.

[1087]
SEMESTER INTERNSHIPS IN GEOSCIENCE PUBLIC POLICY

American Geological Institute
Attn: Government Affairs Program
4220 King Street
Alexandria, VA 22302-1502
(703) 379-2480   Fax: (703) 379-7563
E-mail: govt@agiweb.org
Web: www.agiweb.org/gap/interns/index.html

Summary To provide work experience to Native American and other geoscience students who have a strong interest in federal science policy.

Eligibility This program is open to geoscience students who are interested in working with Congress and federal agencies to promote sound public policy in areas that affect geoscientists, including water, energy, and mineral resources; geologic hazards; environmental protection, and federal funding for geoscience research and education. Applicants must submit official copies of college transcripts, a resume with the names and contact information for 2 references, and a statement of their science and policy interests and what they feel they can contribute to the program. Native Americans, other minorities, and women are especially encouraged to apply.

Financial data The stipend is $5,000.

Duration 14 weeks, during the fall or spring semester. The sponsor also offers a similar program for summer internships.

Additional information This program is jointly funded by the American Geological Institute (AGI) and the American Association of Petroleum Geologists (AAPG). Activities for the interns include monitoring and analyzing geoscience-related legislation in Congress, updating legislative and policy information on AGI's web site, attending House and Senate hearings and preparing summaries, responding to information requests from AGI's member societies, and attending meetings with policy-level staff members in Congress, federal agencies, and non-governmental organizations.

Number awarded 1 each semester.

Deadline April of each year for fall internships; October of each year for spring internships.

[1088]
SEMICONDUCTOR RESEARCH CORPORATION MASTER'S SCHOLARSHIP PROGRAM

Semiconductor Research Corporation
Attn: Global Research Collaboration
1101 Slater Road, Suite 120
P.O. Box 12053
Research Triangle Park, NC 27709-2053
(919) 941-9400   Fax: (919) 941-9450
E-mail: apply@src.org
Web: www.src.org/student-center/fellowship

Summary To provide financial assistance to minorities and women interested in working on a master's degree in a field of microelectronics relevant to the interests of the Semiconductor Research Corporation (SRC).

Eligibility This program is open to women and members of underrepresented minority groups (African Americans, Hispanics, and Native Americans). Applicants must be U.S. citizens or have permanent resident, refugee, or political asylum status in the United States. They must be admitted to an SRC participating university to work on a master's degree in a field relevant to microelectronics under the guidance of an SRC-sponsored faculty member and under an SRC-funded contract. Selection is based on academic achievement.

Financial data The fellowship provides full tuition and fee support, a monthly stipend of $2,186, an annual grant of $2,000 to the university department with which the student recipient is associated, and travel expenses to the Graduate Fellowship Program Annual Conference.

Duration Up to 2 years.

Additional information This program was established in 1997 for underrepresented minorities and expanded to include women in 1999.

Number awarded Up to 30 each year.

Deadline February of each year.

[1089]
SENECA NATION HIGHER EDUCATION PROGRAM

Seneca Nation of Indians
Attn: Higher Education Department, Cattaraugus Territory
12861 Route 438
Irving, NY 14081
(716) 532-3341   Fax: (716) 532-3269
E-mail: carrie.peterson@sni.org
Web: www.sni.org/node/34

Summary To provide financial assistance for college or graduate school to members of the Seneca Nation of Indians in New York.

Eligibility This program is open to members of the Seneca Nation of Indians who are enrolled or planning to enroll in an associate, bachelor's, master's, or doctoral program. They must have applied for all other forms of financial aid for which they qualify, e.g., full-time undergraduates who are New York residents must apply for New York State Indian Aid (NYSIA) and the New York State Tuition Assistance Program (TAP); part-time undergraduates who are New York residents must apply for Aid for Part-Time Study (APTS); non-residents of New York must apply for funding from their state of residence; graduate students must apply for an American Indian Graduate Center (AIGC) fellowship. Applicants with permanent res-

idence on the reservation qualify for level 1 awards; those with permanent residence within New York state qualify for level 2 awards; those with permanent residence outside New York state qualify for level 3 awards. Financial need is considered in the selection process.

Financial data Maximum awards per academic year for tuition and fees are $11,000 for level 1 students, $8,000 for level 2 students, or $6,000 for level 3 students. Other benefits for all recipients include $1,000 per year for books and supplies for full-time students or $100 per 3-credit hours for part-time students; payment of room and board in dormitories or college-approved housing for full-time students; a transportation allowance for commuters of $900 per year for full-time students or $85 per 3-credit hours for part-time students; and a personal expense allowance of $500 per year for full-time students or $50 per 3-credit hours for part-time students.

Duration 1 year; may be renewed.

Number awarded Varies each year.

Deadline June of each year for fall semester; July of each year for fall quarter; October of each year for winter quarter; November of each year for spring semester; January of each year for spring quarter; April of each year for summer semester or quarter.

[1090]
SENECA NATION PROFESSIONAL SCHOLARSHIPS

Seneca Nation of Indians
Attn: Higher Education Department, Cattaraugus Territory
12861 Route 438
Irving, NY 14081
(716) 532-3341   Fax: (716) 532-3269
E-mail: carrie.peterson@sni.org
Web: www.sni.org/node/34

Summary To provide funding to members of the Seneca Nation of Indians in New York who are working on a graduate or professional degree.

Eligibility This program is open to enrolled members of the Seneca Nation of Indians who are enrolled or planning to enroll full time in an advanced degree program, including a master's degree, doctoral degree, or other professional degree (e.g., M.D., J.D.). Applicants must intend to accept employment with the Seneca Nation in their respective discipline. They must apply for financial aid from the Seneca Nation Higher Education Program and the American Indian Graduate Center. Along with their application, they must submit a brief essay on their reason for applying for the scholarship, their career goals, and how the Seneca Nation of Indians will benefit from their gained expertise. Selection is based on that essay, the relationship of desired career goals to current Seneca Nation professional needs, academic performance (minimum GPA of 3.0), and recommendations from faculty and employers. First priority is given to students who reside on the Allegany or Cattaraugus territory of the Seneca Nation; second priority is given to students who live elsewhere in New York State.

Financial data The stipend is $20,000 per year. Recipients must commit to work 1 year in their respective discipline within the Seneca Nation of Indians for each year of support they receive.

Duration 1 year; may be renewed 1 additional year for a master's degree or up to 3 additional years for a doctoral degree. Renewal depends on the recipient's remaining enrolled full time with a GPA of 3.0 or higher.

Additional information This program was established in 2003.

Number awarded 2 each year: 1 in each territory.

Deadline July of each year.

[1091]
SENECA-CAYUGA EDUCATION FELLOWSHIP PROGRAM

Seneca-Cayuga Tribe of Oklahoma
Attn: Tribal Claims Committee
23701 South 655 Road (Highway 10)
Grove, OK 74344
(918) 786-5576   Fax: (918) 786-9245
E-mail: claims@sctribe.com
Web: www.sctribe.com

Summary To provide financial assistance for college or graduate school to members of the Seneca-Cayuga Tribe of Oklahoma.

Eligibility This program is open to Seneca-Cayuga tribal members who are enrolled or planning to enroll as full-time undergraduate or graduate students at a college, university, or vocational training school in any state. Applicants must submit a copy of their tribal membership card; a letter of estimated graduation date from their school; a copy of their class schedule; and either 1) a copy of their high school diploma or GED score; or 2) a college transcript.

Financial data The stipend is $2,500 for the academic year or $1,250 for the summer term. All students also qualify for a 1-time educational supply payment of $1,000. All funds are paid directly to the student.

Duration 1 year; may be renewed, provided the recipient maintains a GPA of 2.0 or higher.

Number awarded Varies each year.

Deadline September of each year for fall semester; January of each year for spring semester; June of each year for summer semester.

[1092]
SEO CORPORATE LAW PROGRAM

Sponsors for Educational Opportunity
Attn: Career Program
55 Exchange Place
New York, NY 10005
(212) 979-2040   Toll Free: (800) 462-2332
Fax: (646) 706-7113
E-mail: careerprogram@seo-usa.org
Web: www.seo-usa.org/Career/Corporate_Law

Summary To provide summer work experience to Native Americans and other students of color interested in studying corporate law.

Eligibility This program is open to students of color who are college seniors or recent graduates planning to attend law school in the United States. Applicants must be interested in a summer internship at a participating law firm that specializes in corporate law. They should be able to demonstrate analytical and quantitative skills, interpersonal and community skills, maturity, and a cumulative GPA of 3.0 or higher. Along with their application, they must submit 1) information on their extracurricular and employment experience; 2) an

essay of 75 to 100 words on how the program area to which they are applying related to their professional goals; and 3) an essay of 250 to 400 words on either an example of a time when they had to operate outside their "comfort zone" or their definition of success. Personal interviews are required.

Financial data Interns receive a competitive stipend.

Duration 10 weeks during the summer.

Additional information This program was established in 1980. Most internships are available in New York City or Washington, D.C.

Number awarded Varies each year.

Deadline December of each year.

[1093]
SEQUOYAH GRADUATE FELLOWSHIPS

Association on American Indian Affairs, Inc.
Attn: Director of Scholarship Programs
966 Hungerford Drive, Suite 12-B
Rockville, MD 20850
(240) 314-7155   Fax: (240) 314-7159
E-mail: lw.aaia@verizon.net
Web: www.indian-affairs.org/scholarships/sequoyah.htm

Summary To provide financial assistance to Native Americans interested in working on a graduate degree in any field.

Eligibility This program is open to American Indians and Alaskan Natives working full time on a graduate degree. Applicants must submit documentation of financial need, a Certificate of Indian Blood showing at least one-quarter Indian blood, proof of tribal enrollment, an essay on their educational goals, 2 letters of recommendation, and their most recent transcript.

Financial data The stipend is $1,500.

Duration 1 year; recipients may reapply.

Number awarded Varies each year; recently, 7 of these fellowships were awarded.

Deadline June of each year.

[1094]
SEVEN STARS GRADUATE SCHOLARSHIP

American Indian College Fund
Attn: Scholarship Department
8333 Greenwood Boulevard
Denver, CO 80221
(303) 426-8900   Toll Free: (800) 776-FUND
Fax: (303) 426-1200
E-mail: scholarships@collegefund.org
Web: www.collegefund.org

Summary To provide financial assistance for graduate school to Native Americans, especially those associated with a Tribal College or University (TCU).

Eligibility This program is open to American Indians and Alaska Natives who can document proof of enrollment or descendancy. Applicants must be working on an advanced degree (e.g., M.A., M.S., J.D., Ph.D., M.D.) at a mainstream institution. They must have a GPA of 3.0 GPA or higher and be able to demonstrate exceptional academic achievement. Preference is given to students, alumni, staff, and faculty of TCUs. Applications are available only online and include required essays on specified topics.

Financial data The stipend is $2,000.

Duration 1 year.

Number awarded Varies each year.

Deadline May of each year.

[1095]
SHEE ATIKA ACADEMIC SCHOLARSHIPS

Shee Atiká, Incorporated
Attn: Shee Atiká Benefits Trust
315 Lincoln Street, Suite 300
Sitka, AK 99835
(907) 747-3534   Toll Free: (800) 478-3534
Fax: (907) 747-5727
E-mail: scholarships@sheeatika.com
Web: www.sheeatika.com

Summary To provide financial assistance to shareholders of Shee Atiká, Incorporated interested in attending college or graduate school in any state.

Eligibility This program is open to Shee Atiká Class A and Class B shareholders enrolled or planning to enroll at a college, university, graduate school, or trade or vocational school in any state. Relatives of shareholders are eligible only if they receive at least 1 share of stock from their family member allowed to make a gift under ANSCA. Students interested in a program of concentrated vocational training may petition for that status. Applicants must submit a statement covering their personal and professional goals, honors and activities, and how this scholarship will assist them. Selection is based on that statement, academic achievement, and financial need.

Financial data The maximum annual stipend is $2,400 for undergraduates, $4,800 for graduate students, or $7,200 for students enrolled in concentrated vocational training.

Duration 1 year; may be renewed up to 3 additional years of undergraduate study or 2 years of graduate study. The maximum that any shareholder may receive for both undergraduate and graduate study is $28,800.

Additional information Shee Atiká, Incorporated is an urban corporation organized under the Alaska Native Claims Settlement Act (ANSCA) to serve the people of the Sitka area of Alaska.

Number awarded Varies each year.

Deadline March, July, October, or November of each year.

[1096]
SHERRY R. ARNSTEIN MINORITY STUDENT SCHOLARSHIP

American Association of Colleges of Osteopathic
  Medicine
Attn: Office of Government Relations
5550 Friendship Boulevard, Suite 310
Chevy Chase, MD 20815-7231
(301) 968-4142   Fax: (301) 968-4101
Web: www.aacom.org

Summary To provide financial assistance to Native Americans and other underrepresented minority students already enrolled in osteopathic medical school.

Eligibility This program is open to African American, mainland Puerto Rican, Hispanic, Native American, Native Hawaiian, and Alaska Native students currently enrolled in good standing in their first, second, or third year of osteopathic medical school. Applicants must submit a 750-word essay on what osteopathic medical schools can do to recruit and retain

more underrepresented minority students, what they personally plan to do as a student and as a future D.O. to help increase minority student enrollment at a college of osteopathic medicine, and how and why they were drawn to osteopathic medicine.

Financial data The stipend is $2,500.

Duration 1 year; nonrenewable.

Number awarded 1 each year.

Deadline March of each year.

[1097]
SHERRY R. ARNSTEIN NEW STUDENT MINORITY STUDENT SCHOLARSHIP

American Association of Colleges of Osteopathic
  Medicine
Attn: Office of Government Relations
5550 Friendship Boulevard, Suite 310
Chevy Chase, MD 20815-7231
(301) 968-4142   Fax: (301) 968-4101
Web: www.aacom.org

Summary To provide financial assistance to Native Americans and other underrepresented minority students planning to enroll at an osteopathic medical school.

Eligibility This program is open to African American, mainland Puerto Rican, Hispanic, Native American, Native Hawaiian, and Alaska Native students who have been accepted and are planning to enroll as a first-time student at any of the 20 colleges of osteopathic medicine that are members of the American Association of Colleges of Osteopathic Medicine (AACOM). Applicants must submit a 750-word essay on what osteopathic medical schools can do to recruit and retain more underrepresented minority students, what they personally plan to do as a student and as a future D.O. to help increase minority student enrollment at a college of osteopathic medicine, and how and why they were drawn to osteopathic medicine.

Financial data The stipend is $2,500.

Duration 1 year; nonrenewable.

Number awarded 1 each year.

Deadline March of each year.

[1098]
SIDLEY DIVERSITY AND INCLUSION SCHOLARSHIP

Sidley Austin LLP
Attn: Scholarships
One South Dearborn
Chicago, IL 60603
(312) 853-7000   Fax: (312) 853-7036
E-mail: scholarship@sidley.com
Web: www.sidley.com

Summary To provide financial assistance and work experience to Native American and other law students who come from a diverse background.

Eligibility The program is open to students entering their second year of law school; preference is given to students at schools where the sponsor conducts on-campus interviews or participates in a resume collection. Applicants must have a demonstrated ability to contribute meaningfully to the diversity of the law school and/or legal profession. Along with their application, they must submit a 500-word essay that includes their thoughts on and efforts to improve diversity, how they might contribute to the sponsor's commitment to improving diversity, and their interest in practicing law at a global firm and specifically the sponsor. Selection is based on academic achievement and leadership qualities.

Financial data The stipend is $15,000.

Duration 1 year.

Additional information These scholarships were first offered in 2011. Recipients are expected to participate in the sponsor's summer associate program following their second year of law school. They must apply separately for the associate position. The firm has offices in Chicago, Dallas, Los Angeles, New York, Palo Alto, San Francisco, and Washington, D.C.

Number awarded A limited number are awarded each year.

Deadline Applications are accepted throughout the fall recruiting season.

[1099]
SIDNEY B. WILLIAMS, JR. INTELLECTUAL PROPERTY LAW SCHOOL SCHOLARSHIPS

American Intellectual Property Law Education Foundation
485 Kinderkamack Road
Oradell, NJ 07649
(201) 634-1870   Fax: (201) 634-1871
E-mail: admin@aiplef.org
Web: www.aiplef.org/scholarships/sidney_b_williams

Summary To provide financial assistance to Native American and other minority law school students who are interested in preparing for a career in intellectual property law.

Eligibility This program is open to members of minority groups currently enrolled in or accepted to an ABA-accredited law school. Applicants must be U.S. citizens with a demonstrated intent to engage in the full-time practice of intellectual property law. Along with their application, they must submit a 250-word essay on how this scholarship will make a difference to them in meeting their goal of engaging in the full-time practice of intellectual property law and why they intend to do so. Selection is based on 1) demonstrated commitment to developing a career in intellectual property law; 2) academic performance at the undergraduate, graduate, and law school levels (as applicable); 3) general factors, such as leadership skills, community activities, or special accomplishments; and 4) financial need.

Financial data The stipend is $10,000 per year. Funds may be used for tuition, fees, books, supplies, room, board, and a patent bar review course.

Duration 1 year; may be renewed if the recipient maintains a GPA of 2.0 or higher.

Additional information This program, which began in 2002, is administered by the Thurgood Marshall Scholarship Fund, 80 Maiden Lane, Suite 2204, New York, NY 10038, (212) 573-8487, Fax: (212) 573-8497, E-mail: srogers@tmcfund.org. Additional funding is provided by the American Intellectual Property Law Association, the American Bar Association's Section of Intellectual Property Law, and the Minority Corporate Counsel Association. Recipients are required to join and maintain membership in the American Intellectual Property Law Association.

Number awarded Varies each year; recently, 12 of these scholarships were awarded.

Deadline March of each year.

[1100]
SITKA TRIBE OF ALASKA HIGHER EDUCATION PROGRAM

Sitka Tribe of Alaska
Attn: Education Department
456 Katlian Street
Sitka, AK 99835
(907) 747-6478   Toll Free: (800) 746-3207
Fax: (907) 747-4915   E-mail: education@sitkatribe.org
Web: www.sitkatribe.org/depts/edu/Scholarships.htm

Summary To provide financial assistance to enrolled members of the Sitka Tribe of Alaska who are interested in attending college or graduate school in any state.

Eligibility This program is open to enrolled members of the Sitka Tribe of Alaska as documented by the Bureau of Indian Affairs. Members of other federally-recognized tribes may also be eligible if funds are available. Applicants must be enrolled full time at an accredited 2-year college (credits must be transferable to a 4-year school) or a 4-year college or university in any state. They must have a high school diploma or GED and be able to demonstrate financial need. Priority is given to eligible Sitka Tribe of Alaska students who have met the minimum requirements in the following order: 1) college seniors; 2) college juniors; 3) college sophomores; 4) entering freshmen; 5) graduate students (provided funds are available); and 6) other qualified applicants (provided funds are available).

Financial data The maximum stipend is $3,000 per year. Payments are made to students through the financial aid office at the college or university they attend.

Duration Up to 10 semesters for students working on a 4-year degree or up to 5 semesters for students working on a 2-year degree. Recipients must maintain a GPA of at least 2.0 as freshmen, 2.2 as sophomores, 2.25 as juniors, and 2.5 as seniors to remain eligible. Graduate students must remain enrolled full time and maintain minimum standards as set by their institution.

Number awarded Varies each year.

Deadline April of each year for students attending the fall semester/quarter or the full year; September of each year for students beginning the spring/winter semester/quarter.

[1101]
SKY PEOPLE GRADUATE SCHOLARSHIP PROGRAM

Northern Arapaho Tribe
Attn: Sky People Higher Education
P.O. Box 8480
Ethete, WY 82520
(307) 332-5286   Toll Free: (800) 815-6795
Fax: (307) 332-9104 E-mail: assistant@skypeopleed.org
Web: www.skypeopleed.org

Summary To provide financial assistance for graduate school to members of the Northern Arapaho Tribe.

Eligibility This program is open to full-time and part-time graduate students who have a GPA of 3.0 or higher. Applicants must be of at least one-fourth Northern Arapaho descent (enrolled or non-enrolled) and must submit a Certificate of Indian Blood or other verification of Northern Arapaho blood with at least one-fourth degree. Along with their application, they must submit a 1-page personal statement that includes a brief history of their background, academic ability and achievement, work or leadership experience, participation in community-related activities, and career goals. Selection is based on that statement, potential to contribute to the community upon graduation, academic ability and achievement, and a letter of recommendation.

Financial data The stipend depends on the availability of funds.

Duration 1 year; may be renewed.

Number awarded Varies each year.

Deadline Deadline not specified.

[1102]
SMITHSONIAN NATIVE AMERICAN INTERNSHIPS

Smithsonian Institution
Attn: Office of Fellowships
470 L'Enfant Plaza, Suite 7102
P.O. Box 37012, MRC 902
Washington, DC 20013-7012
(202) 633-7070   Fax: (202) 633-7069
E-mail: siofg@si.edu
Web: www.si.edu/ofg/Applications/NAP/NAPapp.htm

Summary To support Native American students interested in conducting projects related to Native American topics that require the use of Native American resources at the Smithsonian Institution.

Eligibility Applicants must be Native American students who are actively engaged in graduate or undergraduate study and are interested in working with Native American resources at the Smithsonian Institution. Along with their application, they must submit a 2- to 4-page essay in which they describe their past and present academic history and other experiences which they feel have prepared them for an internship, what they hope to accomplish through an internship and how it would relate to their academic and career goals, and what about the Smithsonian in particular interests them and leads them to apply for the internship.

Financial data Interns receive a stipend of $550 per week and a travel allowance.

Duration 10 weeks.

Additional information Interns pursue directed research projects supervised by Smithsonian staff members. Recipients must be in residence at the Smithsonian Institution for the duration of the program.

Number awarded Varies each year.

Deadline January of each year for summer residency; May of each year for fall residency; September of each year for spring residency.

[1103]
SNA FOUNDATION SCHOLARSHIPS

Seldovia Native Association, Inc.
Attn: SNA Foundation
P.O. Drawer L
Seldovia, AK 99663
(907) 234-7625   Toll Free: (800) 478-7898
Fax: (907) 234-7637
Web: www.snai.com/shareholders/sna-foundation.html

Summary To provide financial assistance to Alaska Natives 1) who are shareholders in Seldovia Native Association (SNA) or their family members and 2) who wish to attend college or graduate school in any state.

Eligibility This program is open to Alaska Natives who are enrolled as shareholders in SNA, their spouses, and their descendants. Applicants must be enrolled or accepted for enrollment as full-time undergraduate or graduate students at an accredited 2- or 4-year college or university in any state. They must have a GPA of 3.0 or higher for achievement scholarships or 2.0 or higher for general scholarships. Along with their application, they must submit a statement of purpose that includes their personal history, a summary of accomplishments, a description of their career goals, and how their degree program fits with their education and career plans. Selection is based on that statement, academic achievement, previous work experience, educational and community involvement, recommendations, seriousness of purpose, major field of study, practicality of educational and professional goals, completeness of the application, and financial need. Alaska residency is not required.

Financial data Achievement scholarships are $2,500 per year; general scholarships are $500 per year.

Duration 1 year; may be renewed.

Number awarded Varies each year.

Deadline June of each year.

[1104]
SOCIETY FOR THE STUDY OF SOCIAL PROBLEMS RACIAL/ETHNIC MINORITY GRADUATE SCHOLARSHIP

Society for the Study of Social Problems
Attn: Executive Officer
University of Tennessee
901 McClung Tower
Knoxville, TN 37996-0490
(865) 689-1531   Fax: (865) 689-1534
E-mail: sssp@utk.edu
Web: www.sssp1.org/index.cfm/m/261

Summary To provide funding to Native Americans and other minority members of the Society for the Study of Social Problems (SSSP) who are interested in conducting research for their doctoral dissertation.

Eligibility This program is open to SSSP members who are Black or African American, Hispanic or Latino, Asian or Asian American, Native Hawaiian or other Pacific Islander, or American Indian or Alaska Native. Applicants must have completed all requirements for a Ph.D. (course work, examinations, and approval of a dissertation prospectus) except the dissertation. They must have a GPA of 3.25 or higher and be able to demonstrate financial need. Their field of study may be any of the social and/or behavioral sciences that will enable them to expand their perspectives in the investigation into social problems. U.S. citizenship or permanent resident status is required.

Financial data The stipend is $12,000. Additional grants provide $500 for the recipient to 1) attend the SSSP annual meeting prior to the year of the work to receive the award, and 2) attend the meeting after the year of the award to present a report on the work completed.

Duration 1 year.

Number awarded 1 each year.

Deadline January of each year.

[1105]
SOCIETY OF AMERICAN ARCHIVISTS MOSAIC SCHOLARSHIPS

Society of American Archivists
Attn: Chair, Awards Committee
17 North State Street, Suite 1425
Chicago, IL 60602-3315
(312) 606-0722   Toll Free: (866) 722-7858
Fax: (312) 606-0728   E-mail: info@archivists.org
Web: www2.archivists.org

Summary To provide financial assistance to Native Americans and other minority students who are working on a graduate degree in archival science.

Eligibility This program is open to minority graduate students, defined as those of American Indian/Alaska Native, Asian, Black/African American, Hispanic/Latino, or Native Hawaiian/other Pacific Islander descent. Applicants must be enrolled or planning to enroll in a graduate program or a multi-course program in archival administration. They may have completed no more than half of the credit requirements for a degree. Along with their application, they must submit a 500-word essay outlining their interests and future goals in the archives profession. U.S. or Canadian citizenship or permanent resident status is required.

Financial data The stipend is $5,000.

Duration 1 year.

Additional information This scholarship was first awarded in 2009.

Number awarded 2 each year.

Deadline February of each year.

[1106]
SOCIETY OF PEDIATRIC PSYCHOLOGY DIVERSITY RESEARCH GRANT

American Psychological Association
Attn: Division 54 (Society of Pediatric Psychology)
c/o John M. Chaney
Oklahoma State University
Department of Psychology
407 North Murray
Stillwater, OK 74078
(405) 744-5703   E-mail: john.chaney@okstate.edu
Web: www.societyofpediatricpsychology.org

Summary To provide funding to minority and other graduate student and postdoctoral members of the Society of Pediatric Psychology who are interested in conducting research on diversity aspects of pediatric psychology.

Eligibility This program is open to current members of the society who are graduate students, fellows, or early-career

(within 3 years of appointment) faculty. Applicants must be interested in conducting pediatric psychology research that features diversity-related variables, such as race or ethnicity, gender, culture, sexual orientation, language differences, socioeconomic status, and/or religiosity. Along with their application, they must submit a 2,000-word description of the project, including its purpose, methodology, predictions, and implications; a detailed budget; a current curriculum vitae, and (for students) a curriculum vitae of the faculty research mentor and a letter of support from that mentor. Selection is based on relevance to diversity in child health (5 points), significance of the study (5 points), study methods and procedures (10 points), and investigator qualifications (10 points).

Financial data Grants up to $1,000 are available. Funds may not be used for convention or meeting travel, indirect costs, stipends of principal investigators, or costs associated with manuscript preparation.

Duration The grant is presented annually.

Additional information The Society of Pediatric Psychology is Division 54 of the American Psychological Association (APA). This grant was first presented in 2008.

Number awarded 1 each year.

Deadline September of each year.

[1107]
SOKAOGON CHIPPEWA COMMUNITY HIGHER EDUCATION GRANTS PROGRAM

Sokaogon Chippewa Community
Attn: Higher Education Director
10808 Sokaogon Drive
Crandon, WI 54520
(715) 478-3830   Fax: (715) 478-0980
Web: www.sokaogonchippewa.com

Summary To provide financial assistance for college or graduate school to members of the Sokaogon Chippewa Community.

Eligibility This program is open to enrolled tribal members of the Sokaogon Chippewa Community who are working on or planning to work on an undergraduate or graduate degree. Applicants must be able to demonstrate financial need.

Financial data The maximum stipend is $1,200 per year.

Duration 1 year; undergraduate grants may be renewed for a total of 10 semesters; graduate grants may be renewed if funding is available; all renewals require the recipient to maintain a GPA of 2.0 or higher.

Number awarded Varies each year.

Deadline June of each year.

[1108]
SOUTHERN REGIONAL EDUCATION BOARD DISSERTATION AWARDS

Southern Regional Education Board
Attn: Coordinator, Program and Scholar Services
592 Tenth Street N.W.
Atlanta, GA 30318-5776
(404) 879-5569   Fax: (404) 872-1477
E-mail: doctoral.scholars@sreb.org
Web: www.sreb.org/page/1113/types_of_awards.html

Summary To provide funding to Native American and other minority students who wish to complete a Ph.D. dissertation, especially in fields of science, technology, engineering, or mathematics (STEM), while in residence at a university in the southern states.

Eligibility This program is open to U.S. citizens and permanent residents who are members of racial/ethnic minority groups (Native Americans, Hispanic Americans, Asian Americans, and African Americans) and have completed all requirements for a Ph.D. except the dissertation. Preference is given to students in STEM disciplines with particularly low minority representation, although all academic fields are eligible. Applicants must be in a position to write full time and must expect to complete their dissertation within the year of the fellowship. Eligibility is limited to individuals who plan to become full-time faculty members at a southern institution upon completion of their doctoral degree. The program does not include students working on other doctoral degrees (e.g., M.D., D.B.A., D.D.S., J.D., D.V.M., Ed.D., Pharm.D., D.N.P., D.P.T.).

Financial data Fellows receive waiver of tuition and fees (in or out of state), a stipend of $20,000, a $500 research allowance, and reimbursement of expenses for attending the Compact for Faculty Diversity's annual Institute on Teaching and Mentoring.

Duration 1 year; nonrenewable.

Additional information This program was established in 1993 as part of the Compact for Faculty Diversity, supported by the Pew Charitable Trusts and the Ford Foundation.

Number awarded Varies each year.

Deadline February of each year.

[1109]
SOVEREIGN NATIONS SCHOLARSHIP FUND GRADUATE AWARDS

American Indian College Fund
Attn: Scholarship Department
8333 Greenwood Boulevard
Denver, CO 80221
(303) 426-8900   Toll Free: (800) 776-FUND
Fax: (303) 426-1200
E-mail: scholarships@collegefund.org
Web: www.collegefund.org

Summary To provide financial assistance for graduate school to Native American students who are interested in working for a tribe or Indian organization after completing their degree.

Eligibility This program is open to American Indians and Alaska Natives who can document proof of enrollment or descendancy. Applicants must be planning to 1) enroll full time in an advanced degree (e.g., M.A., M.S., J.D., Ph.D., M.D.) program at a mainstream institution, and 2) work for their tribe or an Indian organization after graduation. They must have a GPA of 3.0 or higher and be able to demonstrate exceptional academic achievement. Applications are available only online and include required essays on specified topics.

Financial data The stipend is $2,000 per year.

Duration 1 year; may be renewed.

Number awarded Varies each year.

Deadline May of each year.

[1110]
SPECTRUM SCHOLARSHIP PROGRAM

American Library Association
Attn: Office for Diversity
50 East Huron Street
Chicago, IL 60611-2795
(312) 280-5048   Toll Free: (800) 545-2433, ext. 5048
Fax: (312) 280-3256   TDD: (888) 814-7692
E-mail: spectrum@ala.org
Web: www.ala.org

Summary To provide financial assistance to Native American and other minority students interested in working on a degree in librarianship.

Eligibility This program is open to ethnic minority students (African American or Black, Asian, Native Hawaiian or other Pacific Islander, Latino or Hispanic, and American Indian or Alaska Native). Applicants must be U.S. or Canadian citizens or permanent residents who have completed no more than a third of the requirements for a master's or school library media degree. They must be enrolled full or part time at an ALA-accredited school of library and information studies or an ALA-recognized NCATE school library media program. Selection is based on academic leadership, outstanding service, commitment to a career in librarianship, statements indicating the nature of the applicant's library and other work experience, letters of reference, and personal presentation.

Financial data The stipend is $5,000.

Duration 1 year; nonrenewable.

Additional information This program began in 1998. It is administered by a joint committee of the American Library Association (ALA). Units with ALA sponsor a number of other programs aimed at minority recipients, including the LITA/OCLC Minority Scholarship and the LITA/LSSI Minority Scholarship, both offered by ALA's Library and Information Technology Association.

Number awarded Varies each year; recently, 69 of these scholarships were awarded.

Deadline February of each year.

[1111]
SREB DOCTORAL AWARDS

Southern Regional Education Board
Attn: Coordinator, Program and Scholar Services
592 Tenth Street N.W.
Atlanta, GA 30318-5776
(404) 879-5569   Fax: (404) 872-1477
E-mail: doctoral.scholars@sreb.org
Web: www.sreb.org/page/1113/types_of_awards.html

Summary To provide financial assistance to Native American and other minority students who wish to work on a doctoral degree, especially in fields of science, technology, engineering, or mathematics (STEM), at designated universities in the southern states.

Eligibility This program is open to U.S. citizens and permanent residents who are members of racial/ethnic minority groups (Native Americans, Hispanic Americans, Asian Americans, and African Americans) and have or will receive a bachelor's or master's degree. Applicants must be entering or enrolled in the first year of a Ph.D. program at an accredited college or university. They must indicate an interest in becoming a college professor at an institution in the South. The program does not support students working on other doctoral degrees (e.g., M.D., D.B.A., D.D.S., J.D., D.V.M., Ed.D., Pharm.D., D.N.P., D.P.T.). Preference is given to applicants in STEM disciplines with particularly low minority representation, although all academic fields are eligible.

Financial data Scholars receive a waiver of tuition and fees (in or out of state) for up to 5 years, an annual stipend of $20,000 for 3 years, an annual allowance for professional development activities, and reimbursement of travel expenses to attend the Company for Faculty Diversity's annual Institute on Teaching and Mentoring.

Duration Up to 5 years.

Additional information This program was established in 1993 as part of the Compact for Faculty Diversity, supported by the Pew Charitable Trusts and the Ford Foundation.

Number awarded Varies each year; recently, the program was supporting more than 300 scholars. Since its founding, it has supported more than 900 scholars at 83 institutions in 29 states.

Deadline February of each year.

[1112]
ST. CROIX CHIPPEWA INDIANS HIGHER EDUCATION GRANTS PROGRAM

St. Croix Chippewa Indians of Wisconsin
Attn: Education Coordinator
24663 Angeline Avenue
Webster, WI 54893
(715) 349-7709   Toll Free: (800) 236-2195
Fax: (715) 349-7905
Web: www.stcciw.com

Summary To provide financial assistance for college or graduate school to tribal members of the St. Croix Chippewa Indians of Wisconsin.

Eligibility This program is open to enrolled tribal members of the St. Croix Chippewa Indians who are working on or planning to work on an undergraduate or graduate degree. Applicants must be able to demonstrate financial need.

Financial data Stipends range up to $8,000 per year.

Duration 1 year; may be renewed for a total of 10 semesters, provided the recipient maintains a GPA of 2.0 or higher as an undergraduate or 3.0 or higher as a graduate student.

Number awarded Varies each year.

Deadline July of each year for fall term; November of each year for winter term; January of each year for spring term; May of each year for summer term.

[1113]
STOCKBRIDGE-MUNSEE HIGHER EDUCATION GRANT PROGRAM

Stockbridge-Munsee Community
Attn: Education and Cultural Affairs Director
W13447 Camp 14 Road
P.O. Box 70
Bowler, WI 54416
(715) 793-4060   Toll Free: (800) 720-2790
Fax: (715) 793-4830
E-mail: jolene.bowman@mohican-nsn.gov
Web: www.mohican-nsn.gov

Summary To provide financial assistance to members of the Stockbridge-Munsee Community Band of Mohican Indi-

ans who are interested in attending college or graduate school in any state.

Eligibility This program is open to members of the Stockbridge-Munsee Community Band of Mohican Indians who are interested in working on an associate, baccalaureate, or graduate degree at a college or university in any state. Applicants must be able to demonstrate financial need. In the selection process, priority is given to students in the following order: continuing current students, new students, part-time students, students for whom the educational institution has made a determination of no financial need, and students who are repeating a degree level.

Financial data Stipends for full-time study are $2,650 per semester for 2-year college students, $5,000 per semester for 4-year baccalaureate students, or $6,670 per semester for graduate students. Stipends for part-time study are prorated appropriately.

Duration 1 semester; may be renewed up to 4 additional semesters for associate degree students, up to 9 additional semesters for baccalaureate students, up to 4 additional semesters for students in a 2-year graduate program, up to 6 additional semesters for students in a 3-year graduate program, or up to 8 additional semesters for students in a 4-year graduate program. Renewals require students to remain enrolled full time and to maintain a GPA of 2.0 or higher as an undergraduate or 3.0 or higher as a graduate student. Part-time students may renew proportionately.

Additional information This program is offered under contract with the U.S. Bureau of Indian Affairs. Wisconsin residents who attend school in the state must also apply for a Wisconsin Indian Student Assistance Grant.

Number awarded Varies each year.

Deadline May of each year for fall term; September of each year for spring term; April of each year for summer term.

[1114]
STOEL RIVES FIRST-YEAR DIVERSITY FELLOWSHIPS

Stoel Rives LLP
Attn: Professional Development and Diversity Manager
900 S.W. Fifth Avenue, Suite 2600
Portland, OR 97204
(503) 294-9496   Fax: (503) 220-2480
E-mail: lddecker@stoel.com
Web: www.stoel.com/diversity.aspx?Show=2805

Summary To provide financial assistance to Native American and other law students who bring diversity to the profession and are interested in a summer associate position with Stoel Rives.

Eligibility This program is open to first-year law students who contribute to the diversity of the student body at their law school and who will contribute to the diversity of the legal community. Applicants must be willing to accept a summer associate position at Stoel Rives offices in Boise, Portland, and Seattle. Selection is based on academic excellence, leadership, community service, interest in practicing in the Pacific Northwest, and financial need.

Financial data The program provides a stipend of $7,500 to help defray expenses of law school and a salaried summer associate position.

Duration 1 year.

Additional information   This program began in 2004.

Number awarded   3 each year: 1 each in Boise, Portland, and Seattle.

Deadline   January of each year.

[1115]
SUMMER INTERNSHIP PROGRAM FOR GRADUATE STUDENTS

Educational Testing Service
Attn: Fellowships
660 Rosedale Road
MS 19-T
Princeton, NJ 08541-0001
(609) 734-5543   Fax: (609) 734-5410
E-mail: internfellowships@ets.org
Web: www.ets.org/research/fellowships/summer

Summary   To provide an internship opportunity to minority and other doctoral students interested in conducting summer research under the guidance of senior staff at the Educational Testing Service (ETS).

Eligibility   This program is open to doctoral students interested in working on a research project at ETS in 1 of the following areas: measurement theory, validity, natural language processing and computational linguistics, cognitive psychology, learning theory, linguistics, speech recognition and processing, teaching and classroom research, statistics, or international large scale assessments. Applicants must have completed at least 2 years of full-time study for a Ph.D. or Ed.D. Selection is based on the scholarship of the applicant, match of applicant interests with participating ETS researchers, and the ETS affirmative action objectives. An explicit goal of the program is to increase the number of scholars and students from diverse backgrounds, especially such traditionally underrepresented groups as African Americans, Hispanic/ Latino Americans, and American Indians, who are interested in conducting research during the summer in educational measurement and related fields.

Financial data   The award includes a stipend of $5,000, up to $1,000 as round-trip travel reimbursement, and a $1,500 housing allowance for interns residing outside a 50-mile radius of the ETS campus.

Duration   8 weeks in the summer.

Additional information   Fellows work with senior staff at ETS in Princeton, New Jersey.

Number awarded   Up to 16 each year.

Deadline   January of each year.

[1116]
SUMMER TRANSPORTATION INTERNSHIP PROGRAM FOR DIVERSE GROUPS

Department of Transportation
Attn: Summer Transportation Internship Program for
  Diverse Groups
HAHR-40, Room E63-433
1200 New Jersey Avenue, S.E.
Washington, DC 20590
(202) 366-2907   E-mail: lafayette.melton@dot.gov
Web: www.fhwa.dot.gov/education/stipdg.htm

Summary   To enable Native American and other undergraduate, graduate, and law students from diverse groups to gain work experience during the summer at facilities of the U.S. Department of Transportation (DOT).

Eligibility   This program is open to all qualified applicants, but it is designed to provide women, persons with disabilities, and members of diverse social and ethnic groups with summer opportunities in transportation. Applicants must be U.S. citizens currently enrolled in a degree-granting program of study at an accredited institution of higher learning at the undergraduate (community or junior college, university, college, or Tribal College or University) or graduate level. Undergraduates must be entering their junior or senior year; students attending a Tribal or community college must have completed their first year of school; law students must be entering their second or third year of school. Students who will graduate during the spring or summer are not eligible unless they have been accepted for enrollment in graduate school. The program accepts applications from students in all majors who are interested in working on transportation-related topics and issues. Preference is given to students with a GPA of 3.0 or higher. Undergraduates must submit a 1-page essay on their transportation interests and how participation in this program will enhance their educational and career plans and goals. Graduate students must submit a writing sample representing their educational and career plans and goals. Law students must submit a legal writing sample.

Financial data   The stipend is $4,000 for undergraduates or $5,000 for graduate and law students. The program also provides housing and reimbursement of travel expenses from interns' homes to their assignment location.

Duration   10 weeks during the summer.

Additional information   Assignments are at the DOT headquarters in Washington, D.C., a selected modal administration, or selected field offices around the country.

Number awarded   80 to 100 each year.

Deadline   January of each year.

[1117]
SUSAN KELLY POWER AND HELEN HORNBECK TANNER FELLOWSHIP

Newberry Library
Attn: McNickle Center for American Indian History
60 West Walton Street
Chicago, IL 60610-3305
(312) 255-3564   Fax: (312) 255-3696
E-mail: mcnickle@newberry.org
Web: www.newberry.org/mcnickle/powertanner.html

Summary   To provide funding to American Indian doctoral candidates and postdoctorates who wish to use the resources of the D'Arcy McNickle Center for the History of the American Indian at the Newberry Library.

Eligibility   This program is open to Ph.D. candidates and postdoctoral scholars of American Indian heritage. Applicants must be interested in conducting research in any field of the humanities while in residence at the McNickle Center.

Financial data   The stipend is $1,600 per month.

Duration   1 week to 2 months.

Additional information   This program was established in 2002.

Number awarded   1 each year.

Deadline   February of each year.

[1118]
SUSIE QIMMIQSAK BEVINS ENDOWMENT SCHOLARSHIP FUND

Cook Inlet Region, Inc.
Attn: The CIRI Foundation
3600 San Jeronimo Drive, Suite 256
Anchorage, AK 99508-2870
(907) 793-3575   Toll Free: (800) 764-3382
Fax: (907) 793-3585   E-mail: tcf@thecirifoundation.org
Web: www.thecirifoundation.org/designated.htm

Summary To provide financial assistance for undergraduate or graduate studies in the literary, performing, and visual arts to Alaska Natives who are original enrollees to Cook Inlet Region, Inc. (CIRI) and their lineal descendants.

Eligibility This program is open to Alaska Native enrollees to CIRI under the Alaska Native Claims Settlement Act (ANCSA) of 1971 and their lineal descendants. There are no Alaska residency requirements or age limitations. Applicants must be accepted or enrolled full time in a 2-year, 4-year, or graduate degree program in the literary, visual, or performing arts. They should have a GPA of 2.5 or higher. Along with their application, they must submit a 500-word statement on their educational and career goals and how they are contributing, or planning to contribute, to a positive Alaska Native community. Selection is based on that statement, academic achievement, rigor of course work or degree program, student financial contribution, financial need, grade level, previous work performance, community service, and relationship of degree program to career goals.

Financial data The stipend is $2,000 per semester.

Duration 1 semester; recipients may reapply.

Additional information This program was established in 1990.

Number awarded Varies each year.

Deadline May or November of each year.

[1119]
SYNOD OF LAKES AND PRAIRIES RACIAL ETHNIC SCHOLARSHIPS

Synod of Lakes and Prairies
Attn: Committee on Racial Ethnic Ministry
2115 Cliff Drive
Eagen, MN 55122-3327
(651) 357-1140   Toll Free: (800) 328-1880
Fax: (651) 357-1141   E-mail: mkes@lakesandprairies.org
Web: www.lakesandprairies.org

Summary To provide financial assistance to Native American and other minority residents of the Presbyterian Church (USA) Synod of Lakes and Prairies who are studying for the ministry at a seminary in any state.

Eligibility This program is open to members of Presbyterian churches who reside within the Synod of Lakes and Prairies (Iowa, Minnesota, Nebraska, North Dakota, South Dakota, and Wisconsin). Applicants must be members of ethnic minority groups studying for the ministry in the Presbyterian Church (USA) or a related ecumenical organization. They must be in good academic standing, making progress toward a degree, and able to demonstrate financial need. Along with their application, they must submit essays of 200 to 500 words each on 1) their vision for the church, and either 2) how their school experience will prepare them to work in

the church, or 3) the person who most influenced their commitment to Christ.

Financial data Stipends range from $850 to $3,500.

Duration 1 year.

Number awarded Varies each year; recently, 9 of these scholarships were awarded.

Deadline September of each year.

[1120]
SYNOD OF THE COVENANT ETHNIC THEOLOGICAL SCHOLARSHIPS

Synod of the Covenant
Attn: Ministries in Higher Education
1911 Indianwood Circle, Suite B
Maumee, OH 43537-4063
(419) 754-4050
Toll Free: (800) 848-1030 (within MI and OH)
Fax: (419) 754-4051
Web: www.synodofthecovenant.org

Summary To provide financial assistance to Native Americans and other minorities working on a master's degree at an approved Presbyterian theological institution (with priority given to Presbyterian applicants from Ohio and Michigan).

Eligibility This program is open to ethnic individuals enrolled full time in church vocations programs at approved Presbyterian theological institutions. Priority is given to Presbyterian applicants from the states of Michigan and Ohio. Financial need is considered in the selection process.

Financial data Students may be awarded a maximum of $1,500 on initial application. They may receive up to $2,000 on subsequent applications, with evidence of continuing progress. Funds are made payable to the session for distribution.

Duration Students are eligible to receive scholarships 1 time per year, up to a maximum of 5 years.

Number awarded Varies each year.

Deadline August of each year for fall semester; January of each year for spring semester.

[1121]
TANANA CHIEFS CONFERENCE HIGHER EDUCATION GRANTS

Tanana Chiefs Conference
Attn: Education Department
122 First Avenue, Suite 600
Fairbanks, AK 99701-4897
(907) 452-8251, ext. 3184
Toll Free: (800) 478-6822 (within AK)
Fax: (907) 459-3885
Web: www.tananachiefs.org/Higher_Education.shtm

Summary To provide financial assistance to Native Alaskans who have a tie to the Tanana Chiefs Conference (TCC) and are interested in attending college or graduate school in any state.

Eligibility This program is open to Alaska Natives who are enrolled to Doyon, Limited or a member of a tribe or village served by TCC. Applicants must be attending or planning to attend an accredited college, university, graduate school, or vocational training program in any state. They must be able to demonstrate financial need and to apply for all other available financial aid.

Financial data A stipend is awarded (amount not specified).

Duration 1 semester; may be renewed if the recipient maintains a GPA of 2.0 or higher and full-time enrollment.

Additional information TCC serves the following villages in interior Alaska: Birch Creek, Huslia, Minto, Nenana, Nikolai, Rampart, and Tetlin. It also provides funding to 28 other villages that administer the program for students enrolled to their tribe or corporation.

Number awarded More than 200 each year.

Deadline April of each year for fall semester or quarter; November of each year for spring semester or winter or spring quarter; February of each year for summer school.

[1122]
TANAQ FOUNDATION SCHOLARSHIPS

St. George Tanaq Corporation
Attn: Tanaq Foundation
4141 B Street, Suite 301
Anchorage, AK 99503
(907) 272-9886   Toll Free: (888) 811-9886
Fax: (907) 272-9855
Web: stgeorgetanaq.com/foundation.html

Summary To provide financial assistance to Native Alaskans who are shareholders or descendants of shareholders of the St. George Tanaq Corporation and interested in attending college or graduate school in any state.

Eligibility This program is open to shareholders of the St. George Tanaq Corporation and their lineal descendants who are enrolled or planning to enroll full time at a college or university in any state. Applicants must be interested in working on an associate, bachelor's, or master's degree in any field. They must have a GPA of 2.0 or higher. Along with their application, they must submit a 500-word letter of intent that explains how they are doing, their goals, and their expected date of graduation. Financial need is not considered in the selection process.

Financial data Stipends are $2,000 or $1,000. Funds are disbursed directly to the financial aid office of the recipient's school.

Duration 1 year; may be renewed.

Additional information The St. George Tanaq Corporation is an Alaska Native village corporation that serves the island of St. George in the Aleutian chain.

Number awarded Varies each year; recently, 5 of these scholarships (4 at $2,000 and 1 at $1,000) were awarded.

Deadline June of each year for the school year; November of each year for spring semester only.

[1123]
TARGETED OPPORTUNITY PROGRAM (TOPJOBS)

Wisconsin Office of State Employment Relations
Attn: Division of Affirmative Action Workforce Planning
101 East Wilson Street, Fourth Floor
P.O. Box 7855
Madison, WI 53707-7855
(608) 267-1005   Fax: (608) 267-1020
E-mail: Claire.Dehnert@wisconsin.gov
Web: oser.state.wi.us/category.asp?linkcatid=342

Summary To provide an opportunity for Native Americans and other underrepresented students to gain summer work experience with agencies of the state of Wisconsin.

Eligibility This program is open to ethnic/racial minorities (Black or African American, Asian, Native Hawaiian or other Pacific Islander, American Indian or Alaska Native, or Hispanic or Latino), women, and persons with disabilities. Applicants must be juniors, seniors, or graduate students at an accredited 4-year college or university or second-year students in the second year of a 2-year technical or vocational school program. They must be 1) Wisconsin residents enrolled full time at a school in Wisconsin or any other state, or 2) residents of other states who are enrolled full time at a school in Wisconsin.

Financial data Most internships provide a competitive stipend.

Duration Summer months.

Additional information This program was established in 1974. Relevant fields of study include, but are not limited to, the liberal arts and sciences (e.g., history, mathematics, library science, political science, philosophy, physics, psychology, social services, social work, sociology, women's studies); agriculture and natural resources (e.g., animal and dairy science, biology, botany, chemistry, geography, entomology, environmental studies, horticulture, landscape architecture, microbiology, plant pathology, soil science, urban planning, water resources management, wildlife ecology); business (e.g., accounting, business management, economics, finance, human resources, marketing, public administration, real estate); criminal justice; education; health care (including nursing); engineering; information systems and computers; journalism and communications; and law.

Number awarded Varies each year. Since the program was established, it has placed more than 2,500 students with more than 30 different agencies and universities throughout the state.

Deadline February of each year.

[1124]
TBM PROGRAM

Catching the Dream
8200 Mountain Road, N.E., Suite 203
Albuquerque, NM 87110-7835
(505) 262-2351   Fax: (505) 262-0534
E-mail: NScholarsh@aol.com
Web: www.catchingthedream.org/Scholarship.htm

Summary To provide financial assistance to American Indian undergraduate and graduate students interested in studying a field related to economic development for tribes.

Eligibility This program is open to American Indians who can provide proof that they are at least one-quarter Indian blood and a member of a U.S. tribe that is federally-recognized, state-recognized, or terminated. Applicants must be enrolled or planning to enroll full time and major in the 1 of the following fields: business administration, finance, management, economics, banking, hotel management, or other fields related to economic development for tribes. They may be entering freshmen, undergraduate students, graduate students, or Ph.D. candidates. Along with their application, they must submit documentation of financial need, 3 letters of recommendation, copies of applications and responses for all other sources of funding for which they are eligible, official transcripts, standardized test scores (ACT, SAT, GRE, MCAT, LSAT, etc.), and an essay explaining their goals in life, college plans, and career plans (especially how those plans include working with and benefiting Indians). Selection is based on merit and potential for improving the lives of Indian people.

Financial data Stipends range from $500 to $5,000 per year.

Duration 1 year.

Additional information The sponsor was formerly known as the Native American Scholarship Fund. This program was established in 2003.

Number awarded Varies; generally, 30 to 35 each year.

Deadline April of each year for fall term; September of each year for spring and winter terms; March of each year for summer school.

[1125]
TEACHER QUEST SCHOLARSHIP

Brown Foundation for Educational Equity, Excellence and Research
Attn: Scholarship Committee
1515 S.E. Monroe
Topeka, KS 66615
(785) 235-3939   Fax: (785) 235-1001
E-mail: brownfound@juno.com
Web: brownvboard.org

Summary To provide financial assistance to Native Americans and other undergraduate and graduate students of color who are interested in preparing for a teaching career.

Eligibility This program is open to members of minority groups who are enrolled at least half time at an institution of higher education with an accredited teacher education program. Applicants must be enrolled at the undergraduate, graduate, or post-baccalaureate level and have a GPA of 3.0 or higher. Along with their application, they must submit brief essays on 1) their involvement in school, community, and/or other activities and how those activities have prepared them to be an educator; 2) why they aspire to a career in education, their goals, and the level at which they plan to teach; and 3) how they think *Brown v. Board of Education* has influenced their own life experiences. Selection is based on the essays; GPA; school, community, and leisure activities; career plans and goals in education; and recommendations.

Financial data The stipend is $1,000 per year.

Duration 2 years.

Additional information The first Brown Foundation Scholarships were awarded in 1989. The current program replaced the Brown Foundation Academic Scholarships in 2009.

Number awarded Varies each year; recently, 5 of these scholarships were awarded.

Deadline March of each year.

[1126]
TEXAS MEDICAL ASSOCIATION MINORITY SCHOLARSHIP PROGRAM

Texas Medical Association
Attn: Educational Loans, Scholarships and Awards
401 West 15th Street
Austin, TX 78701-1680
(512) 370-1300   Toll Free: (800) 880-1300, ext. 1600
Fax: (512) 370-1630   E-mail: info@tmaloanfunds.com
Web: www.tmaloanfunds.com/Content/Template.aspx?id=9

Summary To provide financial assistance to Native Americans and other underrepresented minorities from any state who are entering medical school in Texas.

Eligibility This program is open to members of minority groups that are underrepresented in the medical profession (African American, Mexican American, Native American). Applicants must have been accepted at a medical school in Texas; students currently enrolled are not eligible. Along with their application, they must submit a 750-word essay on how they, as a physician, would improve the health of all Texans.

Financial data The stipend is $5,000.

Duration 1 year; renewable.

Additional information This program began in 1999.

Number awarded 1 to 8 each year.

Deadline April of each year.

[1127]
THE REV. FRANCENE EAGLE BIG GOOSE MEMORIAL SCHOLARSHIP

United Methodist Church-Arkansas Conference
Attn: Committee on Native American Ministries
800 Daisy Bates Drive
Little Rock, AR 72202
(501) 324-8045   Toll Free: (877) 646-1816
Fax: (501) 324-8018   E-mail: conference@arumc.org
Web: www.arumc.org

Summary To provide book scholarships to Native American Methodist seminary students from Arkansas.

Eligibility This program is open to seminary students of Native American/Indigenous Heritage, including Native Indians, Native Alaskans, Native Hawaiians, and Pacific Island populations. Applicants must be active members of local congregations affiliated with the Arkansas Conference of the United Methodist Church (UMC). If no applications are received from students within Arkansas, the program is open to students from the Oklahoma Indian Missionary Conference. The seminary they are attending must be approved by the UMC University Senate. Along with their application, they must submit brief essays on their educational goals, how they contribute to the Native American community, and a personal accomplishment of which they are particularly proud that relates to their Native American Heritage. They must be able to demonstrate financial need.

Financial data The stipend is $500 per semester ($1,000 per year). Funds are intended to assist in the purchase of books.

Duration 1 semester; may be renewed.

Number awarded 1 or more each year.

Deadline May of each year for fall semester; December of each year for spring semester.

[1128]
THOMPSON HINE DIVERSITY SCHOLARSHIP PROGRAM

Thompson Hine LLP
Attn: Manager of New Lawyer Recruiting
3900 Key Center
127 Public Square
Cleveland, OH 44114-1291
(216) 566-5500   Fax: (216) 566-5800
E-mail: info@thompsonhine.com
Web: www.thompsonhine.com

Summary To provide financial assistance and work experience to Native American and other minority law students from any state who have been accepted as a summer associate with the law firm of Thompson Hine.

Eligibility This program is open to second-year law students who are members of minority groups as defined by the Equal Employment Opportunity Commission (Native American or Alaskan Native, Asian or Pacific Islander African American or Black, or Hispanic). Applicants must first be offered a summer associateship at an office of Thompson Hine in Atlanta, Cincinnati, Cleveland, Columbus, Dayton, New York, or Washington, D.C. Along with their application, they must submit a writing sample (a legal brief or memorandum prepared for their first-year legal writing course or a prior employer), law school and undergraduate transcripts, a current resume, and a list of at least 2 references.

Financial data The stipend is $10,000. Funds are paid to the student after completing the summer associateship and may be used for tuition and other law school expenses during the third year.

Duration 1 year.

Number awarded 1 each year.

Deadline August of each year.

[1129]
TONKON TORP FIRST-YEAR DIVERSITY FELLOWSHIP PROGRAM

Tonkon Torp LLP
Attn: Director of Attorney Recruiting
1600 Pioneer Tower
888 S.W. Fifth Avenue
Portland, OR 97204
(503) 221-1440   Fax: (503) 972-3760
E-mail: Loree.Devery@tonkon.com
Web: www.tonkon.com/Careers/-1LDiversityFellowship.html

Summary To provide financial assistance and summer work experience in Portland, Oregon to Native American and other first-year minority law students.

Eligibility This program is open to members of racial and ethnic minority groups who are currently enrolled in their first year at an ABA-accredited law school. Applicants must be able to demonstrate 1) a record of academic achievement that indicates a strong likelihood of a successful career during the remainder of law school and in the legal profession; 2) a commitment to practice law in Portland, Oregon following graduation from law school; and 3) an ability to contribute meaningfully to the diversity of the law school student body and, after entering the legal profession, the legal community. They are not required to disclose their financial circumstances, but a demonstrated need for financial assistance may be taken into consideration.

Financial data The recipient is offered a paid summer associateship at Tonkon Torp in Portland, Oregon for the summer following the first year of law school and, depending on the outcome of that experience, may be invited for a second summer following the second year of law school. Following the successful completion of that second associateship, the recipient is awarded an academic scholarship of $7,500 for the third year of law school.

Duration The program covers 2 summers and 1 academic year.

Additional information For 2 weeks during the summer, the fellow works in the legal department of Portland General Electric Company, Oregon's largest electric utility and a client of the sponsoring firm.

Number awarded 1 each year.

Deadline January of each year.

[1130]
TOWNSEND AND TOWNSEND AND CREW DIVERSITY SCHOLARSHIP

Townsend and Townsend and Crew LLP
Attn: Diversity Committee
Two Embarcadero Center, Eighth Floor
San Francisco, CA 94111-3834
(415) 576-0200   Fax: (415) 576-0300
Web: www.townsend.com/Who/Who-Diversity

Summary To provide financial assistance to 1) Native Americans, 2) other minorities, and 3) female students attending law school who are interested in preparing for a career in patent law.

Eligibility This program is open to students enrolled at ABA-accredited law schools who are women or members of minority groups that have historically been underrepresented in the field of patent law (American Indians/Alaskan Natives, Blacks/African Americans, Hispanics/Latinos, and Asian Americans/Pacific Islanders). Applicants must have an undergraduate or graduate degree in a field that will help prepare them for a career in patent law (e.g., life sciences, engineering). They must have a demonstrated commitment to preparing for a career in patent law in a city in which the sponsoring law firm has an office. Selection is based on academic performance; work experience related to science, engineering, or patent law; community service; and demonstrated leadership ability.

Financial data The stipend is $2,000 per year.

Duration 1 year; recipients may reapply.

Additional information This program was established in 2005. Townsend and Townsend and Crew has offices in San Francisco, Palo Alto (California), Denver, Walnut Creek (California), San Diego, Seattle, Tokyo, and Washington, D.C.

Number awarded Varies each year; recently, 11 of these scholarships were awarded.

Deadline April of each year.

[1131]
TRAILBLAZER SCHOLARSHIPS

Conference of Minority Transportation Officials
Attn: National Scholarship Program
818 18th Street, N.W., Suite 850
Washington, DC 20006
(202) 530-0551   Fax: (202) 530-0617
Web: www.comto.org/news-youth.php

Summary   To provide financial assistance to Native American and other undergraduate and graduate minority students working on a degree in a field related to transportation.

Eligibility   This program is open to undergraduate and graduate students who are working on a degree in a field related to transportation with a GPA of 2.5 or higher. Along with their application, they must submit a cover letter with a 500-word statement of career goals. Financial need is not considered in the selection process. U.S. citizenship is required.

Financial data   The stipend is $2,500. Funds are paid directly to the recipient's college or university.

Duration   1 year.

Additional information   The Conference of Minority Transportation Officials (COMTO) was established in 1971 to promote, strengthen, and expand the roles of minorities in all aspects of transportation. Recipients are expected to attend the COMTO National Scholarship Luncheon.

Number awarded   2 each year.

Deadline   April of each year.

[1132]
TRIBAL ENERGY PROGRAM SUMMER INTERNSHIP PROGRAM

Sandia National Laboratories
Attn: Photovoltaics and Grid Integration Program
MS-0734
P.O. Box 5800
Albuquerque, NM 87185-0734
(505) 844-5418   TDD: (505) 844-7786
E-mail: skbegay@sandia.gov
Web: apps1.eere.energy.gov/tribalenergy/internships.cfm

Summary   To provide an opportunity for Native Americans to learn more about renewable energy and energy self-sufficiency during a summer internship at Sandia National Laboratories.

Eligibility   This program is open to members of federally-recognized tribes, Alaska villages, and Alaska corporations; members of state-recognized tribes, members of bands or groups, and first peoples of Hawaii or Guam are not eligible. Applicants must be upper-division or graduate students and familiar with Native American cultural and tribal issues. They must be interested in summer employment at Sandia in Albuquerque to learn more about economic development and employment on tribal lands through the use of renewable energy and energy efficient technologies. Along with their application, they must submit a resume indicating their GPA (minimum of 3.2 for bachelor's students, 3.5 for master's students, or 3.7 for doctoral candidates) and 5 essays of 250 words each on assigned topics related to their background and interest in renewable energy at Sandia.

Financial data   The stipend depends on the number of credit hours completed.

Duration   12 weeks during the summer.

Additional information   This program is sponsored by the Energy Efficiency and Renewable Energy Program of the U.S. Department of Energy.

Number awarded   Varies each year; recently, 4 students received these internships.

Deadline   February of each year.

[1133]
TURTLE MOUNTAIN BAND OF CHIPPEWA INDIANS SCHOLARSHIP PROGRAM

Turtle Mountain Band of Chippewa Indians
Attn: Tribal Scholarship Office
P.O. Box 900
Belcourt, ND 58316
(701) 477-8102   Fax: (701) 477-8053
Web: www.tmbci.net

Summary   To provide financial assistance for full-time undergraduate or graduate study in any state to enrolled members of the Turtle Mountain Band of Chippewa.

Eligibility   Applicants must be enrolled members of the Turtle Mountain Band of Chippewa, be full-time students enrolled in an academic program at an accredited postsecondary institution in any state on either the undergraduate or graduate school level, and have a GPA of 2.0 or higher. Undergraduate applicants must be enrolled for at least 12 quarter or 12 semester credit hours (or 6 semester/quarter hours for a summer session); graduate school applicants must be enrolled for at least 1 course. Along with their application, they must submit a Certificate of Indian Blood, a letter of acceptance/admission from their college, the award notice sent by the college's financial aid office, a high school transcript or GED certificate, and any college transcripts. Priority is given to applicants in the following order: seniors who need to attend summer school in order to graduate, juniors who need summer school in order to become seniors, students who need summer school to acquire their 2-year degree, sophomores, freshmen, and graduate students.

Financial data   A stipend is awarded (amount not specified).

Duration   The maximum number of terms the scholarship program will fund a student for an undergraduate degree is 10 semesters or 15 quarters; the maximum number of terms for a student at a 2-year college is 3 years, 6 semesters, or 9 quarters.

Additional information   Once recipients earn 65 or more credit hours at a 2-year college, they must transfer to a 4-year institution.

Number awarded   Varies each year.

Deadline   August of each year.

[1134]
TYONEK NATIVE CORPORATION GRADUATE SCHOLARSHIPS

Tebughna Foundation
1689 C Street, Suite 221
Anchorage, AK 99501
(907) 272-0707   Toll Free: (877) 862-6667
Fax: (907) 274-7125   E-mail: tebughna@tyonek.com
Web: www.tebughnafoundation.com

Summary   To provide financial assistance to original enrollees of the Tyonek Native Corporation (TNC) and their lineal descendants who are interested in attending graduate school in any state.

Eligibility   This program is open to Alaska Native enrollees to TNC under the Alaska Native Claims Settlement Act (ANCSA) of 1971 and their lineal descendants. Applicants must be accepted or enrolled in a graduate degree program at a college or university in any state. They must have a GPA of 3.0 or higher. Along with their application, they must submit a 500-word statement on their educational and career goals and how they are contributing, or planning to contribute, to a positive Alaska Native community. Selection is based on that statement, academic achievement, and financial need.

Financial data   The stipend is $2,500 per semester ($5,000 per academic year) for full-time students; reduced amounts are available to part-time students.

Duration   1 semester; recipients may reapply.

Number awarded   Varies each year.

Deadline   June or November of each year.

[1135]
UDALL FOUNDATION NATIVE AMERICAN CONGRESSIONAL INTERNSHIPS

Morris K. Udall and Stewart L. Udall Foundation
Attn: Program Manager, Internship Program
130 South Scott Avenue
Tucson, AZ 85701-1922
(520) 901-8568   Fax: (520) 670-5530
E-mail: info@udall.gov
Web: www.udall.gov

Summary   To provide an opportunity for Native American upper-division students, graduate students, and recent graduates to work in a Congressional office during the summer.

Eligibility   This program is open to American Indians and Alaska Natives who are enrolled members of recognized tribes and have an interest in tribal government and policy. Applicants must have a GPA of 3.0 or higher as a junior, senior, graduate student, law student, or recent graduate of a tribal or 4-year college. They must be able to participate in an internship in Washington, D.C., where they will gain practical experience in the legislative process, Congressional matters, and governmental proceedings that specifically relate to Native American issues. Fields of study of previous interns have included American Indian studies, political science, law and pre-law, psychology, social work, history, business and public administration, anthropology, community and urban planning, architecture, communications, health sciences, public health, biology, engineering, sociology, environmental studies and natural resources, economics, and justice studies. Applicants must demonstrate strong research and writing skills; organizational abilities and time management skills; maturity, responsibility, and flexibility; interest in learning how the federal government "really works;" commitment to their tribal community; knowledge of Congressman Morris K. Udall's legacy with regard to Native Americans; and awareness of issues and challenges currently facing Indian Country.

Financial data   Interns receive round-trip airfare to Washington, D.C.; dormitory lodging at a local university; a daily allowance sufficient for meals, transportation, and inciden-

tals; and an educational stipend of $1,200 to be paid at the conclusion of the internship.

Duration   10 weeks during the summer.

Additional information   These internships were first offered in 1996.

Number awarded   12 each year.

Deadline   January of each year.

[1136]
UNDERREPRESENTED MINORITY DENTAL STUDENT SCHOLARSHIP

American Dental Association
Attn: ADA Foundation
211 East Chicago Avenue
Chicago, IL 60611
(312) 440-2547   Fax: (312) 440-3526
E-mail: adaf@ada.org
Web: www.ada.org/ada/adaf/grants/scholarships.asp

Summary   To provide financial assistance to Native Americans and other underrepresented minorities who wish to enter the field of dentistry.

Eligibility   This program is open to U.S. citizens from a minority group that is currently underrepresented in the dental profession: Native American, African American, or Hispanic. Applicants must have a GPA of 3.0 or higher and be entering their second year of study at a dental school in the United States accredited by the Commission on Dental Accreditation. Selection is based upon academic achievement, a written summary of personal and professional goals, letters of reference, and demonstrated financial need.

Financial data   The maximum stipend is $2,500. Funds are sent directly to the student's financial aid office to be used to cover tuition, fees, books, supplies, and living expenses.

Duration   1 year.

Additional information   This program, established in 1991, is supported by the Harry J. Bosworth Company, Colgate-Palmolive, Sunstar Americas, and Procter & Gamble Company. Students receiving a full scholarship from any other source are ineligible to receive this scholarship.

Number awarded   At least 10 each year.

Deadline   October of each year.

[1137]
UNITARIAN UNIVERSALIST ASSOCIATION INCENTIVE GRANTS

Unitarian Universalist Association
Attn: Ministerial Credentialing Office
25 Beacon Street
Boston, MA 02108-2800
(617) 948-6403   Fax: (617) 742-2875
E-mail: mco@uua.org
Web: www.uua.org

Summary   To provide financial aid to Native Americans and other persons of color who the Unitarian Universalist Association is interested in attracting to the ministry.

Eligibility   These grants are offered to persons of color who the association is particularly interested in attracting to Unitarian Universalist ministry to promote racial, cultural, or class diversity. Applicants must be in their first year of study. Decisions regarding potential recipients are made in consultation with the schools. Selection is based on merit.

Financial data A stipend is awarded (amount not specified).

Duration 1 year; nonrenewable.

Additional information In subsequent years, recipients may apply for the association's General Financial Aid Grants.

Number awarded Varies each year.

Deadline April of each year.

[1138]
UNITED KEETOOWAH BAND OF CHEROKEE INDIANS EDUCATIONAL SCHOLARSHIPS

United Keetoowah Band of Cherokee Indians
Attn: Department of Education
P.O. Box 746
Tahlequah, OK 74465
(918) 453-2569   Toll Free: (800) 259-0093
Fax: (918) 453-1267
Web: www.unitedkeetoowahband.org

Summary To provide financial assistance for vocational school, college, or graduate school to members of the United Keetoowah Band of Cherokee Indians.

Eligibility This program is open to students who have been enrolled members of the United Keetoowah Band of Cherokee Indians for at least 6 months. Applicants must be working on or planning to work on a vocational certificate, bachelor's degree, master's degree, doctoral degree, or law degree. Along with their application, they must submit a copy of their tribal membership card, a copy of their Social Security card, an official transcript, a class schedule, and documentation of financial need.

Financial data For full-time undergraduate and graduate students, the stipend is $1,500 per semester; for part-time undergraduate and graduate students, the stipend is $750 per semester; for vocational students, the stipend is $1,000 per year.

Duration 1 semester; may be renewed, provided the recipient maintains a GPA of 2.0 or higher.

Number awarded Varies each year.

Deadline August of each year for fall semester; January of each year for spring semester.

[1139]
UNITED METHODIST HIGHER EDUCATION FOUNDATION NATIVE ALASKAN FUND

United Methodist Higher Education Foundation
Attn: Scholarships Administrator
1001 19th Avenue South
P.O. Box 340005
Nashville, TN 37203-0005
(615) 340-7385   Toll Free: (800) 811-8110
Fax: (615) 340-7330
E-mail: umhefscholarships@gbhem.org
Web: www.umhef.org/receive.php?id=endowed_funds

Summary To provide financial assistance to Native Alaskan Methodist undergraduate and graduate students at Methodist-related colleges and universities.

Eligibility This program is open to Native Alaskans enrolling as full-time undergraduate or graduate students at United Methodist-related colleges and universities. Preference is given to United Methodist students at Alaska Pacific University. Applicants must have been active, full members of a

United Methodist Church for at least 1 year prior to applying. They must have a GPA of 3.0 or higher and be able to demonstrate financial need. Along with their application, they must submit a 200-word essay on their involvement and/or leadership responsibilities in their church, school, and community within the last 3 years. U.S. citizenship or permanent resident status is required.

Financial data The stipend is at least $1,000 per year.

Duration 1 year; nonrenewable.

Number awarded Varies each year; recently, 2 of these scholarships were awarded.

Deadline May of each year.

[1140]
UNITED METHODIST NATIVE AMERICAN SEMINARY AWARDS

United Methodist Church
Attn: General Board of Higher Education and Ministry
Office of Loans and Scholarships
1001 19th Avenue South
P.O. Box 340007
Nashville, TN 37203-0007
(615) 340-7344   Fax: (615) 340-7367
E-mail: umscholar@gbhem.org
Web: www.gbhem.org/loansandscholarships

Summary To provide fellowships and fellowship/loans to Native American seminary students preparing for ministry within the United Methodist Church.

Eligibility This program is open to Native Americans accepted and/or enrolled as a full-time student at a school of theology approved by the University Senate of the United Methodist Church. At least 1 parent must be Native American, American Indian, or Alaska Native. Applicants must have been active, full members of a United Methodist Church for at least 3 years prior to applying. They must be able to demonstrate financial need, a GPA of 2.5 or higher, and involvement in their Native American community.

Financial data The average stipend is $12,000. Half of the funds are provided in the form of a grant and half in the form of a loan that is forgiven if the recipient serves at least 2 years in a Native American congregation or ministry/fellowship that is recognized by the United Methodist Church.

Duration 1 year.

Number awarded Varies each year; recently, 12 of these scholarships were awarded.

Deadline March of each year.

[1141]
UNIVERSITY OF NORTH CAROLINA CAMPUS SCHOLARSHIPS

North Carolina State Education Assistance Authority
Attn: Scholarship and Grant Services
10 Alexander Drive
P.O. Box 14103
Research Triangle Park, NC 27709-4103
(919) 549-8614   Toll Free: (800) 700-1775
Fax: (919) 549-8481   E-mail: information@ncseaa.edu
Web: www.ncseaa.edu

Summary To provide financial assistance to Native American and other students at University of North Carolina (UNC)

constituent institutions whose enrollment contributes to the diversity of the undergraduate or graduate population.

Eligibility This program is open to undergraduate and doctoral students who are enrolled or planning to enroll full time at 1 of the 16 UNC institutions. Applicants must have graduated in the top 40% of their high school class, have a weighted GPA of 3.0 or higher, have an SAT score higher than the SAT score of the previous freshman class, and have a record of positive involvement in extracurricular activities. They must be able to demonstrate "exceptional financial need." Their enrollment must "contribute to the intellectual experiences and diversity of the undergraduate population." A portion of the funds are reserved specifically for American Indian students who can provide evidence of tribal affiliation.

Financial data The amount of the award depends upon the financial need of the recipient and the availability of funds; recently, stipends averaged more than $1,900.

Duration 1 year; may be renewed.

Additional information This program was established in 2002 as a replacement for the former North Carolina Minority Presence Grants, North Carolina Freshmen Scholars Program, North Carolina Incentive Scholarship Program, North Carolina Legislative College Opportunity Program, and North Carolina Incentive Scholarship and Grant Program for Native Americans. Students must submit applications to the constituent institution's financial aid office rather than directly to the North Carolina State Education Assistance Authority.

Number awarded Varies each year; recently, a total of 2,793 of these scholarships, with a total value of $5,435,826, were awarded.

Deadline Deadline dates vary; check with the appropriate constituent institution.

[1142]
VARNUM DIVERSITY AND INCLUSION SCHOLARSHIPS FOR LAW STUDENTS

Varnum LLP
Attn: Scholarships
333 Bridge Street N.W.
P.O. Box 352
Grand Rapids, MI 49501-0352
(616) 336-6620   Fax: (616) 336-7000
E-mail: ewskaggs@varnumlaw.com
Web: www.varnumlaw.com

Summary To provide financial assistance to Native American and other law students from Michigan who will contribute to diversity in the legal profession.

Eligibility This program is open to Michigan residents accepted or currently enrolled at an accredited law school in any state or residents of other states attending an accredited Michigan law school. Applicants must be members of an ethnic or racial minority or demonstrate a significant commitment to issues of diversity and inclusion. They must have a GPA of 3.0 or higher. Along with their application, they must submit a 750-word statement on their efforts to promote greater ethnic or racial diversity and inclusion within the legal profession and/or their community.

Financial data The stipend is $4,000.

Duration 1 year.

Number awarded 2 each year.

Deadline January of each year.

[1143]
VIC MATSON, SR. TRIBUTARY SCHOLARSHIP

Sault Tribe of Chippewa Indians
Attn: Higher Education Program-Memorial/Tributary
  Scholarships
523 Ashmun Street
Sault Ste. Marie, MI 49783
(906) 635-4944   Toll Free: (800) 793-0660
Fax: (906) 635-7785   E-mail: amatson@saulttribe.net
Web: www.saulttribe.com

Summary To provide financial assistance to members of the Sault Tribe of Chippewa Indians interested in attending college in any state to work on an undergraduate or graduate degree in a field related to fisheries or natural resources.

Eligibility This program is open to enrolled members of the Sault Tribe who are enrolled full time at a 2- or 4-year college or university in any state. Applicants must be working on an undergraduate or graduate degree in the field of fisheries or natural resources management or a related area. Along with their application, they must submit an essay of 300 to 500 words on how this scholarship will help them realize their goals.

Financial data The stipend is $1,000.

Duration 1 year.

Number awarded 1 each year.

Deadline May of each year.

[1144]
VINE DELORIA JR. MEMORIAL SCHOLARSHIP

American Indian College Fund
Attn: Scholarship Department
8333 Greenwood Boulevard
Denver, CO 80221
(303) 426-8900   Toll Free: (800) 776-FUND
Fax: (303) 426-1200
E-mail: scholarships@collegefund.org
Web: www.collegefund.org

Summary To provide financial assistance for graduate school to Native American students.

Eligibility This program is open to American Indians and Alaska Natives who can document proof of enrollment or descendancy. Applicants must be enrolled in an advanced degree (e.g., M.A., M.S., J.D., Ph.D., M.D.) program. They must be able to demonstrate financial need. Applications are available only online and include required essays on specified topics.

Financial data The stipend is $1,000.

Duration 1 year.

Number awarded Varies each year.

Deadline May of each year.

[1145]
VINSON & ELKINS DIVERSITY FELLOWSHIPS

Vinson & Elkins L.L.P.
Attn: Attorney Initiatives Assistant
1001 Fannin Street, Suite 2500
Houston, TX 77002-6760
(713) 758-2222   Fax: (713) 758-2346
Web: www.velaw.com/careers/law_students.aspx?id=602

Summary To provide financial assistance to Native American and other minority law students who are interested in working in a law firm setting.

Eligibility This program is open to students who are entering the second year at an ABA-accredited law school and are members of a racial or ethnic group that has been historically underrepresented in the legal profession (Asian, American Indian/Alaskan Native, Black/African American, Hispanic/Latino, multiracial, or Native Hawaiian or other Pacific Islander). Applicants must be able to demonstrate a strong undergraduate and law school record, excellent writing skills, and an interest in working in a law firm setting.

Financial data The stipend is $3,500 per year.

Duration 2 years (the second and third year of law school).

Additional information Fellows are also considered for summer associate positions at the sponsor's offices in Austin, Dallas, or Houston following their first year of law school.

Number awarded 4 each year.

Deadline January of each year.

[1146]
VISITING RESEARCH INTERNSHIP PROGRAM

Harvard Medical School
Office for Diversity and Community Partnership
Attn: Minority Faculty Development Program
164 Longwood Avenue, Second Floor
Boston, MA 02115-5810
(617) 432-1892   Fax: (617) 432-3834
E-mail: pfdd_dcp@hms.harvard.edu
Web: www.mfdp.med.harvard.edu

Summary To provide an opportunity for medical students, especially Native Americans and other underrepresented minorities, to conduct a mentored research internship at Harvard Medical School during the summer.

Eligibility This program is open to first- and second-year medical students, particularly underrepresented minority and/or disadvantaged individuals, in good standing at accredited U.S. medical schools. Applicants must be interested in conducting a summer research project at Harvard Medical School under the mentorship of a faculty advisor. They must be interested in a research and health-related career, especially in clinical or translational research or research that transforms scientific discoveries arising from laboratory, clinical, or population studies into clinical or population-based applications to improve health. U.S. citizenship, nationality, or permanent resident status is required.

Financial data Participants receive a stipend (amount not specified), housing, and limited reimbursement of transportation costs to Boston.

Duration 8 weeks during the summer.

Additional information This program, established in 2008, is funded by the National Center for Research Resources of the National Institutes of Health NIH). It is a joint enterprise of Harvard University, its 10 schools, its 17 Academic Healthcare Centers, Boston College School of Nursing, MIT, the Cambridge Health Alliance, and other community partners. Interns attend weekly seminars with Harvard faculty focusing on such topics as research methodology, health disparities, ethics, and career paths. They also have the opportunity to participate in offerings of other Harvard

Medical School programs, such a career development seminars and networking dinners.

Number awarded Varies each year.

Deadline February of each year.

[1147]
WAH-TIAH-KAH SCHOLARSHIP

Osage Minerals Council
813 Grandview
P.O. Box 779
Pawhuska, OK 74056
(918) 287-5433
Web: www.osagetribe.com/education/info.aspx

Summary To provide financial assistance to Osage students who are interested in attending college or graduate school to prepare for a career in the petroleum industry.

Eligibility This program is open to full-time undergraduate and graduate students who can prove Osage Indian blood in any degree. Applicants must be working on or planning to work on a degree in a field related to petroleum. Along with their application, they must submit a copy of their Certificate of Osage Indian Blood, transcripts, 2 letters of recommendation, ACT or SAT scores, and a personal statement of their educational and career goals.

Financial data A stipend is awarded (amount not specified).

Duration 1 semester; may be renewed for up to 7 additional semesters, provided the recipient reapplies each semester and maintains a GPA of 2.0 or higher.

Number awarded Varies each year.

Deadline June of each year for fall term; December of each year for spring term.

[1148]
WAMPANOAG HIGHER EDUCATION SCHOLARSHIP PROGRAM

Wampanoag Tribe of Gay Head
Attn: Education Director
20 Black Brook Road
Aquinnah, MA 02535-1546
(508) 645-9265   Toll Free: (800) 332-7707
Fax: (508) 645-3790
Web: www.wampanoagtribe.net

Summary To provide financial assistance to members of the Wampanoag Tribe of Gay Head who are interested in attending college or graduate school in any state.

Eligibility This program is open to enrolled members of the Wampanoag Tribe of Gay Head who are working on or planning to work full time on a baccalaureate or advanced degree. Applicants must submit a brief essay describing their family ties to Martha's Vineyard (Massachusetts) and their personal reflections about their Wampanoag Heritage.

Financial data A stipend is awarded (amount not specified).

Duration 1 year; may be renewed.

Number awarded Varies each year.

Deadline June of each year.

[1149]
WARNER NORCROSS & JUDD LAW SCHOOL SCHOLARSHIP

Grand Rapids Community Foundation
Attn: Education Program Officer
185 Oakes Street S.W.
Grand Rapids, MI 49503-4008
(616) 454-1751, ext. 103   Fax: (616) 454-6455
E-mail: rbishop@grfoundation.org
Web: www.grfoundation.org/scholarships

Summary To provide financial assistance to Native Americans and other minorities from Michigan who are attending law school.

Eligibility This program is open to students of color who are attending or planning to attend an accredited law school. Applicants must be residents of Michigan or attending law school in the state. They must be U.S. citizens or permanent residents and have a GPA of 2.5 or higher. Financial need is considered in the selection process.

Financial data The stipend is $5,000. Funds are paid directly to the recipient's institution.

Duration 1 year.

Additional information Funding for this program is provided by the law firm Warner Norcross & Judd LLP.

Number awarded 1 each year.

Deadline March of each year.

[1150]
WASHINGTON AMERICAN INDIAN ENDOWED SCHOLARSHIP PROGRAM

Washington Higher Education Coordinating Board
917 Lakeridge Way
P.O. Box 43430
Olympia, WA 98504-3430
(360) 753-7843   Toll Free: (888) 535-0747
Fax: (360) 753-7808   TDD: (360) 753-7809
E-mail: aies@hecb.wa.gov
Web: www.hecb.wa.gov/Paying/waaidprgm/aies.asp

Summary To provide financial assistance to American Indian undergraduate and graduate students in Washington.

Eligibility This program is open to Washington residents who have close social and cultural ties to an American Indian tribe and/or community in the state. Applicants must demonstrate financial need and be enrolled, or planning to enroll, as a full-time undergraduate or graduate student at a Washington state public or independent college, university, or career school. They must agree to use their education to benefit other American Indians. Students who are working on a degree in religious, seminarian, or theological academic studies are not eligible. Selection is based on academic merit, financial need, and documented commitment to return service to the state's American Indian community.

Financial data Stipends range from about $500 to $2,000 per year.

Duration 1 year, may be renewed up to 4 additional years.

Additional information This program was created by the Washington legislature in 1990 with a state appropriation to an endowment fund and matching contributions from tribes, individuals, and organizations.

Number awarded Approximately 15 new and 10 renewal scholarships are awarded each year.

Deadline January of each year.

[1151]
WASHINGTON DIVERSITY FELLOWSHIPS IN ENVIRONMENTAL LAW

American Bar Association
Attn: Section of Environment, Energy, and Resources
321 North Clark Street
Chicago, IL 60654-7598
(312) 988-5602   Fax: (312) 988-5572
E-mail: jonusaid@staff.abanet.org
Web: www.abanet.org

Summary To provide funding to Native American and other law students from underserved groups who are interested in working on a summer project in environmental, energy, or resources law in Washington.

Eligibility This program is open to first- and second-year law students and third-year night students who are members of underrepresented and underserved groups, such as minority or low-income populations. Students may be residents of any state and attending school in any state; preference is given to residents of Washington and to students who are enrolled at law schools in Washington or who have a strong interest in the state. Applicants must be interested in working during the summer at a government agency or public interest organization on a project in Washington in the fields of environmental, energy, or resources law. Selection is based on interest in environmental issues, academic record, personal qualities, and leadership abilities.

Financial data The stipend is $5,000.

Duration 8 to 10 weeks during the summer.

Number awarded 1 each year.

Deadline February of each year.

[1152]
WASHINGTON INDIAN GAMING ASSOCIATION SCHOLARSHIPS

Washington Indian Gaming Association
1110 Capitol Way South, Suite 404
Olympia, WA 98501
(360) 352-3248   Fax: (360) 352-4819
Web: www.washingtonindiangaming.org

Summary To provide financial assistance to members of Indian tribes in Washington who are interested in attending college or graduate school in any state.

Eligibility This program is open to Washington residents who are enrolled members of tribes affiliated with the Washington Indian Gaming Association (WIGA) and to urban Indian students in the state. Applicants must be attending or accepted at a community college, undergraduate institution, or graduate school in any state. Native American students from outside Washington who attend college in the state are also eligible. Along with their application, they must submit a 250-word personal essay on topics that change annually; recently, students were asked to explain why they were considering their intended major, how it would help them reach future career objectives, and how their education would benefit their home community (whether urban or rural). Financial need is also considered in the selection process.

Financial data Stipends are $2,000 per year for graduate or professional students, $1,500 per year for undergraduates at 4-year institutions, or $1,100 per year for students at community colleges or technical schools.

Duration 1 year; may be renewed.

Number awarded Up to 8 graduate and professional scholarships, up to 16 scholarships for 4-year institutions, and up to 9 community college or technical school scholarships are awarded each year.

Deadline March of each year.

[1153]
WASHINGTON INTERNSHIPS FOR NATIVE STUDENTS

American University
Attn: Washington Internships for Native Students (WINS)
4400 Massachusetts Avenue, N.W.
Washington, DC 20016-8083
(202) 895-4900   Toll Free: (800) 853-3076
Fax: (202) 895-4882   E-mail: wins@american.edu
Web: www.american.edu/wins

Summary To provide an opportunity for Native American and Alaska Native undergraduate and graduate students to gain work experience at a federal agency in Washington, D.C.

Eligibility This program is open to members of recognized tribes of Native Americans and Alaska Natives. Applicants must be enrolled at a college or university as a sophomore, junior, senior, or graduate student with a GPA of 2.5 or higher. They must be interested in living in Washington D.C. for a semester or summer and interning at a federal government agency. Along with their application, they must submit transcripts, a letter of nomination from their tribe, a faculty letter of recommendation, a resume, proof of tribal membership, and a 500-word essay on why they want to participate in the program and the contributions they can offer a potential employer.

Financial data Interns receive round-trip travel to Washington, D.C., books, tuition, housing, meals, local transportation, insurance, and a stipend of $140 per week.

Duration Fall and spring internships are for 4 months; summer internships are 2 months.

Additional information This program began in 1994 as a small summer activity and was expanded to a full summer internship in 1999. Spring and fall programs were added in 2001. In addition to work assignments at participating federal agencies, interns take courses on topics of interest to Native communities and receive academic credit.

Number awarded Approximately 25 in each of the semester programs and approximately 100 in the summer.

Deadline May of each year for fall; September of each year for spring; January of each year for summer.

[1154]
WASHOE TRIBE HIGHER EDUCATION GRANT PROGRAM

Washoe Tribe
Attn: Education Department
919 Highway 395 South
Gardnerville, NV 89410
(775) 265-4191, ext. 1136   Toll Free: (800) 76-WASHOE
Fax: (775) 265-6240   E-mail: education@washoetribe.us
Web: www.washoetribe.us

Summary To provide financial assistance for college or graduate school to members of the Washoe Tribe in Nevada and California.

Eligibility Eligible to apply for these scholarships are members of the Washoe Tribe who are working on (or planning to work on) an associate, bachelor's, or graduate degree. Applicants are required to seek all other sources of funding, in addition to applying for this program. In the process, they must complete a Free Application for Federal Student Aid (FAFSA) and receive a Student Aid Report. Awards are grants in the following priority order: 1) continuing students with acceptable grades; 2) new students who reside near or within the boundaries of Washoe tribal colonies (Woodfords, Dresslerville, Carson, Stewart, Reno) and other Nevada and California residents; 3) students outside of Nevada and California; 4) graduate students; and 5) students who have a 4-year degree and are working to obtain a 4-year degree in a different field.

Financial data Recently, stipends were $1,005.

Duration 1 year; may be renewed if the recipient remains enrolled full time with a GPA of 1.8 or higher as a freshman and 2.0 or higher as a sophomore through senior.

Number awarded Varies each year; recently, 10 of these scholarships were awarded.

Deadline July or November of each year.

[1155]
WASHOE TRIBE INCENTIVE SCHOLARSHIPS

Washoe Tribe
Attn: Education Department
919 Highway 395 South
Gardnerville, NV 89410
(775) 265-8600, ext. 1136   Toll Free: (800) 76-WASHOE
Fax: (775) 265-6240   E-mail: education@washoetribe.us
Web: www.washoetribe.us

Summary To provide financial assistance to members of the Washoe Tribe working on an undergraduate or graduate degree at a school in any state.

Eligibility This program is open to members of the Washoe Tribe who are currently working full time on an associate, baccalaureate, graduate, or postgraduate degree at a school in any state. Applicants must have a GPA of 3.0 or higher. Along with their application they must submit proof of Washoe enrollment, a copy of their college grade report, and a copy of their current class schedule. Selection is based on a first-come, first-served basis; financial need is not considered.

Financial data The stipend varies each year; recently, stipends were $1,225 in the spring semester and $890 in the fall semester.

Duration 1 year; recipients may reapply.

Number awarded Varies each year; recently, 8 of these scholarships were awarded in the spring semester and 11 in the fall semester.

Deadline January or September of each year.

[1156]
WATSON MIDWIVES OF COLOR SCHOLARSHIP

American College of Nurse-Midwives
Attn: ACNM Foundation, Inc.
8403 Colesville Road, Suite 1550
Silver Spring, MD 20910-6374
(240) 485-1850　　　　　　　　Fax: (240) 485-1818
Web: www.midwife.org/foundation_award.cfm

Summary To provide financial assistance for midwifery education to Native Americans and other students of color who belong to the American College of Nurse-Midwives (ACNM).

Eligibility This program is open to ACNM members of color who are currently enrolled in an accredited basic mid-wife education program and have successfully completed 1 academic or clinical semester/quarter or clinical module. Applicants must submit a 150-word essay on their 5-year midwifery career plans and a 100-word essay on their intended future participation in the local, regional, and/or national activities of the ACNM. Selection is based on leadership potential, financial need, academic history, and potential for future professional contribution to the organization.

Financial data The stipend is $3,000.

Duration 1 year.

Number awarded Varies each year; recently, 3 of these scholarships were awarded.

Deadline March of each year.

[1157]
WELLS FARGO GRADUATE SCHOLARSHIPS

American Indian Graduate Center
Attn: Executive Director
4520 Montgomery Boulevard, N.E., Suite 1-B
Albuquerque, NM 87109-1291
(505) 881-4584　　　　　　　　Toll Free: (800) 628-1920
Fax: (505) 884-0427　　　　　　E-mail: aigc@aigc.com
Web: www.aigc.com

Summary To provide financial assistance to Native American graduate students interested in preparing for a career in banking, gaming operations, resort management, or administration.

Eligibility This program is open to enrolled members of federally-recognized American Indian tribes and Alaska Native groups who can provide a Certificate of Indian Blood (CIB). Applicants must be working full time on a graduate or professional degree to prepare for a career in banking, resort management, gaming operations, or management and administration, including accounting, finance, human resources, and information systems. They must have a GPA of 3.0 or higher. Along with their application, they must submit an essay on their personal, educational, and professional goals. Financial need is also considered in the selection process.

Financial data A stipend is awarded (amount not specified).

Duration 1 year.

Additional information This program is supported by Wells Fargo Bank.

Number awarded 1 or more each year.

Deadline May of each year.

[1158]
WHITE EARTH SCHOLARSHIP PROGRAM

White Earth Indian Reservation Tribal Council
Attn: Scholarship Program
P.O. Box 418
White Earth, MN 56591
(218) 983-3285, ext. 5304　　　　Toll Free: (800) 950-3248
Fax: (218) 983-3705　　E-mail: highered@whiteearth.com
Web: www.whiteearth.com/education.htm

Summary To provide financial assistance to Minnesota Chippewa Tribe members who are interested in attending college, vocational school, or graduate school in any state.

Eligibility This program is open to enrolled members of the White Earth Band of the Minnesota Chippewa Tribe who can demonstrate financial need. Applicants must be attending or planning to attend a college, university, or vocational school in any state. Graduate students in the fields of business, education, human services, law, and medicine are also eligible.

Financial data A stipend is awarded (amount not specified).

Duration 1 year; may be renewed, provided undergraduates maintain a GPA of 2.0 or higher and graduate students maintain a GPA of 3.0 or higher.

Additional information Applicants for this program must also apply for financial aid administered by their institution and any other aid for which they may be eligible (e.g., work-study, Social Security, veteran's benefits).

Number awarded Varies each year.

Deadline May of each year.

[1159]
WHITE MOUNTAIN APACHE TRIBAL SCHOLARSHIPS

White Mountain Apache Tribe
Attn: Office of Higher Education
205 West Fatco Road
P.O. Box 250
Whiteriver, AZ 85941
(928) 338-5800　　　　　　　　Fax: (928) 338-1869
E-mail: harriethosetoavit@wmat.us
Web: www.wmat.nsn.us/high_ed.html

Summary To provide financial assistance to members of the White Mountain Apache Tribe who are interested in attending college or graduate school in any state.

Eligibility This program is open to members of the White Mountain Apache Tribe who are enrolled or planning to enroll at a college, university, or vocational/technical school in any state. Applicants must be interested in working on an undergraduate or graduate degree. Along with their application, they must submit verification of tribal enrollment, a letter of admission from the college they are attending (graduate students must submit an acceptance letter from their specific graduate program), high school or college transcripts, ACT test scores, and documentation of financial need.

Financial data A stipend is awarded (amount not specified).

Duration 1 year; may be renewed.

Additional information This program is funded by the U.S. Bureau of Indian Affairs (BIA).

Number awarded Varies each year.

Deadline June of each year for fall semester, quarter, or trimester; November of each year for spring semester, quarter, or trimester; May of each year for summer session.

[1160]
WIEA SCHOLARSHIPS

Wisconsin Indian Education Association
Attn: Scholarship Coordinator
P.O. Box 910
Keshena, WI 54135
(715) 799-5110   Fax: (715) 799-5102
E-mail: vnuske@mitw.org
Web: www.wiea.org

Summary To provide financial assistance for undergraduate or graduate study to members of Wisconsin Indian tribes.

Eligibility This program is open to residents of Wisconsin who can provide proof of tribal enrollment. Applicants must fall into 1 of the following categories: 1) entering freshman at a 4-year college or university; 2) new or continuing student at a tribal college or technical/vocational school; 3) undergraduate student at a 4-year college or university; or 4) graduate or Ph.D. student. All applicants must be full-time students. Along with their application, they must submit a 1-page personal essay on how they will apply their education. Selection is based on that essay (25 points), letters of recommendation (10 points), and GPA (15 points if 3.5 or higher, 10 points if 3.00 to 3.49, 5 points if 2.50 to 2.99). Financial need is not considered.

Financial data The stipend is $1,000.

Duration 1 year; nonrenewable.

Additional information Eligible tribes include Menominee, Oneida, Stockbridge-Munsee, Forest County Potowatomi, Ho-Chunk, Bad River Chippewa, Lac Courte Oreilles Ojibwe, St. Croix Chippewa, Red Cliff Chippewa, Sakoagon (Mole Lake) Chippewa, Brotherton, and Lac du Flambeau Chippewa.

Number awarded 4 each year: 1 in each of the 4 categories.

Deadline March of each year.

[1161]
WILEY W. MANUEL LAW FOUNDATION SCHOLARSHIPS

Wiley W. Manuel Law Foundation
c/o Law Offices of George Holland
1970 Broadway, Suite 1030
Oakland, CA 94612
(510) 465-4100
Web: wileymanuel.org/index.html

Summary To provide financial assistance to Native American and other minority students from any state enrolled at law schools in northern California.

Eligibility This program is open to minority students entering their third year at law schools in northern California. Applicants should exemplify the qualities of the late Justice Wiley Manuel, the first African American to serve on the California Supreme Court. Along with their application, they must sub-

mit a 250-word essay on why they should be awarded this scholarship. Financial need is also considered in the selection process.

Financial data The stipend is approximately $1,500.

Duration 1 year.

Number awarded Varies each year; recently, 12 of these scholarships were awarded.

Deadline September of each year.

[1162]
WILLIAM K. SCHUBERT M.D. MINORITY NURSING SCHOLARSHIP PROGRAM

Cincinnati Children's Hospital Medical Center
Attn: Office of Diversity and Inclusion, MLC 9008
3333 Burnet Avenue
Cincinnati, OH 45229-3039
(513) 803-6416   Toll Free: (800) 344-2462
Fax: (513) 636-5643   TDD: (513) 636-4900
E-mail: owen.burke@cchmc.org
Web: www.cincinnatichildrens.org

Summary To provide financial assistance to Native Americans and members of other underrepresented groups interested in working on a bachelor's or master's degree in nursing to prepare for licensure in Ohio.

Eligibility This program is open to members of groups underrepresented in the nursing profession (males, American Indians or Alaska Natives, Blacks or African Americans, Hawaiian Natives or other Pacific Islanders, Hispanics or Latinos, or Asians). Applicants must be enrolled or accepted in a professional bachelor's or master's registered nurse program at an accredited school of nursing to prepare for initial licensure in Ohio. They must have a GPA of 2.75 or higher. Along with their application, they must submit a 750-word essay that covers 1) their long-range personal, educational, and professional goals and why they chose nursing as a profession; 2) any unique qualifications, experiences, or special talents that demonstrate their creativity; and 3) if they are able to pay any college expenses through work and how their work experience has contributed to their personal development.

Financial data The stipend is $2,750 per year.

Duration 1 year. May be renewed up to 3 additional years for students working on a bachelor's degree or 1 additional year for students working on a master's degree; renewal requires that students maintain a GPA of 2.75 or higher.

Number awarded 1 or more each year.

Deadline April of each year.

[1163]
WILLIAM TOWNSEND PORTER FELLOWSHIP FOR MINORITY INVESTIGATORS

Woods Hole Marine Biological Laboratory
Attn: Research Award Coordinator
7 MBL Street
Woods Hole, MA 02543-1015
(508) 289-7171   Fax: (508) 457-1924
E-mail: researchawards@mbl.edu
Web: www.mbl.edu/research/summer/awards_general.html

Summary To support Native American and other minority scientists who wish to conduct research during the summer at the Woods Hole Marine Biological Laboratory (MBL).

Eligibility This program is open to young scientists (senior graduate students and postdoctoral trainees) who are from an underrepresented minority group (African American, Hispanic American, or Native American), are U.S. citizens or permanent residents, and are interested in conducting research with senior investigators at MBL. Fields of study include, but are not limited to, cell biology, developmental biology, ecology, evolution, microbiology, neurobiology, physiology, and tissue engineering.

Financial data Participants receive a stipend and a travel allowance. Recently, grants averaged approximately $1,500.

Duration At least 6 weeks during the summer.

Additional information This fellowship was first awarded in 1921. Funding is provided by the Harvard Apparatus Foundation.

Number awarded 1 or more each year.

Deadline December of each year.

[1164]
WINNEBAGO TRIBE HIGHER EDUCATION ASSISTANCE

Winnebago Tribe of Nebraska
Attn: Education Department
100 Bluff Street
P.O. Box 687
Winnebago, NE 68071
(402) 878-3202   Fax: (402) 878-2632
E-mail: education@winnebagotribe.com
Web: www.winnebagotribe.com/winbagoFrameset=1.htm

Summary To provide financial assistance to members of the Winnebago Tribe of Nebraska who are interested in attending college or graduate school in any state.

Eligibility This program is open to enrolled members of the Winnebago Tribe of Nebraska who are attending or planning to attend an institution of higher education in any state. Applicants must be working on an associate, bachelor's, master's, or doctoral degree or certificate. They must submit a copy of their Certificate of Indian Blood (CIB), transcripts, and documentation of financial need.

Financial data A stipend is awarded (amount not specified). Funding is intended only to supplement other assistance available to the student.

Duration 1 semester; may be renewed.

Number awarded Varies each year.

Deadline April of each year for fall, academic year, or summer school; October of each year for spring or winter.

[1165]
WINSTON & STRAWN DIVERSITY SCHOLARSHIP PROGRAM

Winston & Strawn LLP
Attn: Attorney Recruitment Assistant
35 West Wacker Drive
Chicago, IL 60601-9703
(312) 558-5600   Fax: (312) 558-5700
E-mail: diversityscholarship@winston.com
Web: www.winston.com

Summary To provide financial assistance to Native American and other diverse law students who are interested in practicing in a city in which Winston & Strawn LLP has an office.

Eligibility This program is open to second-year law students who self-identify as a member of 1 of the following groups: American Indian or Alaska Native, Asian or Pacific Islander, Black or African American, or Hispanic or Latino. Applicants must submit a resume, law school transcript, and 500-word personal statement. Selection is based on 1) interest in practicing law after graduation in a large law firm in a city in which Winston & Strawn has an office (currently, Charlotte, Chicago, Los Angeles, New York, San Francisco, and Washington, D.C.); 2) law school and undergraduate record, including academic achievements and involvement in extracurricular activities; 3) demonstrated leadership skills; 4) and interpersonal skills.

Financial data The stipend is $10,000.

Duration 1 year (the third year of law school).

Additional information This program began in 2001.

Number awarded 3 each year.

Deadline October of each year.

[1166]
WISCONSIN INDIAN STUDENT ASSISTANCE GRANTS

Wisconsin Higher Educational Aids Board
131 West Wilson Street, Suite 902
P.O. Box 7885
Madison, WI 53707-7885
(608) 266-0888   Fax: (608) 267-2808
E-mail: Sandy.Thomas@wisconsin.gov
Web: heab.state.wi.us/programs.html

Summary To provide financial assistance to Native Americans in Wisconsin who are interested in attending college or graduate school in the state.

Eligibility Wisconsin residents who have at least 25% Native American blood (of a certified tribe or band) are eligible to apply if they are able to demonstrate financial need and are interested in attending college on the undergraduate or graduate school level. Applicants must attend a Wisconsin institution (public, independent, or proprietary). They may be enrolled either full or part time.

Financial data The stipend ranges from $250 to $1,100 per year. Additional funds are available on a matching basis from the U.S. Bureau of Indian Affairs.

Duration Up to 5 years.

Deadline Generally, applications can be submitted at any time.

[1167]
WISCONSIN MINORITY TEACHER LOANS

Wisconsin Higher Educational Aids Board
131 West Wilson Street, Suite 902
P.O. Box 7885
Madison, WI 53707-7885
(608) 267-2212   Fax: (608) 267-2808
E-mail: Mary.Kuzdas@wisconsin.gov
Web: heab.state.wi.us/programs.html

Summary To provide funding to Native Americans and other minorities in Wisconsin who are interested in teaching in Wisconsin school districts with large minority enrollments.

Eligibility This program is open to residents of Wisconsin who are African Americans, Hispanic Americans, American Indians, or southeast Asians (students who were admitted to the United States after December 31, 1975 and who are a former citizen of Laos, Vietnam, or Cambodia or whose ancestor was a citizen of 1 of those countries). Applicants must be enrolled at least half time as juniors, seniors, or graduate students at an independent or public institution in the state in a program leading to teaching licensure and have a GPA of 2.5 or higher. They must agree to teach in a Wisconsin school district in which minority students constitute at least 29% of total enrollment or in a school district participating in the interdistrict pupil transfer program. Financial need is not considered in the selection process.

Financial data forgivable loans are provided up to $2,500 per year. For each year the student teaches in an eligible school district, 25% of the loan is forgiven; if the student does not teach in an eligible district, the loan must be repaid at an interest rate of 5%.

Duration 1 year; may be renewed 1 additional year.

Additional information Eligible students should apply through their school's financial aid office.

Number awarded Varies each year.

Deadline Deadline dates vary by institution; check with your school's financial aid office.

[1168]
WMACCA CORPORATE SCHOLARS PROGRAM

Washington Metropolitan Area Corporate Counsel
  Association, Inc.
Attn: Executive Director
P.O. Box 2147
Rockville, MD 20847-2147
(301) 881-3018   E-mail: Ilene.Reid@wmacca.com
Web: www.wmacca.org

Summary To provide a summer internship in the metropolitan Washington, D.C. area to Native Americans and other students at law schools in the area who will contribute to the diversity of the profession.

Eligibility This program is open to students entering their second or third year of part- or full-time study at law schools in the Washington, D.C. metropolitan area (including suburban Maryland and all of Virginia). Applicants must be able to demonstrate how they contribute to diversity in the legal profession, based not only on ideas about gender, race, and ethnicity, but also on concepts of socioeconomic background and their individual educational and career path. They must be interested in working during the summer at a sponsoring private corporation and nonprofit organizations in the Washington, D.C. area. Along with their application, they must submit a personal statement of 250 to 500 words explaining why they qualify for this program, a writing sample, their law school transcript, and a resume.

Financial data The stipend is at least $9,000.

Duration 10 weeks during the summer.

Additional information The Washington Metropolitan Area Corporate Counsel Association (WMACCA) is the local chapter of the Association of Corporate Counsel (ACC). It established this program in 2004 with support from the Minority Corporate Counsel Association (MCCA).

Number awarded Varies each year; recently, 11 of these internships were awarded.

Deadline January of each year.

[1169]
WOLVERINE BAR FOUNDATION SCHOLARSHIP

Wolverine Bar Association
Attn: Wolverine Bar Foundation
645 Griswold, Suite 961
Detroit, MI 48226-4017
(313) 962-0250   Fax: (313) 962-5906
E-mail: wbaoffice@ameritech.net
Web: www.wbadirect.org

Summary To provide financial assistance for law school to Native Americans and other minorities in Michigan.

Eligibility This program is open to minority law students who are either currently enrolled in a Michigan law school or are Michigan residents enrolled in an out-of-state law school. Applicants must be in at least their second year of law school. Selection is based on financial need, merit, and an interview.

Financial data The stipend is at least $1,000.

Duration 1 year; nonrenewable.

Additional information The Wolverine Bar Association was established by a number of African American attorneys during the 1930s. It was the successor to the Harlan Law Club, founded in 1919 by attorneys in the Detroit area who were excluded from other local bar associations in Michigan.

Number awarded 1 or more each year.

Deadline April of each year.

[1170]
WOMBLE CARLYLE SCHOLARS PROGRAM

Womble Carlyle Sandridge & Rice, PLLC
Attn: Director of Entry-Level Recruiting and Development
301 South College Street, Suite 3500
Charlotte, NC 28202-6037
(704) 331-4900   Fax: (704) 331-4955
E-mail: wcsrscholars@wcsr.com
Web: www.wcsr.com/firm/diversity

Summary To provide financial assistance and summer work experience to Native Americans and other diverse students at designated law schools.

Eligibility This program is open to students at designated law schools who are members of underrepresented groups. Applicants must be able to demonstrate solid academic credentials, personal or professional achievement outside the classroom, and significant participation in community service. Along with their application, they must submit a 300-word essay on their choice of 2 topics that change annually but relate to the legal profession. They must also submit a brief statement explaining how they would contribute to the goal of creating a more diverse legal community.

Financial data The stipend is $4,000. Recipients are also offered summer employment at an office of the sponsoring law firm. Salaries are the same as the firm's other summer associates in each office.

Duration 1 year (the second year of law school); may be renewed 1 additional year.

Additional information This program was established in 2004. The eligible law schools are North Carolina Central University School of Law (Durham, North Carolina), University of North Carolina at Chapel Hill School of Law (Chapel Hill, North Carolina), Duke University School of Law (Durham, North Carolina), Wake Forest University School of Law (Winston-Salem, North Carolina), University of South Carolina

School of Law (Columbia, South Carolina), Howard University School of Law (Washington, D.C.), University of Virginia School of Law (Charlottesville, Virginia), University of Georgia School of Law (Athens, Georgia), Georgia Washington University Law School (Washington, D.C.), Emory University School of Law (Atlanta, Georgia), and University of Maryland School of Law (Baltimore, Maryland). The sponsoring law firm has offices in Atlanta (Georgia), Baltimore (Maryland), Charlotte (North Carolina), Greensboro (North Carolina), Greenville (South Carolina), Raleigh (North Carolina), Research Triangle Park (North Carolina), Tysons Corner (Virginia), Washington (D.C.), Wilmington (Delaware), and Winston-Salem (North Carolina).

Number awarded Varies each year; recently, 9 of these scholarships were awarded.

Deadline May of each year.

[1171]
WORLD COMMUNION SCHOLARSHIPS

United Methodist Church
General Board of Global Ministries
Attn: Scholarship Office
475 Riverside Drive, Room 1351
New York, NY 10115
(212) 870-3787   Toll Free: (800) UMC-GBGM
E-mail: scholars@gbgm-umc.org
Web: new.gbgm-umc.org

Summary To provide financial assistance to Native Americans, other minorities, and foreign students who are interested in attending graduate school to prepare for leadership in promoting the goals of the United Methodist Church.

Eligibility This program is open to 1) students from Methodist churches in nations other than the United States, and 2) members of ethnic and racial minorities in the United States. Applicants must have applied to or been admitted to a master's, doctoral, or professional program at a university or seminary in the United States. They should be planning to return to their communities to work in furthering Christian mission, whether that be in the local church, the neighborhood clinic, the state rural development office, or the national office on education. Financial need must be demonstrated.

Financial data The stipend ranges from $250 to $12,500, depending on the recipient's related needs and school expenses.

Duration 1 year.

Additional information These awards are funded by the World Communion Offering received in United Methodist Churches on the first Sunday in October.

Number awarded 5 to 10 each year.

Deadline November of each year.

[1172]
WYANDOTTE NATION HIGHER EDUCATION SCHOLARSHIPS

Wyandotte Nation of Oklahoma
Attn: Department of Education
64790 East Highway 60
Wyandotte, OK 74370
(918) 678-2297, ext. 230
Toll Free: (800) 256-2539, ext. 230
E-mail: info@wyandotte-nation.org
Web: www.wyandotte-nation.org/community/education

Summary To provide financial assistance to members of the Wyandotte Nation of Oklahoma who are interested in attending college in any state to work on an undergraduate or master's degree.

Eligibility This program is open to Wyandotte tribal members who are attending or will be attending an accredited college or university in any state to work on an undergraduate or master's degree. Applicants must be able to demonstrate financial need.

Financial data The stipend is $1,500 per semester ($3,000 per year).

Duration 1 semester; may be renewed up to 7 additional semesters by undergraduates or 2 additional semesters by master's degree students.

Number awarded Varies each year.

Deadline Deadline not specified.

[1173]
XEROX TECHNICAL MINORITY SCHOLARSHIP PROGRAM

Xerox Corporation
Attn: Technical Minority Scholarship Program
150 State Street, Fourth Floor
Rochester, NY 14614
(585) 422-7689   E-mail: xtmsp@rballiance.com
Web: www.xeroxstudentcareers.com

Summary To provide financial assistance to Native Americans and other minorities interested in undergraduate or graduate education in the sciences and/or engineering.

Eligibility This program is open to minorities (people of African American, Asian, Pacific Islander, Native American, Native Alaskan, or Hispanic descent) working full time on a bachelor's, master's, or doctoral degree in chemistry, computing and software systems, engineering (chemical, computer, electrical, imaging, manufacturing, mechanical, optical, or software), information management, laser optics, materials science, physics, or printing management science. Applicants must be U.S. citizens or permanent residents with a GPA of 3.0 or higher and attending a 4-year college or university.

Financial data Stipends range from $1,000 to $10,000.

Duration 1 year.

Number awarded Varies each year, recently, 125 of these scholarships were awarded.

Deadline September of each year.

[1174]
YAKAMA NATION HIGHER EDUCATION SCHOLARSHIP

Yakama Nation
Department of Human Services
Attn: Higher Education Program
401 Fort Road
P.O. Box 151
Toppenish, WA 98948
(509) 865-5121, ext. 519   Toll Free: (800) 543-2802
Fax: (509) 865-6994
Web: www.yakama.us/programs.php

Summary To provide financial assistance to Yakama tribal members interested in working on an undergraduate or graduate degree at a school in any state.

Eligibility This program is open to enrolled members of the Yakama nation who are enrolled or planning to enroll in a postsecondary institution in any state. Applicants must be interested in working on an undergraduate or graduate degree on a part-time or full-time basis. Along with their application, they must submit a personal letter describing their educational and employment goals. Financial need is considered in the selection process.

Financial data The stipend is $2,000 per year.

Duration 1 year; may be renewed.

Number awarded Varies each year.

Deadline April of each year for high school seniors; June of each year for current undergraduate and graduate students.

[1175]
YAVAPAI-APACHE NATION HIGHER EDUCATION GRANTS

Yavapai-Apache Nation
Attn: Higher Education Department
2400 West Datsi Street
Camp Verde, AZ 86322
(928) 649-7111   Fax: (928) 567-6485
Web: Yavapai-apache.org/departments.html

Summary To provide financial assistance for college or graduate school to members of the Yavapai-Apache Nation.

Eligibility This program is open to members of the Yavapai-Apache Nation who are enrolled or planning to enroll at an accredited institution of higher education in any state. Applicants must be interested in working full or part time on a vocational certificate or an associate, bachelor's, master's, or doctoral degree. Along with their application, they must submit 1) an academic plan that specifies their course of study or declared major, all classes required for their program, and the expected graduation date; 2) a brief essay on their educational goals and how they will utilize their education; 3) verification of tribal enrollment; 4) copy of high school diploma or GED certificate; and 5) current transcript. Full-time students must also submit documentation of financial need.

Financial data For full-time students, the stipend depends on the need of the recipient. For part-time students, support is limited to tuition, fees, textbooks, supplies, and transportation.

Duration 1 semester; may be renewed up to 5 additional full-time semesters for students working on an associate degree or 9 additional part-time semesters for students working on a bachelor's degree. Renewal requires the recipient to maintain a GPA of 2.0 or higher.

Number awarded Varies each year.

Deadline June of each year for fall and academic year; September of each year for spring only; March of each year for summer; August of each year for vocational/technical school.

[1176]
YUROK TRIBE HIGHER EDUCATION PROGRAM

Yurok Tribe
Attn: Education Department
190 Klamath Boulevard
P.O. Box 1027
Klamath, CA 95548
(707) 482-1350   Fax: (707) 482-0760
Web: www.yuroktribe.org

Summary To provide financial assistance for college or graduate school to members of the Yurok Tribe.

Eligibility This program is open to enrolled members of the Yurok Tribe who are attending or planning to attend an accredited college or university in any state. Applicants must be interested in working full or part time on an undergraduate or graduate degree. They must apply for federal financial aid using the FAFSA. Awards are granted on a first-come, first-served basis.

Financial data A stipend is awarded (amount not specified). Part-time students are funded at half the level of full-time students.

Duration 1 year; may be renewed as long as recipients remain in good standing with their college or university and maintain a GPA of 2.0 or higher.

Number awarded Varies each year.

Deadline Applications may be submitted at any time.

[1177]
ZUNI HIGHER EDUCATION SCHOLARSHIPS

Pueblo of Zuni
Attn: Education and Career Development Center
P.O. Box 339
Zuni, NM 87327
(505) 782-7178   Fax: (505) 782-7223
E-mail: jlucio@ashiwi.org
Web: www.ashiwi.org/highered/higheredhome.htm

Summary To provide financial assistance for college or graduate school in any state to members of the Pueblo of Zuni.

Eligibility This program is open to enrolled members of the Pueblo of Zuni who are high school seniors or graduates. Applicants must have earned a GPA of 2.0 or higher and be interested in working on an associate, bachelor's, or graduate degree as a full-time student at a college or university in any state. They must have also applied for a federal Pell Grant.

Financial data The amount awarded depends on the need of the recipient, up to $5,000 per year.

Duration 1 year; may be renewed if the recipient maintains a GPA of 2.0 or higher.

Number awarded Varies each year.

Deadline June of each year for the fall semester; October of each year for the spring semester; April of each year for the summer session.

Professionals/
Postdoctorates

Listed alphabetically by program title and described in detail here are 207 grants, awards, educational support programs, residencies, and other sources of "free money" available to American Indian, Native Alaskan (including Eskimos and Aleuts), and Native Hawaiian professionals and postdoctorates. This funding can be used to support research, creative activities, formal academic classes, training courses, and/or residencies in the United States.

[1178]
AACAP-NIDA CAREER DEVELOPMENT AWARD

American Academy of Child and Adolescent Psychiatry
Attn: Department of Research, Training, and Education
3615 Wisconsin Avenue, N.W.
Washington, DC 20016-3007
(202) 966-7300   Fax: (202) 966-2891
E-mail: research@aacap.org
Web: www.aacap.org/cs/awards

Summary To provide funding to Native American, women, and other child and adolescent psychiatrists who are interested in a program of mentored training in addiction-related research focused on children and adolescents.

Eligibility This program is open to qualified child and adolescent psychiatrists who intend to established careers as independent investigators in mental health and addiction research. Applicants must design a career development and research training program in collaboration with a research mentor. The program may include prevention; early intervention or treatment research; epidemiology; etiology; genetics, gene-environment interactions, or pharmacogenetics; developmental risk factors; psychiatric comorbidity; medical comorbidity including HIV, Hepatitis C, and STD risk reduction; pathophysiology; services research; special populations (minorities, pregnancy, juvenile justice); health disparities; or imaging studies. U.S. citizenship, nationality, or permanent resident status is required. Women and minority candidates are especially encouraged to apply.

Financial data Grants provide salary support for 75% of the recipient's salary (up to $90,000 plus fringe benefits) and $50,000 per year to cover research and training costs.

Duration Up to 5 years.

Additional information This program is co-sponsored by the American Academy of Child and Adolescent Psychiatry (AACAP) and the National Institute on Drug Abuse (NIDA) as a K12 program of the National Institutes of Health (NIH).

Number awarded 1 or more each year.

Deadline Letters of intent must be submitted in early January of each year; completed applications are due the following March.

[1179]
ADVANCED POSTDOCTORAL FELLOWSHIPS IN DIABETES RESEARCH

Juvenile Diabetes Research Foundation International
Attn: Grant Administrator
26 Broadway, 14th Floor
New York, NY 10004
(212) 479-7572   Toll Free: (800) 533-CURE
Fax: (212) 785-9595   E-mail: info@jdrf.org
Web: www.jdrf.org/index.cfm?page_id=111715

Summary To provide advanced research training to scientists (particularly Native Americans, other minorities, women, and people with disabilities) who are beginning their professional careers and are interested in conducting research on the causes, treatment, prevention, or cure of diabetes or its complications.

Eligibility This program is open to postdoctorates who show extraordinary promise for a career in diabetes research. Applicants must have received their first doctoral degree (M.D., Ph.D., D.M.D., or D.V.M.) within the past 5 years and should have completed 1 to 3 years of postdoctoral training. They may not have a faculty appointment. There are no citizenship requirements. Applications are encouraged from women, members of minority groups underrepresented in the sciences, and people with disabilities. The proposed research training may be conducted at foreign and domestic, for-profit and nonprofit, and public and private institutions, including universities, colleges, hospitals, laboratories, units of state and local government, and eligible agencies of the federal government. Selection is based on the applicant's previous experience and academic record; the caliber of the proposed research; the quality of the mentor, training program, and environment; and the applicant's potential to obtain an independent research position in the future. Fellows who obtain a faculty position at any time during the term of the fellowship may apply for a transition award for support during their first year as a faculty member.

Financial data The total award is $90,000 per year, including salary that depends on number of years of experience, ranging from $37,740 for zero up to $52,068 for 7 or more years of experience. In the first year only, funds in excess of the grant may be used for travel to scientific meetings (up to $2,000), journal subscriptions, books, training courses, laboratory supplies, equipment, or purchase of a personal computer (up to $2,000). Indirect costs are not allowed. Fellows who receive a faculty position are granted a transition award of up to $110,000 for 1 year, including up to 10% in indirect costs.

Duration Up to 3 years.

Deadline January or July of each year.

[1180]
AHRQ INDIVIDUAL AWARDS FOR POSTDOCTORAL FELLOWS

Agency for Healthcare Research and Quality
Attn: Office of Extramural Research, Education, and
    Priority Populations
540 Gaither Road
Rockville, MD 20850
(301) 427-1528   Fax: (301) 427-1562
TDD: (301) 451-0088
E-mail: Shelley.Benjamin@ahrq.hhs.gov
Web: www.ahrq.gov/fund/grantix.htm

Summary To provide funding to underrepresented minorities (including Native Americans) and other postdoctoral scholars interested in academic training and supervised experience in applying quantitative research methods to the systematic analysis and evaluation of health services.

Eligibility Applicants must be U.S. citizens or permanent residents who have received a Ph.D., M.D., D.O., D.C., D.D.S., D.M.D., O.D., D.P.M., D.N.S., N.D., Dr.P.H., Pharm.D., D.S.W., Psych.D., or equivalent doctoral degree from an accredited domestic or foreign institution. They must be proposing to pursue postdoctoral training at an appropriate institution under the guidance of a sponsor who is an established investigator active in health services research. The proposed training should help promote the sponsoring agency's strategic research goals of 1) reducing the risk of harm from health care services by promoting the delivery of appropriate care that achieves the best quality outcomes; 2) achieving wider access to effective health care services and reducing health care costs; and 3) assuring that providers and consumers/

patients use beneficial and timely health care information to make informed decisions. Priority is given to proposals that address health services research issues critical to such priority populations as individuals living in inner city and rural (including frontier) areas; low-income and minority groups; women, children, and the elderly; and individuals with special health care needs, including those with disabilities and those who need chronic or end-of-life health care. Members of underrepresented ethnic and racial groups and individuals with disabilities are especially encouraged to apply.

Financial data The award provides an annual stipend based on the number of years of postdoctoral experience, ranging from $37,740 for less than 1 year to $52,068 for 7 or more years. For fellows sponsored by domestic nonfederal institutions, the stipend is paid through the sponsoring institution; for fellows sponsored by federal or foreign institutions, the monthly stipend is paid directly to the fellow. Institutions also receive an allowance to help defray such awardee expenses as self-only health insurance, research supplies, equipment, travel to scientific meetings, and related items; the allowance is $7,850 per 12-month period for fellows at nonfederal, nonprofit, and foreign institutions and $6,750 per 12-month period at federal laboratories and for-profit institutions. In addition, tuition and fees are reimbursed at a rate of 60%, up to $4,500; if the fellow's program supports postdoctoral individuals in formal degree-granting training, tuition is supported at the rate of 60%, up to $16,000 for an additional degree. The initial 12 months of National Research Service Award postdoctoral support carries a service payback requirement, which can be fulfilled by continued training under the award or by engaging in other health-related research training, health-related research, or health-related teaching. Fellows who fail to fulfill the payback requirement of 1 month of acceptable service for each month of the initial 12 months of support received must repay all funds received with interest.

Duration 1 to 3 years.

Number awarded Varies each year.

Deadline April, August, or December of each year.

[1181]
AIR FELLOWS PROGRAM

American Educational Research Association
1430 K Street, N.W., Suite 1200
Washington, DC 20005
(202) 238-3200   Fax: (202) 238-3250
E-mail: fellowships@aera.net
Web: www.aera.net

Summary To provide an opportunity for junior scholars (especially Native Americans and other underrepresented minorities) in the field of education to engage in a program of research and advanced training while in residence in Washington, D.C.

Eligibility This program is open to early scholars who received a Ph.D. or Ed.D. degree within the past 3 years in a field related to education and educational processes. Applicants must be proposing a program of intensive research and training in Washington, D.C. Selection is based on past academic record, writing sample, goal statement, range and quality of research experiences, other relevant work or professional experiences, potential contributions to education research, and references. A particular goal of the program is to increase the number of underrepresented minority professionals conducting advanced research or providing technical assistance. U.S. citizenship or permanent resident status is required.

Financial data Stipends range from $45,000 to $50,000 per year.

Duration Up to 2 years.

Additional information This program, jointly sponsored by the American Educational Research Association (AERA) and the American Institutes for Research (AIR), was first offered for 2006. Fellows rotate between the 2 organizations and receive mentoring from recognized researchers and practitioners in a variety of substantive areas in education.

Number awarded Up to 3 each year.

Deadline December of each year.

[1182]
AIR FORCE OFFICE OF SCIENTIFIC RESEARCH BROAD AGENCY ANNOUNCEMENT

Air Force Office of Scientific Research
Attn: Directorate of Academic and International Affairs
875 North Randolph Street, Room 3112
Arlington, VA 22203-1954
(703) 696-9738   Fax: (703) 696-9733
E-mail: afosr.baa@afosr.af.mil
Web: www.wpafb.mil/afrl/afosr

Summary To provide funding to investigators at Tribal Colleges and Universities or other institutions (in academia or industry) who are interested in conducting scientific research of interest to the U.S. Air Force.

Eligibility This program is open to investigators qualified to conduct research in designated scientific and technical areas. The general fields of interest include 1) aerospace, chemical, and materials sciences; 2) physics and electronics; 3) mathematics, information, and life sciences; 4) discovery challenge thrusts; and 5) other innovative research concepts. Assistance includes grants to university scientists, support for academic institutions, contracts for industry research, cooperative agreements, and support for basic research in Air Force laboratories. Because the Air Force encourages the sharing and transfer of technology, it welcomes proposals that envision cooperation among 2 or more partners from academia, industry, and Air Force organizations. It particularly encourages proposals from small businesses, Historically Black Colleges and Universities (HBCUs), other Minority Institutions (MIs), and minority researchers.

Financial data The amounts of the awards depend on the nature of the proposals and the availability of funds. Recently, grants averaged approximately $150,000 per year.

Duration Grants range up to 5 years.

Additional information Contact the Air Force Office of Scientific Research for details on particular program areas of interest. Outstanding principal investigators on grants issued through this program are nominated to receive Presidential Early Career Awards for Scientists and Engineers.

Number awarded Varies each year; recently, this program awarded approximately 1,650 grants and contracts to applicants at about 450 academic institutions and industrial firms.

Deadline Each program area specifies deadline dates.

[1183]
AIR FORCE SUMMER FACULTY FELLOWSHIP PROGRAM

American Society for Engineering Education
Attn: Projects Department
1818 N Street, N.W., Suite 600
Washington, DC 20036-2479
(202) 331-5763   Fax: (202) 265-8504
E-mail: sffp@asee.org
Web: sffp.asee.org

Summary To provide funding to science and engineering faculty (particularly those at Tribal Colleges and Universities and other minority institutions) who are interested in conducting summer research at Air Force facilities.

Eligibility This program is open to U.S. citizens and permanent residents who have a full-time faculty appointment at a U.S. college or university in a field of engineering or science of interest to the Air Force. Applicants must be interested in conducting a research project, under the direction of an Air Force research adviser, at an Air Force Research Laboratory, the U.S. Air Force Academy, or the Air Force Institute of Technology. A graduate student may accompany the faculty member. Faculty and students at Historically Black Colleges and Universities ((HBCUs), Minority Institutions (MIs), American Indian Tribal Colleges and Universities (TCUs), and Hispanic Serving Institutions (HSIs) are especially encouraged to apply.

Financial data Stipends are $1,700 per week for full professors, $1,500 per week for associate professors, $1,300 per week for assistant professors, $884 per week for graduate students who have a bachelor's degree, or $1,037 per week for graduate students who have a master's degree. Relocation reimbursement and a daily expense allowance of $50 (for fellows with a commute distance greater than 50 miles) are also available.

Duration 8 to 12 weeks during the summer. May be renewed for a second and third summer, but recipients may not reapply for 2 years after completing a third summer.

Additional information This program first operated in 2005. Research must be conducted in residence at an Air Force facility.

Number awarded Varies each year; recently, 93 of these fellowships were awarded.

Deadline November of each year.

[1184]
ALFRED P. SLOAN FOUNDATION RESEARCH FELLOWSHIPS

Alfred P. Sloan Foundation
630 Fifth Avenue, Suite 2550
New York, NY 10111-0242
(212) 649-1649   Fax: (212) 757-5117
E-mail: researchfellows@sloan.org
Web: www.sloan.org/fellowships

Summary To provide funding for research in selected fields of science to recent doctorates (particularly Native Americans and other underrepresented minorities).

Eligibility This program is open to scholars who are no more than 6 years from completion of the most recent Ph.D. or equivalent in computational and evolutionary molecular biology, chemistry, physics, mathematics, computer science, economics, neuroscience, or a related interdisciplinary field. Direct applications are not accepted; candidates must be nominated by department heads or other senior scholars. Although fellows must be at an early stage of their research careers, they should give strong evidence of independent research accomplishments and creativity. The sponsor strongly encourages the participation of women and members of underrepresented minority groups.

Financial data The stipend is $25,000 per year. Funds are paid directly to the fellow's institution to be used by the fellow for equipment, technical assistance, professional travel, trainee support, or any other research-related expense; they may not be used to augment an existing full-time salary.

Duration 2 years; may be extended if unexpended funds still remain.

Additional information This program began in 1955, when it awarded $235,000 to 22 chemists, physicists, and pure mathematicians. Neuroscience was added in 1972, economics and applied mathematics in 1980, computer science in 1993, and computational and evolutionary molecular biology in 2002. Currently, the program awards $5.22 million in grants annually.

Number awarded 118 each year: 23 in chemistry, 12 in computational and evolutionary molecular biology, 16 in computer science, 8 in economics, 20 in mathematics, 16 in neuroscience, and 23 in physics.

Deadline September of each year.

[1185]
ALZHEIMER'S ASSOCIATION INVESTIGATOR-INITIATED RESEARCH GRANTS

Alzheimer's Association
Attn: Medical and Scientific Affairs
225 North Michigan Avenue, 17th Floor
Chicago, IL 60601-7633
(312) 335-5747   Toll Free: (800) 272-3900
Fax: (866) 699-1246   TDD: (312) 335-5886
E-mail: grantsapp@alz.org
Web: www.alz.org

Summary To provide funding to scientists (particularly Native Americans and members of other underrepresented groups) who are interested in conducting research on Alzheimer's Disease.

Eligibility This program is open to postdoctoral investigators at public, private, domestic, and foreign research laboratories, medical centers, hospitals, and universities. Applicants must be proposing to conduct research with focus areas that change annually but are related to Alzheimer's Disease. They must have a full-time staff or faculty appointment. Scientists from underrepresented groups are especially encouraged to apply.

Financial data Grants up to $100,000 per year, including direct expenses and up to 10% for overhead costs, are available. The total award for the life of the grant may not exceed $240,000.

Duration Up to 3 years.

Number awarded Up to 30 each year.

Deadline Letters of intent must be submitted by the end of December of each year. Final applications are due in February.

[1186]
ALZHEIMER'S ASSOCIATION NEW INVESTIGATOR RESEARCH GRANTS

Alzheimer's Association
Attn: Medical and Scientific Affairs
225 North Michigan Avenue, 17th Floor
Chicago, IL 60601-7633
(312) 335-5747   Toll Free: (800) 272-3900
Fax: (866) 699-1246   TDD: (312) 335-5886
E-mail: grantsapp@alz.org
Web: www.alz.org

Summary To provide funding for research on Alzheimer's Disease to junior and postdoctoral investigators, especially those who are Native Americans or members of other underrepresented groups.

Eligibility This program is open to investigators, including postdoctoral fellows, at public, private, domestic, and foreign research laboratories, medical centers, hospitals, and universities. Applicants must be proposing to conduct research with focus areas that change annually but are related to Alzheimer's Disease. Eligibility is restricted to investigators who have less than 10 years of research experience, including postdoctoral fellowships or residencies. Scientists from underrepresented groups are especially encouraged to apply.

Financial data Grants up to $60,000 per year, including direct expenses and up to 10% for overhead costs, are available. The total award for the life of the grant may not exceed $100,000.

Duration Up to 2 years.

Number awarded Up to 45 each year.

Deadline Letters of intent must be submitted by the end of December of each year. Final applications are due in February.

[1187]
AMERICAN ASSOCIATION OF OBSTETRICIANS AND GYNECOLOGISTS FOUNDATION SCHOLARSHIPS

American Gynecological and Obstetrical Society
Attn: American Association of Obstetricians and
  Gynecologists Foundation
409 12th Street, S.W.
Washington, DC 20024-2188
(202) 863-1649   Fax: (202) 554-0453
E-mail: clarkins@acog.org
Web: www.agosonline.org/aaogf/index.asp

Summary To provide funding to physicians (particularly Native Americans, other minorities, and women) who are interested in a program of research training in obstetrics and gynecology.

Eligibility Applicants must have an M.D. degree and be eligible for the certification process of the American Board of Obstetrics and Gynecology (ABOG). They must be interested in participating in research training conducted by 1 or more faculty mentors at an academic department of obstetrics and gynecology in the United States or Canada. the research training may be either laboratory-based or clinical, and should focus on fundamental biology, disease mechanisms, interventions or diagnostics, epidemiology, or translational research. There is no formal application form, but departments must supply a description of the candidate's qualifica-

tions, including a curriculum vitae, bibliography, prior training, past research experience, and evidence of completion of residency training in obstetrics and gynecology; a comprehensive description of the proposed training program; a description of departmental resources appropriate to the training; a detailed mentoring plan; a list of other research grants, training grants, or scholarships previously or currently held by the applicant; and a budget. Applicants for the scholarship co-sponsored by the Society for Maternal-Fetal Medicine (SMFM) must also be members or associate members of the SMFM. Women and minority candidates are strongly encouraged to apply. Selection is based on the scholarly, clinical, and research qualifications of the candidate; evidence of the candidate's commitment to an investigative career in academic obstetrics and gynecology in the United States or Canada; qualifications of the sponsoring department and mentor; overall quality of the mentoring plan, and quality of the research project. Preference may be given to applications from candidates training in areas currently underrepresented in academic obstetrics and gynecology (e.g., urogynecology, family planning).

Financial data The grant is $100,000 per year, of which at least $5,000 but not more than $15,000 must be used for employee benefits. In addition, sufficient funds to support travel to the annual fellows' retreat must be set aside. The balance of the funds may be used for salary, technical support, and supplies. The grant co-sponsored by the SMFM must be matched by an institutional commitment of at least $30,000 per year.

Duration 1 year; may be renewed for 2 additional years, based on satisfactory progress of the scholar.

Additional information Scholars must devote at least 75% of their effort to the program of research training.

Number awarded 2 each year: 1 co-sponsored by ABOG and 1 co-sponsored by SMFM.

Deadline June of each year.

[1188]
AMERICAN COUNCIL OF LEARNED SOCIETIES FELLOWSHIPS

American Council of Learned Societies
Attn: Office of Fellowships and Grants
633 Third Avenue
New York, NY 10017-6795
(212) 697-1505   Fax: (212) 949-8058
E-mail: fellowships@acls.org
Web: www.acls.org/programs/acls

Summary To provide research funding to Native American and other scholars in all disciplines of the humanities and the humanities-related social sciences.

Eligibility This program is open to scholars at all stages of their careers who received a Ph.D. degree at least 2 years previously. Established scholars who can demonstrate the equivalent of the Ph.D. in publications and professional experience may also qualify. Applicants must be U.S. citizens or permanent residents who have not had supported leave time for at least 2 years prior to the start of the proposed research. Appropriate fields of specialization include, but are not limited to, American studies; anthropology; archaeology; art and architectural history; classics; economics; film; geography; history; languages and literatures; legal studies; linguistics; musicology; philosophy; political science; psychology; religious studies; rhetoric, communication, and media studies; sociology; and theater, dance, and performance studies. Proposals in those fields of the social sciences are eligible only if they employ predominantly humanistic approaches (e.g., economic history, law and literature, political philosophy). Proposals in interdisciplinary and cross-disciplinary studies are welcome, as are proposals focused on a geographic region or on a cultural or linguistic group. Awards are available at 3 academic levels: full professor, associate professor, and assistant professor. Applications are particularly invited from women and members of minority groups.

Financial data The maximum grant is $60,000 for full professors and equivalent, $40,000 for associate professors and equivalent, or $35,000 for assistant professors and equivalent. Normally, fellowships are intended as salary replacement and may be held concurrently with other fellowships, grants, and sabbatical pay, up to an amount equal to the candidate's current academic year salary.

Duration 6 to 12 months.

Additional information This program is supported in part by funding from the Ford Foundation, the Andrew W. Mellon Foundation, the National Endowment for the Humanities, the William and Flora Hewlett Foundation, and the Rockefeller Foundation.

Number awarded Approximately 57 each year: 17 at the full professor level, 18 at the association professor level, and 22 at the assistant professor level.

Deadline September of each year.

[1189]
AMERICAN EDUCATIONAL RESEARCH ASSOCIATION RESEARCH GRANTS PROGRAM

American Educational Research Association
1430 K Street, N.W., Suite 1200
Washington, DC 20005
(202) 238-3200   Fax: (202) 238-3250
Web: www.aera.net

Summary To provide funding to Native American and other faculty members and postdoctorates interested in conducting research on educational policy.

Eligibility This program is open to scholars who have completed a doctoral degree in such disciplines as (but not limited to) education, sociology, economics, psychology, demography, statistics, or psychometrics. Applicants may be U.S. citizens, U.S. permanent residents, or non-U.S. citizens working at a U.S. institution. Underrepresented minority researchers are strongly encouraged to apply. Research topics may cover a wide range of policy-related issues, but priority is given to proposals that 1) develop or benefit from new quantitative measures or methodological approaches for addressing education issues; 2) include interdisciplinary teams with subject matter expertise, especially when studying science, technology, engineering, or mathematics (STEM) learning; 3) analyze TIMSS, PISA, or other international data resources; or 4) include the integration and analysis of more than 1 data set. Research projects must include the analysis of data from at least 1 of the large-scale, nationally or internationally representative data sets, such as those of the National Science Foundation (NSF), National Center for Education Statistics (NCES), or National Institutes of Health (NIH). Selection is based on the importance of the proposed policy issue, the strength of the methodological model and proposed statistical

analysis of the study, and relevant experience or research record.

Financial data Grants up to $20,000 for 1 year or $35,000 for 2 years are available. Funding is linked to the approval of the recipient's progress report and final report. Grantees receive one-third of the total award at the beginning of the grant period, one-third upon acceptance of the progress report, and one-third upon acceptance of the final report.

Duration 1 or 2 years.

Additional information Funding for this program is provided by the NSF and the NCES. Grantees must submit a brief (3 to 6 pages) progress report midway through the grant period. A final report must be submitted at the end of the grant period.

Number awarded Approximately 15 each year.

Deadline January, March, or August of each year.

[1190]
AMERICAN GASTROENTEROLOGICAL ASSOCIATION RESEARCH SCHOLAR AWARDS

American Gastroenterological Association
Attn: AGA Research Foundation
Research Awards Manager
4930 Del Ray Avenue
Bethesda, MD 20814-2512
(301) 222-4012   Fax: (301) 654-5920
E-mail: awards@gastro.org
Web: www.gastro.org/aga-foundation/grants

Summary To provide research funding to young investigators (particularly Native Americans or other minorities and women) who are interested in developing an independent career in an area of gastroenterology, hepatology, or related fields.

Eligibility Applicants must hold full-time faculty positions at North American universities or professional institutes at the time of application. They should be early in their careers (fellows and established investigators are not appropriate candidates). Candidates with an M.D. degree must have completed clinical training within the past 5 years and those with a Ph.D. must have completed their degree within the past 5 years. Membership in the American Gastroenterological Association (AGA) is required. Selection is based on significance, investigator, innovation, approach, environment, relevance to AGA mission, and evidence of institutional commitment. Women, minorities, and physician/scientist investigators are strongly encouraged to apply.

Financial data The grant is $60,000 per year. Funds are to be used for project costs, including salary, supplies, and equipment but excluding travel. Indirect costs are not allowed.

Duration 2 years; a third year of support may be available, contingent upon availability of funds and a competitive review.

Additional information At least 70% of the recipient's research effort should relate to the gastrointestinal tract or liver.

Number awarded 1 or more each year.

Deadline September of each year.

[1191]
AMERICAN INDIAN STUDIES VISITING SCHOLAR AND VISITING RESEARCHER PROGRAM

University of California at Los Angeles
Institute of American Cultures
Attn: American Indian Studies Center
3220 Campbell Hall
P.O. Box 951548
Los Angeles, CA 90095-1548
(310) 825-7315
Web: www.gdnet.ucla.edu/iacweb/pstweber.htm

Summary To provide funding to scholars interested in conducting research in Native American studies at UCLA's American Indian Studies Center.

Eligibility Applicants must have completed a doctoral degree in Native American or related studies. They must be interested in teaching or conducting research at UCLA's American Indian Studies Center. Visiting Scholar appointments are available to people who currently hold permanent academic appointments; Visiting Researcher appointments are available to postdoctorates who recently received their degree. UCLA faculty, students, and staff are not eligible. U.S. citizenship or permanent resident status is required.

Financial data Fellows receive a stipend of $32,000 to $35,000 (depending on rank, experience, and date of completion of the Ph.D.), health benefits, and up to $4,000 in research support. Visiting Scholars are paid through their home institution; Visiting Researchers receive their funds directly from UCLA.

Duration 9 months, beginning in October.

Additional information Fellows must teach or do research in the programs of the center. The award is offered in conjunction with UCLA's Institute of American Cultures (IAC).

Number awarded 1 each year.

Deadline January of each year.

[1192]
AMERICAN SOCIETY FOR CELL BIOLOGY MINORITIES AFFAIRS COMMITTEE VISITING PROFESSOR AWARDS

American Society for Cell Biology
Attn: Minority Affairs Committee
8120 Woodmont Avenue, Suite 750
Bethesda, MD 20814-2762
(301) 347-9323   Fax: (301) 347-9310
E-mail: dmccall@ascb.org
Web: www.ascb.org

Summary To provide funding for research during the summer to Native American and other minority faculty, as well as to faculty members at teaching institutions that serve minority students and scientists.

Eligibility Eligible to apply for this support are professors at primarily teaching institutions. They must be interested in working in the laboratories of members of the American Society for Cell Biology during the summer. Hosts and visitor scientists are asked to submit their applications together as a proposed team. Minority professors and professors in colleges and universities with a high minority enrollment are especially encouraged to apply for this award. Minorities are defined as U.S. citizens of Black, Native American, Chicano/Hispanic, or Pacific Islands background.

Financial data The stipend for the summer is $13,500 plus $700 for travel expenses and $4,000 to the host institution for supplies.

Duration From 8 to 10 weeks during the summer.

Additional information Funds for this program, established in 1997, are provided by the Minorities Access to Research Careers (MARC) program of the National Institutes of Health.

Number awarded Varies each year; recently, 3 of these grants were awarded.

Deadline March of each year.

[1193]
ANDREW W. MELLON ADVANCED TRAINING PROGRAM IN OBJECT AND TEXTILE CONSERVATION FELLOWSHIPS

National Museum of the American Indian
Attn: Head of Conservation
Cultural Resources Center
4220 Silver Hill Road, MRC 538
Suitland, MD 20746-2863
(301) 238-1415   Fax: (301) 238-3201
E-mail: kaminitzm@si.edu
Web: www.nmai.si.edu

Summary To provide Native American and other recent college graduates involved in conservation of museum collections with an opportunity to participate in a training program at the Smithsonian Institution's National Museum of the American Indian (NMAI).

Eligibility This program is open to recent graduates of recognized conservation training programs. Applicants must be preparing for a career in the conservation of material culture of the indigenous peoples of North, Central, and South America. They must be interested in participating in a training program at the NMAI Cultural Resources Center in Suitland, Maryland that involves collaboration with Native people in developing appropriate methods of caring for and interpreting cultural materials. The program is intended to cultivate practical skills as well as foster a solid understanding of the contexts of material culture, the philosophies of conservation at NMAI, and the ethics of the conservation profession. Current projects involved the preparation of artifacts for loans and for exhibits at NMAI sites. Proficiency in English is required.

Financial data Fellows receive a stipend (amount not specified) and funds for travel and research.

Duration 1 year; may be renewed 1 additional year.

Number awarded 1 each year.

Deadline March of each year.

[1194]
ANDREW W. MELLON ADVANCED TRAINING PROGRAM IN OBJECT AND TEXTILE CONSERVATION INTERNSHIPS

National Museum of the American Indian
Attn: Head of Conservation
Cultural Resources Center
4220 Silver Hill Road, MRC 538
Suitland, MD 20746-2863
(301) 238-1415   Fax: (301) 238-3201
E-mail: kaminitzm@si.edu
Web: www.nmai.si.edu

Summary To provide students and professionals involved in conservation of museum collections with an opportunity to participate in a training program at the Smithsonian Institution's National Museum of the American Indian (NMAI).

Eligibility This program is open to 1) students currently enrolled in a graduate program in conservation; 2) recent graduates of such a program; and 3) practicing conservation professionals. Applicants must be preparing for a career in the conservation of material culture of the indigenous peoples of North, Central, and South America. They must be interested in participating in a training program at the NMAI Cultural Resources Center in Suitland, Maryland that involves collaboration with Native people in developing appropriate methods of caring for and interpreting cultural materials. The program is intended to cultivate practical skills as well as foster a solid understanding of the contexts of material culture, the philosophies of conservation at NMAI, and the ethics of the conservation profession. Proficiency in English is required.

Financial data Interns receive a stipend (amount not specified) and funds for housing.

Duration 10 weeks, in summer or winter.

Number awarded Varies each year.

Deadline January of each year for summer; September of each year for winter.

[1195]
ANDREW W. MELLON FOUNDATION/ACLS RECENT DOCTORAL RECIPIENTS FELLOWSHIPS

American Council of Learned Societies
Attn: Office of Fellowships and Grants
633 Third Avenue
New York, NY 10017-6795
(212) 697-1505   Fax: (212) 949-8058
E-mail: fellowships@acls.org
Web: www.acls.org/programs/rdr

Summary To provide funding to recent recipients of doctoral degrees (especially Native Americans, other minorities, and women) in all disciplines of the humanities and the humanities-related social sciences who need funding to advance their scholarly career.

Eligibility This program is open to recent recipients of a doctoral degree in a humanities or humanities-related social science discipline. Applicants must have been 1) a recipient of an Andrew W. Mellon Foundation/ACLS Dissertation Completion Fellowship in the previous year; 2) designated as an alternate in that fellowship program; or 3) a recipient of a dissertation completion fellowship in another program of

national stature (e.g., Whiting, AAUW, Newcombe). They must be seeking funding to position themselves for further scholarly advancement, whether or not they hold academic positions. Appropriate fields of specialization include, but are not limited to, American studies; anthropology; archaeology; art and architectural history; classics; economics; film; geography; history; languages and literatures; legal studies; linguistics; musicology; philosophy; political science; psychology; religious studies; rhetoric, communication, and media studies; sociology; and theater, dance, and performance studies. Proposals in those fields of the social sciences are eligible only if they employ predominantly humanistic approaches (e.g., economic history, law and literature, political philosophy). Proposals in interdisciplinary and cross-disciplinary studies are welcome, as are proposals focused on any geographic region or on any cultural or linguistic group. Applications are particularly invited from women and members of minority groups.

Financial data The stipend is $30,000.

Duration 1 academic year. Grantees may accept this fellowship during the 2 years following the date of the award.

Additional information This program, which began in 2007, is supported by funding from the Andrew W. Mellon Foundation and administered by the American Council of Learned Societies (ACLS). Fellows may not teach during the tenure of the fellowship. If they have a faculty position, they may use the fellowship to take research leave. Fellows who do not have a full-time position may choose to affiliate with a humanities research center or conduct research independently.

Number awarded 25 each year.

Deadline November of each year.

[1196]
ANNE RAY FELLOWSHIP

School for Advanced Research
Attn: Director of Scholar Programs
660 Garcia Street
P.O. Box 2188
Santa Fe, NM 87504-2188
(505) 954-7201   E-mail: scholar@sarsf.org
Web: sarweb.org/index.php?resident_scholars

Summary To provide funding to Native American scholars interested in conducting research in the social sciences, arts, or humanities while in residence at the School for Advanced Research (SAR) in Santa Fe, New Mexico.

Eligibility This program is open to Native American scholars who are interested in conducting research at SAR in the humanities, arts, or the social sciences. Applicants must be interested in providing mentorship to recent Native graduates or graduate students. Along with their application, they must submit a 150-word abstract describing the purpose, goals, and objectives of their research project; a 4-page proposal; a bibliography; a curriculum vitae; a brief statement of tribal affiliation; a 3-page statement identifying their experience and interest in serving as a mentor; and 3 letters of recommendation. Preference is given to applicants whose field work or basic research and analysis are complete and who need time to write up their research.

Financial data The fellowship provides an apartment and office on the school's campus, a stipend of up to $40,000, library assistance, and other benefits.

Duration 9 months, beginning in September.

Additional information Funding for this program, which began in 2009, is provided by the Anne Ray Charitable Trust. In addition to working on their own research, the fellow serves as a mentor to 2 Native interns working at the Indian Arts Research Center on the SAR campus. Participants must spend their 9-month residency at the school in New Mexico.

Number awarded 1 each year.

Deadline October of each year.

[1197]
ANTARCTIC RESEARCH PROGRAM

National Science Foundation
Office of Polar Programs
Attn: Division of Antarctic Sciences
4201 Wilson Boulevard, Room 755S
Arlington, VA 22230
(703) 292-7457　　　　　Fax: (703) 292-9080
TDD: (800) 281-8749　　　E-mail: jlcrain@nsf.gov
Web: www.nsf.gov/funding/pgm_summ.jsp?pims_id=5519

Summary To provide funding to underrepresented minorities (including Native Americans) and other scientists interested in conducting research related to Antarctica.

Eligibility This program is open to investigators at U.S. institutions, primarily universities and, to a lesser extent, federal agencies and other organizations. Applicants must be proposing to conduct Antarctic-related research in the following major areas: aeronomy and astrophysics, organisms and ecosystems, earth sciences, ocean and atmospheric sciences, glaciology, and integrated system science. The program encourages applications from underrepresented minorities and persons with disabilities.

Financial data The amounts of the awards depend on the nature of the proposal and the availability of funds.

Additional information The NSF operates 3 year-round research stations in Antarctica, additional research facilities and camps, airplanes, helicopters, various types of surface vehicles, and ships.

Number awarded Varies each year; recently, the program planned to make 50 awards with a total budget of $22 million for new awards and $30 million for continuing awards.

Deadline May of each year.

[1198]
ANTHC SUMMER INTERNSHIPS

Alaska Native Tribal Health Consortium
Attn: Education, Development and Training Department
4000 Ambassador Drive, Suite 114
Anchorage, AK 99508
(907) 729-1917　　　　　Toll Free: (800) 684-8361
Fax: (907) 729-1335　　E-mail: anthceducation@anthc.org
Web: www.anthc.org/jt/int

Summary To provide summer work experience at the Alaska Native Tribal Health Consortium (ANTHC) to Native Alaskan and American Indian high school, undergraduate, and graduate students.

Eligibility This program is open to Alaska Natives and American Indians who are high school students, undergraduates, graduate students, and recipients during the past 6 months of a GED, diploma, or degree. Applicants must be residents of Alaska and interested in an internship at ANTHC

in such areas as finance, human resources, health records, computer technology, engineering, maintenance, or housekeeping. Along with their application, they must submit a resume, documentation of financial need, and a 1-page personal statement that covers their personal and educational history, accomplishments, educational and career goals, involvement in the Native community, and how this internship corresponds with their career goals.

Financial data These are paid internships.

Duration 9 weeks during the summer.

Number awarded Approximately 25 each year: 20 for high school and undergraduate students and 5 for graduate students.

Deadline February of each year.

[1199]
APA/SAMHSA MINORITY FELLOWSHIP PROGRAM

American Psychiatric Association
Attn: Department of Minority and National Affairs
1000 Wilson Boulevard, Suite 1825
Arlington, VA 22209-3901
(703) 907-8653　　　　　Toll Free: (888) 35-PSYCH
Fax: (703) 907-7852　　　E-mail: mking@psych.org
Web: www.psych.org/Resources/OMNA/MFP.aspx

Summary To provide educational enrichment to Native American and other minority psychiatrists-in-training and to stimulate interest in providing quality and effective services to minorities and the underserved.

Eligibility This program is open to residents who are in at least their second year of psychiatric training, members of the American Psychiatric Association (APA), and U.S. citizens or permanent residents. A goal of the program is to develop leadership to improve the quality of mental health care for members of ethnic minority groups (American Indians, Native Alaskans, Asian Americans, Native Hawaiians, Native Pacific Islanders, African Americans, and Hispanics/Latinos). Applicants must be interested in working with a component of the APA that is of interest to them and relevant to their career goals. Along with their application, they must submit a 2-page essay on how the fellowship would be utilized to alter their present training and ultimately assist them in achieving their career goals. Selection is based on commitment to serve ethnic minority populations, demonstrated leadership abilities, awareness of the importance of culture in mental health, and interest in the interrelationship between mental health/illness and transcultural factors.

Financial data Fellows receive a monthly stipend (amount not specified) and reimbursement of transportation, lodging, meals, and incidentals in connection with attendance at program-related activities. They are expected to use the funds to enhance their own professional development, improve training in cultural competence at their training institution, improve awareness of culturally relevant issues in psychiatry at their institution, expand research in areas relevant to minorities and underserved populations, enhance the current treatment modalities for minority patients and underserved individuals at their institution, and improve awareness in the surrounding community about mental health issues (particularly with regard to minority populations).

Duration 1 year; may be renewed 1 additional year.

Additional information Funding for this program is provided by the Substance Abuse and Mental Health Services Administration (SAMHSA). As part of their assignment to an APA component, fellows must attend the fall component meetings in September and the APA annual meeting in May. At those meeting, they can share their experiences as residents and minorities and discuss issues that impact on minority populations. This program is an outgrowth of the fellowships that were established in 1974 under a grant from the National Institute of Mental Health in answer to concerns about the underrepresentation of minorities in psychiatry.

Number awarded Varies each year; recently, 16 of these fellowships were awarded.

Deadline January of each year.

[1200]
ARCTIC RESEARCH OPPORTUNITIES

National Science Foundation
Office of Polar Programs
Attn: Division of Arctic Sciences
4201 Wilson Boulevard, Suite 755S
Arlington, VA 22230
(703) 292-8577   Fax: (703) 292-9082
TDD: (800) 281-8749   E-mail: phaggert@nsf.gov
Web: www.nsf.gov/funding/pgm_summ.jsp?pims_id=5521

Summary To provide funding to scientists (particularly Native Americans, other underrepresented minorities, and individuals with disabilities) who are interested in conducting research related to the Arctic.

Eligibility This program is open to investigators affiliated with U.S. universities, research institutions, or other organizations, including local or state governments. Applicants must be proposing to conduct research in the 4 program areas of Arctic science: 1) Arctic Natural Sciences, with areas of special interest in marine and terrestrial ecosystems, Arctic atmospheric and oceanic dynamics and climatology, Arctic geological and glaciological processes, and their connectivity to lower latitudes; 2) Arctic Social Sciences, including (but not limited to) anthropology, archaeology, economics, geography, linguistics, political science, psychology, science and technology studies, sociology, traditional knowledge, and related subjects; 3) Arctic System Science, for research focused on a system understanding of the Arctic, understanding the behavior of the Arctic system (past, present, and future), understanding the role of the Arctic as a component of the global system, and society as an integral part of the Arctic system; 4) Arctic Observing Networks, for work related to a pan-Arctic, science-driven, observing system; or 5) Cyberinfrastructure, for projects using high-performance computing for direct and sustainable advances in current Arctic research. The program encourages proposals from underrepresented minorities and persons with disabilities.

Financial data The amounts of the awards depend on the nature of the proposal and the availability of funds.

Number awarded Approximately 75 each year; recently, this program awarded approximately $25 million in grants.

Deadline October of each year.

[1201]
ARMY RESEARCH LABORATORY BROAD AGENCY ANNOUNCEMENT

Army Research Office
Attn: AMSRL-RO-RI
4300 South Miami Boulevard
P.O. Box 12211
Research Triangle Park, NC 27709-2211
(919) 549-4375   Fax: (919) 549-4388
Web: www.arl.army.mil/www/default.cfm?Action=6&Page=8

Summary To provide funding to minority and other investigators (especially those from Tribal Colleges and Universities and other minority institutions) who are interested in conducting scientific research of interest to the U.S. Army.

Eligibility This program is open to investigators qualified to perform research in designated scientific and technical areas. Included within the program are several sites within the Army Research Laboratory (ARL): 1) the Army Research Office (ARO), which supports research in the areas of chemistry, computing and information sciences, electronics, environmental sciences, life sciences, materials sciences, mathematics, mechanical sciences, and physics; 2) the Computational and Information Sciences Directorate; 3) the Human Research and Engineering Directorate; 4) the Sensors and Electron Devices Directorate; 5) the Survivability/Lethality Analysis Directorate; 6) the Vehicle Technology Directorate; and 7) the Weapons and Materials Research Directorate. Applications are especially encouraged from Historically Black Colleges and Universities (HBCUs) and Minority Institutions (MIs).

Financial data The amounts of the awards depend on the nature of the proposal and the availability of funds.

Duration 3 years.

Additional information Although the Army Research Office intends to award a fair proportion of its acquisitions to HBCUs and MIs, it does not set aside a specified percentage.

Number awarded Varies each year.

Deadline Applications may be submitted at any time.

[1202]
ARTIST'S COMMUNITY WORKSHOP PROGRAM OF THE NATIONAL MUSEUM OF THE AMERICAN INDIAN

National Museum of the American Indian
Attn: Artist Leadership Program
Cultural Resources Center
4220 Silver Hill Road
Suitland, MD 20746-2863
(301) 238-1544   Fax: (301) 238-3200
E-mail: ALP@si.edu
Web: www.nmai.si.edu/icap/leadership.html

Summary To provide Native American professional artists with an opportunity to organize and conduct a workshop within their local community.

Eligibility This program is open to Native artists from the western Hemisphere and Hawaii who are recognized by their community and can demonstrate significant artistic accomplishments in any media (e.g., visual arts, media arts, performance arts, literature). Students enrolled in a degree program are ineligible. Applicants must be interested in planning and managing a free workshop for artists in their local community. The workshop may cover such themes as skills that the artist has mastered, new techniques learned during a collections research visit to Washington, D.C., or new or revised cultural art techniques. Along with their application, they must submit a 500-word research proposal, a 500-word project proposal, a digital portfolio of 10 images or 5 minutes, 2 letters of support, a resume, and a 75-word statement describing their purpose, goal, and intended results.

Financial data The grant is $7,000 to cover project costs, supplies, and materials.

Duration Participants first spend 10 days in Washington, D.C. consulting with staff of the National Museum of the American Indian (NMAI), after which they return to their community and complete a project within 1 year.

Additional information This is a 2-part program. In the first part, participants visit Washington, D.C. for 10 days to conduct research in collections of the NMAI and other local museums, participate in interviews with Collections and Education staff, conduct lunch-time presentations for NMAI staff and the museum public, and visit area galleries. Following the completion of that visit, participants return to their community to share the knowledge learned from the experience and research visit and conduct their project. They select the workshop location, create an agenda and syllabus, obtain materials, and facilitate advertising and registration. The workshop they offer should provide 1 to 3 days of instruction to at least 10 community members interested in learning artistic skills.

Number awarded 2 each year.

Deadline April of each year.

[1203]
ASH-AMFDP RESEARCH GRANTS

American Society of Hematology
Attn: Awards Manager
2021 L Street, N.W., Suite 900
Washington, DC 20036
(202) 776-0544   Fax: (202) 776-0545
E-mail: awards@hematology.org
Web: www.hematology.org

Summary To provide an opportunity for Native American and other historically disadvantaged postdoctoral physicians to conduct a research project in hematology.

Eligibility This program is open to postdoctoral physicians who are members of historically disadvantaged groups, defined as individuals who face challenges because of their race, ethnicity, socioeconomic status, or other similar factors. Applicants must be committed to a career in academic medicine in hematology and to serving as a role model for students and faculty of similar backgrounds. They must identify a mentor at their institution to work with them and give them research and career guidance. Selection is based on excellence in educational career; willingness to devote 4 consecutive years to research; and commitment to an academic career, improving the health status of the underserved, and decreasing health disparities. U.S. citizenship or permanent resident status is required.

Financial data The grant includes a stipend of up to $75,000 per year, a grant of $30,000 per year for support of research activities, complimentary membership in the American Society of Hematology (ASH), and travel support to attend the ASH annual meeting.

Duration 4 years.

Additional information This program, first offered in 2006, is a partnership between the ASH and the Robert Wood Johnson Foundation, whose Minority Medical Faculty Development Program (MMFDP) was renamed the Harold Amos Medical Faculty Development Program (AMFDP) in honor of the first African American to chair a department at the Harvard Medical School. Scholars must spend at least 70% of their time in research activities.

Number awarded At least 1 each year.

Deadline March of each year.

[1204]
ASTRONOMY AND ASTROPHYSICS POSTDOCTORAL FELLOWSHIPS

National Science Foundation
Directorate for Mathematical and Physical Sciences
Attn: Division of Astronomical Sciences
4201 Wilson Boulevard, Room 1030S
Arlington, VA 22230
(703) 292-7456   Fax: (703) 292-9034
TDD: (800) 281-8749   E-mail: dlehr@nsf.gov
Web: www.nsf.gov/funding/pgm_summ.jsp?pims_id=5291

Summary To provide funding to recent doctoral recipients in astronomy or astrophysics (especially Native Americans, other underrepresented minorities, and individuals with disabilities) who are interested in pursuing a program of research and education.

Eligibility This program is open to U.S. citizens, nationals, and permanent residents who completed a Ph.D. in astronomy or astrophysics during the previous 5 years. Applicants must be interested in a program of research of an observational, instrumental, or theoretical nature, especially research that is facilitated or enabled by new ground-based capability in radio, optical/IR, or solar astrophysics. Research may be conducted at a U.S. institution of higher education; a national center, facility, or institute funded by the National Science Foundation (NSF), such as the Kavli Institute for Theoretical Physics; a U.S. nonprofit organization with research and educational missions; and/or an international site operated by a U.S. organization eligible for NSF funding, such as Cerro Tololo InterAmerican Observatory. The proposal must include a coherent program of educational activities, such as teaching a course each year at the host institution or an academic institution with ties to the host institution, developing educational materials, or engaging in a significant program of outreach or general education. The program encourages applications from underrepresented minorities and persons with disabilities.

Financial data Grants up to $83,000 per year are available, including stipends of $58,000 per year, a research allowance of $12,000 per year, an institutional allowance of $3,000 per year, and a benefits allowance of $10,000 per year, paid either to the fellow or the host institution in support of fringe benefits.

Duration Up to 3 years.

Number awarded 8 to 9 each year.

Deadline October of each year.

[1205]
ATMOSPHERIC AND GEOSPACE SCIENCES POSTDOCTORAL RESEARCH FELLOWSHIPS

National Science Foundation
Directorate for Geosciences
Attn: Division of Atmospheric and Geospace Sciences
4201 Wilson Boulevard, Room 775S
Arlington, VA 22230
(703) 292-4708   Fax: (703) 292-9022
TDD: (800) 281-8749   E-mail: cweiler@nsf.gov
Web: www.nsf.gov/funding/pgm_summ.jsp?pims_id=12779

Summary To provide funding to postdoctoral scientists (particularly Native Americans, other underrepresented minorities, and individuals with disabilities) who are interested in conducting research related to activities of the National Science Foundation (NSF) Division of Atmospheric and Geospace Sciences.

Eligibility This program is open to U.S. citizens, nationals, and permanent residents who received a Ph.D. within the past 3 years. Applicants must be interested in conducting a research project that is relevant to the activities of NSF Division of Atmospheric and Geospace Sciences: studies of the physics, chemistry, and dynamics of Earth's upper and lower atmosphere and its space environment; research on climate processes and variations; or studies to understand the natural global cycles of gases and particles in Earth's atmosphere. The project should be conducted at an institution (college or university, private nonprofit institute or museum, government installation, or laboratory) in the United States or abroad other than the applicant's Ph.D.-granting institution. Applications are encouraged from underrepresented minorities and persons with disabilities.

Financial data Grants are $86,000 per year, including a stipend of $58,000 per year, a research allowance of $19,000 per year, and a fringe benefit allowance of $9,000 per year.

Duration 2 years.

Number awarded 10 each year.

Deadline January of each year.

[1206]
AWARDS FOR FACULTY AT TRIBAL COLLEGES AND UNIVERSITIES

National Endowment for the Humanities
Attn: Division of Research Programs
1100 Pennsylvania Avenue, N.W., Room 318
Washington, DC 20506
(202) 606-8200   Toll Free: (800) NEH-1121
Fax: (202) 606-8204   TDD: (866) 372-2930
E-mail: FacultyAwards@neh.gov
Web: www.neh.gov/grants/guidelines/AF_TCU.html

Summary To provide funding to faculty members at Tribal Colleges and Universities (TCUs) who are interested in working on a research project in the humanities.

Eligibility This program is open to current and retired faculty members affiliated with a TCU. Applicants must be U.S. citizens or foreign nationals who have resided in the United States or its jurisdictions for at least 3 years. Eligible projects include conducting research in primary and secondary materials; producing articles, monographs, books, digital materials, archaeological site reports, translations, editions, or other scholarly resources; or conducting basic research leading to the improvement of an existing undergraduate course or the

achievement of institutional or community research goals. Support is not provided for graduate course work, but the proposed project may contribute to the completion of a doctoral dissertation. Grants are not provided for curricular or pedagogical methods, theories, or surveys; preparation or revision of textbooks; research leading to the improvement of graduate courses; works in the creative or performing arts; projects that seek to promote a particular political, philosophical, religious, or ideological point of view; or projects that advocate a particular program of social action. Selection is based on: 1) the intellectual significance of the proposed project, including its value to scholars and general audiences in the humanities; 2) the quality or promise of quality of the applicant as a humanities teacher and researcher; 3) the quality of the conception, definition, organization, and description of the project; and 4) the feasibility of the proposed plan of work; and 5) the likelihood that the applicant will complete the project.

Financial data The grant is $4,200 per month of full-time work, to a maximum of $50,400 for 12 months.

Duration 2 to 12 months.

Number awarded Varies each year.

Deadline April of each year.

[1207]
BEHAVIORAL SCIENCES POSTDOCTORAL FELLOWSHIPS IN EPILEPSY

Epilepsy Foundation
Attn: Research Department
8301 Professional Place
Landover, MD 20785-2237
(301) 459-3700   Toll Free: (800) EFA-1000
Fax: (301) 577-2684   TDD: (800) 332-2070
E-mail: grants@efa.org
Web: www.epilepsyfoundation.org

Summary To provide funding to postdoctorates in the behavioral sciences (especially Native Americans, other minorities, women, and individuals with disabilities) who wish to pursue research training in an area related to epilepsy.

Eligibility Applicants must have received a Ph.D. or equivalent degree in a field of social science, including (but not limited to) sociology, social work, anthropology, nursing, or economics. They must be interested in receiving additional research training to prepare for a career in clinical behavioral aspects of epilepsy. Academic faculty holding the rank of instructor or above are not eligible, nor are graduate or medical students, medical residents, permanent government employees, or employees in private industry. Because these fellowships are designed as training opportunities, the quality of the training plans and environment are considered in the selection process. Other selection criteria include the scientific quality of the proposed research, a statement regarding the relevance of the research to epilepsy, the applicant's qualifications, the preceptor's qualifications, adequacy of the facility, and related epilepsy programs at the institution. Applications from women, members of minority groups, and people with disabilities are especially encouraged. U.S. citizenship is not required, but the research must be conducted in the United States.

Financial data Grants up to $40,000 are available.

Duration 1 year.

Number awarded Varies each year.

Deadline March of each year.

[1208]
BEYOND MARGINS AWARD

PEN American Center
Attn: Beyond Margins Coordinator
588 Broadway, Suite 303
New York, NY 10012
(212) 334-1660, ext. 108   Fax: (212) 334-2181
E-mail: nick@pen.org
Web: www.pen.org/page.php/prmID/280

Summary   To recognize and reward Native Americans and other outstanding authors of color from any country.

Eligibility   This award is presented to an author of color (African, Arab, Asian, Caribbean, Latino, and Native American) whose book-length writings were published in the United States during the current calendar year. Works of fiction, literary nonfiction, biography/memoir, and other works of literary character are strongly preferred. U.S. citizenship or residency is not required. Nominations must be submitted by publishers or agents.

Financial data   The prize is $1,000.

Duration   The prizes are awarded annually.

Number awarded   5 each year.

Deadline   December of each year.

[1209]
BYRD FELLOWSHIP PROGRAM

Ohio State University
Byrd Polar Research Center
Attn: Fellowship Committee
Scott Hall Room 108
1090 Carmack Road
Columbus, OH 43210-1002
(614) 292-6531   Fax: (614) 292-4697
Web: bprc.osu.edu/byrdfellow

Summary   To provide funding to postdoctorates (including Native Americans and members of other underrepresented groups) who are interested in conducting research on the Arctic or Antarctic areas at Ohio State University.

Eligibility   This program is open to postdoctorates of superior academic background who are interested in conducting advanced research on either Arctic or Antarctic problems at the Byrd Polar Research Center at Ohio State University. Applicants must have received their doctorates within the past 5 years. Each application should include a statement of general research interest, a description of the specific research to be conducted during the fellowship, and a curriculum vitae. Women, minorities, Vietnam-era veterans, disabled veterans, and individuals with disabilities are particularly encouraged to apply.

Financial data   The stipend is $40,000 per year; an allowance of $3,000 for research and travel is also provided.

Duration   18 months.

Additional information   This program was established by a major gift from the Byrd Foundation in memory of Rear Admiral Richard Evelyn Byrd and Marie Ames Byrd, his wife. Except for field work or other research activities requiring absence from campus, fellows are expected to be in residence at the university for the duration of the program.

Deadline   October of each year.

[1210]
CAREER AWARDS FOR MEDICAL SCIENTISTS

Burroughs Wellcome Fund
21 T.W. Alexander Drive, Suite 100
P.O. Box 13901
Research Triangle Park, NC 27709-3901
(919) 991-5100   Fax: (919) 991-5160
E-mail: info@bwfund.org
Web: www.bwfund.org

Summary   To provide funding to biomedical scientists in the United States and Canada (particularly Native Americans, other underrepresented minorities, and women) who require assistance to make the transition from postdoctoral training to faculty appointment.

Eligibility   This program is open to citizens and permanent residents of the United States and Canada who have an M.D., D.D.S., D.V.M., Pharm.D., or equivalent clinical degree. Applicants must be interested in a program of research training in the area of basic biomedical, disease-oriented, translational, or molecular, genetic, or pharmacological epidemiology research. Training must take place at a degree-granting medical school, graduate school, hospital, or research institute in the United States or Canada. Each U.S. and Canadian institution may nominate up to 5 candidates. The sponsor encourages institutions to nominate women and underrepresented minorities (African Americans, Hispanics, or Native Americans); if a woman or underrepresented minority is among the initial 5 candidates, the institution may nominate a sixth candidate who is a woman or underrepresented minority. Following their postdoctoral training, awardees may accept a faculty position at a U.S. or Canadian institution.

Financial data   For each year of postdoctoral support, the stipend is $65,000, the research allowance is $20,500, and the administrative fee is $9,500. For each year of faculty support, the stipend is $150,000, the research allowance is $3,000, and the administrative fee is $17,000. The maximum portion of the award that can be used during the postdoctoral period is $190,000 or $95,000 per year. The faculty portion of the award is $700,000 minus the portion used during the postdoctoral years.

Duration   The awards provide up to 2 years of postdoctoral support and up to 3 years of support during the faculty appointment.

Additional information   This program began in 1995 as Career Awards in the Biomedical Sciences (CABS). It was revised to its current format in 2006 as a result of the NIH K99/R00 Pathway to Independence program. As the CABS, the program provided more than $100 million in support to 241 U.S. and Canadian scientists. Awardees are required to devote at least 75% of their time to research-related activities.

Number awarded   Varies each year: recently, 5 of these awards were granted.

Deadline   September of each year.

[1211]
CAREER DEVELOPMENT AWARD TO PROMOTE DIVERSITY IN NEUROSCIENCE RESEARCH

National Institute of Neurological Disorders and Stroke
Attn: Office of Minority Health and Research
6001 Executive Boulevard, Suite 2150
Bethesda, MD 20892-9527
(301) 496-3102   Fax: (301) 594-5929
TDD: (301) 451-0088 E-mail: jonesmiche@ninds.nih.gov
Web: www.ninds.nih.gov

Summary To provide funding to neurological research scientists who are Native Americans or members of other underrepresented groups interested in making a transition to a career as an independent investigator.

Eligibility This program is open to full-time faculty members at domestic, for-profit and nonprofit, public and private institutions, such as universities, colleges, hospitals, and laboratories. Applicants must be junior neuroscience investigators making the transition to an independent scientific career at the senior postdoctoral and junior faculty stages under the supervision of a qualified mentor. They must qualify as 1) a member of an ethnic or racial group shown to be underrepresented in health-related sciences on a national basis; 2) an individual with a disability; or 3) an individual from a disadvantaged background, including those from a low-income family and those from a social, cultural, and/or educational environment that has inhibited them from preparation for a research career. Selection is based on qualifications of the applicant, soundness of the proposed career development plan, training in the responsible conduct of research, nature and scientific/technical merit of the proposed research plan, qualifications and appropriateness of the mentor, environment and institutional commitment to the applicant's career, and strength of the description of how this particular award will promote diversity within the institution or in science nationally. Only U.S. citizens, nationals, and permanent residents are eligible.

Financial data Grants provide an annual award of up to $85,000 for salary and fringe benefits and an annual research allowance of up to $50,000 for direct research costs. The institution may apply for up to 8% of direct costs for facilities and administrative costs.

Duration 3 to 5 years; nonrenewable.

Additional information Recipients must devote 75% of full-time professional effort to conducting health-related research.

Number awarded Varies each year.

Deadline February, June, or October of each year.

[1212]
CAREER DEVELOPMENT AWARDS IN DIABETES RESEARCH

Juvenile Diabetes Research Foundation International
Attn: Grant Administrator
26 Broadway, 14th Floor
New York, NY 10004
(212) 479-7572   Toll Free: (800) 533-CURE
Fax: (212) 785-9595   E-mail: info@jdrf.org
Web: www.jdrf.org/index.cfm?page_id=111715

Summary To assist Native American and other young scientists to develop into independent investigators in diabetes-related research.

Eligibility This program is open to postdoctorates early in their faculty careers who show promise as diabetes researchers. Applicants must have received their first doctoral (M.D., Ph.D., D.M.D., D.V.M., or equivalent) degree at least 3 but not more than 7 years previously. They may not have an academic position at the associate professor, professor, or equivalent level, but they must be a faculty member (instructor or assistant professor) at a university, health science center, or comparable institution with strong, well-established research and training programs. The proposed research must relate to Type 1 diabetes, but it may be basic or clinical. There are no citizenship requirements. Applications are encouraged from women, members of minority groups underrepresented in the sciences, and people with disabilities. The proposed research may be conducted at foreign and domestic, for-profit and nonprofit, and public and private institutions, including universities, colleges, hospitals, laboratories, units of state and local government, and eligible agencies of the federal government. Selection is based on the applicant's perceived ability and potential for a career in Type 1 diabetes research, the caliber of the proposed research, and the quality and commitment of the host institution.

Financial data The total award may be up to $150,000 each year. Indirect costs cannot exceed 10%.

Duration Up to 5 years.

Additional information Fellows must spend up to 75% of their time in research.

Deadline January or July of each year.

[1213]
CAREER DEVELOPMENT GRANTS

American Association of University Women
Attn: AAUW Educational Foundation
301 ACT Drive, Department 60
P.O. Box 4030
Iowa City, IA 52243-4030
(319) 337-1716, ext. 60   Fax: (319) 337-1204
E-mail: aauw@act.org
Web: www.aauw.org

Summary To provide financial assistance to Native American and other women who are seeking career advancement, career change, or reentry into the workforce.

Eligibility This program is open to women who are U.S. citizens or permanent residents, have earned a bachelor's degree, received their most recent degree more than 4 years ago, and are making career changes, seeking to advance in current careers, or reentering the work force. Applicants must be interested in working toward a master's degree, second bachelor's or associate degree, professional degree (e.g., M.D., J.D.), certification program, or technical school certificate. They must be planning to undertake course work at an accredited 2- or 4-year college or university (or a technical school that is licensed, accredited, or approved by the U.S. Department of Education). Special consideration is given to women of color and women pursuing credentials in nontraditional fields. Support is not provided for prerequisite course work or for Ph.D. course work or dissertations. Selection is based on demonstrated commitment to education and equity for women and girls, reason for seeking higher education or technical training, degree to which study plan is consistent with career objectives, potential for success in chosen field, documentation of opportunities in chosen field, feasibility of study plans and proposed time schedule, validity of proposed budget and budget narrative (including sufficient outside support), and quality of written proposal.

Financial data Grants range from $2,000 to $12,000. Funds may be used for tuition, fees, books, supplies, local transportation, dependent child care, or purchase of a computer required for the study program.

Duration 1 year, beginning in July; nonrenewable.

Additional information The filing fee is $35.

Number awarded Varies each year; recently, 47 of these grants, with a value of $500,000, were awarded.

Deadline December of each year.

[1214]
CAREER TECHNOLOGY SCHOLARSHIP

Chickasaw Foundation
110 West 12th Street
P.O. Box 1726
Ada, OK 74821-1726
(580) 421-9030   Fax: (580) 421-9031
E-mail: ChickasawFoundation@chickasaw.net
Web: www.chickasawfoundation.org/index_20.htm

Summary To provide financial assistance for vocational school to employees of the Chickasaw Nation.

Eligibility This program is open to employees of the Chickasaw Nation who are currently enrolled at a career technology, vocational/technical, or trade school. Applicants must be at least 18 years of age and have a GPA of 2.0 or higher. Along with their application, they must submit high school or college transcripts, 2 letters of recommendation, a copy of their Chickasaw Nation citizenship card, a copy of their Chickasaw Nation employee identification badge, and a 1-page essay on their long-term goals and plans for achieving them. Financial need is not considered in the selection process.

Financial data The stipend is $1,000.

Duration 1 year.

Number awarded 1 each year.

Deadline August of each year.

[1215]
CAROLINA POSTDOCTORAL PROGRAM FOR FACULTY DIVERSITY

University of North Carolina at Chapel Hill
Attn: Office of the Vice Chancellor for Research
312 South Building, CB #4000
Chapel Hill, NC 27599-4000
(919) 962-4041   Fax: (919) 962-1476
E-mail: susan_walters@.unc.edu
Web: research.unc.edu

Summary To support Native American and other minority scholars who are interested in teaching and conducting research at the University of North Carolina (UNC).

Eligibility This program is open to scholars from underrepresented groups who have completed their doctoral degree within the past 4 years. Applicants must be interested in teaching and conducting research at UNC. Preference is given to U.S. citizens and permanent residents. Selection is based on the evidence of scholarship potential and ability to compete for tenure-track appointments at UNC and other research universities.

Financial data Fellows receive $36,282 per year, plus an allowance for research and travel. Health benefits are also available.

Duration Up to 2 years.

Additional information Fellows must be in residence at the Chapel Hill campus for the duration of the program. They teach 1 course per year and spend the rest of the time in research. This program began in 1983.

Number awarded 5 or 6 each year.

Deadline January of each year.

[1216]
CENTER FOR ADVANCED STUDY IN THE BEHAVIORAL SCIENCES RESIDENTIAL POSTDOCTORAL FELLOWSHIPS

Center for Advanced Study in the Behavioral Sciences
Attn: Secretary and Program Coordinator
75 Alta Road
Stanford, CA 94305-8090
(650) 321-2052   Fax: (650) 321-1192
E-mail: secretary@casbs.org
Web: www.casbs.org

Summary To provide funding to behavioral scientists (especially Native Americans and others who will increase diversity in the field) interested in conducting research at the Center for Advanced Study in the Behavioral Sciences in Stanford, California.

Eligibility Eligible to be nominated for this fellowship are scientists and scholars from this country or abroad who show exceptional accomplishment or promise in the core social and behavioral disciplines: anthropology, economics, political science, psychology, or sociology; applications are also accepted from scholars in a wide range of humanistic disciplines, education, linguistics, and the biological sciences. Selection is based on standing in the field rather than on the merit of a particular project under way at a given time. A special effort is made to promote diversity among the scholars by encouraging participation from groups that often have been overlooked in academia: younger scholars, women, minorities, international scholars, and scholars whose home universities are not research-oriented.

Financial data The stipend is based on the fellow's regular salary for the preceding year, with a cap of $60,000. In most cases, the fellow contributes to the cost of the stipend with support from sabbatical or other funding source.

Duration From 9 to 11 months.

Additional information Fellows must be in residence in a community within 10 miles of the center for the duration of the program.

Number awarded Approximately 45 each year.

Deadline February of each year.

[1217]
CHANCELLOR'S POSTDOCTORAL FELLOWSHIPS FOR ACADEMIC DIVERSITY

University of California at Berkeley
Attn: Office for Faculty Equity
200 California Hall
Berkeley, CA 94720-1500
(510) 642-1935   E-mail: admin.ofe@berkeley.edu
Web: vcei.berkeley.edu/ChancPostdocFellowship

Summary To provide an opportunity for Native Americans and other recent postdoctorates who will increase diversity at the University of California at Berkeley to conduct research on the campus.

Eligibility This program is open to U.S. citizens and permanent residents who received a doctorate within 3 years of the start of the fellowship. The program particularly solicits applications from individuals who are members of groups that are underrepresented in American universities (e.g., women, ethnic minorities, religious minorities, differently-abled, lesbian/gay/bisexual/transgender). Special consideration is given to applicants committed to careers in university research and teaching and whose life experience, research, or employment background will contribute significantly to academic diversity and excellence at the Berkeley campus.

Financial data The stipend is $41,496 per year (11 months, plus 1 month vacation). The award also includes health insurance, vision and dental benefits, and up to $4,000 for research-related and program travel expenses.

Duration 1 year; may be renewed 1 additional year.

Additional information Research opportunities, mentoring, and guidance are provided as part of the program.

Number awarded Varies each year; recently, 5 of these fellowships were awarded.

Deadline November of each year.

[1218]
CHARLES A. RYSKAMP RESEARCH FELLOWSHIPS

American Council of Learned Societies
Attn: Office of Fellowships and Grants
633 Third Avenue
New York, NY 10017-6795
(212) 697-1505   Fax: (212) 949-8058
E-mail: fellowships@acls.org
Web: www.acls.org/programs/ryskamp

Summary To provide research funding to assistant professors (particularly Native Americans, other minorities, and women) who specialize in disciplines of the humanities and the humanities-related social sciences.

Eligibility This program is open to advanced assistant and untenured associate professors in the humanities and related social sciences. Applicants must have successfully completed their institution's last reappointment review before tenure review. They must have a Ph.D. or equivalent degree and be employed at an academic institution in the United States. Appropriate fields of specialization include, but are not limited to, American studies; anthropology; archaeology; art and architectural history; classics; economics; film; geography; history; languages and literatures; legal studies; linguistics; musicology; philosophy; political science; psychology; religious studies; rhetoric, communication, and media studies; sociology; and theater, dance, and performance studies. Proposals in those fields of the social sciences are eligible only if they employ predominantly humanistic approaches (e.g., economic history, law and literature, political philosophy). Proposals in interdisciplinary and cross-disciplinary studies are welcome, as are proposals focused on any geographic region or on any cultural or linguistic group. Applicants are encouraged to spend substantial periods of their leaves in residential interdisciplinary centers, research libraries, or other scholarly archives in the United States or abroad. Appli-

cations are particularly invited from women and members of minority groups.

Financial data Fellows receive a stipend of $64,000, a grant of $2,500 for research and travel, and the possibility of an additional summer's support, if justified by a persuasive case.

Duration 1 academic year (9 months) plus an additional summer's research (2 months) if justified.

Additional information This program, first available for the 2002-03 academic year, is supported by funding from the Andrew W. Mellon Foundation.

Number awarded Up to 12 each year.

Deadline September of each year.

[1219]
CHICKASAW NATION DEGREE COMPLETION INCENTIVE AWARDS

Chickasaw Nation
Attn: Department of Education Services
300 Rosedale Road
Ada, OK 74820
(580) 421-7711   Fax: (580) 436-3733
E-mail: education.services@chickasaw.net
Web: www.chickasaweducationservices.com/index_90.htm

Summary To recognize and reward citizens of the Chickasaw Nation who have completed an undergraduate or graduate degree at a school in any state.

Eligibility This award is available to members of the Chickasaw Nation when they complete a bachelor's degree or higher. Applicants must submit a final official college transcript showing the degree awarded.

Financial data The award is $1,000.

Duration Members of the Chickasaw Nation are eligible for this award each time they complete an academic degree.

Number awarded Varies each year.

Deadline Applications must be submitted within 6 months after graduation.

[1220]
CHIPS QUINN SCHOLARS PROGRAM

Freedom Forum
Attn: Chips Quinn Scholars Program
555 Pennsylvania Avenue, N.W.
Washington, DC 20001
(202) 292-6271   Fax: (202) 292-6275
E-mail: kcatone@freedomforum.org
Web: www.chipsquinn.org

Summary To provide work experience to Native American and other minority college students or recent graduates who are majoring in journalism.

Eligibility This program is open to students of color who are college juniors, seniors, or recent graduates with journalism majors or career goals in newspapers. Candidates must be nominated or endorsed by journalism faculty, campus media advisers, editors of newspapers, or leaders of minority journalism associations. Along with their application, they must submit a resume, transcripts, 2 letters of recommendation, and an essay of 200 to 500 words on why they want to be a Chips Quinn Scholar. Reporters must also submit 6 samples of published articles they have written; photographers must submit 10 to 20 photographs on a CD. Applicants must have a car and be available to work as a full-time intern during the spring or summer. U.S. citizenship or permanent resident status is required. Campus newspaper experience is strongly encouraged.

Financial data Students chosen for this program receive a travel stipend to attend a Multimedia training program in Nashville, Tennessee prior to reporting for their internship, a $500 housing allowance from the Freedom Forum, and a competitive salary during their internship.

Duration Internships are for 10 to 12 weeks, in spring or summer.

Additional information This program was established in 1991 in memory of the late John D. Quinn Jr., managing editor of the *Poughkeepsie Journal*. Funding is provided by the Freedom Forum, formerly the Gannett Foundation. After graduating from college and obtaining employment with a newspaper, alumni of this program are eligible to apply for fellowship support to attend professional journalism development activities.

Number awarded Approximately 70 each year. Since the program began, more than 1,200 scholars have been selected.

Deadline October of each year.

[1221]
CIRCLE OF HONOR AWARD

Tulsa Library Trust
c/o Tulsa City-County Library System
400 Civic Center
Tulsa, OK 74103-3830
(918) 549-7363   Fax: (918) 549-7370
E-mail: trust@tulsalibrary.org
Web: www.tulsalibrarytrust.org/current-projects.php

Summary To recognize and reward American Indians who have enriched the lives of others.

Eligibility This award is available to American Indians whose achievements and contributions have enriched the lives of others. Recipients are inducted into the Circle of Honor at a ceremony in Tulsa, Oklahoma as recognition for their actions in the face of adversity, commitment to the preservation of American Indian culture, and legacy for future generations.

Financial data The award is $5,000.

Duration The award is presented biennially.

Additional information This award was first presented in 2004.

Number awarded 1 each even-numbered year.

Deadline Deadline not specified.

[1222]
CIRI FOUNDATION INTERNSHIP PROGRAM

Cook Inlet Region, Inc.
Attn: The CIRI Foundation
3600 San Jeronimo Drive, Suite 256
Anchorage, AK 99508-2870
(907) 793-3575   Toll Free: (800) 764-3382
Fax: (907) 793-3585   E-mail: tcf@thecirifoundation.org
Web: www.thecirifoundation.org/internships.htm

Summary To provide on-the-job training to Alaska Natives who are original enrollees to the Cook Inlet Region, Inc. (CIRI) and their lineal descendants.

Eligibility This program is open to Alaska Native enrollees to CIRI under the Alaska Native Claims Settlement Act (ANCSA) of 1971 and their lineal descendants. Applicants must 1) be enrolled in a 2- or 4-year academic or graduate degree program with a GPA of 3.0 or higher; 2) have recently completed an undergraduate or graduate degree program; or 3) be enrolled or have recently completed a technical skills training program at an accredited or otherwise approved postsecondary institution. Along with their application, they must submit a 500-word statement on their areas of interest, their educational and career goals, how their career goals relate to their educational goals, and the type of work experience they would like to gain as it relates to their career and educational goals.

Financial data The intern's wage is based on a trainee position and is determined by the employer of the intern with the approval of the foundation (which pays one half of the intern's wages).

Duration Internships are approved on a quarterly basis for 480 hours of part-time or full-time employment. Interns may reapply on a quarter-by-quarter basis, not to exceed 12 consecutive months.

Additional information The foundation and the intern applicant work together to identify an appropriate placement experience. The employer hires the intern. Placement may be with Cook Inlet Region, Inc., a firm related to the foundation, or a business or service organization located anywhere in the United States. The intern may be placed with more than 1 company during the internship period. Interns may receive academic credit.

Deadline March, June, September, or November of each year.

[1223]
CLAIRE M. FAGIN FELLOWSHIP

American Academy of Nursing
Attn: Geriatric Nursing Capacity Program
888 17th Street, N.W., Suite 800
Washington, DC 20006
(202) 777-1170   Fax: (202) 777-0107
E-mail: bagnc@aannet.org
Web: www.geriatricnursing.org

Summary To provide funding to minority and other nurses interested in a program of postdoctoral research training in geriatric nursing.

Eligibility This program is open to registered nurses who hold a doctoral degree in nursing and have a faculty position as an assistant or associate professor at a school of nursing. Recent doctorates in nursing are also eligible. Priority is given to those who received a Ph.D. within the past 7 years. Applicants must demonstrate evidence of commitment to a career in geriatric nursing and education and the potential to develop into independent investigators. They must submit 1) a professional development plan that identifies activities intended to prepare the applicant in research, teaching, and leadership; and 2) a geriatric nursing research project consistent with their interests and previous research or clinical experience, including a mentor who is a geriatric nurse scientist and with whom they will work. Selection is based on potential for substantial long-term contributions to the knowledge base in geriatric nursing; leadership potential; evidence of commitment to a career in academic geriatric nursing; and evidence of involvement in educational, research, and professional activities. U.S citizenship or permanent resident status is required. Members of underrepresented minority groups (American Indians, Alaska Natives, Asians, Blacks or African Americans, Hispanics or Latinos/Latinas, Native Hawaiians or other Pacific Islanders) are especially encouraged to apply.

Financial data The stipend is $60,000 per year. An additional $5,000 is available to fellows whose research includes the study of pain in the elderly.

Duration 2 years.

Additional information This program began in 2001 with funding from the John A. Hartford Foundation. In 2004, the Atlantic Philanthropies of New York City provided additional support and the Mayday Fund added funding for scholars who focus on the study of pain in the elderly.

Number awarded Varies each year; recently, 9 of these fellowships were awarded.

Deadline January of each year.

[1224]
COCOPAH ACHIEVEMENT INCENTIVE AWARDS

Cocopah Indian Tribe
Attn: Education Department
County 15th and Avenue G
Somerton, AZ 85350
(928) 627-2101   Fax: (928) 627-3173
E-mail: cocopah@cocopah.com
Web: www.cocopah.com/education.html

Summary To recognize and reward members of the Cocopah Indian Nation who have completed an academic degree.

Eligibility This program is open to enrolled members of the Cocopah Indian Nation after they have completed an associate, bachelor's, master's or doctoral degree at an accredited college or university in the United States. Applicants must have received financial assistance from the tribal education department during their course of study. They must submit a copy of their diploma.

Financial data Awards are $1,000.

Duration Awards are presented each time an enrolled member completes an academic degree.

Number awarded Varies each year.

Deadline Deadline not specified.

[1225]
COLLABORATIVE RESEARCH FELLOWSHIPS

American Council of Learned Societies
Attn: Office of Fellowships and Grants
633 Third Avenue
New York, NY 10017-6795
(212) 697-1505   Fax: (212) 949-8058
E-mail: fellowships@acls.org
Web: www.acls.org

Summary To provide funding for collaborative research to scholars (particularly Native Americans, other minorities, and women) in any discipline of the humanities and the humanities-related social sciences.

Eligibility This program is open to teams of 2 or more scholars interested in collaborating on a single, substantive project. The project coordinator must have an appointment at a U.S.-based institution of higher education; other project members may be at institutions outside the United States or may be independent scholars. Appropriate fields of specialization include, but are not limited to, American studies; anthropology; archaeology; art and architectural history; classics; economics; film; geography; history; languages and literatures; legal studies; linguistics; musicology; philosophy; political science; psychology; religious studies; rhetoric, communication, and media studies; sociology; and theater, dance, and performance studies. Proposals in those fields of the social sciences are eligible only if they employ predominantly humanistic approaches (e.g., economic history, law and literature, political philosophy). Proposals in interdisciplinary and cross-disciplinary studies are welcome, as are proposals focused on a geographic region or on a cultural or linguistic group. Applications are particularly invited from women and members of minority groups.

Financial data The amount of the grant depends on the number of collaborators, their academic rank, and the duration of research leaves. Funding for salaries is provided at the rate of $60,000 for full professors, $40,000 for associate professors, or $35,000 for assistant professors. An additional $20,000 may be provided for collaboration funds (e.g., travel, materials, research assistance). The maximum amount for any single project is $140,000.

Duration Up to 24 months.

Additional information This program, established in 2008, is supported by funding from the Andrew W. Mellon Foundation.

Number awarded Up to 7 each year.

Deadline September of each year.

[1226]
COMMUNITY ARTS SYMPOSIUM PROGRAM OF THE NATIONAL MUSEUM OF THE AMERICAN INDIAN

National Museum of the American Indian
Attn: Artist Leadership Program
Cultural Resources Center
4220 Silver Hill Road
Suitland, MD 20746-2863
(301) 238-1544   Fax: (301) 238-3200
E-mail: ALP@si.edu
Web: www.nmai.si.edu/icap/leadership.html

Summary To provide Native American professional artists with an opportunity to organize and conduct a symposium on an art-related topic in their local community.

Eligibility This program is open to Native artists from the western Hemisphere and Hawaii who are recognized by their community and can demonstrate significant artistic accomplishments in any media (e.g., visual arts, media arts, performance arts, literature). Students enrolled in a degree program are ineligible. Applicants must be interested in developing a symposium discussing an art-related topic of relevance to their local community. The project must have far-reaching significance and produce new knowledge and understanding. Themes for the symposium may involve identity, language, or the environment. Proposals that reflect intercultural exchanges among indigenous peoples of the Western Hemisphere are strongly encouraged. Applications must include a 500-word research proposal, 500-word project proposal, digital portfolio of 10 images or 5 minutes, 2 letters of support, a resume, and a 75-word statement describing their purpose, goal, and intended results.

Financial data The grant is $6,000, to be used to cover project costs, supplies, and materials.

Duration Participants first spend 10 days in Washington, D.C. consulting with staff of the National Museum of the American Indian (NMAI), after which they return to their community and complete a project within 1 year.

Additional information This is a 2-part program. In the first part, participants visit Washington, D.C. for 10 days to conduct research in collections of the NMAI and other local museums, participate in interviews with Collections and Education staff, conduct lunch-time presentations for NMAI staff and the museum public, and visit area galleries. Following the completion of that visit, participants return to their community to share the knowledge learned from the experience and research visit and conduct their project. They must collaborate with NMAI and community members on the selection of symposium panelists, moderator, and location; draft a press release; refine the symposium content and direction; and outline how the symposium will be documented and posted on the NMAI web site.

Number awarded 1 each year.

Deadline April of each year.

[1227]
CONGRESSIONAL FELLOWSHIPS OF THE AMERICAN ASSOCIATION FOR THE ADVANCEMENT OF SCIENCE

American Association for the Advancement of Science
Attn: Science and Technology Policy Fellowships
1200 New York Avenue, N.W.
Washington, DC 20005-3920
(202) 326-6700   Fax: (202) 289-4950
E-mail: fellowships@aaas.org
Web: fellowships.aaas.org

Summary To provide postdoctoral scientists and engineers (particularly Native Americans, other underrepresented minorities, and individuals with disabilities) with an opportunity to work as special legislative assistants on the staffs of members of Congress or Congressional committees.

Eligibility This program is open to doctoral-level scientists (Ph.D., M.D., D.V.M., D.Sc., and other terminal degrees) in any physical, biological, medical, or social science; any field of engineering; or any relevant interdisciplinary field. Engineers with a master's degree and at least 3 years of professional experience are also eligible. Applicants must demonstrate exceptional competence in some area of science or engineering; have a good scientific and technical background; be cognizant of many matters in nonscientific areas; demonstrate sensitivity toward political and social issues; have a strong interest and some experience in applying personal knowledge toward the solution of societal problems; and be interested in working as special legislative assistants for Congress. U.S. citizenship is required; federal employees are not eligible. Members of underrepresented minority groups and persons with disabilities are encouraged to apply.

Financial data The stipend is $74,872. Also provided are a $4,000 relocation allowance for fellows from outside the Washington, D.C. area, reimbursement for health insurance, and a $4,000 travel allowance.

Duration 1 year, beginning in September.

Additional information The program includes an orientation on Congressional and executive branch operations and a year-long seminar program on issues involving science and public policy. Approximately 30 other national science and engineering societies sponsor fellows in collaboration with this program; for a list of all of those, contact the sponsor.

Number awarded 2 each year.

Deadline December of each year.

[1228]
CURRICULUM DEVELOPMENT, IMPLEMENTATION, AND SUSTAINABILITY GRANTS

United Negro College Fund Special Programs
  Corporation
Attn: Institute for International Public Policy
6402 Arlington Boulevard, Suite 600
Falls Church, VA 22042
(703) 677-3400   Toll Free: (800) 530-6232
Fax: (703) 205-7645   E-mail: iippl@uncfsp.org
Web: www.uncfsp.org

Summary To provide funding to faculty at Tribal Colleges or Universities (TCUs) or other Minority Serving Institutions (MSIs) who are interested in developing new courses or enhancing existing courses focusing on international affairs, international relations, area studies, or Less Commonly Taught Languages (LCTLs).

Eligibility This program is open to full-time and adjunct faculty at Alaska Native Serving Institutions, Hispanic Serving Institutions, Historically Black Colleges and Universities, Native Hawaiian Serving Institutions, and Tribal Colleges or University/Tribally Controlled Colleges and Universities. Applicants must be proposing to conduct a project involving 1) development of new courses focusing on international affairs, international relations, area studies, or LCTLs; 2) enhancement of existing course curricula; 3) development and enhancement of strategic plans; 4) program development assessment; and/or 5) staff development. They may be instructors of international relations, foreign policy, foreign languages (especially LCTLs), political science, sociology, economics, statistics, journalism, world geography, or other relevant disciplines. Selection is based on significance of the project (15 points), quality of project design (15 points), quality of project personnel (10 points), quality of management plan (15 points), adequacy of resources (15 points), quality of project evaluation (15 points), and project budget (15 points).

Financial data The grant is $5,000 per year.

Duration 2 years.

Number awarded 3 each year.

Deadline January of each year.

[1229]
DANIEL H. EFRON RESEARCH AWARD

American College of Neuropsychopharmacology
Attn: Executive Office
5034-A Thoroughbred Lane
Brentwood, TN 37027
(615) 324-2360   Fax: (615) 523-1715
E-mail: acnp@acnp.org
Web: www.acnp.org/programs/awards.aspx

Summary To recognize and reward young scientists (especially Native Americans, other minorities, and women) who have conducted outstanding basic or translational research in neuropsychopharmacology.

Eligibility This award is available to scientists who are younger than 50 years of age. Nominees must have made an outstanding basic or translational contribution to neuropsychopharmacology. The contribution may be preclinical or work that emphasizes the relationship between basic and clinical research. Selection is based on the quality of the contribution and its impact on advancing neuropsychopharmacology. Membership in the American College of Neuropsychopharmacology (ACNP) is not required. Nomination of women and minorities is highly encouraged.

Financial data The award consists of an expense-paid trip to the ACNP annual meeting, a monetary honorarium, and a plaque.

Duration The award is presented annually.

Additional information This award was first presented in 1974.

Number awarded 1 each year.

Deadline Nominations must be submitted by June of each year.

[1230]
DEFENSE UNIVERSITY RESEARCH INSTRUMENTATION PROGRAM

Army Research Office
Attn: AMSRD-ARL-RO-SG-SI(DURIP)
4300 South Miami Boulevard
P.O. Box 12211
Research Triangle Park, NC 27709-2211
(919) 549-4207   Fax: (919) 549-4248
Web: www.arl.army.mil/www/default.cfm?Action=6&Page=8

Summary To provide funding to researchers at colleges and universities in designated states, especially those at Tribal Colleges and Universities (TCUs) or other Minority Institutions (MIs), for the purchase of equipment.

Eligibility This program is open to researchers at colleges and universities in the United States with degree-granting programs in science, mathematics, and/or engineering. Applicants must be seeking funding for the acquisition of major equipment to augment current or to develop new research capabilities to support research in technical areas of interest to the Department of Defense. Proposals are encouraged from researchers at MIs.

Financial data Grants range from $50,000 to $1,000,000; recently, they averaged $235,000.

Duration Grants are typically 1 year in length.

Number awarded Varies each year; recently, 222 of these grants, worth $52.5 million, were awarded.

Deadline September of each year.

[1231]
DEPARTMENT OF DEFENSE EXPERIMENTAL PROGRAM TO STIMULATE COMPETITIVE RESEARCH

Army Research Office
Attn: AMSRL-RO-RI
4300 South Miami Boulevard
P.O. Box 12211
Research Triangle Park, NC 27709-2211
(919) 549-4234   Fax: (919) 549-4248
Web: www.arl.army.mil/www/default.cfm?Action=6&Page=8

Summary To provide funding to researchers at colleges and universities in designated states, particularly those at Tribal Colleges or Universities (TCUs) and other Minority Institutions (MIs).

Eligibility This program is open to researchers at colleges and universities in states and territories that traditionally have not received a large number of research awards (Alaska, Arkansas, Delaware, Idaho, Kansas, Kentucky, Louisiana, Maine, Montana, Nebraska, Nevada, New Hampshire, North Dakota, Oklahoma, Puerto Rico, Rhode Island, South Carolina, South Dakota, Tennessee, Vermont, U.S. Virgin Islands, West Virginia, and Wyoming). Special consideration is given to applications from scholars at MIs. All applying institutions must have an accredited, degree-granting program in science, engineering, or mathematics and a history of graduating students in those fields. Applicants must be proposing a program of research in a science, engineering, or mathematics field of interest to the Department of Defense.

Financial data Grants range from $300,000 to $600,000.

Duration Up to 3 years.

Number awarded Varies; a total of approximately $13 million in new awards is available through the participating Department of Defense agencies each year.

Deadline May of each year.

[1232]
DEPARTMENT OF HOMELAND SECURITY SMALL BUSINESS INNOVATION RESEARCH GRANTS

Department of Homeland Security
Homeland Security Advanced Research Projects Agency
Attn: SBIR Program Manager
Washington, DC 20528
(202) 254-6768   Toll Free: (800) 754-3043
Fax: (202) 254-7170   E-mail: elissa.sobolewski@dhs.gov
Web: www.dhs.gov/files/grants/gc_1247254058883.shtm

Summary To support small businesses (especially those owned by Native Americans, other minorities, disabled veterans, and women) that have the technological expertise to contribute to the research and development mission of the Department of Homeland Security (DHS).

Eligibility For the purposes of this program, a "small business" is defined as a firm that is organized for profit with a location in the United States; is in the legal form of an individual proprietorship, partnership, limited liability company, corporation, joint venture, association, trust, or cooperative; is at least 51% owned and controlled by 1 or more individuals who are citizens or permanent residents of the United States; and has (including its affiliates) fewer than 500 employees. The primary employment of the principal investigator must be with the firm at the time of award and during the conduct of the proposed project. Preference is given to women-owned small business concerns, service-disabled veteran small business concerns, veteran small business concerns, and socially and economically disadvantaged small business concerns. Women-owned small business concerns are those that are at least 51% owned by a woman or women who also control and operate them. Service-disabled veteran small business concerns are those that are at least 51% owned by a service-disabled veteran and controlled by such a veteran or (for veterans with permanent and severe disability) the spouse or permanent caregiver of such a veteran. Veteran small business concerns are those that are at least 51% owned by a veteran or veterans who also control and manage them. Socially and economically disadvantaged small business concerns are at least 51% owned by an Indian tribe, a Native Hawaiian organization, a Community Development Corporation, or 1 or more socially and economically disadvantaged individuals (African Americans, Hispanic Americans, Native Americans, Asian Pacific Americans, or subcontinent Asian Americans). The project must be performed in the United States. Currently, DHS has 7 research priorities: explosives; border and maritime security; command, control, and interoperability; human factors; infrastructure and geophysical; chemical and biological; and domestic nuclear detection. Selection is based on the soundness, technical merit, and innovation of the proposed approach and its incremental progress toward topic or subtopic solution; the qualifications of the proposed principal investigators, supporting staff, and consultants; and the potential for commercial application and the benefits expected to accrue from this commercialization.

Financial data Grants are offered in 2 phases. In phase 1, awards normally range up to $100,000 (or $150,000 for domestic nuclear detection); in phase 2, awards normally range up to $750,000 (or $1,000,000 for domestic nuclear detection).

Duration Phase 1 awards may extend up to 6 months; phase 2 awards may extend up to 2 years.

Number awarded Varies each year; recently, 61 Phase 1 awards were granted.

Deadline February of each year.

[1233]
DEPARTMENT OF HOMELAND SECURITY SUMMER FACULTY AND STUDENT RESEARCH TEAM PROGRAM

Oak Ridge Institute for Science and Education
Attn: Science and Engineering Education
P.O. Box 117
Oak Ridge, TN 37831-0117
(865) 574-1447   Fax: (865) 241-5219
E-mail: Patti.Obenour@orau.gov
Web: see.orau.org

Summary To provide an opportunity for teams of students and faculty from Tribal Colleges or Universities (TCUs) and other minority serving educational institutions to conduct summer research in areas of interest to the Department of Homeland Security (DHS).

Eligibility This program is open to teams of up to 2 students (undergraduate and/or graduate) and 1 faculty from Historically Black Colleges and Universities (HBCUs), Hispanic Serving Institutions (HSIs), Tribal Colleges and Universities (TCUs), Alaska Native Serving Institutions (ANSIs), and Native Hawaiian Serving Institutions (NHSIs). Applicants must be interested in conducting research at designated DHS Centers of Excellence in science, technology, engineering, or mathematics related to homeland security (HS-STEM), including explosives detection, mitigation, and response; social, behavioral, and economic sciences; risk and decision sciences; human factors aspects of technology; chemical threats and countermeasures; biological threats and countermeasures; community, commerce, and infrastructure resilience; food and agricultural security; transportation security; border security; immigration studies; maritime and port security; infrastructure protection; natural disasters and related geophysical studies; emergency preparedness and response; communications and interoperability; or advanced data analysis and visualization. Faculty must have a full-time appointment at an eligible institution and have received a Ph.D. in an HS-STEM discipline no more than 7 years previously; at least 2 years of full-time research and/or teaching experience is preferred. Students must have a GPA of 3.0 or higher and be enrolled full time. Undergraduates must be entering their junior or senior year. U.S. citizenship is required. Selection is based on relevance and intrinsic merit of the research (40%), faculty applicant qualifications (30%), academic benefit to the faculty applicant and his/her institution (10%), and student applicant qualifications (20%).

Financial data Stipends are $1,200 per week for faculty, $600 per week for graduate students, and $500 per week for undergraduates. Faculty members who live more than 50 miles from their assigned site may receive a relocation allowance of $1,500 and travel expenses up to an additional $500. Limited travel expenses for 1 round trip are reimbursed for undergraduate and graduate students living more than 50 miles from their assigned site.

Duration 12 weeks during the summer.

Additional information This program is funded by DHS and administered by Oak Ridge Institute for Science and Education (ORISE). Recently, the available DHS Centers of Excellence were the Center for Advancing Microbial Risk Assessment (led by Michigan State University and Drexel University); the Center for Risk and Economic Analysis of Terrorism Events (led by University of Southern California); the National Center for Food Protection and Defense (led by University of Minnesota); the Center of Excellence for Foreign Animal and Zoonotic Disease Defense (led by Texas A&M University and Kansas State University); the National Center for the Study of Preparedness and Catastrophic Event Response (led by Johns Hopkins University); the National Consortium for the Study of Terrorism and Responses to Terrorism (led by University of Maryland); the Center of Excellence for Awareness and Location of Explosives-Related Threats (led by Northeastern University and University of Rhode Island); the National Center for Border Security and Immigration (led by the University of Arizona and the University of Texas at El Paso); the Center for Maritime, Island and Remote and Extreme Environment Security (led by the University of Hawaii and Stevens Institute of Technology); the Center for Natural Disasters, Coastal Infrastructure, and Emergency Management (led by the University of North Carolina at Chapel Hill and Jackson State University); the National Transportation Security Center of Excellence (consisting of 7 institutions); and the Center of Excellence in Command, Control, and Interoperability (led by Purdue University and Rutgers University).

Number awarded Approximately 12 teams are selected each year.

Deadline January of each year.

[1234]
DEPARTMENT OF TRANSPORTATION SMALL BUSINESS INNOVATION RESEARCH GRANTS

Department of Transportation
Attn: Research and Innovative Technology Administration
John A. Volpe National Transportation Systems Center
55 Broadway, Kendall Square
Cambridge, MA 02142-1093
(617) 494-2051 Fax: (617) 494-2370
E-mail: leisa.moniz@dot.gov
Web: www.volpe.dot.gov/sbir/index.html

Summary To support small businesses (especially those owned by Native Americans, other minorities, veterans, and women) that have the technological expertise to contribute to the research and development mission of the Department of Transportation.

Eligibility For the purposes of this program, a "small business" is defined as a firm that is organized for profit with a location in the United States; is in the legal form of an individual proprietorship, partnership, limited liability company, corporation, joint venture, association, trust, or cooperative; is at least 51% owned and controlled by 1 or more individuals who are citizens or permanent residents of the United States; and has (including its affiliates) fewer than 500 employees. The primary employment of the principal investigator must be with the firm at the time of award and during the conduct of the proposed project. Preference is given to 1) women-owned small business concerns; 2) veteran-owned small businesses; and 3) socially and economically disadvantaged small business concerns. Women-owned small business concerns are those that are at least 51% owned by a woman or women who also control and operate them. Veteran-owned small businesses are those that are at least 51% owned and controlled by 1 or more veterans. Socially and economically disadvantaged small business concerns are at least 51% owned by an Indian tribe, a Native Hawaiian organization, or 1 or more socially and economically disadvantaged individuals (African Americans, Hispanic Americans, Native Americans, Asian Pacific Americans, or subcontinent Asian Americans). The project must be performed in the United States. Selection is based on scientific and technical merit, the feasibility of the proposal's commercial potential, the adequacy of the work plan, qualifications of the principal investigator, and adequacy of supporting staff and facilities, equipment, and data.

Financial data Support is offered in 2 phases. In phase 1, awards normally do not exceed $100,000 (for both direct and indirect costs); in phase 2, awards normally do not exceed $750,000 (including both direct and indirect costs).

Duration Phase 1 awards may extend up to 6 months; phase 2 awards may extend up to 2 years.

Number awarded Varies each year; recently, DOT planned to award 16 of these grants: 1 to the Federal Aviation Administration, 3 to the Federal Highway Administration, 1 to the Pipeline and Hazardous Materials Safety Administration, 2 to the National Highway and Traffic Safety Administration, 3

to the Federal Transit Administration, and 6 to the Federal Railroad Administration.

Deadline November of each year.

[1235]
DIBNER MATH AND SCIENCE TEACHING PROGRAM

Catching the Dream
8200 Mountain Road, N.E., Suite 203
Albuquerque, NM 87110-7835
(505) 262-2351 Fax: (505) 262-0534
E-mail: NScholarsh@aol.com
Web: www.catchingthedream.org/grants.htm

Summary To provide funding to teachers and schools for projects that are designed to improve mathematics and science teaching for Indian high school students.

Eligibility This program is open to teachers at Indian high schools who wish to offer more advanced mathematics and science courses and to enroll more Indian students in advanced classes. Applicants must describe their school, the students to be served, the current number of Indian students enrolling in their advanced mathematics and science classes, how the program will work, how the funds from the grant will be used, the background of the person in charge, and the goals and objectives of the proposed program.

Financial data Grants are $5,000. Some of the previous acceptable uses of funds have included purchase of advanced mathematics or science books, purchase of science supplies, purchase of mathematics supplies, or taking students on field trips.

Duration Grants are awarded annually.

Additional information The sponsor was formerly known as the Native American Scholarship Fund.

Number awarded 1 or more each year.

Deadline October of each year.

[1236]
DIGITAL INNOVATION FELLOWSHIPS

American Council of Learned Societies
Attn: Office of Fellowships and Grants
633 Third Avenue
New York, NY 10017-6795
(212) 697-1505 Fax: (212) 949-8058
E-mail: fellowships@acls.org
Web: www.acls.org/programs/digital

Summary To provide funding to scholars (particularly Native Americans, other minorities, and women) who are interested in conducting digitally-based research in the humanities and the humanities-related social sciences.

Eligibility This program is open to scholars who have a Ph.D. in any field of the humanities or the humanistic social sciences. Applicants must be interested in conducting research projects that utilize digital technologies intensively and innovatively. Projects might include, but are not limited to, new digital tools that further humanistic research (such as digital research archives or innovative databases), research that depends on or is greatly enhanced by the use of such tools, the representation of research that depends on or is greatly enhanced by the use of such tools, or some combination of those features. The program does not support creative works (e.g., novels or films), textbooks, straightforward translations, or purely pedagogical projects. U.S. citizenship or permanent resident status is required. Applications are particularly invited from women and members of minority groups. Selection is based on scholarly excellence (the project's intellectual ambitions and technological underpinnings), the project's likely contribution as a digital scholarly work to humanistic study, satisfaction of technical requirements for completing a successful research project, degree and significance of preliminary work already completed, extent to which the proposed project would promote teamwork and collaboration, and the project's articulation with local infrastructure.

Financial data Fellows receive a stipend of $60,000 and up to $25,000 for project costs.

Duration 1 academic year.

Additional information This program, first available for the 2006-07 academic year, is supported by funding from the Andrew W. Mellon Foundation.

Number awarded Up to 6 each year.

Deadline September of each year.

[1237]
DISCOVERY FELLOWSHIPS

Southwestern Association for Indian Arts, Inc.
3600 Cerrillos Road, Suite 712
P.O. Box 969
Santa Fe, NM 87504-0969
(505) 983-5220   Fax: (505) 983-7647
E-mail: info@swaia.org
Web: swaia.org

Summary To provide funding to American Indian artists, filmmakers, and writers interested in advancing their education and careers.

Eligibility This program is open to American Indian artists whose work conforms to the standards and classification definitions of the Southwestern Association for Indian Arts (SWAIA): jewelry; pottery; paintings, drawings, graphics, and photography; Pueblo wooden carving; sculpture; textiles; basketry; beadwork and quillwork; film and video; writing (poetry and fiction); and diverse arts. Both emerging and established artists are eligible. Their work may be traditional or contemporary. Applicants must be interested in pursuing an opportunity to travel, develop marketing plans, purchase supplies, expand their studies, develop their portfolio, or explore new directions. Funding is not provided to full-time students or for use as a scholarship. Along with their application, they must submit a formal artist statement of 1 to 2 pages explaining and contextualizing their artwork by discussing their motivations to create, materials that they use, or cultural impact they wish to develop with their fellowship. They must also submit samples of their work (4 digital images for visual artists, a 5-minute CD or DVD for filmmakers, or 10 pages of writing for authors), an explanation of how they plan to use the grant, and a formal resume.

Financial data Fellows receive a grant of $5,000 and a complimentary booth at the Santa Fe Indian Market; in lieu of a booth, writers participate in SWAIA's Native literary and performance event during Indian Market Week.

Duration The grants are awarded annually.

Additional information SWAIA established a fellowship program in 1980. Beginning in 2010, it began offering 2 types of fellowships: these Discovery Fellowships (similar to the prior fellowships) and Residency Fellowships (for artists interested in a residency at the Santa Fe Art Institute). The application fee is $25.

Number awarded Varies each year.

Deadline December of each year.

[1238]
DORA AMES LEE LEADERSHIP DEVELOPMENT FUND

United Methodist Church
General Board of Global Ministries
Attn: United Methodist Committee on Relief
475 Riverside Drive, Room 1522
New York, NY 10115
(212) 870-3871   Toll Free: (800) UMC-GBGM
E-mail: jyoung@gbgm-umc.org
Web: gbgm-umc.org/health/doralee.cfm

Summary To provide financial assistance to Methodists and other Christians of Native American or Asian descent who are preparing for a career in a health-related field.

Eligibility This program is open to undergraduate and graduate students who are U.S. citizens of Asian American or Native American descent. Applicants must be professed Christians, preferably United Methodists. They must be attending a college or university to enter or continue in a health-related field. Financial need is considered in the selection process.

Financial data The stipend is $2,000.

Duration 1 year.

Additional information This program was established in 1980.

Number awarded 5 each year.

Deadline June of each year.

[1239]
DUPONT MINORITIES IN ENGINEERING AWARD

American Society for Engineering Education
Attn: Manager, Administrative Services
1818 N Street, N.W., Suite 600
Washington, DC 20036-2479
(202) 331-3500   Fax: (202) 265-8504
Web: www.asee.org/activities/awards/special.cfm

Summary To recognize and reward outstanding achievements by engineering educators who promote diversity in science, engineering, and technology.

Eligibility Eligible for nomination are engineering or engineering technology educators who, as part of their educational activity, either assume or are charged with the responsibility of motivating underrepresented students to enter and continue in engineering or engineering technology curricula at the college or university level, graduate or undergraduate. Nominees must demonstrate leadership in the conception, organization, and operation of pre-college and college activities designed to increase participation by underrepresented students in engineering and engineering technology.

Financial data The award consists of $1,500, a certificate, and a grant of $500 for travel expenses to the ASEE annual conference.

Duration The award is granted annually.

Additional information Funding for this award is provided by DuPont. It was originally established in 1956 as the Vincent Bendix Minorities in Engineering Award.

Number awarded 1 each year.

Deadline January of each year.

[1240]
EARLY CAREER PATIENT-ORIENTED DIABETES RESEARCH AWARD

Juvenile Diabetes Research Foundation International
Attn: Grant Administrator
26 Broadway, 14th Floor
New York, NY 10004
(212) 479-7572   Toll Free: (800) 533-CURE
Fax: (212) 785-9595   E-mail: info@jdrf.org
Web: www.jdrf.org/index.cfm?page_id=111715

Summary To provide funding to physician scientists (particularly Native Americans, other minorities, women, and persons with disabilities) who are interested in pursuing a program of clinical diabetes-related research training.

Eligibility This program is open to investigators in diabetes-related research who have an M.D. or M.D./Ph.D. degree and a faculty appointment at the late training or assistant professor level. Applicants must be sponsored by an investigator who is affiliated full time with an accredited institution, who pursues patient-oriented clinical research, and who agrees to supervise the applicant's training. There are no citizenship requirements. Applications are encouraged from women, members of minority groups underrepresented in the sciences, and people with disabilities. Areas of relevant research can include: mechanisms of human disease, therapeutic interventions, clinical trials, and the development of new technologies. The proposed research may be conducted at foreign and domestic, for-profit and nonprofit, and public and private institutions, including universities, colleges, hospitals, laboratories, units of state and local government, and eligible agencies of the federal government.

Financial data The total award may be up to $150,000 each year, up to $75,000 of which may be requested for research (including a technician, supplies, equipment, and travel). The salary request must be consistent with the established salary structure of the applicant's institution. Equipment purchases in years other than the first must be strongly justified. Indirect costs may not exceed 10%.

Duration The award is for 5 years.

Deadline January or July of each year.

[1241]
EARLY CAREER POSTDOCTORAL FELLOWSHIPS IN EAST EUROPEAN STUDIES

American Council of Learned Societies
Attn: Office of Fellowships and Grants
633 Third Avenue
New York, NY 10017-6795
(212) 697-1505   Fax: (212) 949-8058
E-mail: fellowships@acls.org
Web: www.acls.org/grants/Default.aspx?id=534

Summary To provide funding to postdoctorates (especially Native Americans, other minorities, and women) who are interested in conducting original research in the social sciences and humanities relating to eastern Europe.

Eligibility This program is open to U.S. citizens and permanent residents who hold a Ph.D. degree or equivalent as demonstrated by professional experience and publications.

Priority is given to scholars in the early part of their careers; tenured faculty are not eligible. Applicants must be interested in conducting research in the social sciences or humanities relating to Albania, Bosnia and Herzegovina, Bulgaria, Croatia, Czech Republic, Estonia, Hungary, Former Yugoslav Republic of Macedonia, Kosovo, Latvia, Lithuania, Montenegro, Poland, Romania, Serbia, Slovakia, or Slovenia. Projects comparing more than 1 country in eastern Europe or relating eastern European societies to those of other parts of the world are also supported. Selection is based on the scholarly merit of the proposal, its importance to the development of eastern European studies, and the scholarly potential and accomplishments of the applicant. Applications are particularly invited from women and members of minority groups.

Financial data Up to $25,000 is provided as a stipend. Funds are intended primarily as salary replacement, but they may be used to supplement sabbatical salaries or awards from other sources.

Duration 6 to 12 consecutive months.

Additional information This program is sponsored jointly by the American Council of Learned Societies, (ACLS) and the Social Science Research Council, funded by the U.S. Department of State under the Research and Training for Eastern Europe and the Independent States of the Former Soviet Union Act of 1983 (Title VIII) but administered by ACLS. Funds may not be used in western Europe.

Number awarded Varies each year; recently, 3 of these fellowships were awarded.

Deadline November of each year.

[1242]
EARTH SCIENCES POSTDOCTORAL FELLOWSHIPS

National Science Foundation
Directorate for Geosciences
Attn: Division of Earth Sciences
4201 Wilson Boulevard, Room 785S
Arlington, VA 22230
(703) 292-5047   Fax: (703) 292-9025
TDD: (800) 281-8749   E-mail: lpatino@nsf.gov
Web: www.nsf.gov

Summary To provide funding to minority and other postdoctoral scientists interested in participating in a program of research training and education, in the United States or abroad, in a field relevant to the work of the Division of Earth Sciences of the National Science Foundation (NSF).

Eligibility This program is open to U.S. citizens, nationals, and permanent residents who received a Ph.D. within the past 3 years. Applicants must be interested in a program of research training in any of the disciplines supported by the NSF Division of Earth Sciences: improving our understanding of the Earth's structure, composition, evolution, and the interaction with the Earth's biosphere, atmosphere, and hydrosphere. The project should be conducted at an institution (college or university, private nonprofit institute or museum, government installation, or laboratory), in the United States or abroad other than the applicant's Ph.D.-granting institution. Part of the project should include such educational activities as teaching a course each year at the host institution or an academic institution with ties to the host institution, developing educational materials for formal or informal education venues, or engaging in a significant program of outreach or public education. Applicants must select a sponsoring scientist at the host institution to provide mentoring and guidance with the research and education activities. Applications are encouraged from underrepresented minorities and persons with disabilities.

Financial data Grants are $85,000 per year, including a stipend of $58,000 per year, a research allowance of $15,000 per year, a host institutional allowance of $3,000 per year, and a fringe benefit allowance of $9,000 per year.

Duration 2 years.

Number awarded 10 each year.

Deadline June of each year.

[1243]
EAST EUROPEAN LANGUAGE GRANTS TO INDIVIDUALS FOR SUMMER STUDY

American Council of Learned Societies
Attn: Office of Fellowships and Grants
633 Third Avenue
New York, NY 10017-6795
(212) 697-1505   Fax: (212) 949-8058
E-mail: fellowships@acls.org
Web: www.acls.org/grants/Default.aspx?id=540

Summary To provide financial support to minority and other graduate students, professionals, and postdoctorates interested in studying eastern European languages during the summer.

Eligibility Applicants must have completed at least a 4-year college degree. They must be interested in a program of training in the languages of eastern Europe, including Albanian, Bosnian-Croatian-Serbian, Bulgarian, Czech, Estonian, Hungarian, Latvian, Lithuanian, Macedonian, Polish, Romanian, Slovak, or Slovene. The language course may be at the beginning, intermediate, or advanced level. Normally, requests for beginning and intermediate level training should be for attendance at intensive courses offered by institutions in the United States; proposals for study at the advanced level are ordinarily for courses in eastern Europe. Applications are particularly encouraged from women and members of minority groups.

Financial data Grants up to $2,500 are available.

Duration Summer months.

Additional information This program, reinstituted in 2002, is supported by the U.S. Department of State under the Research and Training for Eastern Europe and the Independent States of the Former Soviet Union Act of 1983 (Title VIII).

Number awarded Approximately 15 each year.

Deadline January of each year.

[1244]
EDUCATION PROJECT GRANTS

Cook Inlet Region, Inc.
Attn: The CIRI Foundation
3600 San Jeronimo Drive, Suite 256
Anchorage, AK 99508-2870
(907) 793-3575   Toll Free: (800) 764-3382
Fax: (907) 793-3585   E-mail: tcf@thecirifoundation.org
Web: www.thecirifoundation.org/project_grants.htm

Summary To provide funding to individuals and nonprofit organizations interested in developing projects that further

the quality of education and life for Alaska Natives, especially of the Cook Inlet region.

Eligibility This program is open to staff at public nonprofit organizations and tribal councils, with preference given to staff at organizations located within Cook Inlet region. Alaska Natives enrolled to Cook Inlet Region, Inc. (CIRI) and their lineal descendants may also submit applications if they are sponsored by a nonprofit organization. Applicants must be proposing projects that 1) promote quality of learning and educational experiences for Alaska Natives from middle school through adulthood; 2) examine educational issues and opportunities and identify possible solutions to eliminate those factors that hinder successful achievement by Alaska Natives in their educational pursuits; or 3) foster educational enrichment programs that improve the quality of life for Alaska Natives. Selection is based on the appropriateness of the applicant's project to the foundation's educational goals and grant guidelines, need for the project, involvement and direct impact upon Alaska Native enrollees and lineal descendants of CIRI, extent to which the project impacts the targeted audience, extent to which the project impacts the general public, clarity of purpose, realistically-defined program and budget plans that can be reasonably accomplished, demonstration of available funds that at least match the amount of funds requested from the foundation, feasibility of project budget and timeline, innovation of project plan, appropriate and clearly-stated project evaluation plan, and ability to complete project within the projected timeline.

Financial data Grant amounts depend on the nature of the project.

Additional information This program was established in 1989.

Number awarded Varies each year; recently, 2 of these grants were awarded.

Deadline Grant applications must be submitted by February, May, August, or October of each year.

[1245]
EDUCATIONAL TESTING SERVICE POSTDOCTORAL FELLOWSHIP AWARD PROGRAM

Educational Testing Service
Attn: Fellowships
660 Rosedale Road
MS 19-T
Princeton, NJ 08541-0001
(609) 734-5543   Fax: (609) 734-5410
E-mail: internfellowships@ets.org
Web: www.ets.org/research/fellowships/postdoctoral

Summary To provide funding to postdoctorates (particularly American Indians and other underrepresented minorities) who wish to conduct independent research at the Educational Testing Service (ETS).

Eligibility Applicants must have a doctorate in a relevant discipline and be able to provide evidence of prior research. They must be interested in conducting research at ETS in 1 of the following areas: measurement theory, validity, natural language processing and computational linguistics, cognitive psychology, learning theory, linguistics, speech recognition and processing, teaching and classroom research, or statistics. Selection is based on the scholarly and technical strength of the proposed research, the relationship between the objective of the research and ETS goals and priorities, and the ETS affirmative action objectives. An explicit goal of the program is to increase the number of scholars and students from diverse backgrounds, especially such traditionally underrepresented groups as African Americans, Hispanic/Latino Americans, and American Indians, who are conducting research in educational measurement and related fields.

Financial data The stipend is $55,000 per year; fellows and their families also receive limited reimbursement for relocation expenses.

Duration Up to 2 years.

Additional information Fellows work with senior staff at ETS in Princeton, New Jersey.

Number awarded Up to 3 each year.

Deadline January of each year.

[1246]
EDWARD A. BOUCHET AWARD

American Physical Society
Attn: Honors Program
One Physics Ellipse
College Park, MD 20740-3844
(301) 209-3268   Fax: (301) 209-0865
E-mail: honors@aps.org
Web: www.aps.org/programs/honors/awards/bouchet.cfm

Summary To recognize and reward outstanding research in physics by Native Americans or members of other underrepresented minority groups.

Eligibility Nominees for this award must be African Americans, Hispanic Americans, or Native Americans who have made significant contributions to physics research and are effective communicators.

Financial data The award consists of a grant of $3,500 to the recipient, a travel allowance for the recipient to visit 3 academic institutions to deliver lectures, and an allowance for travel expenses to the meeting of the American Physical Society (APS) at which the prize is presented.

Duration The award is presented annually.

Additional information This award was established in 1994 and is currently funded by a grant from the Research Corporation. As part of the award, the recipient visits 3 academic institutions where the impact of the visit on minority students will be significant. The purpose of those visits is to deliver technical lectures on the recipient's field of specialization, to visit classrooms where appropriate, to assist the institution with precollege outreach efforts where appropriate, and to talk informally with faculty and students about research and teaching careers in physics.

Number awarded 1 each year.

Deadline June of each year.

[1247]
E.E. JUST ENDOWED RESEARCH FELLOWSHIP FUND

Woods Hole Marine Biological Laboratory
Attn: Research Award Coordinator
7 MBL Street
Woods Hole, MA 02543-1015
(508) 289-7173   Fax: (508) 457-1924
E-mail: researchawards@mbl.edu
Web: www.mbl.edu/research/summer/awards_general.html

Summary To provide funding to Native American and other minority scientists who wish to conduct summer research at the Woods Hole Marine Biological Laboratory (MBL).

Eligibility This program is open to minority faculty members who are interested in conducting summer research at the MBL. Applicants must submit a statement of the potential impact of this award on their career development. Fields of study include, but are not limited to, cell biology, developmental biology, ecology, evolution, microbiology, neurobiology, physiology, regenerative biology, and tissue engineering.

Financial data The fellowship supports a minority scientist's participation in research at MBL. Recently, grants averaged $1,500.

Duration At least 6 weeks during the summer.

Number awarded 1 each year.

Deadline December of each year.

[1248]
EINSTEIN POSTDOCTORAL FELLOWSHIP PROGRAM

Smithsonian Astrophysical Observatory
Attn: Chandra X-Ray Center
Einstein Fellowship Program Office
60 Garden Street, MS4
Cambridge, MA 02138
(617) 496-7941   Fax: (617) 495-7356
E-mail: fellows@head.cfa.harvard.edu
Web: cxc.harvard.edu/fellows

Summary To provide funding to postdoctoral scientists (especially Native Americans, other minorities, and women) who are interested in conducting research related to high energy astrophysics missions of the National Aeronautics and Space Administration (NASA).

Eligibility This program is open to postdoctoral scientists who completed their Ph.D., Sc.D., or equivalent doctoral degree within the past 3 years in astronomy, physics, or related disciplines. Applicants must be interested in conducting research related to NASA Physics of the Cosmos program missions: Chandra, Fermi, XMM-Newton and International X-Ray Observatory, cosmological investigations relevant to the Planck and JDEM missions, and gravitational astrophysics relevant to the LISA mission. They must be citizens of the United States or English-speaking citizens of other countries who have valid visas. Women and minorities are strongly encouraged to apply.

Financial data Stipends are approximately $64,500 per year. Fellows may also receive health insurance, relocation costs, and moderate support (up to $16,000 per year) for research-related travel, computing services, publications, and other direct costs.

Duration 3 years (depending on a review of scientific activity).

Additional information This program, which began in 2009 with funding from NASA, incorporates the former Chandra and GLAST Fellowship programs.

Number awarded Up to 10 each year.

Deadline November of each year.

[1249]
EPILEPSY FOUNDATION RESEARCH GRANTS PROGRAM

Epilepsy Foundation
Attn: Research Department
8301 Professional Place
Landover, MD 20785-2237
(301) 459-3700   Toll Free: (800) EFA-1000
Fax: (301) 577-2684   TDD: (800) 332-2070
E-mail: grants@efa.org
Web: www.epilepsyfoundation.org

Summary   To provide funding to junior investigators (particularly Native Americans, other minorities, and individuals with disabilities) who are interested in conducting research that will advance the understanding, treatment, and prevention of epilepsy.

Eligibility   Applicants must have a doctoral degree and an academic appointment at the level of assistant professor in a university or medical school (or equivalent standing at a research institution or medical center). They must be interested in conducting basic or clinical research in the biological, behavioral, or social sciences related to the causes of epilepsy. Faculty with appointments at the level of associate professor or higher are not eligible. Applications from women, members of minority groups, and people with disabilities are especially encouraged. U.S. citizenship is not required, but the research must be conducted in the United States. Selection is based on the scientific quality of the research plan, the relevance of the proposed research to epilepsy, the applicant's qualifications, and the adequacy of the institution and facility where research will be conducted.

Financial data   The grant is $50,000 per year.

Duration   1 year; recipients may reapply for 1 additional year of funding.

Additional information   Support for this program is provided by many individuals, families, and corporations, especially the American Epilepsy Society, Abbott Laboratories, Ortho-McNeil Pharmaceutical, and Pfizer Inc.

Number awarded   Varies each year.

Deadline   August of each year.

[1250]
EPILEPSY RESEARCH RECOGNITION AWARDS PROGRAM

American Epilepsy Society
342 North Main Street
West Hartford, CT 06117-2507
(860) 586-7505   Fax: (860) 586-7550
E-mail: ctubby@aesnet.org
Web: www.aesnet.org/research/research-awards

Summary   To provide funding to investigators (especially Native Americans, other minorities, and women) who are interested in conducting research related to epilepsy.

Eligibility   This program is open to active scientists and clinicians working in any aspect of epilepsy. Candidates must be nominated by their home institution and be at the level of associate professor or professor. There are no geographic restrictions; nominations from outside the United States and North America are welcome. Nominations of women and members of minority groups are especially encouraged. Selection is based on pioneering research, originality of research, quality of publications, research productivity, relationship of the candidate's work to problems in epilepsy, training activities, other contributions in epilepsy, and productivity over the next decade; all criteria are weighted equally.

Financial data   The grant is $10,000. No institutional overhead is allowed.

Additional information   This program was established in 1991.

Number awarded   2 each year.

Deadline   August of each year.

[1251]
ERIC AND BARBARA DOBKIN NATIVE ARTIST FELLOWSHIP FOR WOMEN

School for Advanced Research
Attn: Indian Arts Research Center
660 Garcia Street
P.O. Box 2188
Santa Fe, NM 87504-2188
(505) 954-7205   Fax: (505) 954-7207
E-mail: iarc@sarsf.org
Web: sarweb.org/index.php?artists

Summary   To provide an opportunity for Native American women artists to improve their skills through a spring residency at the Indian Arts Research Center in Santa Fe, New Mexico.

Eligibility   This program is open to Native American women who excel in the arts, including sculpture, performance, basketry, painting, printmaking, digital art, mixed media, photography, pottery, writing, and filmmaking. Applicants should be attempting to explore new avenues of creativity, grapple with new ideas to advance their work, and strengthen existing talents. Along with their application, they must submit a current resume, examples of their current work, and a 2-page statement that explains why they are applying for this fellowship, how it will help them to realize their professional and/or personal goals as an artist, and the scope of the project they plan to complete during the residency.

Financial data   The fellowship provides a stipend of $3,000 per month, housing, studio space, supplies allowance, and travel reimbursement to and from the center.

Duration   3 months, beginning in March.

Additional information   Fellows work with the staff and research curators at the Indian Arts Research Center, an academic division of the School of American Research that is devoted solely to Native American art scholarship. The center has a significant collection of Pueblo pottery, Navajo and Pueblo Indian textiles, and early 20th-century Indian paintings, as well as holdings of jewelry and silverwork, basketry, clothing, and other ethnological materials. This fellowship was established in 2001.

Number awarded   1 each year.

Deadline   January of each year.

[1252]
EVERYDAY TECHNOLOGIES FOR ALZHEIMER CARE (ETAC) GRANTS

Alzheimer's Association
Attn: Medical and Scientific Affairs
225 North Michigan Avenue, 17th Floor
Chicago, IL 60601-7633
(312) 335-5747   Toll Free: (800) 272-3900
Fax: (866) 699-1246   TDD: (312) 335-5886
E-mail: grantsapp@alz.org
Web: www.alz.org

Summary To provide funding to investigators, especially Native Americans and members of other underrepresented groups, who are interested in developing technology for uses related to Alzheimer's Disease.

Eligibility This program is open to investigators who are full-time staff or faculty at public, private, domestic, and foreign research laboratories, medical centers, hospitals, and universities. Applicants must be interested in conducting research on personalized diagnostics, preventive tools, and interventions for adults coping with the spectrum of cognitive aging and neurodegenerative disease, particularly Alzheimer's Disease. Priority is given to groundbreaking studies on emerging information and communication technologies as well as their clinical and social implications. Research topics may include, but are not limited to, behavioral assessment for early detection, prevention, safety monitoring and support for caregivers, supporting independent function in daily life, social support through face or audio recognition, detecting moments and patterns of lucidity, and privacy and security concerns of Alzheimer's families. Scientists from underrepresented groups are especially encouraged to apply.

Financial data Grants up to $90,000 per year, including direct expenses and up to 10% for overhead costs, are available. The total award for the life of the grant may not exceed $200,000.

Duration Up to 3 years.

Additional information This program is jointly supported by the Alzheimer's Association and Intel Corporation.

Number awarded Up to 4 each year.

Deadline Letters of intent must be submitted by the end of December of each year. Final applications are due in February.

[1253]
FACULTY EARLY CAREER DEVELOPMENT PROGRAM

National Science Foundation
Directorate for Education and Human Resources
Senior Staff Associate for Cross Directorate Programs
4201 Wilson Boulevard, Room 805
Arlington, VA 22230
(703) 292-8600   TDD: (800) 281-8749
Web: www.nsf.gov

Summary To provide funding to new faculty (particularly Native Americans, other underrepresented minorities, and individuals with disabilities) who are working in science and engineering fields of interest to the National Science Foundation (NSF) and intend to develop academic careers involving both research and education.

Eligibility This program, identified as the CAREER program, is open to faculty members who meet all of the following requirements: 1) be employed in a tenure-track (or equivalent) position at an institution in the United States, its territories or possessions, or the Commonwealth of Puerto Rico that awards degrees in a field supported by NSF or that is a nonprofit, non-degree granting organization, such as a museum, observatory, or research laboratory; 2) have a doctoral degree in a field of science or engineering supported by NSF: 3) not have competed more than 3 times in this program; 4) be untenured; and 5) not be a current or former recipient of a Presidential Early Career Award for Scientists and Engineers (PECASE) or CAREER award. Applicants are not required to be U.S. citizens or permanent residents. They must submit a career development plan that indicates a description of the proposed research project, including preliminary supporting data if appropriate, specific objectives, methods, and procedures to be used; expected significance of the results; a description of the proposed educational activities, including plans to evaluate their impact; a description of how the research and educational activities are integrated with each other; and results of prior NSF support, if applicable. Proposals from women, underrepresented minorities, and persons with disabilities are especially encouraged.

Financial data The grant is at least $80,000 per year (or $100,000 per year for the Directorate of Biological Sciences), including indirect costs or overhead.

Duration 5 years.

Additional information This program is operated by various disciplinary divisions within the NSF; for a list of the participating divisions and their telephone numbers, contact the sponsor. Outstanding recipients of these grants are nominated for the NSF component of the PECASE awards, which are awarded to 20 recipients of these grants as an honorary award.

Number awarded Approximately 425 each year.

Deadline July of each year.

[1254]
FACULTY IN INDUSTRY AWARDS

National Science Foundation
Directorate for Engineering
Attn: Division of Industrial Innovation and Partnerships
4201 Wilson Boulevard, Room 550S
Arlington, VA 22230
(703) 292-7082   Fax: (703) 292-9056
TDD: (800) 281-8749   E-mail: dsenich@nsf.gov
Web: www.nsf.gov/funding/pgm_summ.jsp?pims_id=13706

Summary To provide funding to underrepresented minorities and other faculty members in science, engineering, and mathematics who wish to conduct research in an industrial setting as part of the Grant Opportunities for Academic Liaison with Industry (GOALI) program of the National Science Foundation (NSF).

Eligibility This program is open to full-time faculty members at U.S. colleges and universities in science, engineering, and mathematics fields of interest to NSF. Applicants must be U.S. citizens, nationals, or permanent residents. They must present a plan for collaboration between their institution and industry, with a description of the facilities and resources that will be available at the industrial site to support the proposed research. The program encourages applications from underrepresented minorities and persons with disabilities.

Financial data Grants range from $30,000 to $75,000, including 50% of the faculty member's salary and fringe benefits during the industrial residency period. Up to 20% of the total requested amount may be used for travel and research expenses for the faculty and his/her students, including materials but excluding equipment. The industrial partner must commit to support the other 50% of the faculty salary and fringe benefits.

Duration 3 to 12 months.

Additional information This program is also offered by most other NSF directorates. Check the web site for a name and e-mail address of the contact person in each directorate.

Number awarded A total of 60 to 80 grants for all GOALI programs is awarded each year; total funding is approximately $5 million.

Deadline Applications may be submitted at any time.

[1255]
FASEB POSTDOCTORAL PROFESSIONAL DEVELOPMENT AND ENRICHMENT AWARD

Federation of American Societies for Experimental
  Biology
Attn: MARC Section
9650 Rockville Pike
Bethesda, MD 20814-3998
(301) 634-7000   Fax: (301) 634-7001
E-mail: info@faseb.org
Web: www1.faseb.org/postdocprofdevaward

Summary To recognize and reward Native American and other underrepresented minority members of component societies of the Federation of American Societies for Experimental Biology (FASEB).

Eligibility This program is open to postdoctoral members of minority groups underrepresented in the biomedical and behavioral sciences (African Americans, Alaskan Natives, Hispanic Americans, Natives of the U.S. Pacific Islands, and American Indians/Native Americans). Applicants must be U.S. citizens, nationals, or permanent residents and members of a FASEB component society. They must be seeking funding to gain knowledge, skills, and training to assist in becoming competitive for publication in top tier journals and for faculty positions in prestigious research intensive settings. Selection is based on demonstrated research productivity, including publication of first-author papers in scientific journals, mentoring of underrepresented minority undergraduate and graduate students, and service leading to improving and expanding opportunities for minorities in the scientific work force and academia.

Financial data The award consists of a $3,000 career development grant, a certificate of recognition, and a $2,500 travel grant.

Duration This award is presented annually.

Additional information Funding for this award is provided by the Minority Access to Research Careers (MARC) program of the National Institute of General Medical Sciences of the National Institutes of Health (NIH). Member societies of FASEB include the American Physiological Society (APS), American Society for Biochemistry and Molecular Biology (ASBMB), American Society for Pharmacology and Experi-

mental Therapeutics (ASPET), American Society for Investigative Pathology (ASIP), American Society for Nutrition(ASN), American Association of Immunologists (AAI), American Association of Anatomists (AAA), The Protein Society, American Society for Bone and Mineral Research (ASBMR), American Society for Clinical Investigation (ASCI), The Endocrine Society, American Society of Human Genetics (ASHG), Society for Developmental Biology (SDB), American Peptide Society (APEPS), Association of Biomolecular Resource Facilities (ABRF), Society for the Study of Reproduction (SSR), Teratology Society, Environmental Mutagen Society (EMS), International Society for Computational Biology (ISCB), American College of Sports Medicine (ACSM), Biomedical Engineering Society (BMES), Genetics Society of America, American Federation for Medical Research (AFMR), and The Histochemical Society (HCS).

Number awarded 6 each year.

Deadline May of each year.

[1256]
FASSE/CUFA INQUIRY GRANT

National Council for the Social Studies
Attn: Program Manager, External Relations
8555 16th Street, Suite 500
Silver Spring, MD 20910-2844
(301) 588-1800, ext. 106   Fax: (301) 588-2049
E-mail: excellence@ncss.org
Web: www.socialstudies.org/getinvolved/awards/fasse-cufa

Summary To provide funding to minorities and other faculty and graduate student members of the National Council for the Social Studies (NCSS) who are interested in conducting research projects in "citizenship education."

Eligibility This program is open to members of the council who are assistant, associate, or full professors or graduate students with the demonstrated support of a university mentor/adviser. Graduate student applicants must have a mentor/adviser who is also an NCSS member. Researchers from underrepresented groups are encouraged to apply. They must be interested in a project in "citizenship education" that affirms social, cultural, and racial diversity and that addresses issues of equality, equity, and social justice. Proposals that address aims for citizen action are preferred. All proposals should be relevant to school, university, or community-based educational settings. They should either 1) serve student bodies that are socially, culturally, and racially diverse; or 2) involve teachers or prospective teachers who work or will work with diverse student populations. They can address a range of educational levels and settings, from K-12 to collegiate levels, and from school to community settings.

Financial data Grants up to $10,000 are available.

Duration Funded projects must be completed within 1 academic year.

Additional information This program is sponsored by the College and University Faculty Assembly (CUFA) and the Fund for the Advancement of Social Studies Education (FASSE), established by the NCAA in 1984.

Number awarded 1 every 2 or 3 years.

Deadline June of the years in which grants are offered.

[1257]
FDA FACULTY GRANTS

National Science Foundation
Directorate for Engineering
Attn: Division of Chemical, Bioengineering,
 Environmental, and Transport Systems
4201 Wilson Boulevard, Room 565S
Arlington, VA 22230
(703) 292-7942   Fax: (703) 292-9098
TDD: (800) 281-8749   E-mail: lesterow@nsf.gov
Web: www.nsf.gov/funding/pgm_summ.jsp?pims_id=5605

Summary To provide an opportunity for faculty members (especially Native Americans, other minorities, and individuals with disabilities) to conduct research at an intramural laboratory of the U.S. Food and Drug Administration (FDA).

Eligibility This program is open to full-time faculty members at U.S. colleges and universities in science, engineering, and mathematics fields of interest to the National Science Foundation (NSF). Applicants must be U.S. citizens, nationals, or permanent residents. They must present a plan for collaboration between their institution and the FDA, with a description of the facilities and resources that will be available at an FDA laboratory to support the proposed research. The program encourages applications from underrepresented minorities and persons with disabilities.

Financial data Grants range from $25,000 to $150,000, including 85% of the faculty member's salary and fringe benefits during the industrial residency period. Up to 20% of the total requested amount may be used for travel and research expenses for the faculty and his/her students, including materials but excluding equipment. In lieu of indirect costs, up to 15% of the total cost may be allocated for administrative expenses. The fellow's home institution must commit to support the other 15% of the faculty salary and fringe benefits. FDA provides office space, research facilities, research costs in the form of expendable and minor equipment purchases in the host laboratory, and the time of its research staff.

Duration 3 to 12 months.

Additional information This program is also offered by the NSF Directorate for Computer and Information Science and Engineering.

Number awarded A total of 3 to 10 grants for all FDA programs is awarded each year; total funding is approximately $500,000.

Deadline March of each year.

[1258]
FELLOWSHIP PROGRAM IN MEASUREMENT

American Educational Research Association
1430 K Street, N.W., Suite 1200
Washington, DC 20005
(202) 238-3200   Fax: (202) 238-3250
E-mail: fellowships@aera.net
Web: www.aera.net

Summary To provide an opportunity for junior scholars (particularly Native Americans, other underrepresented minorities, and women) in the field of education to engage in a program of research and advanced training while in residence at Educational Testing Service (ETS) in Princeton, New Jersey.

Eligibility This program is open to junior scholars and early career research scientists in fields and disciplines related to education research. Applicants must have completed their Ph.D. or Ed.D. degree within the past 3 years. They must be proposing a program of intensive research and training at the ETS campus in Princeton, New Jersey in such areas as educational measurement, assessment design, psychometrics, statistical analyses, large-scale evaluations, and other studies directed to explaining student progress and achievement. A particular goal of the program is to increase the involvement of women and underrepresented minority professionals in measurement, psychometrics, assessment, and related fields. U.S. citizenship or permanent resident status is required.

Financial data The stipend is $50,000 per year. Fellows also receive relocation expenses and ETS employee benefits.

Duration Up to 2 years.

Additional information This program is jointly sponsored by the American Educational Research Association (AERA) and ETS.

Number awarded Up to 2 each year.

Deadline December of each year.

[1259]
FELLOWSHIP TO FACULTY TRANSITION AWARDS

American Gastroenterological Association
Attn: AGA Research Foundation
Research Awards Manager
4930 Del Ray Avenue
Bethesda, MD 20814-2512
(301) 222-4012   Fax: (301) 654-5920
E-mail: awards@gastro.org
Web: www.gastro.org/aga-foundation/grants

Summary To provide funding to physicians (particularly Native Americans, other minorities, and women) who are interested in research training in an area of gastrointestinal, liver function, or related diseases.

Eligibility This program is open to trainee members of the American Gastroenterological Association (AGA) who have an M.D. or equivalent degree and a gastroenterology-related fellowship at an accredited institution. Applicants must be committed to an academic career; have completed at least 1 year of research training at their current institution; have a commitment from their home institution for a full-time faculty position; and have a preceptor who will supervise their research activities and serve as a mentor. Women and minority investigators are strongly encouraged to apply. Selection is based on the candidate's promise for future success, feasibility and significance of the proposal, attributes of the candidate, record and commitment of the sponsors, and institutional and laboratory environment.

Financial data The grant is $40,000 per year. Funds are to be used as salary support for the recipient. Indirect costs are not allowed.

Duration 2 years.

Additional information Fellows must devote 70% effort to research related to the gastrointestinal tract or liver.

Number awarded 2 each year.

Deadline August of each year.

[1260]
FELLOWSHIPS FOR TRANSFORMATIVE COMPUTATIONAL SCIENCE USING CYBERINFRASTRUCTURE

National Science Foundation
Attn: Office of Cyberinfrastructure
4201 Wilson Boulevard, Room 1145S
Arlington, VA 22230
(703) 292-4766   Fax: (703) 292-9060
TDD: (800) 281-8749   E-mail: citracs@nsf.gov
Web: www.nsf.gov

Summary To provide funding for research training to underrepresented minorities and other postdoctoral scientists interested in working in areas of interest to the Office of Cyberinfrastructure of the National Science Foundation (NSF).

Eligibility This program is open to citizens, nationals, and permanent residents of the United States who are graduate students completing a Ph.D. or have earned the degree no earlier than 2 years preceding the deadline date. Applicants must be interested in a program of research and training in the use of computational concepts, methodologies, and technologies in all sciences (including physical, biological, geological, mathematical, social, behavioral, economic, computer, information, and data). They must identify a host research organization (college, university, privately-sponsored nonprofit institute, government agency, or laboratory) that has agreed to support the applicant's proposed research and educational activities and has identified a mentor to work with the applicant. Selection is based on the applicant's ability to contribute to computational research and educational efforts that integrate distinct theoretical models and computational methodologies to achieve overall goals and lead to a new generation of applications and technologies for solving important real-world problems using cyberinfrastructure (CI). The program encourages applications from underrepresented minorities and persons with disabilities.

Financial data Stipends are $60,000 for the first year, $65,000 for the second year, and $70,000 for the third year. Also provided are a research allowance supplement of $10,000 per year and an institutional allowance of $5,000 per year. Fellows who complete this program and move on to a tenure-track faculty position may apple for a research starter supplement of up to $50,000 to support the setup of their research environment.

Duration Up to 3 years.

Number awarded 6 to 8 each year. Approximately $2.0 million is available for this program annually.

Deadline January of each year.

[1261]
FELLOWSHIPS IN SCIENCE AND INTERNATIONAL AFFAIRS

Harvard University
John F. Kennedy School of Government
Belfer Center for Science and International Affairs
Attn: Fellowship Coordinator
79 John F. Kennedy Street
Cambridge, MA 02138
(617) 495-8806   Fax: (617) 495-8963
E-mail: bcsia_fellowships@ksg.harvard.edu
Web: belfercenter.ksg.harvard.edu/fellowships

Summary To provide funding to Native American and other professionals, postdoctorates, and doctoral students with diverse backgrounds who are interested in conducting research in areas of concern to the Belfer Center for Science and International Affairs at Harvard University in Cambridge, Massachusetts.

Eligibility The postdoctoral fellowship is open to recent recipients of the Ph.D. or equivalent degree, university faculty members, and employees of government, military, international, humanitarian, and private research institutions who have appropriate professional experience. Applicants for predoctoral fellowships must have passed their general examinations. Lawyers, economists, political scientists, those in the natural sciences, and others of diverse disciplinary backgrounds are also welcome to apply. The program especially encourages applications from women, minorities, and citizens of all countries. All applicants must be interested in conducting research in 1 of the 3 major program areas of the center: 1) the International Security Program (ISP), including Religion in International Affairs; 2) the Science, Technology, and Public Policy Program (STPP), including information and communications technology, energy and water policy, managing the atom project, and the energy technology innovation policy research group; 3) and the Dubai initiative.

Financial data The stipend is $34,000 for postdoctoral research fellows or $20,000 for predoctoral research fellows. Health insurance is also provided.

Duration 10 months.

Number awarded A limited number each year.

Deadline January of each year.

[1262]
FIRST BOOK GRANT PROGRAM FOR MINORITY SCHOLARS

Louisville Institute
Attn: Executive Director
1044 Alta Vista Road
Louisville, KY 40205-1798
(502) 992-5432   Fax: (502) 894-2286
E-mail: info@louisville-institute.org
Web: www.louisville-institute.org/Grants/programs.aspx

Summary To provide funding to Native Americans and other scholars of color interested in completing a major research and book project that focuses on an aspect of Christianity in North America.

Eligibility This program is open to members of racial/ethnic minority groups (African Americans, Hispanics, Native Americans, Asian Americans, Arab Americans, and Pacific Islanders) who have an earned doctoral degree (normally the Ph.D. or Th.D.). Applicants must be a pre-tenured faculty member in a full-time, tenure-track position at an accredited institution of higher education (college, university, or seminary) in North America. They must be able to negotiate a full academic year free from teaching and committee responsibilities in order to engage in a scholarly research project leading to the publication of their first (or second) book focusing on an aspect of Christianity in North America. Selection is based on the intellectual quality of the research and writing project, its potential to contribute to scholarship in religion, and the potential contribution of the research to the vitality of North American Christianity.

Financial data The grant is $40,000. Awards are intended to make possible a full academic year of sabbatical research and writing by providing up to half of the grantee's salary and benefits for that year. Funds are paid directly to the grantee's institution, but no indirect costs are allowed.

Duration 1 academic year; nonrenewable.

Additional information The Louisville Institute is located at Louisville Presbyterian Theological Seminary and is supported by the Lilly Endowment. These grants were first awarded in 2003. Grantees may not accept other awards that provide a stipend during the tenure of this award, and they must be released from all teaching and committee responsibilities during the award year.

Number awarded Varies each year; recently, 4 of these grants were awarded.

Deadline January of each year.

[1263]
FREDERICK BURKHARDT RESIDENTIAL FELLOWSHIPS FOR RECENTLY TENURED SCHOLARS

American Council of Learned Societies
Attn: Office of Fellowships and Grants
633 Third Avenue
New York, NY 10017-6795
(212) 697-1505   Fax: (212) 949-8058
E-mail: fellowships@acls.org
Web: www.acls.org/programs/burkhardt

Summary To provide funding to minority and other scholars in all disciplines of the humanities and the humanities-related social sciences who are interested in conducting research at designated residential centers.

Eligibility This program is open to citizens and permanent residents of the United States who achieved tenure in a humanities or humanities-related social science discipline at a U.S. institution within the past 4 years. Applicants must be interested in conducting research at 1 of 12 participating residential centers in the United States or abroad. Appropriate fields of specialization include, but are not limited to, American studies; anthropology; archaeology; art and architectural history; classics; economics; film; geography; history; languages and literatures; legal studies; linguistics; musicology; philosophy; political science; psychology; religious studies; rhetoric, communication, and media studies; sociology; and theater, dance, and performance studies. Proposals in those fields of the social sciences are eligible only if they employ predominantly humanistic approaches (e.g., economic history, law and literature, political philosophy). Proposals in interdisciplinary and cross-disciplinary studies are welcome, as are proposals focused on a geographic region or on a cultural or linguistic group. Applications are particularly invited from women and members of minority groups.

Financial data The stipend is $75,000. If that stipend exceeds the fellow's normal academic year salary, the excess is available for research and travel expenses.

Duration 1 academic year.

Additional information This program, which began in 1999, is supported by funding from the Andrew W. Mellon Foundation. The participating residential research centers are the National Humanities Center (Research Triangle Park, North Carolina), the Center for Advanced Study in the Behavioral Sciences (Stanford, California), the Institute for Advanced Study, Schools of Historical Studies and Social Science (Princeton, New Jersey), the Radcliffe Institute for Advanced Study at Harvard University (Cambridge, Massachusetts), the American Antiquarian Society (Worcester, Massachusetts), the John W. Kluge Center at the Library of Congress (Washington, D.C.), the Folger Shakespeare Library (Washington, D.C.), the Newberry Library (Chicago, Illinois), the Huntington Library, Art Collections, and Botanical Gardens (San Marino, California), the American Academy in Rome, Collegium Budapest, and Villa I Tatti (Florence, Italy).

Number awarded Up to 9 each year.

Deadline September of each year.

[1264]
FRONTIERS IN PHYSIOLOGY RESEARCH TEACHER FELLOWSHIPS

American Physiological Society
Attn: Education Office
9650 Rockville Pike, Room 3111
Bethesda, MD 20814-3991
(301) 634-7132   Fax: (301) 634-7098
E-mail: education@the-aps.org
Web: www.frontiersinphys.org

Summary To provide an opportunity for Native American and other middle/high school life science teachers to participate in a summer research project in physiology.

Eligibility This program is open to science teachers at middle schools (grades 6-9) and high schools (grades 9-12) who do not have recent (within 10 years) laboratory experience in physiology or the life sciences, do not have an advanced degree in laboratory science, and are not a candidate for an advanced degree in a laboratory science. Applicants do not need to have extensive mathematics skills, but they must be able to demonstrate a commitment to excellence in teaching, strong observation skills, and a desire to learn about research first-hand. Teachers who are members of minority groups underrepresented in science (African Americans, Hispanics, Native Americans, and Pacific Islanders) or who teach in schools with a predominance of underrepresented minority students are especially encouraged to apply. Teachers must apply jointly with a member of the American Physiological Society (APS) at a research institution in the same geographic area as their home and school. Selection is based on the quality of the summer research experience and potential long-term impact on teaching and on students.

Financial data For the summer research experience, teachers receive a stipend of $500 per week (to a maximum of $4,000), a grant of $1,000 for completion of online and live professional development, a grant of $600 for development and field testing of inquiry-based lessons and materials, and $100 for completion of project evaluation activities. For the remainder of the year, they receive $2,500 for reimbursement of travel costs to attend the Science Teaching Forum, $1,200 for reimbursement of travel costs to attend the Experimental Biology meeting, $300 for materials to field-test a new inquiry-based laboratory or lesson, and $60 for a 1-year affiliate membership with the APS. The maximum total value of the fellowship is $9,760.

Duration 1 year, including 7 to 8 weeks during the summer for participation in the research experience.

Additional information This program enables teachers to work on a summer research project in the laboratory of their

APS sponsor, use the Internet to expand their repertory of teaching methods and their network of colleagues, and develop an inquiry-based classroom activity or laboratory, along with a corresponding web page. They also take a break from their summer research to attend a 1-week Science Teaching Forum in Washington D.C. where they work with APS staff, physiologists, and mentors to explore and practice effective teaching methods focused on how to integrate inquiry, equity, and the Internet into their classrooms. This program is supported by the National Center for Research Resources (NCRR) and the National Institute of Diabetes and Digestive and Kidney Diseases (NIDDK). both components of the National Institutes of Health (NIH).

Number awarded Varies each year; recently 17 of these fellowships were awarded.

Deadline January of each year.

[1265]
GAIUS CHARLES BOLIN DISSERTATION AND POST-MFA FELLOWSHIPS

Williams College
Attn: Dean of the Faculty
Hopkins Hall, Third Floor
P.O. Box 141
Williamstown, MA 01267
(413) 597-4351   Fax: (413) 597-3553
E-mail: gburda@williams.edu
Web: dean-faculty.williams.edu/graduate-fellowships

Summary To provide financial assistance to Native Americans and members of other underrepresented groups who are interested in teaching courses at Williams College while working on their doctoral dissertation or building their post-M.F.A. professional portfolio.

Eligibility This program is open to members of underrepresented groups, including ethnic minorities, first-generation college students, women in predominantly male fields, and scholars with disabilities. Applicants must be 1) doctoral candidates in any field who have completed all work for a Ph.D. except for the dissertation; or 2) artists who completed an M.F.A. degree within the past 2 years and are building their professional portfolio. They must be willing to teach a course at Williams College. Along with their application, they must submit a full curriculum vitae, a graduate school transcript, 3 letters of recommendation, a copy of their dissertation prospectus or samples of their artistic work, and a description of their teaching interests within a department or program at Williams College. U.S. citizenship or permanent resident status is required.

Financial data Fellows receive $33,000 for the academic year, plus housing assistance, office space, computer and library privileges, and a research allowance of up to $4,000.

Duration 2 years.

Additional information Bolin fellows are assigned a faculty advisor in the appropriate department. This program was established in 1985. Fellows are expected to teach a 1-semester course each year. They must be in residence at Williams College for the duration of the fellowship.

Number awarded 3 each year.

Deadline November of each year.

[1266]
GEORGE A. STRAIT MINORITY SCHOLARSHIP ENDOWMENT

American Association of Law Libraries
Attn: Chair, Scholarships Committee
105 West Adams Street, Suite 3300
Chicago, IL 60603
(312) 939-4764   Fax: (312) 431-1097
E-mail: scholarships@aall.org
Web: www.aallnet.org/services/sch_strait.asp

Summary To provide financial assistance to Native American and other minority college seniors or college graduates who are interested in becoming law librarians.

Eligibility This program is open to college graduates with meaningful law library experience who are members of minority groups and intend to have a career in law librarianship. Applicants must be degree candidates at an ALA-accredited library school or an ABA-accredited law school. Along with their application, they must submit a personal statement that discusses their interest in law librarianship, reason for applying for this scholarship, career goals as a law librarian, etc.

Financial data The stipend is $3,500.

Duration 1 year.

Additional information This program, established in 1990, is currently supported by Thomson West.

Number awarded Varies each year; recently, 5 of these scholarships were awarded.

Deadline March of each year.

[1267]
GERTRUDE AND MAURICE GOLDHABER DISTINGUISHED FELLOWSHIPS

Brookhaven National Laboratory
Attn: Dr. Kathleen Barkigia
Building 460
P.O. Box 5000
Upton, NY 11973-5000
(631) 344-4467   E-mail: Barkigia@bnl.gov
Web: www.bnl.gov/hr/goldhaber.asp

Summary To provide funding to postdoctoral scientists (especially Native Americans, other minorities, and women) who are interested in conducting research at Brookhaven National Laboratory (BNL).

Eligibility This program is open to scholars who are no more than 3 years past receipt of the Ph.D. and are interested in working at BNL. Candidates must be interested in working in close collaboration with a member of the BNL scientific staff and qualifying for a scientific staff position at BNL upon completion of the appointment. The sponsoring scientist must have an opening and be able to support the candidate at the standard starting salary for postdoctoral research associates. The program especially encourages applications from minorities and women.

Financial data The program provides additional funds to bring the salary to $75,000 per year.

Duration 3 years.

Additional information This program is funded by Battelle Memorial Institute and the State University of New York at Stony Brook.

Number awarded Up to 8 each year.

Deadline August of each year.

[1268]
GILBERT F. WHITE POSTDOCTORAL FELLOWSHIP PROGRAM

Resources for the Future
Attn: Coordinator for Academic Programs
1616 P Street, N.W., Suite 600
Washington, DC 20036-1400
(202) 328-5008   Fax: (202) 939-3460
E-mail: white-award@rff.org
Web: www.rff.org/About_RFF/Pages/default.aspx

Summary To provide funding to minority and other post-doctoral researchers who wish to devote a year to scholarly work at Resources for the Future (RFF) in Washington, D.C.

Eligibility This program is open to individuals in any discipline who have completed their doctoral requirements and are interested in conducting scholarly research at RFF in social or policy science areas that relate to natural resources, energy, or the environment. Teaching and/or research experience at the postdoctoral level is preferred but not essential. Individuals holding positions in government as well as at academic institutions are eligible. Women and minority candidates are strongly encouraged to apply.

Financial data Fellows receive an annual stipend (based on their academic salary) plus research support, office facilities at RFF, and an allowance of up to $1,000 for moving or living expenses. Fellowships do not provide medical insurance or other RFF fringe benefits.

Duration 11 months.

Additional information Fellows are assigned to an RFF research division: the Energy and Natural Resources division, the Quality of the Environment division, or the Center for Risk, Resource, and Environmental Management. Fellows are expected to be in residence at Resources for the Future for the duration of the program.

Number awarded 1 each year.

Deadline February of each year.

[1269]
GLORIA E. ANZALDUA BOOK PRIZE

National Women's Studies Association
Attn: Book Prizes
7100 Baltimore Avenue, Suite 203
College Park, MD 20740
(301) 403-0407   Fax: (301) 403-4137
E-mail: nwsaoffice@nwsa.org
Web: www.nwsa.org/awards/index.php

Summary To recognize and reward Native American and other members of the National Women's Studies Association (NWSA) who have written outstanding books on women of color and transnational issues.

Eligibility This award is available to NWSA members who submit a book that was published during the preceding year. Entries must present groundbreaking scholarship in women's studies that makes a significant multicultural feminist contribution to women of color and/or transnational studies.

Financial data The award provides an honorarium of $1,000 and lifetime membership in NWSA.

Duration The award is presented annually.

Additional information This award was first presented in 2008.

Number awarded 1 each year.

Deadline April of each year.

[1270]
GROW YOUR OWN TEACHER SCHOLARSHIP PROGRAM

Idaho State Board of Education
Len B. Jordan Office Building
650 West State Street, Room 307
P.O. Box 83720
Boise, ID 83720-0037
(208) 332-1574   Fax: (208) 334-2632
E-mail: scholarshiphelp@osbe.idaho.gov
Web: www.boardofed.idaho.gov/scholarships/gyo.asp

Summary To provide financial assistance to Native Americans in Idaho who are interested in becoming teachers 1) of bilingual education or English as a Second Language (ESL) or 2) to Native American students.

Eligibility This program is open to Idaho school district employees and volunteers who are 1) interested in completing an associate and/or baccalaureate degree in education with a bilingual or ESL endorsement, or 2) Native Americans preparing to teach in Idaho school districts with a significant Native American student population. Applicants must be attending selected schools in Idaho: Boise State University, the College of Southern Idaho, Lewis-Clark State College, or Idaho State University.

Financial data The stipend is $3,000 per year for full-time students; the stipend for part-time students depends on the number of credit hours and the fee charged to part-time students at the participating college or university.

Duration 1 year.

Number awarded Varies each year.

Deadline Deadline not specified.

[1271]
HEALTH AND AGING POLICY FELLOWSHIPS

Columbia University College of Physicians and Surgeons
Attn: Department of Psychiatry
Deputy Director, Health and Aging Policy Fellows
1051 Riverside Drive, Unit 9
New York, NY 10032
(212) 543-6213   Fax: (212) 543-6021
E-mail: healthandagingpolicy@columbia.edu
Web: www.healthandagingpolicy.org

Summary To provide an opportunity for underrepresented minorities and other health professionals with an interest in aging and policy issues to work as legislative assistants in Congress or at other sites.

Eligibility This program is open to physicians, nurses, and social workers who have a demonstrated commitment to health and aging issues and a desire to be involved in health policy at the federal, state, or local levels. Other professionals with clinical backgrounds (e.g., pharmacists, dentists, clinical psychologists) working in the field of health and aging are also eligible. Preference is given to professionals early or midway through their careers. Applicants must be interested serving as residential fellows by participating in the policy-making process on either the federal or state level as legislative assistants in Congress or as professional staff members in executive agencies or policy organizations. A non-residential track is also available to applicants who wish to work on a policy project throughout the year at relevant sites. The program seeks to achieve racial, ethnic, gender, and discipline diversity; members of groups that historically have been underrepresented are strongly encouraged to apply. Selection is based on commitment to health and aging issues and improving the health and well being of older Americans, potential for leadership in health policy, professional qualifications and achievements, impact of the fellowship experience on the applicant's career, and interpersonal and communication skills. U.S. citizenship or permanent resident status is required.

Financial data For residential fellows, the stipend depends on their current base salary, to a maximum of $120,000 per year; other benefits include a travel allowance for pre-fellowship arrangements and to fellowship-related meetings, a relocation grant of up to $3,500, and up to $400 per month for health insurance. For non-residential fellows, grants provide up to $30,000 to cover related fellowship and travel costs.

Duration 9 to 12 months; fellows may apply for a second year of participation.

Additional information This program, which began in 2009, operates in collaboration with the American Political Science Association Congressional Fellowship Program. Funding is provided by The Atlantic Philanthropies. The John Heinz Senate Fellowship Program, an activity of the Teresa and H. John Heinz III Foundation, supports 1 fellow to work in the Senate. In addition, the Centers for Disease Control and Prevention Health Aging Program sponsors 1 non-residential fellow to work with its staff in Atlanta, Georgia.

Number awarded Varies each year; recently, 4 residential and 5 non-residential fellowships were awarded.

Deadline May of each year.

[1272]
HERITAGE PROJECT GRANTS

Cook Inlet Region, Inc.
Attn: The CIRI Foundation
3600 San Jeronimo Drive, Suite 256
Anchorage, AK 99508-2870
(907) 793-3575   Toll Free: (800) 764-3382
Fax: (907) 793-3585   E-mail: tcf@thecirifoundation.org
Web: www.thecirifoundation.org/project_grants.htm

Summary To provide funding to Alaska Natives and non-profit organizations interested in developing projects that further the heritage of Alaska Native beneficiaries of the Cook Inlet region.

Eligibility This program is open to nonprofit organizations (including, but not limited to, schools, colleges, cultural centers, and museums) and tribal councils, with preference given to organizations located within Cook Inlet region. Alaska Natives enrolled to Cook Inlet Region, Inc. (CIRI) and their lineal descendants may also submit applications if they are sponsored by a nonprofit organization. Applicants must be proposing projects that help promote the sponsor's heritage goals: 1) support educational projects, research, and development of materials on subjects that enhance the understanding and appreciation by Natives and the general public about traditional and contemporary Native history, ethnology,

anthropology, philosophy, literature, the arts, and other related fields; 2) promote enrichment programs about the cultural traditions of Alaska Natives of Cook Inlet region and encourage contemporary Native tradition bearers in pursuit of their work; 3) foster the identification, preservation, curation, and interpretation of traditional and contemporary Alaska Native cultural resource materials of Cook Inlet region; 4) encourage excellence in the development and exhibition of traditional and contemporary Native art, music, literature, and other works for appreciation by the general public; 5) conduct consultation and cooperation to protect traditional and cultural values ascribed to Native lands in the Cook Inlet region; and 6) promote cooperation and involvement of Natives within Cook Inlet region as well as with civic and private organizations to accomplish the foundation's heritage programs. Selection is based on the appropriateness of the applicant's project to the foundation's heritage goals and grant guidelines, need for the project, involvement and direct impact upon Alaska Native enrollees and their lineal descendants of CIRI, extent to which the project impacts the targeted audience, extent to which the project impacts the general public, clarity of purpose, realistically-defined tasks to achieve the project's goals and objectives, demonstration of available funds that at least match the amount of funds requested from the foundation, feasibility of project budget and timeline, innovation of project plan, and appropriateness of a project evaluation plan.

Financial data Grant amounts depend on the nature of the project.

Additional information This program was established in 1996.

Number awarded Varies each year; recently, 2 of these grants were awarded.

Deadline Grant applications must be submitted by February, May, August, or October of each year.

[1273]
HIGH PRIORITY, SHORT-TERM BRIDGE AWARDS IN DIABETES RESEARCH

Juvenile Diabetes Research Foundation International
Attn: Grant Administrator
26 Broadway, 14th Floor
New York, NY 10004
(212) 479-7572   Toll Free: (800) 533-CURE
Fax: (212) 785-9595   E-mail: info@jdrf.org
Web: www.jdrf.org/index.cfm?page_id=111715

Summary To provide funding to underrepresented minorities and other scientists who are interested in conducting diabetes-related research but have not yet received any support.

Eligibility Applicants must have an M.D., D.M.D., D.V.M., Ph.D., or equivalent degree and have a full-time faculty position or equivalent at a college, university, medical school, or other research facility. They must have applied for grants previously and scored within 10% of the funding payline of a research funding agency but failed to receive support. Awards must be used to obtain new data to support the feasibility or validity of the research, address reviewers' concerns, or revise approaches to the research. There are no citizenship requirements. Applications are encouraged from women, members of minority groups underrepresented in the sciences, and people with disabilities. The proposed research may be conducted at foreign or domestic, for-profit or nonprofit, or public or private institutions, including universities, colleges, hospitals, laboratories, units of state or local government, or eligible agencies of the federal government.

Financial data Awards are limited to $50,000 plus 10% indirect costs.

Duration 1 year; may be renewed 1 additional year.

Deadline February, June, or November of each year.

[1274]
HIGH RISK RESEARCH IN ANTHROPOLOGY GRANTS

National Science Foundation
Social, Behavioral, and Economic Sciences
Attn: Division of Behavioral and Cognitive Sciences
4201 Wilson Boulevard, Room 995 N
Arlington, VA 22230
(703) 292-8759   Fax: (703) 292-9068
TDD: (800) 281-8749   E-mail: jyellen@nsf.gov
Web: www.nsf.gov/funding/pgm_summ.jsp?pims_id=5319

Summary To provide funding to scholars (particularly Native Americans, other underrepresented minorities, and persons with disabilities) who are interested in conducting high-risk research in anthropology.

Eligibility This program is open to scholars interested in conducting research projects in cultural anthropology, archaeology, or physical anthropology that might be considered too risky for normal review procedures. A project is considered risky if the data may not be obtainable in spite of all reasonable preparation on the researcher's part. Proposals for extremely urgent research where access to the data may not be available in the normal review schedule, even with all reasonable preparation by the researcher, are also appropriate for this program. Graduate students are not eligible. Applications are encouraged from underrepresented minorities and persons with disabilities.

Financial data Grants up to $25,000, including indirect costs, are available.

Duration 1 year.

Number awarded Generally, 5 of these grants are awarded each year.

Deadline Applications may be submitted at any time.

[1275]
HIGHER EDUCATION GRANTS FOR HOPI TRIBAL MEMBERS

Hopi Tribe
Attn: Grants and Scholarship Program
P.O. Box 123
Kykotsmovi, AZ 86039
(928) 734-3542   Toll Free: (800) 762-9630
Fax: (928) 734-9575   E-mail: tlomakema@hopi.nsn.us
Web: www.hopi-nsn.gov

Summary To provide financial assistance to students of Hopi ancestry who are working on an undergraduate, graduate, or postgraduate degree.

Eligibility This program is open to students who are working on an associate, baccalaureate, graduate, or postgraduate degree. Applicants must be enrolled members of the Hopi Tribe. They must have a GPA of 2.0 or higher and be able to demonstrate financial need.

Financial data The maximum grant is $2,500 per semester ($5,000 per year).

Duration 1 semester; may be renewed for up to 10 terms of undergraduate study or up to 5 terms of graduate study, provided the recipient remains enrolled full time.

Additional information This grant is awarded as a secondary source of financial aid to eligible students who are also receiving aid from the Bureau of Indian Affairs (BIA) Higher Education program.

Number awarded Varies each year.

Deadline June of each year for fall; October of each year for winter; November of each year for spring; April of each year for summer.

[1276]
HO-CHUNK NATION GRADUATION ACHIEVEMENT AWARDS

Ho-Chunk Nation
Attn: Higher Education Division
P.O. Box 667
Black River Falls, WI 54615
(715) 284-4915   Toll Free: (800) 362-4476
Fax: (715) 284-1760
E-mail: higher.education@ho-chunk.com
Web: www.ho-chunknation.com/?PageId=47

Summary To recognize and reward Ho-Chunk students who received financial assistance from the tribe and have completed an associate, bachelor's, graduate, or professional degree.

Eligibility Applicants must be enrolled in the Ho-Chunk Nation and have received financial assistance from the tribe in the past to work on a postsecondary degree. Funds are paid once they have completed any of the following degrees: 1-year certificate or diploma, associate degree (2 years), bachelor's degree (4 years), master's or professional degree, J.D. degree, or doctoral degree.

Financial data Awards are $300 for a 1-year certificate or degree, $750 for an associate degree, $1,000 for a bachelor's degree, $3,000 for a master's or professional degree, $4,000 for a J.D. degree, or $5,000 for a doctoral degree.

Duration Students are eligible for only 1 award per degree.

Number awarded Varies each year.

Deadline Applications must be submitted within 1 year of completion of the degree.

[1277]
HOPI EDUCATION AWARDS PROGRAM

Hopi Tribe
Attn: Grants and Scholarship Program
P.O. Box 123
Kykotsmovi, AZ 86039
(928) 734-3542   Toll Free: (800) 762-9630
Fax: (928) 734-9575   E-mail: tlomakema@hopi.nsn.us
Web: www.hopi-nsn.gov

Summary To provide financial assistance to needy students of Hopi ancestry who are working on an undergraduate, graduate, or postgraduate degree.

Eligibility This program is open to students who are working on an associate, baccalaureate, graduate, or postgraduate degree. Applicants must be enrolled members of the Hopi

Tribe. They must have a GPA of 2.5 or higher and be able to demonstrate financial need.

Financial data   The maximum grant is $2,500 per semester ($5,000 per year).

Duration   1 semester; may be renewed for up to 10 terms of undergraduate study or up to 5 terms of graduate study, provided the recipient maintains a GPA of 2.5 or higher and full-time enrollment.

Additional information   This grant is awarded as a secondary source of financial aid to eligible students who are also receiving aid from the Bureau of Indian Affairs (BIA) Higher Education program.

Number awarded   Varies each year.

Deadline   June of each year for fall; October of each year for winter; November of each year for spring; April of each year for summer.

[1278]
HUBBLE FELLOWSHIPS

Space Telescope Science Institute
Attn: Hubble Fellowship Program Office
3700 San Martin Drive
Baltimore, MD 21218
(410) 338-4574   Fax: (410) 338-4211
E-mail: rjallen@stsci.edu
Web: www.stsci.edu

Summary   To provide funding to postdoctoral scientists (particularly Native Americans, minorities, and women) who are interested in conducting research related to the Hubble Space Telescope or related missions of the National Aeronautics and Space Administration (NASA).

Eligibility   This program is open to postdoctoral scientists who completed their doctoral degree within the past 3 years in astronomy, physics, or related disciplines. Applicants must be interested in conducting research related to NASA Cosmic Origins missions: the Hubble Space Telescope, Herschel Space Observatory, James Webb Space Telescope, Stratospheric Observatory for Infrared Astronomy, or the Spitzer Space Telescope. They may be of any nationality, provided that all research is conducted at U.S. institutions and that non-U.S. nationals have valid visas. Research may be theoretical, observational, or instrumental. Women and members of minority groups are strongly encouraged to apply.

Financial data   Stipends are $58,500 for the first year, $59,500 for the second year, and $60,500 for the third year. Other benefits may include health insurance, relocation costs, and support for travel, equipment, and other direct costs of research.

Duration   3 years: an initial 1-year appointment and 2 annual renewals, contingent on satisfactory performance and availability of funds.

Additional information   This program, funded by NASA, began in 1990 and was limited to work with the Hubble Space Telescope. A parallel program, called the Spitzer Fellowship, began in 2002 and was limited to work with the Spitzer Space Telescope. In 2009, those programs were combined into this single program, which was also broadened to include the other NASA Cosmic Origins missions. Fellows are required to be in residence at their host institution engaged in full-time research for the duration of the grant.

Number awarded   Varies each year; recently, 17 of these fellowships were awarded.

Deadline   June of each year.

[1279]
INDIAN MARKET AWARDS

Southwestern Association for Indian Arts, Inc.
3600 Cerrillos Road, Suite 712
P.O. Box 969
Santa Fe, NM 87504-0969
(505) 983-5220   Fax: (505) 983-7647
E-mail: info@swaia.org
Web: www.swaia.org/awards.php

Summary   To recognize and reward outstanding Indian artists who participate in the Santa Fe Indian Market.

Eligibility   This program is open to artists who have a Certificate of Indian Blood as an enrolled member of a federally-recognized tribe or Alaska Native corporation and a New Mexico Taxation and Revenue CRS Identification Number. Artists must be 18 years of age and older. The 10 divisions are 1) jewelry; 2) pottery; 3) paintings, drawings, graphics, and photography; 4) Pueblo wooden carvings; 5) sculpture; 6) textiles; 7) diverse art forms; 8) beadwork and quillwork; 9); moving images (subdivided into narrative shorts, documentary shorts, animation, and experimental); and 10) basketry. Along with their application, artists must submit slides of each medium that they wish to show at the annual Santa Fe Indian Market. The work must comply with standards of the Southwestern Association for Indian Arts (SWAIA) and be representative of the artwork they plan to sell at the Market.

Financial data   A total of more than $100,000 in prize money is awarded each year. Awards vary each year, but they have included $1,000 for Best of Show and $500 for first place in each category.

Duration   The Market is held on 2 days in August of each year.

Additional information   Special awards include the IAIA Distinguished Alumni Award ($500), the Youth Smile Award ($100), the Artists' Choice Award ($300), and the Innovation Award ($2,500). Standards awards include the Tony Da Award for Pottery ($500), the Joe Cat<A3>3 Award for Beadmaking ($500), the Horse Tack and Attire Award ($500), the Miniature Award ($500), the Jean Seth Award for Basket Making ($500), the Jean Seth Award for Painting ($500), and the Traditional Pueblo Pot Award ($1,000). SWAIA endowed awards include the Helen Naha Award for Hopi Pottery ($200) and the Indian Arts Fund Award ($200). Artists are responsible for payment of a $25 application fee, a $10 city of Santa Fe business license fee, a $10 city of Santa Fe booth permit fee, and a booth fee of $400 to $650.

Number awarded   Varies each year.

Deadline   Applications must be submitted by January of each year.

[1280]
INDIGENOUS CONTEMPORARY ARTS PROGRAM

National Museum of the American Indian
Attn: Expressive Arts Program
Cultural Arts Program Specialist
Fourth Street and Independence Avenue, S.W.
Washington, DC 20024
(202) 633-6653   E-mail: scottv@si.edu
Web: www.nmai.si.edu/icap/expressive.html

Summary To provide funding to Native American artists interested in collaborating to create and present new works.

Eligibility This program is open to collaborations of 2 or more Native artists interested in creating new works for public performance that may include, but are not limited to, music, dance, spoken word (e.g., new scripts, written texts, traditional stories), electronic media, costume design, mask making, set design, performance art, photography, painting, or other forms of expressive culture. Non-Native collaborators may be included, but the proposal must be written by a Native lead artist. All applicants must hold citizenship in the Americas. They are encouraged to use the resources of the National Museum of the American Indian (NMAI), including its collections and exhibitions, for inspiration. Support is not available for film, video production or post-production, concerts or performances of pre-existing work, or any creative art that is not intended for a public performance. Selection is based on the artistic merit of the proposal that clearly shows the collaboration required for completion and public presentation, relationship of the proposed project to the mission of the NMAI and the goals of this award program, project feasibility, and possibility of project's presentation in the lead artist's home community.

Financial data Grants range up to $10,000.

Duration 1 year, beginning in May.

Additional information This program is supported by the Ford Foundation. Upon returning to college, participants are expected to create a new art work and provide photographic documentation that may be used in future NMAI projects or publications. They also provide a short description about the art process or completed art project. Suggested themes include American Indian identity in higher education, language, or the environment.

Number awarded Varies each year.

Deadline January of each year.

[1281]
INNOVATIONS IN CLINICAL RESEARCH AWARDS

Doris Duke Charitable Foundation
Attn: Grantmaking Programs
650 Fifth Avenue, 19th Floor
New York, NY 10019
(212) 974-7000   Fax: (212) 974-7590
E-mail: ddcf@aibs.org
Web: www.ddcf.org

Summary To provide funding to minority and other investigators interested in conducting clinical research that may develop innovations in specified disease areas.

Eligibility This program is open to investigators who have received an M.D., Ph.D., M.D./Ph.D., or foreign equivalent and have a faculty appointment at a U.S. degree-granting institution (although U.S. citizenship is not required). Applicants must be interested in conducting innovative clinical research on a topic that changes annually but recently was limited to sickle cell disease; in other years, research was restricted to cardiovascular disease, stroke, blood disorders, or the development of diagnostics and therapeutic monitoring of AIDS in resource-poor countries. Preference is given to applicants who 1) work in other research areas, in an effort to bring new thinking to the field of sickle cell disease research; 2) are women or underrepresented minorities in medicine (Blacks or African Americans, Hispanics or Latinos, American Indians, Alaskan Natives or Native Hawaiians); or 3) propose the following types of sickle cell disease research: drug discovery, genetic and genomic approaches to study variability in the severity of sickle cell disease, early phase corrective approaches such as gene therapy and transplantation of blood-forming cells, identification of new risks for disease complication, or development of new treatments drawing from innovations in other fields such as cancer research. Selection is based on originality and inventiveness of the concept and approach, relevance of the question posed to the field of sickle cell disease, potential for clinical application, and evidence of the investigator's potential to drive innovation in sickle cell disease clinical research.

Financial data Grants provide $150,000 per year for direct costs and $12,000 per year for indirect costs.

Duration 3 years.

Additional information This program began in 2000.

Number awarded Up to 9 each year. Since this program was established, it has awarded 49 grants worth approximately $12 million.

Deadline Letters of intent must be submitted by June of each year.

[1282]
INTERNATIONAL AND AREA STUDIES FELLOWSHIPS

American Council of Learned Societies
Attn: Office of Fellowships and Grants
633 Third Avenue
New York, NY 10017-6795
(212) 697-1505   Fax: (212) 949-8058
E-mail: fellowships@acls.org
Web: www.acls.org/programs/acls

Summary To provide funding to postdoctoral scholars (especially Native Americans, other minorities, and women) who are interested in conducting humanities-related research on the societies and cultures of Asia, Africa, the Middle East, Latin America and the Caribbean, eastern Europe, and the former Soviet Union.

Eligibility This program is open to U.S. citizens and residents who have lived in the United States for at least 3 years. Applicants must have a Ph.D. degree and not have received supported research leave time for at least 3 years prior to the start of the proposed research. They must be interested in conducting humanities and humanities-related social science research on the societies and cultures of Asia, Africa, the Middle East, Latin America and the Caribbean, eastern Europe, or the former Soviet Union. Selection is based on the intellectual merit of the proposed research and the likelihood that it will produce significant and innovative scholarship.

Applications are particularly invited from women and members of minority groups.

Financial data The maximum grant is $60,000 for full professors and equivalent, $40,000 for associate professors and equivalent, or $35,000 for assistant professors and equivalent. These fellowships may not be held concurrently with another major fellowship.

Duration 6 to 12 months.

Additional information This program is jointly supported by the American Council of Learned Societies (ACLS) and the Social Science Research Council (SSRC), with funding provided by the National Endowment for the Humanities (NEH).

Number awarded Up to 10 each year.

Deadline September of each year.

[1283]
INVESTIGATORS IN PATHOGENESIS OF INFECTIOUS DISEASE

Burroughs Wellcome Fund
21 T.W. Alexander Drive, Suite 100
P.O. Box 13901
Research Triangle Park, NC 27709-3901
(919) 991-5100 Fax: (919) 991-5160
E-mail: info@bwfund.org
Web: www.bwfund.org

Summary To provide funding to underrepresented minorities (including Native Americans) and other physician/scientists in the United States and Canada who wish to conduct research on pathogenesis, with a focus on the intersection of human and pathogen biology.

Eligibility This program is open to established independent physician/scientists who are citizens or permanent residents of the United States or Canada and affiliated with accredited degree-granting U.S. or Canadian medical schools. Applicants must be interested in conducting research projects that hold potential for advancing significantly the biochemical, pharmacological, immunological, and molecular biological understanding of how infectious agents and the human body interact. Although work on AIDS, malaria, and tuberculosis is not excluded, preference is given to research shedding new light on unexplored pathogenesis. Research on understudied infectious diseases, including pathogenic fungi, protozoan and metazoan diseases, and emerging infections, is of especial interest. Candidates must have an M.D., D.V.M., or Ph.D. degree and be tenure-track investigators as an assistant professor or equivalent at a degree-granting institution. Each institution (including its medical school, graduate schools, and all affiliated hospitals and research institutes) may nominate up to 2 candidates. Institutions that nominate a researcher who has a D.V.M. are allowed 3 nominations. The sponsor also encourages institutions to nominate underrepresented minorities and women. Selection is based on qualifications of the candidate and potential to conduct innovative research; demonstration of an established record of independent research; and quality and originality of the proposed research and its potential to advance understanding of fundamental issues of how infectious agents and human hosts interact.

Financial data The grant provides $100,000 per year.

Duration 5 years.

Additional information This program was established in 2001 as a replacement for several former programs: New Investigator and Scholar Awards in Molecular Pathogenic Mycology, New Investigator and Scholar Awards in Molecular Parasitology, and New Initiatives in Malaria Awards. Awardees are required to devote at least 75% of their time to research-related activities.

Number awarded Varies each year; recently, 6 of these grants were awarded.

Deadline October of each year.

[1284]
JAMES A. RAWLEY PRIZE

Organization of American Historians
Attn: Award and Committee Coordinator
112 North Bryan Street
Bloomington, IN 47408-4141
(812) 855-7311 Fax: (812) 855-0696
E-mail: khamm@oah.org
Web: www.oah.org/awards/awards.rawley.index.html

Summary To recognize and reward Native American and other authors of outstanding books dealing with race relations in the United States.

Eligibility This award is presented to the author of the outstanding book on the history of race relations in America. Entries must have been published during the current calendar year.

Financial data The award is $1,000 and a certificate.

Duration The award is presented annually.

Additional information This award was established in 1990.

Number awarded 1 each year.

Deadline September of each year.

[1285]
JAMES H. DUNN, JR. MEMORIAL FELLOWSHIP PROGRAM

Office of the Governor
Attn: Department of Central Management Services
503 William G. Stratton Building
Springfield, IL 62706
(217) 524-1381 Fax: (217) 558-4497
TDD: (217) 785-3979
Web: www.ilga.gov/commission/lru/internships.html

Summary To provide minorities and other recent college graduates with work experience in the Illinois Governor's office.

Eligibility This program in open to residents of any state who have completed a bachelor's degree and are interested in working in the Illinois Governor's office or in various agencies under the Governor's jurisdiction. Applicants may have majored in any field, but they must be able to demonstrate a substantial commitment to excellence as evidenced by academic honors, leadership ability, extracurricular activities, and involvement in community or public service. Along with their application, they must submit 1) a 500-word personal statement on the qualities or attributes they will bring to the program, their career goals or plans, how their selection for this program would assist them in achieving those goals, and what they expect to gain from the program; and 2) a 1,000-word essay in which they identify and analyze a public issue that they feel has great impact on state government. A particular goal of the program is to achieve affirmative action through the nomination of qualified minorities, women, and persons with disabilities.

Financial data   The stipend is $2,611 per month.

Duration   1 year, beginning in August.

Additional information   Assignments are in Springfield and, to a limited extent, in Chicago or Washington, D.C.

Number awarded   Varies each year.

Deadline   February of each year.

[1286]
JDRF SCHOLAR AWARDS

Juvenile Diabetes Research Foundation International
Attn: Grant Administrator
26 Broadway, 14th Floor
New York, NY 10004
(212) 479-7572   Toll Free: (800) 533-CURE
Fax: (212) 785-9595   E-mail: info@jdrf.org
Web: www.jdrf.org/index.cfm?page_id=111715

Summary   To provide funding to established independent physician scientists (particularly Native Americans, other underrepresented minorities, women, and individuals with disabilities) who are interested in conducting basic or clinical diabetes-related research.

Eligibility   This program is open to established investigators in diabetes-related research who have an M.D., D.M.D., D.O., Ph.D., D.V.M., or equivalent degree and an independent investigator position at a university, health science center, or comparable institution. Normally, applicants should have at least 7 years of relevant experience since receiving their doctoral degree. They must be willing to take risks and attempt new approaches to accelerate Type 1 diabetes research. This program is not intended to expand the funding of scientists already well supported for exploring this concept. There are no citizenship requirements. Applications are encouraged from women, members of minority groups underrepresented in the sciences, and people with disabilities. The proposed research may be conducted at foreign or domestic, for-profit or nonprofit, or public or private institutions, including universities, colleges, hospitals, laboratories, units of state or local government, or eligible agencies of the federal government. Selection is based on relevance of the research to and impact on the mission of the Juvenile Diabetes Research Foundation (JDRF); innovation, creativity, and the potential for future innovation relative to the applicant's career stage; and the applicant's motivation, enthusiasm, and intellectual energy to pursue a challenging problem.

Financial data   The total award may be up to $250,000 each year, including indirect costs.

Duration   Up to 5 years.

Number awarded   Up to 4 each year.

Deadline   An intent to submit must be received by August of each year. Completed applications are due in September.

[1287]
JOEL ELKES RESEARCH AWARD

American College of Neuropsychopharmacology
Attn: Executive Office
5034-A Thoroughbred Lane
Brentwood, TN 37027
(615) 324-2360   Fax: (615) 523-1715
E-mail: acnp@acnp.org
Web: www.acnp.org/programs/awards.aspx

Summary   To recognize and reward young scientists, especially minorities and women, who have contributed outstanding clinical or translational research to neuropsychopharmacology.

Eligibility   This award is available to scientists who are younger than 50 years of age. Nominees must have made an outstanding clinical or translational contribution to neuropsychopharmacology. The contribution may be based on a single discovery or a cumulative body of work. Emphasis is placed on contributions that further understanding of self-regulatory processes as they affect mental function and behavior in disease and well-being. Membership in the American College of Neuropsychopharmacology (ACNP) is not required. Nomination of women and minorities is highly encouraged.

Financial data   The award consists of an expense-paid trip to the ACNP annual meeting, a monetary honorarium, and a plaque.

Duration   The award is presented annually.

Additional information   This award was first presented in 1986.

Number awarded   1 each year.

Deadline   Nominations must be submitted by June of each year.

[1288]
JOHN V. KRUTILLA RESEARCH STIPEND

Resources for the Future
Attn: Coordinator for Academic Programs
1616 P Street, N.W., Suite 600
Washington, DC 20036-1400
(202) 328-5088   Fax: (202) 939-3460
E-mail: krutilla-award@rff.org
Web: www.rff.org/About_RFF/Pages/default.aspx

Summary   To provide funding for research related to environmental and resource economics to young scholars, particularly Native Americans, other minorities, and women.

Eligibility   This program is open to scholars who received their doctoral degree within the past 5 years. Applicants must be interested in conducting research related to environmental and resource economics. They must submit a short description of the proposed research, a curriculum vitae, and a letter of recommendation. Women and minority candidates are strongly encouraged to apply.

Financial data   The grant is $9,000.

Duration   1 year.

Additional information   This award was first presented in 2006.

Number awarded   1 each year.

Deadline   February of each year.

[1289]
JUDITH L. WEIDMAN RACIAL ETHNIC MINORITY FELLOWSHIP

United Methodist Communications
Attn: Communications Resourcing Team
810 12th Avenue South
P.O. Box 320
Nashville, TN 37202-0320
(615) 742-5481   Toll Free: (888) CRT-4UMC
Fax: (615) 742-5485   E-mail: scholarships@umcom.org
Web: crt.umc.org/interior.asp?ptid=1&mid=6891

Summary To provide work experience to Methodists who are Native Americans or members of other minority groups and interested in a communications career.

Eligibility This program is open to United Methodists of racial ethnic minority heritage who are interested in preparing for a career in communications with the United Methodist Church. Applicants must be recent college or seminary graduates who have broad communications training, including work in journalism, mass communications, marketing, public relations, and electronic media. They must be able to understand and speak English proficiently and to relocate for a year. Selection is based on Christian commitment and involvement in the life of the United Methodist Church; achievement as revealed by transcripts, GPA, letters of reference, and work samples; study, experience, and evidence of talent in the field of communications; clarity of purpose and goals for the future; desire to learn how to be a successful United Methodist conference communicator; and potential leadership ability as a professional religion communicator for the United Methodist Church.

Financial data The stipend is $30,000 per year. Benefits and expenses for moving and professional travel are also provided.

Duration 1 year, starting in July.

Additional information This program was established in 1998. Recipients are assigned to 1 of the 63 United Methodist Annual Conferences, the headquarters of local churches within a geographic area. At the Annual Conference, the fellow will be assigned an experienced communicator as a mentor and will work closely with that mentor and with United Methodist Communications in Nashville, Tennessee. Following the successful completion of the fellowship, United Methodist Communications and the participating Annual Conference will assist in a search for permanent employment within the United Methodist Church but cannot guarantee a position.

Number awarded 1 each year.

Deadline March of each year.

[1290]
JULIUS AXELROD MENTORSHIP AWARD

American College of Neuropsychopharmacology
Attn: Executive Office
5034-A Thoroughbred Lane
Brentwood, TN 37027
(615) 324-2360   Fax: (615) 523-1715
E-mail: acnp@acnp.org
Web: www.acnp.org/programs/awards.aspx

Summary To recognize and reward members of the American College of Neuropsychopharmacology (ACNP), particularly Native Americans, other minorities, and women who have demonstrated outstanding mentoring of young scientists.

Eligibility This award is available to ACNP members who have made an outstanding contribution to neuropsychopharmacology by mentoring and developing young scientists into leaders in the field. Nominations must be accompanied by letters of support from up to 3 people who have been mentored by the candidate. Nomination of women and minorities is highly encouraged.

Financial data The award consists of a monetary honorarium and a plaque.

Duration The award is presented annually.

Additional information This award was first presented in 2004.

Number awarded 1 each year.

Deadline Nominations must be submitted by June of each year.

[1291]
JUVENILE DIABETES RESEARCH FOUNDATION INNOVATIVE GRANTS

Juvenile Diabetes Research Foundation International
Attn: Grant Administrator
26 Broadway, 14th Floor
New York, NY 10004
(212) 479-7572   Toll Free: (800) 533-CURE
Fax: (212) 785-9595   E-mail: info@jdrf.org
Web: www.jdrf.org/index.cfm?page_id=111715

Summary To provide funding to Native American or underrepresented minorities and other scientists who are interested in conducting innovative diabetes-related research.

Eligibility Applicants must have an M.D., D.M.D., D.V.M., Ph.D., or equivalent degree and have a full-time faculty position or equivalent at a college, university, medical school, or other research facility. They must be seeking "seed" money for investigative work based on a sound hypothesis for which preliminary data are insufficient for a regular research grant but that are likely to lead to important results for the treatment of diabetes and its complications. Applicants must specifically explain how the proposal is innovative. Selection is based on whether 1) the proposed research is innovative; 2) the underlying premise, goal, or hypothesis is plausible; 3) the proposed research can be completed in 1 year; and 4) the proposed research is relevant to the mission of the Juvenile Diabetes Research Foundation and its potential impact. Applications are encouraged from women, members of minority groups underrepresented in the sciences, and people with disabilities. The proposed research may be conducted at foreign or domestic, for-profit or nonprofit, or public or private institutions, including universities, colleges, hospitals, laboratories, units of state or local government, or eligible agencies of the federal government.

Financial data Awards are limited to $100,000 plus 10% indirect costs.

Duration 1 year; nonrenewable.

Deadline January or July of each year.

[1292]
JUVENILE DIABETES RESEARCH FOUNDATION PRIORITY RESEARCH GRANTS

Juvenile Diabetes Research Foundation International
Attn: Grant Administrator
26 Broadway, 14th Floor
New York, NY 10004
(212) 479-7572   Toll Free: (800) 533-CURE
Fax: (212) 785-9595   E-mail: info@jdrf.org
Web: www.jdrf.org/index.cfm?page_id=111715

Summary To provide funding to scientists (especially Native Americans, other minorities, women, and individuals with disabilities) who are interested in conducting research on diabetes and its related complications.

Eligibility Applicants must have an M.D., D.M.D., D.V.M., Ph.D., or equivalent degree and have a full-time faculty position or equivalent at a college, university, medical school, or other research facility. They must be interested in conducting research related to the priorities of the Juvenile Diabetes Research Foundation (JDRF), which currently include 1) restoration and maintenance of normal glucose regulation in Type 1 diabetes, including restoration of beta cell function, immunoregulation, and metabolic control; 2) prevention and treatment of complications of diabetes; 3) improvements in glucose control; and 4) prevention of Type 1 diabetes. Applications are encouraged from women, members of minority groups underrepresented in the sciences, and people with disabilities. The proposed research may be conducted at foreign or domestic, for-profit or nonprofit, or public or private institutions, including universities, colleges, hospitals, laboratories, units of state or local government, or eligible agencies of the federal government. Selection is based on potential to generate new approaches to unsolved scientific problems related to Type 1 diabetes; relevance to the objectives of JDRF: scientific, technical, or medical significance of the research proposal; innovativeness; appropriateness and adequacy of the experimental approach and methodology; qualifications and research experience of the principal investigator and collaborators; availability of resources and facilities necessary for the project; and appropriateness of the proposed budget in relation to the proposed research.

Financial data Grants up to $165,000 (plus 10% for indirect costs) per year are available.

Duration 3 years.

Deadline Letters of intent must be submitted by November of each year.

[1293]
KATRIN H. LAMON FELLOWSHIP

School for Advanced Research
Attn: Director of Scholar Programs
660 Garcia Street
P.O. Box 2188
Santa Fe, NM 87504-2188
(505) 954-7201   E-mail: scholar@sarsf.org
Web: sarweb.org/index.php?resident_scholars

Summary To provide funding to Native American pre- and postdoctoral scholars interested in conducting research in the social sciences or humanities while in residence at the School for Advanced Research (SAR) in Santa Fe, New Mexico.

Eligibility This program is open to Native American Ph.D. candidates and scholars with doctorates who are interested in conducting research at SAR in the humanities or the social sciences. Applicants must submit a 150-word abstract describing the purpose, goals, and objectives of their research project; a 4-page proposal; a bibliography; a curriculum vitae; a brief statement of tribal affiliation; and 3 letters of recommendation. Predoctoral applicants must also submit a brief letter of nomination from their department. Preference is given to applicants whose field work or basic research and analysis are complete and who need time to write up their research.

Financial data The fellowship provides an apartment and office on the school's campus, a stipend of up to $40,000 for scholars or $30,000 for Ph.D. candidates, library assistance, and other benefits.

Duration 9 months, beginning in September.

Additional information Funding for this program is provided by the Katrin H. Lamon Endowment for Native American Art and Education. Participants must spend their 9-month residency at the school in New Mexico.

Number awarded 1 each year.

Deadline October of each year.

[1294]
LEE & LOW BOOKS NEW VOICES AWARD

Lee & Low Books
95 Madison Avenue, Suite 1205
New York, NY 10016
(212) 779-4400   Fax: (212) 683-1894
E-mail: general@leeandlow.com
Web: www.leeandlow.com/p/new_voices_award.mhtml

Summary To recognize and reward outstanding unpublished children's picture books by Native Americans or other writers of color.

Eligibility The contest is open to writers of color who are residents of the United States and who have not previously published a children's picture book. Writers who have published in other venues, (e.g., children's magazines, young adult fiction and nonfiction) are eligible. Manuscripts previously submitted to the sponsor are not eligible. Submissions should be no more than 1,500 words and must address the needs of children of color by providing stories with which they can identify and relate and that promote a greater understanding of each other. Submissions may be fiction or nonfiction for children between the ages of 5 and 12. Folklore and animal stories are not considered. Up to 2 submissions may be submitted per entrant.

Financial data The award is a $1,000 cash grant plus the standard publication contract, including the standard advance and royalties. The Honor Award winner receives a cash grant of $500.

Duration The competition is held annually.

Additional information This program was established in 2000. Manuscripts may not be sent to any other publishers while under consideration for this award.

Number awarded 2 each year.

Deadline October of each year.

[1295]
LIFETIME ACHIEVEMENT AWARD FOR LITERATURE

Native Writers Circle of the Americas
c/o University of Oklahoma
Department of Native American Studies
633 Elm Avenue, Room 216
Norman, OK 73019-3119
(405) 325-2312   Fax: (405) 325-0842
E-mail: nas@ou.edu
Web: www.ou.edu/cas/nas/index.html

Summary   To recognize and reward the lifetime work of outstanding Native American writers.

Eligibility   This award is given to Native American writers who have a long history of outstanding literary activities. The winner is selected by fellow Native American writers. There is no application process.

Financial data   The prize is $1,000.

Duration   The prize is given annually.

Additional information   This award was established in 1992.

Number awarded   1 each year.

Deadline   Deadline not specified.

[1296]
LONG RANGE ANNUAL FUNDING OPPORTUNITY ANNOUNCEMENT FOR NAVY AND MARINE CORPS SCIENCE, TECHNOLOGY, ENGINEERING & MATHEMATICS (STEM) PROGRAMS

Office of Naval Research
Attn: Code 03R
875 North Randolph Street, Suite 1410
Arlington, VA 22203-1995
(703) 696-4111   E-mail: kam.ng1@navy.mil
Web: www.onr.navy.mil

Summary   To provide financial support to investigators at Tribal Colleges or Universities and other schools or companies who are interested in conducting long-range science, technology, engineering, or mathematics (STEM) projects on topics of interest to the U.S. Navy.

Eligibility   This program is open to faculty and staff from academia (colleges and universities), middle and high schools, nonprofit organizations, and industry. Applicants must be interested in conducting long-range projects in STEM fields that offer potential for advancement and improvement of Navy and Marine Corps operations. The projects should help fulfill the mission of the program to foster an interest in, knowledge of, and study in STEM to ensure an educated and well-prepared work force that meets naval and national competitive needs. Applicants at Historically Black Colleges and Universities (HBCUs) and Minority Institutions (MIs) are encouraged to submit proposals and join others in submitting proposals.

Financial data   Grants range up to $200,000 per year.

Duration   12 to 36 months.

Number awarded   Varies each year; recently, a total of $10 million was available for this program.

Deadline   Full proposals must be submitted by September of each year.

[1297]
LONG RANGE BROAD AGENCY ANNOUNCEMENT FOR NAVY AND MARINE CORPS SCIENCE AND TECHNOLOGY

Office of Naval Research
Attn: Acquisition Department, Code BD255
875 North Randolph Street
Arlington, VA 22203-1995
(703) 696-2570   Fax: (703) 696-3365
E-mail: misale.abdi@navy.mil
Web: www.onr.navy.mil

Summary   To provide financial support to investigators (particularly those at Tribal Colleges and Universities and other minority serving institutions) who are interested in conducting long-range science and technology research on topics of interest to the U.S. Navy and Marine Corps.

Eligibility   This program is open to researchers from academia (colleges and universities) and industry. Applicants must be interested in conducting long-range projects in fields of science and technology that offer potential for advancement and improvement of Navy and Marine Corps operations. The proposed research must relate to 1 of the following topic areas: 1) expeditionary maneuver warfare and combating terrorism; 2) command, control communications, computers, intelligence, surveillance, and reconnaissance; 3) ocean battlespace sensing; 4) sea warfare and weapons; 5) warfighter performance; and 6) naval air warfare and weapons. Researchers at Historically Black Colleges and Universities (HBCUs) and Minority Institutions (MIs) are encouraged to submit proposals and join others in submitting proposals.

Financial data   Grant amounts depend on the nature of the proposal.

Number awarded   Varies each year.

Deadline   White papers must be submitted in November of each year.

[1298]
MANY VOICES RESIDENCIES

Playwrights' Center
2301 East Franklin Avenue
Minneapolis, MN 55406-1024
(612) 332-7481   Fax: (612) 332-6037
E-mail: info@pwcenter.org
Web: www.pwcenter.org/fellows_voices.php

Summary   To provide funding to Native Americans and other Minnesota playwrights of color so they can spend a year at the Playwrights' Center in Minneapolis.

Eligibility   This program is open to playwrights of color who are citizens or permanent residents of the United States and have been residents of Minnesota for at least 1 year. Applicants must be interested in playwriting and creating theater in a supportive artist community at the Playwrights' Center. They may be beginning playwrights (with little or no previous playwriting experience) or emerging playwrights (with previous playwriting experience and/or training). Selection is based on the applicant's commitment, proven talent, and artistic potential.

Financial data   Beginning playwrights receive a $1,000 stipend, $250 in play development funds, and a structured curriculum of playwriting instruction and dramaturgical support. Emerging playwrights receive a $3,600 stipend, $1,000 in play development funds, and dramaturgical support.

Duration 9 months, beginning in October.

Additional information This program, which began in 1994, is funded by the Jerome Foundation. Fellows must be in residence at the Playwrights' Center for the duration of the program.

Number awarded 5 each year: 2 beginning playwrights and 3 emerging playwrights.

Deadline February of each year.

[1299]
MATHEMATICAL SCIENCES POSTDOCTORAL RESEARCH FELLOWSHIPS

National Science Foundation
Directorate for Mathematical and Physical Sciences
Attn: Division of Mathematical Sciences
4201 Wilson Boulevard, Room 1025N
Arlington, VA 22230
(703) 292-8132   Fax: (703) 292-9032
TDD: (800) 281-8749   E-mail: devasius@nsf.gov
Web: www.nsf.gov/funding/pgm_summ.jsp?pims_id=5301

Summary To provide financial assistance to postdoctorates (especially Native Americans, other underrepresented minorities, and persons with disabilities) who are interested in pursuing research training in mathematics.

Eligibility Applicants for these fellowships must 1) be U.S. citizens, nationals, or permanent residents; 2) have earned a Ph.D. in a mathematical science or have had equivalent research training and experience; 3) have held the Ph.D. for no more than 2 years; and 4) have not previously held any other postdoctoral fellowship from the National Science Foundation (NSF) or been offered an award from this program. They must be proposing to conduct a program of postdoctoral research training at an appropriate nonprofit U.S. institution, including government laboratories, national laboratories, and privately sponsored nonprofit institutes, as well as institutions of higher education. A senior scientist at the institution must indicate availability for consultation and agreement to work with the fellow. Applications are encouraged from underrepresented minorities and persons with disabilities.

Financial data The total award is $135,000, consisting of 3 components: 1) a monthly stipend of $5,000 for full-time support or $2,500 for half-time support, paid directly to the fellow; 2) a research allowance of $10,000, also paid directly to the fellow; and 3) an institutional allowance of $5,000, paid to the host institution for fringe benefits (including health insurance payments for the fellow) and expenses incurred in support of the fellow, such as space, equipment, and general purpose supplies.

Duration Fellows may select either of 2 options: the research fellowship option provides full-time support for any 18 academic-year months in a 3-year period, in intervals not shorter than 3 consecutive months; the research instructorship option provides a combination of full-time and half-time support over a period of 3 academic years, usually 1 academic year full time and 2 academic years part time. Under both options, the award includes 6 summer months, but no more than 2 summer months of support may be received in any calendar year. The stipend support for 24 months (18 academic year months plus 6 summer months) is provided within a 48-month period.

Additional information Under certain circumstances, it may be desirable for portions of the work to be done at foreign institutions. Approval to do so must be obtained in advance from both the sponsoring senior scientist and the NSF.

Number awarded 30 to 35 each year. A total of $4.8 million is available for this program annually.

Deadline October of each year.

[1300]
MENTOR-BASED MINORITY POSTDOCTORAL FELLOWSHIPS IN DIABETES

American Diabetes Association
Attn: Senior Manager, Research Programs
1701 North Beauregard Street
Alexandria, VA 22311
(703) 549-1500, ext. 2362   Toll Free: (800) DIABETES
Fax: (703) 549-1715
E-mail: grantquestions@diabetes.org
Web: professional.diabetes.org

Summary To provide financial assistance to Native American and other minority postdoctoral fellows working with established diabetes investigators.

Eligibility Applications for these fellowships may be submitted by established and active investigators in diabetes research who wish to supervise the work of a postdoctoral fellow, whom they will select. They must currently hold a grant from the American Diabetes Association. The fellow selected by the investigator must be a member of an underrepresented minority group (African American; Spanish, Hispanic, or Latino; American Indian or Alaskan Native; Native Hawaiian or Pacific Islander); must have an M.D., Ph.D., D.O., D.P.M., or Pharm.D. degree; must not be serving an internship or residency during the fellowship period; and must not have more than 3 years of postdoctoral research experience in the field of diabetes/endocrinology. Applicant investigators and fellows must be U.S. citizens or permanent residents. The applicant investigator must also hold an appointment at a U.S. research institution and have sufficient research support to provide an appropriate training environment for the fellow. The applicant investigator must be a member of the Professional Section of the American Diabetes Association; the fellow must also be, or agree to become, a member. Selection is based on the quality and activity of the applicant investigator's diabetes research program, the likelihood that the fellow trained by the mentor will actively pursue a career in diabetes research, the applicant investigator's past training record, and evidence of sufficient research support and adequate facilities to provide an appropriate training environment for a postdoctoral fellow.

Financial data The grant is $45,000 per year. Within that total, the applicant investigator may determine the salary of the fellow; up to $3,000 per year of the total may be used for laboratory supply costs, up to $1,000 may be used for travel by the fellow to attend diabetes-related scientific meetings, and up to $500 may be used for book purchases.

Duration 2 to 3 years.

Number awarded Varies each year.

Deadline January of each year.

[1301]
MENTORED CAREER DEVELOPMENT AWARD TO PROMOTE FACULTY DIVERSITY/RE-ENTRY IN BIOMEDICAL RESEARCH

National Heart, Lung, and Blood Institute
Attn: Division of Cardiovascular Sciences
6701 Rockledge Drive
Bethesda, MD 20892-7936
(301) 435-0709   Fax: (301) 480-1455
E-mail: silsbeeL@nhlbi.nih.gov
Web: www.nhlbi.nih.gov/funding/inits/index.htm

Summary To provide funding to Native Americans and members of other underrepresented groups interested in developing into independent biomedical investigators in research areas relevant to the mission of the National Heart, Lung, and Blood Institute (NHLBI).

Eligibility This program is open to U.S. citizens, nationals, and permanent residents who are full-time non-tenured faculty members at U.S. domestic institutions of higher education and eligible agencies of the federal government; applications are especially encouraged from faculty at Historically Black Colleges and Universities (HBCUs), Tribally Controlled Colleges and Universities (TCCUs), Hispanic-Serving Institutions (HSIs), and Alaska Native and Native Hawaiian Serving Institutions. Candidates must have received, at least 2 years previously, a doctoral degree or equivalent in a basic or clinical area related to cardiovascular, pulmonary, or hematologic diseases. Applications are especially encouraged from members of a group that will promote greater diversity in scientific research, including 1) members of underrepresented racial and ethnic groups (African Americans, Hispanic Americans, Alaska Natives, American Indians, Native Hawaiians, non-Asian Pacific Islanders); 2) individuals with disabilities; and 3) individuals from disadvantaged backgrounds. Candidates who have experienced an interruption in their research careers for a period of at least 3 but no more than 8 years (e.g., starting and/or raising a family, an incapacitating illness or injury, caring for an ill immediate family member, performing military service) are also eligible. The proposed research development plan must enable the candidate to become an independent investigator in cardiovascular, pulmonary, hematologic, and sleep disorders research with either a clinical or basic science emphasis.

Financial data The grant provides salary support of up to $75,000 per year plus fringe benefits. In addition, up to $30,000 per year may be provided for research project requirements and related support (e.g., technical personnel costs, supplies, equipment, candidate travel, telephone charges, publication costs, and tuition for necessary courses). Facilities and administrative costs may be reimbursed at the rate of 8% of total direct costs.

Duration 3 to 5 years.

Additional information At least 75% of the awardee's effort must be devoted to the research program. The remainder may be devoted to other clinical and teaching pursuits that are consistent with the program goals of developing the awardee into an independent biomedical scientist or the maintenance of the teaching and/or clinical skills needed for an academic research career.

Number awarded Varies each year; recently, 8 to 10 awards were available through this program.

Deadline Letters of intent must be submitted by August of each year; completed applications are due in September.

[1302]
MENTORED NEW INVESTIGATOR RESEARCH GRANTS TO PROMOTE DIVERSITY OF THE ALZHEIMER'S ASSOCIATION

Alzheimer's Association
Attn: Medical and Scientific Affairs
225 North Michigan Avenue, 17th Floor
Chicago, IL 60601-7633
(312) 335-5747   Toll Free: (800) 272-3900
Fax: (866) 699-1246   TDD: (312) 335-5886
E-mail: grantsapp@alz.org
Web: www.alz.org

Summary To provide funding for mentored research on Alzheimer's Disease to junior underrepresented minorities and other investigators who will contribute to diversity in the field.

Eligibility This program is open to investigators who have less than 10 years of research experience after receipt of their terminal degree. Applicants must be proposing to conduct research with focus areas that change annually but are related to Alzheimer's Disease. They must identify a mentor who is experienced in conducting Alzheimer's and related dementia research and in mentoring investigators. Eligibility is restricted to investigators who will contribute to diversity in the field of biomedical research, including members of underrepresented racial and ethnic minority groups (African Americans, Hispanic Americans, American Indians/Alaska Natives, Native Hawaiians, and Pacific Islanders) and individuals with disabilities.

Financial data Grants up to $60,000 per year, including direct expenses and up to 10% for overhead costs, are available. The total award for the life of the grant may not exceed $170,000, including $150,000 for costs related to the proposed research, $10,000 to the fellow upon successful completion of the program, and $10,000 to the mentor upon successful completion of the program.

Duration Up to 3 years.

Number awarded Up to 4 of these and parallel grants are awarded each year.

Deadline Letters of intent must be submitted by the end of December of each year. Final applications are due in February.

[1303]
MENTORED RESEARCH SCIENTIST DEVELOPMENT AWARD TO PROMOTE DIVERSITY

National Cancer Institute
Attn: Center to Reduce Cancer Health Disparities
6116 Executive Boulevard, Suite 602
Bethesda, MD 20852-8341
(301) 496-7344   Fax: (301) 435-9225
TDD: (301) 451-0088   E-mail: ojeifojo@mail.nih.gov
Web: www.cancer.gov/researchandfunding

Summary To provide funding to Native Americans and members of other underrepresented groups who need a period of "protected time" for intensive cancer research career development under the guidance of an experienced mentor.

Eligibility This program is open to U.S. citizens, nationals, and permanent residents who have a research or health professional doctorate and have completed a mentored research training experience. Candidates must be proposing to conduct a research project to prepare for an independent research career related to cancer biology, cancer health disparities, etiology, pathogenesis, prevention, diagnosis, and/or treatment. They must be nominated by a domestic nonprofit or for-profit organization, public or private (such as a university, college, hospital, or laboratory), that can demonstrate a commitment to the promotion of diversity of their student and faculty populations. Institutions must certify that the candidate qualifies as 1) a member of an ethnic or racial group shown to be underrepresented in health-related sciences on a national basis; 2) an individual with a disability; or 3) an individual from a disadvantaged background, including those from a low-income family and those from a social, cultural, and/or educational environment that have inhibited them from preparation for a research career. The mentor must have extensive research experience and an appreciation of the cultural, socioeconomic, and research background of the candidate.

Financial data The award provides salary up to $100,000 per year plus related fringe benefits. In addition, up to $30,000 per year is provided for research development support. Facilities and administrative costs are reimbursed at 8% of modified total direct costs.

Duration 3, 4, or 5 years.

Additional information Recipients must devote at least 75% of their full-time professional effort to cancer-related research and training activities.

Number awarded Varies each year.

Deadline February, June, or October of each year.

[1304]
MICKEY LELAND ENERGY FELLOWSHIPS

Department of Energy
Attn: Office of Fossil Energy
19901 Germantown Road, FE-6
Germantown, MD 20874
(301) 903-4293   E-mail: MLEF@hq.doe.gov
Web: fossil.energy.gov

Summary To provide summer work experience at fossil energy sites of the Department of Energy (DOE) to Native Americans, other underrepresented minorities, and female students.

Eligibility This program is open to U.S. citizens currently enrolled full time at an accredited college or university. Applicants must be undergraduate, graduate, or postdoctoral students in mathematics, physical sciences, technology, or engineering and have a GPA of 3.0 or higher. They must be interested in a summer work experience at a DOE fossil energy research facility. Along with their application, they must submit a 100-word statement on why they want to participate in this program. A goal of the program is to recruit women and underrepresented minorities into careers related to fossil energy.

Financial data Weekly stipends are $500 for undergraduates, $650 for master's degree students, or $750 for doctoral

and postdoctoral students. Travel costs for a round trip to and from the site and for a trip to a designated place for technical presentations are also paid.

Duration 10 weeks during the summer.

Additional information This program began as 3 separate activities: the Historically Black Colleges and Universities Internship Program, established in 1995; the Hispanic Internship Program, established in 1998; and the Tribal Colleges and Universities Internship Program, established in 2000. Those 3 programs were merged into the Fossil Energy Minority Education Initiative, renamed the Mickey Leland Energy Fellowship Program in 2000. Sites to which interns may be assigned include the Albany Research Center (Albany, Oregon), the National Energy Technology Laboratory (Morgantown, West Virginia and Pittsburgh, Pennsylvania), Pacific Northwest National Laboratory (Richland, Washington), Rocky Mountain Oilfield Testing Center (Casper, Wyoming), Strategic Petroleum Reserve Project Management Office (New Orleans, Louisiana), or U.S. Department of Energy Headquarters (Washington, D.C.).

Number awarded Varies each year; recently, 30 students participated in this program.

Deadline January of each year.

[1305]
MILLE LACS BAND ACADEMIC ACHIEVEMENT AWARDS

Mille Lacs Band of Ojibwe
Attn: Higher Education Office
43408 Oodena Avenue
Onamia, MN 56359-2236
(320) 495-3702   Toll Free: (866) 916-5282
Fax: (320) 495-3707
E-mail: mlb.inquiries@millelacsband.com
Web: www.millelacsband.org/Page_Education.aspx

Summary To recognize and reward members of the Mille Lacs Band of Ojibwe after they complete a degree.

Eligibility This program is open to enrolled members of the band, their non-enrolled biological children, and legally adopted children of enrolled band members. Applicants must have just completed their GED certificate or high school diploma, a vocational/technical diploma or certificate (for a program 9 months or more in length), an associate degree, a bachelor's degree, or a graduate (master's or doctoral) degree.

Financial data Awards are $500 for completion of a GED certificate or high school diploma, $1,000 for a vocational/technical diploma or certificate, $1,250 for an associate degree, $1,500 for a bachelor's degree, or $2,000 for a graduate degree.

Duration Awards are presented whenever a student completes a diploma, certificate, or degree.

Number awarded Varies each year.

Deadline Applications may be submitted as soon as an eligible student has completed an educational degree.

[1306]
MINORITY ENTREPRENEURS SCHOLARSHIP PROGRAM

International Franchise Association
Attn: IFA Educational Foundation
1501 K Street, N.W., Suite 350
Washington, DC 20005
(202) 662-0784   Fax: (202) 628-0812
E-mail: mbrewer@franchise.org
Web: www.franchise.org/Scholarships.aspx

Summary   To provide financial assistance to Native Americans and other minority students or adult entrepreneurs enrolled in academic or professional development programs related to franchising.

Eligibility   This program is open to 1) college students enrolled at an accredited college or university, and 2) adult entrepreneurs who have at least 5 years of business ownership or managerial experience. Applicants must be U.S. citizens and members of a minority group (defined as African Americans, American Indians, Hispanic Americans, and Asian Americans). Students should be enrolled in courses or programs relating to business, finance, marketing, hospitality, franchising, or entrepreneurship. Adult entrepreneurs should be enrolled in professional development courses related to franchising, such as those recognized by the Institute of Certified Franchise Executives (ICFE). All applicants must submit a 500-word essay on why they want the scholarship and their career goals. Financial need is not considered in the selection process.

Financial data   The stipend is $3,000.

Duration   1 year.

Additional information   This program is cosponsored by the IFA Educational Foundation and Marriott International.

Number awarded   5 each year.

Deadline   June of each year.

[1307]
MINORITY FACULTY DEVELOPMENT SCHOLARSHIP AWARD IN PHYSICAL THERAPY

American Physical Therapy Association
Attn: Honors and Awards Program
1111 North Fairfax Street
Alexandria, VA 22314-1488
(703) 684-APTA   Toll Free: (800) 999-APTA
Fax: (703) 684-7343   TDD: (703) 683-6748
E-mail: executivedept@apta.org
Web: www.apta.org

Summary   To provide financial assistance to Native American and other minority faculty members in physical therapy who are interested in working on a doctoral degree.

Eligibility   This program is open to U.S. citizens and permanent residents who are members of the following minority groups: African American or Black, Asian, Native Hawaiian or other Pacific Islander, American Indian or Alaska Native, or Hispanic/Latino. Applicants must be full-time faculty members, teaching in an accredited or developing professional physical therapist education program, who will have completed the equivalent of 2 full semesters of post-professional doctoral course work. They must possess a license to practice physical therapy in a U.S. jurisdiction and be enrolled as a student in an accredited post-professional doctoral program whose content has a demonstrated relationship to physical therapy. Along with their application, they must submit a personal essay on their professional goals, including their plans to contribute to the profession and minority services. Selection is based on 1) commitment to minority affairs and services; 2) commitment to further the physical therapy profession through teaching and research; and 3) scholastic achievement.

Financial data   A stipend is awarded (amount not specified).

Duration   1 year.

Additional information   This program was established in 1999.

Number awarded   1 or more each year.

Deadline   November of each year.

[1308]
MISS INDIAN USA SCHOLARSHIP PROGRAM

American Indian Heritage Foundation
P.O. Box 750
Pigeon Forge, TN 37868
(703) 819-0979   E-mail: MissIndianUSA@indians.org
Web: www.indians.org/miss-indian-usa-program.html

Summary   To recognize and reward the most beautiful and talented Indian women.

Eligibility   American Indian women between the ages of 18 and 26 are eligible to enter this national contest if they are high school graduates and have never been married, cohabited with the opposite sex, been pregnant, or had children. U.S. citizenship is required. Selection is based on public appearance (20%), a traditional interview (15%), a contemporary interview (15%), beauty of spirit (15%), a cultural presentation (10%), scholastic achievement (10%), a platform question (10%), and a finalist question (5%).

Financial data   Awards vary each year; recently, Miss Indian USA received an academic scholarship of $4,000 plus a cash grant of $6,500, a wardrobe allowance of $2,000, appearance fees of $3,000, a professional photo shoot worth $500, gifts worth more than $4,000, honoring gifts worth more than $2,000, promotional materials worth more than $2,000, and travel to Washington, D.C. with a value of approximately $2,000; the total value of the prize was more than $26,000. Members of her court received scholarships of $2,000 for the first runner-up, $1,500 for the second runner-up, $1,000 for the third runner-up, and $500 for the fourth runner-up.

Duration   This competition is held annually.

Additional information   The program involves a week-long competition in the Washington, D.C. metropolitan area that includes seminars, interviews, cultural presentations, and many public appearances. The application fee is $100 if submitted prior to mid-April or $200 if submitted later. In addition, a candidate fee of $750 is required.

Number awarded   1 winner and 4 runners-up are selected each year.

Deadline   May of each year.

[1309]
NASA ASTROBIOLOGY PROGRAM MINORITY INSTITUTION RESEARCH SUPPORT

United Negro College Fund Special Programs
  Corporation
Attn: NASA Astrobiology Program
6402 Arlington Boulevard, Suite 600
Falls Church, VA 22042
(703) 205-7641   Toll Free: (800) 530-6232
Fax: (703) 205-7645   E-mail: portal@uncfsp.org
Web: www.uncfsp.org

Summary To provide an opportunity for faculty at Tribal Colleges and Universities (TCUs) and other Minority Serving Institutions (MSIs) to work on a summer research project in partnership with an established astrobiology investigator.

Eligibility This program is open to full-time tenured or tenure-track faculty members at MSIs who have a Ph.D., Sc.D., or equivalent degree in a field of STEM (science, technology, engineering, or mathematics). Applicants must be interested in conducting a summer research project on a topic related to astrobiology. They must identify an established investigator of the National Aeronautics and Space Administration (NASA) Astrobiology Program who has agreed to serve as host researcher. Eligible fields of study include biology, microbiology, astronomy, planetary science, astrochemistry, astrophysics, geology, geochemistry, or geobiochemistry. U.S. citizenship or permanent resident status is required.

Financial data Fellows receive a stipend of $10,000 and an additional grant of $5,000 to cover travel, lodging, and living expenses.

Duration 10 weeks during the summer.

Additional information This program is funded by NASA and administered by the United Negro College Fund Special Programs Corporation.

Number awarded Varies each year.

Deadline March of each year.

[1310]
NASA SCIENCE AND TECHNOLOGY INSTITUTE (NSTI) FACULTY FELLOWSHIP PROGRAM

United Negro College Fund Special Programs
  Corporation
Attn: NASA Science and Technology Institute
6402 Arlington Boulevard, Suite 600
Falls Church, VA 22042
(703) 677-3400   Toll Free: (800) 530-6232
Fax: (703) 205-7645   E-mail: portal@uncfsp.org
Web: www.uncfsp.org

Summary To provide an opportunity for faculty at Tribal Colleges and Universities (TCUs) to work on a summer research project at the Ames Research Center (ARC) of the U.S. National Aeronautics and Space Administration (NASA) in Moffett Field, California.

Eligibility This program is open to full-time Native American faculty members at TCUs who have at least a master's degree or at least 5 years of teaching experience at the college level. Applicants must be interested in working on a summer research project at ARC. Their degree or experience must be in a field of STEM (science, technology, engineering, or mathematics) or education. Along with their application, they must submit an essay detailing how their participation in

the fellowship will benefit them, their institution, and their students.

Financial data Fellows receive a stipend of $12,000 and an additional grant of $3,000 to cover travel, lodging, and living expenses.

Duration 10 weeks during the summer.

Additional information This program is funded by NASA and administered by the United Negro College Fund Special Programs Corporation.

Number awarded Varies each year.

Deadline March of each year.

[1311]
NATIONAL ALUMNI CHAPTER GRANTS

Kappa Omicron Nu
Attn: Awards Committee
4990 Northwind Drive, Suite 140
East Lansing, MI 48823-5031
(517) 351-8335   Fax: (517) 351-8336
E-mail: dmitstifer@kon.org
Web: www.kon.org/awards/grants.html

Summary To provide financial assistance to Native Americans and other members of Kappa Omicron Nu, an honor society in family and consumer sciences, who are interested in conducting research.

Eligibility This program is open to 1) individual members of the society, and 2) research teams where the leader is a member of the society. Applicants must be interested in conducting research in family and consumer sciences or any of its related specializations. The research approach should be integrative in nature and shall make connections across specializations to pursue problems or questions. Special consideration is given to research that studies the cultural and religious differences affecting leadership, Hispanic, Asian, and Native Americans are encouraged to apply. Another topic of interest is the exploration of how minority students "strike out on their own" in career development.

Financial data The grant is $1,000.

Duration 1 year; multi-year funding may be accomplished by including a multi-year management plan in the initial proposal and reporting successful accomplishment of previous objectives annually.

Additional information Funding for these grants is provided by the National Alumni Chapter of Kappa Omicron Nu.

Number awarded 1 or more each year.

Deadline February of each year.

[1312]
NATIONAL CANCER INSTITUTE MENTORED CLINICAL SCIENTIST RESEARCH CAREER DEVELOPMENT AWARD TO PROMOTE DIVERSITY

National Cancer Institute
Attn: Center to Reduce Cancer Health Disparities
6116 Executive Boulevard, Suite 602
Bethesda, MD 20852-8341
(301) 496-7344   Fax: (301) 435-9225
TDD: (301) 451-0088   E-mail: ojeifojo@mail.nih.gov
Web: www.cancer.gov/researchandfunding

Summary To provide funding to Native Americans and members of other underrepresented groups who are interested in a program of training in cancer research under the supervision of an experienced mentor.

Eligibility This program is open to U.S. citizens, nationals, and permanent residents who have a clinical doctoral degree; individuals with a Ph.D. or other doctoral degree in clinical disciplines (such as clinical psychology, nursing, clinical genetics, speech-language pathology, audiology, or rehabilitation) are also eligible. Candidates must be nominated by an eligible institution (e.g., a domestic, nonprofit or for-profit public or private institution, such as a university, college, hospital, or laboratory; a unit of state or local government; or an eligible agency of the federal government) on the basis of their intent to conduct a research project highly relevant to cancer biology, cancer health disparities, etiology, pathogenesis, prevention, diagnosis, and treatment that has the potential for establishing an independent research program. They must qualify as 1) members of an ethnic or racial group shown to be underrepresented in health-related sciences on a national basis; 2) individuals with a disability; or 3) individuals from a disadvantaged background, including those from a low-income family and those from a social, cultural, and/or educational environment that has inhibited them from preparation for a research career. The mentor must be a senior or mid-level faculty member with research competence and an appreciation of the cultural, socioeconomic, and research background of the individual candidate. Selection is based on the applicant's qualifications, interests, accomplishments, motivation, and potential for a career in laboratory or field-based cancer research.

Financial data The award provides salary up to $100,000 per year plus related fringe benefits. In addition, up to $30,000 per year is provided for research development support. Facilities and administrative costs are reimbursed at 8% of modified total direct costs.

Duration Up to 5 years.

Additional information This program was originally established in 2002 as the successor of a program designated the Minorities in Clinical Oncology Program Grants. Recipients must devote at least 75% of their full-time professional effort to cancer-related research and training activities.

Number awarded Varies each year, depending on the availability of funds.

Deadline February, June, or October of each year.

[1313]
NATIONAL CANCER INSTITUTE TRANSITION CAREER DEVELOPMENT AWARD TO PROMOTE DIVERSITY

National Cancer Institute
Attn: Center to Reduce Cancer Health Disparities
6116 Executive Boulevard, Suite 602
Bethesda, MD 20852-8341
(301) 496-8589   Fax: (301) 435-9225
TDD: (301) 451-0088   E-mail: walia@mail.nih.gov
Web: www.cancer.gov/researchandfunding

Summary To provide funding to Native Americans and other underrepresented scientists who are establishing an independent research and academic career in cancer research.

Eligibility This program is open to U.S. citizens, nationals, and permanent residents who have earned a terminal clinical or research doctorate and intend to conduct a research proj-

ect highly relevant to cancer biology, cancer health disparities, etiology, pathogenesis, prevention, diagnosis, and treatment that has the potential for establishing an independent research program. Candidates must be sponsored by a domestic nonprofit or for-profit organization, public or private (such as a university, college, hospital, laboratory, unit of state or local government, or eligible agency of the federal government), that can demonstrate a commitment to the promotion of diversity in their student and faculty populations. They must qualify as a member of a group underrepresented in biomedical research, defined as members of a particular ethnic, racial, or other group determined by their institution to be underrepresented in biomedical, behavioral, clinical, or social sciences, e.g., first-generation college students or graduates, socio-economically disadvantaged persons, or persons with disabilities.

Financial data The award provides salary up to $100,000 per year plus related fringe benefits. In addition, up to $50,000 per year is provided for research support costs. Facilities and administrative costs are reimbursed at 8% of modified total direct costs.

Duration Up to 3 years.

Additional information Recipients must devote at least 75% of their full-time professional effort to cancer-related research and peer review activities. The remaining 25% can be divided among other activities only if they are consistent with the program goals, i.e., the candidate's development into an independent investigator.

Number awarded Approximately 10 each year.

Deadline February, June, or October of each year.

[1314]
NATIONAL CONGRESS OF AMERICAN INDIANS FELLOWSHIPS

National Congress of American Indians
Attn: Internship Program
1516 P Street, N.W.
Washington, DC 20005
(202) 466-7767   Fax: (2020 466-7797
E-mail: ncai@ncai.org
Web: www.ncai.org/Internships-Fellowships.13.0.html

Summary To provide an opportunity for recent college graduates to gain work experience at the offices of the National Congress of American Indians (NCAI).

Eligibility Applicants must have recently completed an undergraduate or graduate degree and be interested in gaining work experience at NCAI. They must describe their previous experience with American Indian and Alaska Native issues; the areas of NCAI's work that are of most interest to them; the relevant work, volunteer experience, or other involvement they have had in the field of Indian affairs or other political, social, or community issues of concern to them; their familiarity with electronic communications, including research and specific software; why they are interested in working with NCAI; what they hope to gain from the fellowship experience; how the fellowship experience relates to their long-range plans; and any special skills or experience they feel they would bring to NCAI. Contact information for 2 references should also be provided; they may be professors, employers, tribal leaders, or personal contacts.

Financial data The stipend is approximately $16,500. Fellows also receive coverage under NCAI's health insurance plan.

Duration 11 months, beginning in September.

Additional information Work assignments cover 3 areas: advocacy, research, and writing.

Number awarded 2 or 3 each year.

Deadline April of each year.

[1315]
NATIONAL HEART, LUNG, AND BLOOD INSTITUTE MENTORED CAREER AWARD FOR FACULTY AT MINORITY SERVING INSTITUTIONS

National Heart, Lung, and Blood Institute
Attn: Division of Blood Diseases and Resources
6701 Rockledge Drive, Room 10135
Bethesda, MD 20892-7950
(301) 435-0052 Fax: (301) 480-1060
TDD: (301) 451-0088 E-mail: mondorot@nhlbi.nih.gov
Web: www.nhlbi.nih.gov/funding/inits/index.htm

Summary To provide funding to faculty investigators at Tribal Colleges and Universities (TCUs) or other minority serving institutions interested in receiving further research training in areas relevant to the mission of the National Heart, Lung, and Blood Institute (NHLBI) of the National Institutes of Health (NIH).

Eligibility This program is open to full-time faculty members at colleges and universities with student enrollment drawn substantially from minority ethnic groups (including African Americans/Blacks, Hispanics, American Indians, Alaska Native, and non-Asian Pacific Islanders). Candidates must have received a doctoral degree at least 2 years previously and be able to demonstrate a commitment to develop into an independent biomedical investigator in research areas related to cardiovascular, pulmonary, hematologic, and sleep disorders of interest to NHLBI. They must identify and complete arrangements with a mentor (at the same institution or at a collaborating research center) who is recognized as an accomplished investigator in the research area proposed and who will provide guidance for their development and research plans. They must also be U.S. citizens, nationals, or permanent residents.

Financial data The awardee receives salary support of up to $75,000 per year plus fringe benefits. In addition, up to $36,000 per year may be provided for research project requirements and related support (e.g., technical personnel costs, supplies, equipment, candidate travel, telephone charges, publication costs, and tuition for necessary courses). Facilities and administrative costs may be reimbursed at the rate of 8% of total direct costs.

Duration 3 to 5 years.

Additional information Awardees must commit 75% of their effort to the proposed project.

Number awarded 2 to 3 each year; a total of approximately $300,000 is available for this program annually.

Deadline Letters of intent must be submitted by July of each year; final applications are due in August.

[1316]
NATIVE AMERICAN LEADERSHIP IN EDUCATION (NALE) PROGRAM

Catching the Dream
8200 Mountain Road, N.E., Suite 203
Albuquerque, NM 87110-7835
(505) 262-2351 Fax: (505) 262-0534
E-mail: NScholarsh@aol.com
Web: www.catchingthedream.org/Scholarship.htm

Summary To provide financial assistance to American Indian paraprofessionals in the education field who wish to return to college or graduate school.

Eligibility This program is open to paraprofessionals who are working in Indian schools and who plan to return to college or graduate school to complete their degree in education, counseling, or school administration. Applicants must be able to provide proof that they are at least one-quarter Indian blood and a member of a U.S. tribe that is federally-recognized, state-recognized, or terminated. Along with their application, they must submit documentation of financial need, 3 letters of recommendation, copies of applications and responses from all other sources of funding for which they are eligible, official transcripts, standardized test scores (ACT, SAT, GRE, MCAT, LSAT, etc.), and an essay explaining their goals in life, college plans, and career plans (especially how those plans include working with and benefiting Indians). Selection is based on merit and potential for improving the lives of Indian people.

Financial data Stipends range from $500 to $5,000 per year.

Duration 1 year; may be renewed.

Additional information The sponsor was formerly known as the Native American Scholarship Fund.

Number awarded Varies; generally, 15 or more each year.

Deadline April of each year for fall term; September of each year for spring and winter terms; March of each year for summer school.

[1317]
NATIVE AMERICAN PUBLIC TELECOMMUNICATIONS PUBLIC TELEVISION PROGRAM FUND

Native American Public Telecommunications, Inc.
1800 North 33rd Street
Lincoln, NE 68503
(402) 472-3522 Fax: (402) 472-8675
E-mail: native@unl.edu
Web: www.nativetelecom.org

Summary To provide funding for the creation of Native American theme programs intended for broadcast to public television audiences.

Eligibility This program invites producers to submit competitive proposals for the research and development, scripting, or completion of culture-specific programs that originate from the Native North American experience and are intended for national public television audiences. All program categories are eligible, except industrial or promotional films and videos, student productions, projects that are commercial in nature, projects for which 4-year exclusive public television broadcast rights are not available, projects or production entities that are foreign-owned or controlled, projects intended solely for theatrical release, and projects funded in part by a government entity or group featured in the content of the program. Applicants must be U.S. citizens or legal residents at least 21 years of age. They must have previous television or filmmaking experience. Applications must be accompanied by a project description, itemized budget, list of key personnel, and sample of a completed work or a work-in-progress by the director. Selection is based on quantity and quality of Native American participation in creative, technical, and advisory roles; power of the finished program to illuminate the Native American experience through public television; originality of concept and style; strength of the production team to complete the project within budget, schedule, and the highest quality standards; sound production and fundraising plans; reasonable budget estimates and considerations; potential interest to a national audience; and strength of sample work.

Financial data   Grants range from $10,000 to $25,000 for research and development or up to $100,000 for production or completion.

Duration   Up to 1 year.

Additional information   This program is underwritten by the Corporation for Public Broadcasting.

Number awarded   Varies each year.

Deadline   March of each year.

[1318]
NAVAL RESEARCH LABORATORY BROAD AGENCY ANNOUNCEMENT

Naval Research Laboratory
Attn: Contracting Division
4555 Overlook Avenue, S.W.
Washington, DC 20375-5320
(202) 767-5227   Fax: (202) 767-0494
Web: heron.nrl.navy.mil/contracts/home.htm

Summary   To provide funding to minority and other investigators interested in conducting scientific research of interest to the U.S. Navy.

Eligibility   This program is open to investigators qualified to perform research in designated scientific and technical areas. Topics cover a wide range of technical and scientific areas; recent programs included radar technology, information technology, optical sciences, tactical electronic warfare, materials science and component technology, chemistry, computational physics and fluid dynamics, plasma physics, electronics science and technology, biomolecular science and engineering, ocean and atmospheric science and technology, acoustics, remote sensing, oceanography, marine geosciences, marine meteorology, and space science. Proposals may be submitted by any non-governmental entity, including commercial firms, institutions of higher education with degree-granting programs in science or engineering, or by consortia led by such concerns. The Naval Research Laboratory (NRL) encourages participation by small businesses, small disadvantaged business concerns, women-owned small businesses, veteran-owned small businesses, service-disabled veteran-owned small businesses, HUBZone small businesses, Historically Black Colleges and Universities, and Minority Institutions. Selection is based on the degree to which new and creative solutions to technical issues important to NRL programs are proposed and the feasibility of the proposed approach and technical objectives; the offeror's ability to implement the proposed approach; the degree to which technical data and/or computer software developed under the proposed contract are to be delivered to the NRL with rights compatible with NRL research and development objectives; and proposed cost and cost realism.

Financial data   The typical range of funding is from $100,000 to $2,000,000.

Duration   1 year.

Additional information   The Naval Research Laboratory conducts most of its research in its own facilities in Washington, D.C., Stennis Space Center, Mississippi, and Monterey, California, but it also funds some related research.

Number awarded   Varies each year.

Deadline   Each program establishes its own application deadline; for a complete list of all the programs, including their deadlines, contact the NRL.

[1319]
NCI MENTORED PATIENT-ORIENTED RESEARCH CAREER DEVELOPMENT AWARD TO PROMOTE DIVERSITY

National Cancer Institute
Attn: Comprehensive Minority Biomedical Branch
6116 Executive Boulevard, Suite 7031
Bethesda, MD 20892-8350
(301) 496-7344   Fax: (301) 402-4551
TDD: (301) 451-0088   E-mail: lockeb@mail.nih.gov
Web: www.cancer.gov/researchandfunding

Summary   To provide funding to Native Americans and members of other underrepresented groups who are interested in a program of research training in patient-oriented oncology under the supervision of an experienced mentor.

Eligibility   This program is open to U.S. citizens, nationals, and permanent residents who have a health professional doctoral degree or a doctoral degree in nursing research or practice; individuals with a Ph.D. degree in clinical disciplines (such as clinical psychology, clinical genetics, social work, speech-language pathology, audiology, or rehabilitation) are also eligible. Candidates must be nominated by a domestic nonprofit or for-profit organization, public or private (such as a university, college, hospital, laboratory, unit of state or local government, or eligible agency of the federal government), that can demonstrate a commitment to diversification of their student and faculty populations. Institutions must certify that the candidate qualifies as 1) a member of an ethnic or racial group shown to be underrepresented in health-related sciences on a national basis; 2) an individual with a disability; or 3) an individual from a disadvantaged background, including those from a low-income family and those from a social, cultural, and/or educational environment that have inhibited them from preparation for a research career. At least 2 mentors are required: 1 who is recognized as an accomplished clinical investigator and at least 1 additional mentor or adviser who is recognized as an accomplished independent basic science investigator in the proposed research area.

Financial data   The award provides salary up to $100,000 per year plus related fringe benefits. In addition, up to $30,000 per year is provided for research development support. Facilities and administrative costs are reimbursed at 8% of modified total direct costs.

Duration   Up to 5 years.

Additional information Recipients must devote at least 75% of their full-time professional effort to cancer-related research and training activities.

Number awarded Varies each year.

Deadline February, June, or October of each year.

[1320]
NEW INITIATIVES GRANTS

Kappa Omicron Nu
Attn: Awards Committee
4990 Northwind Drive, Suite 140
East Lansing, MI 48823-5031
(517) 351-8335   Fax: (517) 351-8336
E-mail: dmitstifer@kon.org
Web: www.kon.org/awards/grants.html

Summary To provide financial assistance underrepresented minorities and other members of Kappa Omicron Nu, an honor society in home economics, who are interested in conducting research.

Eligibility This program is open to 1) individual members of the society, and 2) research teams where the leader is a member of the society. Applicants must be interested in conducting research in family and consumer sciences or any of its related specializations. The research approach should be integrative in nature and make connections across specializations to pursue problems or questions. Special consideration is given to research that studies the cultural and religious differences that affect leadership, especially Hispanic, Asian, and Native American. Another topic of interest is the exploration of how minority students "strike out on their own" in career development.

Financial data The maximum grant is $3,000.

Duration 1 year; multi-year funding may be accomplished by including a multi-year management plan in the initial proposal and reporting successful accomplishment of previous objectives annually.

Additional information Funding for these grants is provided by the New Initiatives Fund of Kappa Omicron Nu.

Number awarded 1 or more each year.

Deadline February of each year.

[1321]
NEW INVESTIGATOR RESEARCH GRANTS TO PROMOTE DIVERSITY OF THE ALZHEIMER'S ASSOCIATION

Alzheimer's Association
Attn: Medical and Scientific Affairs
225 North Michigan Avenue, 17th Floor
Chicago, IL 60601-7633
(312) 335-5747   Toll Free: (800) 272-3900
Fax: (866) 699-1246   TDD: (312) 335-5886
E-mail: grantsapp@alz.org
Web: www.alz.org

Summary To provide funding for research on Alzheimer's Disease to Native Americans and other junior investigators who will contribute to diversity in the field.

Eligibility This program is open to investigators who have less than 10 years of research experience after receipt of their terminal degree. Applicants must be proposing to conduct research with focus areas that change annually but are related to Alzheimer's Disease. Eligibility is restricted to

investigators who will contribute to diversity in the field of biomedical research, including members of underrepresented racial and ethnic minority groups (African Americans, Hispanic Americans, American Indians/Alaska Natives, Native Hawaiians, and Pacific Islanders) and individuals with disabilities.

Financial data Grants up to $60,000 per year, including direct expenses and up to 10% for overhead costs, are available. The total award for the life of the grant may not exceed $100,000.

Duration Up to 2 years.

Number awarded Up to 4 of these and parallel grants are awarded each year.

Deadline Letters of intent must be submitted by the end of December of each year. Final applications are due in February.

[1322]
NEW JERSEY LIBRARY ASSOCIATION DIVERSITY SCHOLARSHIP

New Jersey Library Association
4 Lafayette Street
P.O. Box 1534
Trenton, NJ 08607
(609) 394-8032   Fax: (609) 394-8164
E-mail: ptumulty@njla.org
Web: www.njla.org/honorsawards/scholarship

Summary To provide financial assistance to New Jersey residents who are Native Americans or members of other minority groups and interested in working on a graduate or postgraduate degree in public librarianship at a school in any state.

Eligibility This program is open to residents of New Jersey and individuals who have worked in a New Jersey library for at least 12 months. Applicants must be members of a minority group (African American, Asian/Pacific Islander, Latino/Hispanic, or Native American/Native Alaskan). They must be enrolled or planning to enroll at an ALA-accredited school of library science in any state to work on a graduate or postgraduate degree in librarianship. Along with their application, they must submit an essay of 150 to 250 words explaining their choice of librarianship as a profession. An interview is required. Selection is based on academic ability and financial need.

Financial data The stipend is $1,300.

Duration 1 year.

Number awarded 1 each year.

Deadline February of each year.

[1323]
NEW YORK PUBLIC LIBRARY FELLOWSHIPS

American Council of Learned Societies
Attn: Office of Fellowships and Grants
633 Third Avenue
New York, NY 10017-6795
(212) 697-1505   Fax: (212) 949-8058
E-mail: fellowships@acls.org
Web: www.acls.org/programs/acls

Summary To provide funding to minority and other postdoctorates interested in conducting research at the Dorothy and Lewis B. Cullman Center for Scholars and Writers of the New York Public Library.

Eligibility This program is open to scholars at all stages of their careers who received a Ph.D. degree at least 2 years previously. Established scholars who can demonstrate the equivalent of the Ph.D. in publications and professional experience may also qualify. Applicants must be U.S. citizens or permanent residents who have not had supported leave time for at least 2 years prior to the start of the proposed research. Appropriate fields of specialization include, but are not limited to, American studies; anthropology; archaeology; art and architectural history; classics; economics; film; geography; history; languages and literatures; legal studies; linguistics; musicology; philosophy; political science; psychology; religious studies; rhetoric, communication, and media studies; sociology; and theater, dance, and performance studies. Proposals in the fields social science fields are eligible only if they employ predominantly humanistic approaches (e.g., economic history, law and literature, political philosophy). Proposals in interdisciplinary and cross-disciplinary studies are welcome, as are proposals focused on any geographic region or on any cultural or linguistic group. Applicants must be interested in conducting research at the New York Public Library's Dorothy and Lewis B. Cullman Center for Scholars and Writers. Women and members of minority groups are particularly invited to apply.

Financial data The stipend is $60,000.

Duration 9 months, beginning in September.

Additional information This program was first offered for 1999-2000, the inaugural year of the center. Candidates must also submit a separate application that is available from the New York Public Library, Humanities and Social Sciences Library, Dorothy and Lewis B. Cullman Center for Scholars and Writers, Fifth Avenue and 42nd Street, New York, NY 10018-2788, E-mail: csw@nypl.org. Fellows are required to be in continuous residence at the center and participate actively in its activities and programs.

Number awarded Up to 5 each year.

Deadline September of each year.

[1324]
NEWBERRY CONSORTIUM IN AMERICAN INDIAN AND INDIGENOUS STUDIES FACULTY FELLOWSHIPS

Newberry Library
Attn: McNickle Center for American Indian History
60 West Walton Street
Chicago, IL 60610-3305
(312) 255-3564   Fax: (312) 255-3696
E-mail: mcnickle@newberry.org
Web: www.newberry.org/mcnickle/NCAISFellows.html

Summary To provide funding to faculty at member institutions of the Newberry Consortium in American Indian and Indigenous Studies (NCAIS) who wish to conduct research in American Indian studies at the D'Arcy McNickle Center for the History of the American Indian at the Newberry Library.

Eligibility This program is open to faculty members at NCAIS institutions who are interested in conducting research in American Indian studies at the Newberry Library. Applicants must submit their curriculum vitae; a 300-word project abstract, a 1,500-word project description that discusses the topic, significance, conceptual framework, and specific New-

berry collections to be used; and 3 letters of recommendation.

Financial data Grants provide a stipend of $25,200.

Duration 1 semester.

Additional information The Newberry Library inaugurated the NCAIS in 2009, following the end of its partnership with the 13 universities of the Committee on Institutional Cooperation (CIC). It is limited to 18 universities in the United States and Canada; for a list of those universities, contact the Newberry. Fellows are expected to present research, participate in both the McNickle Center Seminar in American Indian and Indigenous Studies and the Newberry Library Fellows' Seminar, and be available for consultation with the NCAIS Graduate Student Fellows.

Number awarded 1 each year.

Deadline January of each year.

[1325]
NHLBI SHORT-TERM RESEARCH EDUCATION PROGRAM TO INCREASE DIVERSITY IN HEALTH-RELATED RESEARCH

National Heart, Lung, and Blood Institute
Attn: Division of Cardiovascular Diseases
6701 Rockledge Drive
Bethesda, MD 20892-7940
(301) 435-0535   Fax: (301) 480-1454
TDD: (301) 451-0088   E-mail: Commaram@nhlbi.nih.gov
Web: www.nhlbi.nih.gov/funding/inits/index.htm

Summary To provide funding to Native Americans and members of other underrepresented groups interested in conducting a research education program relevant to the mission of the National Heart, Lung, and Blood Institute (NHLBI).

Eligibility This program is open to principal investigators at U.S. domestic institutions (universities, colleges, hospitals, laboratories, units of state and local governments, and eligible agencies of the federal government) who are interested in conducting a research education program related to activities of NHLBI. Applications are especially encouraged from principal investigators who qualify as underrepresented: 1) a member of an ethnic or racial group shown to be underrepresented in health-related sciences on a national basis; 2) an individual with a disability; or 3) an individual from a disadvantaged background, including those from a low-income family and those from a social, cultural, and/or educational environment that has inhibited them from preparation for a research career. The proposed education program must encourage the participation of undergraduate and health professional students who are also currently underrepresented in the biomedical, clinical, and behavioral sciences. Students participating in the program are not required to be enrolled at the sponsoring institution.

Financial data Grants depend on the nature of the project and the number of student participants. Maximum total direct costs should not exceed $311,088. Compensation to participating students must conform to the established salary and wage policies of the institution. Facilities and administrative costs may be reimbursed at the rate of 8% of total direct costs.

Duration Up to 5 years.

Number awarded Up to 8 each year; a total of $900,000 is available for this program annually.

Deadline Letters of intent must be submitted by August of each year; final applications are due in September.

[1326]
NICKELODEON WRITING FELLOWSHIP PROGRAM

Nickelodeon Animation Studios
Attn: Nick Writing Fellowship
231 West Olive Avenue
Burbank, CA 91502
(818) 736-3663　　　　E-mail: info.writing@nick.com
Web: www.nickwriting.com

Summary To provide an opportunity for minority and other young writers and animators to gain experience working at Nickelodeon Animation Studio in Burbank, California.

Eligibility This program is open to writers, whether experienced or not, who are at least 18 years of age. Applicants must submit a spec script, 1-page resume, and half-page biography. The spec script may be either live action (half hour television script based on a current television series) or animation (11- or 30-minute script based on a current animated television series). Scripts should focus on comedy. The program encourages applications from culturally and ethnically diverse writing talent.

Financial data This is a salaried position.

Duration Up to 1 year, divided into 3 phases: a 6-week audition phase in which the fellows write 1 spec script and their talent and progress are evaluated to determine if they are qualified to remain in the program; a 10-week development phase in which they write 1 spec script and are integrated into the activities of the production and development department; and a 34-week placement phase in which they write another spec script and pitch 1 original idea.

Number awarded Up to 4 each year.

Deadline February of each year.

[1327]
NIDDK SMALL GRANTS FOR CLINICAL SCIENTISTS TO PROMOTE DIVERSITY IN HEALTH-RELATED RESEARCH

National Institute of Diabetes and Digestive and Kidney Diseases
Attn: Office of Minority Health Research Coordination
6707 Democracy Boulevard, Room 653
Bethesda, MD 20892-5454
(301) 594-1932　　　　Fax: (301) 594-9358
TDD: (301) 451-0088　　E-mail: la21i@nih.gov
Web: www2.niddk.nih.gov/Funding

Summary To provide funding to Native American and other physicians from underrepresented groups who are interested in conducting a research project in fields of interest to the National Institute of Diabetes and Digestive and Kidney Diseases (NIDDK) of the National Institutes of Health.

Eligibility This program is open to investigators who 1) have a health professional doctoral degree (e.g., M.D., D.D.S., D.O., D.V.M., O.D., Psy.D., Dr.P.H.); 2) have at least 2 to 4 years of postdoctoral research experience; 3) qualify as new investigators; and 4) belong to a population group nationally underrepresented in biomedical or behavioral research, including members of designated racial and ethnic groups (e.g., African Americans, Hispanics, Native Americans, Alaska Natives, Hawaiian Natives, and non-Asian Pacific Islanders), individual with disabilities, or individuals from a disadvantaged background (defined to include those who come from a low-income family and those who come from a social, cultural, and/or educational environment that has inhibited them from obtaining the knowledge, skills, and abilities necessary to develop and participate in a research career). Applicants must be interested in conducting a research project in the area of diabetes, endocrinology, metabolism, digestive diseases, hepatology, obesity, nutrition, kidney, urology, or hematology. They must be sponsored by a domestic for-profit or nonprofit public or private institution, such as a university, college, hospital, or laboratory.

Financial data Direct costs are limited to $125,000 per year. Facilities and administrative costs are reimbursed at 8% of modified total direct costs.

Duration 3 years; nonrenewable.

Additional information This program is also supported by the Office of Dietary Supplements within NIH.

Number awarded Varies each year.

Deadline February, June, or October of each year.

[1328]
NINR MENTORED RESEARCH SCIENTIST DEVELOPMENT AWARD FOR UNDERREPRESENTED OR DISADVANTAGED INVESTIGATORS

National Institute of Nursing Research
Attn: Office of Extramural Programs
6701 Democracy Boulevard, Suite 710
Bethesda, MD 20892-4870
(301) 496-9558　　　　Fax: (301) 480-8260
TDD: (301) 451-0088　　E-mail: banksd@mail.nih.gov
Web: www.ninr.nih.gov

Summary To provide funding for research career development to Native American and other postdoctoral nursing investigators from underrepresented or disadvantaged groups.

Eligibility This program is open to nurses who have a research or health-professional doctoral degree and are employed full time at an institution that conducts research. Applicants must qualify as an individual whose participation in scientific research will increase diversity, including 1) individuals from racial and ethnic groups that have been shown to be underrepresented in health-related science on a national basis; 2) individuals with disabilities; and 3) individuals from disadvantaged backgrounds, including those from a family with an annual income below established levels and those from a social, cultural, or educational environment that has demonstrably and recently directly inhibited the individual from obtaining the knowledge, skills, and abilities necessary to develop and participate in a research career. They must secured the commitment of an appropriate research mentor actively involved in research relevant to the mission of the National Institute of Nursing Research (NINR). Only U.S. citizens, nationals, and permanent residents are eligible.

Financial data The grant provides up to $50,000 per year for salary and fringe benefits plus an additional $20,000 per year for research development support. Facilities and administrative costs are allowed at 8% of total direct costs.

Duration Up to 3 years.

Additional information These grants have been awarded annually since 1998. Grantees are expected to spend at least 75% of their professional time to the program and the other 25% to other research-related and/or teaching or clinical pursuits consistent with the objectives of the award.

Number awarded 3 to 4 new grants are awarded each year.

Deadline February, June, or October of each year.

[1329]
NON-PHARMACOLOGICAL STRATEGIES TO AMELIORATE SYMPTOMS OF ALZHEIMER'S DISEASE

Alzheimer's Association
Attn: Medical and Scientific Affairs
225 North Michigan Avenue, 17th Floor
Chicago, IL 60601-7633
(312) 335-5747   Toll Free: (800) 272-3900
Fax: (866) 699-1246   TDD: (312) 335-5886
E-mail: grantsapp@alz.org
Web: www.alz.org

Summary To provide funding to scientists (especially Native Americans and other underrepresented minorities) who are interested in conducting research on developing non-pharmacological strategies to improve the care of persons with Alzheimer's Disease and related disorders (ADRD).

Eligibility This program is open to postdoctoral investigators at public, private, domestic, and foreign research laboratories, medical centers, hospitals, and universities. Applicants must be proposing to conduct research aimed at the identification, validation, and investigation of non-pharmacological approaches to improve the care of older adults with ADRD. They must have full-time staff or faculty appointments. Proposed research topics may include (but are not limited to) non-pharmacological intervention studies that incorporate state-of-the-science methodologies to investigate outcomes; research on improving methodologies to be employed in non-pharmacological trials; evaluation of new non-pharmacological approaches that have a conceptual and/or empirical basis for potential to impact patient outcomes; or research that moves promising non-pharmacological interventions for treatment of ADRD into the field. Scientists from underrepresented groups are especially encouraged to apply.

Financial data Grants up to $200,000 per year, including direct expenses and up to 10% for overhead costs, are available. The total award for the life of the grant may not exceed $400,000.

Duration Up to 2 years.

Additional information This program began in 2009.

Number awarded Up to 2 each year.

Deadline Letters of intent must be submitted by the end of December of each year. Final applications are due in February.

[1330]
NORTH AMERICAN INDIAN PROSE AWARD

University of Nebraska Press
1111 Lincoln Mall
Lincoln, NE 68588-0630
(402) 472-3581   Toll Free: (800) 755-1105
Fax: (402) 472-6214   E-mail: pressmail@unl.edu
Web: www.nebraskapress.unl.edu

Summary To recognize and reward outstanding book-length nonfiction manuscripts written by authors of American Indian descent.

Eligibility This competition is open to authors of North American Indian descent. They are invited to submit book-length nonfiction manuscripts, including biographies, autobiographies, history, literary criticism, essays, nonfiction works for children, and political commentary. The competition excludes fiction, poetry, drama, collections of interviews, and work previously published in book form. Selection is based on literary merit, originality, and familiarity with North American Indian life.

Financial data The winner receives a cash advance of $1,000 and publication of the award-winning manuscript by the University of Nebraska Press.

Duration The award is presented annually.

Number awarded 1 each year.

Deadline June of each year.

[1331]
NOVEL PHARMACOLOGICAL STRATEGIES TO PREVENT ALZHEIMER'S DISEASE

Alzheimer's Association
Attn: Medical and Scientific Affairs
225 North Michigan Avenue, 17th Floor
Chicago, IL 60601-7633
(312) 335-5747   Toll Free: (800) 272-3900
Fax: (866) 699-1246   TDD: (312) 335-5886
E-mail: grantsapp@alz.org
Web: www.alz.org

Summary To provide funding to underrepresented minorities and other scientists interested in conducting research on developing new pharmacological strategies to prevent or treat Alzheimer's Disease.

Eligibility This program is open to postdoctoral investigators at public, private, domestic, and foreign research laboratories, medical centers, hospitals, and universities. Applicants must be proposing to conduct research aimed at the identification and validation of novel drug targets for prevention or treatment of Alzheimer's Disease, the screening and development of drugs for such targets, and the evaluation of drug safety and efficacy. They must have full-time staff or faculty appointments. Scientists from underrepresented groups are especially encouraged to apply.

Financial data Grants up to $200,000 per year, including direct expenses and up to 10% for overhead costs, are available. The total award for the life of the grant may not exceed $400,000.

Duration Up to 2 years.

Additional information This program began in 2009.

Number awarded Up to 2 each year.

Deadline Letters of intent must be submitted by the end of December of each year. Final applications are due in February.

[1332]
NSF DIRECTOR'S AWARD FOR DISTINGUISHED TEACHING SCHOLARS

National Science Foundation
Directorate for Education and Human Resources
Attn: Division of Undergraduate Education
4201 Wilson Boulevard, Room 835N
Arlington, VA 22230
(703) 292-4627   Fax: (703) 292-9015
TDD: (800) 281-8749   E-mail: npruitt@nsf.gov
Web: www.nsf.gov/funding/pgm_summ.jsp?pims_id=8170

Summary To recognize and reward, with funding for additional research, minority and other scholars affiliated with institutions of higher education who have contributed to the teaching of science, technology, engineering, or mathematics (STEM) at the K-12 and undergraduate level.

Eligibility This program is open to teaching-scholars affiliated with institutions of higher education who are nominated by their president, chief academic officer, or other independent researcher. Nominees should have integrated research and education and approached both education and research in a scholarly manner. They should have demonstrated leadership in their respective fields as well as innovativeness and effectiveness in facilitating K-12 and undergraduate student learning in STEM disciplines. Consideration is given to faculty who have a history of substantial impact on 1) research in a STEM discipline or on STEM educational research; or 2) the STEM education of K-16 students who have diverse interests and aspirations, including future K-12 teachers of science and mathematics, students who plan to pursue STEM careers, and those who need to understand science and mathematics in a society increasingly dependent on science and technology. Based on letters of nomination, selected scholars are invited to submit applications for support of their continuing efforts to integrate education and research. Nominations of all citizens, including women and men, underrepresented minorities, and persons with disabilities are especially encouraged.

Financial data The maximum grant is $300,000 for the life of the project.

Duration 4 years.

Number awarded Approximately 6 each year.

Deadline Letters of intent are due in September of each year; full applications must be submitted in October.

[1333]
NSF STANDARD AND CONTINUING GRANTS

National Science Foundation
4201 Wilson Boulevard
Arlington, VA 22230
(703) 292-5111   TDD: (800) 281-8749
E-mail: info@nsf.gov
Web: www.nsf.gov

Summary To provide financial support to minority and other scientists, engineers, and educators for research in broad areas of science and engineering.

Eligibility The National Science Foundation (NSF) supports research through its Directorates of Biological Sciences; Computer and Information Science and Engineering; Education and Human Resources; Engineering; Geosciences; Mathematical and Physical Sciences; and Social, Behavioral, and Economic Sciences. Within those general areas of science and engineering, NSF awards 2 types of grants: 1) standard grants, in which NSF agrees to provide a specific level of support for a specified period of time with no statement of NSF intent to provide additional future support without submission of another proposal; and 2) continuing grants, in which NSF agrees to provide a specific level of support for an initial specified period of time with a statement of intent to provide additional support of the project for additional periods, provided funds are available and the results achieved warrant further support. Although NSF often solicits proposals for support of targeted areas through issuance of specific program solicitations, it also accepts unsolicited proposals. Scientists, engineers, and educators usually act as the principal investigator and initiate proposals that are officially submitted by their employing organization. Most employing organizations are universities, colleges, and nonprofit nonacademic organizations (such as museums, observatories, research laboratories, and professional societies). Certain programs are open to for-profit organizations, state and local governments, or unaffiliated individuals. Principal investigators usually must be U.S. citizens, nationals, or permanent residents. NSF particularly encourages applications from underrepresented minorities and persons with disabilities.

Financial data Funding levels vary, depending on the nature of the project and the availability of funds. Awards resulting from unsolicited research proposals are subject to statutory cost-sharing.

Duration Standard grants specify the period of time, usually up to 1 year; continuing grants normally specify 1 year as the initial period of time, with support to continue for additional periods.

Additional information Researchers interested in support from NSF should contact the address above to obtain further information on areas of support and programs operating within the respective directorates. They should consult with a program officer before submitting an application. Information on programs is available on the NSF home page. NSF does not normally support technical assistance, pilot plant efforts, research requiring security classification, the development of products for commercial marketing, or market research for a particular project or invention. Bioscience research with disease-related goals, including work on the etiology, diagnosis, or treatment of physical or mental disease, abnormality, or malfunction in human beings or animals, is normally not supported.

Number awarded Approximately 11,000 new grants are awarded each year.

Deadline Many programs accept proposals at any time. Other programs establish target dates or deadlines; those target dates and deadlines are published in the *NSF Bulletin* and in specific program announcements/solicitations.

[1334]
OFFICE OF NAVAL RESEARCH SABBATICAL LEAVE PROGRAM

American Society for Engineering Education
Attn: Projects Department
1818 N Street, N.W., Suite 600
Washington, DC 20036-2479
(202) 331-3558   Fax: (202) 265-8504
E-mail: onrsummer@asee.org
Web: onr.asee.org/about_the_sabbatical_leave_program

Summary To provide support to Native American and other faculty members in engineering and science who wish to conduct research at selected Navy facilities while on sabbatical leave.

Eligibility This program is open to U.S. citizens with teaching or research appointments in engineering and science at U.S. universities or colleges. Applicants must intend to conduct research while in residence at selected facilities of the U.S. Navy. Faculty from Historically Black Colleges and Universities, Hispanic Serving Institutions, and Tribal Colleges and Universities are especially encouraged to apply.

Financial data Fellows receive a stipend equivalent to the difference between their regular salary and the sabbatical leave pay from their home institution. Fellows who must relocate their residence receive a relocation allowance and all fellows receive a travel allowance.

Duration Appointments are for a minimum of 1 semester and a maximum of 1 year.

Additional information Participating facilities include the Naval Air Warfare Center, Aircraft Division (Patuxent River, Maryland); Naval Air Warfare Center, Naval Training Systems Division (Orlando, Florida); Naval Air Warfare Center, Weapons Division (China Lake, California); Space and Naval Warfare Systems Center (San Diego, California); Naval Facilities Engineering Service Center (Port Hueneme, California); Naval Research Laboratories (Washington, D.C.; Stennis Space Center, Mississippi; and Monterey, California); Naval Surface Warfare Centers (Bethesda, Maryland; Indian Head, Maryland; Dahlgren, Virginia; and Panama City, Florida); Naval Undersea Warfare Center (Newport, Rhode Island and New London, Connecticut); Defense Equal Opportunity Management Institute (Cocoa Beach, Florida); Navy Personnel Research, Studies & Technology Department (Millington, Tennessee); Naval Aerospace Medical Research Laboratory (Pensacola, Florida); Naval Health Research Center (San Diego, California); Naval Medical Research Center (Silver Spring, Maryland); and Naval Submarine Medical Research Laboratory (Groton, Connecticut). This program is funded by the U.S. Navy's Office of Naval Research and administered by the American Society for Engineering Education.

Number awarded Varies each year.

Deadline Applications may be submitted at any time, but they must be received at least 6 months prior to the proposed sabbatical leave starting date.

[1335]
OFFICE OF NAVAL RESEARCH SUMMER FACULTY RESEARCH PROGRAM

American Society for Engineering Education
Attn: Projects Department
1818 N Street, N.W., Suite 600
Washington, DC 20036-2479
(202) 331-3558   Fax: (202) 265-8504
E-mail: a.hicks@asee.org
Web: onr.asee.org/about_the_summer_faculty_program

Summary To provide support to Native American and other faculty members in engineering and science who wish to conduct summer research at selected Navy facilities.

Eligibility This program is open to U.S. citizens and permanent residents who have teaching or research appointments in engineering and science at U.S. universities or colleges. In addition to appointments as Summer Faculty Fellows, positions as Senior Summer Faculty Fellows are available to applicants who have at least 6 years of research experience in their field of expertise since earning a Ph.D. or equivalent degree and a substantial, significant record of research accomplishments and publications. A limited number of appointments are also available as Distinguished Summer Faculty Fellows to faculty members who are preeminent in their field of research, have a senior appointment at a leading research university, and are internationally recognized for their research accomplishments. Faculty from Historically Black Colleges and Universities, Hispanic Serving Institutions, and Tribal Colleges and Universities are especially encouraged to apply.

Financial data The weekly stipend is $1,400 at the Summer Faculty Fellow level, $1,650 at the Senior Summer Faculty Fellow level, and $1,900 at the Distinguished Summer Faculty Fellow level. Fellows who must relocate their residence receive a relocation allowance and all fellows receive a travel allowance.

Duration 10 weeks during the summer; fellows may reapply in subsequent years.

Additional information Participating facilities include the Naval Air Warfare Center, Aircraft Division (Patuxent River, Maryland); Naval Air Warfare Center, Naval Training Systems Division (Orlando, Florida); Naval Air Warfare Center, Weapons Division (China Lake, California); Space and Naval Warfare Systems Center (San Diego, California); Naval Facilities Engineering Service Center (Port Hueneme, California); Naval Research Laboratories (Washington, D.C.; Stennis Space Center, Mississippi; and Monterey, California); Naval Surface Warfare Centers (Bethesda, Maryland; Indian Head, Maryland; Dahlgren, Virginia; and Panama City, Florida); Naval Undersea Warfare Center (Newport, Rhode Island and New London, Connecticut); Defense Equal Opportunity Management Institute (Cocoa Beach, Florida); Navy Personnel Research, Studies & Technology Department (Millington, Tennessee); Naval Aerospace Medical Research Laboratory (Pensacola, Florida); Naval Health Research Center (San Diego, California); Naval Medical Research Center (Silver Spring, Maryland); and Naval Submarine Medical Research Laboratory (Groton, Connecticut). This program is funded by the U.S. Navy's Office of Naval Research and administered by the American Society for Engineering Education.

Number awarded Varies each year.

Deadline December of each year.

[1336]
OFFICE OF NAVAL RESEARCH YOUNG INVESTIGATOR PROGRAM

Office of Naval Research
Attn: Code 03R
875 North Randolph Street, Suite 1409
Arlington, VA 22203-1995
(703) 696-4111   E-mail: William.lukens1@navy.mil
Web: www.onr.navy.mil/Education-Outreach.aspx

Summary To provide funding to Native American and other academic scientists and engineers interested in conducting research on topics of interest to the U.S. Navy.

Eligibility This program is open to U.S. citizens, nationals, and permanent residents holding tenure-track faculty positions at U.S. universities who received their graduate degrees (Ph.D. or equivalent) within the preceding 5 years. Applicants must be proposing to conduct research relevant to 1 of the divisions within the Office of Naval Research: expeditionary warfare and combating terrorism; command, control communications, computers, intelligence, surveillance, and reconnaissance; ocean battlespace sensing; sea warfare and weapons; warfighter performance; and naval air warfare and weapons. Selection is based on 1) past performance, demonstrated by the significance and impact of previous research, publications, professional activities, awards, and other recognition; 2) a creative proposal, demonstrating the potential for making progress in a listed priority research area; and 3) a long-term commitment by the university to the applicant and the research. Researchers at Historically Black Colleges and Universities (HBCUs) and Minority Institutions (MIs) are encouraged to submit proposals and join others in submitting proposals.

Financial data Awards up to $170,000 per year are available.

Duration 3 years.

Additional information Approximately 2 recipients of these awards are also nominated to receive Presidential Early Career Awards for Scientists and Engineers to provide an additional 2 years of funding.

Number awarded Approximately 18 each year.

Deadline December of each year.

[1337]
ONLINE BIBLIOGRAPHIC SERVICES/ TECHNICAL SERVICES JOINT RESEARCH GRANT

American Association of Law Libraries
Attn: Online Bibliographic Services Special Interest
   Section
105 West Adams Street, Suite 3300
Chicago, IL 60603
(312) 939-4764   Fax: (312) 431-1097
E-mail: aallhq@aall.org
Web: www.aallnet.org/sis/obssis/research/funding.htm

Summary To provide funding to minority and other members of the American Association of Law Libraries (AALL) who are interested in conducting a research project related to technical services.

Eligibility This program is open to AALL members who are technical services law librarians. Preference is given to members of the Online Bibliographic Services and Technical Ser-

vices Special Interest Sections, although members of other special interest sections are eligible if their work relates to technical services law librarianship. Applicants must be interested in conducting research that will enhance law librarianship. Women and minorities are especially encouraged to apply. Preference is given to projects that can be completed in the United States or Canada, although foreign research projects are given consideration.

Financial data Grants range up to $1,000.

Duration 1 year.

Number awarded 1 or more each year.

Deadline June of each year.

[1338]
PACIFIC ISLANDERS IN COMMUNICATIONS MEDIA FUND GRANTS

Pacific Islanders in Communications
Attn: Program Director
1221 Kapi'olani Boulevard, Suite 6A-4
Honolulu, HI 96814-3513
(808) 591-0059   Fax: (808) 591-1114
E-mail: info@piccom.org
Web: www.piccom.org/resources/funding

Summary To provide funding to producers of public television programs that relate to the Native Pacific Islander experience.

Eligibility This program is open to independent producers and public television stations interested in developing programs that originate from the Pacific Islander experience and are intended for national public broadcast audiences. Applicants must have artistic, budgetary, and editorial control and must own the copyright of the proposed project. They must be at least 18 years of age, be citizens or legal residents of the United States or its territories, and have previous film or television experience. Student productions are not eligible. All projects must be delivered in standard public television lengths and meet accepted technical, ethical, and journalistic standards for national public television broadcast. Programs may be of any genre, but they must be intended for broadcast on national public television. For purposes of this program, Pacific Islanders are defined as descendants of the first peoples of American Samoa, Guam, Hawai'i, and the Northern Mariana Islands. Selection is based on the power of the finished product to shed light on the Pacific Islander experience; ability of the program to provoke thoughtful dialogue about the subject; knowledge and understanding of the subject as well as a thoughtful and sensitive approach; potential of the finished project to be shown on national public television; production and fundraising plans; ability of the producer and the production team to complete the project within budget and on schedule; and extent to which Pacific Islanders hold key creative production positions.

Financial data Maximum awards are $15,000 for research and development grants or $50,000 for production and completion grants.

Number awarded Varies each year; recently, 3 research and development grants, 5 production grants, and 1 completion grant were awarded.

Deadline January, April, or July of each year.

[1339]
PAUL HOCH DISTINGUISHED SERVICE AWARD

American College of Neuropsychopharmacology
Attn: Executive Office
5034-A Thoroughbred Lane
Brentwood, TN 37027
(615) 324-2360   Fax: (615) 523-1715
E-mail: acnp@acnp.org
Web: www.acnp.org/programs/awards.aspx

Summary To recognize and reward minority and other members of the American College of Neuropsychopharmacology (ACNP) who have contributed outstanding service to the organization.

Eligibility This award is available to ACNP members who have made unusually significant contributions to the College. The emphasis of the award is on service to the organization, not on teaching, clinical, or research accomplishments. Any member or fellow of ACNP may nominate another member. Nomination of women and minorities is highly encouraged.

Financial data The award consists of an expense-paid trip to the ACNP annual meeting, a monetary honorarium, and a plaque.

Duration The award is presented annually.

Additional information This award was first presented in 1965.

Number awarded 1 each year.

Deadline Nominations must be submitted by June of each year.

[1340]
PAUL TOBENKIN MEMORIAL AWARD

Columbia University
Attn: Graduate School of Journalism
Mail Code 3809
2950 Broadway
New York, NY 10027-7004
(212) 854-5377   Fax: (212) 854-7837
E-mail: am494@columbia.edu
Web: www.journalism.columbia.edu

Summary To recognize and reward outstanding newspaper writing that reflects the spirit of Paul Tobenkin, who fought all his life against racial and religious hatred, bigotry, bias, intolerance, and discrimination.

Eligibility Materials reflecting the spirit of Paul Tobenkin may be submitted by newspaper reporters in the United States, editors of their publications, or interested third parties. The items submitted must have been published during the previous calendar year in a weekly or daily newspaper.

Financial data The award is $1,000 plus a plaque.

Duration The award is presented annually.

Additional information This award was first presented in 1961.

Number awarded 1 each year.

Deadline February of each year.

[1341]
PAULA DE MERIEUX RHEUMATOLOGY FELLOWSHIP AWARD

American College of Rheumatology
Attn: Research and Education Foundation
2200 Lake Boulevard N.E.
Atlanta, GA 30319
(404) 633-3777   Fax: (404) 633-1870
E-mail: ref@rheumatology.org
Web: www.rheumatology.org/ref/awards/index.asp

Summary To provide funding to Native Americans, other underrepresented minorities, and women who are interested in a program of training for a career providing clinical care to people affected by rheumatic diseases.

Eligibility This program is open to trainees at ACGME-accredited institutions. Applications must be submitted by the training program director at the institution who is responsible for selection and appointment of trainees. The program must train and prepare fellows to provide clinical care to those affected by rheumatic diseases. Trainees must be women or members of underrepresented minority groups, defined as Black Americans, Hispanics, and Native Americans (Native Hawaiians, Alaska Natives, and American Indians). They must be U.S. citizens, nationals, or permanent residents. Selection is based on the institution's pass rate of rheumatology fellows, publication history of staff and previous fellows, current positions of previous fellows, and status of clinical faculty.

Financial data The grant is $25,000 per year, to be used as salary for the trainee. Other trainee costs (e.g., fees, health insurance, travel, attendance at scientific meetings) are to be incurred by the recipient's institutional program. Supplemental or additional support to offset the cost of living may be provided by the grantee institution.

Duration Up to 1 year.

Additional information This fellowship was first awarded in 2005.

Number awarded 1 each year.

Deadline July of each year.

[1342]
PHILLIPS FUND GRANTS FOR NATIVE AMERICAN RESEARCH

American Philosophical Society
Attn: Committee on Research
104 South Fifth Street
Philadelphia, PA 19106-3387
(215) 440-3429   Fax: (215) 440-3436
E-mail: LMusumeci@amphilsoc.org
Web: www.amphilsoc.org/grants/phillips

Summary To provide funding to graduate students and scholars interested in conducting research on North American Indian anthropological linguistics and ethnohistory.

Eligibility Eligible to apply are scholars, preferably young scholars, working in the fields of Native American linguistics and ethnohistory and the history of Native Americans in the continental United States and Canada. Applications are not accepted for projects in archaeology, ethnography, psycholinguistics, or for the preparation of pedagogical materials. Graduate students may apply for support for research on their master's or doctoral dissertations.

Financial data The grants average $2,500 and rarely exceed $3,500. These funds are intended for such extra costs as travel, tapes, films, and informants' fees, but not for general maintenance or the purchase of books or permanent equipment.

Duration 1 year.

Number awarded Varies each year; recently, 18 of these grants were awarded.

Deadline February of each year.

[1343]
POSTDOCTORAL FELLOWSHIP IN MENTAL HEALTH AND SUBSTANCE ABUSE SERVICES

American Psychological Association
Attn: Minority Fellowship Program
750 First Street, N.E.
Washington, DC 20002-4242
(202) 336-6127   Fax: (202) 336-6012
TDD: (202) 336-6123   E-mail: mfp@apa.org
Web: www.apa.org/pi/mfp/psychology/postdoc/index.aspx

Summary To provide financial assistance to postdoctoral scholars (particularly Native Americans and other minorities) who are interested in a program of research training related to providing mental health and substance abuse services to ethnic minority populations.

Eligibility This program is open to U.S. citizens and permanent residents who received a doctoral degree in psychology in the last 5 years. Applicants must be interested in participating in a program of training under a qualified sponsor for research, delivery of services, or policy related to substance abuse and its relationship to the mental health or psychological well-being of ethnic minorities. Members of ethnic minority groups (African Americans, Hispanics/Latinos, American Indians, Alaskan Natives, Asian Americans, Native Hawaiians, and other Pacific Islanders) are especially encouraged to apply. Selection is based on commitment to a career in ethnic minority mental health service delivery, research, or policy; qualifications of the sponsor; the fit between career goals and training environment selected; merit of the training proposal; potential demonstrated through accomplishments and goals; appropriateness to goals of the program; and letters of recommendation.

Financial data The stipend depends on the number of years of research experience and is equivalent to the standard postdoctoral stipend level of the National Institutes of Health (recently ranging from $38,496 for no years of experience to $53,112 for 7 or more years of experience).

Duration 1 academic or calendar year; may be renewed for 1 additional year.

Additional information Funding is provided by the U.S. Substance Abuse and Mental Health Services Administration.

Number awarded Varies each year.

Deadline January of each year.

[1344]
POSTDOCTORAL FELLOWSHIPS IN DIABETES RESEARCH

Juvenile Diabetes Research Foundation International
Attn: Grant Administrator
26 Broadway, 14th Floor
New York, NY 10004
(212) 479-7572   Toll Free: (800) 533-CURE
Fax: (212) 785-9595   E-mail: info@jdrf.org
Web: www.jdrf.org/index.cfm?page_id=111715

Summary To provide research training to underrepresented minorities and other scientists who are beginning their professional careers and are interested in participating in research training on the causes, treatment, prevention, or cure of diabetes or its complications.

Eligibility This program is open to postdoctorates who are interested in a career in Type 1 diabetes-relevant research. Applicants must have received their first doctoral degree (M.D., Ph.D., D.M.D., or D.V.M.) within the past 5 years and may not have a faculty appointment. There are no citizenship requirements. Applications are encouraged from women, members of minority groups underrepresented in the sciences, and people with disabilities. The proposed research training may be conducted at foreign or domestic, for-profit or nonprofit, or public or private institutions, including universities, colleges, hospitals, laboratories, units of state or local government, or eligible agencies of the federal government. Applicants must be sponsored by an investigator who is affiliated full time with an accredited institution and who agrees to supervise the applicant's training. Selection is based on the applicant's previous experience and academic record; the caliber of the proposed research; and the quality of the mentor, training program, and environment.

Financial data Stipends range from $37,740 to $47,940 (depending upon years of experience). In any case, the award may not exceed the salary the recipient is currently earning. Fellows also receive a research allowance of $5,500 per year.

Duration 1 year; may be renewed for up to 1 additional year.

Additional information Fellows must devote at least 80% of their effort to the fellowship project.

Deadline January or July of each year.

[1345]
POSTDOCTORAL FELLOWSHIPS IN POLAR REGIONS RESEARCH

National Science Foundation
Attn: Office of Polar Programs
4201 Wilson Boulevard, Suite 755S
Arlington, VA 22230
(703) 292-8029   Fax: (703) 292-9079
TDD: (800) 281-8749   E-mail: OPPfellow@nsf.gov
Web: www.nsf.gov/funding/pgm_summ.jsp?pims_id=5650

Summary To provide funding to underrepresented minorities and other recent postdoctorates interested in a program of research training related to the polar regions.

Eligibility This program is open to U.S. citizens and permanent residents in appropriate scientific fields who either completed a doctoral degree within the previous 4 years or will complete the degree within 1 year of the proposal deadline. Applicants may be proposing 1) a fellowship, for which they must identify a sponsoring scientist and a U.S. host organization that have agreed to provide a program of research training for fellows, or 2) a travel grant, for travel and per diem expenses to meet prospective sponsoring scientists in their host organizations before submitting a fellowship proposal. The host organization may be a college or university, government or national laboratory or facility, nonprofit institute, museum, or for-profit organization. The proposed or prospective research training should relate to an aspect of scientific study of the Antarctic or Arctic. The program encourages proposals from underrepresented minorities and persons with disabilities.

Financial data The maximum fellowship is $75,000 per year (including $50,000 as a stipend for the fellow, an annual research allowance of up to $11,000, an annual institutional allowance of $5,000, and an annual health insurance allowance of up to $3,600 for a single fellow, up to $6,000 for a fellow with 1 dependent, or up to $9,000 for a fellow with 2 or more dependents). The maximum travel grant is $3,000 for visits to 1 or 2 prospective host organizations. Indirect costs are not allowed for either fellowships or travel grants.

Duration Fellowships are typically 1 to 2 years long; 3-year fellowships may be justified for research and training plans that include field research.

Number awarded 5 fellowships and up to 10 travel grants may be awarded each year; recently, this program awarded approximately $1,000,000 in fellowships and travel grants.

Deadline Applications for fellowships must be submitted by October of each year. Applications for travel grants may be submitted at any time.

[1346]
POSTDOCTORAL FELLOWSHIPS OF THE FORD FOUNDATION DIVERSITY FELLOWSHIP PROGRAM

National Research Council
Attn: Fellowships Office, Keck 576
500 Fifth Street, N.W.
Washington, DC 20001
(202) 334-2872   Fax: (202) 334-3419
E-mail: infofell@nas.edu
Web: www.nationalacademies.org

Summary To provide funding for postdoctoral research to Native Americans and other scholars whose success will increase the racial and ethnic diversity of U.S. colleges and universities.

Eligibility This program is open to U.S. citizens and nationals who earned a Ph.D. or Sc.D. degree within the past 7 years and are committed to a career in teaching and research at the college or university level. The following are considered as positive factors in the selection process: evidence of superior academic achievement; promise of continuing achievement as scholars and teachers; membership in a group whose underrepresentation in the American professoriate has been severe and longstanding, including Black/African Americans, Puerto Ricans, Mexican Americans/Chicanos/Chicanas, Native American Indians, Alaska Natives (Eskimos, Aleuts, and other indigenous people of Alaska), and Native Pacific Islanders (Hawaiians, Micronesians, or Polynesians); capacity to respond in pedagogically productive ways to the learning needs of students from diverse backgrounds; sustained personal engagement with communities that are underrepresented in the academy and an ability to bring this asset to learning, teaching, and scholarship at the college and university level; and likelihood of using the diversity of human experience as an educational resource in teaching and scholarship. Eligible areas of study include most fields of the arts, sciences, humanities, or social sciences or many interdisciplinary ethnic or area studies, but not for most practice-oriented areas. Research may be conducted at an appropriate institution of higher education in the United States (normally) or abroad, including universities, museums, libraries, government or national laboratories, privately sponsored nonprofit institutes, government chartered nonprofit research organizations, or centers for advanced study. Applicants should designate a faculty member or other scholar to serve as host at the proposed fellowship institution. They are encouraged to choose a host institution other than that where they are affiliated at the time of application.

Financial data The stipend is $40,000. Funds may be supplemented by sabbatical leave pay or other sources of support that do not carry with them teaching or other responsibilities. The employing institution receives an allowance of $1,500, paid after fellowship tenure is completed; the employing institution is expected to match the grant and to use the allowance and the match to assist with the fellow's continuing research expenditures.

Duration 9 to 12 months.

Additional information Fellows may not accept another major fellowship while they are being supported by this program.

Number awarded Approximately 20 each year.

Deadline November of each year.

[1347]
POSTDOCTORAL FELLOWSHIPS OF THE MINORITY SCHOLAR-IN-RESIDENCE PROGRAM

Consortium for Faculty Diversity at Liberal Arts Colleges
c/o DePauw University
Academic Affairs Office
305 Harrison Hall
7 East Larabee Street
Greencastle, IN 46135
(765) 658-6595   E-mail: jgriswold@depauw.edu
Web: www.depauw.edu

Summary To make available the facilities of liberal arts colleges to Native American and other minority scholars who recently received their doctoral/advanced degree.

Eligibility This program is open to African American, Asian American, Hispanic American, and Native American scholars in the liberal arts and engineering who received the Ph.D. or M.F.A. degree within the past 5 years. Applicants must be interested in a residency at a participating institution that is part of the Consortium for a Strong Minority Presence at Liberal Arts Colleges. They must be U.S. citizens or permanent residents.

Financial data Fellows receive a stipend equivalent to the average salary paid by the host college to beginning assistant professors. Modest funds are made available to finance the fellow's proposed research, subject to the usual institutional procedures.

Duration 1 year.

Additional information The following schools are participating in the program: Agnes Scott College, Bard College at

Simon's Rock, Bowdoin College, Bryn Mawr College, Carleton College, Centre College, College of Wooster, Colorado College, Denison University, DePauw University, Dickinson College, Gettysburg College, Goucher College, Grinnell College, Hamilton College, Harvey Mudd College, Haverford College, Hobart and William Smith Colleges, Kalamazoo College, Lafayette College, Lawrence University, Luther College, Macalester College, Mount Holyoke College, Muhlenberg College, New College of Florida, Oberlin College, Pomona College, Reed College, Rhodes College, University of Richmond, Scripps College, St. Olaf College, Sewanee: The University of the South, Skidmore College, Smith College, Southwestern University, Swarthmore College, Trinity College, Vassar College, Wellesley College, Whitman College, and Willamette University. Fellows are expected to teach at least 1 course in each academic term of residency, participate in departmental seminars, and interact with students.

Number awarded Varies each year.

Deadline November of each year.

[1348]
POSTDOCTORAL INDUSTRIAL FELLOWSHIPS

National Science Foundation
Directorate for Engineering
Attn: Division of Industrial Innovation and Partnerships
4201 Wilson Boulevard, Room 550S
Arlington, VA 22230
(703) 292-7082   Fax: (703) 292-9056
TDD: (800) 281-8749   E-mail: dsenich@nsf.gov
Web: www.nsf.gov/funding/pgm_summ.jsp?pims_id=13706

Summary To provide an opportunity for recent postdoctorates (especially Native Americans, other underrepresented minorities, and persons with disabilities) to work in industry as part of the Grant Opportunities for Academic Liaison with Industry (GOALI) program of the National Science Foundation (NSF).

Eligibility Applicants for these fellowships must have held a Ph.D. degree in a science, engineering, or mathematics field of interest to NSF for no more than 3 years. They must be U.S. citizens, nationals, or permanent residents. Along with their application, they must submit a plan for full-time work in industry under the guidance of an academic adviser and an industrial mentor. The program encourages applications from underrepresented minorities and persons with disabilities.

Financial data Grants range up to $75,000 per year. Funding, up to $4,000, may also be provided for transportation and moving expenses. Indirect costs are not allowed, but an institutional allowance of $5,000 is provided.

Duration 1 or 2 years.

Additional information This program is also offered by most other NSF directorates. Check the web site for a name and e-mail address of the contact person in each directorate.

Number awarded A total of 60 to 80 grants for all GOALI programs is awarded each year; total funding is approximately $5 million.

Deadline Applications may be submitted at any time.

[1349]
POSTDOCTORAL RESEARCH FELLOWSHIPS IN BIOLOGY

National Science Foundation
Directorate for Biological Sciences
Attn: Division of Biological Infrastructure
4201 Wilson Boulevard, Room 615N
Arlington, VA 22230
(703) 292-8470   Fax: (703) 292-9063
TDD: (800) 281-8749   E-mail: ckimsey@nsf.gov
Web: www.nsf.gov

Summary To provide funding for research and training in specified areas related to biology to junior doctoral-level scientists (especially Native Americans, other underrepresented minorities, and persons with disabilities) at sites in the United States or abroad.

Eligibility This program is open to citizens, nationals, and permanent residents of the United States who are graduate students completing a Ph.D. or who have earned the degree no earlier than 12 months preceding the deadline date. Applicants must be interested in a program of research and training in either of 2 competitive areas: 1) Broadening Participation in Biology, designed to increase the diversity of scientists by providing support for research and training to biologists with disabilities and underrepresented minority (Native American, Native Pacific Islander, Alaskan Native, African American, and Hispanic) biologists; or 2) Intersections of Biology and Mathematical and Physical Sciences, for junior researchers who have conducted doctoral research in biology or physical and mathematical sciences and who present a research and training plan at the intersection of biology with mathematical and physical sciences. They may not have been a principal investigator or co-principal investigator on a federal research grant of more than $20,000. Fellowships are available to postdoctorates who are proposing a research and training plan at an appropriate nonprofit U.S. or foreign host institution (colleges and universities, government and national laboratories and facilities, and privately-sponsored nonprofit institutes and museums).

Financial data The fellowship grant is $60,000 for the first year, $63,000 for the second year, and $66,000 for the third year; that includes 1) an annual stipend of $45,000 for the first year, $48,000 for the second year, and $51,000 for the third year; 2) a research allowance of $10,000 per year paid to the fellow for materials and supplies, subscription fees, and recovery costs for databases, travel, and publication expenses; and 3) an institutional allowance of $5,000 per year for fringe benefits and expenses incurred in support of the fellow.

Duration Fellowships in the area of Broadening Participation in Biology are normally for 36 continuous months; those in the area of Intersections of Biology and Mathematical and Physical Sciences are normally for 24 months (unless the fellow spends more than 1 year at a foreign institution, in which case a third year of support at a U.S. institution may be requested).

Number awarded Approximately 15 fellowships are awarded each year.

Deadline October of each year.

[1350]
POSTDOCTORAL RESEARCH TRAINING FELLOWSHIPS IN EPILEPSY

Epilepsy Foundation
Attn: Research Department
8301 Professional Place
Landover, MD 20785-2237
(301) 459-3700   Toll Free: (800) EFA-1000
Fax: (301) 577-2684   TDD: (800) 332-2070
E-mail: grants@efa.org
Web: www.epilepsyfoundation.org

Summary To provide funding for a program of postdoctoral training to academic physicians and scientists (especially Native Americans, other minorities, women, and persons with disabilities) who are committed to epilepsy research.

Eligibility Applicants must have a doctoral degree (M.D., Sc.D., Ph.D., or equivalent) and be a clinical or postdoctoral fellow at a university, medical school, research institution, or medical center. They must be interested in participating in a training experience and research project that has potential significance for understanding the causes, treatment, or consequences of epilepsy. The program is geared toward applicants who will be trained in research in epilepsy rather than those who use epilepsy as a tool for research in other fields. Equal consideration is given to applicants interested in acquiring experience either in basic laboratory research or in the conduct of human clinical studies. Academic faculty holding the rank of instructor or higher are not eligible, nor are graduate or medical students, medical residents, permanent government employees, or employees of private industry. Applications from women, members of minority groups, and people with disabilities are especially encouraged. U.S. citizenship is not required, but the project must be conducted in the United States. Selection is based on scientific quality of the proposed research, a statement regarding its relevance to epilepsy, the applicant's qualifications, the preceptor's qualifications, and the adequacy of facility and related epilepsy programs at the institution.

Financial data The grant is $45,000. No indirect costs are covered.

Duration 1 year.

Additional information Support for this program is provided by many individuals, families, and corporations, especially the American Epilepsy Society, Abbott Laboratories, Ortho-McNeil Pharmaceutical, and Pfizer Inc. The fellowship must be carried out at a facility in the United States where there is an ongoing epilepsy research program.

Number awarded Varies each year.

Deadline August of each year.

[1351]
PRESIDENTIAL EARLY CAREER AWARDS FOR SCIENTISTS AND ENGINEERS

National Science and Technology Council
Executive Office of the President
Attn: Office of Science and Technology Policy
725 17th Street, Room 5228
Washington, DC 20502
(202) 456-7116   Fax: (202) 456-6021
Web: www.ostp.gov

Summary To recognize and reward the nation's most outstanding young science and engineering faculty members, particularly Native Americans and other minorities, by providing them with additional research funding.

Eligibility Eligible for these awards are U.S. citizens, nationals, and permanent residents who have been selected to receive research grants from other departments of the U.S. government. Recipients of designated research grant programs are automatically considered for these Presidential Early Career Awards for Scientists and Engineers (PECASE). Most of the participating programs encourage applications from racial/ethnic minority individuals, women, and persons with disabilities.

Financial data Awards carry a grant of at least $80,000 per year.

Duration 5 years.

Additional information The departments with research programs that nominate candidates for the PECASE program are: 1) the National Aeronautics and Space Administration, which selects recipients of Early Career Awards based on exceptionally meritorious proposals funded through the traditional research grant process or the unsolicited proposal process; 2) the Department of Veterans Affairs, which nominates the most meritorious recipients of Veterans Health Administration Research Awards in the categories in medical research, rehabilitation research, and health services research; 3) the National Institutes of Health, which nominates the most meritorious investigators funded through its First Independent Research Support and Transition (FIRST) Awards and NIH Individual Research Project Grants (R01) programs; 4) the Department of Energy, which nominates staff members of the national laboratories and the most meritorious recipients of the DOE–Energy Research Young Scientist Awards and DOE–Defense Programs Early Career Scientist and Engineer Awards; 5) the Department of Defense, which nominates outstanding recipients of the Office of Naval Research Young Investigator Program, the Air Force Office of Scientific Research Broad Agency Program, and the Army Research Office Young Investigator Program; 6) the Department of Agriculture, which nominates staff scientists from the Agricultural Research Service, the most meritorious investigators funded through the National Research Initiative Competitive Grants Program (NRICGP) New Investigator Awards, and staff scientists of the Forest Service; 7) the Department of Commerce, which nominates outstanding staff members of the National Oceanic and Atmospheric Administration and the National Institute of Standards and Technology; 8) the Department of Transportation, which nominates the most qualified and innovative researchers in its University Transportation Centers and University Research Institutes programs; and 9) the National Science Foundation, which selects its nominees from the most meritorious investigators funded through the Faculty Early Career Development (CAREER) Program. For a list of the names, addresses, and telephone numbers of contact persons at each of the participating agencies, contact the Office of Science and Technology Policy.

Number awarded Varies each year; recently, 85 of these awards were granted.

Deadline Deadline not specified.

[1352]
PRESIDENTIAL MANAGEMENT FELLOWS PROGRAM

Office of Personnel Management
Attn: Presidential Management Fellows Program
1900 E Street, N.W., Room 1425
Washington, DC 20415
(202) 606-1040   TDD: (202) 606-3040
E-mail: pmf@opm.gov
Web: www.pmf.opm.gov

Summary To offer Native American and other graduate students the opportunity to experience an entry-level career development and training program in Federal public service.

Eligibility This program is open to U.S. citizens and permanent residents who have received or are scheduled to receive a graduate degree (master's, law, or doctoral) during the current academic year. Students first apply online and must then be nominated by an official of their schools. From those applicants, the Office of Personnel Management (OPM) selects a large number of finalists, from whom participating agencies appoint fellows. Appointment of fellows is based on breadth and quality of accomplishments, capacity for leadership, and demonstrated commitment to excellence in the leadership and management of public policies and programs. A preference of 10 points is given to veterans who have a service-connected disability of any rating, recipients of the Purple Heart, widow(er)s or mothers of deceased veterans, or spouses or mothers of disabled veterans. Preference of 5 points is given to veterans who served 1) in a war, campaign, or expedition for which a campaign badge has been authorized or between April 28, 1952 and July 1, 1955; 2) for more than 180 consecutive days, any part of which occurred between January 31, 1955 and October 15, 1976; 3) during the Gulf War period from August 2, 1990 through January 2, 1992; or 4) for 180 or more consecutive days, any part of which occurred since September 11, 2001. In the appointment process, first consideration is to preference eligibles having a service-connected disability of 10% or more; second consideration is to other 10-point preference eligibles; third consideration is to 5-point preference eligibles. A separate preference is given to members of federally-recognized Indian tribes or Native Alaskan villages for positions within the Bureau of Indian Affairs of the Department of the Interior and the Indian Health Service of the Department of Health and Human Services.

Financial data Fellows begin at the GS-9 level (currently, starting at $41,563 per year) and are eligible for promotion to the GS-12 level (currently, $60,274 per year) after the first year of service. Upon completion of the program, they may be eligible for permanent positions at the GS-13 level (currently, $71,674 per year). Their compensation includes health and life insurance, retirement/investment plans, annual and sick leave, and all other benefits of civil service employees.

Duration 2 years.

Number awarded Varies each year; recently, approximately 750 fellows participated in this program.

Deadline October of each year.

[1353]
R. ROBERT & SALLY D. FUNDERBURG RESEARCH AWARD IN GASTRIC CANCER

American Gastroenterological Association
Attn: AGA Research Foundation
Research Awards Manager
4930 Del Ray Avenue
Bethesda, MD 20814-2512
(301) 222-4012   Fax: (301) 654-5920
E-mail: awards@gastro.org
Web: www.gastro.org/aga-foundation/grants

Summary To provide funding to minority and other established investigators who are working on research that enhances fundamental understanding of gastric cancer pathobiology.

Eligibility This program is open to faculty at accredited North American institutions who have established themselves as independent investigators in the field of gastric biology, pursuing novel approaches to gastric mucosal cell biology, including the fields of gastric mucosal cell biology, regeneration and regulation of cell growth, inflammation as precancerous lesions, genetics of gastric carcinoma, oncogenes in gastric epithelial malignancies, epidemiology of gastric cancer, etiology of gastric epithelial malignancies, or clinical research in diagnosis or treatment of gastric carcinoma. Applicants must be individual members of the American Gastroenterological Association (AGA). Women and minority investigators are strongly encouraged to apply. Selection is based on the novelty, feasibility, and significance of the proposal. Preference is given to novel approaches.

Financial data The grant is $50,000 per year. Funds are to be used for the salary of the investigator. Indirect costs are not allowed.

Duration 2 years.

Number awarded 1 each year.

Deadline September of each year.

[1354]
RALPH J. BUNCHE AWARD

American Political Science Association
1527 New Hampshire Avenue, N.W.
Washington, DC 20036-1206
(202) 483-2512   Fax: (202) 483-2657
E-mail: apsa@apsanet.org
Web: www.apsanet.org/content_4129.cfm

Summary To recognize and reward outstanding scholarly books on ethnic/cultural pluralism.

Eligibility Eligible to be nominated (by publishers or individuals) are scholarly political science books issued the previous year that explore issues of ethnic and/or cultural pluralism.

Financial data The award is $1,000.

Duration The award is presented annually.

Additional information This award was first presented in 1978.

Number awarded 1 each year.

Deadline January of each year for nominations from individuals; February of each year for nominations from publishers.

[1355]
READING AWARD PROGRAM

Catching the Dream
8200 Mountain Road, N.E., Suite 203
Albuquerque, NM 87110-7835
(505) 262-2351   Fax: (505) 262-0534
E-mail: NScholarsh@aol.com
Web: www.catchingthedream.org/grants.htm

Summary   To provide funding to Native American and other teachers and schools for projects that are designed to improve the reading ability of Indian students.

Eligibility   This program is open to schools that serve large numbers of Indian students. Applicants must describe the school, the students to be served, the reading habits of those students, how the program will work, how the funds from the grant will be used, the background of the person in charge, and project objectives.

Financial data   Grants are $1,000. Some of the previous acceptable uses of funds have included financial rewards to students for reading heavily, student scholarships, student trips at the end of the year, and even pizza parties for students. Funds cannot be used for the purchase of books, the purchase of computers or reading equipment, or staff training or travel.

Duration   Grants are awarded annually.

Additional information   The sponsor was formerly known as the Native American Scholarship Fund.

Number awarded   10 each year.

Deadline   October of each year.

[1356]
RESEARCH AND TRAINING FELLOWSHIPS IN EPILEPSY FOR CLINICIANS

Epilepsy Foundation
Attn: Research Department
8301 Professional Place
Landover, MD 20785-2237
(301) 459-3700   Toll Free: (800) EFA-1000
Fax: (301) 577-2684   TDD: (800) 332-2070
E-mail: clinical_postdocs@efa.org
Web: www.epilepsyfoundation.org

Summary   To provide funding to Native American and other clinically-trained professionals interested in gaining additional training in order to develop an epilepsy research program.

Eligibility   Applicants must have an M.D., D.O., Ph.D., D.S., or equivalent degree and be a clinical or postdoctoral fellow at a university, medical school, or other appropriate research institution. Holders of other doctoral-level degrees (e.g., Pharm.D., D.S.N.) may also be eligible. Candidates must be interested in a program of research training that may include mechanisms of epilepsy, novel therapeutic approaches, clinical trials, development of new technologies, or behavioral and psychosocial impact of epilepsy. The training program may consist of both didactic training and a supervised research experience that is designed to develop the necessary knowledge and skills in the chosen area of research and foster the career goals of the candidate. Academic faculty holding the rank of instructor or higher are not eligible, nor are graduate or medical students, medical residents, permanent government employees, or employees of private industry. Applications from women, members of minority groups, and people with disabilities are especially encouraged. U.S. citizenship is not required, but the project must be conducted in the United States. Selection is based on the quality of the proposed research training program, the applicant's qualifications, the preceptor's qualifications, and the adequacy of clinical training, research facilities, and other epilepsy-related programs at the institution.

Financial data   The grant is $50,000 per year. No indirect costs are provided.

Duration   Up to 2 years.

Additional information   Support for this program is provided by many individuals, families, and corporations, especially the American Epilepsy Society, Abbott Laboratories, Ortho-McNeil Pharmaceutical, and Pfizer Inc. Grantees are expected to dedicate at least 50% of their time to research training and conducting research.

Number awarded   Varies each year.

Deadline   September of each year.

[1357]
RESEARCH INITIATION GRANTS TO BROADEN PARTICIPATION IN BIOLOGY

National Science Foundation
Directorate for Biological Sciences
Attn: Division of Biological Infrastructure
4201 Wilson Boulevard, Room 615N
Arlington, VA 22230
(703) 292-8470   Fax: (703) 292-9063
TDD: (800) 281-8749   E-mail: amaglia@nsf.gov
Web: www.nsf.gov/funding/pgm_summ.jsp?pims_id=10676

Summary   To provide funding for research to Native American and other scientists underrepresented in the field of biological science.

Eligibility   This program is open to U.S. citizens, nationals, and permanent residents who have a doctoral degree or equivalent experience in a field of biology supported by the National Science Foundation (NSF). Applicants must be able to show how their proposal will increase the participation of scientists from underrepresented groups (African Americans, Hispanics, Native Americans, Native Hawaiians, and Alaska Natives) in biological research and the numbers of such individuals that serve as role models for the scientific workforce of the future. They must be in their first academic appointment as a faculty member or research-related position. Proposers affiliated with Minority-Serving Institutions (MSIs), including Historically Black Colleges and Universities (HBCUs), Hispanic-Serving Institutions (HSIs), and Tribal Colleges and Universities (TCUs), are especially encouraged to apply. Selection is based on the scientific merit of the proposed research and the extent to which the proposed activities will broaden participation of individuals from underrepresented groups in the areas of the biological sciences supported by NSF.

Financial data   Grants provide up to $175,000 over the life of the award, including both direct and indirect costs. An additional $25,000 may be provided for equipment.

Duration   24 months.

Number awarded   10 to 15 each year.

Deadline   January of each year.

[1358]
RIDGE 2000 POSTDOCTORAL FELLOWSHIP PROGRAM

National Science Foundation
Directorate for Geosciences
Attn: Division of Ocean Sciences
4201 Wilson Boulevard, Room 725N
Arlington, VA 22230
(703) 292-7588   Fax: (703) 292-9085
TDD: (800) 281-8749   E-mail: dgarriso@nsf.gov
Web: www.nsf.gov/funding/pgm_summ.jsp?pims_id=5513

Summary To provide opportunities for young scientists (particularly Native Americans, other underrepresented minorities, and persons with disabilities) to conduct geological research on the mid-ocean ridge system as part of the Ridge Inter-Disciplinary Global Experiments (RIDGE) 2000 Initiative.

Eligibility Eligible are U.S. citizens, nationals, or permanent residents who will have earned a doctoral degree within 2 years of taking up the award and who have arranged to conduct research under a senior scientist at an appropriate U.S. nonprofit institution (government laboratory, privately-sponsored nonprofit institution, national laboratory, or institution of higher education). Applicants must be proposing to conduct research that attempts to understand the geological processes of planetary renewal occurring along the mid-oceanic plate boundary and the chemical and biological processes that sustain life, in the absence of sunlight, in the deep ocean. Currently, the program has identified 3 sites as the focus of research: 9-10 degrees North segment of the East Pacific Rise, the East Lau Spreading Center in the western Pacific, and the Endeavor segment of the Juan de Fuca Ridge in the northwestern Pacific. Selection is based on ability as evidenced by past research work; suitability and availability of the sponsoring senior scientist and other associated colleagues; suitability of the host institution for the proposed research; likely impact on the future scientific development of the applicant; scientific quality of the research likely to emerge; and the potential impact of the research on the RIDGE 2000 Initiative. The program encourages applications from underrepresented minorities and persons with disabilities.

Financial data Grants range from $100,000 to $150,000. Funding includes a research allowance of $5,000 per year and an institutional allowance (in lieu of indirect costs) of $300 per month.

Duration 2 years; may be renewed for 1 additional year.

Number awarded 10 each year.

Deadline April of each year.

[1359]
ROBERT WOOD JOHNSON HEALTH POLICY FELLOWSHIPS

Institute of Medicine
Attn: Health Policy Fellowships Program
500 Fifth Street, N.W.
Washington, DC 20001
(202) 334-1506   Fax: (202) 334-3862
E-mail: mmichnich@nas.edu
Web: www.healthpolicyfellows.org

Summary To offer health professionals and behavioral or social scientists (particularly Native Americans and those with diverse backgrounds) who have an interest in health the opportunity to participate in the formulation of national health policies while in residence at the Institute of Medicine (IOM) in Washington, D.C.

Eligibility This program is open to mid-career professionals from academic faculties and nonprofit health care organizations who are interested in experiencing health policy processes at the federal level. Applicants must have a background in allied health professions, biomedical sciences, dentistry, economics or other social sciences, health services organization and administration, medicine, nursing, public health, or social and behavioral health. They must be sponsored by the chief executive office of an eligible nonprofit health care organization or academic institution. Selection is based on potential for leadership in health policy, potential for future growth and career advancement, professional achievements, interpersonal and communication skills, and individual plans for incorporating the fellowship experience into specific career goals. U.S. citizenship or permanent resident status is required. Applications are especially encouraged from candidates with diverse backgrounds.

Financial data Total support for the Washington stay and continuing activities may not exceed $165,000. Grant funds may cover salary support at a level of up to $94,000 plus fringe benefits. Fellows are reimbursed for relocation expenses to and from Washington, D.C. No indirect costs are paid.

Duration The program begins in September with an orientation that includes meeting with key executive branch officials responsible for health activities, members of Congress and their staffs, and representatives of health interest groups; also included in the orientation period are seminars on health economics, major federal health and health research programs, the Congressional budget process, background on the major current issues in federal health policy, and the politics and process of federal decision-making. In November, the fellows join the American Political Science Association Congressional Fellowship Program for sessions with members of Congress, journalists, policy analysts, and other experts on the national political and governmental process. During that stage, fellows make contact with Congressional or executive branch offices involved in health issues and negotiate their working assignments. Those assignments begin in January and end in August, with an option for extending through the legislative term (which normally ends in October or early November). Fellows then return to their home institutions, but they receive up to 2 years of continued support for further development of health policy leadership skills.

Additional information This program, initiated in 1973, is funded by the Robert Wood Johnson Foundation.

Number awarded Up to 6 each year.

Deadline November of each year.

[1360]
ROLLIN AND MARY ELLA KING NATIVE ARTIST FELLOWSHIP

School for Advanced Research
Attn: Indian Arts Research Center
660 Garcia Street
P.O. Box 2188
Santa Fe, NM 87504-2188
(505) 954-7205   Fax: (505) 954-7207
E-mail: iarc@sarsf.org
Web: sarweb.org/index.php?artists

Summary To provide an opportunity for Native American artists to improve their skills through a fall residency at the Indian Arts Research Center in Santa Fe, New Mexico.

Eligibility This program is open to Native Americans who excel in the arts, including sculpture, performance, basketry, painting, printmaking, digital art, mixed media, photography, pottery, writing, and filmmaking. Applicants should be attempting to explore new avenues of creativity, grapple with new ideas to advance their work, and strengthen existing talents. Along with their application, they must submit a current resume, examples of their current work, and a 2-page statement that explains why they are applying for this fellowship, how it will help them realize their professional and/or personal goals as an artist, and describing the project they plan to complete during the residency.

Financial data The fellowship provides a stipend of $3,000 per month, housing, studio space, supplies allowance, and travel reimbursement to and from the center.

Duration 3 months, beginning in September.

Additional information Fellows work with the staff and research curators at the Indian Arts Research Center, an academic division of the School of American Research that is devoted solely to Native American art scholarship. The center has a significant collection of Pueblo pottery, Navajo and Pueblo Indian textiles, and early 20th-century Indian paintings, as well as holdings of jewelry and silverwork, basketry, clothing, and other ethnological materials. This fellowship was established in 2001.

Number awarded 1 each year.

Deadline January of each year.

[1361]
RONALD AND SUSAN DUBIN NATIVE ARTIST FELLOWSHIP

School for Advanced Research
Attn: Indian Arts Research Center
660 Garcia Street
P.O. Box 2188
Santa Fe, NM 87504-2188
(505) 954-7205   Fax: (505) 954-7207
E-mail: iarc@sarsf.org
Web: sarweb.org/index.php?artists

Summary To provide an opportunity for Native American artists to improve their skills through a summer residency at the Indian Arts Research Center in Santa Fe, New Mexico.

Eligibility This program is open to Native American artists; priority is given to individuals who excel in the visual arts that relate to the center's collecting emphasis, but artists who work in the verbal and performing arts are also considered. Along with their application, they must submit a current resume, examples of their current work, and a 2-page statement that explains why they are applying for this fellowship, how it will help them realize their professional and/or personal goals as an artist, and describing the project they plan to complete during the residency.

Financial data The fellowship provides a stipend of $3,000 per month, housing, studio space, supplies allowance, and travel reimbursement to and from the center.

Duration 2 months, beginning in June.

Additional information Fellows work with the staff and research curators at the Indian Arts Research Center, an academic division of the School of American Research that is devoted solely to Native American art scholarship. The center has a significant collection of Pueblo pottery, Navajo and Pueblo Indian textiles, and early 20th-century Indian paintings, as well as holdings of jewelry and silverwork, basketry, clothing, and other ethnological materials. This fellowship was first awarded in 1994.

Number awarded 1 each year.

Deadline January of each year.

[1362]
RUTH L. KIRSCHSTEIN NATIONAL RESEARCH SERVICE AWARDS FOR INDIVIDUAL SENIOR FELLOWS

National Institutes of Health
Office of Extramural Research
Attn: Grants Information
6705 Rockledge Drive, Suite 4090
Bethesda, MD 20892-7983
(301) 435-0714   Fax: (301) 480-0525
TDD: (301) 451-5936   E-mail: GrantsInfo@nih.gov
Web: grants.nih.gov/grants/guide/index.html

Summary To provide funding for mentored research training to minority and other experienced scientists who wish to make major changes in the direction of their research careers.

Eligibility This program is open to U.S. citizens, nationals, and permanent residents who have a doctoral degree and at least 7 subsequent years of relevant research or professional experience. Applications may be submitted on behalf of the candidates by a sponsoring institution, which may be a domestic or foreign, for-profit or nonprofit, public or private institution (such as a university, college, hospital, laboratory, agency or laboratory of the federal government, or intramural laboratory of the National Institutes of Health). Individuals requesting foreign-site training must justify the particular suitability of the foreign site, based on the nature of the facilities and/or training opportunity, rather than a domestic institution. In cases where there are clear scientific advantages, foreign training will be supported. Candidates must have received a Ph.D., M.D., D.O., D.C., D.D.S., D.V.M., O.D., D.P.M., Sc.D., Eng.D., Dr.P.H., D.N.Sc., N.D., Pharm.D., D.S.W., Psy.D., or equivalent degree from an accredited domestic or foreign institution. Members of diverse racial and ethnic groups, individuals with disabilities, and individuals from disadvantaged backgrounds are especially encouraged to apply.

Financial data The award provides an annual stipend based on the number of years of postdoctoral experience, ranging from $37,368 for less than 1 year to $51,552 for 7 or more years. For fellows sponsored by domestic nonfederal institutions, the stipend is paid through the sponsoring institution; for fellows sponsored by federal or foreign institutions, the monthly stipend is paid directly to the fellow. Institutions also receive an allowance to help defray such awardee expenses as self-only health insurance, research supplies, equipment, travel to scientific meetings, and related items; the allowance is $7,850 per 12-month period for fellows at nonfederal, nonprofit, and foreign institutions and $6,750 per 12-month period at federal laboratories and for-profit institutions. In addition, tuition and fees are reimbursed at a rate of 60%, up to $4,500; if the fellow's program supports postdoctoral individuals in formal degree-granting training, tuition is supported at the rate of 60%, up to $16,000 for an additional degree. The initial 12 months of National Research Service Award postdoctoral support carries a service payback requirement, which can be fulfilled by continued training under the award or by engaging in other health-related research training, health-related research, or health-related teaching. Fellows who fail to fulfill the payback requirement of 1 month of acceptable service for each month of the initial 12 months of support received must repay all funds received with interest.

Duration Up to 2 years.

Additional information This program is offered by 16 components of the National Institutes of Health: the National Institute on Aging, the National Institute on Alcohol Abuse and Alcoholism, the National Institute of Allergy and Infectious Diseases, the National Institute of Arthritis and Musculoskeletal and Skin Diseases, the National Cancer Institute, the National Institute of Child Health and Human Development, the National Institute on Deafness and Other Communication Disorders, the National Institute of Dental and Craniofacial Research, the National Institute of Environmental Health Sciences, the National Eye Institute, the National Institute of General Medical Sciences, the National Institute of Neurological Disorders and Stroke, the National Institute of Nursing Research, and the Office of Dietary Supplements.

Number awarded Varies each year.

Deadline April, August, or December of each year.

[1363]
SAR INDIGENOUS WRITER-IN-RESIDENCE FELLOWSHIP

School for Advanced Research
Attn: Indian Arts Research Center
660 Garcia Street
P.O. Box 2188
Santa Fe, NM 87504-2188
(505) 954-7205   Fax: (505) 954-7207
E-mail: iarc@sarsf.org
Web: www.sarweb.org/iarc/dubin/dubin.htm

Summary To provide an opportunity for Native American writers to improve their skills through a winter residency at the Indian Arts Research Center in Santa Fe, New Mexico.

Eligibility This program is open to Native American writers. Applicants must be interested in a program of residence at the Center to work on their creative projects. Along with their application, they must submit a current resume, examples of their current work, and a 2-page statement that explains why they are applying for this fellowship, how it will help them realize their professional and/or personal goals as a writer, and describing the project they plan to complete during the residency.

Financial data The fellowship provides a stipend of $3,000 per month, housing, studio space, supplies allowance, and travel reimbursement to and from the center.

Duration 6 weeks, in January and February.

Additional information Fellows work with the staff and research curators at the Indian Arts Research Center, an academic division of the School of American Research (SAR) that is devoted solely to Native American scholarship. This fellowship was first awarded in 2011.

Number awarded 1 each year.

Deadline January of each year.

[1364]
SARA WHALEY BOOK PRIZE

National Women's Studies Association
Attn: Book Prizes
7100 Baltimore Avenue, Suite 203
College Park, MD 20740
(301) 403-0407   Fax: (301) 403-4137
E-mail: nwsaoffice@nwsa.org
Web: www.nwsa.org/awards/index.php

Summary To recognize and reward members of the National Women's Studies Association (NWSA), particularly Native American and other women of color, who have written outstanding books on topics related to women and labor.

Eligibility This award is available to NWSA members who submit a book manuscript that relates to women and labor, including migration and women's paid jobs, illegal immigration and women's work, impact of AIDS on women's employment, trafficking of women and women's employment, women and domestic work, or impact of race on women's work. Both senior scholars (who have a record of publication of at least 2 books and published the entry within the past year) and junior scholars (who have a publication contract or a book in production) are eligible. Women of color of American or international origin are encouraged to apply.

Financial data The award is $2,000.

Duration The awards are presented annually.

Additional information This award was first presented in 2008.

Number awarded 2 each year: 1 to a senior scholar and 1 to a junior scholar.

Deadline April of each year.

[1365]
SBE MINORITY POSTDOCTORAL RESEARCH FELLOWSHIPS AND FOLLOW-UP RESEARCH STARTER GRANTS

National Science Foundation
Directorate for Social, Behavioral, and Economic
  Sciences
Attn: Office of Multidisciplinary Activities
4201 Wilson Boulevard, Room 907.09
Arlington, VA 22230
(703) 292-4672   Fax: (703) 292-9083
TDD: (800) 281-8749   E-mail: fchowdhu@nsf.gov
Web: www.nsf.gov

Summary To provide financial assistance for postdoctoral research training in the United States or abroad to Native American and other underrepresented minority scientists in fields of interest to the Directorate for Social, Behavioral, and

Economic Sciences (SBE) of the National Science Foundation (NSF).

Eligibility This program is open to U.S. citizens, nationals, and permanent residents who will complete their doctorate within a year or have completed it within the previous 30 months but have not completed more than 12 months in a postdoctoral research position. Applicants must be a member of an ethnic group that is significantly underrepresented at advanced levels of science and engineering in the United States, including Native Americans (Alaska Natives and American Indians), African Americans, Hispanics, and Native Pacific Islanders. They must be seeking fellowship funding for research training that falls within the program areas of the SBE to be conducted at any appropriate nonprofit U.S. or foreign institution (government laboratory, institution of higher education, national laboratory, or public or private research institute), but not at the same institution where the doctorate was obtained. Fellows who accept a tenure-track position at a U.S. academic institution may apply for a follow-up research starter grant.

Financial data The fellowship grant is $60,000 per year, including an annual stipend of $45,000, a research allowance of $10,000 per year, and an institutional allowance of $5,000 per year for partial reimbursement of indirect research costs (space, equipment, general purpose supplies, and fringe benefits). Follow-up research starter grants are $50,000.

Duration Fellowships are for 2 years; applicants who propose to spend their 2-year tenure at a foreign institution may apply for a third year of support at an appropriate U.S. institution. Follow-up research starter grants are for 1 year.

Number awarded Up to 12 each year.

Deadline October of each year.

[1366]
SMITHSONIAN NATIVE AMERICAN COMMUNITY SCHOLAR AWARDS

Smithsonian Institution
Attn: Office of Fellowships
470 L'Enfant Plaza, Suite 7102
P.O. Box 37012, MRC 902
Washington, DC 20013-7012
(202) 633-7070   Fax: (202) 633-7069
E-mail: siofg@si.edu
Web: www.si.edu/ofg/Applications/NAP/NAPapp.htm

Summary To provide opportunities for Native Americans to work on projects related to Native American topics at the Smithsonian Institution.

Eligibility Native Americans who are formally or informally related to a Native American community are eligible to apply. Applicants must be proposing to undertake a project that is related to a Native American topic and requires the use of Native American resources at the Smithsonian Institution.

Financial data Scholars receive a stipend of $150 per day and allowances for travel and research.

Duration Up to 21 days.

Additional information Projects are carried out in association with the Smithsonian's research staff. Fellows are required to be in residence at the Smithsonian for the duration of the fellowship.

Number awarded Varies each year.

Deadline January of each year for summer residency; May of each year for fall residency; September of each year for spring residency.

[1367]
SOCIETY OF PEDIATRIC PSYCHOLOGY DIVERSITY RESEARCH GRANT

American Psychological Association
Attn: Division 54 (Society of Pediatric Psychology)
c/o John M. Chaney
Oklahoma State University
Department of Psychology
407 North Murray
Stillwater, OK 74078
(405) 744-5703   E-mail: john.chaney@okstate.edu
Web: www.societyofpediatricpsychology.org

Summary To provide funding to minority and other graduate student and postdoctoral members of the Society of Pediatric Psychology who are interested in conducting research on diversity aspects of pediatric psychology.

Eligibility This program is open to current members of the society who are graduate students, fellows, or early-career (within 3 years of appointment) faculty. Applicants must be interested in conducting pediatric psychology research that features diversity-related variables, such as race or ethnicity, gender, culture, sexual orientation, language differences, socioeconomic status, and/or religiosity. Along with their application, they must submit a 2,000-word description of the project, including its purpose, methodology, predictions, and implications; a detailed budget; a current curriculum vitae, and (for students) a curriculum vitae of the faculty research mentor and a letter of support from that mentor. Selection is based on relevance to diversity in child health (5 points), significance of the study (5 points), study methods and procedures (10 points), and investigator qualifications (10 points).

Financial data Grants up to $1,000 are available. Funds may not be used for convention or meeting travel, indirect costs, stipends of principal investigators, or costs associated with manuscript preparation.

Duration The grant is presented annually.

Additional information The Society of Pediatric Psychology is Division 54 of the American Psychological Association (APA). This grant was first presented in 2008.

Number awarded 1 each year.

Deadline September of each year.

[1368]
SUBSTANCE ABUSE FELLOWSHIP PROGRAM

American Psychiatric Association
Attn: Department of Minority and National Affairs
1000 Wilson Boulevard, Suite 1825
Arlington, VA 22209-3901
(703) 907-8653   Toll Free: (888) 35-PSYCH
Fax: (703) 907-7852   E-mail: mking@psych.org
Web: www.psych.org/Resources/OMNA/MFP.aspx

Summary To provide educational enrichment to Native American and other minority psychiatrists-in-training and stimulate their interest in providing quality and effective services related to substance abuse to minorities and the underserved.

Eligibility This program is open to psychiatric residents who are members of the American Psychiatric Association (APA) and U.S. citizens or permanent residents. A goal of the program is to develop leadership to improve the quality of mental health care for members of ethnic minority groups (American Indians, Native Alaskans, Asian Americans, Native Hawaiians, Native Pacific Islanders, African Americans, and Hispanics/Latinos). Applicants must be in at least their fifth year of a substance abuse training program approved by an affiliated medical school or agency where a significant number of substance abuse patients are from minority and underserved groups. They must also be interested in working with a component of the APA that is of interest to them and relevant to their career goals. Along with their application, they must submit a 2-page essay on how the fellowship would be utilized to alter their present training and ultimately assist them in achieving their career goals. Selection is based on commitment to serve ethnic minority populations, demonstrated leadership abilities, awareness of the importance of culture in mental health, and interest in the interrelationship between mental health/illness and transcultural factors.

Financial data Fellows receive a monthly stipend (amount not specified) and reimbursement of transportation, lodging, meals, and incidentals in connection with attendance at program-related activities. They are expected to use the funds to enhance their own professional development, improve training in cultural competence at their training institution, improve awareness of culturally relevant issues in psychiatry at their institution, expand research in areas relevant to minorities and underserved populations, enhance the current treatment modalities for minority patients and underserved individuals at their institution, and improve awareness in the surrounding community about mental health issues (particularly with regard to minority populations).

Duration 1 year; may be renewed 1 additional year.

Additional information Funding for this program is provided by the Substance Abuse and Mental Health Services Administration (SAMHSA). As part of their assignment to an APA component, fellows must attend the fall component meetings in September and the APA annual meeting in May. At those meeting, they can share their experiences as residents and minorities and discuss issues that impact minority populations. This program is an outgrowth of the fellowships that were established in 1974 under a grant from the National Institute of Mental Health in answer to concerns about the underrepresentation of minorities in psychiatry.

Number awarded Varies each year; recently, 3 of these fellowships were awarded.

Deadline January of each year.

[1369]
SUSAN G. KOMEN BREAST CANCER FOUNDATION POSTDOCTORAL FELLOWSHIP

Susan G. Komen Breast Cancer Foundation
Attn: Grants Department
5005 LBJ Freeway, Suite 250
Dallas, TX 75244
(972) 855-1616   Toll Free: (866) 921-9678
Fax: (972) 855-1640
E-mail: helpdesk@komengrantsaccess.org
Web: ww5.komen.org

Summary To provide funding to postdoctoral fellows (particularly Native Americans and other minorities) who are interested in pursuing research training related to breast cancer.

Eligibility This program is open to postdoctorates who are no more than 5 years past completion of their Ph.D. or, if an M.D., no more than 3 years past completion of clinical fellowship or 5 years past completion of residency. Applicants may not hold any current faculty appointments and may not currently be or have been a fellow for the same sponsor. They are not required to be U.S. citizens or residents. A principal investigator who is a full-time faculty member at the same institution must sponsor the applicant. Currently, proposals must focus on 4 types of research training activities: 1) basic research that substantially advances progress in breast cancer research and will lead to future reductions in breast cancer incidence and/or mortality; 2) translational research that expands skills and expertise in the application of laboratory, clinical, and applied disciplines to research that translates laboratory, clinical, and/or population discoveries into new clinical tools and applications leading to reductions of breast cancer incidence and/or mortality; 3) clinical research for physicians who wish to pursue a career path that blends patient care with high impact, clinical, and/or translational breast cancer research; expands their skills; positions them for independent careers as physician scientists; and supports high quality research concepts; or 4) disparities research that expands skills and expertise in research exploring the basis for differences in breast cancer outcomes and the translation of this research into clinical and public health practice interventions, particularly among junior scientists from populations affected by breast cancer disparities. The program is especially interested in providing training support for minority scientists; a portion of available funds are designated for minority fellows.

Financial data The grant is $60,000 per year for direct costs only.

Duration 2 years; a third year may be approved, based on an assessment of first-year progress.

Number awarded Varies each year; recently, 56 of these fellowships were awarded.

Deadline Pre-applications must be submitted in September of each year; full applications are due in January.

[1370]
SUSAN KELLY POWER AND HELEN HORNBECK TANNER FELLOWSHIP

Newberry Library
Attn: McNickle Center for American Indian History
60 West Walton Street
Chicago, IL 60610-3305
(312) 255-3564   Fax: (312) 255-3696
E-mail: mcnickle@newberry.org
Web: www.newberry.org/mcnickle/powertanner.html

Summary To provide funding to American Indian doctoral candidates and postdoctorates who wish to use the resources of the D'Arcy McNickle Center for the History of the American Indian at the Newberry Library.

Eligibility This program is open to Ph.D. candidates and postdoctoral scholars of American Indian heritage. Applicants must be interested in conducting research in any field of the humanities while in residence at the McNickle Center.

Financial data   The stipend is $1,600 per month.

Duration   1 week to 2 months.

Additional information   This program was established in 2002.

Number awarded   1 each year.

Deadline   February of each year.

[1371]
SWAIA RESIDENCY FELLOWSHIPS

Southwestern Association for Indian Arts, Inc.
3600 Cerrillos Road, Suite 712
P.O. Box 969
Santa Fe, NM 87504-0969
(505) 983-5220   Fax: (505) 983-7647
E-mail: info@swaia.org
Web: swaia.org

Summary   To provide funding to American Indian artists interested in a residency in Santa Fe, New Mexico.

Eligibility   This program is open to American Indian artists in the visual arts whose work conforms to the standards and classification definitions of the Southwestern Association for Indian Arts (SWAIA): jewelry; pottery; paintings, drawings, graphics, and photography; Pueblo wooden carving; sculpture; textiles; basketry; beadwork and quillwork; film and video; writing (poetry and fiction); and diverse arts. Applicants must be interested in a residency at the Santa Fe Art Institute (SFAI). Along with their application, they must submit a formal artist statement of 1 to 2 pages explaining and contextualizing their artwork by discussing their motivations to create, materials that they use, or cultural impact they wish to develop with their fellowship. They must also submit samples of their work (4 digital images for visual artists, a 5-minute CD or DVD for filmmakers, or 10 pages of writing for authors), an explanation of how they plan to use the residency, and a formal resume.

Financial data   Fellows receive a grant of $5,000; a residency at SFAI that includes lodging, studio space, and basic foods; and a complimentary booth at the Santa Fe Indian Market. In lieu of a booth, writers participate in SWAIA's Native literary and performance event during Indian Market Week.

Duration   The residency lasts 1 month (in August).

Additional information   SWAIA established a fellowship program in 1980. Beginning in 2010, it began offering 2 types of fellowships: these Residency Fellowships and Discovery Fellowships (similar to the prior fellowships). The application fee is $25.

Number awarded   Varies each year.

Deadline   December of each year.

[1372]
SYLVIA TAYLOR JOHNSON MINORITY FELLOWSHIP IN EDUCATIONAL MEASUREMENT

Educational Testing Service
Attn: Fellowships
660 Rosedale Road
MS 19-T
Princeton, NJ 08541-0001
(609) 734-5543   Fax: (609) 734-5410
E-mail: internfellowships@ets.org
Web: www.ets.org/research/fellowships/johnson

Summary   To provide funding to Native American and other minority scholars who are interested in conducting independent research under the mentorship of senior researchers at the Educational Testing Service (ETS).

Eligibility   This program is open to scholars from diverse backgrounds (especially members of traditionally underrepresented groups such as African Americans, Hispanic/Latino Americans, and American Indians) who have earned a doctorate within the past 10 years and are U.S. citizens or permanent residents. Applicants must be prepared to conduct independent research at ETS under the mentorship of a senior researcher. They should have a commitment to education and an independent body of scholarship that signals the promise of continuing contributions to educational measurement. Projects should relate to issues involved in measurement theory, validity, natural language processing and computational linguistics, cognitive psychology, learning theory, linguistics, speech recognition and processing, teaching and classroom research, or statistics. Studies focused on issues concerning the education of minority students are especially encouraged. Selection is based on the scholar's record of accomplishment, proposed topic of research, commitment to education, and promise of continuing contributions to educational measurement.

Financial data   The stipend is set in relation to compensation at the home institution. Scholars and their families also receive reimbursement for relocation expenses.

Duration   Up to 2 years.

Number awarded   1 each year.

Deadline   January of each year.

[1373]
TRAIL OF TEARS ART SHOW

Cherokee Heritage Center
21192 South Keeler Drive
P.O. Box 515
Tahlequah, OK 74465
(918) 456-6007   Toll Free: (888) 999-6007
Fax: (918) 456-6165 E-mail: info@CherokeeHeritage.org
Web: www.CherokeeHeritage.org

Summary   To recognize and reward artists and craftsmen who submit work to a competition with a Native American flavor.

Eligibility   This competition is open to artists 17 years of age and older. All subject matters are eligible, but the show has always retained a distinctively Native American flavor. Artists may submit entries in 8 categories: painting, graphics, sculpture, Trail of Tears theme, miniatures, pottery, jewelry, and basketry. All work must have been completed since January of the competition year, although it may have been started before then. It may not have received a cash award in any other show and must be for sale at a reasonable market price. Each artist may submit only 2 works per category and only a total of 3. The Grand Award is presented to the work judged the most significant expression of art that exhibits the best overall quality, composition, technical achievement, and historical accuracy.

Financial data   Awards vary each year; recently the Grand Award of $1,500 and a total of $10,000 was presented.

Duration   The competition is held annually.

Additional information   This competition was first held in 1971.

Number awarded Varies each year; recently a total of 35 prizes was awarded.

Deadline April of each year.

[1374]
TRAINEESHIPS IN AIDS PREVENTION STUDIES (TAPS) PROGRAM POSTDOCTORAL FELLOWSHIPS

University of California at San Francisco
Attn: Center for AIDS Prevention Studies
50 Beale Street, Suite 1300
San Francisco, CA 94105
(415) 597-9260   Fax: (415) 597-9213
E-mail: Rochelle.Blanco@ucsf.edu
Web: www.caps.ucsf.edu

Summary To provide funding to scientists (especially Native Americans and other minorities) who are interested in conducting HIV prevention research.

Eligibility This program is open to U.S. citizens, nationals, and permanent residents who have a Ph.D., M.D., or equivalent degree. Applicants must be interested in a program of research training at CAPS in the following areas of special emphasis in AIDS research: epidemiological research, studies of AIDS risk behaviors, substance abuse and HIV, primary prevention interventions, research addressing minority populations, studies of HIV-positive individuals, policy and ethics, international research, and other public health and clinical aspects of AIDS. Recent postdoctorates who have just completed their training as well as those who are already faculty members in academic or clinical departments are eligible. Members of minority ethnic groups are strongly encouraged to apply.

Financial data Stipends depend on years of relevant postdoctoral experience, based on the NIH stipend scale for Institutional Research Training Grants (currently ranging from $37,740 for fellows with no relevant postdoctoral experience to $52,068 to those with 7 or more years of experience). Other benefits include a computer, travel to at least 1 annual professional meeting, health insurance, and other required support. The costs of the M.P.H. degree, if required, are covered.

Duration 2 or 3 years.

Additional information The TAPS program is designed to ensure that at the end of the training each fellow will have: 1) completed the M.P.H. degree or its equivalent; 2) taken advanced courses in research methods, statistics, and other topics relevant to a major field of interest; 3) participated in and led numerous seminars on research topics within CAPS, as well as in the formal teaching programs of the university; 4) designed several research protocols and completed at least 1 significant research project under the direction of a faculty mentor; and 5) made presentations at national or international meetings and submitted several papers for publication.

Number awarded Varies each year.

Deadline November of each year.

[1375]
TRAINING PROGRAM FOR SCIENTISTS CONDUCTING RESEARCH TO REDUCE HIV/STI HEALTH DISPARITIES

University of California at San Francisco
Attn: Center for AIDS Prevention Studies
50 Beale Street, Suite 1300
San Francisco, CA 94105
(415) 597-4976   Fax: (415) 597-9213
E-mail: jackie.ramos@ucsf.edu
Web: www.caps.ucsf.edu

Summary To provide funding to scientists (particularly Native Americans and other minorities) who are interested in obtaining additional training at the University of California at San Francisco (UCSF) Center for AIDS Prevention Studies (CAPS) for HIV prevention research in minority communities.

Eligibility This program is open to scientists in tenure-track positions or investigators in research institutes who have not yet obtained research funding from the U.S. National Institutes of Health (NIH) or equivalent. Applicants must be interested in a program of activity at CAPS to improve their programs of HIV-prevention research targeting vulnerable ethnic minority populations. They must be eligible to serve as principal investigators at their home institutions. Selection is based on commitment to HIV social and behavioral research, prior HIV prevention research with communities and community-based organizations targeting communities with high levels of health disparities (e.g., communities with a high proportion of disadvantaged or disabled persons, racial and ethnic minority communities), creativity and innovativeness for a pilot research project to serve as a preliminary study for a subsequent larger R01 grant proposal to NIH or other suitable funding agency, past experience conducting research and writing papers, quality of letters of recommendation from colleagues and mentors, and support from the home institution (e.g., time off for research, seed money). A goal of the program is to increase the number of minority group members among principal investigators funded by NIH and other agencies.

Financial data Participants receive 1) a monthly stipend for living expenses and round-trip airfare to San Francisco for each summer, and 2) a grant of $25,000 to conduct preliminary research before the second summer to strengthen their R01 application.

Duration 6 weeks during each of 3 consecutive summers.

Additional information This program is funded by the NIH National Institute of Child Health and Human Development (NICHHD) and National Institute on Drug Abuse (NIDA).

Number awarded Approximately 4 each year.

Deadline January of each year.

[1376]
UCSB LIBRARY FELLOWSHIP PROGRAM

University of California at Santa Barbara
Attn: Associate University Librarian, Human Resources
Davidson Library
Santa Barbara, CA 93106-9010
(805) 893-3841   Fax: (805) 893-7010
E-mail: bankhead@library.ucsb.edu
Web: www.library.ucsb.edu/hr/fellowship.html

Summary To provide an opportunity for recent library school graduates, especially Native Americans and members of other underrepresented groups, to serve in the library system at the University of California at Santa Barbara (UCSB).

Eligibility   This program is open to recent graduates of library schools accredited by the American Library Association. Applicants must be interested in a postgraduate appointment at UCSB. They must have a knowledge of and interest in academic librarianship and a strong desire for professional growth. Members of underrepresented groups are encouraged to apply.

Financial data   Fellows are regular (but temporary) employees of the university and receive the same salary and benefits as other librarians at the assistant librarian level ($46,164 to $48,029 per year).

Duration   2 years.

Additional information   The program began in 1985. Fellows spend time in at least 2 different departments in the library, serve on library committees, attend professional meetings, receive travel support for 2 major conferences, and participate in the Librarians' Association of the University of California.

Number awarded   1 each year.

Deadline   January of each year.

[1377]
UDALL FOUNDATION NATIVE AMERICAN CONGRESSIONAL INTERNSHIPS

Morris K. Udall and Stewart L. Udall Foundation
Attn: Program Manager, Internship Program
130 South Scott Avenue
Tucson, AZ 85701-1922
(520) 901-8568   Fax: (520) 670-5530
E-mail: info@udall.gov
Web: www.udall.gov

Summary   To provide an opportunity for Native American upper-division students, graduate students, and recent graduates to work in a Congressional office during the summer.

Eligibility   This program is open to American Indians and Alaska Natives who are enrolled members of recognized tribes and have an interest in tribal government and policy. Applicants must have a GPA of 3.0 or higher as a junior, senior, graduate student, law student, or recent graduate of a tribal or 4-year college. They must be able to participate in an internship in Washington, D.C., where they will gain practical experience in the legislative process, Congressional matters, and governmental proceedings that specifically relate to Native American issues. Fields of study of previous interns have included American Indian studies, political science, law and pre-law, psychology, social work, history, business and public administration, anthropology, community and urban planning, architecture, communications, health sciences, public health, biology, engineering, sociology, environmental studies and natural resources, economics, and justice studies. Applicants must demonstrate strong research and writing skills; organizational abilities and time management skills; maturity, responsibility, and flexibility; interest in learning how the federal government "really works;" commitment to their tribal community; knowledge of Congressman Morris K. Udall's legacy with regard to Native Americans; and awareness of issues and challenges currently facing Indian Country.

Financial data   Interns receive round-trip airfare to Washington, D.C.; dormitory lodging at a local university; a daily allowance sufficient for meals, transportation, and incidentals; and an educational stipend of $1,200 to be paid at the conclusion of the internship.

Duration   10 weeks during the summer.

Additional information   These internships were first offered in 1996.

Number awarded   12 each year.

Deadline   January of each year.

[1378]
UNIVERSITY OF CALIFORNIA PRESIDENT'S POSTDOCTORAL FELLOWSHIP PROGRAM FOR ACADEMIC DIVERSITY

University of California at Berkeley
Attn: Office of Equity and Inclusion
102 California Hall
Berkeley, CA 94720-1508
(510) 643-6566   E-mail: kadkinson@berkeley.edu
Web: www.ucop.edu/acadadv/ppfp

Summary   To provide an opportunity to conduct research at campuses of the University of California to Native Americans and other recent postdoctorates who are committed to careers in university teaching and research and who will contribute to diversity.

Eligibility   This program is open to U.S. citizens or permanent residents who have a Ph.D. from an accredited university. Applicants must be proposing to conduct research at a branch of the university under the mentorship of a faculty or laboratory sponsor. Preference is given to applicants 1) with the potential to bring to their academic careers the critical perspective that comes from their nontraditional educational background or their understanding of the experiences of groups historically underrepresented in higher education; 2) who have the communications skill and cross-cultural abilities to maximize effective collaboration with a diverse cross-section of the academic community; 3) who have demonstrated significant academic achievement by overcoming barriers such as economic, social, or educational disadvantage; and 4) who have the potential to contribute to higher education through their understanding of the barriers facing women, domestic minorities, students with disabilities, and other members of groups underrepresented in higher education careers, as evidenced by life experiences and educational background.

Financial data   The stipend ranges from $40,000 to $50,000, depending on the field and level of experience. The program also offers health benefits and up to $4,000 for supplemental and research-related expenses.

Duration   Appointments are for 1 academic year, with possible renewal for a second year.

Additional information   Research may be conducted at any of the University of California's 10 campuses (Berkeley, Davis, Irvine, Los Angeles, Merced, Riverside, San Diego, San Francisco, Santa Barbara, or Santa Cruz). The program provides mentoring and guidance in preparing for an academic career. This program was established in 1984 to encourage applications from minority and women scholars in fields where they were severely underrepresented; it is now open to all qualified candidates who are committed to university careers in research, teaching, and service that will enhance the diversity of the academic community at the university.

Number awarded 15 to 20 each year.

Deadline November of each year.

[1379]
VITO MARZULLO INTERNSHIP PROGRAM

Office of the Governor
Attn: Department of Central Management Services
503 William G. Stratton Building
Springfield, IL 62706
(217) 524-1381 Fax: (217) 558-4497
TDD: (217) 785-3979
Web: www.ilga.gov/commission/lru/internships.html

Summary To provide recent college graduates (especially Native Americans and other minorities) with work experience in the Illinois Governor's office.

Eligibility This program is open to residents of Illinois who have completed a bachelor's degree and are interested in working in the Illinois Governor's office or in various agencies under the Governor's jurisdiction. Applicants may have majored in any field, but they must be able to demonstrate a substantial commitment to excellence as evidenced by academic honors, leadership ability, extracurricular activities, and involvement in community or public service. Along with their application, they must submit 1) a 500-word personal statement on the qualities or attributes they will bring to the program, their career goals or plans, how their selection for this program would assist them in achieving those goals, and what they expect to gain from the program; and 2) a 1,000-word essay in which they identify and analyze a public issue that they feel has great impact on state government. A particular goal of the program is to achieve affirmative action through the nomination of qualified minorities, women, and persons with disabilities.

Financial data The stipend is $2,611 per month.

Duration 1 year, beginning in August.

Additional information Assignments are in Springfield and, to a limited extent, in Chicago or Washington, D.C.

Number awarded Varies each year.

Deadline February of each year.

[1380]
W.E.B. DUBOIS FELLOWSHIP PROGRAM

Department of Justice
National Institute of Justice
Attn: W.E.B. DuBois Fellowship Program
810 Seventh Street, N.W.
Washington, DC 20531
(202) 514-6205 E-mail: Marilyn.Moses@usdoj.gov
Web: www.nij.gov

Summary To provide funding to junior investigators, particularly Native Americans and other minorities, who are interested in conducting research on "crime, violence and the administration of justice in diverse cultural contexts."

Eligibility This program is open to investigators who have a Ph.D. or other doctoral-level degree (including a legal degree of J.D. or higher). Applicants should be early in their careers. They must be interested in conducting research that relates to specific areas that change annually but relate to criminal justice policy and practice in the United States. The sponsor strongly encourages applications from diverse racial and ethnic backgrounds. Selection is based on quality and

technical merit; impact of the proposed project; capabilities, demonstrated productivity, and experience of the applicant; budget; dissemination strategy; and relevance of the project for policy and practice.

Financial data Grants range up to $100,000. Funds may be used for salary, fringe benefits, reasonable costs of relocation, travel essential to the project, and office expenses not provided by the sponsor. Indirect costs are limited to 20%.

Duration 6 to 12 months; fellows are required to be in residence at the National Institute of Justice (NIJ) for the first 2 months and may elect to spend all or part of the remainder of the fellowship period either in residence at NIJ or at their home institution.

Number awarded 1 each year.

Deadline January of each year.

[1381]
WILLIAM TOWNSEND PORTER FELLOWSHIP FOR MINORITY INVESTIGATORS

Woods Hole Marine Biological Laboratory
Attn: Research Award Coordinator
7 MBL Street
Woods Hole, MA 02543-1015
(508) 289-7171 Fax: (508) 457-1924
E-mail: researchawards@mbl.edu
Web: www.mbl.edu/research/summer/awards_general.html

Summary To support Native American and other minority scientists who wish to conduct research during the summer at the Woods Hole Marine Biological Laboratory (MBL).

Eligibility This program is open to young scientists (senior graduate students and postdoctoral trainees) who are from an underrepresented minority group (African American, Hispanic American, or Native American), are U.S. citizens or permanent residents, and are interested in conducting research with senior investigators at MBL. Fields of study include, but are not limited to, cell biology, developmental biology, ecology, evolution, microbiology, neurobiology, physiology, and tissue engineering.

Financial data Participants receive a stipend and a travel allowance. Recently, grants averaged approximately $1,500.

Duration At least 6 weeks during the summer.

Additional information This fellowship was first awarded in 1921. Funding is provided by the Harvard Apparatus Foundation.

Number awarded 1 or more each year.

Deadline December of each year.

[1382]
YERBY POSTDOCTORAL FELLOWSHIP PROGRAM

Harvard School of Public Health
Attn: Office of Faculty Affairs
635 Huntington Avenue, Second Floor
Boston, MA 02115
(617) 432-1047 Fax: (617) 432-4711
E-mail: facultyaffairs@hsph.harvard.edu
Web: www.hsph.harvard.edu

Summary To provide an opportunity for Native American and other minority or disadvantaged postdoctorates to pursue a program of research training at Harvard School of Public Health.

Eligibility This program is open to 1) members of minority groups underrepresented in public health (American Indians or Alaska Natives, Blacks or African Americans, Hispanics or Latinos, and Native Hawaiians or other Pacific Islanders); 2) individuals from socioeconomically disadvantaged backgrounds; and 3) others whose background will contribute to academic diversity. Applicants must have a doctoral degree and be interested in preparing for a career in public health. They must submit 3 letters of recommendation; a curriculum vitae; a proposal for research to be undertaken during the fellowship; a statement of professional objectives in academic public health, including how those objectives would be advanced by research opportunities at HSPH; and a sample publication.

Financial data Fellows receive a competitive salary.

Duration 1 year; may be renewed 1 additional year.

Additional information Fellows are associated with a faculty mentor who assists in the transition to an academic career. With the help of the faculty mentor, fellows develop their research agendas, gain experience in publishing papers in peer-reviewed journals and in obtaining grant support, participate in a variety of professional development workshops, and increase their teaching expertise.

Number awarded Up to 5 each year.

Deadline October of each year.

[1383]
YOUTH PUBLIC ART PROJECT PROGRAM OF THE NATIONAL MUSEUM OF THE AMERICAN INDIAN

National Museum of the American Indian
Attn: Artist Leadership Program
Cultural Resources Center
4220 Silver Hill Road
Suitland, MD 20746-2863
(301) 238-1544   Fax: (301) 238-3200
E-mail: ALP@si.edu
Web: www.nmai.si.edu/icap/leadership.html

Summary To provide Native American professional artists with an opportunity to organize and conduct a collaborative art project focused on youth within their local community.

Eligibility This program is open to Native artists from the western Hemisphere and Hawaii who are recognized by their community and can demonstrate significant artistic accomplishments in any media (e.g., visual arts, media arts, performance arts, literature). Students enrolled in a degree program are ineligible. Applicants must be interested in creating a public art project within their home community in collaboration with a local youth organization. The project must result in a finished product, such as a sculpture, mural, theatrical work, musical performance, or video. Along with their application, they must submit a 500-word research proposal, 500-word project proposal, digital portfolio of 10 images or 5 minutes, 2 letters of support, a resume, and a 75-word statement describing their purpose, goal, and intended results.

Financial data The grant is $7,000 to cover project costs, supplies, and materials.

Duration Participants first spend 10 days in Washington, D.C. consulting with staff of the National Museum of the American Indian (NMAI), after which they return to their community and complete a project within 1 year.

Additional information This is a 2-part program. In the first part, participants visit Washington, D.C. for 10 days to conduct research in collections of the NMAI and other local museums, participate in interviews with Collections and Education staff, conduct lunch-time presentations for NMAI staff and the museum public, and visit area galleries. Following the completion of that visit, participants return to their community to share the knowledge learned from the experience and research visit and conduct their project. They must provide at least 10 art/production lessons to at least 5 community youth during the project schedule.

Number awarded 2 each year.

Deadline April of each year.

[1384]
ZENITH FELLOWS AWARD PROGRAM

Alzheimer's Association
Attn: Medical and Scientific Affairs
225 North Michigan Avenue, 17th Floor
Chicago, IL 60601-7633
(312) 335-5747   Toll Free: (800) 272-3900
Fax: (866) 699-1246   TDD: (312) 335-5886
E-mail: grantsapp@alz.org
Web: www.alz.org

Summary To provide funding to established investigators (particularly Native Americans and other minorities) who are interested in conducting advanced research on Alzheimer's Disease.

Eligibility Eligible are scientists who have already contributed significantly to the field of Alzheimer's Disease research and are likely to continue to make significant contributions for many years to come. The proposed research must be "on the cutting edge" of basic, biomedical research and may not fit current conventional scientific wisdom or may challenge the prevailing orthodoxy. It should address fundamental problems related to early detection, etiology, pathogenesis, treatment, and/or prevention of Alzheimer's Disease. Scientists from underrepresented groups are especially encouraged to apply.

Financial data Grants up to $250,000 per year, including direct expenses and up to 10% for overhead costs, are available. The total award for the life of the grant may not exceed $450,000.

Duration 2 or 3 years.

Additional information This program was established in 1991.

Number awarded Up to 4 each year.

Deadline Letters of intent must be submitted by the end of December of each year. Final applications are due in February.

Indexes

Program Title Index

If you know the name of a particular funding program open to Native Americans and want to find out where it is covered in the directory, use the Program Title Index. Here, program titles are arranged alphabetically, word by word. To assist you in your search, every program is listed by all its known names or abbreviations. In addition, we've used an alphabetical code (within parentheses) to help you determine if a specific program is aimed at you: U = Undergraduates; G = Graduate Students; P = Professionals/Postdoctorates. Here's how the code works: if a program is followed by (U) 241, the program is described in the Undergraduates section, in entry 241. If the same program title is followed by another entry number—for example, (P) 1201—the program is also described in the Professionals/Postdoctorates section, in entry 1201. Remember: the numbers cited here refer to program entry numbers, not to page numbers in the book.

A

AACAP-NIDA Career Development Award, (P) 1178

Accelerator Applications Division Scholarship. *See* ANS Accelerator Applications Division Scholarship, entry (U) 27

Accenture Graduate Fellowships, (G) 650

Accenture Undergraduate Scholarships. *See* AIGC Accenture Undergraduate Scholarships, entry (U) 3

ACLS Dissertation Completion Fellowships. *See* Andrew W. Mellon Foundation/ACLS Dissertation Completion Fellowships, entry (G) 675

ACLS Recent Doctoral Recipients Fellowships. *See* Andrew W. Mellon Foundation/ACLS Recent Doctoral Recipients Fellowships, entry (P) 1195

Acoustical Society of America Minority Fellowship, (G) 651

Adler Pollock & Sheehan Diversity Scholarship, (G) 652

Adolph van Pelt Scholarships, (U) 1

Adrienne M. and Charles Shelby Rooks Fellowship for Racial and Ethnic Theological Students, (G) 653

Advanced Degree Scholarship Fund of the Seminole Nation Judgment Fund, (G) 654

Advanced Postdoctoral Fellowships in Diabetes Research, (P) 1179

Agency for Healthcare Research and Quality Individual Awards for Postdoctoral Fellows. *See* AHRQ Individual Awards for Postdoctoral Fellows, entry (P) 1180

Aging Research Dissertation Awards to Increase Diversity, (G) 655

Agnes Larsen Darnell Scholarship, (U) 2

AHRQ Individual Awards for Postdoctoral Fellows, (P) 1180

AIGC Accenture Undergraduate Scholarships, (U) 3

AIR Fellows Program, (P) 1181

Air Force Office of Scientific Research Broad Agency Announcement, (P) 1182

Air Force Summer Faculty Fellowship Program, (P) 1183

Air Products and Chemicals Scholarship for Diversity in Engineering, (U) 4

Al Qöyawayma Awards. *See* A.T. Anderson Memorial Scholarship Program, entries (U) 41, (G) 690

Alan Compton and Bob Stanley Minority and International Scholarship. *See* BCA/Alan Compton and Bob Stanley Minority and International Scholarship, entry (U) 50

Alaska Library Association Graduate Library Studies Scholarship, (G) 656

Alaska Native Tribal Health Consortium Scholarships. *See* ANTHC Scholarships, entries (U) 28, (G) 676

Alaska Native Tribal Health Consortium Summer Internships. *See* ANTHC Summer Internships, entries (U) 29, (G) 677, (P) 1198

Aleut Foundation Graduate Scholarships, (G) 657

Aleut Foundation Part-Time Scholarships, (U) 5, (G) 658

Aleut Foundation Scholarship Program, (U) 6

Aleut Foundation Vocational Scholarships, (U) 7

Alfred J. Duran Sr. Trust Scholarship. *See* Northern Arapaho Tribe Alfred J. Duran Sr. Trust Scholarship, entries (U) 439, (G) 1013

Alfred P. Sloan Foundation Research Fellowships, (P) 1184

Alice Tonemah Memorial Scholarships. *See* John C. Rouillard and Alice Tonemah Memorial Scholarships, entries (U) 293, (G) 891

Allen Fellowships. *See* Frances C. Allen Fellowships, entry (G) 822

Allogan Slagle Memorial Scholarship, (U) 8

Allogan Slagle Scholarship. *See* California Indian Law Association Allogan Slagle Scholarship, entry (G) 713

Alma Exley Scholarship, (U) 9

Alyeska Match Scholarships, (U) 10

Alzheimer's Association Investigator-Initiated Research Grants, (P) 1185

Alzheimer's Association New Investigator Research Grants, (P) 1186

AMA Foundation Minority Scholars Awards, (G) 659

American Academy of Child and Adolescent Psychiatry-National Institute on Drug Abuse Career Development Award. *See* AACAP-NIDA Career Development Award, entry (P) 1178

American Advertising Federation Fourth District Mosaic Scholarship, (U) 11, (G) 660

Ann Malo Scholarship. *See* Makia and Ann Malo Scholarship, entry (G) 938

Anne Ray Fellowship, (P) 1196

ANS Accelerator Applications Division Scholarship, (U) 27

Antarctic Research Program, (P) 1197

ANTHC Scholarships, (U) 28, (G) 676

ANTHC Summer Internships, (U) 29, (G) 677, (P) 1198

Anzaldúa Book Prize. *See* Gloria E. Anzaldúa Book Prize, entry (P) 1269

APA Minority Medical Student Summer Mentoring Program, (G) 678

APA Planning Fellowships, (G) 679

APA/SAMHSA Minority Fellowship Program, (P) 1199

APS Scholarships for Minority Undergraduate Physics Majors, (U) 30

Aqqaluk Trust Scholarships, (U) 31

Arapaho Educational Trust Scholarship, (U) 32, (G) 680

Arapaho Farm Trust Graduate Scholarship. *See* Nickerson West Shakespeare/Arapaho Farm Trust Graduate Scholarship, entry (G) 1006

Arapaho Farm Trust Undergraduate Scholarship. *See* Nickerson West Shakespeare/Arapaho Farm Trust Undergraduate Scholarship, entry (U) 427

Arapaho Ranch Educational Trust Scholarship, (U) 33, (G) 681

Arctic Education Foundation Scholarships, (U) 34, (G) 682

Arctic Research Opportunities, (P) 1200

Arent Fox Diversity Scholarships, (G) 683

Arkansas Conference Ethnic Local Church Concerns Scholarships, (U) 35, (G) 684

Arkansas Minority Masters Fellows Program, (G) 685

Arkansas Minority Teachers Scholarships, (U) 36

Army Minority College Relations Program Internships, (U) 37, (G) 686

Army Research Laboratory Broad Agency Announcement, (P) 1201

Arnstein Minority Student Scholarship. *See* Sherry R. Arnstein Minority Student Scholarship, entry (G) 1096

Arnstein New Student Minority Student Scholarship. *See* Sherry R. Arnstein New Student Minority Student Scholarship, entry (G) 1097

Arthur E. Jackson Foundation Scholarship. *See* Helen K. and Arthur E. Jackson Foundation Scholarship, entry (U) 239

Artists' Choice Award. *See* Indian Market Awards, entries (U) 269, (P) 1279

Artist's Community Workshop Program of the National Museum of the American Indian, (P) 1202

ASA Minority Fellowship Program, (G) 687

Asche Memorial Scholarship. *See* Elizabeth and Sherman Asche Memorial Scholarship, entries (U) 186, (G) 792

ASCO Medical Student Rotation, (G) 688

ASH-AMFDP Research Grants, (P) 1203

ASLA Council of Fellows Scholarships, (U) 38

Associated Food and Petroleum Dealers Minority Scholarships, (U) 39

Association for Women Geoscientists Minority Scholarship. *See* AWG Minority Scholarship, entry (U) 44

Association for Women in Science Internships, (U) 40

Association of National Advertisers Multicultural Excellence Scholarship. *See* ANA Multicultural Excellence Scholarship, entry (U) 25

Association of Research Libraries Career Enhancement Program, (G) 689

Astronomy and Astrophysics Postdoctoral Fellowships, (P) 1204

A.T. Anderson Memorial Scholarship Program, (U) 41, (G) 690

At-Large Tribal Council Award, (U) 42

Atmospheric and Geospace Sciences Postdoctoral Research Fellowships, (P) 1205

AT&T Laboratories Fellowship Program, (G) 691

Austin Family Scholarship Endowment for Tribal Colleges, (U) 43

Awards for Faculty at Tribal Colleges and Universities, (P) 1206

AWG Minority Scholarship, (U) 44

Axelrod Mentorship Award. *See* Julius Axelrod Mentorship Award, entry (P) 1290

B

Bad River Adult Vocational Training Program, (U) 45

Bad River Higher Education Grant Program, (U) 46, (G) 692

Baker Corporation Scholarship Program for Diversity in Engineering. *See* Michael Baker Corporation Scholarship Program for Diversity in Engineering, entry (U) 371

Baker & Daniels Diversity Scholarships, (G) 693

Baker Donelson Diversity Scholarships, (G) 694

Baker Hostetler Diversity Fellowship Program, (G) 695

Baker Scholarship. *See* Colbert "Bud" Baker Scholarship, entry (U) 123

Balfour Phi Delta Phi Minority Scholarship Program, (G) 696

Bank2 Banking Scholarship, (U) 47

Bank2 Ta-ossaa-asha' Scholarships, (U) 48

Banner Diversity Scholarship. *See* Donald W. Banner Diversity Scholarship, entry (G) 781

Banner Scholarship for Law Students. *See* Mark T. Banner Scholarship for Law Students, entry (G) 940

Baptist Communicators Association/Alan Compton and Bob Stanley Minority and International Scholarship. *See* BCA/Alan Compton and Bob Stanley Minority and International Scholarship, entry (U) 50

Barbara Dobkin Native Artist Fellowship for Women. *See* Eric and Barbara Dobkin Native Artist Fellowship for Women, entry (P) 1251

Barreda Memorial Fellowship. *See* Grace Wall Barreda Memorial Fellowship, entry (G) 841

Barrow Minority Doctoral Student Scholarship. *See* Lionel C. Barrow Minority Doctoral Student Scholarship, entry (G) 932

Barry and Deanna Snyder, Sr. Chairman's Scholarship, (U) 49

BCA/Alan Compton and Bob Stanley Minority and International Scholarship, (U) 50

Beamer Scholarship. *See* Edwin Mahiai Copp Beamer Scholarship, entry (U) 181

Bechtel Undergraduate Fellowship Award, (U) 51

Behavioral Sciences Postdoctoral Fellowships in Epilepsy, (P) 1207

Bendix Minorities in Engineering Award. *See* DuPont Minorities in Engineering Award, entry (P) 1239

Berdach Research Grants, (G) 697

Bering Straits Foundation Higher Education Scholarships, (U) 52, (G) 698

Bering Straits Foundation Vocational Training Scholarships, (U) 53

Bernard Bouschor Honorary Scholarships, (U) 54

Bernbach Diversity Scholarships. *See* Bill Bernbach Diversity Scholarships, entry (G) 699

Bevins Endowment Scholarship Fund. *See* Susie Qimmiqsak Bevins Endowment Scholarship Fund, entries (U) 571, (G) 1118

Beyond Margins Award, (P) 1208

Big Goose Memorial Scholarship. *See* The Rev. Francene Eagle Big Goose Memorial Scholarship, entry (G) 1127

Bill Bernbach Diversity Scholarships, (G) 699

Bill Fryrear Memorial Scholarships, (U) 55

Bill Thunder, Jr. Memorial Scholarship, (U) 56, (G) 700

Billy L. Cypress Scholarship, (U) 57

Biomedical Research Training Program for Underrepresented Groups, (U) 58, (G) 701

Bishop Thomas Hoyt, Jr. Fellowship, (G) 702

Blackfeet Adult Vocational Training Grants, (U) 59

Blackfeet Higher Education Grants, (U) 60

Blitman, P.E. Scholarship to Promote Diversity in Engineering. *See* Maureen L. and Howard N. Blitman, P.E. Scholarship to Promote Diversity in Engineering, entry (U) 363

Blossom Kalama Evans Memorial Scholarships, (U) 61, (G) 703

Blue Spruce Fellowship. *See* Dr. George Blue Spruce Fellowship, entry (G) 786

Bob Stanley Minority and International Scholarship. *See* BCA/ Alan Compton and Bob Stanley Minority and International Scholarship, entry (U) 50

Bois Forte Higher Education Program, (U) 62, (G) 704

Bolden Minority Scholarship. *See* Ethel Bolden Minority Scholarship, entry (G) 799

Bolin Dissertation and Post-MFA Fellowships. *See* Gaius Charles Bolin Dissertation and Post-MFA Fellowships, entries (G) 827, (P) 1265

Bonner Scholarship. *See* Jewell Hilton Bonner Scholarship, entry (U) 290

Bonneville Power Administration Regional Tribal Scholarships, (U) 63, (G) 705

Booker T. Washington Scholarships, (U) 64

Boone Memorial Scholarship. *See* Washington, D.C. Chapter Scholarship Program, entry (U) 615

Boston University Summer Undergraduate Research Fellowship Program, (U) 65

Bouchet Award. *See* Edward A. Bouchet Award, entry (P) 1246

Bouschor Honorary Scholarships. *See* Bernard Bouschor Honorary Scholarships, entry (U) 54

Bradley Scholarship. *See* Ed Bradley Scholarship, entry (U) 178

Brandt Scholarships. *See* Gladys Kamakakuokalani Ainoa Brandt Scholarships, entries (U) 223, (G) 836

Breakthrough to Nursing Scholarships, (U) 66, (G) 706

Bristol Bay Native Corporation Education Foundation Higher Education Scholarships, (U) 67

Broadcast Sales Associate Program, (G) 707

Brock Memorial Scholarship. *See* Cathy L. Brock Memorial Scholarship, entry (G) 720

Brocksbank Scholarship. *See* A.T. Anderson Memorial Scholarship Program, entries (U) 41, (G) 690

Broncheau Memorial Fund. *See* Nez Perce Higher Education Grants, entries (U) 426, (G) 1005

Bronson Fellowship. *See* Ruth Muskrat Bronson Fellowship, entry (G) 1073

Brookhaven National Laboratory Science and Engineering Programs for Women and Minorities, (U) 68

Brotman Student Research Fellowship Awards. *See* Stuart Brotman Student Research Fellowship Awards, entry (U) 564

Brown and Caldwell Minority Scholarship, (U) 69

Brown COREM Scholarships. *See* Richard and Helen Brown COREM Scholarships, entry (G) 1063

Brown Endowment Fund Scholarship. *See* Judson L. Brown Endowment Fund Scholarship, entry (U) 302

Brown Memorial Award. *See* Nell B. Brown Memorial Award, entry (G) 998

Brown Memorial Scholarship. *See* Wilson J. Brown Memorial Scholarship, entry (U) 631

Bud Baker Scholarship. *See* Colbert "Bud" Baker Scholarship, entry (U) 123

Bullivant Houser Bailey Law Student Diversity Fellowship Program, (G) 708

Bunche Award. *See* Ralph J. Bunche Award, entry (P) 1354

Bunche Summer Institute. *See* Ralph Bunche Summer Institute, entry (U) 502

Bureau of Indian Affairs Higher Education Grants for Hopi Tribal Members. *See* Higher Education Grants for Hopi Tribal Members, entries (U) 241, (G) 852, (P) 1275

Bureau of Indian Education Higher Education Grant Program, (U) 70

Bureau of Indian Education Loan for Service Program, (G) 709

Burkhardt Residential Fellowships for Recently Tenured Scholars. *See* Frederick Burkhardt Residential Fellowships for Recently Tenured Scholars, entry (P) 1263

Burlington Northern Santa Fe Foundation Scholarship, (U) 71

Butler Rubin Diversity Scholarship, (G) 710

Byrd Fellowship Program, (P) 1209

C

California Adolescent Nutrition and Fitness Program Culinary Arts Scholarships. *See* Culinary Arts Scholarships, entry (U) 152

California Adolescent Nutrition and Fitness Program Graduate Scholarships. *See* CANFit Program Graduate Scholarships, entry (G) 716

California Adolescent Nutrition and Fitness Program Undergraduate Scholarships. *See* CANFit Program Undergraduate Scholarships, entry (U) 75

California Bar Foundation Diversity Scholarships, (G) 711

California Dietetic Association American Indian/Alaska Native Scholarship, (U) 72

California Diversity Fellowships in Environmental Law, (G) 712

California Indian Law Association Allogan Slagle Scholarship, (G) 713

California Planning Foundation Outstanding Diversity Award, (U) 73, (G) 714

California School Library Association Leadership for Diversity Scholarship. *See* CLSA Leadership for Diversity Scholarship, entries (U) 118, (G) 737

Calista Scholarship Fund, (U) 74, (G) 715

Campbell Graduate Fellows Program. *See* Jeffrey Campbell Graduate Fellows Program, entry (G) 888

Campbell, Jr. Fellowship in Engineering. *See* George Campbell, Jr. Fellowship in Engineering, entry (U) 219

CANFit Program Graduate Scholarships, (G) 716

CANFit Program Undergraduate Scholarships, (U) 75

Cap Lathrop Endowment Scholarship Fund, (U) 76, (G) 717

Capstone Corporation Scholarship Award. *See* Washington, D.C. Chapter Scholarship Program, entry (U) 615

Captain Willie Evans Scholarship. *See* Washington, D.C. Chapter Scholarship Program, entry (U) 615

Cardinal Memorial Scholarship. *See* Heather Cardinal Memorial Scholarship, entries (U) 238, (G) 851

Career Awards for Medical Scientists, (P) 1210

Career Awards in the Biomedical Sciences. *See* Career Awards for Medical Scientists, entry (P) 1210

Career Development Award to Promote Diversity in Neuroscience Research, (P) 1211

U–Undergraduates   **G–Graduate Students**   **P–Professionals/Postdoctorates**

U–Undergraduates   **G–Graduate Students**   **P–Professionals/Postdoctorates**

Innovation Award. *See* Indian Market Awards, entries (U) 269, (P) 1279

Innovations in Clinical Research Awards, (P) 1281

INROADS National College Internships, (U) 273

Inspirational Educator Scholarship, (U) 274

Institute for International Public Policy Fellowships, (U) 275, (G) 874

Intel Scholarship, (U) 276, (G) 875

Intellectual Property Law Section Women and Minority Scholarship, (G) 876

Intermountain Section AWWA Diversity Scholarship, (U) 277, (G) 877

International and Area Studies Fellowships, (P) 1282

International Radio and Television Society Foundation Broadcast Sales Associate Program. *See* Broadcast Sales Associate Program, entry (G) 707

Interpublic Group Scholarship and Internship, (U) 278

Inter-Tribal Council of AT&T Employees Scholarship Program, (U) 279

Investigators in Pathogenesis of Infectious Disease, (P) 1283

Iola M. Henhawk Nursing Scholarship, (U) 280

Iowa Tribe Education Incentive Awards, (U) 281, (G) 878

Iowa Tribe Higher Education Program, (U) 282

Ira L. and Mary L. Harrison Memorial Scholarship, (U) 283, (G) 879

Irene C. Howard Memorial Scholarships, (U) 284

Isaac Broncheau Memorial Fund. *See* Nez Perce Higher Education Grants, entries (U) 426, (G) 1005

Isaac J. "Ike" Crumbly Minorities in Energy Grant, (G) 880

Iwalani Carpenter Sowa Scholarship, (G) 881

J

J. Paris Mosley Scholarship, (U) 285

Jackie Robinson Scholarships, (U) 286

Jackson Foundation Scholarship. *See* Helen K. and Arthur E. Jackson Foundation Scholarship, entry (U) 239

Jacobs Engineering Scholarship, (U) 287, (G) 882

James A. Rawley Prize, (P) 1284

James B. Morris Scholarship, (U) 288, (G) 883

James E. Webb Internships, (U) 289, (G) 884

James H. Dunn, Jr. Memorial Fellowship Program, (P) 1285

Janet Zisk Scholarship. *See* Stanley and Janet Zisk Scholarship, entry (U) 562

JDRF Scholar Awards, (P) 1286

Jean Seth Award for Basket Making. *See* Indian Market Awards, entries (U) 269, (P) 1279

Jean Seth Award for Painting. *See* Indian Market Awards, entries (U) 269, (P) 1279

Jeanette Elmer Graduate Fellowship, (G) 885

Jeanne Spurlock Minority Medical Student Clinical Fellowship in Child and Adolescent Psychiatry, (G) 886

Jeanne Spurlock Research Fellowship in Substance Abuse and Addiction for Minority Medical Students, (G) 887

Jeffrey Campbell Graduate Fellows Program, (G) 888

Jenks Scholarship. *See* Mary K. Moreland and Daniel T. Jenks Scholarship, entry (U) 361

Jewell Hilton Bonner Scholarship, (U) 290

Jimmy Wooten Memorial Scholarship. *See* NNALEA Academic Scholarship Program, entries (U) 434, (G) 1008

Jo Ann Ota Fujioka Scholarship. *See* Dr. Jo Ann Ota Fujioka Scholarship, entry (U) 174

Jo Morse Scholarship, (G) 889

Joe Cat<A3>3 Award for Beadmaking. *See* Indian Market Awards, entries (U) 269, (P) 1279

Joel Elkes Research Award, (P) 1287

John and Muriel Landis Scholarships, (U) 291, (G) 890

John Bennett Herrington Scholarship, (U) 292

John C. Rouillard and Alice Tonemah Memorial Scholarships, (U) 293, (G) 891

John C. Smith Scholarship, (U) 294

John D. Voelker Foundation Native American Scholarship, (G) 892

John Hope Franklin Dissertation Fellowship, (G) 893

John N. Colberg Endowment Scholarship Fund, (U) 295, (G) 894

John Rainer Graduate Fellowship, (G) 895

John Shurr Journalism Award, (U) 296, (G) 896

John Stanford Memorial WLMA Scholarship, (G) 897

John V. Krutilla Research Stipend, (P) 1288

Johnson Health Policy Fellowships. *See* Robert Wood Johnson Health Policy Fellowships, entry (P) 1359

Johnson & Johnson Campaign for Nursing's Future-American Association of Colleges of Nursing Minority Nurse Faculty Scholars Program, (G) 898

Johnson, Jr. Scholarship Program. *See* Lloyd M. Johnson, Jr. Scholarship Program, entry (G) 934

Johnson Memorial Trust Scholarship. *See* Frances Johnson Memorial Trust Scholarship, entries (U) 211, (G) 823

Johnson Minority Fellowship in Educational Measurement. *See* Sylvia Taylor Johnson Minority Fellowship in Educational Measurement, entry (P) 1372

Johnson West Michigan Diversity Law School Scholarship. *See* Miller Johnson West Michigan Diversity Law School Scholarship, entry (G) 956

Joseph A. Sowa Scholarship, (U) 297

Joseph K. Lumsden Memorial Scholarship, (U) 298, (G) 899

Joseph Nawahi Scholarship, (G) 900

Josephine Forman Scholarship, (G) 901

Josephine Nipper Memorial Scholarship, (U) 299

Josephine P. White Eagle Graduate Fellowship, (G) 902

JP Morgan Chase Launching Leaders Undergraduate Scholarship, (U) 300

JTBF Judicial Externship Program, (G) 903

Judd, Jr. Memorial Scholarship. *See* Clem Judd, Jr. Memorial Scholarship, entry (U) 117

Judicial Externship Program. *See* JTBF Judicial Externship Program, entry (G) 903

Judicial Intern Opportunity Program, (G) 904

Judith L. Weidman Racial Ethnic Minority Fellowship, (P) 1289

Judith McManus Price Scholarships, (U) 301, (G) 905

Judson L. Brown Endowment Fund Scholarship, (U) 302

Julius Axelrod Mentorship Award, (P) 1290

June Curran Porcaro Scholarship, (U) 303

June M. Seneca Scholarship, (G) 906

Just Endowed Research Fellowship Fund. *See* E.E. Just Endowed Research Fellowship Fund, entry (P) 1247

Just the Beginning Foundation Judicial Externship Program. *See* JTBF Judicial Externship Program, entry (G) 903

Justine E. Granner Memorial Scholarship, (U) 304

Juvenile Diabetes Research Foundation Innovative Grants, (P) 1291

Juvenile Diabetes Research Foundation Priority Research Grants, (P) 1292

Juvenile Diabetes Research Foundation Scholar Awards. *See* JDRF Scholar Awards, entry (P) 1286

U–Undergraduates G–Graduate Students P–Professionals/Postdoctorates

LeFlore/Grant Foreman Scholarship. *See* Louie LeFlore/Grant Foreman Scholarship, entry (U) 352

Leland Energy Fellowships. *See* Mickey Leland Energy Fellowships, entries (U) 373, (G) 952, (P) 1304

Leonard M. Perryman Communications Scholarship for Ethnic Minority Students, (U) 340

Leonard Memorial Scholarship. *See* NNALEA Academic Scholarship Program, entries (U) 434, (G) 1008

Library and Information Technology Association/LSSI Minority Scholarship. *See* Spectrum Scholarship Program, entry (G) 1110

Library and Information Technology Association/OCLC Minority Scholarship. *See* Spectrum Scholarship Program, entry (G) 1110

Library Systems & Services Inc. Minority Scholarship. *See* Spectrum Scholarship Program, entry (G) 1110

Lifetime Achievement Award for Literature, (P) 1295

Life-Time Scholarships, (U) 341, (G) 928

Lighthorse Scholarship, (U) 342

Liko A'e Scholarships, (U) 343, (G) 929

Lille Hope McGarvey Scholarship Award, (U) 344, (G) 930

Lillian Fowler Memorial Scholarship, (U) 345, (G) 931

LIN Media Minority Scholarship and Training Program, (U) 346

Lincoln Cultural Diversity Scholarship, (U) 347

Lionel C. Barrow Minority Doctoral Student Scholarship, (G) 932

Little River Band of Ottawa Indians Higher Education Scholarship, (U) 348, (G) 933

Little River Band of Ottawa Indians Vocational Education Assistance Program, (U) 349

Lloyd M. Johnson, Jr. Scholarship Program, (G) 934

Long Range Annual Funding Opportunity Announcement for Navy and Marine Corps Science, Technology, Engineering & Mathematics (STEM) Programs, (P) 1296

Long Range Broad Agency Announcement for Navy and Marine Corps Science and Technology, (P) 1297

Lori Piestewa Vocational/Technical or 4-Year Scholarship, (U) 350

Lou Moller Scholarship for Achievement, (U) 351

Louie LeFlore/Grant Foreman Scholarship, (U) 352

Louis B. Russell, Jr. Memorial Scholarship, (U) 353

LSSI Minority Scholarship. *See* Spectrum Scholarship Program, entry (G) 1110

LTK Scholarship, (U) 354, (G) 935

Lumsden Memorial Scholarship. *See* Joseph K. Lumsden Memorial Scholarship, entries (U) 298, (G) 899

M

Mabel Smith Memorial Scholarship, (U) 355

Madison/Kalathas/Davis Scholarship Award. *See* Washington, D.C. Chapter Scholarship Program, entry (U) 615

Mae Lassley/Osage Scholarships, (U) 356, (G) 936

Magnel Larsen Drabek Scholarship, (U) 357, (G) 937

Maher Memorial Fund. *See* Doyon Foundation Competitive Scholarships, entries (U) 172, (G) 785

Makia and Ann Malo Scholarship, (G) 938

Malo Scholarship. *See* Makia and Ann Malo Scholarship, entry (G) 938

Manuel Law Foundation Scholarships. *See* Wiley W. Manuel Law Foundation Scholarships, entry (G) 1161

Many Voices Residencies, (P) 1298

Marathon Oil Corporation College Scholarship Program of the Hispanic Scholarship Fund, (U) 358, (G) 939

Mareyjoyce Green Scholarship. *See* Esther Ngan-ling Chow and Mareyjoyce Green Scholarship, entry (G) 798

Mark T. Banner Scholarship for Law Students, (G) 940

Marks Educational Fund. *See* Richard Marks Educational Fund, entry (U) 509

Marrs Scholarship Fund. *See* Carl H. Marrs Scholarship Fund, entries (U) 81, (G) 718

Martha Miller Tributary Scholarship, (U) 359, (G) 941

Marvin American Indian Scholarship. *See* Frances Crawford Marvin American Indian Scholarship, entry (U) 210

Mary Ball Carrera Scholarship, (G) 942

Mary Ella King Native Artist Fellowship. *See* Rollin and Mary Ella King Native Artist Fellowship, entry (P) 1360

Mary Hill Davis Ethnic/Minority Student Scholarship Program, (U) 360

Mary K. Moreland and Daniel T. Jenks Scholarship, (U) 361

Mary L. Harrison Memorial Scholarship. *See* Ira L. and Mary L. Harrison Memorial Scholarship, entries (U) 283, (G) 879

Marzullo Internship Program. *See* Vito Marzullo Internship Program, entry (P) 1379

Massachusetts Native American Tuition Waiver Program, (U) 362

Matfay Scholarship. *See* Larry Matfay Scholarship, entries (U) 334, (G) 923

Mathematical Sciences Postdoctoral Research Fellowships, (P) 1299

Mathematics, Engineering, Science, Business, Education, Computers Program. *See* MESBEC Program, entries (U) 370, (G) 948

Mathews, Jr. Memorial Scholarship for California Indians. *See* Rodney T. Mathews, Jr. Memorial Scholarship for California Indians, entries (U) 513, (G) 1067

Matson Memorial Endowment Fund Scholarships. *See* Lawrence Matson Memorial Endowment Fund Scholarships, entries (U) 337, (G) 926

Matson, Sr. Tributary Scholarship. *See* Vic Matson, Sr. Tributary Scholarship, entries (U) 606, (G) 1143

Matsuo Takabuki Commemorative Scholarships. *See* Goldman Sachs/Matsuo Takabuki Commemorative Scholarships, entry (G) 837

Maureen L. and Howard N. Blitman, P.E. Scholarship to Promote Diversity in Engineering, (U) 363

Maurice Goldhaber Distinguished Fellowships. *See* Gertrude and Maurice Goldhaber Distinguished Fellowships, entry (P) 1267

McAndrews Diversity in Patent Law Fellowship, (G) 943

McCormick Communications Scholarship for Underrepresented Students. *See* Larry W. McCormick Communications Scholarship for Underrepresented Students, entry (U) 335

McDermott Minority Scholarship, (G) 944

McDonald Education Endowment Scholarship Fund. *See* Kirby McDonald Education Endowment Scholarship Fund, entries (U) 320, (G) 915

McGarvey Scholarship Award. *See* Lille Hope McGarvey Scholarship Award, entries (U) 344, (G) 930

McGhee First Generation Indian Descent Scholarship Program. *See* Fred L. McGhee First Generation Indian Descent Scholarship Program, entries (U) 213, (G) 825

McGhee-Tullis Tuition Assistance Program, (U) 364, (G) 945

McJulien Minority Graduate Scholarship. *See* Patrick D. McJulien Minority Graduate Scholarship, entry (G) 1027

Medical Library Association/National Library of Medicine Spectrum Scholarships. *See* MLA/NLM Spectrum Scholarships, entry (G) 969

U–Undergraduates   **G–Graduate Students**   **P–Professionals/Postdoctorates**

North Dakota Indian Scholarship Program, (U) 437

Northern Arapaho Tribal Scholarships, (U) 438

Northern Arapaho Tribe Alfred J. Duran Sr. Trust Scholarship, (U) 439, (G) 1013

Northern Cheyenne Higher Education Scholarship Program, (U) 440, (G) 1014

Northern Cheyenne Job Training and Placement Grants, (U) 441

Northwest Indian Housing Association Scholarships, (U) 442

Northwest Journalists of Color Scholarship Awards, (U) 443

Nottawaseppi Huron Band of Potawatomi Higher Education Scholarships, (U) 444, (G) 1015

Novel Pharmacological Strategies to Prevent Alzheimer's Disease, (P) 1331

NSF Director's Award for Distinguished Teaching Scholars, (P) 1332

NSF Standard and Continuing Grants, (P) 1333

NSTI Faculty Fellowship Program. See NASA Science and Technology Institute (NSTI) Faculty Fellowship Program, entry (P) 1310

NSTI Summer Scholars Program. See NASA Science and Technology Institute (NSTI) Summer Scholars Program, entry (U) 404

O

Oakerhater Award. See Episcopal Council of Indian Ministries Scholarships, entry (G) 797

Oakerhater Merit Fellowship. See Episcopal Council of Indian Ministries Scholarships, entry (G) 797

OCLC Minority Scholarship. See Spectrum Scholarship Program, entry (G) 1110

Office of Hawaiian Affairs Scholarships, (U) 445, (G) 1016

Office of Naval Research Sabbatical Leave Program, (P) 1334

Office of Naval Research Summer Faculty Research Program, (P) 1335

Office of Naval Research Young Investigator Program, (P) 1336

Oglala Sioux Tribe Higher Education Grant Program, (U) 446

Ohio Newspapers Foundation Minority Scholarships, (U) 447

Olive Whitman Memorial Scholarship, (U) 448

Oliver Goldsmith, M.D. Scholarship, (G) 1017

Oliver W. Hill Scholarship, (G) 1018

Oneida Total Integrated Enterprises College Scholarship Program, (U) 449

Oneida Tribe Higher Education Grant Program, (U) 450, (G) 1019

Online Bibliographic Services/Technical Services Joint Research Grant, (P) 1337

Operation Jump Start III Scholarships, (U) 451, (G) 1020

Oregon Diversity Fellowships in Environmental Law, (G) 1021

Oregon Native American Chamber of Commerce Scholarships, (U) 452

Oregon State Bar Scholarships, (G) 1022

Osage Higher Education Grants, (U) 453, (G) 1023

Osage Scholarships. See Mae Lassley/Osage Scholarships, entries (U) 356, (G) 936

Osage Tribal Education Committee Program, (U) 454, (G) 1024

Ottawa Tribe Higher Education Grants, (U) 455, (G) 1025

Ouzinkie Tribal Council BIA Higher Education Scholarship Grant, (U) 456

P

Pacific Islanders in Communications Media Fund Grants, (P) 1338

Pacific Teacher Scholarship, (U) 457

Page Education Foundation Grants, (U) 458

Parsons Brinckerhoff Engineering Scholarship, (U) 459

Parsons Brinckerhoff Golden Apple Scholarship, (U) 460

Pascua Yaqui Higher Education Scholarship, (U) 461, (G) 1026

Patrick D. McJulien Minority Graduate Scholarship, (G) 1027

Paul and Emily Shagen Scholarship, (U) 462, (G) 1028

Paul D. White Scholarship, (G) 1029

Paul Francis Memorial Scholarship, (U) 463

Paul Hoch Distinguished Service Award, (P) 1339

Paul Tobenkin Memorial Award, (P) 1340

Paula de Merieux Rheumatology Fellowship Award, (P) 1341

Pawnee Nation Higher Education Program, (U) 464

PBS&J Achievement Scholarship, (U) 465, (G) 1030

Pearl Carter Scott Aviation Scholarship, (U) 466, (G) 1031

Pedro Bay Scholarship, (U) 467, (G) 1032

Peet Fellowship. See Gerald Peet Fellowship, entry (G) 835

Pennsylvania Dietetic Association Foundation Diversity Scholarship, (U) 468

Penobscot Nation Adult Vocational Training, (U) 469

Penobscot Nation Fellowship, (G) 1033

Penobscot Nation Higher Education Grant Program, (U) 470

Peoria Tribal Education Program, (U) 471

Peoria Tribe Master's Program Scholarship, (G) 1034

Perkins Coie Diversity Student Fellowships, (G) 1035

Perryman Communications Scholarship for Ethnic Minority Students. See Leonard M. Perryman Communications Scholarship for Ethnic Minority Students, entry (U) 340

Persina Scholarship. See National Press Club Scholarship for Journalism Diversity, entry (U) 406

Peter Doctor Memorial Indian Scholarship Grants, (U) 472, (G) 1036

Peter Kalifornsky Memorial Endowment Scholarship Fund, (U) 473, (G) 1037

PGA Tour Diversity Internship Program, (U) 474, (G) 1038

Phillip D. Reed Undergraduate Endowment Fellowship, (U) 475

Phillip R. Lee Scholarship. See Dr. Phillip R. Lee Scholarship, entry (U) 175

Phillips Fund Grants for Native American Research, (G) 1039, (P) 1342

Pi State Native American Grants-in-Aid, (U) 476, (G) 1040

Picard Scholarship Program. See Truman D. Picard Scholarship Program, entry (U) 587

Piestewa Vocational/Technical or 4-Year Scholarship. See Lori Piestewa Vocational/Technical or 4-Year Scholarship, entry (U) 350

Pistilli Scholarships. See P.O. Pistilli Scholarships, entry (U) 477

P.O. Pistilli Scholarships, (U) 477

Poarch Band of Creek Indians Academic Achievement Bonus, (U) 478, (G) 1041

Pokagon Band Higher Education Scholarship, (U) 479, (G) 1042

Polingaysi Qöyawayma Award. See A.T. Anderson Memorial Scholarship Program, entries (U) 41, (G) 690

Ponca Nation Higher Education Grant Program, (U) 480

Ponca Tribe of Nebraska Educational Grants, (U) 481, (G) 1043

Pope Memorial Scholarships. See Ida M. Pope Memorial Scholarships, entries (U) 261, (G) 867

Porcaro Scholarship. See June Curran Porcaro Scholarship, entry (U) 303

Porter Fellowship for Minority Investigators. See William Townsend Porter Fellowship for Minority Investigators, entries (G) 1163, (P) 1381

Porter Physiology Development Awards, (G) 1044

U–Undergraduates   **G–Graduate Students**   **P–Professionals/Postdoctorates**

Ronald M. Davis Scholarship, (G) 1068

Rooks Fellowship for Racial and Ethnic Theological Students. *See* Adrienne M. and Charles Shelby Rooks Fellowship for Racial and Ethnic Theological Students, entry (G) 653

Rosebud Sioux Tribe Higher Education Grant Program, (U) 514

Rosemarie Maher Memorial Fund. *See* Doyon Foundation Competitive Scholarships, entries (U) 172, (G) 785

Rosemary Gaskin Scholarship, (U) 515, (G) 1069

Rouillard and Alice Tonemah Memorial Scholarships. *See* John C. Rouillard and Alice Tonemah Memorial Scholarships, entries (U) 293, (G) 891

Roy M. Huhndorf Endowment Scholarship Fund, (U) 516, (G) 1070

Royer Memorial Scholarship Fund. *See* Rae Royer Memorial Scholarship Fund, entries (U) 501, (G) 1056

Ruden McClosky Diversity Scholarship Program, (G) 1071

Russ Denomie Criminal Justice/Social Welfare Scholarship, (U) 517

Russell, Jr. Memorial Scholarship. *See* Louis B. Russell, Jr. Memorial Scholarship, entry (U) 353

Ruth Goode Nursing Scholarship, (U) 518

Ruth L. Kirschstein National Research Service Awards for Individual Predoctoral Fellowships to Promote Diversity in Health-Related Research, (G) 1072

Ruth L. Kirschstein National Research Service Awards for Individual Senior Fellows, (P) 1362

Ruth Muskrat Bronson Fellowship, (G) 1073

Ryskamp Research Fellowships. *See* Charles A. Ryskamp Research Fellowships, entry (P) 1218

S

Sac and Fox Nation Higher Education Grants, (U) 519, (G) 1074

Sac and Fox Nation Vocational Technical School Incentive, (U) 520

Saginaw Chippewa Indian Tribe Scholarship Program, (U) 521, (G) 1075

Sahli–Kathy Woodall Minority Student Scholarship. *See* Don Sahli–Kathy Woodall Minority Student Scholarship, entry (U) 169

St. Croix Chippewa Indians Higher Education Grants Program, (U) 556, (G) 1112

St. Croix Chippewa Indians Vocational Grants Program, (U) 557

Salamatof Native Association, Inc. Scholarship Program, (U) 522, (G) 1076

Sally D. Funderburg Research Award in Gastric Cancer. *See* R. Robert & Sally D. Funderburg Research Award in Gastric Cancer, entry (P) 1353

SAMHSA Minority Fellowship Program. *See* APA/SAMHSA Minority Fellowship Program, entry (P) 1199

San Carlos Apache Tribe Higher Education Grants, (U) 523, (G) 1077

Sandia Master's Fellowship Program, (G) 1078

Sandra R. Spaulding Memorial Scholarships, (U) 524

Sankey Minority Scholarship in Meteorology. *See* David Sankey Minority Scholarship in Meteorology, entries (U) 156, (G) 761

SAR Indigenous Writer-in-Residence Fellowship, (P) 1363

Sara Whaley Book Prize, (P) 1364

Sault Higher Education Grant Program, (U) 525

Sault Tribe Higher Education Self Sufficiency Fund, (U) 526

Sault Tribe Higher Education Vocational Training Program, (U) 527

Sault Tribe Special Needs Scholarships, (U) 528, (G) 1079

SBE Doctoral Dissertation Research Improvement Grants, (G) 1080

SBE Minority Postdoctoral Research Fellowships and Follow-up Research Starter Grants, (P) 1365

Scholarship for Diversity in Teaching, (U) 529

Scholarships for Minority Accounting Students, (U) 530, (G) 1081

Scholarships for Social Justice, (U) 531

School for Advanced Research Indigenous Writer-in-Residence Fellowship. *See* SAR Indigenous Writer-in-Residence Fellowship, entry (P) 1363

Schubert M.D. Minority Nursing Scholarship Program. *See* William K. Schubert M.D. Minority Nursing Scholarship Program, entries (U) 628, (G) 1162

Schwabe, Williamson & Wyatt Summer Associate Diversity Scholarship, (G) 1082

Science Applications International Corporation Engineering Scholarship, (U) 532

Science Applications International Corporation Science and Mathematics Scholarship, (U) 533

Science Teacher Preparation Program, (U) 534, (G) 1083

Scott Aviation Scholarship. *See* Pearl Carter Scott Aviation Scholarship, entries (U) 466, (G) 1031

Scotts Company Scholars Program, (U) 535

Sealaska Corporation Internships, (U) 536

Sealaska Endowment Scholarships, (U) 537, (G) 1084

Sealaska Heritage Institute 7(i) Scholarships, (U) 538, (G) 1085

Section of Business Law Diversity Clerkship Program, (G) 1086

Seldovia Native Association Foundation Scholarships. *See* SNA Foundation Scholarships, entries (U) 548, (G) 1103

Semester Internships in Geoscience Public Policy, (U) 539, (G) 1087

Semiconductor Research Corporation Master's Scholarship Program, (G) 1088

Seneca Gaming Corporation Scholarship, (U) 540

Seneca Nation Higher Education Program, (U) 541, (G) 1089

Seneca Nation Professional Scholarships, (G) 1090

Seneca Scholarship. *See* June M. Seneca Scholarship, entry (G) 906

Seneca-Cayuga Education Fellowship Program, (U) 542, (G) 1091

SEO Career Program, (U) 543

SEO Corporate Law Program, (G) 1092

Sequoyah Graduate Fellowships, (G) 1093

Seth Award for Basket Making. *See* Indian Market Awards, entries (U) 269, (P) 1279

Seth Award for Painting. *See* Indian Market Awards, entries (U) 269, (P) 1279

Seven Stars Graduate Scholarship, (G) 1094

Shagen Scholarship. *See* Paul and Emily Shagen Scholarship, entries (U) 462, (G) 1028

Shea Memorial Scholarship. *See* Mellen Shea Memorial Scholarship, entry (U) 366

Shee Atiká Academic Scholarships, (U) 544, (G) 1095

Shell Incentive Fund Scholarships, (U) 545

Sherman Asche Memorial Scholarship. *See* Elizabeth and Sherman Asche Memorial Scholarship, entries (U) 186, (G) 792

Sherry R. Arnstein Minority Student Scholarship, (G) 1096

Sherry R. Arnstein New Student Minority Student Scholarship, (G) 1097

Sholl Memorial Scholarships. *See* Cecil Sholl Memorial Scholarships, entries (U) 86, (G) 723

Shrader Diversity Scholarships. *See* Ralph W. Shrader Diversity Scholarships, entry (G) 1058

Shurr Journalism Award. *See* John Shurr Journalism Award, entries (U) 296, (G) 896

U–Undergraduates   **G–Graduate Students**   **P–Professionals/Postdoctorates**

Sponsoring Organization Index

The Sponsoring Organization Index makes it easy to identify agencies that offer financial aid to Native Americans. In this index, the sponsoring organizations are listed alphabetically, word by word. In addition, we've used an alphabetical code (within parentheses) to help you identify the intended recipients of the funding offered by the organizations: U = Undergraduates; G = Graduate Students; P = Professionals/Postdoctorates. For example, if the name of a sponsoring organization is followed by (U) 241, a program sponsored by that organization is described in the Undergraduates section, in entry 241. If that sponsoring organization's name is followed by another entry number—for example, (G) 1199—the same or a different program sponsored by that organization is described in the Professionals/Postdoctorates section, in entry 1199. Remember: the numbers cited here refer to program entry numbers, not to page numbers in the book.

A

Abbott Laboratories, (P) 1249, 1350, 1356

Academic Library Association of Ohio, (G) 778

Accenture LLP, (U) 3, (G) 650

Accountancy Board of Ohio, (U) 180

Acoustical Society of America, (G) 651

Ad Club, (U) 566

Adler Pollock & Sheehan P.C., (G) 652

Aetna Foundation, Inc., (U) 209, (G) 821

Afognak Native Corporation, (U) 242, (G) 853

Ahtna, Incorporated, (U) 610

Air Products and Chemicals, Inc., (U) 4

Alabama Alliance for Science, Engineering, Mathematics, and Science Education, (U) 534, (G) 1083

Alaska Library Association, (G) 656, 889

Alaska Native Tribal Health Consortium, (U) 28-29, (G) 676-677, (P) 1198

Alaska Village Initiatives, Inc., (U) 257, (G) 862

The Aleut Corporation, (U) 2, 5-7, 26, 164, 214, 344, (G) 657-658, 673, 826, 930

Alfred P. Sloan Foundation, (P) 1184

Alpha Kappa Delta, (G) 687

Alyeska Pipeline Service Company, (U) 10, 89

Alzheimer's Association, (P) 1185-1186, 1252, 1302, 1321, 1329, 1331, 1384

American Academy in Rome, (P) 1263

American Academy of Child and Adolescent Psychiatry, (G) 886-887, (P) 1178

American Academy of Nursing, (P) 1223

American Advertising Federation. District 4, (U) 11, (G) 660

American Advertising Federation. Lincoln, (U) 347

American Antiquarian Society, (P) 1263

American Association for Justice, (G) 1064

American Association for the Advancement of Science, (U) 387, (P) 1227

American Association of Advertising Agencies, (U) 25, 398, 451, (G) 699, 972, 1020

American Association of Colleges of Nursing, (G) 898

American Association of Colleges of Osteopathic Medicine, (G) 1096-1097

American Association of Critical-Care Nurses, (U) 66, (G) 706

American Association of Law Libraries, (G) 832, (P) 1266, 1337

American Association of Petroleum Geologists, (U) 539, (G) 1087

American Association of Petroleum Geologists Foundation, (G) 880

American Association of University Women, (G) 819, (P) 1213

American Bar Association, (G) 1151

American Bar Association. Fund for Justice and Education, (G) 661

American Bar Association. Section of Business Law, (G) 1086

American Bar Association. Section of Environment, Energy, and Resources, (G) 712, 775, 817, 847, 1000, 1002, 1012, 1021

American Bar Association. Section of Intellectual Property Law, (G) 1099

American Bar Association. Section of Litigation, (G) 904

American Bar Foundation, (U) 569

American Board of Obstetrics and Gynecology, (P) 1187

American Chemical Society, (U) 488

American Chemical Society. Department of Diversity Programs, (U) 12

American College of Neuropsychopharmacology, (P) 1229, 1287, 1290, 1339

American College of Nurse-Midwives, (U) 620, (G) 1156

American College of Rheumatology, (P) 1341

American Council of Learned Societies, (G) 675, 770, 788, (P) 1188, 1195, 1218, 1225, 1236, 1241, 1243, 1263, 1282, 1323

American Dental Association, (G) 1136

American Dental Hygienists' Association, (U) 124

American Diabetes Association, (P) 1300

American Dietetic Association, (U) 13, (G) 662

American Educational Research Association, (G) 962, (P) 1181, 1189, 1258

American Epilepsy Society, (P) 1249-1250, 1350, 1356

American Gastroenterological Association, (U) 564, (P) 1190, 1259, 1353

American Geological Institute, (U) 383, 539, (G) 963, 1087

American Gynecological and Obstetrical Society, (P) 1187

American Health Information Management Association, (U) 14

American Hotel & Lodging Educational Foundation, (U) 260

American Indian Chamber of Commerce of Texas, (U) 17, 351

American Indian College Fund, (U) 15, 43, 80, 115, 120, 204-205, 217, 239, 395-396, 425, 431-432, 553-555, 581, 583-585, 599, 638-639, (G) 1094, 1109, 1144

American Indian Education Foundation, (U) 18, 299, 463, (G) 663

American Indian Graduate Center, (U) 3, 215, 622, (G) 650, 664, 709, 786, 793, 835, 841, 885, 895, 909, 1073, 1157

American Indian Heritage Foundation, (U) 390, (P) 1308

American Indian Law Review, (G) 665

American Indian Library Association, (G) 666

American Indian Science and Engineering Society, (U) 21, 41, 71, 227, 276, (G) 668, 690, 840, 875

American Indian Services, (U) 22

American Institute of Certified Public Accountants, (U) 530, (G) 809, 1081

American Institute of Chemical Engineers, (U) 381, 385-386

American Institutes for Research, (P) 1181

American Intellectual Property Law Association, (G) 1099

American Library Association. Library and Information Technology Association, (G) 1110

American Library Association. Office for Diversity, (G) 1110

American Medical Association, (G) 659, 1068

American Meteorological Society, (U) 23, 272, (G) 872

American Nuclear Society, (U) 27, 291, (G) 890

American Philosophical Society, (G) 893, 1039, (P) 1342

American Physical Society, (U) 30, (P) 1246

American Physical Therapy Association, (U) 384, (G) 961, (P) 1307

American Physiological Society, (G) 1044, (P) 1264

American Planning Association, (U) 301, (G) 679, 905

American Planning Association. California Chapter, (U) 73, (G) 714

American Political Science Association, (U) 502, (G) 669, (P) 1271, 1354

American Psychiatric Association, (G) 678, 964-965, (P) 1199, 1368

American Psychological Association. Division 54, (G) 1106, (P) 1367

American Psychological Association. Minority Fellowship Program, (G) 1046, (P) 1343

American Society for Cell Biology, (P) 1192

American Society for Engineering Education, (G) 977, (P) 1183, 1239, 1334-1335

American Society for Microbiology, (U) 374, (G) 1065

American Society of Clinical Oncology, (G) 688

American Society of Hematology, (P) 1203

American Society of Landscape Architecture, (U) 38

American Society of Safety Engineers, (U) 165, 604, (G) 777

American Sociological Association, (G) 687

American Speech-Language-Hearing Foundation, (G) 670

American University, (U) 617, (G) 1153

American Water Works Association. Intermountain Section, (U) 277, (G) 877

Amgen Foundation, (U) 561

Andrew W. Mellon Foundation, (G) 675, 773, (P) 1188, 1195, 1218, 1225, 1236, 1263

Andrew W. Mellow Foundation, (G) 674, (P) 1193-1194

Anne Ray Charitable Trust, (P) 1196

Arctic Slope Regional Corporation, (U) 34, (G) 682

Arent Fox LLP, (G) 683

Arkansas Department of Higher Education, (U) 36, (G) 685

Arkansas State University, (U) 506

Armed Forces Communications and Electronics Association, (G) 1058

Asian American Journalists Association. Seattle Chapter, (U) 443

Asian & Pacific Islander American Scholarship Fund, (U) 215

Associated Food and Petroleum Dealers, (U) 39

Association for Computing Machinery, (U) 477

Association for Education in Journalism and Mass Communication, (G) 932

Association for Educational Communications and Technology, (G) 1027

Association for Women Geoscientists, (U) 44

Association for Women in Science, (U) 40

Association of Black Sociologists, (G) 687

Association of Independent Colleges and Universities of Pennsylvania, (U) 4, 237, 371

Association of National Advertisers, (U) 25

Association of Research Libraries, (G) 689, 873

Association of Schools of Public Health, (G) 721

Association on American Indian Affairs, Inc., (U) 1, 8, 163, 186-187, (G) 792, 816, 1093

The Atlantic Philanthropies, (P) 1223, 1271

AT&T Laboratories, (G) 691

B

Bad River Band of Lake Superior Chippewa Indians, (U) 45-46, (G) 692

Baker & Daniels LLP, (G) 693

Baker, Donelson, Bearman, Caldwell & Berkowitz, P.C., (G) 694

Baker Hostetler LLP, (G) 695, 1029

Bank2, (U) 47-48

Banner & Witcoff, Ltd., (G) 781

Baptist Communicators Association, (U) 50

Baptist Convention of New Mexico, (U) 283, (G) 879

Baptist General Convention of Texas, (U) 360

Battelle Memorial Institute, (P) 1267

Bechtel Group Foundation, (U) 51

Bering Straits Native Corporation, (U) 52-53, (G) 698

Beveridge & Diamond PC, (G) 775

Bill and Melinda Gates Foundation, (U) 215

Black Coaches Association, (G) 802

Black Data Processing Associates, (U) 185

Blackfeet Nation, (U) 59-60

Bois Forte Band of Chippewa, (U) 62, (G) 704

Bonneville Power Administration, (U) 63, (G) 705

Booz Allen Hamilton, (G) 1058

Boston University. Undergraduate Research Opportunities Program, (U) 65

Brigham and Women's Hospital, (U) 209, (G) 821

Bristol Bay Native Corporation, (U) 67, 467, 623, (G) 1032

Brookhaven National Laboratory, (U) 68, (P) 1267

Brown and Caldwell, (U) 69

Brown Foundation for Educational Equity, Excellence and Research, (U) 578, (G) 1125

U–Undergraduates   **G–Graduate Students**   **P–Professionals/Postdoctorates**

Bullivant Houser Bailey PC, (G) 708
Burlington Northern Santa Fe Foundation, (U) 71
Burroughs Wellcome Fund, (P) 1210, 1283
Butler Rubin Saltarelli & Boyd LLP, (G) 710

C

California Adolescent Nutrition and Fitness Program, (U) 75, 152, (G) 716
California Dietetic Association, (U) 72, 83
California Indian Law Association, (G) 713
California Nurses Association, (U) 524
California Rural Indian Health Board, Inc., (U) 175
California School Library Association, (U) 118, (G) 737
California Wellness Foundation, (U) 175
Calista Corporation, (U) 74, (G) 715
Capture the Dream, Inc., (U) 220
Cargill, Inc., (U) 80
Catching the Dream, (U) 198, 370, 411, 577, (G) 812, 948, 988, 1124, (P) 1235, 1316, 1355
Center for Advanced Study in the Behavioral Sciences, (P) 1216, 1263
Center for Scholarship Administration, Inc., (U) 530, (G) 1081
Center for Student Opportunity, (U) 87
CH2M Hill Alaska, Inc., (U) 89
Cherokee Heritage Center, (P) 1373
Cherokee Nation, (U) 42, 90, 119, 296, 512, (G) 738, 896, 998, 1066
ChevronTexaco Corporation, (U) 383, (G) 963
Cheyenne and Arapaho Tribes of Oklahoma, (U) 91, (G) 725
Cheyenne River Sioux Tribe, (U) 92-94
Chickasaw Foundation, (U) 47-48, 55, 77, 95, 123, 135, 167, 197, 284, 292, 342, 345, 361, 392, 436, 466, 559, 580, 631, (G) 726, 789, 931, 968, 1031, (P) 1214
Chickasaw Nation, (U) 96-98, 341, (G) 727-728, 928, (P) 1219
Chippewa County Community Foundation, (U) 462, 515, (G) 1028, 1069
Choctaw Nation, (U) 101, 104-106, 202, 294, 338, 352, 590
Choice Hotels International, (U) 379
Christian Reformed Church, (U) 499, (G) 1054
Chugach Alaska Corporation, (U) 107-108, (G) 730
Cincinnati Children's Hospital Medical Center, (U) 628, (G) 1162
Citigroup Foundation, (U) 115
Citizen Potawatomi Nation, (U) 116, (G) 736
Cleveland Foundation, (U) 285
CNN, (U) 410, (G) 987
Coca-Cola Company, (U) 120
Cocopah Indian Tribe, (U) 121-122, (G) 739-740, (P) 1224
Colgate-Palmolive Company, (U) 124, (G) 1136
College and University Public Relations Association of Pennsylvania, (U) 134
College Scholarships Foundation, (U) 125, (G) 741
Collegium Budapest, (P) 1263
Colorado Education Association, (U) 127
Colorado Educational Services and Development Association, (U) 88
Colorado River Indian Tribes, (U) 129-131, (G) 742-743
Columbia University College of Physicians and Surgeons, (P) 1271
Columbia University. Graduate School of Journalism, (P) 1340
Comanche Nation, (U) 132-133, (G) 744
Community Foundation of Greater New Britain, (U) 9
Community Foundation of Sarasota County, (G) 1071

ComputerCraft Corporation, (U) 135
Confederated Salish and Kootenai Tribes, (U) 136, (G) 747
Confederated Tribes of the Colville Reservation, (U) 85, (G) 722
Confederated Tribes of the Umatilla Indian Reservation, (U) 137, (G) 748
Conference of Minority Transportation Officials, (U) 79, 82, 287, 354, 459-460, 465, 582, (G) 719, 882, 935, 1030, 1131
Connecticut Community College System, (G) 749
Connecticut Department of Higher Education, (U) 138, 621
ConocoPhillips, (U) 383, (G) 963
Consortium for Faculty Diversity at Liberal Arts Colleges, (G) 772, (P) 1347
Consortium for Graduate Study in Management, (G) 750
Constangy, Brooks & Smith LLC, (G) 751
Continental Society, Daughters of Indian Wars, (U) 139
Cook Inlet Region, Inc., (U) 76, 78, 81, 109-114, 184, 256-257, 295, 320, 337, 430, 473, 516, 522, 571, (G) 717-718, 731-735, 861-862, 894, 915, 926, 1037, 1070, 1076, 1118, (P) 1222, 1244, 1272
Cook Inlet Tribal Council, Inc., (U) 10, 140, 366, (G) 753
Copper River Native Association, (U) 141-142, (G) 754
Coquille Indian Tribe, (U) 102, 143-145, (G) 755-756
Cornell University. Weill Cornell Medical College, (U) 216
Corporation for Public Broadcasting, (P) 1317
Costco Wholesale, (U) 146
Courage Center, (U) 188
Crazy Horse Memorial Foundation, (U) 148
Crowell & Moring LLP, (G) 758

D

Dakota Indian Foundation, (U) 154
Dartmouth College, (G) 724
Daughters of the American Revolution. National Society, (U) 20, 210, (G) 667
Daughters of the American Revolution. New York State Organization, (U) 448
Davis Wright Tremaine LLP, (G) 762
DDB Worldwide, (G) 699
Delta Kappa Gamma Society International. Mu State Organization, (U) 158, (G) 763
Delta Kappa Gamma Society International. Pi State Organization, (U) 476, (G) 1040
Denver Museum of Nature & Science, (U) 412
Design Automation Conference, (U) 477
Dickstein Shapiro LLP, (G) 768
Dinsmore & Shohl LLP, (G) 769
Diversified Investment Advisors, (G) 776
DLA Piper US LLP, (G) 824
Doris Duke Charitable Foundation, (P) 1281
Dorsey & Whitney LLP, (G) 783
Doyon, Limited, (U) 171-172, (G) 784-785
DRI-The Voice of the Defense Bar, (G) 787
Duke University. Graduate School, (U) 176

E

Educational Advancement Alliance, Inc., (G) 980
Educational Testing Service, (U) 545, (G) 1115, (P) 1245, 1258, 1372
E.I. duPont de Nemours and Company, Inc., (P) 1239
Eight Northern Indian Pueblos Council, Inc., (U) 182
Eklutna, Inc., (U) 184

U–Undergraduates   **G–Graduate Students**   **P–Professionals/Postdoctorates**

K

Kaiser Permanente, (U) 305, (G) 907
Kaiser Permanente Southern California, (G) 1017
Kansas Board of Regents, (U) 307
Kappa Omicron Nu, (P) 1311, 1320
Katrin H. Lamon Endowment for Native American Art and Education, (G) 908, (P) 1293
Katten Muchin Rosenman LLP, (G) 910
KATU-TV, (U) 309
Kaw Nation, (U) 310-312, (G) 911
Kawerak, Inc., (U) 313
Ke Ali'i Pauahi Foundation, (U) 159, 181, 223, 234, 274, 297, 401, 413, 482, 509, 562, (G) 764, 833, 836-837, 848, 881, 900, 973, 992
Kegler, Brown, Hill & Ritter, (G) 912
Kenaitze Indian Tribe, (U) 316, (G) 913
Keweenaw Bay Indian Community-Lake Superior Band of Chippewa Indians, (U) 314
Kikiktagruk Inupiat Corporation, (U) 317
King & Spalding, (G) 914
Kiowa Tribe of Oklahoma, (U) 318-319
Kirkland & Ellis LLP, (G) 916
Kirkpatrick & Lockhart Preston Gates Ellis LLP, (G) 917
Knik Tribal Council, (U) 321
Koniag Incorporated, (U) 224, 322-326, 334, 357, (G) 918-919, 923, 937

L

Lac Courte Oreilles Band of Ojibwe, (U) 328-329, (G) 920
Lac du Flambeau Band of Lake Superior Chippewa Indians, (U) 330-331, (G) 921
Lagrant Foundation, (U) 332, (G) 922
Landmark Media Enterprises LLC, (U) 333
Landscape Architecture Foundation, (U) 179
Lane Powell Spears Lubersky LLP, (G) 834
Latham & Watkins LLP, (G) 924
Latino Media Association. Seattle Chapter, (U) 443
Lawrence Livermore National Laboratory, (G) 984
LeClairRyan, (G) 1018
Lee & Low Books, (P) 1294
Leech Lake Band of Ojibwe, (U) 339, (G) 927
Library Systems & Services Inc., (G) 1110
Lilly Endowment, Inc., (G) 1011, (P) 1262
LIN Television Corporation, (U) 346
Little River Band of Ottawa Indians, (U) 348-349, (G) 933
Lloyd G. Balfour Foundation, (G) 696
Los Alamos National Laboratory, (G) 984
Louisville Institute, (P) 1262
LTK Engineering Services, (U) 354, (G) 935
The Lullaby Guild, Inc., (U) 335

M

Marathon Corporation, (U) 383, (G) 963
Marathon Oil Corporation, (U) 358, (G) 939
Marriott International, Inc., (U) 382, (P) 1306
Massachusetts Mutual Life Insurance Company, (G) 839
Massachusetts Office of Student Financial Assistance, (U) 362
Mayday Fund, (P) 1223
Mayo Clinic, (U) 66, (G) 706
McAndrews, Held & Malloy, Ltd., (G) 943
McDermott Will & Emery, (G) 944

Medical College of Wisconsin, (U) 166
Medical Library Association, (G) 969-970
Menominee Indian Tribe of Wisconsin, (U) 367-368, (G) 946
Metropolitan Life Foundation, (G) 949
Miami Nation, (U) 400, 558, (G) 950
Michael Baker Corporation, (U) 371
Michigan Department of Civil Rights, (U) 372, (G) 951
Michigan Indian Elders Association, (U) 375
Mid-Atlantic Association for Employment in Education, (U) 529
Milbank, Tweed, Hadley & McCloy LLP, (G) 953
Mille Lacs Band of Ojibwe, (U) 376-377, (G) 954-955, (P) 1305
Miller Nash LLP, (G) 957
Minnesota American Indian Bar Association, (G) 958
Minnesota Department of Education, (U) 191, (G) 800
Minnesota Historical Society, (U) 19
Minnesota Humanities Center, (U) 19
Minnesota Office of Higher Education, (U) 378, (G) 959
Minority Access, Inc., (U) 162, 380, (G) 767, 960
Minority Corporate Counsel Association, (G) 934, 1099, 1168
Minority Educational Foundation of the United States of America, (U) 16
Missouri Department of Higher Education, (U) 391
Mohegan Sun, (U) 209, (G) 821
Montana Guaranteed Student Loan Program, (U) 394, (G) 971
Morgan Stanley, (U) 395-396
Morongo Band of Mission Indians, (U) 513, (G) 1067
Morris K. Udall and Stewart L. Udall Foundation, (U) 397, 595, (G) 1135, (P) 1377
Ms. JD, (G) 672
Muscogee (Creek) Nation of Oklahoma, (U) 149-151, (G) 757
Mutual of Omaha, (U) 399

N

NANA Regional Corporation, (U) 31
National Action Council for Minorities in Engineering, (U) 51, 219, 402, 475, 508, 629-630
National Association for Equal Opportunity in Higher Education, (U) 162, (G) 767
National Association of Black Journalists. Seattle Chapter, (U) 443
National Association of Bond Lawyers, (G) 976
National Association of School Psychologists, (G) 975
National Association of Social Workers, (G) 752
National Business Group on Health, (G) 1068
National Collegiate Athletic Association, (G) 996
National Congress of American Indians, (U) 422, (G) 997, (P) 1314
National Consortium for Graduate Degrees for Minorities in Engineering and Science (GEM), (G) 828-830
National Council for the Social Studies, (G) 808, (P) 1256
National Council of Churches, (G) 1011
National FFA Organization, (U) 64
National Football League Players Association, (U) 414
National Humanities Center, (P) 1263
National Indian Education Association, (U) 293, (G) 891
National Indian Gaming Association, (U) 555
National League of American Pen Women, (U) 240
National Medical Fellowships, Inc., (G) 864, 942, 949, 978-979
National Native American Law Enforcement Association, (U) 434, (G) 1008
National Native American Law Students Association, (G) 1009
National Naval Officers Association. Washington, D.C. Chapter, (U) 421, 532-533, 613, 615

U–Undergraduates　　　　**G–Graduate Students**　　　　**P–Professionals/Postdoctorates**

U–Undergraduates   **G–Graduate Students**   **P–Professionals/Postdoctorates**

U–Undergraduates   **G–Graduate Students**   **P–Professionals/Postdoctorates**

Residency Index

Some programs listed in this book are set aside for Native Americans who are residents of a particular state or region. Others are open to applicants wherever they may live. The Residency Index will help you pinpoint programs available in your area as well as programs that have no residency restrictions at all (these are listed under the term "United States"). To use this index, look up the geographic areas that apply to you (always check the listings under "United States"), jot down the entry numbers listed for the recipient group that represents you (Undergraduates, Graduate Students, or Professionals/Postdoctorates), and use those numbers to find the program descriptions in the directory. To help you in your search, we've provided some "see" and "see also" references in the index entries. Remember: the numbers cited here refer to program entry numbers, not to page numbers in the book.

Tenability Index

Some programs listed in this book can be used only in specific cities, counties, states, or regions. Others may be used anywhere in the United States. The Tenability Index will help you locate funding that is restricted to a specific area as well as funding that has no tenability restrictions (these are listed under the term "United States"). To use this index, look up the geographic areas where you'd like to go (always check the listings under "United States"), jot down the entry numbers listed for the recipient group that represents you (Undergraduates, Graduate Students, Professionals/Postdoctorates), and use those numbers to find the program descriptions in the directory. To help you in your search, we've provided some "see" and "see also" references in the index entries. Remember: the numbers cited here refer to program entry numbers, not to page numbers in the book.

A

Alabama: **Undergraduates,** 534; **Graduate Students,** 751, 1083. *See also* Southern states; United States; names of specific cities and counties

Alaska: **Undergraduates,** 112, 259, 536; **Graduate Students,** 734, 870; **Professionals/Postdoctorates,** 1222, 1231, 1244, 1272. *See also* United States; names of specific cities

Albany, Oregon: **Undergraduates,** 373; **Graduate Students,** 952; **Professionals/Postdoctorates,** 1304. *See also* Oregon

Albuquerque, New Mexico: **Undergraduates,** 283, 586; **Graduate Students,** 879, 984, 1078, 1132. *See also* New Mexico

Allentown, Pennsylvania: **Graduate Students,** 772; **Professionals/Postdoctorates,** 1347. *See also* Pennsylvania

American Samoa: **Professionals/Postdoctorates,** 1338. *See also* United States

Amherst, Massachusetts: **Graduate Students,** 815. *See also* Massachusetts

Anchorage, Alaska: **Undergraduates,** 29, 601; **Graduate Students,** 677, 989, 1139; **Professionals/Postdoctorates,** 1198. *See also* Alaska

Ann Arbor, Michigan: **Graduate Students,** 750, 780. *See also* Michigan

Anniston, Alabama: **Undergraduates,** 37; **Graduate Students,** 686. *See also* Alabama

Appleton, Wisconsin: **Graduate Students,** 772; **Professionals/Postdoctorates,** 1347. *See also* Wisconsin

Arizona: **Undergraduates,** 251, 599. *See also* United States; names of specific cities and counties

Arkansas: **Undergraduates,** 36; **Graduate Students,** 685; **Professionals/Postdoctorates,** 1231. *See also* Southern states; United States; names of specific cities and counties

Athens, Georgia: **Graduate Students,** 1170. *See also* Georgia

Atlanta, Georgia: **Undergraduates,** 79, 451; **Graduate Students,** 699, 750, 811, 914, 1020, 1128, 1170. *See also* Georgia

Austin, Texas: **Undergraduates,** 79, 451; **Graduate Students,** 699, 750, 780, 1020, 1145. *See also* Texas

B

Baltimore, Maryland: **Undergraduates,** 160; **Graduate Students,** 765, 772, 1170; **Professionals/Postdoctorates,** 1233, 1347. *See also* Maryland

Bellingham, Washington: **Undergraduates,** 584. *See also* Washington

Berkeley, California: **Graduate Students,** 750; **Professionals/Postdoctorates,** 1217, 1378. *See also* California

Bethesda, Maryland: **Undergraduates,** 58, 428; **Graduate Students,** 701; **Professionals/Postdoctorates,** 1334-1335. *See also* Maryland

Big Rapids, Michigan: **Undergraduates,** 487. *See also* Michigan

Bloomington, Indiana: **Graduate Students,** 693, 750. *See also* Indiana

Boise, Idaho: **Graduate Students,** 1114. *See also* Idaho

Boston, Massachusetts: **Undergraduates,** 65, 160, 209, 233, 567-568; **Graduate Students,** 765, 780, 821, 944, 1146; **Professionals/Postdoctorates,** 1233, 1382. *See also* Massachusetts

Boulder, Colorado: **Graduate Students,** 989. *See also* Colorado

Browning, Montana: **Undergraduates,** 584. *See also* Montana

Brunswick, Maine: **Graduate Students,** 772; **Professionals/Postdoctorates,** 1347. *See also* Maine

Bryn Mawr, Pennsylvania: **Graduate Students,** 772; **Professionals/Postdoctorates,** 1347. *See also* Pennsylvania

Buies Creek, North Carolina: **Undergraduates,** 487. *See also* North Carolina

Burbank, California: **Professionals/Postdoctorates,** 1326. *See also* California

Subject Index

There are hundreds of specific subject fields covered in this directory. Use the Subject Index to identify these subjects, as well as the recipient level supported (Undergraduates, Graduate Students, or Professionals/Postdoctorates) by the available funding programs. To help you pinpoint your search, we've included many "see" and "see also" references. Since a large number of programs are not restricted by subject, be sure to check the references listed under the "General programs" heading in the subject index (in addition to the specific terms that directly relate to your interest areas); hundreds of funding opportunities are listed there that can be used to support activities in any subject area (although the programs may be restricted in other ways). Remember: the numbers cited in this index refer to program entry numbers, not to page numbers in the book.

A

A.V. *See* Audiovisual materials and equipment

Academic librarianship. *See* Libraries and librarianship, academic

Accounting: **Undergraduates,** 37, 47-48, 63, 81, 162, 177, 180, 204, 289, 358, 395, 420, 427, 474, 495, 530, 538, 543, 576, 605, 622; **Graduate Students,** 686, 705, 718, 767, 809, 884, 939, 995, 1038, 1081, 1085, 1123, 1157. *See also* Finance; General programs

Acoustical engineering. *See* Engineering, acoustical

Acoustics: **Graduate Students,** 651. *See also* General programs; Physics

Acquired Immunodeficiency Syndrome. *See* AIDS

Acting. *See* Performing arts

Actuarial sciences: **Undergraduates,** 399, 495. *See also* General programs; Statistics

Addiction. *See* Alcohol use and abuse; Drug use and abuse

Administration. *See* Business administration; Education, administration; Management; Personnel administration; Public administration

Adolescents: **Graduate Students,** 886-887; **Professionals/ Postdoctorates,** 1178. *See also* Child development; General programs

Advertising: **Undergraduates,** 11, 25, 134, 278, 332, 347, 398, 451, 503, 566; **Graduate Students,** 660, 699, 922, 972, 1020, 1059. *See also* Communications; General programs; Marketing; Public relations

Aeronautical engineering. *See* Engineering, aeronautical

Aeronautics: **Undergraduates,** 292; **Graduate Students,** 974. *See also* Aviation; Engineering, aeronautical; General programs; Physical sciences

Aerospace engineering. *See* Engineering, aerospace

Aerospace sciences. *See* Space sciences

Affirmative action: **Undergraduates,** 271. *See also* Equal opportunity; General programs

African studies: **Professionals/Postdoctorates,** 1282. *See also* General programs; Humanities

Aged and aging: **Undergraduates,** 167; **Graduate Students,** 655; **Professionals/Postdoctorates,** 1271. *See also* General programs; Social sciences

Agribusiness: **Undergraduates,** 56, 427; **Graduate Students,** 700. *See also* Agriculture and agricultural sciences; Business administration; General programs

Agriculture and agricultural sciences: **Undergraduates,** 56, 64, 80, 160, 506, 576; **Graduate Students,** 700, 765, 1123; **Professionals/Postdoctorates,** 1233. *See also* Biological sciences; General programs

Agrimarketing and sales. *See* Agribusiness

Agronomy: **Undergraduates,** 37, 56; **Graduate Students,** 686, 700. *See also* Agriculture and agricultural sciences; General programs

AIDS: **Undergraduates,** 233; **Professionals/Postdoctorates,** 1374-1375. *See also* General programs; Immunology; Medical sciences

Albanian language. *See* Language, Albanian

Alcohol use and abuse: **Undergraduates,** 265; **Graduate Students,** 868, 1046; **Professionals/Postdoctorates,** 1343, 1368. *See also* Drug use and abuse; General programs; Health and health care

Alzheimer's Disease: **Professionals/Postdoctorates,** 1185-1186, 1252, 1302, 1321, 1329, 1331, 1384. *See also* Aged and aging; General programs; Medical sciences

American history. *See* History, American

American Indian affairs. *See* Native American affairs

American Indian language. *See* Language, Native American

American Indian studies. *See* Native American studies

American studies: **Graduate Students,** 675; **Professionals/ Postdoctorates,** 1188, 1195, 1218, 1225, 1263, 1323. *See also* General programs; Humanities

Animal science: **Undergraduates,** 33, 56, 576; **Graduate Students,** 651, 681, 700, 966, 1123. *See also* General programs; Sciences; names of specific animal sciences

Animation: **Professionals/Postdoctorates,** 1326. *See also* Filmmaking; General programs

W

Water resources: **Undergraduates,** 277, 539, 576; **Graduate Students,** 877, 1087, 1123. *See also* Environmental sciences; General programs; Natural resources

Weaving: **Undergraduates,** 269; **Professionals/ Postdoctorates,** 1237, 1279, 1371. *See also* Arts and crafts; General programs

Web design. *See* Internet design and development

Web journalism. *See* Journalism, online

Welfare. *See* Social services; Social welfare

Western European studies. *See* European studies

Wildlife management: **Undergraduates,** 162, 536, 538, 576; **Graduate Students,** 767, 1085, 1123. *See also* Environmental sciences; General programs

Women's studies and programs: **Undergraduates,** 576; **Graduate Students,** 1123; **Professionals/Postdoctorates,** 1269, 1364. *See also* General programs

Worker's compensation. *See* Personal injury law

World literature. *See* Literature

Y

Youth. *See* Adolescents; Child development

Yugoslavian language. *See* Language, Macedonian; Language, Serbo-Croatian; Language, Slovene

Z

Zoning, planning, and land use. *See* Real estate law

Zoology: **Undergraduates,** 162; **Graduate Students,** 767. *See also* Biological Sciences; General programs; names of specific zoological subfields

Calendar Index

Since most funding programs have specific deadline dates, some may have already closed by the time you begin to look for money. You can use the Calendar Index to identify which programs are still open. To do that, go to the recipient category (Undergraduates, Graduate Students, or Professionals/Postdoctorates) that interests you, think about when you'll be able to complete your application forms, go to the appropriate months, jot down the entry numbers listed there, and use those numbers to find the program descriptions in the directory. Keep in mind that the numbers cited here refer to program entry numbers, not to page numbers in the book.

Undergraduates:

January: 24, 27, 66, 124, 134, 160, 174, 177, 210, 215-216, 233, 236, 240, 269, 278, 289, 291, 305, 322, 373-374, 377, 379, 389, 403-405, 448, 477, 485, 492, 502, 547, 561, 567, 570, 595, 614, 619

February: 12-13, 19, 21, 23, 28-30, 34, 38, 58-59, 61, 64-65, 69, 72, 83, 126, 153, 155, 161, 166, 169, 173, 176, 179, 192, 209, 235, 261, 263-265, 272, 275, 290, 302, 306, 332, 335-336, 353, 363, 365, 368-369, 380, 387-388, 391, 406, 428, 433, 440-441, 445, 474, 525, 535, 537-538, 545, 568-569, 576, 586, 636

March: 2, 20, 39-40, 60, 63, 67, 73, 75, 78, 88, 97-98, 112, 114, 122, 127, 133, 148, 152, 159, 171, 181, 223, 232, 238, 257, 267, 271, 273-274, 285-286, 288, 297, 304, 323-325, 340, 346, 367, 383, 397, 401, 410, 413, 421, 423, 426, 442, 447, 457, 467-468, 482, 486, 488, 499, 506, 509, 513, 530, 532-533, 536, 562, 564, 578, 587, 589, 612-613, 615-616, 620, 623, 627, 646

April: 3-4, 14, 16, 18, 42, 51-52, 68, 71, 79, 82, 85-86, 99, 101-102, 118-119, 121, 136, 156, 182, 198, 202, 219, 237, 242, 244-246, 255, 260, 279, 287, 294, 296, 299, 301, 307-310, 314, 343, 351-352, 354, 356, 360, 362, 366, 370-371, 400, 402, 411, 415-420, 435, 443, 458-460, 463, 465, 475, 489, 500, 503, 507-508, 512, 539, 546, 558, 566, 573, 577, 579, 582, 622, 628-630, 632, 644, 649

May: 11, 15, 17, 22, 36-37, 43, 49, 54, 76, 80-81, 84, 87, 91, 109-111, 113, 115, 120, 149-151, 158, 168, 178, 184, 188, 190-191, 195-196, 199, 204-207, 212, 217, 221-222, 234, 239, 256, 295, 298, 303, 312, 315-316, 320, 337, 355, 359, 381, 390, 395-396, 414, 424-425, 430-432, 456, 472-473, 480, 493, 510, 516, 518, 522, 528, 540, 553-555, 560, 563, 571, 581, 583-585, 599, 601, 606, 617, 624, 638-639

June: 1, 5-8, 26, 32-33, 41, 44, 56-57, 70, 74, 90, 93, 100, 117, 129-131, 137, 139, 163-164, 170, 186-187, 193-194, 211, 214, 227, 241, 249-250, 252, 276, 280, 283, 328-329, 339, 341, 344, 375, 378, 382, 385-386, 408-409, 427, 438-439, 446, 449, 454, 462, 469-470, 484, 491, 496-497, 504-505, 511, 519-520, 523-524, 541, 548-551, 565, 574-575, 591-593, 609, 611, 625, 645

July: 45-46, 89, 94, 116, 147, 154, 185, 189, 200-201, 203, 208, 220, 247, 253-254, 270, 313, 327, 330-331, 350, 393, 437, 444, 453, 455, 461, 464, 471, 476, 494, 501, 514-515, 517, 556-557, 572, 596, 610, 618

August: 47-48, 55, 77, 95, 107, 123, 135, 167, 197, 224, 284, 292-293, 321, 326, 334, 342, 345, 357, 361, 392, 436, 466, 481, 559, 580, 588, 600, 631

September: 35, 105-106, 128, 138, 142, 258, 338, 412, 422, 450, 452, 490, 498, 542, 590, 621, 643

October: 9, 103, 277, 300, 347, 399, 526, 647

November: 10, 96, 104, 140, 157, 162, 165, 172, 358, 384, 434, 529, 531, 544, 597, 602, 604-605

December: 50, 125, 175, 225-226, 282, 333, 398, 495, 543

Any time: 31, 53, 62, 92, 108, 180, 213, 243, 317-318, 364, 376, 527, 552, 594, 598, 633, 640, 648

Deadline not specified: 25, 132, 141, 143-146, 183, 218, 228-231, 248, 251, 262, 266, 268, 281, 311, 319, 348-349, 372, 394, 407, 429, 451, 478-479, 483, 487, 521, 534, 603, 607-608, 626, 634-635, 637, 641-642

Graduate Students:

January: 656, 665, 671, 674, 683, 687-688, 691, 706, 708, 724, 745, 762, 765, 773, 780, 783, 788, 806, 810, 813-815, 819, 850, 854, 880, 884, 888-890, 904, 907, 912, 917, 943, 952, 957, 966-967, 977, 981, 991, 1009, 1021, 1029, 1035, 1044, 1046, 1057, 1082, 1086, 1102, 1104, 1114-1116, 1129, 1135, 1142, 1145, 1150, 1155, 1168

February: 653, 655, 661-662, 668, 672, 676-678, 682, 701, 703, 707, 759, 766, 774, 804, 811, 818, 821-822, 849, 867-868, 872, 874, 886-887, 901, 903, 922, 938, 960, 965, 969, 974, 982, 999-1000, 1003, 1007, 1011-1012, 1014, 1016-1017, 1038-1039, 1058, 1084-1085, 1088, 1105, 1108, 1110-1111, 1117, 1123, 1132, 1146, 1151

March: 667, 705, 714, 716, 721, 727-728, 734, 740, 744, 750, 752, 764, 778, 784, 790, 798-799, 809, 817, 832-833, 836-837, 846, 851, 862, 864, 869, 871, 881, 883, 893, 897, 900, 918, 946, 949, 956, 963-964, 973, 980, 987, 992, 1001, 1005, 1018, 1022, 1032, 1048, 1054, 1067, 1081, 1096-1097, 1099, 1125, 1140, 1149, 1152, 1156, 1160

April: 651, 659, 663, 666, 679, 698, 712, 719, 722-723, 737-739, 747, 760-761, 802, 812, 847, 853, 856-857, 876, 882, 896, 902, 905, 929, 935-936, 948, 950, 988, 993-995, 998, 1010, 1030, 1059, 1065-1066, 1068, 1072, 1087, 1100, 1121, 1124, 1126, 1130-1131, 1137, 1162, 1164, 1169, 1174, 1177